ROYAL VISITS AND PROGRESSES
TO WALES,

AND

THE BORDER COUNTIES OF CHESHIRE, SALOP, HEREFORD, AND MONMOUTH,

FROM

THE FIRST INVASION OF JULIUS CÆSAR, TO THE FRIENDLY VISIT OF

HER MOST GRACIOUS MAJESTY QUEEN VICTORIA.

CONTAINING

A SUCCINCT HISTORY OF THE COUNTRY AND PEOPLE,

PARTICULARLY OF THE LEADING FAMILIES WHO FOUGHT AND BLED FOR THEIR KING DURING THE TROUBLESOME TIMES OF

THE CIVIL WARS AND COMMONWEALTH,

THE LATTER PORTION DERIVED CHIEFLY FROM ANCIENT MANUSCRIPTS NEVER BEFORE PUBLISHED,

CHRONOLOGICALLY ARRANGED, WITH NUMEROUS EXPLANATORY NOTES,

AND

Illustrated with an Approved Portrait of Her Majesty, and a Profusion of Pictorial and Historical Engravings.

BY EDWARD PARRY.

SECOND EDITION.

LONDON: CHAPMAN AND HALL, 193, PICCADILLY.

J. H. LEAKE, SHREWSBURY: THOMAS CATHERALL, AND EDWARD PARRY, CHESTER.

MDCCCLI.

LONDON:
BRADBURY AND EVANS, PRINTERS, WHITEFRIARS.

TO

Her Most Gracious Majesty Queen Victoria.

———◆———

MAY IT PLEASE YOUR MAJESTY,

WITH feelings of the profoundest loyalty, pride, and gratitude, I acknowledge your Majesty's gracious condescension in permitting the dedication to your Majesty of the following pages, which, under your Royal and munificent patronage, are now ushered to the world.

From the time that your Majesty ascended the throne of your ancestral realms, Science, Literature, and the Arts, have seemed as it were under your auspices to flourish ; Civil and Religious liberty to expand ; Nature, subdued by the intellect and energy of the Age, has seen achieved the most stupendous undertakings for the benefit and civilisation of Man ; the lightning of Heaven itself has become subservient to extend the intercourse and ensure the amity of nations : manifestly declaring that your Majesty reigns, as well in the affections of your people, as by the might, the splendour, and the authority of your Crown.

But there are still greater glories surrounding and shielding the throne of your Majesty. The endearing virtues of your private and domestic life have spread their benign influences, not merely among the nobility of the land, but to the homes and hearts of the humblest of your subjects ; so that it may truly be said, never was Sovereign of that Island, upon whose empire the sun never sets, raised to a higher pinnacle of glory than your Majesty among the princes of the Earth.

The greatness of England appears in the hands of Providence to be linked with the history of its queens. The valour of ELIZABETH scattered to the winds the Invincible Armada :

the councils of ANNE were crowned with the victories of a Marlborough: but inasmuch as the prosperity and happiness of a people constitutes a nobler diadem for kings than the triumphs of the senate, or the conquests of the sword; so the might of ELIZABETH, and the wisdom of ANNE, are doomed in the Annals of England to pale their lustre before the sceptre of VICTORIA.

By the princes of your Majesty's royal ancestry, the Tudor and the Brunswick families, was maintained, completed, and established, the glorious Reformation in Church and State; and under those constitutional liberties, which flow from it, and which your Majesty so nobly upholds, Great Britain has attained the largest empire of human population that has hitherto been subject under any European and Christian ruler, since the days of Constantine the Great. For of what Western Sovereign, before your Most Gracious Majesty, can it be said, that he has reigned over nearly TWO HUNDRED MILLIONS of subjects; so widely disparted in their territorial localities, yet, united under your protecting sceptre, forming altogether one peaceful, prosperous, and happy kingdom, with every promise and prophecy of continuing for the increasing benefit of mankind, the full enjoyment of their individual felicities, as well as their political and religious freedom.

That Providence may be pleased to prolong a life so important as that of your Majesty, for many, many years, to reign over a happy, contented, and united people, is the earnest prayer of your Majesty's

Most humble and most devoted

Subject and Servant,

EDWARD PARRY.

CHESTER,
   December, 1850.

PREFACE.

———◆———

A HISTORY of the past must of necessity be a work of research and compilation. The writer of this book claims no merit for originality, and happily for him as an annalist, honesty and industry are more desirable qualities than the most florid diction or the most active invention. He aspires to no higher merit than that of a faithful collector, and to the best of his abilities, he has selected with judgment, arranged with care, and abridged with accuracy; and if his endeavours should succeed to the satisfaction of his readers, his utmost ambition will be gratified.

In alluding to the labour consequent upon arranging the scattered information obtained from various archives to enable the Author to illustrate and explain the history of earlier times, and select such facts and incidents as were worthy of attention, he has been cheered and consoled with the hope that he should be enabled to compose a narrative of such striking, important, and interesting events as might not be deemed unworthy of being presented in a connected form to an intelligent reader of the present day.

The work now offered to the public is far however from professing to be complete. The reader will bear in mind that it is simply a concise collection of materials relating to the Principality and the important Border Counties of Cheshire, Salop, Hereford, and Monmouth; and it is now committed to the press with the hope that such records may prove interesting to many, as well as tend to awaken dormant curiosity, and furnish a nucleus for deeper research, and more extended enquiry.

It is worthy of notice, that we are not to look to the English historians for the best accounts of the public transactions of the earlier ages. The historical triads of the ancient Britons supply much valuable information, and the works of foreign writers must be consulted for the most copious accounts of the Middle Ages. Recourse also must be had to Froissart, Philip de Comines, and Monstrelet, for the fullest and the most interesting intelligence concerning the history of our Monarchy.

The Chroniclers of the earliest periods of our history were generally monks—and let it be gratefully borne in mind, that it is almost entirely to them that modern writers owe their knowledge of what are called the darker ages, but which, without their aid, would have been dark indeed. However meanly we may estimate their taste or skill as chroniclers, still their general veracity, on civil affairs at least, and where the immediate interests of their institutions were not concerned, is unimpeachable. In this state of things the facts furnished by them may be safely taken to be such as their opportunities allowed them to collect, and, as far as those facts are concerned, we have unhesitatingly availed ourselves of their labours.

For all errors necessarily incidental to a work of this description, however great the pains and care bestowed upon it, and for all unintentional faults of omission or commission, chronological or otherwise, the Author trusts to the kind and considerate indulgence of the public; to whom, after years of labour and toil in collecting, collating, and abridging that information, which he has gathered (single-handed) from innumerable sources, manuscripts and private records, the work is now most respectfully submitted.

He, however, cannot conclude without acknowledging the very kind and able assistance that has been rendered to him by the gentlemen who superintend that vast repertory of knowledge, the British Museum, as well as by those who have the management of various other libraries to which he has had recourse in the preparation of this work. He would indeed be failing in a sense of duty to those gentlemen, if he were not to express his great obligation to them for the kind attention that he has received on all occasions.

He also begs to acknowledge his grateful thanks to several of the nobility, gentry, and clergy, for their kind permission from time to time to inspect their libraries and manuscripts, particularly to the Most Noble the Marquis of Westminster, Her Majesty's Lord High Steward; the Right Hon. the Lord Mostyn; the Hon. E. Mostyn Lloyd Mostyn, M.P.; Sir Watkin W. Wynn, Bart., M.P., and the Very Rev. the Dean of Bangor, who have not only allowed him the opportunity of inspecting their large and valuable collections of ancient manuscripts, but have entrusted them to his care to enable him to make the necessary extracts.

He must not omit, also, tendering his gratitude to his highly-valued friend, J. B. Henderson, Esq., for nearly the whole of the very clever and original Historical Drawings inserted in this work.

To the engravers and lithographers, Messrs. Fairholt, Reimbault, Nicholls, Wing, Ford, and George, he likewise offers his thanks for the very able and scientific manner in which they have embodied and carried out his suggestions for the various designs and engravings.

CONTENTS.

HISTORIC SUMMARY.

LIST OF MSS., HISTORICAL RECORDS, ANCIENT CHRONICLES,

AND

OTHER AUTHORITIES.

MSS. In the Tower, London.
   " In the British Museum, Royal MSS.
   " Trinity College, Dublin.
   " Arundel Coll. Arm.
   " Bodleian Library.
   " Jesus College, Oxford, "Llyfr-coch" of Hergest, &c. &c.
   " At the Mostyn Library.
   " At the Wynnstay Library.
   " At the Hengwrt Library.
   " At Baron Hill.
   " Pengwern.
   " At Eaton Hall.
   " At Downing.
   " Sub. Ann., 1473-74.
   " In various parts of Wales, by Sir John Leinf, Gyttyn Owen, Gryffyth ap Llywelyn ap Jermy, Fychan, &c. &c.
   " (Peckham) Lambeth.
   " (Cotton.) Cleop.
   " Chronicle of Shrewsbury.
   " In Remembrancer Office.
   " In Harleian Library.
   " (Randle Holmes) Brit. Mus.
   " Salusbury.
   " Rev. Thomas Crane.
   " (Symon's Notes.) Harl.
   " Treatise on the Marches.
   " Lloyd's History of Shropshire.
   " Rowland.
   " Sebright.
   " Bibl. du. Roy. Ambassades.
   " Lambeth.
   " Roberts's Cwtta Cyfarwydd.
   " Shrewsbury Records.
   " Erbistock.
   " (Old French) Brit. Mus.
   " Ambassades.
   " Cathedral Library, Chester.
   " Rymer, Donat.
   " Bangor Cathedral.
   " (Dugdale) Ashmolean Library.
   " (Cotton) Vespas.
Memoirs of the French Academy of Inscriptions.
Fortescue De Laudibus Legum Angliæ.
Cæsar De Bello Gallico.

Pezron's Antiquities Celt.
Hootoman Franc. Gal.
Probert's Gododin.
Rev. D. James's Patriarchal Religion of Britain.
Strabo.
Diog. Laert. in Proem.
Mela De Situ Orbis.
Plin. Hist. Nat.
Iolo Morganwg, Treatise on the Bardic Alphabet.
Diodorus Siculus.
Taciti Annales.
Taciti Vita Agricolæ.
Selden.
Ammianus Marcellinus.
Stillingfleet's Origines Britannicæ.
Horsley's Britannia Romana.
Whittaker's Manchester.
History of Herefordshire.
The Triads.
Archbishop Usher.
Taylor's Fragments.
Martialis Epigrammata.
Tertullian Adv. Judæos.
Origen in Luc.
Clemens Romanus.
Theodoret.
Jerome.
Calmet.
Xiphilin, ex Dione in Neron.
Dion Cassius.
Lipsius.
Itinerary of Richard of Cirencester.
Beauties of Northumberland.
Morant's History of Colchester.
Zosimi Historia.
Gildas Historia de Excidio Britanniæ.
Bede Historia Ecclesiast.
Camden.
Turner's History of the Anglo-Saxons.
Herodian.
Book of Llandaff.
Matthew of Westminster.
Rymer's Fœdera.

Langhorne's Chronicon.
Freculphus Chron.
Cambrian Register.
Saxon Chron.
Vetus Chronicon Holfatiæ.
Vosperus ex Leidensi-Chronico.
Belgic Chronicle.
Nennius.
Geoffrey of Monmouth.
Elegies of Llywarch Hen.
Lady Guest's Translation of the Mabinogion.
Myrddin's Avallennau.
Comment. Brit. Descript.
Owen's British Remains.
Jones's Relics.
Dr. O. Pughe's Essay on Bardism.
Lhuyd's Archæologia Britannica.
Nicholson's Irish Historical Library.
Nicholson's Essay on Welsh Orthography.
Edward Williams's Poems.
Welsh and English Dictionary.
Lucan's Pharsalia.
Caradoc's British History.
Bishop Lloyd's Church History.
Rees's Prize Essay on the Welsh Saints.
Smollet's History of England.
Bowles's History of the Popes.
Leland De Script. Brit.
Blackstone's Commentaries.
Lord Bacon's Historical Discourse.
William of Malmesbury.
Leland's Itinerary.
Bishop Burgess's Second Letter.
Thiers' History of the Norman Conquest.
Verstegan.
Rowland's Mon. Ant.
Williams's Monmouthshire.
Pryse's Preface to Wynne's Caradoc.
Baker's Chron.
J. Fordun's Hist. Scot.
Calendar to the Patent Rolls.
Fabian's Chron.
Grafton's Chron.
Howe's Chron.
Speed's Chron.
Sim. Dunelme.

Spelman.
Wynne's History of Wales.
Asser's Life of Alfred.
Henry of Huntingdon.
Voltaire's Essai Sur les Mœurs.
Herder's Outline of Philosophy.
Humphrey Llwyd's Brev.
Brompton's Chron.
Henry of Huntington.
Roger de Hoveden.
Dr. Campbell's Lives of the Admirals.
Rev. Mr. Lodge's History of Hereford.
Ingulphus.
Lamb's Saxon Chronicle.
John of Salisbury.
Giraldus Cambrensis.
Chroniques Anglo-Normandes.
Henry de Knighton.
King's Vale Royal.
Ormond's Cheshire.
Henshall's Cheshire.
Holinshed.
Matthew Paris.
Coronation Anecdotes.
Pennant's Wales.
Leicester's Cheshire.
Odericus Vitalis.
Robert of Gloucester.
Annales Waverlienses.
Polydore Virgil.
Marianus Scotus.
Camden's Britannia.
Vaughan's British Ant. Rev.
Lord Herbert of Cherbury's Life of Henry VIII.
Warrington's Wales.
Vita Griffith Fil Cynan.
Hume's History of England.
Vit. Lut. Grossi.
Lappenberg's, Geschichte von England.
Domesday Book.
Florence of Worcester.
Lord Lyttleton's History of Henry II.
William of Newburgh.
Dr. Powell's Notes.
Chronica Gerv.
Radulph de Diceto.
Script. Rer. Gallic. et Franc.
Ottley Papers.
Dugdale's Baronage.
Blount's Ancient Tenures.
Brady's England.
Thomas Wykes.
Bishop Fleetwood.
Powell's History of Wales.
Wright's History of Wales.
Evans' Specimens of Welsh Poetry.
Patent Rolls.

Close Rolls.
Disraeli's Curiosities of Literature.
Wright's History of Ludlow.
Dugdale's Monasticon.
Jones's History of Brecon.
Bingley's Welsh Tour.
Issues of the Exchequer.
Dodsworth's Collections.
Chronicle of Chester Abbey.
Annales Cestrenses.
Rishanger's Chron. (Ed. Halliwell).
Chron. Abendon. (Ed. Halliwell).
Yorke's Royal Tribes.
History of the Mortimers.
Prynne's Records.
Episcopal Register of Lichfield.
Piers Langtoft.
Guthrie's Hist. Eng.
J. Rossi's Ant. Warw.
Hen. de Knyghton de Event. Ang.
Carte's Hist. Eng.
Peckham Register.
Mill's Catalogue of Honour.
Browne Willis's Bangor.
Evans's Dissertatio de Bardis.
Williams's Dictionary of America.
Gray's Poems.
Arch. Prys's Psalms.
Bishop Percy's Reliques of Ancient Poetry.
Bradshaw's Life of St. Werburgh.
Leges Walliæ.
Llwyd's Archæology.
Rot. Wallia.
Boswell's Antiquities.
Pennant's Wales.
Walter de Mapes.
Thomas Walsingham.
Leland's Collectanea.
Pipe Rolls.
Cambria Triumphans.
Tanner's Notitia Monastica.
Royal and Noble Authors.
Foxe's Acts and Monuments.
Visions of Piers Ploughman.
Nicholas's Proceedings of the Privy Council.
Monstrelet.
Drake's Parliamentary History.
Polychronicon.
Shakespeare.
Wilkins' Concilia.
Accounts and Extracts.
Camden's Annals of Ireland.
Froissart.
Mezeray.
Vit. Richard II.
Chaucer.
Rapin's History of England.
Cotton's Abridgment.

Burney's History of Music.
Merlin's Prophecies.
Warton's History of English Poetry.
Otterbourne.
Le Labonneur Hist. Charles VI.
Hallam's History of the Middle Ages.
Devon's Pell Rolls.
Calendar to the Patent Rolls.
Proceedings of the Privy Council.
Ellis's Original Letters.
Hackluyt.
Hardynge's Chronicle.
Archæologia Cambrensis.
Gale's Scriptores.
Villaret's Hist. of France.
Recollections of Royalty.
Sir Harris Nicholas.
Sir Frederic Madden.
Habington's Hist. of Edward IV.
Annales Wilhelmi Wyrcestre.
Lewis Glyn Cothi.
Warkworth Chronicle (Ed. Halliwell).
Chronicle of Croyland.
Paston Correspondence.
Owen and Blakeway's History of Shropshire.
Philip de Comines.
Clarendon's State Papers.
History of Whalley.
Strype's Memorials.
Crapelot.
Dr. Davies's Address.
Rev. Griffith Jones's Welsh Piety.
Rev. Walter Davis's Life of Hugh Morris.
Tracts in the British Museum.
Williams's Tourists Guide.
Antiquities of Cheshire.
Myfyrian Archæology.
Husband's Collections.
Burghah's Journal.
Perfect Diurnall.
Mercurius Aulicus.
Parl. Hist.
Collectanea Curiosa.
Cambro-Briton.
Chambers's Worcester.
Randle Holmes's Narrative of the Siege of Chester.
Archæologia Cambrensis.
Burnet's History of His Own Times.
Hunter's Notes to Bp. Cartwright's Diary.
Lord Somer's Tracts.
Observations on the Landed Revenues of the Crown.
Gentleman's Magazine.
Book of Basinwerk Abbey.
Sir James Mackintosh.
Lamartine.

CHRONOLOGICAL TABLE.

NORMAN DYNASTY.

	NAMES.	BORN.	ACCESSION.	REIGNED.	DIED.	WHERE BURIED.
NORMAN LINE.	WILLIAM THE CONQUEROR . . .	1027	Dec. 26, 1066	Years. 21	Sept. 9, 1087	Caen in Normandy.
	WILLIAM II. . . . . Third son of William the Conqueror.	1057	Sept. 19, 1087	13	August 2, 1100	Winchester.
	HENRY I. . . . . Fourth son of the Conqueror.	1068	August 5, 1100	35	Dec. 2, 1135	Reading.
BLOIS.	STEPHEN . . . . Nephew of Henry I.	1105	Dec. 26, 1135	19	Oct. 5, 1154	Feversham.

SAXON LINE RESTORED.

	NAMES.	BORN.	ACCESSION.	REIGNED.	DIED.	WHERE BURIED.
PLANTAGENET.	HENRY II. . . . . . . Grandson of Henry I.	1133	Dec. 8, 1154	35	July 6, 1189	Fontevrault.
	RICHARD I. . . . . Son of Henry II.	1156	August 13, 1189	10	April 6, 1199	Fontevrault.
	JOHN . . . . Brother to Richard I.	1165	April 6, 1199	17	Oct. 19, 1216	Worcester.
	HENRY III. . . . . . . Son of John.	1207	Oct. 17, 1216	56	Nov. 16, 1272	Westminster.
	EDWARD I. . . . . . . Son of Henry III.	1239	Nov. 16, 1272	35	July 7, 1307	Westminster.
	EDWARD II. . . . . . . Son of Edward I.	1284	July 7, 1307	20	Sept. 21, 1327	Gloucester.
	EDWARD III. . . . . . . Son of Edward II.	1312	Sept. 22, 1327	50	June 21, 1377	Westminster.
	RICHARD II. . . . . . . Grandson of Edward III.	1366	June 21, 1377	22	Jan. 10, 1400	Westminster.

HOUSE OF LANCASTER.

	NAMES.	BORN.	ACCESSION.	REIGNED.	DIED.	WHERE BURIED.
PLANTAGENET. **LANCASTER.**	HENRY IV. . . . . Son of John, Duke of Lancaster, who was fourth son of Edward III.	1367	Oct. 1, 1399	14	March 20, 1413	Canterbury.
	HENRY V. . . . . Son of Henry IV.	1389	March 20, 1413	9	August 31, 1422	Westminster.
	HENRY VI. . . . . Son of Henry V.	1421	August 31, 1422	39	April 21, 1461	Windsor.

HOUSE OF YORK.

	NAMES.	BORN.	ACCESSION.	REIGNED.	DIED.	WHERE BURIED.
PLANTAGENET. **YORK.**	EDWARD IV. . . . . . . Son of the Duke of York.	1442	April 21, 1461	22	April 9, 1482	Windsor.
	EDWARD V. . . . . . . Son of Edward IV.	1470	April 9, 1483	Three months	June, 1483	Unknown.
	RICHARD III. . . . . . . Brother to Edward IV.	1443	June, 1483	2	August 23, 1485	Leicester.

c

UNION OF THE ROSES.

	Names.	Born.	Accession.	Reigned.	Died.	Where Buried.
				Years.		
TUDORS.	HENRY VII. . . . . Son of Tudor, Earl of Richmond.	1456	August 23, 1485	24	April 22, 1509	Westminster.
	HENRY VIII. . . . . Son of Henry VII.	1492	April 22, 1509	37	Jan. 28, 1547	Windsor.
	EDWARD VI. . . . . Son of Henry VIII.	1537	Jan. 29, 1547	6	July 16, 1553	Westminster.
	MARY . . . . Daughter of Henry VIII.	1516	July 16, 1553	5	Dec. 1, 1558	Westminster.
	ELIZABETH . . . . Daughter of Henry VIII.	1533	Nov. 7, 1558	45	March 24, 1603	Westminster.

UNION OF THE ENGLISH AND SCOTCH CROWNS.

	Names.	Born.	Accession.	Reigned.	Died.	Where Buried.
STUARTS.	JAMES I. . . . . Son of Mary, Queen of Scots.	1566	March 24, 1603	22	March 27, 1625	Westminster.
	CHARLES I. . . . . Son of James I.	1600	1625	24		Windsor.
	COMMONWEALTH . . . . Under OLIVER CROMWELL and his son, lasted from Jan., 1649, to May, 1660.	—	1649	11		
	CHARLES II. . . . . Son of Charles I.	1630	May 29, 1660	25	July 6, 1685	Westminster.
	JAMES II. . . . . Brother to Charles II.	1633	Feb. 6, 1685	4	Abdicated, Jan. 22, 1688	Paris.
	WILLIAM, PRINCE OF ORANGE, AND MARY Daughter of James II.	1650	Jan. 22, 1689	13	March 8, 1702	Westminster.
	ANNE . . . . Second daughter of James II.	1664	March 8, 1702	12	August 1, 1714	Westminster.

HOUSE OF HANOVER.

	Names.	Born.	Accession.	Reigned.	Died.	Where Buried.
LINE OF BRUNSWICK.	GEORGE I.	1660	August 1, 1714	13	June 11, 1727	Hanover.
	GEORGE II. . . . . Son of George I.	1683	June 11, 1727	33	Oct. 25. 1760	Westminster.
	GEORGE III. . . . . Grandson to George II.	1738	Oct. 25, 1760	60	Jan. 29, 1820	Windsor.
	GEORGE IV. . . . . Son of George III.	1762	1820	10	1830	Windsor.
	WILLIAM IV. . . . . Son of George III.	1765	1830	7	1837	Windsor.
	VICTORIA . . . . Grand-daughter of George III., niece to George IV. and William IV., and daughter of the Duke of Kent.	1819	1837			

LIST OF ILLUSTRATIONS.

THE ABORIGINAL BRITONS.

*" To be the Heralds of our Country's fame,
Our first ambition, and our dearest aim."—GOUGE.*

N the history of an ancient nation each of her children holds a proud birthright of inheritance,—to trace the noble current of antiquity; to contemplate with a holy eye, fidelity and loyalty; and to review, in the dim light of half-forgotten annals, that fortitude and conduct which proved the guardian of his individual freedom and the bulwark of his individual faith.   In the heroic actions of his ancestors, he reads a lesson of gratitude and duty; and in the love of country, he feels that he is descended from those who, like their protecting rocks, however assailed by storms, yet stand superior to the conflicts of two thousand years, unmoved and unsubdued.

It appears from "Hén Drioedd Cenedl y Cymry," (the old Triads[1] of the nation of the Cymry,) which were in use among the ancient Bards and Druids of this island in very early times, (and which are the most precious and authentic remains of history we possess,) that the colony of the Cymry, or Britons, who first inhabited this island, came originally from Defrobani, or Summer Land, a country in Asia. (Triad IV.)

Hu THE MIGHTY, led the Cymry to the island of Britain, and first established them in a civil community. (Triad v.)   Hu was one of the three national pillars, and was celebrated for having taught the Cymry the mode of tilling the land; for having made poetry and song the vehicle of memory and record; (Triad XCII.) for having made several implements for the improvement of agriculture,[2] and for other useful arts. (Triad LVI.)

This venerable patriarch appears to have been endowed with uncommon qualifications for the arduous task of conducting a colony over the Hazy Sea, or German Ocean, to the utmost region of the then known world, where, for many ages afterwards, the Romans considered their descendants as,

" Penitus toto divisos orbe Britannos."

These authorities are corroborated by the poems of the ancient bards, which are also of very great antiquity.   Taliesin, who flourished from A.D. 520 to 570, in his poem called "The Appeasing

---

[1] The term, Triad, is an artificial association of three unconnected ideas or events, for the purpose of aiding the memory.   The Welsh have their poetical and historical Triads, which are remarkable for their singular strength, clearness, and historical brevity.

[2] A very curious stone was found in France, with a bas-relief of *Hu*, in the act of cutting down a tree, as an emblem of his being the first who taught the cultivation of the earth.   A print, representing this·relic, is given in the Memoirs of the French Academy of Inscriptions, vol. ii. p. 370.

B

of Lludd," has the following singular passage, translated from the original in the Myfyrian Archæology of Wales:—

> " The original colonist of Britain's first of isles
> Were a numerous race, natives of Gaffis,
> A country in Asia.—Clad in their own dress,
> Who could equal them! Their skill is celebrated;
> They were the dread of Europe.

The island itself is said to have had three names. The first, Y Fel Ynys, or the Honey Island; then Clas Meiddin, or Meityn, the rocky or water-guarded island, which was its name when the first colony settled in it, under Hu the Mighty; the third and last name, which it has since retained, is that of Prydain, or Britain, having been so called in honour of the chief of that name, who, according to the Triads, is celebrated for having given the settlement a regular form.

The traditions and science of the first settlers were improved upon by their successors, who made no inconsiderable progress in the cultivation of poetry. (Triad xcii.) In the Triads we also find vestiges similar to those of some of the most ancient and celebrated nations of antiquity. They are few in number, it is true; but they are so strikingly characteristic, as to leave no reasonable doubt of the fact of their common origin.

Before we enter on the subject of the Royal Visits to Wales, it is necessary that we should give a short account of the first inhabitants of this island, their laws, constitution, manners, and also of their heroic conduct in defence of their country.

Though little now remains to enable us to form a just idea of the internal policy by which the island was governed in those early times, it is still possible to perceive one general principle which prevailed up to the time of Vortigern, which is, that though the island was in three original divisions, and afterwards in subdivisions, governed by kings or princes of each division or subdivision, some one of them possessed sovereign power over the whole island. These had the authority of making laws, and of levying the whole power of the kingdom in case of invasion. Their exercise of power was limited by a common law, under the name of the custom of the country. The laws of " Dyfnwal Moelmud," the patriarchal legislator, who is supposed to have lived about 400 years before Christ, are said to contain the principles of the Common Law of England.[3]

The Triads make mention of National Institutes and laws as being in existence in this island for ages previous to the Christian era; and the names of the kings and princes[4] are given, who freed the country from the horrors of anarchy, and taught the Britons the necessity of wise and just regulations, and acknowledged principles of equity and right.

These laws were always enacted by the general suffrage of what were afterwards called *Uchelwyr*, or noblemen, and the *Gwyr dá*, men of small estate, or such as we would call freeholders; the common people being in a state of villenage, or slavery to the great men. It is probable that the general principles, and many of the particular usages established by the laws of Prince Hywel, were derived from those old National Institutes.

In very early times the island of Britain was divided into three grand territories, Cymry, Lloegr,

---

[3] Fortescue, " De Laudibus legum Angliæ."

[4] Our Welsh records furnish us with a list of the names of fifty-nine kings and princes who governed in Britain before the invasion of Julius Cæsar. Our most ancient British History is called *Brut y Brenhinoedd*, or the Chronicle of the British Kings, because it concludes with Cadwaladr the last King; and to distinguish it from the continuation by Caradog, which is called *Brut y Tywysogion*, or the Chronicle of the Princes. It begins with the Trojan colony, and ends with the reign of Cadwaladr, the abdicated King of the Britons. It hath gone among us under the name of Tyssilio, a bishop, the supporter of the British Church against the usurpations of Austin the monk, and the son of Brochwel Ysgythriog;[*] but he seems to have been only the continuer of it, from the Roman conquest to his own time, about the year 660. It was afterwards continued to the death of Cadwaladr, by some other hand. Caradog, of the Abbey of Llancarfan, collected and continued this history to the year 1156. The monks of Conway, and Ystrad-fflur pursued it

[*] A.D. 606.—Brochwel commanded the Britons at their memorable defeat near Chester, which led to the massacre of the monks of Bangor Monachorum. His son Tyssilio, besides his Welsh work, wrote an Ecclesiastical History of Britain, which Archbishop Usher said he had seen.

and Alban, and to each of these pertained the honour of monarchy. "There is one supreme authority in union with the arbitration or voice of the country and community, agreeable to the distribution of Prydain, the son of Aedd the Great; and to the nation of the Cymry does the supreme authority pertain, according to the voice of the country and the nation, because of natural right and equity; and subject to this constitution ought the sovereignty to be regulated in every territory of Britain, and every sovereignty is subject to the voice of the country: on that ground is the proverb founded, 'Trechgwlad nag Arglwydd:' The country is greater than its lord." Such is the language of our ancient documents on the subject of government, and civil liberty. Another Triad is as follows: "The three pillars of the common weal of the isle of Britain, the voice (or decision) of the country, the sovereignty, and the law, according to the distribution of Prydain, the son of Aedd the Great."

There are three characters mentioned as men of the first consequence among the primitive Britons; the first is *Hû* or *Huis* the Mighty, who first conducted the Cymry to Britain; the second is Prydain, the son of Aedd the Great, who first established a regular government in this island; for, before that time, there were no fixed principles of equity (that is, every one did as "seemed good in his own eyes"); and no law but that of force: the third was Dyfnwal Moelmud; and he was the first who made a proper distribution of the laws, institutes, and customs, national and territorial rights. In another Triad, three supreme rulers, or persons invested with monarchy by the general suffrage, are mentioned; the first is Prydain, the second the celebrated Caractacus, and the third is Owain, the son of the usurper Maximus; when the Cymry had their rights of sovereign power restored to them in consequence of the abdication of the Romans, these were styled monarchs, chosen by general suffrage, because they were exalted to that dignity by the states of the whole country; through all the territories of the nation of the Cymry, in all the lordships, commots, and hundreds of the isle of Britain, and its appended islets. Thus we find that Prydain, or Brito, was the first legislator of the Britains; and the Cymry, or first settlers, considered all the succeeding colonies bound, by right and compact, to acknowledge their supreme authority. Prydain formed the coming tribes into a regular community. Dyfnwal made further improvements in legislation, and settled the constitution of government and the grand principles of jurisprudence; he fixed the boundaries of the various divisions and subdivisions of the country, and adjusted the rights and claims of the various classes of the community.

When the Romans first invaded Britain under Julius Cæsar, its inhabitants, particularly the Druids, were famous, even among foreign nations, for their superior knowledge of the principles, and their great zeal for the rites of their religion. This we derive from the best authority—the writings of that illustrious and observing general, Julius Cæsar, who informs us, "That such of the Gauls as were desirous of being thoroughly instructed in the principles of their religion (which was the same as that of the Britons), usually took a journey to Britain for that purpose."[5]

This religion, in the knowledge of which the Britons of that age so much excelled, could justly boast of very high antiquity. Its first and purest principles at least descended to them, together with their language, and many other things, from Gomer, the eldest son of Japhet; from whom the Gauls, Britons, and all the other Celtic nations[6] derived their origin. For it is not to be imagined that this renowned parent of so many nations, who was but grandson from Noah, could be unacquainted with the knowledge of the true God, and of the most essential principles of religion; or that he neglected to communicate this

---

to 1270, just before the death of the last prince. Humphrey Llwyd translated this book from Welsh into English, adding some things from Matthew Paris and Nicholas Trivet, but died before he published; and it was left in the hands of Sir Henry Sidney, President of Wales, who recommended Dr. Powel to augment and print it, which he did, and dedicated to Sir Philip Sidney, the son of Sir Henry, in 1584. The monks of Ystrad-fflur and Conway seem purposely to have discontinued their history, unwilling to relate the final conquest of their country, and the death of Llywelyn. This part was completed by Humphrey Llwyd himself, assisted by the collections of Guttyn Owain.

[5] Cæsar de Bel. Gal. lib. vi., c. 23.

[6] Pezron's Antiquities Celt. c. 3.—Hootoman Franc. Gal. c. 2.

knowledge to his immediate descendants, through whom it passed to succeeding ages. But, unhappily, the method by which this religious knowledge was handed down from Gomer to his numerous posterity, was not calculated to preserve it pure and uncorrupted. This was tradition, which, like a stream, however limpid it may be near its fountain head, is very apt to swell and become turbid in its progress.

But though these streams of religious knowledge flowed through different channels into very distant countries, yet they long retained a strong tincture of their original fountain. The secret tenets of the Druids, and all the different orders of priests and bards, were more agreeable to primitive tradition and right reason, than their public doctrines; as they were not under any temptation in their private schools to conceal or disguise the truth. It is not improbable that they still retained, in secret, the great doctrine of " One God, the creator and governor of the universe."[7] This was originally the doctrine held by all the orders of priests and their followers, and it was retained by some of them long after the period we are now considering. We may, therefore, reasonably conclude that it was not unknown to the Druids at this period. " That there is one God, the creator of heaven and earth," is one of the doctrines which the Brachmans of India are sworn to keep secret. Cæsar acquaints us, that the Druids taught their disciples many things concerning the nature and perfections of God. Some writers are of opinion, and have taken much learned pains to prove, that our Druids, as well as other orders of priests, taught their disciples many things concerning the creation of the world—the formation of man—his primitive innocence and felicity—his fall into guilt and misery—the creation of the angels—their rebellion and expulsion out of heaven—the universal deluge—and the final destruction of this world by fire; and that their opinions on all these subjects were not very different from those which are contained in the writings of Moses, and in other parts of Scripture.

" There are three classes of men," says Strabo, "who are highly and universally esteemed among the Britons. These are the Bards, the Ovates, and the Druids. The Bards are poets and musicians; the Ovates are priests and physiologists; and the Druids add the study of moral philosophy to that of physiology."[8] If it were necessary, the testimony of several other authors of antiquity might be produced, to prove that the Druids of Britain and Gaul applied themselves with great assiduity to the study of the sciences.

When we reflect on the great antiquity and prodigious number of the Druids, the many immunities which they enjoyed, the leisure and tranquillity in which they lived, and the opportunities and encouragements which they had to study, we are rationally inclined to believe, that they had made considerable progress in several branches of learning before they were destroyed by the Romans. We shall be confirmed in this opinion if we observe the respectful terms in which the Greek and Roman writers speak of their learning. Diogenes Laertius places them in the same rank, in point of learning and philosophy, with the Chaldeans of Assyria, Magi of Persia, and the Gymnosophists and Brachmans of India.[9] Both Cæsar and Mela observe, that they had formed very extensive systems of Astronomy and of Natural Philosophy, and these systems, together with their observations on other parts of learning, were so voluminous, that their scholars spent no less than twenty years in making themselves masters of them,[1] and getting by heart that infinite multitude of verses in which they were contained. The Bards had also a secret, like the Free Masons, by which they knew one another; and, indeed, it has been supposed by some, that Masonry is Bardism in disguise. Both Bards and Druids made use of a term, known only to themselves, to express the

---

[7] The following short but comprehensive prayer of Talhaiarn, who flourished in the beginning of the fifth century, is an indisputable proof that the Britons were in the possession of the divine knowledge of their maker, and of the Sacred Scriptures, long before the great St. Augustine arrived in this country :—

" O God ! grant thy protection, and in the protection strength ; and in strength discretion ; and in discretion justice, and in justice love ; and in love, to love God ; and in loving God, to love all things."—*Notes to Probert's Gododin.*

[8] For a full account of the religion of our forefathers, we beg to refer our readers to our friend the Rev. D. James's Patriarchal Religion of Britain.

[9] Strabo, lib. iv., p. 197.

[1] Diog. Laert. in Proem.

unutterable name of the Deity; and the letters O. I. W. were used for that purpose. In this they resemble the Jews, who always say Adonai when the name Jehovah occurs.

"The Druids"[2] says Cæsar, "hold numerous disquisitions concerning the heavenly bodies and their motions, in which they instruct their disciples." Taliesin, who flourished in the sixth century, in one of his poems, says :—

> " Mi a wn enwau'r ser
> O'r Gogledd hyd Auster."

" I know the names (another copy has it "the number") of the stars from north to south;" and in another poem, "Dyhuddiant Elphin," he challenges the rival poets to trace the mysteries of nature in their competition with him. He has also left a poem on the Universe. It is merely an enumeration of the elements, planets, and the greater divisions of the globe, in verse, of which this is the substance:

" The elements are seven, viz., fire, earth, water, air, mist, atoms, and the animating wind. The sources of our ideas, seven: perception and volition, and the five senses."

This is the more singular, as it corresponds exactly with the position of the great Locke.

"There are seven spheres of the planets, and three aqueous ones, varying in their motions. The planets are seven: Sola, Luna, Marcarucia, Venerus, Severus, Jupiter, and Saturnus; and the zones five, two uninhabited, because of the cold, and one because of the heat."

The above extracts are sufficient to prove that science was cultivated with considerable attention in the time of our Bard, and the enumeration of objects indicate a respectable progress for the age he lived in.

The learned Dr. Halley hath demonstrated that Cæsar arrived in Britain, in his first year's expedition, on the 26th of August; and Cæsar himself informs us that, on his arrival, the harvest was finished, except in one field, which, from some cause or other, was more backward than the rest.[3] This is a proof that the British husbandmen were acquainted with, and used, the proper seasons for ploughing, sowing, and reaping.

The Britons seem also to have understood rural economy; for the fact of their Keepers of Cattle having a distinct appellation, evinces that numbers of others were occupied in the labours of the field. They appear, in consequence, to have had sufficient corn for their own support: and their pastures were abundantly stocked with cattle, sheep, and hogs; besides which, they bred, for amusement, hares, geese, and poultry.

When the people of any country come to be engaged in agriculture, architecture, commerce, and the study of the sciences, they have daily occasions to measure some things, as well as to number others. Hence, we may reasonably conclude that some of the Britons, particularly the Druids, had made considerable progress in geometry and arithmetic, before they were subdued by the Romans. This conclusion is confirmed by the best historical evidence: for we have the authority of Cæsar, that the Druids were all acquainted with geometry, properly so called, or the measuring of land. "When any disputes arise," says he, "about their inheritances, or any controversies about the limits of their fields, they are entirely referred to the decision of the Druids."[4]

With respect to the naval power of our ancestors, nothing certain is known, although the learned Selden has attempted to establish its existence. We have, however, reasonable ground to conjecture that they were not deficient in this particular. As to small vessels (and the mention of them does not exclude the probability of their having others of larger dimensions), Cæsar bears ample testimony to the ingenuity of their construction, and their great convenience; and he acknowledged himself indebted to the Britons for several useful improvements in the Roman navy. The facility with which these instruments of water conveyance were made, and their peculiar portability, has occasioned a continuance of their use; and coracles still form the fishing boats which ply on some of the rivers of Wales, particularly on the Dee.

Of the state of mechanical science, it is not easy to say much with any degree of precision. The

---

[2] Cæsar de Bel. Gal., lib. vi., c. 13, 14 ; Mela de Situ Orbis, lib. iii., c. 2.   [3] Plin. Hist. Nat., lib. xvi., c. 44.
[4] Cæsar de Bel. Gal. lib. vi., c. 13.

principle of the lever, the screw, and inclined plane, was well understood by the ancient Britons: and we have abundant proofs of the application of their knowledge of these subjects in their monumental and religious structures. Witness their immense Carnedds, and Cromlechs, burial places, and altars, which are to this day seen in various parts of the Principality and England—particularly Stonehenge, that triumphant monument of ancient British skill, which is attributed, by very many ancient and able writers, to the Britons. If that enormous stone in the Parish of Constantine, Cornwall, was really moved by art from its original place, and fixed where it now stands (as one of the most learned and diligent antiquaries thinks it was), it is a proof that the Britons could perform the most astonishing feats by their skill in mechanics. Dr. Borlase, in his "Antiquities of Cornwall," gives a particular description of that stone. "I measured the circumference of this," says the Doctor, "and found it to be 97 feet in circumference, about 60 feet across the middle, and, by the best information I can get, it contains at least 750 tons of stone. This stone is no less wonderful for its position than for its size; for, although the under part is semi-circular, yet it rests on two large rocks; and so light and detached does it stand, that it touches the two under stones but, as it were, on their points."

It is certain that writing was known among the Britons in the time of Cæsar, who describes their letters as being similar to the Greek.[s]

The remarks of Martial and Juvenal, in their allusions to the learning of the Britons, are applicable to the effect which may be attributed to the plans of Agricola, at the periods in which those authors wrote. The former corroborates the affirmation that the Latin language was well understood in this island, not very long after its subjugation :—

" Dicitur et nostras cantare Britannia versus."

And Juvenal, in his fifteenth satire, mentions the general diffusion of the Greek and Latin languages, and adverts to the proficiency among judicial advocates in the exercise of oratory :—

" Nunc totus Graias nostrasque habet orbis Athenas,
Gallia causidicos docuit facunda Britannos.
De conducendo loquitur jam rhetore Thule."

That the inhabitants of this island, particularly those of Cornwall, carried on an extensive foreign commerce, is beyond a doubt; for the people of Brittany, or Bretagne, traded here in large ships, and the ports of Britain were visited by merchant vessels from the Levant. Tin, which was esteemed the most valuable production of this island, was exported by the Britons many ages antecedent to the encroachment of the Belgæ. The discovery of this valuable metal induced the visits of foreign merchants, and led to a series of commercial interchanges, highly important in the early annals of Britain. The first nation which opened a trade with the inhabitants of this island was undoubtedly the Phœnician. That enterprising people, the founders of navigation and of extensive commerce, are supposed to have commenced a trade with Britain about 500 years before the Christian era. This country produced great quantities of brass, copper, lead, and iron ores, but in those days tin appears to have been the principal article, in which the Phœnicians enjoyed an exclusive trade for nearly three centuries, when they reluctantly admitted the Greeks to a participation in their advantageous traffic. From such a competition of purchasers, the Britons derived considerable benefit.

" Phœnicians forced me in the mines to toil,
The fossils did my fair complexion spoil.
Though dark my hue, and frightful garb I wear,
But then my parts are bright, my mind sincere."—*MS. Verse from Samm's Britannia.*

The British kings and chieftains, who were educated by the Druids, were famous for their eloquence.

[s] See Iolo Morganwg's treatise on "Coelbren, y Beirdd," the Bardic alphabet.

This is evident from the many noble speeches which are ascribed to them by the Greek and Roman writers.[6] Tacitus expressly tells us, "The British chieftains, before a battle, fly from rank to rank, and address their men with animating speeches, tending to inflame their courage, increase their hopes, and dispel their fears."[7]

The ancient Britons were no less remarkable than the other Celtic nations, for their love of liberty and their abhorrence of slavery, and for the bravery which they displayed in preserving the one, and in defending themselves from the other. They submitted with pleasure to the government of their own princes, which was mild and legal, but they were struck with horror at the thought of being reduced to servitude. It was to this well known passion of theirs for liberty that their leaders constantly addressed themselves in all their harangues, to excite them bravely to fight against the Romans;[8] and it was this powerful passion that actually animated them to oppose so long and obstinate resistance to that all-subduing people, as well as to make many bold attempts to shake off their yoke.[9]

The character which Tacitus gives the ancient Britons, even after they had submitted to the Roman government, is probably very just, and certainly very honourable: "The Britons are a people who pay their taxes and obey the laws with pleasure, providing no arbitrary or illegal demands are made upon them; but these they cannot bear without the greatest impatience, for they are only reduced to the state of subjects, not of slaves."[1]

They possessed an established government, consisting of a princely aristocracy, united in times of danger under one head, as expressed by one of our ancient bards :—

> " Un pen ar Gymru wen wedd,
> Ac un enaid gan Wynedd."

> " One head, let hoary Cambria lead ;
> One soul, let Gwynedd's sons pervade."

In accordance with this system, Cassivellaunus and Caractacus were elected to oppose the Romans, Arthur to oppose the Saxons, and Owen Gwynedd and Llywelyn to oppose the Normans. The British army, in the time of the Romans, was composed of regular and well disciplined troops, divided into charioteers, cavalry, and infantry, and their horses were admirably trained for the purposes of war.

The Britons were not unacquainted with the scientific mode of warfare or with the destructive implements of war, which struck terror to their enemies.

The war-chariot of the Britons formed the most remarkable feature in their military arrangements, and was found even by the firmest phalanx of the Romans to be a vehicle of tremendous operation. These were of two kinds, both of which had two wheels and were drawn by two horses. The chariots were armed with sharp blades, or scythes and hooks; and were driven furiously upon the ranks of an enemy, destroying or maiming all who unsuccessfully endeavoured to interrupt their progress.

The war-chariots of the second class contained the chieftains, and most honourable persons in command, who cast their darts around while they inspired the respective troops with energy in the fight. The skilful mode in which the British conducted the assault, and arranged their horses, is described by Cæsar in words to the following effect :—"They first divide their chariots on all sides, and throw their darts; often by the noise of the wheels and horses, putting the foremost ranks of the enemy into disorder. When they have forced their way into the midst of the cavalry, they quit their chariots and fight on foot. Meanwhile, the drivers retire a little from the combat, and place themselves in reserve, to favour the retreat of the warriors,

---

[6] Diod. Sicul., lib. v., c. 8.

[7] See Tacit. Annal., lib. xii., c. 37, 54 ; Vita Agric., c. 30—32.

[8] Valour in war was the most admired and popular virtue of the ancient Britons. Their natural courage arising from the soundness and vigour of their constitutions, was raised to an enthusiastic height by many powerful incentives. They were accustomed almost from their infancy to handle arms and to sing the glorious actions of their ancestors. This inspired their young hearts with impatient desires to be engaged in war. The ancient Britons were undoubtedly brave,

but they wanted unanimity and discipline, and to these causes must be attributed the success both of the Romans and the Saxons. Had their prudence been as great as their courage, and their unanimity as strong and lasting as their love of liberty, no enemy durst have landed, or if they had, it would have been only to find a speedy grave.—*Sharon Turner.*

[9] Tacit. Vita Agric., c. 38.

[1] Tacit. Vita Agric., c. 38.

should they be too much oppressed by the enemy. Thus in action, they perform the part of nimble cavalry and stable infantry; and by practice they have arrived at such expertness, that in the most steep and difficult places they can stop their horses when at full speed, turn them which way they please, run along the pole, rest on the harness, and throw themselves back with the most surprising dexterity."[2]

Ancient British War-chariot armed with Scythes.

It is allowed by Cæsar, that the most hardy of his veteran troops were disconcerted by this mode of attack; and if we may rely on the testimony of the same writer, the number of chariots was truly formidable. Cæsar asserts that no less than four thousand war-chariots were retained by Cassivellaunus, after that prince, hopeless of success in the field, had disbanded the remainder of his forces.

The accounts which have descended to us from their enemies, the Romans, afford sufficient evidence of the personal courage, discretion, and skill of the British chiefs. They usually chose their ground with great judgment, on the ascent of a hill; and they turned their superior knowledge of the country which they defended to the greatest possible advantage. In drawing up their troops, as we are informed by Tacitus, they commonly placed the infantry in the centre, in several lines, and in distinct corps; each division of warriors, consisting of the members of one clan, being commanded by its chieftain.

These bodies of infantry were so disposed that they could with ease support and relieve each other, as exigency might demand. The cavalry and chariots were stationed on either side, with small detached parties, spreading along the front of the line; and this part of the army, rushing forward on a signal, commenced the action, encouraged by the war-cry of the whole force.

Accustomed to a limited theatre of warfare, amidst woodlands and morasses, with rival and contiguous tribes, the British commanders evinced a consummate skill in the arts of stratagem and surprise.

On such arts, indeed, depended their best hope when they were opposed by the veteran legions, for their valour, however great, and their tactics, though far from contemptible, were not sufficient to enable them to cope in the open field with the superior arms and refined discipline of the Romans.

[2] Cæsar, de Bel. Gal. lib. iv., c. 33.

The history of Britain, after the defeat of Caractacus to the departure of the Romans from the island, is still such as to show, that the national spirit was not broken, though the power was at different times reduced to a state bordering on despair. The noble effort of Boadicea was an instance glorious in itself, however unfortunate in the event.

Some of the native princes displayed eminent abilities in the conduct of war. According to the Roman writers, Cassivellaunus, Caractacus, and Galgacus, all formed combined movements and enlarged plans of operation, and contrived stratagems and surprises which would have done honour to the greatest captains of Greece and Rome. Their choice of ground for fighting was almost invariably judicious, and they availed themselves of their superior knowledge of the country on all occasions.

It is evident, however, that the Britons, collectively, possessed more than the untutored tumultuary valour ascribed to them by many writers. The skill in stratagem and retreat displayed by the Britons, greatly perplexed, if it did not entirely baffle, the illustrious Cæsar, one of the most consummate generals of Rome, the victorious mistress of so many nations. And in after ages of that contest, whence we date the commencement of our national annals, the arts of the Romans assisted, in no mean degree, the success of their arms over the general population of Britain. Such a triumph renders subjugation attractive; but still it must not be forgotten, that, after a struggle of more than four centuries, the conquerors of the continent left a portion of this island unsubdued, and sacred to rude but honest and indignant patriotism.

> " Such are the sons of Cambria's ancient race,
> A race that checked victorious Cæsar and
> Imperial Rome ; and forced mankind to own
> Superior virtues Britons only knew,
> Or only practised, for they nobly dared
> To face oppression ! And where freedom finds
> Her aid invoked, there will the goddess fly."— ROLT.

An eminent sage of the law hath affirmed, that the ancient Britons, before they were subdued by the Romans, were in possession of that admirable system of jurisprudence, the present Common Law of England, and that no material changes have been made in that system either by the Romans, the Saxons, Danes, or Normans. His words are these:—" The realm of England was first inhabited by the Britons; next after them it was ruled by the Romans; then again by the Britons; after whom the Saxons possessed it, and changed its name from Britain to England : then the Danes for some time had the dominion of it; then again the Saxons; last of all the Normans, whose posterity governs it at present. Yet in the time of all these different nations and kings, this kingdom hath always been governed by the same customs by which it is governed at present. If these ancient British customs had not been most excellent, reason, justice, and the love of their country, would have induced some of these kings to change or abolish them; especially the Romans, who ruled all the rest of the world by the Roman laws." [3]

These facts respecting the first inhabitants will suggest to the reflecting mind that the Romans on their arrival did not find our ancestors hordes of ignorant savages as Hume and other historians would have us believe; but a people, though widely different from their invaders in temper, customs, and manners, yet having all the necessaries, and some of the conveniences of life, and what is most valuable of all possessions, contentment in their condition.[4] It will also further appear, that as early as their actions furnished materials for history, the Britons breathed a spirit of genuine freedom; had imbibed rational notions of its political advantages; and of the miseries resulting from despotic

---

[3] Sir John Fortescue, Chief Justice of England, in his celebrated work on the constitution of England, " De laudibus legum Angliæ," with notes by Selden, c. xxvii., pp. 38, 39. Sir John at this time had the care of Edward, Prince of Wales, son of Henry VI. and Margaret of Anjou. He wrote this book for the use of his royal pupil, to instruct him in a higher kind of knowledge, the true science of Royalty, which he considered preferable to martial exercises, which the prince at that time was so much taken up with.—*Life of Sir John Fortescue.*

[4] For the documents on which these are founded, see the Triads of the Cymry—Brut y Brenhinoedd ; the works of the ancient Bards ; Cæsar de Bell. Gal. lib. i. iv. v. et vi.; Ammianus Marcellinus, lib. xv.; Diodorus Siculus, lib. vi.; Tacitus in Vita Agricolæ ; and Stillingfleet's Origines Britannicæ.

power.   Upon this principle, therefore, they always studied to procure and preserve their liberty; and whenever they were deprived of it by any undue extension of arbitrary power, they never ceased struggling, till the galling yoke of despotism was removed.   The same spirit animated their minds, and the same temper pervaded their actions, when their country was invaded by the Romans.[a] Excited by a patriotism never exceeded in the annals of man, and stimulated by a noble ambition, never to be satisfied except by victory, and never extinguished but by death, they fought with a degree of bravery that astonished the legionary troops; performed prodigies of valour, which nearly represented them as invincible;[b] and disputed every inch of ground with a tenacity and obstinacy that extorted from their victors the tribute of admiration and esteem.

Such were the inhabitants of the Isle of Britain when the Romans first entered it with an hostile army.   Respecting the condition or state of these Britons, at the period in question, there has been a great discrepancy of opinion among the most learned of our writers.   Some, without possessing that impartiality which should ever accompany the enquirer after truth, and in despite of the most unexceptionable authorities, treat these people as naked, illiterate, wretched savages, destitute of clothes, and without any shelter from the inclemency of the weather; fierce by nature, rude in their manners, unacquainted with the arts, and far removed from civilisation.   Others, following the British history, describe them as a martial, potent, learned, flourishing, and trading nation, well-known in other countries by their commercial and military relations; as a people who possessed a foreign trade, equipped large fleets, sent out powerful armies, and achieved numerous conquests abroad; and who, at home, erected stately edifices, founded large cities, and instituted seminaries of learning, so as to obtain respect from surrounding countries.   This may, and probably is, a picture possessing too little that is real in its general outline; not sufficiently accurate in its figures, and too high and glowing in the colouring.   But, waving the testimony of authorities, which in some respects may be considered doubtful, and adopting as guides reason and experience, it will be readily discerned that the ancient Britons need not be degraded into absolute savages, merely because the Greeks and Romans chose to give them, as they did to all strangers, the contemptuous name of "Barbarians."   There can be no doubt but that the Britons brought with them the knowledge of the arts and sciences, to whatever extent they were possessed by the parent country at the time of their emigration; and these they must have had abundant opportunities of exercising in a country, which could administer little to their subsistence or comfort, without the application of both labour and skill.

> " The ancient Britons are a hardy race,
> Averse to luxury, and slothful ease ;
> Their necks beneath a foreign yoke ne'er bow'd,
> In war unconquered, and of freedom proud ;
> With minds resolved they lasting toils endure,
> Unmixed their language, and their manners pure.
> Wisely does nature such an offspring choose,
> Brave to defend her wealth, and slow to use ;
> Where thirst of empire ne'er inflames their veins,
> Nor avarice, nor wild ambition reigns."—YALDEN.

---

[a] Tacitus describes this spirit of resistance by the emphatic term *pervicacia*," a stubborn immobility of character.

[b] "Anorchfygol" (Invincible).   This was the motto adopted by some of the early princes of Wales.

ROMAN VISITS—ARRIVAL OF JULIUS CÆSAR.

B.C. 55.

ULIUS CÆSAR was prompted either by the insatiate lust of gain, or by the impulse of an unbounded ambition, rather than any desire to serve his country by enlarging her territories, to invade Britain. Rome was in the height of her glory about fifty-five years before the Christian era. At that time Cæsar was so much elated with his conquest of Gaul and other countries, that he resolved upon invading Britain.

The circumstances of the invasion of Britain by Julius Cæsar, as far as they regard the Romans, and are related by himself, are well known. From his narration, it appears that the Britons had frequently sent auxiliaries to Gaul—a measure to which they might have been induced by the connection subsisting between the two countries, in order to repel a foreign power. This alone might have been thought sufficient to induce Cæsar to invade this country; but at this time there was another cause, to which the Triads attributed the hostilities of Cæsar against this country. "Casibelan, enamoured of Flur, the daughter of Mygnach Gorr, finding that she had been carried off by a prince of Gascony, called Mwrchan, and presented to Julius Cæsar, made a descent on Gaul; and having slaughtered 6000 of the Cæsareans,' rescued and brought her back. Cæsar to avenge himself came to Britain." (Triad cii., civ.)

In this expedition his best troops, to the number of 61,000, are said to have accompanied Casibelan [8] into France, of whom very few returned. The strength of the island was therefore considerably diminished, but the spirit of the nation was unimpaired.

According to Dr. Halley's calculations, the Roman army, with their legions and infantry, approached the British shore on board of eighty ships, on the morning of the 26th of August, fifty-five years before the Christian era. Cæsar [9] arrived opposite the cliffs of Dover, about the worst possible point to effect a landing in the face of an enemy; the Britons were not disposed to be friends; and when the Romans looked from their ships, to the steep white cliffs above them, they were astonished to see them covered all over by the armed Britons. Finding that this was not a convenient landing-place, Cæsar resolved to lie by till the third hour (afternoon), in order, he says, to wait the arrival of the rest of his fleet. Some haggard vessels appeared to come up; but the eighteen transports, bearing the cavalry, were no where seen. Cæsar, however, favoured by both wind and tide, proceeded at the appointed hour, and sailing about seven miles further along the coast, prepared to land his forces on an open, flat shore, between Walmer Castle [1] and Sandwich.

[7] The appellation Cæsareans, here, and in some other Triads, given to the Romans, is uncommon, if not peculiar to the Triads.

[8] Caswallon of the Britons, and Cassivellaunus of the Romans.

[9] Cæsar de Bel. Gal., lib. vi., c. 23.

[1] Horsley (Britannia Romana) shows that Cæsar must have proceeded to the north of the South Foreland, in which case the landing must have been effected between Walmer Castle and Sandwich. Others, with less reason, think he sailed southward from the South Foreland, and landed on the flats of Romney Marsh.

c 2

The Britons, in vast bodies, under the command of their brave prince Caswallon (Cassivellaunus), were prepared to receive them, and what with the infantry, cavalry, and their celebrated war-chariots, they made a very imposing and formidable appearance, so much so, that Cæsar himself confesses, that the opposition of the Britons, under the leadership of Cassivellaunus their principal chief, and his brave followers, was a bold one, and that the difficulties he had to encounter were very great on many accounts; but superior skill and discipline, and the employment of military engines on board the war-galleys, to which the British were unaccustomed, and which projected missiles of various kinds, at last triumphed over them, and Cæsar disembarked his two legions. While the Roman soldiers were hesitating to leave their ships, the standard-bearer of the Tenth Legion proved himself worthy to be a Roman citizen. He came forward, and exclaiming

Landing of Julius Cæsar.

with a loud voice, said, " Follow me, my fellow-soldiers, unless you will give up your eagle to the enemy! I at least will do my duty to the Republic and to our general ! " He leaped into the sea as he spoke, and dashed with his ensign among the enemy's ranks. The men instantly followed their heroic leader, and the soldiers in the other ships, excited by the example, also crowded forward along with them. The two armies for some time mixed in combat, but at length the Britons withdrew in disorder from the well-contested beach. As their cavalry was not yet arrived, the Romans could not pursue them, or advance into the island, which Cæsar says prevented his rendering the victory complete. Tacitus, in his Life of Agricola, expressly says, that Cæsar, on this occasion, gave the Romans a view only, and not a possession of Britain.

It is evident that the first descent of Cæsar on Britain, even by his own account, was attended with very little success; by that of Tysilio, which is confirmed by Lucan, he was completely routed in battle; in which, says the former, the mould was drenched with the blood of the slain,

" As it is when the south-wind disorders the snow on the coast of the sea—"

driven to his ships, and obliged to return to France. While he meditated a second descent with forces more adequate to the enterprise, the treachery of a petty chieftain facilitated a success which otherwise he might have sought in vain.[1]

In the following spring Cæsar made a second descent upon Britain, with eight hundred ships. He found the natives here and there prepared to receive him, and perceiving his design, they followed his motions, and sending their cavalry and war-chariots[2] before, marched on rapidly with their main force to oppose his landing.

Many and desperate were the conflicts that ensued. The battle often raged with fury, sometimes one party appeared to have the advantage, sometimes the other. Eventually the Britons retired with precipitation to the woods, and the assailants remained masters of the shore. Winter was approaching; and after a short campaign of three weeks Cæsar hastened back with his legions to Gaul.

When relieved from the second hostile visit of Julius Cæsar, Britain remained free from invasion for the term of ninety-seven years. During this period the island continued nominally tributary to Rome, and an occasional interchange of friendly communications appears to have taken place between the two countries. But the Romans, in their pride of empire, looked with repugnance on an intercourse with any people who were not the slaves of their authority. They often threatened hostility for the purpose of subjugation, and in the year A.D. 43, they commenced a war destined to produce events of a highly important nature in the British annals.

A.D. 43.—In this year Aulus Plautinus, by the command of the Emperor Claudius, led from Gaul into Britain an army of four legions, with their auxiliaries and cavalry. Vespasian (afterwards Emperor) was appointed second in command, and in this situation gave the first proof of his extraordinary talents. If we may credit Suetonius, he fought thirty battles, in all of which he was victorious, and took more than twenty towns.

The Britons, divided by faction, and perhaps not sufficiently aware of the serious intention of the enemy, failed to adopt suitable measures for the defence of their coast. But Caractacus, Togodumnus, and the sons of the deceased King, Cunobeline, assembled their respective subjects, opposed and overcame the Romans in several battles. They afterwards sustained a defeat, and Togodumnus was slain; but the Britons still remained in arms, and offered no proposals of peace or submission.

The Emperor Claudius soon after arrived in Britain, and took the command of the army.

---

[1] This was the defection of Avarwy, nephew of Cassivellaunus, and at this time chief of the Island of Thanet.

[2] The war-chariot, the use of which seems at that time to have been peculiar to the Britons, several times produced tremendous effects on the Romans; this chariot would of itself prove a high degree of mechanical skill, and an acquaintance with several arts. These cars were of various forms and sizes, some being rude, and others of curious and even elegant workmanship. Those most commonly in use, and called *Esseda* or *Essedæ*, by the Romans, were made to contain each a charioteer for driving, and one, two, or more warriors for fighting. They were at once strong and light; the extremity of their axles and other salient points were armed with scythes and hooks for cutting and tearing whatever fell in their way, as they were driven rapidly along. The horses attached to them were perfect in training, and so well in hand, that they could be driven at speed over the roughest country, and even through the woods, which then abounded in all directions. The Romans were no less astonished at this dexterity than at the number of the chariots. The way in which the Britons brought the chariots into action, was this: At the beginning of a battle they drove about the flanks of the enemy, throwing darts from the cars; and, according to Cæsar, the very dread of the horses, and the noise of the rapid wheels, often broke the ranks of his legions. When they had succeeded in making an impression, and had winded in among the Roman cavalry, the warriors leaped from the chariots, and fought on foot. In the meantime, the drivers retired with the chariots a little from the combat, taking up such a position as to favour the retreat of the warriors in case of their being overmatched. "In this manner," says Cæsar, "they perform the part both of rapid cavalry and of steady infantry; and, by constant exercise and use, they have arrived at such expertness, that they can stop their horses when at full speed, in the most steep and difficult places, turn them which way they please, run along the carriage-pole, rest on the harness, and throw themselves back into their chariots with incredible dexterity." For a long time the veteran legions of Rome could not look on the clouds of dust that announced the approach of these war-chariots without trepidation.

He stayed for a short 'time only, but received the submission of several princes, and appointed Aulus Plautinus governor of the new province. Plautinus is reported to have conducted the whole of the war with much success, but his victories do not appear to have advanced the design of the invaders in any material degree.

A.D. 50.—Octavius Scapula was this year named governor of the Roman province in Britain. On his arrival, he found that the most patriotic of the Britons were so far from being in a state of terror and retreat at his approach, that they were engaged in committing acts of devastation on such of the nations as had formed alliances with the Romans. He commenced his administration with equal bravery and policy. He defeated the predatory Britons with considerable slaughter, and, as a means of protecting the province from future incursions, he constructed a chain of forts along the northern border of the province, which appears to have been then formed by the rivers Severn,[4] Upper (or the Warwickshire) Avon, and Nen or Nyne. But an additional measure of precaution adopted by Octavius, that of ordering the inhabitants of every suspected district to surrender their arms, led to a revolt, during which the Iceni, assisted by some neighbouring nations, hazarded a battle, and were defeated.[5]

A.D. 51.—The government of Octavius was of short duration, but prolific of memorable events. The Silures under the command of the renowned Caractacus, made a desperate struggle for their liberties. Even at that early period, the zeal of the Britons for their country's independence was enthusiastic. Their leader, Caractacus, maintained his ground for the space of nine years in the most patriotic manner. Many of his followers bound themselves with an oath to conquer or to die; and, impatient of delay, they defied the attacks of the enemy with shouts that rent the air.

To their natural ferocity, says Tacitus, these people added the courage which they now derived from the presence of Caractacus.[6] His valour and the various turns of his fortune had spread the fame of this heroic chief throughout the island. His knowledge of the country, his admirable skill in the stratagems of war were great advantages; but he could not hope, with inferior forces, to beat a well-disciplined Roman army with their warlike and defensive accoutrements. He therefore retired to the territory of the Ordovices, which included within its limits nearly all North Wales. Having drawn thither to his standard all those who valued British liberty in preference to Roman slavery, he resolved to wait firmly the issue of a battle. According to the great historian, he chose his ground with admirable art. It was rendered straight by steep and craggy hills. In parts, where the mountain opened, and the easy acclivity afforded an ascent, he raised a rampart of massive stones. A river flowed between him and the enemy, and a part of his forces showed themselves in front of his ramparts.

As the Romans approached, the chieftains of the confederate British clans rushed along the ranks, exhorting their men, and Caractacus animated the whole, exclaiming, "This day must decide the fate of Britain. The era of liberty or eternal bondage begins from this hour! Remember your brave ancestors who drove the great Cæsar himself from these shores, and preserved their freedom, their property, and the persons and honour of their wives and children!"

There is a lofty hill in Shropshire, near to the confluence of the rivers Coln and Teme, which is generally believed to have been the scene of the last battle fought by our hero. Its ridges are furrowed by trenches, and still retain fragments of a loose stone rampart; and the hill, for many centuries, has been called by the people, "Caer Caradoc," or the Castle or fortified place of Caradoc, which is the British name for Caractacus. The Roman General, Ostorius, was astonished at the excellent arrangements and spirit he saw displayed. The rolling river, the flinty rampart, the hanging crags, and the high embattled ranks of the enemy presented a succession of obstacles; but he was a Roman, and his troops were impatient to engage. The river was easily passed; but at the ramparts, a long and sanguinary conflict took place. The

---

[4] See Tacitus, and Whittaker's Manchester, vol. ii. p. 529.

[5] See History of Herefordshire, Article "Early Britons."

[6] "When the British hero Caractacus went to battle," says the Triad, "none would stay at home: they followed him freely, and maintained themselves at their own expense. Unsolicited and unsoliciting they crowded to his standard." (Triad LXXIX.) Such was their admiration of his character, on which adversity in the extreme could alone shed greater lustre.

Britons defended themselves with the utmost resolution, and a multitude of the Romans fell. Tacitus says, that the Britons, having neither breast-plates nor helmets, could not maintain their ground, and at length discipline and perseverance prevailed. On the Romans, covered with armour, the sword of the Britons could not make any destructive impression, while death attended every blow struck by a Roman arm. The ramparts were thrown down, and the Britons, after a fierce and glorious resistance, were pursued to their camp on the top of the hill. Despair gave them fresh courage, and in their camp another obstinate stand was made; glory on one side, and unconquerable love of liberty on the other, gave birth to extraordinary feats of valour. The result is well known; Rome once more conquered, and the standard of British liberty fell.

Caractacus himself escaped from the carnage, but his wife and daughter were taken prisoners, and his brothers surrendered. Soon after the battle Caractacus was betrayed; he took refuge with his stepmother, Cartismundua,[7] Queen of the Brigantes, who basely violated the rites of hospitality, and delivered to Ostorius, loaded with chains, the hero who for nine years had arrested the flight of the Roman eagle, and defended his native land. He was carried, with his wife and family, prisoner to Rome.

At the Imperial City this illustrious chief showed to what degree of elevation a great mind can soar. He and his family were sent thither to adorn the triumph of the conqueror, and gratify the curiosity of the Roman populace. All Rome—all Italy, were impatient to gaze on the indomitable Briton, who for so many years had bid defiance to the masters of the world. His name was everywhere known, and he was everywhere received with marked respect. A day was appointed for the British captive to appear before Claudius, and every measure was taken which could heighten the contrast between the victors and the vanquished.

The Emperor and the Empress were seated upon two splendid thrones, and surrounded with senators, guards, and all the apparatus of civil and military pomp; and the infinite multitudes of Rome crowded to be spectators of the scene.

The procession began with the vassals and subjects of Caractacus, and an exhibition of the spoils and trophies taken from the Britons. Next followed the brother of Caractacus, with his wife and daughter, whose tears and abject behaviour formed a striking contrast with the modest but firm and dignified deportment of Caractacus himself. In the presence of Claudius, the friends of the British chief and their families quailed and begged for mercy; while he alone, superior to misfortune, marching with a firm step and an undismayed countenance, approached the tribunal, fixed his eyes on the Emperor, and addressed him in the following emphatic manner:—

" Had the measure of my success been equal to my birth and fortune, I had come to this city as a friend rather than a captive; nor would you have disdained to have received me as an ally, since I am by birth a Prince, and by fortune the chief of many free and warlike nations. My present state is as humiliating to me as it is glorious to you: with these chains you can confine my person, but heaven has given me a mind out of the reach of human power to enslave. I once had horses, men, arms, and riches— was it strange I should be unwilling to part with them? If your ambition aims at universal sway, it does not follow that mankind are all obliged to submit to the yoke. Had I fallen in battle, or sooner been betrayed, neither my misfortune nor your success would at this time have been so renowned. If to defend my life, my liberty, and my country, be a crime, punish me with death, and my misfortunes will end with it. If I am suffered to live, then to future ages I shall remain a monument of your clemency."

Claudius, deeply affected with the behaviour of his noble captive, ordered the chains to be instantly taken off Caractacus and his whole family, and both he and the Empress not only treated them with the greatest kindness, but set them at full liberty.

---

[7] This Cartismundua was Queen of the Brigantes. As the Welsh name of Foeddawg, or Boeddawg in sound, appears to be the British name of Boadicea, some of our most learned authors have confounded this princess with the infamous Cartismundua; but Tacitus plainly enough distinguishes the one from the other; the one being Queen of the Iceni, and the other reigned over the Brigantes.

" Here, brave Caradoc ! the recording Muse,
Thy virtues, conflicts, and thy fall, reviews ;
Thy manly eloquence, thy adverse fate,
The act that made a Claudius *truly great*.
Thine, liberal Roman ! be the hero's fame,
And Britain's muse still venerates thy name :
Pours, with a grateful flow, this verse to thee,
That bade, with generous voice, thy foe be free."

Disastrous as the fate of Caractacus was to Britain at the time, He, whose providence brings good out of evil, made his family, even in their captivity, a blessing to their country. We learn from the ancient British Triads,[*] which contain historical fragments of undoubted authority and credit, though but little known until comparatively late years, that Caractacus, after a war of nine years in opposing the Roman army and in defence of the liberties of his country, was basely betrayed by

Moses and the Prophets.   Apostles.   Bran the Blessed and his Disciples.

First Introduction of Christianity into Britain, from a very Ancient Engraving.

Argwedd Foeddig, the Queen of the Brigantes, and that he, his father Bran, and his wife and family were delivered into the hands of Ostorius, the Roman General, and afterwards carried captive to Rome, about A.D. 52 or 53, where they were detained seven years or more as hostages. At this time the Gospel of Christ was preached at Rome, and Bran, with others of his family, became converts to Christianity, and afterwards a reformer of the manners of his countrymen. His name with the apt epithet "blessed," is therefore joined with those of *Prydain* and *Dyfnwal Moelmud*, as one of the three who healed the discords of the kingdom.—(Triad xxxvi.)

It is a remarkable and interesting fact, that the detention of the British hostages should have been coincident with the Apostle Paul's residence, as a prisoner, at Rome ; and it is a no less remarkable coincidence, that they should be released from confinement in the same year in which St. Paul was

---

[*] The following is a translation of the Triad quoted above : "Bran the Blessed, the son of Llyr Llediaeth, was one of the three blessed sovereigns of the Island of Britain, who first brought faith in Christ to the race of the Cymry from Rome, where he had been seven years hostage for his son Caractacus," &c. (See Triad xxxv.) The family of Bran the Blessed was long distinguished as one of the holy lineages of the Britons.

set at liberty. Caractacus and his family went to Rome A.D. 51, and remained there seven years; Paul was sent there in A.D. 56, and staid there two years. Nothing could be more convenient for St. Paul's mission to the Gentiles than the opportunity which their return must have afforded him; and nothing more probable than that he should embrace so favourable an opportunity of extending the knowledge of Christianity. Be that as it may, however, as Bran and Caradoc, otherwise Brennus and Caractacus, were Welch princes, we may safely conclude that Christianity made its way into Wales as early as into any part of this kingdom. When Bran returned to his native land, some of his family, it is thought, staid behind and settled at Rome. Of these, Claudia,[1] mentioned with Pudens and Linus, (2 Timothy iv. 21), is deemed to have been one, and supposed to be the same with Claudia, the wife of Pudens, upon whose marriage Martial the Poet,[1] composed one of his epigrams. Martial's Claudia was undoubtedly a British lady, as appears by the poet's encomium upon the graces of her person, the honour of which he seems to envy her native isle.

> " Claudia ceruleis cum sit Ruffina Britannis
> Edita, cur Latiæ pectora plebis habet I
> Quale decus formæ ! Romanum credere matres
> Italides possunt, Attides esse suas,"[2] &c.—Lib. ii. Ep. 54.

Besides these, Pomponia Græcina, the wife of Aulus Plautinus, Claudius's lieutenant, and the first Roman Governor of Britain, has been also thought a Briton and a Christian—consequently one of the earliest British Christians. Of her, Tacitus says :—"An illustrious lady, married to Plautius, who was honoured with an ovation (or lesser triumph) for his victories in Britain, was accused of having embraced a strange foreign superstition; and her trial for that crime was committed to her husband. He, according to the ancient law and custom, convened her whole family and relations, and having, in their presence, tried her for her life and fame, pronounced her innocent of anything immoral."[3]

Both Tertullian and Origen speak of Christianity as having made its way into Britain, and they do not represent its introduction as a recent event; so that it may be presumed to have taken place long before their time. The former says, "that there are places among the Britons which were inaccessible to the Romans, but yet are subdued by Christ."[4] The latter says, "The power of God our Saviour is even with them in Britain, who are divided from our world."[5] It was usual with the ancients, long before Origen's time, to speak of Britain as *divided from the world*. Even King Agrippa, according to Josephus, in his speech to the Jews at Jerusalem, about the beginning of the revolt, uses a similar language. Eusebius is more explicit: speaking of the pious labours of the Apostles, he declares that some of them "had passed over the ocean, and preached to those which are called the Britannic Islands." From his connexion with the Imperial Court, and his intimacy with the Emperor Constantius, who was himself a native of Britain, he may well be supposed to have possessed the best information; and as much of his reasoning depends upon the truth of the above allegation, it is natural to presume that he was well assured of the fact. Theodoret, also, another ancient and respectable ecclesiastical historian, expressly names the Britons among the nations whom the Apostles (the fishermen, publicans, and tent-makers, as he calls them) "had persuaded to embrace the religion of Him who was

---

[1] Claudia, according to the decision of the learned Usher, was the daughter of Caractacus; and Taylor, in his Fragment, No. 608, has rendered this highly probable.

[1] Martialis Marcus Valerius, one of the poets of that age, and who was in Rome at that time, speaks of Claudia as a lady of extraordinary beauty and virtue.

[2] This tribute of admiration of the poet, paid to the British matron, is thus imitated by the late learned and Rev. Peter Roberts :—

> "If Claudia's of the woad-stained British race,
> Whence is that lovely form and heavenly face ?

> Why does the Roman and the Grecian dame
> Dispute her birth, and urge a jealous claim ?
> Thus blest, ye Gods, still bless the happy pair,
> And make their offspring your peculiar care.
> Her love his only ; mutual be their will,
> And may her sons* her latest wish fulfil."

[3] Annal., lib. xii., c. 32.
[4] Adv. Judæos, cap. 7.
[5] In Luc., cap. i., Hom. 6.

---

* Epig. lib. iv. 13, lib. xi. 54.

D

crucified." ⁶   To these testimonies may be added that of Gildas, the earliest of our British
historians.   According to him, the Gospel began to be published at the time of the memorable
revolt and overthrow of the Britons under Boadicea (A.D. 60 or 61), and was followed by a long
interval of peace.   Speaking of this revolt, with its disastrous termination and consequences, Gildas

The Druids, or the Conversion of the Britons to Christianity by Bran and his Disciples.

adds, " In the meantime, Christ, the true Sun, afforded His rays, that is, the knowledge of His precepts, to
this island, benumbed with extreme cold; having been at a great distance from the sun, not the sun in the
firmament, but the Eternal Sun in heaven."

   "That St. Paul did go to Britain," says Dr. Burgess, late Bishop of Llandaff, "we may collect from the
testimony of Clemens Romanus, Theodoret, and Jerome, who relate that, after his imprisonment, he
preached the Gospel in the Western parts; that he brought salvation to the islands that lie in the ocean;
and that, in preaching the Gospel, he went to the utmost bounds of the West."   What was meant by the
West, and the islands that lie in the ocean, we may judge from Plutarch, Eusebius, and Nicephorus, who
call the British Ocean the Western; and again from Nicephorus, who says that one of the Apostles went
to the extreme countries of the ocean, and to the British isles; but especially from the words of Catullus
who calls Britain "the utmost island of the West;" and from Theodoret, who describes the Britons as
"inhabiting the utmost part of the West."   When Clement, therefore, says that Paul went to the utmost
bounds of the West, "we do not conjecture," says Calmet, "but are sure, that he meant Britain, not only
because Britain was so designated, but because Paul could not have gone to the utmost of the West

⁶ Tom. iv., serm. 9.   ⁷ Epist., c. 1.

without going to Britain." * It is almost unnecessary, therefore, to appeal to the express testimony of Venantius, Fortunatus, and Sophronius, for the Apostle's journey to Britain.

There is a force in the expression of Clemens Romanus' that is justly appreciated, inasmuch as he repeats his assertion. His words are: "Paul receiveth the reward of his patience. He suffered both in the East and in the West; and having taught the whole world righteousness, and for that end, travelled to the *utmost bounds of the West* . . . . he suffered martyrdom." Had not the writer been well assured of his facts, he would have been contented with his first assertion, "he preached in the West;" whereas, he greatly strengthens this assertion by repetition and addition: "He travelled to the UTMOST BOUNDS OF THE WEST '—a mode of expression rising greatly in energy above the former; and evidently intended to mark out to the reader a determinate, specific, and well-known proposition, as the object of the phrase.

In addition to these facts, we learn that the ancient British Bishops attended the Council of Arles, A.D. 314. We have no proof of their being at the Council of Nice, A.D. 325, but it is recorded that at the Council of Ariminum, A.D. 359, there were four hundred Bishops of the West, and amongst them those of Britain. At the Council of Antioch, A.D. 363, testimony was borne to the orthodoxy of the British Bishops, though the Arian heresy had found its way across the Channel. Both St. Jerome and St. Chrysostom speak often of the orthodoxy of the British Church in their writings.

Their late sanguinary defeat, and the loss of Caractacus, did not break the spirit of the Britons. They fell upon the Romans soon after, broke up their fortified camp, and prevented them from erecting a line of forts across their country. The prefect of the camp, with eight centurions and the bravest of his soldiers, was slain; and, but for the arrival of reinforcements, the whole detachment would have been sacrificed. A foraging-party, and the strong detachments sent to its support, were routed; this forced Ostorius to bring his legions into action; but, even with his whole force, his success was doubtful, and the loss of the Silures very inconsiderable. Continual and most harassing attacks and surprises followed, till at length Ostorius, the victor of Caractacus, sunk under the fatigue and vexation, and expired, to the joy of the Britons, who boasted that, though he had not fallen in battle, it was still their war which had brought him to the grave.

A.D. 52. — Claudius appointed Aulus Didius as Governor of Britain. Before his arrival, Manlius Valens had an engagement with the Silures, in which one legion of the Roman army was entirely cut off.

Veranius succeeded Aulus Didius, but died in less than one year after his arrival, without performing any action worthy of record.

A.D. 57.—Nero succeeded to the Roman Empire, and sent Suetonius Paulinus, an officer of distinguished merit, to Britain. In A.D. 59-61, he revived the spirits of the conquerors. Being well aware that the island of Mona, now Anglesea, was the chief seat of the Druids, and the place of refuge of the defeated British warriors, and of the disaffected generally, he resolved to subdue it. In order to facilitate his approach, he ordered the construction of a number of flat-bottomed boats. In these he transported his infantry over the Menai Straits, while the cavalry were to find their way across, partly by fording and partly by swimming. The Britons added the terrors of their superstition to the force of their arms, for the defence of this sacred island. "On the opposite shore," says Tacitus, "there stood a wildly-diversified host; there were armed men in dense array, and women running among them, who, in dismal dresses and dishevelled hair, like furies, were carrying flaming torches. Around were Druids pouring forth curses; lifting up their heads to heaven, and, by the novelty of their appearance, striking terror into the hearts of the Roman soldiers, who, as if their limbs were paralysed, exposed themselves motionless to the blows of the enemy. At last, roused by the exhortations of their leader, and, stimulating one another to despise a frantic band of women and priests, they made their onset, overthrew their foes, and burnt them in the fires which

---

³ Mr. Taylor's Fragments to Calmet.   ⁹ 1st Epist. Cor., cap. 5.

they themselves had kindled for others. A garrison was afterwards placed there, among the conquered, and the groves, sacred to the cruel superstition, were cut down."

The attack of Suetonius upon the Druids, and the destruction of the groves of Mona, could not fail to exasperate all the British tribes that clung to their ancient worship; besides, there were other recent causes of provocation in particular states. The Roman colonists too freely indulged their avarice and love of plunder. They treated the Britons with cruelty and oppression, drove them from their houses and homes, and looked upon them as slaves and captives. Besides these injuries, Tacitus says that "the Romans introduced priests of their own creed, trained up to their way of thinking, who, with a pretended zeal for religion, devoured the substance of the land."

While Suetonius was thus engaged in Anglesea, a most formidable rebellion broke out among the British tribes under Boadicea, the widowed Queen of the Iceni,[1] who, with her virgin daughters, had been treated with great cruelty and indignity by the Romans.

This warlike princess, like Semiramis and Zenobia, is entitled to be classed among the heroes of the human race. The Romans seized upon the territory left to her by her husband, and because she remonstrated against such an act of injustice and resisted their plunder, they treated her with the utmost barbarity. Catus, the Procurator, caused her to be scourged, her daughters to be violated, and the relations of her deceased husband to be reduced to slavery. These unheard-of wrongs,—the dignity of her birth,—the energy of her character,—drew round Boadicea the disaffected from all parts of the kingdom.

An immense army of daring and devoted adherents rallied round her person and invested her with supreme command. Her dauntless heart swelled within her, and her eyes flashed like those of a tigress, thirsting for blood. Her own subjects were joined by the Trinobantes and the neighbouring states, in all amounting to upwards of 200,000 men. The proudest castles of the Romans were battered down, their most flourishing settlements and colonies were laid waste; the most splendid and opulent seats of their power were reduced to ashes, and 70,000 persons of the enemy, without distinction of sex, or age, or rank, were swept away from the face of the earth.

In a short time Suetonius recruited his army, which was not considerable in point of numbers, though in other respects very formidable, being composed of the bravest, the best armed, and best disciplined troops in the world, under the command of a general of great courage and long experience. When the Britons drew near their enemies and were ready to engage, Boadicea, mounted on a lofty chariot, dressed in royal robes, a spear in her hand, and her two unhappy daughters seated at her feet, drove through the whole army, and addressing herself to each nation, conjured them to fight bravely, and take vengeance on the Romans, for the loss of their own liberties, the stripes inflicted on her person, and the violated honour of her virgin daughters. She encouraged them to hope that Heaven would espouse their cause against their abandoned enemies; she put them in mind of their late victory over the ninth Legion; she desired them to take courage from their own prodigious strength and numbers, whose very shouts were sufficient to confound so weak an enemy, and concluded with declaring "that she, though a woman, was fully determined to conquer or to die; the men, if they pleased, might live and be slaves." On the other hand, the Roman general being sensible that everything depended upon the event of this battle, encouraged his soldiers to despise the clamour and multitude of their enemies, who were ill armed and worse disciplined, and would betake themselves to flight as soon as they felt the edge of their swords. He directed them to keep firm in their ranks, and after they had discharged their javelins to rush upon the enemy with their swords.[2]

The signal for battle being given, the Britons advanced to the charge with dreadful shouts, and poured a shower of darts and arrows upon the enemy. The Romans stood firm, sheltering themselves with eir shields, until the Britons had exhausted all their darts, and advanced within reach of their javelins, which

---

[1] The Iceni inhabited Suffolk, Norfolk, and Cambridgeshire.   [2] Tacit. Annal., lib. xiv., c. 35, 36 ; Xiphilin, ex Dione in Neron.

they discharged with great force. The legions, supported by their auxiliaries, then rushed upon the Britons, with their shields and swords, and their cavalry with their pikes, with such impetuosity and force as bore down all resistance. They procured their victory with the slaughter of 80,000 men. The unhappy Queen would not survive such calamities, but in utter despair put an end to her life by poison.

As no historian has attempted to show where this great battle took place, and where such an immense slaughter and carnage was committed, the author hopes that, though the question at this distant period must be involved in great obscurity, he may be permitted to presume to point out by conjecture the district where such a lamentable catastrophe took place. He knows tolerably well every portion of the Principality, as well as several districts in England, but he knows of no place where so many striking

Boadicea addressing her People.

circumstances and coincidences, are calculated to point out the field of battle where such a tremendous carnage took place, as in the joint parishes of Caerwys, Newmarket, and Llanasa in Flintshire, which are situated within about three miles of Bodfarus, (Bodfarry,) one of the Roman stations in that part of the country.

In support of this conjecture he would remark, in the first place, that in no part of Wales are to be seen such an assemblage of ancient and verdant tumuli[3] as in the above parishes: they are quite

---

[3] We are informed by our venerable and much respected friend, the Rev. H. Parry, Vicar of Llanasa, that the number of large ones may be called twenty-seven, the great mound above Newmarket being the largest, but there are a great quantity of smaller ones.

observable, and their view (particularly the large one above Newmarket,) called Cop Paulinus[4] (Copalini,) must be a high treat to the curious observer, or antiquarian traveller. Those that have been examined are found to contain the remains of a vast quantity of human bones, which, with the soil that covers them, the neighbouring farmers occasionally carry to manure their land. Coins and urns have been discovered in some, which prove them to be sepulchral. The author, when a boy, recollects hearing of one Thomas Jones, of Axton, having digged into one of the tumuli and found an urn full of silver coins, which he disposed of, and with the money received built himself a house; from this circumstance he was called Twm y Pot Coch, or Tom the Red Pot.

The author has been informed by an eye-witness, that on Axton mountain he saw a common spade put down into the earth up to the handle in nought else but a mass of human bones; from this it would appear that a great slaughter took place in the immediate neighbourhood. Not far from the great tumulus above Newmarket there is a place to this day called "Bryn y Saethau," or the Hill of Arrows, probably from being the station of the archers in the engagement. Close to this is "Bryn-y-Lladdfa," or the Hill of Slaughter, a name peculiarly appropriate to the site of a battle. A little below this again is "Pant y Gwae," the Hollow of Woe, and close by is "Bryn y Coaches," the Hill of the War-chariots. In the same parish, and in the immediate neighbourhood, are also the following singularly applicable places to such an event:—"Braich y Dadleu," the Hillock of Contention; "Pwll y Crogwyn," the Hollow of Execution; "Coetia yr Orsedd," the Tribunal Field, and "Pant Erwin," the Hollow of Severity.

Between Newmarket and Mostyn, and not more than half a mile from some of the places alluded to, there is, on a gentle elevation, a very singular antiquated stone cross, or monument, called "Maen Achwynfan," or the Stone of Lamentation. This is of an elegant form and sculpture—is twelve feet high, two feet four inches broad at the bottom, and ten inches thick. Of this piece of antiquity, Mr. Pennant observes:—"I do not presume (after the annotator on Camden has given up the point) to attempt to guess at the age. Only, I must observe, that it must have been previous to the reign of gross superstition among the Welsh, otherwise, the sculptor would have employed his chisel in striking out legendary stories instead of the elegant knots and interlaced work that cover the stone. Those who suppose it to have been erected in memory of the dead slain in battle on the spot, draw their argument from the number of the adjacent tumuli, containing human bones and skulls often marked with mortal wounds; but these earthly sepulchres are of more ancient times than the elegant sculpture of this pillar will admit. The former were only used in Pagan days."

The late learned Edward Lhwyd, in his additions to Camden, calls it "Maen y Chufan," and our friend, the Rev. Henry Parry, one of the best antiquarians we have in Wales, states it to be "a cross erected to St. Chwyfan," the patron saint of Diserth; in the church-yard of which place, as well as that of Newmarket, similar crosses, but of smaller dimensions, are still to be seen. When such high and learned authorities disagree, we must leave the matter undecided, and proceed with our next point.

On the road to Caerwys, (the adjoining parish), are also to be seen a great number of verdant tumuli; and formerly a large unhewn stone, called "Carreg Bedd Buddig," the grave-stone of Buddig or Boadicea, was pointed out to travellers, on which was the following inscription, cut in very rude letters, in Latin, to the following effect:—HIC JACET ERBO . . . OBIT. This stone was used as a gate-post; but the late Mr. Pennant, the historian, had it removed to his seat at Downing, now the residence of Lord Fielding.

A few years ago, a splendid golden torque was found at Bryn Sion, a small farm between Caerwys and Newmarket, such as we are told in history[5] was worn by Queen Boadicea, when she took the command of

[4] Cop Paulinus might have taken its name after Suetonius Paulinus, who commanded the Roman army at the time.

[5] We learn from the historian Dion Cassius, that such an ornament was worn by Boadicea when leading the Britons to battle against the Romans; and taking all circumstances into consideration, the probability is that this valuable and highly interesting antique gem, was worn by the celebrated Amazon herself on that occasion. This ancient decoration is of pure gold, and was purchased from

the Britons, and led them to battle in her war-chariots against Suetonius Paulinus, who commanded the Roman army. These circumstances strongly indicate the fact, that this neighbourhood was the scene of an eventful battle between the Britons and Romans, when, alas, upwards of 60,000 of the former was slain by the latter, and from the surrounding tumuli there cannot be a doubt but these monuments of antiquity were erected as memorials of the dead who were slain in this or some other battle at a very early period.

> "Rest, ye brave dead! 'midst the hills of your sires;
> Oh! who would not slumber when Freedom expires!
> Lonely and voiceless your halls must remain,
> The children of song may not breathe in the chain."—HEMANS.

The Romans were not satisfied with merely depriving the Britons of their lands, but they also imposed upon them a variety of obnoxious taxes, which were exorbitant in their amount, and very arbitrarily collected. It appears that the land and poll taxes were established at this time, and a tax was levied upon the bodies of the dead before they were allowed to be buried, which occasioned great discontent. The famous Boadicea complained bitterly of these taxes in her harangue to the British army before the battle with the Romans under Suetonius.—"Have we not," said she, "been deprived of our most valuable possessions, and do we not pay many heavy taxes for what remains? Besides all the various impositions on our lands and goods, are not our bodies taxed, and do we not pay for the very heads on our shoulders? But why do I dwell on the living, when even the dead are not exempt from their exactions? Do you not all know how much we are obliged to pay for the bodies of our departed friends? Those who are subject to other nations are subject only for life, but such is the exquisite tyranny and insatiable avarice of the Romans, that they extort taxes even from the dead." [6]

Though much weakened by the defeat they had sustained under Boadicea, the Britons still remained in arms; and, about the end of this year, or in the early part of A.D. 62, Suetonius was finally recalled. Between the date of his recall and the commencement of the reign of the Emperor Vespasian, the successive governors of Britain were named *Petronius Turpilianus; Trebellius Maximus*; and *Vectus Bolanus*. They all passed their time in inactivity, which must be attributed chiefly to the distracted state of politics at Rome.

The comparative tranquillity of the Britons terminated soon after the accession of Vespasian to the imperial throne. *Petilius Cerealis* was the first governor appointed by this Emperor; and in the year 72 or 73, the Romans, under his command, made war upon the numerous and powerful tribe of the Brigantes, which they subdued after several sanguinary battles.

Julius Frontinus, who succeeded to the government in the year 75, carried the Romans against the Silures, an enemy difficult of conquest, from the situation of the country, and from their native valour and love of liberty. This brave nation, which had often been the foremost in opposing the invader, was at length compelled by Frontinus to submit to the Roman power.

A.D. 79.—Titus Vespasian, being Roman Emperor, sent his deputy, *Julius Agricola*, into Britain.

A bright era now occurs in the annals of the Roman connection with Britain. The sword had hitherto been used as the undisguised instrument of ambition and avarice; but at this time, a man, no less renowned for his military talents than for his wisdom and humanity, arrived in this island, who

---

the farmer who found it while ploughing, by the late Marquis of Westminster, for 400*l.*, and it is now carefully preserved in a glass case at Eaton Hall, by its present noble proprietor, who values it above price. There is another golden torque at Mostyn Hall, the seat of the Hon. E. M. Ll. Mostyn, M.P., which was found in the neighbourhood of Harlech in 1692 (See Camden). We are told that the Welsh Prince Aneurin, who flourished in 540, and who bore such a conspicuous part at the Battle of Cattraeth, with others, wore similar torques on that occasion. The privilege of wearing the golden torque was limited to those only who were distinguished by the highest rank of valour. Nor was the practice confined to the ancient warriors of this country; they were worn by the chieftains of Gaul. The custom was also common to other nations; we find by the prophet Daniel, v. 7, that a chain of gold was a mark of high rank in Babylon. It is also alluded to in the Song of Solomon, i. 5.

[6] If the calculations of Lipsius concerning the Roman revenues be true, they would amount to no less than two millions sterling annually. They were so great that they enabled generals to assume the imperial purple with great dignity, without any other income.

permanently secured the various triumphs of the Roman arms, by introducing the arts of polished life among the Britons, and by teaching them to forget the opprobrium of subjugation while emulous of imitating the manners of their conquerors. Julius Agricola was fortunate in having his actions recorded by *Tacitus*, one of the most eloquent historians of antiquity; famous in adding a large part of Britain to the map of the empire; and glorious in the clemency of his administration. Agricola extended the Roman Empire in Britain beyond all his predecessors. He equally divided the importation of corn; he instituted many good laws, and caused the youth of Britain to be educated in the liberal arts, and had a peculiar excellency in the science of fortification. He was recalled from Britain in A.D. 85. We have seen that he considerably extended the geographical boundaries of the Empire, and, by the mildness and wisdom of his government, he laid the foundation of a permanent obedience to the Roman sway in the south of Britain, now termed England. From the time of his administration is to be dated a great alteration in the manners of the inhabitants of this district. Roman learning, customs, and fashions met with favour amongst the conquered, and the adoption of these produced a sociality of intercourse, and a growing unity of interests. While Agricola held command in Britain, three successive Emperors filled the throne of Rome: *Vespasian, Titus,* and *Domitian.* He was succeeded in the government of the British province by *Sallustius Lucullus,* of whom little is said, but that he invented a lance of a new form, and that he was put to death by the tyrant Domitian, for bestowing on his weapon the name of the "Lucullian Lance."

Hadrian succeeded to the imperial power, on the death of Trajan, in the year 117. *Julius Severus* was governor of Britain in the early part of his reign, and was succeeded by *Priscus Licinius.* The Emperor visited Britain in person, but not for the purpose of extending the limits of the province by force of arms. His chief object in personally exploring this, in conjunction with other provinces of the Empire, was in order to make such a careful examination into the state of civil and military affairs, as might assist in preserving peace on a secure basis. In pursuit of this noble object, he caused a wall of earth to be raised, as an additional defence of the south and conquered part of Britain against its northern and unsubdued neighbours. This rampart extended from the mouth of the Tyne on the east to the Solway Frith on the west, nearly occupying the line of Agricola's first chain of forts.[7]

In the reign of *Antoninus Pius,* which commenced A.D. 138, *Lollius Urbicus* was Governor of Britain. He was an able general, and one who was compelled by circumstances to exercise his talents with activity. The Caledonians in the vicinity of Hadrian's wall provoked a war, and Lollius, after having, in several engagements, defeated the Mætæ, a tribe which inhabited the level country near the wall, built a strong rampart farther towards the north, which extended from the Frith of Forth to the Clyde.

Similar commotions on the borders of the wall occurred in the reign of the succeeding Emperor, *Marcus Aurelius Antoninus,* but they were quelled, without great difficulty, by his lieutenant, *Calpurnius Agricola;* and the south of Britain happily remained in a state of tranquillity, the inhabitants intermingling with the Romans by slow but sure degrees, and gradually adopting their arts and manners.

Pertinax, who was afterwards Emperor, was sent to Britain for the purpose of redressing some grievances, but he met with great difficulties in restoring quiet and discipline among the tumultuous soldiery; he, at length, in some measure succeeded, and then resigned the government, as is believed, to *Clodius Albinus,* who possessed this command during the latter part of the reign of Commodus, and throughout the two following short and troubled reigns.

On the death of the Emperor *Didius Julianus,* this general ventured to contend for the diadem. He assumed in Britain the insignia of empire, and led an army, consisting of British Romans and Romanised Britons, to the Continent, where he hazarded a battle, but was defeated, and subsequently destroyed himself in despair, thus leaving *L. Septimus Severus* in undisputed possession of the throne.

---

[7] In a note on the Itinerary of Richard Cirencester (Mr. Hatcher's edition, p. 52), it is judiciously observed that this rampart of earth was evidently nothing more than a line, intended to obstruct the passage of an enemy between the stations, which constituted the real defences of the frontier.

A.D. 182.—During the reign of Commodus the Emperor, Lucius, a king in some part of Britain (and the first Christian King in Europe we read of), received the Christian faith, and this nation was the first that by public authority professed it. He was tributary to the Romans, and was the son of Lles ap Coel (King Coelus), who built Colchester, and was great grandson to King Arviragus, who married the Emperor Claudius's daughter. This King Lucius altered the three Arch-Flamens and twenty-eight Flamens into so many Archbishopricks and Bishopricks. The Archbishopricks were London, York, and Caerlleon in Wales. The heathen temples were all destroyed, and privileges and means were granted to sacred places then erected.

About the year 207, the Emperor Severus repaired to Britain in person; at that time he was aged and afflicted with disease, but he entered on the war with alacrity, for the love of military glory lent a youthful ardour even to his latest exertions. In the present undertaking, he is said to have been additionally stimulated by a wish for removing from the dissolute pleasures of Rome his two sons *Caracalla* and *Geta*. Both these princes attended him in his expedition, and the events of this imperial visit are of considerable weight and value in the annals of Roman operations in Britain.

Severus deputed the government of South Britain to *Geta*, his youngest son, and proceeded against the allied northern nations at the head of a formidable army. He passed the wall of Hadrian, and, notwithstanding the natural difficulties presented by the country, and the pernicious opposition of the enemy, who declined meeting him in the open field, but often decoyed his troops into destructive ambushes, he penetrated into the heart of Caledonia, and compelled the inhabitants to sue for peace, which was granted to them only on condition of their relinquishing a portion of territory, and delivering up their arms.

After concluding this peace, Severus marched his army into the northern parts of the Roman province; and it was now that he carried into execution a great and memorable work, some vestiges of which still remain to proclaim his activity, perseverance, and grandeur of design. Convinced of the inefficacy of Hadrian's rampart of earth, he employed the soldiers in erecting a wall of solid stone, defended by numerous stations for the residence of garrisons, massive towers for the annoyance of assailants, and intervening watch-turrrets, in which sentinels continually kept guard. This wall ran nearly parallel with Hadrian's rampart, at a small distance towards the north, and was in height fifteen feet, and eight or nine feet in breadth. Its length was rather less than seventy-four Roman miles, and the whole of this stupendous work, the greatest effort of Roman skill in Britain, is believed to have been completed in two years.[s] Severus died at York, in 211.

A.D. 211.—The Emperor Antoninus Caracalla concluded a peace with the Britons, took hostages, and returned to Rome.

A.D. 282.—Marcus Aurelius Carus being Emperor, sends his deputy, Carausius, into Britain, who made a peace with Maximus (Dioclesian's adopted son), and kept it until he was overthrown by Constantius Chlorus. He was afterwards assassinated by Alectus.

A. D. 287.—Dioclesian being Emperor, sends Alectus into Britain to quiet the commotions there, who, after three years' reign was killed by Asclapiodatus, Duke of Cornwall, and one of Constantius Chlorus's captains, and many thousand Romans with him. This Dioclesian was a great persecutor of the Christians, for in his time was St. Alban, the proto-martyr of England, beheaded at Holmehurst, now St. Albans; Aaron and Julius suffered at Leicester; and about 1000 Christians at Lichfield.

Dioclesian and Maximian resigned the imperial dignity about the year 290, and were succeeded by their Cæsars, *Constantius* and *Valerius*. On the partition of government which followed this occurrence, Britain was allotted to *Constantius*, who resided in this island for many years.

---

[s] For a statement of many contradictory opinions with regard to the history of the wall attributed to Severus, the reader is referred to the Beauties of Northumberland, pp. 2—7. This famous wall reached from the German Ocean to the Irish Sea. It was eighty miles long. One of our ancient Bards notices this rampart thus :—

" Gorug Severus waith Cain
   Yn drais draws Ynys Brydain
   Rhag gwerin gythrawl, gwawl-fain."

A.D. 291.—Constantius Chlorus relieved Britain in an expedition against the Scots. He afterwards married the fair Helena,[*] by whom he had a son, Constantine the Great, who succeeded his father in 312. He was at the city of York at the time of his father's death; and he there commenced his bright and auspicious reign, a memorable epoch in the history of Europe at large.

When these contests were terminated by the submission of the refractory tribes, a general peace prevailed through the provinces for the remainder of Constantine's reign. The blessings of this tranquil era were incalculably augmented by the aid which the governing power afforded to the cause of Christianity, and, through that medium, to an improvement in the morals and manners of the Britons.

Constantine is said to have been the first Christian Emperor, as Lucius was the first Christian King. Ancient Britain glories in the honour of the birthright of them both. In his time the first general council of Nice against Arius the heretic, took place; it was proclaimed by him, and was attended by 318 bishops. In 314 he called another council at Arles in France, to which he sent the Archbishops of London, York, and Caerlleon in Wales. Constantine died on the 22nd of May.

After the death of this successful ruler, the provinces of the empire were divided between his three sons, Constantine, Constans, and Constantius. Britain, together with Gaul, Spain, and part of Germany, became the portion of Constantine, the eldest of these princes; but he was dissatisfied with the arrangement and entered upon active hostilities, and in 340 he invaded the territories of his brother Constans, where he fell into an ambush and was slain.

Constans then seized on his dominion, and thus obtained the government of the whole western provinces. He passed into Britain in the year 343, for the purpose of chastising the Scots and Picts, who had renewed their depredations to the south of the wall. Firmicus celebrates this voyage of Constans from Gaul to Britain in the following words:—" In winter (which never had been nor will be done again) your oars triumphed over the swelling, furious waves of the British ocean." Constans, who had committed many acts of tyranny, was murdered on the continent in A.D. 350, by Magnentius, who, in the month of August A.D. 353, destroyed himself at Lyons.

The whole of the Roman empire then fell under the sway of Constantius, who deputed the administration of affairs in Britain to several successive governors. The only military occurrences of this reign, in which the British provinces were implicated, relates to incursions of the Scots and Picts. Some formidable irruptions of these people took place in the year 360. Julian, termed the Apostate, who was afterwards Emperor, was then intrusted with the government of the western part of the empire; and during his short reign the inhabitants of South Britain remained free from any serious disturbance.

A.D. 367.—Theodosius was appointed governor of Britain, and his conduct in this high office was equally applauded by the imperial court and by the tributary inhabitants. Theodosius quitted Britain in A.D. 369, honoured with the approbation of the Emperor, and rewarded by the blessing of the people to whom he was so eminent a benefactor; for he had corrected many abuses in the mode of collecting taxes, and materially improved the internal polity and condition of the province.

A profound tranquillity prevailed in Britain for several years subsequent to the departure of the last general. This was interrupted by an event, the ill effects of which were felt by the inhabitants for many successive ages. This took place in the year 379, and was caused by Gratian, the son of Valentinian. In A.D. 381, Maximus, whose valour was well known to the natives, assumed the purple in this island; he had married the daughter of a British chief, and was in other respects so acceptable to the nation, that they warmly attached themselves to his cause. He made his son by the British lady whom he had married his partner in the imperial purple; and thus bound the Britons, who now first appear with distinction in a

---

[*] Constantine was the son of Constantius, by Helena, the first wife of that emperor. Many writers assert that Helena was a native of Britain; some suppose her to be the daughter of a British king, and others that she was of mean origin, and was mistress of Constantius. Several of these writers affirm that her illustrious son Constantine, was also born in Britain; but it may be observed that neither of the above assertions is corroborated by the testimony of contemporary authors. See these questions amply discussed in Morant's History of Colchester, B. i. p. 28—34.

martial character under the Roman standard, still more closely to the interests of his family. The prosperity of Maximus, however, was only short-lived. He experienced two signal defeats, and was put to death by Theodosius, son of the general of that name who obtained great renown in Britain.

The Britons were not present at the two engagements which decided the fortune of their chosen leader, having been sent into Gaul, under the conduct of Victor, their youthful countryman; but they were speedily attacked, and were defeated with the loss of their general. In this calamitous situation, in a foreign country, exposed to a triumphant enemy, and without ships to convey them home, the fugitive adventurers were so fortunate as to meet with a friendly reception in Armorica, where considerable numbers settled, and their descendants continue to this day[1] to resemble the Welsh both in language and manners.

Immediately after the death of the Emperor Maximus, such a scene of confusion succeeded in the imperial affairs, that it would occupy too much room to attempt a brief discussion of the discordant accounts given by writers,[2] respecting the revolutions and consequent devastations which happened at that eventful period. The Romans were miserably harassed on all sides by the surrounding barbarians; and the Britons, unable to derive their usual protection from the legionary troops, shared a similar fate. At the period when the invaders bade a final adieu to this island, the country was exposed to the inroads of numerous enemies. Assailed on the north by the Picts and Scots, it was equally invested by the Irish on the west. The native strength of the country had been exhausted in the support of foreign wars; the number of its inhabitants further diminished by famine and pestilence; and the grand bulwark of its safety, the navy, was fallen into decay. Under these disadvantages, the people were also in want of that unanimity so essential to become powerful in times of emergency. They had recourse to their ancient form of government, and elected for their governors certain reguli, or chieftains; but those princes, instead of uniting to oppose the common enemy by well-concerted plans of co-operation, and to ward off the impending danger by combined force, were principally occupied in securing their separate interests. It has been remarked by a very judicious writer,[3] that the great source of the misfortunes which happened to the Britons, was the political error committed by the Romans in not making an entire conquest of the island. This had been the design of Julius Agricola, and if Domitian had suffered him to have effected what he was very near accomplishing, then would the Romans, at their departure, have left the whole of the inhabitants in a similar, or better condition than what they found them in; as of course, by reverting to their aboriginal constitution, they would have been united under one supreme monarch, or Pendragon; and being free from intestine divisions they would have found their united strength sufficient to repel the attempts of invasion, by any foreign enemy. But enervated by luxury, and weakened by dissensions, they found themselves in a worse state, as to self-defence, than on the arrival of Julius Cæsar. In this sad situation, without union, order, or discipline, and attacked on all sides by inveterate foes, through infatuation or despair, they adopted the most impolitic of all expedients for national safety, that of calling in the assistance of one barbarous nation to drive out another, which quickly, in the sequel, subjected them to a new and heavier yoke.

Of the melancholy effects which took place during those times of confusion and trouble, the British historians, Gildas and Nennius (indisputable authorities),[4] give ample testimony; and their narratives are

---

[1] The New Testament has lately been printed in the Breton language, which any one well acquainted with the Welsh language will be able to read with little difficulty.

[2] Zosimi Historia, lib. vi.; Gildas, Historia de Excidio Britanniæ; Bede, Historia Ecclesiast., lib. i.

[3] Stillingfleet's Origines Britannicæ.

[4] In the leading particulars of their narration of the affairs of this period, they are followed by Camden and by several modern writers, amongst whom may be noticed Dr. Henry; but Mr. Turner, in his History of the Anglo-Saxons, dissents from the propriety of an appeal to the "querulous Gildas," and takes a very different view of the affairs of this important era. According to Mr. Turner,[*] the Britons were so far from renewing a timid allegiance to Honorius,

[*] We are informed that Mr. Turner was supplied by our late learned countryman, Dr. Owen Pugh, with some very curious and authentic information on this portion of our history from ancient Welch MSS. Poems, the works of the early bards, never before published, and which would enable him to give an independent and impartial statement.

not simply relations, but pictures of the period, drawn by men who depict as though they have been eye-witnesses, and seem to speak of the different scenes as though they had both seen and felt, and that in language correspondent to the circumstances they relate.

The progressive advantages derived by the Britons from intermixture with their polished invaders, are unquestionable, although, as a nation, they were subject to some humiliation, and to many penalties. We view, indeed, in every step, the progress of mind of the conquering legions; and whilst contemplating so attractive a picture, subjugation itself loses all deformity of aspect.

Inspired by the lessons and example of the Romans, the inhabitants of the more inland districts applied themselves to agriculture, and so successful were their efforts that Britain soon exported annually large quantities of corn, and assisted greatly in supplying with grain the Roman armies on the Continent.

The progress of agriculture was followed by the establishment of manufactures; and commerce received a new and powerful impulse. Fresh ports were opened; and the Briton was roused from his inactivity, and taught to turn to advantage the great natural resources of his country. Induced by precept and example to prefer social interchange to sullen and ferocious seclusion, he quitted, by slow degrees, his gloomy solitude, and began to enjoy the pleasures of civilised society. The city arose on the site of dark woodland huts; and the Briton was courted even by his conquerors to become its inmate. The Roman language, with its stores of literary treasure, was imparted to the rude natives; and thus, with a suddenness almost unprecedented in the annals of nations, ignorance and superstition gave way to sound learning and philosophy. With the literature of the conquerors was introduced a relish for the elegant indolence of the portico and the bath; a fondness for delicate attire; and a love of the refinements and pleasures of society.

These rapid improvements in art and science were necessarily productive of a striking change in the general face of the country. Large tracts of land were cleared of their unprofitable burthen of thickly matted trees; and the thriving towns and villages were rendered easy of communication by lines of solid roads, formed on the model of those great military highways which, under the guidance of the Romans, were made to intersect the island in various directions—the most distinguished vestiges of this important era.[5] The first remove from an extreme rudeness of Divine worship, was quickly succeeded by the introduction of Christianity. The enlightening beams of this beneficent religion were communicated to Britain before the close of the first century. Their diffusion, however, was gradual, and the poverty of the early Christians debarred them from adorning the country with edifices proportional in splendour to their religious zeal.

The Roman territories in Britain for more than one hundred and fifty years made only one province, but about the beginning of the third century they were divided into two provinces by the Emperor Severus.[6] At length, when the authority of the Romans extended over all that part of this island, which lies south of the wall between the firths of Forth and Clyde; the whole country was divided into five provinces, of whose names, situations, limits, and inhabitants, it may be proper to give the following brief account :—

I.—FLAVIA CÆSARIENSIS. This province extended over the whole breadth of the island, where it is broadest, from the Land's End in Cornwall, to the South Foreland in Kent, and was bounded on the south by the English Channel; on the north by the Bristol Channel, the Severn and the Thames. It comprehended the present counties of Cornwall, Devonshire, Dorsetshire, Somersetshire, Hampshire, Wiltshire, Berkshire, Surrey, Sussex, and Kent.[7]

II.—BRITANNIA PRIMA. This province was bounded on the south by the Thames; on the east by the British Ocean; on the north by the Humber; and on the west by the Severn; and comprised the

after the death of Constantine, that, "in this extremity, they displayed a magnanimous character; they remembered the ancient independence of the island and their brave ancestors, who still lived enrolled in the verses of their Bards; they armed themselves, threw off the foreign yoke, deposed the imperial magistrates, proclaimed their insular independence, and with the successful valour of youthful liberty and endangered existence, they drove the fierce invaders from their cities."

[5] Roman Roads.   [6] Herodian, lib. iii., c. 24.
[7] See the Map of Britain according to the "Notitia."

present counties of Gloucester, Oxford, Buckingham, Bedford, Herts, Middlesex, Essex, Suffolk, Norfolk, Cambridge, Huntingdon, Northampton, Leicester, Rutland, Lincoln, Nottingham and Derbyshire.[8]

III.—BRITANNIA SECUNDA. This province was bounded on the south by the Bristol Channel, and the Severn; on the west by St. George's Channel; on the north by the Irish Sea; and on the east by Britannia Prima. This province contained the countries of the Carnavii, Silures, Demetæ, and the Ordovices, which are now Warwickshire, Worcestershire, Staffordshire, Cheshire, Herefordshire, Radnorshire, Breconshire, Monmouthshire, Glamorganshire, Carmarthenshire, Pembrokeshire, Cardiganshire, Montgomeryshire, Merionethshire, Caernarvonshire, Denbighshire, and Flintshire.

IV.—MAXIMA CÆSARIENSIS. This province was bounded on the south by the Humber; on the east by the German Ocean; on the west by the Irish Sea; and on the north by the wall of Severus; and embraced the countries of Parisi and Brigantes, which are now the counties of York, Durham, Lancaster, Cumberland, and Northumberland.

V.—VALENTIA. This was the most northerly province of the Romans in Britain. It was erected A.D. 369, by the victorious general Theodosius, and called Valentia, in honour of the Emperor Valens. This province contained all that extensive tract of country which lay between the walls of Severus and Antoninus Pius, and was inhabited by several British nations, which, besides their particular names, were called by the general name of Macatae.

Eventually this great Empire, the mistress of the world, exhibited symptoms of decay; its sun was about to go down in darkness. Rome was no longer the envy of the surrounding nations; and nothing can be clearer than that she had well earned her recompense. She had drained that cup of intoxication which, if it but touch the lips, is seen to fill the heart with alternate foolishness and frenzy. Her recovery became hopeless. The enemy was at the gate, and she was torn by intestine feuds. The people were turbulent and intractable; her rulers were unprincipled and vacillating; the bonds and relations of society were broken. In this desperate state of things the Emperors felt themselves obliged to withdraw the military from the remoter districts.

Though the Romans, by means of their distinguished generals, and through the bravery of their soldiers, had conquered and given laws to distant kingdoms, the time was near at hand, when they themselves were to experience that humiliation, which they had so constantly imposed on others. Being obliged to recal their legions from Britain to defend their own capital, this island was restored to its ancient privileges and freedom. Though, however, it enjoyed the name of liberty, it did not possess the means of preserving it, inasmuch as the great majority of the youths of Britain, capable of bearing arms, had been induced to follow the fortunes of the Romans, and fight their battles to the neglect of their own country.

Time after time the Roman legions were called from Britain to fight the imperial battles of Gaul; and on each of these occasions they took with them detachments of young British soldiers, whom they had studiously trained to the art of war. Thus the Roman forces in this country gradually decreased; and about the middle of the fifth century they quitted the island never to return.[9]

It is the opinion of Mr. Turner, that Britain never was subject to Rome after the year 410: yet he seems to admit that application might have been made to the Romans for assistance from some particular districts; and we may indeed conceive that all the country was not of the same sentiment with respect to the dependence on Roman authorty, and having recourse to Roman aid.

If the Britons of the province had now acted their part well, they had it in their power to become a happy and flourishing people, but mutual jealousies and discord disturbed them incessantly; and this was one great reason that they had no well-concocted plans of defence, and were so liable to be overrun by the barbarians from the north.

It is supposed, by writers best entitled to credit, that the Romans finally quitted Britain in the year

---

[8] Hist. Brit. Rom., p. 480.

[9] Bishop Stillingfleet makes the first supplies to have been sent between the death of Maximus and the year 407, the second in the year 425, and the third in the year 443.

of the Christian era 446, which was five hundred and one years after their first descent upon the island, and four hundred and three years after their first settlement in the country.[1]

The Britons were now left to the management of their own affairs, to their own councils, and to their own protection and defence. In a few years, every trace of the Roman administration had vanished away; and all the provinces which had belonged to the Roman empire were divided among a multitude of petty princes, chiefly British, but in part of Roman origin, who, being dignified with the title of Kings, were haughty in proportion to their power, and dared to believe themselves great enough to be released from the bonds of humanity and justice.

As soon, therefore, as the Roman troops were withdrawn, the Britons became unable to defend themselves. The Picts and Scots, taking advantage of this helpless condition, made frequent invasions of their dominions, and pursued their ravages with increased barbarity. At last, harassed with these repeated incursions, we find that very people, who had so bravely held out against the Roman valour, begging in the most humiliating strains to exchange freedom once more for protected servitude. "The Barbarians," say they in their petition, "drive us to the sea, the sea again back to the Barbarians; thus bandied between two deaths we either perish by the sword or by water."

In the course of one of these incursions, which took place in the year 448, the Picts and Scots extended their ravages as far as Mold, in Flintshire, where, at that time, the two Bishops Garmon and Lupus (who, about two years before, had been sent to this country to confute the Pelegian heresy) were teaching[2] and baptising the British[3] Christians every Easter week.

Tradition informs us that the prelates, being apprised of the enemy's approach, placed themselves at the head of their disciples, whom they were now about to lead in their temporal as well as their spiritual warfare—the Britons being more disposed to rely on the prayers of these holy men, and to follow their councils, than to confide in their own valour. The Welsh do not seem to have made any preparation to oppose their invaders, in a hostile way; the enemy were aware of this, and designed to fall upon them whilst they were engaged in their religious exercises, and preparing to celebrate Easter, according to the usual practice of the Church at that time.[4] The Christian army, wet with their recent baptism in the River Alun, were led by their holy commanders against the Pagan host. Germanus instructed them to attend to the word he gave, and repeat it. Accordingly, he pronounced the word *Hallelujah.*[5] His soldiers caught the sacred sound, and repeated it with such ecstatic force, that the hills, re-echoing with the cry, struck horror into the enemy, who were seized with a sudden panic, as if heaven was about to pour down vengeance upon them for attempting to violate the devout exercise of the Christians; for it appeared to their terrified imaginations that the rocks and mountains were ready to fall upon and overwhelm them. The depredators threw down their arms, and fled on all sides. The British pursued, and left but few alive to relate the dismal story. Many of the fugitives, in their confusion, were drowned in the River Alun, which they had to cross, and many perished by the sword. Such is the relation given by "Constantius of Lyons," who wrote the life of St. Germanus, within thirty-two years after the death of the saint; and the ancient narrative adds: "Thus the Britons obtained a bloodless victory, won by faith, and not by force of arms."

---

[1] See some conclusive remarks on this subject in Whittaker's History of Manchester, 4to ed., vol. ii., and Horsley's Britannia Romana, p. 75.

[2] In the Book of Llandaff, as referred to by Bishop Usher, p. 182. It appears that the British Church had frequently sent over to France to implore the assistance of their brethren previous to the coming over of Garmon and Lupus, which is a proof that they were in possession of the knowledge of divine truth long before that time.

[3] Garmon not only established schools, where the youths were taught astronomy and geometry, and other sciences agreeable to the learning of those ages, but furnished the Churches with pastors, and regulated the exercise of public worship by presenting the British Christians with proper forms of doctrines according to the usage of the Gallican Church, and which are, in a great part, retained to the present age, in the liturgy of the established Church of England. The last named circumstance is worthy of the regard of those who are too forward in attributing all forms of prayer to a popish origin.

[4] The early British churches were founded at a time when the Britons were not in communion with the Church of Rome, and before the practice of dedicating to Saints according to the usual mode had become customary.

[5] Brit. Eccles. Antiquitates, 335; Paulinus Diaconus, lib. xv. c. 12, and Bede, lib. i. c. 20, describes the action.

We can easily conceive that a superstitious people would impute this singular victory to the extraordinary interposition of the Almighty, and that they esteemed their leader, like Gideon, to be armed with celestial power. But the mind, at the present period, not seeing objects through the medium of either superstition or enthusiasm, will conclude this event to have arisen out of natural causes, always under the direction of Divine Providence. The invaders, it is possible, from the nature of the outcry, might suspect an ambush, or that the number of the Britons was increased : besides, the mind of man, in an uncultivated state, is liable to fears the most sudden, absurd, and contagious. *Maes Garmon*, which takes its name [6] from this celebrated victory, lies near Rhual, the seat of Colonel Phillips (one of the heroes of Waterloo). It is situated about a mile from Mold, Flintshire. Nehemiah Griffith, one of his ancestors, erected a column to commemorate this remarkable event, on which he placed a Latin inscription. The following is a translation :—

A D 420.[7]
The Picts & Saxons with united force,
made War against the Britons in this Valley,
to this Day call'd Mæs Garmon.
When the Host descended to the Battle,
Garmon & Lupus being Apostolic Generals of
the Britons,
And Christ . . . present in yᵉ Camp,
They shouted Hallelujah, Hallelujah, Halᵇ.
Terror discomfits the hostile Troop :
The Britons triumph :
Their Enemies being destroy'd without blood⁴:
A Victory gain'd by Faith & not by force of Arms.
N.   G.
In memory of th. Halleluᵇ. Vict'ry erectᵈ. this Monᵗ.

---

[6] It bore that name in the age of Archbishop Usher, as he informs us, and the learned primate was much struck with the coincidence.

[7] The date of this battle seems to have been agreed upon both by Mr. Griffith and Mr. Pennant, who each fix it in 420. Matthew of Westminster, says expressly that it took place in 448, p. 152—154. In Rymer, vol. i. p. 443, it is said to have taken place in the year 447.

SAXON VISITS.—ARRIVAL OF HENGIST AND HORSA, A.D. 449.

E have now to contemplate new scenes and new transactions, in consequence of the arrival of the Saxons and Angles in this island. They landed here first as auxiliaries to the Britons; they afterwards became their enemies, then their masters, and ultimately their friends, after they had established their dominion over the most important as well as the largest portion of Britain, and imposed their own laws and language on the inhabitants. "All this fulfilled the purposes of Divine Providence, who sees the final result of all things; the land was first to undergo a severe scourge from internal conflicts, and the dreadful concomitants of war, until in the end, the general happiness shall be effected thereby in the fulness of time."

At the period of which we are now speaking, A.D. 449, Britain was torn asunder by factions which contended for superiority. At the head of one of these was Vortigern, a weak and luxurious prince. During these contentions, the Picts and Scots made another expedition, and desolated the country wherever they went. Vortigern was clamorous for foreign aid. He wished to have a force at his command that would enable him to repel not only the foreign enemy, but also to overawe those princes who were hostile to his claims. He sought a universal sway over his countrymen, but the great body of the people were desirous of raising to the supreme authority a prince endowed with great abilities, and full of youthful ardour, named Aurelius Ambrosius, whom, therefore, Vortigern viewed with considerable jealousy.

At this juncture, three Saxon *cyules*, or small ships, arrived² off the coast full of armed men, under the command of two leaders, Hengist and Horsa. They were asked, "what was their object, whence they came, what were their tribes and their country?" Hengist and Horsa made reply, that they had been exiled from their native shores; and that, in obedience to a domestic law, which enacted, that when there was a superabundance of population, the youths should decide by lot who should emigrate, they had become the necessary exiles.

Whether the Council of Vortigern preceded this event, or whether it was in consequence of it that he proposed accepting the aid of these foreigners, is uncertain, but be that as it may, their admission into the kingdom was approved of, and the Isle of Thanet³ was the place assigned for them. It was agreed that they were to fight¹ the enemies of the Britons, to receive the necessary supplies, and that their valour should be rewarded by an assignment of teritory for their future residence. It is hardly to be supposed that the nation

---

² The year in which Hengist arrived is contested. The authorities for A.D. 449 preponderate. See Langhorne's Chronicon, p. 5, and Usher's Primord., p. 401.

⁹ Hengist begged as much ground of King Vortigern as the hide of an ox would compass, which being easily granted, the hide was cut into thongs, which took in so much ground, that a fort was built upon it, called Thong Castle, where Hengist settled himself.

¹ "From the British evidence," says Sharon Turner, "I have made the arrival of the Saxons not in consequence of invitation. Many foreign writers sanction me; among others, Freculphus, Chron. t. 2, lib. v., c. 16, who lived in the ninth century."

in general acceded to this measure; it may more rationally be considered as originating with Vortigern, and a few chiefs with whom his influence preponderated; and indeed it may be questioned whether the honour he had long been aspiring to, was not self-assumed, and not conferred upon him by the princes and states of the island.

Hengist and Horsa, the ancestors of Englishmen, arrived in England, A.D. 447, at Elbsfleet in the Isle of Thanet, not far from the ancient Richborough. Our engraving, is taken from a very old print published by Verstegan, in his "Decayed Intelligence," about 200 years ago. It will show the manner of the apparel which they wore, the weapons which they used, as well as the banner[2] which they first spread in the field.

The sword of the Saxon was ready for any enterprise; war and booty were his high-prized pleasures. The Picts and Scots were scattered by Hengist, assisted by the Britons, as far as Caer Wair, probably on the Were in Durham. His success was honoured with the triumphant acclamation of the Britons, and several parties in the island were reconciled to this settlement.[3] But the ambition of Hengist began to show itself; he envied the wealth and possessions of the Britons; and he could not but feel that he was only a retained mercenary, whose services would be forgotten when the exigency had passed.

He justly represented to Gwrtheyrn (Vortigern), that if he and his small band were expected to serve against the Picts and Scots and his enemies, they must be allowed to invite more of their countrymen to come to their aid. The King assented, and an express embassy was sent to their native land, inviting more Saxons to come over.

The following is given by Wittichind as the speech of the ambassadors when addressing the Saxon youths:— " The Britons intend to reward liberally those who will devote themselves to chastise the Picts and Scots. Hengist and his friends have accepted the proposal, but they want succours." Hengist may have added as a lure, the probability of greater aggrandisement. Ethelward asserts that Hengist pointed out to the Saxons "the fertility of the soil, and the cowardice of the natives."[4] The Britons beheld with dissatisfaction the gradual increase of the Saxon army, which was revealed by the increased supplies required, and they demanded its immediate departure; but Hengist possessed the confidence of Gwrtheyrn, and the increased supplies which he needed were provided.

"Whether Hengist won the confidence of Gwrtheyrn," says Turner, " by his use in stimulating rebellion, or whether he had a daughter, the blue-eyed Rowena, who taught the aged bosom of the British chief to forget the claims of his country, and to indulge his passion, though Britain was the victim, and whether Kent was the price of her beauty, are circumstances not yet decisively ascertained. Nennius and Geoffrey mention the incident, but no Welsh bard has been published who seals them with his attestation. The beauty of his daughter, Rowena, no doubt captivated the heart of the aged monarch, in consequence of which the Saxon then became bold in his demands; and perceiving the dissensions that so fatally prevailed among the native princes, he turned the Saxon arms against the Britons, and aimed at the conquest of the whole country. In order to this, he secretly sent over for fresh reinforcements; he set the King at variance with his nobles; and became so insolent in his demands, as to render himself insupportable to the Britons. Being confident of their own strength, which they knew how to augment at pleasure, the Saxons soon made it appear what their ambition aimed at. They entered into a secret compact with the Picts, and received supplies from Germany, so that they now considered themselves in a position to carry out their ambitious project. These things, together with the perfidiousness of Vortigern, opened the eyes of the British nobles to the public danger."

The chieftains, however, instead of boldly insisting on the departure of the Saxons, smothered their resentment, though additional numbers were incessantly pouring in, and Hengist clamoured for fresh supplies in proportion to the increase of his adherents. Seventeen *cyules*, or longboats, filled with warriors came to the aid of the Saxons in Kent, besides forty which went to the north of the island under Octa and

---

[2] They bore on their standard the white horse, blazoned in the same manner as now borne by the Duke of Brunswick.

[3] See Arymes Prydain Fawr: or, The Great Armed Confederacy

of Britain. Camb. Reg., vol. ii. p. 555.

[4] Ethelward, 833; Sax. Chron. 12; and others affirm "that the first band were rovers; the next were invited."

F

Abira. All this, it is said, met with the sanction of Vortigern, who was easily wrought upon by the specious insinuations of Hengist.

The British nobles at length remonstrated strongly with the King, on the danger to which he was exposing the country, by admitting these foreigners in such great numbers to dwell in the land, as they would soon be able to overpower the inhabitants. Vortigern paid little attention to these complaints; and though aware of the dissatisfaction of the nobles, he continued to support the Saxons, regarding them as a powerful guard against the discontent of his subjects, or the attempts of a rival. His infatuated connexion with Rowena, the daughter of Hengist, strengthened the Saxon interest, while, at the same time, it served to render him completely odious to his subjects. The Britons now resolved to depose Vortigern, and to invest his son *Vortimer* with the administration of the kingdom.

This the Saxons could not fail to consider as a rupture between the two nations. The British chiefs now roused to fury, with Vortimer at their head, prepared for war with the Saxons, who had already commenced hostilities. In the meantime the clergy, seeing Vortigern's dissolute life, as well as being moved with his treachery to his country, solemnly excommunicated him, in a public synod convened for that purpose.[1]

The first engagement between the Britons and the Saxons is said to have been fought at Darwent, in the sixth year after the arrival of Hengist and Horsa, A.D. 455. The second was fought at Ailsford, according to the British chronicle, but the Saxon writers make this to be the first. Horsa, the brother of Hengist, and Cattigern, the son of Vortigern, fell in this action by wounds mutually inflicted. Two other battles soon ensued, in which the Saxons sustained a severe defeat, and were compelled to take refuge in the Isle of Thanet, whence they embarked for Germany.

That the Saxons at this time sustained an overwhelming defeat, appears from the circumstance that Hengist did not again venture to land on the shores of Britain until after the expiration of five years. About that time Vortigern resumed the government (Vortimer having been poisoned by his stepmother, Rowena), and he probably sent an invitation to Hengist, to come once more to Britain.

Be that as it may, Hengist landed with a powerful force under his command; but having had proof of the valour of the Britons, and knowing how formidable they might prove, he had recourse to a subtle stroke of policy. He pretended in a message dispatched to the King, that his return was connected with no hostile design; that being ignorant of the death of Vortimer, his intention was to come to the aid of his son-in-law, and establish him on the throne; and that seeing that he was once more raised to that dignity he was entirely at his disposal, and would retain or dismiss any number of his forces, according to his desire.

The weak and perfidious monarch admitted this specious plea; and he, moreover, consented to the proposal that a national congress of the chiefs of the island should be convened, in order to concert the terms upon which a treaty of amity and alliance should be formed between the two nations. The Britons, on the first of May, were accustomed to hold a grand festival in a place suitable for a general assemblage. Such a situation they had on Salisbury Plain, where the performance of certain sacred rites was celebrated, in conjunction with every kind of festivity.

The British chiefs, trusting to the sacredness of the occasion, and the honour of treaties, came unarmed. The Saxon chief, on the other hand, had commanded his adherents to conceal their weapons under their sleeves; and directed that, at a signal to be given in the season of joy and festivity, every man should act his part with cool and undaunted resolution. At an hour when the Britons were lost to every thought but that of pleasure, in the midst of the mead-horns, Hengist exclaimed, in the language of his country, *Nemed eure seaxes*—"*Draw your daggers.*" A dreadful carnage ensued, in which four hundred and sixty British chieftains are said to have fallen at the feet of the perfidious Saxons. The Britons did not, however, fall altogether unrevenged. One nobleman, Eidiol, the Earl of Gloucester, is said to have

[1] In the Triads, Vortigern is called Gwrtheyrn or the " Gainsayer," because of the detested advice which he gave, to invite the Saxons over; and his afterwards assigning them the Isle of Thanet for a residence. On that account he, along with *Avarwy*, who befriended Julius Cæsar and the Romans; and *Medrod*, who proved treacherous to his uncle Arthur, and was the cause of his ruin, are considered as names consigned to perpetual execration as the betrayers of their country.

performed feats of heroic valour; he slew no less than seventy Saxons with a truncheon. One of our ancient bards alludes to this circumstance in the following couplets:—

> "Gwae ddydd, annedwydd anwir!
> Gwae rhag yr hell, gyllell hir!
> Cyllell hir cuell a llem,
> Callestr-fin, holl-drin hyll-drem.
> Dagr garnwen, gethren gythrawl
> Neddai ddu a naddai ddiawl!"—IOLO GOCH.

Another account states that Hengist invited Vortigern, with three hundred and sixty nobles, to a superb banquet. The scene of this festivity was on Salisbury Plain, not far from Stonehenge, the most magnificent relic of the early worship of our ancestors. A temporary wooden building was erected for that purpose. The tables were spread out with all the profusion that Saxon taste was capable of displaying; and the guests took their seats with unsuspecting confidence, with warmth of heart, full of enthusiasm, full of enjoyment, full of gaiety; but, alas! they were to return to their homes no more. The Saxons, who had been artfully distributed among them, waited for the appointed signal; and at the words, "Nemed eure seaxes," uttered by Hengist, each drew his short sword, which he had concealed under his sleeve, and plunged it up to the hilt in the bosom of his neighbour.[6]

In order that we may not appear partial in our account of this transaction, we subjoin that given by Mr. Turner, the learned author of the History of the Anglo-Saxons:—"One transaction of our ancestors was so foul that we should eagerly assume the right to blot it out of history, if the fair laws of evidence had discredited it. While it remained only in the pages of Nennius and Geoffrey, the funeral scroll might be contemplated as a possible fiction, because no great crime should be suffered to stain the reputation of the great names who have outlived their day, unless a moral certainty impresses it on our belief; and the charge of authors so incorrect as Nennius and Geoffrey would not authorise the detraction; but the expressive indignation of the bard Golyddan, his energetic strains, pour on the fact an attestation which we cannot, in candour, disavow; he lashes the memory of his Britons into revengeful activity; he points to the intoxication of the great Banquet of Mead—to the bleeding guests violently slain; he recals the tears of the matrons; he remembers the moaning which the cruel pagan excited."[7]

From this pathetic lay we may turn, with some belief, to the unanimous consent of Nennius and Geoffrey. Hengist appointed a meeting of peace; weapons were not to intrude. The perfidious German counselled his friends to conceal their swords in their garments, and, at his request, to use them against the Britons. The conference began, the horns of festivity went round; when, at the terrible exclamation of "Nemed eure seaxes," out rushed the Saxon weapons; the disarmed Britons fell before the execrable assassins, and three hundred of the bravest chiefs of the country are stated to have perished. Of all crimes, those perpetrated in abuse of generous confidence are most to be abhorred; they break the noblest bonds of society, and tend to deliver up mankind to the government of suspicion, one of the most malignant fiends which human misery can foster.

The object of such a massacre was to enfeeble the opposition of British valour; and it proves that the ferocity imputed by the classics to our ancestors was not a calumny. The purposes of Hengist were now avowed; and after such an event, the sword of ruthless vengeance must have been raised upon the one side, while ambition and rapacity confronted it on the other.

The Saxons, according to British history, now insisted on their own terms, and four of the principal towns were delivered into their hands, the King being speciously detained as a prisoner, as if

[6] Cambrian Register, vol. ii. 557. The learned Usher, p. 415, says that Vorperus ex Leidensi-Chronico; Kimpius, Rev. Fris, lib. ii., c. 22; and Gerbrandus, in his Belgic Chronicle, lib. i., c. 9, mention the assassination, and make the number slain 300. Ubbo Emmius says on the subject, "auctoritatem nec adjicio, nec demo." Hist. Fris. 41.

[7] Nennius, c. 48; Geoffrey, lib. vi., c. 15. This incident seems to have pleased the world, for Wittichind gives a similar advice against the Thuringians, p. 3, to which the Vetus Chronicon Holfatiæ, published by the great Leibnitz, adds the "Nemed eure seaxes." Wittichind says: some maintain that the name of the Saxons arose from this incident, "qui cultellis (Saks) tantam multitudinem fudissent," as if Ptolemy and the Roman authors had never existed.

reluctant to comply with their demands. In the meantime Ambrosius, called by the Welsh, Emrys Wledig, the rival of Vortigern, being supported by the chiefs of Cornwall and the Armoric Britons, was preparing to put in his claim to the supreme command, as Pendragon, or Standardholder of the Britons. Among other persons of consideration, the clergy gave their support to this young chieftain, who met now with no opposition, Vortigern being generally abhorred by all ranks.

The perfidious Vortigern, now completely detested, fled to his own hereditary dominions, among the Silurians, and shut himself up in a place called Gronow Castle, in Herefordshire, on the banks of the Wye. This last retreat of the monarch was set on fire, and he was consumed in the flames, at the instigation, it is said, of Ambrosius, his rival, whom the Britons preferred to the command of the army and the government of the country. It is uncertain at what time *Emrys*, or Ambrosius, was elected sovereign or Pendragon of the Britons. Dr. Owen Pughe gives the date of A.D. 481, but it must have been considerably earlier. The battle of Wyppotsfleet, in Kent, was fought in the year 465; twelve British chieftains of distinction, with several thousands of inferior warriors, fell in that conflict.

"The name of Hengist," says Mr. Turner, "has been surrounded with terror, and his steps with victory : from Kent he is affirmed to have carried devastation into the remotest corner of the island, to have spared neither age, sex, nor condition ; to have slaughtered the priests at the altar; to have butchered in heaps the people, who fled to the mountains and deserts." In contradiction to all this, our author ventures to affirm, that all the battles of Hengist were either fought in Kent, or at no great distance from that territory which he acquired for himself, and left to his posterity.

When Hengist and his son Esca found themselves competent to resume their attacks upon the Britons, they carried havoc and desolation into the neighbouring territories, until the inhabitants flew to arms and checked their ravages.

In about three years after the last incursions of the Saxons, under Hengist and his son Esca, Emrys and the Britons had a new set of enemies to oppose; for the spirit of emigration had now seized the German tribes. These looked to Britain as the proper field for the exercise of their valour, where, like their countrymen, they expected to obtain settlements for themselves.

It was about A.D. 477, that Ella and his three sons landed in Sussex, and, notwithstanding the stoutest opposition of the natives, succeeded in establishing themselves there and in Hampshire, driving the Britons into the forest of Andoria, where there was a city strongly fortified, called by the Saxons Andrewcester. In the eighth year after the arrival of Ella, that place was taken, and the Britons, who had bravely defended it, were all put to the sword. The maxim of these heathens in the present instance was " utter extermination," and they appeared determined to make an entire slaughter of the Britons wherever they went.

Ella was now rising into great note among the Saxon chiefs, and his name carried terror with it. Hengist fell in an engagement in Yorkshire, where he had gone to join the Angles of that quarter.[a] His son Octa fled, and was taken prisoner, and spared, says the British history, by the clemency of Ambrosius, as the Saxon chieftain threw himself on the mercy of the conqueror.

In the year 495, eighteen years after the landing of Ella, Venric came with five ships. Though his force was small, the impression he made was powerful. He was opposed for five and twenty years, and at last met with an overwhelming defeat at Badon Mount.

While Kerdic and his son were extending their conquests, and profiting, no doubt, by the want of union among the native chiefs, who seldom came forward to oppose the common foe, unless their own territories were invaded, a band of Saxon auxiliaries came over from the continent, under the conduct of Porta, and landed in Hampshire, where that leader sustained a vigorous attack from the natives, before he could obtain a footing in the country.

On the death of Ambrosius, the Britons inhabiting the Western coast elevated Uthr to the throne,

---

[a] The British History states that he was taken prisoner in the midst of the fight, and doomed to death by the sentence of the British chiefs and clergy.

who thereupon added the title of Pendragon, or Commander-in-Chief, to the royal dignity, and the supreme command of their armies. According to some accounts this prince was brother of Ambrosius, had fought under him, and thereby recommended himself as a man of bravery and military talents.

During his reign Venric erected his conquests into a kingdom, which went under the name of the Kingdom of Wessex, and being now assisted by Porta as well as Ella, King of Sussex, Esca, King of Kent, and all the Saxon colonies in Britain, the Britons had to contend with a most powerful confederacy. The combined force of the Saxons was met in the West of England by a British army, some say, under the command of Llew ap Cynvarch, whom the Saxon annalists call *Natanleod.* The event of the battle* proved disastrous to the Britons, who left five thousand men dead on the field. The Saxons abroad heard of this defeat of the Britons and came over in numerous shoals to try their fortune in Britain.

Although the Saxons met with various repulses from the bravery of Uthr, the increasing numbers that were continually pouring in upon the Britons emboldened them to hope for ultimate success.

Uthr Pendragon having died from the effect of poison, treacherously administered to him by one of his attendants, as we have it in the British history, he was succeeded in the supreme command of the army by his son, the renowned Arthur.[1]

The Saxons had by this time obtained a firm footing, and established themselves in various parts of Britain. The kingdoms of the South Saxons, of East Anglia, and Wessex, were established, previous to the year 520, about which time Arthur began to reign as Prince of Siluria, and afterwards had the supreme command conferred upon him.

The Loegrian Britons had in general submitted themselves, and it was chiefly the natives of Cornwall, Wales, Cumberland, and Strath-Clyde, that now opposed the Anglo-Saxons.

According to William of Malmesbury, Kerdic was established in the kingdom of the West Saxons in the year 519: and Arthur was raised to supreme power in the tenth year of Kerdic's reign; but according to Powell and Dr. Owen Pughe, the date of Arthur's elevation was, A.D. 517.

The fame of this distinguished and celebrated chieftain has been celebrated throughout the continent of Europe, while his praises have been the noble theme of our most distinguished bards, Taliesin, Merddin, and Llywarch, who were his cotemporaries. He is also honoured in the Triads as one of "The three brave Sovereigns of the Isle of Britain."

According to Nennius, he was one of the most successful opponents of the Saxons, whom he defeated in twelve battles. The battle of Badon Mount, near Bath, in which he defeated the Saxons, under Kerdic, was one of the most decisive ever fought between the Welsh and Saxons. This, according to Usher, took place in A.D. 520, or 530, according to other accounts. The last agrees with the old chronology preserved in the Red Book of Hergest. In consequence of the success of Arthur in this engagement, the Silurian territories were preserved inviolate, and the natives left in possession of the country to the west of the Severn. This famous battle is noticed by Llywarch, thus:—

> " Gwae hwynt-hwy yr ynfydion
> Pan fu waith Faddon.
> Arthur Ben haelion
> (Y Llafnau by gochion)
> Gwnaeth ar ei alon
> Gwaith gwyr gewynion
> Gewynion gwaed daredd,
> Mach deyrn y gogledd."[2]

---

[2] According to Nennius, this battle was fought during the sovereignty of Arthur; and if so, it must be what Llywarch Hên celebrates as the Battle of *Llongborth*, and where Geraint, a Damnonian chieftain, fell. His elegy is one of the finest pieces of that Bard. See Elegies of Llywarch Hên.

[1] The name of Arthur implies either a person of high renown or undaunted courage. This might be well applied to our modern Arthur,—the Duke of Wellington.

[2] Englished thus:—

" Woe to them, the miserable ones, because of the action at Badon:
Arthur was at the head of the brave, when the blades were red with blood:
He avenged on his enemies the blood of warriors;
Warriors who had been the defence of the Kings of the North."

Llongborth is another celebrated battle recorded by the muse of the venerable Llywarch. A chieftain of Devonshire, called Geraint ap Erbin, fell in that contest; and his elegy is preserved among the remains of the Cumbrian Bard,[3] who gives a poetic description of the battle in all the horrors that attend war and slaughter. Another of Arthur's battles is mentioned by Llywarch; it was fought at Llongborth, when the Bard lost Gwên, his favourite son. The bravery of this youth is set forth in expressive and laconic terms by his father. "As he was my son, he did not recede."

Arthur, according to the fictions of Geoffrey of Monmouth, is said to have achieved the highest renown by his battles on the Continent, and in Ireland, as well as in his native isle; and even as to his invincible prowess at home, it has been greatly exaggerated, so that his very existence has been called in question. But the Arthur we have been speaking of is a very different character to Geoffrey's hero of romance of the same name, who performs so important a part in the Mabinogion,[4] although they are confounded together. In the popular account, our Arthur is distinguished in the ancient British Triads as one of the "brave sovereigns of the Isle of Britain."

It has been calculated that twenty-two years intervened between the battle of Badon and that of Camlan, which was the last battle our hero fought, and it was also the scene of that disastrous conflict that caused his death, in which Medrod[5] dared to meet his injured uncle, with the sword of wrath, to consummate the crime of incest with murder. The battle lasted two days.[6] The poem of Myrddin adds that seven only escaped from the slaughter. The traitor fell; but Arthur also received a mortal wound.

The grave of Arthur was the mystery of the world; his death was concealed, and a wild tale was diffused among the populace, that he had withdrawn from the world into some magical region, from which, at a future crisis, he was to reappear and to lead the Cymry in triumph through the island. This marvellous tale was believed by many in those superstitious times, and even Henry II. believed it. When that monarch was in Wales[7] he heard the tradition of the Welsh bards; he had the expression from the mouth of one of them as to the exact spot where King Arthur was interred at Glastonbury, and for his own satisfaction he ordered a proper search to be made. Giraldus Cambrensis, who flourished in the time of Henry II., affirms that he was present at the abbey when a leaden cross was taken up, with an inscription in rude, but legible characters, to this effect:—

HIC JACET SEPULTUS
INCLYTUS REX ARTHURUS
IN INSULA AVALONIA.

Arthur was not only celebrated for his valour as a warrior, but for every trait forming the character of a great prince. He is particularly held up to our view as possessing great zeal for the Christian religion; the defence of which against the pagan Saxons, was used as a powerful argument to animate

---

[3] Arthur himself was a poet as well as a warrior. He sang the following Englyn to three of his cavaliers:—

"Sef ynt fy nhri Chadfarchawg,
Mael Hir, a Llyr Lluyddawg,
A cholofn Cymry Caradawg." *

Englished thus :
"Those are my three cavaliers of battle,
Mael the tall, and Llyr the armipotent,
And that pillar of the Cymry, Caradawg."

[4] See Lady Guest's translation of these interesting tales, just published, with numerous historical notes. Rees, Llandovery.

---

* Caradawg here mentioned was a Prince of the Cornish Britons during the sixth century, of which period was also Llyr and Mael. They were all three, cotemporaries of Arthur, and fought under him, as may be inferred from the Englyn here quoted, from the Archæology of Wales.

[5] Medrod was nephew to Arthur. He seduced his uncle's queen, and eloped with her to Cumberland, where he raised a civil war, and thus the British princes who ought to have had one common interest, spent their strength in domestic feuds. The consequence of this state of discord, was the ruin of the native Britons and the loss of the brave Arthur, who fell by the hands of the perfidious Medrod.

[6] Myrddin's Avallennau. This battle is said by Geoffrey to have taken place, A.D. 542. By Wharton, in his Anglia Sacra, and many authors cited by Usher, in 521. The years 542 and 543 have been also selected; but the chronology in the Red Book of Hergest places it in 576.

[7] It was at an entertainment given at Kilgeran Castle in Pembrokeshire, that Henry received the information. In allusion to this, the Rev. C. Morgan has written a fine poem, intituled "The Shrine of Arthur."

the courage of the Britons. Sir Richard Blackmore has made fine use of this in his poem on Arthur;[8] and the interview between this hero and Howel, the Armorican King, is well conceived.

Arthur's greatest achievement was the battle of Badon Hill. That victory not only stopped the progress of Kerdic, but gave repose to the Silurian territory to the end of his days. This alone entitles him to be ranked as the most gallant of all the British princes, and his name deserves to be enrolled among the ancient heroes of the Isle of Britain. No wonder that during the twelfth century his fame had been unbounded. According to Alanus de Insulis, "He was more known in Asia than in Britain; our pilgrims returning from the east and west talk of him; Egypt and the Bosphorus are not silent; Rome, the mistress of cities, sings of his actions; Antioch, Armenia, Palestine, celebrate his deeds." If Alanus answers for the eastern hemisphere, Humphrey Llwyd gives evidence for the western world: "Not only our writers, but the Spaniards, Italians, Gauls, and Swedes, beyond the Baltic, sing to this day, in their books, the illustrious actions of this most valiant King."[9]

"The conquest of the Anglo-Saxon," says Mr. Turner, "did not exterminate the Britons. It is true, however, that many submitted to the invaders; others disdained their slavish yoke, and emigrated to other countries. Armorica or Bretagne was the refuge to many; Cornwall and Wales received a large accession of population; and some are even said to have visited Holland."[1] The most indignant of the Cymry retired into Wales. There the Bards, fugitive like the rest, consoled the expatriated Britons with the hope that the day would arrive when they would have their full revenge by driving out the Saxon hordes. This animating prediction was not only sung by Taliesin, but Myrddin also promised the Britons that they should again be led by their majestic chief, and be again victorious. He boldly announced that in this happy day should be restored to every one his own; that then the horn of gladness should proclaim the song of peace, the serene days of Cambrian happiness.[2] The proud invaders mocked the vaunting prophecy, and to render it nugatory, they unpeopled some of their native coasts on the Baltic, and filled Britain with an active and hardy race, whose augmenting population and persevering valour at length carried the hated Saxon sceptre even to the remotest corners of venerated Anglesea.

It has been very usual with some writers to impute every fiction, that they discover, connected with our ancient history, to the Welsh Bards; but such persons should be informed, that truth, "Y Gwir yn erbyn y byd," (the truth against the world) has always been the motto of the Bards,—"I honour the veracity of the Welsh Bards," says Mr. Turner in his Anglo-Saxons, "and admit their facts into history."[3] It is true, that in the fragments of the very ancient Bards, we have a great deal of mythology, but that was never designed to pass for history. The fabulous narratives, which found their way into our old

[8] Whatever may be thought of the general merit of that work, the author has succeeded admirably in distinguishing between the Britons and their forces, ranged under their various tribes, and the Saxons and their auxiliaries on the other hand.

[9] Comment. Brit. Descript., frag. p. 75.

[1] See Turner's Anglo-Saxons, vol. ii., p. 246.

[2] See the poem of Taliesin translated into a Latin Sapphic, in Owen's British Remains, p. 127. The Welsh is translated thus :—

"A serpent with chains
  Towering and plundering
  With armed wings
    From Germania.
"This will overrun
  All Lloegria and Brydon
  From the land of the Lochlin sea
    To the Severn."

After mentioning that the Britons will be exiles and prisoners to Saxony, he adds :—

"Eu Ner a folant,
  Eu hiaith a gadwant,
  Eu tir a gollant
    Ond gwyllt Walia."
Thus Englished,
"Their Lord they will praise,
  Their language preserve,
  Their country lose
    Except wild Wales."
Till the destined period of their triumph revolves;
"Then the Britons will obtain,
  Their crown and their land,
  And the strange people
    Will vanish away."

He concludes by declaring that Michael has predicted the future happiness of Britain. See his Avallenau in Jones's Relics. Golyddan also predicts the unanimity of the Britons, Lloegria in flames, and the pagans put to flight. See his Arymes Prydain, in Camb. Reg., vol. ii., p. 561.

[3] Vol. i., p. 148, note.

chronicles, are in prose, and were brought over from the continental Bretons. It is from thence we have these tales, which transport us into fairy regions, beyond the limits of all historical probability. The Armoric fictions of King Arthur, and his famous Caliburno, Sir Launcelot, Sir Tristram, and all the rest of the Knights of the Round Table, are not found in the simple fragments of our ancient poetry.

The Welsh Bards must not be confounded with the romance writers. They were the surviving branch of that wonderful system which has been popularly known by the name of Druidism, though the present professors of Bardic science assure us that the Druids, or "Derwyddon" did not compose the principal order, but were only such of the Bards as were appointed to officiate in religious rites.[4]

The Bards were also the conservators of the knowledge of the ancient Britons; they were the priests, the teachers of morality and of science. Song was one of their principal methods of giving permanency to their traditionary maxims and institutes. The most prominent trait in the ancient British poetry, was, its being *consecrated as the vehicle of truth*, whilst other nations had consigned it to the ornament of fiction; it was therefore in common with the Triads, employed as a systematic medium of tradition, and considered as less liable to error than the use of letters.

The Bards having thus laid claim to poetry as an appendage to their system, all the powers of genius were exerted in bringing it to perfection; hence their poetical criticism has been surpassed by none other, "and their system of versification is superior to anything of the kind perhaps in the world; it is reduced to twenty-four elementary classes, and there is not in any language, ancient or modern, any kind of verse to be found, that is not used in the Welsh language, and deducible from one or other of those primary classes. All the principles, all the varieties, all the combinations of verse that exist in nature, belong to one or other of these; and we have in common use many kinds so singularly different from what has ever yet been known in any part of ancient or modern Europe, that no conception of them can well be conveyed to one unacquainted with the Welsh language."[5]

The copiousness of the Welsh language is very great; it may be safely affirmed, that it has no rival as to the variety of its synonymous forms of expression, principally arising from the rich combination of its verbs, for every simple verb has twenty modifications, by means of qualifying prefixes; and in every form it may be conjugated either by inflexions like the Latin, or by auxiliaries, as in English.

Having thus given a brief view of the mechanism of Welsh versification, we shall now proceed to give a few specimens of the Bards, who flourished from the earliest ages to the close of the bloody struggle maintained against the Saxons, to preserve the nominal sovereignty of the island, and this period may be said to have lasted from the fifth to the eighth century. The names of the Bards of this epoch, of whose works there are now any remains preserved, are Aneurin, Taliesin, Merddin, Llywarch, and Meigant.

Aneurin, who is usually stiled Monarch of the Bards, was a chief of the Ottadini. His poem on the battle of Cattraeth is recorded as the masterpiece of that period. The following passage is given, together with a literal translation, as a specimen of the poem :—

> "Gwyr a aeth Gattraeth, oet ffraeth y llu,
> Glasved eu hancwyn a'u gwenwyn fu,
> Trychant trwy beiriant yn catau,
> A gwedi elwch, tawelwch fu,
> Cyd elwynt y llafnau i benydu,
> Dadl diau, angau i eu treitu."

---

[4] See Dr. O. Pughe's Essay on Bardism, prefixed to his translation of Llywarch Hên. p. 37.—Lhuyd's Archæologia Britannica is a most valuable attempt at a thesaurus of the Celtic languages and literature; he used Greek characters for the peculiar sounds of the Welsh language. See his Preface to "At y Cymry," a translation of which is in the appendix to Nicholson's Irish Historical Library, p. 100. See also his curious Essay on Welsh Orthography, Archæol. 225. It is a great pity that Lhuyd's collections for a second volume, which now exist, are not published, as it would give us a complete thesaurus of Celtic literature and antiquities, which are now buried in oblivion.

[5] See Edward Williams's Poems, Lyric and Pastoral, vol. ii., p. 226.

> " Men went to Cattraeth, eloquent the host,
> Green sparkling mead their dainty and their bane.
> With arms they hastened, panting after wounds,
> And after acclamation's silence reigned,
> Whilst lurid blades proceed in dealing pain
> To yield sure triumph, by their thrusts, for death."

There is much of the poetry of Taliesin still preserved. That poet makes more frequent allusions to the Bardic maxims and mythology than any others of the ancients, of whose works we have any remains. His verses in general are peculiar for being short and comprehensive, like the following :—

> " Gwelais wyr gorfawr
> A dygyrchynt awr ;
> Gwelais waed ar lawr
> Rac ruthr cletyfawr ;
> Glesynt esgyll gwawr
> Esgorynt ynn waewawr." [6]

Of Merddin's poetry there have been only a few pieces preserved ; the *Avallennau* and the *Hoiunau* are the principal ones. These are published with a literal translation in Jones's Poetical and Musical Relics of the Welsh Bards.

We have nothing of Meigant, except an elegy upon Cynddylan, Prince of Powys.

We have more of the poetry of Llywarch preserved than of any other bard of this first period, excepting Taliesin. These have been published by our old and much respected friend, the late Dr. Owen Pughe,[7] under the title of " Heroic Elegies of Llywarch Hên" Prince of the Cumbrian Britons, from which we extract the following fragment, entitled " Elegy upon Geraist ap Erbin, Prince of Devon."

> " Pan aned Geraint oedd agored pyrth nef,
> Rhoddai Grist a arched,
> Pryd mirain Prydain ogoned.
>
> " Moled pawb y rhudd Eraint,
> Arglwydd ; molaf innau Eraint,
> Gelyn i Sais, câr i saint," &c. &c.[8]

We shall here close our specimens of the Bards and our mountain Greek ; the next epoch shall conclude with the fall of the ancient British government by the death of David, the last Prince of Wales, in the year 1283.

[6] " I saw the mighty host of men who hastened together at the shout ; I saw blood imbue the ground from the assault of swords ; they tinged with blue the wings of the morning, when they sent the ashen messengers of pain."

[7] The ingenious author of the Welsh and English Dictionary— a work of immense labour and deep research, which will long stand a splendid monument to the industry, the learning, and the talent of its author. We are indebted for a considerable portion of the account of the Bards to a writer under the assumed name of " Meirion," in the Cambrian Register, which we strongly opine is the production of our late lamented friend.

[8] " When Geraint was born, the gates of heaven were open ;
Christ then granted what was requested,
A countenance beautiful, the glory of Britain.

" Let all celebrate the red-stained Geraint,
Their lord ; I will also praise Geraint,
The Saxon's foe, the friend of saints."

The following elegant lines, by the Rev. John Walters, are taken from the Welsh of Llywarch Hên's Lament of Cynddylan, Prince of Powys, who fell in battle in the vicinity of Shrewsbury, then called Pengwern, the Seat of Royalty :—

> " Come forth and see, ye Cambrian dames,
> Fair Pengwern's royal roof on flames,
> The foe the fatal dart hath flung,
> (The foe that speaks a barbarous tongue),
> And pierced Clynddylan's princely head,
> And stretched your champion with the dead ;
> His heart which late, with martial fire,
> Bade his loved country's foes expire ;
> Such fire as wastes the forest hill,
> Now like the winter's ice is chill ;
> O'er the pale corpse, with boding cries,
> Sad Argoed's cruel eagle flies ;
> He flies exulting o'er the plain,
> And scents the blood of heroes slain," &c. &c.

The concise abruptness of the original shows a heart overloaded with sorrow, and forms the strongest evidence of their being the genuine remains of Llywarch.

"The Druids," says Mr. Turner, "were anciently known to, and celebrated by Cæsar; [*] both they and the Bards are mentioned by Diodorus Siculus,[1] by Strabo, by Posidonius, by Lucan, and by Ammianus Marcellinus.[2] These authors represent them as employed, amid their occupations, in celebrating the actions of the great by the arts of poetry and music.

The superstitions of Druidism were terrible, but they fell before the gentle spirit of the Christian dispensation; as the benignant precepts of this system attracted the adoration of the natives, the class of Druids, already wounded by the Roman sword, completely expired;[3] but the principal order of the Bards survived their pagan rights, and a regular succession is continued, though with many changes as to number and popularity, to the present day.[4]

"The Bardic System, as at present known," says Mr. Turner, "expresses an ardent benevolence, a sublime theology, mixed with the peculiar notion of transmigration—which, however, is put into its most plausible shape—and a valuable morality."[5] "When we recollect that the poems of Taliesin show him to have been a pious Christian, as well as a bard, and that the family of Aneurin were monks; and that the poetry of Meigant, and other bards, is deeply imbued with Christian ideas, I cannot but imagine that we see Bardism as it was after Christianity had enlightened the Welsh muses."[6]

The Saxons, by degrees, possessed themselves of the greatest portion of the kingdom, and established seven kingdoms, which went under the name of the Heptarchy. Their boundaries were as follows:—

1. MERCIA contained sixteen counties, Huntingdon, Rutland, Lincoln, Northampton, Leicester, Derby, Nottingham, Oxford, Chester, Salop, Gloucester, Worcester, Stafford, Warwick, Buckingham, and Bedford. The Angles had chiefly settled in this district. Leicester was its metropolis. Continued 220 years; governed by twenty kings.

2. NORTHUMBERLAND was also inhabited by Angles. It was originally composed of two kingdoms, Bernicia, and Deira. Of these Bamborough and York were the capitals. Begun by Ella and Ida. Continued 370 years, during the reigns of twenty-three kings.

3. WESSEX composed Hants, Bucks, and Wilts, Somerset, Dorset, Devon, and part of Cornwall, with the Isle of Wight. Winchester was the chief place. Continued under nineteen kings, for 561 years.

4. SUSSEX had only itself and Surrey. Chichester was its chief town. Begun by Ella, and continued seventy-six years during the reign of five kings only.

---

[*] De Bel. Gal. lib. vi., c. 13, is an invaluable sketch, to which we are greatly indebted. Pliny also mentions the Druids, lib. xvi., c. 95.

[1] Diod. Siculus. lib. v., p. 213—308, ed. Rhod.; Strabo, lib. iv., p. 197 —302. The passages of these two authors have greatly contributed to our certainty of the Bardic antiquity.—*Turner.*

[2] Amm. Marcell, l. xv., c. 9, p. 75, ed. Gronov. Lucan's beautiful verses, lib. i.; and Rowe's musical translation, v. 784—811, are worth remembering. It is curious that Mr. Park, in his adventurous travels, should have found men in Africa in some respect answering to the Bards of Northern Europe.

[3] Though the Druidical priesthood was abolished, the Bards retained the valued honour of their name. Taliesin says, that "pleasing to the sovereign is the love of the Derwyddon." See Dr. Pughe's Dictionary, under *Derwyddon.*

[4] From 1681 a remnant only of the Bards has existed, little known, but occasionally holding a gorsedd for Glamorgan, the only provincial chair extant. Those members were until lately reduced to two. See Dr. Pughe's Essay, p. 62. Mr. E. Jones, author of the "Ancient Relics," revived the custom of the congress at Corwen, in Merionethshire. Since that time it has been held alternately in many towns in North and South Wales.

[5] See Extracts from the Welsh Bardic Triads, annexed to E. Williams's Poems, vol. ii., pp. 227, 256; Dr. Pughe's Account of Bardism, prefixed to Llywarch Hên, pp. 28, 31, 54.

[6] The following beautiful lines on Taliesin, from the pen of the Nightingale of the Vale of Clwyd,[*] claim insertion here, as illustrative of bygone days, and is applicable to that beautiful plaintive Welsh air, "Toriad y Dydd"—The Break of Day:—

A voice from time departed yet floats thy hills among,
Oh Cambria! thus thy prophet-bard, thy Taliesin sung!
The path of unborn ages is traced upon my soul,
The clouds that mantle things unseen away before me roll.

A light, the depths revealing, hath o'er my spirits pass'd;
A rustling sound, from days to be, swells fitful in the blast,
And tells me that for ever shall live the lofty tongue,
To which the harp of Mona's woods by Freedom's hand was strung.

Green island of the mighty! I see thine ancient race
Forced from their father's realm to make the rocks their dwelling place.
I see from Uthyr's kingdom the sceptre pass away,
And many a line of bards, and chiefs, and princely men decay.

But long as Arvon's mountains shall lift their sovereign forms,
And wear the crown to which is given dominion o'er the storms,
So long, their empire sharing, shall live the lofty tongue,
To which the harp of Mona's woods by Freedom's hand was strung.

---

[*] The late Mrs. Hemans.

5. KENT had Canterbury for its capital. Hengist was the first King; Ethelbert was another (of whom more anon). This kingdom continued 372 years.

6. ESSEX comprised itself, Middlesex, and part of Hertfordshire. London was the capital. This kingdom commenced in 527; continued 281 years, during the reign of fourteen kings, the last of whom built St. Paul's, in London.

7. EAST ANGLIA included Cambridgeshire, Suffolk, Norfolk, and the Isle of Ely. Begun by Offa in 575, and continued 353 years, during the reign of fifteen kings.

It must not, however, be supposed that the Britons made no resistance to the Saxon establishments. Inured, by degrees, to war, and roused, at length, by the bitterest wrongs, they opposed the invaders with spirit, and often with success. Aurelius Ambrosius, a prince of great valour, and particularly Arthur (Uthr), who conquered the Saxons in no less than six battles in one year, were two of the bravest heroes recorded as defenders of their country. Arthur fell at length, when full of years, in a civil contest with his own nephew, Medrod. After his death, the Britons retired to the mountainous districts of North and South Wales, and Cornwall; from these stations (until their total but successive subjection), they continued to annoy their powerful neighbours, the Saxons, with a vigour which, had it been united and energetically exerted, might have saved their country.

The kindred race of petty sovereigns who governed the Anglo-Saxons were employed during the next three hundred years in waging perpetual war on each other, or the original natives of the islands, indiscriminately, until the year 828, when a royal warrior and statesman united these petty states into one great monarchy.

A.D. 607.—Ethelfred, the fierce King of Northumberland, renewed the war with the Cymry. The ostensible cause of the renewal of hostilities was the refusal of the ancient British bishops to comply with the demands of Augustine the monk, who required them to alter their mode of worship, and to conform with the Church of Rome, particularly in their time of keeping Easter.[7] Augustine had, about A.D. 603, been sent to England, by Pope Gregory, with the object of converting the Saxon pagans to Christianity. He was afterwards taken under the especial care and patronage of Ethelbert, King of Kent, who showed him much favour. Augustine was made Archbishop of Canterbury, and Ethelbert became his patron and defender in all things appertaining to his mission;[8] and on the refusal of the British bishops to comply with his demands, that monarch at the instigation of Augustine, prevailed upon Ethelfred, King of Northumbria, which kingdom borders upon the Principality, to enter the territory of Brochmael Ysgythriog,[9] the then Prince of Powys, in whose dominion the celebrated monastry of Bangor-is-y-Coed, was situated, and in which the ancient British bishops and their humble followers resided.

The Pope directed Augustine to accommodate the ceremonies of the Christian worship as much as possible to those of the heathens in Britain, that the people might not be too much startled at the change; and, in particular, he advised him to allow the Christian converts at certain festivals to kill and eat a great number of oxen to the glory of God, as they had formerly done to the honour of the Devil. It is quite unnecessary to make any remark upon this mixture of pious zeal and worldly policy. There is one question, however, deserving especial notice, wherein Augustine requests

---

[7] The old Britons did not want for the forms of Christianity, for they had regular diocesan Bishops, besides the various orders of inferior clergy, sent out in general from the religious houses, with which Wales and Cornwall then abounded. The Bishops of Llandaff, Margam, Llanbadarn, St. David, St. Asaph and Bangor, with that of St. Keïbius, in the Island of Anglesea, were now established, and endowed; Columbia, Kentigern and Anian had evangelised the northern Britons.

[8] Brut y Brenhinoedd—The British History.

[9] This Brochmael, by the Latin writers named Brochmaelus, was a very considerable prince in that part of Britain called Powys Land, and lived in the town then called Pengwern Powys, now Shrewsbury, in the house where since the College of St. Chad stands. He was a great prince and patron of the monks of Bangor, whose part he took against the Saxons that were set on by St. Augustine the Monk, to prosecute them with fire and sword, because they would not forsake the customs of their own Church and conform to those of Rome. *Caradoc of Llancarvan's British History.* Wynne's edition, 1702, p. 23.

Gregory to inform him, "How he ought to deal with the bishops of Gaul and Britain?" To which Gregory replies, "We give thee no power over the bishops of Gaul," they being under the Archbishop of Arles: "but all the bishops of the Britons we commit to thy fraternal care, that the unlearned may be taught, the weak strengthened by persuasion, and the perverse corrected by authority."

Augustine, now enjoying the protection of so powerful a monarch as Ethelbert, and having had the British bishops (without their knowledge) committed to his "fraternal care," he soon conceived the ambitious project of subjugating the old British clergy to his metropolitan authority, and so placing the whole island under the jurisdiction of the Roman See.

They were accordingly summoned to attend Augustine, to hold a conference with him, somewhere on the banks of the Severn or Dee, which afterwards, according to Bede, received the name of the "*Augustine Oak.*"

Augustine opened this conference with admonishing and entreating the Britons to lay aside those ecclesiastical usages of theirs that were contrary to the practices of the Romish Church, and to unite with him and his brethren in preaching the Gospel to their neighbours, the Saxons. He told them that they did not keep Easter at its proper time, and did many other things contrary to the unity of their Church. But Augustine could not prevail either by entreaties or threats; the Cymry still adhered to their own mode of worship and traditions, which with great tenacity they refused to give up. Augustine upon this "told them, in a *threatening tone,* that, if they would not be at peace with their brethren, they must expect war with their enemies, and look for the vengeance of the English, towards the conversion of whom they had refused their co-operation."

The British Church having, as we have stated, received the Gospel from the Apostles themselves, had hitherto continued independent of the Church of Rome, and would not acknowledge any other authority over them except that of their own Primate. Leland says that "*Dynoth, Abbot of Bangor,* did, in a spirited speech, at *large dispute with great learning and gravity,*" against receiving the authority of the Pope, or of Augustine. He maintained the authority of the Archbishop of St. David's, and declared that it was not to the interest of the Welsh to submit either to Roman pride or to Saxon tyranny.[1]

[1] In a curious old manuscript belonging to the Cottonian collection at the British Museum, marked Claudius 8, 8, this celebrated speech is preserved in Welsh, with a note showing that it was transcribed from another manuscript, written in the tenth century, in the possession of Roger Mostyn, gentleman, ancestor of the Hon. E. M. Lloyd Mostyn, who is in possession of several others of equal rarity, which he values above price. And as it will serve to illustrate the independency of the British church, we shall here give a transcript of this curiosity :—" Bid ysps a diogel i chwi, yn bod ni holl un ac arall yn uvydd ac yn ostyngedyg i Eglwys Duw ac ir Pab o Ruvain, ac I boob kyur grisdion dwyuol, i garu pawb yn i radd mewn kariad perffaith, ac i helpio pawb o honaunt a gair a gweithred y vod ynn blant i Dduw: Ac am genach uvydddod na hwn nid adwen i vod ir neb ir yddych chwi yn henwi yn Baab yn ne yn Daad o daade yw gleimio ac yw ovunn : Ar uvydddod hwn ir yddym ni yn barod yw roddi ac yw dalu iddo ef, ac i pob Kywir Krisdion yn dragwyddol. Hevyd ir ydym ni dan lywodraeth Esgob Kaerllion ar wysc yr hwn ysydd yn olygwr dan Dduw arnom ni y wneuthud i ni gadw yr ffordd ysbrydol." That the English readers may not be strangers to the sense of this speech, we here present them with a literal translation of it :—" We would have you know and be assured that we, all and every one of us, are subject to and owe a deference of perfect charity to the church of God, the pope of Rome, and every pious Christian in their respective degrees, and to help every one in word and in deed to make them the children of God. Other obedience than this I know not to be due to him whom ye call pope, or father of fathers, nor can he claim or require it. Such obedience or deference as this we are ready to pay him and every Christian for

ever. Besides, we are under the government of the bishop of Carlleon upon the Usk, who is our superior, or superintendent, under God, to oblige us to preserve ourselves uncorrupted with respect to spirituals."

See Dr. Hammond, on Denoth the Abbot of Bangor's answer to Augustine. See also Bishop Lloyd's Church History, p. 67, and Archbishop Usher.

The following Chronology of the time when churches were built in Anglesey.*—Translated from an old MS. 500 years old.—That Christianity had taken deep root among the Britons in the second century is clear from the testimony of Tertullian, a cotemporary writer, who states that certain parts, inaccessible to the Romans, were subdued by Christ, and we learn from Blunt's History of the Reformation, chap. i., " The Britons had churches of their own, built after a fashion of their own Saints, their own hierarchy."— Llanrhyddlad and Llanrhwydrus were built in the year 570 ; Llanbadric in 440 ; Llan Elian, 450 ; Llan Degvan and Llan Dyfrydog in the year 500 ; Llan St. Dygwl in 530 ; Llan Ddyfnan Llan Geinwen, and Llanddwyn, 590 ; Llan Allgo, Llan Eugrad, Llan Vaelog, Llan Gaffo, and Llan Gwillog in 605 ; Llan Gristiolus and Llan Ddona in 610 ; Aberffraw, Trewdraeth, Llan Aedan, and Llanddaniel Fab in 616 ; Llan Enghenel, Llanfinnan, Llanjestin, and Llangefni in 620 ; Llan Flewin, Llan Gredivel or Penmynydd, Penmon, Cappel Seiriol, Llanbeulan, Rhoscolyn, Coedanna, Cappel

* On referring to Rees's Prize Essay on the Welsh Saints, we find that there are other churches in various parts of Wales quite as ancient as those in Anglesey.

Augustine still endeavoured to persuade them to a conformity to the Church of Rome, particularly with respect to the keeping of Easter. However trivial this circumstance may seem to our readers, it was considered an important point, and made the subject of a long debate at this time. The Saint, seeing that his argument had little effect, is introduced by Bede as descending even to prayers, and from them to

Interview between Augustine the Monk and the ancient British Bishops.

reproaches. But the Britons still continuing tenacious of their ancient custom, Augustine cut the dispute short by a challenge. "Come then," says Augustine, "we will put the truth of our opinions to this test; whosoever of us shall, by his prayers, heal a sick or infirm person, let his opinion be looked upon as having the sanction of the Deity, and be embraced as such by the opposite party." The Britons having with great reluctance agreed to this text of their orthodoxy, a blind person (a *Saxon*) was brought in. He was first offered to the British bishops, without meeting with relief, and he was carried to Augustine, who kneeled down in the sight of the whole assembly, and restored him instantaneously to his sight by

Ceidio, and Llech Gynvarwy in 630, and Oriron the same year; Prince Pabo, commonly called Post Prydain, from his being a great support to the Britons against the Picts and Scots (about the time of Caswallon Law Hir) built his church at Llanbabo in the year 460. He was buried at Llanerchymedd, and left a stone with this inscription at Llanbabo church :—

"Yn Llanerchymedd yn Mondo
Y claddwyd Brenin Pabo,
A'i frenines, teg ei gwedd,
Yn Llanerchymedd mae hono."

Llandysilio was built by Tysilio, the son of Brochmael Yscythriog, in the year 655; Edwen, niece or daughter of King Edwin, built her church at Llan Edwen; King Cadwaladr, who was a saint as well as a monarch, built his church at Llan Cadwaladr, in the year 650; St. Mechell was the son of Echwid, son of Gwyn, who was nephew to "Gloew Gwlad Sydyn," Lord of Glo'ster; he was christened by "Maelos," in Brittany, his church was dedicated to his name; he died in Anglesey, and was buried in the churchyard of Penrhos Lligwy. The following inscription was on his tombstone :—

"St. Mechell built his church A.D. 630; St. Dygwel, 530.

"Peirio, Eugred, gwyr, o'n bro,
Ac Allgo, Capho, a Maelog,
Oedd feibion cawr o Frydain gain,
A chwaer i rhai'n oedd Cwyllog."

his prayers.[2] The poor Britons were unable to perform any wonders of this kind; but their own eyes were, however, sufficiently open without a miracle to discern pride and arrogance. They submitted no farther than this, that they should consult the great body of their brethren, without whom they could engage to do nothing; and they proposed that a fuller assembly than the present should be convened. This proposal was agreed to; and accordingly, at the next conference, seven bishops and many divines were present, and in particular Dinoth, Abbot of Bangor, and several of his monks. Archbishop Parker gives a list of the names of these divines that were present at this Synod, as well as the dioceses supposed to be at that time within the jurisdiction of the Cambrian metropolitan, including Powys, of which Chester was at that time the capital.

The British divines, previous to their entering upon their conference with Augustine, applied to a certain aged archbishop of great repute, for his wisdom and sanctity. They consulted him as to whether it would be proper for them to give up their traditions at the persuasion of Augustine? "If he be a man of God," said the anchorite, "follow him." "But how," they enquired, "are we to be assured of this?" "The Lord hath said," rejoined he, "'Learn of me, for I am meek, and lowly in heart,' if this Augustine be meek and lowly in heart you may believe that, as he bears the yoke of Christ himself, he will impose no other on you; but if he shows himself haughty and proud, that affords you proof that he is not of God; and you are therefore not to give heed to him."[3] "But how," they asked, "shall we be able to make the distinction?" To this the holy man replied: "When you meet him at the place appointed for holding the Synod, if he rises up to you on your approaching him, be assured of his being a servant of Christ; and it behoves you, therefore, to attend to him with deference. If, on the contrary, he treat you with scorn, and rises not up to salute you, seeing you are the greater number, then let him be despised of you." They resolved to act according to his advice. Augustine, when they approached him, instead of rising to greet them, kept his seat. When they perceived his pride, they became so angry, that they rejected every proposal he made to them.[4]

"If," said they, "he will not now as much as rise up to us, being the greatest number, what can we expect if we become subjects to his authority." They peremptorily told him that they would not have him for their bishop, and *that they would not* have the rites of their ancient Church perverted by him. They also told him of the great injustice done to them by the Saxons, with whom they wished to have no intercourse, until they restored to the native Britons, what they had taken from them by usurpation. "And, no doubt," says Bishop Stillingfleet, "the British bishops looked upon this attempt of Augustine upon them, as adding one usurpation to another: it was this that made them so averse from any communication with the missionaries, which otherwise had been inexcusable."

"This," as Lord Bacon says, "was the Britons' resolution, and they were as good as their word; for they maintained the liberty of their Church five hundred years after this time, and were the last of all the churches of Europe that gave up their power to the Roman beast, and in the person of Henry VIII., that came of that blood by *Owen Tudor*, the first that took that power away again."[5]

The invasion of the Saxons drove the Britons into Wales, and the Christianity of the latter receded before the Paganism of the former. In the middle of the sixth century the endowed bishopricks of Wales

---

[2] Smollet suggests, not without some degree of reason, "that the person was tutored for this purpose, and in all probability was not blind."

[3] Origines Britannicæ, c. 8.

[4] Laurentius, the successor of Augustine, endeavoured, by expostulary epistles, to gain over the Britons and the Scots to conform to all the ceremonies and submit to the authority of Rome, but without success. Laurentius complains that the Scots were equally obstinate with the Britons of Wales in opposing the custom of the universal Church. The Bishop Laurentius says, "We thought that the Scots had been better, but we found them no way to differ from the Britons in their behaviour. For their Bishop (Dagon) coming

to us, not only refused to eat with us, but even to take his repast in the same house where we were entertained, nor lodge under the same roof."—*Bowles' History of the Popes.*

"The Britons maintained their orthodoxy 150 years after Augustus's conference uncontaminated with the errors of the Church of Rome."—*Leland de Scrip. Brit.*, p. 99.

"The ancient British Church, by whomsoever planted, was a stranger to the Bishop of Rome, and all his pretended authorities."—*Blackstone's Commentaries*, vol. iv., p. 105, ed. 1795.

[5] Lord Bacon, Historical Discourse on the Uniformity of the Government of England, 4to, 1647, p. 20.

were Llandaff, Margam, Llanbadarn, St. David's, St. Asaph, and Bangor, with St. Kebius, in Anglesea. St. David[6] was elected the primate in 519, at the Synod of Brevi, afterwards Llanddewi Brevi, called to suppress the Pelagian heresy, which had made rapid progress in the Cambro-British churches.

Thus nobly did the Cambro-Britons stand up for the independence of their Church, and refused to submit to the encroachment of the Bishop of Rome, and his legate Augustine the monk, who now forgot the advice given him by Pope Gregory, that it was not necessary that all churches should exactly use the same external ceremonies; for he was a man of a different spirit from the pontiff, and evinced too much of that temper which has, in subsequent ages, marked all the proceedings of the Roman pontiffs and their adherents. The time was now come when the saying of that prelate and martyr was being fulfilled, who being asked if it were proper to administer the sacred ordinance in wooden vessels, replied, "*We once had golden priests, who made use of wooden vessels; but now we have wooden priests, who make use of vessels of gold.*"

Augustine was greatly annoyed at receiving such a peremptory refusal,[7] and did not forget his threats which he had uttered. He informed his patron of what had taken place.

The King was not unwilling to see the Cambro-Britons chastised; he therefore instigated Ethelbert, King of Northumberland, to march his army into the territory of Brochwel Ysgythriog, Prince of Powys, within whose dominions the synod had been held.

Ethelfred, the King of Northumberland, having obtained a victory over the Northern Britons, turned his arms against the Welsh, who were at that time in possession of Chester. On his arrival near that city, his army being drawn up in front of

The Slaughter of the Monks of Bangor.

the enemy, he perceived a body of men, without military appearance, who were stationed in a place of security. Struck with the novelty of the sight, he enquired the cause, and was told that they were monks from the monastery of Bangor, who had come to offer up their prayers for the prosperous event of the day.

The monarch said, " If they cry to their God against us, then they fight against us with their prayers." Enraged at an opposition so singular in its nature, and stimulated by hatred of a religion which threatened the destruction of paganism, Ethelfred ordered his army to assault this defenceless and pious troop, who had already fasted and prayed for the space of three days.[8] Twelve hundred of these unfortunate religious men

[6] It is a remarkable fact that three distinguished prelates of the present century should immortalise their names by the defence of their religion : Bishop Bull defended the Nicene creed ; Bishop Horsley vindicated the Catholic Faith against the attacks of Dr. Priestly ; while Dr. Burgess stepped forward to vindicate the truth of the independency of the ancient British Church, and against the restless spirit of Socialism, thus forming a triad of Divines from the same diocese, celebrated for their defence of the Catholic Faith.

[7] See Brut y Brenhinoedd—The British History.

[8] " Ethelfrid, King of Northumberland, having besieged Chester in 607, and Brochmael, a British prince, advancing to relieve it, the monks of the neighbouring monastery of Bangor marched in pro-

cession to pray for the success of their countrymen. But the British being totally defeated, the heathen victor put the monks to the sword, and destroyed their monastery. The air to which these verses is adapted is called *Ymdaith Mwngc*, the Monks' March, and is supposed to have been played at their ill-omened procession."— *Walter Scott.*

" When heathen trumpets' clang
  Round beleaguer'd Chester rang,
  Veiled nun and friar grey
  Marched from Bangor's fair abbaye :

were cut to pieces; fifty only of the whole number present in the battle having escaped the enemy's sword. The army of the Northumbrian King was composed of so vast a number of men, that Brochmael[9] was soon defeated.

This unfavourable omen might naturally have cooled the ardour of a people less superstitious than the Welsh; but it seems that they regarded this act of Ethelfred as an impious sacrilege, and though in the action which ensued, or in the pursuit, they were terribly slaughtered, it appears, however, by the great loss which their enemies sustained, that they made a spirited resistance.[1] After the battle, the Saxon prince marched to Bangor, a British monastery, situated on the banks of the river Dee; and with a barbarism peculiar to the Goths, destructive of those arts which soften and improve human nature, he entirely laid waste that ancient and celebrated seminary of learning, and committed to the flames its valuable library.[2]

In consequence of this act of sacrilegious barbarism that noble institution never afterwards raised its head. It was the largest of all the *Bangors*, or religious houses among the Britons, but even the very ruins cannot now be traced. Giraldus Cambrensis, mentions that in his day, the vast pile of ruins then to be seen bore testimony to the ancient fame and extent of this monastery.[3] But we have now only the name of this once celebrated place, which is said to have contained accommodation for seven courses of monks, containing three hundred in each course.

Dr. Hammond, in writing on the subject of the intercourse between Augustine and the Abbot of Bangor, has fully cleared up this subject, and shown satisfactorily that Augustine was not dead (as some say) at the time of the battle of Bangor. Some old writers have even asserted that he was present[4] at the battle; but, be that as it may, the whole circumstances of the history show that Ethelbert, incited by him, urged the Northumbrian King, Ethelfred, to bring an army against the Britons of Wales; and from so powerful an enemy, and a fierce heathen, no compassion could be expected.

Ethelfred then attempted to penetrate into Wales; but his passage over the Dee, at Bangor, was

High their holy anthem sounds,
Cestria's vale the hymn rebounds,
Floating down the sylvan Dee.
    O miserere Domine!

On the long procession goes,
Glory round their crosses glows,
And the Virgin Mother mild
In their peaceful banner smiled;
Who could think such saintly band
Doom'd to feel unhallow'd hand?
Such was the Divine decree.
    O miserere Domine!

Bands that masses only sung,
Hands that censers only swung,
Met the northern bow and bill,
Heard the war-cry wild and shrill.
Woe to Brochmael's feeble band,
Woe to Olfrid's[*] bloody hand,
Woe to Saxon cruelty.
    O miserere Domine!

Weltering amid warriors slain,
Spurn'd by steeds with bloody mane,
Slaughter'd down by heathen blade,
Bangor's peaceful monks are laid:
Words of parting rest unspoke,
Praise unsung, and bread unbroke,
For their souls, for charity,
    O miserere Domine!

Bangor, o'er the murder wail,
Long the ruins told the tale;
Shatter'd towers, and broken arch,
Long recalled the woful march: †
On thy shrine no tapers burn,
Never shall thy priests return;
The pilgrim sighs and sings for thee,
    O miserere Domine! "

[9] Brochmael Ysgythriog.

[1] Langhorne, Chr. Reg. Aug., p. 150; Bede, lib. ii., cap. 2, p. 80; Saxon Chron. p. 25; William of Malmesbury, lib. i., p. 17.

[2] Humphrey Llwyd, p. 71.

[3] Leland says, "That the cumpace of the Abbay was a wallid toune; and yet remaineth (in Henry VIII.'s reign) the name of a gate caulid *Porth Hogan* by north; and the name of another *Porth Clais* by south. Dee syns changing the bottom rennith now thro the mydle, betwixt thes two gates; one being a mile drive from the other."—*Itinerary*. Turner, vol. i. 135.

[4] See Bishop Burgess, of St. David's, second letter to his clergy. The conference with Augustine took place A.D. 607, and was attended by seven bishops and a great number of religious men, chiefly from the great monastery of Bangor on the Dee.—See M. Thiers's History of the Norman Conquest, vol. i. p. 68. This distinguished foreign writer has entered fully into this subject.

[*] Ethelfrid.

† William of Malmesbury says that in his time the extent of the ruins of the monastery bore ample witness to the desolation occasioned by the massacre:—" Tot semiruti parietes ecclesiarum, tot anfractus porticum, tanta turba ruderum quantum vix alibi cernas."

disputed by the Prince of Powys, who gallantly sustained the charge until relieved by Cadvan,[5] the King of North Wales; by Meredyth, the King of South Wales; and Bledus, the Sovereign of Cornwall.[6] When the confederated princes had joined their forces they called in religion to their aid.

Demothus,[7] the Abbot of Bangor, made an oration to the army; and, before the action, gave orders that every soldier should kiss the ground, in commemoration of the communion of the body of Christ; and should take up water in their hands out of the river Dee, and drink it in remembrance of His sacred blood, which was shed for them.[8] Animated by this act of devotion, which in these times had a powerful influence on the mind, and stung with resentment for the disgrace and injuries they had lately received, the Welsh encountered the Saxons with great bravery, entirely defeated them with the loss of above ten thousand men, and obliged Ethelfred, with the remainder of his army, to retreat into their own country.[9] There was something singular in the fortunate event of that day as an act of retaliative justice, and as it severely punished, in the sight of Bangor, the recent desolation of its monastery.

The exertions of the British having failed, eight Anglo-Saxon governments were established in the island. This state of Britain has been denominated, with great impropriety, the Saxon Heptarchy. When all the kingdoms were settled, they formed an Octarchy. Ella, supporting his invasion in Sussex, like Hengist in Kent, made a Saxon duarchy before the year 500. When Cerdic erected the state of Wessex, in 519, a triarchy appeared; East Anglia made it a tetrarchy; Essex, a pentarchy. The success of Ida, after 547, having established a sovereignty of Angles in Bernicia, the island beheld an hexarchy. When the northern Ella penetrated, in 560, southward of the Tees, his kingdom of Deira produced an heptarchy. In 586, the Angles branching from Deira into the regions south of the Humber, the state of Mercia completed the Anglo-Saxon Octarchy. These states warred with each other; sometimes one state was absorbed by another; sometimes, after an interval, it emerged again.

It was in slow progression that the nations, comprised under the title of Anglo-Saxons, possessed themselves of the different districts of the island. The Britons yielded no post, until it had been purchased by blood; and almost a century and a half passed away from the first arrival of Hengist to the full establishment of the Octarchy. It is difficult, during this dark period, to give an account of the conquests these states made on each other.

A.D. 610.—Misfortune flew upon all sides to assail the persecuted Cymry, but they sometimes triumphed. Ceolwulph advanced with the warriors of Wessex, not merely to the Severn, but crossed it into the province of Glamorgan. Affrighted at his force, the inhabitants hastened to Tewdric, their former king, who had quitted his dignity, in behalf of his son Mowric, to lead a solitary life among the beautiful rocks and woodlands of *Tintern*. They solicited him to resume the military command, in which he had never known disgrace, if he sympathised in the welfare of his countrymen or of his son. The royal hermit beheld the dreaded Saxons on the Wye, but the remembrance of his own achievements inspired him with hope. He put on his forsaken armour, conducted the tumult of battle with his ancient skill, and drove the invaders over the Severn. A mortal wound on the head arrested the pulse of life, whilst he was in the full enjoyment of his glory, and he breathed his last wishes for his country's safety at the confluence of the Severn and the Wye. The local appellation, Methern, the abbreviation of Merthern Tewdric,[1] points out his remains to the sympathy of posterity. In the sixteenth century his body was found in a good state of preservation, and the mark of the fatal blow on the head was still visible.[2]

[5] In consequence of this victory, Cadvan, King of North Wales, was elected at Chester to the sovereignty of Britain; but in the present loss of the Empire that dignity could extend no further than to command the united forces of the remaining Britons. In 617 according to Matthew of Westminster—the furious King of Northumberland—the great afflictor of Chester and the Britons, was slain by Redwold, the King of the East Angles.

[6] Humphrey Lhuyd, p. 72; Geoff. Monmouth, p. 396.

[7] Dinoeth.   [8] Langhorne, p. 151; Humphrey Lhuyd, p. 72.

[9] Verstegan, c. v. p. 132; Geoff. Monmouth, p. 371; Humphrey Lhuyd's Brev., p. 72; Rowland's Mon. Ant., p. 188; Langhorne, Chr. Reg. Aug., p. 151.

[1] Merthyr Tewdric, the martyr of Tewdric. Usher quotes the Register of Llandaff for this conflict, p. 562. Langhorne, Chron., p. 148.

[2] Godwin, præsul. ap. Usher, 563. In the chancel of Mathern Church an epitaph mentions that he lies there entombed.—*Williams's Monmouthshire.* Appendix, No. 17.

H

"The condition of the Cambro-Britons at this juncture," says Mr. Turner (History of Anglo-Saxons), "calls for our most compassionate anxiety. They had been driven out of their ancient country; they had retired into those parts of the island which were divided by mountains, woods, marshes, and rivers, from the rest; yet, in this retreat they lived, with their hands against every man, and every man's [3] hand against them; they were the common butt of enterprise to the Angles of Bernicia and Deira and Mercia—to the Saxons of Wessex, and to the Gwyddelians of Ireland; and yet they were always as eager to assail as to defend. The wild prophecies of enthusiasts, who mistook hope for inspiration, having promised to them, in no long period, the enjoyment of the soil from which they had been exiled, produced in them a perpetual appetite for war. Their independent sovereignties, fed by their hostile ambition the flames of domestic quarrels, supplied new hecatombs to the demons of destruction, and accelerated the ruin of their independence. The Cymry maintained the unequal conflict against the Anglo-Saxons with wonderful bravery, and did not lose the sovereignty of their country until the improvements of their conquerors made the conquest a blessing!"

A.D. 617.—King Ethelfrith being dissatisfied with his kingdom of Bernicia, and the trophies that he had won in Scotland and Wales, invaded Deira, to which Edwin, the son of Ella, at the age of three years, had succeeded, and by expelling the little infant, converted the Saxon states in England into an hexarchy. Edwin was carried into North Wales, and was generously educated by Cadvan, prince of Wales. He afterwards succeeded Ethelfrith in his kingdom, and was driven by Cadwallon, the son of Cadvan, to engage in hostilities against his former protector. Cadwallon had invaded his dominion, and had penetrated as far as Widdrington, eight miles north of Morpeth; but Edwin defeated him, and not content with his victory, he pursued his enemy into Wales, and thence into Ireland. He reigned with great prosperity for eighteen years, during which time a considerable portion of Wales and the Menavian [4] Islands submitted to his power.

So severely did he exercise his advantages, that the British Triads characterise him as one of "three plagues that befel the island of Anglesea."

For seven years his authority continued over Gwynedd. But the spirit of ambition was only flattering him to his ruin. A slow but unerring retribution always avenges the violations of morality. Cadwallon besought the aid of Penda, and the restless sexagenary armed with all the activity of youth. The confederated kings met in Hadfield Chase, in Yorkshire, on the 12th of October, A.D. 633. A desperate battle ended with the death of Edwin, in his forty-sixth year; one of his children and most of his army perished. The royal widow fled in terror under the protection of Paulinus and a valiant soldier, with some of her children, to her kinsman in Kent.

On the death of Edwin, the ancient divisions of Northumbria again prevailed, and an heptarchy re-appeared. His cousin Osric, the nephew of Ella, succeeded to Deira, and Eanfrid, the long exiled son of Ethelfrith, to Bernicia; both restored paganism. The Welsh King, Cadwallon, full of projects of revenge against the nation of the Angles, continued his war.[5] Osric rashly ventured to besiege him in a strong town, but an unexpected sally from Cadwallon destroyed the King of Deira, and then the victor desolated Northumbria.

The swords of Cadwallon and his army seemed the agents destined to fulfil their cherished prophecy.[6] The fate of the Anglo-Saxons was now about to arrive; three of their kings had been already offered up to the shades of the injured Cymry, and Arthur had revived in Cadwallon. Alas! how erroneous are all human calculations! We never know but that the same moon which silvers our most gorgeous trophies,

---

[3] Matthew of Westminster paints this very forcibly: he says the Britons retired to Cornwall and to Wales, which he describes as their impregnable country.

[4] The Menavian Islands were Euborica and Mona, or Mann and Anglesea. Bede states, c. 9, that Anglesea contained 960 hides of families, and of men 300. The fertility of Anglesea occasioned the proverb, "Môn Mam Cymry;" Mona the mother of Wales.—*Pryse's Preface to Wynne's Caradoc.* The King of Gwynedd had his royal seat at Aberffraw, which is now a small village.—*Lhuyd's Frag.*, 52.

[5] Bede, lib. iii. c. 1. The town was a municipium; in all probability, York.

[6] The men of Powys so distinguished themselves in this battle that they obtained from Cadwallon a boon of fourteen privileges. The Welsh call the scene of conflict Meigen. See *Cynddelw* cited in Owen's Llywarch Hên.

may also make visible the chilling prison of our tomb. This moment we smile and vaunt, one more, and tears bedew our high-plumed hearse.

Triumphant with the fame of fourteen great battles and sixty skirmishes, Cadwallon despised the rash youth who presented himself in arms to impede his full success. The blood of Earfrid, his brother, and the cries of desolated Northumbria, demanded of Oswald to be the deliverer of the land; with humble confidence he committed his cause to the arbitration of Providence,[7] and calmly waited the decision on the banks of the Denise.[8] There

> "The enthraller of Lloegr, the fierce aflictor of his foes, the prosperous lion fell;
> The wrath of slaughter hastened to make the Eagles fall."[9]

Cadwallon and the flower of his army perished. The return to the Cymry of their ancient country never became probable again.[1]

Penda, King of Mercia, is the first prince who holds an important place in our Bardic history. He obtained supreme power in A.D. 626; and, during a reign of twenty-nine years, was engaged in continual wars with his neighbours. In A.D. 642, he gained a great victory over the Northumbrians, at a place called Maserfield, where the pious King Oswald was slain by Penda, who with the "mountain dwellers of Wales," at that time his allies, completely routed the Northumbrians. Oswalddestren, now Oswestry in Shropshire, takes its name from this transaction. Insatiable in acts of ferocity, Penda caused the head and limbs of Oswald to be severed from his body, and exposed on stakes, but they were removed by Oswy, his successor.[2]

On the death of Cadwallon, A.D. 676, his son, Cadwaladr, succeeded to the kingdom of North Wales and to the ideal sovereignty of Britain.[3] In the course of his reign, the irruptions of the Saxons had become more frequent, and a famine, with its usual attendants, a pestilential distemper, had raged[4] in Britain. To avoid the common dangers of his country, a conduct which did not mark a magnanimous spirit, Cadwaladr, with numbers of his nobility and other subjects, retired, A.D. 689, to Alan, his kinsman, the King of Bretaigne, in whose Court he found a hospitable reception.[5] From an uniform, and perhaps a singular principle of affection, we have seen this country afford an asylum to the Britons in every season of adversity.

Shortly afterwards, this weak and superstitious king abdicated his throne, went to Rome, and was kindly received by Pope Sergius. He, for the good of his soul, submitted to have his head shaven and to be initiated into the order of the White Monks. He lived in this state eight years, a situation very unworthy of a prince, as it secluded him from the practice of active virtue.

A.D. 703.—The death of Cadwaladr, which took place this year, put an end to the dignity which had been annexed for many ages to the British government.[6] The Welsh princes of later times usually resided at Diganwy,[7] on the water of Conway, and at Caer Seiont,[8] near Caernarvon.

A.D. 741.—The next monarch that paid a visit to the principality was Ethelbald; the object of his visit was to annex the pleasant region between the Severn and the Wye to his Mercian territories; he entered Wales with a powerful army at Carno Mountain, near Abergavenny, where his progress was checked by the Britons under the command of Prince Roderic Molwynog, grandson of King Cadwaladr. A fierce battle took place, which, however, was not decisive to either party.

A.D. 746.—Ethelbald, elated with his partial successes attempted another invasion of Wales, and advanced

---

[7] The piety of Oswald, prior to the battle, is expressed by Bede. To his arrayed army, he exclaimed, "Let us kneel to the Omnipotent Lord, the existing and the true, and unite to implore his protection against a fierce and arrogant enemy. He knows that we have undertaken a just war for the safety of our people." The army obeyed the mandate, lib. iii. c. 2.

[8] Camden places this battle at Dilston, on a small brook which empties itself into the Tyne, 854, Gib. ed. Smith marks Erringburn as the rivulet on which Cadwallon perished.

[9] Llywarch Hên., pp. 115, 117. This Bard composed an elegy upon his friend.

[1] Turner.
[2] Bede, lib. ii. c. 12.
[3] Rowland's Mona Ant., p. 188; Verstegan, c. v. p. 132.
[4] Wynne's Wales, p. 8.
[5] Baker's Chron., p. 4; J. Fordun's Hist. Scot; Gale, p. 647.
[6] Welsh Chron., p. 5; Rowland's Mona, p. 188; Lhuyd, p. 66.
[7] Famous in Tacitus by the name of Cangorum.
[8] Called by the Romans, Segontium.

H 2

as far as Henfern.[9] At that place, he again met with the spirited resistance of the Welsh, and by the assistance of their allies they gave him a signal overthrow.

A.D. 763.—King Offa succeeded to the throne of Mercia. The Saxons at this time were daily encroaching upon South Wales. The inhabitants of this country, filled with indignation at the repeated injuries they had suffered, rose up in arms, entered Mercia with fire and sword, and retaliated on their enemies for the devastations they had made in Wales; and, animated by their success, they continued to make frequent incursions into Mercia, committing at the same time great ravages therein. Offa, determined to endure these injuries no longer, entered into a league with the other Saxon princes to check their enterprising spirit. He raised a considerable army, with which he passed the Severn into Wales; but the Welsh being too weak to encounter so great a force, quitted the even country and retired into the mountains, where they knew they would be secure from the vengeance of the combined Saxons, who, when they found themselves unable to penetrate with advantage these strong and natural fortifications, returned into Mercia. As soon

Battle of Rhuddlan Marsh.

as they had retired, the Welsh renewed their incursions into newly acquired Saxon territories. Offa, to prevent these inroads, planted a colony of Saxons near the Severn and the Wye; and as a further security against the reiterated invasions of the Welsh, he caused a deep dyke and a high rampart to be made, which extended one hundred miles over rocks and mountains, and across deep vallies and rivers. This great work is still to be traced, and it retains its name, " *Clawdd Offa*," Offa's Dyke,[1] to this day. An interval of peace

[9] Commonly called by the Welsh Henffordd, or the Old Road.— *Humphrey Lhuyd*, p. 74.

[1] This dyke extended from the River Wye to the *Dee*, along the counties of Hereford, Radnor, and Montgomery, Denbigh, and Flint. It may be traced between Bishop Castle and Newtown, thence northward by Mellington Hall, Caerddin, Limor Park, Forden Heath, Nant y Criba, Layton Hall, and Buttington Church, in Montgomeryshire. It then crosses the Severn and passes by the churches of Llandysilio and Llanymynach; from this place it runs by Tref-y-Clawdd, Cefn y Bwch race-course above Oswestry, then above Selatyn, from thence to the River Ceiriog, the Glyn, Cefn y Bedd, where there is a large breach, supposed to be the places of interment of the English who fell in the Battle of Crogen; it then goes by Chirk Castle, and below Cefn y Wern; crosses the Dee and the Ruabon road, near Plâs Madoc, forms part of the turnpike-road to Wrexham, thence by Plâs Power Adwy'r Clawdd near Minera, by Brymbo crosses Cagidog river, thence to Bryn Yorkyn, Coed Talwrn, Treuddyn Chapel near Mold, pointing towards the Clwydian Hills; beyond which there can be no further traces discovered.

gave Offa the opportunity of completing this celebrated dyke; but the Welsh were not insensible to the dishonour and injury thus done by the Mercian King to their country. They concealed their feelings under the mask of indifference, but secretly concerted a plan for the destruction of the work, which they carried into effect on the night of St. Stephen's day. They broke down the rampart and levelled the dyke to the length of a bow-shot. They afterwards, in conjunction with the Northumbrians and the South Saxons, attacked the camp of Offa and slew a considerable number of his army before any resistance could be made. Offa's troops, unable to sustain the onset of the Welsh, were obliged to retreat to save themselves from destruction. Offa immediately retired into his own dominions, meditating vengeance against his enemies. His anger was first directed against the hostages given by the Welsh. He ordered them to be more strictly confined; and afterwards their wives and families were consigned to perpetual slavery. Soon afterwards he marched with a formidable army into the confines of Wales, breathing vengeance; but several years elapsed before a general engagement took place.

A.D. 795.—At this time, however, a general action took place between these parties upon Rhuddlan Marsh, Flintshire. The Welsh, who were commanded in this memorable conflict by Caradoc, King of North Wales, were defeated with dreadful slaughter, and their leader was killed in the field. All who fell into the hands of the Saxon Prince were ordered to be massacred. According to tradition, the Welsh who escaped the sword of the conqueror in their precipitous flight across the marsh, perished in the water by the flowing of the tide. According to some historians, Offa died soon after this action; but others say that he, as well as Meredydd, Prince of Dyfed, were slain in the battle of Rhuddlan Marsh.[1]

> " On Morva Rhyddlan's plain the rivals stood,
> Till Morva Rhyddlan's plain was drench'd in blood :
> Not all the Saxon's might could Cymry quell,
> Till, foremost of his band, Caradoc fell."

---

[1] We have been favoured with the following verses by Mr. J. M. Jones, of Trefriw: they are a free translation of the original verses in Welsh by the Rev. Evan Evans, of Ince, one of the Chaired Bards of Gwynedd. The original verses, which are very beautiful, are adapted to the fine old plaintive Welsh air, " Morva Rhuddlan :"—

> " O'er Arvon's heights the sun sank low,
>   The veil of night doth all invest,
> The zephyr's breath hath ceas'd to blow,
>   And distant waves are lull'd to rest.
> My heart within my heaving breast,
>   Oh! deeply throbs with grief and pain,
> Whilst musing on that scene unblest,
>   On Morva Rhuddlan's fatal plain!

> " Break through the gloom upon my sight,
>   The massive shields! Ha! now I hear
> The clash of blades—the hissing flight
>   Of arrows—and the charging cheer;
> But, hark! 'bove all, both loud and clear,
>   Caradoc's voice above the slain—
> ' Turn we their battle's wild career,
>   Or sink on Morva Rhuddlan's plain!'

> " Each Briton's heart with courage swells,
>   Each British cheek 's with fury red;
> Each nervous arm a foeman fells,
>   Each blade a fiercer death hath sped;
> Lo! frightful gaps—and dead on dead!
>   Whilst Cambria prays that Heaven would shield
> Her hearths and homes—her warriors aid
>   In fight on Rhuddlan's bloody field!

> " By solemn dread my soul 's assail'd :
>   The victors' shouts now louder grow!
> Boast not; 'twas numbers that prevailed,
>   And not thy might, exulting foe!
> But, oh! of those the grief and woe,
>   And wailing as they fly to gain
> The mountain heights, and leave below
>   Their dead on Rhuddlan's bloody plain.

> " Old Snowdon's crags—each stream and dell,
>   Loud echoes bear to British wail;
> And rocks to rocks responsive tell
>   Of Cambria's loss the fearful tale;
> And now upon the rising gale
>   Is borne Caradoc's fate along,
> And weeping Bards his fall bewail
>   In Morva Rhuddlan's mournful song!

> " I seek the warriors' lowly bed
>   On Rhuddlan's Marsh; but cannot trace
> A vestige of the noble dead,
>   Or aught to mark their resting-place;
> Green rush and reeds are all that grace
>   The graves of those in fight who fell,
> For freedom—for their land and race.
>   Oh, fatal field! farewell, farewell!"

The translator found it too difficult to follow the measure of the original, namely the ancient national air, said to be composed immediately following and to commemorate the carnage of Morva Rhuddlan.

A.D. 819.—After the death of Cynan Tindacthwy, Mervyn Vrych and Essyllt succeeded to the sovereignty of North Wales[3]; annexing the island of Man to their other dominions.[4] In the early part of their reign,[5] Egbert, King of the West Saxons, invaded Wales with a powerful army, desolated the country as far as the mountains of Snowdon,[6] and seized on the lordship of Rhyvonioc.[7] He then advanced to Mona, and took possession of that island, having fought a bloody battle with the Welsh at Llanvaes, near Beaumaris,[8] and though the island was soon recovered by King Mervyn, and the Saxons were driven out, it lost at this period the ancient name of Mona, and was afterwards by the Englishmen called Anglesey, or Englishman's Isle.[9] This formidable inroad was no sooner over, as if the Welsh were to enjoy no interval of peace, than Kenulph, King of Mercia, in two successive inroads, committed great devastation in West Wales and in Powys.[1]

A.D. 828.—The valour and policy of Egbert, at this period, had united the Saxon Heptarchy into one kingdom;[2] and such an union, under a vigorous administration, might have proved fatal to the Welsh, if the attention of the Saxon Prince had not been diverted from foreign conquests to the security of his own territories. To consolidate more closely the various parts of his dominions, he gave the whole of his new kingdom the common name of ENGLAND;[3] and at this juncture every species of union was necessary to oppose the formidable and increasing invasions of the Danes.

A.D. 833.—A large body of these people landed about this time in West Wales,[4] and such was the animosity of the Welsh, and such the wretched alternative left them, that they united with the Danes in a common interest as the less and most distant evil, to wreak their vengeance upon the Saxons, and to establish the Danish power on the ruin of more immediate and hereditary enemies.

The Welsh, in consequence of this alliance, joined their forces with the Danes, and after having ravaged a great part of his dominions, and destroyed many of his castles and fortified towns, they fought a severe battle with the Saxon Prince, upon Hengist Downs, but in this action they sustained a terrible defeat, with the slaughter of a great part of their army.[5]

A.D. 835.—Incensed at this invasion, and alarmed at the consequence of such alliances in future, Egbert made war upon the Welsh, and invested the city of Chester, determined that they should feel the utmost effects of his resentment and power. This city had hitherto remained in possession of the Welsh,[6] and was regarded as an important post upon the frontier. It was taken at this time by Egbert.[7] Among other marks of his indignation against the very memory of the Britons, he gave orders that the brazen statue of Cadwallon should be taken down and defaced;[8] he likewise issued a proclamation that all the men, with their wives and children, who were descended from British blood, should depart his territories in six months, on pain of death;[9] and to add injury to insult, he made another law, as savage as it was unavailing, which affixed the penalty of death to every Welshman who passed the limits of Offa's Dyke, and should be taken on the English borders.[1] Those coercive restraints were more necessary than such a feeble barrier and futile law; though the hand of power had drawn an arbitrary line, which insulted the feelings, and entrenched upon the rights of a warlike and irascible people.

A.D. 838.—The Saxon Prince died soon after the siege of Chester, and his death probably suspended for several ages the destiny of Wales.

A short cessation of the Danish inroads gave leisure to Bertred, the tributary sovereign of Mercia, to renew hostilities against the Welsh,[2] and a severe battle was fought by the two princes, at a place

---

[3] Rowland's Mon. Ant., p. 188.　　　[4] Ibid., p. 173.

[5] Matth. Westm., pp. 224, 227, recites three different invasions of Wales by Egbert, in which he subdued that country and made its king tributary, A.D. 810, 811, 830.

[6] Eryri in the Welsh, signifying Mountains of Snow. Humphrey Lhuyd, p. 65.

[7] Welsh Chron., pp. 24, 25.　　　[8] Ibid.

[9] Rowland's Mon. Ant., pp. 172, 173.

[1] Welsh Chron., p. 25.

[2] Fabian, p. 184 ; Rowland's Mon. Ant., p. 172.

[3] Humphey Lhuyd, Brev., p. 13 ; Verstegan, c. v. p. 125.

[4] Grafton's Chron., p. 132 ; Welsh Chron., p. 27.

[5] Saxon Chron., p. 72.　　　[6] Welsh Chron., p. 27.

[7] Grafton's Chron., p. 132 ; Fabian, p. 184.

[8] Howe's Chron., p. 77.

[9] Welsh Chron., p. 27, from Ranulph Cestr.

[1] Speed's Chron., p. 318.

[2] Saxon Chron., p. 75.

called Kettel, upon the frontiers, in which Mervyn, the King of North Wales, was slain, A.D. 843, who left his eldest son, named Roderick, to succeed to his dignity.[3]

A.D. 843.—The prospect now opens under a new point of view,—the unenviable reign of Roderick. This young prince succeeded to his father's throne with a greater extent of territory than had fallen to the share of any Cambrian sovereign. He enjoyed, by right of his father and mother, the sovereignty of the Isle of Man, with the territories of North Wales and Powys, and having married Angharad, the heiress of South Wales, the whole province of Cambria centred in his person.[4] The firmness resulting from this union, the nature of the country and valour of its inhabitants, their inveteracy against the Saxons, and the perilous situation of that people, were important advantages which opened with the reign of Roderick.

If this fortunate combination of circumstances had been directed agreeably to a wise policy, it would probably have secured the independency of Wales, and have fixed its government upon a basis so solid and permanent that it might have sustained the storms of ages, and have fallen at length amidst the ruins of time, unless undermined by the refinements and luxury of a bordering and more civilised and powerful people.

Instead of taking advantage of this fortunate conjuncture, a crisis which will never more return in the annals of Wales, a fatal and irreparable measure took place. For Roderick, early in his reign, divided his dominions into three principalities, which, during his life, were governed by chieftains acting under his authority; and this singular event seems to have arisen from the narrow idea, that the Welsh, accustomed to be ruled by their native princes, ought not to yield obedience to a common sovereign.[5]

The death of Mervyn Vrych, the youth and inexperience of Roderick, and the late victory obtained over the Welsh, flattered Berthred, the Mercian prince, with the hopes of further success. Agreeably to this design, and strengthened by the aid of Ethelwulph, the King of England, he entered North Wales with a powerful army,[6] A.D. 846, and advanced as far as Anglesea, which he laid waste in a cruel manner.[7] The young Prince Roderick, on this trying occasion, neglected no exertion, which was due to his own honour and to the defence of his country. By the spirited resistance he made, the King of Mercia was prevented from making any great progress in the island; and, soon after, fortunately for the Welsh, the attention of that prince was called to the protection of his own dominions from the power of the Danes.[8] The inroads of these people increasing every day, the English fully employed in attending to their own safety, left the Welsh to enjoy many years of unusual tranquillity.

If Roderick had possessed the qualities of a truly great prince, he would, at least at this fortunate period, have attempted to provide against future evils; and the nature of his country, intersected by rivers fortified with mountains, and almost surrounded by the ocean, might have pointed out the rational means of defence.

Had this prince made a proper use of the leisure which the troubles in England had given him, he would have placed garrisons in the frontier towns; would have collected magazines, and fortified the passes; and he would have exerted his utmost ability to secure his country from foreign invaders, by forming a naval power: he would also have endeavoured to reduce his subjects to a just subordination, by promoting among them a spirit of union, and a steady obedience to the laws. Instead of these regulations, that period seems to have been distinguished by a total neglect of every measure, which, if steadily pursued, might have given security to his kingdom.

A.D. 872.—The Danes, having received a repulse in England, and being, by treaty, obliged to relinquish that country, made a descent on the island of Anglesea, where in two battles they met with a very spirited opposition from Roderick; one of which was fought at Bangole, and the other at Menegid.

[3] Welsh Chron., p. 27, 28.
[4] Rowland, p. 173, 188; Welsh Chron., p. 35.
[5] Rowland's Mon. Ant., p. 174.
[6] Sim. Dunelme, pp. 120, 139; Hist. Angl. Script.; Matth. West., p. 231.

[7] Welsh Chron., p. 85.
[8] Sim. Dunelme, Ann. 874; Saxon Chron., p. 82; Welsh Chron., p. 31.

At the same time South Wales was invaded by another body of Danes, who desolated the country and laid the churches and religious houses in ruins.[9]

About this time Roderick changed the royal residence from Caer Segont[1] to Aberffraw in Anglesea. It is strange that he should desert a country where every mountain was a natural fortress; and in times of such difficulty and danger, should make a choice of a residence so exposed and defenceless.

A.D. 872.—Alfred the Great ascended the English throne. We could dwell with delight upon the virtues and glorious actions of this prince. He was one of the most renowned scholars of the day, as well as one of the greatest monarchs that ever sat on the throne of these realms. And it is with pleasure that we record, that his learned preceptors, John and Asser Menaviensis, received, in a seat of learning in Wales, those bright endowments which qualified them to render such important service to their royal pupil.

This prince is celebrated as the founder of the English navy. The most brilliant incident in his history was, perhaps, his defence of England against the formidable Hastings. In his struggles against the Northmen, over whom he prevailed at Eddington, he had to oppose power rather than ability; but in resisting Hastings he had to withstand a skilful veteran, versed in all the arts of war by thirty years practice of it, renowned for his numerous successes in other regions, and putting in action a mass of hostility which might have destroyed a man of less ability than the Saxon king.

> "Would'st thou gain thy country's loud applause,
> Be thou the bold assertor of her cause;
> Her voice in council, in the fight her sword.
> In peace, in war, pursue thy country's good,
> For her bare thy bold breast, and pour thy generous blood."—*Choice of Hercules.*

"Before the winter," says an old writer, "had fettered animated nature with its icy bands, the indefatigable Hastings had raised a large army from the East Anglians and Northumbrians. Their wives, their shipping, and their wealth, they confided to the East Anglians; and marching with that vigorous rapidity from which Hastings had so often derived his surest advantages, they rested neither night nor day until they had reached and fortified Chester in the Wiral.[2] Alfred was active to pursue, but he did not overtake them till they had embosomed themselves in military defences, which the military knowledge of that day respected as impregnable, though which, perhaps, our attainments might despise. Alfred, for two days, besieged them, drove away all the cattle in the vicinity, slew every enemy who ventured beyond the encampment, and burnt and consumed all the corn in this district."[3]

Why the siege was prosecuted so long, has not been explained to us. Perhaps, as Chester was at the extremity of the dominions which the King considered as his own, he was satisfied with taking measures that should keep the enemy beyond his frontiers.

A.D. 895.—They had now been nearly two years in England, exerting a courage and activity which might have overwhelmed a monarch who wielded his sceptre with a less wise and steady hand. But Alfred's talents augmented with his emergencies. Hastings began to feel their superiority: his future activity was rather depredation than personal competition. From Chester he led his bands, for sustenance, into North Wales; he plundered, and then quitted it: but not daring to molest West Saxony or Mercia, where the troops of Alfred were watching his progress, he made a circuit through Northumbria and East

---

[9] Welsh Chron., p. 34.

[1] Near the present town of Caernarvon.

[2] Spelman, who in his life of Alfred is generally accurate, construed Lego-ceaster to mean Leicester, but this town is spelt with an *r* before ceaster, as Leger-ceaster, Legra-ceaster, Sax. Chron., pp. 25, 106. The Wirall is thus described by Camden: "From the city (Chester), there runneth out a chersonese into the sea, inclosed on the one side with the estuary of the Dee, and on the other with the River Mersey: we call it Wirall; the Welsh, because it is a corner, call it Cilgwri. This was all hithertofore a desolate forest, and not inhabited (as natives say); but King Edward disforested it; now it is well furnished with towns."

[3] Sax. Chron., 95.

Anglia, and proceeded till he reached Mersey in Essex. Hastings, before the winter, drew his ships from the Thames up the Lea.[4]

The sovereignty of Alfred was not only established over the Anglo-Saxons, but even the Cymry in Wales acknowledged his power, and sought his alliance. Many petty kings still reigned in Wales, who were always fighting against each other, with various success. Roderic the Great, who fell in battle, in A.D. 876, and who had the dominion of all Wales, divided it into three sovereignties; North Wales, South Wales, and Powys, whose seats of power were at Aberffraw, Dinevor, and Mathraval. He devised these kingdoms to his three sons, of whom Anarawd had Gwynedd, or North Wales; Cadell, South Wales; and Mervyn, Powys.[5]

But, notwithstanding the predominance of Roderic in Wales, and the dignity which he conferred on his sons, the inferior kingdoms still continued, although oppressed by the usurping claims of ambition. It is asserted by Asser, that Hemeid, and all the inhabitants of South Wales, were harassed by the sons of Roderic; and that, in this exigency, they submitted themselves to Alfred, to have the benefit of his protection. Helised, son of Tewdwr, King of Brecon, distressed also by the son of Roderic, sought the patronage of Alfred. Nor were these the only Welsh princes who sheltered themselves under the power of the West Saxon king. Howel, the son of Rhys, King of Glegnenig, and Brochmael and Fermail, the sons of Meiric, the Kings of Gwent and Monmouthshire, to escape the oppression of the Earl Eadred and of the Mercians, submitted themselves to Alfred to enjoy his protection against their enemies. Even Anarawd, the King of Gwynedd, and his brothers, abandoning the friendship of the Northumbrians, whose alliance had been rather injurious than profitable, made a personal visit to Alfred, and besought his friendship. The King received Anarawd honourably, became his sponsor at his confirmation, and enriched him with ample presents. He submitted himself to Alfred, and conditioned to be obedient to the royal pleasure, like Ethered, the commander of Mercia.[6]

The friendship of Alfred was never sought in vain. All who demanded his aid experienced the vigilance and protection with which the king defended himself and those attached to him. To what a noble eminence does this fact and these submissions exalt his character. *He never raised a weapon against the Welsh*, and yet the Princes of Wales requested his sovereignty, in order to enjoy the benefit of his wisdom and power. It was a generous confidence which they conceded: but what must have been the popular reputation of Alfred? How pure the life of justice and virtue which would induce such trust, and, in an age of plunder, could possess it without encroachment and without blame!

One circumstance was a constant source of regret in Alfred's mind. He had passed the early period of his youth without instruction. This was caused by the absurdity and over-fondness of his father, combined with the ignorance, which was the fashion of the day, to deprive the young prince of any education. His biographer states that he was twelve years of age before he was even taught to read.

When Alfred began his own education, his principal obstacle was the want of an instructor; and from the period of his father's death, in A.D. 858, to his accession in A.D. 871, he had no opportunity of acquiring that knowledge which he coveted. But when he succeeded to the throne, which invested him with the wealth and influence of the West Saxon Kings, he sent, at various intervals, to different parts at home and abroad, for instructors capable of translating the learned languages. "Like the sagacious bee, which springs in the dawn of summer from its beloved cells, wheels its swift wings through the trackless air, descends upon the shrubs and flowers of vegetable nature, selects what it prefers, and brings home the grateful load; so Alfred, directing afar his intellectual eye, sought elsewhere for the treasure which his own kingdom did not afford."[7]

The merit and learning of Asser and John Menaviensis soon reached the King's ear. He sent for these two distinguished scholars from St. David's College in Wales. "I was called by the King," says Asser, in

---

[4] Hor. Lig., 333. The Lea (Ligan) is a little river which divides Essex from Middlesex, as the Stour separates it from Suffolk, and the Stort from Hertfordshire.

[5] Wynne's Wales, 27—34.
[6] Asser's Life of Alfred, pp. 49, 50.
[7] Asser, p. 45.

I

his plain but interesting biography, " from the western extremities of Wales. I accompanied my conductors to Sussex, and first saw him in the royal city of Dene. I was benignantly received by him ; among other things he asked me earnestly to devote myself to his service, and to become his companion. He requested me to leave all my preferments beyond the Severn, and he promised to compensate me for them by greater preferments." Asser expressed his regret at quitting without necessity, and merely for profit, the place where he had been brought up, and where he had taken orders. Alfred replied, " If this will not suit you, accommodate me with at least half your time. Be with me six months, and pass the rest in Wales." Asser declined to engage himself until he had consulted his friends. The King condescended to repeat his solicitations, and Asser promised to return to him within half a year ; a day was fixed as a pledge for his visit, and on the fourth day of their interview, Asser quitted him to go home.'

The Saxon clergy, as well as the rest of the population, were at this time overwhelmed in the grossest ignorance. " Very few were they," says Alfred, " on this side of the Humber (the most improved parts of England), who could understand their daily prayers in English, or translate any letter from the Latin. I think there were not many beyond the Humber ; they were so few, that I cannot recollect one single instance on the south of the Thames when I took the kingdom."'

A fever seized the learned Welshman at Winton, and continued to oppress him for a year. The King, not seeing him on the appointed day, sent letters to inquire into the cause of his tarrying, and to accelerate his journey. Asser, unable to stir, wrote to inform him of the state he was in, but on his recovery, he advised with his friends, and on receiving their assent, he attached himself to Alfred for a .moiety of every year. The clergy of St. David's expected that Alfred would preserve their patrimony from the depredations of Herneid. " I was honourably received in the royal city at Leonaford," says Asser, " and at that time stayed eight months in his court. I translated and read to him whatever books he wished, which were within our reach ; for it was his peculiar and perpetual custom, day and night, amidst all his other afflictions of mind and body, either to read books himself, or to have them read to him by others."'

It was about this period that Asser suggested to his royal master the propriety of establishing seminaries of learning in his kingdom for the education of his people, who were then in total ignorance, as he himself acknowledges. Asser further recommended the King to establish a university at Oxford, for the education of the higher classes of his subjects. The King appointed John of St. David's to the professorship of that university, to the foundation of which the King contributed very liberally. Asser, his biographer, further mentions the profuse donations with which Alfred remunerated his attachment.' " No eloquence," says the author of the Anglo-Saxon History, " can do more honour to any human character than this unadorned narrative. The condescension, benignity, the desire of improvement, and the wise liberality of Alfred, are qualities so estimable, as to command the veneration of every reader."

A.D. 887.—Alfred obtained the happiness he had long coveted, of reading the Latin authors in their original language. Asser noted the date of the circumstance, and described its occurrence. Soon afterwards the King was enabled to write several useful works, and to translate the works of the learned fathers, and other authors of antiquity.

The most exquisite luxury which aged parents can enjoy, when the charms of life, and all the pleasures of sense are fast fading around them, is to see their parental care rewarded by a dutiful, affectionate, and intelligent offspring. Alfred enjoyed this happiness, which he had so well merited. Ethelfleda, his eldest

---

' Asser, pp. 47, 48.

' Alfred's Preface, p. 82 ; Wise's Asser.

' Asser, p. 49 ; Herneid was one of the Welsh princes contiguous to St. David's.

' Asser, p. 50. On the morning of Christmas eve, when Asser had determined to visit Wales, the King gave him two writings, containing a list of the things that were in the two monasteries at Ambresbury in Wiltshire, and Banwell in Somersetshire. On the same day Alfred gave him those two monasteries, and all that they contained : he also gave him a silk pall, very precious, and as much incense as a strong man could carry ; adding that he did not give him these trifles as if he was unwilling to give him greater things. On Asser's next visit the King gave him Exeter, with all the parishes belonging to it in Saxony and Cornwall, besides innumerable daily gifts of all sorts of wordly wealth. He gave him immediate permission of riding to the two monasteries ; and then of returning home.

daughter, was a woman of very superior mind, and such were its energies, that they even reached a masculine strength. She is extolled in the ancient chronicles as the wisest lady in England.[3] Her brother Edward allowed himself to be guided by her counsels in the most important transactions of his life. The reign of Edward was distinguished by vigour and prosperity. Some of the last instructions of Alfred to his son have been popularly preserved, and they deserve to be quoted for their pathetic simplicity, their political wisdom, and the proof which they offered of this monarch's anxiety for the welfare of his subjects.[4]

Thus said Alfred: " My dear son, set thee now beside me, and I will deliver thee true instructions. My son, I feel that my hour is coming—my countenance is wan—my days are almost done. We must now part. I shall go to another world, and thou shalt be left alone in all my wealth. I pray thee (for thou art my dear child), strive to be a father and a lord to thy people. Be thou the children's father and the widow's friend. Comfort thou the poor and shelter the weak; and, with all thy might, right that which is wrong: and, son, govern thyself by law; then shall the Lord love thee, and God above all things shall be thy reward. Call thou upon him to advise thee in all thy need, and so shall he help thee the better to compass that which thou wouldst.[5]

Kings and queens are placed on an eminence so lofty that their actions can effect the whole nation which contemplates them. The fortunes of human nature are in their hands. Virtue and intellect flourish as their conduct is wise; and nations prosper or decay according as the measures of executive authority are salutary or ignoble.

No sovereign ever shaped his conduct with more regard to the public happiness than Alfred. He seems to have considered his life but as a trust to be used for the benefit of his people, and his plans for their welfare were intelligent and great.

His predominant wish was their mental and moral improvement. This is no speculation of a modern fancy; it is his own assertion in his most deliberate moments. His letter to his bishops, prefixed to his translations of Gregory's Pastorals, breathes this principle throughout. To communicate to others the knowledge which we possess, he states, is even a religious duty. He laments the ignorance which overspread his land; he desires that all the youths who had pecuniary means, should learn to read English: he devoted his own leisure, and he calls upon his literary clergy to devote theirs, to the translating into English the books they possessed. He led the way with taste and judgment in his historical and philosophical transactions; he seems to have placed his glory in the intellectual advancement of his rude countrymen.

By mild expostulation, by reasoning, by gentle flattery, or by express command, or in case of obstinate disobedience, by severe chastisements; he overcame the pertinacity of vulgar folly, and wisely made his bishops, earls, ministers, and public officers exert themselves for the common benefit of all his kingdom.[6] Among other things he was inflexible in exacting from all a competency for their offices. To produce this he compelled them to study literature; even they who had been illiterate from their infancy, earls, governors, and ministers, were compelled to learn to read and write, choosing rather to endure the painful toil than to lose their preferment.[7] Why is the fair influence of true religion lessening among us, but

---

[3] Elfleda, daughter of King Alfred, restored the City of Chester, that had felt the fury of the Danes, to its former splendour. Of which most excellent Princess, the following encomium, in Latin verse, is to be found in Henry of Huntingdon, lib. v., p. 354. Translated thus :—

" Glorious Elfleda, born to victory,
The master-piece of Nature shines in thee;
Thy outward form for beauty was designed,
But Heaven informed thee with a manly mind:
The virtues of both sex in thee is seen—
A king in fact, though a vicegerent queen.
Cæsar the conquered world subdued; but thou
Wouldst make the Conqueror himself to bow."

[4] This is the conclusion of the Cotton MS. of the precepts and instructions of Alfred in Galba, A. 19, now spoilt.

[5] This great monarch's morals are worth reading.—See Spelman's translations of the same.

[6] Asser, p. 69.

[7] One of the most ardent desires of our late patriarchal King George III., was, " that every one in his dominions should be able to read his Bible." Her Most Gracious Majesty Queen Victoria has followed Alfred's plan in several of his good works and examples ; to wit—the Commission appointed to enquire into the State of Education in England and Wales, &c. &c.

because the appointed guardians of our morals are not always careful to acquire the talents and the manners which interest the thoughtless, impress the dissolute, and satisfy the doubting? In every age the world requires from its moral teachers, example, persuasion, and conviction.

At last the progress of human destiny deprived the world of this most beneficent luminary. This victorious warrior; this sagacious statesman; this friend of distress; this protector against oppression; this mighty intelligence; who in an age of ignorance loved literature, and diffused it; who in an age of superstition, could be rationally pious; and in the station of royalty, could discern his faults and convert them into brilliant virtues; was at last called away from the world on the 26th of October, in the year 900-1.

If a Frenchman[8] of a difficult taste, of satirical humour, but of distinguished talents, has doubted whether a man ever lived more worthy of the respect of mortality than Alfred;—if a German,[9] of elaborate research and comprehensive thought, has declared him to be a pattern to kings in times of extremity; a bright star in the history of mankind, and even exalts him above Charlemagne;—an Englishman cannot be accused of undue partiality, if he contemplates this applauded monarch with an affectionate enthusiasm; neither can a Welshman[1] be denied the glory and satisfaction in the manner his countrymen conducted the education of one of the most renowned monarchs in Christendom!

We now resume the history of the Visits to the Principality and the Border Towns since the Division by Roderick the Great.

A.D. 877.—Anarawd, the eldest son of Roderick the Great, succeeded to the sovereignty of North Wales.[2] This territory was the *Venedocia* of the Romans,[3] and was by the Britons called Gwynedd.[4] The residence of the sovereigns of this district was at Aberffraw in Anglesea, in a palace which had been erected during the life of King Roderick.[5] The kingdom of North Wales, in the four divisions of Anglesea, Arvon,[6] Meirionydd, and Perfeddwlad,[7] containing fifteen *cantreds*, subdivided into thirty-eight *commots*,[8] was bounded on the west and north by the Irish Sea, and on the south by the River Dyvi, which separated it from South Wales, and on the south and east was divided from Powys and England by mountains and rivers, particularly by the *Dee*.[9] The language spoken in this country is esteemed the most pure, and comes the nearest to that of the ancient Britons. Its inhabitants, from a variety of causes, preserved their independency longer than either of the other principalities. Besides the valour of the people, and in general the public virtue of their princes, the natural situation of the country of Snowdon,—a range of mountains, and extending from one sea to the other, and guarded by two rivers discharging themselves into the ocean at Traeth Mawr and Conway,—formed a rampart exceedingly strong, over which the Welsh usually retreated when they were pressed by the English arms. The principal defiles, likewise, which opened through that range of vast mountains, were secured by strong fortifications. The castle of Dinganwy was placed opposite to the water of Conway, an arm of the sea which opened into the country; that of Caer Rhun was situated at the pass of Bwlch y ddau Vaen, with a fort at Aber; Dolwyddelen Castle, and a watch-tower was placed at Nantfrancon; Dolbadern Castle at Nant Peris, and the fort at Cidom was fixed at Nant tal y Llyn. The other pass of Traeth Mawr was guarded by the strong Castles of Harlech on one side of the bay, and of Cricieth on the other, with a watch-tower at Cesel Gyvarch, and a fort at Dolbenmaen.[1] These various fortifications, all of them placed in the most advantageous situations, marked, for a rude age, great military sagacity.

Cadell, the second son of the late prince, succeeded to the sovereignty of South Wales,[2]

[8] Voltaire, Essai sur les Mœurs, vol. xvi. c. xxviii., p. 473, ed. 1785.

[9] Herder, Outline of Philosophy of the History of Man, pp. 547, 548, living a century after Charlemagne; he was perhaps a greater man in a circle happily more limited.

[1] By the instruction of the learned Asser of St. David's, Alfred had the felicity of being made acquainted with all the learned works of antiquity, which enlightened his understanding, and prepared the way for his glorious reign.

[2] Rowland, p. 174. [3] Humphrey Llwyd, p. 64. [4] Ibid.

[5] Welsh Chron., p. 56; Rowland, p. 174.

[6] Signifying "above Mona."

[7] "The inward or middle part." Humphrey Llwyd, pp. 64, 66.

[8] Wynne's Wales, pp. 5, 8.

[9] Humphrey Llwyd, p. 64.

[1] Rowland's Mon. Ant., p. 148. [2] Ibid. p. 174.

distinguished by the name of Deheubarth, as lying to the south of the other provinces.[3] The residence of the princes of this country was at Dinevawr,[4] on the banks of the river Tywi,[5] in Caermarthenshire, where a palace had been erected by Roderick,[6] in a situation strongly fortified by woods and mountains; and more convenient on that account, than their ancient abode at Caermarthen, upon the same river, which was probably at this time in possession of the English.[7] This district, the *Demetia* of the Romans, was composed of the present counties of Cardigan, Pembroke, Caermarthen, Glamorgan, Monmouth, and Brecknock; it consisted of twenty-six *cantreds*, subdivided into eighty-one *commots*;[8] and was encompassed by the Irish Sea, by the Severn, by the Rivers Wye and Dyvi.[9] The continual influx of foreigners into this country has been the means of corrupting the language from its original purity.[1*]

Mervyn, the youngest son of Roderic the Great, succeeded to the principality of Powys.[2] The residences of the princes of this country was at Mathraval, in Montgomeryshire; at which place a palace had been built by the late prince.[3] The principality of Powys, afterwards divided into Powys Vadoc and Powys Wenwynwyn,[4] had fourteen *cantreds*, subdivided into forty *commots*.[5] It was bounded on the north by North Wales; on the east by the country which lies between Chester and Hereford; and on the south by England; on the west by the river Wye, and by mountains which divide it from South Wales.[6] The fertility and open situation of this country subjected it to continual invasions: and having more to dread from the arms of the English than to expect from the regular support of their countrymen, the princes of Powys took an early and frequent part in the affairs of England.

Early in the reign of Anarawd, that prince had an opportunity of affording the northern Britons the like friendly protection which his ancestors had so often received from their countrymen in Armorica. The remains of the Strath-Clyde Britons having been more harassed by the Danes, Saxons, and Scots; and, after severe conflicts with them, having lost Constantine, their King, in battle, applied to Anarawd for an asylum in his dominions.[7] This prince agreed to receive them on the only tenure incident to these turbulent ages, which was to obtain and preserve a settlement by the power of the sword.

Under the conduct of Hobart, these Britons came into Wales; and, having every motive of resentment and interest to urge them to valour, they easily disposed of the Saxons of that country which is situate between the Dee and the Conway.[8]

A. D. 878.—These people remained for a time in quiet possession of their new kingdom, until Eadred, the Earl of Mercia, mortified with the disgrace his arms had sustained, made preparations to recover the country which had been so easily torn from him.[9] The Britons, having early intelligence of his design, removed their cattle and other valuable effects beyond the River Conway. To support his allies, and to expel from the bosom of his country its hereditary enemies, Anarawd exhibited a spirit and activity suitable to the importance of the occasion; and having encountered the Saxons at Cymryd, A.D. 880, about two miles from the town of Conway,[1] by his own gallantry and the bravery of the troops, he entirely defeated them. With a pious and honest exultation, the young Prince called this memorable action, *Dial Rodri*,[2] expressive of the vengeance he had taken for his father's death.[3] Pursuing their victory, the Welsh followed the Saxons into Mercia, laid waste the borders, and returned into their own country loaded with valuable spoil.[4]

Anarawd, agreeably to the piety of those days, and to express his gratitude for the late prosperous

---

[3] Humphrey Llwyd's Brev., p. 64.
[4] Dinas Vawr or the Great Palace.   [5] Towy.
[6] Wynne's Wales, p. 34.
[7] Humphrey Llwyd, p. 79.   [8] *Ibid.*
[9] Wynne's Wales, pp. 16, 20.
[1] Humphrey Llwyd, p. 76.
[2] Rowland's Mona, p. 175.   [3] *Ibid.*
[4] Humphrey Llwyd, p. 70.   [5] Wynne's Wales, pp. 10, 11.
[6] Humphrey Llwyd, p. 70.
[7] Humphrey Llwyd's Brev., p. 31.
[8] Wynne's Wales, p. 38; Humphrey Llwyd, pp. 31, 32.

[9] Wynne's Hist. of Wales, p. 38.
[1] Cymryd is situated between Conway and Caer Hên, the Conovium, of the Romans, and is noted for a bloody battle between Anarawd Prince of Wales, and the Saxons under Edred, Duke of Mercia. The Britons were victorious, and drove the invaders back to their own country. Anarawd styled the battle "Dial Rhodri," or the revenge of Roderic, for his father, Roderic the Great, had the year before been slain by the Saxons. Camden, ii, 802-3; Powell, 38.
[2] Or "Roderic's Revenge."
[3] Wynne's Hist. of Wales, p. 38.   [4] *Ibid.*

event, endowed the collegiate church of Bangor, and that of Clynnogvawr, in Arvon, with lands and great possessions.[5] These northern Britons, by an unaccountable and singular policy, were allowed to establish a separate state in the Vale of Clwyd, in *Rhos*, and in the conquered country.[6] Part of this country had been called Tegenel by the Romans, Englefeld by the Saxons, and Tegeingl by the Welsh; but being now united with other territories, the northern Britons gave their new kingdom the name of Strath-Clwyd,[7] part of it being situated on the banks of the River Clwyd.[8]

A.D. 893.—Civil dissension, an evil naturally springing out of the conduct of Roderic, and which soon set aside his futile regulations, had already taken root in the breast of his sons. For Anarawd, after the late storm was dispersed, probably on account of the tribute not having been paid,[9] united with the English against his brother, the Prince of South Wales; and with their joint forces, invaded the territory and laid waste the country of Cardigan, and the vale also which borders upon the Wye, in Radnorshire.[1]

A.D. 896.—The Danes being obliged to flee before the arms of Alfred, made a descent upon the coast of Wales, and advanced into the country as far as Builth; and some time after, being again discomfited by that truly great prince, they laid waste the country of Brecknock, and other districts in South Wales.[2]

A.D. 900.—A large body of the same people landed again in Anglesea; but this invasion seems only to have been distinguished by a battle fought at Meilon, and by the death of Mervyn, Prince of Powys.[3]

The fatal policy of Roderic again became conspicuous. Cadell, the Prince of South Wales, on the death of Mervyn, his brother, took possession, by force, of the principality of Powys; incited by ambition or jealousy, natural to brothers who enjoy an equal share in their father's dominions and dignity.[4]

A.D. 907.—Cadell, the Prince of South Wales, dying in this year, was succeeded by his eldest son, Howel, who likewise annexed the sovereignty of Powys, to his hereditary dignity.[5]

A.D. 908.—The city of Chester, which had lain some years in ruins since it had been demolished by the Danes,[6] was rebuilt and much improved by Elfreda, the wife of the tributary sovereign of Mercia:[7] she likewise repaired the walls, and enlarged their circuit round the castle, which, before this time, had been situated without the city.[8]

A few years after this event, Anarawd, the King of North Wales, died, and left two sons; Edwal Voel, and Elis.

A.D. 913.—Edwal Voel, the eldest son of the late prince, succeeded to the sovereignty of North Wales, and was married to the daughter of his uncle Mervyn, the late Prince of Powys.[9] Early in his reign, the Irish made a descent upon the island of Anglesey, which they laid waste in a cruel manner.[1]

A.D. 933.—Athelstane, the King of England, having in several victories triumphed over the Danes and Scots, marched with an army into Wales, and at Hereford imposed upon the princes of that country a yearly tribute of twenty pounds in gold, three hundred pounds in silver, and two thousand five hundred head of cattle, besides, a certain number of hawks and hounds.[2] This arbitrary tribute was no longer regarded by the Welsh, than while the kings of England had the power of enforcing its observance.[3]

A.D. 940.—A Welsh chieftain had been imprisoned in England; and his confinement being resented by Edwal Voel, probably as an insult offered to the independence of his crown, that prince, with his brother Elis, attempted by hostilities to avenge the affront; but in the contest they were both slain,

[5] Wynne's Wales, p. 301 ; Camden's Brit., p. 671.
[6] The country from Conway along the Dee to Chester. Welsh Chron.
[7] *Istrad Clwyd.*
[8] Hum. Llwyd, p. 69.
[9] Brit. Ant. revised by Vaughan of Hengert, p. 13.
[1] Welsh Chron., p. 41.
[2] Wynne's Wales, pp. 41, 42.   [3] *Ibid.*
[4] Welsh Chron., p. 42.   [5] Welsh Chron., p. 35.
[6] Welsh Chron., pp. 44, 46.   [7] Saxon Annals, p. 95.

[8] Math. Westm., Flor. Hist., p. 269.
[9] Brompton's Chron., p. 838 ; Fabian's Chron., p. 224, printed at London, A.D. 1559.
[1] Brit. Ant. revised by Vaughan of Hengwrt, p. 4.
[2] Welsh Chron., pp. 45, 47.
[3] Brompton's Chron., p. 838, with respect to the tribute, with the difference only of doubling the number of cattle stores. Chron., p. 82 ; Welsh Chron., p. 50 ; Grafton's Chron., p. 149, pub. 1569.

fighting against the English and Danes.⁴ The King of North Wales left six sons, Meyric, Jevav, Jago, Cynan, Edwal, and Roderic; and his brother had a son, named Cynan, and a daughter, Eawst.⁵

The love of power is an active and commanding principle in man: to obtain and preserve it, he will employ his utmost sagacity, and bend the full force of his various faculties. Even the wise and temperate mind of Howel, Prince of Wales, was not exempt from its influence. The great esteem into which this prince had arisen from a just administration, had probably gained him some years before, the sovereignty of Powys; and enabled him at this time, A.D. 940, by the concession of North Wales, to unite into one kingdom the three principalities.⁵

To reduce his subjects to a sense of order, and to render them subordinate to civil authority, Howel determined to collect into one code the ancient customs and laws of Wales, which, in the lapse of ages, and in the confusion and turbulence of the times, had nearly lost their efficacy and weight. In pursuance of this design, he convened the Archbishop of St. David's, and other bishops and clergy, to the number of one hundred and fifty, with the principal chieftains of Wales: out of every *commot* were likewise summoned six persons, distinguished by their talents and virtues. This assembly, forming a great national council, met upon the banks of the Tâf, at the White Palace belonging to King Howel.⁷

As soon as this preparation was finished, Howel selected twelve persons who were eminent for wisdom, gravity and experience: and he joined in the commission Blegored, the Archdeacon of Llandaff, a person highly distinguished for his learning, and a knowledge of the laws. This committee entered into a strict examination of the customs and ancient institutions of Wales. With a judicious and discriminating eye, they abolished every law become injurious or unnecessary; those, likewise, which time had rendered confused and unintelligible, were explained with greater perspicuity; and, by a proper digest of the whole, a system was framed, which, allowing for limited ideas on jurisprudence, was wisely adapted to the genius of the Welsh.⁸

The famous code of laws of Howel Dha, "the Good," consist of three divisions, and relate to the regulation of the royal household, the claims of the king, the distinctions of rank, the courts of law, the modes of proceeding in them, and the general police of the country. Certain baronial and manorial courts are acknowledged; but in matters of inheritance, and disputes respecting territory, the judgment of the King's Court must be resorted to. The prince is acknowledged as the supreme head, but not as possessing any direct authority over particular lordships. The lower class, as Cæsar says respecting the Gauls, were but *in servorum loco;* and the fine for killing a slave was according to its value, like an ox or a sheep. Murder was generally punished by a fine, which amounted to a fixed sum of money, according to the rank of the person; and, if this were not paid, any of the family had a right to avenge the death of his kinsman. The disgrace of any crime was attached to the whole family of the person who had been guilty. In various cases they had their juries; and these differed in number according to the occasion. In general the oaths of fifty substantial freemen were requisite to form a verdict; but in some cases a still greater number were required. No offence was capital unless it was considered to amount to the value of one hundred pounds, which shows the great leniency of their punishments, and the humane spirit of their laws.

In a MS., found among the Cotton Collection in the British Museum, and which does not appear to have been consulted by Dr. Wotton, although considered to be, as far as it goes, one of the fairest and most complete copies of the code of Howel Dda, or Howel the Good, extant, that legislator thus introduces the code:—

"The King of Wales, Hywel the Good, son of Cadell, hath done this by the grace of God, prayer, and fasting, when Wales was in his possession according to its boundary; the sixty-four hundreds of South Wales, the eighteen hundreds of North Wales, the sixty townships of Trachyrchell, and the

⁴ Welsh Chron., p. 51.
⁵ Welsh Chron., p. 51; Brit. Ant., revised by Vaughan of Hengwrt, p. 14.
⁶ Welsh Chron., p. 52.
⁷ Welsh Chron., p. 53. ⁸ *Ibid.*

sixty townships of Buallt.   And within that limit nobody's word was before his word; but his was superior to all.'

"As bad customs and bad laws existed before his time, he thereupon summoned six men out of every commot in Wales, and brought them to him to the White House, together with seven score crosiers, between bishops, archbishops, abbots, and good instructors, to frame wholesome laws,—to annul those that were become corrupt before his time, and to enact good ones in their stead, and thus to give stability to his name.   And out of that number, twelve of the wisest laymen, and one of cleri were selected to make the laws.   The business of the assembly was ended by a denunciation of the vengeance of God, of the assembly, and of Wales, upon all who dare to violate the provisions of the code.

"This system was formed on the basis of the ancient national laws.'

"After the new code of laws had been read, proclaimed, and ratified by public approbation; three copies of them were put into writing, one of which was designed for the use of the prince, and to follow his court; and the others were deposited in the palaces of Aberfraw and Dinevawr.

"Influenced, likewise, by the spirit of the age, or desirous of rendering such a ceremony subservient to his views, Howel, attended by the Archbishop of St. David's, the Bishops of Bangor and St. Asaph, and thirteen other persons of distinction, proceeded to Rome, where the new system of legislation was solemnly ratified by the Pope; and having thus given the last sanction to his laws, he returned into Wales." '

The mild temper of this prince seems in some measure to have influenced the transactions of his reign; few military incidents having disturbed it during a period of forty years.   At this time, however, the English, with a considerable force, invaded North Wales; and after they laid waste the small territory of Strath-Clwyd, returned into their own country.'

A few years after this event, King Howel died, A.D. 948, leaving four sons, Owen, Rhun, Roderic, and Edwyn, who, dividing among themselves the principalities of South Wales and Powys, relinquished North Wales to the right heirs, Jevav and Jago, the sons of Edwal Voel.'

The death of this amiable prince, who had long enjoyed the mild honours resulting from peace and the public esteem, spread universally the deepest sorrow.   As a grateful memorial of his virtues, posterity have given him the surname of *Dda*, or "the Good."   His code of laws is the best eulogium to his memory, and raises him as much above the rest of the Cambrian princes,' as peace and gentleness of manners, and a regulated state, are preferable to the evils inseparable from war, to the fierceness of uncivilised life, and to the habits of a wild independency.

Edward the Elder succeeded to the throne of his father Alfred.·   After two or three battles, in which he defeated his enemies, he pursued the plans which his father had devised for the protection of his throne.   He built fortresses in different parts of the country, in which he was vigorously assisted by his sister Ethelfleda, Queen of Mercia.

The position of these fortresses demonstrate their utility.   Wigmore in Herefordshire; Bridgenorth and Chirbury in Shropshire; Eddisbury, Runcorn, and Thallwall in Cheshire; Stafford and Wednesbury in Staffordshire, and Bakevile in Derbyshire, answered the double purpose of awing Wales, and protecting that part of the frontier of Mercia.   Both Edward and Ethelfleda had many struggles with the Northmen, but their triumphs were easy.   The Welsh suffered from the warlike Ethelfleda.   On one occasion she took Brecon and a Welsh queen.   She died, A.D. 920.'

Edward the Elder must be ranked among the illustrious founders of the English monarchy.   He executed with judicious vigour the military plans of his father, and not only secured the Anglo-Saxons from the Danish yoke, but even proposed the way for that destruction of the Anglo-Danish power which

* Said to have been originally framed by Moelumtius, who reigned in Britain 441 years before Christ ; Holinshed, p. 177.

¹ Welsh Chron., p. 54.   ² *Ibid.*   ³ *Ibid.*, p. 58.

⁴ Saxon Chron.

⁵ From this comparison it is the author's meaning to except

those British and Cambrian princes who defended their country from the rapacity or ambition of foreign enemies—a conduct than which nothing can be more meritorious, or scarcely anything have a higher claim on the respect and gratitude of mankind.

⁶ Saxon Chron.

his descendants achieved. Some writers wish to attribute greater power and glory to Edward than to his father Alfred. His own merit, indeed, was luminous of itself; but as his course was in the direct path of his father's radiance, he can only be ranked as an illustrious planet, which derives its glory from the beams of the other orbs. He died at Farrington, A.D. 924.

A.D. 924.—Athelstan succeeded to the throne: this brave and warlike king is represented to have been a great benefactor to the monastic institutions. He rebuilt many monasteries, and endowed them liberally with funds, books, and ornaments.[7]

Besides making the Welsh tributary, he turned his arms on the Cornish. He made Tamar the boundary of his dominions, as he had already made the Wye the limits of North Wales. He died A.D. 941, and was succeeded to the throne by his brother Edmund the Elder.

A.D. 959.—Edgar, at the age of sixteen, succeeded to the throne which his conduct had contributed to make vacant. The boyish age, at which he was inducted into his power, transfers the crime of its acquisition to the agents who prompted it. Edgar was rather the king of a great nation in a fortunate era than a great prince himself; and he was indebted to the successive triumphs of his predecessors for that brilliant peace by which his reign was distinguished. His actions display an ambiguous and mixed character. His policy sometimes breathes a large and liberal spirit, but he was oftener near, arrogant, and vicious.

Raised to the throne of his brother by vindictive monks, his reign became theirs, rather than his own. Dunstan, not Edgar, was the monarch of England during the greatest portion of his life; and the sublime policy of the government was to convert the clergy into monks, and to fill the nation with Benedictine institutions. For this Edgar toiled. He warred, not with opposing armies, but with unprotected gownsmen! His associates were not generals, or philosophers, or statesmen, but Dunstan and his monks!

A.D. 960.—At this time the kings of North Wales had neglected to pay the tribute which was due to the crown of England, agreeably to the great impolitic institution of Roderick the Great, and the more recent, but no less imprudent regulations, in some respects, in the laws of Howel Dda. To preserve such an ornament to his crown, and a badge of subordination so flattering to his pride, Edgar, the King of England, invaded North Wales; and as he marched through the country spread around the usual devastation.

A.D. 961.—The King being acquainted with the injuries both countries had received from the wolves, which then abounded in North Wales, and destroyed sheep and other cattle, he remitted, with some degree of liberality, the ancient tribute, and only exacted the yearly payment of the heads of three hundred of those animals.[8]

This demand, so singular in its nature, was paid by the Welsh princes during three or four years. After that time, the wolves being nearly extirpated, their country, agreeable to the liberal design of Edgar, ought to have been released from payment of any future tribute.[9] Soon after this the Irish made a descent upon the island of Anglesea, destroyed the palace at Aberffraw, and slew Roderick the youngest son of Edwal Voel.[1]

A.D. 966.—The union, so long subsisting between the princes of North Wales, in a joint administration of twenty years, was at this period dissolved. An event soon followed by a series of crimes, the consequence of a divided sovereignty, and of bosom friendship turned into deadly hatred.

King Edgar had a palace at Chester, which he appears to have visited several times. Its site is referred to in many ancient writings, and is marked on several old maps, and particularly in one, executed

[7] William of Malmesbury, p. 48. There are two curious MS. in the Cottonian library, which were presents from Athelstan. One, Tiberias, A. 2, is a MS. of the Latin Gospels. It is beautifully illuminated, and is declared to have been used for the coronation oath of our Anglo-Saxon Kings. There is also in the Cottonian library a MS. Claudius, B. 5, which contains the proceedings of the fifth synod at Constantinople in the seventh century. A marginal note is inserted by Sir Robert Cotton that the synod was held in 681. Sergius was Pope in 970.

[8] Stowe's Chron., p. 83, printed at London, A.D. 1614; Fabian's Chron., p. 249.

[9] William of Malmesbury, p. 50; Fabian, p. 249; Stowe's Chron., p. 83; Welsh Chron., p. 62.

[1] Welsh Chron., p. 62.

K

in the time of Queén Elizabeth, by the words, "*Ruinosa domus Comitis Cestriensis*," which appear on a space representing a field in Handbridge, in which there is to this day the remains of a cell, called Edgar's cave. Full details have been handed down to us of the manner in which, on one of his visits in A.D. 971, he was rowed from his palace near Chester, to the monastery of St. John, by eight tributary kings,[2] viz., Kenneth of Scotland, Malcolm of Cumberland, Malanze, King of the Isles, Donald, Seffrith, Howel, Iago, and Ilhed,

King Edgar rowed by eight Kings on the River Dee.

Kings of Wales. "He caused them to enter a barge, and sitting four on one side, and four on the other, they rowed him while he steered the helm, passing thus in triumph on the river Dee, from his palace to the monastery of St. John, where he landed, and received their oath to be his faithful vassals, and to defend his rights by land and sea; and then, having made a speech to them, he returned to his barge, and passed in the same manner back to his palace."[3]

Edgar's ostentatious display of his power, and useless humiliation of other sovereigns, because they were less fortunate, cannot but offend the reflecting mind. "He was not satisfied," says the author of the History of the Anglo-Saxons, "with the mere confession of his power, but his puerile vanity demanded a more painful sacrifice. He ascended a large vessel with his nobles and officers, and he stationed himself at the helm, while the eight kings who had come to do him honour, were compelled to take the seats of

---

[2] There is a difference of opinion about the number of kings; William of Malmesbury, p. 56; Henry of Huntington, and Roger de Hoveden, p. 426, state the number to be six; but the monk of Chester calls them eight, and is followed by Webb.

[3] Dr. Campbell, in his Lives of the Admirals, and the state of the maritime forces of that period.

The following lines are extracted from Webb's account of Cheshire :—

"Edgar, England's famous king of nations, great commander,
About the northern British coast did pass the seas with wonder;
With navy great he did at last the City of Legions enter,
To whom eight other petty kings their homage there did tender;
The first of them was Kenneth called, and King of Scotts was then,

And Malcolm of Cumberland, with Macon King of Man,
The other five were called thus: Donald, South Wales ruling,
Siffrith and Howel, both of them North Wales then commanding;
King James, a man of great renown, did Galloway command,
And Inkel, then a famous king, did rule all Cumberland.
All these at Edgar's high command made haste, and did them swear
To serve him truly, sea and land, and put their foes in fear;
These all at once a barge did take, and Edgar took the helm,
And placed the rest at each oar one; he being then supreme
Did guide his course, tho' rowing hard upon the river Dee,
Thereby he well might boast himself the English king to be;
Thus by so many under kings, which he had then ordain'd,
His royal state and dignity with honour was maintain'd."

the watermen and to row him down the Dee,—a most arrogant insult to the feelings of others, whose titulary dignity was equal to his own. Such actions are not the evidence of true greatness, and never confer dignity."[4]

Notwithstanding the great care taken by the four succeeding monarchs, from Edward the Martyr, A.D. 975, to Canute and Harold, A.D. 1017, to repress the invasion of the Welsh, that valiant people continued to harass them and their successors for a long time afterwards.

A.D. 1045.—Edward the Confessor having banished Algar, son of Leofric, Duke of Mercia, for some misdemeanours, the Duke found his way into Wales, and entered into a conspiracy with Griffith, Prince of South Wales, with whom he made an inroad into Herefordshire, laying the whole district waste with fire and sword.[5]

Edward having collected an army to repel this invasion, gave the command of it to Ralph, the first Earl of Hereford, who was the son of Walter de Maunt, by Goda, the King's sister. The armies met within two miles of the city of Hereford, on the 24th of October, 1055. Ralph gave orders for the English to fight on horseback, which was contrary to their usual custom. On this occasion the Earl was not only guilty of misconduct, but also of cowardice; for when the attack should have been made, he betook himself to flight, together with the French and Normans that were in his army, by which means the battle was lost, and great slaughter made among the English.[6]

The Welsh were so elated with their victory, that they immediately proceeded to storm Hereford, which after some opposition was delivered into their hands. Having got possession of the city, they attacked the cathedral, whither most of the citizens had fled for protection, with their wives, children, and the most valuable part of their property. The bishop, Earl Agelnoth, and the canons, supported by the citizens, attempted to defend it, but were soon overpowered by numbers. The conquerors having satiated themselves with slaughter, pillaged the church of every curious relic, and then set fire to the building. The flames communicated to the city, which was almost entirely reduced to ashes; Leoffegar, the bishop, was the only person who was spared. Nor was his fate much to be envied; for, being carried away captive, he suffered every kind of indignity and torture which ingenuity could devise; at last he was put to death, and in consideration of these sufferings he was afterwards enrolled among the saints.

The King, who was then at Gloucester, hearing of the overthrow of his forces, collected another army, and appointed Harold, Earl of the West Saxons (afterwards King Harold), general. He advanced against the enemy, and pursued them for some time without any great advantage or loss on either side, but Griffith and Algar, not finding themselves in a condition to oppose him, thought it prudent to make a retreat to the mountains of Eryri. Harold followed them, and pitched his camp at the foot of Snowdon, and stayed there for some time; this gave occasion to a treaty; the Welsh laid down their arms; and peace ensued.

Edward was succeeded on the throne by Harold, the son of Godwin. During his reign the Welsh actively carried on hostilities against the Anglo-Saxons. If any other feeling than personal ambition had actuated the British leader, they must have discovered that however feeble the Saxon King may have been, yet from the comparative state of the two nations, the most brilliant success of the Welsh could only have a transient effect: such consideration did not, however, affect the conduct of the Welsh princes. Gryffyth, Prince of South Wales, continued for many years to make successful inroads into those portions of England which bordered on his dominions.

In the year after, he reinstated Algar; the new insults which he offered and which caused the death of Harold's priest just raised to the bishopric,[7] were again connived at by a peace; and, in 1058, he again

[4] Malmesbury, p. 56; Mailros, p. 150; Hoveden, p. 426; Sim. Dun., p. 159. Nothing can more strongly display Edgar's vanity than the pompous and boastful titles which he assumed in his charters. They sometimes run to the length of fifteen or sixteen lines. How different from Alfred's " *Ego occidentalium Saxonum Rex.*"

[5] The Welsh were driven to those rebellions by the severe exactions demanded of them by the English. William of Malmesbury informs us that Athelstan made the Prince of Wales pay a yearly tribute of 20lb. of gold and 300lb. of silver, which continued to be exacted for some years.

[6] Rev. Mr. Lodge's History of Hereford.

[7] Flor., p. 418. The MS. Tib., B. 1, says of this bishop, that he would forego his spiritual arms and take to his spear and sword, and go against Griffith.

K 2

restored Algar; but in 1063 the storm of vengeance broke out. Harold resolved upon his punishment. He marched into Wales at the head of a numerous army; Gryffyth fled. Harold burnt his palace, and his ships, and returned.

In the beginning of the following summer Harold circumnavigated Wales with a marauding fleet, while his brother Tostig marched over it by land. The Welsh submitted, gave hostages, agreed to pay tribute, and banished the obnoxious Gryffydd, who soon after perished.[8]

The means by which Harold obtained such immediate and decisive success, are stated to have been a change of the armour of his soldiers. Heavy armed troops were unable to pursue the Welsh to their mountainous retreats. Harold observed this impediment to their success, and commanded the soldiers to use leathern armour and lighter weapons. By this arrangement, wherever the Britons could retreat, his men could pursue. He crossed their snowy mountains, Snowdonia, and the Plinlimmon hills, defeated them in the plains, and multiplied destruction till terror and feebleness produced general subjection.[9] He raised a heap of stones on the hills and other places where he obtained a victory, with this inscription,

" HERE HAROLD CONQUERED."—

Such a depopulation of Wales ensued from this invasion, that to this disastrous cause, Giraldus ascribes the tranquil acquiescence of the Britons under the Norman yoke.[1] Harold closed his efforts by passing a law that every Briton found beyond "Offa's Dyke," with a missile weapon *should lose his right hand!*[2]

The principality of Wales and its borders were connected with the name of the last Anglo-Saxon king, long after the fatal conflict at Hastings. A report was widely prevalent during the twelfth century, that Harold had escaped from the slaughter. It was said, that after seeking in vain for assistance from the people of the continent who were nearest in the family of nations to his own, he returned to England to pass the remainder of his life in religious retirement—that disguising his name and face, he passed many years as a hermit on the borders of Wales, exposed to the insults of the people over whom he had so often triumphed, and who knew not the humble individual whose religious habit they derided; that he afterwards settled at Chester, where he ended his days, and on his death-bed revealed the secret to his confessor. The monks of Waltham, Harold's rich monastic foundation, received the legend with joy, and consigned it to writing in a manuscript which is still extant.[3]

Giraldus Cambrensis mentions it as the tradition of the place, that Harold, having survived his wounds at the battle of Hastings, spent the remainder of his days as an anchorite in a cell near St. John's Church, at Chester. The same tradition is mentioned by John Brampton, who adds that his tomb was shown in the middle of the area behind the cross at St. John's Church: and there were those who asserted that he was yet alive when King Henry the First, returned through Chester from Wales, and that he had an interview with that monarch. The historian himself inclines to the more generally received opinion that King Harold died in battle, and was buried at Waltham. Henry de Knighton, and other historians, relate that Queen Algitha, after the Conqueror's success, was, for a while, removed to Chester, as a place of security, by her brothers Earl Edwin and Earl Morcar.[4] Giraldus also relates a tradition, that Henry, Emperor of Germany, spent the latter part of his days as a hermit in a desert place near Chester, and was buried in that city, having confessed his rank when on the point of death.

Camden, in noticing this tradition, speaks of Henry the Fourth as the Emperor of whom it was told; but all the circumstances mentioned by Giraldus, (who only calls him "*Imperatorem Romanum, Henricum,*") apply to Henry the Fifth. There has been a tradition, of very long standing, that the Emperor led a

---

[8] Flor., p. 424; Ingulph, p. 68; Lamb's Saxon Chronicle, p. 270. The head of Gryffydd was brought to Harold. Turner's Anglo-Saxons.

[9] Ingulph, p. 68. This invasion is fully stated by the elegant John of Salisbury, whose writings give so much credit to the twelfth century. See his *De Nugis Curialium*, lib. vi., c. vi., p. 285.

[1] Giraldus Cambrensis's Wallic., c. vii., p. 431.

[2] J. Salisbury, p. 185.

[3] The Vita Haroldi of the MS. alluded to has been lately printed in the second vol. of the Chroniques Anglo-Normandes, edited by M. Murphy. Rouen, 1836.

[4] Henry de Knighton, inter Dee, p. 2344; Roger de Hoveden John Brompton, &c.

very retired life under the borrowed name of Godescallus, or Godstallus; and a lane near the Cathedral, called Godstall-lane, is said to have obtained that appellation from him.[5] In an ancient chronicle, called the "Red Book of the Abbey of Chester," was the following passage, which seems to give some countenance to these traditions:—"A. 1110, Rex Henricus dedit filiam suam Godescallo imperatori Alemannæ, qui nunc Cestriæ jacet." Notwithstanding the authority of this passage, and that the time when Giraldus Cambrensis found the tradition current at Chester was about sixty years after the death of Henry the Fifth, Emperor of Germany, yet it seems evident, from the authority of the best historians, that it was wholly void of foundation; since we are told that the Emperor Henry the Fifth, died at Utrecht, and that our monarch, Henry the First, who was then in Normandy, sent immediately for his daughter Maud, the Empress, and brought him with her to England.[6] Speaking of the latter days of the Saxon dominion in England, Stow thus describes the dress and manner of the inhabitants:—"The Englishmen were then apparelled in garments to the mid knee, their hair rounded, and their beards shaven, all save the upper lip, their arms adorned with golden bracelets, and their skin marked, painted, and printed; at meat they forced themselves to surfeit, and drank until they vomited. These last qualities they dealed to them that overcame them, but I would not you should think I speak these evils of all England, for I know that many of the clergy did singly observe the paths of holiness, and also of the lay people did endeavour to serve God. But generally speaking the English in those days gave themselves up to all sort of vice and immorality, which made them effeminate and womanish; whereof it came to pass that, running headlong against Duke William, they lost themselves and their country, with one, and that an easie and light battaile."[7]

---

[5] King's Vale Royal, part ii., p. 22; Godstall-lane is spoken of in a survey of the streets of Chester. Temp. Edw. III. It is described as near the walls on the north side of East Gate-street, adjoining the churchyard of St. Wisburgh, and it is said to have been the habitation of one Godescallus, who having been an Emperor, led in his latter days a holy and religious life, and died at Chester. See Harleian MSS. Brit. Mus., No. 2111, f. 53, b. 56, A.

[6] Holinshed; Matthew Paris, &c.

[7] Whatever merits the ancient Saxons might possess as warriors and freemen, yet it appears a few centuries made a considerable change in their moral, whatever it did in their physical, character. For, when about the ninth century, England was invaded by the *Danes*, the Saxons were so far from resisting them, like a brave and spirited people, that, on the contrary, they for many years submitted to their tyranny, in a manner the most abject and slavish, while those barbarians were traversing the land at their pleasure, exacting the most oppressive tribute. Amongst the Welsh, the Danes, with all their tactics, were never able to effect even a settlement, much less the imposition of taxes.

Again, when the Normans invaded Britain, the *Welsh* resisted their aggressions and those of their successors in England with the most determined bravery for upwards of two hundred years. Whereas the *Saxons* were subdued completely in one single battle: and such was their spiritless conduct, that they never once as a nation attempted to release themselves from the galling yoke imposed upon them by their conquerors, though of the most repulsive and degrading nature. Even the tyranny of the *Curfew Bell* could not rouse them, nor the oppression of the *Forest Laws*. Surely this is not a people to be proud of as the parent stock of the English nation. And if mixture of blood has any influence upon the moral character, it is well for Britain that such streams of Celtic blood have flowed into the veins of the English for the last few centuries. Since then they have conquered the whole of Europe.

NORMAN PERIOD.

MMEDIATELY after the decisive battle of Hastings, which took place A.D.1066, William, Duke of Normandy, mounted the English throne.[1] During the war which ended in the conquest of England by that prince, the Welsh remained inactive spectators of the scene before them, viewing it with the same indifference as if it had been a struggle between two foreign nations. Indeed it was not likely that they should interest themselves in the prosperity of either side; knowing, that whatever the event might be, they themselves might in their turn become the victims of the conquerors.

William, unwilling to entrust so vast an extent of country as the kingdom of Mercia to any one of his barons, divided that province into separate governments, corresponding in a great measure with the counties into which it has been since formed; and thereby he at once destroyed that power which had so often endangered the throne, and was enabled to bestow honours and emoluments on a greater number of his followers. The city and county of Chester, in the first instance, was given to Gherbard, a noble Fleming, who had attached himself to the fortune of the Conqueror, and had been greatly distinguished by his bravery at the battle of Hastings, and subsequently in various encounters against the Welsh. The title of Earl of Chester was also granted to him, but not accompanied by the palatinate dignity conferred upon his successors.

In maintaining these possessions the Earl was exposed to great dangers from the English as well as from the Welsh. Being called into Flanders soon after he had taken possession of his new territories, he unfortunately fell into the hands of his enemies, and, by reason of a long captivity, was obliged to resign them to another. The Conqueror appointed his nephew, Hugh Lupus, the first Norman Earl of Chester in his stead.[2] To him he delegated a fulness of power; he made him a County Palatine, and conferred upon

---

[1] After William had taken the coronation oath, to protect the Church, prohibit oppression, and execute judgment in mercy, the archbishop put the question, "Will ye have this prince to be your king?" The people answered with loud shouts, and the noise gave so much alarm to the Norman garrison in the city, that the soldiers, believing the English to have revolted, without waiting to make any investigation, immediately set the next houses on fire, which spreading and giving a general alarm, most of the congregation rushed out of the church, the English hastening to stop the fire, and the Normans to plunder. The bishops, clergy, and monks, who remained within the church, were in such confusion, that they were scarce able to go through the office of crowning the king; William himself, who saw the tumult, and could not conjecture its cause, sate trembling at the foot of the altar, and, though no great mischief was done by the fire, it laid the foundation of a long and inveterate enmity between the English and the Normans.—*Coronation Anecdotes.*

[2] The following is the grand charter of William the Conqueror to his nephew, Hugh Lupus, the first Earl of Chester, written in old English metre by H. Bradshaw, monk of Chester, author of the life of St. Werburgh in 1521:—

> " The King gave to him for his inheritance
> The county of Chester with its appurtenance—
> By victory to win the aforesaid Earldom,
> Freely to govern it by conquest right;
> Made a sure charter to him and his succession,
> By the sword of dignity to hold it with might,
> And call a parliament at his will and sight,
> To order his subjects after true justice,
> As a perpotent prince, and statutes to devise.

" By virtue of this grant," says the great antiquary Camden,[*] " Cheshire enjoyed all sovereign jurisdiction within its own

---

[*] Camden's Britannia, vol. i. p. 662.

him extensive sovereign power, insomuch, that the ancient Earls of Chester held their own parliaments, and had their own courts of law, in which any offence against "the sword of Chester" was cognisable in the same way as the like offence against the dignity of the Royal Crown was in the courts at Westminster,[3] for William allowed Lupus to hold this country, *tam liberé ad gladium, sicat ipse* REX *tenebat Angliam ad coronam.* The sword by which he was invested with his dignity is still to be seen in the British Museum, with the inscription "*Hugo Comes Cestriæ*"[4] upon it.[5] Another inferior office was held by the Earls by virtue of this sword, that of sword-bearer of England at the time of the coronation.

Lupus instantly took possession of his new dominions. It is probable that he was invested in them by William himself; for we find the Conqueror at Chester,[6] in person, in A.D. 1069, when he repelled the Welsh, and finally reduced the Mercian province, which appears to have been in arms up to this period.

As soon as Lupus was firmly established in his government he began to exert his regal prerogative. He formed his parliament by the creation of eight barons, viz., Nigel, Baron of Halton; Robert, of Monthault (Mold); William Malbederg, Baron of Nantwich; Vernon of Shipsbrook; Fitzhugh of Malpas; Haman de Massie; Venebles of Kindestan; and Nicholas of Stockport; these were to assist the Earl with their advice: *Ego Comes Hugo et mei Barones* was the form of his writs. They were obliged to attend the Earl, and to repair to his court to give it the greater dignity. They were bound, in time of war with Wales, to find for every knight's fee a horse with caparison and furniture, or two without furniture, in the division of Cheshire. Their knights and freeholders were to have corselets and habergeons, and were to defend their lands with their bodies. Every baron had also four esquires; every esquire one gentleman, and every gentleman one valet.[7]

They had besides the power of life and death. The earls had their chamberlain, who supplied the place of a chancellor; a baron of the exchequer, and other officers, (which were continued until within these few years) conformable to those of the Crown at Westminster. He had also justices, before whom causes were tried, which would otherwise have been triable only in the Superior Courts at Westminster.

One of the immediate results of the Norman Conquest was a long period of complicated disorders in the Marches of Wales. The Welsh were instigated by the Saxon refugees to make frequent incursions. In A.D. 1068-9 they ravaged Shropshire and laid siege to Shrewsbury, and King William was obliged to go in person to drive them from the border. He appointed Roger de Montgomery, one of his great barons, to rule Shropshire, which he did with vigour and justice (such justice at least as might be expected from a conqueror). He made considerable encroachments on the territory of the independent Welsh, and one of his retainers, named Baldwin, established a post, which, from him, received the name of Baldwin's-town, and at which, Earl Roger afterwards built a castle, and gave it his own name, viz, Montgomery, called by the Welsh to this day Trefaldwyn.[8]

During William's absence in Normandy, whither he had gone to settle some affairs that required his presence, it appears that the Welsh princes as usual grumbled among themselves, and one portion of them, in conjunction with Edric, Earl of Mercia, had made considerable inroads into the Marches of England.

---

precincts; and that in so high a degree, that the ancient earls had parliaments of their own barons * and tenants; and were not obliged by the English Act of Parliament. These high and otherwise unaccountable jurisdictions were through necessity on the marches and borders of the kingdom, as investing the governors of those provinces with dictatorial power, and enabling them more effectually to subdue the common enemies of the nation." And agreeable to these high powers, when the style in all legal proceedings of the Court at Westminster ran, *Contra coronam et dignitatem Regis,*

in the County Palatine these pleas were constantly expressed, *Contra dignitatem gladii Cestriæ.*

[3] Pennant's Wales, vol. i., p. 169.

[4] Leicester's Cheshire, 108.

[5] This famous sword of dignity is in length about four feet, and so unwieldy, as to be handled with great difficulty by a strong man with both his hands. The blade is two edged, and has this inscription immediately beneath the hilt, "*Hugo Comes Cestriæ;*" the hilt itself is decorated with pearls.

[6] Odericus Vitalis, lib. iv., p. 516.

[7] Enderbie's MSS. quoted by Dr. Gower, p. 22.

[8] Dr. Gower's Materials, p. 22.

---

* Every baron had four squires, every esquire had one gentleman, and every gentleman one valet, for their attendants.—*Erdeswicke's MSS.*

72

On his return from Normandy, William invaded the Principality with a powerful force in order to chastise the inhabitants for their late aggression. The Welsh princes were unable to oppose his arms, and awed by the influence of his mighty name, they wisely submitted, without any resistance, and consented to pay him homage, and to take the oath of fealty. Having been induced by the submission of the inhabitants to lay aside his hostile intentions, William, agreeably to that spirit of piety, which in those days tinctured the mind of the fiercest warrior, marched with his army to the City of St. David, and offered up his devotions at the shrine of that Saint.[9]

William the Conqueror paying his devotion at the Shrine of St. David's.

It appears that towards the latter part of his reign, the Conqueror again led an army into Wales. He was doubtless provoked to this by the ravages of the Welsh, who are said to have over-run the southern part of the border, as far as the city of Worcester, A.D. 1086. We, however, find no details of these transactions, and we only know from the assertions of old writers that William left Wales to his successors, as an appendage to the English crown, and that he had compelled the Welsh to acknowledge his supremacy; but the peace that was thus established by the king's vigorous government, seems to have been first broken by the Anglo-Norman barons.[1]

The changes produced in England during this reign were very great. A contemporary writer says, "William mitigated our barbarous manners, and amplified our cultivation of Christianity, which, before his coming, had been in a very low state."

The sound of the "Curfew Bell," which William caused to be tolled in every part of the kingdom at 8 o'clock every evening, was very galling to the feelings of the English; as by the sound of this bell they were compelled to put out all fires and lights, otherwise they became liable to fine and imprisonment. The most important financial operation of William was his Survey of England, to ascertain the legal rights of the Crown, and a knowledge of the state of the property of the country. The facts required, were, for the most

[9] Welsh Chron., p. 15.

[1] "The land of the Britons was in the Conqueror's jurisdiction,
He built castles therein and ruled that people."—*Saxon Chron.*

part, ascertained by the oaths of a competent number of persons in every district; the record of the information they collected and returned to the Exchequer, is the celebrated Doomsday-Book.[2]

The King's great object in instituting this survey, was to form an exact calculation of his own revenues, and, especially, how much money he might be enabled to raise by way of a land tax. Accordingly, he laid an impost of six shillings on every hide of land[3] throughout England, as soon as he had ascertained this point; which tax affected the Normans, who had become, generally speaking, the lords of the soil, far more than it did the English, who were for the most part reduced to abject poverty.

William the Conqueror, at his death, which took place in September, A.D. 1087, a few years after his expedition into Wales, left the succession of his crown to be disputed by his two sons, William Rufus and Robert Curthose, who was then in possession of the Dukedom of Normandy. Bishop Odo, who had been in prison in the latter years of the preceding reign, organised a party in England in favour of Duke Robert. The great barons on the Welsh border immediately espoused the same cause, and in A.D. 1088, Roger de Montgomery, Ralph de Mortimer, Roger de Lacy, and their neighbours, armed their dependants, and called in the aid of the Welsh princes to make war against William.

The spirit and genius of the Welsh nation revived, and with it revived also the variety of evils which are incident to intestine divisions. The three sons of Bleddyn ap Cynfyn were desirous of recovering their lost sovereignty, which they had been deprived of by the murder of their father, and by the usurpation of Trahaearn ap Caradoc; they raised an insurrection in South Wales against Rhys ap Tewdwr.[4] Numerous battles were fought between the contending princes, and victory declared itself first for one party and then for the other, until at last Prince Rhys obtained a complete victory, after which he dismissed his numerous auxiliaries with rewards expressive of his gratitude.[5]

A.D. 1088.—Early in the reign of William Rufus, an insurrection broke out upon the borders, excited by the Earls of Hereford and Shrewsbury. The Welsh, eager to embrace the first opportunity for the recovery of their liberties, joined the mal-content lords; and rushing with great fury upon the English Marches, like a torrent which had long been pent up, they ravaged and laid waste the country about Worcester[6] to the gates of that city. They were, however, in the event, repulsed with great slaughter, by the valour of the citizens, excited by the spirited conduct of Wulston, their Bishop.[7]

At this time an incident happened, springing from a trivial occurrence, which produced an awful change in the affairs of South Wales, and which, in some measure, produced the final ruin of Cambria. Llywelyn and Einion, chieftains of eminence in South Wales, and the sons of the Lord of Pembroke, rose in rebellion against Rhys ap Tewdwr, their sovereign; and they likewise drew into their treasonable designs Gruffydd ap Meredydd, another chieftain of that country. Having joined their forces, they marched to attack Prince Rhys, who then resided at Llandudoch, in the County of Pembroke, where an action ensued, in which the rebels were defeated, and Gruffydd taken prisoner; the two other leaders having saved themselves by flight. The rebel chieftain was instantly put to death as a traitor,[8]—the first instance we have seen, in these miserable times, of legal justice having dared to assert her prerogative. Einion, rendered desperate by the late event, and afraid to trust his safety with any of his own kindred, associated with Jestyn ap Gwrgaint, Lord of Glamorgan,[9] between whom there was a similarity of situation and interest, he being at that time in arms against his sovereign. To bind themselves still more closely to each other,

---

[2] Hoveden, p. 460. Robert of Gloucester, in his Rhyming Chronicle, gives the following quaint description of the Domesday Book :—

"Then King William to learn the worth of his land,
Let enquiry stretch throughout all England;
How many plough land, and hidden also,
Was in every shire, and what they were worth thereto;
And the rents of each town, and the waters each one,
The worth, and woods, eke, and wastes where lived none.
By that he wist what he were worth of all England,
And set it clearly forth that all might understand,
And had it clearly written, and that *script* he put, I wis,
In the treasurie of Westminster, where it still is."

[3] This was called Hydage.
[4] Welsh Chron., p. 117.
[5] Wynne's Wales.
[6] Called by the Romans, Brangonia; by the Britons, Caer-Wrangon; and by the Saxons, Worcestre. Hump. Lhuyd, p. 26.
[7] Annales Waverlienses.
[8] Welsh Chron., p. 119.
[9] The territory of Morganwg or Morgan.

L

it was agreed that Einion should marry the daughter of Jestyn, on condition that he procured a body of Normans to assist in their enterprise, as that chieftain had served in the English armies, and had formed acquaintance with the Norman nobility.[1] Influenced by those powerful motives, Einion hastened into England.

The design was agreeable to the enterprising spirit of the age. The English princes, too, had always employed, in their various attempts at subjugating Wales, this principle of Machiavelian policy—*Divide et Impera.* And at this time, the treason of two men, coinciding with the views of Rufus, infused a fatal poison into the bosom of their country.

Robert Fitzhammon, a gentleman of the King's privy chamber, and baron of the realm, undertook the adventure. He selected for this enterprise twelve knights of considerable note, who agreed to serve under him with a large body of forces.[2] These troops, early in the following year, landed in Glamorgan, and were received with great honour by Jestyn, the lord of that country; who, joining his forces with the Normans, laid waste the territories of Rhys ap Tewdwr. At the time of this invasion, the Prince of South Wales was above ninety years old. With a spirit and activity uncommon at his age, he marched in person against the rebels; and meeting them upon the Black Mountain[3] near Brecknock, after a severe and bloody conflict, his army was vanquished, and this ancient and gallant prince was himself slain in the action.[4] He left two sons by his wife, the daughter of Rhiwallon ap Cynvyn, Gruffydd, and another son, who, at his father's death, was a prisoner in England.[5] In this manner died Rhys ap Tewdwr, attempting to resist the deepest oppression, and fighting for the independence of his country. With this warrior, sunk the glory of the Principality of South Wales;[6] after whose death, betrayed by the vices of its own princes, and torn in pieces by foreign adventurers, it lost its ancient importance, and gradually fell into decay.

The treason of the Welsh chieftains having thus attained so unfortunate an issue, Jestyn kept all his engagements with the Normans very faithfully; not only dismissing them with the stipulated pay, but with presents suitable to the importance of their service. Einion demanded of Jestyn his daughter in marriage, agreeably to the promise he had made; but prosperity having rendered that chieftain proud and insolent, he rejected his suit, and even embittered the refusal by treating him with disdain. Resenting a conduct so faithless and ungrateful, Einion hastened after the Normans, in hopes of overtaking them before they had sailed. On his arrival at the sea shore, he found that they were already embarked; and as he might not be heard at so great a distance, he waved his mantle as a signal for them to return. Fitzhammon and his knights immediately put to shore, to know the cause of so extraordinary a proceeding. As soon as they had landed, Einion laid open his grievances, and likewise the facility of subduing a territory likely to remain unprotected by the Welsh princes; who must have seen with an eye of indignation the late conduct of Jestyn. Touched in some measure with the injuries of their friend, but still more, it is probable, with the prospect of possessing so fertile a country, Fitzhammon and the knights readily engaged in the views of Einion, and, contrary to every principle of honour, suddenly invaded the territory of Glamorgan. Little expecting such a turn of fortune, Jestyn was easily dispossessed of his territory.

They then proceeded to parcel out the domain agreeably to feudal ideas. Fitzhammon, reserving to himself the principal parts, with the seigniory of the whole, gave the remainder of that province, to be held as fiefs under himself, to the twelve knights who had shared in the adventure,[7] leaving the rough and barren mountains the property of Einion.[8]

---

[1] Welsh Chron., p. 119.   [2] *Ibid.*

[3] On Hirbrain, between Neath and Merthyr Tydfil.

[4] Wynne's Wales, p. 112; Humphrey Llwyd, p. 80; Polydore Virgil, lib. x., p. 71.

[5] Humphrey Llwyd's Brev., p. 81; Welsh Chron., p. 120.

[6] Humphrey Llwyd's Brev., p. 80; Welsh Chron., p. 120, from Ran. Cest., lib. vii., c. 7; Marianus Scotus.

[7] The castle and manor of Ogmore was given to William de Londres; the lordship of Neath to Richard Greenfield; that of Coyty to Paine Tuberville; Llan Blethyan to Robert St. Quintine; Talavan to Richard Syward; the castle and manor of Penmarc to Gilbert Humfrevile; the castle and manor of Sully to Reginald Sully; the manor of East Orchard to Roger Berkrolles; that of Peterton to Peter le Soor; that of St. George to John Fleming; that of Fonmon to John St. John; and the manor of Donats to William le Esterling. Wynne's Wales, p. 115.

[8] Camden's Britannia, p. 609, Gibson's Ed.; Humphrey Llwyd's Brev., p. 80; Welsh Chron., p. 120.

In this manner were the Lords of the Marches [a] established in Wales; possessing, in all cases, with the exception of the power of granting pardons for treason, *Ima regalia*. In the castle of Caerdiff [1] the lords of Glamorgan usually kept their chancery, exchequer, and court, where the twelve knights, by their tenures, were obliged to attend one day in every month, having separate apartments in the castle for that purpose. [2] Each of the other lordships had a distinct jurisdiction, enjoying the same rights with that of Glamorgan, except in cases of wrong judgment, when an appeal might be made to the superior court. [3] All disputes in matters of equity, arising in the several lordships, were determined by the chancellor in the Chancery court of Glamorgan. [4]

The fortunate issue of the late adventures raised among the Norman nobility an ardent spirit of enterprise. The King of England threw powerful incentives in their way; alluring them by motives of interest and power, those strong incitements to human conduct. Several barons petitioned the King for license to possess, under homage and fealty, those territories which they might conquer in Wales. This liberty given to the English lords of obtaining at their own charge the territories of the Welsh, though springing out of a wise policy, was apparently founded on the absurd idea of forfeiture; because the people had renounced the allegiance to which they had submitted through necessity, during the wars of Harold, and the decisive reign of the Norman conqueror.

The situation of South Wales, rendered defenceless by the death of Rhys ap Tewdwr, favoured the designs of these military adventurers, among the foremost of whom was Bernard de Newmarche, [5] who easily took possession of the province of Brecknock, containing three cantrevs; and to colour his title with some degree of popularity, he married Nest, the granddaughter of Gruffydd ap Llywelyn. [6] Roger de Montgomery, Earl of Shrewsbury, was the next who did homage to the King for Caerdigan. Arulph, the younger son of that nobleman, obtained likewise the great lordship of Pembroke. [7] In this easy manner, by the desultory enterprises of a few Norman lords, was the principality of South Wales subdued.

Hugh Lupus, Earl of Chester, likewise did homage for Englefield and Rhyvonioc, with the country extending along the sea shore from Chester to the water of Conway. Ralph Mortimer did the same for the territory of Elvel, as did Hugh de Lacie for the lands of Euas, and Eustace de Cruer for Mold and Hopedale. [8] These barons endeavoured to secure their conquests by erecting fortresses, [9] and, as far as they were able, by settling in them English or Norman inhabitants. At this time Bristol, Gloucester, Worcester, Shrewsbury, and Chester were re-built and fortified, and formed a line of military posts upon the frontiers. [1] Thus the last asylum of the Britons was invested on every side, or broken by their enemies. The ancient seats of the Dimetæ, &c. &c., who, supported only by native bravery, had given a check to the Roman arms, and whose descendants had baffled until this period the utmost efforts of the Saxon and Norman princes, having been thus subdued.

The kingdom of North Wales, and the Principality of Powys, were not long secure from the encroaching spirit of the times. The Earl of Shrewsbury did homage for all Powys, and brought under his subjection some districts in that territory, particularly the town and castle of Baldwyn. This important fortress he fortified more strongly, and called it Montgomery, after the name of his family. [2] The Principality of Powys from this period had little concern in the interests of Wales. The policy of England soon rendered that territory, which had been for ages a barrier of defence, a dangerous neighbour upon the confines; and it

---

[a] An old English word, signifying "boundary."

[1] Caerdâf, or City on the Tâf.

[2] Wynne's Wales, p. 115.

[3] Welsh Chron., p. 122.

[4] Several gentlemen came at this time to Brecknock, with Bernard de Newmarche, to whom he gave the following manors, which their heirs enjoy to this time; the manor of Abercynric and Slowch to the Aubreys; the manor of Llanhamlach and Tal. y Llyn to the Walboifs; the manor of Gilston to the Gunters; and the manor of Pontwilym to the Havards, &c. See Welsh Chron., p. 150; Camden's Brit., p. 599. Gibson's Ed.

[5] Welsh Chron., p. 148.

[6] *Ibid.*, p. 151.

[7] Welsh Chron., p. 152.

[8] *Ibid.*, p. 151.

[9] Built by Baldwyn, lieutenant of the Welsh Marches in the reign of William I. See Camden's Brit., p. 650. Gibson's Ed.

[1] Vaughan's British Ant. Rev., p. 18.

[2] Manuscript relating to the Marches of Wales in the possession of Philip Lloyd Fletcher, Esq., of Gwernhaeled in Flintshire.

became, by the defection of its princes, an instrument of mischief in the hands of the English against the national quiet and safety.

The kingdom of North Wales, at this time reduced to the island of Anglesea, the counties of Merionydd and Caernarvon, and a part of the present counties of Denbigh and Cardigan, still preserved the national character and importance. The natives of that country, aided by the virtue of their princes, became more formidable than ever to the English; and at times acquiring union with additional vigour from despair, their enemies, instead of being able to make new conquests, held those which they had already obtained, by a precarious tenure.

The late incidents having produced a striking change in the situation of Wales, and the Lords of the Marches having introduced into that country a new system of jurisprudence, some account of those lords, and of the system they introduced, may be interesting to the reader. The conquest of Wales had always been a leading object in the politics of England; not only from the desire of more extensive dominions, but as a means of preventing in future the devastation and misery, which the animosity of a warlike and an injured people had produced on the English borders. The utility of employing likewise in foreign enterprises a martial nobility, inclined the Norman princes to encourage, by every incitement of advantage and honour, the dangerous designs of subduing, or of making settlements in Wales.

To enable the English lords to preserve the obedience of the people they had subdued, the kings of England allowed them to assume in their several territories, an absolute jurisdiction.[3] But they did not hold this authority under any grant from the Crown; it was only for the present connived at by the prince, and arose, as a wise measure, out of their particular situations.

There is not, it is said, any record to be found in the Tower, or in any other part of England, of a grant having been given to any Lord of the Marches, to possess the authority annexed to that dignity. The King's writ, issuing out of the courts at Westminster, did not extend into any parts of Wales, except into Pembroke, accounted at this time a portion of England; neither did the sheriffs, nor other officers of the King, execute his writs or precepts in any other part of the country.

The high privileges incident to the Lords of the Marches could not, for many reasons, be held by charter.

The kings of England, when they gave to any baron such lands as they might conquer from the Welsh, could not fix those immunities on any certain precinct; not knowing which, or whether any, would be eventually subdued. The lords themselves were not solicitous to procure such immunities; as it frequently happened that those estates of which they had taken possession were afterwards recovered by the Welsh, either by composition with the kings of England, or by force of arms. Another cause of their not possessing any charters of prerogative was, that such privileges, so high in their nature, so royal and united to the Crown, could not, by the laws of England, be disunited from the same. It was therefore thought a wiser course to suffer them to establish, of their own authority, such royal jurisdictions rather than to hold them under a grant from the sovereign, which, if at any time called into question, might be adjudged of no force. Those lordships which were conquered at the expense of the English princes themselves, were subject to a more regular jurisdiction; being governed, in general, by the laws of England.[4]

The Lords of the Marches, selecting the most agreeable and fertile part of the territories, erected castles for their own residence, and towns for the accommodation of their soldiers. It was in this manner that most of the present towns and castles on the frontier of Wales were built. This appears, by the ancient charters given to such towns by those lords who first conquered or founded them, expressive of the immunities to the burgesses and freemen; few or none of them having purchased such liberties from the kings of England till many years after; and when this was done, which was seldom the case, they were only confirmations of privileges granted by their ancient lords.

Among other towns and castles about this time built in Wales, were Pembroke, Tenby, and Haverford-

---

[3] Lord Herbert of Cherbury's Life of Henry VIII.   [4] *Ibid.*

west, erected by Strongbow, William de Valence, and the Hastings. Newport was built by Martin, Lord of Cemaes; the town and castle of Cydweli by Londres, and afterwards enlarged by the Duke of Lancaster; the towns and castles of Swansea, Oystermouth, Longhor, Radnor, Buellt, and Rhaiadr, were erected by the Bruces, Mortimers, Beauchamps, Herberts, Abergavenny by Dru de Baladon; and in after times Ruthin by the Lords Grey, and Denbigh by Lacie, Earl of Lincoln. The greater part of these were ancient towns and castles before the Norman conquest, which had been either injured or destroyed by the devastations of war, or in the lapse of time.

The Lords of the Marches held under the kings of England, by the tenure of serving in war with a certain number of their vassals, and of furnishing their castles with strong garrisons, and with all military implements. The English laws were, for the most part, administered in the Marches of Wales; their tenures likewise were principally English, being transmitted by fine, recovery, feoffment, and livery of seisin.

Some lords, from motives of prudence, permitted their tenants, who were natives of the country, to enjoy many of their ancient laws, which were not repugnant to those of England, or injurious to their own interest. Among other concessions in favour of the Welsh were the usage of gavel-kind, and the transfer of lands by surrender in court, which gained admission into the jurisdiction of those lordships under the names of "customs," though anciently they had formed part of the common law of Wales. A sufficient number of people not being easily obtained to colonise the conquered countries, it was obviously the interest of the Lords of the Marches to sooth the asperity of the conquest by allowing the Welsh to retain many of their ancient customs. As the mode of transfer, as well as the principles of succession, were different among the two people, two courts were established in many lordships, in which the custom of each nation prevailed. There were, however, a few lordships, though entirely held by English tenures, in which the tenants were permitted the custom of gavel-kind, although they transmitted their lands by feoffment. These estates were said to be held by English tenure and Welsh *dole*. In those lordships where the land was thus divided, and which were held by knight's service, the lord had the wardship of all the sons, as well as the daughters; and this was a point of great advantage; it might induce such lords to encourage their tenants in the custom of dividing their estates among their sons. In many lordships the Welsh laws were not in use, and English customs entirely prevailed. The whole jurisprudence depended entirely upon the will of the first conquerors.

The chief qualifications of a Lord of the Marches was that he should hold of the king *in capite*. Though conquest was the general principle on which his right was founded, in some instances his dignity proceeded from a different cause; as in the case of Powys, a great part of which was never gained by conquest but changed into Lordships' Marches by the following means:—

The Princes of Powys, seeing the perilous situation of their country, and actuated by fear or interested motives, made their submission to Henry I., and agreed to hold under him their several territories, paying the same obedience and duties which the Lord of the Marches owed to the crown of England. Thus did several of the lordships of Powys differ from the others. In one point, however, they agreed—that they did, and of necessity, must hold of the king *in capite*.[b] This circumstance, together

---

[b] It appears from various ancient documents, that after the conquest of England by the Normans, King William placed several of his Norman nobility on the confines of Wales, and gave them power to make such conquests in that country as they were able. By this piece of policy a double end was answered: those whom he had brought over into England, were thus left to provide territory for themselves; and their power tended in some degree to reduce the Welsh people into subjection. The lands thus seized were holden *in capite*, of the crown of England: several of the English nobility who possessed property on the borders of Wales, found it worth their while to aid these incursions. Such of the Welsh as had seigniories or lordships here, were invited by the king to acknowledge a dependence on the crown, under ample promises and full reservation of all their rights and privileges.—All the lands rendered thus dependent on the English crown were denominated Baronies Marches, and a kind of palatine jurisdiction was erected in them, with power to administer justice in the respective territories, and the king being supreme lord, wherever their own jurisdiction failed, redress was sought in the English courts of law. This scheme was continued with considerable success for several reigns, till at length a wide strip of frontier country extending all the way from Bristol to Chester, which formerly belonged to the Welsh, became subject,

with their renouncing obedience to the Princes of Wales, was all that was at first expected by the kings of England or by the Lords of the Marches.⁶ The barony of Powys had not any manors which held under it like other lordships which were obtained by conquest; and for the same reason there were neither knights' fees, nor plough, nor ox-lands in these lordships; these divisions being introduced into Wales by the English and Norman lords, were entirely unknown to the ancient Britons.

under a certain tenure to the English crown. This tenure was, that, in case of war, the lords should send to the army a certain number of their vassals; that they should garrison their respective castles, and keep the Welsh people in subjection. In return for these services, the lords seem to have had an arbitrary and most despotic power in their own domains. They had the power of life and death in their respective courts, in all cases except those of high treason.

In every frontier manor a gallows was erected, and if any Welshman passed the boundary line that was fixed between the two countries, he was immediately seized and hanged; every town within the Marches had a horseman armed with a spear, who was maintained for the express purpose of taking these offenders. If any Englishman was caught on the Welsh side of this line he suffered a similar fate from them. The Welsh esteemed everything that they could steal from their English neighbours as lawful prize. On this account many of the latter were compelled to have their dwellings moated round, and to have pallisadoes or stakes on the edge of the moat: and these inhabitants every night, for better security, drove their cattle within the fence. If a Welshman could but get a horse or cow over the boundary line, he had only to cry out " My own," to prevent the claims of his countrymen, for the horseman could not dare to follow, lest he should be hanged.

After the conquest of Wales by Edward I., the Baronies Marches were continued, but under regulations somewhat different from the former. In the reign of Edward IV. they were governed by a lord president, and a council, consisting of the Chief Justice of Chester, and three justices of the peace of Wales. In cases of emergency, other persons were allowed to be called in.

By a statute passed in the reign of Henry VIII., the principality and dominion of Wales became formally annexed to the realm of England; and the same jurisdiction and government, and a similar administration of justice was adopted. All the Welsh laws and most of their peculiar customs and tenures, were by this statute entirely abolished. By this statute also, four new counties were made, Radnorshire, Brecknockshire, Montgomeryshire, and Denbighshire. The Marches became annexed partly to England, and partly to these new counties of Wales. The president and council of the Marches were however allowed to continue as before, and their general court was holden at Ludlow.

A statute, however, was passed in the year 1689, the second of William III., after the death of the Earl of Macclesfield, the last lord president, by which the government of the entire principality was divided between two peers of the realm, who had the titles of Lords Lieutenant of North and South Wales. From this period the Marches were entirely abolished.

⁶ There were twenty-one Lords Marchers who sat among the English lords, and had the titles of those places they had won from the Welsh. They had originally regal jurisdiction in their several baronies, where the king's writs did not run. This was intended as a strength against the neighbouring enemy; but Edward I., in his statute of Rhuddlan, withdrew this power, for he was able of himself to rule our countrymen. None were erected after that period; they held of the king immediately, that is, *in capite*, and were accordingly bound to him in personal suit and service, and to find him a certain number of soldiers.

Henry VIII. finally reduced their broken power. Many of

these baronies had fallen to the Crown from purchase, inheritance, or forfeiture. He resumed all or most of the jurisdictions that were left, and deprived the Marchers of the same, leaving them in effect but as lords of manors in England. He then ordained justices* of assize himself, and justices of the peace, sheriffs, and other officers; and divided the country more correctly into counties; and erected great sessions and other courts for its government, by officers of his own, and according to the laws of England, and left little or no authority to the Lords Marchers. The former policy and presents of the Kings of England to their nobles had continued from the Norman Conquest, until Edward I.; insomuch, that at that time Wales was almost come into the possession of divers English lords, who held the same of the Kings of England, and not of the Princes of Wales.

There were no representatives in the Commons House of Parliament from Cheshire or Wales till the Welsh Incorporating Acts of Henry VIII.

We would remind our readers that the Lords Marchers were not to be considered as possessing their dignity by a Royal grant from their superior lord, the King of England; their territories were held by assumption and an implied permission. Indeed, it would appear that these licensed land-pirates were not particularly desirous of procuring any specific charters of liberties; for their tenure was precarious, and possessions so gained, says a writer on this subject, are not always peaceably enjoyed.—But the dangerous tendency of *such* a jurisdiction appeared evident to Henry III. For in consequence of the league entered into between John, Earl of Chester, the Earl of Pembroke, and the Prince of Wales, Henry resolved on the conquest of the country by his own forces. The Earl of Chester dying, the king compromised with his four sisters, and assumed the title and dominion of the County Palatine, first granted by the Conqueror to his kinsman, Hugh the Wolf, " Tenendum sibi et heredibus suis adeo libere ad gladium, sicut ipse Rex tenebat totam Angliam et coronam;" and, says Owen, " This resumption was not occasioned so much upon that fair pretence commonly received, ' *Ne tam præclara dominatio divideretur,*' as to draw to the Crown such a checking jurisdiction, and which is the greatest part of the county of Flint, which the Earls of Chester, as Lords Marchers, had won from the Welsh; and to make way thereby for his entrance into Wales, and to prosecute his intended conquest with more facility."—On the annexation of the territory to the immediate control of the English Crown, Henry conferred the earldom on his son Edward. He formed Flint into a separate county, but annexed the government thereof to the County Palatine of Chester. Edward, on his accession to the throne, made further conquests, and erected five new counties, viz., Caermarthen, Cardigan, Anglesea, Caernarvon, and Merioneth; and for the government thereof, those laws were established which bear the title of *Statutes of Wales*, and ordained the three courts of Chancery, Session, and Exchequer.

---

* Henry VIII. gave us but four judges to the whole Principality; the Puisnes were added by Elizabeth. Only eight justices of the peace were allowed to each shire by Henry, who formed the new counties of Monmouth, Denbigh, Montgomery, Brecknock, and Radnor.

We think it best in this place to introduce some account of the Royal Tribes of Wales established about the middle of the 11th century.

Genealogy was in no nation, except the Hebrew, considered of so much importance, or carried to an equal extent, as in the Principality of Wales. Indeed family distinction is pursued so far, that perhaps it induces the Cambrian to think more highly of himself than he ought to think. Pride of ancestry was a delicate and essential point among the ancient Britons, and consequently they were more desirous of noble than of rich connexions. So deeply was this principle rooted, that even the lowest class of the people carefully preserved the direct and collateral descents' of their families, and were in general able from memory, not only to recite the names of their proximate proprietors, but to trace their various relations back, through numerous generations. This custom, amongst the hereditary prejudices of the Welsh, has been supposed to arise from the mountainous nature of the country, and the circumstances of the inhabitants living long in the same district. But a more rational cause may be found in the peculiar mode of their ancient government, and legal tenures. The laws of gavel-kind, so dispersed property, and ramified heritable relations, that it was essential to correctly ascertain the consanguinity of affinity through the male and female lines, to the utmost possible latitude. The following particulars are extracted from York's "Royal Tribes."

"The five regal Tribes, and the respective representative of each, were considered as of royal blood. The fifteen common Tribes, all of North Wales, and the respective representative of each, formed the nobility; were lords of distinct districts, and bore some hereditary office* in the palace. Gruffydd ap Cynan, Prince of North Wales, Rhŷs ab Tewdwr, of South Wales, and Bleddyn ab Cynfyn, of Powis, regulated both these classes, but they did not create them; as many of the persons placed at their head, lived before their time, and some, after. The precedence, as it stands, is very uncertain, and not governed by the dates; the last of them were created by Dafydd ab Owain Gwynedd, who began his reign in 1169. We are left ignorant of the form by which they were called to this rank. Mr. Vaughan of Hengwrt informs us that 'Gruffydd ab Cynan, Rhŷs ab Tewdwr, and Bleddyn ab Cynfyn, made diligent search after the arms, ensigns, and pedigrees of their ancestors, the nobility and kings of the Britons. What they discovered by their pains in any papers and records was afterwards by the Bards digested, and put into books, and they ordained five Royal Tribes, there being only three before, from whom the posterity to this day, can derive themselves, and also fifteen special tribes, of whom the gentry of North Wales are for the most part descended.'

"The founder of the first of the 'Five Royal Tribes' was Prince GRUFFYDD AP CONAN, who ranked amongst the most celebrated of them. He received his crown of North Wales in 1077, from Trahaern ap Caradoc, at the battle of Carno,' who had been elected by the people without the merits of descent, on the assassination of Prince Bleddyn ap Cynfyn. Gruffydd[1] was descended in a direct line from Anarawd, the eldest son of Roderick the Great, and was entitled not to the Principality of the North alone, but the supremacy of Wales vested in him; for it was the condition in the tripartition of Roderic, and

---

[7] As long as a Welsh pedigree, is a proverbial adage for tenacity and tediousness in narration.

[8] By the laws of Howel Dda it appears there were twenty-four great officers of the Welsh Court.

[9] The mountains of Carno, like the mountains of Gilboa, (says Pennant), were celebrated for the fall of the mighty. The fiercest battle in our annals happened in 1077, amid these hills, when Gruffydd ap Cynan, supported by Rhys ap Tudor, Prince of South Wales, disputed the sovereignty of North Wales with Trahaern ap Caradoc, the reigning prince, followed by Caradoc ap Gruffydd and Meilio, sons of Rhywallon ap Gwyn, his cousins german. After a most bloody contest, victory declared itself in favour of the first; Trahaern and his kinsman disdaining flight, fell on the spot; and Gruffydd ap Cynan was put into possession of his rightful throne, which he filled during fifty-seven years with great dignity.

[1] Gruffydd had personal rather than political courage (often political villainy). He had fought hand to hand with that hardy baron, Fulke Fitzwarren, who was entrusted by Henry I. with the care of the Marches, and was wounded by him in the shoulder, and fled; but in the end wrested from Fulke his castle and lordship of Whittington. There was another action in which he was personally engaged; and the circumstances are very extraordinary. Robert of Rhuddlan, nephew to Hugh Lupus, and the possessor of that castle, where he then resided, received in it a visit from Gruffydd, who came to solicit his assistance against his Welsh subjects. This he obtained; but on some quarrel attacked Robert in his castle, took and burnt the baily or yard, and killed such a number of his men, that but few escaped into the towers.

confirmed by his grandson, Howel Dda, that the Princes of South Wales and Powys should be tributary to the North. He beareth arms, gules, three lionels passant in pale, barry argent, armed azure.

"The founder of our second royal tribe, was RHYS AP TEWDWR, distinguished by the name of Mawr, or the Great.' In him the legal succession of South Wales was restored. He was, moreover, the choice of the people, on the murder of the usurper, Rhys ap Owain. With Gruffydd ap Cynan, he shared the victory at Carno; and the fortunes of that field set them both on their hereditary thrones. He beareth arms, gules, a lion rampant, Or, within a border indented.

"BLEDDYN AP CYNFYN ranks the third royal tribe. He had a title to Powys in female succession from his great grandmother, Angharad;' but his crown of North Wales was usurpation, in common at first with his brother, Rhiwallon, who fell four years after in the battle of Mechain, and the whole was then his own. He beareth arms, Or, a lion rampant, gules armed and lacquered, Or. This warlike prince was put to death by his own subjects,' and his head sent to Harold, who commanded the armies of the Confessor Edward with success against our countrymen. Harold brought Gruffydd's widow out of Wales, and married her; she was sister to the powerful Saxon Earls, Edwyn and Morcar, the sons of Algar, and grandsons of Leofric, Earl of Mercia; which latter led an army against Sweyn, King of Denmark, in 1003, and died in 1057, being the husband of the famous Godiva, who freed Coventry from an heavy tax, and gave rise to the well-known story of Peeping Tom.

"ATHELSTAN GLODRYDD was the founder of the fourth royal tribe. He was Prince of the country between Wye and Severn, which he inherited as the heir of Tudor Trevor, from whom he derived the title to the Earldom of Hereford. Athelstan, King of England, was his god-father. Athelstan bore two coats, quartered azure, three boars' heads, cabouched sable, lacquered gules, tusked Or.

"JESTYN AP GWRGANT, the fifth royal tribe, was Prince or Lord of Glamorgan. He descended, in the twenty-ninth generation, from our great Caractacus,—a sorry slip (says Mr. York) from such a stock.

"There is a dispute among our genealogists respecting the fourth and fifth royal tribes. Some historians assert that Jestyn ap Gwrgant is the fourth royal tribe, and that Athelstan Glodrydd is the fifth; others state *vice versâ*. The uncertainty of dates at this period is very perplexing. Mr. Vaughan, of Hengwrt, says that 'Gruffyth ap Conan, Rhys ap Tewdwr, and Bleddyn ap Cynfyn, being the only royal tribes then existing, founded two more.' As far as this relates to Jestyn ap Gwrgant, the matter may be clear; for these four may be said to have been cotemporaries, about the year 1073."

A.D. 1093.—This year the Normans, who inhabited the country of Glamorgan, fell upon and destroyed the countries about Gwyr, Kidwely, and Ystrâd Tywy, which they harassed in such a cruel manner that they left them bare of inhabitants. And to increase, as it was thought, the miseries of the Welsh, King William Rufus, being informed of the great slaughter which Gruffydd ap Cynan and the sons of Bleddyn ay Cynfyn, had lately committed upon the English within Shropshire, Cheshire, Worcestershire, and Herefordshire, entered Montgomery, which place, having been some time before demolished by the Welsh, King William had rebuilt. But the Welsh kept all the passes so well, that the King could not penetrate into the country, and he returned with no great honour to England.

A.D. 1096. — The late disasters, and the disgrace which he in person had received, excited in the fierce mind of Rufus the keenest indignation. He entered Wales a second time, at the head of a royal army. During his march the activity of the Welsh cut off his provisions, harassed his troops, and considerably diminished his numbers both in men and horses; for, keeping aloof in the woods and marshes, or at the tops of mountains, they suddenly attacked the English with great advantage in the defiles of the country, and the passages of rivers.' And such was the valour of the Welsh, and

---

' Rhys was the son of Tewdwr, the son of Einion. the son of Owain, the eldest son of Howel Dda, the legal Prince of South Wales; but elected to the North, in preference to the sons of Idwal Yoel, the right heirs.

' " Bleddyn ap Cynfyn bob cwys,
     Ei hun bioedd hen Bowys."

' Welsh Annals, p. 3; Welsh Chron., p. 102; and Warrington's Wales, p. 348.

' Brompton's Chron., p. 992; Matthew of Westminster, lib. ii. fol. 12; Polydore Virgil, p. 174.

such the conduct of their leaders; so great were the difficulties likewise which Rufus found in attempting to penetrate through the country, or in drawing the enemy to battle, that in despair he gave up the enterprise, and, after re-fortifiying some castles on the Borders, returned with additional disgrace into England.[6]

Discomfiture and disgrace having of late attended the arms of England, a different mode of conducting the war was adopted. Many of the Norman nobility were encouraged to undertake, at their own charge, the conquest of the Welsh; and about this time, or before, many barons had acquired considerable settlements in those parts of Wales which had lately been subdued, or along the frontiers of the country. Among others, Peter Corbet settled on the lordship of Cawrs; Mortimer, on Wigmore; Fitz-Allen, on Clun and Oswestry; Monthault, on Hawarden; Fitzwarren, on Whittington; Roger le Strange, on Elesmere; Drude Baladon, on Abergavenny; and Gilbert, on Monmouth.[7]

A.D. 1098.—At the secret instigation of Owen ap Edwyn, Lord of Engerfield, and of other chieftains in North Wales, a very formidable army invaded that country, under the command of the Earls of Chester[8] and Shrewsbury.[9] Gruffydd, the King of North Wales, and Cadwgan ap Bleddyn, not being able on a sudden to collect a force sufficient to oppose them, and not having the necessary confidence in their troops, gave way for a time, and retired to the mountains for security. The two earls, meeting with no resistance, continued their march into that part of Caernarvonshire which lies opposite to Anglesea. Gruffydd ap Cynan, seeing the danger which threatened the seat of his government, passed over the water of the Menai, attended by his associate Cadwgan, and having received a slight reinforcement out of Ireland, he seemed determined to defend the island.[1] At this critical moment, Owen ap Edwyn, whose daughter had married the Welsh King, and who was likewise his principal minister, openly avowed his treason, and joined the English army with his forces. The Welsh prince astonished at the perfidy and revolt of so powerful a chieftain, and unable to oppose the united force of the enemy, withdrew into Ireland.[2] No longer protected, the island of Anglesea fell an easy prey to the English, who poured upon the inhabitants a full measure of retaliation for the cruelties which had lately been committed on the borders of England. It is painful to relate the singular and savage barbarities exercised upon this occasion, resembling more the deliberate malice of ruffians than the impetuosity of soldiers. Some of the people had their hands cut off, others their feet; some had their eyes pulled out, others were castrated, and great numbers massacred. A priest of the name of Hearred, venerable for his years and his wisdom, having taken sanctuary in a church, the Earl of Shrewsbury commanded him to be taken from hence, ordered one of his eyes to be pulled out, his tongue to be cut, and caused him likewise to be deprived of his manhood.[3]

We should have drawn a veil over such a scene of barbarity, if the design of history had only been to adorn a story, and not to point the instructive moral, or to delineate with a faithful pencil the portraiture of men and manners.

The safety of North Wales, at this perilous crisis, depended upon a train of fortuitous circumstances. Magnus, the son of Harold, King of Norway, having taken possession of the Orkneys and the Isle of Man, arrived accidentally on the coast of Anglesey. Hearing of the cruelties committed by the English, and touched with a sense of generous pity, he determined to land his forces, and to preserve the miserable inhabitants from destruction.[4] The English endeavoured to oppose the Norwegians; in the attempt the Earl of Shrewsbury was slain. The Prince of Norway, observing that nobleman, whose impetuous valour had carried him into the sea, resolute in opposing his landing, levelled an arrow at him, which, through the opening of his armour, pierced his right eye, and, reaching his brain, he fell down convulsed into the water. The Norwegian Prince, on seeing him fall, exultingly cried, "Let him dance!"[5] This accidental stroke of

---

[6] Brompton's Chron.; Matthew of Westminster; Polydore Virgil.

[7] Manuscript treatise on the Marches, in possession of Philip Lloyd Fletcher, Esq.

[8] Hugh Vrâs, or the fat Earl of Chester.

[9] Called by the Welsh, Hugh Goch, or Hugh with the Red Head.

[1] Welsh Chron., p. 155.   [2] Ibid.

[3] Brompton's Chron., p. 994; Fabian, p. 315.

[4] Welsh Chron., p. 156; Vita Griffith Fil Conain.

[5] Girald. Camb. Itin., cap. vii.; Simon Dunelme, p. 223.

justice, seen by the eyes of superstition, made the Welsh to conclude that the arrow had been directed by the immediate hand of the Almighty.

The death of the Earl of Shrewsbury produced some disorder amongst the English, and obliged them to abandon the shore. The Earl of Chester, on this disaster, suddenly retreated into England, leaving Owen ap Edwyn to enjoy for a time the fruits of his treason.

The Norwegians, finding that the English had not left anything to plunder, immediately re-embarked.[6] This attempt was the last enterprise of any of the Northern nations to plunder or subdue this country.[7]

William Rufus met with his death while hunting in the New Forest. He was accidentally struck by an arrow, which was found broken, and a part sticking in his breast. "He died," says Malmesbury, "meditating great things, and would, probably, have achieved them." He does not disclose what he alludes to, but we learn from the French Minister of the time, that his object was believed to be no less than the crown of France.[8]

HENRY was hunting in a different part of the New Forest when Rufus fell. He was informed by the cries of his attendants of his brother's calamity; one might have expected that the claims of fraternal sympathy would have drawn him to the fatal spot, and have led him to pay the last tribute of affection to his remains.[9] But ambition extinguished sensibility. He left the body to the casual charity of a passing rustic, and rode precipitately to Winchester, to seize the royal treasure. According to the compact between Robert and Rufus, the succession had now devolved upon Robert, who was abroad on a crusade; and the baron into whose care the treasury had been committed, came breathless to the castle to anticipate Henry's purpose. With honourable fidelity, he asserted the right of the absent Robert, to whom both he and Henry had sworn fealty. The discussion grew fierce, and Henry became outrageous at the resistance, and, unsheathing his sword, declared that no foreigner should presume to withhold from him his father's sceptre. Mutual friends interfering, the treasure was surrendered to Henry, who proceeding to London, was, on the following Sunday, the third day after William's death, created king and crowned.[1] An account of the ceremony of his coronation, is preserved in MS. Cott. Claudius, A. 3. Henry soon established himself in the popular favour, and the barons and clergy assembled to support him. When Robert heard of his brother's death he made preparations to return, and effected a landing at Portsmouth, but the formidable army collected by Henry, gave no encouragement to his hopes, and produced a panic which enabled the councillors of both to mediate a peace.

Robert, whose passions were versatile, who acted by paroxysms, and who was as easily tranquillised as he was excited, was satisfied with the honour of invading his brother's territories, with the chance of succession that was promised him, and with an agreement from Henry to pay him two thousand pounds of silver every year; the friends of each were to enjoy their properties in England and Normandy undisturbed. The brothers embraced each other in sight of both armies, and the reconciliation was so cordial that Robert became Henry's guest for two months.[2] A quarrel subsequently took place, the result of which was that Robert was imprisoned in Cardiff Castle.

It is stated that Henry treated Robert in his captivity, which lasted twenty-eight years, with every delicacy of food, and with royal robes; he allowed him permission to play at chess and dice, and to visit the neighbouring gardens, woods, and pleasant places. Some historians however deny that his confinement was only a sort of honourable restraint. Henry himself, in a letter to the Pope, gives the following account of the circumstances:—"I have not," says he, "imprisoned him as an enemy, but I have placed

---

[6] Welsh Chron., p. 156 ; Hume's History of England.

[7] In the course of this expedition, the Earl of Chester rebuilt the castle of Diganwy, the seat of the ancient princes of Wales. King's Vale Royal of Cheshire, p. 48.

[8] Segar mentions this as the common opinion. Vit. Lut. Grossi, p. 96.

[9] Some rustics saw the body, and carried it in their cart to Winchester. Malmesbury, p. 126.

[1] Ordericus Vitalis, pp. 782, 783.

[2] Saxon Chron., p. 209 ; Ord. Vit., p. 788. Robert absolved Henry from the homage, and entered into a treaty to furnish his brother with 1000 knights if required. See Rymer, p. 4.

him in a royal castle, as a noble stranger, broke down with many troubles; and I supply him abundantly with every delicacy and enjoyment."

Henry and Matilda kept their Easter this year at Bath, and during the summer introduced the popular custom of making a Royal Progress through different parts of England.[3]

Several important measures were adopted during this reign to repress the turbulence of the Welsh. The king seems to have been extremely dissatisfied with the conduct of his allies in the war with Robert de Belesme, and soon afterwards he caused their Prince, Jorwerth, to be seized, and detained in close prison about four years. During this period, says Wright, the Ludlow historian, a destructive guerilla warfare was constantly kept up on the southern border. At this time numbers of Flemings, a hardy and industrious race of men, came over to England. Some of their countrymen had already settled in this country in the days of the Conqueror, and we find them established about Downton at the period of the Domesday survey. An irruption of the sea into Flanders compelled the inhabitants to emigrate in great numbers; a large portion went to Germany, but many sought a refuge in England, and were allowed to inhabit the border of Scotland. Shortly afterwards, A.D. 1107-9, the King moved this colony to the Welsh border, and gave the Flemish refugees the district about Ross in Herefordshire, and Haverfordwest and Tenby in Pembrokeshire. They were, however, chiefly settled about the former place, and they brought there their manners and language, of which many traces remained even as late as the time of Queen Elizabeth. Giraldus has given us an interesting account of their superstitions.[4] They were beneficial in many respects to the country; they laid the foundation of the trade in wool for which Herefordshire was afterwards celebrated; and, equally ready to handle the plough or the sword, they enriched the county by their industry, and tamed the Welsh by their courage.[5] Checked in their depredations in the south, the latter now turned their fury against the northern boundary.

The King, on more than one occasion, was obliged to lead an army against them, and in one of these expeditions he narrowly escaped with his life. As he was carefully making his way through the woods, Henry was struck in the breast with an arrow, which was fortunately turned off by the mail with which he was covered; and the King asserted that the blow had been treacherously aimed by one of his own men. The Welsh always escaped by carrying their goods to the tops of the least accessible mountain. Taking advantage of the death of Richard, Earl of Chester, who was drowned in the celebrated wreck of the White-ships, they entered Cheshire, A.D. 1119, massacred many of the inhabitants, and burnt two castles. Henry hastened to the Border, and an English army, after a "painful march," again encamped at the foot of Snowdon, where the Welsh, according to the English chronicles, sued for peace. The King took hostages and returned home; but within a dozen years, in spite of the severe chastisement which they had received on this occasion, the Welsh were again in arms and invading Herefordshire: they burnt Cans, a town belonging to Paine Fitz John, who was still sheriff of that county, and treated the inhabitants with cruelty. The King, who was in Normandy, hastened to England to punish their contumacy; but death stopped him on the road. He left the crown of England to be seized upon by another usurper, and the kingdom to be torn by a new contest for the succession, more fatal than any that had gone before.

This year, 1237, the military command of the city and county of Chester were confided to Hugh Le Despenser, Stephen de Seagrave, and Henry de Audley; while the civil jurisdiction was given to the barons of the Earldom; for, as Camden[6] observes, "The King himself, after the Earldom came into his hands, for

---

[3] Saxon Chron.

[4] Girald. Camb. Itin., lib. xi. Compare the account there given with the very similar superstitions of the Tartar invaders of Europe in the following century, as related by William de Rubruquis.

[5] Girald. Camb. Itin.; William of Malmsb., p. 158; Robert Hovedon; Rad. Dicet. (in the Decem Scriptures),&c. Lappenberg, Geschichte von England, ii. 283. Giraldus describes these Flemings as being in his time—Gens fortis et robusta, continuoque belli conflictu gens

Cambrensibus inimicissima; gens, inquam, lanificiis, gens mercimoniis usitatissima; quocunque labore sive periculo terra marique lucrum quærere gens pervalida; vicissim loco et tempore nunc ad aratrum nunc ad arma gens promptissima; gens utique felix et fortis, si vel regibus ut deceret Cambria cordi fuisset, vel præstitutis saltem et præfectis injuriarum dedecus animo vindice displicuisset.

[6] Camden's Britannia, 1667, p. 454.

to maintain the Palatinateship, continued here the ancient rights and Palatine privileges and courts, like as the King of France did in the county of Champagne." In the following year, letters patent, dated 10th of May, 1238, were issued; a translation of which, extracted from the records of the Court of Chancery, reads thus :—

"THE KING, to the Barons, Knights, and Freemen of the City of Chester, greeting: Know ye that the aforesaid Earldom of Chester, together with our castles of Gannock and Dincolyn, in Wales, and all things to the same appertaining, we have commanded to be retained in our bounds, as always belonging to our Crown. And that there may be manifest proof to you that the same Earldom, without any separation at any time, we will retain annexed to our Crown, we have now assigned the same to our Queen [7] in dower." [8]

In testimony, &c. &c.

Henry retained the Earldom.

Gruffydd ap Cynan, King of North Wales, a popular prince, had not long enjoyed the pleasure of sitting on the throne of his ancestors, when a sudden calamity befell him, which, for a long time, deprived him of his kingdom and his liberty. A native of Wales, called Merion Gôch, entered into a conspiracy to betray him into the hands of the English. Agreeably to the plan which had been previously concerted with the Earls of Chester and Shrewsbury, a strong body of infantry and horse were stationed at Rûg, in Edeyrnion. The snare being laid, Gruffydd ap Cynan was desired by the treacherous Welshman, at the instance of the two English lords, to give them the meeting, under the colour of a friendly conference. With a simplicity which neither agrees with the character of the times, nor with the dictates of prudence, the Welsh king came to the place appointed, attended only by a few retainers, whom he had brought out of Ireland. He had no sooner made his appearance, than he was seized and carried in chains to the castle of Chester. His attendants were allowed to depart, without receiving any other injury than the loss of a thumb, which was cut from the right hand of each. This instance of whimsical barbarity might arise from the instigation of Merion Gôch, who, from the prejudices of his country, would detest them as foreigners, and who might also resent the partiality which this prince had always entertained for the Irish.

Gruffydd remained many years in captivity—a confinement, no doubt, that was rendered more bitter from a sense of his own inability to afford protection to his subjects, or to prevent the fatal consequences which, during that period, were taking place in South Wales and in Powys. The Earl of Chester having disarmed so formidable an enemy, committed dreadful ravages in North Wales; and in order to preserve the conquests he had made, and render his inroads more safe, he erected a fortress at Aberllienawg, in Anglesea; one also at Caernarvon, another at Bangor, and another in Merionydd, all of which he furnished with strong garrisons.

North Wales having been left many years without a sovereign in the power of the Earl of Chester, and exposed to his merciless ravages, since the death of Rhys ap Tewdwr, no chieftain had arisen in South Wales to rekindle the spirit of patriotism; and that country, wrested in great measure from the

---

[7] The following are the particulars of the amount of this dower, extracted from the Saxon Chronicle :—

For the Lady Catharine, Queen of England, mother of Henry VI., A.D. 1422, 1 Hen. VI. :—
Castle and vill. of Rothelane to the value of 42l. 12s. 2d.
Castle and town of Flynt to the value of 46l. 3s. 4d.
The vill. of Colshull to the value of 60s.
The vill. of Baghogre, with the mill, to the value of 9l. 0s. 4d.
The vill. of Wagnol (*Vaynol*) to the value of 100s.
The vill. of Kyons, with the mill there, to the value of 12l.
The vill. of Moston beyond 13l. 6s. 8d., granted to John Chittewynd, to the value of 6d.

The manor and lordship of Eglesed beyond 100s., for the fee of

the Escheator, and 45l. 0s. 2½d., paid to Nicholas Saxton to the value of 45l. 5s. 3½d.
The county of Flynt beyond 103s. 4d., for the fee of the Escheator of the said county, to the value of 7l. 7s. 2½d.
The office of Shrievalty there beyond 21l. for the fee of the said sheriff, twenty marks granted to Nicholas Holland, and 42s. 1d. for rent resolute to Nicholas Saxton, to the value of 105l. 0s. 12d., in the county of Flynt in Wales, which said mine, castles, vills, manors, lordships, commotes and offices, beyond the annuities, fees and rents aforesaid, and beyond 60l. in the fees of the constables of the said castles of Rothelane and Flynt to be received yearly, are worth clear 138l. 6s. 8d.; castle and lordship of Hawarden and Mohanddale, Flintshire, 66l. 13s. 4d.

[8] Camden's Brit., p. 665 ; Vita Griffith Fil Conain.

hands of its native princes, had been parcelled out among Norman adventurers.[*] In this state of things, when the prosperity of Wales appeared irretrievably lost, her fortunes were changed on a sudden by the enterprising spirit of a few individuals, possessed of neither power nor consequence.

Gruffydd ap Cynan had languished twelve years in captivity,[1] neglected by his subjects, or what is more probable, without their having had the ability to procure his release. The situation of this prince excited the compassion of a young man, named Kynric Hir, a native of Edeyrnion, who determined, if possible, to effect his escape out of prison, though at every hazard to himself. The enterprise was bold, generous, and full of danger. Attended by a few followers, he repaired to Chester, under the pretence of purchasing necessaries; gaining admittance into the castle while the keepers were deeply engaged in feasting, he carried on his back the captive prince, loaded with chains, with safety into his own dominions. It is with pleasure we contemplate an action like this, heroic in itself, and directed by a principle of masculine virtue.

Though Gruffydd ap Cynan had thus fortunately escaped out of the hands of his enemies, he had many difficulties still to encounter, as his own subjects were either dispirited or alienated from him, and the English were masters of his country. His danger was sometimes so great that he was obliged to lie concealed in woods and other places of security, but after he had endured a variety of evils, and taken those castles which the Normans had erected during his captivity, he recovered the entire possession of his kingdom.[2]

It was not likely that the impatient spirit of the Welsh, their sovereign having obtained his liberty, would remain quiet under the late usurpations. Gruffydd ap Cynan, fired with resentment for the miseries which he himself and his country had endured, with Cadwgan, the son of Bleddyn ap Cynvyn, invaded the territory of Cardigan, and slew great numbers of the English, who had settled in that country.[3] After this enterprise, the two princes returned into their own territories.

A.D. 1135.—STEPHEN, son of the Earl of Blois, and a grandson of the Conqueror, by Alice his daughter, by means of great promises, obtained the crown,[4] notwithstanding the States had sworn allegiance to the Empress Maud, widow of the Emperor Henry V. Stephen was the last of the Norman monarchs.

The Welsh continued in arms after the accession of Stephen, but they were occupied in domestic quarrels, and in attacking the castles, which were very numerous at that time, and which had been built in the interior of the country by Stephen's predecessors. The great barons of Herefordshire and Salop were engaged in more important projects than the prosecution of border warfare. It was here that the conspiracy was formed against the King, in favour of the claims of the Empress Matilda, which soon afterwards involved the whole kingdom in the horrors of civil war. In the third year of Stephen's reign, A.D. 1138, nearly all the castles and strong towns on the Border were fortified against him. Robert, Earl of Gloucester (the illegitimate son of Henry I.) occupied Bristol, which formed the head-quarters of the rebellion, and Gloucester; Geoffrey Talbot garrisoned his own castle of Weobly and seized upon Hereford; William Fitz Alan, the sheriff of Shropshire, established himself in the castle of Shrewsbury; Ralph Paganel, an active and influential partisan of the Empress, fortified himself in his castle of Dudley; and Gervase Paganel, probably the brother or kinsman of Ralph, seized upon that of Ludlow. William Peverel, in like manner, raised the standard of rebellion in his castles of Ellesmere, Whittington, &c. From these strongholds the revolted barons sent out their emissaries, who ravaged and plundered the surrounding country in the most ruthless manner.

Stephen was no less active than his enemies; he quickly made himself master of Hereford, and Geoffrey Talbot sought refuge in the castle of Weobly, from which also he was driven by the King. After placing

---

[*] Brady relates, out of Domesday, that William the Conqueror granted to Hugh Lupus, Earl of Chester, North Wales, in farm, at the rent of 40l. per annum, besides Rhôs and Rhynvonioc, p. 201.

[1] Camden's Brit. Gibson's ed., p. 656.   [2] Vita Griffith Fil Conain.

[3] Welsh Chronicle, p. 152; British Antiq. revised by Vaughan of Hengwrt, p. 22.

[4] The coronation of Stephen, after he had sworn allegiance to the Empress Matilda, was viewed with great anxiety in an age when it was supposed that the punishment of perjury was immediate and visible. The ceremony was performed by William, Archbishop of Canterbury; and it is said that a dreadful storm arose, which threw all the parties into such confusion, that the consecrated wafer fell on the ground, the kiss of peace after the sacrament was omitted, and even the final benediction forgotten.—*Coronation Anecdotes.*

a garrison in both these fortresses, the King quitted the Border. In these cruel wars, the towns as well as the country suffered equally from both parties. In the attack upon Hereford by the King, all the city on one side of the Wye bridge was burnt; and, as soon as he was gone, Geoffrey Talbot with his army, consisting in great part of Welshmen, came and burnt that part of the city which stood on the other side of the bridge.[5] On this occasion the assailants were beaten off with loss by Stephen's garrison; afterwards Stephen turned his attention towards Shrewsbury castle, which he besieged with the most powerful warlike engines which were then in use; the besieged were almost suffocated with clouds of thick smoke which were thrown into the place, and at length, one of the gates being driven in, the place was taken by storm. Part of the garrison escaped, many were slain, and a few of the prisoners of rank were hanged by order of the King.

The siege of Shrewsbury occurred in the year 1138. Probably the lesser fortress of Shropshire yielded without much struggle, for we hear nothing of his proceedings until he reached Ludlow Castle, which was then under the charge of Gervase Paganel, and, being a strong place, made an obstinate resistance. Two forts were erected by the assailants, and the siege was prosecuted with great vigour, yet it was not successful, and it needed all the prudence of the monarch to hinder sanguinary feuds from breaking out among the besiegers.[6] In one of the attacks, the Scottish prince, approaching rashly too near to the walls, was seized by an iron grapple thrown out from the castle, and would have been taken prisoner, but the King with his characteristic bravery rushed to the spot, and saved his hostage at the imminent peril of his own life. The King soon afterwards raised the siege, and repaired to Oxford, where his presence was necessary.

After the arrival of Matilda in England, her army was strengthened by ten thousand Welsh auxiliaries, raised by Robert, Earl of Gloucester. Her cause was sustained in Herefordshire by Geoffrey Talbot and Gilbert de Lacy, with Milo, constable of Gloucester, the son of Walter, constable of Shropshire, in the preceding reign. At the end of the autumn of 1139, they plundered and partly burnt the city of Worcester. Immediately afterwards Talbot attacked Hereford, set fire to the cathedral, slaughtered the monks, and sacked the town. The king hastened to Worcester, and then pushing forwards encamped his army at Little Hereford and Leominster. In the following year he again occupied Little Hereford,[7] not far distant from Ludlow, which we may suppose to have been still held by Gervase Paganel. Stephen's progress in this quarter was arrested by other events. In 1141, Earl Robert's Welshmen took part in the battle of Lincoln, where the King was made captive.[8] Milo de Gloucester, for his conduct in this engagment, was rewarded by Matilda with the Earldom of Hereford; and among the witnesses to the grants are the signatures of Ralph Paganel and Gilbert de Lacy.[9]

[5] In the king's attack, "Civitas Herefordensis infra pontem fluminis Wegæ comburitur igne." Contin. of Florence of Worcester, p. 520. In Talbot's attack the part "ultra pontem Wegæ" was burnt. *Ibid.*, p. 521.

[6] The account of this siege is chiefly taken from the Continuator of Florence of Worcester, pp. 527, 528. He spells the name *Ludelawe.* The orthography in other accounts of the same event is, *Ludlaue* in Henry of Huntingdon; *Ludelawe* in Roger de Hovedon; *Ludehlawe* in Mathew Paris; *Lodelowe* in Ralph de Dicet. and in Robert of Gloucester.

[7] These particulars are given by the Continuator of Florence of Worcester, pp. 531—533.

[8] Two of our most valuable Border historians end with this year, Ordericus Vitalis, a native of Shropshire, whose father was a trusty minister of Roger de Montgomery, and the anonymous monk of Worcester, who continued the Chronicle of Florence of Worcester from the year 1118.—*Wright's Ludlow.*

[9] This grant is printed in Rymer's Fœdera, last edition, p. 14, vol. i.

PLANTAGENET PERIOD.

NE of the first acts of the government[1] of HENRY II., relating to Wales, was to banish out of England the Flemish soldiers who had followed the fortunes of Stephen, and actuated by sound principles of political wisdom, he gave permission to these foreigners to settle among their countrymen, who had settled as a colony, and had acquired an accession of strength in the province of Pembroke, in South Wales.

Several causes conspired with the motives of ambition and glory in engaging the King of England to use at this time the utmost exertion in attempting the conquest of Wales. Madoc ap Meredydd, Prince of Powys, conscious of having joined the enemies of his country, and dreading that resentment which such conduct had excited in the breast of Owen Gwynedd, endeavoured, as a means of his future security, to incite the English king to the invasion of North Wales.

Cadwaladr likewise having, since the fatal issue of the combat with his nephew, been treated with severity by his brother Owen and by the sons of that prince, had fled into England, and in that court had employed, in the prosecution of the same design, his own solicitation, supported by the powerful influence of the House of Clare.[2]

The glory to be acquired, and the importance of the object, with the apparent facility of the enterprise from the defection of such powerful princes, determined Henry to exert every means which his great power afforded, for the conquest of the country.

A.D. 1157.—Henry collected from different parts of England a very formidable army, with which he marched to Chester; thence advancing into Flintshire, he encamped his forces on a marsh called Saltney, which borders on the River Dee. Such were the mighty preparations which this prince had made for the conquest of Wales, that he compelled every two of his military vassals throughout England,[3] to find one soldier to reinforce his army and enable him with greater vigour to prosecute the war. Owen, the Prince of North Wales, with his usual activity, advancing to the frontier of his dominions, took post at Basingwerk, near Holywell, in the county of Flint. An unsuccessful attempt to take the castle of Mold greatly provoked Henry, and on this occasion he resolved, by one great blow, to atone for all previous failures. He projected the entire subjugation of the country. During his encampment on Saltney Marsh, near Chester, he seemed to challenge the Welsh chieftains to the unequal contest; and the Prince

---

[1] Henry II. was crowned at Westminster on the Sunday before Christmas-day, A.D. 1154, by Theobald, Archbishop of Canterbury: although his hereditary right was unquestionable, he was formally elected by the clergy and people. It is said that Henry was crowned again with his queen, A.D. 1159; but this report arose from his having worn the crown during the ceremony.

[2] Welsh Chronicle, p. 208.

[3] Matt. Paris, p. 81. There were 60,000 knights fees created by the Conqueror, which must make the levy Henry raised at this time to amount to 30,000 men.—*Hume's Hist.*, vol. ii. p. 2 ; Appendix, p. 141.

of Gwynedd, on the other hand, was neither unprepared for this invasion nor slow to oppose it. He advanced with a powerful force from Basingwerk Castle, on the Dee, in order to give battle to the English monarch. He sent his two sons, with a strong detachment of his forces, to Euloe Castle wood, Flintshire. After they had reconnoitred for some time, some skirmishes commenced; the Welsh suffered the enemy to advance along the straits, and Henry, too confident in the strength and discipline of his troops, ordered them to move forward, till at length his forces got entangled in the wood, and other snares that were laid for them.

The Welsh in the meantime sprang upon the enemy all of a sudden, and so fierce and unexpected was the attack, that the cries of the English were horrible, and the slaughter equally dreadful; the remaining part of English were routed in all directions, and followed even to Henry's camp, which then lay on Saltney Marsh, near Chester. Alarmed at the danger, and mortified by the disgrace, the King of England broke up his camp, and marched along the sea-shore to the town of Flint, intending by this manœuvre to deceive the Welsh prince, and by leaving him on the left, to penetrate by a nearer road into the interior of the country; but in passing through a long and narrow defile at Coleshill, he was intercepted by Owen.

The design was conducted with temper and judgment; the English were permitted to enter unmolested so far into the Strait as to render their advance or retreat both difficult and dangerous. The Welsh then rushing with terrible outcries from out of the woods, assaulted them with pikes, swords, arrows, and other missile weapons. Struck with dismay, encumbered with heavy armour, and unaccustomed to fight in such situations, the English were again thrown into the utmost disorder, being unable either to retreat or to resist so unexpected an onset.[4] In the general confusion Henry himself was obliged to fly. Eustace Fitz-John, and Robert de Courcy, with other noblemen of distinction, were slain.[5]

The few of the rear-guard who had escaped the sword, fell back upon the main body of English, who were advancing in regular order to the entrance of the defile.

A rumour instantly prevailed of the death of the King, and the Earl of Essex,[6] hereditary standard-bearer of England, threw to the ground the royal standard; at the same time crying aloud, "The King is slain!"[7] The terror then became universal. The Welsh perceiving their disorder, attacked the English with such impetuosity that a general rout must have ensued, if at this moment the King, at length extricated from his perilous situation, had not made himself known to the army, by lifting up the visor of his helmet. His presence in an instant changed the scene. The English acquiring fresh ardour from the gallantry of their sovereign, who with alacrity led them on to the charge, gave a check to the Welsh forces, and drove them back into the woods.[8]

The Prince of Wales, after this slight disaster, from a hill above Bagillt, to this day called *Bryn-dy-chwelwch*, retired to a post near St. Asaph, called from this event "*Cil Owen*," or Owen's Retreat. On

[4] Welsh Chron., p. 207 ; Holinshed's Chron., p. 67 ; Girald. Camb. Itin., lib. ii. cap. x.

[5] Stowe's Chron., p. 149.

[6] Henry de Essex was disgraced for his conduct in the Battle of Coleshill. Six years afterwards, in a quarrel with Robert de Montford, the latter openly accused him of treason, in throwing down the standard, with the intention of betraying the king. Henry de Essex retorted the charge, and the cause was decided by judicial combat in an island on the Thames near the Abbey of Reading. The standard-bearer was vanquished, and left for dead, and his body was carried by the monks to the church to be buried there. But when released from the weight of his armour, he recovered, and soon afterwards became one of the shorn monks of the Abbey of Reading.—*Chronica Joscelini de Brakelonda* (Edited by John George Rokewood, Esq., for the Camden Society), pp. 50, 52. This account differs from that commonly given, but Josceline de Brakelonda

received it from Henry de Essex's own mouth, after the latter had taken the cowl at Reading. The standard-bearer assured him that he really believed that the king had been slain.

[7] Annales Waverlienses, p. 159.

[8] Notwithstanding the dreadful slaughter and drubbing Henry's army met with in this instance by the Welsh, he bore a very honourable testimony to their valour and extraordinary courage in defending their country's honour and liberty. When writing to Emanuel Comnenus, the Greek Emperor, he says, "*the Welsh are not afraid to fight unarmed with enemies armed at all points, willingly shedding their blood in the cause of their country, and purchasing glory at the expense of their lives.*"—*Lord Lyttleton's Hist. Henry II.*

The same historian, when speaking of the hospitality of the Welsh, says that "every man's house was open to all, and thus no wants were felt by the most indigent, nor was there a beggar in the nation."

the nearer approach of the King he retreated to *Bryn-y-pin*, a stronger post, situate five miles west of St. Asaph. At the same time, by orders of Henry, an English fleet, which he had assembled at Chester, infested the coast of North Wales. The King of England meeting with no resistance, advanced to

Retreat of Henry the Second from Euloe Wood.

Rhuddlan, where he erected a house for the Knights Templars, a new kind of military garrison in Wales, and established, it is probable, for a purpose similar to the original institution of that order in Palestine. He likewise more strongly fortified the castle of that town with the fortress at Basingwerk; and that he might secure the conquests he had made, by rendering more easy the marching of armies, he cut down the woods and constructed new roads through the country he had subdued.[9] Owen did not remain an indifferent spectator of transactions so inimical to the interests of his country. He descended frequently from his post on the hill to skirmish with the King's troops, and to molest them in their designs;[1] but no general action ensued; the two princes having been taught prudence by their past experience, did not choose to risk the fate of their separate armies by engaging in improper situations. At the same time the English fleet, under the conduct of Madoc ap Meredydd, the Prince of Powys, made a descent on the island of Anglesea, ravaged a great part of the country, and plundered two churches; on returning to their ships the party was attacked by the whole strength of the island, and entirely cut to pieces. Dismayed by the fate of their associates, the English fleet weighed anchor and sailed back to Chester.[2] Owen derived but little advantage from these fortunate incidents, as the English were in force, and in the meantime had strongly fortified in the parts of Flintshire. The wise measure likewise which Henry had employed in having stationed a fleet on the coast of Wales, gave the Welsh prince reason to fear that his army, cooped up in the interior parts of the country, might be in danger of perishing for want of necessary sustenance, as his

[9] Matth. Paris, p. 81.
[1] MS. of Caradoc, ut supra; Stowe's Chron.

[2] Welsh Chron.; Girald. Camb. Itin., lib. ii. cap. vii.; William Newburgh, lib. ii. cap. v.; Brompton's Chron., p. 1048.

N

kingdom had been accustomed to receive from foreign countries a great part of its provisions. These motives, cogent as they may be, will scarcely justify Owen as a magnanimous and independent sovereign, in concluding a peace with the King of England, upon terms so injurious to his country, and to his own particular honour and interests. By this treaty, both he himself and his chieftains submitted, A.D. 1157, to do homage to Henry, which ceremony was performed on Snowdon;[3] he agreed to yield up those castles and districts in North Wales, which, in the late reign, had been obtained from the English;[4] to take Cadwaladr, his brother, into favour, and to restore him his territories.[5] And what contributed still more to complete the humiliating scene, he was obliged to deliver up two of his sons as pledges of his future obedience.[6]

Thus have we seen the Welsh nation, by a solemn act of its sovereign, and by the means of an English fleet, reduced again to a dependence on the crown of England. If the long and gallant resistance these people had made for freedom against a power so very unequal, excite our admiration and wonder, we shall be no less surprised that a nation like the English, so much further advanced in political wisdom, should not have been able sooner to terminate the contest.

The year after this important event, a general peace took place between England and Wales.[7] The princes and all the chieftains of South Wales repaired to the court of England; when Henry granted them peace, on the terms of doing homage for their own territories; and on their ceding to him those districts, which in the late reign had been recovered from the English.[8]

Rhys, the son of Gruffydd ap Rhys, the immediate heir to the sovereign dignity of South Wales, was not included in the general pacification.

Animated with the same spirit which had hitherto distinguished his family, this prince was not willing tamely to yield up to ambitious foreigners, a sovereign dignity, which had descended to him through a long line of ancestors. Under the just fears that Henry would employ his force against him, he commanded his vassals to remove their goods and cattle into the forest of Towi; from whence, unsupported by any confederate, he made war against the English.[9]

Pleased with his gallant spirit, or afraid of his power, Henry sent him an invitation to his court, under an assurance of a gracious reception; but threatened at the same time, if he rejected the friendly overture, that the whole force of Wales and of England should be employed to convey him thither.[1]

The high spirit of the Welsh prince was obliged to submit to so alarming a summons, and by the advice of his friends he repaired to Henry's court, where, having done homage, and given up two of his sons as hostages for his fidelity, the district of Cantrev Mawr, the ancient demesne of his family, was promised him.[2] But, contrary to that promise, the King gave him only a few lordships, remote from each other, and intermixed with the English territories, intending, no doubt, by such a disposition of his property, to render his power less dangerous. Necessity obliged Rhys to remain quiet under such unjust and mortifying treatment.[3]

The situation of this prince, though little to be envied, excited the rapacious spirit of Walter Clifford, and of another English lord; who making an inroad into his territories, slew many of his vassals, and carried away considerable spoils. Rhys sent immediate intelligence to the King of this outrage, desiring satisfaction for the injury he had received.[4] But Henry, partial to the conduct of his English subjects, and regarding with a jealous eye the Welsh, paid no other attention to his complaints than holding out to him fallacious assurances of redress. Incensed at a conduct so faithless, Rhys threw off his allegiance, determined that his sword should do him that justice which had been denied him by the English King.[5]

[3] Probably at Conway, where the district of Snowdon began. Matth. Paris, p. 81.
[4] Annales Waverlienses, p. 159.
[5] Welsh Chron., p. 288.
[6] Lord Lyttleton's History of Henry II., vol. ii. p. 79.
[7] Welsh Chron., p. 108.
[8] Lord Lyttleton's History of Henry II., vol. ii. p. 80.

[9] Welsh Chron, p. 208.
[1] Ibid.
[2] Lord Lyttleton's History of Henry II., vol. ii. p. 81. The like security was exacted from all other Welsh chieftains and princes.
[3] Welsh Chron., p. 208.
[4] Ibid.
[5] Dr. Powel's notes on Girald. Camb. Itin., lib. i. cap. x.

He began his revolt by laying siege the castle of Llandovery,[6] in Caermarthenshire, of which he soon gained possession. At the same time Einion, nephew to the Welsh prince, alike eager to throw off the ignominious yoke, flew to arms; regarding the oath of allegiance which his uncle had taken as dissolved, as the obligation on the part of the King of doing justice and affording protection had not been observed. He invested the castle of Homfrey, which he took by storm, and put the garrison to the sword. In the fortress he found a number of horses, and instruments of war, sufficient to equip a considerable body of men. Rhys likewise, with equal rapidity and success, spread over the whole country of Cardigan, which he soon brought under his subjection, after having levelled to the ground every fortress belonging to the English.[7]

A.D. 1158.—Henry regarded this revolt of sufficient importance to demand his presence in South Wales, and entered that country by the sea coast of Glamorgan.[8] But finding all his efforts ineffectual, he was under the necessity of giving up the enterprise[9] and of leaving Rhys ap Gruffydd in possession of his conquests, without any other condition than that of giving hostages for the preservation of the peace during the King's absence in Normandy.[1] Thus did the Prince of South Wales, deserted by all his confederates, baffle the efforts of a mighty monarch.

His subsequent conduct by making a sudden inroad into Pembroke, though only contending for his hereditary rights, yet threw some stain upon his honour, as it was likely to expose the hostages in Henry's hands to the cruel treatment usual in these times.[2]

A.D. 1159.—Having laid siege to Caermarthen, the Earl of Bristol, natural son to Henry, with the Earl of Clare, and the Welsh Prince, Cadwaladr, his brother by marriage, besides two other barons, came to the relief of that place. Howel and Cynan, the sons of the Prince of North Wales, joined also in the unnatural alliance.

Unable to resist so formidable an opposition, Rhys retreated to the mountains of Cern-Rester, in which strong post he remained in security. The confederate army encamping for some time at Dynnyllie, built there a castle; after which, having no intelligence of Rhys ap Gruffydd, they broke up their camp, and returned to their respective countries.[3]

A.D. 1160.—Madoc ap Meredydd, the last Prince of Powys, dying at Winchester, his remains were

---

[6] Llanymddyvri.

[7] Welsh Chron., p. 209.

[8] The following poem, to the war song of the Men of Glamorgan, is from the pen of Sir Walter Scott. It is interesting, as exhibiting the peculiarities of his style.

THE NORMAN HORSE-SHOE.

The Welsh, inhabiting a mountainous country, and possessing only an inferior breed of horses, were generally unable to encounter the shock of the Anglo-Norman cavalry. Occasionally, however, they were successful in repelling the invaders; and the following verses celebrate a supposed defeat of Clare, Earl of Striguil and Pembroke, and of Neville, Baron of Chepstow, Lords Marchers of Monmouthshire. Rymny is a stream which divides the counties of Monmouth and Glamorgan; Caerphili, the scene of the supposed battle, is a vale upon its banks, dignified by the ruins of a very ancient castle.

"Red glows the forge in Striguil's bounds,
And hammer's din, and anvil sounds,
And armourers, with iron toil,
Barb many a steed for battle's broil.
Foul fall the hand which bends the steel
Around the courser's thund'ring heel,
That e'er shall dint a sable wound
On fair Glamorgan's velvet ground.

"From Chepstow's towers, ere dawn of morn,
Was heard, afar, the bugle horn,

And forth in banded pomp and pride,
Stout Clare and fiery Neville ride.
They vow'd their banners broad should gleam
In crimson light on Rymny's stream;
They swore Caerphili's sod should feel
The Norman charger's spurning heel.

"And sooth they swore; the sun arose,
And Rymny's wave with crimson glows,
For Clare's red banner, broad and wide,
Roll'd down the stream to Severn's tide.
And sooth they vow'd; the trampled green
Show'd where hot Neville's charge had been;
In every sable hoof-tramp stood
A Norman horseman's curdling blood.

"Old Chepstow's brides may curse the toil
That arm'd stout Clare for Cambrian broil;
Their orphans long the art may rue,
For Neville's war-horse forg'd the shoe.
No more the stamp of armed steed
Shall dint Glamorgan's velvet mead,
Nor trace be there in early spring,
Save of the fairies' emerald ring."

[9] Girald. Camb. Itin., lib. ii. cap. x.

[1] Welsh Chron., p. 209.

[2] Brompton's Chron., p. 1059.

[3] Welsh Chron., p. 210.

N 2

removed from thence and interred at Meivod in Montgomeryshire, the usual burying-place of his family. After his death, that Principality, one half of which, called Powy's Vadoc, he had held entire,[4] underwent several divisions, according to the principles of the Welsh law of descent, and was never again united under one sovereign.[5] This prince left three sons, Gruffydd Maelor, Owen, and Elis; besides a daughter by Susannah his wife, who was the daughter of Gruffydd ap Cynan; he had also Owen Brogyntyn, and two other sons who were illegitimate; all of whom shared, agreeably to the custom of Wales, the paternal inheritance. Likewise Owen, his nephew, the son of Gruffydd ap Meredydd, stiled Owen Cyveilioc, had a district called by that name, which contained near half of Powys.[6] The sovereignty of England was acknowledged by all these chieftains.

A.D. 1163.—Henry having returned from Normandy, and having reduced the other Welsh princes to his obedience, turned all his attention to the affairs of South Wales; and to the hostilities lately committed against him by Rhys ap Gruffydd.

That prince, still remaining unsubdued, had, during the absence of the English monarch, continually infested the adjacent country from his strong posts on the mountains of Brecknock, encouraged by some prophecies then current in Wales, that the King would never return to England.[7] Incensed at the frequent violations of the peace, Henry invaded South Wales,[8] and advancing as far as Pencader, received the

---

[4] Welsh Chron., pp. 210, 211.

[5] *Ibid.*

[6] The boundaries of ancient Powys appear to have been at one time very extensive, if we may judge from the following Englyn :—

TERVYNAU ARGLWYDDIAETH POWYS.

" O Gevn yr Ais, dur-ais a drig, O Gaer
    I Eisteddva Gurig,
O Garn Gynnull ar Gonwy
    Hyd y Rhyd Helig ar Wy."

Literally rendered into English—

From Cevn yr Ais, and from Chester to Eisteddva Gurig,
And from Garn Gynnull on the River Conway, to Rhyd Helig on the River Wye.

[7] Lord Lyttleton's Hist. Henry II., vol. ii. p. 152.

[8] Giraldus Cambrensis says, that Henry II. when planning an expedition against South Wales, at a place called Pencadair, in that country, consulted an antient Welshman as to the strength and number of forces in that part of the Principality, and the probability of his success against them; the old man thus pithily replied :—This nation, oh King ! may suffer much, and be in great measure ruined, or at least weakened by your present or future attempts, as formerly it has often been; but we assure ourselves it will never wholly be destroyed by the anger or power of any mortal man, unless the wrath of heaven concur in that destruction; nor (whatever changes happen as to any other part of the world) can I believe that any other *language beside the Welsh* shall answer at the last day for the greater part of this corner of the globe !" To the same effect prophesied Taliesin :—

" Eu Nêr a volant
    Eu hiaith a gadwant,
Eu tir a gollant,
    Ond gwyllt Wallia."

Which may be translated thus :—

" Still shall they chaunt their great Creator's praise,
And still preserve their language and their lays;
But nought preserve of all their wide domains,
Save Wallia's wild uncultivated plains."

To this patriotic partiality for their language and *natale solum,* we may venture to attribute all that nationality of character, which, sur-

viving the ravages of time, still continues undiminished in the Cambro-British breast. The sequestered peasant who rarely quits the vicinity of his mountain, who speaks no other language than his mother tongue, still adheres with infinite attachment to all the habitudes and customs of his ancestors; on all occasions he adopts their sentiments, and dwells with fond delight upon the traditions of old times. Arthur, Llywelyn, and Glyndyfrdwy's lord will ever be the themes of Cambro-British admiration, whilst Offa, Edward and Henry will never cease to create disgust. Uneducated in the refinements of that new philosophy which ostentatiously affects an universal citizenship, the Welshman thinks no country equal to his own, and even in the midst of poverty is happy to acknowledge as his proudest boast that he was born an *Antient Briton :—*

" Whilst every good his native wilds impart
    Imprints the patriot passion in his heart,
And e'en the hills which round his mansion rise,
    Enhance the bliss his scanty fund supplies.
Dear is that shed to which his soul conforms,
    And dear that hill which lifts him to the storms.
And as a babe, when scaring sounds molest,
    Clings close and closer to his mother's breast;
So the loud torrent and the whirlwind's roar,
    But bind him to his native mountains more."

Giraldus relates another occurrence which took place about sixteen years before his Itinerary, in the following words, which are translated from the Latin by Lord Lyttleton :—" 'We traversed the sands of Niwegal, where (at the time that Henry II. was compelled on account of the storms to winter in Ireland), and in many other parts of the western shore, occurred an extraordinary phenomenon; for a very violent tempest drove the sands from the beach, and exposed land to view, which had been covered for many ages. Here were now seen trunks of trees standing in the sea, with the marks of the axe as visible on them as if they had been lately felled; the earth was extremely black, and the wood of the trunks resembled ebony both in colour and hardness.'

" I have been more particular," (says his lordship), " in citing this extract, because I have heard from good authority that the same circumstance, though in a less degree, has been sometimes observed in modern times. The whole country is now so barren of wood, that scarcely a tree is to be seen within some miles of Niwegal."

submission of Rhys, who, despairing of being able any longer to resist his power, a second time did him homage, and delivered up hostages likewise for his future fidelity.[9] This ceremony was also performed the year following, A.D. 1164, at Woodstock, where Rhys ap Gruffydd, attended by the other princes and chieftains of Wales, did homage to the King of England, and to Henry, his son.[1]

The submissive demeanour of Rhys ap Gruffydd was of no long continuance. His impatient spirit was again set on fire by an outrage, marking equally the ferocity of the times, and the weak or partial government of the English king. Cynon, the nephew of the Welsh prince, and a gallant youth, had been lately murdered in his bed, by his own servant, at the instigation of the Earl of Gloucester.[2] Finding no protection in the English, or safety in submission, Rhys at once determined to trust his fortune to the decision of arms. In his first enterprise he obtained possession of the territory of Dinevawr, and a large district of Cantrev Mawr. Having recovered the ancient demesnes of his family, he then invaded the territory of the Earl of Gloucester, destroying on his progress the castle of Aberrheidiol,[3] and other fortresses belonging to the enemy; and at length he reduced likewise the entire province of Cardigan. Eager to recover his hereditary honours, and receiving, no doubt, an additional incentive from the place where he then resided, which had been the royal seat of his ancestors, Rhys carried his arms into Pembroke, and making many inroads on the estates of the Flemings, and ravaging their country, he returned to the castle of Dinevawr, enriched with spoils, and high in the esteem of his country.[4]

Fired by his gallant example, a spirit of revolt sprung up in Wales. With great judgment this prince, during the winter, either by deputies or in person, had conferences with the different Welsh princes. He awakened their sleeping virtue and roused it into action by such incentives as were likely to touch a warm, free, and spirited people. He pointed out the prospects of asserting their freedom, which had of late opened on their country, from the dissensions which had arisen in England between Henry and the Archbishop of Canterbury, and from the probability likewise that this prince would soon be engaged in a war with France; that country, as well as the Pope, having espoused the cause of Thomas à Beckett.[5]

Animated by his generous spirit, by the prosperity which had attended his arms, and by such a favourable conjunction, the Prince of North Wales and all his sons, his brother Cadwaladr, and the chieftains of Powys, joined Rhys ap Gruffydd, in hopes of gaining the independence they had lost, and of recovering that honour, which of late they had forfeited. At no period had the Welsh nation united into a confederacy like this, concentrating with so much energy and force, the various policies and interests, the different tempers and abilities, of the princes of Wales.[6] The first enterprise, under the conduct of David, the son of Owen Gwynedd, was an inroad into Flintshire, where he committed most grievous devastations, carrying away the cattle and inhabitants to the Vale of Clwyd.[7]

A.D. 1164.—During the absence of the King in Normandy, some forces had been levied by parliament for the reduction of Rhys ap Gruffydd.[8] Henry on his arrival marched with these troops into Flintshire, for the protection of Rhuddlan Castle, which fortress he was afraid the Welsh would besiege. The enemy having retired, and the King not being sufficiently in force to pursue them, stayed only a few days to augment his garrisons, and marched back into England, in order, by raising new levies, to prosecute the war with greater vigour.[9] His British dominions, and the different territories he possessed in France, furnished him with their choicest troops; from Normandy, Anjou, and Gascony, from Guienne, Flanders, and Brittany; and with this combined and formidable force, he marched into Powys, with the full resolution of exterminating the inhabitants.

[9] Welsh Chron., p. 220.
[1] V. Diceto Ymag. Hist., sub ann. 1136 ; Matth. Paris, p. 84.
[2] Wynne's Wales, p. 189 ; Chron. of Wales, p. 220.
[3] On the confluence of the rivers Rheidiol and Ystwyth.
[4] Welsh Chron., p. 220.
[5] Lord Lyttleton's History of Henry II., vol. ii. p. 439.

[6] Welsh Chron., p. 220 ; British Antiq. revised by Vaughan of Hengwrt, p. 23.
[7] Welsh Chron., p. 221.
[8] Lord Lyttleton's History of Henry II., vol. ii. p. 440.
[9] Welsh Chron., p. 221 ; Brompton's Chron., sub ann. 1165 ; Chronica Gerv., p. 1398 ; Girald. Camb. Itin., lib. ii. cap. x.

The English army entered the Welsh confines at Oswestry, where Henry encamped for some time,[1] in expectation that the terror of his arms might, by shaking the firmness of the confederate princes, call them back to their allegiance, or at least that the protection which such a power would naturally afford might detach from the common cause the chieftains of the house of Powys, the usual adherents of his family. It might have been expected that a confederacy like this, heterogeneous in itself, and forming its union from a sudden impulse rather than from steady principles of either policy or patriotism, would have shrunk from so formidable an armament; but, determined to rescue their country from a foreign domination or to perish in the attempt, the Welsh princes remained firm and intrepid.

A.D. 1165.—Henry II. at the head of a well appointed and numerous army (for on this occasion he availed himself of all his resources, not only in England, but also in France and Flanders), and eager for conquest, and thirsting for revenge, marched for the third time against North Wales, and having reached Oswestry, on the confines of Wales, there pitched his camp in the vicinity of the Welsh prince. Owen, upon being apprised of the approach of the English monarch, repaired with his brother Cadwaladr, and the whole strength of his country to Corwen, in Merionethshire, where he was joined by Rhys ap Gruffydd, and Owen Cyveiliog, princes of South Wales and Powys, as well as by several other subordinate chiefs, with all the forces they could muster within their respective districts.[2] Thus it may be presumed that the Welsh were in possession of an army, formidable at least by its numbers, if not equal in discipline and appointments, to that of the enemy; and whatever they may have wanted in these respects seems to

---

[1] Welsh Chron., p. 221; Brompton's Chron. sub ann. 1165; Chron. Gerv., p. 1398; Girald. Camb. Itin., lib. ii. cap. x.

[2] The following panegyric upon Owain Gwynedd, Prince of North Wales, by Gwalchmai, the son of Melir, in the year 1157, is translated from the original Welsh by the late Rev. Evan Evans (Ieuan Brydydd Hir), author of the early specimens of ancient British poetry:—

"I will extol the generous hero descended from the race of Roderic,* the bulwark of his country, a prince eminent for his good qualities, and the glory of Britain, Owain the brave and expert in arms, a prince that neither hoardeth nor coveteth riches. Three fleets arrived, vessels of the main, three powerful fleets of the first class, furiously to attack him on a sudden. One from Iwerddon,† the other full of well-armed Llochlynians,‡ making a grand appearance on the floods; the third from the transmarine Normans, which was attended with an immense though unsuccessful toil."

The following poetic address, supposed to be delivered by Prince Owain Gwynedd to his army, at the gallant stand he made at Corwen against the forces of Henry the Second, appeared in the pages of the Cambrian Quarterly. The words are composed to that fine martial air, "The March of the Men of Harlech," the melodious sound and bold grandeur of which fires the soul of every Cambrian when played by a skilful hand on the trembling strings of his native harp:—

"Cymmry! here we take our station,
Daring Henry's fierce invasion;

---

* Owain Gwynedd, Prince of North Wales, was descended in a direct line from Roderic the Great, Prince of all Wales, who divided the Principality amongst his three sons.

† Iwerddon, the British name of Ireland; hence the Hibernia of the Latins, and Ιερη and 'Ιουερνια of the Greeks, probably so called from the British "Y Werdd Ynys," i.e., the Green Island.

‡ Llochlynians, the Danes; so called from the Baltic, which our ancestors called Llychlyn. Llychlyn is the name of Denmark and Norway, and all those Northern regions mentioned in the works of our Bards.

Be the war-cry of the nation,
    Death or liberty.
Draw your swords with fire,
Bend your bows in ire;
    Advance your spears,
    With freedom's cheers,
And make our foes retire.
Burst upon their ranks like thunder,
Strike their dastard souls with wonder,
Drive them back and far asunder;
    Teach them we are free.

"Coward fears cannot affright us,
Jealousy no more shall blight us,
Knaves no more to feuds excite us
    In fierce campaigns.
Our sons in torture lying,
Our wives in anguish crying;
    Our mothers' cares,
    And daughters' prayers,
To us for succour crying.
Shall we tamely see their anguish,
As in tyrants' chains they languish,
No! we will invaders vanquish,
    And break their chains.

"Warriors! see the war descending;
Gleaming spears and swords are blending;
Stand we firm with souls unbending,
    For we will be free.
The storms of battle lour,
And we within this hour,
    Must stand or fall,
    Like warriors all,
Against this mighty power.
Where you see my standard streaming,
Where you hear the foe wild screaming,
There am I midst swords thick gleaming;
    Cymmry! follow me."

have been in a great measure supplied by the prudence of their commanders, who encamping on the mountainous lands in the vicinity of Corwen, resolved to wait the assault of the English, rather than risk a battle in a less advantageous situation.

Henry, on the other hand, as soon as he was aware of the formation of this patriotic league within so short a distance from his army, determined upon an immediate attack. With this view he broke up his camp, having first given directions that the woods should be cleared along his projected route, in order to avoid an ambuscade, which his former contests with Owen had given him so much reason to apprehend.

Skirmish in the Vicinity of Chirk Castle.

This precaution, however, could not secure him from a surprise. His advanced guard was suddenly attacked on its way through a defile by a small body of the Welsh, though not with any final advantage; for after much bloodshed on both sides, the pass was forced by the English, who proceeded without further opposition, towards the spot where the Welsh army was stationed.

The English, by this time, had become acquainted with the particular mode of warfare adopted by their opponents, and, accordingly, avoiding the glens and defiles, confined themselves to the open grounds. While in this situation, and the two armies in sight of each other, Henry, it is probable, unable to dislodge the Welsh from their strong position, strove to tempt them to a general engagement; but the latter, acting with their accustomed caution, and profiting by their more intimate knowledge of the country, contented themselves by harassing the outposts of the enemy, and by intercepting their supplies, which they did so effectually that the English were reduced to the most wretched extremities: and the weather being, at the same time, particularly unfavourable, Henry was driven to the humiliating necessity of abandoning an enterprise on which he had entered with so determined a spirit, and with such flattering hopes. Thus foiled in his most vigorous attack on the independence of Wales, he returned home in a state of the deepest mortification; and, in a barbarous ebullition of revenge, caused his Welsh hostages, among whom were two sons of Prince Owen, to be immediately deprived of their eyes. And this wanton and indefensible act of cruelty was the only consolation he could administer to his disappointed ambition!

This expedition, however, was not the last of Henry's attempts against North Wales. For soon after its failure, he again set out for the purpose of invading the country; but after having conveyed his troops by sea as far as Chester, he suddenly relinquished his design and disbanded his army. This formidable enemy of Wales died in 1189; and Richard, surnamed Cœur de Lion, succeeded.

"The Dragon of Mona's sons' were so brave in action, that there was a great tumult on their furious attack; and before the Prince himself, there was vast confusion, havock, conflict, honourable death, bloody battle, horrible consternation, and upon Tal Moelore a thousand banners. There was an outrageous carnage, and the rage of spears, and hasty signs of violent indignation. Blood raised the tide of the Menai, and the crimson of human gore raised the brine. There were glittering cuirassiers, and the agony of gashing wounds, and the warriors prostrate before the chief, distinguished by his crimson lance. Lloegria was put in confusion; the contest and confusion was great; and the glory of our Prince's wide-wasting sword shall be celebrated in a hundred languages, to give him his merited praise."[4]

Weak as the Welsh were at the close of the twelfth century, they still hoped not only to recover the conquered portion of their own immediate country, but a return of the time when they possessed the island of Britain. Their immovable confidence in this chimerical hope made such an impression upon those who observed it, that in England, and even in France, the Welsh were considered to possess the gift of prophecy.[3] The verses in which the ancient Cambrian poets had expressed, with effusion of soul, their patriotic wishes and expectations were looked upon as mystic predictions, the exposition of which it was sought to discover in the great events of the day.[4] Hence the singular celebrity which Myrdhin, a bard of the seventh century, enjoyed five hundred years after his death, under the name of Merlin the Enchanter. Hence also the extraordinary renown of King Arthur, the hero of a petty nation, whose existence was scarcely known upon the Continent; but the books of this petty nation were so full of poetry, they had so powerful an impress of enthusiasm and conviction, that once translated into other languages, they became most attractive reading for foreigners, and the theme upon which the romance writers of the middle ages most frequently constructed their fictions. It was thus that the old war-chief of the Cambrians appeared in the fabulous histories of the Norman and French trouvères, the ideal of a perfect knight and the greatest king that ever wore a crown.

Not content to adorn this personage with every knightly perfection, many foreigners believed in his return well nigh as firmly as did the Welsh themselves. This opinion gained ground even among the conquerors of Wales, whom it terrified, despite all their efforts to conquer the impression; various reports, each more fantastic than the rest, nourished this belief. Now it was said that pilgrims, returning from the Holy Land, had met Arthur in Sicily, at the foot of Mount Etna; now that he had appeared in a wood in Lower Brittany, or that the foresters of the King of England, in making their rounds by moonlight often heard a great noise of horses, and met troops of hunters, who said they formed part of the train of King Arthur. Lastly, the tomb of King Arthur was no where to be found; it had often been sought but never discovered, and this circumstance seemed a confirmation of all the reports in circulation.

The contemporary historians of the reign of King Henry II. admit that all these things formed for the Welsh a groundwork for national enthusiasm, and great encouragement in their resistance to foreign rule. The stronger minded among the Anglo-Normans ridiculed what they called the Breton Hope; but this hope so vivid, so real, that it communicated itself by contagion even to the enemies of the Cambrians, gave umbrage to the statesmen of the Court of England. To give it a mortal blow, they resolved to discover the tomb of Arthur, and this they did in the following manner :—About the year 1189, a nephew of the King, named Henry de Sully, ruled the Abbey of Glastonbury, raised on the site of the

---

[3] Owain Gwynedd had many sons noted for their valour, especially Howel, who was born of Finnog, an Irish lady. He was one of his father's generals in the wars against the English, Flemings, and Normans, in South Wales; and was a noted Bard, as several of his poems now extant, testify.

[4] It seems that the fleet landed in some part of the Frith of Menai, and that it was a kind of mixed engagement, some fighting on shore, others from the ships; and probably the great slaughter was owing to its being low water, and that they could not set sail, otherwise I see no reason why, when they were worsted on land, they should continue to fight in their own ships. It is very plain that they were in great distress, and that there was a great havoc made of them, as appears from the remainder of this very spirited poem.

[5] Radulf. de Diceto, ut sup. p. 534.

[6] Script. Rer. Gallic. et Franc., xii. et seq.; passim.

building, whither popular tradition related that the great Cambrian Chief had retired, to await the cure of his wounds. This Abbot all at once announced, that a bard of Pembrokeshire had had a revelation as to the sepulchre of King Arthur; and hereupon extensive excavations were commenced within the walls of the monastery, care being taken the while to keep apart all persons who were likely to raise doubts on the subject. The desired discovery was of course made, and there was found, say the contemporaries, a Latin inscription engraved on a metal plate (see page 38), and bones of an extraordinary size. These precious remains were raised with great marks of respect, and Henry II. had them placed in a magnificent coffin, of which he did not grudge the expense, thinking himself amply repaid by the injury done to the Welsh, in depriving them of their long cherished hope, of the superstition which animated their courage, and shook that of their conquerors.

The patriotic determination of the Cambrians, however, survived the hope of King Arthur's return, and they were still far from resigning themselves to a foreign rule. This disposition of mind gave them confidence in themselves, so undoubting that it seemed to partake of insanity. In an expedition which King Henry II. made in person to the south of Wales, a Cambrian chief, under the influence of one of those family feuds which were the capital vice of the nation, came to his camp and joined him. The King received him as a valuable auxiliary, and questioned him as to the probable chances of the war: "Dost thou think," he said, "that the rebels can withstand my army?" At this question patriotic pride awakened in the heart of the Welshman. Looking at the King with an air at once calm and assured, he answered: "King, your power may to a certain extent, weaken and injure this nation, but utterly to destroy it requires the anger of God. In the day of Judgment, no other race, no other tongue, than that of the Cymry, will answer for that corner of the earth to that Sovereign Judge."

The historians do not say in what terms Henry II. replied to these words, so impressed with imperturbable conviction; but the idea of the prophetic skill of the Welsh was not without power over him, at least, so his flatterers thought, for his name is found by interpolation, in many old poems attributed to the Bard of Myrdhin.

One day, as the same king, returning from Ireland, passed through Pembrokeshire, a countryman accosted him, to communicate an entirely religious prediction, remarkable only for the circumstances which accompanied it. The Welshman thinking that a King of England must needs understand English, addressed Henry II. with language, thus; "*God holde ye, King.*" This salutation was followed by an harangue of which the King understood but a few words; wishing to answer and unable to do so, he said, in French, to his Squire, "Ask this peasant if he is telling us his dreams." The Squire, whose less elevated position enabled him to converse with Saxons, served as an interpreter between his master and the Cambrian. Thus, to the fifth King of England, the English language was almost a foreign tongue.

A.D. 1189.—RICHARD THE FIRST having made all necessary preparations for his coronation,' came to London, where he assembled the Archbishops of Canterbury, Rouen, and Tours, who had given him absolution in Normandy for waging war against his father, after he had taken the cross as a crusader. First, the archbishops, bishops, abbots, and clergy, wearing their square caps, and preceded by the cross and holy-water bearers and deacons burning incense, went to the door of the royal bed-chamber, and led the Duke in solemn procession to the great altar in the church of Westminster. When they reached the altar, Richard swore, in the presence of the clergy and people, on the Holy Gospel and the sacred relics, that he

---

' The festivities at this coronation were sullied by a sanguinary and disgraceful riot. Numbers of Jews had flocked to England in the reign of Henry II., where they were honourably protected by that liberal and enlightened sovereign. Grateful for such unusual favours, they assembled at London to subscribe among themselves, in order to make Richard a splendid present on the day of his coronation. Unfortunately Richard was persuaded by some of the bigots who surrounded him that the Jews were accustomed to practise magic on sovereigns during the time of the coronation, and he therefore issued an edict, prohibiting any Jew from entering the church while the ceremony was performed, or appearing at the palace during dinner. Curiosity overcame prudence; several of the most formidable Jews mingled with the crowd, and gathered round the gates of the palace. One of them, endeavouring to force an entrance, was struck in the face by an over-zealous Christian; this signal roused the fanaticism of the multitude; a general assault was

would observe peace, honour, and respect, all the days of his life, to God, holy Church, and its ordinances. His attendants then stripped him to his trousers and shirt, the latter of which was left open between the shoulders on account of the anointing. Baldwin, Archbishop of Canterbury, who wore rich buskins of cloth of gold, then anointed the King in three places; on the head, between the shoulders, and on the right arm. A consecrated linen coif and a cap of estate were then placed upon his head, and he was vested with the royal robes, the dalmatic, and the tunic; the Archbishop then delivered him a sword, to restrain the enemies of the Church. Two earls then buckled on his spurs, and invested him with the pall of state. After which, Baldwin conjured him, in the name of God, and forbade him to take the crown, unless he were firmly resolved in his heart and soul to observe all the promises to which he had sworn.

We do not find that this monarch was ever on the Borders of Wales; but our old chronicles state that Prince Rhys ap Gruffyth, in the first year of this King's reign, took a journey into England, and that he travelled as far as Oxford, conducted by the Earl of Morton; where, on the refusal of Richard to meet him in person, as his father, King Henry, had done before, he flew into a violent passion, and returned into his own country; afterwards led an army into the Marches, and took several castles. Richard was much annoyed at this, and ordered the Archbishop of Canterbury, whom he had appointed his lieutenant in England, to march with a powerful army into Wales. The Archbishop besieged the castle of Gwenwynwyn,[7] near Welshpool; but the garrison made such a vigorous defence, that he lost a great many of his men, and all his attempts proved ineffectual.

A.D. 1199.—KING JOHN succeeded his brother Richard. This monarch ascended the throne to the prejudice of the hereditary right of his nephew Arthur, by virtue of a form of election by the archbishops, bishops, earls, barons, and other the estate of the realm, assembled in the church of Westminster, May 27th. "The reign of King John," says Mr. Turner, the author of the Anglo-Saxons, "was a series of disgraces, originating from the vice and imbecility of the sovereign. The defects of his character appeared so early in his father's lifetime, that his clerical tutor, Giraldus Cambrensis, then describes him as a prey to the follies of youth; impressible as wax to vice; rude to his better advisers; remarkable rather for juvenile levity, than for the promise of that manly maturity towards which he was hastening."

On the accession of this weak and worthless king, the country was filled with gloomy apprehensions; he neither loved nor was he loved by his people, who had already anticipated the evil days which were fast approaching. Even the doctors of the Church were carried along by the general feeling, and went about preaching that the thousand years mentioned in the Revelations were now completed, and the old Dragon was about to be let loose upon the earth.[8] Nothing shows us more distinctly the unsettled state of the kingdom in the time of King John than his constant movement from one part of the island to the other; for during the whole eighteen years of his reign he scarcely ever remained more than a few days in the same place. During this period the Welsh were in a continual state of hostility, either among themselves or with their neighbours; and, fearing their inroads, the King frequently approached the Border.

The Princes of North Wales had long been very uneasy neighbours to the Kings of England: always ready to afford refuge to their rebellious subjects and to co-operate with their enemies. The prince now on the throne of North Wales was Llywelyn the Great, an enterprising and spirited youth, who had, in 1195, asserted his just claim to the sovereignty that had been wrested from him by his uncle David.

made upon the Jews, who fled in confusion towards the city. Some wretches, eager for plunder, raised a cry that the king had given orders for the extermination of the unbelieving Jews; and, as this was by no means improbable, when the king was a crusader, it received implicit credit. The city mob, swelled by the multitudes who had come from the country, attacked the houses of the Jews, which the inhabitants defended with great courage and obstinacy. The enraged populace, when night came on, finding that they could not break into the houses, hurled brands and torches on the roofs and through the windows. Conflagrations burst forth in various parts of the city, which consumed not only the houses of the Jews, but those of the Christians adjoining. Richard caused several of the ringleaders and most notorious malefactors to be apprehended the next day; they were hanged as a terror to others, a proclamation was issued taking the Jews under the royal protection, and the tranquillity of the city was restored.—*Coronation Anecdotes.*

[7] Powys Castle, now the residence of the Right Hon. the Earl of Powis.

[8] Roger Hoveden, Annal. An. 1201, p. 18.

King John judged it expedient to win Llywelyn over to his party if possible: accordingly he went to Hereford on the 11th July, A.D. 1201, and entered into a treaty of peace, the terms of which may be seen in Rymer. Among other articles it was agreed that if any further dispute arose between the contracting powers, Llywelyn was to make his election whether it should be decided by the Welsh or by the English law; if he chose the latter, the King "shall put his case in England" *in loco competenti*, i. e., in a convenient situation for the Prince.

These terms were sufficiently favourable to the Welshman; still further, however, to conciliate him, the King, in the following year, 1202, gave him in marriage his natural daughter Johanna;[*] and in March 1204-5, settled upon him the lordship of Ellesmere.[1] Nay, so far did he carry his compliances, that when Llewelyn revived the obsolete claims of his ancestors to a supremacy over all the Welsh princes; and Gwenwynwyn, Prince of Powis, indignantly rejected this pretension; the King, in 1207, insidiously invited the son of Cyveilioc to Shrewsbury, to treat with his council, and there threw him into prison. Nor was the captive prince released till he had consented to certain articles of accommodation. These are dated on the Eve of St. Denis, in the 10th year of John's reign, 1208, the King being then in person at Shrewsbury.[*] The Prince, who is there called Gwenwynwyn ap Hugh de Keveilioc, covenants to send twenty hostages: if he does not procure twelve of them to come in the course of a week, he is to remain with the King as a forfeited captive, "*tanquam forisfactus suus*," and he shall abide for the eight others: but after all the twenty are arrived, then the Prince shall be delivered up.

If we might believe an old Chronicle of the Fitz Warines,[*] the Prince of Powis soon after took ample revenge on the perfidious monarch, uniting his forces with the lord of Whittington, (Fulke Fitz Warine,) defeating the King with great loss, and obliging him to retire with disgrace to Shrewsbury. It is more certain, because we know it from Rymer, that the territories of this unfortunate Prince had suffered greatly during his captivity: for on the 16th of December in the same year, 1208, the King, being then at Bristol, remits to Llywelyn, his anger for all the injuries committed on the lands and goods of Gwenwynwyn, " while he was in our custody," and promises hereafter to treat him as a beloved son.

Llywelyn was not of a temper to be softened by these advances of the King: his darling object was the independence of his Principality, and in the pursuit of this he disregarded the ties of affinity and the obligations of gratitude.

On his return from Normandy in 1207, the King again visited the Borders of Wales. On the 22nd of August he was at Worcester and Tewkesbury. On the 17th of September he had approached as far as Bristol. Two months afterwards John was again in progress towards Wales; on the 12th and 13th November he was at Tewkesbury and Gloucester, where we find him signing documents; from the 15th to the 17th he was at St. Briavel's, and from the 18th to the 22nd we find him at Hereford. In 1208 we find the King travelling backwards and forwards to and fro the different towns on the Borders. He was at Hereford on the 22nd and 23rd of April, and again at Hereford from the 1st to the 3rd of July. We find him at Shrewsbury on the 8th and 9th of October, and on the 20th at Oxford, on his way to Westminster.

The King's progresses were not less frequent in the year 1209. On the 20th of January he was at Gloucester; at Tewkesbury on the 21st and 22nd; at Worcester on the 23rd; at Shrewsbury from the 26th to the 29th. He was backwards and forwards very often to the end of the year.

---

[*] By Agatha, daughter of Robert, Earl Ferrars: for John did not scruple to pollute the noblest families of his realm by his licentious amours. It is observable, that the Princess of Wales, in her charter to Ellesmere, calls King Henry, her brother-in-law, " frater in lege :" from which she probably intended it to be supposed, that the nuptial ceremony had passed between her father and mother.

[1] Among the Ottley papers is a note of this grant : " Johannes, &c. concedit Lewelino principi Norwalie in maritagium cum Johanna filia nostra castrum de Ellesmara, &c. anno. 6." From the terms of this extract, it should seem that Ellesmere was part of the marriage portion. The grant appears to have been made at Worcester on the 23rd of March. " Rex vicecomiti Salop, salutem. Scias quod dedimus dilecto filio nostro Leuilino manerium de Ellesmere cum omnibus pertinentiis suis in maritagium filie nostre. Teste meipso apud Wygorn, 23 Marcii." Rot. Clau. 6 Joh. m. 7. (in Dodsw. MSS. vol. 103.)

[*] Rymer's Fœdera, vol. i. p. 150.

[*] Inter MSS. Dugdale, vol. xxxix. in Museo Ashmol. Oxon. This document is of respectable antiquity, having been written when Ludlow belonged to the family of Lacy, and, consequently, not later than 1240; but no dependence whatever can be placed upon it.

These frequent visits are evidence of the unquiet state of the Welsh Border; they were probably caused as much by the turbulence of the English lords of the Marches as by the hostilities of the Welsh. On one of these occasions Gwenwynwyn, Prince of Powys, is said to have come to confer with the King's council at Shrewsbury, and was there detained a prisoner, whilst Llywelyn, Prince of North Wales, invaded his territory. In the latter part of 1209 King John was probably drawn to the Border by the rebellious conduct of the families of Breose and Lacy, who fled to their possessions in Ireland. From the 14th to the 17th of May, 1210, the King was at Bristol with an army drawn together for the purpose of pursuing his fugitive barons; he was at Swansea on the 28th and 29th, and at Haverfordwest on the 31st, from whence he passed over to Ireland in the beginning of June, and was engaged in hostilities there during that month and July.

A.D. 1210.—This year, says the Welsh Chronicle, King John levied a powerful army, with which he embarked for Ireland. Whilst he was on the borders of Wales, on that journey, a man was brought before him who was charged with the murder of a priest. The officer desired to know the king's pleasure as to the manner in which he would have the criminal punished; but, the King, instead of ordering any punishment to be inflicted upon him suitable to the heinous offence, discharged him with a *" Well done thou good and faithful servant, thou hast slain mine enemy;"* for such he esteemed the clergy of those days! It should be understood, however, that the Pope at this time had excommunicated King John and the realm of England.

On the 27th of August the King was at Haverfordwest, on his road to Bristol.

About this time, says Matthew Paris, died Fitz Petre, lord chief justice of England, who was much dreaded by John, though he dared not remove him from his high office. When John heard of his death he exultingly cried, " And is he dead then? Well, let him go to hell and join Archbishop Hubert; by God's foot, I am now, for the first time, King of England."

The courage of the Welsh appears to have been raised by the absence of the King, and they commenced hostilities against the famous Ranulph, Earl of Chester. It was probably on this occasion that the Earl being attacked suddenly was obliged to take shelter in the Castle of Rhuddlan, in Flintshire, where he was besieged by a numerous army of Welshmen.[4]

The hostilities of the Welsh continued during this year and the year following. In the month of March, 1211, King John marched to the Borders of Wales; we trace him by the signatures on the records, at Bristol, on the 4th of March; at Gloucester on the 6th and 7th; at Hereford on the 9th; at Kilpeck

---

[4] Tradition has connected with this event the origin of a singular office or dignity which long existed in the Principality of Chester, of which the title may be translated into English by *Master of the Rogues and Strumpets*, and which seems to have had some affinity with the office of the *Rex Ribaldorum* in France. According to the story, when the Earl of Chester found himself in danger of being taken by the Welsh, he sent for aid to his constable of Cheshire, Roger de Lacy, Baron of Halton, who by his fiery courage (and perhaps for other causes) had obtained the surname of Hell. It happened to be the time of one of the great fairs held at Chester (in Midsummer), where was assembled a vast concourse of people of the class above mentioned, who came to join in and profit by the festivities of the occasion, and among them no small number of wandering minstrels, who were considered as belonging to the same class. Roger de Lacy collected these people, and hastened with them to Rhuddlan; and the Welsh, astonished at the numerous army (as they supposed it to be) which was approaching, raised the the siege. The Earl, we are told, in gratitude for his constable's timely arrival and as a memorial of the event, made Roger de Lacy ' Master of the Rogues and Strumpets of Cheshire,' an office which he or his successor transferred to their steward, Hugh de Dutton, and his heirs.* This singular office was continued up to a late period. In the 14th Henry VII. (A.D. 1498), Lawrence Dutton, Lord of

Dutton, in answer to a quo-warranto on behalf of Prince Arthur as Earl of Chester, claimed that all minstrels inhabiting or exercising their office within the county and city of Chester ought to appear before him, or his steward, at Chester, at the feast of St. John the Baptist yearly, and should give him at the said feast four flagons of wine and one lance; and also every minstrel should pay him fourpence half-penny at the said feast; and that he should have from every strumpet residing and exercising her calling within the county and city of Chester four-pence yearly at the feast aforesaid; for all which he pleaded prescription. It is also certain that the Duttons used to keep a court every year upon the above feast, being the fair day, where all the minstrels of the county and city attended and played before the lord of Dutton or his steward, upon their several instruments, to and from divine service, after which the old licences granted to the minstrels, &c., were renewed, and new ones granted.†

---

* The words of the charter are, " Magisterium omnium peccatorum et meretricum totius Cestreshire, sicut liberius illum magisterium teneo de comite, salvo jure meo mihi et hæredibus meis."

† See Dugdale's Baronage, and Blount's Ancient Tenures for further information concerning this singular custom.

on the 11th; at Abergavenny on the 12th; again at Hereford on the 16th and 17th; and at Ledbury on the 18th, from whence he returned to London. The official records for the remainder of the year and a part of the year following, appear to be for the greater part lost, and we can only ascertain from what remains that the King was at Hereford on the 12th and 18th of November. This is the more to be regretted, as some of the most important events connected with the history of Wales in this reign occurred during that year. According to the Welsh accounts, the King at the urgent solicitations of the Lords Marches, came to Chester with a great army in the spring or in the beginning of summer of that year, and marched by the coast to Rhuddlan, the Welsh retiring to the mountains as he advanced. John pursued his course, crossed the river Clwyd, and encamped under the castle of Diganwy, which had been built by the Earl of Chester in the preceding year. There his army suffered much from fatigue and disease, and being surrounded by the Welsh and in danger of being deprived of provisions, he was obliged to make a hasty retreat into England.

According to Giraldus Cambrensis, Prince Llywelyn "cut off his victuals from behind him, so that he could not get more from England. His army was reduced to a starving state, and were glad to take horseflesh from pure need. The King had no remedy; he returned with great rage, leaving the country full of dead bodies."

John, enraged at the failure of his first attempt, again assembled a numerous army at Oswestry, (Album Monasterium), the castle of John Fitz Alan, and on the 8th of July, marching into Wales, he devastated the country over which he passed in the most cruel manner. He crossed the river Conway; he himself halted at Aber, and sent the Brabanters of his army to burn Bangor, which they did effectually, and took Robert of Shrewsbury,[5] then bishop of that see, prisoner, and carried him to the English camp. From Bangor he pursued the Welsh princes, and penetrated as far as the district lying round Snowdon. In consequence of these vigorous steps the princes were compelled to submit, and Llywelyn obtained peace by the intercession of his wife, Princess Joan, King John's daughter, and by the delivery of twenty thousand head of cattle, and twenty-eight hostages from among the principal families, with which the King returned to Oswestry,[6] in great triumph, on the Assumption of the Virgin, August 15, 1211.

A.D. 1211.—The King at this time was greatly embroiled in quarrels and disputes with Pope Innocent III., who, disgusted with John's conduct, detached one of his nuncios to Wales, to absolve Prince Llywelyn, Gwenwynwyn, and Maelgwyn from their oaths of allegiance to King John, and withal, gave them a strict command, under the penalty of excommunication, to molest and annoy him with all their endeavours, as an open enemy to the Church of God.[7]

A.D. 1212.—The Welsh availing themselves of this circumstance, and invited by the Sovereign Pontiff, made an incursion into England, and took several of the King's castles, burned many towns, and then returned with their booty. This infraction of all good faith may somewhat palliate, though it never can justify, the violence of the King's usage. In his fury, he determined to exterminate the whole nation; and with this view he summoned his army to meet at Nottingham. But nothing can excuse the horrible cruelty of which he was there guilty, so congenial with the tenor of his character. The moment he arrived at that place he commanded the twenty-eight or thirty-two hostages (for historians differ as to the number,) who had been delivered to him at the late peace, all children, and allied to the most distinguished nobles of Wales, to be

---

[5] This prelate was afterwards ransomed for two hundred hawks: a good riddance of rapacious birds! He was however suffered to remain here, although totally incapable of performing his duty, on account of his ignorance of the language of the people. At his death, he was, in accordance with his own request, buried in the market place at Shrewsbury. He was the original compiler of the Legend of St. Wenefrede, afterwards enlarged by Bishop Fleetwood.

[6] Mr. Carte makes Whitchurch the town to which King John returned after his successful inroads into Wales (v. i. p. 813). In the records of that age both these towns are designated by the same name, Album Monasterium; so that it is not easy to distinguish them unless we are assisted by extrinsic evidence, which in this case induces us to fix the king's return at Oswestry, from which he set out, as Dr. Powell expressly affirms. The road from Carnarvonshire to that town lay through the friendly county of Powis (friendly as far as hostility to the Prince of Wales could make it,) and it was a town capacious enough to entertain the English army; which could not then be said of Whitchurch.

[7] Matthew Paris, p. 194; Brady's England, p. 482; Annales Waverliensis, p. 173; Thomas Wykes, p. 37; Holinshed, p. 176.

instantly hanged; and the inhuman monarch refused to take any refreshment until the horrid deed was perpetrated. In the same detestable spirit of impotent revenge he issued his orders to Robert de Vipont, his governor or castellan of Salop, to execute the young Prince of South Wales, Rees ap Maelgwyn, a youth of seventeen years,[8] which to the utter disgrace of humanity was complied with.

The King received several messages from various parts of the country, informing him that a conspiracy had been laid against his person. The King of Scotland sent a messenger to warn him, while one day at dinner, and before he rose from the table, another messenger brought a letter from his daughter, Joan, Princess of Wales, also warning him of treasons meditated against him. The King despised these warnings, and continued his progress to Chester, but he was there met by other messengers, who brought him more distinct information, that if he proceeded with his enterprise he would either be killed by his own soldiers or be delivered to his deadly enemies the Welsh; and struck with consternation he disbanded his army and returned to London. It was just at this time that the Pope had excommunicated the contumacious monarch, and offered his kingdom to the King of France, and shortly afterwards John, distrustful of his own people, surrendered his crown to the Papal Legate, and consented to receive it again as a vassal of the Romish See.[9]

During the war between King John and the barons, Giles de Breose, Bishop of Hereford, son of William de Breose, a great baron and an ecclesiastic of much power and wealth, opposed the King, and entered into an alliance with Prince Llywelyn. Mortimer, although strongly solicited by them, adhered to John, upon which Llywelyn, with Alen Wyn Alen, Prince of Powys, Maelgwyn, another potent Welshman, and the Bishop of Hereford, entered his castle of Camaron and utterly demolished it, for which he was afterwards compensated; for Gualdo, the Pope's Legate, pronounced excommunication against all who had taken anything from the King and his friends, unless they made timely satisfaction.

The thirteenth century, (says Mr. Wright, the author of the History of Ludlow,[1]) is one of the most important and interesting periods in our national annals. In the reign of the cunning and worthless John, began the great struggle for the English liberties, to which the course of events had long tended. The period to which more particularly belongs the title of *Anglo-Norman* was now ended; during the first century after the Conquest, the King and his Norman barons had been closely tied together by their common opposition to the native English; but in the latter end of the twelfth century the two races were already joining in a community of interests and blood, and the alliance was completed and rendered durable by the continual attempts of King John to strengthen his power by the introduction of strangers. After this time the descendants of the Norman barons who had come in with Duke William called themselves Englishmen, and became distinguished by their hatred to foreigners.

The King's apprehensions having been calmed by the exaction of hostages from his barons, he returned towards the Borders of Wales, but with what retinue we have no information. He was at Tewkesbury on the 30th of July, 1212; at Worcester on the two following days; at Bridgenorth on the 2nd and 3rd of August; at Shrewsbury on the 4th; and at Bridgenorth on his return, on the 5th. He again came to Bristol in October, and was there on the 18th and 19th of that month. He made a third progress towards Wales in the beginning of November, and was at Flaxley in the Forest of Dean on the 8th and 9th of that month; at St. Briavel's from the 10th to the 12th; at Flaxley again on the latter day; at Tewkesbury on the 13th; at Hereford from the 13th to the 18th; and he went from thence by Tewkesbury to Warwick and London. King John did not again visit the Border till November 1213; on the 20th and 21st of which month he was at Tewkesbury; he was at Hanley Castle from the 22nd to the 24th; at Hereford from the 25th to the

[8] Powell's History of Wales, sub ann. Other authorities make this unfortunate youth only seven years of age. Mr. Carte calls the merciless instrument of John's cruelty, *John* de Vipont (v. i. 815): and there was an officer of this name, Castellan of Mathrafal; but the governor of Shrewsbury Castle was *Robert*, Robertus de Veteri Ponte, who attests this king's charter to the town in 1205.

[9] Matthew Paris, sub ann.

[1] We beg here to acknowledge our obligation to our learned friend, the author of the History of Ludlow, for much valuable information, on this portion of our work, from Mr. Wright's extensive correspondence with the various literary societies of Europe. No gentleman is better able to gain such authentic information, nor have we found any more willing to impart it. His History of Ludlow, now in course of publication, is an exceedingly interesting work, from which we have made several extracts, not to be found elsewhere.

27th; at Kilpeck on the 26th and the 27th; at St. Briavel's on the 28th and 29th; at Monmouth on the 29th and 30th; and on the latter day he returned to St. Briavel's on his way to London.

In the great struggle between the King and the barons during the latter years of John's reign, the Welsh entered into a close alliance with the baronial party. Immediately after his return from Normandy, in 1214, John repaired to the Border; from the 14th to the 17th of December he was at Gloucester; he was at Monmouth on the 18th; at Kilpeck on the 18th and 19th; at Hereford from the 21st to the 23rd; at Worcester from the 25th to the 27th; and at Tewkesbury on his return on the 27th. Some of the most powerful of the Border families, as the Mortimers and the Lacies, were staunch adherents to the Royal cause, but many others, and among the rest the Fitz Alans and the well-known Fulk Fitz Warine, were as firm adherents to the baronial confederacy. John upon this occasion, appears to have seized on many of the castles of his enemies, and garrisoned them for his own use; before he left the Border he gave the castle of Grosmont, and probably Screnfrith and the other fortresses in the neighbourhood to John de Monmouth. He had previously given a strong castle in the Marches to Falcasius de Breauté, one of the most violent and cruel of his foreign mercenaries.

In November, 1214, the barons, taking advantage of the distracted state of their sovereign's affairs, and the contempt he had incurred by his homage to Rome, met at Bury, in Suffolk, to concert measures for obtaining a relaxation of the services due to the Crown by the feudal law. The names of two great lords of the Marches, John Fitz Alan, and Fulke Fitz Warine, occur in the list of nobles assembled on that occasion. The latter had even the honour in the following year of being excommunicated by the Pope (who had now taken his abject vassal, the wretched John, under the protection of the Holy See) for his perseverance in this confederacy, by which the barons, who merely intended to vindicate the privileges of their own order, unconsciously laid the corner stone of the beautiful fabric of English liberty.

Llywelyn, glad of an occasion to embarrass his father-in-law, espoused with eagerness the cause of the barons, in which he was joined by Gwenwynwyn, Bleddyn ap Owen, of Porkington, and other Cambrian chieftains, who, in 1215, under the command of the Prince of Wales, marched with a powerful army until they appeared before the gates of the stone bridge at Shrewsbury. The inhabitants at that time, in gratitude for favours formerly received from the wretched John, adhered to that base and cruel monarch, and had fortified the town in the best manner they could. The Welsh Prince set fire to the house of the abbot, and, carrying the town without much resistance, re-entered into the possession of Pengwern, four hundred and fifty years after it had been wrested from his ancestors.[2]

" The entrance of Llywelyn into the ancient metropolis of Powis," says the Salopian historian, "must have been a moment of triumphant gratulation. That spirited prince was not ignorant of the ancient glories of his line, nor devoid of vigour and activity to assert and reclaim its lost rights. A period of four centuries and a half had elapsed, since Pengwern had been wrested from the hands of his progenitors; and we may well conceive the pride and satisfaction with which he surveyed the lofty spires and embattled turrets of his recent conquest; while every bard of his household would new string his harp, and in his native verse proclaim, that now was the period arrived when the descendant of Cadwaladr would avenge the robberies of the Saxon spoiler, upon the feeble princes of the House of Plantagenet. This is not mere imagination. The bard of Llywelyn the Great intimates that his hero grasped in imagination the sceptre of England. 'He is for recovering the government of all Britain.'[3] 'He puts Lloegr (England) to flight, and is fully bent to conquer the land that was formerly in the possession of Cadwallon, the son of Cadfan.'[4] Cadwallon was father of Cadwaladr, the last king of the Britons.

" Such were the topics of panegyric resounded by the British muse on the occupation of Pengwern by its ancient possessors. But history is silent on the subject. All we know with certainty is, that Llywelyn

[2] For this account of the capture of Shrewsbury by the Prince of Wales, we are indebted to Dr. Powell's History of Cambria, which is confirmed, in part, by writ 6 Henry III., quoted by Mr. Lloyd, MS. History of Shropshire, p. 31, and also by Messrs. Owen and Blakeway, to whose vast researches we acknowledge our obligation.

[3] Evans, Specimens of Welsh Poetry, p. 33.   [4] P. 35.

continued at Shrewsbury, while his partisan Giles de Breose, Bishop of Hereford (whose brother had espoused the Prince's daughter), was employed in the disposal of Clun Castle, and in the conquest of Mid-Wales[5]: and records prove that Shrewsbury did not long continue in the hands of the Welsh. For in the next year, 1216, the Bishop being dead, and the King having succeeded in seducing many of his barons from the party of Prince Louis of France, marched a powerful army into these parts, to chastise the insolence of his son-in-law, and to support Gwenwynwyn, whom Llywelyn had expelled from all his possessions, for his adherence to the King of England.[6] In the course of this expedition, John passed from Hereford by Hay and Radnor, both which he destroyed, then to Oswestry, where, after reposing three days, August 7th, 8th, and 9th, A.D. 1216, he, in the true spirit of a tyrant, reduced it to ashes,[7] probably to prevent its falling into the hands of his great enemy, Fulke Fitz-Warine, lord of the neighbouring castle of Whittington; hence he marched to Shrewsbury, where we find him on the 14th of the same month, and which, therefore, was then in his possession."

On the 15th of June, 1215, Magna Charta, that invaluable document, the foundation of the liberties and of the glorious constitution of England, was signed by King John.[8]

By this charter the liberties of England were established on a solid basis, and the rights and privileges of all classes, with the exception of the unfortunate villeins, who were considered as the property of their more fortunate masters, were solemnly sanctioned and confirmed.

A.D. 1215.—At the end of the month of July, the King made another brief visit to the Borders, and was at Shrewsbury on the 30th and 31st of July; at Bridgenorth on the 1st of August; and at Worcester the next day. Throughout the records of this year we trace the King's anxiety to store the castles which were in his hands, and to place them in safe custody against the impending contest. On the 19th of July the castle of Hereford was committed to the custody of the Grand Justiciary, Hubert de Burgh. On the 14th of August, it was transferred, at his request, to the younger Walter de Clifford,[9] and in the October following, we find payments made to Clifford for his expense in fortifying it.[1] About this time the Bishop of Hereford died, and on the 18th of November, the King ordered his castle to be delivered into the hands of the younger Walter de Clifford.[2] The King appears also to have obtained possession of the castle on the south-western border of Herefordshire, for he restores Grosmont to John de Monmouth[3] on the 1st of December.

A.D. 1216.—It was not until the summer of 1216, that King John, after having ravaged with fire and sword a large portion of his kingdom, came with his foreign mercenaries to the Border, which we may suppose to have suffered all the worst effects of their cruelty. On the 19th and 20th of July, we find him at Bristol and Berkeley; on the 21st he was at Gloucester; on the 22nd and 23rd at Tewkesbury; and on the 24th to the 27th at Hereford. At this time he ordered Thomas de Erdington to deliver up the castle of Bridgnorth and the county of Salop to the custody of the Earl of Chester.[4] From Hereford he is said to have written to Llywelyn, Prince of Wales, and to Reginald de Breose (brother of the late Bishop of Hereford, and third son of the famous William de Breose), offering them favourable terms if they would join him against Louis of France, who had been called in by the barons. Being unsuccessful in his

---

[5] Powell's History of Wales, sub ann.   [6] Ibid.

[7] The inhabitants of Shrewsbury seem to have been accessory to the destruction of Oswestry. In the Pipe Rolls of Henry III., 12, is this entry, "John le Strange renders an account of 28l. raised from the Burgesses of Shrewsbury for stores sold by them, and 32l. for like stores sold by himself."

[8] This important document of human liberty has a rare history of its own, and of the providence that saved it from utter destruction. Sir Robert Cotton, being one day at his tailor's, discovered that the man held in his hand, ready to be cut up for measures, the original Magna Charta, with all its appendages of seals and signatures. He bought this singular curiosity for a trifle, and recovered in this manner what had long been given over for lost.—Curiosities of Literature, ed. 1791.

[9] Patent Rolls, pp. 149, 153. The family of the Cliffords possessed large estates on the Border. The Walter de Clifford here mentioned, was the brother of Rosamond de Clifford, the mistress of Henry II., better known by the more celebrated name of "Fair Rosamond."

[1] Close Rolls, p. 231. Honey was still a very important portion of the produce of lands on the Border. It appears by an entry this year, that Stephen D'Evereux (de Ebroicis) held Badlingham of the king by the tenure of paying thirty-two gallons of honey yearly to the king's use in the castle of Hereford. Close Rolls, p. 219. This probably formed part of the stores for the use of the garrison.

[2] Patent Rolls, p. 159.   [3] Ibid., p. 160.

[4] Patent Rolls, p. 175.

attempt to detach them from the alliance of the baronial party, he marched to Hay Castle, which he took and destroyed.

The King was at Hay on the 27th and 28th of July, and on the latter day he wrote again to some of the Welsh nobles, inviting them to an interview, and declaring that he was come to the Border for their benefit, and not with any intention to injure them.[5] From Hay Castle the King returned to Hereford, where he remained from the 29th to the 31st of July. On the latter day he went to Leominster, where he was on the 1st of August. On the 2nd of August he was at Radnor, where also he destroyed the castle, and he went the same day to Kingsmead. On the 3rd he was at Kingsmead and Clun, and on the 4th at Shrewsbury. From the 6th to the 10th of August the King was at Oswestry, the castle of John Fitz Alan, which he burnt to the ground. From this place, on the 7th of August, John sent another safe-conduct to the Prince of Wales to repair to his presence.[6] From the 11th to the 14th, the King was again at Shrewsbury. On the 12th he granted to Robert de Mortimer a market to be held weekly, and a fair to be held yearly on St. Owen's day (March 4), and the five following days, in his town of Richard's Castle.[7] From the 14th to the 16th of August, the King was at Bridgenorth, and on the latter day he gave into the hands of the Earl of Chester, the custody of Shrewsbury, Bridgenorth, and the county of Salop. From Bridgenorth, John went to Worcester, where he was on the 16th and 17th of August, and thence to Gloucester, which he reached on the latter day. The whole of the King's movements on this occasion show that his chief object was to tamper with the Welsh, and with the Lords of the Marches, in whom lay his last hope of raising an army sufficient to afford any solid prospect of opposing the progress of his enemies. He had taken the opportunity of wreaking his vengeance on a few of the barons on the immediate Border who were opposed to him, and before he left this part of the kingdom for the last time, on the 18th of August he took the castle of Hereford from Walter de Clifford, and gave it to the keeping of Walter de Lacy, with orders for fortifying and storing it, and on the 20th he again gave to John de Monmouth the castles of Grosmont, Screnfrith, and Lantely. From Gloucester, King John proceeded on that Progress which ended at Newark-upon-Trent, where he died on the 10th of October. At his own request his body was carried to Worcester, where it was deposited in the cathedral. One of his last acts connected with the Border of Wales was his grant, on the 10th of October, of three carucates of land in the forest of Acornbury to Margaret de Lacy for the foundation of her monastery.

Thus ends the life of this wretched hunted monarch, after having been the victim of contending passions, baffled tyranny, defeated fraud, and wounded pride.

A.D. 1216.—HENRY THE THIRD succeeded to the throne upon the death of his father, King John. London being in possession of the French Prince, Louis, an assembly of the principal authorities was convened at Winchester, under the presidency of Gualdo, the Papal Legate. They unanimously resolved that the young king should be crowned on the 28th of October. The ceremony was performed in the Cathedral of Winchester. The Papal Legate compelled Henry to do homage to the holy Roman Church and Pope Innocent, for his kingdom of England and Ireland; he also made him swear that he would pay an annual tribute of one thousand marks to the Papal see. The ceremony of coronation was repeated by Stephen Langton, Archbishop of Canterbury.

Early in the year 1236, Henry married the lady Eleanor, daughter to the Earl of Provence, whose beauty is celebrated by all the chroniclers.

The ceremony of her coronation was performed with extraordinary pomp on the 22nd of January. Holinshed's account of it will no doubt gratify our readers.[8]

---

[5] Patent Rolls, p. 191. [6] Ibid., p. 192.
[7] Rot. Claus. p. 281.
[8] " At the solemnitie of this feast and coronation of the quene, all the high peeres of the realm both spirituall and temporall were present, there to exercise their offices as to them apperteined. The citizens of London were there in great arraie, bearing before hir in solemn wise three hundred and three score cups of gold and silver, in token that they ought to wait upon hir cup. The Archbishop of Canterbury (according to his dutie) crowned hir, the Bishop of London assisting him as his deacon. The citizens of London served out wine to everie one in great plentie. The feast was plentifull, so that nothing wanted that could be wished. Moreover in Tothill-fields roiall justes were holden by the space of eight daies together."—Coronation Anecdotes.

P

The annals of the fifty years, which immediately preceded the conquest of Wales, display a terrible tissue of conspiracies, proscriptions, and bloodshed. The strong arm of England had already reduced the Welsh to a state of absolute and oppressive bondage; and it is probable that Henry III. might have claimed the honour of effectually subduing our nation had he succeeded in quenching that high-born spirit of enthusiastic patriotism, which glowed in the hearts of our ancient nobility. But this was an achievement reserved for time and oppression only to accomplish; and for nearly two centuries after the subjugation of their country, we find sparks of this fiery volume occasionally emitted, in attempts to regain that freedom so congenial to the wild habits of the mountaineers. "History," says Hume, at the commencement of his history of the reign of Henry III., "being a collection of facts which are multiplying without end, is obliged to adopt some act of abridgment to retain the more material events, and to drop all the minute circumstances, which are only interesting during the time, or to persons engaged in the transactions." The whole of Henry's reign is intimately connected with our subject, and is full of interest, but we shall take his advice and endeavour not to be prolix in our detail.

A Cambrian may regret the loss of the independence of his country, and even an indifferent reader may sympathise with the generous struggles of Llywelyn, or detest the insidious policy of Henry; but when we compare the general insecurity that prevailed during those protracted hostilities, with the safety which he now enjoys, he cannot fail to be thankful for the result which has united both nations into one people; and has enabled him to sleep without the precaution of moats and battlements; to take his excursions without a retinue of armed followers; and to sow his fields without the fear that a merciless invader may reap his harvests.

Henry, at the death of his father, King John, was only a boy nine years of age, with a competitor to the throne, and a confederacy of rebellious subjects arrayed in arms against him, and Llywelyn, Prince of Wales, did not fail to seize this happy opportunity of consolidating and enlarging his dominion. He quickly became master of every part of the Principality; and had the English barons, his confederates, continued faithful to their engagements, the consequences might have proved fatal to the Crown of England, or at least a large portion of its domains might have been transferred into the hands of Llywelyn. Fortunately for the young king, the successes of his guardian, the Earl of Pembroke, had expelled the French prince; had broken the confederacy, and compelled the barons to return to their allegiance; and the Prince of Wales was obliged to enter into a treaty with his royal brother-in-law. The conference was holden at Worcester, in the second year of that king. By this treaty, which is extant in Rymer,[9] the Prince of North Wales agrees to surrender the castles of Caermarthen and Cardigan; and engages not to receive any of the King's enemies. In consideration of these concessions to the Protector, (for the castles just mentioned were the possessions of the Earl of Pembroke), it is engaged that the Prince shall have the custody of all the land which belonged to Wenhunwen (so the name is there written) in Wales and Mungumer, of which he was disseised on account of the war between King John and his barons, to hold to the full age of the heirs of Gwynwynwyn. Llywelyn contracting on his part to provide reasonable sustenance for the said heirs, whether they be educated in England or Wales, and to pay the dower of M. (Margaret, daughter of Rhys ap Gryffyth, lord of South Wales), widow of Gwenwynwyn. By this arrangement the kingdom was restored to peace for a short time only.

By the treaty with Louis and his adherents, in September, 1217, Llywelyn, Prince of Wales, who with his barons had been excommunicated, were to deliver up to the King all the fortresses on the Border which he had taken during the baronial wars, and he came to Hereford on the Octave of St. Martin (Nov. 18), probably for the purpose of negotiating on that subject. As the King could not meet him at that time, Llywelyn received a safe-conduct to come to meet him at Worcester, on the second Sunday after Ash Wednesday, (March 11, 1218.[1]) Accordingly we trace the King in his progress to the place of meeting by his signature to the documents of the period. He was at Gloucester on the 8th of March, and

---

9 Rymer's Fœdera, v. ii. p. 227.   1 Rymer's Fœdera, vol. i. p. 149.

Tewkesbury on the 11th, on which day he probably reached Worcester, where he remained till the 17th. Llywelyn came there at the appointed time, and bound himself to certain conditions of peace and alliance which were then agreed upon.[2]

"The Welsh Border of the counties of Hereford, Monmouth, and Salop, during the thirteenth century, was covered with castles and monastic houses.[3] These numerous castles may be divided into three or four principal groups, of which the largest was formed by the line of fortresses running along the Welsh boundary of the south-western part of Herefordshire. Beginning with Monmouth, we have, in continued succession, White Castle, Screnfrith, and Grosmont, within Monmouthshire; and in Herefordshire, Kilpeck, with the two Ewyases, Wilton, Clifford, Whitney, Eardesley, the chain being thus continued to Radnor. It will be observed that the castles on this line are nearly all Anglo-Norman; it formed the basis of the operations of the early Norman barons in the interior of Wales. Another line of castles skirted the Roman road from Hereford to Shrewsbury. These, after the entry of the Normans, became of less importance, and, with the exception of Wigmore, the importance of which arose from its being the chief seat of the great and powerful family of the Mortimers, are scarcely mentioned in history. Wigmore, with Richard's Castle, and perhaps Croft Castle, were originally Saxon buildings. To this group was added by the Normans the castle of Brampton Bryan, built by Bryan de Brampton in the twelfth century. Ludlow formed part of a line of castles which stretched from Richard's Castle along Corvedale, and included the castles of Corfham and Holgate. Another group, including Knighton, Clun, Bishop's Castle, &c., defended the Welsh border on the north-west.

"With the exception of Ludlow, the most interesting ruins of the castellated buildings of the Norman period belong to the first of these groups, and are scattered along the southern and western Borders of Herefordshire. In general the remains of the castles which were built before the Conquest are very unimportant. Goodrich Castle is a fine and remarkable ruin; but the site of the castle of Hereford is covered with streets, and of Wigmore Castle and Richard's Castle the foundations and a few fragments of the walls are all that remains. Of the history of Caynham Castle which appears to have been deserted from a remote period, we are entirely ignorant. It occupied the summit of a hill about two miles to the south of Ludlow."[4]

[2] Rymer's Fœdera, vol. i. p. 150.

[3] A manuscript * preserved in the British Museum, written in the early part of Henry III.'s reign, furnishes us with the names of the most important of such buildings then existing., viz., Hereford, Kilpeck, Ewyas Harold, and Ewyas Lacy, Grosmont, Screnfrith, White Castle, Monmouth, Goodrich Castle, Wilton, Clifford, Whitney, Huntington, Keueuenleis, &c. &c. Among those in Shropshire the following are mentioned:—Shrewsbury, Bridgnorth, Holgad, Corfham, Ludlow, Ellesmere, Cause, and Blancmuster or Oswestry. Of these castles those of Hereford, Monmouth, Goodrich, Wigmore, Radnor, Bridgnorth, and Shrewsbury, were originally Saxon fortresses, and formed the defence of the Border previous to the Norman Conquest. There are no traces now left of some of the above castles, but the greater number, with others omitted in it, adorn the country by their imposing and picturesque ruins.

* The following is a portion of the MS. preserved in Cotton Vespas. A. xviii., fol. 159, which relates to the castles and monasteries of Hereford and Salop:—

HEREFORD.

Episcopatus. Hereford. S. Mr. et St. Atheberti. Canonici seculares.
Abbatia. Wiggemore. S. Jacobi. Canonici nigri.
Abbatia. Dore. S. Mariæ. Monachi albi.
Prioratus. Leomenstre. S. Jacobi. Monachi nigri ne Redinge.
Prioratus. Hereford. S. Petri et Pauli. Monachi nigri.
Prioratus. Bartone. S. ——— Monachi nigri.

Prioratus. Clifford. S. Mar. Monachi nigri de Cluniaco.
Prioratus. Hereford. S. Petri et Pauli, et S. Guthlaci. Moniales nigræ.
Prioratus. Monemue. S. Mar. et S. Florent. Monachi nigri de Saumer.
Prioratus. Acornebery. S. Katerinæ. Moniales albæ.
Prioratus. Lingebroke. S. ——— Moniales albæ.
Prioratus. de Kilpek.
Prioratus. Ewyas Haraldi.
Castella. Hereford. Kilpek. Ewyas Haraldi. Ewyas Laci. Grosmund. Skenefreid. Castrum Album. Monemue. Gotrige. Wiltone. Clifford. Witesneic. Huntindone. Herdeleye. Wigmorre. Radenowere. Keueuenleis. Ledebure north. Seynt Brevel.

SALOPESYRE.

Abbatia. Salopesbery. S. Petri et S. Milburgæ. Monachi nigri.
Abbatia. Beldewas. S. Mar. Monachi nigri.
Abbatia. Cumbemere. S. Mar. Monachi albi.
Abbatia. Lilleshelle. S. ——— Canonici nigri.
Abbatia. Hageman. S. Mar. Canonici albi.
Prioratus. Wenelok. S. Milburgæ. Monachi nigri de Cluniaco.
Prioratus. Stone. S. Michaelis. Monachi nigri.
Prioratus. Dudelege. S. ——— Monachi nigri.
Prioratus. Brumfeld. S. ——— Monachi nigri.
Prioratus. Wyggemor. Canonici albi.
Castella. Bruges. Salopesbery. Holgod. Corfham. Ludelawe. Ellesmere. Caus. Blancmuster. ij°.

[4] Wright's History of Ludlow.

The feuds between the Welsh and the Lords of the Border, which had originated, or been cherished, during the baronial contest, were not, however, easily extinguished, and many years passed away before this part of the kingdom ceased to be the scene of a continual succession of predatory warfare. At the commencement of the year 1220, these hostilities had taken a character which called for active interference of the King. On the 1st of May in that year, the King wrote to Llywelyn inviting him to meet him at Shrewsbury on the Monday after the Ascension;[5] on the 25th of April he had ordered sixty pounds to be paid out of his treasury to defray the expenses of his journey,[6] and we find him at Shrewsbury on the 7th of May, where it is probable that the Welsh prince sent excuses for not attending to his invitation. On the 9th the King returned to Bridgenorth, where he granted licenses to the burgesses of Shrewsbury and Bridgenorth to cut down timber in his forests for the strengthening of their respective towns.[7] On the 10th he had reached Worcester, and on the 17th he arrived at Westminster, where he appears to have taken immediate measures for raising a considerable army. The especial objects of Llywelyn's enmity were William Mareschal, Earl of Pembroke, (the son of King Henry's guardian), and Reginald de Breose, and he was preparing to invade their lands with a powerful army. Henry appeared again on the Border in August; he was at Berkeley on the 15th and 16th of that month; at Monmouth on the 17th; at Screnfrith on the 19th; at White Castle on the 20th, and at Striguil on the 21st; where he appears to have heard first of the real extent of Llywelyn's preparations, and he learnt that he was then marching against Reginald de Breose.[8] On the 23rd, the King was at Bristol on his return from the Border, and the Welsh proceeded with their hostilities, but before the end of September their progress had been arrested by Henry's interference, who, on the 5th of October, wrote to the Welsh prince, citing him to appear before him at Worcester on the Octaves of St. Andrew (December 7th).[9] It does not appear that this meeting took place, but Llywelyn had agreed to make amends for the damages he had committed. A new appointment was probably made and kept in the year following, as the King came to Shrewsbury on the 28th of June, when a truce, if not a reconciliation between the hostile parties, was agreed upon. Early in the following year the Welsh appear to have again assumed a threatening attitude, and we find the English monarch at Screnfrith from the 4th to the 7th of March, but the truce was finally prolonged on the 30th of April.

Llywelyn appears to have taken advantage of the truce to prepare on a large scale for a new invasion of the English Border. In the beginning of March, 1223, the King was called from a Progress in the northern part of England by the intelligence that the Welsh prince was besieging Whittington, the castle of Fulke Fitz Warine.[1] Henry reached Shrewsbury on the 7th of March, and on his approach it is probable that the Welsh retired; and he proceeded by Bridgenorth, Kidderminster, Worcester, and Gloucester, towards the capital. After the King's departure the Welsh renewed their hostilities; a letter of safe-conduct, sent on the 22nd of June to Llywelyn, to meet the King at Worcester on the Monday after the feast of St. John the Baptist,[2] was disregarded; and when the King arrived at Worcester with an army at the beginning of July, he learnt that the Welsh had taken Whittington as well as the castle of Kinardsley, or Kinnersley, belonging to Baldwin de Hodnet. He immediately sent orders to put Shrewsbury in a state of defence, and after staying at Worcester till the 16th, and at Gloucester till the 22nd, he returned to Windsor, where, on the 12th of September, he received intelligence from Reginald de Breose that he was closely besieged in his own castle of Buellt, and that the English forces were insufficient to withstand the progress of Llywelyn and his army.[3] The King immediately called together a powerful army, which was to meet at Gloucester, and on the 19th of September he reached Hereford in person. He caused the fortifications of that city to be put in a good condition, and remained there till the 25th; on the 26th he was with his army at Leominster; on the 29th he was at Shrewsbury; and the next day he

[5] Rymer's Fœdera, p. 159.

[6] " Liberate etiam de thesauro nostro eidem Willelmo sexaginta libras deferendas nobiscum ad expensas nostras versus Salopesbir." Close Rolls, p. 416.

[7] Close Rolls, pp. 417, 418.   [8] *Ibid.*, p. 428.

[9] Rymer's Fœdera, p. 164.

[1] Close Rolls, p. 537.   [2] Rymer's Fœdera, i. p. 168.

[3] Fœdera, i. p. 170 ; Matt. Paris, Hist. Maj. sub ann. 1221. The historian is entirely wrong in the date he gives to these occurrences. Wright's History of Ludlow.

marched with his army to Montgomery. Here, having terrified the Welsh by the greatness of his preparations, and by the ravages which he began to commit upon them, he received hostages from Llywelyn for their future submission.[4] But the King determined to put a check upon their incursions on this part of the Border, by building a new and strong castle at Montgomery. Immediately after his arrival he wrote to the sheriff of Shropshire for arms, and to Hereford for stores. At the same time he restored to Baldwin de Hodnet and Fulke Fitz Warine their castles of Kinardsley and Whittington. On the 7th of October he sent for twenty "good miners" from the Forest of Dean, to make the fosses and lay the foundations.[5] Having remained at Montgomery till the 11th, he returned to Shrewsbury on that day, or on the 12th, and passed through Bridgenorth on the 13th, and Kidderminster on the 14th, to Worcester, where he remained from the 14th to the 16th, and from thence he went to Gloucester. From both these cities he sent to Montgomery, money and materials for the works, with abundance of stores and arms. On the 18th of November he ordered six hogsheads of Gascon wine and fifty "bacons" to be sent from Bristol to the castle of Hereford. On the 22nd, he sent to Montgomery six thousand quarells, or cross-bow arrows, which had been made at St. Briavel's, where there appears to have been an extensive manufactory of these weapons. On the 23rd, the King appointed a chaplain to serve in the "new castle" of Montgomery. During the whole of the year 1224, the King was occupied in strengthening the Border, and in building his castle, which appears to have been finished in September. On the 19th of that month he arrived at Worcester, where he was met by his sister Joan, Llywelyn's wife;[6] on the 21st he was at Kiddermister; on the 22nd, at Bridgenorth; and from the 24th to the 30th, at Shrewsbury; where he strengthened the fortifications of the castle. On the 1st of October the King visited the castle of Montgomery, which he entrusted to Baldwin de Hodnet. On the 2nd he was at Ludlow, on the 4th at Hereford, and on the 7th at Gloucester.

At this period, the family of the Mortimers was increasing fast in power and importance; and their possessions on the Border were repeatedly enlarged by alliances with the heiresses of the old Lords of the Marches, whose families were becoming extinct. Three successive lords of Wigmore intermarried with the house of the Breoses; Hugh de Mortimer, the grandson of Roger, who founded Wigmore, married Annora, the daughter of William de Breose; Ralph de Mortimer married the widow of Reginald de Breose; and his son, Roger de Mortimer, married Maude, the daughter and co-heir of Reginald's son, the second William de Breose. At this time all the barons were distinguished by their loyalty, and by their hostility to the Welsh. Hugh de Mortimer died in November, 1227, in consequence of wounds which he had received in a tournament. His brother Ralph, who succeeded to his estates, was remarkable throughout the whole of his life for his hatred towards the Welsh, which appears to have been founded partly on resentment for personal injuries. In 1221, according to a chronicle of the abbey of Wigmore,[7] while Ralph was a prisoner in France, the Welsh invaded his estates, and, ravaging as far as Wigmore, they entered the abbey on the first Sunday in Lent, plundered it of everything worth carrying away, and then burnt all the houses and offices to the ground, leaving no part of the building entire except the church.

The year after that in which the new castle of Montgomery was completed, we find Llywelyn again in arms. While William Mareschal was absent in Ireland, the Prince suddenly invaded his lands, seized upon two of his castles, and, having massacred the defenders, garrisoned them with Welshmen. William Mareschal returned in haste, and soon recovered his castles; and, in revenge, he invaded the lands of Llywelyn, who raised a large army to oppose him. The hostile parties engaged on the banks of the Tivy, and, according to the English chronicles, the English obtained a decisive and sanguinary victory.[8] But the Earl's success must have been partial, for Llywelyn continued to harass the English during the remainder of the year. He was, probably, encouraged by the inability of the King, who was occupied with other affairs, to come to the assistance of the barons. Henry cited the Welsh prince to meet him at Worcester fifteen days after the feast of St. John the Baptist (July 9th);[9] in June he sent to inform him that other matters

[4] Rymer's Fœdera, v. i. p. 170.
[5] "Ad operationes castri nostri quod ibidem construimus faciendas." Close Rolls, p. 565.   [6] Close Rolls, p. 622.
[7] In the Monasticon, last edition, vol. vi. p. 350.
[8] Matthew Paris, who places these transactions in the year 1223.
[9] Rymer's Fœdera, i. p. 179

of importance then occupied him, and he changed the day of meeting to the Assumption of the Blessed Virgin (August 15th). In spite of the King's threats and expostulations, Llywelyn proceeded with his hostile preparations, which had assumed so serious a character in the autumn of the same year that Henry obtained from the Pope a bull of excommunication against the person of his refractory kinsman.[1] This war appears to have been partly excited by Hugh de Lacy, and some other barons, who had withdrawn their allegiance from the King, and joined their forces with those of the Welsh.[2] According to some accounts, a peace was at length concluded between Henry and Llywelyn, who met at Ludlow.[3]

But at this period no peace between the English and Welsh was lasting; and for many years the Border was the scene of continual strife. The grounds of the great baronial confederacy were already laid, which soon afterwards humbled the Crown at its feet. During the thirteenth century the turbulence of the Welsh was in no small degree a safeguard to the liberties of England. When the defenders of the Great Charter were defeated or overpowered, they found a never-failing refuge in the mountains on the other side of the Border, and they could there hold their councils and raise their forces for future operations; while the first notice of an insurrectionary movement among the English barons was the signal for a rising among the Welsh, who were led by the love of liberty to join their banners. In 1226, feelings of mistrust arose between the King and William Mareschal, who retired to his castles in Wales; and on the 28th of July, in that year, we find Henry at Worcester sending a safe conduct to Llywelyn to meet him at Shrewsbury.[4]

A.D. 1226.—The young king appears to have just arrived at the age of nineteen years, and was anxious to have a friendly interview with the Prince of Wales, his sister the Princess of Wales, and his nephew their son. The safe conduct (a necessary precaution in that period of animosity) is dated at Worcester, July 28th; and it was, probably, in the course of this visit to Shrewsbury, that the King granted to his sister the manors of Ruckley and Condover, to hold during pleasure, since we find them in his hands just before, and in hers soon after it.

The Prince and the King continued friends till at least the commencement of 1228, as the manors of Condover and Ruckley, which Henry III. had granted to his sister, the wife of Llywelyn, to hold during the royal pleasure, still remained in her possession in the March of that year.[5] In the following August this friendship sustained an interruption. The King had granted the honour and castle of Montgomery to his Justiciary, the great Hubert de Burgh; and the garrison there having received orders to cut down a large wood, not less than five miles in length, says Matthew Paris, which offered too convenient a shelter to the depredations of robbers, were unexpectedly assailed by the Welsh, and driven into their castle, where they were closely besieged, and whence they sent pressing messengers to their lord, supplicating his aid. The young king, enraged at this affront to his favourite, and eager to try his maiden sword, hastened with a small band to Montgomery, raised the siege;[6] and being strongly reinforced, destroyed the wood; after which, advancing into the heart of the country, he burned a house of White Monks,[7] on the site of which

[1] Rymer's Fœdera, i. p. 180. The bull is dated in October. It is there said of the Prince of Wales, " Nunc vero idem, tanquam homo prævaricationi assuetus et facilis ad fallendum, se simul, et famam et promissa confundens, Regi obedire recusat, et castra sibi ab eo commissa diruens, arma contra ipsum Regem erexit, et ei et ejus fidelibus, præcipue nobili viro W. comiti Penebrocensi, balivo regio, guerram movet."

[2] Matthew Paris.

[3] Caradoc of Llancarvan. As the Rolls of this period have not yet been printed, we are no longer able to trace the king in his progresses, except by a few isolated documents printed by Rymer.

[4] Rymer's Fœdera, i. p. 182.

[5] Pat. 11 Hen. III. n. 7. dorso. Rex probis hominibus, &c. The king to the good men of Ralegh and Cunedour, greeting. Because we make all our cities, burghs, and demesnes to be talliated; and have granted to our beloved sister Johanna lady of North Wales: (domine Norwallie) to whom we committed our said manors to hold as long as it should please us, Know ye, that in place of the said tallage which we might take of you, it is our intention that you shall make a reasonable aid to her.

[6] The Welsh Chronicles make the King of England aggressor in this business, and assert, that having determined to subdue the Principality, he advanced into the Marches, and encamped at Ceri, i.e. Kerry, Montgomeryshire.

[7] Habitaculum albi ordinis, Cridia vocatum. We are unable to state the situation of this monastery. Mr. Carte calls it a religious house at Kery: but Tanner mentions nothing of the kind there. Mr. Jones (Hist. of Brecon, v. i. p. 129) conjectures Cridia to be a corruption of Creigiau, the rocks: but he throws no light upon its situation. A writer in the Cambrian Register (i. 326) considers it as a generic term, Crefydd-dy, a religious house: while Mr. Bingley, in his Welsh Tour (ii. 35) and Mr. Caley (Cambrian Register, ii. 283) place it at Kymmer, near Dolgelle; and the former quotes M. Paris and Dr. Powell as confirming this assertion, which, however, is certainly not the case. It is highly probable that Henry went too far into Wales on this occasion.

the Justiciary erected a castle, with which he was so highly pleased, that, according to a custom which is not quite obsolete, he called it *Hubert's Folly*.

A.D. 1227.—The Border appears to have been more tranquil, but it was the scene of new trouble in 1228. The building of Montgomery Castle was not tamely viewed by the Welsh. Many skirmishes took place between the two armies; in one of these William de Breose was taken prisoner, and carried away captive by Llywelyn: and the King of England became so weary of the contest, that, in the end, he was glad to retreat; being compelled thereto, as the Monk of St. Alban's suggests, by the treachery of certain of his nobles, who held a secret correspondence with his enemies; in consequence of which Hubert was obliged, on receiving three thousand marks from the Prince of Wales, to dismantle the castle so recently constructed. This was, perhaps, the compensation which had been the subject of so much negotiation; and by this slight payment, which in the next year Llywelyn extorted from Breose for his ransom, and by an external show of respectful submission to his brother-in-law, at their meeting, the Welsh prince soon pacified the easy king: and we find a safe conduct (Oct. 13, 1229) for the Princess of Wales to visit Shrewsbury.

This fair and frail princess was Joan Plantagenet, daughter of King John. Except in the misunderstanding caused by the supposed amour with the unfortunate de Breose, she is said to have lived on friendly terms with her husband, was an amiable woman, interposed her good offices with her father, King John, and effected peace between him and her husband; particularly when the latter was encamped upon a mountain adjoining Ogwen's Pool, called Carnedd Llywelyn, from which he saw his country in ruins, and Bangor in flames, which John had kindled.[s]

The conjugal infidelity of Joan laid the foundation of the succeeding rupture, and led the way to the hostilities which ensued. Isabel, one of the daughters and coheirs of Breose, had been married to David, son of Llywelyn; who thus obtained a pretext, which he did not neglect, of seizing her lands (May 1231) with an armed force. These estates lay chiefly in the district now known as the county of Brecon. This insult on the part of Llywelyn was aggravated by the circumstances under which it was committed. It was at the moment when a treaty was on foot for a peaceable accommodation of all matters in dispute between the two countries. For, on the 27th of the same month, information of this irruption not having yet, it should seem, reached the English court, a safe conduct was issued, authorising the ambassadors of the Prince of Aberfraw and Lord of Snowdon, (so he is therein styled,) to come to Shrewsbury on Wednesday next after the quindene of the Holy Trinity. But the outrage committed by the Prince in Brecknockshire interrupted the proposed interview.

Shortly afterwards, Princess Joan died, and, at her request, she was interred in the monastery of the

---

[s] Pennant quotes from Dugdale, that the above knight was William de Breose, a potent baron in the reign of Henry III. We examined the mound where Llywelyn's castle stood: it is elevated about twenty-four feet, tapers, and is about sixty feet in diameter. The vestiges of a moat and its feeder from the river are also yet visible. The following couplets are well known to all in the vicinity:—

" Diccyn doccyn gwraig Llywelyn,
 Beth a roit am weled Gwilim ?"

" Cymru, Lloegr, a Llywelyn,
 Oll a rown, am weled Gwilim."

Translated thus :—

" Lovely princess, says Llywelyn,
 What will you give to see your Willim ?"

" All Wales and England, and Llywelyn,
 I 'd give to see my dearest Willim."

On a mountain, about four miles south of Llywelyn's castle, and in a field called Cae Gwillim Ddu, is an artificial cave, where William de Breose was interred. This melancholy incident happened in 1229. Llywelyn died in 1240. His son afterwards married de Breose's daughter. The following singular tradition connected with the

Princess is thus rendered into verse by the late Mr. Hutter of Birmingham :—

" To a tragical incident let us remove,
 Of deception and conquest, destruction and love.
 At Aber resided a prince of high state,
 His moat is yet standing, Llywelyn the Great.
 In his wars with the English, success was his doom,
 He took a knight prisoner, and kept him at home.
  Soon after they parted some acts came to light
 Between the fair Princess and late captured knight.
 Llywelyn a letter determined to send,
 To invite back to Aber his late worthy friend.
 Arriving, the dungeon must hide him from day,
 Till a gallows was built in full view by the way;
 Where, on a small eminence, down in the dell,
 Six score yards from the castle, I know the spot well,
 The valiant knight suffered ! What heart would not move !
 The victim of treachery, victim of love.
  While hanging, the Prince to his lady applied :
 Then on towards the window he took her aside;
 And while a sarcastic smile you 'd discover,
 Asked ' what she would give for a sight of her lover !' "

Dominican friars, at Llanfaes, near Beaumaris, A.D. 1237. Llywelyn erected a monument over her, where she lay at rest two hundred and ninety-three years, till Henry VIII., who may justly be said to have murdered the living and sold the dead, disposed of this house to one of his courtiers, when the church was converted into a barn, which still remains. Joan was ejected from her narrow tenement; her coffin of stone was placed in a small brook, and lay there for two hundred and fifty years longer, being used as a watering trough by the farmers. The coffin is now carefully preserved and may be seen in the park of Baron Hill, Anglesea, the elegant seat of Sir R. B. W. Bulkely, Bart., M.P.

Princess Joan's Coffin-lid.

A.D. 1231.—Llywelyn, as appears by the Welsh Chronicle, having ravaged the Marches of South Wales, and taken the castles of Rhayader, Radnor, and several others, Henry III. came against him with a great army as far as Hereford, and sent his nobles with a part of it to attack the Welsh prince, who had, by that time, fled to North Wales. A remarkable circumstance took place during this expedition, with which Cwmlin Abbey became intimately connected; and as it was of considerable importance in the history of the place, it is thought proper to give a translation of the account of the particulars as they are related by Matthew Paris, the historian.[9]

"The king removing his army came to the city of Hereford; Llywelyn was, at that time, with his forces not far from the Castle of Montgomery, in a certain meadow, where was a river, whose banks consisted of marshes, and where he craftily prepared an ambuscade for the soldiers of the said castle. For it is said that Llywelyn directed a certain friar of the Cistercian Abbey, which was near, to go towards the castle, whom, when the soldiers of the castle saw pass by, they went out to speak to him, and enquired if he had heard anything about King Llywelyn. He answered, that he had seen him with a small attendance in a neighbouring meadow, where he waited for a larger number of men. The soldiers then asked the friar whether the horsemen might pass through the river and meadow with safety? And he answered, that the bridge, on which the travellers were accustomed to pass over the river, had been broken down by Llywelyn, because he dreaded an attack; but that they might safely pass through the river, and enter the meadow on horseback, and with a few horsemen either overtake or put to flight the Welshmen; which being heard, Walter de Godarvilla, the governor of the castle, believed the false assertions of the friar, and ordered the soldiers and sergeants to be armed, who, having mounted their horses, came speedily to the place; whom, when seen coming in force, the Welshmen betook themselves to flight in a neighbouring wood, and the soldiers of the castle pursuing them rapidly with their horses, and especially those who were foremost, became immersed in the river, and marshy portion of the meadow, up to their horses' bellies; but those who were following, being warned by the immersion of their companions, escaped, and condoled with them on their misfortune. Then the Welshmen, being informed of the immersion of their enemies, returned against them in great force, and, with their lances, slew the horses and soldiers floundering in the mud. A dreadful conflict was the consequence, and many were slain on both sides, but the Welshmen gained the victory.

"When the misfortune that had happened to the soldiers was at length made known to the King, he speedily went in a hostile manner to the abbey, whose friar had betrayed the soldiers, and, in revenge for such criminal conduct, plundered and burnt a grange belonging to the abbey, and ordered the abbey itself to be similarly plundered and destroyed by fire. But the abbot of the place, that he might save the

[9] Matth. Paris, Hist. Angl., p. 492, 493.

buildings, which he had erected at such very great expense and labour,[1] gave the king three hundred marks, and thereby assuaged his indignation.

These things having been accomplished, the King caused Maud's Castle, in Wales, which had been demolished by the Welsh, to be elegantly rebuilt with stone and mortar, and when the work was completed, which was done at a great expense, the King placed therein soldiers and dependants, who should restrain the incursions of the Welshmen.

Henry had intimated his intention of holding a personal interview with the Prince of Wales, but our restless chieftain gave the English government little repose. He complained of the incursions of Thomas Corbet of Caus, a powerful baron; and alleged other grievances. These representations produced a letter to him from the King of England, dated at Guildford, Feb. 20, 1231-2. Its singular preface, "*Wishing to the prince the spirit of wiser counsel,*" does not promise an epistle of a nature so conciliating as follows. For Henry proceeds to state, that after his departure from Castle Matilda, in Eleuein, a truce was established to last to November 30th, "for the performance of which," says he, "I sent in the parts of Eleuin, the Archdeacon of Salop and Nicholas de Molis, and into the parts of Shropshire, John Fitz Alan and John le Strange, the younger." He further states that the Prince had represented to him that he had received no satisfaction for the injuries committed by Thomas Corbet, an English subject, and thereupon his Majesty apologises for this omission; and for his inability to meet the Prince, on account of the arrival of Peter, Duke of Bretagne; adding, that he intends either to come himself to the March in person, or else to send his brother Richard, Earl of Cornwall and King of the Romans, in his room; requesting the Prince not to be displeased that Corbet had declared, that those of whom the complaints were made, did not belong to his lordship; "for," concludes the King, "it is our wish and desire to give you full satisfaction."

This sounds like the language of conciliation; but its sincerity may reasonably be doubted. The court of England had resolved to refer this embroiled and angry dispute to the Pope, and a copy of this letter would be very useful to lay before the commissaries of the holy father. If the Papal authority was often exerted to the detriment of Christendom, we must own that it was also occasionally beneficial. Turbulent and independent sovereigns, who would hearken to no other call, were sometimes obliged to lay down their weapons at the command of the sovereign pontiff, who could enforce his orders by the terrors of excommunication. To call in the aid of this spiritual ally was a favourite measure of the feeble Henry; who did not disdain to flatter the Roman see by professions of that vassalage which his father had done all in his power to entail upon the realm of England, and thus he seldom failed to engage the Pope on his side.[2]

St. Mary's church in Shrewsbury was the place appointed for the court of the papal legates; and the King himself intended to visit this town on the same business, as a round table or tournament is prohibited, and those who intended to partake of that martial sport are commanded forthwith to follow him (July 20,) because he was going to the parts of Salop, to hold parley with the Prince. With a view of settling preliminaries for this adjudication, letters of safe conduct were issued, to remain in force to the Eve of St. Lawrence, (Monday, Aug. 9,) and authorising Llywelyn and his men to come to Shrewsbury, for the purpose of meeting the King and his council. On Friday next before St. Luke's day (Oct. 18) we find

---

[1] "Sumptuosis valde laboribus constructa." Matth. Paris, p. 493.

[2] The Archbishop of Canterbury, and the Bishops of Lichfield and Rochester, received orders to repair to Shrewsbury on the Monday after Trinity. At the same time Henry wrote to Llywelyn, requesting him, as he valued the King's friendship, to meet those prelates on the following day, "in some secure and convenient place," for the purpose of negotiating a firm and lasting peace between the two countries: the Prince of Aberfraw (for he received no higher title at this time) probably not thinking it prudent to trust his person within the walls of that town, which had so recently suffered from his destructive invasion. Llywelyn refused to enter into any treaty unless the confederate barons were included; and to this condition the bishops, who desired to heal the wounds of the kingdom, were not very averse. They endeavoured, however, to impress their sovereign with an idea that they had much difficulty in procuring even these terms. Matthew Paris has preserved a story, which proves that if Henry was deficient in most of the qualities of a king, he was yet esteemed even by his foes for his beneficence and charity. The archbishops, finding Llywelyn obstinate, threatened him with the resentment of the King and clergy. The Prince replied, "I fear the alms of the King of England more than all his soldiers and priests put together."

Q

the legates, so they are styled in the patent, actually assembled in St. Mary's church; and about the same time Henry renewed his intention of visiting Shrewsbury on this important business; letters of safe conduct being issued for the Prince Llywelyn and his chiefs to meet for purposes of conference in that city.

On the 6th of December the King's proxies appear before the legates in the sacred edifice mentioned above, to press their charge against Llywelyn for infraction of treaties. But it must have been on this very day that the legates determined to shift the decision from themselves to certain arbitrators: six on the King's side, R. bishop of Chichester, chancellor; R. bishop of Coventry and Lichfield; R. Marescall, earl of Pembroke; J. de Lacy, earl of Lincoln, and constable of Chester; S. de Segrave, justiciary of England; R. Fitz Nichol, seneschall of the king. And four on that of the Prince, J. Denevet, seneschall of Llywelyn; Wrenoc, his brother; Ivan Vychan; David the clerk. For on the day following, Henry, who was then at Shrewsbury, undertakes to acquiesce in the determination of the referees, and "to ratify the provision which they are to make concerning reparation of damages, and refunding of money to us, and of restitution to be made to him, the said Llywelyn," and engage to assign to Isabel de Breose, the wife of his nephew, David, her property in the hands of her father; "provided that sufficient surety be made to us, that the said David shall perform his service due to us, and shall keep the peace in future." Having concluded this business, the King did not continue much longer in Shrewsbury, but repaired to Worcester where he kept his Christmas.

"A.D. 1223-25.—The repeated satisfaction required of Llywelyn, Prince of Wales, at this time, was strongly prognosticated by the English council. They seem to have been conscious of their inability to enforce it; though they choose to save the dignity of their master, by stipulating that it should be a preliminary to the absolution of the Prince. However this be, Rymer has preserved a notification from the King to Llywelyn (24th April, 1224) informing the Prince that he had intended to be at Shrewsbury on the 3rd of May, being Sunday next after the Invention of the Holy Cross, in order to receive from him the stipulated satisfaction: but that he now found it necessary to defer the journey for a week, and that he should not be able to come to Shrewsbury before the end of a month from Easter last past. This visit never took place; perhaps was never designed: since nearly a twelvemonth[3] after the last mentioned letter (viz. 14th of April, 1225,) another occurs of similar import, informing the Prince that the King of England, on account of the pending treaty with France, would not be able to reach Salop on the day appointed, viz., at the end of a month from Easter last past, but had deferred receiving the satisfaction to the quindene of St. John Baptist (July 9), on which day he appointed the Prince to meet him at Worcester: and their interview is again put off, by letter dated June 30th, to the Assumption of St. Mary (Aug. 15)."

The motive for these repeated delays, all of which originated with the English monarch, appears to have been the absence of the legate, who was expected over with a supply of spiritual artillery from the papal storehouse; and accordingly we find in Rymer, a bull of Honorius III. (3 Non. Octob., in the 8th year of his pontificate, 5 Oct. 1225,) again excommunicating Llywelyn for his frequent violations of solemn treaties.

The troubles which marked the year 1233 are said to have been preceded by extraordinary natural phenomena; when the sun rose over the counties of Hereford and Worcester on the morning of the 8th of April, the inhabitants of those districts were astonished at beholding it accompanied by four other suns, arranged in a visible circle, which appeared to have embraced within its circumference the whole of England; this larger circle being cut by four smaller ones, the four smaller ones forming the point of intersection.[4] The apprehensions excited by this prodigy were heightened by the knowledge of the distrust which already appeared between the ill-advised monarch and his barons.

---

[3] In the intermediate space, however, another interview with Llywelyn seems to have been at least projected: for, in Aug. 13, 1224, the King informs the Earl of Pembroke's bailiffs, that he cannot be at Shrewsbury on Sunday next after the feast of St. James, which day he had appointed, to meet Llywelyn there, to receive from him compensation, as was provided, for all damages from the day of taking Kinardesle Castle, but had prorogued the meeting to the day of the Nativity of the Virgin (Sept. 8), and therefore in the meantime enjoins them to observe the truce with the Prince.

[4] Rymer's Fœdera, pp. 201, 202.

"Henry daily inclined more and more to his foreign favourites, to the injury of his subjects, and the great and just Hubert de Burgh had already fallen a sacrifice to his own integrity, and was a close prisoner in the Castle of Devizes. The English barons [1] began to confederate together, and the King, full of fears and suspicions, invited them to a grand meeting at London on the kalends of August. He had already deprived several barons of their estates to bestow them on the Poitevins who surrounded his court, and Richard Mareschal was now the object of his jealousy. The wife of Richard Earl of Cornwall (the King's brother) was the Earl Mareschal's sister, and when he paid her a visit on his way to the appointed meeting, she took him aside and informed that a plot had been laid to seize upon his person. The Earl immediately turned back, and never stopped till he found himself safe on the Border of Wales, where he was joined by others who had fallen equally with himself under the King's displeasure; amongst whom were Gilbert Basset, Richard Suard, and Walter de Clifford, with many other knights distinguished for their influence and personal bravery. The King then summoned the refractory barons to appear before him at Gloucester on the Sunday before the Assumption of the Virgin Mary, and on their refusal to obey, gave orders to invade and ravage their lands as the possessions of traitors to his crown. At the same time he declared them outlaws, and gave their confiscated estates to his Poitevins, on which Richard Mareschal and his friends entered into an alliance with the Prince of Wales.

"The King immediately marched to Hereford with a formidable army, consisting chiefly of foreigners, more especially of Flemings. He was at Hay Castle on the 2nd of September, when he sent messengers to Llywelyn to try to detach him from the confederacy. From Hereford he sent his defiance, or declaration of war, to the Earl Mareschal, and laid siege to one of his castles, but with so little success that he saw himself on the point of being obliged to retire from before it. Humiliated by this check, he opened negotiations with the Earl, offering, on condition the castle should be immediately placed in his hands, to take him again into favour, and to reform the corruptions in the government of which the barons complained, or to restore the castle in a fortnight. On these conditions the Earl gave up the castle, and the King appointed the Sunday before Michaelmas to receive the outlawed barons at Westminster. When that day arrived, the King had fulfilled none of his promises, and in defiance of the advice of his best counsellors, he treated with contempt the Earl's claim for the restitution of his castle. The latter took up arms and, after a very brief siege, made himself master of his own fortress. At the same time the aged justiciary, Hubert de Burgh, was carried away by force from his prison by some of his friends, who armed him according to his rank, and conducted him to the Border, where he joined the revolted barons, and strengthened their cause by his experience and influence, as well as by the sympathy excited by his injuries.

"The King was furious when he received intelligence of these events. He assembled in haste a formidable army at Gloucester, and marched with it to Hereford; but the barons had carried all their cattle and other effects from the open country into their castles, and, unable to support his vast host in a country which thus afforded no provisions, he retired to the Castle of Grosmont, intending to remain there some days, and, confident in his numbers, encamped negligently in the fields without the castle. The barons, who had good intelligence, were informed of his position; the Earl Mareschal refused to join in an attack upon the person of the King, but the other confederates marched during the night with a numerous army of English and Welsh, and at daybreak on the feast of St. Martin (November 11), fell upon the royal camp, drove away the knights and soldiers without striking a blow, and made themselves masters of above five hundred horses, and all the equipages and baggage of the camp. The King was safely lodged in the Castle of Grosmont, but he lost all his money and provisions, and many of his principal men were obliged to fly almost in a state of nudity."

After this reverse the King felt himself no longer secure at Grosmont, and retired to Gloucester, having garrisoned all the castles in his possessions on the Border with bands of hungry Poitevins and Flemings under the command of John de Monmouth and Raoul de Thony, to the latter of whom he had given the Castle of Matilda. These garrisons of strangers soon became the terror of the peasantry, for they did

---

[1] For a fuller account of these times, see Mr. Wright's History of Ludlow.

nothing but plunder and ravage the country round. But Henry's departure increased the boldness of the confederate barons, who now retaliated by invading the lands of John de Monmouth and the other partisans of the King. Richard Mareschal, at the head of the united army of the outlaws, marched towards Monmouth at the latter end of November, intending to lay siege to the castle, which was entrusted to the care of a Flemish knight, named Baldwin de Guines. While the army was moving to its quarters, the Earl, attended only by a hundred knights, approached to reconnoitre the castle. He was observed and recognised by Baldwin de Guines, who assembled a thousand of his bravest warriors, and sallied out to capture his enemy. The companions of Richard Mareschal advised him to make his escape with as much speed as possible; but their gallant leader told them that he had never yet turned his back on an enemy who offered him battle, and, he added, "I shall not change my custom to-day." For several hours, in spite of the inequality of numbers, the Earl Mareschal and his men defended themselves valiantly with their spears and swords. At length, despairing of overcoming the whole party collectively, Baldwin de Guines chose twelve of his companions to single out the Mareschal, while the rest were engaged in the attack upon his knights; and, although the Earl slew most of his assailants, his horse was at length killed under him, and he was thrown in his heavy armour on the ground. Baldwin de Guines, furious at his obstinate resistance, threw himself on the Earl, and tore his casque from his head with so much violence, that Richard's face was covered with blood; then, having placed him on a horse, he drew it by the bridle towards the castle of Monmouth, while some of his men held him and pushed him from behind. At this critical moment one of Richard Mareschal's arbalestriers, seeing the danger of his master, aimed an arrow at Baldwin de Guines, which pierced through his armour, made a dangerous wound in his breast, and stretched him apparently lifeless on the earth. His men, believing him dead, left their captive to attend to their lord; and at the same time the Earl Mareschal's army, having received intelligence of the combat, arrived at the spot. The soldiers of Baldwin de Guines now sought safety by flight, but when they came to the river which they had to pass, they found the bridge broken down, and a few only with their wounded leader reached the castle. The rest were either drowned in attempting to pass the river, or were slain by their pursuers, or were taken prisoners, and obliged to pay heavy ransoms for their liberty. The field of battle was covered with the dead. "From the time of this skirmish," says Matthew Paris, who is our authority for this episode in the Border history, "the Earl Mareschal, Gilbert Basset, Richard Suard, and the other exiles and those who were in league with them, laid fatal snares for the Poitevins who occupied the castles of the King of England, so that whenever one of them issued forth to pillage the country, they laid hold of him and would accept no other ransom than his head. It soon came to that point, that the roads and other places were strewed with the bodies of these foreigners, in such numbers that the air was corrupted by them."

The King, humiliated by these reverses, endeavoured vainly to entrap the Earl Mareschal by specious offers of pardon. His failure in this attempt, and the representations of his foreign favourites, embittered still more his hatred against the confederate barons. Henry held his Christmas at Gloucester, with a small attendance of English nobles, for he had been abandoned by most of the barons who had been with him at the memorable defeat at Grosmont. On the Monday after Christmas-day, John de Monmouth, the King's most zealous partisan in these parts, collected a large army to attack the Earl Mareschal by surprise. But his vigilant antagonist had received intimation of his design, and when the soldiers of John de Monmouth were making their way with difficulty through the intricacies of a forest they had to pass, the confederates fell upon them suddenly with terrible shouts, drove them out of the forest, and pursued them with so much fury, that John de Monmouth was almost the only one who escaped. Richard Mareschal, emboldened by his success, invaded the lands of John de Monmouth, and ravaged them with such persevering hostility, that "from a rich man he became suddenly poor and needy." At the same time his partisans carried on a similar kind of destructive warfare against the other royalists. Richard Suard burnt the lands of the King's brother, Richard Earl of Cornwall, near Brehull, rooting up and destroying utterly even the woods and single trees. They treated in the same manner the domain of

Segrave, belonging to the grand justiciary Stephen de Segrave, and a manor near it belonging to the Bishop of Winchester. who was one of Henry's evil counsellors. In the midst of these ravages, the confederates made a rule to injure none but the evil advisers of the King.

Soon after these occurrences, a little before the Octaves of the Epiphany (January 13th), Richard Mareschal and Prince Llywelyn, with their united armies, marched to Shrewsbury, destroying the country in their way. After having collected an immense booty, and having burnt a large part of the town of Shrewsbury, they returned into Wales. The King, finding it impossible to put a stop to these ravages, left Gloucester and went towards Winchester. Unable to succeed by open force, he had recourse to treachery, and a plot was formed in Ireland against the Earl, who, called thither to defend his positions in the sister island, became a victim to the treachery of his own friends. When the King heard of his death, he is said to have burst into tears, and to have declared the Earl of Pembroke had not left behind him a knight who was worthy even to be second to him in courage and military skill.

The death of this able baron was followed by a reconciliation between the King and the rest of the exiles. Among the first of those who were restored to favour was the aged justiciary, Hubert de Burgh. On the 16th of June, 1234, the King, when at Tewkesbury, took into his grace Gilbert Mareschal, Richard's brother and heir; and on the 30th day of the same month he concluded a truce with Llywelyn.[6] This was followed by a treaty of peace between Henry and the Welsh prince towards the end of November.

During the remainder of Llywelyn's life, his transactions with the English king were of a more pacific character. It appears, indeed, from a document bearing date the 18th of February, 1236,[7] that the Welsh prince had infringed the peace, or rather truce, concluded in the preceding year; but a new one was signed by the King at Tewkesbury on the 11th of July following,[8] when Llywelyn came to Shrewsbury and Wenlock to renew his oaths of allegiance and fidelity.[9] The truce was prolonged at the beginning of June, 1237, and again in March, 1238, the King being then at Tewkesbury, and in the July of the same year.[1] In the following year the King again quarrelled with the family of the Mareschals, who retired to their possessions on the Border. Soon afterwards the King treated with equal indignity Simon de Montfort, who was destined shortly to play so distinguished a part in the history of the time; and the same year Henry brought a new accusation against the aged Hubert de Burgh, which served as a pretext for extorting from him four of his castles, White Castle, Grosmont, Scenfrith, and "Hanfeld."[2] The two following years were still more fruitful in events which influenced the fate of the Border. On the 11th of April, 1240, Llywelyn died, and left his Principality to be contended for by his children, David and Griffith. The former called his brother to a pacific conference, and there treacherously seized upon him and committed him to close prison. Early in 1241, died Walter de Lacy, overcome with age and infirmities, leaving his extensive possessions to be divided among heiresses. Near the same time Gilbert Mareschal was slain at a tournament, and was succeeded in the title and estates, first by his brother Walter Mareschal, and then by the remaining brother Anselme, who died at the end of the year 1245. Thus two of the most powerful families on the Border became extinct.

At the latter end of October, 1240 (the Tuesday after St. Dunstan's day), the King renewed with David the truce, or peace, which had been made with Llywelyn, and in the following month we find the King and the Prince deciding by arbitration a dispute which had arisen between them. The domestic quarrels of the Welsh, as might be expected, did not fail to affect the peace of the Border. In the following spring David was at war with Ralph de Mortimer, and attempted to seize a ship belonging to the city of Chester.[3] At the same time Griffith and his friends were urging the King of England to interfere in his behalf, and release him from his chains. On the 11th and 12th of February, Henry was at Worcester,[4] called thither doubtlessly by the affairs of Wales, for not long afterwards he summoned all

---

[6] Rymer's Fœdera, pp. 212, 213.
[8] Rymer's Fœdera, p. 229.
[1] Rymer's Fœdera, pp. 232, 235.
[7] Rymer's Fœdera, p. 223.
[9] Rymer's Fœdera, p. 230.
[2] Matthew Paris, sub ann. 1239.
[3] Rymer's Fœdera, pp. 242, 243.
[4] Issues of the Exchequer, ed. by Devon, 1838, pp. 17, 18.

his fiefs who held of the Crown by military service, to assemble with arms and baggage at Gloucester at the beginning of autumn. On the 2nd of August he held a council at Shrewsbury, and, David having refused to attend, he ordered the army which he had taken with him to Shrewsbury to advance against his refractory nephew.[5] We find the King with his numerous and well provisioned host at Rhuddlan on the 31st of August.[6] The Prince, terrified by the formidable preparations of the invader, made no attempt to resist, but gave up his brother, with an earnest recommendation to the King to keep him closely confined, if he wished to retain Wales in peace. Henry willingly agreed to this condition, and Griffith with the Welsh hostages were sent to London and committed to safe custody in the Tower. David himself came to London in November, and took a solemn oath of allegiance and fidelity to the English crown.

Griffith remained in confinement till the year 1244, when David, having sufficiently strengthened his power in Wales, conceived the idea of withdrawing from his dependence on the crown of England. He appears to have been partly urged to this measure by the Pope, who was dissatisfied with the English, and absolved the Welsh from their oath to the King. Negotiations had been opened for the purpose of obtaining Griffith's liberty, but these having failed, he and the other hostages made an attempt to escape from the Tower. His companions succeeded in their enterprise, but Griffith fell from the wall to the ground, and, being fat and heavy, he was killed on the spot. This event occurred at the end of April:[7] it was followed by an active war between the Welsh and the English Lords of the Marches who were encouraged by the promises of the King to assist them. On the 15th of July, a truce appears to have been made,[8] but it was of short duration; for, immediately afterwards, to use the words of Matthew Paris, " the Welsh issuing from their retreats like a swarm of bees," spread desolation over the Border. The King, who was just returned from Scotland with a powerful army, instead of hastening to repress their rebellion, sent an insufficient force under Herbert Fitz Matthew, dispersed the rest of his host, and resigned himself to idle repose at London. On his arrival, Herbert found that Ralph de Mortimer and the Earl of Hereford, who had joined their forces to withstand the invaders, had sustained a severe defeat. The next day he made an attempt to retrieve the honour of the English, but with no better success; his army was almost destroyed, and he sought a precarious asylum in his castles. From this time the audacity of the Welsh knew no bounds. David formally withdrew himself from the allegiance of the King of England, and placed himself under the protection of the Pope; and Henry, in return, caused him to be excommunicated by his bishops on the 29th of November, and prepared to invade Wales in the following year.

On the 6th of January, 1245, the King summoned David and his adherents to appear in his court at Westminster, to make amends for the devastation which they had caused on the Borders of Wales.[9] On the 10th of the same month he sent orders to the justiciary of Ireland, Maurice Fitz Gerald, to invade the Welsh coasts. In March, an ineffectual attempt appears to have been made to negotiate.[1] But hostilities continuing, during Lent, a body of Welsh fell into an ambush in the neighbourhood of Montgomery, and above three hundred were slain by the garrison of that place. David revenged this check by a long series of sudden and sanguinary incursions, scarcely a night passing in which the Welsh did not enter some part of the Border, and put everything they met to fire and sword. In these invasions they were frequently repulsed by the Borderers; and on one occasion, the English having engaged the Welsh in a wooded pass, the brave Herbert Fitz Matthew was slain.[2]

Several complaints were laid against Prince David to the King by the barons whose land he had injured during his late depredations. The King not wishing to excite any alarm in the mind of the Prince whom he had marked for his prey, summoned his nephew to appear before him at Worcester, to answer the complaints of the Lords Marches and others. As the Prince paid no attention to his command, a second writ was issued by the King in 1241. In this, after reprimanding him for his neglect, " which," says the

---

[5] Matthew Paris, sub ann. 1241.   [6] Rymer's Fœdera, p. 243.   [1] Fœdera, p. 259.
[7] Rymer's Fœdera, p. 256.   [8] Ibid.   [2] Matthew Paris, sub ann. 1245.
[9] De homicidiis, incendiis, depraedationibus, &c. Fœdera, p. 258.

King, "has been thought by some premeditated," he directs him to appear at Shrewsbury on the fourth Sunday in Lent, before the Royal Commissioners; or to send proxies, with full powers, to answer all the complaints laid against him. On the 27th of March, another writ was issued to convoy him to Montfort Bridge for the same purpose. In the May following, the King sent Sir S. de Segrave to hold a court at Shrewsbury, to hear evidence and to give judgment in the cause between the Prince and the Lords Marches. This was afterwards adjourned, for the purpose of hearing further evidence. After this, the King sent solemn messengers, the Bishop of Lichfield, John Fitz Geoffrey, and Henry de Audley, to Shrewsbury, to meet the Prince, and to receive satisfaction from him for all the grievances of which complaint had been made against him. But David's intelligence in the English court, as well as the warnings of his own conscience, intimated to him the danger of putting himself into the King's power. David appears to have been aware that he would have been, in his turn, cast into prison, if he had ventured to enter the gates of Shrewsbury. Accordingly, he declined to meet the Royal Commissioners, or even to send any on his part. This produced an angry letter from the King, dated at Marlborough,[3] July 14, reciting the above particulars, and finally summoning David to attend him on the Feast of St. Peter ad Vincula, August the 1st.

This summons had perhaps no other view than the hopes of amusing David a little longer: for Henry was now preparing to enter Wales at the head of an army. Having assembled it at Gloucester, he marched to Shrewsbury, where he arrived before the 2nd of August, as we find him holding a council there, on that day, where he halted his army for a fortnight. The King and his barons, with the tenants by knight service and their retainers, would alone have made a formidable host. But besides these, here were also many of the Welsh nobles, who came to tender their services to the King of England, and to settle their differences with him and with the Marchers. Hither also repaired Senana,[4] the wife of the captive Griffith, to solicit the affairs of her husband. The negotiation between her and the English ministry did not occupy much time; and while it evinces the paltry venality of Henry, exhibits a curious picture of the indigence and want of specie which prevailed in the Principality. By deed, dated at Shrewsbury, on the Monday before the Assumption of the Virgin (Aug. 15), the King engages to procure the liberation of Griffith for the sum of six hundred marks, and the restitution of his inheritance for three hundred more : of which sum one third part is to be paid in money, the remainder in cattle and horses, to be appraised by "lawful men," and to be delivered to the sheriff of Shropshire, at Shrewsbury, for his Majesty's use. Several of the chief Marchers and Welsh nobles, as Ralph de Mortimer, Walter de Clifford, Roger de Montalt, seneschall of Chester; Griffith ap Madoc, of Bromfield; and others who were then at Shrewsbury, also give their security for these payments. Every thing, in short, was conspiring to render David an easy prey to his uncle Henry; who, leaving Shrewsbury, proceeded to Chester; and having advanced into Wales as far as Rhuddlan Castle, the Prince found it necessary to submit, and by deed executed at Alnet, on the river Elwy, near St. Asaph (Aug. 29), and confirmed by him in the King's tent at Rhuddlan, two days later, also to surrender all the lands which his father, Llywelyn, had wrested from the late King in the war between him and his barons; also to resign the territory of Englesmere, and to submit all differences between him and Griffith to the English courts of judicature.[3]

These concessions, far from satisfying the cupidity, or interesting the generosity of Henry, only inflamed his desire for more.

Amongst the muniments of the Earl of Bridgewater is another charter of David, making further grants to the King of England. It has no date, but belongs to this or the following year, as one of the witnesses, Hugh de Albini, Earl of Arundel, died in 1243. In the charter executed at Alnet, David

[3] Powell, p. 355.

[4] She was also of royal descent : her father Caradoc being grandson of Rodri, Lord of Anglesey, a younger son of Owain Gwynnedd the Great, King of North Wales. From Griffith, brother to this lady, proceeded a line of posterity, which after seven descents assumed the surname of Wynn, in the person of John Wynn of Gwydir, grandfather of the famous Sir John Wynn, and ancestor, through females, of the present Lord Gwydir and Sir Watkin Williams Wynn, Bart.

promises to restore Monthaut (Mold); this states him to *have restored* it: that promises to surrender to the King all the homages which King John had; this speaks of them as *being so surrendered*. The former charter speaks of the detention of Griffith by David; from the silence of this deed on that head, it may be concluded that he was now in the custody of the King.

Henry having obtained possession of the person of Griffith, no longer regarded the solemn contract into which he had entered at Shrewsbury with his wife Senana; but committed him to the Tower of London, where he perished (March 1, 1243-4) in endeavouring to make his escape. Weary of his tedious confinement, to which neither the company of his consort, with which he was indulged, nor the liberal allowance of a noble (6*s.* 8*d.*) a day, which he received from the King, could reconcile him; he endeavoured to obtain his liberty by letting himself from the window by a rope made of the hanging of his apartment and the furniture of his bed; but the weight of his corpulent and bulky person broke the rope, and the next morning he was found dead in the Tower-ditch by the guards, a miserable and lamentable sight, his head being literally forced into his body by the violence of the fall.[1]

Griffith thus removed; his son,[6] the companion of his prison, detained in stricter confinement; and David childless; the King of England no longer concealed his intentions of utterly subjugating the Principality. He even conferred upon his eldest son, afterwards King Edward I., then a child of four years old, the title of *Prince of Wales*,[7] together with the dominions belonging to that title; and though David, in resentment of this insult, withdrew his allegiance, and threw himself into the arms of the Pope, he did not desist from his pretensions. In the Lent of 1245, we find the two nations in arms at Montgomery[8] and elsewhere; and Henry commanded his army to meet on the 1st of July,[9] for the purpose of subduing the country. He had not, however, himself left London by that time; for on that very day he writes from Westminster to the justice of Chester, and to the sheriff of Staffordshire and Shropshire, commanding the latter to raise in his bailiwick 50 oxen and fat cows, 1000 quarters of wheat, and 500 of oats, and to deliver them at Chester by the feast of St. Peter ad Vincula (Aug. 1), or within the Octaves of the said feast, against the expedition of the King's army in Wales;[1] and three days later, he again writes to the same persons, directing the sheriff to provide 1000 bacons by the same time, for the same purpose, and adding that he will undertake to pay for them.[2] Notwithstanding these precautions, however, the army appears to have been wretchedly supplied. Matthew Paris[3] has preserved a letter written by a nobleman in the English army, dated Sept. 24, descriptive of the want of necessaries which prevailed in the camp,[4] and of a slight engagement between a detachment of the Welsh on one side, and of three hundred Welshmen, Marchers of Cestreshire and Salopesburgshire on the other, to gain possession of an Irish vessel, laden with provisions, which had been stranded.

A.D. 1246.—In the spring of this year Prince David ap Llywelyn, broken in spirit and tormented by his subjects, died at his palace at Aber. He was buried with his father at Aber Conway. In this season of common calamity, the Welsh nobility immediately elected Prince Llywelyn ap Gruffydd, the nephew of the late prince, to the vacant throne, giving him the strongest assurance of perpetual allegiance. The wisdom of the choice was evinced in the noble stand Llywelyn made in defence of the liberty of his country. The firmness of his mind and his dignified deportment raised him in the eyes of his enemies, to whom he spoke in the

---

[3] Math. Paris, sub. ann.

[6] This was his eldest son Owen. He was soon after released out of prison, and "became faithful to the king." Pat. 29 Hen. III. Leland, v. 45.

[7] "Intituled his eldest son Edward to the Principality of Wales." Dr. Powell's History, 1584, p. 309; quoting the records in the Tower, 29 Hen. III. I cannot find this fact in any of our contemporary historians.

[8] Math. Paris, p. 654.   [9] *Ibid.,* 660.

[1] Claus. 29 Hen. III. m. 7. in Dodsworth's Collections, vol. 108.

[2] *Ib.* in coll. W. Mytton.   [3] P. 682.

[4] One of his courtiers, then in the camp, most pathetically describes the miseries of the English armies. In a letter written to his friends, dated September, 1245, he states: " The King with his army lieth at Gannock, fortifying of that strong castell. We lie in our tents, thereby *watching, fasting, praying,* and *freezing* with cold ! We watch for fear of the Welshmen, who are wont to invade us and come upon us by night-time. We fast for want of meat, for the halfpenny loaf is worth fivepence. We pray to God to sende us home againe speedily. . We starve for cold, wanting our winter garments, having no more but a thin linnen cloth betwyxt us and the wind."—See Matthew of Westminster, f. 294.

language of a free and independent prince, whom they attempted by cruelty to deprive of the dominion of his ancestors.

We learn from the Sebright MSS. that Prince Llywelyn was at this time with Henry III. in London, where he had been for some months; and that upon hearing the news of his elevation to the Principality he stole privately away.

A.D. 1251.—An arbitrary grant of all the lands between Chester and Conway, not included in his realm or jurisdiction, was made by Henry III. as an appendage to his son, and made " to appertain to the sword and dignity of Chester," of which place his son was lately made Earl. Prince Edward farmed all this land to Adam de la Zouch, an English baron, for the small sum of one hundred marks.[1] This baron greatly oppressed the country, and the cruel laws of England at that time so pressed the natives, that they had neither spirit nor opportunity to carry on commerce nor to cultivate the lands, for by this grant they were deprived of the usual pasturage for their cattle, and they were, in consequence, in constant danger of famine. It was not in the nature of Llywelyn, when the dearest concerns of his people were mingled with his own, to remain inactive or unmoved by the repeated solicitations to attempt one more effort to throw of the English yoke. Driven by necessity and invigorated by despair, Llywelyn at length determined to rescue his country from its vile dependence on England, or bravely perish amidst the ruins of its fortunes.

Llywelyn assembled his armies and prepared for the invasion of England. In order to raise the hopes and pious confidence, as well as to diffuse through every bosom the prospect of better days, Llywelyn addressed his countrymen in the following consolatory and animatory language :—

" Thus far," said he, " the Lord God of Hosts hath helped us; for it must appear to all that the advantages we have obtained are not to be ascribed to our own strength, but to the favour of God, who can as easily save by a *few* as by *many*. How should we, a poor, weak, and unwarlike people, compared with the English, dare to contend with so mighty a power if God did not patronise our cause? His eye has seen our affliction; not only those injuries which we have suffered from Geoffrey de Langley, but those also which we have received from other cruel instruments of Henry and of Edward. From this moment our all is at stake; if we fall into the hands of the English we are to expect no mercy. Let us then stand firm to each other! It is our union alone that can make us invincible! You see in what manner the King of England treats his own subjects; how he seizes their estates, impoverishes their families, and alienates their minds. Will he, then, spare us, after all the provocation we have given him, and the farther acts of hostility and ravage which we meditate against him? No; it is evidently his intention to blot out our name from under the face of heaven. Is it not better, then, at once to die and go to God, than to live for a time at the capricious will of another, and at last to suffer some ignominious death assigned us by an insulting enemy ?"

Animated by this oration, the Welsh infested the English Border with incessant inroads, and by fire and sword they rendered the frontier a scene of desolation.

The oppressions exercised by Henry towards the inhabitants of Wales, as well as his own subjects, and the lavish and injudicious profusion towards his favourites, which compelled him to apply, and to apply in vain, to his parliament for assistance, and the projects he had in view had well nigh terminated in the subversion of the monarchy. The proceedings of the "Mad Parliament," held at Oxford, June 11, 1258, by which the King was virtually deposed, and the regal power vested in the hands of a despotic junto, are too well known to be here detailed. In the meanwhile, Llywelyn, the young Prince of Wales, whose character was not less vigorous and active than that of his grandfather and namesake, had succeeded in deposing[2] his brother and colleague in the Principality. Being now more at liberty to act for himself, he became impatient of the narrow limits within which he was confined by the late treaties, and was exasperated by the insults and oppressions exercised over his subjects by the bailiffs and officers of Prince Edward. Hence he

[1] Rymer's Fœdera, p. 43.

[2] He threw him into Dolbadarn Castle, on the Lake of Llanberis, in the very bosom of Snowdon. Leland describes its situation very precisely, and had certainly been there. "Dolebaterne, a v mile from Caerarvon by est south est, hard by [a] Llynne : it is on a rok bytwixt two linnys : ther is yet a pece of a toure, wher Owen Goch, brother to Lluelen last prince, was yn prison." Itin., v. 45.

was engaged in almost continual warfare with the English Marchers. Though he was by no means deficient in policy, and knew how to recede as well as to advance, his incursions were occasionally intercepted by offers of satisfaction, and often were the King and parliament of England obliged to direct their attention to his proceedings.

A.D. 1256.—Prince Edward, who two years before had been created Earl of Chester, came to the city on the festival of St. Kenelan. He was met on the road by the clergy and citizens in grand procession, who conducted him to the city. He stayed there three days receiving the homage and fealty of the nobles of Cheshire and Wales, after which, having visited his castles and land in the latter provinces, he returned through Chester and went to Darnhall.[7]

A.D. 1257.—The King summoned his barons, spiritual and temporal, to meet him at Chester, with their vassals, on a certain day, in order to revenge the inroads of the Welsh and invade their territories.[8] He now assumed his father's duties, and made heavy exactions upon the territory between Chester and Conway. Thus this young prince soon became intimately acquainted with the country which was afterwards to form so important a portion of his dominions. Henry III. again resolved to invade Wales in person during the year 1257, but after a fruitless effort, at the head of a powerful force, he was compelled to retreat ingloriously to Chester with the shattered remains of his army. He also advanced a second time in this year against Llywelyn, but without success.

A.D. 1264.—During the King's war with the barons, William de le Zouch, then justice of Chester, and the citizens, fearing lest the city should be besieged either by the barons or the Welsh, began to render it more secure by digging a deep ditch, for which purpose they destroyed some houses and gardens belonging to the Abbey of Chester in Bogg-lane.[9] It appears that the fears of the citizens were not without cause, but their precautions seem to have been ineffectual, for we are told by our historians, that the Earl of Derby, in the course of the same year, came to Chester with a great army, and took possession of the city and castle for the barons.[1]

On the 7th of June, we find the King hastening to make fresh preparations for the invasion of Wales. About the beginning of July, he summoned all his nobles and military fiefs to assemble on the Border;[2] and on the 20th of August he was at Chester.[3] Instead of marching into the interior, Henry began by cutting off all communication between the Welsh and their neighbours; and by this measure, assisted with the ravages of war, he reduced a great portion of the country to a state of extreme misery. He encamped on the northern coast at "Gannoc" (the name given by the English at that period to Diganwy, in Caernarvonshire), where he spent nearly three months in fortifying a strong castle, which became, as Matthew Paris observes, a sore in the eyes of the Welshmen. At the approach of winter, the King, taking a lesson by his former dilemma, left the castle well stored and garrisoned, and returned to London. The campaign had been most disastrous to the Welsh; vast numbers had fallen by the swords of the English, and of the Irish who had been landed on their coasts, and the numbers who perished by starvation and by the hardships of war were scarcely less numerous. The greater part of those who remained were reduced to the greatest distress. On the 10th of November, the King was at Worcester, where he issued a new proclamation forbidding his subjects to hold any communication with his enemies the Welsh.[4] At the beginning of spring, David, the cause of all these disasters, died, heart-broken, as it was said, by the misfortunes of his countrymen. They were too much exhausted to continue their hostilities against the English, and, for two years the whole of North Wales remained in a state of extreme desolation.

---

[7] Extract from the Chronicle of Chester Abbey, in Bp. Gastrale Notitia.

[8] Mr. Pennant justly observes, that Chester appears to have been a constant rendezvous of troops for every expedition on that side of the kingdom, from the time of the Romans to the reign of William III.

[9] On the Patent Roll of the 52 Henry III. (1267) is an order for enquiring into the extent of the damage, and making compensation; the Justice having promised the abbot an equivalent for the damage.

[1] Holinshed.

[2] Matth. Paris, sub ann. 1245.

[3] Rymer's Fœdera, p. 263.

[4] Rymer's Fœdera, p. 264.

The Welsh were moved by a two-fold incitement to take part with the English barons in the great struggle which was now approaching. The plunder of the lands and possessions of the adverse party was a sufficient temptation to them to join in the quarrel, as they had done before on similar occasions; but at the present time the extortions and oppressions under which the English themselves suffered, pressed with double weight on the unfortunate inhabitants of the Principality, who had been placed at the mercy of the King and his favourites by their disastrous war under David. The country was distributed like Turkish pashaliks, to the highest bidders, who ground the wretched inhabitants to dust, that they might extract from them their last piece of money to pour into the King's treasury, and into their own. It was thus thus Alan de la Zouch, who had succeeded John de Grey in the government of the country bordering on Cheshire, drew in 1251, eleven hundred marks of annual revenue from a district which, in the time of his predecessor, had paid only five hundred. In the year following, when Alan de la Zouch passed through St. Albans with a number of carriages heavily laden with the produce of his extortions, which he was carrying to the treasury, he declared publicly that the whole of Wales was now at length reduced to absolute obedience to the English laws, and that it was in a state of profound tranquillity.[5]

But this peace, although it lasted for two or three years afterwards, could not be of long duration; it was the silence of despair. After having supported the tyranny of a succession of paltry exactors, the patience of the Welsh was at length exhausted, and in 1256 they were forced into rebellion by the oppressions of Geoffrey de Langley, then collector of the revenues for the King. At first the rising appears to have been partial, and it was disowned by their Prince Llywelyn, who demanded a personal interview with the King, who was at Gloucester on 22nd of July,[6] probably on his way to the Border for that purpose. But the meeting did not take place, and as winter (the season most favourable to the Welsh) approached, the insurrection became more general. They began by attacking the possessions of Prince Edward, to whom the government of Wales had been entrusted. Their first efforts were attended with complete success, for they were not only favoured by the unusual humidity of the weather which rendered it impossible to enter Wales with a regular army, but they appear to have been secretly assisted and encouraged by the English barons. Nevertheless, it was Peter de Montfort (one of Simon's sons), who was governor of Abergavenny, who made the most vigorous resistance against their inroads. On the Thursday after the Feast of St. Matthew (September 21st), the Welsh advanced in considerable force against the castles held by this baron, who, assisted by John de Grey, Roger de Mortimer, Reginald Fitz Peter, Humphrey de Bohun, and other Lords of the Marches, defeated them in several encounters;[7] yet not many days after, Peter de Montfort gives the King an account of these successes, he writes another letter, begging for speedy assistance, and describing his own position as being extremely critical.[8] The retreat of Prince Edward increased the courage of the Welsh, who crossing the northern Border, carried their devastations up to the walls of Chester. At the same time they drove from his lands their countryman Griffith de Bromfield, who had merited their hatred by his obsequiousness to their English oppressors. During the winter and the following spring the Marches of Wales continued thus to present a scene of rapine and bloodshed.

It is said that at first the King refused to pay any attention to the messages of his son Edward and the barons of the Border, alleging that they ought to be able to take care of what was their own. But, on the 18th of July, he summoned a great army to assemble on the Border in two divisions, one to join the English barons on the borders of Herefordshire and Gloucestershire, while the other repaired to Chester, where he was to join them in person,[9] and on the 11th of September we find him encamped at Diserth, in Flintshire.[1] The Welsh, however, had carried into the most inaccessible part of Snowdon their families and flocks, and Henry's expedition had so little effect, that his disappointment threw him into a fever, by which he was confined to his bed for some time after his return. During the remainder of the autumn, and the following winter, the Marches continued to be in a lamentable state of distraction, and several castles on the southern

[5] Matth. Paris, sub ann. 1251-2.
[6] Rymer's Fœdera, i. p. 344.
[7] Rymer's Fœdera, i. p. 339.
[8] Rymer's Fœdera, i. p. 341.
[9] Rymer's Fœdera, i. p. 361; Matth. Paris.
[1] Rymer's Fœdera, p. 363.

Borders were taken and plundered, and some of them occupied, by the Welsh.[1] Evan Griffith de Bromfield, who had suffered so much for his fidelity to the English, found it necessary to desert the King, and was received into the confederacy of the Welsh barons. At the beginning of the year 1258, the Marches of Wales were literally reduced to a desert.[2]

The time was now come when the English barons found it necessary to make open resistance to the King and his foreign favourites; and the supposition that the Welsh were in secret league with the former seems to be confirmed by the circumstance that they now made eager proposals for peace. It may be observed that their ravages had extended chiefly to the lands and possessions of Prince Edward and of some of the Lords Marchers who were zealous royalists. In the spring of 1258, Henry again summoned his baronage to attend him into Wales, but they answered with complaints of the fatigues and losses which they had already sustained in this service. Yet, after a brief and stormy meeting at Westminster, they all came in warlike array to the parliament held at Oxford in July, with the excuse that it was necessary they should be in readiness to march against the Welsh. This parliament may be considered the proclamation of war against the barons. The messengers of Prince Llywelyn were conducted to it by Peter de Montfort, and a truce for one year was concluded on the 17th of July.[4] Yet on the 18th of August the Welsh had already infringed the truce, and Peter de Montfort and James de Alditheley were sent to require amends. After this the peace was observed with little interruption for some years.

Llywelyn prevented the storm just ready to burst upon him, by soliciting a renewal of the truce, which was accordingly protracted to Midsummer. Three days before its expiration, the King, taking advantage of the pacific state of his dominions, embarked for France. Lywelyn availed himself of this absence, in concert, as it seems, with Montfort, to violate the peace between the two countries. For it appears, from a writ of the King on the Close Rolls of his 47th year, 1262, addressed to Ralph Bassett, of Drayton, that, upon his landing at Dover, with his queen and retinue, on Wednesday, in the Eve of St. Thomas the Apostle, Dec. 20, he was informed at Canterbury that Llywelyn and his " accomplices," unmindful of their fealty pledged to him, and in violation of the truce, had hostilely siezed certain castles, &c., of his liege subjects. In consequence of this, he summons Bassett to be at Hereford on the third day after this instant Epiphany, Jan. 9, 1262-3; and he afterwards called upon certain of the Lords Marchers to meet James de Aldithle at Ludlow, on the Octaves of Purification.[5] So furious was this invasion, that it was found necessary to recall Prince Edward from the continent. He returned immediately; and in the same month in which his father summoned his army to Hereford, we find the Prince writing to Griffith ap Gwenwynwyn, Prince of Powis, enjoining him to assemble his forces, and attack Llywelyn for having invaded the Marches.[6] The English prince was not contented with these commands to others. He repaired himself with promptitude towards the country which most demanded his presence; and, on the 15th of April, 1263, at the latest, he visited Shrewsbury; whence he writes to his royal father, requesting his interference to compel the Bishop of Hereford[7] to residence in his castle of Lidbury North, for the greater defence of that country. And though this gallant prince, pushing his advantages, soon compelled Llywelyn to take refuge in the fastnesses of Snowdon, yet such was the ferment into which the kingdom was thrown by the artifices of Leicester and his party, that Edward was unable effectually to restrain the incursions of the Welsh, being under a necessity of repairing hastily to London to secure the throne which he was born to inherit.

The struggles made by the King to free himself from the disgraceful shackles imposed upon him

---

[2] In 1258, William de Abetot was slain at the siege of Ewyas Castle.

[3] Matth. Paris, sub ann. 1257.   [4] Rymer's Fœdera, i. p. 372.

[5] Roger and Hugh de Mortimer, John Fitz Alan, both the John Le Stranges, elder and younger, Hamo Le Strange, Thomas Corbet, Griffin ap Wennewin, Fulke Fitz Warin, Ralph le Botiler, and Walter de Dunstanville.

[6] Dugd. MSS. B. i.

[7] This was Peter, a Burgundian. He was soon after taken prisoner by the rebels in his cathedral church, spoiled of all his treasures, and carried to Ordeley Castle. Matth. Paris, p. 992. For Ordeley, Lelands reads Erdesley, Baskervile's Castle. It is near Kinnersley.

by the Constitutions of Oxford, divided the whole nation into two parties; royalists, and those who adhered to the faction of the barons. Shropshire, in general, espoused the cause of the monarchy, and was, therefore, grievously infested by the incursions of Llywelyn, who entered its western border in the beginning of February with a large army. He had succeeded in persuading Griffith ap Gwenwynwyn, Prince of Powis, to desert the royal standard, and co-operate with him in this foray, which was undertaken with the avowed design of laying waste the March, especially the lands of Roger de Mortimer, that firm supporter of the throne,[s] and indeed Llywelyn's rival for the Cambrian sceptre: and it was with the view, probably, of co-operating with his active ally, that the rebel leader, Montfort, marched his army from Worcester to the Border counties, in the spring of 1264. He took Bridgnorth, and afterwards Shrewsbury, with very little resistance.

These acts of insolence, aggravated by declarations of regard and veneration for the royal person, were quickly followed by the fatal *mise*, or Convention, of Lewes, May 14, which threw the King a prisoner into the hands of the Earl of Leicester, making this latter master, for a time, of the whole of England.

The refractory Earl of Leicester entered into a conspiracy with Llywelyn, and they invested England with an army of thirty thousand men, and, advancing into Cheshire, committed great depredations upon the Earl of Chester's territories, and took the Earl himself prisoner.

Simon de Montfort, the eldest son of Simon, the potent Earl of Leicester, met Llywelyn at Hawarden [*] Castle, Flintshire, where they entered into a treaty establishing peace between Cheshire and North Wales, in order to promote their respective designs; and in the year following, 1265, on the 22nd of June, Montfort obliged the captive monarch to make an absolute cession to the Welsh prince not only of this fortress,[1] but, what was still more mortifying to Henry's feelings, he was obliged to make an absolute cession of the whole sovereignty of Wales, and its baronial suffrages, with several others of his unjustly acquired possessions on the Borders. By this treaty, the barons were compelled to make their submission for their tenures, to Llywelyn, the Prince of Wales, instead of to Henry, the King of England.

The war between the King and the barons began on the Border, where the partisans of each had numerous castles. Roger de Mortimer raised his tenantry, and invaded and ravaged the land of Simon de Montfort. The latter, who had already been affianced to Llywelyn's daughter, whom he afterwards married; sent also a portion of the baronial army, to retaliate on the possessions of Mortimer, and they laid siege to Wigmore Castle. They seized upon Macy de Bezile, a foreigner whom the King had made sheriff of Gloucestershire, and the obnoxious Bishop of Hereford, whom they dragged from the altar of his cathedral church, and imprisoned them both in the castle of Eardisley.[2] Macy de Bazile was taken in the castle of Gloucester, after an obstinate defence. Simon de Montfort, who had directed the siege, then marched with his army to Worcester, which, already taken and rudely treated by Robert de Ferrers, Earl of Derby, willingly opened its gates to the barons. From thence Montfort marched to Bridgenorth and Shrewsbury, both of which he garrisoned against the King. The citizens of Shrewsbury shut their gates, and at first defended themselves stoutly, but hearing that the Welsh were approaching on the other side, they gave up the town.

Towards the end of February, 1264, Edward, with an army consisting in a great measure of foreigners, hastened to the Border, to relieve Roger de Mortimer, who was closely besieged in Wigmore Castle. Edward came to Hereford, and took the castles of Hay, Huntingdon, and Brecknock, which he gave to Roger de Mortimer, who fled secretly from Wigmore to join him at Hereford; but Wigmore Castle fell into the hands of the barons,[3] who then pursued the Prince from Hereford to Gloucester, where he took refuge in the castle, which was delivered up to him by Roger de Clifford. The barons immediately took possession

---

[s] These particulars, new to history, are derived from the singular attestation of a deed belonging to Alberbury priory in the archives of All Souls' College, Oxford, for which, as for innumerable other favours, the authors of the Salopian History acknowledge their obligation to the Rev. Edward Williams, formerly Fellow of that College.

[*] Annales Cestrenses, quoted by Carte, vol. ii. p. 151.
[1] Rymer's Fœdera, i. 814.
[2] Rishanger's Continuat. of Matth. Paris; Robert of Gloucester, pp. 535, 537; Rishanger's Chron., ed. Halliwell, p. 11.
[3] Chron. Abendon. ed. Halliwell, p. 16.

of the town, and after some bickerings and negotiations, Edward agreed to make his peace with them, and swore to observe the statutes which had been made at Oxford. The baronial army then moved towards London. No sooner were they gone, than Edward showed how little he intended to keep his engagements; as a punishment for having received his enemies, he treacherously imprisoned many of the burgesses, severely amerced the town, and hanged the porters who had opened the gates, one of whom was named Hobkin of Ludlow;[4] and then he marched towards Northampton, ravaging the lands of the barons as he went. On the other hand, Llywelyn and his Welshmen, who had been called to the aid of the barons when they marched against Roger de Mortimer, laid waste the lands of Prince Edward, and took and destroyed his two castles of Gannoc (Diganwy) and Diserth. A little before Easter they defeated, near Kerry, the younger John L'Estrange, who held Montgomery for the King; but shortly afterwards they received a severe check at Clun.

These events were followed by a short cessation of arms, during which some of the barons deserted their cause, and the King began to take courage. Next came the attack upon Northampton, the siege of Rochester, and the decisive battle of Lewes, which placed the King and his son Edward at the mercy of the barons.

After the battle of Lewes, the Marchers were the first to raise their heads in opposition to the party who were now in power. In the autumn of 1264, the most influential of the Border barons, Roger de Mortimer, James de Aldittheley or Audeley, Roger de Leyburne, Roger de Clifford, Hamo L'Estrange, Hugh and Roger de Turberville, and others, were in arms, and were encouraged and supported by the Earl of Gloucester. Simon de Montfort immediately marched with his army towards the Border, taking with him the King and Prince Edward, who had been kept a prisoner at Dover. They were at Worcester on the 15th of December.[5] From thence Simon de Montfort marched to Hereford, and joined himself with the Welsh under Llywelyn, his ally. They took Hay Castle, and Simon de Montfort invaded the lands of the Mortimers; captured, first, Richard's Castle, which he delivered to his partisan, John Fitz John; and, afterwards, the castle of Ludlow, and pursued Roger de Mortimer to Montgomery Castle, where the latter was obliged to make his peace.[6]

One of the first steps adopted by Montfort for the consolidation of his authority, was to summons a parliament upon a new system. Having appointed conservators of the peace in every county, he directed to them writs in the King's name, commanding them to send four of the most "loyal and discreet" knights of their respective bailiwicks, to meet at London on the Octave of the Holy Trinity.[7] During this eclipse of the monarchy several of the principal barons of Shropshire, as Roger de Mortimer, James de Audley, Roger de Leyburne, Roger de Clifford, Hamo le Strange, John, Robert, and Hugh de Turberville took up arms to rescue their captive sovereign, in whose name letters were written to them and their co-Marchers from Worcester, December 15, commanding them to desist. In these, the King was made to express his astonishment that they should permit their men to make prey, damage, and tort (wrong): the more so, as he reminds them that certain of their number were gone to Kenilworth to speak with "our dear son Edward" (where, be it noted, this *dear son* was in prison), and to make a firm peace. The Lords Marches knew too well who it was that dictated this letter, to pay any regard to its contents: they continued their hostilities against Montfort; who, uniting his forces with Llywelyn, took Hereford, Hay, and Ludlow Castle, and ravaged the estates of Mortimer. But this transient interruption to the despotism of the rebellious Earl only served to strengthen his power, and the barons laid down their arms in pursuance of a treaty concluded at Montgomery.[8]

---

4 " Sir Roger of Clifford tho porter's vaste nom
    That porters were atte gate tho Jon Giffard in com,
    As Hobekin of Ludlowe, and is felawes also,
    And let hom upe the west gate an-honge bothe to."
                                    Robert of Gloucester, p. 544.
5 Rymer's Fœdera, i. p. 449.
6 Rishanger's Chron., ed. Halliwell, p. 35; Ejusd. contin. Matth. Paris.

7 In fact, this parliament never met. At the commencement of the next year, Leicester modelled it upon somewhat more of a popular basis; commanding two knights from each county instead of four, and directing certain cities and boroughs in his interest to send each two deputies.
8 Rymer's Fœdera, sub ann.

In consequence of this incurable loyalty of Shropshire, a considerable portion of it was upon the point of being severed from the crown of England.[*] Llywelyn had now a prospect of accomplishing that object which his grandfather had once transiently enjoyed, the including of Shrewsbury within the Principality of Wales. The critical ground on which the Earl of Leicester stood, compelled him to use every means to attach his allies to his cause; and Llywelyn was now to be gratified for the part he had taken in the contest. Besides agreeing to give him his daughter in marriage, the Earl expedited to him enormous grants by the royal authority, of which he then held the supreme control. By letters patent, dated at Hereford, June 22, 1265, the captive king, in consideration of a fine of thirty thousand marks, which in all probability was never paid, or meant to be paid, is made to "remit his anger" against the British prince, whom he distinctly terms "Prince of Wales:" wills, that all "literal obligations" (the charters, no doubt, described above) which the said Prince, or David his predecessor, have made to "Us" against their rights and liberties, be annulled; grants to the Prince of Wales the "lordship" of all the great men of Wales, with the "Principality;" also Castle Matilda, the hundred of Ellesmere, and the castle of Hawarden, and that of Montgomery, when it shall be subdued (to which the King promises to be assisting) : the Prince is also to have the lordship of Wytenton Castle, so as the heir of the said castle shall do to the Prince the service which his ancestors have been accustomed to perform and ought to have performed to the predecessors of the said Prince. Nor was this all; for, if we may believe a contemporary writer,[1] the Earl of Leicester also signed to the Prince a charter, under the royal seal, of all the lands to which his predecessors might have claimed any title by the most ancient pretensions, "jure vetustissimo :" and Henry was obliged to consent that the future boundaries of Wales should include the country in a direct line from Holt to Shrewsbury.[2]

Whether Llywelyn would have elevated Pengwern to its ancient rank as a metropolis, or whether its English inhabitants would have submitted to what they must have regarded as a foreign yoke, it is vain to inquire. The victory gained at Evesham, August 5, by the gallantry of Prince Edward, who had effected his escape[3] from Hereford, had confederated that county with those of Worcester, Salop, and Chester, their villages and towns, cities and castles;[4] restored the royal authority, and of course annulled all the proceedings which Henry had been compelled to sanction during his captivity : a single instrument of a private nature will show us the dreadful condition into which the kingdom was thrown by these sudden revolutions of the state :—"August the 14th, 49 Hen. III. Prince Edward at Chester grants and assigns ' in tenenciam' to his beloved and faithful Sir Ivo Paunton all the lands in Ashele which Hugh Bedell our enemy had, to hold during pleasure, *unless any one* who was personally present with us in the conflict at Evesham, on the 4th of August, shall *first* have laid his hands (*manus posuerit*) thereupon."[5]

Simon de Montfort then moved with his royal prisoners towards the south, but he was soon called back by new movements on the Border. The Earl of Gloucester had entirely broken his alliance with the party in power, and was, with John Giffard, gathering strength in the forest of Dean ; Roger de Mortimer again raised the standard of revolt at Wigmore ; Robert Walerand, Warine de Bassingburn, and others seized upon the castle of Bristol ; and at the same time two powerful nobles who had escaped from the battle of Lewes, and taken refuge on the continent, John de Warrenne, Earl of Surrey, and William de Valence, Earl

[*] Matth. Paris, sub ann. 1265.   [1] T. Wikes, p. 69.

[2] This was, in fact, restoring the ancient limits of Wales. Dr. Powell, in his learned notes on the Itinerary of Wales by Giraldus, lib. ii. cap. 11, writes, "where Giraldus says that the Dee is the boundary between Cambria and Lloegria (England) ; this is to be understood from Hilcuria to Castle Lyons : but from thence to the south the boundary is a line drawn from the same castle to Pengwern Powys, i.e. Salop ; and afterwards to Castle Isabel on Severn's bank ; so that the cantreds of Trefred and Maelor are included within Wales ; as may be seen in the articles of pacification made at Montgomery between Henry III. and Llywelin ap Griffith." See also Yorke's Royal Tribes, p. 58.

[3] See the curious account of this escape in the Chronicle of the Mortimers. Dugdale's Monastic., art. Wigmore. It took place on Thursday in Whitsun week about the hour of vespers. Rymer, vol. i. p. 810. Matth. Paris places it two days later, viz. on the vigil of the Trinity, p. 662.

[4] Matth. Paris, 997.

[5] Lacon evid. 1583. in Dugd. MSS. vol. 39. Ashm. Libr. What confusion this must have created in the country, when every royalist thought himself at liberty to seize upon the possessions of the other party !

of Pembroke, landed at Pembroke and joined the confederacy.   Simon de Montfort, after holding a council at Oxford, marched again to Worcester.   The barons of the opposite party attempted to oppose him, and broke down the bridges over the Severn, but the Prince of Wales had also called together his army, and the Borderers were obliged to make their submission, and were again deprived of many of their castles.   A temporary reconciliation was at the same time effected between the Earl of Gloucester and Simon de Mortimer.   But this was of very short duration, and Simon was soon recalled to the Marches.[6]

Simon de Montfort was again at Worcester in May, and on the 18th of that month he was at Hereford, with the King and Prince Edward, and he remained there till the latter end of June.[7]   A plot was formed by the Marchers to deliver the Prince from his confinement.   Roger de Mortimer, one day towards the end of May, sent the Prince a present of a very swift steed,[8] with a private intimation that he should ask permission of his keepers to try it on a certain day on the Widemarsh (Wydmersh), and that the moment he saw a person on a white horse make a signal from the hill towards Tullington, he should leave his attendants and ride in that direction at his utmost speed.   The required permission was easily obtained, and on the day appointed the stratagem was carried into effect, and the knight who made the signal, who was the lord of Croft, led the Prince to the park at Tullington, where Roger de Mortimer, with Roger de Clifford, John Giffard, and five hundred men in arms, were waiting to receive him.   The Prince was closely pursued, for the whole country (tota patria) was up to guard him; but when the pursuers saw the forces of Roger de Mortimer, they returned in dismay.   Edward was conducted to Wigmore, where he was received joyfully by dame Maude de Mortimer (Roger's wife), and from thence he went to Pembroke, where John de Warenne and William de Valence were raising forces.[9]   The Borderers were encouraged by the success of their stratagem, and soon raising a large army, they took successively Chester, Shrewsbury, Bridgenorth, and Ludlow,[1] and shortly afterwards Worcester and Gloucester.   Earl Simon, in retaliation, took the castle of Monmouth and levelled it with the ground, and then joining with the army of Prince Llywelyn in Glamorganshire, proceeded to ravage and lay waste the lands of the confederates.   Immediately afterwards he prepared to return into England to strengthen his party, and came to Hereford.

In the mean time Prince Edward and his friends, being at Worcester, learned that the younger Simon de Montfort, with many influential men of the party, were at Kenilworth, and by a forced march from Worcester, they fell upon them by surprise, and made the greater number prisoners.   Earl Simon, with the King in his company, was on his way to join his son, and arrived at Kempsey, near Worcester, on the feast of St. Peter-ad-Vincula, August 1st, when he learnt that Prince Edward was arrived at Worcester with forces far superior to his own.   He marched the same night to Evesham, where, on the 5th of August, was fought the celebrated battle which ruined the baronial cause, and in which Simon de Montfort, with two of his sons, and most of the leading men of his party, were slain.   The body of the Earl was barbarously mutilated, and his head was carried to Worcester, and presented to dame Maude de Mortimer, who was

---

[6] Rishanger, ut supra ; Robert of Gloucester, pp. 551, 552.

[7] Rymer's Fœdera, i. pp. 445—457.

[8] This story is differently told by others (Henry de Knighton, p. 452, and Dugdale's Baronage) ; who mention that Roger Mortimer seeing his sovereign in this great distress, took no rest till he contrived some way to rescue him, and for that purpose sent a swift horse to the Prince, then prisoner with the King at the castle of Hereford, for the purpose before-mentioned ; that the Prince obtaining leave of Montfort to try if the horse was of use for the great saddle, first wearied out the horses, and then got on this (a boy with two swords, whom this Roger had sent, being near with another horse,) and so turning himself to Robert de Ros, then his keeper, and other bystanders, said, " *I have been in your custody for a time*, but now I bid you *Farewell!* " and so rode away, adding that this Roger, with his banner displayed, received him at a hill called Dunomoir (Dinmore) and so conveyed him to Wigmore.

[9] History of the Mortimers in the Monasticon, tom. vi. p. 351. Conf. Rishanger and Robert of Gloucester.

[1] It appears probable that the last and successful insurrection against Simon de Montfort was planned at Ludlow. Simon de Montfort was reverenced as a saint after his death, and we are told, in the collection of his miracles, that he appeared in a dream to the vicar of Wardon, telling him to warn Geoffrey de Stalares that if he did not repent and make amends for his seditious plots at Ludlow against the Earl Simon, he would fall into some sudden misfortune (ut Galfridum de Stalares militem ex parte suâ moneret, quod seditiones et machinamenta quæ contra comitem Symonem et suos complices apud Luddelow fecerat, emendaret). Geoffrey neglected this admonition : and soon after, being on his way to London, he was burnt with all his retinue in a house where he had taken up his lodgings. Halliwell's Rishanger, p. 80.

staying there. Among the prisoners were John Fitz John, the younger Humfrey de Bohun, with two sons of Simon de Montfort, and several other barons.

The King, now at liberty and restored to power, was at Worcester on the 7th of August, the second day after the battle.[2] He removed thence to Gloucester, where, on the 24th of August, he levied a heavy fine on the citizens of Hereford for their attachment to the baronial cause.[3] On the 28th of November following, a truce was made with the Welsh; but they still continued in arms for many months. On the 21st of September, 1266, the King was at Shrewsbury, negotiating with Llywelyn; and on the 25th he was at Montgomery, where, four days afterwards, a peace was agreed to.[4] This peace was confirmed at Michaelmas, 1268, when Henry again went to Shrewsbury with an army; yet, on the 21st of May, in the year following, we find Edward once more obliged to meet the Welsh prince at Montgomery.

Although the party of Simon de Montfort was destroyed in the battle of Evesham, the civil war was not ended. The remains of the great baronial confederacy held out at Kenilworth, Chesterfield, and especially in the Isle of Ely. Even the Earl of Gloucester, whose defection had been the cause of the overthrow of the barons, turned round again, and forced the royalists to give ground before the popular feelings of the nation. The immediate consequences of this great revolution were large confiscations of estates, and changes of possessors of landed property. None benefited more by these confiscations than the Borderers who had stood firmly by the King, and particularly the already powerful family of the Mortimers, who, after a few generations, will be found contending for the crown itself. Roger de Mortimer of Wigmore, the bitter enemy of Simon de Montfort, received immediately after the battle of Evesham, grants of lands in Wales, of which, in the troubles which preceded, he had taken forcible possession, and his extensive territory was increased by the addition of Kerry and Kedewyn, and the castle of Dolvorwyn.[5]

As far as England was concerned, the liberties for which the barons had fought were not lost in the carnage at Evesham: they not only survived the slaughter of their defenders, but they triumphed even in their defeat. During the struggle between the King and the barons, a party which had lain dormant during the times of Anglo-Norman tyranny, the commonalty, stepped into the field and gained an influence which no victories or intrigues could afterwards destroy: in the destruction of the barons, it was partly relieved from a power which might have been more fatal to its interests than that of the most despotic of monarchies. The feudal aristocracy of the Anglo-Norman barons had ceased to exist in the force which it possessed in the twelfth century, but the aristocracy itself survived a little longer to perish by the sword in the sanguinary wars of the Roses, or by the axe, under the peaceful but no less sanguinary reigns of the first Tudors.

It is thus that the fatal conflict at Evesham closes a distinctly marked period of English history. Its effect on the history of Wales was still more remarkable. Since the reign of the Conqueror, the Welsh had enjoyed a precarious independence, which was equally useless and equally injurious to both parties, English as well as Welsh. Wales, as the smaller power, lived only by the internal quarrels of the greater power; and it lived in a state of existence which could only be tolerated because the greater power had too much to do at home to apply a remedy to it.

The remainder of this reign was not productive of many important events. In 1267, it became necessary for the King to march against Llywelyn, who, probably, insisted on the performance of the last treaty made with him. We find Henry and his son at Shrewsbury from the 4th to the 27th of September, at which town, on the Sunday before Michaelmas, a treaty was concluded, under the auspices of Cardinal Ottoboni, between " the excellent Lord Henry King of England, and the noble man Lewelin son of Griffin." Such a change had the battle of Evesham made in the style of the Cambrian prince: for *noble man* was the addition of barons in that age.

By Michaelmas-day Henry was advanced to Montgomery, where he appoints Roger Gumeri, Hugh de Mortimer, and Roger de Hopton, Sheriff of Salop and Stafford, his commissioners to complete the peace.

---

[2] Rymer's Fœdera, i. p. 458.
[3] *Ibid.*

[4] Rymer's Fœdera, i. p. 473.
[5] History of the Mortimers, printed in the Monasticon, vi. p. 351.

8

This actually took place at Montgomery on the 3rd of the calends of October, Sept. 29. On the payment of a large sum of money, and the surrender of certain castles, Llywelyn was, in future, to receive the homage of all the Welsh nobles, and to bear the title of Prince of Wales, which, as has been said, Henry had conferred upon his own son. The Prince of Wales was eager to conclude a negotiation so much to his own advantage: and on the same day (Thursday, in the Feast of St. Michael) he swore to the observance of the peace in the presence of the King and his sons.

Edward, however, felt the necessity of keeping a strict watch over the proceedings of so restless a neighbour, and was able to appreciate the importance of Shrewsbury, as a post from which he might attend to this quarter of the realm. He saw, moreover, the necessity of providing it with a governor, on whose vigilance and fidelity he could depend during his absence in Palestine; and, therefore, procured a grant from his father, dated at Winchester, the 23rd of September, 1269, whereby the King notifies to the bailiffs and good men of Salop, that he had committed their castle and town to his dear son Edward, to be kept during pleasure, and commanding them to be obedient to him or to his certain attorney, whom he shall depute by his letters patent for the custody of the same: and this grant appears to have continued in force to the death of Henry.

We now enter on the most important of our Royal Visits, and we may say the most important in their results, particularly as they have turned out to the mutual benefit of both nations, England as well as Wales.

Edward the First distinguished the commencement of his reign by immense preparations for a most vigorous attack upon Llywelyn, Prince of Wales, and his hitherto unconquerable people.[*] The death of his father opened the way to this dexterous and ambitious prince to carry out the great object he had in view, which was to unite the whole island under one head, and to the attainment of this object it may be feared that he occasionally sacrificed those immutable rules of morality, which ought to bind all men. The contest between Edward and Llywelyn was disputed with mutual spirit and bravery. The rival princes were both young. Edward, indeed, when he first appeared in arms against the Welsh, had scarcely numbered seventeen summers; and Llywelyn was only a few years his senior. The one fought for conquest, the other for life and liberty, for his crown and his country; and, as both were actuated by motives which spurred them to exertion, it was not likely that the contest would terminate either tamely or speedily. The event has proved how long was its duration, how fatal and unfortunate to Wales its termination and consequences.

It is impossible to contemplate the patriotic struggles of our ancestors, during this period, without pity and admiration. They were heroically contending for their birthrights—for the ancient and revered laws of their forefathers; and the most noble feelings of patriotism and loyalty animated them to defend those laws, and to preserve them from violation by a cruel and detested enemy. But in vain did they contend against the overwhelming force of England. After a succession of unhappy and delusive vicissitudes, they submitted to the yoke of the conqueror, and lamented on the gloom and solitude of their mountains the loss of their loved independence.

Mr. Warrington, in his History of Wales, has eloquently commented on the conduct of the Cambro-British, in the following spirited passage:—"The fall of nations," he observes, "distinguished only by misfortunes, or merely illustrious for conquests, may raise, for a moment, a sigh of pity on the transient effusions of applause; but a people like the Welsh, satisfied with their mountains—who had been forced into a long and unequal contest in defence of their native rights, with few other resources than their valour

---

[*] Edward I. and his queen were crowned at Westminster on the 15th of August, 1274, by the Archbishop of Canterbury. Holinshed relates the following particulars:—"At this coronation were present, Alexander King of Scots, and John Earle of Bretaine, with their wives, that were sisters to King Edward. The King of Scots did homage unto King Edward for the realme of Scotland, in like manner as other the Kings of Scotland before him had doone to other Kings of England, ancestoures to this King Edward. At the solemnitie of this coronation there were let go at libertie (catch them that catch might) five hundred great horsses by the King of Scots, the Earles of Cornewall, Glocester, Pembroke, Warren, and others, as they were allighted fro their backs."—*Coronation Anecdotes.*

and a fond attachment to their liberty, though falling in the ruins of their country, will have a claim upon the esteem and admiration of the world, as long as a manly sentiment and freedom shall remain. But, in reflecting upon the history of this nation with a just and discriminating spirit, we are frequently led to survey its manners and national character with the opposite emotion of pleasure and disgust. We are not, however, to estimate this character too nicely by the refined standard of civilised judgment. It is true there are traits in the genius of this people marking in their manner the deepest ferocity; it is true that caprice and levity, and the spirit of discord, too often predominated in their councils, and governed their conduct; and it is also true, that striking defects may be traced in their policy and laws, ruinous to themselves and disgraceful even to a less cultivated period. But the vices of an uncivilised people are in some degree softened, and even balanced by their virtues. A spirit unsubdued by danger and misfortune, hospitable manners, and eager friendships, a high relish of the arts of music and poetry, with a principle of justice inherent with their laws, are qualities to be thrown into the opposite scale. And, no doubt, the influence of these, blending the lighter with the darker shades, softened the asperity of ruder features, and tempered into a milder mass the colouring of the whole. But the spirit of freedom and ardent love of their country were the distinguishing characteristics of the Cambro-British. These were the animating spring of their genius, which enabled them to sustain, through a long succession of ages, the most striking and discouraging reverses of fortune. And it is the collision of such vicissitudes, by calling into exertion public virtue and heroism, which imparts dignity to the character of man, and constitutes the true glory of a nation."

Edward had seen the dangerous pretensions of the Prince of Wales, and seems from the first to have been bent upon his subjugation. He was absent at the death of the King his father, but either in consequence of orders left by him before his embarkation for Palestine, or from the Lord Chancellor's own knowledge of his new sovereign's views, that officer, as guardian of the realm, within less than a fortnight after the accession of the new monarch, issued a commission,[7] November 29th, to the abbots of Dore and Haghemon to receive the oath of fealty from Llywelyn ap Gryffydd, Prince of Wales. This demand was very grating to a gallant and aspiring prince; proud of his ancestry, which he was fond of tracing up to the Trojan Brutus; and not at all disposed to admit the superiority of the English monarch, whose kingdom he regarded as his own inheritance.[8] Accordingly the negotiation concerning the performance of this trifling ceremony was drawn out to a great length. Early in the following year, 1273, the abbots above mentioned proceeded to meet the Prince. The result of their journey we learn by a letter from R. Sprenghose, Constable of Montgomery, to the Lord Chancellor Merton,[9] informing him, that according to his lordship's precept, the abbots of Dore and Haghemon, with certain of his (the constable's) bailiwick, advanced to the ford of Montgomery to receive from the Lord L., son of Griffin, Prince of Wales, the oath of fealty to the King: but that after waiting a long time after noon (*ultra horam none*) " the Lord L. neither came himself, nor sent any excuse."

Thus the matter rested till the next year, 1274, when, though the King was not yet returned from abroad, a writ was issued in his name, April 14th, wherein, " having heard of divers trespasses committed in the March of Wales against the peace concluded between the late King and Llywylyn ap Griffin" (he gives him no higher title), he directs William de Beauchamp, Earl of Warwick; Roger de Clifford, Prior of St. Thomas without Stafford; William Bagot, and Odo de Hodenet, to go to the Ford of Montgomery on Sunday after St. Philip and James, where, says the King, *"I have commanded Llywelyn to meet you."*

---

[7] Rymer's Fœdera. Four days earlier is an acquittance on the patent rolls to the Prince of Wales for 3000 marks, due from him to the late King in conformity to the treaty of peace. " Rex omnibus, &c. Sciatis nos recepisse a dilecto nobis Leulino filio Griffini principe Wallie tria millia marcarum de termino Natalis Domini, A.D. 1272, in quibus idem Leulinus nobis tenebatur solvend' in termino predicto per formam pacis inter celebris memorie d'nm H. regem patrem nostrum & ipsum Leulinum inite & firmate, de quibus Leulinum

quietamus. T. E. Abor. Archiep'o & E. Comite Cornubie. 25 Nov." Pat. 1 E. I. M. 20.

[8] See the curious correspondence between Llywelyn and the Archbishop of Canterbury, in Powell's Hist. of Wales, ed. 1697, p. 395. His Grace feeling himself pressed by the sovereignty of Brutus and Camber, alleges their usurpation on the rights of Corineus the giant.

[9] Rymer's Fœdera, sub ann ; Prynne, Records, iii. 119, a.

s 2

These *commands*, however, the Prince of Wales thought proper still to disobey: and we cannot wonder that this contumacy from one whom Edward regarded so much beneath him, should give umbrage to a youthful and spirited monarch. Llywelyn, to shelter himself from the effects of Edward's resentment, (aggravated by his refusal to perform homage at the coronation, August 19,) procured from the Pope[1] a bull directed to the Archbishop of Canterbury, 15 Cal. September (Aug. 18,) directing that prelate to dispense with the Prince's attendance, on his undertaking to appear in Wales before the archbishop's commissaries. The King of England did not wish to show any disrespect to the sovereign pontiff, yet he was determined to bend the haughty Llywelyn to the performance of homage; that galling mark of submission, by which, kneeling down unarmed and bareheaded before his sovereign, he was, with closed and uplifted hands, to acknowledge himself the "man" of Edward, to do unto him homage, and to be faithful and true to him during life.[2] In order, therefore, to deprive the Prince of the only reasonable pretext for non-compliance with this stipulated ceremonial, he directed the Welsh ambassadors[3] to notify to their master, his royal intention of taking a journey to Shrewsbury; at which town he proposed to arrive on the quindene of St. Martin (*i.e.* November 26), and where by writ of the 3d of that month, dated from Northampton,[4] he summoned Llywelyn to appear and perform homage, on the Sunday after St. Andrew. (30th Nov.) On his road to Shrewsbury, however, the King was taken ill of a violent and sudden abscess, and obliged to stop at Clyve (probably Cliff, in the county of Warwick), by which he was so much weakened, that he notifies[5] to the Prince his inability at present to continue his journey; informing him, that he intended to repair hither as soon as possible, and in the meanwhile directing him to pay certain sums duty, by treaty.[6]

A.D. 1275.—The King repaired to Chester with the same view of exacting the homage of the Welsh prince, but Llywelyn still broke his appointment with the King as he had done before with his minister, and the English monarch, indignant at this affront, no longer took any pains to accommodate the British prince, but by writ, Sept. 10, summoned him to appear at Westminster, in three weeks from Michaelmas-day; whereupon the Prince, the next day, applied again to the Pope for his protection against the insidious designs of Edward, who had appointed so distant a place for the performance of homage; but the death of his Holiness, which happened at this time, deprived the Prince of the support of this arbitrer of Christendom.

Whether Prince David, Llywelyn's brother, had at that this time left the court of Wales seems not clear: the first mention we have seen of that fact is in a letter[7] written by the dean and chapter of Bangor to the Archbishop of Canterbury, on Sunday next, after the close of Easter, 1276, wherein they pray his grace "*not to condemn Llywelyn unheard.*" From this last expression it appears that Edward had applied to the primate for a sentence of excommunication against his adversary.[8] The fugitive prince was received with open arms by the King of England; who, eager to embrace any measure which might sow dissension in the court and councils of Llywelyn, conferred upon his brother ample estates and a wealthy marriage.

---

[1] Rymer's Fœdera. The Prince demanded, as hostages for his security, in case he attended the coronation, our King's son, Robert Earl of Gloucester, and Robert Burnell the Lord Chancellor. Walsingh. p. 46.

[2] The following account of the manner of performing homage is taken from an ancient manuscript of the see of Lichfield, drawn up while that practice continued in force; viz. in 1847. "Verba dicenda cum quis faciet homagium. Ille debet esse discinctus [unarmed], & genuflectet ambobus genubus, & tenebit manus suas inter manus domini, & ita dicebit (sic) I become yor man from this tyme forward, and to yowe do homage, and shal be feythfull and trewe duryng my lyffe, except the feyth that I owe unto my soverayn lorde the Kynge. And the serves appertaynyng to my londe wheche I hold of yowe I shall truly do to my power, so helpe me God and my holy dame." Episcopal Register of Lichfield, A.D. 1487.

In the Sundorn statute roll, which was written about 1283, it is thus set down,

"Modus faciendi homagium

"Modus qualit' lib' faciet homag' d'no suo de quo tenet capitale mesuagiu'. Tenebit manus suas attentas inter manus domini sui sub gremio suo dicens sic, Jeo Devens vostre home de eeo jour enavant de vie e de membre e de terene honur a vous fei portere del ten' q' Jeo tens ou clayme tenere de vous en la vile de N. sauve la fay q' Jeo dey a nostre seignur le Roy e a mes autre seignurag'."

[3] Rymer's Fœdera.

[4] Dodsworth, vol. iii.

[5] Rymer's Fœdera, ii. 42; and Lloyd's MS. History of Shropshire.

[6] Rymer's Fœdera, ii. 65.   [7] Rymer's Fœdera, ii. 37[?]

[8] It is certain he did so in the subsequent war. See his letter in Rymer, dated 28th March, 1282. regni 10.

This step was not likely to diminish the jealousy or disgust of the Prince of Wales. He still continued refractory on the proposal of visiting London; where a parliament having been summoned in the beginning of October, the peers sent letters to Lylwelyn, persuading him to obey the royal summons. In reply, he offers, Oct. 14, to repair to Montgomery, or to " the White Monastery of John Fitz Alan," as Oswestry was then called; but declines a journey to the metropolis of England. On the receipt of this answer, by which Edward, resolute to exact a personal obedience, was, or affected to be, greatly enraged; the parliament immediately condemned Llywelyn as a rebel for his non-appearance; and at the King's request, the spiritual lords addressed a letter to him. This document, dated from Westminster on the Friday · after St. Martin hiemalis, Nov. 11, prays Llywelyn to abstain from molesting the " peaceful " king of England.

These diplomatic forms were only the prelude to military operations. The monarch having, Nov. 15, constituted Roger de Mortimer his general against the Welsh, and having on the following day issued a pardon to all of that nation who would desert Llywelyn ap Gryffydd " our rebel" (as he styles him): by writ issued at Windsor, Dec. 12, he summoned the army to meet at Worcester in the Octave of St. John Baptist, and, in order to collect as large a force as possible, also directed that the bishops and abbots should not be excused from doing their service; and further directed the sheriffs to summon all the tenants in capite. At the same time, to intimidate Llywelyn by an unequivocal declaration of his intentions to continue the contest till he had carried his point, he determined to transfer the seat of government to Shrewsbury; and actually removed thither some of the supreme courts of justice.

During the next two years, five or six mandates of a similar nature were sent by Edward to Llywelyn, which the latter thought proper to disobey. The Welsh prince resolutely persisted in his refusal, unless some English nobles of distinction were delivered as hostages for his security. Llywelyn had, indeed, undertaken, by his treaty with Henry, to do homage for the Principality, upon condition that the Welsh lords should remain feudatories to himself only; and, while Henry lived, this condition was strictly observed. Edward, however, animated, no doubt, by his old enmity against the natives of Wales, had thought proper to violate the treaty both in this respect and in some others. For, he had not only made a violent seizure of some Welsh baronies, but had openly countenanced several of Llywelyn's subjects, who had revolted against him. Under such circumstances, the latter was fully justified in refusing to risk his person at the English court, without proper indemnity;* for a monarch, who had already shown his disregard of the solemn engagements of a treaty, might not be very scrupulous in his observance of more ordinary duties.

Llywelyn accordingly transmitted a spirited memorial[1] to England, explaining, with firmness and moderation, yet with proper respect, the motives that influenced his conduct, and offering, at the same time, to perform homage at any place where his personal safety might be ensured.

This resolute conduct on the part of Llywelyn had the natural effect of exasperating Edward, who was, however, in all probability, rejoiced at the pretext afforded him of renewing his designs against the independence of Wales. And to the execution of these he received an additional incitement, the' zeal with which he was seconded by his parliament and prelates, at whose suggestions the penalties of outlawry and

* On one of these occasions the following remarkable circumstance took place. Edward being at Aust Ferry on the Severn, and knowing that the Prince of Wales was on the opposite side, sent him an invitation to come over the river that they might confer together and settle some matter of dispute. This being refused by Llywelyn, King Edward threw himself into a boat, and crossed over to the Prince, who, struck with the gallantry of the action, leaped into the water to receive him, telling the King at the same time that his humility had conquered his own pride, and that his wisdom had triumphed over his own folly.

[1] This memorial, which is still preserved, is addressed to the Archbishops of Canterbury and York, and the rest of the bishops in Convocation. After detailing his various complaints in the most dispassionate manner, as well as the obvious hazard of his personal attendance in England, Llywelyn thus concludes : " We, therefore, desire your lordships earnestly to weigh the dismal effects that must happen to the subjects both of England and Wales, upon the breach of the articles of peace, and that you please to inform the King of the sad consequences of another war, which can in no way be prevented, but by using us according to the conditions of the former peace, which, for our part, we will in no measure transgress. But, if the King will not hearken to your counsel, we hope that you will hold us excused if the nation be disquieted and troubled thereupon, which as much as in us lieth, we endeavour to prevent.

excommunication were awarded to the alleged contumacy of the Welsh prince, without any regard to the justice of his cause, or the patriotism of his motives.

During the progress of these proceedings, which occupied a period of more than three years, Llywelyn formed the resolution of claiming the hand of Eleanor de Montfort, who had formerly been betrothed to him by her father. Eleanor was, at this period, the inmate of a French convent;[2] and Llywelyn, accordingly, made application to the King of France for her release. This request met with immediate compliance, not only from the King, but likewise from the widow of his late friend, the Earl of Leicester; and Eleanor was, in consequence, sent with her brother for the purpose of becoming the bride of Llywelyn. The vessel, however, which bore them, in passing the point of Cornwall, fell, unfortunately, into the hands of the English; and Eleanor and her brother were made prisoners. They were both conducted to Edward, who felt, it is probable, a secret delight in this unexpected advantage over his enemy, though only to be retained at the expense of his honour. But Edward wanted the chivalrous generosity to part with such a prize; and the fair Eleanor was accordingly detained at the English court, where she remained in easy captivity for three years.

This incident was calculated at once to wound the pride and awaken the indignation of Llywelyn, and his first impulse was to avenge the insult by an immediate appeal to arms. But, upon cooler reflection, he preferred trying previously the effect of negotiation. With this view he made the offer of a large sum for the ransom of Eleanor, but the overture was rejected, unless the money was to be accompanied by a compliance with the arbitrary demand, to which Llywelyn had already refused to accede, and which he still resolved to resist. Even his love, however ardent and sincere, could not bribe him from the duty he owed to his country. There was now, therefore, no alternative but arms, and the mutual exasperation of both princes was likely to communicate to the approaching contest a character of peculiar obstinacy.

The first campaign against the Welsh, however, either languished or was attended with trifling results; but, in 1277, the English monarch summoned all his vassals to take the field, and meet him with their retainers at Chester, from which city he issued a proclamation, commanding all persons in the county that possessed 20*l.* per annum to attend him there, to be made knights at their own expense. In his advance,[3] Edward repaired the castles of Flint and Rhuddlan, opened roads into almost all the inmost fastnesses of Snowdon, and manifested the prudence of a statesman and a commander preparing for the subjugation of a brave people.

Edward's presence was rendered necessary on the Borders by the invasion of the lands of the Lords Marches. He was joined by a numerous body of vassals, who had assembled at Worcester, with which he entered North Wales in the summer of 1277, and such was the superiority of his forces, and the celerity of his movements, or the want of preparation on the part of his antagonist, that the latter was compelled without a battle, to take refuge among the inaccessible defences of Snowdon, and that, unluckily, without having made provision for such an emergency.

The isle of Anglesea, too, was in the hands of the English, so that Llywelyn, who perhaps had depended upon that quarter for supplies, was deprived of his usual resource. In addition to this, there had been a general defection among the chieftains of South Wales, which destroyed the hope of any effective co-operation from them. In this extremity, urged by the suffering of his famishing soldiers, and without any chance of relief, the Welsh prince was under the mortifying necessity of offering to capitulate; some tender recollections, also, with respect to his beloved Eleanor, may at length have had their share in contributing to this unfavourable result.

---

[2] At Montgargis.

[3] A.D. 1278.—In the sixth year of his reign, Edward the First invaded Wales according to his usual practice, on the side of Chester. We find by a MS. in the Harleian collection, Bibl. 2003, ff. 781, 785, kindly pointed out to us by Sir John Hanmer, Bart., M.P., that Edward on this occasion crossed the estuary of the Dee on horseback, at Shotwick Forde, "which forde," says the MS., "dothe still continue." The distance across the estuary is about two miles; the ford has long been done away with, and the place, which in those days was covered with the briny ocean, is now solid ground, called the "Wild Marsh," the water being confined to a narrow compass.

Edward, upon receiving these overtures, refused to listen to any terms that were not founded on an unconditional surrender on the part of Llywelyn, who was to be indebted to the clemency of his conqueror for any indulgence he might receive. Arbitrary and humiliating as this proposal was, the Welsh prince did not feel himself in a condition to reject it. A treaty was, accordingly, concluded on this basis; and such was the severity of the terms, that it is difficult to conceive how a prince of such acknowledged valour and spirit as Llywelyn, could have been forced, by any circumstances, to submit to them. He was not only to do homage annually in London, as had formerly been stipulated, but he was to deliver up all his prisoners; to restore all forfeited lands; to grant amnesties to his rebellious brothers; to resign the feudal supremacy over the barons; to pay a tribute of fifty thousand marks;[4] and even to surrender to Edward a portion of his dominions, including nearly the whole of the counties of Denbigh and Flint, while ten of the most considerable Welsh chieftains were to become hostages for the due observance of this degrading convention. Such form a part only of the conditions which the generous clemency of Edward imposed upon his unfortunate adversary; but it is scarcely to be doubted that the present triumph of the English monarch was rendered more insolent by a remembrance of his past defeats. In return for the sacrifices thus exacted from Llywelyn, certain concessions were made to his subjects, which related chiefly to the administration of justice according to the forms usual in Wales, and to the enjoyment of their ancient customs and privileges.

In compliance with the terms of this treaty, Llywelyn accompanied the King to London, for the purpose of performing the stipulated homage. He was attended on the occasion by several Welshmen of distinction with their retinues. The language and manners of the party appear to have been a subject of much merriment or derision to the English; a circumstance which, considering the irascible temper of the Welsh, could not have had a very conciliatory effect. Its results were indeed quite of an opposite nature; yet whatever may have been Llywelyn's particular feelings, he chose to disguise them for the present, with the view, it would appear, of securing an object, who at this juncture must have engrossed his chief thoughts. This was his marriage with Eleanor de Montfort, who still continued in honourable captivity at the English court; and there can be little doubt that the same motive must have had an important influence on the Welsh prince in his assent to the humiliating treaty he had recently concluded..

Soon after Llywelyn's return to Wales from the English metropolis, he received somewhat imperative orders from Edward to meet him at Worcester. This injunction at any other season the Welsh prince might have hesitated to obey; but on the present occasion, the private reason already noticed left him no choice. He hastened to the presence of the King, and, whatever mortification he endured, he considered himself, perhaps, amply remunerated by being put in possession of the hand of his betrothed bride. The marriage took place on the 12th of October, 1278, in the presence of Edward and his queen, but not before the former, with his usual policy, had made the occasion a pretext for exacting some new submissions from the Welsh prince. He extorted from him a promise on the very eve of the nuptial solemnity, not to afford protection to any one who might have incurred the displeasure of the English crown. As soon as Llywelyn had secured the possession of his bride, he departed with her in haste to Wales, probably to his house at Aber, near Conway, where about this time he generally resided.

In the year 1277, the barons of Snowdon, with other noblemen of Wales, had attended Llywelyn to London, when he came thither at Christmas to do homage to Edward, for the four cantreds of Rhôs, Rhyfoniog, Tegeingl, and Dyffryn Clwyd; and bringing, according to their usual custom, large retinues with them, were quartered at Islington and the neighbouring villages. These places did not afford milk for such numerous trains; they liked neither the wine nor the ale of London; and though plentifully entertained, were much displeased at the new manner of living, which did not suit with their taste: they slighted the English bread, and their pride too was disgusted by the perpetual staring of the Londoners, who followed them in crowds to gaze at their uncommon garb. "No," cried the indignant Britons,

---

[4] These were Rhodri and David, to the former of whom he was to pay an annuity of 1000 marks, and the latter one of 500. Besides this he was to reinstate his brother Owain in the lands which his treason had forfeited.

" we never again will visit Islington, except as conquerors;" and from that instant they resolved to take up arms.[5]

Having brought the Prince under his severe yoke, Edward was content to take him into some degree of favour. He remitted the fine,[6] which the Prince of Wales could never have paid. Yet Llywelyn still neglected to make his personal appearance at a parliament holden at Easter the following year, 1278,[7] and this induced the King again to visit the Marches with a small force; but he was appeased by the submission and respectful demeanour of Llywelyn.

For the next two years the Welsh prince appears to have relinquished himself entirely to the enjoyment of his conjugal felicity, and might have remained so for the remainder of his days, but for the calamity of the death of his fair bride, which took place in 1280, after having given birth to a princess.[8] This event was, no doubt, the source of much affliction to Llywelyn, and appears to have had an effect of another nature, in dissolving all the ties that had bound him to England; and, it is probable, that the grief, natural to the occasion, subsided, only to give place to a revival of the ancient animosity, heightened as it had been by recent events, that existed between the two nations. While Eleanor lived, she had, perhaps, been able to conciliate his feelings upon this subject, if indeed the remembrance of her father's fate and her own wrongs had predisposed her to such a task. But whatever part she may have acted in this respect, Llywelyn appears to have considered himself, when she was no more, as at once liberated from all restraint. And it is more than probable, that this notion was encouraged by a reflection upon the arbitrary conduct pursued towards him by Edward, while his fortunes were in a certain degree at that monarch's disposal.

Llywelyn reproached himself for the sacrifice of his country; and he read reproof in the countenances of every faithful subject. To restrain the indignation of his people he found to be impracticable, and he probably felt his condition to be intolerable. The brave people of Snowdon declared, that though their prince gave the English king possession of their country, they would never submit to the yoke of strangers.

Prince Llywelyn began to reflect upon his unfortunate position, and he was urged by the songs of the bards and by the indignation of his subjects, to make a sudden invasion of England. The ambiguous words of a prophecy of Merlin, also, asserting, that a " prince, born in Wales, should be acknowledged king of the whole British Island," was an additional stumulus to urge him onwards. The Welsh people, as a body, had never acquiesced in the proceedings of their prince, and the natural consequence of all treaties of submission were soon exhibited.

But these were not the only considerations that tended to exasperate Llywelyn. The inhabitants of that part of North Wales, which had been ceded to Edward by the late treaty, had been since exposed to many innovations, as impolitic as they were vexatious. The people unable and unwilling to submit any longer to such a system of tyranny, united in an appeal to David, Llywelyn's brother, to assist them in the redress of their wrongs. David, who had also been a sufferer from the same cause, at once sympathised with their grievances, and undertook, as far as he could, to avenge them; and, as a preliminary measure, he renounced his unnatural allegiance to Edward, and became reconciled to his brother. He likewise engaged several other chieftains to unite in his cause. Llywelyn, animated by these events, disclaimed further submission to the conditions of the late treaty, and seemed by the vigour of his present conduct determined to atone for the weakness of his former concessions.

Llywelyn in his own person had cause to complain of injuries the most humiliating and poignant, of which the following is an instance: There was a suit depending between him and Grufydd ap Gwenwynwyn,

[5] Carte, from a MS. in the Mostyn Collection.
[6] Rymer's Fœdera, ii. p. 88.
[7] Wykes, p. 106.
[8] The only issue of this marriage was one daughter, who, with her cousin, a daughter of David, spent the greatest part of her life in an English convent. Rymer, vol. ii. p. 429. This child, whose name was Gwenddolen, was brought to Edward a captive in her cradle: she was reared and professed a nun in the convent of Sempringham, with her cousin Gwladys, the only daughter of Prince David, brother to Llywelyn, which Prince was afterwards executed by Edward. Thus ended the line of Roderick the Great—*Piers Langtoft*. Piers mentions his personal acquaintance with these royal votaresses.

respecting an estate which he held of the King, and lying in the Marches. Contrary to the custom established in Wales and in the Marches that all causes of this nature should be tried on the very land which was the subject of dispute, the Prince of Wales received an order from the judges to attend the hearing of that suit at Montgomery. Llywelyn felt highly displeased at this usage, and sternly refused to obey it, conceiving that such a measure would yield up an essential article of the peace, and would derogate from his dignity as a sovereign prince.

The idea that this demand might in future be drawn into a precedent, at last awakened Prince David to a sense of his own situation, who might hope to succeed to the sovereignty upon the death of his brother. He had himself already experienced many causes of complaint, of fear, and of jealousy, respecting the property which he held under Edward. He was sued by William Venables, an Englishman, before the justiciary of Chester, for the villages of Hope and Estyn, contrary to the custom of the Welsh, and the spirit of agreement under which he had held them under the English King. That officer had likewise cut down his woods of Lleweni, with those about Hope, and had sold the timber and carried it into Ireland. He was also threatened, when Reginald de Grey, the other justiciary, came into the country, that the Castle of Hope should be taken from him, and that his children should be secured as pledges of his fidelity in future. Many of the most eminent chieftains in the country had likewise much reason to complain of injuries which they themselves had received. The rigorous exactions of the English officers in Wales, partial and oppressive, and repugnant to the manners of the people, heightened their sufferings to an insupportable degree.

In this season of national misery, when their common fate depended solely upon a virtuous union, the Welsh chieftains besought Prince David that he would be reconciled to his brother Llywelyn; calling on him by every incitement which might act upon a brave or an angry spirit, to desert the English cause, to return to the duty which he owed his country, and to shield her in the hour of danger. The sentiments of David were agreeable to his countrymen, and his present views congenial with their own. Feeling for those miseries, which, in some measure, he himself had produced, and a ray of patriotism springing up in his bosom, he consented to be reconciled to his brother, and to engage in the common cause. Sensible of the peril that awaited him if success did not justify the revolt, or too suspicious of Llywelyn to confide in his firmness, he required from that Prince an assurance that he would never again yield obedience to the English king or relax in his enmity against him. Llywelyn having agreed to this condition, David withdrew privately from the court of England, and arrived with safety in Wales.

The concert being for a general insurrection, David opened the campaign by a gallant exploit at Hawarden, which was performed late in the evening of Palm Sunday, March 22, 1282. The night was extremely dark and stormy, which favoured his design. He surprised the castle, put the garrison to the sword, and wounded and took prisoner Roger de Clifford, justiciary of Chester. After the action the two brothers, David and Llywelyn, having united their forces, invested the castles of Flint and Rhuddlan, the only fortresses which were then in the possession of the English. These exploits were regarded as signals of revolt; the Welsh rising from every quarter were instantly in arms. The gallant spirit of their forefathers seemed to animate every bosom. Rhys ap Maelgwyn and Gruffydd ap Meredydd surprised the castle of Aberystwyth, and committed great devastation in the present counties of Cardigan and Caermarthen. Many chieftains likewise of other fortresses in South Wales, numerous parties of the Welsh, all on fire for revenge, poured suddenly upon the English Marches, and in their progress levelled destruction on all around them.

The King of England, at this period, was at Devizes, where he was keeping his Easter, not suspecting the event which had happened. On being informed of the revolt he expressed the deepest indignation, and determined to proceed without delay into Wales, to make an entire conquest of that country. All other concerns were immediately laid aside, and his talents and the strength of his kingdom were rendered subservient to this great design.

How severely the King of England felt what he considered to be the ingratitude of the Welsh Prince,

T

we learn from his letter to the King of Castile, apologising for his inability to assist that monarch against the Saracens. " Before your messengers came," says he, " namely, in the time of the Lord's passion, when Judas betrayed our Lord, our traitors, Llywelyn ap Griffith and David his brother who was our familiar and counsellor, traitorously rose against us with all their Welsh, invading the lands of our March, killing our lieges, burning villages and towns." But Edward lost no time in unavailing complaints, which one can scarcely imagine serious: he forthwith adopted the most vigorous measures: again assembling his army, and repairing to Shrewsbury, whence, on the 2nd of June, he constituted Roger Springhos, captain of the *munition* (or fortress) of White Minster (Oswestry), in the absence of Roger de Mortimer.

Previous to his military operations he dispatched letters to the two archbishops, commanding them to issue spiritual censures against the Welsh prince and all his adherents. John Peckham, Archbishop of Canterbury, before he proceeded to extremities, unknown to the King, and in a true spirit of benevolence, undertook a journey to Wales, to endeavour to recal Llywelyn and the Welsh chieftains to a sense of their duty.

In the meantime Edward sent part of his forces to the relief of those castles to which the Welsh princes had laid siege; and he also issued out orders that his military tenants should assemble at Worcester without delay. He obtained from the nobility and prelates a promise of a fifteenth of their moveables, and afterwards a thirtieth. The clergy likewise gave him a twentieth of their temporalities to enable him to carry on the war. As these aids might not be raised so soon as they might be required, he borrowed money of all the trading towns in England, to answer his present necessities; and he desired a like loan out of Ireland, from the merchants, the prelates, and nobility of that kingdom. Such was the esteem in which the English king was held, that Gaston de Bern desired to have the honour of serving in the Welsh expedition; and even the Scots, on this occasion, offered their services.[9]

As soon as he had concerted his measures, the King of England commenced his march for the confines of Wales at the latter end of April. Finding that the war was likely to become more difficult than he had at first conceived, he issued out summonses from Worcester, that all his military tenants should meet him at Rhuddlan in the ensuing month of June; the prelates of England, also, and twenty-four abbots holding of the Crown, were included in these orders.

The English king, on his march to Chester, was joined by the country people inhabiting the Borders, whom he employed as before, in opening roads through the enemy's country. After remaining a fortnight at Chester, to refresh his troops, he, about the middle of June, invested the Castle of Hope. This fortress, which had been some time in David's possession, was yielded up to the King almost as soon as he appeared before it. On the approach of Edward, the Welsh Prince raised the siege of Rhuddlan Castle, and retreated slowly towards Snowdon, thinking it more prudent to seize every opportunity of cutting off detached parties, than, with unequal force, to fight him in the open field. Seizing a favourable opportunity, he put to flight a detachment of the English army. Fourteen ensigns were taken in the action; the Lords Audley and Clifford, the son of William de Valence, Richard de Argenton, with many others, were slain; and the King himself, defeated and in disgrace, was obliged to retire for protection into Hope Castle.

Edward was not able to perform any action of moment, until the latter end of autumn.[1] In the middle of July, he resided in Rhuddlan Castle, and issued orders from thence to the sheriffs of the neighbouring counties, to send him, in proportion to the extent of each, a number of hatchet-men, who were to cut down woods, and open passages for his army, before he could advance any further with convenience and safety. He also gave, to several English barons, grants of land in the four counties, the late ceded country.

---

[9] In April, 1282, the king writes from the Devizes to the justices of the bench, informing them of his will, that his bench of pleas of Westminster be held at Salop during his pleasure, and commanding them to adjourn all their proceedings to that town by the octave of the Holy Trinity.

[1] On the 16th of August, he writes from Rochelle to his treasurer and barons of the exchequer, directing them to remove all pleas of the exchequer, rolls, memoranda, and tallies to the same place, under the safe conduct of his beloved cousin (the name left in blank).

During these transactions, the Archbishop of Canterbury went a second time into Wales, and transmitted the following monitory letter to Llywelyn and his adherents :—

Artycles sent from the Archbishop of Canturburie to be intimated to Llywelyn, Prince of Wales, and the people of the same Countrie.

" 1. Because we came to those parts for the spirituall and temporall health of them whom we have ever loved well, as divers of them have knowne.

" 2. That we come contrarie to the will of our Lord the King, whom our said coming (as it is said) doth much offend.

" 3. That we desire and beseech them, for the bloud of our Lord Jesus Christ, that they would come to an unitie with the English people, and to the peace of our Lord the King, which we intend to procure them so soon as we can.

" 4. We will them understand that we cannot long tarrie in these quarters.

" 5. We would they considered, that after our parting out of the countrie, they shall not, perhaps, find anie that they will so tender in the preferring of their cause, as he would doo, if it pleased God (with our mortall life), we might procure them an honest, stable, and firme peace.

" 6. That if they do contemne our petition and labour, we intend forthwith to signifie their stubbornes to the High Bishop and the Court of Rome, for the enormitie that manie waies hapneth by occasion of this discord this daie.

" 7. Let them know, that unlesse they doo quicklie agree to a peace, that warre shall be aggravated against them, which they shall not be able to sustain, for the King's power increaseth dailie.

" 8. Let them understand that the realme of England is under the speciall protection of the See of Rome ; that the See of Rome loveth it better than anie other kingdome.

" 9. That the said See of Rome will not in anie wise see the State of the realme of England quaile, being under speciall protection.

" 10. That we much lament to heare that the Welsh men be more cruell than Saracens : for Saracens, when they take Christians, they keep them to be redeemed for monie. But (they saie) that the Welshmen, by and by, doo kill all that they take, and are onlie delighted with blood, and sometimes cause to be killed them whose ransome they have received.

" 11. That whereas they were ever wont to be esteemed, and to reverence God and ecclesiastical persons, they seeme much to revolt from that devotion ; moving sedition and warre and committing slaughter, and burning in the holie time, which is great injurie to God, wherein no man can excuse them.

" 12. We desire that, as true Christians, they would repent ; for they cannot long continue their begun discord, if they had sworne it.

"13. We will that they signifye unto us, how they will or can amend the trouble of the King's peace, and the hurt of the common wealth.

"14. That they signifye unto us how peace and concord may be established ; for in vain were it to forme peace to be dailie violated.

"15. That granting they were injured, as they saie (which we no waies doo know), they which were judges in the cause might so have signifyed to the King's Majestie.

"16. That unless they will now come to peace, they shall be resisted by decree and censure of the Church, besides warre of the people."

The Primate expostulated with Llywelyn upon his having broken the late agreement ; and the Welsh Prince returned an answer to the following effect :—That he was obliged to take up arms in defence of his people, who were cruelly harassed and oppressed ; but that he was ready to lay them down immediately, and live in perpetual amity and concord with England, provided Edward would agree to redress their grievances, which, he said, were many and intolerable. He particularly observed, that the King had detained several lands betwixt the rivers "Dywi and Dalus," and refused to give him satisfaction, unless he would suffer his cause to be tried by the laws of England, in direct violation of the articles of the late treaty; that the Lord Grey, when appointed justice, had prosecuted the Welsh for some misdemeanours committed in the late reign, and of which they had been acquitted by the act of indemnity passed at the late pacification; that Rhys ap Meredydd had been stripped[2] of his lands and earth, contrary to all the dictates of justice and equity; that many new customs had been introduced into the four cantreds held by his Majesty, notwithstanding the solemn assurance he had given that nothing of that nature should be attempted; that the inhabitants of Anglesea were tried by the laws of England, in direct contradiction of the articles of the peace; that Prince Llywelyn was forced to pay sums of money to the queen mother under the title of *Aurum Reginœ*, which was an intolerable grievance.

The determined resolution on the part of the two brothers was followed by a general insurrection, and Llywelyn and David opened the campaign with signal results. The Welsh assembled in great numbers, overrun the Marches with incredible rapidity, and committed terrible havoc wherever they came, devastating all the country with fire and sword, and investing the Castle of Rhuddlan.

The King was no sooner informed of these proceedings, than he summoned his nobility and military tenants to meet him at Worcester by the ensuing midsummer, and, in the meantime, removed his courts of justice from Westminster to Shrewsbury. At length, having assembled a numerous army, he advanced against Llywelyn and his brother, who, at his first approach, abandoned the siege of Rhuddlan and retired into the mountains of Snowdon, whither it was impossible to pursue them, and he therefore allowed the Archbishop[3] of Canterbury again to treat with them concerning the articles of a peace, who, actuated by a real or affected desire to serve Llywelyn, made an offer of his mediation between him and the King of England. His overtures to Llywelyn combined a singular mixture of admonition and menace; exhorting him on the one hand to a declaration of his grievances, and threatening him, on the other, with the severest penalties, both spiritual and temporal, in the event of his contumacy; alleging at one moment his lively interest in the fortunes of Llywelyn, and consigning him at another to the utmost vengeance of his hostility. To this extraordinary address Llywelyn replied in a tone of manly moderation, representing the injurious infraction of the late treaty on the part of the English, together with his own anxiety for the preservation of the peace so long as it could be maintained without the sacrifice of his own honour, or the security of his subjects, and offering satisfaction for any wrongs committed by the Welsh, provided a corresponding disposition were manifested on the part of their enemies. This temperate answer was accompanied by a specification of the injuries of which the Welsh had to complain.

Nothing could be more equitable than these propositions; but Edward, conscious of his strength, disdained to treat with his opponents on terms of equality. In answer therefore to the suggestion of the

---

[2] Among the wrongs urged by Llywelyn, were the murder of religious persons, the wanton destruction of monasteries and convents, and many unwarrantable exactions committed by the English functionaries throughout the districts over which they had any control.

[3] The following is a copy of the mock conciliatory terms that were offered by the archbishop in the king's name in his usual spirit of diplomacy, to Llywelyn and his brother David, the heir apparent to the Cambrian throne, with a view of inducing them to resign the little remaining territory and shadow of royalty, which they still most tenaciously withheld. The three documents contain various illusive items. The title of the first runs thus: "These are to be said to the Prince before his *councell*." The second: "These following are to be said to the Prince *in secret*." The third: "These are to be said to David, brother to Llywelyn, *in secret*." The latter is worthy to be recorded, as exhibiting the domineering spirit of ecclesiastical bigotry at the time :—

"*First Item*. That if he (David) for the honour of God, will go to the Holie Land, he shall be provided for according to his degree, so that he doth not returne unless he be called by the King, and we entrust the king to provide for his child.

"*Second Item*. And these things we tell ourselves to the Welshmen, that a great deal greater peril will hang over them than we told them by mouth when we were with them. These things which wee write become greevious, but it is a great deal more greevious to be oppressed with armes, and finally to be rooted out because everie daie more and more their danger doth increase.

"*Third Item*. It is mere hard to be alwaies in warre, in anguish of minde and danger of bodie, alwais sought and besieged, and so to die in deadly sinne, and continual rancour and malice.

"*Fourth Item*. We fear (whereof we be sorrie) unless you doo agree to peace, we most certainly will aggravate the sentence ecclesiastical against you for your faults, of the which you cannot excuse yourselves, whereas yee shall find both grace and mercie if you will come to peace."

The Bishop of St. David's was the bearer of these generous conditions.

Archbishop, who wished him to consider the subject of Llywelyn's complaint, and to allow the Welsh chieftains to plead their cause in his presence, he observed in equivocal terms that they were at liberty to come and depart again, if it should appear in justice they ought to return in safety ! With this ungenerous reply, the Archbishop hastened to apprise Llywelyn of the King's answer, but the Welsh prince, aware perhaps of its duplicity, refused to accede to any conditions that might compromise his conscientious duty towards his subjects, or his respect for the dignity of his own station.

This spirited resolve of Llywelyn was not calculated to bring the negotiation to an amicable issue. The pride of the English monarch naturally took the alarm, and he declared his determination not to be satisfied with anything short of an unconditional surrender on the part of the Welsh. The Archbishop, however, either of his own accord, or with the secret connivance of Edward, made another effort to mediate between him and Llywelyn, but as the terms proposed in the letter were of the same dictatorial strain, offering mercy on the one hand, and threatening vengeance on the other, there was little probability that they should be attended with any success.

In addition to what Llywelyn advanced before, he said, that when his marriage was celebrated at Worcester, the King had compelled him to sign and confirm a writing, by which he engaged that he would never give shelter or protection to any person contrary to the pleasure of Edward; a most unreasonable article, which might deprive him of the assistance of his most faithful friends and servants; that the justices of Chester had levied a distress upon his goods as an equivalent for the profits of a certain shipwreck, which he had seized in the course of the late war; that the King's officers, instead of administering justice to the Welsh with candour and impartiality, oppressed and imprisoned them out of mere wantonness and cruelty; and that the articles of the treaty in favour of himself and his subjects were never observed, but grossly violated in almost every instance by the very persons who were bound to see them executed.

David also complained that he had been stripped of certain towns belonging to the cantreds, which had been conferred upon him as a reward for the many faithful and important services he had performed to his Majesty; that he was forced to answer suits, concerning Welsh affairs, in the King's court at Chester, contrary to the laws of the country; that the Justice of Chester had destroyed his woods, oppressed his tenants, subjected the Welsh to an English jurisdiction, and haughtily rejected his remonstrance, when he demanded reparation for these injuries; that he was threatened in the King's court with the loss of his lands, cattle, and children; and that in order to prevent such terrible calamities, he had been obliged to take up arms for his own safety and protection.

The Archbishop, well knowing that many of these complaints were but too well founded, again interposed his good offices on behalf of the Welsh, and entreated that they might have free access to the throne, and liberty to depart without molestation. Edward replied that he was willing to do justice to all his subjects, that they might freely come and lay down their complaints before him in person, and, at the same time depart in safety, provided it should appear that they deserved that favour.

Meanwhile he proposes the following terms, which the Archbishop transmitted to the Welsh prince, by the hands of Joannes Wallensis :—"The King will hearken to no treaty about the four cantreds, and the Isle of Anglesey; Llywelyn shall submit at discretion, in which case his Majesty will give him a pension of one thousand pounds, with some county or earldom in England, and make an honourable provision for his daughter; the subjects of Llywelyn shall be treated according to their rank, and in whatever manner the King shall be pleased to order. If David, brother of Llywelyn, will agree to go to Palestine, he shall be maintained by the King according to his quality, but shall not presume to return without the permission of his Majesty." [4]

The Archbishop advised them to comply with these terms, as the only means of preserving themselves

<hr>

[4] There were three propositions made in this instance by the archbishop ; one of a public nature, and two others addressed in private to Llywelyn and David respectively. The public proposals related chiefly to the unconditional capitulation of Llywelyn and his nobles, and the private one suggested the surrender of Snowdon on the part of Llywelyn, in exchange for an English county, and with reference to David, proposed his future residence in the Holy Land during the king's pleasure.

from utter ruin and destruction; adding, that should they be so imprudent as to reject them, he should be obliged to subject them to the highest censures of the Church.

Llywelyn replied that he would cheerfully agree to any reasonable conditions, but the terms now offered were utterly inconsistent with the safety of his person, the dignity of his station, and the welfare of his subjects.

The Welsh noblemen declared that they would consent to no terms of accommodation, unless Edward would agree to a treaty concerning the four cantreds and the Isle of Anglesey, the inhabitants of which were afraid of submitting to the King's mercy, because he had violated every oath, promise, and covenant, which he had made to the Prince and his subjects, and his officers had always oppressed the Welsh with equal cruelty and injustice.

David told the Archbishop that when he should be inclined to engage in a crusade, he would go to Palestine voluntarily and of his own accord, but that he would not be compelled to such a step by any power on earth; that, as he had taken up arms in defence of life and liberty, he depended upon the providence of God, to protect them from the cruelty of the English, who, in the most impious and sacrilegious manner, had destroyed their churches, profaned their sacraments, butchered their priests at the altar, murdered their countrymen without distinction of either sex or age, and even stabbed the tender and innocent babes hanging at the breasts of their mothers.

A.D. 1282.—The Archbishop had no sooner received Llywelyn's answer than he pronounced the sentence of excommunication against that Prince and all his adherents; and, in the beginning of the year, Edward, at the head of a powerful army, invaded Wales, which he now resolved to reduce to entire subjection.

In this undertaking, however, he met with several obstructions. He was worsted in divers petty encounters, with the loss of many of his principal nobility; and returning in the autumn to the castle of Rhuyddlan, he issued writs for assembling two extraordinary councils and as many synods, in order to concert more effectual measures for accomplishing the enterprise in which he had embarked.

Shortly afterwards the King advanced towards the Island of Anglesey, having crossed the River Conway on a bridge of boats, and his army being transported to the island by a fleet of the Cinque Ports, the inhabitants submitted without resistance.

From thence he ordered another bridge of boats to be formed to cross the Menai, to the Island of Anglesea, and, before the work was finished, three hundred men-at-arms, under the conduct of Lord William Latimer and Lucas de Thong, went over to the other side of the river, to keep the enemy in play, and allow the bulk of the army to cross the bridge without molestation.

But the tide flowing beyond the bridge and swelling to such a height as to prevent this detachment from retreating or receiving any assistance, the Welsh rushed down from the mountains with horrid yells and attacked the English with such fury and impetuosity, that they were instantly routed, and either slain or drowned in the river. No less than fifteen knights, two and thirty esquires, and about a thousand common soldiers perished on this occasion, nor indeed was there a single person of this detachment who survived to carry back the news of their catastrophe, except Lord William Latimer, who owed his life to the goodness of his horse, which swam with him across the river. The English were so dispirited by this disaster that they neither completed the bridge nor attempted any other enterprise in that part of the country.

After the defeat of Edward and the English army on this occasion, Llywelyn is said to have spent the evening with his friends at Aber, and in the hilarity of the moment composed the following witty and appropriate verse :—

> " Mae'n Don llawer bron, llu'r brenin,—heddyw,
> Er hawdded ein chwerthin ;
> Llawer Sais, leu-bais libin,
> Ar gro yn dô ar ei din."

From the lavish terms of praise in which Llywelyn is commemorated by several cotemporary Bards, we may infer that he was a friend and patron of the national muse, and, indeed, it is traditionally related that his social hours, at his palace at Aber, were often dedicated to her service.

The late disaster paralysed for a moment the operations of the English monarch, and elevated in proportion the spirits of his rival. Llywelyn, indeed, on the elation of success, regarded his triumphs as almost complete. Although still confined to his mountain fastnesses, he was abundantly supplied with provisions, and, as the year was far advanced, he relied upon the certain retreat of the English in the course of a short time; and the superstitious notions of his followers, who applied to their situation some pretended predictions of Merlin, served to inspire a general confidence. Such was the deceitful gleam that radiated the evening of Welsh independence; the lingering light was as yet above the horizon, but the tempest was at hand in which it was to be for ever obscured.

The period we have just been considering was obviously the crisis of Llywelyn's fate, and, had he evinced during it any of that prudent caution for which he had been remarkable on former occasions, he might have ensured for some years a peaceful and prosperous reign. But, seduced by his recent success, he resolved upon tempting his fortune still further, and this resolution was the cause of his ruin.

Edward, it has just been seen, had been unexpectedly baffled in his expedition against North Wales, and it will afford us some idea of the extent of his disaster to learn that he found it necessary to raise fresh levies[5] throughout his dominions for the purpose of supplying his losses. While these preparations were going on, the King appears to have retired from the advanced post he occupied in the direction of Snowdon, and Llywelyn profiting by the circumstance, set out in an evil hour with a part of his forces for South Wales, with the intention of encountering the English in that quarter. The defence of the mountainous position he had imprudently quitted was entrusted to his brother.

The late success of the Welsh, in the action on the Menai, had set fire to their enthusiastic spirit; they considered it as a miracle that had been wrought in their favour. Confident in the faith of the ancient prophecies, that, in the person of Llywelyn, the empire of their fathers would be restored, they urged that Prince to act with intrepidity, to seize this fortunate moment, and to assault the English in their turn, separated and dispirited by the loss which they had lately sustained.[6] Llywelyn thought this an enterprise of too much importance to engage in it without further reinforcements, which he was not without the hopes of receiving, as he had entered into an extensive correspondence with many of Edward's subjects in the Marches, and in South Wales.[7] In hopes by these means of drawing together a great body of troops, to enable him to strike so decisive a blow, or by his presence to reanimate his party, he determined to go into South Wales. Thinking the quarter of Snowdon safe for the winter, he left his brother David to guard the passes of those mountains, and the Prince of Wales himself, with a body of forces, marched to the aid of his adherents who favoured his cause in that country,[8] where, having overrun the counties of Caerdigan and Strath Tywi, he ravaged the estates of Rhys ap Meredydd.[9]

The King having intelligence of the sudden movement of the Welsh prince, dispatched orders to Oliver de Dinham, and other noblemen in the west, to pass over the mouth of the Severn to Caermarthen, and to give their support to his generals in that country.[1]

Llywelyn having so far succeeded in his enterprise, proceeded with his forces to the cantred of Buellt, where, by agreement, he was to hold a conference with some of the lords of that district.[2] As he had not anything to fear from the southern quarter, his only anxiety was to secure the principal pass into the country, that no danger might arise from the north. With this design, having posted the main part of his army on the summit of a mountain, near the River Wye, he stationed a body of troops at a bridge called Pont Orewyn, which commanded the passage over that river.[3] Having thus secured himself as he

---

[5] The taxes that were imposed upon this occasion were not confined to England, but extended also to Ireland.

[6] Matth. Westm., p. 176; P. Virgil, p. 324; Brady, vol. ii. p. 9.

[7] Guthrie's Hist. Eng., p. 897.

[8] *Ibid.* Annal. Waverleiensis, p. 235; Polydore Virgil, p. 324;

Matth. Westm., p. 176.

[9] J. Rossi's Ant. Warw. p. 165; Welsh Chron., p. 373.

[1] Rymer's Fœdera, vol. ii. p. 223.

[2] Welsh Chron., p. 373.

[3] Holinshed, p. 281.

thought from the sudden attack of an enemy, the Prince of Wales, unarmed, and attended by his esquire alone, proceeded into the valley where it had been agreed that the conference should be held.[4] There is every reason to suppose that the design was betrayed by the very lords whom Llywelyn had appointed to meet.[5] In a moment after his departure the bridge was attacked by John Gifford and Sir Edmund Mortimer, at the head of a body of men, who were natives of Buellt, the latter nobleman or his father being lord of that country.[6] The post was maintained with such spirit by the Welsh, that the English lords were not able to make any impression, until Helias Walwyn, who was probably a native of the country, decided the contest, by pointing out to the enemy a passage through the river, though somewhat dangerous, which lay below, at a little distance from the bridge.[7] A detachment was sent under Walwyn to ford the river, and with some difficulty they made good their passage. Assaulted in the front and rear, the Welsh relinquished their post, and the remainder of the English army passed over the bridge.[8]

The Prince of Wales all this time was waiting in a small grove, the place which had been appointed for the meeting of those chieftains with whom he was to hold the conference. On the enemy's first assault his esquire came to inform him that he heard a great outcry at the bridge. The Welsh prince enquired with eagerness if his soldiers were in possession of that post, and being informed that they were, he calmly replied, "he then would not stir from thence though the whole power of England was on the other side of the river." This confidence, not improperly placed, lasted only for a moment, the grove being in an instant surrounded by the enemy's horse.[9] Beset on every side, and cut off from his army, Llywelyn endeavoured as he could to make good his retreat, and to join the troops which he had stationed on the mountain, who, drawn up in battle array, were eagerly expecting the return of their Prince. In making this attempt he was discovered and closely pursued by Adam de Francton, an English knight, who perceiving him to be a Welshman, and not knowing his quality, plunged his spear into the body of the Prince of Wales, being unarmed and incapable of defence.[1]

This being done, Adam de Francton, regardless of the person he had wounded, instantly rejoined his own army, which had then descended the mountain in order to dislodge the enemy from their post.[2] The Welsh on this occasion were steady and acted with great spirit, neither animated by the presence of their Prince, nor dispirited by a knowledge of his fate. They poured upon their enemies, as they advanced up the mountain, a shower of arrows and darts, but the English having placed bodies of archers in the intervals of their horse, annoyed them in their turn, and at length reached the summit.[3] The action continued doubtful for more than three hours, and was maintained on both sides with great resolution and valour,[4] until at length the Welsh were obliged to give way, entirely defeated, and left two thousand men,[5] a third of their number, dead on the field.[6]

All this while Llywelyn had lain on the ground, faint and almost expiring. He had just life enough remaining to ask for a priest, and a white friar, who chanced to be present, administered to the dying Prince the last sacred duties of his office.[7]

The hurry of the action having ceased, Adam de Francton, now at leisure, returned into the valley to strip the person he had wounded. On viewing the body, which was still breathing, it was found, to the great joy of the English army, that the dying person was no other than the Prince of Wales.[8] Elated with the triumph he had thus achieved, Adam de Francton severed the Prince's head from his body, and despatched it to Edward, who was then at Conway Castle. The bleeding trophy was received by the King with barbarous

[4] Hen. de Knyghton de Event. Aug., p. 246.

[5] Humphrey Lhuyd, p. 57; Welsh Chron., p. 373.

[6] Welsh Chron., p. 373.

[7] Holinshed, p. 281; Welsh Chron., 373.   [8] *Ibid.*

[9] Welsh Chron.

[1] Hen. de Knyghton, p. 2464; Humphrey Lhuyd's Brev., p. 60; Welsh Chron., p. 374; Holinshed, p. 281.   [2] *Ibid.*

[3] Hen. de Knyghton, p. 2464; Welsh Chron., p. 374; Holinshed, p. 281.   [4] Polydore Virgil, p. 324.

[5] Carte's Hist. Eng, vol. ii. p. 194, from Chron. Dunstable.

[6] Polydore Virgil, p. 324. This action was fought on the 10th of December.

[7] Rymer's Foedera, vol. ii. p. 224.

[8] Hen. de Knyghton, p. 2464; Guthrie's Hist. Eng., p. 879; Welsh Chron., p. 374. The following is the account preserved by tradition amongst the inhabitants of Buellt respecting this event:— "Llywelyn had posted his army on a hill near Mochryd, a village about three miles below Buellt, on the south side of the Wye. On

exultation, totally unworthy of a magnanimous prince. That he should rejoice in the fall of such a formidable enemy, was not unnatural; but the insult offered to his mangled remains was unpardonable—a true picture of cruelty and tyranny. Upon stripping Llywelyn, there were found in his trousers

The Head of Llywelyn brought to Edward at Conway Castle.

his privy seal, a paper that was filled with dark expressions, and a list of names which were written in a kind of cypher; a letter or two was discovered at the same time, all of which evidently proved that he had engaged in a confederacy with several lords, who were Edward's subjects in the Marches. A transcript of these was sent by Sir Edmund Mortimer to the Archbishop of Canterbury, who was then in Pembrokeshire, and who transmitted them immediately to the King, as a necessary precaution to guard against their designs. But the King thought it not prudent to make any further enquiries, being desirous of not adding to a flame which he thought must now die away of itself.

The following is a translation of the letter from the Archbishop of Canterbury to the King, alluded to above, which, we believe, has not before appeared in English :—

the north side of the river, two miles below Buellt, the Prince had a house called Aberadwy, to which he came for the purpose of conferring with some chieftains of the country. During his stay there he was alarmed by the approach of some English troops, who probably had intelligence of his situation. The Prince, to extricate himself from the danger that threatened him, caused his horse's shoes to be reversed, in order to deceive his pursuers, as the snow was on the ground; but this circumstance was made known to the enemy through the treachery of the smith, and they followed so closely, that Llywelyn had but just time to cross the draw-bridge at Buellt, which being drawn up secured his retreat. In the meantime, the English posted at Oberedwy had information of a ford a little lower down, called *Cefn Ium Bach*, which they crossed, and by that means came between Llywelyn and his army stationed at Mochryd. The only means of safety now offered to Llywelyn was to secrete himself. But the enemy were so vigilant in the pursuit, that the Welsh Prince was soon found in a narrow dingle, in which he had concealed himself, three miles north of Buellt, and about five miles from his army, and which place was called from this event, *Cwru Llywelyn*. The Prince was put to death and his head cut off. He was buried where he fell, and the spot is still known by the name of *Cefn y Bedd*, or the " Mound of the Grave."

U

" To our Very Dear Lord Edward, by the Grace of God, King of England, Lord of Ireland, Duke of Aquitaine ; Brother John, by the Sufferance of God Archbishop of Canterbury, Primate of all England, with Great Reverence, Greeting.

SIRE,—Know that these were at the death of Llywelyn found on his person, most carefully concealed, things that we have seen, and amongst others a letter disguised in false words of treason, and that you may be thereof informed, we send the transcript of the letter of the Bishop of *Ba,*[*] which letter is in the possession of Edmund de Mortimer, as is also the privy seal of Llywelyn, which things you may have at your pleasure ; and this we send you for information, and not that any one may suffer in consequence, and we pray you that none may be put to death because of our report, nor suffer imprisonment (?) and that our request may be (fully) granted.

Know, then, Sire, that Dame Maude Longespeye besought us by letters that we would absolve Llywelyn, so that he might be buried in consecrated ground ; and we replied we would do nothing unless it could be proved that he showed signs of true repentance before death ; and Edmund de Mortimer told me that he had heard from his vassals who were at the point of death that he (Llywelyn) had asked for the priest before his death.

But without perfect certainty we would do nothing. On this account, know then ; that the day he was wounded, a white monk chanted him a mass, and Sir Roger de Mortimer took his vestments.

Therefore, Sire, we beseech you take pity on the priests and suffer not that they be slain, nor that any bodily harm befal them.

And know, Sire, that God will defend you from evil if you do not displease him, and cherish the maxim that to grant that one has the power to withhold is worth consent.

And for this reason, Sire, we pray you to be pleased to allow the priests who are in Snowdon (*ia*) to withdraw and seek their fortunes with their goods in France or elsewhere ; and since we believe Snowdon (*ia*) will be yours, if it happen that during, or after the conquest, harm is done to the priesthood, God will hold you responsible, and your fair name will be tarnished, while we ourselves are condemned as cowards ; and should it please you to make known to us your pleasure concerning these matters, we will give them whatever consideration there will be in our power, and will either go ourselves or take other steps.

And know, Sire, that if you grant us not our prayerful requests, you will bring sorrow on us, the poignancy of which we can show you in this mortal life.

Sire, may God watch over you and all that belongs to you."

This letter was written at Pembroke on the Thursday after the Feast of Saint Lucy, 1282.[1]

Thus fell, Llywelyn, Prince of Wales, in defence of the noblest and most glorious cause, the liberty and independence of his country, after a reign of thirty-six years. Had he survived the fatal day it is hard to say what might have been the consequence.

He has been accused by some historians of inconstancy and ingratitude, but with what shadow of justice let the reader determine, after having perused the long list of grievances which he urged in excuse for his hostilities against the English, and the little regard that was paid to his complaints.

Every generous Briton should here drop a tear over the ruins of a brave and heroic people, who for so many

---

[*] Einion, Bishop of Bangor.

[1] See Peckham Register, f. 100 b. in Bibl. Lambeth. This letter was translated by William Harling, Esq., of Chester, from a copy of the original, several parts of which are obscure and difficult to render into English, from the quaint construction of the old French and Italian words gallicised, in consequence of which the translator has been obliged to depart considerably from the construction of several sentences to make the meaning intelligible. The faults in grammar were more easily got over. The archbishop addressed another letter (from Pembroke, Dec. 13, 1282) to the king himself on the subject of the papers. His grace adds, that Dame Mahaud Longespeye prayed him to pronounce sentence of absolution upon the Prince, to the intent that he might be interred in holy ground : but that he declined it, unless she could bring evidence that Llywelyn discovered signs of repentance in his last moments: Rymer. This benevolent lady was cousin-german to the deceased, being daughter and sole heiress of Walter de Clifford, Lord of Corfton and Culmington in Shropshire, by Margaret, daughter of Llywelyn the Great. Her first husband, William Lonspe, was son of William Earl of Salisbury ; but she was at this time the wife of John Giffard of Brimsfield.

centuries maintained their freedom against all the efforts of the English monarchs. And, indeed, whether we consider the length of the contest, the inequality of the forces, the motives that prompted the English to attack, or the principles that animated the Welsh to resist, we will hardly find a similar case in history.

The cause of the Welsh was the cause of liberty and independence, and, therefore, the common cause of mankind. Accursed, therefore, be the partiality and injustice of those historians, who, blinded by national prejudices, and dead to the finer feelings of humanity, refuse to the memory of a brave and generous people, that tribute of praise and commendation which their virtues so amply deserve.

It will ever redound to the honour of the Welsh that, placed as they were, in the most disadvantageous circumstances, they yet maintained their freedom for such a length of time, and that when they fell, they fell into a state, not of slavery, but of dependence, and into such a state of dependence as seems rather to be the result of an union than a conquest.

Had Edward considered the matter in this light, he would never have treated the remains of Llywelyn with that cruelty and barbarity with which he used them.

He sent his head immediately to London, where it was received with the most extravagant demonstrations of joy, and the citizens carried it through Cheapside, erected upon the point of a spear, and adorned with a silver circlet or crown, as a burlesque accomplishment of the soothsayer's prediction; then it was placed in the pillory to glut the revenge of a brutish rabble, to shock the delicacy of every person of sentiment, to move the compassion of the humane and generous, and to fill every thoughtful and considerate mind with serious reflections upon the instability of all earthly greatness.

Such was the end of the most illustrious man of the age in which he lived, who deserved to be compared with the most celebrated characters of ancient times; both for his greatness of mind in meeting dangers, and for his wisdom and valour in overcoming them. In love for his country he was equalled by none, for in defence of the public cause he was neither to be seduced by rewards nor intimidated by power; and whilst some of the land had submitted to the yoke of Edward, he was determined to be free!

This brave and heroic prince reigned thirty-six years, universally beloved by all his subjects. He died leaving only one daughter[2] to survive him. The English historians of these times are silent respecting the character or personal qualities of this Prince. But the conduct of his life was the best illustration of his character. And if the valour of Llywelyn, his talents, and his patriotism, had been exerted upon a more splendid theatre, on the plains of Marathon, or in the Straits of Thermopylæ, his name would have been recorded in the classic page, and his memory revered, as that of an illustrious hero, and a gallant assertor of the rights of nature. But no trophies have been raised to celebrate his fame. The vindictive spirit or policy of his conqueror found an interest in burying amidst the ruins of freedom almost every trace or monumental record which might preserve the memory of this Prince, or perpetuate his glory. Gratitude however could pay no tribute so expressive as the tears which his country shed over the tomb of their fallen sovereign.

An elegy, composed by a bard who lived in the court of Llywelyn, in wild and plaintive notes, and with a seemingly prophetic spirit, finely expresses the sorrow and despair of the Welsh.

"The voice of lamentation is heard in every place as heretofore in Camlan. The copious tears stream down every cheek; for Cambria's defence, Cambria's munificent lord, is fallen. O Llywelyn, the loss of thee is the loss of all. At the thought of thee a horror chills my blood, exhausts my spirits, and consumes my flesh. Behold how the course of nature is changed! How trees of the forests furiously rush against each other! See how the ocean deluges the earth; how the sun deviates from its course; how the planets start from their orbits. Say, ye thoughtless mortals, do not these things portend the

---

[2] It appears that the daughter of Llywelyn, and the daughter of his brother David, were confined in a nunnery in England; as an order was sent by Edward seven years after the deaths of their parents, to Thomas de Normanville, to enquire minutely into the state and safe custody of the said Princesses. Rymer, vol. ii. p. 429. This daughter of Llywelyn and Eleanor de Montfort, whom he called Catherine Lackland, was sent by Edward, attended by a nurse, to be educated in England. She was afterwards married to Malcolm, Earl of Fife. Llywelyn is also said to have had a son of the name of Madoc; but he must certainly have been illegitimate, as that Prince had been only once married. Mill's Catalogue of Honour, p. 310. It is most probable that David's daughter remained in England and died a nun.

dissolution of nature? And let it be dissolved! Let kind heaven hasten the grand catastrophe. Let a speedy end be put to the incurable anguish of our spirits; since now there is no place to which we, miserable men, may flee; no spot where we may securely dwell; no friendly counsel; no safe retreat; no way by which we can escape our unhappy destiny." [3]

PRINCE DAVID, after the death of his brother, Prince Llywelyn, assumed the reins of government, and attempted to renew the war to recover the Principality; but the same superstition which had formerly inspired his men with courage now filled them with despair. On the death of their favourite prince they either abandoned his cause or followed it with reluctance. The same event gave additional courage to the English; and before the Welsh could recover from the effect of their recent and irreparable loss, the enemy followed up their victorious career, took possession of a portion of Snowdonia, and routed the Welsh in all directions.

The Earl of Warwick now received orders to explore the recesses of the Snowdon hills, and secure the stability of the conquest by putting to death every person found in arms. He obeyed the injunctions of his sovereign but too well. In a pass on the mountain (the "Thermopylæ of Cambria") he attacked a numerous body of the Welsh; and, after a sanguinary conflict, by a superiority in numbers and tactics, he vanquished the gallant patriots, who, struggling for their expiring liberties, when they failed to conquer, chose to fall.

A quaint but generally faithful historian gives the following account of the action:—

" Whilst the King remained at Conway, the Earl of Warwick being informed that a great number of Welsh were assembled, and had lodged themselves in a certain valley betwixt two woods, chose out a troop of horse, together with some cross-bowmen and archers, and set upon them in the night time. The Welsh being thus surprised, and unexpectedly encompassed about by their enemies, made the best haste they could to oppose them; and so pitching their spears in the ground, and directing the points towards the enemy, endeavoured by such means to keep off the horse. But the Earl of Warwick having ordered his battle, so that between every two horses there stood a cross-bowman, did so gall the Welsh with the shot of their quarrels, that the spearmen fell apace, and then the horse, breaking in easily upon the rest, bare them down with so great a slaughter as the Welsh had never received before."

The Cymry fled precipitately and took shelter in their mountains and fastnesses. They were vigorously pursued with fire and sword, and the unresisting natives were slaughtered without mercy. An ancient historian [4] has observed that more than three thousand perished in this dreadful carnage. What generous lover of his country, who reads this tragic history, but would pronounce over the names of these brave defenders of their country the emphatic sentiment of the poet—

> " Rest, ye brave dead! 'midst the hills of your sires;
> Oh! who would not slumber, when freedom expires!
> Lonely and voiceless your halls must remain,
> The children of song may not breathe in the chain."—HEMANS.

Prince David managed to conceal himself and family for some time after this event, though he suffered extremely from want of provisions. At length one of his countrymen who served the King as a spy, discovered the place of the Prince's retreat, and on the night of the 21st of June he treacherously delivered him up to Edward.[5] The King sent a detachment of his army and took David in a morass.[6] This Prince with his wife, two sons and seven daughters, were brought prisoners to Rhuddlan

---

[3] Gryffydd ap yr Ynad Côch wrote the poem from which this passage is extracted, and if it were possible for a translation to transfuse half the excellence of the original, it would show the Bard was equally inspired with the true spirit of poetry, as affected by the fate of his beloved Prince.

[4] Polydore Virgil, p. 282.

[5] This was Einion ap Evan, afterwards made Bishop of Bangor by Edward I. This prelate was well paid for his treachery, for according to a MS. belonging to the Bangor Cathedral, which was lent to us by the courtesy of the very Rev. Dean Cotton, it appears that Edward bestowed upon him and his successors for ever, the ferries of Borthwen and Cadnant, three manors in the County of Caernarvon, and two in the Isle of Anglesea. Einion had the honour of baptising the King's son, born at Caernarvon, afterwards Edward II., and the above MS. intimates that the above property was given for performing that office; but other historians differ.

[6] Rymer's Fœdera, vol. ii. p. 247.

Castle, where the King then resided.[7] This unfortunate Prince was examined at Rhuddlan, and several very curious relics were found upon him; among the rest was one called *Croesenydd,*[8] or a part of the real cross of Christ, highly venerated by the Prince of Wales, and the crown of the celebrated King Arthur,[1] which, with several others, were taken from him and delivered to the King.

In this deserted situation, David early entreated for liberty to speak to the King, but, in spite of frequent solicitations, this small favour was denied him. He also implored for mercy, which also was denied him. How striking is the contrast formed by the conduct of Edward towards the unfortunate David, when compared with the mild and noble behaviour of the Emperor Claudius to the brave, yet unsuccessful, Caractacus, the celebrated Silurian and Ordovicean chief, or, as Tacitus says he described himself, "*plurium gentium imperator,*" who was taken and carried prisoner to Rome about the year 50, after having bravely defended his country against the Roman power for nine years. The eloquence and dignified deportment of Caradoc, or Caractacus,[2] so affected the congenial Claudius, that he was liberated, and permitted to return with his family to Britain, leaving his father Brân as hostage.[3]

Edward caused David to be removed from Rhuddlan Castle to Chester Castle, from whence he was sent in chains to Shrewsbury. Here the King summoned a Parliament to meet on the 30th of September, 1283. By the first writ the lords only were summoned to appear, but the second writ was directed to the commonalty of every county, directing them to choose two knights each; the third to the cities and boroughs; the fourth to the judges. The King himself appeared in person, together with eleven earls and one hundred barons, who were commissioned to try him.

Before this august assembly, David, Prince of Wales, was tried as a vassal of the Crown and a peer of the realm, though we believe that, in reality, he was neither the one nor the other; for, after making every research and inquiry, we have not been able to find out any traces of his ever having been created baron of the realm; and he always claimed a sovereignty independent of the Crown of England. During this time, the King was staying at Acton Burnel, near Shrewsbury, the seat of his Chancellor, but, according to our Welsh records, he presided at the trial in person.

The trial, we may suppose, did not occupy much time. The prisoner would not be permitted to dispute the fact of his vassalage; that of his revolt could not be denied: it was not the usage of that period to allow any advocates to plead his cause, and he was soon condemned to an ignominious and most cruel death: this last part of the transaction appears to us to call for unqualified reprobation on the conduct of the King. Had he respected the patriotism of David, or his proximity to the aboriginal throne of North Wales, and spared his life, every one would have applauded conduct so noble and magnanimous. But his conduct in devising, or in permitting his nobles or lawyers to devise, and to carry into act, a new and most barbarous mode of execution,[4] deserves the execration of mankind.

There is something singular in the sentence pronounced against the Prince by John Vaux, Chief Justice of England. He was condemned to five different kinds of punishment: to be drawn at the tails of horses through the streets of Shrewsbury to the place of execution, because he was a traitor to the King; to be hanged, for having murdered Fulk Trigald and others, in the Castle of Hawarden; his heart[5] and

[7] Matthew Westminster, p. 177.—" For his treacherous conduct to David the last Prince of Wales, Einion was promoted to the See of Bangor. In his new and official capacity, the first duty he had to perform was to excommunicate his countryman, Prince David. But so generally was he hated for this act that he was obliged to quiet his diocese and retire to Reading or St. Alban's, in one of which convents he ended his days."—*Browne Willis's Bangor.*

[8] J. Rossi's Ant. Warw., p. 202. See Annales Waverlienses, p. 238.

[1] Nennius says that Prince Arthur brought a part of the real cross from the Holy Land.

[2] Vide Tacitus, lib. 13.　　[3] See pages 16, 17.

[4] Trivet thus relates it. " 1283. Ante festum S. Joannis Bapt. captus est David frater principis, et Rodolanum adductus: quem

Rex ad sui conspectum admittere renuens, licet hoc ipse David instantius flagitaret, Salopiam transmisit carceri mancipandum. Parliamentum post festum S. Michaelis est habitum Salopiæ: in quo, per deputatos ad hoc justitiarios, David judicialiter condemnatus, tractus, et suspensus est; visceribusq; combustis, corpus capite truncatum, et in quatuor partes est divisum: quibus in civitatibus Angliæ majoribus suspensis, caput Londoniis super palum fixum est ad terrorem consimilium proditorum." P. 259.

[5] There is a tradition extant, that when David's heart was thrown into the fire, one of Edward I.'s courtiers was ordered to superintend this part of the sentence. He took his sword and turned it in the fire; the heart being very much swollen with heat, caused it to explode, and it flew with great force from the fire, and struck the

bowels to be burnt, because those murders had been perpetrated on Palm Sunday; his head to be cut off; his body to be quartered, and to be hung in four different parts of the kingdom. This sentence, cruel in the extreme, the rigour of which had refined into novelty, was executed on David in all its severity. To feast still more the eyes of the people, his head was sent to the Tower of London, and, being fixed on a pole, was placed opposite that of his brother Llywelyn.*

Every generous idea and every sentiment of delicacy seemed to have been extinguished in national hatred, and in the frenzy of joy which had seized on the English. Here was a Prince of royal descent, bred up with tenderness, and one shining amongst the nobles of the English court, dragged by horses through the streets and lanes of Shrewsbury, without, it is probable, the accommodation of a hurdle, afterwards hung up for a short time, then taken down while yet alive, for the purpose of taking his heart and bowels from his body, to be burnt. This cruel barbarity is not only a disgrace to the memory of that monarch, but a severe satire upon human nature.

The death of David closed the sovereignty of the ancient British empire, which, according to the Cambrian Records, continued from the first coming of Brutus, 1136 before Christ, to 1282 after Christ, a period combining not less than *two thousand four hundred and eighteen years!* When we consider this, we cannot be surprised at the resolute courage with which they rallied around the standard of their independence; a reflection on their patriotic perseverance, even at this distant period, is enough to awaken in our breasts the emotions of sympathy and regret.

The ancient Britons bravely withstood the army of Imperial Rome, and ably resisted the utmost efforts of the Picts, Scots, and Saxons, and, through various degrees of fortune, afterwards successfully resisted the Norman princes.

Having been so long occupied with the history of the Castle of Rhuddlan, the scene of so much that was important in our past history, in the days of its glory, we cannot refrain, in the spirit of sympathy, from making a few reflections on its decay.

The ruins of this castle exhibit a picture of faded prosperity, a scene of havoc, ruin, and desolation, and who that is capable of reflection, or that is alive to human feelings, can muse on it with indifference.

How often has this spot, now peopled only with images of gloom, been enlivened by the array of all that was magnificent and splendid in feudal pomps; by groups of "high-born beauties and enamoured chiefs;" by whatever could delight the imagination, or awaken the most powerful emotions of the heart! Beneath these mouldering arches how often have the sweetest notes of minstrelsy broken upon the ear! How often have those ivy-mantled walls witnessed the sprightly dance and resounded to the voice of mirth, to the festive and the choral song! so well expressed in the following distich, by one of the Welsh bards :—

"Y llwybrau gynt lle bu'r gân,
Yw lleoedd y ddyllan!"
"What formerly were musical walks of song,
Are now the dreary habitations of the owl."

Amid these deserted and silent towers, how often has despotism unsheathed its sword and rioted without control in cruelty and bloodshed! How often has oppression here set at nought every tender sentiment of pity, and doomed the simple, the unoffending, and the helpless, to famine and to death! How often, too, has abject servility bowed its knee and hugged its degrading chain! All these have vanished!

courtier in the eye, which blinded him for life. Thus, David, as it were, even in death, had the last blow, and resented the cruelties and injuries to which in life he had been subjected. The following couplet by one of our Bards commemorates the event :—
"Cof o'r golwyth Amwythig
O'r tan a fwriai naid dig," &c.
Anglicised thus :—
"His heart from the fire with fury did jump,
And gave the foul courtier a glorious good thump;

Let this be a lesson, to the foe that would fry
The heart of another—to take care of his eye!"

* This was done to fulfil a prophecy current among the natives of Wales, which stated that "a Prince of their own people should be crowned in London." To accomplish this prediction in the same spirit in which many similar predictions have been fulfilled, his head was tauntingly surrounded by a crown of paper gilt.

Well may the contemplation inspire the lonely wanderer with awe; well may it touch their bosom, and realise in them the conviction that there is only One Being whom age cannot reach nor change affect; that earthly glory is but as the mockery of a dream;[7] that the baser passions of our nature, though they may revel for a season, amidst crowns and canopies of state, will not eventually triumph; and that every thing which depends for its support on the children of Adam, bearing the stamp of mortal vanity, is hastening to decay, and will soon be buried in forgetfulness.

The Ruins of Rhuddlan Castle.

On looking over the present ruins of this once important castle, involuntary reflections start up at every footstep, particularly when we lingeringly pass through the desolate spaces which once glittered with all the trappings of state, and had been occupied as the fine courts, the royal apartments, and the magnificent halls of not only the ancient Princes of Wales, but of England; all now lies open and abandoned. Except where turned into little gardens, weeds and grass cover all the lower rooms, the mantled ivy creeps up the sides of the walls, twines round the pillars, forces its way through the fissures, and becomes, in many places, not merely an ornamental but a defensive girdle to the crumbling walls. How irresistibly does the sentiment " *Sic transit gloria mundi*," force itself upon the mind in such situations as these ! Here we might say, "how are the mighty fallen !"

In contemplating these majestic ruins, ideas of by-gone days rush like ghosts of grandeur upon the mind, and we murmur the pathetic verse of the poet :—

> " Oh, what are pomp and sublunary power !
> And what is man that boasts himself so high !
> The sport of fate—the tenant of an hour—
> Dust, animated dust, that breathes to die ! "—HOOLE.

---

[7] The late Emperor of France, in speaking of the ambition which proved his ruin, said with equal truth and eloquence, " I willingly resign myself to every brilliant dream."

THE FOLLOWING IS THE COPY OF A ROLL CONTAINING AN ACCOUNT OF THE EXPENSES OF KING EDWARD THE FIRST, AT RHUDDLAN CASTLE, FLINTSHIRE, IN THE TENTH AND ELEVENTH YEARS OF HIS REIGN, 1281—1282.

THIS interesting document was discovered in 1805 among the unsorted records in the White Tower, London, by Samuel Lysons, Esq., F.R.S. It has since been translated by the Rev. John Brand, late Secretary of the Royal Antiquarian Society. The Roll consists of four membranes, containing the particulars of the sums paid to the workmen employed at the Castle, in making considerable additions to it on that occasion. The wages of the archers, sailors, workmen, the officers of the household, &c., are also detailed under proper heads, besides a great variety of curious items, arranged under the head of necessaries. Rhuddlan, or as it is called in the records, Rothelan Castle, appears to have been the headquarters of the King during his expedition against Prince Llywelyn; and most of his orders entered on the Rotuli Walliæ of the 10th and 11th year of his reign are entered thence.

	£	s.	d.
Imprimis the said Richard (de Bures) charges himself with having received from the King's Wardrobe in his tenth year, at several times	858	6	8
From the same, by Peter de Welles	37	4	0
From the same, by the Mayor of York	233	6	8
In the same year, by the fine of Lady de Baliol for her Welsh service	26	13	4
By the fine of the Baron of Greystock	80	0	0
By the fine of the Abbot of Glastonbury	23	6	8
The same acknowledges that he has received from the King's Wardrobe in his eleventh year	934	2	4½
From Sir William de Perton	40	0	0
Total of Receipt	£2232	19	8½

Necessary Expenses.—Carpenters.

	£	s.	d.
On Friday next after the Feast of the Assumption of the Blessed Mary at Rothelan, paid to Master Richard Lengingam receiving by the day 12d. for his wages, and the wages of three overseers of twenty, each receiving 6d. per diem, and sixty-three carpenters, each receiving 4d. by the day, going to Anglesey for sixteen days; viz., from Sunday the 23rd of August to the 7th day of September, each day being reckoned	18	16	0
On the Sunday next ensuing, paid to Master Peter de Brompton, for the wages of an hundred carpenters, each receiving 4d. per diem, and their constable receiving 8d. by the day; of which, five are overseers of twenty, and each receives 6d. per diem for his wages, from Sunday 23rd of August, for the seven following days	12	3	9
Sunday the 30th of August, paid to fourscore and six carpenters of the above number, with their overseers of twenties, for their wages, from Sunday August 30th, for the seven following days, and for the wages of Master Henry of Oxford, carpenter, their captain, receiving 8d. per diem for the same time, by the hands of P. de Brompton	10	10	0
Sunday the 6th of September, paid to Master Henry of Oxford, and fourscore and fourteen carpenters,			

	£	s.	d.
with their overseers of twenties, from Sunday the 6th of September, for the seven following days, by the hands of Master P. de Brompton	11	8	8
For the wages of seven carpenters newly received, by the hands of John of London, for the said seven days, one of them receiving 6d. and each of the others 4d.	0	17	6
For the wages of fifteen carpenters and shoeing-smiths, each receiving 4d. a day, except one, who only received 3d. per diem, from Sunday 30th of August, for the seven following days	1	14	5
Sum	55	10	5

Carpenters.

	£	s.	d.
Item for the wages of twelve of the aforesaid carpenters, from Sunday 6th of September, for the seven following days	1	8	0
Sunday 13th day of September, paid to an hundred and eight carpenters, the constable and overseers of twenties being accounted for, and two smiths and two shoeing-smiths. The constable to receive per diem 8d. the overseers of twenties 6d. and each of the others 3d. except one, who receives 3d. for their wages, from Sunday the 13th day of September, for the seven following days, by the hands of P. de Brompton	12	12	7
Monday, the 22nd of September, paid to an hundred and eight carpenters and others aforesaid, for their wages, from Sunday 21st day of September for the seven following days	12	12	7
Tuesday, the Feast of St. Michael, paid to one hundred and twenty carpenters, and one overseer of twenty, with the constable, overseers of twenties, smiths, and others aforesaid, being accounted for, for their wages, from Sunday 28th of September to the 3rd day of October, each day being reckoned, for seven days, by the hands of Master P. de Brompton	15	5	0
Item, for the wages of twelve carpenters and one overseer of twenty, from the Tuesday next after the Feast of All Saints, to the Monday next following, each day being reckoned, for seven days	1	11	6

	£	s.	d.
For the wages of twenty carpenters, with the overseers of twenty, two shoeing-smiths and two smiths, from the Tuesday next before the Feast of All Saints to the Monday next following, for seven days . .	2	16	7
For the wages of the same, from the Tuesday next after the Feast of All Saints, for the seven following days	2	16	7
Sum . .	48	18	3

Carpenters.

	£	s.	d.
Wednesday, 21st day of October, at Rothelan, paid to sixty carpenters (the constable and overseers of twenties being included) for their wages, and the wages of two smiths and two shoeing-smiths, each receiving 4d. a day ; the constable and overseers of twenties as before, from Tuesday next after the Feast of St. Luke to Monday on the morrow of All Saints, for fourteen days	15	10	4
Tuesday, the 3rd of November, paid to three overseers of twenties . . . . . and shoeing-smiths for their wages, from Tuesday next after the feast of All Saints to the Monday next following, for seven days	6	16	6
Item, paid to William Bird, carpenter, receiving 4d. per diem for his wages, from Friday, 2nd of April, to the Vigil of Easter for sixteen days .	0	5	4
To the same for the wages of one carpenter, receiving 4d. by the day, from Friday, 2nd April, for the seven following days	0	1	9
Tuesday in Easter week, paid to a carpenter working in the castle, for his wages for three days . .	0	1	0
To William Bird for his wages, from Friday next after the feast of St. Peter ad Vincula, for the four following days	0	1	4
For the expenses of nine carpenters going from Maclesfield to Aberconway, by the King's order . .	0	6	0
To William de Tiringham, clerk, appointed for the payment of the carpenters wages, from Sunday 23rd day of August to Sunday the 21st of September, for twenty-eight days, at 4d. per diem . .	0	9	4
To two smiths, one receiving 4d. per diem, and the other 3d. for their wages, from Sunday 23rd of August to Sunday 12th of September, each day being reckoned, for twenty-one days	0	12	3
To the same for their wages from Tuesday next after the feast of All Saints, and for two shoeing-smiths, from that same day, each of the shoeing-smiths receiving by the day 3d. for the nine following days	0	9	9
Sum . .	24	13	7

Sailors.

	£	s.	d.
Friday next after the feast of the Assumption of the Blessed Mary, at Rothelan, paid to forty-seven sailors of the King, conducting ships to Anglesey, for their wages, from Sunday 23rd day of August, for seven days, each receiving per diem 3d. except seven, each of whom received per diem 6d. . .	4	14	6
For the wages of seven boys, serving the said seven masters for the same time, each receiving 2d. per diem	0	8	2
To the master of the King's galley, receiving 6d. by the day, and to nine sailors of the said galley, each			

	£	s.	d.
receiving 3d. per diem for their wages, for the said seven days	0	19	3
Monday, the last day of August, paid to the said fifty-six sailors, with eight masters and six boys, for their wages for seven days, from Sunday 30th of August to Saturday the 5th day of September, by the hands of Symon le Rous	6	0	2
For the wages of nine sailors, with the master of the ship, called the Marye of Lyme, the master receiving 6d. a day, for the said seven days . . .	0	17	6
To the master of the galley of Chester, and his nine sailors for their wages, from Sunday the 28th day of September, for the four following days . .	0	11	0
To a certain sailor bringing the King's venison from Chester to Rothelan, for his wages . .	0	6	8
To a certain servant, keeping the said venison at sea, for his wages for seven days	0	1	2
Sum . .	13	18	5

Archers.

	£	s.	d.
Saturday next after the Feast of the Assumption of the Blessed Mary, at Rothelan, paid to Geoffry le Chambelin, for the wages of twelve crossbow men, thirteen archers, for twenty-four days, viz., from the day of the Assumption of the Blessed Mary to the Vigil of her Nativity, each day being reckoned, each cross-bow man receiving by the day 4d., and each archer 2d.	7	8	0
Thursday, 27th of August, paid to Robert Giffard for the wages of eight constables of cavalry, each receiving per diem 12d., and of eight hundred and fifty-seven archers, each receiving by the day 2d., and of their forty-three captains of twenties, each receiving 4d. per diem, from Tuesday the 25th day of August, for the seven following days . .	55	6	0
To Master R. Giffard, for the wages of six archers, newly come, from Friday 27th of August, for the six following days	0	6	0
Thursday, 3rd day of September, paid to Guillemyn and his companion, cross-bow men, for their wages, from Thursday 20th day of August to Wednesday the 2nd day of September, each day being reckoned, each receiving 6d. a day	0	13	0
To Master R. Giffard, for the wages of eight constables and eight hundred and twenty-six archers, with forty-one captains of twenties, from Wednesday the 2nd day of September to the Wednesday next after the Feast of the Nativity of the Blessed Mary, for seven days	53	7	6
Friday next after the Feast of the Nativity of the Blessed Mary, paid to Master R. Giffard, for the wages of one thousand and forty archers, and ten constables, and fifty-two captains of twenties, from the Thursday next after the Feast of the Nativity of the Blessed Mary to the Wednesday next after the Feast of the Exaltation of the Holy Cross, each day being reckoned	67	4	0
Friday next after the Feast of the Exaltation of the Holy Cross, for the wages of a thousand and sixty archers, with fifty-three captains of twenties, from the Thursday next after the Feast of the Exaltation of the Holy Cross, to the Wednesday next after the			

x

	£	s.	d.
Feast of St. Matthew the Apostle, each day being reckoned, for seven days, with the wages of ten constables of cavalry	68	8	6
Sum .	252	14	0

Archers.

	£	s.	d.
Friday next after the feast of St. Matthew the Apostle, paid to Master R. Giffard for the wages of a thousand and twenty archers, with fifty-one captains of twenties, from Thursday next after the feast of St. Matthew the Apostle, to Wednesday next after the feast of St. Michael, for seven days following, each day being reckoned, with ten constables of cavalry .	65	19	6
To Guillemine and his companion, cross-bow men, for their wages, from Wednesday, the 2d day of September to Wednesday next after the feast of St. Matthew the Apostle, for twenty-one days, at 2d. by the day.	1	1	0
Wednesday next after the feast of St. Michael, paid to eight constables and one hundred archers, being in the fortification of the castle of Flint, for their wages, from Tuesday on the feast of St. Michael to the Monday next following, for the seven days ensuing, by the hands of Master William Pyforer .	6	9	6
To Master R. Giffard, for the wages of the same archers, from the Tuesday next after the feast of St. Michael to the Monday next following, for seven days, by the hands of Master William Piforer . . .	6	9	6
To Master R. Giffard, for the wages of a thousand archers, from Thursday next after the feast of St. Michael to the Wednesday on the morrow of St. Faith, each day being reckoned, for seven days, reckoning the constable and captains of twenties .	63	15	0
Monday 25th day of October, at Rothelan, paid to Master R. Giffard, for the wages of four constables, four hundred archers, from Sunday 24th day of October, to Wednesday the 4th day of November, for eleven days	40	14	0
To Master William de Audeley, for the wages of five constables, five hundred and forty archers, with twenty-seven captains of twenties, from Saturday next after the feast of St. Luke to Thursday on the morrow of the Apostles Simon and Jude, for six days	29	17	0
To Master R. Giffard, for the wages of three hundred and fifty-eight archers, with seventeen captains of twenties, or constables, from the Friday next after the feast of the Apostles Simon and Jude, for three days, to Sunday on the morrow of All Saints	9	7	6
Sum .	224	13	0

Archers.

	£	s.	d.
To Master Giffard, for the wages of one constable of foot, receiving 6d. per diem, and of fifty-three archers, with two captains of twenties, from Monday on the feast of All Souls to the Wednesday following, for three days	1	9	0
Thursday the 14th of January, paid to Master R. Giffard for the wages of five constables, five hundred and twenty archers, with twenty-six captains of twenties, from Thursday aforesaid to Wednesday next after			

	£	s.	d.
the feast of the Conversion of St. Paul, for the fourteen days following	67	4	0
To Master William le Botiller for the wages of one constable, two hundred and six archers, with ten captains of twenties, from Saturday 16th day of January to Wednesday 27th day of the same month, for twelve days	22	4	0
Tuesday next after the feast of the Ascension of our Lord, paid to Master R. Giffard for the wages of two hundred archers, with two constables and ten captains of twenties, from Sunday on the feast of St. Benedict to Saturday the 15th day of May, for fifty-six days .	103	12	0
Sunday on the feast of Pentecost, paid to Master R. Giffard, for the wages of one constable and one hundred archers, from the said Sunday 16th day of May, to Saturday next after the octaves of the Holy Trinity, for twenty-one days	19	8	6
St. John Baptist's day, paid to Richard de Estham for the wages of fifty-seven archers, with three captains of twenties, from the Sunday next after the feast of St. John the Baptist to the Saturday next following, for seven days	3	10	0
Sunday on the feast of the Translation of St. Martin, paid to Master R. Giffard for the wages of fifty archers and one constable of cavalry, with three captains of twenties, from the said Sunday to Saturday the 10th day of July, for seven days .	3	8	10
Sunday on the feast of the Translation of St. Benedict, paid to the same for the wages of fifty archers, from the said Sunday to Saturday on the Vigil of St. James, each day being reckoned, for sixteen days	6	5	0
Saturday the 4th day of September, at Chester, paid to Richard de Daneport, receiving 12d. per diem for his wages, and of sixty archers, conducting David de Rothelan to Chester, for two days . .	2	3	0
For the wages of R. Clerk of Master R. Giffard, from Friday next before the feast of St. Bartholomew, to Wednesday on the morrow of St. Faith, each day being reckoned, for forty-nine days, at 4d. per diem, the Lord Bishop of Bath being voucher .	0	16	4
Sum .	229	0	8

Masons.

	£	s.	d.
Sunday next after the feast of the Assumption of the Blessed Mary, paid to one master mason, receiving 6d. per diem, and five masons each receiving 4d. and one workman receiving 3d. a day for their wages, from the said Sunday to the Saturday next before the feast of St. Matthew the Apostle, for twenty-eight days	3	7	8
To the same master for his wages, and his four masons and one workman, from Sunday on the Vigil of St. Matthew, for the seven following days . . .	0	14	7
To the same for his wages, and of his three masons and one workman, from Sunday next before the feast of St. Michael to the third day of October, for seven days	0	12	3
To the same for his wages, and of three masons and two workmen, from Sunday on the feast of St. Luke to Saturday next after the feast of All Saints, each day being reckoned, for twenty-one days .	2	2	0

	£	s.	d.
Saturday the 15th day of January, paid to eleven masons sent to the King, for their wages of three days, by order of Master W. de Luda	1	2	0
Sum . .	7	18	6

Mowers.

	£	s.	d.
Sunday next after the feast of St. John Baptist, paid to twenty-two mowers, each receiving 1d. ¼ per diem for their wages, from St. John Baptist's day, for four days following	0	11	0
Wednesday following, paid to twenty-three mowers, each receiving 6d. per diem for their wages of two days	1	3	0
Thursday following, paid to the said mowers for Thursday	0	11	6
Item, to twelve spreaders for their wages, during the said three days, viz. Tuesday, Wednesday, and Thursday, each receiving 2d.	0	6	0
Friday 2d day of June, paid to twenty-three mowers for their wages that day	0	11	6
Item, to the said twelve spreaders of hay for their wages that day	0	2	0
Wednesday on the feast of the Translation of St. Thomas the Martyr, paid to fourscore and sixteen spreaders of hay for their wages that day, whereof fourscore received each per diem 1d. ¼, and each of the others 2d.	0	12	8
For the wages of eighteen mowers, each receiving 2d. per diem for Wednesday and Thursday . . .	0	18	0
For the wages of nine spreaders of hay, each receiving 2d. per diem for the said two days . .	0	3	0
On the Sunday following, paid to thirteen mowers for their wages on Friday and Saturday . . .	0	13	0
For the wages of six spreaders of hay, on the said two days	0	2	0
Monday following, paid to one hundred and sixty spreaders of hay for their wages on Saturday and Monday	0	16	6
Tuesday 19th day of June, paid to thirteen mowers for their wages, on Monday, Tuesday, Wednesday, Thursday, Friday, Saturday, Monday, and Tuesday, each 6d. per diem	2	12	0
For the wages of thirty-three spreaders of hay, during the said eight days, each receiving per diem 2d.	2	4	0
Wednesday following, paid to sixteen mowers for their wages that day	0	7	9
For the wages of thirty spreaders of hay on that day .	0	5	1
On the Saturday following, paid to eleven mowers for their wages on Friday and Saturday . . .	0	1	2
To three spreaders of hay on that day	0	0	6
Sum . .	13	1	6

Necessaries.

	£	s.	d.
Tuesday next before the feast of the Blessed Mary Magdalen, for six carts, each with three horses, hired to carry the hay from the meadows to the castle of Rothelan, for one day . . .	0	6	10
For eight carts, each with two horses, hired for the carriage of the King's hay at Rothelan . .	0	6	8
Wednesday following, paid to twenty-four men raking			

	£	s.	d.
together and putting the hay in a mow, for their wages for one day	0	4	0
For the wages of two men mending the road, by which the hay was carried from the meadows . . .	0	0	10
Friday following, paid for twenty carts, hired for the carriage of the King's hay from the meadows to the castle, during three days	3	0	4
Item, to seventy-seven men, preparing, raising, raking together, and stacking the hay, during the said three days	1	14	4
For the carriage of turf, with which the house was covered, in which the hay was placed . . .	0	1	5
For mending the road for carrying the hay . . .	0	0	10
For an iron fork bought to turn the hay . . .	0	0	3
Saturday next before the feast of St. Peter ad Vincula, paid for three carts, hired for the carriage of the King's hay, on Friday and Saturday . . .	0	6	4
For the wages of thirty-one men, collecting and stacking the hay on the said two days	0	10	4
For the wages of twelve mowers, mowing the King's hay, for eight days	0	6	0
On the Sunday following, paid for one cart, with three horses, and one with two horses, hired for the carriage of the Queen's hay, for eight days . .	0	2	0
For the wages of seventeen spreaders of hay, for one day	0	2	10
For the making of a ditch about the house, where the said hay was put	0	1	8
For mending the hay-house	0	1	6
For three hundred and a half of nails to mend the said house	0	0	8
To eight men preparing the hay that day . . .	0	1	4
For five carts, each with three horses, for carrying the hay from the meadows to the castle, one day .	0	5	2
Sum . .	7	13	4

Necessaries.

	£	s.	d.
Monday next after the feast of St. Lawrence, paid to a certain workman for making a ditch about the Queen's hay-house	0	1	8
To a certain workman, for his wages for seven days, to clean the house in which the King's hay was put .	0	1	9
For putting and piling up one rick of hay in the house .	0	1	8
For taking hay out of the house, and drying it and putting it in again	0	1	10
To a certain servant, watching the hay in the meadows during seventy-six days	0	12	8
Saturday on the Feast of St. Ambrose, paid to William the Plumber, receiving 12d. per diem for his wages, from Sunday on the Feast of St. Benedict to Sunday the 18th of April, for twenty-nine days . .	0	1	9
To his boy, receiving 1s. 6d. per week for his wages during the same time	0	6	0
For eight cart loads of lead, price by the cart load 5s. bought to cover the King's chamber, in the castle of Rothelan	2	0	0
For twelve pounds of tin, bought for soldering . . .	0	2	5
For a melting-pot and brushwood, bought to cast the said lead	0	0	11
Monday 19th day of April, paid to the said William for his wages for sixty-seven days, viz. from Monday aforesaid to the day of the Nativity of St. John Baptist, each day being reckoned . . .	3	7	0

x 2

	£	s.	d.
For the wages of his boy nine weeks, during the said time	0	13	6
For the wages of another boy, six weeks of the said time	0	9	0
For one hundred and six pounds of tin, bought for soldering during the said time	1	1	3
For brushwood bought to melt the said lead during the same time	0	1	4
To the said William, for his wages of seventy-one days, viz. from Friday on the morrow of St. John Baptist to Friday 3d day of September, each day being reckoned	3	11	0
To his two boys for their wages during the said ten weeks	1	10	0
For brushwood bought to fuse the said lead during the same time	0	2	0
For carriage of tin from Chester to Rothelan	0	0	6
Sum	15	13	7

Necessaries.

	£	s.	d.
To John the Chandler for wick, brushwood, tallow, colour, and other things necessary in the office of the chandlery, from the Feast of the Assumption of the Blessed Mary to the Feast of St. Michael, at several times	3	1	5
Saturday next after the Feast of the Assumption of the Blessed Mary, at Rothelan, paid to Ranulph Foleschank for the wages of four charcoal-makers, one receiving 4d. and each of the others 3d. a day, from Sunday 23d day of August to Saturday the 12th day of September, each day being reckoned, for twenty-one days	1	1	9
To the same for the wages of four plasterers for the same time	1	2	9
For the wages of three servants serving the carpenters, and three serving the plumbers, for the same time, each receiving 3d. per diem	1	10	6
To David of Waltham and his companion, each receiving, 4d. a day; and to fifteen workmen, each receiving 3d. per diem for their wages, during the said time	4	12	9
For the wages of twenty-two workmen and one turf-cutter, receiving 5d. a day for their wages, from the Tuesday next after the Feast of the Exaltation of the Holy Cross to the Saturday next after the Feast of St. Michael, each day being reckoned, for nineteen days	5	12	5
To two men keeping the King's mill for their wages, from the Friday next after the Feast of St. Bartholomew, to the Tuesday on the morrow of the Holy Cross, each receiving 2d. per diem for nineteen days	0	6	4
For the wages of thirty workmen, working on the Vigil of the Holy Cross, each receiving 3d. per diem	0	15	0
To a certain plaisterer for his wages on these two days	0	1	0
Sum	18	4	11

Necessaries.

	£	s.	d.
To Henry de Greneford for timber, nails, and boards, bought for him, and for carts hired for the carriage of timber from Rhudland to the ships sailing towards Anglesey, with other minute expences	3	2	4½
To the same for large nails, small boards, and laths, and for the carriage of timber from the castle to the mill	1	16	0
To the same for eight thousand nails bought by him, and for divers carriages of timber and boards bought for the Queen's chamber, and for several houses of the castle, and to the King's hall	2	17	8
To the same for thirteen carts, four whereof with three horses each, and the other with two each, hired to carry timber from the wood of St. Asaph to the castle, and for loading and unloading of the same for one day	0	13	0
To the same for eleven carts, hired for one day, four of them with three horses, and seven with two horses, and for the wages of three men loading the said carts	0	10	2
To Ranulph Folescanks for timber bought for the workshop at Maclesfeld, by the King's command	0	2	0
For a certain mill-stone, with an iron axle-tree, bought for the workshop of the castle	0	7	1
For seven empty casks for making paling for the bridge of Rothelan	0	3	8
For locks bought to fasten the bars of the town and bridge by night	0	1	6
To Henry de Greneford for three thousand nails, and the wages of thirty men loading the ships with timber towards Anglesea, and for five carts hired for the same for one day	0	12	8
To the same for the wages of a boy watching the said timber, receiving 2d.¼ per diem from Friday next after the Feast of St. Bartholomew, for eighteen days following	0	3	9
Sum	10	9	10½

Necessaries.

	£	s.	d.
Tuesday on the Feast of St. Michael, paid for the wages of two turf-cutters for seven days, each receiving 5d. per diem	0	5	10
For the carriage of turves to cover the King's kitchen	0	7	6
For cradles and machines bought for the plaisterers of the houses of the castle	0	0	8
For a boat bought for the Queen's use, by Reginal Fikeis	0	14	0
For the carriage of dung out of the castle, and the carriage of turves to cover to houses of the castle, for six days, by the hands of David	1	1	4
For twenty-nine carts hired to seek litter in the field, for three days; and for the wages of twelve mowers and five men helping them, and gathering together the said litter, and of twelve men leading the said carts	2	16	11
To Henry Sparwe, the crier, receiving 4d. per diem for his wages from Sunday the 23rd day of August to Wednesday on the morrow of St. Michael, for thirty-nine days	0	13	0
To Master William, the King's baker, for five carts hired by him, to carry meal from Chester to Rothelan	0	5	10
For two carts to carry timber, for eighteen days	1	13	6
For the wages of three Welshmen working in the castle, three days	0	4	2
For the carriage of four casks filled with beans, ex-			

	£	s.	d.
pended in the household, from the water to the castle	0	2	0
For the making of the kitchen	0	10	6
Tuesday next before the Feast of the Ascension of our Lord, paid for the carriage of thirty-four casks of wine, from the water to the castle	1	0	5
For the carriage of Wheat ; viz., for 145 quarters, from Good Friday to the Vigil of the Ascension of our Lord, from the water to the castle	1	3	1
Sunday 24th day of October, at Rothelan, to David de Waltham, receiving 4d. per diem, and to one plaisterer receiving 4d. per diem, and nineteen workmen, each receiving 2d.¼ per diem for their wages, from Sunday on the Feast of St. Luke to the day next before the Feast of St. Martin, for twenty-three days	5	6	4½
Sum . .	16	5	1½

Necessaries.

	£	s.	d.
Monday the 25th day of October, paid to a certain Welsh workman in the castle, in different ways, receiving 2d. per diem for his wages, for sixteen days	0	3	4
To a certain turf-cutter, receiving 5d.¼ a day for his wages, for ten days	0	4	7
To six men carrying shingles to cover the hall of the castle, each receiving 2d.¼ per diem for their wages, for seven days	0	8	9
For the different carriage of timber, turves, boards, and old houses, to the castle, by the hands of David de Waltham, at different times	3	18	10
For the carriage of corn from the sea to the castle .	0	0	8
For the reparation of the bakehouse, by Richard de Paris	0	10	0
For thirty-nine thousand four hundred of nails, bought for the boards and laths for the houses of the castle	2	7	8
For a chain and lock bought for the boat, by the hands of Randal Foleschank	0	0	8
For lime bought for the Queen's chamber in the castle .	0	1	8
For twenty-two empty casks, bought to make paling for the Queen's court-yard	0	18	4
For making a house for the use of the King's fisherman	0	13	4
To Stephen, the painter, painting the King's chamber, and for colours bought by him, and for his pay .	0	14	0
For the carriage of venison from Chester to Rothelan .	0	0	9
To Wildebor, the fisherman, receiving 10d. per diem, and his six companions, the Queen's fishermen, each receiving 3d. per diem, fishing in the sea, for their wages, from Sunday 10th day of January to Sunday 21st of February, for forty-two days .	4	18	0
To the same for buying bait to catch fish .	0	2	6
To John of the Queen's Salsary, going to fish in the lakes of Stafford, for his wages, from Tuesday 19th day of January to the first day of February, for fourteen days, at 2d. per diem . . .	0	2	4
Sum . .	15	5	5

Necessaries.

	£	s.	d.
To John of the Queen's Salsary, for things wanted by him for sending fish to the King from Stafford into Wales	0	3	0
To William, the King's fisherman, and a boy, fishing in the lake of Stafford, for their wages of fourteen days ; viz., from the 19th day of January to the 1st day of February	0	4	1
To Richard le Forester, going to catch rabbits for the King's use, for his wages, and the keeping of his ferrets during the said time	0	3	6
To the three shoeing-smiths of the King returning to the King towards Standon, for their expences .	0	3	0
Monday on the morrow of St. Benedict, paid to William Bird for work about the Stewpond of the castle .	0	8	0
To William the Plumber making seats about the said Stewpond, for his pay	0	1	0
For the pay of four men filling the said Stewpond with water	0	0	8
The Tuesday following, paid for two carts with six horses hired to carry wheat from the water to the castle	0	2	4
For the reparation of a cart of the King's, conveying a pipe of honey from Aberconway to Rothelan .	0	1	4
For the carriage of figs and raisins sent to Aberconway	0	0	1
For two carts hired with six horses, bringing wheat from Chester to Rothelan	0	2	4
Thursday the 1st day of April, paid to John of the Queen's Salsary, for doing such things as were necessary for the sending of fish to the King from Stafford	0	5	0
For one cart with four horses, hired to convey the Queen's baggage from Rothelan to Aberconway .	0	2	0
For six hundred turves, bought to place about the Queen's Stewpond in the castle	0	1	0
For the carriage of the said turf into the castle, for three days	0	2	6
To Peacock and his boy, laying the said turves, for his wages for four days	0	1	8
Sum . .	2	1	6

Necessaries.

	£	s.	d.
Thursday the 1st day of April, paid for the carriage of figs and raisins from Rothelan to Aberconway .	0	0	8
Tuesday on the Feast of the Invention of the Holy Cross, paid to the King's tent-maker to buy such things as were necessary for mending the tents .	0	1	0
For timber bought for the works of the castle, by William Bird	0	2	0
For the carriage of three thousand pounds from the King's wardrobe to the wardrobe of the Queen .	0	0	5
For the carriage of the King's fruit from Rothelan to Aberconway	0	1	0
For the reparation of saddles and other harness belonging to the Queen's chariot	0	10	4
Tuesday 11th day of May, paid for the carriage of cheese from Rothelan to Aberconway . . .	0	0	4
For the carriage of Master Oto's robe to Master Oto .	0	0	5
For cleansing the Queen's Stewpond in the castle .	0	0	6
For filling the said Stewpond with water . . .	0	4	8
For one lock bought for the same Stewpond . .	0	0	4

	£	s.	d.
For removing and mending of two locks in the Queen's chamber	0	0	1½
For cleansing the court of the castle	0	1	4
For the passage of the Lady Joan, the King's daughter, at Aberconway	0	2	0
For carriage of the baggage of the King's daughter from Aberconway to Rothelan	0	3	8
For forks and rakes bought for the King's hay	0	1	5
For three tankards bought for the use of the Lady Elizabeth, the King's daughter	0	0	6
For the pay of four men carrying water to the King's Stewpond, within the castle	0	2	8
For the expenses of Richard de Foxcote, carrying wax from Rothelan to Karnarvan	0	0	8
To Henry de Montepesson for the carriage of wax and almonds from Chester to Rothelan	0	2	0
To a certain smith going to Maclesfeld for making the King's works there, for his expenses	0	2	0
For a posnet bought for the Lady Elizabeth, the King's Daughter	0	0	6
Sum	1	18	6½

Necessaries.

	£	s.	d.
On Friday next after the Feast of St. Lawrence, paid for the carriage of fourscore casks of wine from the water to the castle	1	2	0
For the carriage of nine quarters of wheat from Chester to Rothelan	0	3	0
For parchment bought for the Queen's wardrobe	0	1	4
For a cart bringing lances and crossbows from Rothelan to the Hope, going and coming	0	1	4
For mending the locks of the castle	0	4	0
To Hudde the baker, for the carriage of three hundred quarters of wheat, at different times, from the water to the castle	1	4	3
To the same for the repair of the granary where the wheat was placed	0	2	0
To the same for twelve horses, hired for the carriage of wheat from Ruthyn to Rothelan, for one day	0	4	0
To the same for one cart with three horses, hired for the same for one day	0	1	0
For a coffer, a posnet, a tankard, and a bucket, bought for the Lady Elizabeth, the King's daughter	0	2	1
Friday, the 3rd of September, paid for two carts, each with three horses, hired for the carriage of the baggage of the Queen's daughter from Rothelan to Flint, Chester, Wich,[1] and Macclesfield, for four days	0	9	4
For a cart with two horses, hired for the carriage of the baggage of Margaret de Burgh, for the said four days	0	3	4
For a cart with two horses, hired to carry the baggage of Maids of Honour of the Queen	0	3	4
For a cart with three horses, hired for the carriage of the baggage of the Lady de Hach	0	4	4
For a cart with four horses, hired for the carriage of the baggage of the Queen's wardrobe, for the said four days	0	6	0

[1] Wiz, in the original, must have been intended for *Wich*, meaning Norwich, on the road to Macclesfield.

	£	s.	d.
For a cart with two horses, hired for the carriage of the chapel of the King's daughter	0	3	4
For a chariot, hired to help to carry the baggage of Joan Ferre, for one day	0	0	6
For a cart with five horses, and one with two horses, hired for the carriage of the Queen's baggage from Bromburgh to Macclesfield, for five days	0	10	0
Sum	5	1	7

Necessaries.

	£	s.	d.
Friday, the 3rd day of September, paid for one cart with four horses, hired for the carriage of the coffers of the wardrode of the Queen, from Rothelan to Macclesfield, for four days	0	4	8
For the carriage of the baggage of the wardrobe robes of the Queen, from Carnarvon to Rothelan	0	8	6
For two carts, each with three horses, hired for the carriage of the said baggage from Chester to Macclesfield	0	7	0
To Geoffry of the Queen's butlery, for wines brought into the castle	0	10	6
To Matthew de Horne, in part of payment of 30l. due to him for the carriage of corn from Anglesey to Chester, by sea, by order of Thomas de Gonneys	13	6	8
To Baldwin, door-keeper, for making the hall of the castle	5	0	0
To the same for the carriage of timber of the hall	2	0	0
To William the Plumber, in part of payment of his wages	1	0	0
To the King's tent-maker, in part of payment of his wages	0	10	0
To Master Thomas the marshal, for the repair of the harness of the Queen's horses	0	12	0
Sum	23	18	10

Gifts.

	£	s.	d.
On the day of the Queen's churching, at Rothelan, paid to divers minstrels attending there by the Queen's Gift	10	0	0
To a certain female spy, as a gift	0	1	0
To Robert de Veteriponte, (Master W. de Luda being voucher), by way of gift	1	0	0
Tuesday on the Feast of the Nativity of the Blessed Mary, paid to William the Plumber retiring, by way of gift	0	13	4
To the messenger of the Lord Earl Gueldres, returning to his own country, as a gift	0	13	4
To a certain female spy, to purchase her a house, as a gift	1	0	0
To John Picard, for the restoration of a nag of his that was dead	2	0	0
To Admet the Taylor, for the restoring a nag of his that was dead	2	0	0
To certain servants of the Queen staying at Ruthyn, to the carriage of a cask of wine, by way of gift	0	2	8
Sunday on the Vigil of the Conversion of St. Paul, paid to Ralph le Vavassour, bringing news to the Queen of the taking of the castle Dolinthalein, as a gift	5	0	0
To John de Moese, coming immediately with the same news, with letters of the Earl of Gloucester, by way of gift	5	0	0
To Reginald, the boy of W. de Monterebello, coming with the same news, with letters of his Lord, by way of gift	0	6	8

	£.	s.	d.
On Friday next after the Feast of St. Benedict, paid to Boz, being sick, after the departure of the messengers of Arragon, by way of gift	0	2	0
To a certain poor woman, by way of gift, from the Queen	0	2	0
To certain sailors for the salvage of wines in a ship wrecked at sea, by way of gift	1	0	0
To a certain player, as a gift	0	1	0
To a certain boy, bringing to the Queen a palfrey, on the part of Master John de Bonn, by the Queen's gift .	0	2	6
Sum . .	19	4	6

Wardrobe.—Necessaries.

	£.	s.	d.
Tuesday on the Feast of the Nativity of the Blessed Mary, paid for six ells of web cloth, and six ells of strong fine linen, bought for pennons and Welsh standards of Ewyas, and for the making of the same	0	13	4
For twenty-two ells of web cloth, bought for divers offices the day of the Queen's uprising . . .	0	6	3
For the carriage of two casks, and one bale of almonds, from the sea to the castle	0	0	10
Thursday following, paid for cotton, bought for making Paris Candles, for the Queen's use . .	0	1	1
For one pomegranate, bought and given to Master Henry de Newerk[2]	0	8	0
For six ells of canvas, bought for the windows of the King's chapel	0	1	9
For one pound of galingale, two pounds and a half of cinnamon, three pounds of pepper, one pound of ginger, half a pound of cubeb cloves and nutmegs, eight pounds and a half of fennel and anise seed, one pound of sugar, and one quarter of carraways .	1	3	10
For medicines, taken of Richard de Montepesson, for the King's use	0	10	0
For twelve pounds of figs and raisins, bought for the same	0	12	9
For twelve ells of black canvas, for mending the King's tent	0	3	6
For mending the Queen's tent	0	10	0
For thread, bought for mending the tents . .	0	1	4
For a frail of figs, and a frail of raisins, bought of John Banquer	1	6	8
To the same for oxysaccharum,[3] for the use of the Queen	0	8	0
To the same, for one quarter of wax, for the Queen's use	0	15	2
To the same, for twelve pounds and a half of wick .	0	2	1
To the same, for one pound of cotton . . .	0	0	10
To the same, for one pound of saffron . . .	0	6	0
To the same, for twenty-three pounds of wax . .	0	13	4
To the same, for one pound of pepper . . .	0	1	0
Thursday the 2d day of September, paid for eight pounds of wax	0	4	8
For one pound of saffron, bought of John Banquer .	0	5	0
For different spices and sirups, bought for the use of Viscount Tartasen	0	9	0

[2] Either there must be a clerical error in the sum, or this must have been some jewel or ornament; as it is not to be conceived that a sum exceeding ten pounds of our money should have been given for a pomegranate.

[3] A composition of vinegar, sugar, and the juice of sour pomegranates.

	£.	s.	d.
For different medicines, bought for the use of the Queen, by Master Nicholas	1	7	1
Sum . .	10	1	6

Alms and Oblations.

	£.	s.	d.
Friday next after the Feast of St. Lawrence, paid for the pittance of the preaching friars of Rothelan . .	0	7	8
For the brethren of the hospital at Rothelan . . .	0	1	0
On the day of the Queen's churching, in oblations at mass	0	3	0
For the moulding the Queen's wax that same day .	0	0	11½
For the oblations of the Queen, and those that stood round at mass, on the birth day of the Blessed Virgin	0	1	2
Friday the 22d day of October, at Rothelan, paid in oblations at the celebration of mass for the soul of William de Bigorr	0	1	10
In oblations on Good Friday	0	1	2
In oblations on the day of Pentecost	0	1	8
In oblations of mass for the soul of the Queen of Norway	0	1	8
In oblations on the birth-day of the Blessed Mary .	0	2	8
Sum .	1	2	9½

Minute Expences.

	£.	s.	d.
On the day of the Queen's churching, paid to the Queen's William going to Chester to seek prunes for the Queen's use, for his expences	0	0	6
Monday on the morrow of St. Benedict, paid to a boy carrying letters of the King to Master William de Perton at Chester	0	0	4
To a boy bringing letters of the King to Macclesfield to seek for archers	0	0	8
To William the messenger, carrying letters of the King to London, which were to be sent to the court of Rome, for his expences	0	0	3
To a boy bringing letters to Aberconway . . .	0	0	3
Sunday next after the Feast of St. John the Baptist, paid to a boy carrying letters of the King to Aberconway, for his expenses	0	0	3
Sum .	0	3	0

For the Wages of Knights, Soldiers.—Sum 24l. 9s.

	£.	s.	d.
Saturday the 5th day of January, paid to the Lord Engolrane, serving with the Lord John de Deynile, and his four Esquires, for their wages from the 1st day of April to the 4th day of June, for sixty-five days	19	10	0
To the same, for the pay of his fifth Esquire, from the 12th day of May to the 4th day of June, for twenty-four days	0	1	4
To the said five Esquires for their pay, for fifteen days following the 4th of June	3	15	5
To master Richard de Brus, on account of his wages, by the hands of Robert de Edenham, by order of Master William de Luda	10	0	0
Tuesday on the Feast of the Nativity of the Blessed Mary, paid to Master G. de Picheford in advance of his pay	2	0	0
Monday on the Feast of the Conversion of St. Paul, paid to Master John Weston, on account of his pay, by order of the treasurer	6	0	0
Sum .	42	9	0

	£	s.	d.
Of Bailiffs Wages.			
Friday next after the Feast of the Assumption of the Blessed Mary, paid to William de Hertfield for his wages	1	0	0
To John Artald for his wages	1	0	0
To Robert de Clopton for his wages	1	0	0
To Stephen le Burgullon for his wages	1	0	0
To Robert de Vilers for his wages	0	10	0
Sum . . .	4	10	0
Wages of Esquires.			
To Robert de Cantelu for his wages	1	0	0
To Peter de Welles for his wages	1	0	0
To Henry de Qwetel for his wages	0	16	8
To William Fitz-Glay for his wages	1	0	0
To William de Wydsore for his wages	1	14	0
To Roderick of Spain for his wages	1	0	0
To Robert le Despencer for his wages	2	0	0
To John de Silvestrod for his wages	2	10	0
To Matthew of the Exchequer for his wages	0	17	6
To Symon de Chiltenham for his wages	0	10	0
To Richard de Burgh for his wages	0	2	6
To Master J. de Clifford for his wages	0	4	8
Sum . .	12	15	4
**Advance Money.*			
To William the Taylor of the Earl of Mar'. in advance for the Manucaption of G. de Aspal . . .	0	10	0
To the G. Lord de Genevill, by the hands of Sir J. his chaplain, in advance, by the command of the Lord Bishop of Bath	20	0	0
To Anthony Beck,[4] by the hands of Sir Hugh his chaplain, in advance	2	0	0
To the Lord Bishop of Bangor, by the hands of Sir J. his chaplain, by order of the Lord Bishop of Bath .	0	10	0
To Master W. de Luda, for divers advance moneies . .	2	5	0
To the Lord Bishop of Bath, by the hands of Master W. de Marchia, in advance	3	6	8
To the Lord Bishop of Waterford, by the hands of Master W. de Luda, advance	60	0	0
To John de Beauchamp of Essex, in advance . . .	0	6	8
To the John Lord de Vescy, in advance, by the hands of Roger de Stratton, Master W. de Luda being voucher	5	0	0
To the Lord Bishop of Bath, by the hands of Master W. de Marchia, in advance	6	13	4
To Anthony Bek, by the hands of a boy of his, by order of Master W. de Luda, in advance . . .	0	10	0
To H. Earl of Lincoln, by his canon, by the King's command	113	6	8
To Walter Sauvage, by his boy, for the keeping of his horse	0	6	8
To Master G. de Picheford by the particulars . . .	7	17	6
To Master W. de Luda, in advance, by particulars .	3	15	2¼
Sum of the Advance Money, besides the last particulars	227	3	2¼

[4] Anthony Bek was promoted to the Bishoprick of Durham, in the year 1283.

The Sum of the Expenses of this Roll, 1325*l.* 10*s.* 4*d.*½.

Sum total of this Roll, with the Expenses of the other Roll of the Queen's household, 2220*l.* 2*s.* 10*d.*¼.

And the Sum of the Receipt, as appears above, is 2232*l.* 19*s.* 8*d.*¼.

And so the Sum of the Receipt exceeds the Sum of the mises 12*l.* 16*s.* 10*d.* which are placed to the Queen in the Book of Advance Money, in the 13th year, which Master Richard de Bures acknowledges to have delivered to the same on his private account.

Indorsed on the Roll.

The Sum of Sums of this Roll, 1318*l.* 10*s.* 8*d.*½.

In a former part of our work, we stated that the second epoch of the account of our Welsh Bards[5] should conclude with the fall of the ancient British Government, by the death of David, the last Prince of Wales, in the year 1283.

The destruction of manuscripts at the White Tower, &c., &c., has deprived us of many works of genius of the beginning of this epoch; and it is singular that we have not one piece which can be ascertained to have been written in the time of our law-giver, Howel Dda, (the Good). We must, therefore, descend to the reign of Gruffydd ap Cynan, about the commencement of the twelfth century, to begin the list of the authors of whose works there are any considerable remains. This Prince was a great patron of the Bards and Minstrels; he was passionately fond of Welsh Music, and caused a statute to be passed for the better regulation of the minstrels. Some parts of this law had respect also to the bards.

[5] The Bards were designated "the guardians of celestial truth," and adopted as their motto, "Y gwir yn erbyn y byd." Truth was held so sacred by the ancient British Bards and Druids, that they would never admit into their poetical compositions anything whatever of a fictitious nature; their fundamental maxim was to search for truth, and to adhere to it with the most rigid severity: hence in all the genuine works that are extant of our ancient Welsh Bards, from *Meugant*, about the close of the fourth century, we do not meet with a single poem founded upon fiction; and, singular as it may appear, contrary to the practice of all other nations, the most authentic historians of the Welsh are in *verse*, and all their fabulous writings in prose.

The chief bard of Gruffydd ap Cynan was Meilyr, whose elegy upon the death of that Prince, A.D. 1137, is extant, and also two or three other pieces by him. One of them is the following, and is entitled, "The Death-bed of the Bard":—

" REX REGWM, rybit rwyt i foli :
Ym arglwyt uchaf archaf weti.
Gwledic gwlad orfod
Goruchel Wenrod ;
Gwyrda gwna gymmod,
Ryngod a mi !" &c., &c., &c.[6]

We are fortunate in possessing many remains of the poetry of the bards, who lived in the age succeeding that of Meilyr. These were *Gwalchmai*, the son of Meilyr ; *Cynddelw, Daniel Llosgwrn, Mynyw, Owain Cyfeiliog*, a Prince of Powys ; and *Llywarch*, the son of Llywelyn, generally called *Prydydd Moch*.

There are fourteen poems by Gwalchmai preserved ; and the admirers of ancient Welsh poetry would have had cause to rejoice if the number had been greater : for the energy of the British language was never, perhaps, displayed by an equal master of its powers. It is to be regretted that the peculiar excellence of his compositions is lost in translation, wherein nothing more than a dimmed representation of his general ideas appears. Such we infer from the specimen before us, being a poem addressed to Owain Gwynedd, upon the battle of Tal y Foel, A.D. 1151 :—

" Ardwyreif hael i hil Rodri,
Ardwyad gorwlad, gwerlin teithi.
Teithiawc Prydein
Twyth afyrdwyth Ywein,
Teyrnein ni grein,
Ni grawn rei.

" Tair lleng y daethant, liant lestri ;
Tair praf prif lynges wy bres brofi,
Un o Iwerton ;
Arall erfogion
Or Llychlynigion,
Llwrw hirion lli."[7]

Of the works of Cynddelw there are about forty pieces remaining upon various subjects, mostly of great length and considerable merit, particularly the poem to Owen Cyfeiliog, Prince of Powys, who died in

[6] Translated thus :—"The King of Kings is accessible to be adored : To my Lord Supreme I will prefer a prayer. Sovereign of the religion of necessity [a phrase from the Bardic mythology], the most exalted circle of bliss ; beneficent Being, make a reconciliation between Thee and me ! Returning memory iterates a groan that thou shouldst be condemned for my sake,—yet repenting it was done ! I deserved shame in the presence of God, the universal ruler, in not serving truly in my duty of devotion ! "

[7] Translated thus :—"To the radiancy of light I will exalt the bounteous one of the offspring of Rodri, guardian of the country's bounds, endowed with the gifts of an illustrious line.

" Britain's throne is Owen's right ; the active in the course of wrath ; the princely one that submits to none ; that hoards no treasures.

" Three legions the vessels of the torrent brought three grand and first of fleets, bent on the quick assault. One from the West green Isle (Ireland) ; another teeming with armed ones, of the men of Lochlin, long burdens of the flood ; the third over the sea from Normandy with mighty bustle came, with unpropitious fate."

These lines have been rendered into immortal verse by Gray, in his " Three Triumphs of Owen, a Fragment :"—

" Owen's praise demands my song,
Owen swift, and Owen strong :

Fairest flower of Rodri's stem,
Gwyneth's shield and Britain's gem ;
Lord of every regal art,
Liberal hand, and open heart.

" Big with hosts of mighty name,
Squadrons three against him came ;
This the force of Erin hiding
Side by side as proudly riding ;
On her shadow long and gay
Lochlin ploughs the wat'ry way ;
There the Norman sails afar
Catch the wind, and join the war.

" Dauntless on his native sands
The Dragon son of Mona stands ;
In glittering arms, and glory drest,
High he rears his ruby crest.
There the thundering strokes begin,
There the press and there the din ;
Talymoelfra's rocky shore
Echoing to the battle's roar.'

Y

A.D. 1197. This Prince was a distinguished patron of Cynddlelw and the bards in general. A translated specimen of his animated muse has already appeared in Evans's "Dissertatio de Bardis," and from it has been copied into subsequent publications.

The next in succession was Hywel, one of the sons of Owen Gwynedd, who aspired to the throne after his father's death in A.D. 1169. This raised an unnatural contest, and he fell before the conclusion of the same year in opposing the claims of his brother David.[*] Hywel was a high-spirited young man, and possessed talent, as appears by his poetical compositions, of which there are eight preserved. His muse seems to have been principally devoted to the fair sex; at least the following lines may be considered a fair specimen of the fragments of his works we have remaining :—

> " Fyn dewisi riain firiain feindeg,
> Hirwen yni ller lliw ehoëc;
> A'm dewis synwyr, syniaw arwreiciait,
> Ben dywaid o frait wetait wovec," &c., &c., &c. [9]

The next Bard whose works we shall notice is *Llywarch*, denominated *Prydydd Moch*, for what reason is not now known. He was the laureate bard to several of the princes. There are about thirty pieces composed by him now extant, which display a superior energy of character to most, if not all, of the poets of the middle ages. One of his poems must be deemed of considerable importance and curiosity : it is an invocation when undergoing the fiery ordeal, to exonerate himself from having any knowledge of the fate of Madoc, the son of Owen Gwynedd.[1] In addition to this piece, the same author has another remarkable allusion to the same event, in a panegyric addressed to Roderic, another son of Owen, wherein he recounts what befel his brothers. The passage commences thus :—

> " Dau deyrn derwyn dydores yn llid ;
> Llu daiar o'n hoffes ! " &c.[2]

The following translation of a poem by Llygad Gwr, a bard who flourished about the year 1270, is translated from the original, at Jesus College, Oxford, by the late Rev. Evan Evans, (*Ieuan Brydydd Hir*) :—

" I address myself to God, the source of joy, the fountain of all good gifts, of transcendent majesty. Let the song proceed to pay its tribute of praise, to extol my hero, the Prince of Arllechwedd,[3] who is stained with blood, a prince descended from renowned kings. Like Julius Cæsar is the rapid progress of the arms of Gruffudd's heir. His valour and bravery are matchless, his crimson lance is stained with gore. It is natural to him to invade the lands of his enemies. He is generous ; the pillar of Princes. I never return empty-handed from the North. My successful and glorious Prince, I would not exchange on any conditions. I have a renowned Prince, who lays England waste, descended from noble ancestors. Llywelyn, the destroyer of thy foes, the mild, the prosperous governor of Gwynedd ; Britain's honour in the field, with thy sceptered hand extended on the throne, and thy gilt sword by thy side. The lion of Cemaes,[4] fierce in the onset, when the army rushes to be covered with red. Our defence, who slightest alliance with strangers ; who with violence maketh his way through the midst

---

[*] Two other brothers, Madoc and Ririd, disgusted with the scenes of violence they had witnessed, are recorded to have emigrated in A.D. 1172, to a land discovered far to the westward by Madoc in a former voyage, in A.D. 1170. This afterwards has been proved to be America, which was thus discovered *some centuries before Columbus was born!*

[9] Translated thus :—" My choice is a lady, elegant, slender, and fair, whose lengthened white form is seen through the blue thin veil, and my choicest faculty is to muse on superior female excellencies, when she with diffidence utters the becoming sentiment ; and my choicest participation is to become united with the maid, and to share mutual confidences as to thoughts and fortune. I choose the bright hue of the spreading wave, thou who art the most discreet of thy country, with thy pure Welsh speech. Chosen by me art thou : What am I with you! How! dost thou refrain from speaking! Ah! thy silence even is fair ! I have chosen a maid, so that with me

there should be no hesitation ; it is right to choose the choicest fair one."

[1] The same as is mentioned before to have discovered a new country to the westward. See Dr. Williams, Author of the Discovery of America, and founder of the Literary Fund.

[2] Translated thus :—" Two Princes of strong passion broke off in wrath ; the multitude of earth did love them. One on land in Arfon, allaying of ambition ;* and another a placid one, on the bosom of the vast ocean, in trouble great and immeasurable, prowling after a possession easy to be guarded, estranged from every one, for a country."

[3] Arllechwedd, a part of Caernarvonshire.

[4] Cemaes, the name of several places in Wales. The Bard means a cantred of that name in Anglesea.

---

[*] This was Hywel, most likely, who was slain in the year 1169, fighting against his brother David.

of his enemies' country. His just cause will be prosperous at last. About Deganwy[5] he has extended his dominion, and his enemies fly from him with maimed limbs, and the blood flows over the soles of men's feet. Thou dragon of Arfon,[6] of resistless fury, with thy beautiful well-made steeds, no Englishman shall get one foot of thy country. There is no Cymro thy equal.

"There is none equal to my Prince with his numerous troops in the conflict of war. He is a generous Cymro, descended from Beli Hir, if you inquire about his lineage. He generously distributeth gold and riches. An heroic wolf from Eryri.[7] An eagle among his nobles of matchless prowess; it is our duty to extol him. He is clad in a golden vest in the army, and setteth castles on fire. He is the bulwark of the battle with Greidiæn's courage.[8] He is a hero that with fury breaketh whole ranks, and fighteth manfully. His violence is rapid, his generosity overflowing. He is the strength of armies arrayed in gold. He is a brave Prince, whose territories extend as far as Teivi,[9] whom nobody dares to punish. Llywelyn, the vanquisher of England, is a noble lion, descended from the race of kings. Thou art the king of the mighty, the entertainer and encourager of bards. Thou makest the crows rejoice, and the Bryneich to vomit blood; they feasted on their carcases. He never avoided danger in the storm of battle, he was undaunted in the midst of hardships. The Bards prophesy that he shall have the government and sovereign power; every prediction is at last to be fulfilled. The shields of his men were stained with red in brave actions from Pulford[1] to the farthest bounds of Cydweli. May he find endless joys, and be reconciled to the love of God, and enjoy heaven by his side.

"We have a prudent Prince, his lance is crimson, his shield is shivered to pieces; a Prince furious in action, his palace is open to his friends, but woe is the lot of his enemies. Llywelyn, the vanquisher of his adversaries, is furious in battle, like an outrageous dragon; to be guarded against him availeth not, when he cometh hand to hand to dispute the contest. May he that made him the happy governor of Gwynedd and its towns strengthen him for length of years to defend his country from hostile invasion. It is our joy and happiness that we have a brave warrior, with prancing steeds; that we have a noble Cymro, descended from Cambrian ancestors, to rule our country and its borders. He is the best Prince that the Almighty made of the four elements. He is the best of governors, and the most generous—the Eagle of Snowdon, and the bulwark of battle. He pitched a battle where there was a furious contest, to obtain his patrimony on Cefus Gelowydd: such a battle never happened since the celebrated action of Arderydd.

"He is the brave lion of Mona, the kind-hearted Venedotian, the valiant supporter of his troops in Bryn Derwyn. He did not repent the day in which he assaulted his adversaries; it was like the assault of a hero descended from undaunted ancestors. Now a hero disputing with hosts of men like a man of honour in avoiding disgrace. He that saw Llywelyn, like an ardent dragon, in the conflict of Arson and Eiddionydd,[2] would have observed it was a difficult task to withstand his furious attack by Drws Daufynydd.[3] No man has ever compelled him to submit: may the Son of God never put him to confusion.

"Like the roaring of a furious lion in search of prey, is thy thirst of praise; like the wind of a mighty hurricane over the desert main, thou warlike Prince of Aberfraw.[4] Thy courage is furious, thy impetuosity irresistible, thy troops are enterprising in brave actions; they are fierce and furious, like a conflagration. Thou art the warlike Prince of Dinefor,[5] the defence of thy people, the divider of spoils. Thy forces are comely and neat, and of one language. Thy proud Toledo sword is gilt with gold, and its edge broke in war. Thou Prince of Mathraval,[6] extensive are the bounds of thy dominions; thou rulest people of four languages. He staid undaunted in the battle field against a foreign nation and its strange language. May the great King of Heaven defend the just cause of the warlike Prince of the three provinces.

---

[5] Deganwy, the name of an old castle near the mouth of the River Conwy to the east; it was formerly one of the regal palaces of Maelgwyn Gwynedd, King of Britain; and was, as our annals relate, burnt by lightning, A.D. 811, but was afterwards rebuilt and won by the Earls of Chester, who held it for a considerable time, but was at last retaken by the Prince of North Wales.

[6] Arfon: the county now called Caernarvonshire.

[7] Eryri: Snowdon, which some suppose derived from Mynydd Eryrod, the hill of Eagles, but more probably the hill of Snow. Snowdon in English signifies literally the hill of snow, from Snow and Down; that being still a common name for a hill in England, as Barham Downs, Oxford Downs, Burford Downs, &c. &c.

[8] Greidiawl: the name of a hero mentioned by Aneurin Gwawdrydd in his Gododin.

[9] Teivi, the name of a large river in Cardiganshire. It was the policy of the British princes to make the Bards foretel their success in war, in order to spirit up their people to brave actions, upon which account the vulgar supposed them to be real prophets. Hence the great veneration they had for the prophetical Bards—Myrddin Emrys, Taliesin, and Myrddin Wyllt. This accounts for what the English writers say of the Welsh relying so much on the prophecies of Myrddin. There are many of these pretended prophecies still extant. The custom of prophesying did not cease till Henry VIII.'s time, and the reason is obvious.

[1] Pwlffordd is the name of a place in Shropshire. There is a bridge of that name still in that country. There is another Pullford near Chester.

[2] Eiddionydd, now Eifionydd, the name of a Commot, or district in Caernarvonshire.

[3] Drws Daufynydd is the name of a pass between two hills, but where it lies we know not. Drws Daufynydd signifies, literally, the door of the two hills. There are many passes in Wales denominated from Drws, as Drws Ardudwy, Drws y Coed, Bwlch Oerddrws, &c.

[4] Aberffraw, a royal palace in Anglesea.

[5] Dinefor, the name of the Prince of South Wales's palace, pleasantly situated upon the hill above the river Tywi.

[6] Mathrafal, the seat of the Prince of Powys, not far from Welshpool, in Montgomeryshire, now in the possession of the Earl of Powys.

"I make my address to God, the source of praise, in the best manner that I am able, that I may extol with suitable words the chief of men, who rageth like fire from the flashes of lightning, who exchangeth thrusts with the burnished steel. I stand in armour by the side of my Prince, with the red spear in the conflict of war; he is a brave fighter, and the foremost in action. Llywelyn, thy qualities are noble, I will valiantly make my path broad with the edge of my sword. May the prints of the hoofs of my Prince's steeds be seen as far as Cornwall. Numerous are the persons that congratulate him upon his success, who is a sure friend. The lion of Gwynedd, and its extensive territories, the governor of the men of Powys, and the South, who hath a general assembly of his armed troops at Chester, who ravageth Lloegr to amass spoils. In battle his success is certain, in killing, burning, and in overthrowing castles. In Rhos and Penfro, and in the contests with the Normans, his impetuosity prevaileth. The offspring of Gruffydd, of worthy qualities, generous in distributing rewards for songs. His shield shines, and the strong lances quickly meet the streams of the gushing gore. He extorteth taxes from his enemies, and claimeth another country as a sovereign Prince. His noble birth is an ornament to him. He besiegeth fortified towns, and his furious attacks, like those of Fflamddwyn, reach far. He is a prosperous chief with princely qualities; his Bards are comely about his tables; I have seen him generously distributing his wealth, and his mead horns filled with generous liquors. Long may he live to defend his brothers with a sharp sword, like Arthur with the lance of steel. May he who is lawful King of Cymru, endued with princely qualities, have his share of happiness at the right hand of God."

Poetry and good language was in greater perfection in Wales a little before and a little after the Norman Conquest, than it hath been since; and the historical part of our poems is a great light to historians, both English and Welsh, Irish and Scotch. Goronwy Owain on this subject says, "I find the old metres were, what all compositions of that nature should be, that is, lyric verses adapted to the tunes and music then in use. Of this sort were the several kinds of Englynion, Cywyddau, Odlau, Gwawdodyn, Toddaid, Trybedd y Myneich, and Glogyrnach, which appear to have in their composition the authentic stamp of genuine lyric poetry, and of true primitive antiquity. As to the rest, I mean Gorchest y Beirdd, Huppynt hîr and byrr, being the newest, they were falsely thought the most ingenious and accurate kind of metres. But I look upon them to be rather depravations than improvements in our poetry. What a grovelling, low thing that Gorchest y Beirdd is? And I would have an impartial answer, whether the old, despised, exterminated Englyn Milwr hath not something of antique majesty in its composition. Now, when I have a mind to write good sense in such a metre as Gorchest y Beirdd, and so begin, and the language itself does not afford words that will come in to finish with sense and Cynghanedd too, what must I do? Why, to keep Cynghanedd (i. e., the alliteration) I must write nonsense to the end of the metre, and cramp and fetter good sense, whilst the dictionary is overturned and tormented to find out words of a like ending, sense or nonsense; and besides, suppose our language was more comprehensive and significant than it is (which we have no reason or room to wish), what abundance of mysterious sense is such a horrid jingling metre of such a length able to contain! In short, as I understand, that it and its fellows were introduced by the authority of an Eisteddfod, I wish we had another Eisteddfod, to give them their dimittimus to some peaceable acrostic land, to sport and converse with the spirits of deceased puns, quibbles, and conundrums of pious memory; then would I gladly see the true primitive metres reinstated in their ancient dignity, and sense regarded more than a hideous jingle of words, which hardly ever bear it."

The Welsh poetry had great compass and variety. Dr. John David Rhys, the physician and grammarian, who took his degree in Italy, introduces a comparison between the Welsh and Italian poetry, and inserts a whole Italian poem, marked in the manner he has done the Welsh. In Metastasio is a poem similar to a very favourite metre in Welsh poetry, viz.,

"Sopra il santissima."—*Natale Ode*, vol. ix.

In this the end of the first line rhymes to the middle of the second, and the end of the second to the middle of the third.[7]

We could easily fill a volume with similar specimens of the beautiful composition of our ancient Bards who flourished about a thousand years ago, but with regard to their intrinsic merits we refer our readers to

7 See Arch. Prys's Psalms.

the learned Bishop Percy, who in one of his letters to the Rev. Evan Evans, (*Ieuan Brydydd Hïr,*) author of the *Dissertatio de Bardis*, has the following remarks :—"From the translation (of the ancient British poetry) you have already favoured me with a sight of, I conceive a very favourable idea of the merit of your ancient Bards, and should be sorry to have their precious relics swallowed up and lost in the gulph of time. I can readily conceive that many of their most beautiful peculiarities cannot possibly be translated into another language, but even through the medium of a prose translation one can discern a rich vein of poetry, and even classical correctness, infinitely superior to any other compositions of that age that we are acquinted with—*Certain I am that our own nation at that time produced nothing that wears the most distant resemblance to their merit ;* I have lately been collecting specimens of English poetry, from the time of the Saxons down to that of Elizabeth, and am ashamed to show you what wretched stuff our Rhymers produced at *the same time that your Bards were celebrating the praise of Llywelyn with a spirit scarce inferior to Pindar*. Inclosed I send you a specimen of an Elegy on the death of Edward the First[1]—that cruel Edward who made such havoc among the Cambrian Poets. I know not whether you will be able to decypher these foul scrawls, or distinguish them from the marginal explanations with which I have accompanied them, but you will see enough to be convinced of the infinite superiority of your own Bards, nor do I know that any of the nations of the Continent (unless perchance Italy, which now about begun to be honoured by Dante) were able at that time to write better than the English. The French I am well assured were not ; one thing is observable in the Elegy of Edward the First, which is, that the Poet, in order to do honour to his hero, puts his eulogium in the mouth of the Pope, with the same kind of fiction with which a modern Bard would have raised up Britannia, or the Genius of Europe—sounding forth his praises. Considering the destruction which our merciless monarch made among the last sons of ancient genius, it may be looked upon as a just judgment upon him that he had no better than these miserable Rhymers to disgrace his memory."[2]

. " The Saxons," says Mr. York, in his " Royal Tribes," " at least for some time, were no poets ; they landed here *without* an *alphabet*. The Normans had their Jongleurs,[1] Troubadours, and Provençal Songs ; the monks jingled their Latin doggerel : but, until the days of Gower, Chaucer, and Lydgate, native English numbers were, in a manner, unknown.[2] The scholar, since, hath excelled his master :—

> " ' Nosque ubi primus equis Oriens afflavit anhelis,
> Illic sera rubens accendit lumina Vesper.'

" The Britons had taught the Saxons to read, and given them the first of all things, even Christianity itself, which they spread with true Celtic ardour."

---

[2] The following is an extract from the miserable poem alluded to by the Bishop, in his Reliques of Ancient English Poetry :—

> " Now is Edward of Carnarvon
> Kyng of Engelande al aplyht,
> God lete him ner be worse man
> Than his Fader, ne lasse of myht
> To holden his pore men to rhyt,
> And understande goode counsail,
> At Engelande for to wysse and dyht,
> Of gode knyhtes dark him not fail."

Speaking of Horace, Lewis Morris (when writing to the Rev. Evan Evans, the author of the *Dissertatio de Bardis*), says, " He was a stranger to our methods handed down to us by his masters, the Druidical Bards, who knew how to sing before Rome had a name. So never hereafter mention such moderns as Horace and Virgil when you talk of British Poetry. Llywarch Hen, Aneurin, and the followers of the Druids, are our men, and Nature our rule."

[2] Mr. Andrews has well observed, that the tale of Edward I.'s cruelty to the Bards has no foundation, but an obscure tradition,

and a hint in the Gwydir history. Edward has been also accused of having destroyed all the ancient records and writings in Scotland. This is ably refuted by Sir David Dalrymple. But an order at that time existed to silence the Welsh Bards. Our countrymen were most severely treated by the fourth Henry, when the Welsh were rendered by an Act of Parliament incapable of purchasing lands, or of performing any office in any town, or of having any castle or house of defence. English judges and juries were to decide between English and Welsh ; Englishmen that married Welshwomen[*] were disfranchised, and no Welshman might bind his child to any trade, nor breed him up to literature. The absurdities of those ordinances counteracted their virulence, and the moderation of the fifth Henry having laid them to sleep, if not repeated, they were in a great measure forgotten.

[1] " This species of minstrels ended in the conjuring art ; hence our jugglers."—*Yorke.*

[2] " We must not wonder if the English verse in these early cen-

---

[*] Henry no doubt was jealous of the charms of our countrywomen, and fearful of their influence on his English subjects.

In the month of September, 1284, King Edward and his queen stayed in Chester for four days, during which time the Royal pair heard mass in St. Werburgh's Church on St. Augustine's day, on which occasion he presented the Convent with a cloth of great value.[3]

A.D. 1287.—Although Wales had at length been subdued by the superior prowess of England, the measures pursued to crush the proud and gallant spirit of her people, contributed largely to the fostering of that enmity which had been engendered by the cruelty and oppression of the English, and which the Mountaineers entertained towards their conquerors with vindictive and terrible malignity. Notwithstanding the destruction of the regal power, there yet existed a number of brave and resolute patriots, who, headed by chieftains, as remarkable for their nobility as for their valour and military experience, boldly determined to regain their independence, or to sink among the ruins of their country's freedom. Rhys ap Meredydd, therefore, a chieftain of great influence in South Wales, was the first who rebelled against the domination of the English; and during Edward's absence at Guienne, he appeared in arms against the ruling power at the head of six thousand followers. For a short time Rhys was successful; but at length after having been proclaimed traitor, he fell into the hands of the enemy and was executed at York, his castles and domains having been previously confiscated.[4]

The King of England having at length reached the height of his ambition in the final conquest of Wales, annexed it to the kingdom of England, and in order to secure the obedience of the newly subdued country, and rivet the fetters he had imposed on the Welsh, Edward introduced English jurisprudence, divided North Wales into counties, and appointed proper officers to enforce the obedience of his reluctant subjects.

In order to further his designs and accomplish his projects, the King took up his residence at Rhuddlan Castle, and there promulgated the famous body[5] of laws called "Statutes of Rhuddlan."[5] From this ancient fortress he issued a proclamation to all the inhabitants of Wales, pledging himself that he would take them under his protection, and at the same time giving them assurances, that they should enjoy their ancient land and liberties, as heretofore, reserving for himself only the same rents, duties, and services which were always claimed by the Princes of Wales.

Edward soon forfeited his hollow promises, for he granted to his followers a considerable portion of the best land in the Principality. He gave the Lordship of Ruthin to Reginald de Grey, the Lordship of Denbigh to the Earl of Lincoln, and all his other adherents were amply rewarded for their service by the grants of vast estates: this puts us in mind of the old adage,

"Hael Hywel ar eiddo'r wlad."

"How generous Hywel with the property of the country!"

With a view to conciliate the Welsh Clergy, Edward sent for the Archbishop of Canterbury to come to Rhuddlan, who issued out orders for repairing the different churches, that had been injured by the late war. The King also made a recompence to "Master Richard Barnard, Parson of Rhuddlan," for some land taken from him previous to his enlarging the castle.[7]

For the injuries done to the inhabitants of Rhuddlan during the war, Edward made this town a free borough, and granted it great privileges; as a further proof of his good will, he attempted to remove the See of St. Asaph to Rhuddlan, but to this the Pope would not give his consent.

These liberal and lenient measures were a wise policy in Edward, but the subsequent introduction of

---

turies appear uncouth. The Bard had to do with a harsh though nervous language, frowned on by the Court, neglected by the gentry, and disguised by a most unintelligible mode of spelling."—*J. P. Andrews.*

[3] Bradshaw's Life of St. Werburgh.

[4] History of Wales, vol. ii. p. 289.

[5] Leges Walliæ, p. 542 ; Welsh Chron., p. 377.

[6] Though these statutes are very little attended to, either by lawyers or historians, the learned Judge Barrington says that they deserve particular attention. They not only inform us what were the customs in Wales at that time, but likewise the remedy by the law of England. There is a MS. of this law in the Hengwrt Collection—Llwyd's Archæology.

[7] Rot. Wallia, p. 75.

foreign laws and rigorous treatment, supported by other harsh and oppressive measures, were not at all likely to suit a people sore with injuries, and so attached to their native Princes. It may still be affirmed, however, that in no part of the busy transactions of Edward's life, did he display a greater depth of policy than he did in the preservation of his newly acquired territory. Sometimes he flattered and soothed the vindictive spirit of the fiery Cambrians, and at other times he punished with rigour their unbending obstinacy; in these alternate fits of kindness and severity, he experienced much difficulty in curbing the eager patriotism of our countrymen. Though he had done away with the royal power of Wales,—vanquished the brave and generous Llywelyn,—exposed his lifeless head to the derision of the multitude,—and cruelly murdered his brother David,[8]—he still found that the Welsh would not willingly bend their knee to one whom they looked upon as an usurper of their rights and privileges. They promised him submission, however, providing he would govern them in person, or they were willing to be governed by a chieftain of their own country; but firmly declared that they would yield no obedience to any person, who was not born in Wales and resided among them. At last their wishes were gratified; the idea struck Edward that his Queen was pregnant, and he instantly sent orders for Eleanor to come to Wales. Though it was then in the depth of winter, and the season severely cold, he caused her to be removed to Caernarvon Castle, the place designed for her accouchement. Notwithstanding her advanced state of pregnancy, her delicate and critical situation, *she performed her journey on horseback!*

The Queen reached the newly built Castle of Caernarvon early in the spring of A.D. 1284. This truly royal fortress, which was built to overawe the insurgents of the Principality, appears at present in its external state very nearly the same as when Queen Eleanor first entered the stupendous gateway so many centuries ago. The walls are studded with defensive octagonal towers, they have two principal gates, the east facing the Snowdon mountains, the west commanding the Menai. The entrance to the castle is very stately; beneath a noble tower, on the front of which appears the statue of the great Edward, finely carved from life, drawing a dagger, with a stern air, as if menacing his unwilling subjects. The entrance has four portcullises, with every requisite of strength.[9]

To this mighty castle Edward brought Eleanor, at a time when her situation promised an increase to the royal family. The Eagle Tower, through whose gate the affectionate Eleanora entered, is at a prodigious height from the ground, and at the farthest end, and could only be approached by a drawbridge, supported on masses of opposing rock. Every one who beholds it must be struck with its grand position; it is still, by the tradition of the district, called Queen Eleanor's gate; nor was the Eagle Tower (Twr yr Eryr) by any means too lofty for the security of the royal Eleanor and her expected infant, since most of the Snowdon barons still held out, and the rest of the Principality was fiercely chafing at the English curb. This consideration justifies the tradition which points out a little dark den, built in the thickness of the walls, as the chamber where the faithful Queen gave birth to her son Edward. The chamber is twelve feet in length and eight in breadth, and is without a fireplace. Its discomforts were somewhat modified by hangings of tapestry, of which some tenter marks still appear in the walls.[1] Queen Eleanor was the first person who used tapestry as garniture for walls in England, and she never needed it more than in her dreary lying-in chamber at Caernarvon.[2]

---

[8] It is said, indeed, that David was faithless and ungrateful. The king had conferred on him the honour of knighthood, had been the means of his marrying the daughter of the Earl of Derby, a rich widow, and had given to him the Castle of Denbigh, with 1000l. per annum. But candour requires us to bear in mind that every Welshman was at all times ready to shed his last drop of blood for the independence of his country, and that in David's opinion the sceptre was the inalienable hereditary right of his family. The feeling has been acknowledged and honoured by patriots and philosophers in all ages :—

"Jove fix'd it certain that the fatal day
Which makes men slaves takes half their worth away."—POPE.

[9] Stow. His noble portrait, engraved by Vertue in Carte, is taken from this statue.

[1] It was the duty of the grooms of the chamber to hang up the tapestry, which was always carried in progress with the royal baggage, and sent forward with the purveyor and grooms of the chamber, so that the queen found the stone walls of her sleeping chamber in comfortable order for her reception.

[2] Among the memorials of Queen Eleanor's sojourn at Caer-

The Prince was born April 25th, when fires were not indispensable in a small close chamber. As a soldier's wife, used to attend her lord in all campaigns, from Syria to Scotland, the Queen had, in all probability, met with far worse accommodations than in the forlorn chamber in the Eagle Tower. The Queen certainly provided a Welsh nurse for her infant.[3] She thus proved her usual good sense by complying with the prejudices of the country.

Edward the First was at Rhuddlan Castle, negotiating with the despairing magnates of Wales, when news was brought him by Gruffydd Llwyd, a Welsh gentleman, that the Queen had made him the father of a living son, of surpassing beauty. The King was transported with joy; he knighted the Welshman on the spot, and made him a magnificent donation of lands.[4]

Edward the First presenting the Welsh Chieftains with a Prince born among them, at Rhuddlan Castle.

The King hastened directly to Caernarvon, to see his Eleanor and her boy; and a short time after he issued a proclamation that he would hold his parliament at Rhuddlan Castle, for the purpose of taking into consideration the best mode of securing the public welfare of Wales, and he particularly desired all the Welsh chieftains to meet him there, when he practised his well-known fraud and deceit. He commenced his harangue by stating, "that in consequence of their long expressed desire to have a prince, a native of

narvon Castle, the cradle of her infant son is still shown. It is hung by rings and staples to two upright pieces of wood, like a cot; it is of rude workmanship, yet with much pretence to ornament, having many mouldings, though the nails are left rough; it is made of oak, and is in length three feet two inches; its width is one foot eight inches at the head, and one foot five at the foot; it has rockers, and is crowned by two birds, whether doves or eagles, antiquaries have not yet decided.—*Boswell's Antiquities.*

[3] There is an entry in the household book of Edward II., of twenty shillings, which the king presented to Mary of Caernarvon, his nurse, for coming all the way from Wales to see him.

[4] Pennant's Wales.

their own country, if they promised obedience to the one he named he would indulge them by nominating a person, whose life had hitherto been irreproachable, one that was born among them, and could not speak a word of English." [5]   The Welsh eagerly assented to acknowledge such a person for their future ruler, but little did they think, when expressing their acclamations of joy, and tendering their unbounded promises of obedience, who this prince should be; when the King presented his own son, born a few days before at Caernarvon Castle! "This, says he, shall be your future prince! *Wele eich dyn!* Behold your man!" The Cambrian chiefs little expected such a ruler, and their surprise was great; they had, however, no alternative but submission, and with as good a grace as they might, kissed the tiny hand which was to sway their sceptre, and vowed fealty to the babe of the faithful Eleanor.[6]

Soon after Edward and his Queen and a great part of the English nobility spent their Christmas at the magnificent palace at Conway Castle,[7] they were attended by a great part of the English nobility, who assembled round them in all the joyous festivity that a luxurious court could boast of. The splendid hall, crowded with warriors, knights, and damsels, echoed the rude merriment of feudal days. The cup passed quickly round, and tales of feats of arms, of slaughtered foes, and strange adventures seemed to beguile the time. Here were they protected in the very heart of an enemy's country, fallen, indeed, but still powerful. From hence were issued the edicts of the sovereign against the brave and patriotic natives.

Many traces of this Queen's (the most accomplished of her day) abode at Conway Castle still exist; among others her state bed-chamber[8] retains some richness of architectural ornament; it opens on a terrace commanding a beautiful view. Leading from the chamber is an arched recess, called by tradition "Queen Eleanor's Oriel"; it is raised by steps from the floor, and commands a beautiful view. Here the Queen of England, during her *levée* or rising, sat to receive the ladies qualified to be presented to her, while her tire-woman combed and braided those long tresses which are the glory of a Spanish donna, and which her statues show Eleanor of Castille to have possessed. A poem, contemporary with this Queen, minutely describes these state toilet-places.

> " In her oriel there she was,
> Closed well with royal glass ;
> Filled it was with imagery,
> Every window by and by."

But how desolate now is the appearance of the shattered walls and grass-grown towers, the broken arch and the tangling ivy!

> "The turrets o'ermantled with ivy around,
> Shall echo to music no more;
> No longer the chords of the harp shall resound,
> And the carol of gladness is o'er."

---

[5] Stow's Annals, 203. Powell, 376.

[6] Stow minutely details this incident, the authenticity of which is not only supported by the local traditions of North Wales, but by the great authority of Selden.

[7] The ruins of this castle and its vicinity have a fine appearance from whatever point of view they may be seen, and are in themselves solemn and impressive. They proclaim its former magnificence ; they remind us of the pomp and grandeur of its possessors, now gone down to the dust; they show us the decay to which sublunary objects are destined, in spite of every effort to rescue them from the all-devouring gulph of oblivion :—

> "'Tis *now* the raven's bleak abode,
> 'Tis *now* the apartment of the toad,
> And *there* the fox securely feeds,
> And *there* the poisonous adder breeds,
> Conceal'd in ruins, moss, and weeds;

> While ever and anon there falls
> Huge heaps of hoary moulder'd walls!
> Yet time has been, that lifts the low,
> And level lays the lofty brow,
> Has seen this *broken pile* complete,
> Big with the vanity of state!
> But transient is the smile of fate—
> A little rule, a little sway,
> A sunbeam in a winter's day,
> Is *all* the PROUD and MIGHTY have
> Between the cradle and the grave!"—DYER.

[8] As a proof of the progress of rational refinement, and the habits of different ages, it may not be amiss to mention here that an order was issued in the reign of Edward I., as history informs us, "that the chambers of that monarch should be furnished with *clean straw once a week!*"

Having settled the affairs of North Wales, Edward, to gratify a martial nobility, and to amuse or flatter his new subjects by a spectacle not unknown to the Welsh, gave orders that a tournament * should be held at Nevyn, a town in Caernarvonshire, and situate on the Irish Channel. This joust was in imitation

Tournament at Nevyn, in Caernarvonshire.

of that species of military entertainment supposed to have been instituted by King Arthur, and which was called the *Round Table*,[1] from the knights who resorted to these martial exercises being seated at a table

9 This custom is said also to have been in use amongst the Gauls and ancient Britons.

1 The following anecdote of Sir Tudor ap Goronwy, and Edward I. is preserved in the Welsh records :—

"The King (Edward I.), hearing that Sir Tudor had assumed the honour of knighthood without his permission, called him to account for so extraordinary a procedure; Sir Tudor replied, that by the laws of the Round Table he had a right to do so, having the three requisites :—first, he was a gentleman ;—secondly, he had an ample fortune ;—and, thirdly, as to his prowess, he was ready to fight any man, be he whom he would, that was hardy enough to dispute it. The king, admiring the dignity of his manner, confirmed to Sir Tudor the honour he had so justly assumed, and so well deserved."— *Wynn's History.* From this Sir Tudor was lineally descended, Henry VII., King of England, who was the son of Edmund, Earl of Richmond, the son of Sir Owen Tudor, son to Meredith the son of this Sir Tudor ap Goronwy. Sir Tudor was one of the great proprietors who, holding their estates *in capite*, did homage to Edward Prince of Wales, at Chester, the 29th of Edward I. His three sons were, in their time, styled the three temporal Lords

of Anglesey : viz., Ednyved of Tre'r Castell, Goronwy of Pen-mynydd, and Rhŷs of Arddreiniog. The three spiritual being the Archdeacon of Anglesey, the President of Holyhead, and the Prior of Penmon. On this demesne is supposed to have been fought, in 818, the "sore battle of Llanvaes," as Caradoc of Llangarven calls it ; and this event, like that of Battle-field in Shropshire, between Henry IV. and the gallant Hotspur, seems to have given name to the parish. Egbert, the West Saxon, having invaded Wales with a great army, ravaged the country even unto Snowdon, took possession of the isle, and called it Anglesey (Anglorum Insula) ; but was soon driven out of it by Mervyn Vrych, who had married Esyllt, heiress of North Wales, daughter of Cynan Tindaethwy, son of Rhodri Molwynog, King of Wales, who resided at Penrhyn, near Bangor. Lewis Morris, in his ode to Sir William Gruffydd, of that house, in 1500, says, that the ponderous arms of Mervyn Vrych were in the great hall there, and the curious antiquary of the eighteenth century will, perhaps, seriously regret that they are not now to be found.

Edward I. in the eighth year of his reign formed the project of examining every man's title to his land by a *quo warranto.* This arbitrary measure was resisted with admirable spirit by John Earl

of that form. A great number of knights, English as well as foreigners, came from different countries, to share in this splendid and military entertainment.' And here the English king had an opportunity of showing his Welsh subjects, that he was not inferior to Arthur, their celebrated warrior, in feats of arms, and in knightly accomplishments. This diversion being ended, he made a progress through Caerdigan, where he remained a month to settle the affairs of South Wales; from thence he proceeded into the county of Glamorgan, on a visit to the Earl of Gloucester, to whom that country belonged; and having been nobly entertained by that lord,' he arrived at Bristol, in which city he remained during the Christmas holidays.' On the 2nd of January he issued a writ from thence, of a conciliatory nature, by which the inhabitants of Rhuddlan, Conway, Caernarvon, and other towns were declared to be free from any liability to pay talliages for ever.' King Edward then returned to London after an absence of nearly three years.' On his arrival in his capital, he rode in great solemnity through London to Westminster, attended by the Archbishop of Canterbury, and his suffragan bishops dressed in their sacred vestments, besides an infinite multitude which attended the procession. The King upon this occasion carried a part of our Lord's cross which he had brought out of Wales, and which was gilded and ornamented with precious stones, and placed it upon the altar in Westminster Abbey.

After his conquest of Wales Edward the First spent some days during the summer of 1294 at a place called Bala-deulyn, at the foot of Snowdon,' which is said to have been in the possession of the Welsh princes from time immemorial. Edward issued several edicts from Bala-deulyn.

Edward, apprised of fresh hostilities, sent the Earls of Lancaster and Lincoln, with a strong body of forces, to suppress the rebellion; but, when they had advanced as far as Denbigh, they were attacked by the Welsh, and entirely defeated. The King, afraid of losing the only conquest he had ever made, resolved to march against the enemy in person; and his presence produced an immediate change in the face of affairs. The Welsh, though they fought with surprising bravery, were worsted in several engagements, and compelled to retire to the mountains of Snowdon, whither they were instantly pursued by Edward, in the depth of winter.

Madoc, flying before the King, returned to the Marches, where he gained some petty advantages; but at last, being routed, with the loss of the best part of his forces, on the hills near Caus Castle, he submitted to Edward, and was sent prisoner to the Tower of London. Most of the Welsh barons, seeing no other means of saving themselves from utter destruction, followed his example, and were committed to close custody in different castles.

The rest of the rebels were indulged with a pardon; but Edward swore that, if they should presume to raise another rebellion, he would extirpate the whole race without mercy.

He continued for some time longer in the country, until he had rebuilt the Castle of Beaumaris, cut down the woods on the inland parts, and erected some fortresses on the sea-coast. He then returned to London about the latter end of July.

Warren, who drew his sword in the face of the writ, saying that "he held his land by his sword, and by his sword he would make his tenure good." The king and his judges were alarmed, and gave up the attempt. Of the nobleman who thus dared to snap asunder the oppressor's rod, little else is known, but it is impossible that his heroism can ever be forgotten while justice, independence, and liberty are sacred. We have seen a large engraving by Strut, from a painting by Lambert, which represents the Earl in the Exchequer Court unsheathing his trusty sword.

² Matth. Westm., p. 178; Camden's Brit., p. 664. Gibson's edition.

³ Carte, vol. ii. p. 197.

⁴ Chron. T. Wyke, p. 110; Holinshed, p. 282.

⁵ Rymer's Fœdera, vol. ii. p. 248.

⁶ Annales Waverleiensis, p. 238.

⁷ Snowdon was held sacred by the ancient Britons, and they believed that if a person slept upon its top the most beautiful forms and images would float before him, and he would awake in possession, and under the influence, of a poetical spirit. It was formerly also a royal forest and abounded with red deer; they were driven from their haunts early in the 17th century; a few remains are still preserved in the parks of our nobility. The wolf, so much dreaded by our ancestors, maintained its ground on Snowdon to a comparatively late period. The eagle had from time immemorial regarded the Snowdonian cliffs as his own dominion; but he has long since shifted his abode. Few tourists are satisfied without climbing the steeps of Snowdon; and not seldom has the visitor on reaching its summit stood for some time motionless and silent. Those hills, those rocks, those vallies, those streams, those lakes, have laid strong hold on his feelings, and thrilled him with ecstatic wonder. The perpendicular height of Snowdon, ascertained by the latest trigonometrical survey is 3571 feet above the level of the sea; two or three other points by which it is surrounded are of nearly equal elevation.

Morgan was still in arms in the county of Glamorgan, which he held of the Earl of Worcester; who, by his haughty and overbearing behaviour, had rendered himself so odious to the natives, that they refused to own his superiority, though they offered to submit, if they might be permitted to hold their lands immediately of the Crown of England. They were, accordingly, gratified in this particular; laid down their arms; swore fealty to the King; and gave hostages for their good behaviour. In order to prevent the like commotion for the future, Edward endeavoured to conciliate the affections of the Welsh, by granting them some new privileges and immunities. The fines commonly paid by the tenants to their lords, for the marriage of their daughters, were moderated: freeholders were allowed to put their sons (if they had more than one) into holy orders, without the King's licence; and to alienate their lands for three years, to any of their own countrymen, except monks and other religious corporations; and orders were given for observing the ordinances of Kennington, all over the Principality.

A.D. 1294.—The King passed through Chester on St. Nicholas's Day, being on his march to North Wales to quell another rebellion. Soon after the suppression of this revolt, Edward, being then at war with the King of France, attempted an experiment of taxation on his newly acquired subjects; and, anticipating considerable resistance on their part, he appointed, as the collector of this impost (which was to consist of a fifteenth of all moveables), Roger de Puleston, a man high in the monarch's favour, and of a brave and daring spirit. No sooner, however, did he attempt to execute this commission than he was indignantly and outrageously opposed, and three insurrections sprung up, in consequence, in different parts of the Principality, and nearly all at the same time. The revolt commenced with acts of hostility which evinced an inveterate and decided resolution that the sword alone should decide the dispute. Roger de Puleston, and his colleagues in the collection of the odious tribute, were the first who became a sacrifice to the fury of the rebels. They were hanged, and afterwards beheaded. A considerable number of English, assembled at Caernarvon, were the next victims who fell into the hands of the enraged insurgents; and this hazardous and unfortunate experiment had well nigh effected a complete restitution of liberty to Wales. A resolute spirit of resistance and patriotism seemed once more diffused throughout the Principality; and such of the Welsh as had not already embraced the cause of their country, flocked readily to the standard of the rebel chieftains, and, by their numbers and success, became so formidable, that Edward, then on the point of embarking with his army for France, thought it expedient to recall his forces, and march at their head directly into Wales. After encountering many difficulties, he succeeded in stationing the greater part of his troops in Conway Castle, in Caernarvonshire, where he was closely besieged by the enemy. Deficiency of provisions was the principal evil that befel the English garrison; indeed, the distress of the English soldiers was so great in this respect, that Edward, in common with his men, was obliged to eat the coarse viands that were found in the castle, and to use, for his drink, water sweetened with honey. It is said that, on this occasion, a single flagon of wine only remained in the fortress, which was reserved for the King's use. But he could not be prevailed upon to taste it, till it was mixed with water, and distributed among the garrison, declaring, with a manly spirit, that he would share every extremity with the meanest of his soldiers.

The consequence of this misfortune might have proved fatal to Edward's ambition, had not a reinforcement of troops, bringing with them a plentiful supply, remedied the evil, and enabled them to hold out the siege with bravery and spirit. After a short time the insurgents were driven to the mountains, and the royal army merrily spent its Christmas in the Castle of Conway.

A.D. 1295.—In order to enable Edward to defray the expenses of the French War, the merchants of England and Ireland agreed to an additional duty upon all the merchandise that would be exported during the continuance of the war. The prelates and clergy indulged him with a moiety of all their revenues for one year. The parliament granted an aid, amounting to a tenth of all moveables, and the King issued a commission for levying a sixth in all the cities, boroughs, and towns of the royal demesnes.

But all those measures, however well concerted, were rendered ineffectual by a number of untoward circumstances. The people of Wales, were cruelly tortured by the Lords of the Marches; besides other hardships, they considered these extra taxes an intolerable grievance; and hearing that Edward was on the point of embarking for the Continent, where he would probably be detained a considerable time, they thought it a favourable opportunity to shake off the English yoke, and attempt the recovery of their liberties.[s]

Edward the First and Queen Eleanor keeping their Christmas at Conway Castle. See page 169.

Accordingly, the King's commissioners had no sooner begun to levy a fifteenth, which had been lately granted, than they flew to arms, and seizing several English officers, hanged them without form or trial. This disturbance was considered at first no more than a sudden eruption of popular fury, but it soon increased to such a degree that the rebels overran the whole country, and murdered all

[s] Our ancient Chronicles inform us that from this time the Welsh laid aside much of their rudeness, and settling peaceably in towns they began to amass wealth and indulge in the luxuries of life, until their manners became assimilated to those of their English neighbours.

"A quo tempore werræ in Wallia quieverunt, et Wallenses more Anglicorum pene vivere incœperunt, thesauros congregantes et rerum damna de cætero formidantes." Tho. Walsingham, p. 63. A similar account of the manners of the Welsh is given in the rythmical *Cambriæ Epitome*, printed among the poems of Walter Mapes, l. 185 :—

"Mores brutales Britonum
jam, ex convictu Saxonum,
commutantur in melius,
ut patet luce clarius.
Hortos et agros excolunt;
ad oppida se conferunt;

et loricati equitant,
et calceati peditant;
urbane se reficiunt;
et sub tapetis dormiunt;
ut judicentur Anglici,
nunc potius quam Wallici.
Hinc si quæratur ratio,
quietius quam solito
cur illi vivant hodie;
in causa sunt divitiæ,
quas cito gens hæc perderet
si passim nunc confligeret.
Timor damni hos retrahit;
nam nil habens nil metuit,
et, ut dixit Satyricus,
cantat viator vacuus
coram latrone tutior,
quam phaleratus ditior."

the English who fell in their way. These revolters were headed in South Wales by one Morgan; in West Wales by Maelgwyn Vaughan; and in North Wales by Madoc, a near relation of their last Prince, Llywelyn. Morgan being joined by the most powerful of the neighbouring barons, drove the Earl of Gloucester out of the country; Maelgwyn ravaged the counties of Cardigan and Pembroke; and Madoc, taking advantage of a fair in Caernarvon, surprised the town, took the castle, and afterwards made himself master of Snowdon and Anglesea. But the victorious Edward again led his army against the Welsh, and in this campaign he retook Anglesea, and followed the Britons to the very heart of Snowdonia and again brought them to subjection.

The philosophical historian, Sir James Mackintosh, in his History of England, thus expresses himself of the conquest of Wales :—

"The mind is often perplexed about estimating the comparative demerits of both parties in such contests as that between Edward and Llywelyn. But the only principle by which a just judgment can be formed is that of invariable regard to the intention of the contending chiefs. Edward's object was aggrandisement. Whatever occasional breaches of treaty or violations of humanity the Welsh may have committed, their deliberate aim never could have reached beyond the defence of their rights. His ambition tainted all his acts, and renders his conformity to the letter of the law a fraudulent evasion of the rules of justice. Their cause was in itself sacred, and entitles them to some excuse for having maintained it by those means of warfare which the barbarity of that age deemed lawful."

Mr. Turner, the learned author of the History of the Middle Ages, makes the following remarks also on this reign :—

"The reign of Edward the First was that of a prince whose sedate judgment and active talents advanced the civilisation of his country. It may be considered under four heads:—his incorporation (not the conquest) of Wales; his wars in Scotland; his foreign transactions; and his internal regulations. The Welsh, as the descendants of the original population of Britain, must always be an interesting people. Their very name and patriotism so long perpetuated in their ancient Principality, renders them of more antiquarian value, because it occasioned their language, their poetry, and their customs to continue for many ages in their ancient state, because wilfully unimproved. They were too proud to deviate into the civilisation of their country; and the Welsh of the thirteenth century, with whom Edward conflicted, seem to have differed little from the Cymry who with noble bravery withstood and manfully defended their country against the Roman army, and afterwards, under their venerated Arthur, laboured so unavailingly to drive the Saxon and the English to the Eyder and the Elbe."

EDWARD THE SECOND.—This Prince was born at Caernarvon Castle on the 25th of April, 1284.[9] He was the first English Prince born in Wales, and the first who bore the title of Prince of Wales. He ascended the throne on the 7th of July 1307. He married Isabella, daughter of Philip, the fourth King of France; and on the 24th of February in the following year, he was crowned at Westminster.[1] Although he was a monarch who had the highest reputation for military talents and political sagacity, he proved himself the most incapable ·and unfortunate monarch probably that ever sat on the throne of England.

Historians differ as to the reasons which called for the Queen's removal from the English coast to Caernarvon. Some ascribe it to her natural desire of being near the King, who had made arrangements for taking up his residence in Wales, that he might, if possible, enthrone himself in the affections of the people, and establish his conquest on a secure and permanent basis. Others allege that it was a measure of

[9] The infant was baptised by Einion, Bishop of Bangor. For this office, and to perpetuate the remembrance of it, Edward bestowed upon the prelate and his successors for ever the ferries of Borthwen and Cadnant, three manors in the county of Caernarvon, and two in the isle of Anglesea.

[1] Holinshed informs us, "There was such presse and throng at this coronation, that a knight, called Sir John Bakewell, was thrust or crowded to death." The bishops also were incommoded, and forced to hurry through the service in a slovenly manner; and yet it was not concluded before three in the afternoon."—*Coronation Anecdotes.*

state policy. The Welsh had suffered much from the insolence and cruelty of the English officers set over them by Henry the Third, and had resolved and avowed their resolution not to acknowledge any prince unless he were a native of Wales. As the most effectual method of satisfying their wishes, the Queen, who expected soon to become a mother, was brought to Caernarvon.

The Queen engaged for the young Prince a Welsh nurse, the mother of Sir Hywel y Pedolau, who, being a foster brother to the King, was in great favour, and was knighted by him. Sir Hywel was so strong a man that he could, it is said, straighten horses shoes with his hands, whence his name, *y Pedolau*, i.e., "of the Horseshoe." "And here," says Mr. York, "I am led to doubt the policy of Edward the First in making his second son, Edward, a Welshman, and bringing his Queen for that purpose to lie in at Caernarvon, his elder son Alphonsus being then alive; and since the union of England and Wales was a great object, and for which eventually we are much obliged to him, it seemed to be made more difficult by this measure, as the Welsh might not have easily resigned their countryman and adopted King."

The Eagle Tower at Caernarvon Castle, the Birth-place of Edward the Second.

In the castle of this place are the remains of a spacious apartment, believed by some historians to be that in which Queen Eleanor gave birth, on St. Mark's day, to Edward the Second, the first Prince of Wales of English descent. Mr. Pennant, assuming that in those times the consorts of kings were regardless of pomp and of nice accommodations, supposes the Prince was born in a small room adjoining, which has much the appearance of a closet; but Mr. Hartshorne, in his splendid work on Caernarvon Castle, recently published, and illustrated with some beautiful engravings, enters into the question at some length to prove that the Prince was not born in the Eagle Tower, but in another part of the Castle.[2]

The principal gate had four portcullises, and was of adamantine strength. The exterior walls, now in many places overhung with ivy and creeping shrubs, are seven feet nine inches thick, and inclose between two and three acres of ground, part of which was occupied by various castellated buildings, and the rest formed the court of the noble edifice, into which a plentiful supply of water was conveyed, by leaden

[2] Great improvements have recently been made in repairing the walls of this fortress, under the superintendence of a Committee of the Woods and Forests. We should be glad to hear of its being made a Royal residence, so as to induce Her Majesty to pay an occasional visit, to her loyal and devoted subjects in the Principality.

pipes, from a well about half a mile to the east. On entering the spacious inclosure, we find the dilapidation to be more considerable than the outward appearance of the walls might lead us to expect—

" All, all within
Proclaims that nature has resumed her right."

When this immense fabric was in its perfect state, a corridor, or gallery, attached to the outward walls, and surrounding the courts, facilitated the communication (which must have been of great importance during a siege,) between the towers and the other buildings. A portion of it only, on the south side, has escaped the ravages of time, and this is by no means a narrow intricate passage; two persons may with ease walk along it together, and it is uncommonly elegant in its structure. The towers are high and angular. The largest among them, the Eagle Tower, with its three mellowed turrets, has been the admiration of ages. It takes its name, tradition says, from the figure of an eagle having been placed on its pinnacle. Some centuries ago, the superb monarch of the feathered tribe was frequently to be seen in this district. An aërie was every year built upon the rocks of Snowdon:[3]

" And from the summit of that craggy mound
The perching eagle oft was heard to cry,
Or on resounding wings to shoot athwart the sky."—BEATTIE.

From the summit of the Eagle Tower, which may be reached by a close winding staircase, the prospect is magnificent. The eye wanders over Caernarvon Bay, harbour, and shipping, the Menai Straits, the Isle of Anglesea, with its gently rising hills, its meadows, and its cottages; the Seiont, and a diversified and enchanting tract of country, bounded by the Caernarvonshire Mountains. At the opposite extremity of the court is the "Queen's Gate," so designated from Eleanor, the Queen of Edward the First, having passed through it when she first entered the castle. It is at a great height above the ground, and could be approached from the outer side only by a "jealous drawbridge," which was occasionally dropped over a wide foss.

A.D. 1312.—King Edward the Second came to Chester to meet his favourite, Piers Gaveston, on his return from Ireland.[4]

During the short reign of this monarch, Wales and the Border towns were the scene of several important events. The King by his injudicious partiality for particular favourites exasperated the barons; nay, the affections of his Queen, Isabella, became alienated. His inglorious and unsuccessful war against the Scots served to render Edward still more unpopular; and the evils of the State were aggravated by famine, which prevailed throughout England, A.D. 1316, and was so dreadful that the people were ready to devour each other. Gaveston, Edward's favourite, became so unpopular that the parliament petitioned the King to banish him. Edward consented with great reluctance, and appointed him Governor of Ireland.

A.D. 1317.—Sir Gruffydd Llwyd,[5] indignant and annoyed at the sufferings of his countrymen under the English yoke, meditated a revolt, and attempted to form an alliance with Sir Edward Bruce, the short-lived King of Ireland. Letters passed between them, but without effect.[6] At length, moved by his own noble spirit, he determined alone to free his country from the slavery to which he himself had probably in some manner contributed. He took up arms,[7] and for awhile overran the country with resistless impetuosity. At length he was subdued, taken, and undoubtedly underwent the common fate of our gallant insurgents. Sir Gruffydd had fortified his house at Tregarnedd in Anglesea with a very strong foss and rampart, and made another stronghold about three-quarters of a mile distant, in the morass of Malltraeth, called "Ynys Cefni," which he insulated by bringing round it the waters of the

[3] These birds, as is not unusual with them, have now changed their haunts.   [4] Leland.

[5] This gentleman received from Edward I. the honour of knighthood for bringing him the news of the birth of his son Edward of Caernarvon. He did homage for his lands in Wales to the young Prince at Chester.

[6] Wynne's Hist. Wales, p. 311.

[7] Powell's Wales, p. 383.

River Cefni.' Both still remain; the foss is nearly perfect; it is near four yards deep and eight wide. His daughter Morfydd, one of his coheiresses,' conveyed by marriage this estate, being her portion, to Madoc Gloddaeth.'

A.D. 1321.—This infatuated monarch met at Flint Castle the haughty but insidious favourite, Piers Gaveston, who, a short time before, had been banished from the country for his evil deeds. In consequence of his attachment to Gaveston, a confederacy of the Barons of England rose against him, headed by the Lord Badlesmere,' a man who owed his honours and nearly the whole of his ample estates to the power of his misguided sovereign. The Mortimers, at the instance of the rest of their associates, made themselves masters of Bridgenorth Castle, and held it against the King. Their resistance was however of no long duration; Edward soon took the castle, and thence proceeded to Shrewsbury, accompanied by the Earls of Richmond, Pembroke, Arundel, Surrey, and other nobles.'

A.D. 1321.—Edward's II.'s reception at Shrewsbury ' denotes the loyalty of its inhabitants in this crisis. On his coming near the town, he was honourably received by the burgesses, who went out to meet him, clad in armour, and so conducted him into the town, which was strongly fortified.' He continued there several days, at least from the 15th to the 23rd, during which time he was busily employed in appointing governors, on whose fidelity he could depend, to various castles, the owners of which were in open hostilities to him. Thus, on the 18th of January, he commits Red Castle to John de Felton; on the 19th, the castle of La Pole and the land of Powys to Robert Sapy; on the 22nd, Chirk Castle to Peter Giffard; and on the 23rd, being still in this town, he commits the castle and town of Lodelaw (Ludlow) to Ralph le Botiller.'

Notwithstanding the respectable posture of the King's affairs, and his possession of this strong and steady town, he thought proper still further to keep on the mask. Accordingly, he here issued a proclamation of general amnesty to all his subjects, Badlesmere only excepted:' and in consequence of this assurance, Roger de Mortimer of Wigmore (who figures in history as Earl of March, and was afterwards so instrumental in the disposal of this monarch), together with his uncle Roger de Mortimer of Chirk, repaired hither,' and threw themselves at the King's feet. It is lamentable to think that a

³ Rowland's MSS.   ⁹ Sebright's MSS.

¹ It remained in this branch of that house till 1750, when it was sold by the late Sir Thomas Mostyn, Bart., M.P., to the late Owen Williams, Esq., M.P.

² The following is Edward's own account, or, what modern journalists would denominate the *court version* of the transaction. It bears date from Shrewsbury, Jan. 15, and is addressed to Richard Lovel, constable of the castle of Bristol. "Whereas Humphrey Earl of Hereford and Essex, Roger de Mortuo Mari of Wigmore, Roger de Mortuo Mari of Chirk, Roger Damory, Hugh Daudele senior and junior, Bartholomew de Badlesmere (ten more are enumerated, two of whom are Talbots) have taken and burned Briggenorth, to which we had sent our servants, 'cum providentiis nostris ibidem faciendis,' (to make purveyance for us); and whereas they afterwards invaded the castles of Elmle and Henle, being in our hands, detaining the said town and castles, &c."—it commands Lovel to arrest any of the above if they be found within his bailiwick.

³ That all the peers mentioned in the text attended Edward II., appears from his charter of Newport in this county, dated at Salop, 23rd January, 15ᵐᵒ regni (1321-2), and witnessed by "John de Britanne Earl of Richmond, Adam (*i.e.* Adomar) de Valence Earl of Pembroke, Edmund Earl of Arundel, John de Warren Earl of Surrey, John de St. John, Ralph de Camois, Gilbert Perrse steward of our household, and others."

⁴ Edward must therefore have taken Newport in his way from Bridgenorth to Shrewsbury: perhaps it was to secure in his interests that town, so important for the transmission of his troops through the Wild Moors; for its proprietor, James de Audley, was an infant of

only eight years, whose near kinsmen, the two Hugh Audleys, were in arms against the king. This would make his charter a measure rather of policy, than a mere boon accorded to the merriment of his landlord; though Edward was of a temper by no means insensible to this species of merit. In fact, he had a great turn for low buffoonery: we learn from the curious document of his private expenses in the Antiquarian Repertory, vol. ii. p. 57, that "Jak of St. Alban's" was paid no less a sum than 2*l.* 10*s.* for "dancing before him on a table;" and Morris Ken, a servant in his kitchen, 20*s.* for "riding before him when he was hunting the deer, and falling often from his horse," thereby "causing the king heartily to laugh:" of Mr. Levere's talents for acquiring the royal favour, we are not informed. It must be observed that Mr. Skrymsher is mistaken in his chronology of the Royal Visit to Newport: the battle, as he calls it, of Burton, was several weeks after.—*Owen and Blakeway.*⁎

⁵ Lloyd's MS. quoting Chronicle, f. 329.

⁶ Rotuli finium istius anni, m. 16, 17. In Dugdale's MSS. vol. O. The lord of Red Castle (near Hawkstone), James de Audley, was, as has been observed, a minor: Chirk and Ludlow were possessions of the two Roger Mortimers, the king's open enemies: but we cannot account for the appointment to Pole (now Powis) Castle, for it does not appear that its lord, John de Charleton, was a partisan of the rebels.

⁷ Leland Coll. i. 274.

⁸ Walsingham, p. 115. These were not the only branches of this potent house, who experienced the frowns of the sovereign. We

⁎ We are indebted to the great industry of these gentlemen for much valuable information connected with this portion of our work.

A A

sovereign should have conceived himself at liberty to break his faith with these suppliants, apparently without the smallest scruple: he instantly sent them to the Tower of London;[*] and having weakened his adversaries by the seizure of those two powerful and valiant lords, the chief support of the baronial faction, and having also arrested Sir Hugh de Audley, senior, and Sir Maurice de Berkeley,[1] he quitted Shrewsbury and went southwards.

"A.D. 1325.—Edward designing an expedition to his duchy of Guyenne, on which the French monarch had made some aggressions, determined to raise a body of men in Wales. Those of the northern part of that Principality were ordered to muster on Midlent Sunday, in Shrewsbury, whither Giles de Beauchamp and Aleyn de Cherelton were commanded to repair, for the purpose of reviewing them, and conducting them to Portsmouth. The deposal and murder of Edward, which soon ensued, originated in his consent to abandon this expedition, and in the permission which he unwarily gave his Queen to visit the court of France, under the pretext of endeavouring to accommodate the differences which had occasioned him to take up arms.

"On that revolution, the inhabitants of Shrewsbury took an active part against the King. Edmund, Earl of Arundel, was one of the few peers who had preserved their loyalty to the crown. He assembled a multitude of his Welsh tenantry at Oswestry, with a view of seizing Shrewsbury for the King. In this emergency, the bailiffs and burgesses sent a pressing entreaty to Whittington, requesting the aid of Fulke Fitz Warin, lord of that place. We have not seen whether Fitz Warin complied with this message. It is not very probable that he should do so; as we find him not long afterwards displaying his loyalty to his dethroned sovereign: but another potent baron, Sir John de Charlton, of Powys, marched to their aid; and the burgesses, by his assistance, apprehended Arundel near Shrewsbury, with certain of his adherents, after an obstinate struggle, Nov. 17th, 1326, the day after the capture of his sovereign. The Earl was taken from thence to Hereford, where he expiated his loyalty to his sovereign and affinity to the Despensers on a scaffold. For this service, the burgesses received an immediate grant under the great seal, which was now in the hands of the Queen, of all the goods and chattels found upon the Earl and his adherents, apprehended within their liberties."

About the latter part of the unfortunate reign of Edward the Second, his Queen, Prince Edward, and the principal barons met in Hereford, to concoct measures for the good of the State, and having called together the great council of the realm, they declared the Prince, afterwards Edward III., Protector of the Kingdom, although his father, King Edward II., was then alive.

The Queen on her entrance into the city was welcomed with joyful acclamations, and, in the insolence of triumph, very unworthy of her sex and station, she obliged the unfortunate Despenser, the King's favourite, to attend her progress. He was placed upon a lean deformed horse, clothed in a taberee, a dress worn in those days by thieves and the lowest of men.

When the unfortunate King found himself deserted by his subjects, he fled directly to Wales, but he met with so few friends that he was obliged to conceal himself among the woods in the neighbourhood of Glamorgan. Roger de Mortimer with the Queen hastened to the Border; and passed the last days of the year 1327 at Hereford. Thither the unfortunate King was brought a prisoner; and before they left that city several of his partisans were beheaded or hanged.

learn from the pipe rolls of the 18th of this reign, (after the suppression of the revolt) that Hugh de Mortimer (who seems to have been the Lord of Chelmarsh) accounted for 200*l.* as a fine for the safety of his life, and restoration of his lands, because he adhered to Thomas, late Earl of Lancaster.

[2] Enderbie tells us, if we understand him aright, that the Welsh proved loyal to the crown upon this occasion. Mortimer of Chirk was deservedly odious to them: for he obtained that castle and domain by the murder of its young lord, Llywelyn, the last Prince of Powys. "About the year 1322," says he, " one Sir Griffith Lloyd,

knight, gathered a great number of Welshmen, and took divers castles in Wales, which were kept by the people of the Lord Mortimer, the elder: he took also the castles of Mould, Chirk, &c.: the keepers whereof coming to Prince Edward at Shrewsbury, who was then King of England, submitted themselves to him, and were shortly after sent to the Tower of London." Cambria Triumphans, p. 332. The author calls Edward II, Prince, because he considers him Prince of Wales.

[1] Both these barons had large estates in Shropshire: it was at the castle of the latter, Edward was afterwards murdered.

Few monarchs more completely forfeited "all fair renown," few have been more deplorably weak, profligate, and selfish. He was obliged to surrender his crown in January, 1327, and from that period, till he closed his dishonoured life in agonies, he was recognised only as "Edward of Caernarvon."[1]

The Welsh people were warmly attached to this unhappy Prince. With all his faults, they remembered that he was born among them, and looked upon him as their countryman. Their partiality towards him knew neither change nor decay.[2] Through all his misfortunes, he never ceased to be an object of their compassion, and they honoured his death with plaintive and melancholy songs.

The favourite, Hugh Despenser, was condemned to the same cruel punishment to which the Welsh Prince, David, had been subjected, at Shrewsbury; with this difference, that the English traitor was suspended on a gallows fifty feet high.

It is to the honour of the female sex, that we have but few, if any, instances on record of cruelty equal to that, which, if not directed was sanctioned by Isabel, Queen of Edward II. In this case the Queen made head against her husband, and led an innocent son to plot the destruction of his father. After Edward had been for some time in custody of his enemies, and his patient sufferings were known and commiserated by the people, his persecutors became alarmed and were determined to destroy him; for this reason they removed him from the fortress in the dead of night. On the occasion of his removal from Bristol to Gloucestershire, one of the wretches, his conductors, crowned him with a wisp of hay, in derision of his former dignity, and forced him to alight in a filthy puddle that he might have his hair and beard cut off, for which purpose a wretched barber was engaged, who appeared with his implements carrying water in an old helmet, at the same time rudely apologising for it not being warm. The manliness of Edward for a moment forsook him, and he let fall a shower of tears, adding, "these will supply the lack of warm water." He was then again mounted on a sorry nag, and conveyed to Berkeley Castle. His treatment there was inhuman beyond expression, but though every privacy was observed his condition was not unknown. So much did the country feel, that one William Aylmer, a neighbouring loyal gentleman, with some friends, attempted to break into Berkeley Castle, but their design failed in the execution, and the sympathising leader of this little band was taken prisoner. After this attempt orders were sent from the Queen and Mortimer, her paramour, that the King should be dispatched, on which account the Earl of Berkeley was suspended as his keeper, and the villains Gourney and Maltravers lodged him in a damp turret, on a level with the battlements and leads of the Castle, where he was obliged to stand up to his knees in water, surrounded by carrion, putrid carcases, &c., intended to infect the air and occasion his death. There he uttered many loud complaints, which were heard and commiserated by some workmen and the surrounding neighbourhood. This mode of destruction proved too slow, and it was resolved that the 21st of September should be his last. On the night of that day he had an extraordinary indulgence of a supper, and much apparent kindness; this was to induce him to sleep soundly, and it had the desired effect. About midnight, Gournay and Maltravers, with fifteen others entered his bed-chamber, where they put him to death in a manner too shocking to be related in these pages.[4] Thus fell Edward II. by the hands of murderous traitors. His head was put into a silver vessel, and the Berkeley family attended his corpse to Gloucester for interment. His son, Edward III. afterwards caused a marble tomb to be erected over his remains.

Within a few months after the deposition of Edward, Roger de Mortimer was created an Earl, by the title of Earl of March. Immediately afterwards he imitated his grandfather in holding a " Round

---

[2] In the Herald's office, according to Bishop Tanner, Notitia Monastica, p. 253, is a MS. Latin poem, written by this ill-fated prince, while a prisoner. Its title is, " Lamentatio gloriosi Regis Edwardi Karnarvan, quam edidit tempore suæ incarcerationis." There is every reason to believe that the verses are not genuine. See Royal and Noble Authors, vol. i. p. 8, ed. 1789.

[3] We find that in the third year of Edward II., the following supplies were sent from Wales to assist him in his Scotch wars.

The barony of Powys sent four hundred; Rhos and Rhyfoniog, that is Denbigh, two hundred; Nanhandwy and Glyndyfrdwy two hundred; Bromfield and Yale two hundred—numbers exceeding the generality of Militia proportions.

[4] " Mark the year, and mark the night,
When Severn shall re-echo with affright
The shrieks of death, through Berkeley's roof that ring,
Shrieks of an agonising king."—GRAY.

A A 2

Table;" and he conducted the Queen and the young King to the Marches of Wales, where he welcomed them with magnificent festivities, accompanied with tournaments and other princely recreations, in his Castles of Ludlow and Wigmore.' Roger de Mortimer was now blinded by his ambition, and set no bounds to his ostentation. He scarcely took pains to conceal his familiarity with the Queen; he usurped all the powers of the government, and offended many of the nobles by his haughtiness. It is said that his own son Geoffrey was accustomed to speak of him as the "King of folly." A conspiracy was formed against him, headed by the King, who was desirous of taking the government of his country into his own hands; and the powerful nobleman was captured by surprise in the Castle of Nottingham, and having been convicted' of high treason, by a parliament called for that purpose, in 1331, he was hanged on the common gallows in London. The sentence was perhaps one rather of vengeance than of justice: the chief charge brought against him was that of having usurped the sovereign power, and having injured the country by mal-administration. In most of the particular cases specified, the accusations were general and indefinite. In some he had perhaps adopted the best measures which the circumstances would admit.' Several of Mortimer's friends were condemned along with him.

The character of this unhappy King seems to have been a compound of indolence, effeminacy, weak judgment, and self-will. His person was tall and strong, and his countenance handsome. His natural capacity was so enervated by indulgences that, though a reflective contemporary says, "that if he had exercised himself in arms, he would have excelled the Cœur de Lion; and that if he had not followed the advice of bad men, he might have been more noble than all his predecessors;"' yet his reign was more disgraceful and calamitous than that of any preceding sovereign of the Norman Line. Infirm in spirit and devoted to his enjoyments, he showed no energy but in striving to be arbitrary, and in supporting his favourites, against the united feelings of his nobility and the common sense of his people. Son of one of the most able of the English kings and father of one of the most celebrated, his reign intervenes like a narrow and rugged isthmus between two great continents; barren itself, but the connecting passage between regions of great produce and renown. It is the opinion of an able writer, that from a wiser education, he would have derived a stronger judgment, and then might have become an applauded and happy King; but blighted in the spring-time of life, his character became such as chiefly serves,

> "To point a moral or adorn a tale!"

EDWARD THE THIRD' enjoyed a long and glorious reign, but it presents us with no historical feature, either general or local, connected with the subject of this work. Wales had to some extent been pacified, and the importance of the Border towns of Chester, Shrewsbury, Ludlow, Hereford, and Monmouth, no longer existed. The petty transactions that took place in these parts are lost in the blaze of the conquest, which beamed from the subjugation of Scotland and France. In both these wars the Welsh and the inhabitants of the Marches took a prominent part, particularly at the great battles of Poictiers and Cressy.

' "Exinde rex Edwardus tertius ad Marchiam transiit, et in castris dicti domini Rogeri comitis de Loddelowe et de Wyggemore, forestisque et parcis, cum maximis expensis in communiis, hasti-ludiis, et aliis solaciis, munificisque donariis sibi et suis largiter effusis, regaliter per nonnullos dies tractatus," &c. Monasticon, vi. p. 352.

' On Mortimer's impeachment, the first charge was, that "he had procured Edward of Caernarvon to be murdered in a most heinous and tyrannous manner within the Castle of Berklie."

' The charges against Roger de Mortimer, specified in the Rolls of Parliament, 4 Edward III., are, that he had been, by his intrigues, instrumental in the fall of Edward II.; that he had caused him to be removed from Kenilworth to Berkeley Castle, where he had been at least privy to his murder, &c. &c.

' Mon. Maln. p. 136. This author seems to have penned his thoughts in his chronicles, as if writing a diary from day to day.

In this part he exclaims, "Grant, O Lord! peace in our days, and may the king be harmonious with his barons."

' On the deposition of Edward II., his son, Prince Edward, was brought to a general assembly by the nobles and clergy in the abbey church of Westminster, on the 20th of January, 1327, and Walter Raynold exhorted all present to choose the young prince for their sovereign. All assented; but the prince himself declared that he would not accept the crown until it had been voluntarily resigned by his father. A remarkable coronation medal was struck on this occasion: on one side the young prince was represented crowned, laying his sceptre on a heap of hearts, with the motto "Populo dat jura volenti" (He gives laws to a willing people); and on the other was a hand held out to save a falling crown, with the motto "Non rapit, sed recipit." (He seizes not, but receives.)

We have no account of a Royal Visit to Wales during the reign of Edward III.,[1] but after the parliament of November, A.D. 1342, when that victorious monarch, celebrated his entering on the fiftieth year of his age, he made an excursion with his chief nobles, as well as the French hostages, then in his Court, to several great forests, where he hunted all sorts of noble game. Burns says that his expenditure on this occasion averaged 100l. a day.[2]

Clun Forest on the Borders of the Marches in Shropshire was one of those he visited at that time, and it is highly probable that the important town of Shrewsbury was also honoured with the Royal presence on that occasion.

A.D. 1336.—Whilst Edward was engaged in his wars in Scotland, tidings were brought to him that the Welsh were getting turbulent; and fearful lest they should break the peace, he sent orders[3] that all the castles in that country should be visited and stored. This order was repeated in A.D. 1337.[4]

During the rest of the reign of Edward III., the Welsh seem to have continued in quiet obedience to the English laws. They appear in history chiefly as furnishing continual levies to increase the English armies in Scotland and France. The materials for Border history during this period are very scant, yet they afford evidence that the submission of the Welsh did not altogether insure the tranquillity of the English Marches. It appears that towards the middle of the fourteenth century the English counties beyond the Severn were overrun by bands of outlaws. In Gloucestershire they had joined together and elected themselves a chieftain, to whom they gave sovereign power, and in whose name they issued proclamations; and, setting in defiance the King and his laws, they infested equally the sea and the land, capturing and plundering the King's ships on one element, and murdering and robbing the King's subjects on the other. In A.D. 1347, the King sent a commission to Gloucester to concert means of discovering the offenders and bringing them to justice.[5]

The King's suspicions of the fidelity of his Welsh subjects, appear, however, not have decreased, and we find him ordering frequent precautionary measures against a rebellion. The Border fortresses were kept in a good state of defence. In A.D. 1369 an order was issued forbidding the men of Shrewsbury to quit their houses on the pretence of attending the foreign wars, lest by their absence the town should be weak of defence in the case of a sudden rise of the Welsh.

A.D. 1370.—The sheriffs were ordered to put the castles of Wales in a state to support sieges, and to arm the English population, for the purpose of withstanding the French, who threatened an invasion towards Christmas of that year.

A.D. 1377.—The same fears of the French invasion appear to have been entertained, and similar orders were repeated, for the defence of the coasts of Wales.[6]

RICHARD THE SECOND.—With respect to this reign Hume observes that "there is no part of the English history since the Conquest, so obscure, so uncertain, so little authentic or consistent, as that of the wars between the Roses: historians differ about many material circumstances."[7]

---

[1] A.D. 1353.—Edward the Black Prince, with the Earls of Warwick and Stafford, at the head of an armed force, came to Chester to protect the justices itinerant, Sir Richard Willoughby and Sir Richard Snareshall, in the execution of their duty, from the violence of the populace. The occasion is not mentioned; but it is probable that there had been some commotion on account of the dearness of provisions; that year being recorded as a year of great scarcity. See Dugdale, Baronage, i. p. 141; Walsingham.

[2] Burns, p. 626.

[3] Rymer's Foedera, pp. 895, 913, &c. A singular occurrence is alluded to in a document of the year 1336 (ib. p. 937). It appears that Edward II., in his flight into Wales, had carried with him his treasure, which, in his last perils, he had buried. The document just mentioned is an order for an inquisition relating to the discovery of this treasure, "in florenis, denariis numeratis, vasis aureis et argenteis, jocalibus, armaturis, victualibus, et aliis rebus," to the amount of sixty thousand pounds, found "in partibus de Glamorgan et Morgannok in Wallia," and dispersed and carried away by "divers malefactors."—Wright.

[4] In the second year of this reign, Roger de Mortimer, and Joan his wife, obtained a license from the monarch to hold a fair in Ludlow on the eve of St. Catherine (25th of Nov.) and four days following, for ever.

[5] Rymer's Foedera, iii. p. 126.

[6] Rymer's Foedera, iii. pp. 869, 901, 1075.

[7] The coronation of this king was more magnificent than any of the preceding. The procession of the king from the Tower of Westminster, on the day preceding the coronation, is thus described by Holinshed: "The citie was adorned in all sorts most richlie. The water-conduits ran with wine for the space of three hours

The seeds of discord, from which sprang the wars between the rival houses of York and Lancaster, were first sown in the reign of Richard II. The primary cause of these bloody wars may, in some measure, be found in the weakness of the King, who allowed himself to become the dupe of favourites who took an undue advantage of his tender age, he being only eleven years old when he ascended the throne. They had insinuated themselves into his favour; and, by flattery and intrigue, so won his confidence during his minority, that the King ruled according to their will and caprice. Thus, by their ill-advised counsels, they led him into the commission of several rash acts whereby the love of his subjects became daily alienated from him, while a strong and powerful opposition was raised against his ministers, his favourites, and himself.

The King was naturally of a gentle and amiable disposition; and was possessed of a noble and generous spirit. But these qualifications, through want of parental care and proper education, proved of no advantage either to himself or to the nation. The evil habits which he had contracted during his minority, and in which he was indulged by his favourites, completely unfitted him for sovereign power; so that when he attained his majority (May 1389), and took the reins of government into his own hands, he had neither the mind, nor the resolution, to act for himself and independently of the advice of those whom he suffered to monopolise his favours and affections. Those favourites had but too well succeeded in poisoning his tender mind, and filling it with prejudice and suspicion against his real well-wishers, who lamented the thraldom in which he was holden, and the disrepute into which the government of the kingdom was fast sinking. He therefore never lost sight of those whom he had been taught to look upon as his opponents, until by intrigue and treachery they were ensnared and murdered. Among the wretched sufferers from his tyranny, was his own uncle Thomas, Duke of Gloucester, son of Edward III. That Prince was betrayed into the hands of the Earl of Nottingham, who took him under his custody, and immediately shipped him for Calais. There, after being kept a close prisoner for some time, he was secretly strangled.

When the King had succeeded in his dark and unnatural purposes, and had as he thought triumphed over his enemies, his next project was to seat himself firmly on his throne. With this view, he liberally conferred new honours upon divers individuals, hoping by so doing to gain their affections, and to render them more constant and faithful in their attachment to his person. He created five dukes, among whom were Henry, Earl of Derby, and Thomas Mowbray, Earl of Nottingham. The former was made Duke of Hereford, and the latter as a reward for the services which he rendered in the matter of the Duke of Gloucester, became Duke of Norfolk.

We have no means of ascertaining how far the Borderers took part in the popular insurrections of the opening years of the reign of Richard II. These movements were chiefly confined to the eastern parts of the island: but we have many reasons for believing that the inhabitants of the English counties on the Borders of Wales shared largely in the reforming spirit of that age. Even before the preaching of Wiclyffe, this neighbourhood had produced the bold satirical poem which is so well known under the title of Piers Ploughman. In the reign of Richard II., the Border had already become the stronghold of the Lollards.[8]

together. In the upper ende of Cheape was a certain castell, made with foure towers; out of the which castell, on two sides on it, ran forth wine abundantly. In the towers were placed foure beautifull virgins, of stature and age like to the king, apparelled in white vestures, in every tower one, the which blew in the king's face, at his appearing neere to them, leaves of gold; and as he approached also, they threw on him and his horsse counterfeit florens of gold. When he was come before the castell they tooke cups of gold, and, filling them with wine at the spouts of the castell, presented the same to the king and to his nobles. On the top of the castell, betwixt the foure towers, stood a golden angell, holding a crowne in his hands, which was so contrived, that when the king came, he bowed downe and offered to him the crowne. In the midst of the king's pallace was a marble pillar, raised hollow upon steps, on the top whereof was a great gilt eagle placed, under whose feet in the chapiter of the pillar divers kinds of wine came gushing forth at foure several places all the daie long, neither was anie forbidden to receive the same, were he never so poor or abiest."

[8] One of the most remarkable men of this sect, the history of whose persecutions in 1393 will be found in Foxe's Acts and Monuments, was a native of Herefordshire; his name was Walter Brut, or Bright, probably a member of one of the families of that name which still have their representatives in Herefordshire and Shropshire. The mode in which his contemporaries spoke of this early

King Richard appears to have used all occasions of showing favour to the Welsh, and to have looked to them for support and aid in case of need. He also placed great dependence on the people of Cheshire, who were governed by one of his creatures, Thomas Molineux, Constable of Chester. We have already seen how obnoxious the people of Cheshire were at this time to the inhabitants of the neighbouring counties. It is probable that the favourable eye with which Richard regarded them tended not a little to render him unpopular on the Border.

A.D. 1387.—When the great barons had begun to enter into hostile league against the King's favourite, Robert de Vere, then newly created Duke of Ireland, Richard and the favourite repaired into Wales, in order to consult with more security on means to crush the conspiracy. They returned from thence to Nottingham, where a parliament was called, and the barons were cited to appear and answer the charges which were brought against them. But they called together their tenants, and prepared to meet the favourite in arms. The Duke of Ireland raised the men of Cheshire, and joining with them some Welsh levies, he marched into Oxfordshire, where he was met by the barons at Radcote Bridge, on the Isis. But the courage of the favourite forsook him in the moment of danger, and, seeing no other way of escape, he quitted his armour, threw himself into the river, and swam down the stream. His army was easily put to the rout, and the leader of the Cheshire men, Thomas Molineux, was slain by one of the baronial party, named Thomas de Mortimer. The Duke of Ireland escaped to the Continent; and in his absence he was attainted and outlawed.[9]

The interest which the people of the Welsh Border took in these events is proved by the political poem in alliterative verse (written in imitation of the Vision and Creed of Piers Ploughman), on the deposition of Richard II., which is a strong declaration of the principles and motives of the party which placed Henry IV. on the throne. It appears to have been composed at Bristol.[1] In the first parliament of the new monarch, the Commons presented a vigorous petition against the outrages committed by the people of Cheshire against their neighbours, and they were probably, after this, effectually restrained. It is certain that the complainants had found little redress during Richard's reign;[2] and the men of Chester appear to have been in open rebellion at the beginning of that of his successor.[3]

The Welsh, who had remained quiet while King Richard was in need of their assistance, took up arms in his cause after his death, and remained during several years in open rebellion against King Henry.

A.D. 1387.—The town of Shrewsbury was honoured by a visit from the sovereign, during which time some transactions occurred of a remarkable nature, and intimately connected with the train of events which led to the deposition and murder of that unhappy King. Tired with the restraints created by the opposition which was headed by his uncle, the Duke of Gloucester, he made a progress to the Marches of Wales, in

champion of the Reformation may be seen in the following specimen of a political poem, resembling in style the Visions of Piers Ploughman, and probably, like it, written on the Border, under the title of the Creed of Piers Ploughman.—*Wright.*

" Alle that persecution
In pure liif suffren,
They han the benison of God,
Blissed in erthe.
I pray, parceyve now
The pursut of a frere,
In what mesure of a mekenesse
Thise men deleth.
Byhold upon Water Brut
Hou bisiliche thei pursueden,
For he seid hem the sothe,*
Hy may no marren hem,
But men telleth

That he is an heretik,
And yvele byleveth,
And precheth it in pulpit
To blenden the puple.
They wolden awyrien that wight
For his wel dedes,
And so they chewen charité,
As chewen shaf houndes."

A few years later, the celebrated Sir John Oldcastle (Lord Cobham), the head of the Lollard party, took refuge on the Welsh Border from the enmity of his persecutors, and was there discovered and arrested by his pursuers.

[9] See Mr. Wright's History of Ludlow.
[1] This poem has been published by the Camden Society.
[2] The commons, in their petition for redress of this grievance, 1 Henry IV., say, " come sovent avant ses heures ad esté pursuez et montrez et plusours parlementz en temps Richard le Secounde jadys roy d'Engleterre, sanz aucune remedie." Rot. Parl. vol. iii. p. 440.
[3] See Nicholas's Proceedings of the Privy Council, vol. i. p. 113.

* *i.e.* Because he told them the truth.

the month of August, with the view, as it seems, of cultivating an interest in that quarter.   He proceeded through Coventry to Shrewsbury, where, being attended by the Chief Justice, Sir Robert Tresillian, and certain other judges and eminent lawyers, he consulted them on the validity of those proceedings in the late parliament which had so greatly encroached upon the royal authority.   Having secured such answers as were favourable to the prerogative, he dismissed his lawyers, and proceeded into Wales and Cheshire, but enjoined their attendance at Nottingham, to deliver their opinions in writing, which they did on the 25th of the same month.   It cannot be denied that these opinions were in the main highly unconstitutional; and equally so were the means which had been used to fetter the regal power.[4]

A.D. 1394.—King Richard II.[5] came to Chester, with the Duke of Gloucester, and the Earls of March, Salisbury, Arundel, Nottingham, Rutland, and others on his way to Ireland.   This monarch, towards the close of his reign, testified a great partiality towards the inhabitants of Cheshire; in the year 1397, when he scarcely knew whom to trust about his person, he appointed a corps of two thousand Cheshire archers for his body guard.[6]   The next year, "for the love he bore to the gentlemen and commons of the shire of Chester, he caused it to be ordained, in the parliament holden at Shrewsbury, that from henceforth it should be called and known by the title, Principality of Cheshire."[7]   From this time he took the title of "*Prince of Chester.*"   The act for making Cheshire a principality, was revoked in the next reign.

A.D. 1397.—"The King having succeeded in putting down all opposition to his measures, having murdered his uncle of Gloucester, and condemned the Earl of Arundel, associated with that patriotic prince, to the block, and having secured such elections as were favourable to his designs, convened a parliament at Westminster in September, which he afterwards adjourned to Shrewsbury.   His view in calling this assembly was to establish his authority upon the firmest basis; indeed upon the ruin of his country's freedom.   As he might expect to accomplish this unhallowed project with greater facility in a remote provincial town, than in the metropolis of the kingdom, this was probably his true reason for that adjournment: though the ground actually stated was the peculiar affection which he entertained for the people of Shropshire.   An apprehension of tumult among Arundel's tenantry in this country, and the design of seizing his estates, were likewise, it is probable, among the motives for making Shrewsbury the scene of that national assembly."

The parliament met at Shrewsbury pursuant to its adjournment, January 29th, 1397-8.[8]   It was the fashion of that age to assign distinguishing epithets to any remarkable assemblies of the nation.   This of Shrewsbury, was denominated the GREAT PARLIAMENT, from the important state affairs which were transacted in it.   The King lodged at Lilleshull Abbey on the 25th of January on his way hither, and soon after entered the town in state.   At the opening of the session, he indulged his taste for magnificence, by entertaining the members with a sumptuous feast.   Intending to dazzle by the splendour of monarchy, he was attired in his royal robes; and to awe by military display, he was attended by a numerous guard of

---

[4] For the particulars of these new regulations, we would refer our readers to Messrs. Owen and Blakeney's excellent History of Shropshire, to whose indefatigable exertions and deep researches we are indebted for much valuable and curious information.   For the account of the great parliament, see pp. 175-8.

[5] Richard of Bourdeaux succeeded to the title of Prince of Wales, Duke of Cornwall, and Earl of Chester, having had a special grant of that of Cornwall, in consequence of his father, the Black Prince, having died during the lifetime of Edward III.

[6] The many charters now in Chester, granted by Richard during his frequent visits to Chester, show how much he was attached to the capital of his favourite county, in which he was so highly popular; and in a moment of great extremity, when he could not collect any troops upon whom reliance could be placed, he adopted two thousand Cheshire archers for his body guard.   21 Richard II. cap. xix.

[7] At the latter part of his reign, he erected the earldom into a Principality, annexing to it the lands of Bromfield, Yale, Chirk Castle, and other possessions forfeited (under legal forms that were a mockery of justice) by the condemnation of the Earl of Arundel. Richard himself assumed the title of Prince of Chester; and it was ordained that no grant should hereafter be made of the new Principality to any person except the eldest son of the king, if it should so please the king to advance him.   21 Richard II. cap. xix.

[8] This parliament was held at Shrewsbury on the Monday after hilary 1397, in pursuance of an adjournment from Westminster, which as the king expressly said, was made "on account of the great love he bore the inhabitants of these parts."   Here the unfortunate Richard obtained from his obsequious senate a stretch of authority unknown before; and by a strange concession they enacted that the whole power of the nation should devolve on the king, twelve peers, and six commoners.   But luckily for the kingdom the Pope's bull was required to confirm so irregular a proceeding.

Cheshire men; over whom, however, he had so little control, that they conducted themselves in a most disorderly manner, and actually plundered the burgesses of all their armour to a great amount.

The first transaction of the parliament was the case of Sir John de Cobham: he had been engaged with the Earl of Arundel, in opposition to the King; as was alleged, in treason against him. Having been, on these grounds, impeached by the commons, he was now tried, and found guilty of high treason. But the King changed his sentence into imprisonment for life in the island of Jersey.

They next entered into the consideration of those opinions which Tresillian and his brethren had originally given in this town eleven years before: and for the illegality of which they had suffered such condign punishment. The present assembly being completely under the King's control, now found those opinions to be perfectly constitutional, and all the proceedings of the parliament which had condemned them, were declared to be null and void: nay, as if to degrade any assembly which had ever exerted itself in opposition to the crown, and vindicate the honour of his great-grandfather Edward II., whom in many respects he so nearly resembled, this opportunity was also taken for reversing the attainder of the Despensers, after the lapse of nearly a century. This obsequious parliament further continued the subsidies on wool and leather for the King's life, and granted a fifteenth and a half, for the purpose of making some compensation to those persons who had suffered for their attachment to the royal cause.

To fix all this, as no doubt he thought, upon the firmest basis, the King caused the lords spiritual and temporal to be sworn in parliament on the cross of Canterbury (which was brought to Shrewsbury for that purpose), that they would keep for ever the statutes and ordinances now made: " And also a great part of the commons and others," says the roll, " stretched out their right hands in affirmance of their oaths: and so did all the proxies of the clergy, and so did the knights (of shires) standing round the King: and then, after proclamation made in the hearing of all the people, to know if they would consent hereunto, (so little did this infatuated prince regard the dangers he might entail on the constitution, if he could secure for a moment the shouts of a mob,) they also answered, lifting up their hands on high,[*] and crying with loud voices, that it pleased them well, and they are said to have hereto fully assented."

The Duke of Hereford (afterwards King Henry the Fourth,[1]) finding the popular stream set so strongly in favour of the crown, with a view, as it should seem, of providing for his own security, took, what would now be deemed, a very extraordinary step. On the last day of the session, leaving his place, he advanced into the middle of the house; and there, falling on his knees before the King, acknowledged his having engaged in several of the tumultuous meetings, which had arisen since the commencement of the present reign: for all of which he craved mercy and pardon, though he had actually received one under the great seal only two days before.[2] The King accepted his excuses, promised to be good lord to him, and declared to all the estates there present, that he granted the Duke full pardon for all his past offences. This singular scene was intended by the crafty Henry to be the prelude to a measure still more unprecedented, and which drew after it consequences the most important and fatal to the crown and life of Richard.

There is perhaps no reign in our annals, say the learned authors of the History of Salop, concerning which a greater diversity of opinion prevails among historians, than this on which we are now engaged. Mr. Carte has undertaken to rescue the character of Richard from the obloquy with which succeeding generations have loaded it. According to him, the misfortunes for which it is notorious, and its melancholy termination, are solely to be attributed to the ambitious designs of his uncles; who, with a view of making

---

[*] Rot. Parl. iii. 360. This was a mode of swearing usual in that age. In 1451, when the Bordelois swore allegiance to Charles VII., on their surrender, the commonalty joined by " extending their hands towards Heaven, as is usual in such cases." Monstrelet, v. ix. ch. 26.

[1] Dugdale says, the Earl of Derby was created Duke of Hereford in the parliament of Shrewsbury upon Michaelmas-day (the king sitting crowned) by girding him with a sword, and putting a cap of honour on his head. Baronage iii. 120, from the Parl. Rolls : but

this is a mistake occasioned by a hasty view of them. The creation took place in London on Saturday the 29th of Sept., 1397, before the adjournment to Shrewsbury. See the printed Rolls, iii. 355.

[2] Rymer's Fœdera, viii. 32. One of the articles of accusation on which this king was deposed a year or two after, charged him with procuring many oppressive acts to be passed this time at Shrewsbury. Besides making himself Prince of Chester, he had lately created five dukes, one marquis, and four earls, who first took their seat at this adjournment at Shrewsbury.

B B

themselves masters of the crown, most culpably neglected his education, and adopted every factious means to embarrass his government. Much of all this is undoubtedly true: both parties were highly culpable, and it is not easy to say which was most so. Gloucester, Arundel, and their allies, exercised their power, when they had it, with intolerable insolence and cruelty; but an impartial peruser of our history must allow, that Richard was by no means of a character fitted to inspire respect, especially in a race of hardy and martial peers, who had witnessed the glorious exploits of his ancestors. Elegant and accomplished manners were in their eyes a poor substitute for courage in the field, and wisdom in the cabinet; and when he resolved to annul the enactments of a lawful, however violent, parliament, by his own single authority out of parliament, it was surely their duty to bring him back within his constitutional limits. From all these causes his history presents a succession of remonstrances and impeachments, of plots and executions, of accusations, defiances, and challenges. The last scene of this kind which took place during his reign occurred in the Parliament of Shrewsbury.

The Dukes of Hereford and Norfolk had been jointly concerned in the impeachment of Arundel and his fellow-sufferers, in the parliament at Westminster. But a quarrel[2] soon broke out between these two noblemen. Norfolk, either touched by remorse for his share in the ruin of a patriotic peer, or, as seems more probable from his character, with a view of ensnaring his late confederate, in a conversation which he held with Hereford after the adjournment of parliament, expressed himself in very disrespectful terms of the King. This conversation the Duke of Hereford immediately divulged to his sovereign, and in the parliament of Shrewsbury made it the subject of a public accusation against the Duke of Norfolk. The King was extremely unwilling that any discourse about himself should be made the subject of open discussion; and accordingly this unexpected transaction hastened the conclusion of the parliament, which sate but four days, and then broke up, after delegating its authority to a committee of twelve lords and six commoners, who were to dispatch all its business which could not be concluded in that short session.

The King, however, continued in these parts. He was resident in Shrewsbury on the 5th and 6th of February: on the last of which days he revoked the pardon of the Earl of Arundel: and we find him attended by the extraordinary committee of parliament on the 23d of February at the town of Oswestry, which he had just acquired by the attainder of that Earl. It was there that Henry de Lancaster and Thomas Mowbray (so the contending Dukes are styled on the rolls of parliament) appeared, preparatory to their intended duel at Coventry.

After the dissolution of the Parliament of Shrewsbury,[4] Richard held the committee of parliament at Oswestry, where the Dukes of Hereford and Norfolk appeared before him, in order to have their quarrel adjusted. It appears that the Duke of Hereford[5] had basely betrayed a private conversation, in which he said that Mowbray had dropped several expressions of a treasonable nature. The accusation was denied, and, according to the barbarous usage of the times, Mowbray demanded the privilege of acquitting himself by single combat. Each of the dukes, agreeably to the laws of chivalry, flung down his glove, which was taken up before the King and sealed. The King appointed Coventry for the place of combat,[6] and caused,

---

for that purpose, a vast and magnificent theatre to be erected on Gossford Green. The rival dukes made some requisite preparations, particularly with reference to the essential article of armour.

Froissart relates what steps they took in order to secure the most effective armour; and the preference given to foreign armourers in those days, may be seen from the fact that the Earl of Derby[7] sent messengers to Lombardy; and that the Earl Marshall, on his part, sent to Almayn, to procure the armour required for the combat. "The charges of these two lordes," says Froissart, "was greate, but the Earle of Derby was the mooste charge."

The armour of these great men was unusually splendid and expensive. It was inlaid with gold and silver, of elegant devices and patterns. Besides beauty, the utmost regard was paid to the essential requisite of its being proof. This was to be the result of the skill of the armourer, not of art-magic; for the combatants were to clear themselves by oath from having recourse to any incantations, or rendering their armour or bodies invulnerable by any charm. Let their cause be ever so bad, they determined to die like good Christians, disavowed all dependence on the power of Satan, and supplicated the prayers of the pious spectators :—

> " Add proof unto my armour with thy prayers,
> And with thy blessing steel my lance's point." [8]

Holinshed minutely describes this important affair, as well as the ceremony preceding the resolution taken by the unfortunate monarch, which, in the end, cost him his crown and life. We shall insert the account in the very graphic words of honest Holinshed himself.

" At the time appointed the King came to Coventrie, where the two dukes were readie, according to the order prescribed therein; coming thither in great arraie, accompanied with the lords and gentlemen of their linages. The King caused a sumptuous skeffeld, or theatre, and roial listes, there to be errected and prepaired. The Sundaie before they should fight, after dinner, the Duke of Hereford came to the King (being lodged about a quarter a mile out of the town, in a tower that belonged to Sir William Bagot), to take his leave of him. The morrow after, being the daie appointed for the combat, about the spring of the day, came the Duke of Norfolke to the Courte to take leave likewise of the King. The Duke of Hereford armed him in his tent, that was set up neere to the lists; and the Duke of Norfolke put on his armour betwixt the gate and the barrier of the town, in a beautefal house, having a fair perclois of wood towards the gate, that none might see what was done within the house.

" The Duke Aumarle that daie being High Constable of England, and the Duke of Surrie, Marshall, placed themselves betwixt them, well armed and appointed; and when they saw their time, they first entered into the lists with a great company of men, apparelled in silke sandal, imbrodered with silver both richlie and curiouslie; everie man having a tipped staff, to keep the field in order. About the houre of prime came to the barriers of the lists, the Duke of Hereford, mounted on a white courser, barded with green and blew velvet, imbroidered sumptuously with swans and antelopes of goldsmith's worke, armed at all points. The constable and marshall came to the barriers, demanding of him what he was; he answered, 'I am Henrie of Lancaster, Duke of Hereford, which am come hither to do mine indevor against Thomas Mowbraie, Duke of Norfolke, as a traitor untrue to God, the King, his realme, and me.' Then incontinentlie he sware upon the holie Evangelists, that his quarrel was true and just; and upon that point he required to enter the lists. Then he puts up his sword, which before he held up naked in his hand, and putting down his visor, made a cross on his horsse, and with speare in hand entered into the lists, and descended from his horsse, and set him down in a chaire of green velvet, at the one end of the lists, and there reposed himself, abiding the comming of his adversarie.

" Soone after him, entered into the field, with great triumph, King Richard, accompanied with all the peeres of the realme; and in his companie, was the Earle of Saint Paule, which was come out of France, in post, to see this challenge performed. The King had there above ten thousand men in armour, least

---

[7] Duke of Hereford.   [8] Shakspeare. Richard II., in the speech of Hereford on this occasion.

some fraie or tumult might rise amongst his nobles, by quarrelling or partaking.   When King Richard was set in his seat, which was richly hanged and adorned, a King at Arms made open proclamation, prohibiting all men, in the name of the King, and of the High Constable and Marshall, to enterprise or attempt to approach, or touch any part of the lists, upon pain of death, except such as were appointed to order or marshall the field.   The proclamation ended, another herald cried, ‘ Behold here Henrie of Lancaster, Duke of Hereford, appelant, which is entered into the lists roiall, to do his devoir against Thomas Mowbraie, Duke of Norfolke, defendant, upon paine to be found false and recreant.’

“The Duke of Norfolke hovered on horsseback at the entrie of the lists, his horse being barded with crimson velvet, imbroidered richlie with lions of silver and mulberie trees; and when he had made his oth before the constable and marshal, that his quarrel was just and true, he entered the field manfullie, saieing aloud, ‘ God and him that hath the right;’ and then he departed from his horsse, and sate him downe in his chaire, which was of crimson velvet, continued about with red and white damaske.   The lord marshal viewed their spears, to see that they were of equal length, and delivered the one speare himself to the Duke of Hereford, and sent the other to the Duke of Norfolke by a knight; then the herald proclamed, that the traverses and chaires of the champions should be removed, commanding them, on the King’s behalf, to mount on horssebacke, and address themselves to the battel and combat.

“The Duke of Hereford was quicklie horssed, and closed his barrier, and cast his speare into the rest; and when the trumpet sounded, set forward couragiouslie towards his enemie six or seven passes.   The Duke of Norfolke was not fullie set forward, when the King cast downe his warder, and the heralds cried, ‘ Ho! ho!’   Then the King caused their speares to be taken from them, and commanded them to repaire againe to their chaires; where they remained two long houres, while the King and his councell deliberatlie consulted what order was best to be had in so weightie a cause.   Finallie, after they had devised, and fullie determined what should be done therein, the heralds cried, ‘ Silence;’ and Sir John Bushie, the King’s secretarie, read the sentence and determination of the King and his councell, in a long roll; the effect whereof was, that Henrie, Duke of Hereford, should, within fifteene daies, depart out of the realme, and not to returne before the term of ten yeares were expired, except by the King he should be repealed againe; and this upon paine of death : and that Thomas Mowbraie, Duke of Norfolke, because he hath sowen sedition in the relme by his words, should likewise avoid the realme, and never returne againe into England, nor approch the borders or confines thereof upon pain of death; and that the King would staie the profits of his lands, till he had levied thereof such summes of monie as the duke had taken up of the King’s treasuror, for the wages of the garrison of Calis, which were still unpaid.

“When these judgments were once read, the King called before him both parties, and made them to sweare that the one should never come in the place where the other was, willinglie, nor keepe any companie togither in any forren region; which oth they both received humblie, and so went their waies. The Duke of Norfolke departed sorrowfullie out of the realme into Almanie, and at last came to Venice, where he for thought and melancholie, deceassed; for he was in hope (as writers record) that he should have beene borne out in the matter by the King; which, when it fell out otherwise, it greeved him not a little.   The Duke of Hereford took leave of the King at Eltham, who there released foure yeares of his banishment; so he took his journie over into Calis, and from thence he went into France, where he remained.

“ A woonder it was to see what a number of people ran after him, in everie towne and street where he came, before he tooke the sea, lamenting and bewailing his departure, as who should saie, that when he departed, the onlie sheild, defense and comfort of the commonwealth was vaded and gone.” [*]

Norfolk was exiled during life, and his lands were confiscated; but he did not long survive his disgrace.   He went first into Germany, and then to Venice, where, in a short time, he died broken-hearted.

[*] Holinshed’s Chron., p. 494.

Hereford went over to France, and was honourably received by the French king. But he had not been absent many months before his father, the Duke of Lancaster, died. On his demise the crown claimed his estate, which the court lawyers declared to be forfeited.

From Oswestry, Richard, accompanied by many of his principal nobility, proceeded to Chester, where he was present at the installation of his chaplain, John Burghill, Bishop of Lichfield and Coventry, in the Church of Saint John, then a cathedral of that diocese.

A.D. 1399.—At this period Richard undertook an expedition against Ireland to avenge the death of Roger Mortimer, Earl of March, lord lieutenant of that island, who had been slain there by the rebels. Hereford, now Duke of Lancaster, took advantage of Richard's absence. By the concurrence of fortunate circumstances, he was enabled to land at Ravenspur, in Yorkshire, in the month of July, 1399, and in September following, he succeeded in deposing Richard. He was accordingly proclaimed King, by the title of Henry the Fourth.

The following exceedingly curious and interesting account of Richard's troubles in Wales, and his downfal afterwards, are taken from an illuminated French MS. in the British Museum. It was written by a French nobleman, who accompanied Richard, and was an eye-witness to the sudden and tragical fate of this monarch. It appears that he, like many others of his countrymen, was attracted to England by Richard's marriage with a princess of France.

He came over to London in the spring of the year 1399, and remained in close attendance on King Richard for about seven months; and until that unhappy monarch was brought to London as a prisoner by Henry Bolingbroke, Duke of Lancaster. His manuscript, which formerly belonged to Charles of Anjou, Earl of Main and Mortmain, is now among the treasures preserved in the British Museum. It is written in French rhyme or verse, which was common at that time. As a poem its merits are considered slender, but as a narrative of facts it is *exceedingly valuable*, and the facts themselves are of the most moving and interesting nature. It supplies an original and circumstantial account of the misfortunes of Richard the Second in Wales and on the Borders; it bears sufficient internal evidence of its authenticity. Its value has been well appreciated by many English writers. Among our old annalists both Holinshed and Stow have quoted it, and from Holinshed Shakespeare drew many of the materials which he wove into his grand and pathetic historical play. In modern times, Tyrrell, Rapin, Turner, Lingard, and other historians have made great use of this French history, quoting it as an authoritative document of an otherwise very obscure part of English history. But the manuscript itself was never published in a perfect form, until of late years, when the Rev. Mr. Webb published an admirable English translation of it, with numerous explanatory notes, and we are indebted to that gentleman's labours for the following :—

" Richard's expedition to Ireland, in the summer of 1399, opened the way into England to the exiled Henry Bolingbroke. Our French knight attended Richard to Milford Haven, and from thence he was requested to accompany the King to Ireland, and wrote an account of the short but difficult campaign in that country. He was with Richard at Dublin, when the fatal news was brought to him that Bolingbroke had landed on the English coast, that the Archbishop of Canterbury had publicly preached a sermon in his favour, and that the great body of the nobility, as well ecclesiastic as lay, had joined him. He describes how the King's face turned pale thereat, and how many of the nobles who were with him had treacherously detained him in Ireland for many weeks, with the view of facilitating the progress of Bolingbroke. He heartily sympathises with Richard, and still more heartily curses his rivals and the nobility and people of England, like one that has forgotten, or that has never known, the enormous faults and errors of the sovereign. Yet he honestly confesses, that his partiality is owing, in good part, to Richard's fondness for Frenchmen."

After detailing minutely the account of the wars in Ireland, the writer goes on to state :—

" Thus were we in joy and delight in Dublin, where full six weeks very pleasantly passed away without having any certain tidings from England, for no peril or pain that could be undergone, could bring vessels of any size over in safety, so contrary were the winds, and so outrageous the tempest at sea, that to my thinking our Lord was wrath with the King, for in the meantime the Duke of Lancaster seized the greater part of England by the strangest and foulest treachery I ever knew, as you shall hear. However, to proceed; the sea soon after became calm, when it pleased the Sovereign Ruler of all below, a barge arrived which was the occasion of much sorrow.[1] Those who were in her related to the King how the Duke had caused his treasurer to be beheaded,[2] and how when he first arrived in this country he made the proud Archbishop of Canterbury preach to the people to this effect:—'My good people, hearken all of you here: you well know how the King most wrongfully, and without reason, banished your Lord Henry; I have, therefore, obtained of the holy father, who is our patron, that those who shall forthwith bring aid this day, shall every one of them have remission of their sins, whereby from the hour of their baptism they have been defiled. Behold the sealed bull that the Pope of renowned Rome hath sent me, my good friends, in behalf of you all. Agree then to help him to subdue his enemies, and you shall for this be placed, after death, with those who are in Paradise.'[3] Then might you have beheld young and old, the feeble and the strong, make a clamour, and, regarding neither right nor wrong, stir themselves up with one accord, thinking that what was told them was true. They all indeed believed it, for such as they have little sense or knowledge.

"The archbishop invented this devise because no one dared to stir through dread, dear sire, of your wrath. This sermon ended, they began to flee towards the Duke that they might confound and injure you, and waste your country by conquest. Taking towns and castles for his own, he brings young and old under subjection; they leave nothing for the poor people that can be carried away. 'Resolve, sire, to make haste that you may quickly set aside his enterprise, who doeth much to blame.' It seemed to me that the King's face at this turned pale with anger, while he said: 'Come hither, friends; good Lord, this man designs to deprive me of my country.' He caused the young and old of his council to assemble, that they might consider what was best to be done in this affair. Now they agreed, on a Saturday, to put to sea on next morning, without waiting longer than a day and a half; and when the Duke of Aumarle heard of the departure, he slily resolved upon a trick, thinking that if he could, he would make it otherwise. He went with great secresy to the King that he might defeat every thing that all of them could do, saying, 'Sire, do not vex yourself, for never did I hear a matter so much belied; be not in such haste now to set out; it were much better to take good time, and send first for the whole of the navy; for we have not a hundred barges; how shall we go, seeing that in this place there are many huge rooks in the sea, and the bottom is dangerous. But look here, it were better to send over the Earl of Salisbury,[4] who shall hold the field against the Duke, and sufficiently make war upon him; he will have all the Welsh to conquer him. And, in the meantime, we will go by land to Waterford, where you shall send to every port for your navy, so that weak and strong, and all your host, may then pass over. You shall soon see your enemies captive, dead, or discomfitted, of the whole of this be well assured.' The King put more trust in him than all his friends;[5] by this counsel was the whole of the other set aside. A certain aged person, who truly loved

---

[1] This might be the vessel in which Sir William Bagot passed over, for while the duke was wreaking his vengeance upon the other lieutenants of the king, Bagot made his escape to Chester, and thence to Ireland. Walsingham, p. 358.

[2] William Scroope, second son of Henry Lord Scroope of Masham. Among his other titles, he was at that time Chamberlain of Ireland, Justice of Chester, North Wales, and Flint. Henry took him at Bristol, with Sir John Bussy and Sir Henry Green, and beheaded him in compliance, as he professed, with the wishes of the people. This very act was treason by the statute 25 Edward III. 5, c. 12, "If a man slay the treasurer of the king, it ought to be judged treason."

[3] The archbishop who read this pretended Bull was Thomas Fitz Alan, third son of Richard Earl of Arundel and Warren, by Eleanor, his second wife, daughter of Henry Earl of Lancaster.

He appears to have been elevated step by step to his high position with unprecedented haste by Richard himself, and by way of gratitude acted as the principal leader in the deposition of his royal master in favour of his relation the Duke of Lancaster.

[4] This Earl of Salisbury was John de Montacute, who had borne arms in France with distinguished bravery under the Black Prince. He was a nobleman of high character and great accomplishments. His eldest son, Thomas, was that renowned Earl of Salisbury, who was slain in the wars of France at the siege of Orleans. Dugdale.

[5] His overweening confidence in the duke completely blinded him. Froissart says, that if he had stated "black was white, the king would not have said to the contrary." Hastiness, irresolution, and procrastination were his bane, and this brought him into contempt with his people.

the King, was displeased at it, telling him, 'Dear sire, surely in such a case it is useless to delay.' Nothing that could be said to him was of any avail. His good friends thereat checked their smiles, and were greatly grieved and wrath at heart. Without further discourse, he sent for the Earl of Salisbury, saying, 'Cousin, you must go to England, and resist this mad enterprise of the Duke, and let his people be put to death, or taken; and learn too, how, and by what means, he hath thus troubled my land, and set it against me.' The Earl said, 'Sire, upon mine honour, I will perform it in such manner, that in a short time you shall hear of this disturbance, or I will suffer the penalty of death.' 'Fair cousin, I know it well,' said the King; 'and will myself pass over as speedily as I may, for never shall I have comfort or repose so long as the false traitor, who now hath played me such a trick, shall be alive. If I can but get him into my power, I will cause him to be put to death in such a manner, that it shall be spoken of long enough, even in Turkey.' The Earl caused his people and vessels to be made ready for immediate departure, gravely took leave of the King, and entreated him to proceed with all possible haste. The King acting upon his advice, said, 'That whatsoever might happen he would put to sea within six days.'[6] At that time the Earl, who had great desire to set out in defence of King Richard, had earnestly prayed me to go over with him, for the sake of merriment and song,'[7] and thereto I heartily agreed; my companion and myself went over the sea with him. Now it came to pass, that the Earl landed at Conway. I assure you it was the strongest and fairest town in Wales.

"There we were told of the enterprise of the Duke's; a more cruel one, shall, I think, never be spoken of in any land; for they told us that he had already conquered the greater part of England, and taken a great many towns and castles;[8] that he had displaced officers, and everywhere set up a different establishment in his own name; that he had put to death, without mercy, as a sovereign lord, all those whom he held in displeasure. When the Earl heard those doleful tidings it was no wonder that he was alarmed, for the Duke had gained over the greater part of the nobles of England, and we were assured there were full sixty thousand men ready for war. The Earl then quickly sent his summons throughout Wales and Chester, that all gentlemen archers and other persons, should come to him, without delay, upon pain of death, to take part with King Richard, who loved them.

"This they were desirous to do, thinking of a truth that the King had arrived at Conway; I am certain that forty thousand were trained and mustered in the field within four days, every one eager to fight with all who wished ill to the ever preux and valiant King Richard.'[9]

"Then the Earl, who endured great pain and trouble, went to them all, and declared to them, with a solemn oath, that before three days were ended he would straiten the Duke and his people, that for this time they should advance no further to waste the land. Soon after he found his friends assembled together

---

[6] The king stopped eighteen days after the departure of the Earl of Salisbury, and thus threw all his affairs into disorder. Respecting this fatal delay in Ireland, Otterbourne states that all things were made ready, and even the horses were put on board. These were ordered to be disembarked and taken to another port, which caused great delay.

[7] Singing and dancing in those days were considered great accomplishments, and in all probability our author was a good performer in both.

[8] The seizure of castles was a great object with the Duke of Lancaster, and the number that descended to himself by inheritance might excite surprise. Besides the castellated mansions of various sizes, with which doubtless many of his manors and towns were furnished, there are eighteen strong castles distinctly specified as appertaining to the family at that time, among which there were several in South Wales and the Marches. See Dugdale's Baronage.

[9] From the predatory dispositions and habits of the people of North Wales and Cheshire, they were ever ready to arm; and in 1387, they had furnished the king with troops in his contest with his nobles. No part of the island was so well affected towards him, or continued more unshaken in its fidelity after his misfortune. On Cheshire, as we have shown, he had conferred marks of special favour. In the summer of the above-mentioned year, he had visited it, and ingratiated himself with persons of all ranks in the county: they adopted his livery, and bound themselves by oath, to stand in his defence against all manner of men. In the parliament held in 1398 at Shrewsbury, Richard ordained that from thenceforth, in consequence of the love he bore to the gentlemen of Cheshire, it should be called and known by the name of the *Principality of Cheshire*, from the time he took the title of "Prince of Chester." This act was revoked in the next reign.

Henry diligently watched the Cheshire men, and one of the statutes of his first parliament was enacted against them. He had sufficient reason to be suspicious of them. Chester, Flint, and Denbigh were afterwards conspicuous in the insurrection of the Percies in 1403. The goods, lands, and chattels of thirty-four Cheshire gentlemen were forfeited to the king, and two hundred knights and squires of that county lay dead upon the field of battle at Shrewsbury.

in the field, he spoke to them well-advisedly. 'My good gentlemen, let us all make haste to avenge King Richard in his absence, that he may be satisfied with us in the time to come; for mine own part, I purpose neither to stop nor to take rest, till such time as I shall have made my attempt upon those who are so traitorous and cruel towards him. Let us go hence, and march directly towards them. God will help us if we are diligent in assaulting them; for according to our law, it is the duty of every one, in many cases, to support the right until death.'

"When the Welshmen understood that the King was not there, they were all sorrowful, murmuring to one another in great companies full of alarm, thinking that the King was dead of grief, and dreading the horrible and great severity of the Duke of Lancaster and his people. They were not well satisfied with the Earl, saying, 'Sir, be assured that for the present we will advance no further, since the King is not here; and do you know wherefore? Behold the duke is subduing everything to himself, which is a great trouble and terror to us; for indeed, we think that the King is dead since he has not arrived with you at the port: were he here, right or wrong, each of us would be eager to assail his enemies; but now we will not go with you.' The Earl at this was so wroth at heart, that he had almost gone out of his senses with vexation; he shed tears. It was a pity to see how he was treated. 'Alas,' said he, 'what shame befalleth me this day. Oh death! come unto me without delay; put an end to me, I loath my destiny. Alas! now will the King suppose that I have devised treason.'

"While thus he mourned, he said, 'My comrades, as you hope for mercy, come with me, I beseech you; so shall we be champion for King Richard, who within four days and a half will be here, for he told me when I quitted Ireland, that he would upon his life embark before the week was ended: Sirs, I pray you, let us hasten to depart.' It availed nothing, they stood all mournful, like men afraid; a great part of them were disposed to betake themselves to the Duke for fear of death. But the Earl kept them in the field fourteen days expecting the coming of King Richard. Many a time, said the good Earl apart, 'Small portion will you have of England, in my opinion, my rightful lord, since you delay so long. What can this mean? certes (*certainly*) I believe you are betrayed, since I hear no true tidings of you by word or deed. Alas! I see these people are troubled with fear, lest the Duke should hem them in (*or hate them*). They are but common[1] ignorant people, they will desert me.' So said the good Earl to himself in the field, while he was serving with those who in a little time all abandoned him; some went their way straight to the Duke, and the rest returned to their homes; so they left the Earl encamped, with none but his own men, who did, I think, not amount to one hundred. He lamented it greatly, saying, in a sorrowful manner, 'Let us make our retreat, for our enterprize goeth on very badly.'

"Thus does the Earl make little account of his life, for he saith well, that he hath neither death nor good report; the people of the Duke stir up so much vexation in his heart. The enemy advanced without farther delay, for they had been told that the Earl had gathered his troops, to come to the point against them. The Duke was glad of it, he desired nothing so much as to combat all those would defend or wait for King Richard. He made his way as straight as he could, towards the Earl, who withdrew himself to Conway, full of grief, sadness, and dismay.[2] Great hurt it did me, for I sincerely loved him, because he heartily loved the French: and, besides, he was humble, gentle, and courteous in all his doings, and he had every one's word for being loyal and prudent in all places. He gave most largely, and his gifts were profitable. Bold he was and courageous as a lion. Right well and beautiful did he also make ballads, songs, roundels, and lays.[3] Though he was but a layman, so gracious were all his deeds, that never,

---

[1] The earl did not know the Welsh people so well as the writer, otherwise he would not have said so. The Welsh were always considered a brave, courageous people. They might be ignorant; but were not the generality of the English, and indeed almost every other nation, equally so! There were no very learned men in those days. They were "like angels' visits—few and far between."

[2] This intimates that the Earl of Salisbury had first advanced beyond Conway, and that the duke made some demonstrations against

him in that direction. It is probable that the latter was now at Chester; but how far Salisbury had pushed towards him, or whether the other had actually passed the Dee, does not appear, no further notice being taken of this operation. Flint and Rhuddlan were still in Richard's possession till Northumberland brought up his detachment towards Conway, treacherously to deceive and to seize the king's person.

[3] Ballad-making was much in fashion in those days, and the

I think, shall that man issue from his country, in whom God hath implanted so much worth as in him. May his soul be placed in paradise with the saints for ever, for they have sinned foully, put him to a painful death, like a martyr, loyally maintaining reason and the rightful cause.' How this happened, if God preserve, you shall hear; but first I must tell you of the arrival of King Richard; too late for him, for he tarried eighteen days after our departure from Ireland. It was very great folly. Accursed be the man by whom this happened; well did he prove the love that he had for the King, who so loved him. Throughout his host he gave order for lading barges and ships, and for those who could bear arms to embark.

"Thus King Richard passed the sea in a little time, for the weather was fair and bright, and the wind good, which brought him within two days to Milford. He did not stop there, considering the distress, complaints, and lamentations of the poor people, and the mortal alarm of all.

"Then the King resolved⁵ that, without saying a word, he would set out at midnight from his post, attended by five⁶ persons, for he would on no account be discovered. In that place he clad himself in another garb,⁷ like a poor priest of the Minors, and disguised his features by colouring his face, for the fear that he had of being known of his foes. Alas! he thought that the Earl was still keeping the field with his warriors, wherefore he rode hard towards him in sad and pensive mood.

"It is now right that you should know what friends he took with him into the country. I saw and

French took the lead in composition of this kind. According to Warton a new species of poetry was introduced to this country in 1380, from France.

⁴ He was an eminent patron of the disciples of Wycliff; their doctrines had spread so rapidly, that they made their way into the court, the church, and the universities. The great towns of London, Leicester, and Bristol, in particular, cherished them with avidity; and, according to Knighton, a man could scarcely meet two persons on the road without one of them being a Wycliffite.* As their religious assemblies were subject to interruption, Sir John Montacute and others, about 1387, used to attend them in armour.†

⁵ It would appear that the panic and disorganisation that prevailed among the troops, caused Richard's resolution of quitting his army. The author assigns no reason, but we learn from other sources that desertion had taken place to a serious extent before he withdrew. Some days after his arrival in Wales, when the king arose in the morning, and was about to say his orisons, he leaned on a window that looked to the field where his army was encamped, and when he saw the smallness of the number he was quite dismayed. His army of thirty-two thousand was reduced to six thousand, the rest having during the night joined the Duke of Lancaster.‡

The account of the discussion that took place in the council at Milford is supplied by the MS. Ambassades, and is curious, inasmuch as it is characterised by the speakers, and shows the reasons for which the king was determined to retire to Conway. He consulted with his friends what course he had best pursue. Then said the Earl of Salisbury, "Sir, this man, truly, as I have heard, hath already stirred up many people against you by false reports and artful words (paroles entrouvées); you now see and may perceive that four parts of your men, and all those of high rank, have left you in a single night. So it seemeth to me that it were well, saving the correction of your good opinion, since we are few in number (and, moreover, we know not whether those who are with us will remain), that on the approach of night we should take four or five hundred of the best and most faithful of those that are left: put to sea, for our navy is ready to go wherever you please, and make straight for

Bordeaux: there we shall be well received, and you will also have aid, if it be needful, from France, from Brittany, or from Gascony; for it is better to withdraw a little from an enemy than to throw oneself on his protection." The Earl of Huntington replied: "By Saint George, if my lord trusts to me he will go this very night to Ballicaldit* or Ballicaldric, and thence to the strong castle of Conway; there he will be in a state of security in his kingdom, and in his rightful inheritance." And the king made answer, "So we should at Bordeaux." "That is true," said the earl; "but if you go to Bordeaux, every one will say you have fled without being pursued, and that if you had not felt yourself guilty in some respects, you would not have gone away; and if you are in the castle of Conway you will be secure from any one; for, in spite of Henry of Lancaster, and all his friends, at all times, and at any time you please, you may embark and go where you choose, and, peradventure, while you are in the castle, some good agreement may be made." Then said the king, "You speak well: we will do so; and tomorrow yourself shall go to Henry of Lancaster to know what he would have." The Bishop of Carlisle, the Earl of Salisbury, Sir Stephen Scroope, Ferriby, Janico, and Maudelaine would have preferred going to Bordeaux; but it pleased the king to listen to his brother.†

⁶ According to other MSS. about one hundred horse accompanied the king in his flight. If it were so, many of these might have fallen away from him by the road. That he went off secretly, and abandoned the remains of his army, all the MSS. agree.

⁷ The habit of the Franciscan, or Minor Friar, was a loose garment, of a grey colour, reaching down to the ancles, with a cowl of the same, and a cloak over it, when he went abroad. They used to gird themselves with cords and to go barefoot. Tanner, Notit. Monast. preface, p. 18. The dresses of the clergy about this time was the subject of much episcopal animadversion. "Any clerk wearing buttons in public was subject to a fine." The seventy-fourth canon of the Church of England, as it now stands, is in part but a more modern edition of the above regulations adapted to the Reformation.

---

* Fox, i. p. 576; Wilkin's Concilia, iii. p. 265; Knighton Col. 2661.

† Yfrod Nuestr, p. 540.

‡ Accounts and Extracts, ii. p. 216.

---

* A strong castle thirty miles from Milford, and it is said he reached there the first night; from thence he made straight to Conway, on the road to which he went off secretly and abandoned his army.

† Bibl. du Roy. MS. Ambassades, pp. 131, 132.

observed the Duke of Exeter,[8] and with him the good Duke of Surrey,[9] who was loyal and true to his death; together with the brave Earl of Gloucester. Three bishops were also with them, two of whom, as you shall hear, were not (did not behave) like men of worth. But I will first tell you their names : one was the Bishop of St. David's ;[1] the other was my lord of Carlyle; he was the best of them, for he never would desert the good King, nor did he ever change his mind about it for anything that was said to him. The third was the Bishop of Lincoln, who cared nothing (not a rotten pear) for all their doings, for he was the Duke's own brother, and thought he could easily make his peace with him at any time. Of laymen, there were two knights, right worthy in arms, valiant and bold.

"The first was named Stephen Scroope ;[2] the other Ferriby,[3] who was well made and active; they had also Jenico,[4] who bore the character of a good soldier, for, according to common reports, he undertook very great feats.

" Thus the King set out that very night with only thirteen others ; he travelled hard, desiring quickly to find the Earl of Salisbury, who took no account of his life, for the evil treatment and shame that he had of the Duke, who thus, go where he will, surmounteth everything.

" The King rode on without any disturbance, so that he arrived at Conway, where the houses are covered with tiles,[5] by break of day.[6]

" At the meeting of the King and the Earl, instead of joy there was great sorrow. Tears, lamentations, sighs, groans and mourning, quickly brought forth. Truly it was a piteous sight to behold their looks and countenances, and woful meeting. The Earl's face was pale with watching ; he related to the King his hard fate, and how he had made his muster when he landed in England, and that he had straightway sent through the country for the Cheshire men and the Welsh, who were heartily willing to conquer their enemies.

" ' Forty thousand of them were brought together. Then said I to them often: My good friends, let us go forward; the King hath sent me over hither to lead you on. Be sure that I will not desert you till I die. But I could not dissuade them from going, each of them when he saw his danger (his tail on fire), some to the Duke, others elsewhere ; thinking because they saw you not directly there, that you were of a truth dead beyond the sea. So after I had kept them for nearly a fortnight in the field, they left me all alone in the plain. Alas ! very little doth he love you who hath so long detained you in Ireland. All is lost; without the help of our Lord, I surely think that we are delivered over to our latter end.' No one would believe how much the King grieved at it. His mortal misfortune was not light, neither (was) his wrath, while he often said :—' Glorious and merciful God, who didst endure to be crucified for us, if by sin I have greatly trespassed against thee, with folded hands I cry thee mercy. Suffer me not to lose my

---

[8] John de Holland, third son of the Earl of Kent, by Joan, daughter of Edmund of Woodstock. His mother, one of the most beautiful women of the age, was afterwards the wife of the Black Prince ; and hence John de Holland was uterine brother to Richard II. He was also brother-in-law to Henry Duke of Lancaster, having married his sister Elizabeth. His advancement to the title of the Earl of Huntington bears date, 2nd June, 2 Rich. II., and to that of Duke of Exeter, 29th Sept., 21 Rich. II. He was celebrated for his valour and enterprise, and he himself confessed to the Duke of Lancaster, " I love nothing better than fighting."

[9] This young nobleman was nephew of John de Holland, son of Thomas Holland, Earl of Kent, by Alice, daughter of Richard Earl of Arundel.

[1] Guido de Mona or Mohun. He was treasurer of England, 21 Rich. II., and was one of the witnesses to the will of the king. Walsingham, in recording his decease, briefly observes, that " in his life he was the cause of much mischief."

[2] Sir Stephen Scroope, eldest son of Henry Lord Scroope of Masham, in the county of York : he had served in France and Flanders during the last and present reign.

[3] In the Lambeth MS. (margin) he is called William Fireby. Some say he was a knight : some, that he was chaplain to the king. He was beheaded for his fidelity to Richard.

[4] Jenico de Artois was a captain of great renown. He was a German or Gascon ; he had the good fortune to please and be promoted by Henry IV.

[5] The reader who has visited this town and district, and remarked the abundance of slate with which the country is furnished, will recognise the author's talent for observation, in the insertion of this circumstance. Conway, through it has suffered by war and time, still presents the same material features that it did in those days.

[6] This passage of the text on first inspection might seem even to go beyond the idea held out in one of the MSS., that he performed the distance from Milford to Conway in less than thirty-six hours. This would include two nights and a day. On looking at the Ordnance Maps I find that the distance from Milford to Conway is about 135 miles, which, bad as the roads undoubtedly were, might easily be accomplished in that time, being upon an average (stoppages included) not quite four miles an hour.

country and my life through these perfidious traitors, full of envy, who would thrust me out, and deprive me of mine inheritance. Alas! I know not what they would require of me. According to my ability, I have desired to observe (have respect unto) justice and righteousness. That Sovereign King, who sitteth above and seeth afar, I call to witness it, so truly, that my sad heart could wish that all mortals, past, present, and to come, could know my thoughts and desires. If I have been most invariable in preserving right, reasons demand it; for a king should be firm and steady, both in keeping himself notable for the punishment of the wicked, and for holding to the truth in every place. Alas! and because I have followed this righteous course as far as I was able for these three years past, yea for eight or ten, do these people keep me in this affliction. O, God of Glory! I humbly beseech thee, that as I have never consented, according to my ability, to bring evil upon any one who had not deserved it, be pleased to have mercy upon me. Alas! a poor king; for I know right well that unless thou shouldst speedily deign to regard me, I am lost.

"I will now tell you in what manner the constable who commanded his (the King's) people basely went off without waiting for him, and took away all his men. On that night, in which the good King set out from the sea-port at midnight, there arose a murmur and report in the army that the King had fled without saying a word. Then the constable much rejoiced at it, for he could not well find out any method of departing; but when he saw that the host were alarmed, he spoke so loud as to be plainly heard:—'Let us begone, since my lord is so careful to secure himself; we are all lost.' Presently he caused the trumpets to sound, and commanded that every man should forthwith prepare for departure, for he knew not when the King would return. There was most wonderful confusion in packing up and loading waggons; every one soon made ready his baggage to depart. They carried off all that belonged to the King,—robes, jewels,[7] fine gold, and pure silver, many a good horse[8] of foreign breed, many a rich and sparkling precious stone,[1] many a good mantle, and whole ermine, good cloth of gold, and stuff of foreign pattern.[2] One whose name was Sir Thomas Percy, had the charge of the whole of this; he was the King's steward, and had been long in his service, to speak properly in French, he was chief grand-maitre d'hôtel. The constable and he discoursed together; they set out shortly after, and took their way straight through Wales; but the Welsh, who saw their treason, opposed them here and there in companies of one or two thousand, often saying, 'Wretched traitors, you shall advance no further this way, and shall surrender all the stolen jewels you are carrying away; for the King has not given them to you.' Thus were the English all robbed by the Welsh. They kept back their waggons, and all the harness, gold and silver, and jewellery set in gold.[3] Then were the

---

[7] The king's apprehensions, love of display, or probable intention of holding a parliament, had induced him to take the Regalia with him on the expedition,* and they brought forward, as one of the offences charged against him, that he had carried with him towards Ireland, without the consent of the states of the kingdom, the treasures, reliques, and jewels of the crown.† The holy oil of anointing, used at coronations, and reputed to have been handed down from Beckett's time, he kept about him during the remainder of his difficulties, till it was wrested from him at Chester by the duke, who entertained, or affected to entertain, the same superstitious value for it.

[8] Among other showy things, Richard was very fond of fine horses. Shakspeare turned this to good account in the incident of the groom and Roan Barbary (See Rich. II. act. v. sc. 5). The young man attendant upon Richesse in the Romaunte of the Rose is a counterpart of this and other particulars:—

> "Hys luste was moche in householdyng;
> In clothing he was full fetyse,
> And loved well to have horse of pryse;
> He wonde to have reproved be
> Of thafte or murdre, yf that he
> Had in hys stable an hackenay."

---

* Twenty-fourth article of Accusation.
† Waling, ut supra, pp. 360, 361.

---

[1] Richard from the chain of his shoe to the plume upon his casque, was perhaps the greatest fop of his day. He had one coat at this time estimated at thirty thousand marks, the value of which must chiefly have arisen from the precious stones with which it was adorned.

[2] Most writers who gave given an account of these times have descanted upon the luxury and extravagance that extended more or less to all arts of life, and affected the whole of society. Even menial servants indulged in the absurd shoes called *cracows*, and in *pokys* (pouches), enormous sleeves which the Monk of Evesham compares to bagpipes, and tells that they were oft dipped into the broth when attendants were waiting at table. "The vanity of the common people in their dress was so great," says Knighton, "that it was impossible to distinguish the rich from the poor, the high from the low, the clergy from the laity, by their appearance. Fashions were continually changing in novelty and form." We are no friends to a sumptuary law, and are of opinion, that the evil of indiscriminate dress, is one, in the present day, which rectifies itself.

[3] It appears that a considerable portion was recovered by the exertions of Henry IV., who issued a proclamation for this purpose, and took great pains to get all he could of Richard's property into his hands. Rymer's Donat. MSS. i. 4596, p. 157, dated Nov. 6th.

English greatly troubled and enraged, for a thousand of them were spoiled, who were sent to the Duke with their doublets, with nothing but a staff in their hands and barefoot. For moreover, he that was not mounted must there tell whence he come, or whither he was going, and right or wrong, must pay his smart or die. This, though it should seem hard to be believed, is true; for with one accord, they (the Welsh) pitied the very great wrong and outrage that the English did to the King. Alas! what a spirit! God will some time reward them for it; for he who willingly doeth injury to another is often sure to be greatly punished of God, who is powerful above the present race of men as well as the past.

"Behold how the English were treated by the Welsh, who had no mercy on them, as they marched like people put to the rout, here ten, here twenty, there forty, there an hundred. They were obliged to abandon their prey, for these Welshmen came from the mountains without number; and it also happened very ill for them, that out of two or three roads they had taken the narrowest, and the most dangerous. It was the way that Heaven disposed them to go, for it was full of rocks and stones, so that they marched through it with difficulty. I heard eight days after that the English lost all their plunder, seeing that the Welsh, who were able men, closely pursued them. Certes, to my mind, it was exceedingly well done. Where the English then made their retreat, or which way they went, I know not, but I tell you that in less than a month, I saw the constable in the host of the Duke, as well as Lord Percy, who had been steward to the noble King Richard, bearing the order of the Duke;[4] and on the other hand I was told that they came straight to him early and late, without delay; and more than five hundred others, all naked, whom the Welsh had stripped to their doublets, and well beaten, as, if you remember, you have heard before. I will now tell you of the King, who remained at Conway, all sorrowful and astonished, saying, 'Sirs, I solemnly beseech you, advise me according to your opinion, since it is usual for a man in time of need to look to his friends.' The Duke of Exeter spoke first, for he was the King's brother, saying, 'It were good to send quickly to the Duke to know what he means to do, what is his desire, or for what reason he would take and keep your kingdom, your body, and your goods; or whether he wants to be king and sovereign master of England, Prince of Wales, and rightful Lord of Chester.' Thus spoke the noble Duke of Exeter to his brother. 'Let him be told he was banished by consent of his own father;[5] let him also consider well what he is about, for it would be a very great disgrace to him for ever, if it should appear that his rightful King was undone by him or by his doings. Never throughout his life would he recover this shame (let him reflect) too, how that all Kings in being, all nobility, and knighthood, would be displeased and disgusted at him, with good reason; and that throughout the world he would be said to be the true mirror of treason, if thus he wished to destroy and quite undo his lord. Let him take pattern from his father,[6] who all his life was gentle and courteous and would never think or act disloyally against you, and hated falsehood. Let him be well informed of all these matters, and that his race were never reproached with any treason or outrage, so that it were a great injury for him to disgrace his noble line by this undertaking; and how God hateth and condemneth him who maintaineth falsehood in any shape; such is our belief, as Holy Church teacheth concerning us, and he may take all his land again, on condition, that for your honour, he will at

[4] The badge of the house of Lancaster was the antelope and red rose; a fox's tail dependant; a swan argent gorged and chained Or, from the De Bohun.

[5] Because his father was of the council, and seneschal of England, it was his duty officially to pronounce sentence * upon his own son. Merks in his speech before the parliament in behalf of Richard II., has been made to say, that "the duke was banished the realm by King Richard and his council, and by the judgment of his own father."†

[6] Henry must have given his father some trouble, as by Richard's own account of him, John of Gaunt had passed sentence of death upon his son two or three times, and he was himself obliged once to intercede for his life. Henry on one occasion had to ask Richard's pardon on his bended knees; afterwards he held a threat to the king; and on another occasion he personally insulted him by offering to draw a sword upon him in the palace. When Richard heard in Ireland that Henry had landed, he used these expressions: "Ah, dear uncle of Lancaster, had I believed you, this man would not now have offended me; you told me truly that I did wrong to pardon him so often, for he would still continue to offend me. Three times have I pardoned his misdeeds, and this is the fourth offence he has committed against me."—Accounts and Extracts, ii. p. 222, 266.

* He did this in the case of the Earl of Arundel in 1396. Stow's Annals, p. 17.   † Merks, Bishop of Carlisle.

least come and sue for pardon. If he design not to come, it will be needful that any one who is able, should offer some other counsel. Thus shall it be said unto him, if it seem good to you; and let us consider who shall go to him, for it is needful that we dispatch him without further delay, provided you will agree to what I have spoken; else let any one who can find out a better plan declare it, for there should be no partiality amongst us, we are but few, and as you see the severity of the Duke is so great and perilous for us.' Then the King replied with a sorrowful voice: 'Fair brother, you speak the truth, you have found an excellent way; for my part I think we could take no better counsel. Fair cousins and loyal friends, let every one, I pray you, give his opinion, seeing it toucheth our honour and our life, for Duke Henry hateth us mortally, and hath moreover certainly done us much wrong. Let us now see whether we are of accord, and whether each of you will keep to his agreement.' Then they all said, 'Yea, we can find no better method in the world. For he who is sick must look for a remedy, and if he stirs before the time, he runs the risk of death, or of bearing all the blame.' Thus did they at this time agree, as I tell you, to send to Duke Henry. Now it came to pass that the Duke of Exeter was chosen by them, for they could not there find a man who knew how to speak so wisely, or set forth or relate a great matter. The King caused his fair cousin the Duke of Surrey to go with him. They left the King in the morning, who heartily besought them to shorten their journey, and act well; and to set before him all the matter that you have already heard, to the end that they might draw from him agreements of peace.

"Thus they departed from the King, but they had not much liberty to return, for Duke Henry kept them at bay, as you shall presently hear. Now the King continued all sorrowful at Conway, where he had no more with him than two or three of his intimate friends, sad and distressed. Ferriby was also with him, who was not very secure, for the Duke hated him; I cannot tell the reason, but I think Ferriby greatly dreaded him. Moreover there was another good friend, whom I have called Sir Stephen Scroope; I saw him frequently with the King at that time. My companion and myself were there. Every one was very uneasy for himself, with sufficient cause. Reckoning nobles and other persons, we were but sixteen in all. Now consider the power, possessions, and grandeur of King Richard, who was so great a lord; reflect what mischief, torment, and grief, must it be for him to be thus dealt with by treason, and by fortune, who at all times hath power and authority, severe as she is, to undo those whom she pleases. She is a mistress passionate and proud, most changeable and impetuous; for she is so restless, no bond can stop her, and when she resolves to act according to her nature, which, to some persons is often severe, be it bad or good, it must be endured, for no one can make resistance to her gifts. I shall now come to the conclusion of King Richard, who from sport of fortune, together with treason, as I have said, was all alone at Conway, full of sorrow, mourning, and dismay. I know full well that he and the Earl said that it would be a great thing to send to his people, whom he lately left at the sea port, to come thither without delay. But in the meantime, by chance, there arrived a horseman, who set aside the measure, for he related to the good King the whole that the constable had done, which was not very honourable to him, since he declared without falsehood or fable, that he appeared to be unsteady towards him, and as soon as the King had left Milford that he had heard the news of it, he set out upon his departure from that place; neither would the steward remain behind him, but packed up all that belonged to the King that was hitherto on board, and then afterwards they went away; but the Welsh, who were stout and fresh, closely pursued them. 'These,' said he, 'took all your substance, and slew a great number of them; such as escaped thence have gone straight to the Duke. This dear sire, have I been told for truth.' And when the King had let him say the whole, you may be sure he was not fain to smile, for on all sides, one after another, came pouring in upon him mischief and trouble. 'O Virgin Mary, sovereign queen, pure and unblemished mother of Jesus,' thus spoke the King, 'fortune dealeth very harshly with me.' Then said he to the Earl of Salisbury, "How shall we prevail over the Duke and his people; the Duke who by his power treateth us in so grievous a manner? Alas! if this man tell the truth, they have not done their duty towards us, seeing we have ever mightily benefitted them all, and if they fail in loyalty,

God will look to their doings. He who knoweth how to punish the misdeed of the sinner, is the righteous judge. For well I know, that when the latter day shall come, and he shall hold his judgment, the wicked shall have neither refuge nor reprieve, but shall find what they have done and spoken; and then shall they be accursed from his mouth, as we are told, in pain infernal. Such is our belief. Wherefore in every respect we take heed unto ourselves; and thus it is often said, Power hath no law.' Then said the Earl, ' Sire, by my honour, you speak the truth.'

"They then agreed to make no further stay at Conway,' for they were greatly afraid, and with good reason. They went straight to Beaumaris, which was ten[8] miles from Conway. This is a castle that could not be taken in ten years, provided it were victualled for that time, and furnished with some good defenders. One side of it was seated on the champaign country; the other is on the sea. Saint Edward[9] caused it to be built, as I have heard the English tell. The King was here, but would not stop long, for he thought that himself and his people would be more secure at Caernarvon; it is a town, and has a fine noble castle, a place of strength. On one side is abundance of woods for the chase, and the tide comes up on the other quarter. There was the King, whose face was often pale, as he regretted his hard fate, and condemned the hour, and the day, that he ever crossed the salt sea into Ireland. ' Gentle Virgin Mary,' would he often say, ' Succour me, Lady; I cry thee mercy; since truly I have never deserved, with regard to the Duke, that he should thus pursue me and my people, whom greatly and undeservedly he hateth, and falsely betrayeth, as may be seen. Every one knoweth and may discern it. Alas! and when the truth shall be known in gentle France, I firmly hope that my father-in-law will also bitterly grieve[1] at heart for it. For truly it will be a great scandal for him, and, indeed, for every living mother's son among kings; considering the outrage and very great distress, the poverty, and condition in which I am; and that I am thus concealing myself on account of those who have ever been on my side. Now they are turned, I know not why. Alas! what treachery! It will be a reproach to them for ever, so long as the world shall endure, or the deep ocean be able to cast up tide or wave. This action redounds with great evil to them all. Glorious God! who didst die for us, suspended on the cross, look mercifully upon me; none other than thou can aid my present need, and I must lose my land and my life, should fortune will it; I must take it all in good part, for her authority must be obeyed.' Thus oftentimes spoke King Richard, sighing piteously from his heart, so that I solemnly protest more than a hundred times, I shed many a tear for him. There lives not a man so hard-hearted, or so firm, who could not have wept at sight of the disgrace brought upon him.

"What is still worse, in the castles, to which he retired, there was no furniture, nor had he anything to lie upon but straw; really he lay in this manner for four or six nights; for, in truth, not a farthing's worth of victuals or anything else was to be found in them. Certes, I dare not tell the great misery of the King, who stayed not long at Caernarvon, for he had little rest there on account of his misfortunes and great poverty.[2]

[7] Otterbourne agrees in the account of the king's wanderings from one castle to another, in search of refuge; that he was in Anglesea, Beaumaris, Caernarvon, and Conway, is certain; but we question his stating that he was in Flint and Holt, which contained great part of his treasure. Both these places are within a short distance from Chester, not more than ten or twelve miles; and as Duke Henry had reached Chester by the time Richard threw himself first into Conway, he would have obstructed him, as he had already driven the Earl of Salisbury into that fortress. The author had been with the king when he inspected Rhuddlan Castle, and charged the governor to defend it. Stow tells us that he shifted to Beaumaris by advice of the Earl of Salisbury.

[8] This is a mistake, the distance by sea cannot be less than fifteen miles, and by land, over the Menai, twenty-three miles.

[9] Our author confounds Edward I. with Edward the Confessor; the former built Beaumaris during his wars in Wales in 1294.

(Camden's Annals of Ireland.) He gave it the name of Beaumaris. (Walsingham, Hist. Angl., p. 63.) William Scroope, Earl of Wiltshire, beheaded at Bristol, was appointed governor in 20 Rich. II. (Dugdale's Baronage, i. p. 279.) Henry IV. granted it with the whole county and dominion of Anglesea to Hotspur for his life.

[1] This proved true, according to Froissart. "The king was much afflicted at the melancholy account he heard; for he knew the English to be determined and hard to appease; and although he had been for some time in good health, the rage he got into on learning the events passing in England, brought back his frenzy." And again, after Richard's decease. "The King of France was not in good health, nor had been, ever since he heard of the misfortunes of his son-in-law Richard, and his disorder was greatly increased when he was told of his death." Charles VII. was afflicted with fits which brought on derangement. Froissart, xii. pp. 28, 32.

[2] Richard must have felt his distress and humiliation very great in

"The King returned to Conway, where he thus greatly bewailed his wife: 'My mistress and my consort! Accursed be the man, little doth he love us, who thus shamefully separateth us two. I am dying of grief because of it, my fair sister, my lady, and my sole desire. Since I am robbed of the pleasure of beholding thee, such pain and affliction oppresseth my whole heart, that oftentimes I am hard upon despair. Alas! Isabel,[3] rightful daughter of France, you were wont to be my joy, my hope, and my consolation; I now plainly see that through the great violence of fortune which hath slain many a man, I must wrongfully be removed from you. Whereat I often endure at heart so severe a pang, that day and night I am in danger of bitter and certain death, and it is no wonder, considering my misfortunes, who from such a height, have fallen thus low, and lose my joy, my solace, and my consort.[4] I plainly see that no one maketh a secret of vexing and cheating me. Alas! every one attacketh or hateth me; still praised be God in his holy heavens above.' Thus spoke the King while his eyes wept piteously; for he could do no better at the time.

"I will now tell you how the Duke dealt with the King's brother, who went to him with the Duke of Surrey, a most loyal lover of King Richard, inasmuch as he was afterwards put to death for it, as, if Heaven preserve me, you shall very presently hear. The two dukes travelled early and late till they came to Chester, which the Duke of Lancaster, on his part, had already taken by his art and cunning without assault.[5] They both entered: when they got in, a great number of persons were with them, who thought they were changing the service of the King, and that they were coming to sue for mercy to Henry, Duke of Lancaster; but great folly caused them to think so, for they would not have crouched to him for all the gold of England. They were straightway led to Duke Henry[6] in the castle, which is a regular

this instance, for during that age great attention was paid to the comfort and decoration of bedding : here he had neither a pillow for his head, nor scarcely a morsel to appease his hunger. The following lines by Chaucer are peculiarly applicable to the condition of the king :

"Gone is thy joy, and all thy myrth on erth ;
Of all thy blythnesse, now art thou black and bare ;
There is no salve may help thy sore :
Fell is thy fortune, wicked is thy werth ;
Thy blisse is banished, and thy bale unberde.

Where is the chambre wantonely besene
With burly bed and bankers brouded bene,
Spyces and wyne to thy collatione,
The cups all of gold and sylver shene,
Thy sweetemeats served in plates clene,
With savoury sauce of good facience,
Thy gay garments ?—
All is arere, thy great royal renoune ;
——For thy bed take now a bunch of stro."

Complaynt of Cresseyde.

[3] "Isabel was eldest daughter of Charles VI., King of France, whom Richard had espoused, Oct. 31st, 1396. At that time she was but eight years old, and he was in his twenty-seventh year ; and the disparity of their ages had given rise to much discussion and dissatisfaction among his subjects, who were averse to his alliance with France. But the king despised public opinion, and overruled all the remonstrances of their friends. Sir John Grailly, the captal of Buch, ventured to tell him, "that it was no way agreeable to the English that he should connect himself by marriage with France." Others told him, "the lady was far too young." But he replied, "that every day she would increase in years." In addition to this, he gave pleasantly his reason for preferring her, that since she was so young, he should educate her and bring her up to his own mind, and to the manners of the English, and that for himself he was young enough to wait till she was of a proper age to be his wife.*

* Froissart, xi. c. 23.

They were accordingly married in St. Nicholas's Church at Calais. Her dowry, as settled by the conventions, was 800,000 livres, 300,000 to be put down upon the day of marriage, and 100,000 annually, till the whole should be paid. This was never done, and soon after the death * of the king she was restored to her father. Richard spent in the festivities of his nuptials, not including presents, 300,000 marks and more.—*Walsingham's Hist. Angl.*, p. 356.

[4] "To many readers these piteous lamentations of a husband of thirty, over a baby-wife in her eleventh year, couched in terms, which would better apply to a female of his own age, may appear weak and absurd. Be this as it may, he certainly was much attached to her, and by the confession of the French had behaved very affectionately and honourably towards her." Accounts and Extracts, ut supra. Mezeray.

[5] Sir Robert and Sir John a Legh, were sent with a deputation to treat for Chester, and to surrender everything to the Duke. He met him at Shrewsbury.† Sir Robert was sheriff of Cheshire, 21 Rich. II.‡ Henry entered Chester on the 8th of August, where he was received in a royal manner, with solemn processions of all the religious orders.§

[6] On his arrival before the Duke, Huntington bent one knee to the ground, and said, "It is but reasonable, sir, that I should pay you reverence ; for your father was a king's son, and my wife also is your sister." "Rise, brother-in-law," said the duke, coldly ; "you have not always acted thus." Then taking him by the hand, he drew him aside, and they conversed together for a long time, but I know not what they said. From the last expression, as well as from what has been noticed before, Gaillard conjectures the author of the MSS. Ambassades to have been an eye-witness. See MS. Account and Extracts in the library of the King of France, ii. p. 218.

* When Richard was prisoner in the Tower he earnestly requested that he might be allowed to see her, but Henry refused him. Accounts and Extracts, vol. ii. p. 227.
† Vita Rich. II., p. 154.   ‡ Carte, ii. p. 633.
§ MSS. Harl 5171.

building; he was heartily rejoiced and delighted when he saw them; right welcome he seemed to make them. And afterwards he said to the Duke of Exeter: 'Come, brother-in-law, tell us, I pray you, without further controversy, what news you bring.' 'None, brother-in-law, that is very good for my lord, but such as is disgraceful and bad, whereat I am most sorrowful and distressed.'

"And then he went on to tell him very prudently, what you have already heard at their parting with the King; that it would be most disgraceful for him thus to break his fidelity to his lord; and that he was banished by the will and consent of his good father, so that he should well weigh the whole of the matter; also that he would bring great shame and reproach upon every king alive; and that he would be hated by those who are his good friends, and that all would be his enemies who loved honour, loyalty, worth, and vassalage; and if he should commit such an outrage, it would be a scandal to his lineage for ever, seeing that he ought to be a great lord in wisdom and moderation; but, should it happen that his rightful king should be disinherited, by his will or by his force, he would be compared to Guendolen,' who, in his time, committed much treason, through which many a worthy knight died. So that he earnestly besought him not to bring on this comparison. He told him he should also have his land and substance, provided he would henceforth do his duty; and that the King would freely pardon him the whole of the outrage he had committed against him. Thus right well and handsomely did the Duke of Exeter tell him of his doings, and dared too, to speak boldly to him, for he had married his own sister, and was thus his equal. Moreover, the Duke of Exeter said to him: 'I beseech you, brother-in-law, give us immediately the whole or part of our answer; for my lord is expecting us, who is not in very good plight.'

"Then said the Duke Henry: 'You have spoken to me much to the purpose, but if God grant me health and happiness, you shall neither go to-day nor for a week to come. It is not right that I should send you back so soon; you are not messengers for hire, and it is not wise in my lord to send you here; could he find none to send but you two; it is but a mean service for a gentleman of such high birth to send you here.' So the Duke resolved to retain them, but his brother-in-law continually besought him that he would give them leave to depart, saying: 'Sire, the King may think that treason causeth us to abide here. We should never recover this disgrace. Wherefore, brother-in-law, for God and honour's sake, to the end that we may have no dishonour, we lovingly entreat you to suffer us to be gone.' Then spake the Duke, who was as bold as a lion: 'Brother-in-law, talk no more of this; at a proper season I will send you back to the King; and come no more into my presence; for I swear, and assure you, upon mine honour, that you shall go from me upon no such message for a month to come.'[8]

"Thus were the two dukes detained, who were greatly vexed at heart, considering that Duke Henry was with them at the time, and bewailing the King, who remained alone without a soul, to aid or support him. Thus each of the two dukes often wept; but, like, or dislike it, they were obliged to endure it all. Duke Henry separated them; he kept his brother, the Duke of Exeter, about him; and caused the Duke of Surrey to be shut up in the Castle of Chester. It had many fine windows and lofty walls. When I saw it, it put me in mind of the Castle of Namur, it is so high and strong. The good duke was in no great safety there. Six[9] miles from the city was another fortress that they called Holt; it stood very lofty upon a rock. In the meantime, the Duke went against it with all his army. Those who were in it were so much afraid, that they knew not what to do; though they were certain that the Duke could not

[7] "The false Genallon;[*]
    He that purchased the treason
    Of Roulande and Olivere."—CHAUCER.

[8] "Henry farther alleged as his reason for detaining Huntington, that he must wait for the return of Northumberland, who had been sent to the king with a message from him. Such is the account given in the MS. Ambassades; though, according to our author, the resolution to send that nobleman was not yet adopted. Huntington was not only kept against his will, but made to wear the cognisance of Henry, and write a letter to Richard, requesting him to place entire confidence in the Earl of Northumberland." MS. Ambassades, p. 133.

[*] A celebrated character in the middle ages: he caused the death of Rolando, and the defeat of the French army at Roncevalles, and was torn in pieces by horses at Aix-la-Chapelle, by order of Charlemagne—the name afterwards became proverbial for any insincere person.

[9] Our author mistakes the distance; there are eight good miles between Chester and Holt.

hurt them in the least at any time; for the castle is so strong and sound, that in my opinion, considering the height upon which it is seated, it could not have been taken by force in ten years.[1] It was also garrisoned with good men.

"There were an hundred picked men-at-arms within it, carefully provisioned on the part of the King. But they were not diligent in keeping good guard at the entrance of the pass, which is narrow, and must be ascended on foot, step by step; but faint-hearted and cowardly as they were, they gave it up to the duke, who made haste to enter, more delighted than ever; for it contained a hundred thousand marks sterling in gold, and upwards, which King Richard caused to be treasured up there, besides a great quantity of other precious things. By Saint Mor (Maurice?), I heard it said that what could be found there might fairly be reckoned at two hundred thousand marks.[2] Duke Henry took it all away with him. Thus was Holt surrendered, as I have told you; and all the subsistence of King Richard seized. It was likewise stored with military provisions, bread, wine, fresh water, and cattle, for six years. Such fellows are not worth a straw; for, without fighting a battle or defending themselves, they were presently ready to give it up to Duke Henry. I heartily wished that he had hanged them all!

" Duke Henry did not stop long at Holt, but returned straight to Chester, where he summoned the whole of his council, and desired each of them to say what he thought good to be done. The Archbishop of Canterbury answered first, and said, ' Fair Sirs, King Richard hath retired into Wales, where there are many dangerous mountains, over which neither waggon nor baggage can pass; on the other hand is the sea, where abundance of fish may be taken. Your army could not approach him; but it were good to send to him, to swear unto him, and make a covenant to be at peace with him for ever, on condition that he will swear that a parliament shall be called by him, in which those wicked men shall be punished, by whom his uncles were put to death; so shall ye henceforth be good friends; and let him appoint such a day as shall seem good to him, and in such place, that every one, clerk or layman, knight, prince, or monk, may visit it; for you cannot take him by any other means, since he hath the power, in spite of us, at any time, to put to sea and begone: because I have heard say that he hath caused vessels to be obtained at Conway. So that I think you ought to advise upon this matter. Now speak upon it, my lords and friends.' Every one then said, ' Better counsel than this I never heard.' Then said Duke Henry, ' The thing will do well, and it will be a good method. It is my advice that the aged Earl of Northumberland,'

---

[1] It would appear from the engraving of Holt Castle by Norden in 1610, when it was entire, that its form was pentangular, having a bastion tower at each angle, four of them circular, and that facing the river, square. The entrance was by a drawbridge, over a deep moat, communicating with a gateway upon which stood a square tower, strengthened by portcullises and machicolations. John Earl Warren, who murdered Madoc, the heir to these lands, began to build it in the reign of Edward I., and it was finished by his son William. It afterwards belonged to the Fitz Alans, and was in the hands of Richard Fitz Alan, Earl of Arundel,* who was resident there with armed men in 17 Richard II. The Earl of Albemarle obtained it of the king, with several other fortresses in that county, for his life; but it was restored to the family of Fitz Alan by Henry IV. It has since, at different times, been made the depository of wealth and military stores in the reigns of Henry VII. and Edward VI. by Sir William Stanley and Thomas Seymour † of Sudley, Lord High Admiral of England. On the execution of Stanley, Henry VII. seized upon his effects, and found in this fortress, among a variety of valuables, money and plate to the amount of forty thousand marks. ‡ This of itself would be sufficient to account for the tradition of treasure; but does not at all invalidate

the fact of the hoard that Richard II. had laid up there. It was demolished by order of parliament. The castle of Holt, and the adjoining ground, is now the property of the Rt. Hon. Lord Kenyon, who purchased it some years ago from the crown.

[2] " Kynge Richarde," says Fabyan, " fande grete rychesse, that before tyme to Kynge Richarde belonged." He then quotes Poly-chronicon for different items, adding, " so it should seeme that Kynge Richarde was ryche when his money and jewellery amounted to VII. C. M. li." See Fabyan by Ellis, pp. 550, 551.

[3] A brief account of this veteran negotiator and warrior will convey some idea of the manner in which his life was spent. He was eldest son of Henry Percy, by Mary, daughter of Henry Earl of Lancaster, married 22 Edward III. to a daughter of Lord Nevill, by whom he had three sons, one of whom was the celebrated Hotspur. In the 42 Edward III. his father died. In that year he accompanied the king to Calais, when peace was made with France. In 43 Edward III. he took an active part in the wars with France. In 46 Edward III. he accompanied the king to France to the relief of Thouars. In 47 Edward III. he purchased Milford Castle in Northumberland for 760l. during the minority of the Earl of Athol, and attended the king to Flanders; 50 Edward III. he was made marshal of England, and went officially to inspect the castle of Calais and the marches thereof. He appeared now a protector of Wycliff, to whom he showed much respect. At the coronation of Richard II. he acted as marshal of England, and was advanced ot

* Walsingham, Hist. Angl., p. 350.
† Dugdale's Baronage, iii. p. 368.
‡ See Pennant's Wales, vol. i. pp. 205, 210, 212.

my fair cousin, set out to-morrow in the morning, and that he return not until, by truces or by force, he bring back the King. Let him also take with him four lances, and a thousand archers, who must be very diligent: for there is nothing in the world that I so much desire as to have the King in my keeping.' Then he said to the Earl, 'Fair cousin, be careful to depart, and accomplish well your enterprise; for you can do me no greater pleasure in the world. I pray you now make haste; and I shall stay at Chester till you return, or till I have news from you, which may revive my heart with joy.' 'God grant it may be such,' said the Earl; 'by reason or by craft will I bring him.' So the Earl set out without delay; he took his road as straight as he could for Conway, pondering and full of care as to how he might take the King. Thus he and his men travelled till they reached a very strong castle, called Flint. He sent in an order, on the part of Duke Henry, to give up the fort to him, or all of them, without favour or respite, should be delivered over to death. So King Richard's people opened the gate to him through fear: he turned them out, and committed the keeping of it to a great party of his own men. In this castle, that you have heard me call Flint, was the King taken, as shall be hereafter related. Northumberland now made his people hasten straight from that place to another stronghold called Rhuddlan, whither he found a toilsome and heavy road; many a mountain and great rock are between them. He got over as fairly and well as he could; and mightily rejoiced he was. He sent to the castellan,[4] who was an old knight, commanding him instantly to surrender the fortress in the name of the Duke, or he, and all who might be taken therein, should be hanged without mercy: not for all the wealth of the realm should they escape. Doubtless, he would make them taste of death, if they gave not up to him the castle and the place. At this menace of the Earl, the castellan turned pale with fear; for he had not long kept the castle and approach in the name of the King. It is very strong, because the sea comes into the passes; and on the other side it is posted very loftily upon a rock; its walls are strong and thick, well provided with large towers.[5]

"But such was the fear of the old man from morning till night, that, coward-like, he gave up the keys to him, although King Richard had gently besought him to keep the fortress, seeing it was well stored with wine and corn; *for he had very lately been there, and myself with him.* The castellan bargained with the Earl to surrender it in the name of Duke Henry, upon condition that he should continue castellan of that

---

the dignity of the Earl of Northumberland; shortly afterwards he entered Scotland at the head of ten thousand men against the Earl of Dunbar, and wasted his lands: 2 Richard II., he entered that country again and took Berwick: 7 Richard II., he again chastised the Scots: 10 and 11 Richard II., Ambassador to Scotland: 13 Richard II., commissioner to treat of peace between France and Flanders, at the interview between France and Flanders. He afterwards invited Charles VI. to his pavilion. In consequence of some rupture between Richard II. and his eldest son, Hotspur, he absented himself from Court, put himself in communication with Henry of Lancaster, who was then across the seas, and during Richard II.'s absence in Ireland, he and his son Hotspur joined Henry of Lancaster on his arrival at Doncaster. The zeal that he had shown in the cause of Henry IV. procured his advancement to the office of Constable of England for life, and the gifts of the Isle of Man, to hold by bearing the sword of Lancaster at the coronation. He was besides made constable of the castles of Chester, Flint, Conway, and Caernarvon. In 2 Henry IV., he was commissioned to treat respecting a marriage between Blanch, eldest daughter of the king, with Lewis Duke of Bavaria: 3 Henry IV., he defeated the Scots in a decisive battle at Halidon-Hill, and here his services and intimate connexion with Henry IV. ceased. In the fourth year of Henry IV., his dissatisfaction began to show itself. Some say this was caused by a dispute about the prisoners taken at Halidon-Hill. The Percy took up arms, and Sir Thomas and young Henry lost their lives at the Battle of Shrewsbury, before Northumberland could bring up his force which he had collected for their aid. The earl afterwards appeared before the king and disavowed the actions of his son: 7 Henry IV., he appeared with the insurgents in Yorkshire, and when they were quelled he was pursued into Scotland. With a resolution unbroken by these reverses, he next retired into Wales, and concerted with Owen Glyndwr the means of deposing Henry IV. He afterwards appeared in Yorkshire, and at the head of a considerable number of men proclaimed liberty to all that would follow him. He was slain by the sheriff of the county after rebelling against the king whom he had placed upon the throne. His head and quarters were distributed in London and elsewhere.

[4] Whoever the governor of this fortress might be, he does not appear to have been at his post. His office had a peculiar authority attached to it by an express provision: 10 Richard II., he was constituted for the time being sheriff of the county. "Constabularius castri de Flint pro-tempore existenti debet esse vice-comes comitatus de Flint."—Calend. Rot. Pat., p. 214; 1 Pat. 10. Rich. II.

[5] The vestiges of this castle prove its original strength; the walls are flanked by six strong round towers, three of which remain tolerably entire. The ditch is wide and deep, and on both sides faced with stone; the steep encampment towards the river was defended with walls, in which were square bastions—one of them is still standing. It was originally built by Llywelyn ap Seisyllt,* 1015-20. Harold burnt it in 1053, and it was restored by William the Conqueror, or Henry II.

---

* Orderic. Vit., p. 36.

place all his life, to which the Duke agreed.' They were now but ten miles distant from Conway, by a direct road.' There was the King in sorrow and dismay: he knew nothing of the coming of the Earl, but he often said, 'I cannot tell what this can mean: O, glorious God, my Maker! what can become of my brother-in-law of Exeter? It is eight days since he went to Chester, to bring the Duke and myself to an agreement. I certainly believe they are suffering pain or mischief. I know not what to think or say of it.' Thus the King was sore troubled, because of the evil that continually pressed upon him, to his further undoing; yet still he gave thanks to the Almighty. It is now right to tell you of Northumberland, and what he meditated, as he went on his way, for the better taking of King Richard: for he was sure that if the King was aware of his force and power, he would, on no account, stir from his castle.

"He formed his men* into two bodies under the rough and lofty cliffs of a rock (Penmaen Rhôs); they were fresh and eager, persecuting traitors as they were, to take the King. Alas! what men were they, and what could be their thoughts? When for two-and-twenty years they had upheld him in great joy and honour, to ruin him afterwards, is in my mind so great a error, that they ought to be looked upon as the wickedest of mortals; and recorded in chronicles, that their deeds and their reproof might be seen in distant times. The subtle Earl said to his people, 'Keep well this pass, I am going on with five others to the opposite shore, and, or please God, I will ere to-morrow dawn, in some way or other (in prose or rhyme), tell the King such tidings, that unless he be harder than file or tempered steel, I think I shall make him leave his quarters. But beware that ye stir not, for your lives, till you see the King or myself return.' So they put themselves in good array; and the Earl, without making any stir, went on to Conway to fulfil his word. There is an arm of the sea, before the town; but when the Earl came in front of it he sent a herald to King Richard, to ask if he would be pleased to grant him safe conduct, that he might pass over to tell him how the Duke was desirous of coming to an agreement with him. Then the herald crossed the water, and found the King aloft in the castle hardly assailed by sorrow. He said cheerfully to him. 'Sire, the Honourable Earl of Northumberland hath sent me hither to relate to you how desirous he is immediately to be at peace with you. May it please you, for the better knowledge of the truth, to grant him safe conduct, and leave to come here, for otherwise he will not presume to stir.' Salisbury, who was there, then said, it would be a good thing to make him come thither alone.' Then the King said aloud to the messenger in his own language, 'I heartily give the Earl of Northumberland permission to pass.' He thanked him a hundred times, descended from the castle, and passed the water, where the Earl had been long expecting him. Then he related to him how King Richard had freely granted him safe conduct, and besought him to make haste.

"On his entrance into the castle, the Earl of Northumberland found King Richard, and the Earl of Salisbury with him, as well as the Bishop of Carlisle. He said to the King, 'Sire, Duke Henry hath sent me hither, to the end that an agreement might be made between you, and that you should be good friends for the time to come. If it be your pleasure, Sire, that I may be heard, I will deliver to you the message and conceal nothing of the truth. If you will be a good judge and true, and will bring up all those I shall

---

⁶ That the agreement was kept appears from the grant of the constableship of the several castles of Chester, Flint, Conway, and Caernarvon, all upon the same line, to the Earl of Northumberland in Henry IV.* Rhuddlan, which forms a link in the chain, is omitted in the list, and we may therefore conclude that the old castellan retained it.

⁷ Our author is again mistaken in the distance; but perhaps French miles were longer in those days than our present English miles. The distance from Rhuddlan to Conway is seventeen miles.

⁸ "These men were commanded by Sir Thomas Erpingham, (MS. Ambassades, p. 136), who came over with Henry from France. He was also one of the commissioners that passed sentence of depo-

sition upon Richard II., and in his advanced age gave the signal for the Battle of Agincourt."—*Rapin,* i. p. 113.

⁹ His little retinue perhaps remained on the other side of the water, because Northumberland is admitted into the castle alone. And this should be particularly noted, since we shall endeavour to show that a studied misrepresentation of the whole affair was made by the Lancastrians for an obvious end. Walsingham * tells us, that the first proposition towards a treaty came from Richard, and that he desired to confer with the Earl of Northumberland and Archbishop Arundel at Conway. So much of the true circumstances of the case kept out of sight.

---

* Hist. Anglia, p. 358.

* Dugdale's Baronage, i. p. 278.

here name to you, by a certain day for the end of justice;[1] listen to the parliament which you shall lawfully cause to be held between you at Westminster, and restore him to be Chief Judge of England, as the Duke his father[2] and all his ancestors had been for more than a hundred years. I will tell you those who shall await the trial, may it please you, Sire, it is time they should.' 'Yes, tell me then, I desire to know who they are.'—'Know, Sire, that the first is your brother. The second, who hath behaved amiss, is the Duke of Surrey, who is indeed imprisoned in the Castle of Chester, for some offences committed against Duke Henry. Another is the Earl of Salisbury, together with the Bishop of Carlisle; the fifth, as I have heard my lord say, is Maudelaine;[3] these are they who agreed and counselled you to put your uncle most wrongfully to death, and if they deny it, they await the judgment of your parliament. There also shall Duke Henry be Chief Judge. Those who have been guilty of crime or treason shall be punished without partiality. Such is the determination of my lord. Certes, my lord, he would do nothing that is foolish or unreasonable. I would moreover speak to you of another thing; that you will speedily appoint a day, for there is nothing in the world that he desireth more, I know it well; and he wishes for nothing but his land, and that which appertaineth to him; neither would he have anything that is yours, for you are his immediate rightful King; and he regretteth in his conscience the great mischief and wrong he hath done unto you through the evil persuasion of the enemy, who never slumbereth nor sleepeth, but is ever watchful to tempt mankind. It is he that hath whispered to him all that he hath done. Wherefore for the sake of Him who suffered unparalleled death for us upon the cross, may it please you to be gentle unto my lord, who is sorrowful and afflicted, and for once lay aside your wrath; and he will most humbly come on his knees before you and sue for mercy. This done, together shall ye go to London, like devout and peaceful men; or if you choose to go by a different road, you shall take it, and then shall the parliament be proclaimed throughout the land. Be sure of all this: I will swear it upon the body of our Lord, consecrated by the priest's hand, that Duke Henry shall most faithfully observe all that I have said, and everything as I have told you; for he solemnly pledged it to me upon the Sacrament, when last we parted. Now consider, Sire, how you will act, for I have tarried long.'

---

[1] We are here supplied with some additional matter from the MS. Ambassades. Huntington (Duke of Exeter), by the command of the duke, sent one of his retinue after Northumberland with two letters, one for the king, and the other for Northumberland, when he appeared before the king with seven attendants. He was asked by him if he had not met his brother on the road! "Yes, sire," he answered, "and here is a letter he gave me for you." The king looked at the letter and the seal, and saw it was the seal of his brother; then he opened the letter and read it; and all that it contained was this: "My very dear lord, I commend me to you, and you will believe the earl in everything that he shall say unto you; for I found the duke at my city of Chester, who has a great desire to have a good peace and agreement with you, and has kept me to attend upon him until he shall know your pleasure." When they had read the letter, he turned to Northumberland and said: "Now tell me what message you bring." To which the earl replied: "My very dear lord, the Duke of Lancaster hath sent me to you to tell you that what he most wishes for in this world, is to have peace and agreement with you; and he greatly repents with all his heart of the displeasure he hath caused you now, and at other times; and asks nothing of you in this living world, save that you may account him your cousin and friend; and that it may please you only to let him have his land, and that he may be chief judge of England, as his father and predecessors have been, and that all other things of times past may be put into oblivion between you two, for which purpose he hath chosen umpires (judges) for yourself and for him; that is to say, the Bishop of Carlisle, the Earl of Salisbury, Maudelaine, and the Earl of Westmoreland; and charges them with the agreement that is between you and him. Give me an answer, if you please, for all the greatest lords of England and the commons are of this opinion." On which the king desired to withdraw a little, and he should have an answer soon.[*]

The latter part of this speech contains an important variation from the MS. Metrical History, worthy of the artifice of the earl; but the opposite account of our eye-witness, confirmed by Richard's subsequent address to his friends, is doubtless the true representation. The writer of the MS. Ambassades may have been at this time at Chester; but admitting that he had been in the train of Northumberland, on the journey, he could not have been present at the conference.

[2] "The style of the duke his father was; John, the son of the King of England, Duke of Guienne and Lancaster, Earl of Derby, Lincoln, and Leicester, Steward of England."—*Cotton's Abridgment*, p. 343.

[3] Maudelaine was a priest of the Chapel Royal, who resembled the king so much in size, feature, and speech, that he was employed by the insurgents at Christmas to personate him in the army. He had served the king in several confidential and difficult undertakings. He was a witness to Richard's will, and went with him upon the Irish expedition. On their return to Milford he was among those of his counsel who advised him to withdraw from his army to France. He was afterwards missing. When he was taken to London for execution, he asked the mayor should he be quartered. "No," said the mayor, "but your head will be cut off." He thanked God that "he should die in the service of his sovereign lord and king."—*Walsingham, Hist. Angl.*, p. 363.

[*] MS. Ambassades, pp. 134, 135; Mr. Allen's Extracts.

"Then King Richard wisely replied : 'Northumberland withdraw; ere it be long you shall have your answer, that you may speedily depart.' Then might you see them separate. They discoursed long upon the matter of which they heard the Earl speak, till at last the King said :'—'Fair sirs, we will grant it to him, for I see no other way. You perceive as well as I do, that all is lost; but I swear to you that whatever assurance I may give him, he shall for this surely be put to a bitter death for the outrage and injury that he hath done unto us. And, doubt it not, no parliament shall be held at Westminster upon this business, for I love you so entirely that I would not suffer you to come to parliament to die for the fulfilment of his pleasure, for I know full well that he would make you suffer a most heavy penalty, and that you would be in very great danger of being put to bitter, certain death, seeing many murmur against you. Yet fear not, my good friends, but in spite of them you shall ever be my nearest friends, for I have always found you without evil intention, good and loyal. Moreover, I tell you that I will summon and bring together men throughout Wales that may be ready for us on a certain day. When we have spoken to Duke Henry, we will then take our way through Wales; and if he should ask us wherefore we do so, we will tell him that there are no victuals (not a pennyworth) the other way, since his people and his army have wasted everything, and that we are going that way lest provisions fail us. Thus will we say to him, if it seems good unto you, and I believe that he will readily agree to it; the Earl hath told us so. And when we shall have found our people assembled, we will display our banners to the wind, and suddenly march with vigour against him. For, I am sure that when they shall behold my arms, they will be so sorry at heart for the wrong they have done unto me, and that the half of those who have gone along with him will desert him, and come over to us; for a good and faithful heart can never prove false, and return will bring to their remembrance that, during my life, they ought to hold me as their rightful lord. You will then see them come to us straightway, and you will know that we have *right on our side*. God, if we trust in him, will aid us. If we are not so much in our place as they shall be, yet, please God, they shall not choose, but fight for us; and if they be in anywise discomfitted, they shall be put to death. There are some of them whom I will flay alive. I would not take all the gold in the land for them, if it please God that I continue alive and well.

"Thus the King spoke unto them, and they all agreed thereto, saying, 'Sire, let the Earl of Northumberland be sent for, and let him forthwith be made to take the oath, as he hath declared he will, if we will consent to all he hath said.' Then was the Earl called in without further parley, and the King said to him, 'Northumberland, the Duke hath sent you hither to reconcile us two, if you will swear upon the body of our Lord, which we will cause to be consecrated, that the whole of the matter related by you is true; that you have no hidden design therein of any kind whatsoever, but, that like a notable lord, you will surely keep the agreement; we will perform it; for well I know that you are honourable (*preudoms*) and would not perjure yourself for any bribe; for the man who perjureth himself, knoweth that he must live in disgrace, and die of it at last in great sorrow.' Then replied the Earl, 'Sire, let the body of our Lord be consecrated. I will swear that there is no deceit in the affair; and that the Duke will observe the whole as you have heard me relate it here.' Each of them devoutly heard mass ;' then the Earl, without further hesitation, made oath upon the body of our Lord. Alas! his blood must have turned (at it), for he well knew to the contrary.

"Yet would he take the oath, as you have heard, for the accomplishment of his desire, and the performance of that which he had promised the Duke, who had sent him to the King.

' Another account states that he consulted with his friends, Carlisle, Salisbury, Scrope, Ferriby, and Jenico, in the chapel at the castle at Conway, and said to them, "Gentlemen, you have heard what the earl says; what think you of it ?" To which they replied, "Sir, do you speak first." The king answered, "It seems to me that a good peace might be made between us two, if it be as the earl says. But in truth whatever agreement or peace he may make with me, if I can ever get him to my advantage I will cause him to be foully put to death, just as he hath deserved." MS. Ambassades, p. 135.

* The translator in the course of his enquiries some time ago took the Metrical History and compared it on the spot with the Castle of Conway. There he recognised the venerable arch of the eastern window of the chapel still entire, where must have stood the altar, at which this mass was performed, when the fatal oath was taken.

"Thus was the agreement made between them. One had bad intentions, the other still worse;* but as for the King, his offence was not so great, for it is often said, 'Necessity has no law,' neither did he make oath or agreement like the Earl; hereafter he will come to a shameful death for it, unless he make reckoning with God by repentance, because of that which he did surpasseth all other evil deeds, for in my opinion, when you have heard the whole, no other deed beareth resemblance to it, and because he goes on with success, he ruleth and liveth in great prosperity and governeth in peace, until death cometh, which awaiteth each of us every hour, and before whose stroke nothing can stand.

"To return to our former affair. The Earl besought the King to set out, saying, 'Sire, I pray you let us think of our journey, for well I know that the Duke hath great desire to know if peace is made.' Alas! the King knew nothing of the mischief, nor of the Earl's desire, who wished to deceive him in a manner as you may here behold. The King said to him, 'We can set out when you will; but I think it right that you should go on before to Rhuddlan, that dinner may be prepared there.' 'Just as you please,' replied the Earl, and departed. King Richard soon followed him. The Earl rode on till he saw his men under the mountain, and then was he well pleased when he saw that they were careful with good order and prudence to guard the pass. So he related unto them the whole matter, how he had succeeded, and that the King presently would come to them. Every one of them was much rejoiced at it, for they had very great desire to get possession of their lord. The King set out after him from Conway, and on his road to Rhuddlan, he passed the very broad and great water, and then rode on four miles till he mounted the rock where the Earl was concealed at the descent.' When he beheld them he was greatly astonished, saying, 'I am betrayed; what can this be?' Lord of Heaven help me!' Then were they known by their banners that might be seen floating. 'I think,' said he, 'it is the Earl who hath drawn us upon his oath.' Then were all in bitter dread. I could wish myself then in France, for I saw them almost in despair; and by good right one ought not to be surprised that they were all in distress, for not a man of them could get away from that place to flee without being stopped or taken. But that I may be understood, I must tell you how that the King had come so near to them, that it was much nearer to return to the town than to descend the rock, which was washed by the main sea. We could not get away the other side, owing to the rock; so, cost what it might, we were forced either to die or pass into the midst of the Earl's people.' He appeared armed in mail. Then did the King demean himself so sorrowfully, that it was a pity to behold. Often times did he say, 'O true God, what mischief and trouble do I undergo! Now do I plainly see that this man is taking me to the Duke, who loves us not. O Virgin Mary! sovereign queen, have mercy upon me, for if thou deignest not to look upon me, I know I am lost.' Thus spoke the King, who on that spot had no power, for as it appeared to me, we were but twenty or two-and-twenty.' So every one descended the lofty rock to the great grief of the King. And Salisbury said to him frequently,

* The event strangely verified this prediction, as the Earl of Northumberland, some few years afterwards, suffered an ignominious death as a traitor to Henry of Lancaster.

7 Thomas, the author of the Memoirs of Glyndwr, places the scene in one of the bottoms near Llandulas. Pennant conjectures it to be near Penmaen Rhôs, which is more probable. Much of the coast to the eastward of the " Orme's head," partakes of this rocky character.

8 " And here, in hidden cliffs, concealed lay
        A troop of armed men, to intercept
        The unsuspecting King; that had no way
        To free his foot, that into danger stept:
        The dreadful ocean on the one side lay;
        The hard encroaching mountain the other kept."
                                        Civil War, B. 1.

9 The principal persons composing Richard's followers, as distinctly enumerated shortly after their capture, were, exclusive of the king, the Earl of Salisbury, the Bishop of Carlisle, Sir Stephen Scroope,

Jenico, Ferriby, the author and his companion : the famous Owen* Glyndwr, at that time a squire in Richard's† service ; and probably Gwilim ap Tudor, another Welsh squire, about his person, whom he had retained with a pension of ten pounds the preceding year ;‡ and who afterwards, together with his brother Rhys, as generals under Glyndwr struggled against Henry IV. in the Welsh war ; the others might be inferior servants of the court, or mere domestics. Hall § introduces two others, John Pallett and Richard Seimer, as assured servants of the king, endeavouring at Flint to favour his escape. Pennant introduces Perkyn Legh among them ; but the head of the unfortunate Perkyn was already set upon one of the gates of Chester.

* Pennant's Wales, p. 304.

† Dugdale's Baronage, i., p. 716, b. He says Owen had been squire to the Earl Arundel. Pennant, however, *ut supra*, concludes that he was knighted before the disposal of Richard.

‡ Calend. Rot. Pat., p. 234, Rich. II., No. 30.

§ Union of the families of Lancaster and York. Introduction, p. 6.

as one utterly astounded, 'Now see I well that I am certain to be a dead man, for Duke Henry surely beareth a great hatred towards me. Alas, wherefore have we trusted the Earl upon his faith? Certes, it hath been our utter ruin: but it is too late. May Jesus, in whom I believe, vouchsafe to help us.' While thus they discoursed, it came to pass that we drew near to them, as it might be the distance of a good bow-shot.

"The Earl came and kneeled quite to the ground, saying to the King: 'Be not displeased, my rightful lord, that I should come to seek you for your better security; for the country, as you know, is disturbed by war.' Then said the King: 'I could very well go without so many people as you have brought here. I think this is not what you promised me. You told me that you had been sent with only five others. This is very ill done, considering the oath that you made. You do not seem to be sound in your loyalty, having thus taken post around this place. Depend upon it I shall return to Conway, which I left this day.' Then said the Earl: 'My lord, you accuse me of dishonour, but I solemnly declare,[1] that since I have you here, I will bring you to Duke Henry as directly as I may, for you must know that I made him such a promise these ten days past.'[2]

"Then he caused bread and wine to be brought, which he himself presented to the King, who, considering his power, durst not refuse what the Earl chose to command. When this was over, they remounted, went on straight to Rhuddlan, and dined sumptuously in the strong castle there.

"Dinner being ended, Northumberland drew out his people, being very diligent to ride on directly to Chester, where Duke Henry was awaiting the Earl with a great number of men. He was much surprised at his delay, for he knew nothing of the business that the Earl had achieved, or how he was bringing the King with him. From Rhuddlan, immediately after dinner, without further delay, we went on straight to Flint, where we stopped. That fortress had been yielded to the Duke without any resistance; and we came into this castle on the morrow, to take King Richard and the whole of his party, as you shall presently hear. Alas! you may imagine how he mourned that day in private.[3] He had reason enough for so doing, seeing that on every side his enemies, like tyrants, are all ready and desirous to put him to death. On that night greatly did he call upon his consort, the daughter of the King of France, saying thus: 'My dearest heart, my sister, I bid you farewell. For love of you am I thus detained, for never have I deserved of my people to be basely ruined. But if it be thy pleasure that I should die, ah Jesu Christ! vouchsafe to guide my soul safe to heaven, for escape or fly I cannot. Alas! father-in-law of France, never shall I see you more. Your daughter I leave unto you amongst these false, wicked, and faithless people. Wherefore I am almost in despair; for she was my joy and delight. Heaven grant that as soon as you shall know this affair, you may one day speedily avenge it, that no one may blame you for it. The matter concerneth you; soon may you hear of it. Alas! I have neither vassals, men, nor money at present to send to you; but I leave it to you. It is now too late. Alas! wherefore did we trust Northumberland, who hath delivered us into the hands of wolves? I fear that we are all dead men, for these people here have no pity. May they be utterly confounded!'

"Thus spake the King at that time to Salisbury, who made greater lamentation than ever I beheld. So did the Bishop of Carlisle. As for all the rest, not one of them went to sleep that night.[4]

---

[1] He repeats the oath taken in the chapel at Conway in the most revolting manner.

[2] This account is fully corroborated by the MS. Accounts and Ambassades, p. 220.

[3] The lamentations of Richard given in the MS. Ambassades agree in the main with these in the text; but are rather larger, and involve some curious particulars intermixed, with invocations to the Deity, the Virgin Mary, and St. John the Baptist, and many appeals to his friends in France. Among other things, he exclaims, "Ah! dear cousin of Brittanny! Alas! you said truly, at your departure, that I should never be safe while Henry of Lancaster was alive. Alas! thrice have I saved his life! for, once, my dear uncle of Lancaster (on whom God have mercy!) would have put him to death for the treason and villainy he had been guilty of. All night did I ride to preserve him from death, and his father yielded him to my request, telling me to do with him as I pleased. How true is the saying that we have no greater enemy than the man we save from the gallows! Once he drew his sword on me in the chamber of the queen, on whom God have mercy! He was of the council of the Duke of Gloucester and the Earl of Arundel; he consented to my death, that of his father, and all my council. All his offences towards me have I pardoned; nor would I believe my uncle, his father, who two or three times condemned him to death." See Account and Extracts, vol. ii. p. 222.

[4] "At one o'clock the Bishop of Carlisle exhorted them to submit to their fate with resignation; on which they ceased bewailing themselves, and went to bed." MS. Ambassades, p. 139; Mr. Allen's Extracts.

"Northumberland sent word that very night to the Duke, that he was bringing the King. The messenger came to Chester about break of day. He related to the Duke the whole. He gave the Duke a full account of King Richard, who was left at Flint. It gave him great pleasure and joy at heart, and with good reason, for there was nothing in the world that he more desired.

"The whole of Duke Henry's army was encamped about Chester, and spread themselves over a considerable extent of country. There he caused it to be proclaimed, that every one should be ready to accompany him wherever he might lead them, and the English sounded many a trumpet. Now will I tell you of the taking of the King, without seeking any more rhymes, that I may the better set down the whole of the words that passed between these two at their meeting, because I think that I thoroughly remember them. So I shall relate them in prose; for it seems that (*in verse*) one sometimes adds or brings together too many words to the matter whereof one is treating. Now, may He who made us in his own likeness, punish all those who committed this outrage!

"I shall treat in this part, of the afflictions and sorrows of King Richard in the Castle of Flint, when he waited the coming of the Duke of Lancaster, who set out from the City of Chester on Tuesday, the 22nd day of August, in the year of the Incarnation of our Lord, 1399, with the whole of his forces, which I heard estimated by many knights and squires, at upwards of one hundred thousand men, marshalled in battle array, marching along the sea-shore with great joy and satisfaction, and eager also to take their rightful and natural lord, King Richard; who early in the morning, on the said Tuesday, arose, attended by sorrows, sadness, afflictions, mourning, weeping, and lamentations; he heard mass most devoutly, like a true catholic, with his good friends the Earl of Salisbury, the Bishop of Carlisle, Sir Stephen Scroope, and other knights, who for no adversity, nor any disaster that befel the King, would desert him. There was, moreover, with them one who was son of the Countess of Salisbury, whom King Richard had knighted in Ireland; together with the eldest son of the Duke of Lancaster, and many others. There was there likewise, Janico, a Gascon squire, who showed well the true love he had for King Richard; for never, for threats of knights or squires, nor for any entreaty whatever, would he put off the service of his lord, the King, to wit, the heart, saying: 'Now, God forbid that for mortal man I should put off the order of my rightful lord, save at his own command.' So that at last it came to the knowledge of the Duke of Lancaster, who caused him to be led shamefully and basely to the Castle of Chester, expecting that from day to day they would cut off his head, for such was the common report of the people; and yet, as I have since heard, he was not put to death for it, but I can assure you, he was the last who bore the order of King Richard in England; and there he plainly showed that he was not easily inclined to treason, nor descended from a race of traitors. As to their breed and nature they are readily disposed to treason, as they evermore side with the most powerful, and him that maketh the best show, without regard to right, law, reason, or justice. Neither is this any new thing; for many a time have they undone and destroyed their king and lord, as may be known from divers histories and chronicles. And in order that I may not go too far from the matter that I have opened, I will say no more at present of their nature and condition, but return to King Richard, who, having heard mass, went upon the walls of the castle, which are large and wide on the inside, beholding the Duke of Lancaster as he came along the sea-shore with all his host. It was marvellously great, and showed such joy and satisfaction, that the sound and bruit of instruments,' horns, buisines, and trumpets, were heard even as far as the castle.

"Then did he commend himself to the holy keeping of the Lord of all the saints of Heaven in this manner:—

"'Alas! now see I plainly that the end of my days draweth nigh, since I must needs be delivered into the hands of mine enemies, who mortally hate me that never deserved it. Surely, Earl of Northumberland, thou shouldest have great fear and dread of heart, lest our Lord God take vengeance

---

' The band would have received a strong accession of military   ii. pp. 358, 359. The family of Northumberland had always several
musicians from the famous minstrels of Chester. See Burney,   minstrels in pay.

upon the sin which thou didst commit when thou vowedst so foully by him to draw us forth from Conway, where we were right secure. Now, for this, may God reward thee!'

"Thus spake King Richard to the Earl of Salisbury, to the Bishop of Carlisle, and to two other knights, Sir Stephen Scroope and Ferriby, weeping most tenderly, and greatly lamenting upon the said walls of the castle. So that, I firmly believe, no creature in this mortal world, let him be who he would, Jew or Saracen, could have beheld these five together without being heartily sorry for them. While they were in this distress, they saw a great number of persons quit the host, pricking their horses hard towards the castle to know what Richard was doing. In this first company was the Archbishop of Canterbury, Sir Thomas Percy, and the Earl of Rutland, whom Duke Henry had removed from the office of Constable of England, and from the dukedom of Aumarle, which he held aforetime of King Richard. But I firmly believe that he took them away from him for a pretence, and to blind the world, that no one might think that he knew anything of the affair or of the treason, rather than for any other cause: and yet I know not whether he was at all acquainted with it; but I am quite sure that he and Sir Thomas Percy, who had been steward to the King, that is to say, in French, 'Grand Maistre d'Ostel,' set out from the port of Milford, and carried off his men and his property, in consequence of which, as I told you before, they were robbed in Wales,' and they went over to the Duke, as it appeared; for they came the very first to the Castle of Flint, bearing the order of Duke Henry, not the heart. The archbishop entered first, and the others after him; they went up to the donjon. Then the King came down from the walls, to whom they made very great obeisance, kneeling on the ground. The King caused them to rise, and drew the archbishop aside, and they talked together for a very long while. What they said I know not, but the Earl of Salisbury afterwards told me that he had comforted the King in a very gentle manner, telling him not to be alarmed, and that no harm should happen to his person. The Earl of Rutland, at that time, said nothing to the King, but kept at as great a distance as he could from him, just as though he had been ashamed to see himself in his presence. They mounted their horses again, and returned to Duke Henry, who was drawing very nigh; for between the City of Chester and the castle, there are but ten short miles, which are equal to five French leagues, or thereabouts. And there is neither hedge nor bush between them; nothing but the sea-shore; and on the other side lofty rocks and mountains. And he assured that he made a fine show of them as he came; for they were right well marshalled, and their numbers were such, that, for my own part, I never saw so many people together. I think that the chief captain of the Duke's army was Sir Henry Percy, whom they hold to be the best knight in England.' The King went up again upon the walls, and saw that the army was two bow shots from the castle. Then he, together with those who were with him, began anew to make great lamentations, bewailing most piteously his consort, Isabel of France, and calling upon our Lord Jesus Christ, saying, 'Good Lord God! I commend myself into thy holy keeping, and cry thee mercy, that thou mayest pardon all my sins; since it is thy pleasure that I should be delivered into the hands of mine enemies; and if they cause me to die, I will take death patiently as thou didst for us all.' While he thus spoke, the host approached the castle, and entirely surrounded it even to the sea, in very fair array. Then the Earl of Northumberland went to Duke Henry, who was drawn up with his men at the foot of the mountains.' They talked together rather a long while, and concluded that he should not enter the castle,

---

⁶ He is rather guarded in speaking of the conduct of Sir Thomas, whose reputation stood high; and perhaps for this reason he never indulges in any expressions personally derogatory to him. Carte says, "the Earl of Leicester was really concerned for the king; but seeing no remedy, broke his rod in the great hall of that castle, and dissolved the household. He did it, according to Walsingham, by desire of Richard, bidding them preserve themselves for better times."

⁷ Henry could not have selected a better captain to command under him. He continued in his situation at Berwick: 1 Henry IV. made him governor of Roxburgh Castle, sheriff of Northumberland, with a grant of the castle and lordship of Bamborough for his life, justice of Chester, North Wales, and Flintshire, and constable of

the castles of Chester, Flint, Conway, and Caernarvon. The next year saw him in opposition to Henry IV. under colour of advancing into Scotland: he raised and trained a force in the Marches, and drew southward, probably over the ground he had traced in 1399, with the captive king through Cheshire to Lichfield, and thence to Shrewsbury. His uncle, Sir Thomas Percy, joined him, and the fatal issue of their attempt is familiar to every reader. Never for a time was field more severely contended than at Shrewsbury.

⁸ Flint Castle stands upon a rock at the bottom of the town; but we cannot make out the mountains which he speaks of, unless he means the rising ground to the westward, which is now all cultivated, and which after various undulations terminate in the Clwydian Hills.

till such time as the King had dined, because he was fasting. So the Earl returned to the castle. The table being laid, the King sat down to dinner, and caused the Bishop of Carlisle, the Earl of Salisbury, and the two knights, Sir Stephen Scroope and Ferriby, to be seated, saying thus, ' My good, true, and loyal friends, being in point of death for maintaining loyalty, sit down with me.' In the meantime a great number of knights, squires, and archers, quitted the army of Duke Henry, and came to the said castle, desiring to behold their King, not for any goodwill that they bore him, but for the great thirst that they had to ruin him, and to put him to death. They went to see him at dinner, and published throughout the castle that, as soon as the Duke should come, all those that were with him, without any exception, would have their heads cut off. And they, moreover, said, that it was not at all certain whether the King would escape. At the hearing of this news, every one had great fear and dread at heart for himself. Because nature teacheth every creature to fear and dread death more than anything else besides. For my own part, I do not think that I ever was so much afraid as I was at that time; considering their great contempt, and how unwilling to listen to right reason or loyalty. And forasmuch as nature constrained me to dread death, my companion and myself consulted Lancaster, the herald, who, with a great number, had come to the castle to the King: so I besought him, for the love of our Lord, that he would help us to save our lives, and that he would be pleased to bring us to Duke Henry, his master. Then he answered us, that he would do it right willingly.' The King was a very long time at table, not for anything he ate; but because he well knew that, so soon as he had dined, the Duke would come for him, to carry him off, or put him to death. They also let him remain a long time at table because he was fasting. After he had dined, the Archbishop of Canterbury and the Earl of Northumberland went in search of the Duke of Lancaster. He quitted his men, who were drawn up in a very fair array before the castle, and with nine [1] or eleven of the greatest lords, who were with him, came to the King. At the entrance to the castle, Lancaster, the herald, brought us before the Duke, kneeling on the ground: and the herald told him, in the English language, that we were from France, and that the King had sent us with King Richard into Ireland, for pleasure, and to see the country; and earnestly entreated him to save our lives. Then the Duke made answer in French: ' My young men, fear not, nor be dismayed, at anything that you behold; keep close to me, and I will answer for your lives.' This reply was most delightful to us. After this the Duke entered the castle, armed at all points, except his basinet, as you may see in this history. Then they made the King, who had dined in the donjon, come down to meet Duke Henry, who, as soon as he perceived him at a distance, bowed to the ground; and as they approached each other, he bowed a second time, with his cap in his hand; and then the King took off his bonnet, and spoke first in this manner:—
' Fair cousin of Lancaster, you be right welcome.' Then Duke Henry replied, bowing to the ground, ' My lord, I come sooner than you sent for me; and I will tell you why I did so. The common report of your people is, that you have, for the space of twenty, or two-and-twenty years, governed them very badly, and very rigorously, and in so much, that they are not well contented therewith. But if it please our Lord, I will help you to govern them better than they have been governed in time past.' King Richard then answered him. "Fair cousin, since it pleaseth you, it pleaseth us well.' And be assured, that these are the very words that they two spoke together, without taking away or adding anything, for I heard and understood them very well. And the Earl of Salisbury, and another aged knight who was one of the council of Duke Henry, told me the same in French. He told me as we rode to Chester, that Merlin,[2] and Bede, had, from the time in which they lived, prophesied of the taking and ruin of the King,

---

[*] They probably recognised this herald from having seen him in the suite at Paris. His style was " Lancaster King at Arms."

[1] " He brought over with him the Archbishop of Canterbury, the young Earl of Arundel and Lord Cobham ; and had been joined at different places on his march by the Earl of Northumberland, the Earls of Worcester, Rutland, and Westmoreland; Lords Bardolf, Beaumont, Berkeley, Carleton, Darcy, Loval, Ross, Scales, and Willoughby ; Sir John Stanley, Sir Henry Percy, Sir Edmund

Mortimer.[*] Lord Berkeley was certainly one of these." See Dugdale's Baronage, i. p. 360.

[2] The prophecies of Merlin in those days had their practical influence throughout Wales and England, and were widely circulated through the Continent. They were printed at Paris, in French, A.D. 1498 ; in London, by Wynkyn de Worde, A.D. 1529 ; and

[*] Vita Ric. II. p. 154 ; Walsingham, Baker, and Carte.

and that if I were in his castle, he would show me the prophesy, in manner and form, as I had seen it come to pass, saying thus :—

" ' There shall be a King in Albion, who shall reign for the space of twenty or two-and-twenty years in great honour, and in great power, and he shall be allied and united with those of Gaul; which King shall be undone in the parts of the North, in a triangular place.' Thus, the knight told me, it was written in a book belonging to him. The triangular* place he applied to the town of Conway : and for this he had a very good reason, as though it had been so laid down by exact measurement. In the said town of Conway was the King sufficiently undone, for the Earl of Northumberland drew him forth as you have heard before, by the treaty which he made with him; and from that time he had no power. Thus the knight held this prophecy to be true, and attached thereto great faith and credit, for such is the nature of the people of that country that they thoroughly believed in prophesies, phantoms, and witchcraft, and had recourse to them very willingly. Yet in my opinion this is not right; but shows a great want of faith.

" Thus, you have heard, came Duke Henry to the castle and spake unto the King, to the Bishop of Carlisle, and the two knights, Sir Stephen Scroope and Ferriby; howbeit, unto the Earl of Salisbury he spake not at all, but sent word to him by a knight in this manner :—' Earl of Salisbury, be assured that no more than you deigned to speak to my lord the Duke of Lancaster, when you were in Paris, at Christmas last, will he speak unto you.' Then was the Earl much abashed, and had great fear and dread at heart, for he saw plainly that the Duke mortally hated him. The said Duke Henry called aloud, with a stern and savage voice, ' Bring out the King's horses;' and then they brought him two little nags⁴ not worth forty franks;' the King mounted one, and the Earl of Salisbury the other. Every one got on horseback, and we set out from the said castle of Flint about two hours after mid-day.

" In form and manner as you have heard, did Duke Henry take King Richard, his lord, and he brought him with great joy and satisfaction to Chester,⁶ which place he had quitted in the morning. And know that with great difficulty could the thunder of heaven have been heard, for the loud noise of their instruments, horns, buisines, and trumpets; insomuch that they made the sea-shore resound with them.

" Thus the Duke entered the City of Chester, to whom the common people paid great reverence, praising our lord, and shouting after the King, as it were in mockery. The Duke led him straight to the castle, which is right fair and strong, and caused him to be lodged in the dungeon. And then gave him in keeping to the son of the Duke of Gloucester,⁷ and the son of the Earl of Arundel, who hated him more than any man in the world, because King Richard had put their fathers to death. There he saw his brother the Duke of Exeter, but neither durst nor was able to speak to him. Presently after the Duke sat down to dinner, and made the Archbishop of Canterbury sit above him, and at some distance below

at Venice, in 1554.—See *Warton's History of English Poetry*, iii. p. 146.

³ The triangular shape of the town of Conway may be well distinguished from a small terrace or rampart at the western entrance, which commands the whole of the walls. Here Richard with proper precaution and a moderate force might have felt secure, or, as a last resource, might have found means of escaping to sea. Conway must have been neglected or very ill defended after the king was enticed out of it. Gwilym ap Tudor and Rhys, his brother, received a pardon, 2 Henry IV., for having, with many of his people, taken the castle and burnt the town.—Col. Rot. Parl., 3, p. 2, 2 Henry IV. This fortress had been, or was afterwards, used as a prison. John Claydon, a Lollard of London, was confined in it for two years, in 1404, by Braybrook, Bishop of London. See Concilia, iii., p. 372. Goodwin in Braybrook.

⁴ This studied mortification was particularly hurtful to the feelings of Richard, whose taste and fondness for fine horses were proverbial;

and it was the custom at this period to mount criminals of high rank upon the most miserable jades that could be found ; it was one of the final acts of degradation before execution. Thus the Duke of Lancaster, in 1322, and Archbishop Scroope, in 1405, were led to the places where they suffered death. With respect to the latter, the celebrated Judge Gascoigne firmly refused to obey the orders of Henry IV. in passing judgment upon Scroope. " Neither you, my lord king, nor any of your lieges in your name, can legally, according to the laws of the kingdom, sentence any archbishop to death." Fulthorp, however, was more complying.

⁵ The value of a franc at this time was 3s. 4d. *Anderson.*

⁶ According to some authors the king was brought to Chester on the 20th of August. Carte places this event on the 19th of August.

⁷ When Henry gave the king in charge of these young men, he said to them, " Here is the murderer of your fathers ; you must be answerable for him." MS. Ambassades ; Accounts and Extracts, ii., p. 225.

him the Duke of Exeter, brother to King Richard, the Earl of Westmoreland, the Earl of Rutland, the Earl of Northumberland, and Sir Thomas Percy: all these were seated at Duke Henry's table. And the King abode in the tower, with his good friends, the Earl of Salisbury and the Bishop of Carlisle, and the two knights; and from thenceforth we could never see him, unless it were abroad on the journey; and we were forbidden to speak to him any more, or to any of the others.

" Duke Henry stayed three days at Chester, and held a very great council: they determined that they had too great a number of people, since the King was taken; and that thirty or forty thousand men were sufficient to take the King to London; and that otherwise the country would be too much distressed, seeing that it had been very greatly wasted as they came. So the Duke sent back the greater part of his people, and set out from the city on the fourth day after the taking of the King, taking the direct road to London.[8] He arrived at Lichfield, a very fair little city, and there poor King Richard thought to escape from them by night,[9] and let himself down into a garden, through the window of a large tower, in which they had lodged him. But I believe it was not our Lord's pleasure that he should escape; and he was perceived and most villainously thrust back into the tower; and from that time forth, at all hours of the night, he had ten or twelve armed men to guard him without his being able to sleep.[1]

" Now it came to pass that they of London heard the news of the taking of their rightful lord, King Richard, who set out in a very fair company, to wit, five or six of the greatest burgesses, governors of the City. They came to meet Duke Henry, and know that I heard it related by many knights and squires, that as soon as they were arrived in the presence of the Duke, they requested of him, on the part of the commons of London,[2] that he would cut off the head of their rightful lord, King Richard, and all those who were taken with him, without bringing him any further, which request Duke Henry would not grant, and he excused himself as prudently as he could, saying, ' It would be a very great disgrace to us for ever if we should thus put him to death; but we will bring him to London, and then he shall be judged by the parliament.'

When they drew within six or seven miles of London, the mayor, accompanied by a very great number of the commons, marshalled and clad, each trade by itself, in different garments, drawn up in rows and armed, came to meet Duke Henry, with a great number of instruments and trumpets, showing great joy and great satisfaction. The sword was borne before the said mayor as before the King. When they came together they saluted him (the King), and Duke Henry afterwards, to whom they paid much greater respect than they had done to the King,[3] shouting in their language, with a loud and fearful voice, ' Long live the good Duke of Lancaster;' and they said, one to another, that God had showed them a great miracle when he sent the said Duke to them, and how that he had conquered the whole kingdom of

[8] The route of the army is thus laid down by the Evesham historian, and the line he has given seems right: "After the capture, to Chester, Nantwich, Newcastle, Stafford, Lichfield, Coventry, Daventry, Northampton, Dunstable, St. Alban's, London. The king never changed his clothes during the whole of the way."

[9] The recollection of what had passed a few months back in this city, must have affected the wretched king. Lichfield seems to have been a favourite spot with him. Here, on his way to Shrewsbury, he had kept the Christmas of 1398, accompanied by foreign noblemen, and the Pope's nuncio, with magnificent tournaments and feasting. The Monk of Evesham states the daily consumption to have been twenty-eight oxen, and three hundred sheep. The king was also present at the installation of two bishops at this city, which made him acquainted with the place, and accounts for his attempts to escape.

[1] The MS. Ambassades states that "he was guarded as a thief or a murderer. Of his wailings and complaints no one knew anything except those who guarded him."* According to Otterbourne he was watched every night by a thousand men; but that writer gives too favourable an account of the duke's treatment of him. The king requested that he might not be intruded upon nor insulted by the common people at meals or on the journey, and his friends were permitted to sup and pass * the night with him.

[2] The Londoners had not forgotten the quarrel they had with him in 1392, when, upon their refusal to lend him money, he threatened to deprive them of their rights and privileges and fleeced them of ten thousand pounds. Hist. Angl., p. 347. Froissart enlarges upon their disaffection, and Walsingham gives them a very bad character; he says that an account of their iniquities would be sufficient to fill a volume, p. 348.

[3] " The Earl of Derby was a hundred times more beloved than King Richard. The mayor and principal citizens had accompanied him to Dartford on his departure into banishment." Ib. xii. c. 13; Ib. c. 7.

* Accounts and Extracts, ii., p. 225.

* Otterbourne, p. 208.

England in less than a month, and that he well deserved to be King who thus knew how to conquer; and they most devoutly gave loud thanks to our Lord for it, saying that it was his will, and that otherwise he could not have done it.

"When within about two miles of London, the Duke caused the whole army to halt on the one side and the other. Then he spoke thus aloud to the commons of the said city: 'Fair sirs, behold your King; consider what you will do with him:' and they answered with a loud voice, 'We will take him to Westminster.'⁴ And so he delivered the King unto them, much in a like manner as did the Jews deliver our Saviour, did Duke Henry give up his rightful lord to the rabble of London, in order that, if they should put him to death, he might say, 'I am innocent of this deed.'

"Thus did the commons and rabble of London carry their lawful King to Westminster. The MS. Ambassades states, that the King was, on the next day, carried through the City of London on a sorry horse, with an open space around him. Some felt pity for him, but others expressed great joy, abusing him, and saying, 'Now are we avenged upon this little bastard who has governed us so ill.'⁵ Several citizens had contrived to kill him as he passed through the city, but the mayor and aldermen having timely notice of their design, prevented it by their vigilance. Richard and his compeers were kept in prison until the month of October, on the first Wednesday of which he was prevailed upon to call the parliament together.

"So they all assembled with an evil intention at Westminster, without the City of London. This is the truth. First (came) all the prelates, archbishops, and bishops. Alas! what were their thoughts, what their resolution? They must have wrath in their hearts to agree to such a parliament. The dukes came foremost, then marquises, earls and knights, squires, varlets, and archers; with many sort of folk, who were neither noble nor gentle, but all false and traitors; there they were in such great heaps, and determined to elect another king, which they did most wrongfully, as you shall hereafter be told. The prelates were seated on one side, and on the other, as says my informant (for at this time our author had left England), sat all the lords, of all degrees, great and small.

"First of all, on the right sat Duke Henry, and next to him the Duke of York, his fair cousin, whose heart was not right faithful towards his nephew, King Richard; after him, on the same side, sat the Duke of Aumarle, the son of the Duke of York; and then the Duke of Surrey, who was ever loyal and true. Next to him sat the Duke of Exeter, who had no reason to rejoice, for he now saw before him preparations made for the ruin of the King, his brother. The next was the Marquis of Dorset, and the Earl of Arundel, who was right young and active. The Earl of Norvic (Warwick?) was not forgotten in the account, neither he of la Marche. There was one who was Earl of Stamford, and another called the Earl of Pembroke, and close to him was seated the Earl of Salisbury, who so faithfully loved the King to the last. The Earl of Devonshire was there, as I heard. All other earls and lords, the greatest in the kingdom, were present at this assembly; their pleasure and desire being to choose another king. There in fair fashion stood the Earl of Northumberland and the Earl of Westmoreland the whole of the day; and for the better discharge of their duty, they kneeled very often; wherefore, or how, I cannot tell.

"The Archbishop of Canterbury next arose, and preached before all the people in Latin. The whole of his sermon was upon this, 'Habuit Jacob benedictionem a patre suo:—How Jacob had gotten the blessing instead of Esau, although he were the eldest son.' This he set forth as true. Alas! what a text for a sermon! He made it to prove in conclusion, that King Richard ought to have no part in the Crown of England, and that the Prince ought to have had the realm and territory. These were very ungrateful people; after they had all held him to be rightful king and lord for two and twenty years, by a great error they ruined him with one accord.

---

⁴ The duke then sent for the king, who arrived with his face bathed in tears, and delivered him up to them, who carried him up to Westminster.

⁵ MS. Ambassades, pp. 143, 144; MS. 635, p. 23; vol. xii. p. 26. Froissart explains the origin of this charge of illegitimacy.

"When the Archbishop had finished his sermon, a lawyer, who was a most sage doctor, arose and commanded silence. Then he began to read aloud an instrument, which related how Richard, some time King of England, had avowed and confessed, of his own will,[6] without compulsion, that he was neither capable nor worthy, wise nor prudent, nor gentle (enough) to bear the crown; and that it was his wish to resign it into the hands of another worthy man (*prudomme*) of noble birth and greater wisdom than himself. Thus, right or wrong, they by argument caused King Richard to make a declaration, in the Tower of London, in a most wicked manner; and then this parliament read the instrument before all. Its witnesses were bishops[7] and abbots who affirmed and testified that the instrument was entirely true. Now consider this testimony: never was such an outrage heard of.

"When the reading of the instrument was ended, all kept silence, and the Archbishop then rose, and took up anew his discourse, laying his foundation upon the instrument aforesaid, and speaking so loud that he was plainly heard of the people. 'Forasmuch as it is thus, and that Richard, some time King of England, hath by his words, and of his own good will, acknowledged and confessed that he is not sufficiently able, worthy, or well skilled to govern the kingdom, it were right good to advise and choose another king.'

"Alas! fair sirs, what an evil deed! There they were, judges, and also the party accusing. It is not a thing justly divided, nor of legal right; because there were no men in that place for the old King, save three or four, who durst upon no account gainsay them. All that they said or did was the greatest mockery, for great and small, they all agreed, without any dividing, that they should have a king who better knew how to discharge his duty than Richard did. And when the Archbishop had finished declaring his will and his evil intention, and the people had replied according to that which they had heard, he began to interrogate and question each man by himself. 'Will you, that the Duke of York be your king?' All in good order answered, 'No.' 'Will you, then, have his eldest son, who is Duke of Aumarle?' They answered aloud, Let no one speak to us of him.' Once more he again asked: 'Will you then have his youngest son?' They said, 'Nay, truly.' He then asked them concerning many others, but the people stopped at none of those that he had named; and then the Archbishop ceased to say much. He next enquired aloud: 'Will you have the Duke of Lancaster?' They all at once replied, with so loud a voice, that the account which I heard appeared marvellous to me, 'Yea, we will have him and no other.' Then they praised Jesus Christ.

"Then did Duke Henry, who at that time was on his knees, most solemnly rise and declare before all, that he accepted the regal power, since it was thus ordained of God; he himself afterwards questioned them all, and asked them if it was their will. With a marvellously loud voice they answered, 'Yea.' This so quickened him, (put such a flea in his ear,) that without further delay he accepted and took possession of the Crown of England.

"Soon after they made good King Richard acquainted with the truth of this melancholy business, which was piteous for him to hear. Then he wept and said: 'Make ready death and assault me; no one can aid me more, since I have lost my friends. Gracious Lord, who wast crucified, deign to have mercy upon me; for I can live thus no longer.'"[8]

Richard had not long been a prisoner when he met with an untimely death. Henry the Fourth despatched Sir Piers Exton to rid him of his rival, which he executed in the manner commonly related.[9] The accounts given of the manner and cause of his death by different chroniclers vary considerably;

---

[6] This is, however, contradicted by Northumberland himself, who ought to have known what passed.

[7] The Archbishops of York and Canterbury, the Bishop of Hereford, the Prior of Canterbury and Abbot of Westminster, were witnesses to the formal act of resignation; and the Bishop of St. Asaph and Abbot of Glastonbury, among the commissioners in the sentence of deprivation.

[8] The following entry occurs at the end of the MS. from which the text is taken. "This book of the taking of King Richard of England belongeth to my Lord Charles of Anjou, Earl of Maine and Montaign, and Governor of Languedoc. CHARLES." The latter word is an autograph.

[9] See Fabian, Hall, Hayward, MS. Ambassades, and most of the other MSS. in Bibl. du Roy; Le Labonneur, Hist. Charles VI.

but the version given by Fabian is the most probable, and thus dramatised by Shakespeare in his *Richard the Second* :—

SCENE IV.

Enter EXTON *and a* Servant.

Exton. Didst thou not mark the king, what words he spake !
Have I no friend will rid me of this living fear !
Was it not so !
  Serv. Those were his very words.
  Exton. Have I no friend ! quoth he : he spake it twice.
And urg'd it twice together ; did he not !
  Serv. He did.
  Exton. And, speaking it, he wistfully look'd on me ;
As who should say,—I would thou wert the man
That would divorce this terror from my heart ;
Meaning, the king at Pomfret. Come, let 's go ;
I am the king's friend, and will rid his foe.

SCENE V.

   *   *   *   *   *   *
   *   *   *   *   *   *

Enter KEEPER, *with a dish.*

  Keep. Fellow, give place ; here is no longer stay.
                               [To the Groom.
  K. Rich. If thou love me, 'tis time thou wert away.
  Groom. What my tongue dares not, that my heart shall say.
  Keep. My lord, will it please you to fall to !
  K. Rich. Taste of it first, as thou art wont to do.
  Keep. My lord, I dare not ; Sir Pierce of Exton, who
Lately came from the king, commands the contrary.
  K. Rich. The devil take Henry of Lancaster and thee !
Patience is stale, and I am weary of it. *[Beats the* Keeper.

Enter EXTON, *and* Servants, *armed.*

  K. Rich. How now ! what means death in this rude assault !
Villain, thy own hand yields thy death's instrument.
                 [Snatching a weapon, and killing one.
Go thou, and fill another room in hell.
        [He kills another, then EXTON *strikes him down.*
That hand shall burn in never-quenching fire,
That staggers thus my person.—Exton, thy fierce hand
Hath with the king's blood stain'd the king's own land.
Mount, mount, my soul ! thy seat is up on high ;
Whilst my gross flesh sinks downwards, here to die. *[Dies.*
  Exton. As full of valour, as of royal blood :
Both have I spilt ; O, would the deed were good !
For now the devil, that told me—I did well,
Says, that this deed is chronicled in hell.
This dead king to the living king I 'll bear ;
Take hence the rest, and give them burial here.

SCENE VI.—WINDSOR. *A Room in the Castle.*

Flourish. Enter BOLINGBROKE *and* YORK, *with* Lords *and*
Attendants.

  Boling. Kind uncle York, the latest news we hear
Is—that the rebels have consumed with fire

Our town of Cicester in Glostershire ;
But whether they be ta'en, or slain, we hear not.

Enter NORTHUMBERLAND.

Welcome, my lord : What is the news !
  North. First to thy sacred state wish I all happiness.
The next news is,—I have to London sent
The heads of Salisbury, Spencer, Blunt, and Kent :
The manner of their taking may appear
At large discoursed in this paper here. *[Presenting a paper.*
  Boling. We thank thee, gentle Percy, for thy pains ;
And to thy worth will add right worthy gains.

Enter FITZWALTER.

  Fitz. My lord, I have from Oxford sent to London
The heads of Brocas, and Sir Bennet Seely ;
Two of the dangerous consorted traitors,
That sought at Oxford thy dire overthrow.
  Boling. Thy pains, Fitzwalter, shall not be forgot ;
Right noble is thy merit, well I wot.

Enter PERCY *with the* BISHOP OF CARLISLE.

  Percy. The grand conspirator, abbot of Westminster,
With clog of conscience, and sour melancholy,
Hath yielded up his body to the grave ;
But here is Carlisle living, to abide
The kingly doom, and sentence of his pride.
  Boling. Carlisle, this is your doom :—
Choose out some secret place, some reverend room,
More than thou hast, and with it joy thy life ;
So, as thou liv'st in peace, die free from strife :
For though mine enemy thou hast ever been,
High sparks of honour in thee have I seen.

Enter EXTON, *with* Attendants, *bearing a coffin.*

  Exton. Great king, within this coffin I present
Thy buried fear : herein all breathless lies
The mightiest of thy greatest enemies,
Richard of Bordeaux, by me hither brought.
  Boling. Exton, I thank thee not ; for thou hast wrought
A deed of slander, with thy fatal hand,
Upon my head, and all this famous land.
  Exton. From your own mouth, my lord, did I this deed.
  Boling. They love not poison that do poison need,
Nor do I thee ; though I did wish him dead,
I hate the murderer, love him murdered.
The guilt of conscience take thou for thy labour,
But neither my good word, nor princely favour :
With Cain go wander through the shade of night,
And never show thy head by day nor light.
Lords, I protest my soul is full of woe,
That blood should sprinkle me to make me grow.
Come, mourn with me for what I do lament,
And put on sullen black, incontinent ;
I 'll make a voyage to the Holy Land,
To wash this blood off from my guilty hand :—
March sadly after ; grace my mournings here,
In weeping after this untimely bier. *[Exeunt.*

HOUSE OF LANCASTER.

ENRY THE FOURTH was crowned by Archbishop Fitzalan on the 13th of October, 1399; and on this occasion the ampulla was first employed. After Henry had gone to the Tower, he created forty-six knights of the Bath, among whom were three of his own sons. The procession from the Tower to Westminster was unusually spendid, no less than six thousand horses having been employed on the occasion.[1]

An extreme desire of swaying the British sceptre, was the most prominent feature in this King's character. Deterred by no difficulties, and awed by no scruples of humanity, he obtained the crown by means the most unjustifiable; and the murder of Richard will be an indelible and eternal blot on his memory. His tumultuous reign, and his unsuccessful military operations, especially against the Welsh, detract greatly from his fame, both as a warrior and as a statesman. His reign was short and disturbed. He had gained the sceptre through the unpopularity of the preceding King, and not through his plodding and ambitious pretensions. He acquired power by force without right, and contrary to the national rules of hereditary descent. His claim could not stand upon its own merits; it rested upon the necessities caused by the vices of others; it succeeded by the temporary support of a few of the great and of the populace, and principally through the assistance of the Earl of Northumberland and the clergy, and it had no foundation if their humours changed. It was, therefore, naturally mutable[2] and insecure. He had not been long on the throne before a conspiracy was entered into, to assassinate him at Oxford; and afterwards another conspiracy to seize him at Windsor, and to destroy him. The King was privately informed of the plot, and eluded the blow by withdrawing secretly to London. Those ill-advised noblemen, the Earls of Salisbury and Huntington, as well as others, flew upon their expected prey with vain attempt. They had dressed up an impostor somewhat resembling Richard, to personate that Prince, and they were joined by many. But finding Henry prepared with twenty thousand men to encounter them, they retreated towards Wales. At Cirencester, they were defeated by the citizens, who took the Earl of Salisbury and put him to death, and shortly afterwards the Earl of Huntington was taken and beheaded. Many of their adherents were

---

[1] Froissart gives the following account of Henry IV.'s procession. " The Duke of Lancaster left the Tower this Sunday after dinner, on his return to Westminster; he was bare-headed, and had round his neck the order of the King of France. The Prince of Wales, six dukes, six earls, eighteen barons, accompanied him, and there were of knights and other nobility from eight to nine hundred horse in the procession. He passed through the streets of London, which were all handsomely decorated with tapestries and other rich hangings: there were nine fountains in Cheapside and other streets he passed through, that ran perpetually with white and red wines. The whole cavalcade amounted to six thousand horse, that escorted the Duke from the Tower to Westminster."

[2] The embarrassment of his title probably produced the farce acted on his coronation. He was anointed with oil, stated to have been given by the Virgin Mary to Becket. It had lain hid until it was found in Richard's reign, with an inscription, predicting that the sovereigns anointed with it should be champions of the Church. The Archbishop refused to apply it to Richard, but poured it upon Henry, to create a popular impression that he was appointed by, and chosen of heaven. Walsingham details this miracle, p. 401.

executed. The death of Richard, dreadful in its nature, mysterious as to its cause, and suspicious from the time of its occurrence, followed these events.[3]

The Scots attempted an invasion under the brave Earl Douglas, whom the Earl of Northumberland and his gallant son, Hotspur, confronted at Halidon Hill. The flower of the Scottish chivalry was taken or destroyed, and its celebrated leader became the captive of the Percies.

A more dangerous movement occurred in Wales, under the celebrated Owen Glyndwr, who complained to Henry that some of his lands had been taken from him by Lord Grey de Ruthin, one of the King's favourites. He attempted, by peaceful means, but unsuccessfully, to recover his possessions. The King, instead of listening to Glyndwr's complaint, directed him to be pursued as a disturber of the public peace, without a hearing. Fired with indignation at such partiality and injustice, Owen flew to arms, and the Welsh, delighted at seeing a Cambrian of abilities resenting the wrongs of himself and his countrymen, and waging war with the English, rallied round him by thousands. The mountains of Snowdon afforded him a refuge against Henry's forces; and when the King retired, he emerged from his fastnesses to achieve new successes, new devastations, and increased popularity. As he approached Herefordshire, Earl Mortimer, a nobleman whose title to the throne preceded Henry's, led out its militia to chastise him, but was beaten and taken prisoner. Owen's talents and activity, the means of defence afforded by the mountains of Wales, the internal disturbances of England, and Henry's personal disquietudes, combined to give Glyndwr so many advantages to continue his triumphs. Our hero enjoyed another advantage, which arose from some misunderstanding or dispute between the King and the Duke of Northumberland, who had so materially assisted in placing Henry on the throne: any solicitations for favour from such parties seem a demand; and delay or refusal of the concession will be thought an insult and a wrong. Hence Northumberland[4] and his family could not avoid seeming presumptuous, intruding, insatiable, and dangerous to Henry; while he would always be supposed by them to be more or less ungrateful, envious, treacherous, and malignant. The recollection of the deceit which Northumberland practised upon Richard, would also preclude all confidence in his future demeanour, however specious, or even truly honourable. Such fair semblance had he shown to his former master, when he was practising to betray him. What could give his new lord an assurance against his future instability, or distinguish his allegiance from his hypocrisy? The wicked man must submit to be suspected, and expect to be sacrificed by his companions in iniquity.

"It is to these general causes of mutual dissatisfaction," says Mr. Turner, "between parties so situated, that we must look for the origin of the warfare between the Percies and the throne.[5] The King had not been a niggard in his favours to them. He made the head of the house, and his son, lords of the northern parts of Wales, and his brother, the Earl of Worcester, governor of the Prince of Wales.[6] This man is stated to have abandoned his charge, and to have incited his nephew, the famous Hotspur, to rebel. In his young mind, proud of the undeviating favours of fortune, animated by its own love of enterprise and gallant daring, too sensible of its own merit, stimulated to ambition by deserved popularity,[7] and constitutionally warm and excitable, it was not difficult for a respected kinsman, to rouse irritability and dissatisfaction. He refused to bring his Scotch prisoner to the King, and was offended that he would not ransom Mortimer.[8] The family united in a determination to rebel. Douglas joined them. They spread a report that Richard

---

[3] See Walsingham, p. 105.

[4] Northumberland brought some of them before the king at Westminster. The Parliament Rolls mention the Stewart, son and heir to the Duke of Albany; the King of Scotland's brother, three other Scotchmen, and three French. But Douglas was not among them. Their reception is thus described :—"They were led by the Earl of Northumberland and several lords, before our lord the king in his palace at Westminster, and knelt three times to his royal person. Henry was requested to treat them honourably and graciously, which he did. He told them they need not be troubled for what had happened, they were taken in the field like valiant knights; they were ordered to another room and to eat with the king. Walsingham, p. 407, 408.

[5] History of the Middle Ages, vol. ii. p. 263.

[6] Ibid.

[7] Walsingham says, that in him "spes erat reposita totius populi," p. 409.

[8] Thus Harding, who was with the Percies, states,

> "But Sir Henry his sonne there would not bryng
> His prisoners in no wise to the kyng.
> But the kyng he prayed for Mortimer
> That ransomed might he been with him so;
> He said him nay, for he was taken prisoner
> By his consent and treason for his foo."—*Chron.* p. 360.

F F

was alive. Their public manifestoes were as empty, and probably as false, as such productions usually are; they seem to have produced no general sympathy. Hotspur now resolved to raise Mortimer, his wife's brother, to the throne. But the country appears to have considered it more as a personal quarrel between two great families, than as a national concern; for the force with which the King went down to the battle at Shrewsbury, where Hotspur met him (and chose to fight before his father, who was detained by sickness, had joined him), was but fourteen thousand men.[9]

One of the most distinguished men of this period was Owen Glyndwr. He was fifth in descent from Gruffydd, to whom Edward I., in 1282, made a grant of Glyndyfrdwy, and who wrote himself, in 1279, "Griffinus Vychan, filius Griffini ap Madog, dominus de Yal." Gruffydd, or Griffin ap Madog, the father of this Griffin, is the same whom Mathew Paris, in 1241, calls "potentissimus Wallensium," and who was great grandson of Madog, the last prince of Powys Fadog. Besides this high descent on his father's side, Ellen, the mother of Glyndwr, was great grand-daughter of Llywelyn, the last prince of North Wales; and thus he united in his person, and was not slow to nourish in his mind, pretensions upon the two ancient Principalities of North Wales and Powys.[1] To the pride of high birth, he added the advantage of an acute mind, an ardent courage, and a cultivated understanding. He was born in the year 1364, had received the best education that the age could afford, at what Fortescue[2] calls the university of London, and had actually been called to the bar, a distinction conferred at that time only on men of the first families. He was afterwards introduced into the family of the Duke of Hereford,[3] where he held the post of an esquire, till the hereditary claims of his princely lineage involved him in a dispute with Lord de Grey of Ruthin, who had taken possession of a great portion of Glyndwr's estates. He left the court and retired to his native fastnesses on the banks of the Dee. Sycharth was the name of Owen's seat; it was situated at Glyndwrdwy, between Llangollen and Corwen. Iolo Goch, the celebrated poet of this period, resided here for some time. He came on a pressing invitation from Owen, who, knowing the mighty influence of this order of men over the ancient Britons, made his house, as Iolo says, a sanctuary for the bards. He made them the instruments of his future operations, and to prepare the minds of his people against the time of his intended insurrection. In one of his poems Iolo gives a splendid description of Owen's mansion; he compares it in point of magnificence to Westminster Abbey, and says his hospitality was unbounded.

The bard speaks feelingly of the wine, the ale, the bragod, and the white bread; nor does he forget the kitchen, nor that important officer, the cook. Such was the hospitality of this house that the place of porter was useless, nor were locks nor bolts known. To sum up all, no one could be *hungry* or *dry* at Sycharth.

The bard pays all due praise to the lady of the house and her offspring.[4] The original in Welsh is beautifully worded according to the rules of alliteration. The following is a translation:—

> "His wife, the best of wives!
> Happy am I in her wine and metheglin.
> Eminent woman of a knightly family.
> Honourable, beneficent, noble.
> His children came in pairs;
> A beautiful nest of chieftains."

---

[9] " With Percy was the Erle of Worcester,
   With nine thousand of gentyls all that wer,
   Of knyghts, squyers, and chosen yeomanry,
   And archers fyne withouten raskaldry."
                    Ellis Hardyng's Preface.
Otterbourne states that Hotspur had 14,000 choice troops, p. 239.

[1] His estates, however, were not large. The manors and lordships of Glendourdy in Edernyon, Sycharth and Kentlith, in North Wales, Hiscote and Guyoneth in South Wales, were granted by Henry IV. in his second year (8th Nov. 1400) to his brother John Earl of Somerset (ancestor of the Dukes of Beaufort), by the name of all

the manors, lands, and tenements, which were of Owyn de Glyndourdy in North and South Wales, and which were forfeited to the king by the high treason of the said Owen. Rot. Parl. iv. p. 440.

[2] De laudibus legum Angliæ, cap. xlix.

[3] Most of our writers, as Gough, Hall, Camden (ii. p. 473), Pennant, in his elaborate biography of the Welsh chieftain at the end of his Tour, Robert Burton (History of Wales, 1730, p. 154), even Carte (ii. 650), have represented Glyndwr as esquire to Richard II., and have ascribed his hatred of the usurper to his attachment to his late sovereign and master.

[4] The lady whom he thus celebrates, was Margaret, daughter of

Lord de Grey of Ruthin, one of Henry's most powerful barons, had, as we have stated before, taken a large portion of Owen's lands; some historians state that it was done with the King's permission. Owen sought justice repeatedly without having recourse to violence; at length he laid his case before parliament, but his suit was dismissed without redress. Injury was added to this insult. When Henry was preparing an army for his expedition against the Scots, Owen Glyndwr was summoned among other barons to attend the King;[1] the writ for that purpose was entrusted to Lord de Grey, who designedly neglected to deliver it till the time had elapsed within which it was possible to obey. Lord de Grey returned it to the King, and falsely represented the absence of Owen as an act of wilful disobedience, and by this piece of treachery he took possession of all his land, and under pretence of his having incurred a forfeiture, he invaded such parts of Glyndwr's estates as lay adjacent to his own.

The danger of driving into desperate measures a person of his interest, spirit, and abilities, was foreseen by John Trevor, Bishop of St. Asaph, who advised more temperate proceedings; adding, that Owen was by no means a despicable enemy, and that the Welsh would certainly be provoked into a general insurrection.[1] The bishop's advice was rejected, and he was told that there could be nothing to apprehend from such a *"bare-footed rabble."* This last sentence caused Owen's Welsh blood to rise, and as became an injured man, he flung off the English yoke. Ambition now joined with revenge, he revolved in his mind his own genealogy; he traced his descent from the ancient race of British princes; and apparently laying aside all sense of private wrong, made open claim to the throne of Wales. By the universal aid of his countrymen, he raised himself in a few months to the rank of a sovereign prince, and restored the ancient limits and independence of his country.

Owen's first act of open hostility took place in the summer of 1400. He naturally directed his attack against the lands of his enemy, Lord de Grey, and immediately recovered what he had been unjustly dispossessed of. As soon as the news had reached the King, he sent Lord Talbot and Lord de Grey to reduce him. They arrived with such speed that they surrounded his house before he had any notice of their approach, but he had the good fortune to escape into the woods. Owen immediately raised a powerful band of men, and on the 20th of September, surprised, plundered and burnt to the ground the town and castle of Ruthin, at the time when a great fair was held there. After this exploit he returned to his fastnesses among the mountains, whence he made occasional sallies and ransacked the Borders.

In January, 1401, a parliament was summoned at Westminster, and the twelfth chapter of the statute passed therein evinces the alarm excited by these daring inroads. The original is in French, but it runs thus in English :—

"Also, be it ordained and established, that henceforth no Welshman, entirely born in Wales, and having father or mother born in Wales, do purchase lands or tenements, in the towns of Cestre, Salop, Briggenorth, Ludlowe, Leomynster, Hereford, &c. &c., nor other market towns whatever adjoining the Marches of Wales, nor in the suburbs of such towns, on pain of forfeiture : and also, that no such

---

Sir David Hanmer, of Hanmer, in the county of Flint, one of the Justices of the King's Bench by appointment of Richard II., in 1383, and ancestor to Sir John Hanmer, Bart., the present Member for the Flintshire Boroughs.

[1] He gave evidence in the case of the Scroope and Grosvenor controversy in 1386, as Owen, Lord of Glyndyfrdwyr, aged 22.

[1] Of Glyndwr's personal courage, bravery, and other qualifications, for to head such an undertaking, we may judge from the following passages from the works of Gruffydd Llwyd, his chief bard :—

"With thy bright shining helmet thou art the brave and ever conquering son of the renowned Gruffydd Vychan. Thou art equal to nine heroes : thou hast in battle a generous heart : thou Owen, impetuous in onset, didst force thy way with thy trusty sword : thou shalt be esteemed for thine actions. When thy toils prest heaviest upon thee, in besieging hostile walls, thy ashen lance, terrible in battle, with its steel head, was, from the force of thine attack, shivered in pieces. Much to thy praise, quitting the grasp, thy hand eagerly seized the upper part, and by a firm hold, intrepidity of heart, strength of arm, shoulder, and breast, thou didst cause splinters and flashes of lightning to sparkle from the steel. Thou art a wise and able warrior, equal to a two-edged sword. In thy white-garment (the jupon) thy onset in the field of battle is terrible. Not only with thy sharp-piercing lance, hast thou struck terror and amazement into hundreds, but by thy glorious name and valour. Thou art secure and undaunted as steel, and a Cambrian with every excellence. No sooner did the terrible fight discontinue than thy fame was swiftly wafted into Wales, and all knew of your successful toils and wounds in battle."

Making every allowance for the enthusiasm of poetry, there is enough here to show that Owen was the life and soul of all the brilliant encounters with the English, which history has recorded ; and we find the splendid bassinet and trusty sword, given by the King of France, thought worthy of notice.

Welshman be henceforth chosen or received to be citizen or burgess in any city, burgh, or market town; and that those Welshmen who now are enfranchised in any such city, town, &c., find sufficient surety, as well towards our lord the King and his heirs, and his realm of England, &c. &c."

It was evidently the object of this enactment to drive Welsh settlers from the above towns into their own country; a measure, the policy of which may be questioned. It would surely have been wiser to attach them by confidence, than to alienate them by vexatious restrictions.

The year 1401 saw the British chieftain, nothing daunted, continuing his predatory warfare against the English government, and to this date must be referred a letter' from Glyndwr to one of his friends, an esquire of ancient birth, in the County of Chester, declaratory of his views and hopes.

"GREETING AND LOVE:—We tell you that we hope by the help of God and you to be able to deliver the offspring of Wales out of the captivity of our English foes, who have for a long time now passed, oppressed us and our ancestors. And ye may know of your own sense that their time draws to a close, and the victory turneth towards us, according to the ordinance of God from the beginning; so that no one needs to doubt that there will be a good end, unless it be lost by sloth and disagreement: and because all the offspring of Wales is in doubt and danger as to the subjection which we have heard is in the power of your enemies against them: According to this, we command and require and entreat, that you would be ready to come with all the force you can to us, to the place where you hear we are burning and oppressing our enemies and journeying: and this shall be shortly, by God's help. And do not omit this as you would have your freedom and honour in future. And do not wonder that you had no warning of the first rising; seeing that out of much fear and danger it was necessary we should rise without giving warning: Farewell, and God defend you from evil.

"By Yweyn ap Gruffydd, Lord of Glyndyfrdwy.

"To our most dear and most entirely beloved Henry Don."[8]

In pursuance of the intentions announced in this letter, Glyndwr mustered his forces in great numbers in 1402, and became so formidable by the defeat and capture of his enemy Lord de Grey, and Sir Edmund Mortimer, uncle to the young Earl of March, that Henry determined to march against him in person, and resolved to assemble three several armies, which should enter Wales as nearly as possible at the same time, from as many different quarters. The principal of these, to be commanded by himself, was to meet at Shrewsbury on the 27th of August. The event of this expedition was very unfavourable to

---

[7] This letter is preserved in a MS. of Edward Lhuyd's (inter coll. W. Mytton) and said by him to be "wrytten by Owen Glyndwr with his own hand, and lately seen by Mr. Owen Lloyd in London:" at the end is another attestation to its authenticity: but the contents of it speak sufficiently for themselves :—

"SALUTEM ET AMOREM. Vobis narramus quod speramus auxilio Dei et vestro posse liberare progeniem Wallicanam de captivitate inimicorum nostrorum Anglicorum, qui oppresserunt nos et antecessores nostros a multo tempore jam elapso. Et sciatis ex sensu vestro proprio quod tempus illorum desinit, et triumphus vertit versus nos, secundum ordinaco'em Dei a principio quod non refert alicui dubitare; quin finis eveniet bona nisi amittat [ur] per desidiam et discordiam : et quod omnes [omnis] progenies Wallicane est in dubio et periculo * secu'm [f. secundum] objectionem† [f. subjectionem]

---

* Glyndwr uses *periculum* in the ancient and we believe primary sense of *danger*, to denote *fear*. So Chaucer:

"In *danger* had he all the younge girls."

C. E. 665. et passim.

† This part of the letter is very obscure and unintelligible : "objectionem" seems an error of the transcript, which is very faulty, for

quam audivimus esse penes inimicos vestros predictos versus ipsos : Secundum hoc vobis mandamus et requirimus et supplicamus quatenus satis [f. sitis] p'ati venire in maxima fortitudine quam possitis ad nos ad locum ubi audieritis quod sumus comburentes opprimendo inimicos nostros itinerando : et hoc erit infra breve per auxilium divinum : Et hoc non omittatis sicut velitis habere libertatem vestram et honorem de cetero : Et non admiramini quod non habuistis premonicionem primæ surrectionis : nam ex nimio timore et periculo oportuit nos surgere non premonentes. Valete, et Deus vos defendat à malo.

"A n're tresch'r et   "P' Yweyn ap Gruffydd Dn'm de
tressentierement b'n   Glyn Dyfrdwy
aime Henry Don."

E Cod. MS. escod. in Chart. penes Dn' Robert Pugh de Keon y garlleg in paroch. Ll. St. ffraid ap'd Denbigh.

[8] Henry Done, Esq., of Utkinton, in Cheshire, was the representative of that ancient family at that time, and to him undoubtedly this letter was addressed.

"subjectionem :" *ob* and *sb* (sub) in ancient MSS. are scarcely distinguishable.

the English monarch. His army was harassed by inclement seasons in that mountainous region. On the 7th of September the atmosphere seemed to have recovered its serenity, and the King had pitched his tent on a pleasant spot; when, in the beginning of the night, a sudden tempest arose, which laid it prostrate; his lance, which was fixed in the ground near him, fell down with a violent crash, and pierced some armour that lay beside it: and the King himself must inevitably have perished, had he not slept that night completely armed. We cannot wonder that the ignorant and superstitious multitude of the English army attributed this war of elements to the necromancy of Glyndwr; with whom certain friars of the order of St. Francis were supposed to be leagued in a diabolic covenant. Henry was compelled to retire with loss and dismay: and the disgrace which his arms essayed upon this occasion, was among the motives which hastened on the insurrection of the Percies.

The following is the conclusion of a letter of defiance sent ~~by~~ Gruffydd ap David, one of the most active of the insurgents, ~~to~~ Lord de Grey of Ruthin:—

> "We hope we shall do the a privy thing,
> A rope, a ladder, and a ryng;
> High on gallows for to hyng.
> And thus shall be your endyng:
> And he that made the be ther to helpyng:
> And we on our behalf shall be well-willyng,
> For thy lettres knowledging."

The same person in another letter, says, "Hit was told me that ye ben in purpos for to make your men bran (burn) and sle in qwatesoever cuntré that I be, and am sesened in. Withowten doubt as mony men that ye sleu and as mony howsin that ye bran for my sake, as mony wol I bran and sle for your sake; and doute not that I wolle have both bredde and ale of the best that is in your lordschip." [*]

The letters of the reign of Henry IV. in the Cotton Collection relate entirely to Owen Glyndwr's rebellion. They are fourteen in number, and with one exception new to history; several of these are from constables of castles, and show not only the mode of keeping the fortresses of that time, but the nature of the warfare that was waging against them. The Welsh hated Henry IV. for his ill-usage to Richard II.; they had furnished Richard with troops in his contest with his nobles, and remained unshaken in their fidelity to him as long as they believed him to be alive.

Independently of their historical worth, these letters are curious as philological specimens. The eighth letter is from the mayor and burgesses of Cairleon to those of Monmouth, upon the defeat of a part of Owen Glyndwr's army by the Lord of Carew.

This letter is curious on two accounts. It acquaints us with the defeat of a portion of Glyndwr's forces by the Baron of Carew,—a fact unknown to our historians; and it details a conference between Owen Glyndwr and one Hopkins ap Thomas, (whom he held to be "Master of Brut,[1]") as to what should be his fate hereafter.

The following is the letter:—

"GRETYNG TO YOU OUR GODE FREENDES AND WORCHIPFUL BURGEIS OF MONEMOUTHE:—We do yow to understonde of tydynges the weche we have yherd of Owen Glyndwr, that is, to wete, of letter under seel, the wheche were y sende to us by the capteyne of the towne of Kadewelly, and in the lettres wer y wrete wordes

---

[*] There are several letters illustrative of this period in MS. Cotton. Mus. Brit. Cleop. E., folio 116, orig.

[1] "Master of the Brut" means skilled in the prophecies of Merlin, whose vaticinations form a part of the *Brut* of Geoffrey of Monmouth. Henry IV. and Glyndwr were both worked upon by ancient predictions; and each, it is probable, sought the type of the other in those numerous prophecies which our ancestors, in the thirteenth, fourteenth, and fifteenth centuries, were so fond of considering as in a state of progressive accomplishment. By the parties who met at the house of the Archdeacon of Bangor, Henry IV. was represented as the "Moldewarpe" accursed of God; while Glyndwr, Sir Henry Percy, and Sir Edmund Mortimer, were represented as the dragon, the lion, and the wolf, which should divide the realm between them. "Such," says Hall, "was the deviation, and not divination, of that Mawmet Merlin." The sequel of Glyndwr's history shows that Hopkin ap Thomas of Gower was not infallible as a seer.

that ther was a day of batell ytake by twyxt the worthy Baron of Carewe and Owein Glyndor; and we do yow to understonde that thys day of batell schuld have be do the xij. day of Jule; and the nyzt be fore that thys batell schulde be do, Oweyne wes y purpos to have yvordede yon to the Hull azeenward; and for he wold y wete wher his wey wer clere y nowe to passe, zyf he hede nede, to the Hull, he sende vii. c. of his meine (company) to serche the weyes, and thes vii. c. menne went to serche thys weyes, and ther thys vii. c. menne were y mette with the barons menne of Carew, and I slay up everychone that ther was nozt on that sc * * * * * alyve; and ther words buth (be) y do us to understonde that it is sothe with owte lesying. And fforthmor we do yow to understonde that Oweine the * * * * * es in the ton (of Kairm'then) he sende after Hopkyn ap Thomas of Gower to come and speke with hym upon trewes; and when Hopkyn come to Owein, he piede (prayed) hym, in as meche as he huld hym Maister of Brut, that he schuld do him to understonde how and what maner hit schulde be falle of hym; and he told him wittliche that he schold be take with inne a bref tyme; and the takyng schold be twene Kayrmerthen and Gower; and the takyng schold be under a black baner: knowelichyd that thys blake baner schold dessesse hym, and nozt that he schold be take undir hym. No more con (can) we say to yow at thys tyme, but buth (be) glad and merry, and drede yow nozt for we hopethe to God that ze have no nede. And we do yow to understonde that al thys tydyngs buth sothe with oute doute.

"Per Le Maire and Les Burgeis de Kairlyon."

When Sir Edward Mortimer announces to his tenantry his coalition with Glyndwr, which is written in French,[1] he sets out, very curiously, by expressing a doubt whether Richard II. is dead or alive.

"Tres chier et bien amez:—Vous salue mielx souvent, et vous face a entendre que Oweyn Glydor ad moeue une querelle la quelle est tielle, qe si le Roy Richard soit en vie de luy restorer a sa couronne, et senour qe mon honore neuewe q'est droit heir al dit coronne serroit Roy d'Engleterre, et qe le dit Owyen avoieit son droit in Gales."[2]

When speaking of the division of the kingdom, in this letter, Mortimer makes no allusion to the portion which was to fall to the Percies. Opinion certainly wavered at this time, as to Richard's positive fate, which, though conjectured, was not known. There can be no doubt that the proclamation of Henry IV. against the inventors of false reports, dated at Westminster, June 5th, in this very year, was intended to satisfy those who continued uncertain. It states, that rumour had been hinted to the ears of the foolish, that King Richard, his last predecessor, was still alive in Scotland, and that he was coming with the Scots to invade the realm; whereas, in truth, the said Richard was *dead* and *buried*:—"quod Dominus Ricardus nuper Rex Angliæ, ultimus prædecessor noster, adhuc vivit in Scotia, quodque in manu forti, ac vexillo protenso, veniet una cum Scotis in dictum regnum nostrum, ipsum, et nos, ac ligneos nostros protimis invasurus, cum *in rei veritate præfatus* Ricardus, sit *mortuus et sepultus.*"

As regards the omission of the Percies, it need only be observed that Sir Edmund Mortimer's letter is dated December 14th, and that the tripartite indenture of partition was not finally agreed upon till the middle of the next year.

---

[1] Some of the letters of this period are a singular mixture of French and English; for example: that of Richard Kyngeston, Archdeacon of Hereford, to Henry IV. It begins, "Notre tres redoute et Soverein Seigneur le Roy, Je me recommande humblement a votre hauteire comme petit creature et centinuel oratour;" and ends, "Escr. grant haste en haste a Hereford le viij⁰ jour de Juyle.

Votre petite creature Richard Kyngeston,
Ercedeake Hereford.

And the postscript is completely English, as a man in earnest might drop his best for his natural style: "And for Gode's love, my lyge Lord, thinketh en zour self and zour astat, or bemy (by my) trowthe all is lost elles; but and ze come zoure selfe with haste, all other wille folwine aftor. And at (on) Fryday last,

Kermerdyn town is taken and brent, and the castle zolden (yielded) be mo. Wygour, and the castle Emelyn is y zoldin; and slayn of the toune of Kermerdyn mo than l. persones. Writen in ryght haste on Sunday; and y cry zow mercy, and putte in zoure hye grace that y write so schortly; for by my trowthe that y owe to zow, it is needful."

[2] Translated thus :—" Very dear and well beloved, I greet you much, and make known to you, that Owen Glyndwr has raised a quarrel, of which the object is, if King Richard be alive to restore him to his crown; and if not, that my honoured nephew, who is the right heir to the said crown, shall be King of England, and that the said Owen will assert his right in Wales."

The negotiation for the partition of the kingdom seems to have originated with Mortimer and Glyndwr only. The battle of Shrewsbury was fought on July 21st, 1403. The manuscript chronicle whence these accounts are extracted, compiled by one of the chaplains of Henry V., gives the particulars of the final treaty, signed at the house of the Archdeacon of Bangor, more amply than can be found elsewhere. The Severn, the Trent, and the Mersey, were to shut in Owen's territory; while the Percies were to have not only all that was north of Trent, but Leicestershire, Northamptonshire, Warwickshire, and even Norfolk. Sir Edmund Mortimer (not the nephew whom he speaks of in his letter) was to content himself with the remainder. The expectation declared in this treaty, that the contracting parties would turn out to be the persons spoken of by Merlin, who were to divide the *greater Britain*, as it was called amongst them, corroborates the story told by Hall.

The following are the letters[4] alluded to :—

Letters from Sir Henry Percy (Hotspur) to the Council relative to the affairs of Wales.
Dated 10th April, 2 Hen. IV., 1401.

"REVEREND FATHERS IN GOD AND VERY HONOURED LORDS :—You will please to know that I have received a letter under the Privy Seal of our Lord and King, by the advice of his Council, with certain ordinances under the Great Seal; and I am charged to proclaim the said ordinances within the limits of the jurisdiction of my office of Justice, according as it seems best to me in the matter. And I have also received another letter under the said Privy Seal, charging me that I do not allow any Welshman to be Justice, Chamberlain, Chancellor, Seneschal, Receiver, Master of the Forest, Viscount Escheator, nor Constable of the Castle, nor Custos Rotulorum of Wales, but that English are to be in the same offices, and that they are to remain over them in their own persons, excepting the Justice and his Lieutenant, which ordinances I am charged to enforce immediately, as it appertains to me in virtue of my office. As to which matters, Rev. Fathers in God and very honoured Lords, I will do my loyal devoir to the best of my ability, aided by the advice of the others of the Council. My very honoured and very redoubtable Lord the Prince being in these parts, has had consideration of those who bore themselves well to the King and my Lord the Prince at the time of taking of the Castle of Conway, above mentioned, and such consideration it is best to give at this time if you look to the keeping of the castle in time to come. And Reverend Fathers in God and very honoured Lords, as to what has been written in the said two letters, that I do well and safely guard all the castles which I have in keeping for the term of my life or otherwise, in the said parts, so that from my negligence, no pillage, damage, or loss happen to either the castles or the country; and I am charged in the said two letters, on my faith and allegiance, and upon pain of forfeiting the said castles and the profits appertaining thereto, without ever after being restored or admitted to the keeping of any of them. I wish you to know that I have not in Wales any castle in my keeping, for which I cannot answer and will answer for. As I have done and mean to do as loyally my duty as any subject that the King has in these said parts, trusting in you my Lords, that in case such mischief happen, as never shall, please God, by my fault, that you will be as lenient to me as to others of my little estate in like case. And if I have done or could do in time to come, here or elsewhere, good service to the King, my Sovereign Lord, that you will aid me to obtain such assistance as I shall be entitled, and justice shall require, for it seems to me that I have nothing in these parts, but what the King of his gracious favour has frankly given me, and on account of his being satisfied that I have well deserved of him.

"Reverend Fathers in God and very honoured Lords, nothing more to write at present, but you will inform me of your noble pleasure on this and other matters which I will perform to the best of my power.

"I pray to God to keep you in health. Written at Denbigh, the 10th day of April.

"HENRY PERCY."

---

[4] Bibl. Cotton: Cleopatra, f. 16, contemporary MS.

4th May, 2 Henry IV., 1401.

"REVEREND FATHERS IN GOD AND VERY HONOURED LORDS:—I recommend myself to you, and wish you to know that the country of North Wales, in which I hold my sessions, is well-intentioned and obedient in all points to the law: excepting those rebels who are in the castles of Conway and Rees, which is in the mountains, and whom I hope will be well chastised, if God pleases, by the forces and authorities which my redoubtable brother the Prince has sent there, as well of his counsel as of his retinue, to hold the siege before the rebels in the said castles; which siege if it can be continued until the said rebels are taken, will be a great ease and comfort to the governance of this country in time to come. And also Reverend Fathers in God and very dear Brethren, the peasantry of the said country of North Wales, that is to say, the counties of Caernarvon and Merioneth, have just presented themselves before me and humbly thanked my redoubtable brother, the Prince, for his very great kindness in supplicating our Lord, the King, for his gracious pardon, and they humbly beg for the confirmation thereof under his seal, offering to give him of their own will (besides the usual dues) and without any other request, as great a sum as they gave to King Richard when he was King and Prince, as the bearer will fully declare unto you. And you will remember how many times I have besought you for the payment of the soldiers of the King in the City of Berwick and in the East Marches of England, who are in such great poverty that they cannot bear arms for the want of their pay, and for them you are supplicated to order that they be paid in manner as was settled between the Treasurer and me at our last meeting, if better payment cannot be obtained for them. For otherwise I must come to you for the said payment, everything else being of minor importance. Reverend Fathers in God and very honoured Lords, I have nothing more to say to you at present, but I pray the Holy Spirit that you be maintained in all honour and joy according to your true desires.—Written at Caernarvon, the 3rd day of May.

"HENRY PERCY,
" Guardian of the East Marches of England towards Scotland."

17th May, 2 Henry IV., 1401.

"VERY REVEREND FATHER IN GOD, AND VERY HONOURED AND VERY DEAR LORDS:—I recommend myself to you, and let it please you to know that I send to my very redoubtable sovereign Lord the King and to you, my well beloved friend James Strangways, who will declare unto you the state of the marches, and country, and I pray for your commands as to the governance of the rebels, as well for the comfort as for my guidance how to act, * * * * *¹ and from my proposal before, according to my power and the great labour and cost that I have sustained, and the great want and necessity that I saw in the country, the latter, in good faith, are to me so insupportable that I cannot bear them any longer than the end of the month, or three or four days afterwards. You will be pleased to proclaim such ordinances as you will see necessary, when you have learned the state of the country; and, in the meantime, I will do all in my power, by land and by sea, with my body and my goods, to render service, and beseech that you will, according to your wise discretion, consider all my said labour and cost, and adopt such measures for the country so that the expected mischief may not ensue, which God defend. Very Reverend Fathers in God, and very honoured and very dear Lords, I have nothing more to say now than I trust you will continue in health. Written at Denbigh, the 17th day of May.

" HENRY PERCY."

" *4th June, 2 Henry IV.* 1401.

 " VERY REVEREND FATHERS IN GOD, AND VERY HONOURED AND VERY DEAR LORDS:—I recommend myself to you, and as to the news, if you wish to know them, I have already written and certified by my well-beloved friend, James Strangways, the news and state of this country; but since his departure, I see so much pillage and mischief in the country, that good and hasty measures ought to be immediately adopted

---

¹ Obliteration in the MS.

by sea as well as by land. All the country is, without doubt, in great peril of being destroyed by the rebels if I should leave before the arrival of my successor, the which will be an affair of necessity; for I cannot bear the cost that I am put to without other ordering from you. And touching this that has been done by my very honoured uncle, and the other forces in his company, I hope that it has been certified unto you and of my doing in this * * by land and by sea, for my soldiers' pay, and my own expenses, and for the journey that I had on the 13th of May last to Cader Idris, God be praised. The bearer, John Irby, was present with me, and can acquaint you with the particulars. Monsieur Hugh Browe was with me, with twelve lances and one hundred archers of my right honourable cousin, the Count of Arundell, without any other aid, at my proper charges; and by such governance as you may see meet to order for this answer, for I do not here await your answer by the aforesaid James Strangways of the undermentioned and other matters; and please to know that news have reached me this day from the Sieur of Powis, as to his combat with Owen de Glyndwrdwy, whom he had discomfited, and wounded many of his men on his way to my much honoured uncle and myself, as he certified, for which I thank God. And also I have news this day that my people, whom I had ordered on the sea, how they have taken * * * to Bardsey; that was taken from the English by the Scotch * * *[6] they pursued a Scotch ship to the Milford coast, and took her, the said ship, with 300 men, well accoutered prisoners, for which I thank God. Very Reverend Fathers in God, and very honoured and very dear Lords, with nothing more to say at present, I pray God to keep you in good health. Written at Denbigh, the 4th day of June.

"HENRY PERCY."

In the spring of 1401, William ap Tudor and his brother Rees ap Tudor had obtained possession of the Castle of Conway, where they were immediately besieged by Henry Percy, so well known to the readers of Shakespeare by the name of Hotspur, who held the office of Justice of North Wales and Chester. On the 10th April and the 4th of May, Percy writes to the privy council from Caernarvon,[7] that all North Wales was quiet and submissive, with the exception of Conway Castle, and those who were with Rees ap Tudor in the mountains.[8] Soon after this the Welsh garrison of Conway appear to have entered into negotiations with Percy and the Prince of Wales, who had joined in the siege, for conditions of surrender. On the 17th of May his position had become more gloomy; he speaks of the pride and intractability of the insurgents, and complains of the difficulties and expenses of his office, which he subsequently resigned. On the 4th of June, Percy again complains of the increasing turbulence of the country in which he was stationed; he speaks of having defeated the insurgents in Cader Idris, complains of receiving little aid from any of the Lords Marchers except the Earl of Arundel and Sir Hugh Bowe,[9] and sends news that the Lord of Powys (Edward de Cherlton) had fought and defeated Owen Glyndwr in person.[1]

Glyndwr appears to have been occupied at this time in invading the English side of the border; and his proceedings were of such a threatening character that the King thought it necessary to march against him in person. In his letters to the sheriffs of counties for the assembling of his army, he states that he had received intelligence on the 26th of May, that Owen Glyndwr and his Welsh rebels had assembled in the Marches of Caermarthen, and that they had proclaimed it as their intention to enter England with an armed force for the purpose of destroying the English people and language.[2] The King was then at

[6] Obliterations in the MS.

[7] Devon's Pell Rolls, p. 283. Proceedings of the Privy Council, vol. i. p. 147.

[8] Owen, chief bard of Gruffydd Llwyd, after regretting his absence from home, chaunts his praise, and predicts success of the war. The Cywydd, or poem, begins thus: "Eryr digrif afrifed Owen," &c. &c. The following is a specimen of the poem, paraphased by the late Rev. Mr. Williams, of Vron, near Mold:

"Cambria's princely eagle hail !
Of Gruffydd Vychan's noble blood !

Thy high renown shall never fail,
Owen Glyndwr, great and good!
Lord of Durdwy's fertile vale—
War-like—high-born Owen, hail!"

[9] The king gave about this time to Hugh Bowe all the lands in Cheshire and Salop which had belonged to Robert de Puleston, who had joined himself with Owen Glyndwr. See Calendar to the Patent Rolls, p. 242.

[1] Proceedings of the Privy Council, x. pp. 150—152.

[2] Proceedings of the Privy Council, ii. p. 54.

Wallingford, and with his characteristic activity he prepared to move towards the Border on the following day. He was at Worcester on the 8th of June, on which day he wrote two letters to his privy council, one directing them to prepare a fleet to repel an invasion, the other informing them that on his approach the Welsh had retired from the Border, although they were increasing in numbers, and that he was determined to advance.[3] The King returned from Wales late in September or early in November; but we have no narrative of his operations. Some of the Welsh chiefs stood firm to their allegiance; others had submitted and received pardon; and many of the castles were strengthened, and put into better hands.[4] But Glyndwr still stood out, and with him the larger part of those who had taken up arms. After his return, the King appointed Percy's uncle, the Earl of Worcester, captain of Cardigan Castle, and his lieutenant in Wales.

A.D. 1402.—This year was ushered in by a comet or blazing star, which the bards interpreted as an omen favourable to the cause of Glyndwr. "And in the iiii yere of Kynge Henri's reigne, ther was a starre seyn in the firmament, y[t] showed himself through the worlde for di'use tokenynges y[t] should befal sone after, the whiche starre was named and called by *Clargie*, Stella Comata."[5]

The star at that time served to inspire a superstitious people with courage, and the first success of their chieftain confirmed their belief and gave new vigour to their actions.

Lord de Grey, who had before felt the effect of Owen's power, now raised a considerable army, and encountered our hero, but was defeated and made prisoner. He was taken and carried, fast bound, into confinement amidst the savage fastnesses of the Snowdon.[6] Lord de Grey remained a long time in captivity, nor did he gain his liberty until he paid the enormous sum of ten thousand marks. He was such a personal favourite with the King, that, pitying the severity with which he was treated, and admiring the firmness with which he resisted the offers of Glyndwr, to make him swerve from his loyalty, he issued out a special commission, dated the 10th of October, 1402, empowering Sir Walter de Roos, Sir Richard de Grey, Sir William de Willoughby, Sir William de Zouch, John Henry, William Vaus, John Lee, John Langford, Thomas Payne, and John Elnstow, to treat with Owen and his council about his ransom. It was agreed to pay six thousand marks on the day of St. Martin following,[7] and to give as hostages, for the payment of the remainder, his eldest son and some other persons. And in order to raise the money, Henry granted a

---

[3] Proceedings of the Privy Council, i. p. 133, and ii. p. 56.

[4] At this time the famous Lollard, Sir John Oldcastle, was made captain of Builth: in the year following (1402) he had the command of Kidwelly Castle.

[5] Caxton's Chronicles, printed at St. Alban's. This circumstance has been turned into poetic verse by the elegant pen of the late Mrs. Hemans, the sweet nightingale of Wales—it is designated very properly "Owen Glyndwr's War Song," and arranged to the favourite air of "Codiad yr Hedydd," or the "Rising of the Lark," by Mr. John Parry, London.

"Saw ye the blazing star;
The Heavens look down on freedom's war,
    And light her torch on high!
Bright, on the dragon crest,
It tells that glory's wing shall rest
    Where warriors meet to die!
Let earth's pale tyrants read despair
    And vengeance in its flame!
Hail ye, my Bards! the omen fair
    Of conquest and of fame;
And swell the rushing mountain air
    With songs to Glyndwr's name.

"At the dead hour of night,
Mark'd ye how each majestic height

Burn'd in its awful beams.
Red shone th' eternal snows,
And all the land, as bright it rose,
    Was full of glorious dreams.
O, eagles of the battle, rise,
    The hope of *Gwynedd* wakes;
It is your banner in the skies
    Through each dark cloud which breaks,
And mantles with triumphant dyes
    Your thousand hills and lakes!

"A sound is on the breeze,
A murmur as on swelling seas,
    The foe is on his way!
Lo! shield and spear and lance,
From Deva's waves with glittering glance
    Reflected to the day!
But who the torrent wave compels
A tyrant's chain to bear!
Let those who wake the soul that dwells
    On our free wind beware;
The greenest and the loveliest dells
    May be the lion's lair."

[6] Vita Ricardi II., p. 178.   [7] Rymer's Fœdera, p. 279.

license to Robert Braybrook,[8] Bishop of London, and two other feoffees of divers lordships for Lord de Grey, to sell the lordships of Herteleigh, in Kent.

After this Lord de Grey was set at liberty. It is probable that Owen engaged him to observe a neutrality as an additional condition of redemption. Lord de Grey, on the other hand, seems to have thought it necessary to secure his tenants and himself by an alliance with Owen, for no sooner was he released, than he married Jane, third daughter of the Welsh chieftain. He had no issue by this lady.

Owen after securing this potent enemy began to give a free scope to his revenge by punishing such of his countrymen as he considered to have acted as traitors to the generous cause of freedom, by an unnatural adherence to the English, whose yoke they had borne for such a length of time. He burnt the dwellings of several of those parties, and otherwise punished them. He afterwards overran the Borders on his way to South Wales, for Glyndwr's interest and fortune lay both in the North and South of Wales. During the summer of 1401, he posted himself, with his army, on Plinlimmon, a lofty mountain situated between Cardiganshire and Montgomeryshire. He acted with great policy here, for the situation was admirably adapted for receiving succours from his vassals and friends, both in North and South Wales. From hence his followers made plundering excursions, and were the terror of all that declined espousing his cause.

The Flemish inhabitants of Ross, Pembroke, and Cardigan, suffered greatly from Glyndwr's invasion. A severe engagement took place between them at a place called "Mynydd Hyddgant," where a vast number of the Flemings were left dead on the spot. This victory added greatly to the reputation of Glyndwr; multitudes in consequence gathered to his standard, and greatly contributed to his power and importance.

Henry, alarmed at his success, marched against him a second time in person. He entered Wales with a great army about the beginning of June,[9] destroyed the abbey of Ystrad Ffur, in Cardiganshire, and ravaged the country, but was obliged to make a disgraceful retreat, after his forces had suffered greatly by famine and the fatigues they continually underwent.

The English council gave orders for strengthening the Border castles; and the Welsh spent the winter (the season which had always been favourable to them) in preparing for active operations at the first break of spring.

The insurrection at this time had reached its greatest force. At the approach of spring the operations of Glyndwr had become more extensive, and there remained but a few ill-garrisoned castles to hinder his crossing the Border. Early in the year the Prince of Wales, afterwards Henry V., had been sent to Shrewsbury, where he was organising an army to hold North Wales in check. A letter which he wrote[1] to the privy council on the 15th of May, and of which the following is a translation, gives a curious picture of the kind of warfare carried on between the rival parties :—

A.D. 1402

"VERY DEAR AND ENTIRELY WELL BELOVED : We greet you earnestly with our entire heart, thanking you very dearly for the good care which you have had of the businesses which concern us in our absence, and we pray you very affectionately for your good and friendly continuance, as our trust is in you. And for news in this part, if you will know, among others, we were lately informed that Oweyne de Glyndourdy assembled his forces of other rebels, his adherents, in great number, purposing to make an incursion, and to fight if the English would resist him in his purpose, and so he boasted to his people. Wherefore we took our forces and went to a place of the said Oweyn, well built, which was his principal mansion, named Saghern, (Sycharth) where we expected to have found him, if he had had will to fight in manner as he said; and at our coming hither, we found nobody, and therefore we caused the whole place to be burnt, and several other houses thereabouts of his tenants. And then we went straight to his other place of Glendourdy, to seek him there, and there we burnt a fair lodge in his park, and all the country there about. And we lodged ourselves by there all that night, and certain of our people sallied forth there into the country, and took

[8] Dugdale, i. 717.   [9] Vita Ricardi II., p. 174.   [1] The original is in French.

a great gentleman of the country who was one of the said Oweyn's chieftains, who offered five hundred pounds for his ransom to have had his life, and to have paid the said sum within two weeks; nevertheless it was not accepted, but he was put to death, as well as divers others of his companions who were taken in the said expedition.   And then we went into the Commote of Edeyrnion, in the county of Merionnyth, and there we ravaged with fire a fair country, and well inhabited.   And thence we went to Powys, and there being a scarcity of provender for horses in Wales, we caused our men to carry oats with them, and we remained. . . . days.   And to inform you more fully of this expedition, and of all other news here at present, we send to you our very dear esquire, John de Waterton, to whom you will be pleased to give entire faith and credence in what he shall report to you from us touching the news above mentioned.   And may our Lord have you always in his holy keeping.   Given under our signet, at Shrouesbury, this 15th day of May."

Soon after the return of their prince from this "foray," Owen Glyndwr, whose strength was evidently increasing, approached the English border, with the intention of ravaging Herefordshire and Shropshire. Edmund de Mortimer, the uncle of the young Earl of March, hastily levied the men of Herefordshire, and met the Welsh on the hills in the neighbourhood of Radnor, at Maelienydd.   In this battle, which was fought on the 12th of June, the men of Herefordshire were entirely defeated, and Mortimer himself taken prisoner.   The contemporary chroniclers give us no particulars of this battle beyond recording the savage barbarity of the Welsh women who followed their countrymen,[2] but it was afterwards the tradition of the place that Edmund de Mortimer was taken after a long and desperate personal combat with Glyndwr himself.   The victors are said to have advanced as far as Leominster, where they established themselves, and from whence they issued to plunder and lay waste the neighbouring country.   The house at Leominster is still shown, in which, according to tradition, Glyndwr deposited his prisoner; and he is said to have robbed the priory church, as well as several churches in the vicinity, some of which were nearly destroyed by his men.   He appears to have returned in haste to Caermarthenshire, to collect there his forces for the reduction of the strong places in that country which were still in the hands of the English.

The state of Wales at this time will be best pictured by two or three other contemporary letters which have escaped the ravages of time.   The first was written to John Fairford, receiver of Brecknock, by John Scudamore, who held the castle of Carregcynnen for the King.

"WORSCHIPFUL SIR, I recomand me to yow, and forasmoche as I may nought spare no man from this place away fro me, to certefie neyther the king ne[3] my lord the prynce, of the myschefs of these countrees aboute, ne no man may pass by no wey hennes, I pray yow and require yow that ye certefie hem how al Kermerdyn schire, Kedewely, Carnwaltham, and Yskenyn, ben sworen to Oweyn yesterday, and he lay to night yn the castel of Drosselan, with Rees ap Gruffuth.   And ther I was, and spake with hym upon truys, and prayed of a sauf-conduyt[4] under his seal to send home my wif and her moder and their mayne,[5] but he wolde none graunte me.   And on this day he is about the towne of Kermerdyn, and ther thinketh to abide til he may have the towne and the castel.   And his purpos ys from thennes into Pembroke schire; for he halt hym siker[6] of all the castell and towns in Kedewelly, Gowerslonde, and Glamorgan, for the same countrees have undertaken the sieges of hem til thei ben wonnen.   Wherfore wryteth to Sir Hugh Waterton, and to alle thilke that ye suppose wol take this matter to hert, that thei excite the king hederwardes in al haste to vengen hym on summe of his false traytors the whyche he hath overmoche cherischid, and to rescewe the townes and casteles in these countrees; for I drede ful sore ther be too fewe trewe men in hem. I can[7] no more as nowe; but pray God help yow and us that thinken to be trewe.   Written at the castel of Carreckennen, the .v. day of Juil., yowres, John Skydmore."

---

[2] Thomas Walsingham, Hist. Angl.   [3] Nor.   [4] Safe-conduct.

[5] Household.   [6] Holds himself sure.   [7] Know.

The attack upon Caermarthen was successful. On the 7th of July[8] the constable of Dynevor Castle, "Jankyn Hauard," writes thus to the receiver of Brecknock:[9]—

"DEARE FRENDE, I do yow to wetyn[1] that Oweyne Glendour, Henri Don, Res Duy, Res ap Griffith ap Llywelyn, and Res Gethin, han y-won the town of Kermerdyn, and Wygmor, constable of the castell, had yeld up the castell of Kermerdyn to Oweyn: and [they] han y-brend[2] the town, y-slay[3] of men of [the] town more than fifty men; and thei budd in purpos[4] to Kedweli; and a siege is ordeynyd at the castell that I kepe, and this is gret peril for me, and all that buth wydden;[5] for thei han y-made har avow[6] that thei will algate[7] have us dead therein. Wherfore I pray yow that ye nul not bugil us, that ye send to us warning wythin schort time whether schul we have any help or no: and but ther be help coming,[8] that we have an answer, that we may come bi night and steal away to Brecknock; cause that we faylyth vitals and men, and namely men. Also Jenkyn ap Llywelyn hath yeld up the castell of Enclyn wyth free wyll; and also William Gwyn, Thomas ap David ap Griffith, and moni gentils ben in person wyth Owen. Warning herof I pray that ye send me bi the berer of this letter. Fareth well, yn the name of the Trinitie. Y-wrigt at Dynevour, yn haste and yn drede, yn the feast of Seint Thomas the Martir."

The following undated letter from the same person, appears to have been written a few days later:—

"DEARE FRYND, I do you to wetyn that Owyn was in purpos to Kedewely, and the Baron of Carewe was that day comyng wyth a grete retenu towards Seint Cler, and so Owyne changed his purpos and rode to-genes[9] the baron; and that night a lodged hym at Seint Cler, and destruyed al the contrie about. And a Tuesday they weren at tretys[1] al day; and that nyght he lodged him at the town of Locharn, six miles out of the town of Kermerdyn. His purpose is, if so that the Baron and he acordeth in tretys, than a turneth agein to Kermerdyn for his part of the goods, and Res Duy his part; and mony of these grete maisters stond yet in the castell of Kermerdyn, for they have not y-made har ordinance whether the castell and the town shall be brend or no, and therfore, if ther is any help comyng, haste hem with al haste toward us, for they mowe have goodes and vytelles plentie; for every hous is full aboute us of her[2] poultrie, and yet wyn and hony ynow in the contrie, and wheat and beanes, and al maner of vytells. And we of the castell of Dunevor had tretys of ham[3] Monday, Tuesday, and Wedynsday, and now a woll[4] ordeyn for us to have that castell, for there a casteth to ben y-circled thence, for that was the chef place in old tyme. And Oweyn's muster a Monday was, as they seyen hemselven, seven thousand and twelve score speres, such as they were. Other tidyng I not[5] now, but God of hevene send yow and us from all enemies. Y-wryten at Dynevor, this Wedynsday, in haste."

The next letter is written from Hereford, on the 8th of July, by Richard Kingston, Archdeacon of Hereford. It is addressed to the King, and gives us a singular picture of the fears of the people on the English side of the Border, who had already suffered from Glyndwr's incursion in the preceding month. The original of the Archdeacon's letter is written in French.

"OUR VERY REDOUBTED AND SOVEREIGN LORD THE KING: I recommend myself humbly to your highness as your lowly creature and continual bedesman. And our very redoubted and sovereign lord the King, please you to know that from day to day letters come from Wales containing intelligence by which you may learn that the whole country is lost, if you do not come as quickly as possible. For which reason may it please you to direct yourself towards our parts with all the power you can, riding day and night for the salvation of these parts. And please you to know that it will be a great disgrace, as well as loss, if you should lose or suffer to be lost, at your commencement, the country which your noble ancestors have won and for so

---

[8] The date of this letter (the feast of St. Thomas the Martyr) must be intended for the feast of the Translation of St. Thomas, July 7.

[9] Ellis's Original Letters, second series, i. p. 13. These letters are partly modernised in the spelling.

[1] I give you to know.   [2] Burnt.   [3] Slain.

[4] Remain in purpose; i.e. continue in the intention to go.
[5] All that are within [the castle].
[6] Made their vow.   [7] At all events.
[8] And if there be no help coming.
[9] Against.   [1] At treaties; i.e. a-treating.
[2] Their.   [3] Them.   [4] He will.   [5] Know not.

long a time peaceably held; for people talk very ill-favouredly. And I send to your Highness the copy of a letter which came from John Scudamore this morning. Our most redoubted and sovereign lord the King, I pray to the Almighty that he grant you a good and holy life, with victory over your enemies. Written in haste, great haste, at Hereford, the 8th day of July."

About this time the Percies, dissatisfied at the King's conduct about the Scotch prisoners taken at Homildon, and at the non-payment of the great expenses they had incurred in the King's service, suddenly revolted, having previously come to some understanding with Owen. The popular story alluded to by Shakespeare is, that at a secret conference, they divided England between them by anticipation, and that Owen was to have all the country west of the Severn. It is said that the meeting was held at the house of David, Dean of Bangor, lineally descended from Caradoc ap Iestyn, who was outlawed in 1406, as a partisan of Owen's. This tradition has in it nothing improbable; but is not, as far as historical researches can discover, supported by any reliable evidence.

It is clear that the revolt was entirely unforeseen by the King, who was actually on his march to join the Percies. He appears to have received the news at Burton-on-Trent about the 16th of July.' He decided, with his usual promptitude, on instantly attacking Hotspur, who had joined his uncle, the Earl of Worcester, on the Borders of Wales, and on the 23rd of July fought and won the battle of Shrewsbury, in which Hotspur and the Earl of Worcester were killed, and the rebellion completely crushed. Owen certainly was not in the battle in person, nor is the story, of his having seen it from a tree on the other side of the river, supported by any evidence better than vague tradition. It is possible that he may have marched to join the confederates, and that the promptitude of the King prevented his junction; but it is rather imagined that he was engaged in the siege and blockade of Lampadern, Harlech, Carnarvon, Carmarthen, and other strongholds in the South and West of Wales. Many Welsh insurgents were of course in the battle, which naturally may have given rise to the reports alluded to. Two days after the battle, the Prince was empowered to pardon those of Chester, Flint, and Denbigh.'

In March, 1405,' an attempt was made to carry off from Windsor Castle, where they were confined, the young Earl of March and his brother; Constance, Lady Despenser, who held the strong Castle of Caerphilly, contrived their escape, but they were retaken. There seems great reason to suppose that they intended to have joined Owen. We find that at a council, held on the 1st of March, 1405, strict measures of precaution were taken with respect to these state prisoners.'

On the 11th of March, Prince Henry, with a very inferior force, defeated at Grosmont, in Monmouthshire, an army of eight thousand of the insurgents of that part of the country, and took a prisoner of great importance, whose name is not given, but whom the Prince intended to send to the King as soon as his wounds would allow him to travel; this success was thought of sufficient importance for the King to forward the intelligence to the council.' According to Carte,' the Welsh were again defeated, on the 15th, at Mynydd y Pwll Melin, in Breconshire, where a brother of Owen was slain, and his son taken prisoner; but there are considerable doubts as to the accuracy of this date.

The King prepared slowly for his expedition into Wales, for his attention was diverted to other quarters. The Scots attempted to favour the Welsh by an incursion into the northern counties of England: and the French were threatening a simultaneous invasion. Henry's first proclamation declaring his intention of marching in person against "Owen Glyndwr and the other rebels of Wales" is dated on the 25th of June, when he had just received intelligence of the capture of Edmund Mortimer.' On the 31st of July he issued another proclamation, fixing the 27th of August for the day of meeting of the army at Chester.' A letter

⁶ Rymer's Fœdera, viii. p. 313. ⁷ Ibid., p. 320.

⁸ Sir H. Nicolas, i. p. 221, ii. p. 83. Ellis's Original Letters, Second Series, i. p. 33. See also, in Sir H. Nicolas, ii. p. 77, a letter from the inhabitants of Shropshire, perhaps to be referred to this date, alluding to the French as lately landed.

⁹ Sir H. Nicolas, i. p. 223, 229—235.

¹ Rymer's Fœdera, viii. p. 405. Sir H. Nicolas, i. p. 248. Rymer makes a curious mistake, corrected by Sir H. Nicolas. The word "j'envoia" he puts as the name of a lordship, near Monmouth, "Jennoia." ² Vol. ii. p. 625; Sir H. Nicolas, ii. p. 665.

³ Rymer's Fœdera, iv. p. 30; Proceedings of the Privy Council, i. p. 185. ⁴ Rymer's Fœdera, ib. p. 39.

from Edward Cherlton, Earl of Powys, dated from the Castle of Pool, on the 5th of August (apparently of this year), represents the Welsh as becoming every day more active in their incursions on the Border in his neighbourhood, and presses urgently for assistance.[5] The chroniclers[6] state that the King moved towards Wales just before the Feast of the Assumption of the Virgin (August 15); the insurgents retired at his approach, and left the English army to pursue a course of plunder and devastation uninterrupted, except by the elements. These appeared as though they had conspired with the Welsh; so tempestuous a season had not been witnessed for many years; and the English army, after considerable loss, although it had committed terrible havoc and carried away much plunder, was obliged to return without having effected much of that for which it was called together. It is said that the King himself was on one or two occasions exposed to personal danger by the inclemency of the weather. This check confirmed the common people in a belief which had already gained some ground, that Owen Glyndwr added to his other qualities that of being a powerful magician, and they attributed to his unholy incantations the storms which had baffled his enemies.[7]

Edmund Mortimer remained still a prisoner: it is said that the King was unwilling to pay his ransom, and that, in revenge, he entered into a confederacy with the Welsh chieftain. On the 13th day of December, Mortimer proclaimed to his tenantry that he had taken up the quarrel of Owen Glyndwr, and that his design was to dethrone King Henry in favour of his nephew, the rightful heir of the house of York, and secure, at the same time, the independence of the Welsh.[8] This alliance was cemented by the marriage of Edmund Mortimer and Glyndwr's daughter. The accession of Edmund Mortimer, probably, was rather a nominal than a physical addition to the force of the insurgents; but a few months later, success appeared to be rendered certain by the addition of the powerful family of the Percies to the confederacy. A triple league was formed between Glyndwr, Henry Percy (Hotspur), and Edmund Mortimer. The latter fought no longer for his nephew: he laid claim to his own share of the spoils. It was agreed that if it should appear, by the success of their enterprise, that the three parties of the league were the three persons who, according to the prophecies of Merlin, were to obtain possession of the Isle of Britain, and divide it between them, the partition should be made in the following manner:—Owen Glyndwr, as Prince of Wales, was to have the whole of Wales and the adjoining Border up to the banks of the Severn, Trent, and Mersey; the Percies were to have in their sovereignty all the counties north of the Trent, with those of Leicester, Northampton, Warwick, and Norfolk; and Edmund Mortimer was to take the remainder for himself and his successors.[9]

The less important events of this period have been forgotten amid the great events which followed. A letter is addressed by the inhabitants of Shropshire to the privy council, and dated on the 21st of April, probably in 1403, by which it appears that the Welsh were then threatening the Border with devastation.[1] We learn that the custody of Ludlow Castle at this time was considered of sufficient importance to be entrusted to the care of Sir Thomas Beaufort, one of the most eminent statesmen and soldiers of the age, afterwards Earl of Dorset and Duke of Exeter;[2] while Richard's Castle, as well as the Castle of Montgomery, were in the charge of Sir Thomas Talbot.[3] On the 16th of June, the King wrote to the sheriffs

---

[5] Proceedings of the Privy Council, ii. 70.

[6] Thomas of Walsingham, p. 365.

[7] Shakespeare puts these words into the mouth of Glyndwr :—

"——————————— At my birth,
The front of heaven was full of fiery shapes;
The goats ran from the mountains, and the herds
Were strangely clamorous to the frighted fields.
These signs have mark'd me extraordinary;
And all the courses of my life do show,
I am not in the roll of common men.
Where is he living,—clipp'd in with the sea
That chides the bounds of England, Scotland, Wales,—
Which calls me pupil, or hath read to me?
And bring him out, that is but woman's son,

Can trace me in the tedious way of art,
And hold me pace in deep experiments."

[8] The original proclamation is printed in Ellis's Original Letters, second series, i. p. 24.

[9] See the particulars of this treaty stated in an extract from a MS. Chronicle printed in Ellis, ib. p. 27.

[1] Proceedings of the Privy Council, ii. p. 77.

[2] Pell Rolls, p. 295. 7th December. To Sir Thomas Beaufort, Knight, Keeper of "Lodelowe" Castle, in money paid to him by the hands of Matthew Penketh, &c., for the wages of himself, his men-at-arms, and others, dwelling with him in the garrison of "Lodelowe Castle in Wales," to resist the invasion of the rebels there, 88l. 18s. 9d. [3] Ibid, p. 298.

of the English counties on the Border, that he had learnt that Owen Glyndwr " and his other rebels " were marching in great force towards the English Border, to carry away the stores, burn the country, and destroy the inhabitants.[4]   Henry was himself preparing to visit the north, when, in the middle of July, he received certain information of the great confederacy formed against him, and learnt that young Henry Percy was marching to join the Welsh with an army of English and Scots, which, when increased by the men of Cheshire led by his uncle, the Earl of Worcester, amounted to nearly fourteen thousand men.   The King was then at Burton-upon-Trent; with singular rapidity he marched towards the Border, and entered Shrewsbury when the army of the Percies were already near the town, and before the Welsh had time to join them.   The decisive battle of Shrewsbury, fought the next day, in which not less than ten thousand men are said to have fallen, destroyed the hopes of the confederates.   Most of the leaders of the rebels were killed or taken : Henry Percy was slain in the battle; and his uncle and one or two others were captured and immediately beheaded.

There are no less than five contemporary, and perhaps independent, accounts of the famous and severely contested battle which took place under the ancient walls of Shrewsbury, and which was the awful prelude to so many more between the rival houses.   We shall avail ourselves of the narrative drawn up from a comparison of the whole by the erudite historians of Salop.

"We are unable to trace the progress of Hotspur's long march from the north to Shrewsbury, a journey of not less than two hundred and fifty miles.   He, probably, set out in the beginning of July; and skirting along the eastern side of Cheshire, where his army received a considerable augmentation, passed through Stafford,[5] and was joined there by his uncle, the Earl of Worcester.[6]   The King, aware of his intention to gain possession of Shrewsbury, and desirous of cutting off his junction with Glyndwr, pursued him with hasty marches.   We find his Majesty, on the 16th of July, at Burton-upon-Trent, and on the 17th at Lichfield: whence, finding that he could not overtake his enemy, he hastened on to reach Shrewsbury before him.   He would naturally take the Watling-street road, and enter this town over the Abbey Bridge.   The route of Hotspur was more to the north, in order to keep up a communication with the Severn, so important for his junction with Glyndwr.   In all probability, he marched through Newport, by High Ercall and Haghmond Hill ; and hoped to gain admittance through the North or Castle Gate.   The King arrived just in time to save the town : he entered it only a few hours before Hotspur, who reached the Castle Foregate on the evening of Friday, July 19th, and the King's forces could not have advanced from Lichfield before the morning of that day.   They were certainly here before Percy : for, aware of the intention of that young nobleman, and desirous to save the castle from his attack, they set fire to that extensive suburb, and marched out of the castle gates to offer him battle.   Hotspur, unwilling to bring his army into action at the close of a toilsome march, and learning, from the royal banner[7] which waved on the walls, that the King was in possession of the town, called off his followers from the attack, and retired to the Bull-field, an extensive common which stretched from Upper Berwick[8] to the East.   He

---

[4] Rymer's Fœdera, iii., part 1, p. 46.

[5] Mr. Pennant brings him through Cheshire and Lichfield. But if he was at Stafford, Lichfield seems an unnecessary deviation from his route. That he touched on some part of Cheshire there can be little doubt, from the great numbers of that county who joined his forces. This, which is abundantly proved by other authorities, is further confirmed by the following entry on the patent rolls:

Pat. 4 H. IV., p. 2. m. 7. "Pro Henrico principe Wallie, De tractando cum gentibus comitatus Cestriæ de finibus et redemptionibus suis faciendis pro rebellionibus suis apud bellum de Salop in comitiva Henrici de Percy."

[6] Hall, sub ann.   [7] Walsingham, 368.

[8] Hence this engagement was sometimes called the Battle of Bulfield. In the Calendar of Inquisitions ad quod damnum, 4 Henry V., is the following entry : " Johannes Massy de Tatton chivaler defunctus in villa de Harlescote juxta Salop proditorie insurrexit cum armaturis, &c., contra Henricum nuper regem Anglie, et apud bellum de Bolefeld idem Johannes interfectus fuit."

It is also sometimes called the Battle of Berwickfield : and Upper Berwick was also entitled (nor is the name yet quite obsolete) " Berwick of the Bull-field," to distinguish it from Lower Berwick, the manorial residence of the Thurnhams and Leybournes, the Enderbies and Lacies, and in later times, of the families of Jones, Hosyer, and Powys.

It was also called the Battle of Husseyfield, from the ancient family who possessed the site on which it was fought. " Rogero Acton armig' Regis de extenta omnium terrarum et tenementorum que fuerunt Johannis Russale armig' tam in com' Salop. quam in com' Ebor. que quidem D'ni Regis forisfact' existunt eo quod idem Joh'es contra Regem et fideles suos cum Henrico Percy proditore et in bello de Husifelde interfectus extitit." Original. ex offic. rememorator. thesaurar. in scacc. 5 Hen. IV. rot. 19.

thus protected his rear by the woody and impervious precipices extending to Leaton-shelf, and had the river not only on his side, but also, if it had not entirely deserted its ancient channel under Cross-hill (as there is reason to believe it had not), in its front also. This position enabled him likewise to communicate readily over that stream by the ford of Shelton with the forces of Glyndwr, when they should arrive, as he hoped, on the opposite bank. Here he passed the night in council. His army consisted of fourteen thousand chosen men, of whom a considerable part were of the county of Chester, at that time eminent for its skill in archery; but, if Hall is correct, the royal army was nearly double that number; for he writes that above forty thousand men were assembled on both parts, and every circumstance of the battle proves that the King was at the head of a very superior force. His situation was, however, by no means devoid of anxiety. He must have been conscious how slender the title was which he possessed to the throne: and how ill-disposed the peerage of his realm were to maintain him upon it. From the castle he might view, as the dawn arose, the plain which stretched to the north, glittering with hostile arms: while the dreadful Glyndwr was believed to be in full march from Oswestry, to join the rebels with his Welsh forces. But the difficulties of the crisis only sufficed to call forth his energies and display his talents.

Henry was himself a distinguished warrior. In earlier life he had, in company with his princely uncle the Duke of Gloucester, travelled into the north of Europe in quest of martial glory;[1] and under the banners of the renowned Teutonic order had made a glorious campaign against the Pagans of Lithuania.[2] He was still in the vigour of life, being much under forty years of age, and an adversary every way worthy of the gallant Percy; whom, relying upon the superiority of his numbers, he determined, if possible, to force to an engagement, before that young nobleman should receive his reinforcements from Wales or the north. By break of day, therefore, he dispatched, it is probable, a strong force, under the nominal command (for it could be no more) of the young prince, the future hero of Agincourt, but then a youth of fourteen years, to come up with Hotspur at Berwick, if possible. He himself, with the main body, appears to have marched out on the Hadnall-road, ready to proceed as occasion might demand, either to the north of Cross-hill and Almond Pool, and close the rebels between his two divisions; or else to advance further on upon that road, where it branches off to Shawbury, with the view of cutting off their retreat, if Hotspur, aware of his design, should attempt to march to the east. It happened as the King anticipated. Hotspur, on his advance, broke up in some disorder, and marched by Harlescot and Abright Hussey to Hateley-field, which stretches from thence eastwards. Here, however, finding it impossible to avoid an engagement, on account, as we may suppose, of the obstruction to his retreat presented by the King's movement above mentioned, he made his stand in the rear of a field of pease nearly ripe; behind which he stationed his army, and hoped thereby to deter the King from advancing over a tract which must necessarily impede his operations.

He then addressed his little army in a short harangue, of which Walsingham has preserved the heads.

---

[1] Hackluyt, i. 122.

[2] The following notice is from Hardyng's Chronicle, chap. cciii. fol. cci. ccii.

"Howe for therle of Marche his right Sir H. Percy & Sir Tho. P. his uncle earl of Worc' faught with the king & were slaine at the battaile of Shrewsbury, where al the lordes deceyved them the yr. of Xt. mcccciii & of his reigne the 4th y. that were bound to them by their seales except therle of Stafforde which letters I saw in the castel of Werkeworthe when I was constable of it under my lord Sr Rob. Umfraville who had that castel of K. H. his gift by forfeiture of therle of Northd.

"On Maudleyn even was on the Saturday
After long treate the prince began to fight
The yere of Xt. a M. was no nay
Four hundreth also & thre therto ful right
When the battaile was stryken of mekyl might

And of the kyng then was the fourth yere
Of his reigne accompted wel & clere."

This is all that Hardyng says on the subject of the battle. Hall, who had evidently read, and indeed quotes this chronicle, confounds and totally misconceives his information. After relating that the Percies showed their articles of confederacy to diverse noble men and prelates of the realm, who promised them aid and succour, not only by wordes but by their writing and seals, he proceeds: "al the confederates them abandoned, & at the daie of the conflict left alone, the Erle of Stafford only excepte, which beyng of a haute corage & hye stomache kept his promise & ioined with the Percies to his destruccion." xx. b. Thus Hall makes Stafford, who according to Hardyng was the only peer who kept his faith to the king, and whom we know to have fallen in his quarrel, the only peer who kept his faith to Hotspur, and perished on his side!

H H

" We must desist," said he, " from any further attempt to retreat,' and turn our arms on those who come against us.   Ye see the royal banner, nor is there time to seek a passage even though we wished it.   Stand, therefore, with stedfast hearts : for this day shall either promote us all, if we conquer ; or deliver us from an usurper, if we fall : and it is better to die in battle for the common wealth, than after battle by the sentence of our foe :" and with this, to support the courage of his men by proving his design to fight to the outrance,' he dispatched two of his esquires, Kynaston and Salvayn, with that strange letter of defiance, in which he loads the King with the most horrid crimes : and of which, though it sadly interrupts the order of our narration, an abstract must be laid before the reader.   It runs in the names of himself, his father, and his uncle :—

" WE, Henry Percy, Earl of Northumberland, Constable of England, and Keeper of the West March of England against Scotland, Henry Percy, our first-born son, Keeper of the East March of England against Scotland, and Thomas Percy, Earl of Worcester, Stewards and Protectors of the State, before our Lord Jesus Christ, our Supreme Judge, aver, say, and intend to prove with our hands, personally, on this day, against you, Henry, Duke of Lancaster, your accomplices and supporters, that you have unjustly assumed and named yourself King of England without a just title, but by thy treachery and the violence of thy supporters ; because, when you entered England after your exile, you swore to us at Doncaster, upon the Holy Gospels, held and likewise kissed by you personally, that you would not lay any claim to the kingdom, or to the Royal Estate, but only to your own heritage, and the heritage of your wife in England, and that Richard, at that time our Lord and King, should reign to the end of his life, guided by the good counsel of the Lords Spiritual and Temporal.   You imprisoned that same Lord, thy King and ours, beneath the Tower of London, until, through fear of death, he resigned the Kingdoms of England and France, and renounced all his right in the aforesaid Kingdoms, and his other dominions and lands beyond the sea.   Upon the plea of which resignation and renunciation, by the advice of your supporters, and by the public clamour of the vulgar populace, collected together at Westminster by you and your accomplices, you crowned yourself King of the aforesaid Kingdoms, and took possession of all the citadels and Royal domains, contrary to your oath ; wherefore you are perjured and false.

" Likewise we aver, say, and intend to prove that, although you swore to us upon the Sacred Gospels at the same time and place, that you would permit no tenths from the clergy, no fifteenths from the people, nor any other imposts to be levied in the Kingdom of England for the Royal use, so long as you should live, except by the advice of the three estates of the Kingdom in Parliament, and not then, except under the greatest necessity, for the resistance of enemies only, and not otherwise : you, contrary to your oath so given, have caused to be levied very many tenths, fifteenths, and other taxes and imposts, from the clergy, the community of England, and the merchants, through fear of your Royal Majesty ; wherefore you are perjured and false.

" Likewise we aver, say, and intend to prove that, although you swore to us upon the same Holy Gospels, at the same time and place, that Richard, our Lord and King and yours, should reign in his own royal right as long as he should live : you treacherously caused our Lord the King and yours to be imprisoned in your Castle of Pontefract without his consent, or the decree of the Lords of the Kingdom,

---

³ Walsingham has certainly misplaced this brief and characteristic address. He supposes it to have been spoken on the evening before the battle : but it is plain, from the tenour of it, that he must be mistaken ; no general would exhort his followers to make a vigorous resistance, and immediately march them off to a distance. As we have no wish to sacrifice historic truth to a favourite hypothesis, it must be observed that the words " to retreat " are not in the original. That runs thus : " Henricus autem (i. e. Percy) subito conspecto vexillo regio cum jam instaret effringere villam, mox destitit ab infestatione villanorum, dicens suis, *Desistere nos oportet ab inceptis et*

arma vertere," &c. The historian evidently conceived the " attempt " from which Hotspur counselled his troops to desist, to be the attack of the townsmen : but it does not appear that he ever could attack them ; before he reached the castle gates, the king marched out to meet him. The attempt which he told them to relinquish was doubtless that of retreating.

⁴ Hall, quoting the same authority with ourselves, Hardyng, represents this manifesto as sent the night before the battle. But Hardyng is express : it was " sente to kynge Henry in the felde."

and to suffer hunger, thirst, and cold for fifteen days and as many nights, and to perish by murder, which is horrible to be heard amongst Christians; wherefore you are perjured and false.

" Likewise we aver, say, and intend to prove that, as soon as Richard, our Lord the King and yours, was so horribly murdered as above stated, you seized, usurped, and took forcible possession of the Kingdom of England, and the name and honour of King of France, unjustly and contrary to your oath, from Edmund Mortimer, Earl of March, then the nearest and direct heir of England and France, immediately and hereditarily to succeed after the decease of the aforesaid Richard; wherefore you are perjured and false.

" Likewise we aver, say, and intend to prove, as before, that although you swore at the same time and place to support and maintain the laws and good customs of the Kingdom of England, and afterwards, at the time of your coronation, you swore to defend and preserve them uncorrupted, you craftily and contrary to the law of England, wrote to your supporters to elect in every county in England, for each Parliament, representatives such as were favourable to you, so that in your Parliaments we could gain no justice in these our complaints now mentioned, contrary to your will, although we have often complained to you, according to the consciences given to us by God, without avail, as God is our witness, and also the venerable fathers, Thomas Arundell, Archbishop of Canterbury, and Richard Scroope, Archbishop of York; therefore it now behoves us, before our Lord Jesus Christ, to seek redress with a strong hand.

" Likewise we aver, say, and intend to prove, that when Edmund Mortimer, brother of Roger Mortimer, late Earl of March and Ulster, was captured by Owen Glyndwr in open war in thy cause, and still kept in prison and iron chains, you proclaimed that he was captured by stratagem, and would not allow any treaty for his liberation, neither through himself nor us, his relations and friends, wherefore we treated for his liberation with the above mentioned Owen Glyndwr for the sake of peace between thee and the same Owen, with our own property, on which account you have regarded us as traitors, and likewise have craftily and secretly compassed and imagined the death and final destruction of our persons. Therefore we have the greatest distrust in you and your accomplices and supporters, as being traitors, and the destroyers of the Royal Estate, and the invaders, oppressors, and spoilers of the true and rightful heir of England and France, and we here intend to prove it, with our own hands, on this day, with the assistance of Almighty God." [5]

No one has informed us how the King received this furious manifesto. He had something else to engage his attention. He proceeded [6] to marshal his forces, dividing them into two columns, or wedges. Of one of these he took the command himself, and entrusted the other to his son. The front rank of his own column was led on by his nephew, the young Earl of Stafford, a soldier of conspicuous valour, on whom he had that morning conferred the high office of Constable of England, recently enjoyed by the Earl of Northumberland. Previous to the final onset, the King, in compliance with the customs of chivalry, bestowed the honour of knighthood on certain of his most distinguished esquires. [7] Hotspur, perceiving that an engagement was unavoidable, called for his favourite sword. His attendants informed him that it was left behind at Berwick, of which village it does not appear that he had till then learned the name. At these words he turned pale, and said, " I perceive that my plough is drawing to its last furrow, for a wizard told me in Northumberland that I should perish at Berwick: which I vainly interpreted of that town in the North." [8] His courage did not, however, yield to the impressions of superstition; he rallied his spirits,

---

[5] Archæologia, xvi. 139. seqq. from a MS. of Hardyng in the British Museum.

[6] It is very probable that this division had taken place at an earlier hour, and that the king made this disposition, as we have supposed, before his troops quitted Shrewsbury: but we have unfortunately no details on the subject.

[7] The learned M. de la Curne de Ste Palaye, in his curious historical notes on the Vow of the Heron (Mem. sur l'anc. Chev. v. iii. p. 79) records this practice, and adds, " one may easily conceive with what courage this honour must inspire those who obtained it:

and with what ardour they would maintain the glory of their recent title." So in Lawrence Minot's 6th poem on the successes of King Edward III.

" Knights war ther wale to score,
That war new dubbed two that dance."

See Shakspeare, Hen. V., act iv., sc. ult.

[8] It is immaterial to our present purpose whether any part of this incident be authentic or not. The calling for the sword may be derived from the *notum efflagitat ensem* of the Æneid, xii. 759; the form of expression (the *furrow* and the *plough*) may have been a

and arranged his troops with his usual ability: assigning their respective stations to his uncle Worcester, the Scottish Earl of Douglas,[*] his recent captive at Halidon; Sir Richard Venables, Baron of Kinderton; Hugh Brow, Hugh Vernon, and others. His troops appear to have been chiefly stationed on the north side of the spot now occupied by the church, in a field still called the Hateleys: on the east side of the church is a field denominated the King's Croft, in which, it may be presumed, were ranged those which the King commanded in person. These positions exactly agree with the objects which we have assigned above to the respective leaders; and lend, it is hoped, some confirmation to the conjectural part of the preceding narration.

While the hostile armies, drawn up in battle array facing each other, waited, with mute expectation, the sound of the trumpet, the dreadful signal for combat, two venerable divines, Thomas Prestbury, Lord Abbot of Salop, and the Clerk of the Privy Seal, advanced out of the royal army, and proceeded towards that of Percy. The King, desirous to spare the blood of his subjects, offered him and his adherents pardon and peace, and redress of all grievances of which they could justly complain. Hotspur was touched by these unexpected overtures, made under circumstances of such numerical inequality, and requested his uncle of Worcester to repair to the royal presence in company of these holy men, and state the grounds on which he had taken up arms. The King, we may suppose, was in his turn somewhat softened by the sight of the Earl, who had been so recently engaged in the domestic office of Governor to the Prince of Wales; and a recollection of the obligations he had received from the Percy family might mix itself with his other reflections. It is certain that to the remonstrances of Worcester, delivered in a fierce and haughty tone, he listened with respect, and replied with a condescension which, in the opinion of the spectators, was somewhat unbefitting the royal dignity.[1] A contemporary writer[2] has preserved, though with a mistake of the person,[3] the dialogue supposed to have passed between them. The King "counselled him to put himself on his grace." To which the other replied, "I trust not in your grace."—"I pray God," rejoined the King, "that thou mayest have to answer for the blood here to be shed this day, and not I. March on, standard-bearer!" and the battle was set.—It is certain that the stern temper of Worcester rejected all attempts at conciliation: he was conscious how deeply he had been engaged in fomenting the quarrel; and, on his return to his friends, he misrepresented the demeanour of Henry in such a manner to his nephew, that the latter, with whatever reluctance, was compelled to relinquish all hopes of accommodation. At length, therefore, much of the day having been consumed in these fruitless negotiations, both parties flew to arms, and the air was rent with the war-cries of "St. George" on one side, and "Esperance Percy" on the other. In the meanwhile, Glyndwr had advanced as far as Shelton, on the opposite bank of the Severn, where he awaited the issue of the contest, determined to proceed or retire according to its event.[4] He is said, by the

---

common monastic metaphor, (see Gale's Scriptores, i. 281); and what Otterbourne calls the "*equivocation*" of Berwick, may be paralleled by twenty similar tales from the Acherusia of the Epirot (Livy, viii. 24) to the Jerusalem chamber of this very King Henry: (See Malone's Shakspeare, edited by Boswell, xvii. 197.) All that is material of the incident in an historical view, is the support which it gives to the position we have assigned to the army of Hotspur on the night of the 19th of July.

It was at Upper Berwick in all probability that this sword was left: the other would have been too remote from the body of the army, for the head-quarters of the general: and as it appears from a statute-merchant on the records of Shrewsbury exchequer (liber A.) that William Betton of Berwick was obliged to borrow a sum of money in this very year, it is not unreasonable to conclude, that this necessity was created by the compulsory hospitality he was forced to display upon the present occasion towards the Northumbrian leader.

[*] This was Archibald, the third Earl of Douglas, so unfortunate in all his enterprises, that he acquired the epithet of Tineman, because he "tined" or lost his followers in every battle which he fought.

See the Lady of the Lake: and note ix. on Canto 2. He was scarcely recovered from the loss of an eye at Halidon; nor did he escape unmutilated from the field of Shrewsbury. ·

[1] "Cum rex omni rationi condescendisset, et humiliasset se, secus quàm personam regiam, decuisset." Walsingham, p. 368.

[2] The author of Eulogium, as quoted above. Leland's Collectanea, i. 312.

[3] The fragment just mentioned represents Hotspur himself as holding this interview with the king; but we are certain from Walsingham that such was not the fact.

[4] "Owen Glendour promised Henry Percy to have joined with him at that batttaile." Leland. But the British chieftain acted upon this occasion in the spirit of the Tassillon of a late epic:—

"Hardi dans les complots, mais incertain, perfide;
    Alors qu'il faut tirer le glaive au champ d'honneur,
Tassillon veut savoir quel sera le vainqueur,
    Avant de deployer sa banniere timide."
                                Charlemagne, xvii. 12.

Mr. Warrington has made a fine use of this failure in his tale of

constant tradition of the country, to have ascended there the branches of a lofty oak, whose venerable trunk yet remains, for the purpose of viewing the battle; at least, of gaining, from personal inspection, the earliest intelligence of its event.

The fight began by furious and repeated volleys of arrows from Hotspur's archers, whose ground, as may be seen, greatly favoured that kind of warfare: and they did great execution on the royal army. The King's bowmen were not wanting in return, and the battle raged with violence. The military art had not yet attained that perfection which almost supersedes the effect of individual exertion; and Hotspur, with his associate Douglas, bent on the King's destruction, rushing through the midst of the hostile arrows, pierced their way to the spot on which he stood. To adopt the vivid language of a contemporary,[5] "in the ardour of his spirit, he assembled a band of thirty warriors, broke into the royal army, and made a great alley in the midst thereof," such was the terror which his presence inspired "even to the stoutest of the King's guards." Monstrelet says, Henry was thrice unhorsed by the Scottish Earl, and would have been taken or slain had he not been defended and rescued by his own men. And the fortune of the day would have been forthwith decided, if the Scottish Earl of March[6] had not withdrawn him from the danger; for the royal standard-bearer was slain, his banner beaten down; and many of the chosen band appointed to guard it (among whom were the Earl of Stafford and Sir William Blount), were killed by these desperate assailants,—while the young Prince of Wales was wounded in the face by an arrow. In short, notwithstanding all the exertions of the royalists,[7] victory seemed inclined to favour the rebel army, who fought with renewed ardour, from an opinion, naturally derived from the overthrow of his standard, that the King himself had fallen,[8] and animated each other to the combat with cheering and redoubled shouts of "*Henry Percy, King! Henry Percy, King!*"

In this critical moment, the gallant Percy, raging through the adverse ranks in quest of his sovereign,

Howel and Glyndwr, which forms one of the brightest ornaments of the pages of Marmion :—

> "Ev'n from the day, when, chain'd by fate,
>   By wizard's dream, or potent spell,
> Ling'ring from sad Salopia's field,
>   Reft of *his* aid the Percy fell;
>
> "Ev'n from that day, misfortune still,
>   As if for violated faith,
> Pursued him with unwearied step,
>   Vindictive still for Hotspur's death."

[5] Eulogium, ut supr.

[6] This nobleman is generally called the Earl of Dunbar: but Dunbar was his family name. He wrote himself *Le Count de la March d'Escoce*. He quitted his country in disgust, on the Duke of Rothsay's refusal to marry his daughter who had been affianced to that prince, and afterwards resided in the court of Henry IV., to whom he was related : "Ane of yhour poer kyn," as he calls himself, in a letter addressed to the king: "and, excellent prince," he proceeds, "syn that I claim to be of kyn tyll yhow, & it peraventour nocht knawen on yhour parte, I schew it to your lordship be this my lettre, that gif Dame Alice the Bewmont was yhour graunde dame, Dame Marjory Comyne hyrr full sister was my graund dame on the tother syde : sa that I am bot of the feirde degré of kyn tyll yhow, the quilk in alde tyme was callit neir."—Pinkerton's Hist. of Scotland, vol. i., Appendix. A descent is omitted in this statement. The Duke of Lancaster, maternal grandfather to the king, married a daughter of the Lord Beaumont by Alice Comyn, the Earl of Buchan's daughter : and when Henry invaded Scotland, he took care to remind the natives of the Scottish blood which flowed in his veins.

[7] According to Monstrelet, the king slew thirty-six men at arms with his own hands. Vol. i. c. 7.

[8] Some of our historians relate that, at this famous battle, Henry IV.

caused several persons to be clothed in royal armour similar to his own, in order that he might elude the pursuit of his assailants : and such an expedient we find recorded on other occasions. Thus, in the battle between Chunibert, king of the Lombards, and the rebel Alachis, a priest is said to have been killed in consequence of having dressed himself in Chunibert's habit, (Origines Langobard., p. 32) : and at a much later period, 1513, one Elphinstone, wearing the same arms as the Scottish monarch, is supposed to have fallen at Flodden fight. (Lord Herbert's Life of Hen. VIII. p. 44). But Walsingham takes no notice of this device in his account of the battle of Shrewsbury, and we may therefore reasonably doubt whether it was practised on this occasion. It certainly does not accord with our general idea of the gallantry of the king : though, on the other hand, motives of prudent policy might justify its adoption. Montaigne, in his Essays, (vol. i. c. 47), "*De l'incertitude de nostre jugement*," discusses the question of the expediency of such disguises at some length. "When we consider how much depends on the safety of the commander, it seems as if we could not doubt that it is right to adopt them : on the other hand," says he, "the inconvenience which we incur thereby, is not less than that which we would avoid : for the general not being recognised by his followers, the courage which they would receive from his example and presence begins by degrees to fail ; and losing the sight of his marks and accustomed ensigns, they judge him either to be dead, or to have retired despairing of success." He subjoins several instances of this practice : to which he might have added that of Ahab, (1 Kings, xxii. 30). Trajan, we are told, was very nearly being wounded in his expedition against the Agarenes, καιπερ την βασιλικην στολην αποθεμενος ινα μη γνωρισθη. Xiphilin. e Dione, c. lxviii. p. 785. The conduct of Henry IV. of France at the battle of Ivri (1590) was decidedly the reverse. "Si vous perdez vos enseignes, cornettes, ou guidons, ne perdez point de vue mon panache blanc, vous le trouverez toujours au chemin de l'honneur et de la victoire." Perefixe, Hist. d' Hen. IV. part 2.

fell by an unknown hand; alone, and hemmed in by foes. The King lost no time to avail himself of this event. Straining his voice to the utmost, he exclaimed aloud, *"Henry Percy is dead!"* The sound was heard by either army: into those it struck dismay, while these it animated and encouraged. The rebels fled in every direction, nor could the King, anxious as he was to terminate the slaughter, restrain the impetuous pursuit of his own troops, till the flower of Cheshire, two hundred knights and esquires (besides pages and footmen), were slain. Douglas broke through, and endeavoured to escape in the direction of Haghmond-hill:[9] being closely pursued, and leaping from a crag, he experienced a severe injury, and was captured: but the King, in admiration of his valour, set him at liberty.[1]

The loss in both armies was great: in the judgment of that age, it was the severest field that had ever been fought. But the estimates of the numbers slain vary, as might be expected, in a very great degree. One authority[2] names sixteen; another,[3] eighteen hundred. Walsingham gives no precise number. "On the royal side," he says, "*many* esquires and valets, and *a large body* of private soldiers were slain, besides ten knights.[4] On the same side three thousand were severely wounded. On the adverse part, most of the knights and esquires of Cheshire were killed, to the number of two hundred; besides damosels[5] and footmen, whose number, I have not been able to learn." An ancient manuscript rates the number of gentlemen at two thousand two hundred and ninety-one, besides commons.[6] They were chiefly buried, says that authority, in a great pit, the dimensions of which are there specified, and over which the present church of Battlefield was afterwards erected: but many are stated[7] to have lain dispersed in various directions for the space of three miles about the field of battle: a fact which confirms what has been said above of the desultory nature of the conflict. Others of the more distinguished rank, were interred in the neighbouring town, chiefly in the cemetery of the Dominican, or St. Mary's Friars.[8]

The Sunday was, no doubt, occupied in devout thanksgiving in all the parochial and conventual churches of Shrewsbury, and in the decent offices of sepulture: and on the spot wherein the armies

---

[9] Tradition says that the queen was stationed on Haghmond-hill; where a thicket called "The Queen's Bower," is yet shown. Henry is not likely to have brought her to Shrewsbury on such an occasion: and the tale is disgraced by a foolish etymology of the name *Haghmond* from her exclamation, "Hey, man!" to a messenger, whose announcement of the victory she had heard imperfectly, which is utterly unworthy of notice, and throws suspicion over the whole. Haghmond is unquestionably derived from the High Mount (haut mont), midway of which the venerable abbey was placed.

[1] For this our only authority is Mr. Philips, p. 38. But if Douglas did fall from a crag, it must have been from Haghmond-hill, as there is no other in the neighbourhood; and this is just in the direction which Hotspur would gladly have taken, and which the *Tineman* would therefore naturally pursue. Hall, however, is the first writer who introduces this circumstance respecting the Scottish Earl. None of the contemporaries mention it. All that Walsingham says of him is, "verenda transfixus perdidit paulo minus loculum." P. 369. Whether Hall had any authority for the crag, or Philips for placing it at Haghmond, does not appear.

[2] Eulogium ut supra.

[3] Registrum de Lacok in Ashmole MSS. vol. 866, p. 320—this is expressed to be *ex utraque parte.*

[4] These appear to have been the Earl of Stafford, Sir Hugh Stanley, Sir John Clifton, Sir John Kokaine, Sir Nicholas Gansell, Sir Walter Blount, Sir John Calveley, Sir John Massey of Puddington, Sir Hugh Mortimer, and Sir Robert Gonsill, which last had received the honour of knighthood that morning.

[5] Domicellos, Damoisel, Damoiseau, is expounded by Cotgrave, "A young gentleman professing arms and not yet knighted:" or as Chifflet, quoted by Du Cange (in v.) and the Abbé de Sade (Mem. de Petrarque, i. 130, n.) have it, "the son of a knight, not yet knighted." Curne de Ste Palaye, however, considers the term as merely synonymous with esquire: (Mem. sur l'ancienne Chevalerie, t. i. p. 36;) and it is plain that Walsingham could not have considered it in the exclusive sense of Chifflet. Mr. Hallam (Hist. of Midd. Ages, i. 150) who adopts the definition of De la Curne, says that the title was unknown before the thirteenth century. In the Cæremoniale Episcoporum (Rome, 4to, 1606, lib. i. cap. 23) "barones et domicelli sine titulo," are to be censed, "post magistratus omnes."

[6] "Bellum Salopiæ in campo vocato Haitlefeld alais Berwyefeld ——pridie festum be. Mariæ Magd. 1403. Ubi interfecti sunt procerum 2291, præter communes, quorum corpora inibi sunt tumulata in quodam tumulo sive puteo in longitudine 160 ped. in latitudine 68, ac in profunditate 60: supraque corpora——idem rex constrxi fecit collegium de 6 capellanis et 6 pauperibus—concessis ad idem indulgentiis graciosis per Romanos pontifices et episcopos provinciæ Anglicanæ." Mr. Godolphin Edwards, from a MS. That the church was built over the remains of the slain is confirmed by its dimensions; in length 126 feet; in breadth (with the cemetery) 65.

[7] See the charter of 5 Dec., 24 Henry VI. to the College of Battlefield. "Quorum corpora circa tria miliaria et ultra in eodem campo et circiter eundem campum jacent humata."

[8] In the year 1801, when the upper part of the Friars was partially levelled, many remains were disinterred. A gentleman was present when a skeleton was dug up seven feet two inches in length, and another saw there five skeletons laid close together, without any appearance of a coffin. These were probably some of those who fell at Battlefield. Our latter informant, an eminent physician, says, what he saw were young subjects, the teeth firm in their heads.

were chiefly engaged, and which from this destructive contest has borne to after-ages the name of Battlefield,* a collegiate establishment was soon after erected to pray for the souls of all those who fell therein.

The body of Hotspur was at first delivered to his kinsman, Lord Furnival,¹ for interment, and it was by him committed to the ground with the suffrages of the Church, and with all the honours which, in that haste, could be procured as due to his rank. It is painful to reflect, that the King afterwards repented him of this generous attention to the remains of deceased valour. He caused the corpse to be taken out of the tomb in which it had been laid, and to be placed between two mill-stones in the public street, near the pillory;² where, as if he feared lest the general sympathy should rescue it from its ignominious situation, it was kept under military guard, till the head was severed from the body, which was divided into quarters, and transmitted to several cities of the realm. There is no need to waste many words on this transaction, disgraceful only to its author.

On the following Monday, after the form of a trial, the inhabitants of Shrewsbury beheld the execution of certain prisoners of note,—the Baron of Kinderton, Sir Richard Vernon, and, chief of all, the Earl of Worcester, who paid for his complicated offences of treason and perfidy by the loss of his head, which by the King's order was set upon London bridge.³

The King quitted the Border immediately after the battle of Shrewsbury, in order to secure the northern counties. Early in the spring he had appointed Prince Henry his lieutenant in Wales,⁴ and now on quitting the Marches, on the 25th of July, the King then at Stafford, gave him authority to pursue the rebels, as well as to pardon and receive into favour those that would turn to their allegiance.⁵

Although Glyndwr did not succeed in joining the Percies before their engagement with the King's army, he nevertheless invaded the neighbouring English counties with a formidable army. On one occasion the rival armies encamped within a short distance of each other, in the neighbourhood of Leominster, but no engagement took place. It appears that the English merely drove the Welsh over the Border. After the King had repressed the presumption of his northern barons, he returned to direct the operations of his army in the Borders, in person. We find him at Worcester on the 8th of September, giving orders for strengthening the Welsh castles, the neglect of which he says had been the cause of Glyndwr's success.⁶ From Worcester he proceeded to Hereford, where we find him on the 14th, giving power to William Beauchamp to take into his grace the rebels about Abergavenny, and Ewyas Harold. From Hereford the King marched directly into Wales. On the 15th of September he was at Devynork, in the neighbourhood of Brecknock, granting a commission similar to the one just mentioned, to Sir John Oldcastle, John ap Henry, and John Fairford, clerk, to pardon and disarm the inhabitants of the districts of Brecknock, Buelth, "Cancresselly," Hay, "Glynbeng," and Dynas.⁷ On the 27th of September the King proclaimed a general pardon to such of the people of Cheshire, with few exceptions, as had been active in the rebellion, and had fought against him at the battle of Shrewsbury.

It is probable that the King, during this expedition, found means by favour and promises to corrupt⁸

* The field on which the Battle of Evesham was fought bears the same appellation.

¹ Thomas Nevile, Lord Furnival, was grandson of Matilda Percy, the great aunt of Hotspur: he was also nephew to King Henry.

² "Corpus de tumulo exhumari precepit et inter duas molas asinarias in quodam vico de Shrewsbury juxta collistrigium reponi fecit." Anglia Sacra, ii. p. 366. One of the horse-mills of which we have formerly read, was probably employed on this disgusting occasion.

³ The writ to this effect bears date at Lichfield, July 25. Rymer's Fœdera, v. iv. pt. 1. p. 52. Monstrelet, whose brief account of this battle is full of errors, writes "the Lord Thomas Percy was there slain, and his nephew Henry made prisoner, whom the king ordered

instantly to be put to death before his face." We are sure that it was the nephew who was slain, and the uncle who was made prisoner; but with this change of persons, the story is like enough to be true. The age was barbarous, and the earl had sinned in a deep measure.

⁴ Rymer's Fœdera, iv. part 1, p. 41.

⁵ Ibid., p. 52.   ⁶ Ibid., p. 55.   ⁷ Ibid., p. 56.

⁸ There is one instance, however, recorded by the Monk of Evesham at this time, which shows true paternal affection, and adds much to the honour of our countrymen. A Welshman (he might have been one of the above) had made a rash promise to the king when in Wales, to betray Glyndwr, but on second consideration he afterwards refused to perform it, and, eagerly stretching out his

the fidelity of several of the friends of Glyndwr; for we find a free pardon granted to William ap Tudor (a gentleman who had been excepted in the pardon of last year), and to thirty-one others of the inhabitants of the country. The pardon is dated at Westminster, on the 8th of July, 1401.[9] This defection seemed to have very little effect on the spirit of Glyndwr. He acquired new friends, and such addition of strength, that the King resolved to go again in person against him. He issued out his orders to the sheriffs of Devonshire, and one and twenty other counties, to repair with their forces to Worcester, on the 1st of October, from whence he proceeded with thirty thousand men to the mountains of Wales, where he hoped to take Glyndwr by surprise; but the Welsh chieftain, with his accustomed skill and tact, was prepared to meet him. The elements again favoured him on this occasion, which augmented the misery of the English army. They were watched so narrowly, that neither forage nor victuals could pass to the King's camp. Torrents of rain, swollen rivers, and precipitous rocks, were unusual difficulties to soldiers from flat and fertile regions. The torrents of rain that fell nightly disturbed their encampments, and, on account of the slippery nature of the ground, Henry, at last, was forced to decamp. A shameful and rapid retreat was the only alternative; and a disastrous one he made, after having suffered a considerable loss in men and ammunition, as well as fifty of his carriages.[1] Shakespeare puts the following ostentatious words into Glyndwr's mouth, in consequence of Henry's repeated defeats:—

> " Three times hath Harry Bolingbroke made head
> Against my pow'r; thrice from the banks of the Wye
> And sandy bottom Severn have I sent
> Him bootless home, and weather-beaten back."

Glyndwr was now in the meridian of his glory. He assembled the estates at Machynlleth, a town in Montgomeryshire, where he caused his title to the Principality to be acknowledged, and was formally crowned, Prince of Wales.

At this meeting he narrowly escaped assassination. Among the chieftains who appeared to support his title, came a gentleman from Brecknockshire, David Gam,[2] or the Crooked David; "a man," says Mr. Carte,[3] "who held his estate of the honour of Hereford, who had long been in the service of Bolingbroke, and was firmly attached to his interest. Notwithstanding he had first married a sister of Owen Glyndwr, yet such a furious hatred had he conceived to his cause, that he appeared at the assembly with the secret and treacherous resolution of murdering his Prince and his brother-in-law. Carte says he was instigated to it by King Henry. He was a man of unshaken courage; and party zeal, or hopes of reward, probably determined him to so nefarious a deed. The plot of David against his Prince was, however, discovered. He was arrested and imprisoned, and would have met with his merited punishment, if he had not been saved by the intercession of Owen's best friends and warmest partisans.[4] He was pardoned, on a solemn promise of adherence to the cause of Glyndwr and his country. It appears that our chieftain did not choose to rely on his promise, but kept him in close confinement till the year 1412, as will appear in the transactions of that period.

1404.—War was daily expected to break out with France. The parliament took the safety of the King's

---

neck to the headsman, told him to strike, for he had two sons at that time in the service of his chieftain; therefore, would on no account reveal his councils, which would prove penal to them.

[9] Rymer's Fœdera, viii. p. 209.

[1] Walsingham, p. 556.

[2] David Gam afterwards, in 1215, accompanied Henry V. to the Battle of Agincourt, and was selected by that monarch to go and ascertain the numbers of the enemy before the action. On his return he informed the king, " An't please you, my liege,* there are

---

* The numbers of the French army on this occasion amounted to 100,000, being ten times the number of the English forces.

---

enough to kill, enough to be taken prisoners, and enough to run away." The king was pleased with the reply; and in the battle, David, his son-in-law, Roger Vychan, and his relative Roger Lloyd, rescued his majesty when surrounded by his foes (viz. eighteen French cavaliers who had encompassed him), and whose life they saved at the risk of their own, and killed the eighteen Frenchmen. The king, after the victory, visited the spot where they lay in the agonies of death, and bestowed on them the only reward that could be then paid to their valour—the honour of knighthood. Shakspeare designates Sir David Gam by the name of Fluellyn.

[3] Carte, ii. p. 654.

[4] Wynne's Hist. Wales, p. 321.

person into consideration. His household was regulated; and, in particular, it was ordered that no *Frenchman* or *Welshman* should remain about his Majesty's person.[5]

There was at this time every appearance of a correspondence being carried on between the French King and the English and Welsh insurgents. The French fleets hovered around our coasts, and some effected a landing in the Isle of Wight. A league, offensive and defensive, was formed between Charles and Owen Glyndwr. Owen sent his Chancellor, Gryffyth Young, Archdeacon of Merioneth, and his kinsman, John Hanmer, ambassadors to the French Court. Their appointment is dated at Dolgelle in a princely style:—"Datum apud Dolguielli, 10 die mensis Maii MCCCC. quarto et principatus nostri quarto," and begins, "Owinus, Dei gratiâ Princeps Walliæ, &c."[6]

The French King received them with open arms. The treaty itself, which is worded as being a league between the King of France and the Prince of Wales, against the usurper Henry, Duke of Lancaster, was signed at Paris, on the 14th of June; and Glyndwr ratified it on the 12th of January, 1405, in his Castle of Llanbadarn.

During this year Owen Glyndwr appears to have been almost undisturbed master of Wales, with the exception of the stronger castles that were garrisoned and provisioned by the English. According to Thomas of Walsingham, "all this summer he plundered, burnt, and destroyed the districts around him, and by means either of treachery or open force made many prisoners, slew many of the English, and took many castles, some of which he levelled with the ground, while he fortified others as strongholds for himself."[7] The King seems to have satisfied himself with keeping a small force distributed over the counties of Hereford and Salop to protect the English side of the Border. As summer approached, this force was found insufficient, and Prince Henry repaired to the Border in person. On the 10th of June, the sheriff, escheator, and gentry of Herefordshire write from Hereford that the Welsh rebels had invaded and plundered "Inchonefelde" (Irchingfield) in that county, and that they threatened a more general invasion the following week with a force which the few English troops there were unable to withstand.[8] They appear to have effected their threat, and were only driven back by the arrival of Prince Henry. On the 26th of June, the latter writes to the King, who was then marching towards Scotland, that he had just arrived at Worcester, where he learnt that the Welsh had entered the county of Hereford in great force, burning and destroying on every side, that they were provisioned for fifteen days, and that they had already committed great havoc, when his approach had compelled them to retire; but he states that the insurgents were threatening to enter the county again in still greater numbers, and that he had called the chief men of the Border to meet him at Worcester, for the purpose of concerting measures to avert the danger.[9] The Prince appears to have made Worcester his head quarters; and we trace him there or in other parts of the Border during the summer and autumn.

During the latter part of the year 1404, the French had made some ineffectual attempts to carry over an army to Wales, which were frustrated by storms and other impediments; and the promised aid did not arrive till the beginning of the year following, which was perhaps the cause of the delay in Glyndwr's ratification of the treaty. A French army, said to have amounted to twelve thousand men, was then landed at Milford Haven, from a fleet of one hundred and twenty, or, according to some accounts, one hundred and forty ships.

The arrival of the French auxiliaries struck consternation into the English inhabitants of the Border.

---

[5] Carte, ii. 256.

[6] The King of France, Charles VI., seeing that the Cambrians were at open hostility with the King of England, resolved to fulfil towards them his promises, and those of his predecessors. He concluded with Owen Glyndwr a treaty, the first article of which ran thus:—

"Charles, by the grace of God, King of France, and Owen, by the same grace, Prince of Wales, will be united, confederated, and bound to each other, by the ties of true alliance, true friendship, and good and solid union, especially against Henry of Lancaster, the enemy of the said Lords, King, and Prince, and against all his aiders and abettors."—Rymer's Fœdera, iv., para. 1, p. 69.

[7] Walsingham, p. 562.

[8] Proceedings of the Privy Council, i. p. 223.

[9] *Ibid.*, p. 229. "Je feu certiffiez que les Galoys feurent descenduz en le countée de Hereford ardantz et destruantz mesme le countée en tresgrandz povoirs, et feurent vitaillez pur xv. jours, et voirs est q'ils ont arz et fait grand destruccioun en les bordures du dit countée."

They first took and burnt the town of Haverford West, but were defeated in their attempt upon the castle. They then marched towards Caermarthen, burning and destroying on the way. From a letter written from Conway on the Saturday after the Epiphany, we learn that the French were then preparing for a second attack upon the town of Caernarvon, having failed in their first attempt. Letters from Chester dated a few days later (15th and 16th of January) describe Harlech and Conway Castles as being likewise in great danger of falling into the hands of the Welsh.[1] In March their successes were interrupted for a moment by a severe defeat on the borders of Herefordshire. A body of eight thousand Welsh had come suddenly to Grosmont, where they burnt part of the town; the Prince, who was at Hereford, collected a small body of men, marched rapidly against them, and, on the 11th of March, defeated them with great slaughter. Eight hundred or a thousand of the Welsh are said to have been left dead on the field, amongst whom was Glyndwr's brother, Tudor; and his eldest son, Griffith, who commanded the expedition, was taken prisoner.[2] He, however, soon repaired his disgrace; for, collecting his forces again, he pursued the victors with such expedition, that he overtook them at a place called Craig y Dorth, near Monmouth, and entirely defeated them.[3] It appears that the King, alarmed by the successes of his enemies, intended to proceed in person against the Welsh about the end of April, and that he was at Worcester on the 8th of May; but he was called off to the north by the rebellion of the Earl of Northumberland and the Archbishop of York, and was again compelled to leave the prosecution of the war against Owen Glyndwr to the management of his son.[4]

At Caermarthen the French were joined by Glyndwr with about ten thousand Welshmen. The combined army, after having gained some other advantages in Wales, advanced towards England; and Prince Henry, pressed by superior numbers, was compelled to retreat to Worcester, pursued almost to the gates of the city by the invaders. This was late in the summer. The King, who had reduced to obedience his rebellious subjects in the north, hastened to the relief of his son. On the 8th of August he had sent directions to the sheriffs to raise the forces of the Border counties, and meet him at Hereford. On the 27th of August he was at Worcester.[5] The Welsh and French retired before him, and we find him with his army at Hereford on the 4th of September. It appears that there was some fighting, in which the French suffered considerable loss; and it is said that on one occasion the hostile armies lay in view of each other during eight days, separated only by a deep valley, but that the French and Welsh were at length obliged to retreat for want of provisions. King Henry made but a short stay at Hereford, for on the 10th of September we find him again in the north, at Beverley, in Yorkshire. The French appear to have reaped little satisfaction from the kind of warfare in which they were engaged: they had hardly landed in Wales when the ships of the cinque ports attacked and partly destroyed their fleet, and every attempt of the French government to send them stores and provisions had been defeated: and now, disheartened probably by a painful retreat, they re-embarked and left the Welsh to their own resources.

The latter, more habituated to their mountain warfare, defended themselves bravely, but they were no longer able to act on the same extensive scale. The English army had penetrated into Wales, and, by the 22nd of September, it had laid close siege to the Castle of Llanbedarn. The King, in a document of the date just mentioned, describes this as the last strong-hold of the rebels, the fall of which would ensure the pacification of the country, and he speaks of his intention to proceed thither and push forward the

[1] These letters are printed in Ellis's Original Letters, sup. cit. pp. 30—38. They certainly belong to 1405 and not as there supposed to 1404.

[2] The letter of Prince Henry to his father, describing this affair, is printed in Rymer's Fœdera, iv. part 1, p. 79 ; in Ellis, ib. p. 38, and in the Proceedings of the Privy Council, i. p. 248.

[3] The English historians mention this defeat of Glyndwr, and they tell us that the English army was commanded by Richard Beauchamp Earl of Warwick, who, according to the Dugdale Baronage, took the

banner of Glyndwr; but they are silent with respect to the revenge that so immediately followed. Owen's standard-bearer was Ellis ap Richard ap Howel ap Morgan Llwyd of Althrey, descended from Rhiwallon ap Durgad ap Tudor Trevor. This information is from some ancient MS. pedigrees, formerly in the possession of Thomas Griffith, Esq., of Rhual, Flintshire.

[4] Proceedings of the Privy Council, i. p. 251.

[5] Rymer's Fœdera, ib. pp. 85, 87.

siege in person.' Accordingly, we find him again at Worcester on the 6th of October. In the course of the month he entered Wales, but we have an indistinct and confused account of his operations. On the 3rd of November, he was at Dunstable, on his return to his capital. According to some accounts, he had been compelled to retreat through want of money and provisions; others say that he had experienced a rude check from the enemy by incautiously involving his army among the mountain passes. It is certain, however, that after this year the Welsh insurrection never presented the same formidable character which it had previously assumed.

But Owen Glyndwr still preserved his independence, and for several years he kept Prince Henry constantly occupied. It appears that he had nourished the hope of obtaining, by means of his French allies, a formal acknowledgment of his independence from the English monarch, whose weakness and embarrassments were much overrated by his foreign and domestic enemies. In 1406, the Welsh were again encouraged by the prospect of assistance from France, but they were, as before, disappointed in the results which they anticipated from it. A fleet of nearly thirty ships put to sea, but many of them were taken or rudely treated on the way, and those which succeeded with difficulty in reaching the Welsh coast exerted little influence on the war. Fifteen ships laden with provisions, which followed them, were all captured by the English. Prince Henry drove the rebels gradually out of South Wales, and many of Glyndwr's most faithful partisans were taken and committed to prison. In April we find the King issuing more general orders for taking the rebels into grace, and a few months later, the inhabitants of South Wales were ordered by proclamation to return to their houses. Prince Henry established himself at Caernarvon, from whence he directed this petty but desolating warfare, which was continued without interruption during the following year. We learn from the contemporary chroniclers that in the summer of 1407, the Prince besieged and took the Castle of Aberystwyth, which was however almost immediately retaken by Glyndwr.' In the latter months of the same year King Henry held his parliament at Gloucester.

In 1408, some kind of an insurrection appears to have taken place in Shropshire in favour of Glyndwr, for it is stated that John Talbot, Lord Furnival, who went at that time with two hundred men towards Caernarvon against Owen Glyndwr and his adherents, was stopped at Shrewsbury by the constable of the castle and town, who shut the gates against them.' In the year following Shropshire became the seat of still greater troubles. On the 16th of May the King directed letters to Edward de Charlton, Lord of Powys, and other barons on the Border, stating that he had heard that Owen Glyndwr and "John, the pretended bishop of St. Asaph" had collected together many rebels and traitors and joined themselves with "our enemies of France, Scotland, and other parts in the Principality of Wales, continuing their rebellion and committing great havoc."' The Welsh chieftain, about this time, sent a strong party headed by Rhys Ddu and Philpot Scudamore, his nephew, who overran and plundered a great part of Shropshire, till they were entirely defeated by the English. Rhys Ddu was taken, and executed in London.

From this period we know very little of Glyndwr's personal history. It is clear that he continued to hold a certain degree of precarious power, though tradition represents him as being frequently reduced to the most distressing expedients to escape the pursuits of his enemies. In the last year of the reign of King Henry IV., the English monarch authorised John Tiptoft, seneschal of Brecknock, and William Botiller, receiver of Brecknock, to treat with Owen for the ransom of David Gam, a Welsh gentleman who has rendered himself famous in history as the enemy of Glyndwr.' Yet at this period the hardy chieftain must have felt severely the desolation attendant upon civil strife; his bravest and most faithful friends had been slain in battle, or they had perished more ignominiously on the scaffold; even his nearest relations, the members of his own household, were lingering in English prisons.' As early as 1408 we find his own secretary and his son Gryffudd prisoners at Nottingham, in the custody of Richard Grey of Codnor; and

⁶ Rymer's Fœdera, ib. p. 90.
⁷ Thomas of Walsingham, p. 568.
⁸ MS. Addit. Mus. Brit. No. 4599, art. 30.
⁹ Rymer's Fœdera, iv. part 1, p. 154.   ¹ Ibid.   ² Ibid.

we learn among the records of the first year of King Henry V., that on the 27th of June in that year (1413) thirty pounds were paid to John Weale " for the expenses of the wife of Owen Glyndwr, the wife of Edmund Mortimer (Glyndwr's daughter), and others their sons and daughters, in his custody in the city of London at the King's charge."[3] On the 19th of February following, one pound was paid to " a certain Welshman, coming to London, and there continuing for a certain time, to give information respecting the conduct and designs of Owen Glyndwr."[4]

The manner and place of Glyndwr's death are extremely doubtful, but that event is said to have occurred in 1416. Twice in that year Sir Gilbert Talbot was commissioned to negotiate directly or indirectly with him and the other insurgents who had not yet submitted, for their pardons.[5]

The results of this long insurrection were visible in Wales and on the Border for many years. During more than a century afterwards, the inhabitants of the walled towns and castles pointed out the ruins which had been made by Owen Glyndwr. The people of Herefordshire and Shropshire had suffered much from the parties of marauders who carried off everything that they could find in the shape of plunder, and destroyed what they could not remove. In the parliament held at Gloucester in 1407, the people of Shrewsbury presented a petition setting forth their losses and grievances, by which it appears that all the sheep and other live stock in the neighbourhood of the town had been repeatedly carried away by the Welsh ; and that Glyndwr had burnt no less than eight villages within the liberties of the town, as well as the suburbs of the town up to the gates, from whence he had been driven by the exertions of the burgesses.

On the other hand, the Welsh had lost in the war all the advantages of social position which they had gained during the preceding century. They had become again a persecuted people—and were placed under severe laws, which deprived them of most of the political rights of Englishmen, particularly the capability of holding lands or offices in the English counties. Their condition was a frequent subject of petition and debate in the ensuing parliaments. Many Welshmen who had served the King in the war, and distinguished themselves by their attachment to the English party, and others who had since gained the good will of the court, obtained marks of freedom, emancipating them from the restrictions under which their less fortunate countrymen laboured.

The Border remained long in a state of excitement. Many Welsh and Englishmen joined together as outlaws and bandits, and infested the woods and highways. The restless inhabitants of the mountains persecuted the people of the counties of Hereford and Salop in the same manner as the people of Cheshire had done in the reign of Richard II :—they crossed the Border in small parties, surprised and carried away prisoners, men of substance, and retained them in captivity for months, till themselves or their friends procured their redemption by the payment of a heavy ransom.[6] A remarkable instance of such personal attacks is related in the Rolls of Parliament of the 4th of Henry V. (A.D. 1416). As Robert Whittington, Esq., and his son Guy were riding home from the city of Hereford to their own house, in company with their three valets and two pages, on Monday before the Feast of St. Simon and St. Jude (the latter end of October), they were suddenly attacked in the village of Mordiford by about thirty men " armed and arrayed in manner of war," among whom they recognised Philip Lyngeyn, John Crew, Richard Loutley, Laurence Smith, William Kervere (Carver), Walter Bradford, John Bradford, and Walter Walker, who are described as the servants of Richard Oldcastle, Esq. These men led them forcibly to " a mountain named Dynmorehille," where they robbed them of their horses and harness and retained them till night, when they carried them on foot to a chapel which their prisoners did not know, at a distance of about two leagues, and in this chapel they imprisoned them all night, threatening them vehemently, either to kill them immediately or to carry

[3] Devon's Pell. Rolls, p. 321.   [4] Ibid.

[5] The date, 1415, assigned to the death of Owen Glyndwr, in the before-mentioned Memoirs, by the Rev. Thomas Ellis, rector of Dolgelle, is not correct, as in the following year Henry V. tested a writ directed to Sir Gilbert Talbot, of Goodrich Castle, " de recipiendo Glendourdy et Wallenses ad gratiam." He probably

passed the remainder of his days in Herefordshire, as is asserted, and died at the house of one or other of his daughters, in that country, for his own estates had been confiscated to the crown, and bestowed, by Henry IV. on the Earl of Somerset.

[6] Rolls of Parliament, iv. p. 52.

them prisoners into Wales.   On the Tuesday they carried their prisoners from one wood to another, all of which were equally unknown to them, till they came to an old mill, where they passed the second night, and there they renewed their threats of carrying them into Wales, unless they freed themselves by sufficient sureties in the country to the amount of six hundred pounds, to cease and let fall all personal actions against the parties concerned for this or any other personal trespass.   Guy Whittington was sent in search of the necessary securities, whilst his father and the others were kept prisoners in the mill, and at length he found three gentlemen of Gloucestershire, John Brown, John Paunton, and John Rich, who each of them gave a bond of a hundred and eleven pounds that Robert Whittington should, after his release, give under his seal to the said Philip Lyngeyn and his companions, and to Richard Oldcastle and Walter Huckluyt, Esqrs., two general acquittances and releases of all manner of personal actions from the beginning of the world to the Feast of All Saints following, upon which they were set at liberty.'   The petition of the parties aggrieved gives us no information relative to the origin of this Border feud.

Although the character of this Cambrian chief furnishes problems, on which the learning and ingenuity of modern writers have been abundantly exercised, and in regard to which the disputants have arrived at the most opposite conclusions ; yet there is something about it that has a sacred charm for the imagination. Very remotely descended, through females, from the royal stock of North Wales, unconnected with any of the Norman nobility, and unaided by any peculiarly favourable circumstances, he raised himself in a few months to the rank of a sovereign prince, and restored the independence and the ancient limits of his country.   At the head of a people who, after more than a century of subjection, must have been almost unfitted for military success, he frequently carried the war across the Borders, and, animated by the presence of their sovereign, compelled large bodies of the enemy's forces to retreat before him.   Destitute of any resources but those created by himself, he either won from his opponents, or obtained from his allies, treasure, arms, troops, and fortresses, by means of which he baffled the policy of Henry IV., rivalled the military genius of his son, backed by the chivalry and bowmen of Agincourt, and for fifteen years defied the whole power of England.   His name must ever hold the first place in the memory of his countrymen, who may reflect with pride, that even the conquerors of France were unable to reduce to submission one who may justly be styled, the last of the Welsh princes.   His exploits form one of the most imposing chapters in the page of history, and his name, like that of Wallace, will be respected by the generous as long as valour and constancy shall be appreciated upon earth !

The revolt of Owen Glyndwr was one of the last efforts of the ancient Britons to recover their independence.'   Henry IV.'s usurpation and Owen Glyndwr's insurrection were both alike indefensible. The one, through unheard-of success, retained his crown ; while the other witnessed, through uncommon disasters, a second subjugation of his country.   The former, during a short reign, was hailed Henry IV. of England, while the latter is branded with no milder epithets than *a rebel*, a most *profligate rebel*.   Thus, one murder makes a felon, thousands a hero : good fortunes transform the usurper into a legal sovereign, and one luckless event dooms the real hero to disgrace and oblivion, defrauds him of his merited fame, and brands him with infamy.   Those who regard Owen Glyndwr as a traitor, ought to keep in mind that his

---

7 Rolls of Parliament, iv. p. 99.

8 From a MS. in old French, preserved in the British Museum, MS. Cotton. Cleop. f. iii. fol. 3, which was written in Glyndwr's time, it appears that the Welsh castles at that time were not very extensively garrisoned, and it furnishes the actual state of many of them.   " Caernarvon had John Bolde for its constable, with twenty men-at-arms and eighty archers ; the annual maintenance amounted to 900*l*. 6*s*. 8*d*.   Crukkith Castle had Roger de Accon for constable, with six men-at-arms and fifty archers ; annual maintenance, 416*l*. 14*s*. 2*d*.   Hardelagh had Dycon de Macy for constable, with ten men-at-arms and thirty archers ; annual maintenance, 398*l*. 6*s*. 8*d*. These were castles in North Wales belonging to the prince ; the total of these charges amounting to 2421*l*. 3*s*. 6*d*.   Denbigh Castle belonged to the Earl of March, and had been granted to Henry Percy ; Beaumaris also belonged to Henry Percy, with the Isle of Anglesea.   Of these castles Monsieur de Rutland, with thirty men-at-arms, and one hundred and twenty archers, kept Denbigh at the annual expense of 1672*l*. 18*s*. 4*d*.   John de Pulle, with fifteen men-at-arms and one hundred and forty archers, kept Beaumaris at the yearly expense of 988*l*. 10*s*. 10*d*.   The castles which belonged to the prince, as chamberlain of Cheshire, were Ruddhlan and Flint ; of Ruddhlan Henry de Coueney was constable, who kept it with nine men-at-arms and forty archers, at the expense of 422*l*. 15*s*. 10*d*. Of Flint Nicholas Hanteck was constable, with four men-at-arms and twelve archers ; expense, 146*l*. per annum." Ellis's Original Letters, i. second series.

sword was only drawn against an usurper; and, whatever excesses mark his military career, may find ample palliation in the injustice that had provoked him.

From this period their indomitable spirit and high ambition, in attempting to recover their lost territories, became a subject of grave consideration. The blood of their princes was nearly exhausted, and their patriotic feelings gradually declining; and had it not been for the cruel and oppressive enactments of Henry IV., they would have been, in some measure, satisfied with their condition. No opportunity, however, was offered them to shake off the despotic yoke which had so long galled them, until their gallant countryman, Henry, Earl of Richmond, grandson of Sir Owen Tudor, of Penmynydd, Anglesea, overcame that sanguinary tyrant, Richard III., on the field of Bosworth, in which conflict he was principally assisted by them; two-thirds of his army being Welsh. They crowned him on the field of battle, and he ascended the throne as Henry VII., on the 22nd August, 1485, a day which ought never to be forgotten by the Principality.

"Such," says Mr. Harding, in his Prize Essay on the Castles of Glamorgan and Monmouth, "was the fate of the last Welsh prince, and such the termination of the independence of the Principality: but the page which closes the annals of the British race is disfigured by no cowardice, and disgraced by no corruption. Her warriors fought out her battle with the courage of despair, and only threw down their arms when they had neither a leader to follow nor a country to defend. And if, politically speaking, Wales be indeed no more, yet poetry and tradition, in preserving from oblivion the records of her most vigorous existence, and the tragic story of her fall, have kept alive a national spirit, which the lapse of centuries of foreign dominion have failed materially to weaken. The chord struck by her slaughtered bards yet vibrates in the breasts of their countrymen; unchanged by the closest contact with their conquerors, they speak her language, cherish her customs, and fondly cling to her soil. The Cymry are, to this hour, a peculiar people; identified with their Saxon neighbours only by a participation of those equal laws and free institutions, by which they have been more than repaid for the loss of a turbulent and sanguinary independence, and by a loyalty, which, in changing its object, has lost none of that fond and fearless devotion, which has, in all times, so brilliantly illuminated the chequered pages of their history.

> " ' So kindly mixed, and up together grown,
> As severed they were here, united still their own.' "—Drayton's Polyolbion.

Henry IV., on his death-bed, when tortured, both in body and mind, was seized with doubts respecting his title to the throne, but gave no charge to his son to relinquish his claim. As his reign had been founded in usurpation, so his death was unlamented.

Henry the Fifth.—This monarch,[2] surnamed of Monmouth, was born at Monmouth.[1] On his father's exile, he was taken by Richard II. to his palace, and, in his twelfth year, accompanied him to Ireland. He

---

[2] Henry V. was crowned on the 9th of April 1413. Katherine of France, the Queen of Henry V., was crowned on the 24th of February 1420; the account which Holinshed gives of the magnificence displayed upon this occasion is far too characteristic of the age to be omitted :—"After the great solemnisation of the foresaid coronation in the church of St. Peter's, at Westminster, was ended, the queene was conveied into the great Hall of Westminster, and there set to dinner. Upon whose right hand sat, at the end of the table, the Archbishop of Canterbury, and Henrie, surnamed the Rich, Cardinall of Winchester. Upon the left hand of the queene sat the King of Scots in his estate, who was served with covered messe, as were the foresaid bishops, but yet after them. Upon the left hand, next to the cupboord, sat the maior and his brethren, the aldermen of London. The bishops began the table, against the barons of the Cinque Ports; and the ladies against the maior. These, with others, ordered the service; and, for the first course, brawne in mustard, eeles in burneur, pike in herbage, fuiment with balien, lamprie powdered, trout, codling, plaice fried, martine fried, crabs, leech

lumbard flourished tartes, and a devise called a pellican, sitting on hir nest with hir birds, and an image of St. Katharine holding a booke, and disputing with doctors.

"The second course was, gellie coloured with columbine flowers, white potage or creame of almonds, breame of the sea, conger, cheuen, barbill and roch, fresh salmon, halibut, gurnard, rochet broiled, smelts fried, crevis or lobster, leech-damaske, with the king's poesie flourished thereon.

"The third course was, dates in compost, creame motle, carpe deore, turbut, tench, pearch with goion, fresh sturgion with welks, porperous rosted, crevesse de eau doure, pranis, eeles rosted with lamprie, a leech, called the white leech, flourished with hawthorn leaves and red hawes; a marchpane garnished with diverse figures of angels."

[1] Speaking of Monmouth, it is impossible not to recollect that our earliest Brittsh historian, Geoffrey of Monmouth, was a native of this place, and derived from it his surname. Leland conjectures that Geoffrey of Monmouth was educated in a Benedictine convent at that

is there described by a person in the expedition, as a young, handsome, and promising "bachelor." The King made him a knight, with this address, "My fair cousin, be noble and valiant;" and to do him honour, and to fix the favour in his memory, at the same time raised eight or ten others to this dignity. When the news arrived of his father's landing in England, Richard expressed his feelings to the young prince, but Henry reminded the King of his own innocence and youth, and Richard acquiesced in the propriety of his self-justification.

On his father's obtaining the Crown, he was declared Prince of Wales, Duke of Cornwall, and Earl of Chester, and afterwards Duke of Aquitaine, and heir apparent to the kingdom of England. It is related that he received some part of his education at Oxford, under the care of his uncle, the well known Cardinal Beaufort. In his thirteenth year, he attended his father into Scotland, being his second expedition, in which he became personally acquainted with military movements. When the King went into Wales, to attack Glyndwr, Henry was acting under him, while his brother was sent to govern and preserve Ireland. In the next summer that rebellion of the Percies occurred, which shook his father's throne. In the furious battle of Shrewsbury, he felt that upon its issue depended the fortunes of his house, and his soul rose to an energy equal to the greatness of the struggle.

Though wounded in the face, he refused to quit the field, as he was desired. "With what spirits will the others fight," he exclaimed; "if they behold me, the son of their King, retiring frightened from the battle: lead me to the foremost ranks, that I may animate my fellow-soldiers by my conduct, and not merely by my words." They made a fiercer attack, and assisted to win the hard-fought victory.

Having thus had four times the experience of military affairs in Ireland, Scotland, Wales, and England, his father deemed him competent, though but sixteen, to conduct the troublesome war in Wales, against Owen Glyndwr; and appointed him lieutenant of the forces directed against this obstinate and active chieftain. In this petty, but difficult, warfare, all the qualities of an able general were exercised and formed. Privations, vigilance, enterprise, patience, and perseverance, were successively required. In the second year of his campaign, he petitions parliament for supplies to guard the Marches effectually; and in the following spring he defeated, with an inferior force, a Welsh army of eight thousand men from Glamorgan and its neghbourhood. He details his success in a respectful and modest letter to his father:—

"MOST DREAD SOVEREIGN LORD AND FATHER:—In the most humble manner that I may in my heart devise, I recommend myself to your royal Majesty, humbly praying your gracious blessing. Most dread Sovereign Lord and Father, I sincerely beseech God graciously to show his providence towards you in all his works! For on Wednesday, the 11th of this instant month of March, your rebels of the Glamorgan, Morgamock Usk, Netherwent, and Oscruent, drew together to the number of eight thousand men, by their own account, and went in the morning of the same day, and burnt part of your town of Grosmont, within your lordship of Monmouth and Jennoia." [After mentioning his opposing force, he adds] : "And there, by the aid of the blessed Trinity, your men won the field and overcame all the said rebels; of whom they slew on the field, by fair reckoning upon our return from the pursuit, some say eight hundred, and some, one thousand, being questioned upon pain of death. Nevertheless, be it one or the other, in this account I will not dispute : and to give you full information of the whole affair, I send you a person worthy of credit therein, one of my faithful servants, the bearer hereof, who was in the battle, and very satisfactorily performed his duty, as he has ever done. Now, such amends hath God ordained you for the burning of

place, and that he became a monk of that order. He was Archdeacon of Monmouth, and was made Bishop of St. Asaph in the reign of King Stephen, about the year 1151. His history, which was probably finished after the year 1138, is the chief foundation of Milton's, a work on which even the illustrious name of the author of Paradise Lost could confer no value. Geoffrey's work is a fabulous account of British Kings, from the Trojan Brutus, the grandson of Æneas, to the reign of Cadwalader, in the year 688. Milton brings his history down to the Norman Conquest. It is observed that Geoffrey was not the inventor of all the stories he relates. The main part of his work is a translation from a MS. written in the British language, and brought to England by his friend Gwallter, Archdeacon of Oxford. To Geoffrey, however, we are indebted for the account of the achievements of King Arthur, Merlin's Prophecies, and many of the speeches and letters. As an apology, Mr. Warton observes, "that fabulous histories were then the fashion, and popular traditions a recommendation to his book."

your one hundred houses in the town aforesaid. And no prisoners were taken, except one, who was a great chieftain among them, whom I would have sent to you, but that he is not able yet to bear the journey. And with respect to the course I propose to hold hereupon, please your Highness to give credence to the bearer hereof, in what he will himself inform your Highness on my part. And pray God ever keep you in joy and honour, and grant that I may shortly have to comfort you with more news. Written at Hereford, the said Wednesday at night.

> "Your most humble and obedient son,
> "HENRY."

The date of this letter being from Hereford, and the scene of the conflict in Monmouthshire, we may infer that he had not been able to penetrate effectually into the interior of Wales; but was contented to watch the Border counties. Though he was then but seventeen, his services in the war were so highly thought of, that the House of Commons, by their Speaker, requested of the King that, for the safeguard of his subjects, and to resist the malice of the Welsh rebels, the Prince might be continually residing, and attending to those hostilities. They also requested the King to send his letters under the Privy Seal, thanking him for his good and unceasing labour and diligence, which he had endured and continually sustained, in his honourable person, to conquer that revolted country. In the same year the Speaker prayed that the Prince might be ordered to go with all possible speed to Wales, on account of the news which had arrived of the rebellion of the Earl of Northumberland; and, in 1407, requested that he might be graciously thanked for his labour, diligence, and diseases which he had many times suffered, in resisting the great rebellion of the Welsh. The Prince, kneeling, immediately afterwards, before his father, graciously interceded for the Duke of York, whom the King had imprisoned; avowed his obligations to him, and that, if it had not been for his good counsel, both he and his army would have often been in great perils and desolations.

Henry, from his very infancy, signalised his valour against the French. Two victories which he gained over them, excited his father's jealousy to such a degree, that from that time he removed him from all public affairs, and from the command of the army. The young Prince, left to himself without employment, conformed to his own active and fiery disposition. He gave himself up, without scruple or discretion, to the greatest excesses: nothing was talked of but his debaucheries. He waylaid the receivers of his father's revenues, in order to rob them of their treasure. Designed by nature for a conqueror or a robber on the highway, he seemed to acknowledge no other rights but those which were given by force and courage. His outrages, and the abandoned extravagance in which he had lived, had lost him the esteem of the nation: a remarkable accident restored it to him. Having entered a court of justice in order to support, by his presence, the cause of one of his favourites, who, nevertheless, was condemned, he gave the judge[2] on his tribunal a box on the ear. The magistrate immediately ordered him to be committed to prison. The Prince, coming to himself, obeyed without replying. This reparation of his fault, and his submission to the laws, did him great honour. After his father's death, he refused the homage which the nobles would have paid him before his coronation, by saying that it was not right that they should oblige themselves to be faithful to him, before he had engaged himself by a solemn oath to govern them equitably, and according to law. When he was settled on the throne, he sent for all who had been concerned with him in his disorders, and who had already depended on his favours. He publicly exhorted these accomplices of his youthful follies to acknowledge their faults, and reform their conduct; he made them presents, and forbade them ever again to appear before him. Thus—

> "Consideration, like an angel came,
> And whipped the offending Adam out of him;
> Leaving his body as a paradise
> To envelope and contain celestial spirits."

"All the nation rejoiced at seeing on the throne a prince who gave at his accession such promising expectations, adorned with many accomplishments of both mind and body, a majestic stature, a noble figure,

[2] Judge Gascoigne.

strength, address, incomparable valour, genius, and activity: he proved himself the greatest politician in Europe." [3]

Henry V. created Richard de Breos, Earl of Worcester, who married Isabel, one of the sisters and coheiresses of Richard le Despenser. He died early, in 1420, in consequence of a wound, and left an only daughter, Elizabeth, who married Sir Edward Neville, fourth son of Ralph, Earl of Westmoreland, to whom she conveyed by her marriage all her father's lands, except the Castle of Abergavenny, which, by virtue of the entail, came to Richard (son of Thomas), Earl of Warwick, the companion in arms of Henry V., who made him guardian of his son. He was highly distinguished at the battle of Shrewsbury, and in the French wars. He travelled through Europe, and to the Holy Land, performed many feats of arms, and died at Rouen, in 1439, in command of the English forces then in France. His son was created Duke of Warwick, who died in 1445,[4] leaving an only daughter, Anne, who died an infant. On her death, the possession was long disputed by two branches of the Neville family, Sir Edward and Sir Richard; the one claiming it in right of his wife, Elizabeth Beauchamp; the other, as having married Anne, sister of the late Duke.

The following curious letter is an illustration of the era of Henry V., and relates to the apprehension of Sir John Oldcastle, who was in Wales, and executed, in 1418, as a follower of Wickliffe's doctrines :—

"We, Jevan and Gruffuth, sons of Gruffuth ap Jevan ap Madoc ap Gwennoys, of Powys Londe, Gentilmen, and Hoel ap Gruffuth ap David ap Madoc and Dero ap Jevan ap Jorum ap Ada of the same Londe, reman tenauntz to Sir Edward Charletoun Knyght, Lord of Powys, and tatheres of Sir John Oldcastell, that was myscreant and unbuxome to the lawe of God, and traitour convicte to our gracious Soveraigne Lord and his Henry Kyng of England aftyr the conquest the V.th thonken oure said Soveraigne Lord in as lowely wyse, and with as hole hert as we in our semple manner condeuyse, that it hath liked him of his gracious goodnesse for to remember his notarie proclamation made thorgh his Roialme by his hie commaundement of the Guerdon and reward by his hie discression appoynted to him that mizt haue that fortune and grace to ben takers of the said John Oldcastell, for the which guerdon and reward oure said Lord of Powys, by the graciouse governance and assent of our said Soveraigne Lord, hase compownyd with us and fynaly accorded, so that we and everych of us ben fully satisfied and agreond, after oure own desire and plaisir, in pleyn accomplissement and excusation of the Proclamation aforesaid; of the wych Guerdon and rewarde we hold us fynaly agrart and content for evermore."

This document settles a discrepancy, if it does not correct an error, in some of our historians. Lingard, in endeavouring to do so, falls into a blunder. He says, "In the rolls, the capture of Oldcastle seems to be attributed to Lord Powis; but Hearne has published a writ, dated Dec. 1, in which it is expressly asserted that he was taken by Sir Edward Charlton." But the fact established by the foregoing letter is, that Sir Edward Charlton and Lord Powis were one and the same person. Sir John Oldcastle's execution was attended with circumstances of unusual barbarity. He was burnt, suspended by a chain from a gallows. Till burning became a more frequent punishment for heretics, the mode appears to have varied. In one instance, in the reign of Henry IV., the sufferer was inclosed in a cask. Prince Henry afterwards King Henry V., was present at the execution, and hearing the wretched moans of the victim in the barrel, ordered the fire to be drawn away, and the cask to be opened, offering the half-dead sufferer his life, and a daily allowance of threepence from the exchequer, if he would recant. The heretic refused. He was again enclosed in his cask, and consumed. Henry VIII. and Queen Mary chained their sufferers openly to a stake.[5] It may not be uninteresting, as a trait in the history of this country, to know that, prior to the reign of Henry V., specimens of English correspondence are rare. Letters previous to that time were usually written in French or Latin. The reader who desires to see original specimens of the earlier periods, will find plenty preserved in the Cottonian volumes in the British Museum.

---

[3] Villaret's Hist. of France.   [4] Dugdale's Baronage, i. 244.   [5] Recollections of Royalty.

During this period, Meredith, son of Owen Glyndwr, capitulated and went to England, and received his pardon from the King. The other chiefs of the late insurrection were also pardoned, and several of them even obtained posts of honour at the Court of London, in order that they might not return to Wales, which, indeed, had ceased to be inhabited by the Welsh nobility, from the increased tyranny and vexatious oppression of the English authorities. "Among these Cambrian exiles," says the author of the Norman Conquest,[6] "either by necessity or ambition, was a member of the family of Tudor, named Owen ap Meredith ap Tudor, who, during the reign of Henry V., lived with him as Groom of the Chamber, and was very much in grace with the King, who granted him many favours, and deigned to address him as '*nostre chièr et fogal*.' His manners, and handsome form and deportment, made a vivid impression on Queen Catherine of France, who, after the death of her husband, Henry V., secretly married him."

This Owen was the father and founder of the ancient and royal House of Tudor. The family residence was at Pen Mynydd, Anglesea. The Tudors were a very ancient family, and a branch of the family continued to occupy their ancient seat for ages after the elevation of the other branch to the throne of England. The former branch, for some time before it became extinct, assumed the name of Owen. Richard was the last of the family, and was sheriff of the county in 1637. The estate is now the property of Sir Richard B. W. Bulkely, Bart., the worthy and popular member for his native county.

The Ruins of the ancient seat of the Tudor Family in Anglesea.

There are still to be seen some remains of the ancient residence of the ancestors of the Tudors at this place. The door of the gateway, part of the house, and the great chimney-piece of the hall, are to be seen in the present farm-house. Some of the coats of arms, dates of the building, or time of repairs, are to be seen with the initial letters of the owners. The celebrated Owen Tudor was born here in 1385. Our Cambrian records state that, after a scholastic education, Owen went to London to study the law, but, not liking his profession, he travelled abroad. After visiting several countries, he returned to the metropolis, and got admission into the English court. Soon after the death of Henry V., his widow, Catherine of France, was enamoured with Owen, and the Dowager Queen became a subject's wife. His introduction was rather singular: being an active gentleman, very comely in person, and courtly in his behaviour, he was once commanded to dance before the Queen; but, in footing it, down he slipped, and, unable to recover himself, he fell into her lap as she sat on a stool, with the maids of honour around her, admiring his agility; "the Queen," as honest Hall informs us, "beyng young and lustye, followyng more her owne appetyte than frendely counsaill, and regardyng more her private affection than her open honour, toke to husband privily (in 1428) a goodly gentylman, and a beautiful person, garniged with many godly gyftes both of nature and of grace, called Owen Teuther, a man brought furth and come

---

[6] Monsieur Thiers.

of the noble lignage and auncient lyne of Cadwalader, the laste kynge of the Britonnes." This match, important in its consequences, restored the British race of princes to the throne of this kingdom.

> "If Britain saw her regal fire
> In brave Llywelyn's breast expire,
> Her pride to dust return;
> A day, though distant, cheers my view,
> A spark in Mona's hearth renew—
> A brighter blaze shall burn."

They lived happily together until 1437, when Owen lost his royal consort at Bermondsey, where she was buried. The issue of this marriage were three sons, Edmund, Jasper, and Owen, and one daughter. Owen embraced a monastic life in the Abbey of Westminster, and died soon after; the daughter died in her infancy. During the life of the Queen, the marriage had been winked at, notwithstanding a law had been made after that event, enacting that no person, under severe penalties, should marry a Queen Dowager of England, without the special licence of the King. On the death of Catherine, all respect ceased to her spouse. The King's uncle assumed the reins of government, to whom this match was disagreeable. He caused Owen to be apprehended and committed to the Tower, because, contrary to the statute (which was made six years *after* his marriage) he had married the Queen without the King's consent! He escaped from prison by the assistance of his confessor and servant. On being retaken, he was delivered to the custody of the Earl of Suffolk, constable of the Castle of Wallingford, and after some time was again committed to prison. He made his escape a second time. The length of his second imprisonment does not appear. After a considerable period, high honours were conferred on his two eldest sons, half brothers to the King. In the year 1452, they were both created Earls; Edmund was made Earl of Richmond, and Jasper, Earl of Pembroke. Henry, about this time, was disturbed by the open claim of the Duke of York to the succession, and found it prudent to strengthen his interest by all possible means. The Welsh, flattered by the honours bestowed on their young countrymen, ever after faithfully adhered to the House of Lancaster.

Owen had besides, a natural son, called Davydd, knighted by his nephew, Henry VII., who also bestowed on him in marriage Mary, the daughter and heiress of John Bohun, of Midhurst, in Sussex, and with her a great inheritance. Owen himself was taken no notice of till the year 1460, when, as a patent expresses it, in regard of his good services, he had a grant of the parks in the lordship of Denbigh, and the wood-wardship of the same lordship. The year following, he fought valiantly under the banners of his son Jasper, at the battle of Mortimer's Cross; he would not quit the field, but was taken with several other Welsh gentlemen, and beheaded with them soon after at Hereford, and interred in the Church of the Grey Friars in that city.

It was a descendant of the ancient House of Tudor that Lord Bacon eulogised as "England's best son and greatest of sovereigns," from whose wise policy may be traced the elements of those enlightened institutions that have made England the freest of nations, and the pride of the sea. It is to a princess of the House of Tudor that she owes her commerce and her dominion of the seas: "Elizabeth shivered the sword of Spain, paralysed the power of Roman idolatry," and restored the British race of princes to the throne of these realms.

"In visiting Plas Pen Mynydd, the ancient remains of the family of the Tudors," says Mr. Hutton, the Birmingham historian, "I walked thirty-three miles to examine it, at the age of seventy-seven, and spent two days in making inquiries." His remarks are as follows:—"The chief that is said of Owen is, that he was an 'accomplished and handsome Welsh gentleman.' And is this all that such a man merits, who furnished England with a numerous race of Kings and Queens?

> "'A beautiful nest of chieftains.'
> "'Nyth teg o bennethiaid da.'

Shall such a nobleman be consigned to oblivion, whom history has not charged with errors? Let him live, then, in my page, since he has not found another."

Whether Tudor was a gainer or a loser by his elevation, the reader will determine. His private fortune would have supplied every necessary of life, and something more. Perhaps, if he had lived in these enlightened and liberal days, he would have fared better; be that as it may, the restoration of the British dynasty in the House of Tudor was an event highly to be hailed. To this, doubtless, Taliesin alluded in the sixth century—

> " I Vrython dymbi
> " Gwared, gwnedd ovri."
>
> " There will be to the Britons
>   A deliverance of exalted power."

The following letter[7] from Henry V., but to which we can assign no date of the year, was evidently written after apprehensions began to be entertained by the government of disturbances within the realm.

" *To oure Trusty and Welbeloved the Baillifs and Inhabitants of oure Towne of Shrouesbury.*
    " *By the King.*

"TRUSTY AND WELBELOVED: We grete you wel, and late you wite that we have wel understanden by youre letters late sent unto us youre dewe obeissance and trouwe acquitaille unto us, and howe faithfully ye be disposed to do that myght growe to our wel and pleas[r], of whiche wee can you right good thankes, and trust verraly that ye wol so continue. Desiring and in al wise willing and charging you, that in caas any personne wol make any sturing, insurrection, or gadering within oure Towne of Shrouesbury under what colour or pretense so evir it be, withoute oure especial commaundement, that thenne ye with al diligence do him to be putte in sure warde unto the tyme it be determined by us and oure counsail what shal be doon with him in that behalve: and spareth[8] not so to do as ye desire to stande in the favour of oure good grace. Yeven under oure signet at our palois of Westmynstr the XVI day of Janievr."

The next letter[9] appears to have been written by Henry, on his return to Worcester after the battle of Ludford. The leading members of the corporation of Shrewsbury at that time must have been able politicians, since they contrived to keep well with the Court, notwithstanding their attachment to the opposite party.

" *To our Trusty and Welbeloved the Baillifs and Inhabitants of oure Towne of Shrouesbury.*
    " *By the King.*

"TRUSTY AND WELBELOVED: We grete you wele. And forasmuch as we nowe late yave you in strait commaundement surely to kepe the passage of oure Towne of Shrouesbury; to thexecuting whereof, as we have undurstande by the report of oure cousin therl of Shrouesbury, ye have doon youre trewe and faithful diligence, whereof we can you right good thankes; and in especial that ye have doon your effectuel devoir to the resistence of Edward Bourgchier to entre or passe by oure said towne; whereby we understande the gret zele and affection that ye have tobey and execute oure highe commaundements and plaisirs. Lating you wite that we shall in such wise reknowlege your said faithful demening as shall be for youre wele proffit and honnour in tyme to come. Yeven under oure signet at oure Cite of Worcestre the XVII day of Octobre."

On the death of Henry V., his son, then only nine months old, succeeded to the throne by the title of Henry VI. In his reign the seed of discord which had been sown in the time of Richard II., produced so abundant an harvest that scarcely a family in the whole kingdom escaped from the direful effects of

---

[7] Extracted from a curious MS. in possession of T. F. Duke, Esq., Salop, by Messrs. Owen & Blakeway.
[8] *i. e.* Spare not. The second person plural of the imperative mood had not yet lost its ancient termination.
[9] From MS. previously quoted.

the desolation which ensued. So turbulent indeed were those times, that history in a great measure throws a mantle over the bloody scene.[1]

HENRY THE SIXTH was crowned at Westminster, November 6th, 1429, being then only in the ninth year of his age.[2]

In the year 1450, the whole of France, excepting Calais, was lost to England. Soon after this misfortune symptoms of discontent began to manifest themselves throughout England. The people were loud in their outcries against the government, and attributed the loss of their foreign possessions to the mal-administration of the ministers. Under the influence of these feelings the people turned their attention to Richard Plantagenet, Duke of York, who was then in Ireland, whither he had been sent to quell a rebellion. Here, as well as in France, he gained great reputation for wisdom, moderation, and valour. His fame for those qualifications soon spread far and wide, and his friends in consequence began now to entertain strong and sanguine hopes of seeing him one day placed on the British throne; and the imbecility of the King, his utter incapacity to govern, and the factious discontent and rebellion with which he was environed, seemed to warrant such an expectation.

The Duke on his return from Ireland finding that his popularity was become great, and was likely to increase still more, and that his friends had been successful in forming a strong party in his favour, began to think seriously of enforcing his claims to the crown. He determined to take up arms under pretence of affecting a change in the ministry, and repairing to his estates on the Borders of Wales, he, in conjunction with the Earls of Salisbury and Warwick, raised there an army of ten thousand men. With this army the Duke of York advanced towards London by a circuitous route in order to avoid an army which the King was leading in person against him; but before he reached the capital he received certain intelligence that the Londoners were not willing to admit him, probably rendered cautious by the violence committed by the rebels under Jack Cade, two years before. The Duke crossed the Thames at Kingston bridge, marched into Kent, where the popular cause was always strong, and on the 1st of March encamped in a strong position at Brent-heath, near Dartford. The royal army followed, and soon after was encamped on Blackheath, the same place which had been occupied by Jack Cade and the insurgents under him. This was the first time that the two opposing political parties had faced each other in warlike array, and neither side appears to have been anxious to fight. The Duke's forces were very considerable, for a contemporary,[3] who was perhaps present, informs us that, "there was my Lorde of Yorke's ordinaunce iij thousand gownners, and himself in the middle warde with viij thowsand, my Lorde of Devenshere by the south side with vi thowsand, and Lorde Cobbame with vi thowsand at the water side, and vii shippers with their stuffe." A brief negotiation, in which the Bishops of Winchester and Ely acted for the King, and the

[1] Lewis Glyn Cothi, a celebrated Welsh bard of this period, has, however, preserved several interesting circumstances not to be found elsewhere. These poems were published in 1837, by the Royal Cambrian Society, edited by our late and venerable friend, the Rev. Walter Davis, (Gwallten Mechain) Rector of Llanrhaiadr, and our excellent friend, Rev. John Jones (Tegid) one of the Prebends of St. David, with numerous historical and interesting notes. The work is valuable on account of some particulars given of the leading and influential characters of these times, particularly in Wales and the Border countries. Our bard himself was not an inactive spectator ; for he was but too successful in several instances in kindling into a flame the latent sparks of bravery, which, had it not been for his spirit-stirring poems, would in all probability have lain dormant in the bosom of its possessor. It appears, however, from his compositions, that he was not actuated by any fixed political principles, nor by any genuine attachment to either of the contending parties. To him it was a matter of indifference whether the House of York or that of Lancaster should finally triumph. His bitter and rancorous hatred towards the whole of the English nation, as exhibited in his poems,

was so desperate, that he cared not in the least by whom the kingdom was governed, if the sovereign must be an Englishman. Mindful, perhaps, of the late untoward struggles of Owen Glyndwr, as well as many others of the native princes before his time, he rejoiced that the English were now at war among themselves.

[2] The coronation feast was celebrated at Westminster, with great splendour. In the first course, Fabian tells us, there were, among other royal viands, "Bore hedes in castellys of gold and enarmed," "Custard royall, with a lyopard of gold syttyng therein, and holding a floure de lyce." The pageant for this course was, " A sotyltie of Seynt Edwarde and Seynt Lowys armed, and upon eyther his cote armoure, holdyng atwene them a figure lyke unto Kynge Henry, standynge also in his cote armoure, and a scripture passynge from them both, sayinge,—' Beholde I perfyght kynges', under one cote armoure."

[3] Taken from some contemporary notes of a Yorkist partisan, in a MS. in the British Museum, communicated by Sir Frederic Madden to the Archæologia, xxxix. p. 326.

Earls of Shrewsbury and Warwick and others, for the Duke, ended by the King acquitting the Duke of treason, promising to listen to all his complaints, and by his agreeing to put the Duke of Somerset under arrest, and calling a new council, in which the Duke of York was to have a place. The latter on these conditions disbanded his army; but when he came before the King he found that he had been deceived, for Somerset was at liberty, and charged him with being a traitor, and the Duke was detained as a prisoner and sent to London to stand his trial. The court however suddenly stopped further proceedings, alarmed as it is said by a report that the Duke's eldest son, Edward Earl of March, was marching towards London at the head of a powerful army of Welshmen to rescue his father; and, after having on the 10th of March made his submission and taken his oath in St. Paul's to be a true, faithful, and obedient subject in the presence of the King and most of the nobility, he was allowed to retire to his Castle of Wigmore, "where," says Grafton, "he studied both howe to displease his enemies, and to obteyne his purpose. And so by meanes of the absence of the Duke of York, which was in maner banished the court and the King's presence, the Duke of Somerset rose up in high favour with the King and the Queene, and his worde onely ruled and his voyce was onely heard."

It appears that some of the men of Kent suffered for the favour they had shown to the Duke of York in this affair, and that his actions were looked upon with suspicion and jealousy after his return to Wigmore Castle. We learn this from the following note by the same contemporary writer mentioned above, who also speaks of tumults which had arisen at Ludlow, in which a messenger of the King was slain.—" Then affter, the kynges yeman of his chambure, namyde Fazakerley, with letteris was sent to Ludlow to my lorde of Yorke, chargynge to do forthe a certeyne of his mayny,[4] Artherne, squiere, Sharpe, squiere, etc., the whiche Fazakerley hylde in avowtry[5] Sharpus wiff, the whiche Sharpe slowe Fazakerley; and a bakere of Ludlow roos and the commyns, etc.;[6] the which bakere is at Kyllyngworthe (Kenilworth) castelle, etc. Affter this my lorde of Shrousbury, etc. rode into Kent, and set up vi. peyre of galowes, and dede execucione upone Johan Wylkyns, taken and broght to the towne as for capteyne, and with othere mony mo,[7] of the whiche were hangede and behedede, the which hedes were sent to Londone, and Londone said ther should no mo hedes be set upone there."

We find the Duke of York at Ludlow Castle on the 3rd of July, 1451-2, from whence he writes to the bailiffs of Shrewsbury,[8] acquainting them with his design, and requesting their assistance, in terms expressive of much reciprocal cordiality between himself and the town. Indeed he would never have opened so fully his secret views, if he had not been secure of their cordial co-operation. He addresses himself to their national feelings, on the loss of the Continental dominions of the crown; alarms their fears by the danger of a French invasion; excites their sympathy for the oppression under which he had so long laboured; and in the true spirit of a politician, who admits no apology, however cogent, for the misfortunes of an adversary, he points their indignation against the obnoxious minister, (who really appears to have been nowise culpable in the loss of Normandy): at the same time he is lavish in his professions of loyalty and submission to the sovereign at whose seat he grasped.

" To my Right Worshipful Frendes, The Baillys, Burgeys, and Comuns of the good Town of Shroesbury.

"RIGHT WORSHIPFUL FRENDES.—I recomande me unto you, And I suppose it is wel knowen unto you aswel by exp'ance (experience) as by comun langage saide and rapported through oute al Cristendome, what laude, what worship, honeur and manhood, was ascribed of all nacons un to the poeple of his royaune whiles the King oure souv'ain lord stood possessed of his lordships in his Roy^me of ffrance and duchie of Normandie, and what derogacon, losse of marchandisse, lesion, deshoneur, and vilanie, is said and rapported gen'ally un to this Englyshe nacon for losse of the same, namely un to the Duc of Som'set which had the

---

[4] Dismiss a certain number of his household retainers.

[5] Held in adultery.

[6] i.e. A baker of Ludlow rose up, and the commons or townspeople with him, he led an insurrection of the town.

[7] Many more.

[8] This letter was copied from a MS. formerly in the Bodleian Library, now unfortunately missing. See Ellis's Original Letters, with modern translations.

gouv'nance and charge ther'of. The whiche losse hathe caused and encouraged the Kyngs enemis for to conquere and gete Gascoigne and Gyenne, and now daily thay make thaire avance for to leye siege unto Calais and to other places in the marches there, for to applye them to theire obeissance; And so for to come into this lande with greet puissances to the final distrucon thereof yif thay myght obteen yaire entent, and to put the lande in their subjection (whiche God defende).

"And on the other parte (hit is to bee supposed) hit be not unknowen unto you, how that, after my comyng out of Irland, I, as the King's trew liege man and servant, and ever schal bee to my lyues ende, for my trewe acquitale, perceyuyng the inconvenients afore reherced, advertissed his roial magestie of certain articles concerning the wel and sauvegarde as wel of his mooste roial personne, as the tranquillite and conservacon of al this his royme. The whiche advertissements, how bee hit that hit was thought that thay were ful necessary, were leyed apart, and to be of noon effect, thourgh envye, malice, and untrouthe of the said Duc of Somerset; whiche for my trouthe, feith, and ligeance, that I owe un to the Kyng, and the good wille and *sauans* that I have to al this Royaume, laboureth continuelly about the Kyngs highnesse for myn undoing, and to corrupt my blood and to *deshorte* it me and myn heires and such personnes as been about me, withouten any desert or cause doon or attempted on my part, or thairs, I make our Lord juge.

"Wherefore, worshipful frendes, to thentent that every man shal know my pourport and desir, for to declare me such as I am; I signifie un to you, that with the help and supportacon of Almighty God, and of our Lady, and of all the compaigne of Heven, I, after sufferance and delayes, not in wille ner entent or [f. to] desplaise my sou'ain lord, seying that the saide Duc ever prevaleth and ruleth about the Kyngs personne, that by his meene the lande is likely to bee betrayed, am fully concluded for to procede in al haste agenst hym, with the helpe of my kynnesmen and frendes, in suche wise that hit shal growe to the more ease, pees, tranquillitee, and sauve gard of al this lande (even more keeping me within the boundes of my ligeance, as hit parteeneth to my duetee). Prayeng and exhorting you to fortifie, enforce, and assiste me, and to come to me with all diligence, where so ever I shall bee or drawe, with as many goodly and likly men as ye may make, to execute thentent abovesaide.

"Written under my signet at my cestel of Lodelowe the iij^d day of ffeuver.

"Fferthermore I pray you that suche streyte appointment and ordonance bee made, that the peuple whiche shal come in your feloship, or bee sent un to [me] by youre agreement, bee demeened in such wise by the weye, that they doo noon offense nor robberie nor oppression uppon the peuple, in lesion of justice. Written as abouv. Youre goode frend,

"R. YORKE."

Ludlow being a very important fortress as well as a stronghold, the Duke of York selected it as his chief place of residence for himself and family. The following letter from his two sons, written probably at the commencement of the political intrigues which led eventually to the civil war, is curious, as connecting with Ludlow two names which afterwards hold so prominent a position in the annals of history.[2]

"RYGHT HIEGH AND RYGHT MYGHTY PRINCE, Oure ful redoubted and ryght noble lorde and ffadur, as lowely with alle oure hertes as we youre trewe and naturell sonnes can or may, we recomaunde us unto your noble grace, humbly besechyng your nobley[1] and worthy ffaderhode[2] daily to geve[3] us your hearty blessyng, thrugh which we trust muche the rather to encrees and growe to vertu, and to spede the bettur in alle matiers and thinges that we schalle use, occupie, and exercise. Ryght high and ryght myghty Prince, our ful redouted lorde and ffadur, we thanke our blessed Lorde not oonly of your honourable conduite[4] and good spede in alle your matiers and besynesse, and of your gracious prevaile[5] agenst thentent

---

[2] See Ellis's Original Letters, i. p. 9.
[3] Give.
[1] Nobleness.
[4] Conducting.
[2] Fatherhood.
[5] Success, prevailing.

and malice of your evilwillers, but also of the knowelage that hit pleased your nobley to lete us nowe late have of the same by relacion of Syr Watier Devreux, knyght, and Johan Milewatier, squire, and Johan at Nokes, yemon of your honorable chambur. Also we thonke your noblesse and good ffaderhode of oure grene gownes nowe late sende unto us to our grete comfort; beseching your good lordeschip to rembre our porteux,[6] and that we myght have summe fyne bonettes sende unto us by the next seure messige, for necessité so requireth. Overe this, ryght noble lord and ffadur, please hit your highnesse to witte that we have charged your servant William Smyth, berer of thees, for to declare unto your nobley certayne thinges on our behalf, namely, concernyng and touching the odieux reule and demenyng[7] of Richard Crofte and of his brother. Wherefore we beseche your graciouse lordeschip and fulle noble ffaderhode to here him in exposicion of the same, and to his relacion to yeve ful faith and credence. Ryght hiegh and ryght myghty prince, our ful redouted and ryght noble lorde and ffadur, we beseche almyghty Jhesu yeve yowe as good lyfe and long, with as muche contenual perfite prosperité, as your princely hert con best desire. Writen at your castill of Lodelowe, on Setursday in the Astur Woke.[8]

"Your humble Sonnes,

"E. Marche, and

"E. Rutlonde."

The Duke's constant opposition to the unpopular measures of the court, although it procured him the enmity of the government, made him beloved by a large portion of the people.

A.D. 1453.—The ferment was so great at this time throughout the country that the people, without any just cause, threw all the blame occasioned by the loss of France, on the ministry. The Queen (the celebrated Margaret of Anjou) and her party finding that they were unable to contend with York, sent Somerset to the Tower, and the King being seized with one of his fits of sickness, York was made Protector of the Kingdom.

The course of events soon opened a new path to the ambition of the Duke of York. In the October of 1453, the unfortunate King was attacked by a malady which was attended with mental as well as bodily weakness. We learn from an interesting letter of intelligence, dated the 19th of January, 1454, that when the Prince of Wales, then three months of age, was presented to his father, neither the Duke of Buckingham nor the Queen could obtain any sign of recognition.—"At the Princes comyng to Wyndesore, the Duc of Bukingham toke hym in his armes, and presented him to the Kyng in godely wise, besechyng the Kyng to blisse hym; and the Kyng yave no maner answere. Natheles the Duc abode stille with the Prince by the Kyng; and whan he coud no maner answere have, the Queen come in and toke the Prince in hir armes, and presented hym in like fourme as the Duke had done, desiryng that he shulde blisse it; but all their labour was in veyne, for they departed thens without any answere or countenance, savyng onely that ones he loked on the Prince, and cast doune his eyene ayen, without any more."[9] It appears that the real state of the King's health was kept secret as long as possible, and the Queen, chiefly by the assistance of the Archbishop of Canterbury, retained for a while the executive government in her own hands. We learn from the letter just mentioned, that Margaret was at that time taking steps to obtain an act of parliament, giving her the sole Regency of the kingdom, while a bill of attainder against the Duke of York was at the same time in preparation; and that the latter was preparing to meet his friends at London with a powerful retinue. Two months later, the death of the Archbishop on the 22nd of March, led to an immediate change in the position of the different parties. A deputation of the lords forced their way into the royal presence to consult the King on the election of a new primate. Shortly afterwards the parliament elected the Duke of York, Protector; the Duke of Somerset, the Queen's favourite, had already been committed to the Tower. The Duke of York's first Protectorship lasted only nine months. At the end of the

[6] A breviary or service book.   [7] Demeanour.   [8] Easter week.   [9] Archæologia, xxix. p. 307.

year, the King recovered his reason and was restored to the full exercise of his royalty, and the Queen regained her influence; the first act was to liberate the Duke of Somerset, which was followed by other acts equally unpopular. The Duke of York, as a necessary measure of personal safety, retired again to the Castle of Ludlow, where he was joined by the Duke of Norfolk, the Earls of Warwick and Salisbury, and other powerful friends.

Having assembled a small but trusty army of Borderers and Welshmen, the Duke again marched towards London, and on the 22nd of May surprised the King at St. Alban's, where a battle took place between the contending parties, which ended in the entire defeat of the Royalists, who fled in the utmost disorder. The King himself was slightly wounded in the neck with an arrow, and had taken shelter in the house of a tanner, where he was found by the victors. Although the King was now a prisoner in the hands of the Yorkists, the Duke as yet laid no distinct claim to the crown. Henry being still considered from his bodily health incapable of governing the kingdom, the lords were compelled by the urgent remonstrances of the commons and the people, in the parliament, which met in November, to appoint the Duke of York a second time Protector, and he placed some of his tried friends in the most important offices of the state. The Queen, however, was busy in her intrigues, and the Battle of St. Alban's had given rise to personal feuds which were not likely to end without further bloodshed.

A.D. 1455.—Margaret of Anjou, Queen of Henry VI., visited Chester, "upon progresse, with many great lordes and ladyes, and was most graciously received by the mayor and citizens." But the royal " progresse " was not one of pleasure alone; the real object of Margaret was to enlist the gentry of the country in the cause of her husband, and her visit was again repeated the year before the battle of " Bloreheath," when she distributed *white swan badges* among the principal partisans of the King, as cognisances of the House of Lancaster. The Queen won the hearts of the citizens by her royal courtesy and hospitality. In the former great conflict at Shrewsbury, the gentry of Cheshire were nearly all enrolled on one side; but at this period the feelings of the inhabitants appear to have undergone considerable change, for the chief houses were arrayed in almost equal numbers under the banners of the two contending parties.

The Duke, who appears to have been beset on every side with the plots and snares of his enemies, spent the leisure which he could snatch from the cares of government in strengthening his cause on the Borders of Wales, where we frequently trace his presence. Yet at the end of 1456, when the King in parliament demanded the restoration of all his rights, the Duke resigned the protectorate without a murmur. A reconciliation afterwards took place, and both parties joined lovingly together in a public procession to St. Paul's, amid the joyful acclamations of the populace. This took place on the 25th of March, 1457. A pompous description of the ceremony is given by the old chroniclers, and particularly by the poets of that day; several interesting songs by whom are preserved in a contemporary MS. in the British Museum.* Some of these documents, however, prove the insincerity of the reconciliation between the rival parties. It was evident that the Queen and her party had only smothered their enmity until the arrival of a favourable moment for vengeance, and the leaders of both parties found it necessary to surround themselves with armed men. The first public outbreak was a serious affray at Westminster, when the Earl of Warwick was attacked by some of the Queen's household, and narrowly escaped by a boat on the river. The Earl, after a conference with his father, the Earl of Salisbury, and the Duke of York, proceeded to Calais, which, under the government of Warwick, had became the stronghold of the Yorkists. Alluding to the above circumstance, Polydore Virgil says, "The Duke and the Erle of Salesbury were much moved with this offence, spake openly betwixt themselves in bitter and sharpe termes, that the matter was nothing els but the ' fraude and fury of a woman,' who thinking she might do whatsoever she listed, sought nor minded any thing, so much as by womanish slight to torment, consume, and utterly destroy all the nobility of the land." Accordingly the great Yorkist leaders began again to raise their vassals, with the intention of marching towards London.

* See Cotton. MS. Vespas. B. xvi. fol. 4.

L L

The following is a copy of the letters patent of King Henry VI., creating Edward, his son, Prince of Wales and Earl of Chester :—

"HENRY, BY THE GRACE OF GOD, KING OF ENGLAND AND FRANCE, LORD OF IRELAND, &c. To all archbishops, bishops, abbots, priors, dukes, earles, barons, justices, viscounts, governors, ministers, and all our balives and faithful subjects, Greeting. Out of the excellency of royal preheminence, like as beame from the sun, so do inferior honours proceed: neither doth the integrity of the royal luster and brightnesse by the naturall disposition of the light affording light fro light, feele any loss or detriment by such borrowed light : yea, the royal scepter is also the much the more extolled, and the regall throne exalted, by how much the more nobles, preheminences, and honours are under the command and power thereof.

"And this worthy consideration allureth and induces us, which desire the increase of the name and honour of our first begotten and best beloved son, Edward, in whom we behold and see ourselves to bee honoured, and our royal house also, and our people subject unto us: hoping by the Grace of God, and by coniecture taken of his gratious future preceeding to be more honourably strengthened, that wee may with honour present, and with abundant grace prosecute him, who in reputation of us, is deemed the same person with us.

"Wherefore, by the counsell and consent of our prelates, dukes, earles, viscounts, and barons of our kingdom, being in our present parliament, we have made and created, and by these presents make and create him, the said *Edward, Prince of Wales and Earle of Chester*. And unto the same Edward we give and grant, and by this charter have confirmed, the name, style, title, state, dignity, and honour of the said principality and county, that he may therein in governing rule, and in ruling direct and defend, We, by a garland upon his head, by a ring of gold upon his finger, and a verge of gold, have, according to the manner, invested him, to have and to hold the same, unto him and our heires, the Kings of England, for ever. Wherefore we will and straightly command, for us and our heires, that Edward, our son, aforesaide, unto him and his heires, the Kings of England aforesaide, for ever. These being witnesses :—

"The reverend fathers John, Cardinal and Archbishop of Canterbury, Primate of all England; our Chancellor, and William, Archbishop of York, Primate of England ; Thomas, Bishop of London; and William, Bishop of Norwich ; our well-beloved cosins Richard, Duke of Yorke, and Humfrey, Duke of Buckinghame ; our well-beloved cosins Richard, Earle of Warwick, Richard, Earle of Salisbury, John, Earle of Wiltshire, and our beloved and faithful Raffe Cromwell, Chamberlain of our House; William Faulconbridge, and John Stourton, Knights.[1]

"Dated at our Pallace of Westminster, the xv. day of March, and in the yeare of our reigne XXXII."

At the beginning of September, A.D. 1457, we find the Duke at Shrewsbury, just at the period when the bailiffs were elected, and possibly with a view of promoting a choice favourable to his views. According to the corporation books, we find he received a present at that time of money and wine, amounting in value to 2l. 3s. 8d., and two oxen worth 26s. 8d. His son, the Earl of March, afterwards Edward IV., accompanied him on that occasion, and had a gift of bread and wine, "for the honour of the towne," to the

[1] Things required unto the creation of the Prince of Wales : —
First, an honourable habite (viz.) a rose of purple veluet, having in it aboute xvii elnes, more or less, garnished about with a fringe of gold, and lined with ermines.

A surcoat or inner gowne, having in about xiii elnes of velvet, of like couler. Fringe and furre.

Laces, buttons, and tassels (as they cal them) ; ornaments made of purple, silk, and gold.

A girdle of silk also to girdle his inner gowe.

A sword, with a scabbard made of purple, silke, and gold, garnished with the like girdle he is girt withall, thereby showing himself to be Duke of Cornwall by birth and not by creation.

A cap of the same velvet that his robe is of, firred with ermines,

with laces, and a button, and tassels on the Crown hereof made of Venice gold.

A garland, or a little coronet of gold, to be put on his head, together with his cap.

A long golden serge or rod, betokening his gouerment.

A ring of gold also, to be put on the third finger of his left hand, whereby he declareth his marriage with equity and justice.

All these things were almost with royall sumptuousnesse prepared for Edward, soune to King Henry VI. to have been created Prince of Wales, but preuented by his father's death, he was crouned King Sixt of that name. Yet the forme, with the rites and ceremonies belonging to the inuesting of the prince unto the principality of Wales, you may perceive by that which is before declared.

amount of 7*s*. 5*d*. Wine was, at that time, also bestowed on "divirs knights, esquires, and other gentlemen of the Duke of York and Earl of March, for the honour of the Towne."[2] Other extracts from the accounts of the same bailiffs, which we copy from the learned authors already quoted, evince a continued intercourse between this great Duke and the town of Shrewsbury.

A.D. 1459.—The battle of Blore-heath took place, on the 23rd September, near Market-Drayton, Shropshire. The Duke of York had arrived at Ludlow in the preceding month, and Richard Neville, Earl of Salisbury, was now on his march from the north, to join him there. Hereupon the veteran royalist, James Touchet, Lord Audley, whose fortress of Red Castle lay near the Earl's line of march, advanced with an army of ten thousand men to oppose him, but was defeated with great loss. The Lancasterian leader himself fell by the hand of Roger Kynaston, Esq., of Hordley, who afterwards received the honour of knighthood for his gallant exploits in the service of the House of York.

"In the great battail of Blore Heath," says the old Chronicles of Hall, "wer slayn xxiiij c persons. But the greatest plague lighted on the Cheshire men, because one halfe of the shire was on the one parte, and the other on the other parte, but the Erle's (the Earl of Salisbury) two sonns, the one called Sir John Nevill, and the other Sir Thomas, were sorely wounded, which soberly jorneing into the North country, thinking there to repose themselves, were on their jorney apprehended by the Queen's friendes, and conveyed to Chester, but their keepers delivered them shortly, or elles the March men had destroyed the gaytes. Such favour had the commons of Wales to the Duke and his affinitie, that they could suffre no wrong nor evil words to be spoken of hym or his friendes." After the battle, the Earl of Salisbury continued his march to Ludlow.

The Court had also been making great exertions to avert the threatened danger, and had raised a much more numerous army than their opponents. The King hastened to Worcester with sixty thousand men; as he advanced towards Ludlow, the army of the Yorkists had drawn up into an intrenched camp in the fields of Ludford. They had been joined by the Earl of Warwick, who brought a body of veteran troops from Calais, under an old and experienced commander, Sir Andrew Trollop. Some attempt was made at negotiation, and the Yorkist leaders addressed a letter to the King, which is printed by Stowe. They knew that King Henry, whom they were opposing, reigned in the hearts of his subjects, and, in order to do away with the people's attachment to the King, they caused a report of his death to be spread, and made the most revered offices of religion bend to human policy, by ordering mass to be celebrated for the repose of his soul, though they knew that the King was then alive and well!

Henry, however, roused himself on this occasion with a spirit and energy which were not generally supposed to belong to him. "He made exhortation, by his own mouth, to all the lords, knights, and nobles in his host, so witty, so knightly, so manly, so comfortable wise, with so princely apport and assured manner, of such the lords and people took such joy and comfort, that all their desire was only to fulfil his courageous knightly desire."[3] Stowe says, "On the 13th of October the King's army came in view of the intrenchments of Ludford, and were received with a brisk cannonade, which compelled them to retire, and no further attack was made on that day. In the evening, the Duke of York and the two Earls, the father

---

[2] Paid for a breakfast to Thomas Acton and Thomas Hoord for their good council touching the return of a precept of the Duke of York directed to the bailiffs for surety of the peace.

Money paid for the expenses of Thomas Hoord and William Lyster riding to the lord Duke of York at Ludlow, to get the said precept dissolved.

Extracts from the accounts of Fitzherbert and Adys the bailiffs:

In denariis solutis et vino dato in exhenniis datis domino duci Ebor' in sua essentia hic die martis post festum Sci Michaelis . . . . XLIIIs. VIIId.

Pro duobus bobus datis eidem duci eodem die . . XXVIs. VIIId.

Pro vino dato comiti Salop eodem tempore . . XIIIs. IIIId.

In denariis solutis pro vino et pane in exhenniis dat' comiti del March pro honestate ville . . . . VIIs. Vd.

In denar' solut' pro vino exp'nd' super diversos milites armigeros et alios generosos homines ducis de Ebor' & comitis March pro honestate ville . . . IIIIs. VId.

Denar' solut' p' jantaclo Thome Acton Thome Hoord expendit' p' suo bono consilio h'end' p' ret'no cuiusdam p'cepti ducis Ebor' ball' direct' p' sec' pacis . VIIs. Vd.

Denar' solut' p' exp'ns' Thome Hoord et Willi Lyst' equitanciu' d'no duci Ebor' pro disolvcacoe pcepti pdci de secur' pac' ad vill' de Ludlowe . . . IIIIs. Xd.

[3] W. Wyrc. ap Hearne, Lib. Nig., p. 483.

and son, and the Setter up of Kings, held a council of war, at which it was determined to attack the enemy, and take them by surprise early in the morning, which probably would have been attended with success, had not Sir Andrew Trollop, the marshall of the Yorkist army, deserted during the night to the Royalists, carrying with him the veteran troops under his own particular command, and betrayed all their councils to the King. The Yorkists, dismayed by this defection, broke up their camp in the night and fled, the Duke of York and his youngest son, the Earl of Rutland, escaping to Ireland, while the Earls of Warwick and Salisbury, with Edward, Earl of March, succeeded in reaching Calais in safety." The Lancastrians entered Ludlow, and wreaked their vengeance upon the town and castle, which, as the old historians inform us, were plundered "to the bare walls." The Duchess of York, with her two youngest sons, were taken and placed in safe custody, and many of the richer partisans were executed, and their estates confiscated.

On the 20th of November, a parliament met at Coventry, in which the Yorkist leaders were attainted,[4] and they are thus enumerated in a contemporary letter in the Paston Correspondence :—"The duc of York, therle of Marche; therle of Rutland; therle of Warrwyk; therle of Salusbury; the lorde Powys; the lorde Clynton; the Countesse of Sarr; Sir Thomas Nevyle; Sir John Nevyle; Sir Thomas Haryngton; Sir Thomas Parre; Sir Joan Convers; Sir Joan Wenlock; Sir William Oldhall; &c. As for lorde Powys, he came inne and hadde grace as for his lyf, but as for his godes, the forfeiture passid." Notwithstanding all this disaster, the Yorkists did not lose their courage. The Earl of Warwick at Calais entirely defeated the attempt to drive him from his government, and the fleet, having revolted to him, made him master of the English coasts, and enabled him to hold easy communication with the Duke in Ireland. One of the letters in the Paston Correspondence, dated January, 1460, says, "the Duke of York is at Dublin, strengthed with his earls and homagers;" and that the Court was in dread of further danger, appears by another letter in the same collection, dated 29th of January, from which we learn that the King, on his

---

[4] In the subsequent act of attainder, the following account is given of the transactions at Ludlow :—

"And the Friday, in the vigill of the fest of the translation of seint Edward kying and confessour, the xxxviiith yere of youre moost noble reigne, at Ludeford in the shire of Hereford, in the feldes of the same, the seid Richard duc of York, Edward erle of Marche, Richard erle of Warrewyk, Richard erle of Salesbury, Edmond erle of Rutlond, Johan Clynton lord Clynton, Johan Wenlok, knyght, James Pykeryng, knyght, the seid Johan Conyers, and Thomas Parre, knightes, John Bourghchier, Edward Bourghchier, squires, nevues to the seid duc of York, Thomas Colt Edward late of London, gentilman, Johan Clay late of Chesthunt in the shire of Hertford, squier, Roger Eyton late of Shrouesbury in Shropshire, squire, and Robert Boulde, brother to Herry Boulde, knight, with other knyghtes and people, such as they had blynded and assembled by wages, promyses, and other exquisite meanes, brought in certeyn persones bifore the people, to swere that ye were decessed, doyng masse to be said, and offeryng all to make to people the lesse to drede to take the feld. Neverthelesse, after exortation to all the lordes, knyghtes, and nobley in youre host, made by youre owne mouth, in so witty, so knyghtly, so manly, in so comfortable wise, with so pryncely apporte and assured maner, of which the lordes and the people toke such joye and comfort, that all their desire was oonly to hast to fulfill youre corageous knyghtly desire, albe the ympedyment of the weyes and streitnesse, and by lette of waters, it was nygh evyn or ye myght come to take grounde covenable for youre felde, displaied youre baners, raunged youre batailles, pighted your tentes ; they beyng in the same feldes the same day and place, traiterously raunged in bataill, fortefied their chosen ground, their cartes with gonnes sette bifore their batailles, made their escarmysshes, laide their enbusshmentes there, sodenly to have taken the advauntage of youre host. And they entendyng the destruction of youre moost noble persoon, the same Friday and toune, in the feld there falsely and traiterously

rered werre ayenst you, and than and there shotte their seid gonnes, and shotte as wele at youre most roiall persone, as at youre lordes and people with you than and there beyng. But God, in whos handes the hertes of kynges been, made to be knowen, that they whos hertes and desires were oonly sette to untrouth, falsenesse, and cruelté, subtily coloured, and feyned zelyng justice, ment the grettest falseness and treason, most ymmoderate covetise that ever was wrought in any realme : insomoche that by Robert Radclif, oon of the felanship of the seid duc of York, and erles of Warrewyk and Salesbury, it was confessed at his dying, that both the coroune of Englond and duchie of Lancaster they wold have translated at their wille and pleasure. But Almyghty God, that seth the hertes of people, to whome is nothyng hidde, smote the hertes of the seid duc of York and erles sodenly from that most presumptuouse pryde, to the most shamfull falle of cowardise that coude be thought, so that aboute mydnyght than next suyng they stale awey oute of the felde, under colour they wold have refreshed theym awhile in the toune of Ludlowe, levyng their standardes and baners in their bataill directly ayenst youre feld, fledde oute of the toune unarmed with fewe persones into Wales ; understondyng that youre people hertes assembled, was blynded by theym afore, were the more partie converted by Goddes inspiration to repent theym, and humbly submytte theym to you, and aske youre grace, which so didde the grete part ; to whome, at our lordes reverence and seint Edward, ye ymparted largely your grace. But, soverayne lorde, it is not to be thought, but they and it had been possible to theym by eny meane, their wille was to have accomplished their cruell, malicious, and traiterous entent, to the fynal destruction of your moost roiall persone. And to shewe forthermore the contynuance of their most detestable fixed traiterous purpose and desire ayenst you, soveraine lorde, and you and youre magesté roiall, and the wele of youre realme and subgettes, some of theym been arryved in your toune of Caleis, wharby the toune stondeth in jupartie, as wele as all the goodes of all your marchauntes beyng of the staple there."

way to London, was "raising the people; that great activity was displayed in preparing a powerful army for immediate service, and the vindictive measures of the Court left no alternative to the Yorkist leaders but to seek safety in open war. In the month of July, both the contending armies met at Northampton, and, after an obstinate battle, the Lancastrians were entirely defeated, and the King himself was left in the hands of the victors. The Earl carried the King to London, and immediately called a parliament.

On receiving intelligence of this victory, the Duke of York returned from Ireland, in order openly to prosecute his claim to the crown in the parliament of October. Hall describes the haste with which he posted from Dublin to that assembly in London, but we are sure, from a better authority,⁵ that he landed at Chester in the middle of August, whence he passed through Shrewsbury and Ludlow to Hereford, and where he had appointed the Duchess to meet him. They reached London on the 10th of October. When the Queen (Margaret of Anjou) heard that the King was taken prisoner, she retired to Durham, but, not thinking herself safe there, she then, together with her son and eight persons, fled to Harlech Castle,⁶ in Merionethshire. She soon again left this fortress, and returned to the north, where she used every effort to collect her scattered adherents.

Harlech Castle, Merionethshire.

The King, aware of the danger that threatened him, caused, on the 9th day of August, A.D. 1460, letters⁷ to be written to the constables of Beaumaris, Conway, Flint, Hawarden, Holt, and Ruthin,

⁵ Holinshed Chron., vol iii. p. 566.

⁶ Called also Caer Collwyn, and Twr Bronwen. This fortress is a noble object, situated upon a rock of great elevation above the sea, where formerly stood its western base. According to the British historians, the castle was originally built by Maelgwyn Gwynedd, Prince of North Wales, about 350. It was formerly called Twr Bronwen, from Bronwen (the Fair-necked), sister to Bran ap Llur, Duke of Cornwall, and subsequently King of Britain. In the eleventh century it obtained the name of Caer Collwyn, from Collwyn ap Tango, founder of one of the fifteen tribes of North Wales, and lord of Eifionydd, Ardudwy, and part of Llueyn. He lived in the time of Anarawd, about A.D. 877, and resided in the square tower of the original building. The remains are still apparent, as are also a part of the old walls: the modern work in some places resting upon them. The present structure was built by Edward I. in 1282. In 1283 he appointed Hugh de Wlonkeslow constable, with an annual allowance of 100l.

In 1404, it was taken by our gallant countryman, Owen Glyndwr. In the civil wars, this fortress more than once changed masters: Major Hugh Pennant defended the place with spirit against a large force under General Mytton, to whom, in March 1647, it surrendered on good terms. It had the honour of not only being the last place that held out for the House of Lancaster, but also for King Charles I.

In 1692, a golden torque was dug up in a garden near this place. A long disquisition is given by Camden, on this celebrated piece of antiquity, which is preserved with several other objects of curiosity at Mostyn Hall, the seat of the Hon. E. M. Lloyd Mostyn, M.P. It is about four feet long, flexible, and hooked at both ends.

⁷ Nicholas, Proceedings, &c., of the Privy Council of England, vol. vi. p. 303.

commanding them to provide for the security of those places; also to Jasper Tudor, Earl of Pembroke, assuring him of the King's belief of the loyalty of Richard, Duke of York, and commanding him to deliver Denbigh Castle to the Duke, or to the Duke's deputy; and likewise to the Lord Powys, commanding him to surrender the castle of Montgomery.

On the 17th of the month, Henry himself wrote a letter (as if suspecting their loyalty) to Sir William Herbert, knight, Walter Devereux, and Roger Vaughan, esquires, giving them power to prevent all unlawful assemblies, to arrest all such persons as should attempt to victual or fortify castles or places of strength in South Wales, and to adopt measures for the safety of those castles, until the King should give further directions.

At the parliament holden in the autumn of this year, the Duke threw off the mask, and openly stated his claim to the Crown. The parliament hesitated, and ordered it to be taken into consideration; and it was finally agreed that Henry should enjoy the throne during his life, and that the Duke of York should be acknowledged his heir, and appointed Protector of the kingdom till Henry's death. Being thus armed with royal authority to sit in judgment on those who trangressed the laws, we can scarcely doubt that he would employ his powers to the furtherance of his own views. "My lord of York," says Paston, who wrote a short time after the fight, (London, Oct. 12, 1460), "hath divers strange commissions from the Kyng, for to sitte in dyvers townys comyng homewarde, that is for to say in Ludlow, Schroffysbury, Hereford, Leycestre, Coventre, and in other dyvers townys, to punish them by the fawtes to the Kyng's lawes."

For a time the new order of things went on smoothly, at least in appearance; but there was little solidity under the surface. We have abundant evidence of fears and suspicions in the Paston Letters, those interesting memorials of the popular feelings of the fifteenth century. John Brackly, a priest and very popular preacher of this period, says in a letter written from Norwich to Sir John Paston, soon after the events just described, "God save our good lord Warwick, all his brethren, Salisbury, &c. from all false covetise and favour of extortion, as they will flee utter shame and confusion. God save them and preserve from treason and poison; let them beware thereof, for the pity of God; for if aught come to my Lord Warwick but good, farewell ye, farewell I, and all our friends; for, by the way of my soul, this land were utterly undone, as God forbid; their enemies boasting with good (i. e. with money, by bribery) to come to their favour. But God defend them, and give them grace to know their friends from their enemies, and to cherish and prefer their friends, and lessen the might of all their enemies throughout the shires of the land."

Events were now marching on with fearful rapidity. .The Queen, who had fled to the north, was actively employed in raising another army, and had been joined by the most powerful of the Lancastrian lords. Hitherto the contest had been chiefly maintained by the family feuds of the great barons of the realm, but the commons were every day made more and more parties in the cause. It is stated by the old chroniclers that the Queen held forth a promise of free permission to plunder the whole country south of the Trent, as an inducement to march against the triumphant Yorkists.

The Duke of York was aware of the Queen's proceedings, and marched somewhat precipitately to anticipate the attack. In the December following we find the Duke in his own castle of Sandal, in Yorkshire, and the Queen also in the neighbourhood with a superior force. The Duke, provoked at the Queen's challenge, risked an engagement with an inferior force. After fighting for some time, the Yorkists were thrown into fatal disorder by an unexpected attack in the rear from a fresh body newly arrived. The result was in the highest degree disastrous to the Yorkists. The Duke himself was slain, and two thousand of his men left dead on the field. His son, the Earl of Rutland, was put to death after the battle; his friend, the Earl of Salisbury, with several others, were taken prisoners and sent to Pomfret, where they were beheaded, and their heads, together with that of the Duke, being fixed on poles, were placed over the gate of the City of York.

The Queen marched directly upon London, and the conduct of her troops seemed to verify in every point the report that the Northern men had covenanted for the plunder of the South. She met with no serious check till her arrival at St. Alban's, where she was opposed by the Yorkists, under the Earl of Warwick; but having turned their position, she attacked the main body of the Earl's army between that town and Barnet, and completely defeated it, the last stand being made by the men of Kent, on Barnet Common. The King was left on the field, and was thus again liberated from the party who had been acting in his name.

The Lancastrians annulled all the acts of government passed since their defeat at Northampton, proclaimed the leaders of the Yorkists as traitors, and set a price on the head of Edward, Earl of March, who now, by the death of his father, had become the immediate pretender to the throne.

Edward, Earl of March, the Duke of York's eldest son, was on the Welsh Border when he heard of the death of his father. Upon hearing the news he removed to Shrewsbury, whence he proceeded to other towns along the Severn, publishing wherever he went the murder of his father, his own danger, the instability of the government, and the danger with which the nation was threatened.

Edward's appeal was not in vain,[8] for the people in the Marches of Wales were firmly and faithfully attached to the house of Mortimer; he soon found himself at the head of an army of twenty-three thousand men, ready to march against the Queen and the murderers of his father; but when he was preparing to proceed, news was brought to him that Jasper Tudor, Earl of Pembroke, and James Butler, Earl of Ormond and Wiltshire, had assembled together a great number of Welsh and Irish in order to surprise and take both him and his friends, and then bring them in triumph to the Queen.

After receiving this intimation he fearlessly marched against them. The hostile parties met at Mortimer's Cross, near Wigmore, in Herefordshire, where on the 2nd of February, 1461, a great battle was fought. It is said that before the battle commenced three suns appeared in the sky, which approached each other until they joined in one, and that Edward taking this as a favourable omen, subsequently adopted a bright sun as his badge, in remembrance of this circumstance. After an obstinate struggle the Yorkists obtained a complete victory, and nearly four thousand of their enemies were slain. All the prisoners of rank were beheaded at Hereford, in retaliation for the Queen's cruelties after the battle of Wakefield. The Earl of Pembroke escaped by flight, but his father, Sir Owen Tudor, was taken prisoner, and immediately beheaded by Edward's orders.

Among those who fell on Edward's side was a celebrated Welsh chieftain, Griffith ap Nicholas,[9] of Newtown, who was originally a Lancastrian, and was governor of Kilgerran Castle under Henry VI., but was induced by the following circumstances to change sides:—Jasper, Earl of Pembroke, coveting the governorship of the castle, at this time holden by Griffith, used all the interest which he and his brother, Edmund, Earl of Richmond, possessed with Henry VI. to have him superseded. This attempt on the part of Jasper so exasperated Griffith that he never forgot the insult. When Richard Duke of York was appointed Protector, on the Yorkists gaining the battle of Northampton, he sent commissioners to different parts of the kingdom with power to arrest and punish all persons guilty of any misdemeanour against the laws of the realm.[1] Among such persons was Griffith ap Nicholas, who on a former occasion had withholden from the Duke of York some land in Herefordshire, and had refused to obey the sheriff's warrant then issued against him; and now, in addition, had committed several depredations on the Marches. When, therefore, Griffith heard of a fresh storm that was brewing against him, he lost no time in breaking off with the court; and by tendering his services to the Duke, which were readily accepted, to support the

[8] All the men of power who inhabited the country between Gloucester and Shrewsbury had dependence on him as heir to Mortimer; or held in chief of his mighty confederate, the Earl of Warwick. Habington's Hist. of Edward IV., 4to. p. 3. 1569.

[9] Griffith ap Nicholas was possessed of great property, and allied to the principal families in North and South Wales, and maintained princely establishments. A contemporary bard addressing him, said:

"Saith gastell sy ith gostiaw,
A saith lys sy ith law."

that is:

"Thou holdest seven palaces in thy hands,
And castles seven, with domain lands."

[1] "The Duke of York, who had escaped to Ireland, returned in consequence of the victory gained at Northampton over the king's army, and landed at Chester; from thence he proceeded to the different towns as above stated.

claims of the house of York to the throne, he escaped the threatened punishment. He was faithful to his promise, for on the death of the Duke at Wakefield, he united his forces with those of his son, the Earl of March, and fell, bravely fighting by his side, in the battle of Mortimer's Cross.[2]

The Duke of York, after he had received his commission from the King, appears to have used the powers entrusted to him, principally for the furtherance of his own ambitious views. This we judge to have been the case not only from his conduct with respect to Griffith ap Nicholas, in his proceedings against whom he had no justice on his side; but, from a poem addressed to Rice ap John,[3] of Aberpergwm, and from another to Henry ap Gwilym (both of whom were staunch Lancastrians), and according to the solemn attestation of the poets here referred to, innocent of the charge preferred against them. Rice ap John, however, made a manly and successful resistance to the commissioners; for when they came to arrest him, they were compelled by him, with the assistance of his adherents, to make a hasty retreat. There is also a poem by Jerwerth Vynglwyd, dated A.D. 1460, addressed to him, in which the poet writes in anticipation both of his arrest and of the confiscation of his lands. It is an excellent and well-written poem, and contains a graphic description of the sad state of affairs, as well as a noble vindication of Rice ap John:

But to return to our narrative. Margaret compensated the defeat sustained by the Royalists at Mortimer's Cross, by a victory which she obtained over the Earl of Warwick at St. Alban's; but she made no great advantage of this victory. For Edward,[4] who was then in Gloucestershire, hearing of the disaster, advanced against her; and, meeting with the Earl of Warwick and the remains of his army, at Chipping Norton, in Oxfordshire, was soon in condition to give her battle with superior force. Previous to his meeting with Warwick, Edward had, in his train, Walter Devereux, William Herbert, John Wenlock, and William Hastings, and others from the Marches of Wales, with an army of eight thousand men.

A.D. 1441.—Edward continued his march towards the east, his forces continually increasing by the way, until, at Chipping Norton, he joined the Earl of Warwick, who was retreating from Barnet.

The Lancastrian army remained at the latter place and at St. Alban's, plundering the country about, and not sparing even the ancient abbey and church of St. Alban's. The Queen hesitated in moving towards London, because she was well aware that the citizens were unfavourable towards her. She sent to the lord mayor for some carts of victuals for her army, and he did not venture to disobey her order: but Hall informs us, "the moveable commons, which favoured not the Queen's part, stopped the cartes at Cripplegate, and boldely sayd, that their enemies, which come and spoyle and robbe the citizens, should neither be relieved nor victayled by them."

While the Queen was concerting measures for punishing the stubbornness of the Londoners, news arrived of the approach of Edward and the Earl of Warwick, and the Lancastrian army immediately commenced its retreat towards the north.[5]

Edward, less scrupulous than his father, took advantage of the favourable disposition manifested towards him, and entered the capital amid the acclamations of the citizens. He took up his residence at Baynard Castle; where, on the third day of March, the Archbishop of Canterbury, the Bishops of Salisbury and Exeter, the Duke of Norfolk, Richard Earl of Warwick, William Herbert, with many others, held a council, when it was unanimously agreed upon to bestow the crown of England on Edward, Duke of York; and accordingly, on the following day, he was proclaimed King, by the title of Edward IV.

---

[2] In his death his countrymen had a severe loss, for he was firmly attached to the Welsh people, and to the Welsh bards he was the Mæcenas of his day. He held an Eisteddfod at Caermarthen, over which he presided for the space of twelve months and one day, and gave a splendid entertainment to the bards. A lineal descendant of his, the present noble Lord Dynevor, was, like him, the President of the Eisteddfod held in the same town in the year 1823.

[3] See Lewis Glyn Cothi's Works, Dosparth i.—xxiv, lines 23—44.

[4] Annales Wilhelmi Wyrcestre, ed. Hearne, 488, 489.

[5] For further particulars, see Hall's Chronicle.

HOUSE OF YORK.

HE accession of EDWARD IV. to the throne took place on the 4th of March, 1461, when he had not yet reached his twenty-first year; his title was confirmed by the forms of a popular election. Immediately after his victory over Henry VI., he came to London, and returned thanks to God at St. Paul's Church. He was then conducted in solemn procession to Westminster, and placed on the King's Bench, in the Hall, which was filled with people. It was then demanded of the commons whether they would accept this Prince to be their sovereign; to which all assented. He was crowned by Archbishop Bouchier, June 29th, 1461.

"On Thursday, the first week in Lent," a manuscript at Lambeth informs us, "came Edward to London with thirty thousand men, and so in field and town every one called 'Edward King of England and of France.'" In the eyes of the populace the loss of the French conquests was a sore blot in the character of the unfortunate Henry.

We agree with our friend, the erudite historian of Ludlow, that nothing gives us so striking a picture of the spirit of these great national struggles as the popular songs of the age. A contemporary manuscript in the archiepiscopal library at Lambeth, has preserved a song composed on the occasion of Edward's entrance into London, which gives us some notion of the joy with which he was received.[1]

The young king took every precaution, and had need of the utmost activity to secure his new position. The Queen, in her retreat, had kept her forces together, and was busily employed in strengthening herself in the north, where, by the middle of March, she had collected an army of sixty thousand men. On the other hand, the Duke of Norfolk and the young king's friends were "using all diligence in preparing for

[1] Communicated by Mr. Halliwell to the Society of Antiquaries, and printed in the Archæologia, vol. xxix. p. 130:—

"Sithe God hathe chose the to be his knyght,
And posseside the in this right,
Thoue him honour with al thi myght,
            Edwardus Dei gratia.

"Oute of the stoke that longe lay dede,
God hathe causede the to sprynge and sprede,
And of al Englond to be the hede,
            Edwardus Dei gratia.

"Sithe God hath yeven the, thorough his myghte,
Owte of that stoke birede in sight
The floure to springe and rose so white,
            Edwardus Dei gratia.

"Thoue yeve hem lawde and praisinge,
Thrue vergyne knight of whom we synge,
Undefiled sithe thy bygynyng,
            Edwardus Dei gratia.

"God save thy contenewaunce,
And so to prospede to his plesaunce,
That ever thyne astate thou mowte enhaunce,
            Edwardus Dei gratia.

"*Rex Angliæ et Franciæ,* y say,
Hit is thine owne, why saist thou nay?
And so is Spayn, that faire contrey,
            Edwardus Dei gratia.

"Fy on slowtfulle contenewauance!
Where conquest is a noble plesaunce,
And registerd in olde rememberance,
            Edwardus Dei gratia.

"Wherefore, prince and kyng moste myghti,
Remembere the subdene of thi regaly,
Of Englonde, Fraunce, and Spayn, trewely,
            Edwardus Dei gratia."

M M

the warre;" and on reaching Pontefract, his army had increased to forty-nine thousand men; Edward left London the 12th of March, and soon joined the advancing army. On the 27th, the contending parties came in sight of each other at Towton, near York, where an engagement took place. They fought with unrelenting fury from three o'clock on Saturday till three o'clock on Sunday, when the Yorkists gained a decisive victory. In this savage contest, in which neither side gave quarter, from thirty to forty thousand men were slain, of which number twenty-eight thousand belonged to the Lancastrian party. The Earls of Northumberland and Westmoreland, with several other barons of the Queen's party, and Sir Andrew Trollop, who had deserted the Yorkists at Ludlow, were among the dead; and the Earls of Devonshire and Wiltshire were taken and beheaded. The Dukes of Somerset and Exeter escaped to York, and fled thence with the Queen, King Henry, and their son, Prince Edward, closely pursued by their enemies to Scotland. Edward entered York immediately after, where he found the heads of his father and younger brother still exposed on the walls, and a number of Lancastrian heads were put up in their place. After remaining in the north a sufficient time to secure the effects of his victory, he returned to London. Soon after his return, he created his brother, George, Duke of Clarence; and his brother, Richard, Duke of York; and shortly afterwards he made a tour through the southern parts of the kingdom, where he was received with unusual rejoicings.

A curious Yorkist ballad on the battle of Towton, and the events which preceded it, written immediately after Edward's coronation, is preserved.[2] It not only pictures the spirit of the times and the

---

[2] This ballad is preserved in a manuscript in the library of Trinity College, Dublin, from which it was copied by Sir Frederick Madden, and communicated to the Archæologia, xxix. p. 343. During the war between the two Houses of Lancaster and York, it is well known a White and Red Rose were their respective badges. On the union of the two Houses in the person of Henry VII. it was customary to have a white and red rosette painted on the ceiling of the taverns in London, with the motto "Persevere under the Rose," which being alternately white and red, was emblematical of the union, and an invitation to forget all past distinctions of party. It is reported, that when roses were first brought from Italy to England, they were consecrated as presents from the Pope, and placed over the gates of confessionals as the symbols of secresy. Hence the meaning of the phrase "Under the Rose":—

"Now is the Rose of Rone growen to a gret honoure,
　Therfore syng we everychone, i-blessed be that floure!

"I warne you everychone, for [ye] shud understonde,
　There sprang a Rose in Rone, and sprad into Englonde;
　He that moved oure mone, thoroughe the grace of Goddes sonde,
　That Rose stonte alone the chef flour of this londe.
　　I-blissid be the tyme that ever God sprad that floure!

"Blissid be that Rose ryalle that is so fresshe of hewe!
　Almighty Jhesu blesse that soule that the sede sewe!
　And blissid be the gardeyne ther the Rose grewe!
　Cristes blessyng have thei alle that to that Rose be trewe!
　　And blissid be the tyme that ever God sprad that floure!

"Betwixt Cristmas and Candelmas, a litel before the Lent,
　Alle the lordes of the northe thei wrought by oon assent;
　For to stroy the sowthe cuntré thei did alle hur entente;
　Had not the Rose of Rone be, al Englond had he shent.
　　I-blissid be the tyme that ever God sprad that floure!

"Upon a Shrof Tuesday, on a green leede,
　Betwixt Sandricche and Saynt Albons many man gan blede;
　On an Aswedynsday we levid in mykel drede,
　Than cam the Rose of Rone downe to halp us at oure nede.
　　Blissid be the tyme that ever God sprad that floure!

"The northern men made her bost, whan thei had done that dede,
　'We wol dwelle in the southe cuntrey, and take al that we nede;
　These wifes and hur doughters oure purpose shal thei spede.'
　Than seid the Rose of Rone, 'Nay, that werk shal I forbede.'
　　Blissid be the tyme that ever God sprad that floure!

"For to save al Englond the Rose did his entent,
　With Calays and with Londone, with Essex and with Kent;
　And all the southe of Englond unto the watyr of Trent;
　And whan he sawe the tyme best, the Rose from London went.
　　Blissid be the tyme that ever God sprad that floure!

"The way into the northe cuntré the Rose ful fast he sought,
　With hym went the Ragged Staf, that many man dere bought;
　So than did the White Lyon, ful worthely he wrought,
　Almighti Jhesu blesse his soule that tho armes ought!
　　And blissid be the tyme that ever God sprad that floure!

"The Fisshe Hoke cam into the fielde with ful egre mode;
　So did the Cornysshe Chowghe and brought forthe alle hir brode;
　Ther was the Blak Ragged Staf, that his bothe trewe and goode,
　The Brideld Horse, the Watyr Bouge by the Horse stode.
　　Blissid be the tyme that ever God sprad that floure!

"The Grehound and the Hertes Hede, thei quyt hem wele that day,
　So did the Harow of Caunterbury, and Clynton with his Kay;
　The White Ship of Brystow, he feryd not the fray,
　The Blak Ram of Coventré, he said not one nay.
　　Blissid be the tyme that ever God sprad that floure!

"The Fawcon and the Fetherlok was ther that tyde,
　The Blak Bulle also hymself he would not hyde;
　The Dolfyn cam fro Walys, iij. Carpis be his syde,
　The prowde Libert of Salesbury, he gapid his gomes wide.
　　Blissid be the tyme that ever God sprad that floure!

"The wolf cam fro Worcetre, ful sore he thought to byte,
　The Dragon cam fro Glowcestre, he bent his tayle to smyte;
　The Griffon cam fro Leycestre, fleyng in as tyte,
　The George cam fro Notyngham with spere for to fyte.
　　Blissid be the tyme that ever God sprad that floure!

exultation of the victors, but it enumerates by their banners the chief towns which sent men to aid the victorious party, and to avenge the invasion of the South by the Northerns, as well as the barons who took part in this sanguinary contest.[1] Some of these banners or badges cannot now be easily appropriated.

In the summer after his coronation King Edward made a tour through the southern parts of the kingdom, beginning at Canterbury, and passing through Winchester, and other places until he reached Bristol, where he was received with unusual rejoicings :—"Deinde Rex Edwardus, Cantuarium peregre profectus, partes meridionales pertransiit, ubi Willielmum Episcopum Wintonie de manibus querentium animam ejus eripuit, insectatores suos graviter redarguit, et eorum capitaneos carcerali custodi emancipavit. Bristollie apperians, a civibus ejus cum maximo gaudio honoratissimè receptus est."[2] At the Temple Gate he beheld a figure representing William the Conqueror, who was made to address him in the following doggrell verse,—

> " Wellcome, Edwarde, oure son of high degré !
> Many yeeris hast thou lakkye owte of this londe.
> I am thy forefader, Wylliam of Normandye,
> To see thy welefare here through Goddys sond."

A giant over the gate appeared in the act of delivering up the keys. As the king marched into the town other pageants were ready to receive him, and prove the attachment of the citizens to his person. While he remained here, Sir Baldwin Fulford and other Lancastrians were brought before him, and beheaded on the 9th of September. The King soon after left Bristol to prepare for his first parliament, which met at London in the beginning of November.

A contemporary writer observes that, on this occasion, "forsomoche as he fande in'tyme of nede grete comfort in his comyners, he ratyfied and confermyd alle the ffraunsches yeve to cyteis and townes, &c., and graunted to many citeis and townes new ffraunschesses more than was graunted before, ryghte largly, and made chartours thereof, to the entent to have the more good wille and love in his londe."[4]

A.D. 1468.—In October of this year we find Edward master of all England and Wales, except three strongholds, one of which was Harlech Castle, in Merionethshire. At that time, Davydd ap Einion, a friend to the house of Lancaster, and a man as much distinguished for his valour as for his handsome person and great stature, possessed this place. Finding the governor determined to keep the castle, the King sent an army under William Herbert, Earl of Pembroke, who, after imitating the course of Hannibal over the Alps, invested the place. The Earl finding that he could not succeed, appointed his brother, Sir Richard, a man described as being equal in size and military prowess to the British commandant.

> " Sir Richard came, his legion led,
> To bid the chief surrender ;
> For well he knew, that Einion's son
> Was Harlech's brave defender."

" The Boris Hede fro Wyndesover with tusses sharp and kene,
The Estriche Fader was in the felpe, that many men myght sene !
The Wild Rat fro Northamptone, with hur brode nose,
Ther was many a fayre pynone wayting upon the Rose.
Blessid be the tyme that ever God sprad that floure !

" The northern party made hem strong with spere and with shielde;
On Palmesonday affter the none thei met us in the felde ;
Within an owre thei were right fayne to fle, and eke to yelde,
xxvij. thousand the Rose keyld in the felde.
Blissid be the tyme that ever God sprad that floure !

" The Rose wan the victorye, the feld, and also the chace ;
Now may the housband in the southe dwelle in his owne place ;
His wif and eke his fair doughtre, and al the goode he has ;
Soche menys hath the Rose made, by vertu and by grace.
Blissid be the tyme that ever God sprad that floure!

" The Rose cam to London ful ryally rydyng,
ij. erchebisshops of England thei crouned the Rose kyng;
Almighti Jhesu save the Rose, and geve hym his blessyng,
And all the reme of England joy of his crownyng,
That we may blisse the tyme that ever God sprad that floure !
Amen, pur charite."

[3] MS. Arundell, Coll. Arm. 5, fol. 169, r°. This Chronicle in the College of Arms was first used, as far as I know, for an historical purpose, in a MS. note in a copy of Carte's History of England in the Bodleian Library, where it is referred to on the important testimony of the death of Henry VI. Mr. Black quotes it in the *Excerpta Historica*, but its value does not appear to be fully appreciated by that author ; it is the diary of a contemporary writer on the side of the House of York, and extends to the execution of the Bastard of Fauconberg, and Edward's celebration of the feast of Pentecost which took place immediately afterwards.

[4] Warkworth's Chronicle, ed. Halliwell, p. 2.

He sent peremptory orders to surrender the place: to which the governor promptly replied, "I held a tower in France till all the old women in Wales heard of it; and now the old women of France shall hear how I defend this castle." The assailing army found that the place was so strong, both by nature and art, as only to be reduced by famine. Sir Richard was, therefore, under the necessity of compounding for its surrender, by promising the heroic defender to intercede with his royal master for life and liberty. This promise he religiously fulfilled. The King at first indignantly refused to grant Sir Richard's request. "Then, Sire," said Sir Richard, "you may if you please take my life in lieu of the Welsh chieftain's; if you don't comply, I will most assuredly replace Davydd in his castle, and your highness may send whom you please to take him out."[a]

A.D. 1469.—Harlech Castle was the last place that surrendered to King Edward, and as a reward for the taking of it, Sir William Herbert was, on the 27th of May, created Earl of Pembroke, of which dignity Jasper Tudor was now deprived. The Earl of Warwick who had been privately fomenting discontent, when he had gained to his side his brothers, the Marquis of Montague and the Archbishop of York, and also Edward's brother, George Duke of Clarence, departed for Calais; where in the month of July, in order to secure the friendship of the Duke, he gave him his eldest daughter, Isabella, in marriage. Shortly after Warwick's departure an insurrection broke out in the North, the origin of which there is reason to believe was attributable to the joint art of Clarence and Warwick. An attack was made by the rebels on the City of York, which was repulsed, and the ringleaders taken and beheaded. In despite of this they continued in arms, and being soon headed by men of greater distinction, Sir Henry Neville, son of Lord Latimer, and Sir John Coniers, they advanced southward, and began to appear formidable to the government.

William Herbert, now Earl of Pembroke, was ordered by Edward to march against the insurgents at the head of a body of Welshmen. When he arrived at Banbury he was joined by five thousand archers, under the command of Humphrey, Lord Stafford, lately created Earl of Devonshire; but the two chiefs quarrelling about lodgings, Lord Stafford deserted in the night. The two armies met at Danesmoor, about four miles from Banbury. Before a general battle had taken place, Pembroke, in a skirmish, had succeeded in taking Sir Henry Neville prisoner, and ordered him immediately to be put to death. This summary execution enraged the rebels; a fiercely contested battle ensued, in which the Welshmen were vanquished, leaving about five thousand dead on the field.[b] Pembroke, his brother, Sir Richard Herbert, Thomas Vaughan, John Donne of Kidwely, with several other eminent persons, were taken prisoners and beheaded.

After this battle the northern troops marched towards the town of Warwick, to join the Earl who had arrived there from Calais. The Duke of Clarence, also, who was not far distant, hastened at the express request of the Earl, to the place of rendezvous. Edward, who was in pursuit, advanced at the head of his army. When both parties met, a parley ensued; the King who was at Woolney, about four miles from the town of Warwick, expecting a reconciliation would be the result, apprehended no danger to his person, until he was surprised, taken prisoner, and conveyed to Warwick Castle; thence he was conducted to Myddleham Castle, and placed under the custody of the Earl's brother, the Archbishop of York. He had not been there long, before, by the assistance of Sir William Stanley, Sir Thomas Borough, and others, he effected his escape and made his way to York, where he was well received by the citizens. After remaining in this city two days, during which he mustered a small army to accompany him on his journey, he proceeded towards London, but afterwards fearing lest with so small an army he should be unable to make his way there without hazard to his person, he returned to Lancaster. Here he found the Lord Hastings his chamberlain, at the head of a body of troops, ready to assist him, and thus reinforced, he retraced his

---

[a] The compliment, high in sentiment, and beautiful in words, was paid to Herbert by a bard of that day:—

"Gwrol tragwrol, trugarog wrol,
Ni vu drugarog na vai dragwrol."

"The manly mind, the truly brave,
Loves mercy, and delights to save."

[b] See notes to Lewis Glyn Cothi's Poems, Dosp. 6, 7, 8.

steps towards London, where he arrived in safety. The intelligence of his arrival in the capital greatly perplexed Clarence and Warwick, to whom, after consulting with their friends, it appeared advisable to send to the King, requesting him, with the safety of their persons, to grant them an audience with a view of explaining themselves and settling their differences amicably.

This was granted by the King, and they met at Westminster. The meeting proved anything but satisfactory. They separated; the King went to Canterbury; the Duke and the Earl retired to Warwick Castle. This interview was shortly afterwards followed by an insurrection in Lincolnshire. It was, however, soon quelled by the King, who marched in person against the rebels. He fought them near Stamford, took their leaders prisoners, and ordered them to be beheaded immediately.

The Duke of Clarence and the Earl of Warwick, on hearing the result of this battle, fled to France, where they were well received by the King; they were also furnished by him with men and money, so that in the September following they landed at Dartmouth. No sooner was the news of their landing made known, than a great number rallied around their standard, and their army daily increasing, they marched against Edward. The King, through his own previous neglect in not preparing for the event by having an army in readiness, found himself in no condition to risk a battle. He, therefore, by the advice of his friends, escaped from the country. He arrived at Lynn, went on board of a Dutch vessel, with difficulty landed in Holland, and there placed himself under the protection of the Duke of Burgundy.[7] Clarence and Warwick, finding that Edward had made his escape, marched to London, released Henry VI. from the Tower, and, in the month of October, had him again proclaimed King! A parliament being assembled in November, Edward was declared an usurper, and he and his adherents were attainted.

Pennant, who quotes Leland, says that Edward IV., while Duke of York, was besieged at Denbigh Castle by the army of Henry VI., and the King declared it his intention, if Edward was taken, to give him his life, but on condition only that he should for ever banish himself from the realm.[8] However, he escaped. For their services in taking this castle from the Yorkists, Henry granted to Jasper, Earl of Pembroke, and the Duke of Bedford, a thousand marks, to be paid out of the Lordships of Denbigh and Ruthen.

This event of Edward's life is not noticed by any other historian, and the only time that Prince was constrained to abdicate his dominions, was in 1470, when he took shipping at Lynn, not by reason of any capitulation with his enemies, but through the desperate situation of his affairs at that period.

A.D. 1470.—On the 24th of June, Jasper Tudor landed with three French ships at Harlech. He was accompanied by fifty persons. In his progress through North Wales, there flocked to his standard two thousand men; he marched to the town of Denbigh, which he ransacked and set fire to. Upon hearing of his proceedings, William Herbert, with his brother Richard, hastened against him with an army of ten thousand men. Jasper was attacked by Sir Richard, and his army routed; several were taken prisoners, of whom twenty were beheaded, but Jasper himself escaped by flight. William Herbert laid siege to the Castle of Harlech, which held out till the 14th of August, when it was surrendered by its gallant defender, Davydd ap Jevan ap Einion.[9] Jasper Tudor, who was now restored to his titles, lost no time in visiting his county of Pembroke, where he found his nephew, Henry, son of Edmund, Earl of Richmond, in the custody of Lady Herbert, wife of the late Sir William Herbert, Earl of Pembroke.[1] Henry found in her a kind and careful guardian, one who watched over his education and the improvement of his mind. Jasper, taking Henry along with him, returned to London, and introduced him at Court.

Edward, in consequence of the aid he received from his brother-in-law the Duke of Burgundy, and relying upon the promised assistance of his friends in England, landed, on the 14th of March in the

---

[7] Charles the Bold, Duke of Burgundy, married Edward's sister on the 3rd of July, 1468. It was to this marriage that Edward owed his preservation abroad, and the final recovery of his kingdom.

[8] Leland's Itin. v. 58. The words are, " King Edward IV. was besiged in Dinbigh Castle, and their it was pactid between King Henry's men and hym (self) that he should with lyfe departe the realme never to returne. If they had taken King Edward there, *debellatum fuisset.*"

[9] Annales Wilhelmi Wyr., ed. Hearne, vol. ii. p. 506.

[1] Grafton.

following year, at Ravenspur, in Yorkshire. Among those who went to meet Edward on his arrival, we find, according to Gytto'r Glyn[2] (a contemporary bard), the brave Kynaston, of Hordley, in Shropshire, one of whose descendants has thus rendered the words of the bard:

> "————This dread hero ran with haste
> To meet his king, his kinsman, and his friend :
> Proffered his life, his all, to aid the cause
> Of injured majesty."

Lewis Glyn Cothi records another warrior, Llywelyn ap Rees ap John, of New Radnor, who also with his men hastened to meet Edward after his landing. From the same person we learn that he was also present at the battles of Barnard and Tewkesbury.

Edward, after his landing, proceeded unmolested towards York, where, after a long parley, he was received into the city. From thence he went to Doncaster, on the way to which he had some accession to his army. From Doncaster he marched to Nottingham, where he was joined by Sir William Parr and Sir John Harrington, at the head of six hundred men. He next arrived at Leicester, where three thousand more joined his standard. On the 29th of March, he appeared before Coventry, in which town the Earl of Warwick, with an army of six thousand men, was quartered. Edward, after several fruitless attempts to draw the Earl out of the town into the open field, withdrew himself from Warwick. At this time, the Duke of Clarence abandoned the Earl of Warwick, and, going over to his brother, brought to his aid an army amounting to more than four thousand men. Edward, by the advice of his friends, marched through Northampton, where he was well received, towards London. The gates of the city being thrown open to him, he went first to St. Paul's, and thence to the bishop's palace, where the archbishop presented himself to the King, and also the unfortunate Henry, who again fell into Edward's hands.[3]

The Earl of Warwick, trusting to the fidelity of his brother, the archbishop, and the citizens of London, advanced towards the capital; but, unexpectedly, on Easter even, he was met by Edward and his army at Barnet. The following morning, the 14th of April, a battle was fought. After a long and hard contest, victory at last declared itself on Edward's side. Among the slain left on the field, were found the Earl of Warwick, and his brother, the Marquis of Montague. The Duke of Somerset[4] and the Earl of Oxford escaped into Wales, to Jasper, Earl of Pembroke.

On the same day on which this battle was fought, Queen Margaret, and her son Edward, the Prince of Wales, landed at Weymouth, supported by a small body of French forces. When she received intelligence of her husband's captivity, and of the defeat and death of the Earl of Warwick, she took sanctuary in the Abbey of Beaulieu, in Hampshire. Whilst she was there, the Duke of Somerset, the Earl of Devonshire, Jasper, Earl of Pembroke, John Lord Wenlock, and others, presented themselves to her, and, consulting as to what steps should be taken in the present crisis, they came to the resolution of still prosecuting the war against Edward. They then separated: the Earl of Pembroke went to Wales, to his Earldom, to collect and rally his adherents; the Queen went to the southern counties of England, and having, with the assistance of her son, the Prince, and other noblemen, collected a considerable addition to her forces, she marched to Bath; but there receiving intelligence that Edward was advancing against her, she went to Bristol, intending from thence, after having been joined by the Earl of Pembroke, to proceed to the counties of Lancaster and Chester. She had not, however, gone further than Tewkesbury, when King Edward overtook her and gave her battle, in which the Queen and her forces were defeated. She was taken prisoner, and her son, the Prince, in his endeavour to escape to the town, was taken and murdered.[5]

---

[2] See, Arwyrain neu gerdd foliant i Syr Roger Kynaston, in Gytto'r Glyn's Poems.

[3] See History of Edward IV., arrival in England, p. 30.

[4] This was not the first time the Duke of Somerset took refuge in Wales : see Paston's Letters, by which we find that some of our countrymen were impeached for adhering to the House of Lancaster.

"The men's names that be impeached are these, John Hanmer, and William his son, Roger Puliston, and Edward ap Madoc ; these be the men of worchip that shall come in." Paston's Letters, dated at Holt Castle, Denbighshire, 1st of March, 1463-4.

[5] Prince Edward was only eighteen years of age when he was put to death. Historians differ as to the mode ; but according

The Duke of Devonshire fell in the field, but the Duke of Somerset, with many others, were made prisoners, and afterwards beheaded. The Queen was conveyed to London, and thrown into the Tower, and King Henry, on the 23rd of May, only a few days after the battle, expired in his confinement.

The Earl of Pembroke, who was levying his forces in Wales, disbanded his army when he received the intelligence of the battle of Tewkesbury, and fled into Brittany with his nephew, the young Earl of Richmond.[6]

A.D. 1476.—Edward was now firmly established on his throne, yet, for all that, and although all the hopes of the House of Lancaster seemed to be utterly extinguished, he could not help entertaining some inward apprehensions for the final destiny of the House of York, as long as Henry, Earl of Richmond, was alive. He, therefore, in 1476, endeavoured to have him delivered up to him, but in this his purpose failed.

Through the whole of his reign, Edward regarded the town of Shrewsbury with much affection. When he was firmly settled on the throne by the second and final expulsion of his rival, he sent his queen there to be delivered of her second son, Richard of Shrewsbury, in 1473-4.[7] The place which he chose for her residence was the house of the Dominican or Preaching Friars, on the banks of the Severn, below the collegiate church of St. Mary, where he had been entertained himself on a former occasion. He probably considered this situation to be less exposed to sudden attack than the monastery of St. Peter, on the other side of the river. She was also delivered here of her third son, George. Indeed, on the first of these occasions, the King seems to have accompanied her thither: it is at least certain that he was resident in Shrewsbury during some part of the year 1473.[8] It was probably in consequence of some such occasional residence of the royal family in this town, that in 1475 it was visited by two of the Queen's sons by her former husband, Thomas Gray, recently created Marquis of Dorset, and the Lord Richard, his brother.

It appears, from the archives of the corporation of Shrewsbury, that "the xᵒ daye of April the xviijᵒ yer of the Regne of oʳ sov'eign lord kyng E. the iiijth the right reu'ent fadʳ in god John Byshop of Worcestr p'sident of my lord prince councell, and the right noble lord Antony Erle Rivirs uncle and gou'noʳ to the said Prince and other of hys honerable councell beynge in the Town of Shrouysbury, for the wele rest and tranquillity of the same town, and for good rule to be kept by the officers mynystres and inhabitants thereof."[9]

The Queen of Henry VI., Margaret of Anjou, was conveyed to London, and continued a prisoner till A.D. 1475, when she was ransomed by her father for fifty thousand crowns, which he borrowed of Louis XI.

---

to "Master Flyghtwod's boke, Recordar of London," it was as follows, "Edward, Prince of Wales, was taken flynge to the towne wardes, and slayne in the fielde."

[6] See Paston's Letters, vol. ii. p. 74, 75.

[7] So he is called in a patent, 19 Edw. IV. m. 28. "Richardus Salop Dux Ebor." "This yeare the ducke of Yorke was borne in the Blacke Friars within the towne of Shrewsbury. The which Friars stande the vnder Sainct Mary's churche in the sayde towne estward." Taylor's MS. sub. ann. 1473—1474.

[8] This appears from the account of the sequestrators of Alberbury, still remaining in the archives of All Souls College, and entitled, "He sunt expense quas Will. ap David (and three others) procuratores administrationis sequestri fructuum et proventuum ecclesie de A. expenderunt circa ipsam administraco'em, A.D. M.CCC.LXI.III. Item Will'us ap David, Gryff. ap David, pro essendo apud Salop. quum dominus Rex erat ibi."

[9] We learn from the same ancient source (the accounts of the Bailiff of Shrewsbury,) that the King visited this town the next year, 1478; in these the following items occur:—

"Money paid for the honour of the town in divers costs and expenses done in the hostel, upon a certain French gentleman sent by the Lord Prince to the bailiffs and community, and paid to the hands of Maurice Montgomery, Sergeant to the Lord Prince, 13s. 4d.

"To William Harper, minstrel of the Lord Prince, 3s. 4d.

"Reward to a messenger of the Lord Prince bearing a letter to the bailiff, and another to all the artificers of the town, 3s. 4d.

"Wine given to Master Hawt, comptroller of the Lord Prince, 3s. 8d.

"Wine given to William Yong, Knt., and other gentlemen of the Lord Prince, 6s."

From the following items it would appear that the king took up his abode at the abbey.

"Money paid for bread in presents, given to the Lord Prince, with two carts at the abbey, 20s.

"Two pipes of ale to the Lord Prince, 17s.

"One pipe of wine for the Lord Prince. (The price is torn).

"Wine given to the Lord of Powys, 7s. 9d.

"Reward to a minstrel of the Duke of Gloucester called Taborer, 3s. 4d.

"Ale given to dyvers for the honour of the town, in the removal of the Lord Prince, 12d.

"For a pipe of red wine, given to the Lord Prince, 23s. 3d.

"Rewards of six minstrels for the honour of the king, 20s."

From an old deed of the Mercers' Company it would appear that the Prince was at Shrewsbury in 1480. It ends thus, "Given in our presence at Schrewysbury, the eleventh day of May, in the xx of the reyne of my most drede lord and fader Kinge Edward the Fourth."

of France. She afterwards lived in private life, and died in A.D. 1482. It is remarkable that no complete or authentic memoir of this extraordinary queen had ever been presented to the public, until the clever authoress of the Queens of England took it in hand. Miss Strickland has produced an exceedingly interesting narrative of the most extraordinary events, out of which we have extracted such portions of her work as relate immediately to the subject we are engaged in.

On the 6th of October, A.D. 1472, the King created his eldest son, Prince of Wales and Earl of Chester, and immediately sent him and his youngest brother to the Castle of Ludlow, in company with his half brothers, the Marquis of Dorset and Sir Richard Grey, and under the guardianship of his uncle, Antony Woodville, Earl Rivers. Hall, in his Chronicle, tells us the royal child was sent to Ludlow, "for justice to be doen in the Marches of Wales, to the end that by the authoritie of hys presence the wilde Welshemenne and evill disposed personnes should refrain from their accustomed murthers and outrages." The Prince's council, over which Alcock, Bishop of Worcester, was appointed president, were actively occupied in carrying out these objects. In the following official letter, dated in 1475, when the Prince was still hardly four years of age, we find his two half brothers occupied in putting down one of these not unfrequent acts of turbulence.

" *To our Trusty and Welbeloved the Baillies of Shrewsbury, and to either of them.*
" *By the Prince.*

"TRUSTY AND WELBELOVED, We grete you wele: and where as oftentymes heretofor ther have be made as well unto our moost drad lorde and fadre, as unto us, greet and haynes complaynts of robberies, murdres, manslaughters, ravysshments of women, brennyng of houses, and othir horrible dedys and misbehavyngs, by thenhabitants of the Marches adjoinant unto you; and in especiall now late greet murdre, brennyng, and manslaughter doon by errant theves and rebellious of Oswestre hundred and Chirkes lond in dispite of my said lord and fadres lawes and us, as the said misdoers fere nor shame opynly to sey, as we be credibly enformed. For the redresse of the same, my said lorde and fadre hath commanded us by his speciall lettres to assemble and reise his liege people, and to se the punisshment of the said malefactours. For thexecution whereof we have substitute our right entierly and welbeloved brethern uterynes Thomas Markes Dorset and Richard Grey, knight, with power sufficient unto thoes parties. Wherfor we desire and pray you, and natheless in my said lordes name charge you, that fortwith, upon the sight of this our writyng, ye do make opyn proclamacion in our said lorde and fadres name, that all manner men within your baillyweke betwix lx. and xvj. arredie themselfs, sufficiently harneysed, and drawe toward our said brethern, there to give their attendaunce in all hast possible. And that ye ne faile herof as ye will answere to my said lorde. And that ye put you in effectual devoir to se that vitelers purvey and bring brede, ale, flessh, and other vitail for the sustentacion of our said brethern and their felawship, and they shal be wele and truly content therfor. Yeven undre our signet, at the castle of Ludlowe, the viij. day of June."

The two Princes remained at Ludlow during the life of their father. We find them paying visits to Shrewsbury in 1478 and 1480. On King Edward's death in 1483, they were still at Ludlow Castle, under the guardianship of their maternal uncle, Lord Rivers, and their half brother, Lord Richard Grey, and were immediately recalled to London, to perish there, within a few weeks, amid the mysterious events which attended the accession of Richard III. to the throne. After having celebrated at Ludlow the then high festival of St. George's Day, they left that town, on the 24th of April, 1483, on their way to the capital.

Edward IV. possessed eminent talents for government, and many of the qualities of a great King. He bestowed much attention on the improvement of commerce. The intelligent author of the second continuation to the Chronicle of Croyland writes, that he purchased merchant vessels, laded them with wools, cloths, tin, and other commodities of his realm, as one of those who lived by merchandise; and bartered them by his factors both in Italy and Greece. By incorporating the fraternity of drapers of Salop, he led to most important effects on the opulence of the town and county for the three succeeding centuries; and by preparing for the institution, if he did not himself institute the Council in the Marches of Wales, he laid the foundation of a subordination to authority, and a regular administration of justice in this quarter of his dominions, which it had never known before. To this he was naturally led by the circumstances of his early life. Much of it had been spent in the Marches of Wales. The very title which he bore till he ascended the throne, was derived from that district. Ludlow had been the favourite scene of his infancy and childhood[1] and to that castle he took the resolution of sending his son the Prince of Wales at an early period, attended by a council to regulate the affairs of these Marches.

The court of the president and council of the Marches of Wales were established at Ludlow by King Edward IV., in honour of the Earls of March, from whom he was descended (as the court of the Duchy

Ludlow Castle, the Judicial Seat of the Lords Marchers.

of Lancaster had been before by Henry IV., in honour of the House of Lancaster), and owed its first institution to the prerogative-royal transacting business and acting judicially by virtue of that authority, to the entire satisfaction of the subject for about the space of sixty years (till the 34th of Henry VIII.); that court was confirmed by act of parliament, which was thought convenient to be done, by reason of the other laws relating to Wales, which at that time were further explained and enlarged.

Besides a list of the officers of the court, there is extant a roll of the names of knights and esquires "appointed by the King's most noble grace, in the Marches of Wales, to gyff attendance with such number of hable persons deffincibly as they may make to assist the King's Commissioners at Lodelowe, from time to time, the fees of each of them was 100s." For this roll the reader may consult Lloyd's History of Shropshire,

[1] The learned Camden says of Ludlow, that it was a town "majore elegantiâ quam vetustate;" but that it was a town of note in the time of the Britons, is evident from the name it bore, "Dinam," though we have no particular records left of the matter. Since the Conquest a noble knight assumed the surname of Dinam in honour of the place. We have not found how it came to be called Ludlow, a word of no affinity with Dinam, nor is there any mention of either in Doomsday. While the court of the president and council of the Marches stood, this was a town of great resort, and in a flourishing condition, and though its importance has been diminished, still the situation and conveniences of the place, render it a place of consequence to the adjacent country, which will ever support its trade and commerce.

N N

which further states: "Be it remembered that the book whereof this copy is taken forth, was assigned with the hand above and under of our late sovereign, Henry VII." 44th of Elizabeth: Edward, Lord Zouch, Lord President, among other instructions had in charge as follows:—"And further her majesty's pleasure is, that there shall be one benefice with cure of souls, to preach and to use the common prayer, for the Lord President and the household, and shall always be resident with the said council and not to be absent to serve any other cure or function." The Lord President had an allowance to live in great state and grandeur, and had a numerous household to attend him and the rest of the officers of the court, with fees and salaries suitable to their several ranks. We may easily form an idea of the splendour of the preceding presidents from the order in which his Grace the Duke of Beaufort, Lord President of Wales, made his entry into the Castle of Ludlow, on Thursday, July 17th, 1684.

The magnificent Castle of Ludlow is situated on a rock and commanding a delightful prospect. It was in every respect, according to the taste of former times, fit for a royal residence. Its battlements were high and thick, and its towers lofty and strong. Formerly it had in its front a spacious lawn of nearly two miles in extent, most of which is now enclosed and applied to more useful purposes. This castle was a palace of the Prince of Wales in right of his Principality. As this castle is peculiarly connected with our subject, a brief history of the edifice will not be uninteresting, and is as follows:—

"It was built by Roger de Montgomery, soon after the Conquest, in the centre of a large tract of country given him by King William. Roger Belesme, son of the founder, having rebelled against Henry I., it was seized by that monarch and remained the property of the crown in the time of Stephen. Notwithstanding this, Gervase Pagnal, having joined the Empress Maude, governed this place against his sovereign, Stephen;[2] besieged, and according to some accounts, took it, in 1139; but others say that he was unsuccessful and obliged to raise the siege.

In the reign of Henry VI., this castle belonged to Richard Plantagenet, Duke of York, who there drew up that declaration of his allegiance to the King, which pretended that the army of ten thousand men, which he had assembled in the Marches of Wales, "was for the public weal of the realm."

Another apology, much of the same nature, was likewise dated from this place, by the same Duke of York, eight years after; when his associate, Lord Audley, had been defeated at the battle of Blore-heath, in Staffordshire; and Andrew Trollop and John Blunt had deserted his party. As might be supposed this declaration was of no avail; a parliament was shortly after convened at Coventry, and there he and his adherents were attainted of treason.

Upon the triumph of the Yorkists, in the person of Edward IV., Ludlow Castle became again the property of the Crown, and here, under the tuition of Lords Wodeville and Scales, young Edward, who afterwards enjoyed the title of Edward V., for a little while kept his court.

The manner in which Lord Chief Justice Hale mentions this circumstance, includes a severe reflection on the manners of the Principality at that period. He was sent there, says the Judge, "for justice to be done in the Marches of Wales, to the end that by the authority of his presence, the wild Welshmen and other evil-disposed persons should refrain from their accustomed murders and outrages."

In one of the outer buildings, Butler is said to have composed the first cantos of his celebrated and unique poem of Hudibras, when he was secretary to Lord Carbery, then Lord President.

In the first of William and Mary, it having been clearly proved that this court was become a great grievance instead of a benefit, it was dissolved by act of parliament: soon afterwards the building was deserted and suffered to fall into decay. It at present belongs to the Crown; but though a governor is still appointed, no care is taken of it.

---

[2] A curious anecdote is preserved of one of these attacks: Prince Henry, son of King David, King of Scots, being newly created Duke of Northumberland, was present at the siege as a vassal of Stephen. One day, rashly approaching too near the walls, he was snatched from his horse by a grappling iron, one of the instruments of defence, and would have been dashed to pieces, had it not been for Stephen himself; who, with great presence of mind, and considerable personal risk, rescued him from his perilous situation.

The courts and royal apartments are stripped of their curious and valuable ornaments. The arms of Queen Elizabeth and others, however, are yet remaining in the hall. In the inner bailey of the castle is a curious Saxon chapel, of circular form, with numerous armorial ensigns carved upon the panels.[3]

" Here royal and noble youths and damsels tasted of all the delights, and drank of all the sorrows incidental to their exalted, but not in the eye of reason, enviable situations. Here ambition has balanced its hopes and its fears; the proud feudal chief has, in these courts, disdained the idea of a superior, assembled his vassals in arms, and issued those mandates to which success or defeat have affixed epithets of honour or disgrace. The insolence of triumph has at one time flushed the cheek and swelled the bosom of its inhabitants, and at another time, the fearfully glancing eye and the humble tone of supplication, has testified how low it is frequently possible for subdued haughtiness to sink. In some of these chambers, perhaps, the prayer of sincere penitence has frequently been uttered, and the flights of a mistaken, but ardent devotion, have risen to the throne above. With all the rites of superstition, the *extreme unction* has been given to many a dying wretch; and in many cases we hope the Divine mercy has overlooked the weakness of mortality, forgiven the absurdities of an erroneous formulary, and accepted the little pure grain of humility and goodness which existed, though in the midst of so much rubbish and folly.

" Here, perhaps, as thought took a different direction and our eyes glanced upon another part of the ivy and moss-clad walls, was the spot in which the Court of Marches assembled. In an instant, the president, the judges, the secretaries, the attorneys, with all the apparatus of maces and swords, and the splendid drapery of a court of justice, contrasted with the pale faces, the haggard looks, and the dirty and perhaps tattered garbs of a few forlorn wretches, dragged before them, rose into view. In some instances the scales of justice were poised with an equal hand; but in a much greater number, it is to be feared, they were raised or depressed by the caprice or the interest of those who held them; especially we may suppose this to have been the case in the latter period of its existence, as we know, that by a solemn act of the legislature, its longer continuance was declared incompatible with the welfare of the neighbourhood.

EDWARD THE FIFTH.—Edward IV. died on the 9th of April, 1482. At that time his son, Prince Edward, was at Ludlow Castle with his uncle and governor, the Earl Rivers. The Queen sent for him to London, where he had been proclaimed King by the title of Edward V. But he did not long enjoy the sovereign dignity; for his paternal uncle, Richard, Duke of Gloucester, whose ambition was only exceeded by his cruelty and treachery, pursuing that hatred which he had always manifested towards the Queen and her relatives, first deprived the young king of the protection of his governor and maternal uncle, the Earl Rivers, whom, together with Lord Richard Grey and Sir Thomas Vaughan,[4] he caused to be arrested and shortly afterwards beheaded at Pomfret Castle.

We learn from an ode, written by Glyn Cothi in the spring of 1483, that Edward IV. sent his son, then only thirteen years of age, with his governor and uncle, Earl Rivers, into the Principality with a body of troops to quell some disturbances. Before they returned, however, they were informed that the King was no more. The Queen requested the Earl, her brother, to disband his troops, and hasten to London with her son, the prince. Rivers accompanied the young king to Northampton to meet Richard, Duke of Gloucester, who set off from York for the same place, apparently anxious to pay his homage and his congratulations to his royal nephew as soon as possible: but, in reality, it was with a view to separate the young king from his retinue; which he did, and sent him with his domestics to London. His uncles, the Earl Rivers, Lord Grey, and Sir Thomas Vaughan, who possessed a considerable office in the King's

---

[3] Visitors who wish to visit these magnificent ruins may obtain permission by applying to Mr. Jones, agent to Lord Clive, who resides at the house nearly adjoining, and which was formerly the residence of *Lucien Bonaparte.*

[4] This Sir Thomas was son of Sir Roger Vaughan of Tretower. The following anecdote is related of this aged person when on the scaffold:—" I appeal," said he, " to the high tribunal of God against the Duke of Gloucester, for this wrongful murder, and our real innocence." Ratcliffe, with a sneering insensibility that does no credit to the gentry of that day, remarked, " You have made a goodly appeal; lay down your head." The knight replied, " I die in the right; take heed you die not in the wrong;" and submitted to the blow.

household, and others of the King's friends, he caused to be arrested, and conducted to different castles in Yorkshire, and they were afterwards executed by his command, as has been just narrated.

Richard thus paved the way for despatching the young king and his brother, whom he soon after put to death by an obscure and an unnatural assassination. This circumstance is recorded by a Welsh Bard[5] who lived at that time, and the following is a translation by the late Right Hon. Mr. Justice Bosanquet[6] of that portion of the poem to which we allude :—

> " Old London saw, in evil hour,
> A Jew usurp the British power ;
> The boar, on murder foul intent,
> Brave Edward's sons in durance pent :
> His tender wards, his nephews two,
> By lawless, ruthless force he slew.
> Out on his Saracen, savage face !
> Who angels killed of Christian race,
> And brought (by holy Non[7]) the shame
> Of Herod on a manly name !
> I marvel that the wrath of Heaven
> Had not the earth beneath him riven.

RICHARD THE THIRD.—After the murder of these innocents, and of others whom he thought stood in the way of his gaining his ambitious ends, Richard succeeded to the throne on the 10th of June by the above style and title. He and his queen, Anne, daughter to the Earl of Warwick, were crowned on the 5th of July, 1483, "with the selfe same provision," says Grafton, "that was appointed for the coronation of his nephew." The King and Queen received the sacrament from the hands of the Cardinal Archbishop of Canterbury, and one host, or consecrated wafer, was divided between them.

The character of this monarch, as well as the events of his brief reign, being so well known, we will only notice such incidents as are connected with our subject, and which brought about his overthrow and death.

On the 4th of July, two days before he was crowned, Richard held his court in the Tower of London. On this occasion many new earls were created, and several gentlemen received the order of knighthood. But John Martin, Bishop of Ely, the most adroit statesman in the country, and who had been a great favourite with King Edward, was on the same day delivered up to the Duke of Buckingham, to be kept in irons. The Duke sent him to his manor in Brecknock in Wales. However, it was not long after the coronation, before the Duke himself, who had been chiefly instrumental in placing Richard on the throne, thought it expedient to quit the court, and entered into a conspiracy to dethrone his royal master. Among the causes which led him to this was Richard's uncourteous conduct towards him, especially in not rewarding him for his services, as he had promised he would do on his accession to the crown. The Duke on leaving the court returned to his castle of Brecknock where the bishop was still in custody, and here it was that he conceived the project of deposing Richard and placing Henry, Earl of Richmond, on the throne. He opened his mind gradually to the bishop, whom he knew to favour the House of Lancaster. The bishop at first hesitated to give his opinion on the subject, fearing lest the Duke intended to betray him to the King; but when he was assured that the Duke had no such intention, but was, on the contrary, determined to carry his plan into execution, he no longer concealed his real sentiments, which happened to be in union with those of the Duke. The first step taken after this was, that of the Duke sending for his tried friend and confidant, Reginald Bray, who was then in Lancashire, in the service of the Countess of Richmond and Lord Thomas Stanley.[8] He arrived at Brecknock, and after a consultation, it was agreed, that he should return and communicate to the Countess the message entrusted

[5] Davydd Llwyd in an ode to Henry VII.

[6] That learned judge, though an Englishman, understood the Welsh language very well.

[7] Non was the mother of David, a saint of credit in Wales, whose anniversary is celebrated on the first of March.

[8] The Dowager Countess of Richmond, Henry's mother, had married Lord Stanley.

to him. She, on hearing what was in agitation, and how it was intended in the event of success, that the Earl should marry Elizabeth, Edward IV.'s daughter, immediately avowed her approval of the Duke's design. After Bray had departed, the bishop, to the great mortification of the Duke, effected his escape; and going to Ely, where he found money and friends, he was enabled from thence to make his escape to Flanders, in order to join the Earl of Richmond, and thereby to become still further instrumental in promoting his cause.

The Dowager Countess of Richmond, after she had received the intelligence as above related from Bray, sent her physician, Dr. Lewis, a Welshman, to Queen Elizabeth, who was then in sanctuary at Westminster. He was fixed upon because he was not only trustworthy, but was also possessed of superior talents; and besides that, in his character of physician, he was less liable to suspicion. He went accordingly and acquainted the Queen with the intended project, which was to dispose of Richard and make the Earl of Richmond king in his room, provided she would consent that he, upon his accession, should be united to the Princess Elizabeth, or, in case of her death, to her sister Cicely. The Queen having signified her approbation, Dr. Lewis then waited upon the Countess of Richmond, who was not only pleased with the result, but also sent a special messenger, Hugh Conway, into Brittany to inform her son of what was going on in England. At the same time, to insure safety, Thomas Ram was dispatched by Richard Guilford, and Richard Cyffyn Dean of Bangor by the North Wales chieftains; the latter was conveyed in an open fishing-boat. The messengers upon their arrival had an audience with the Earl, who acquainted the Duke of Brittany with the object of their coming. The Duke rejoiced on hearing the intelligence, and more especially as he had, a little previously, refused to acquiesce in King Richard's solicitation to have the Earl delivered up to him. The messengers returned with an assurance from Richmond of his hearty concurrence in the proceedings of his friends in England, and of his readiness to land amongst them as soon as they thought it proper and prudent for him to undertake the enterprise.

At the time the Duke of Buckingham was concerting his revolutionary measures, he and Sir Rice ap Thomas were at variance one with another; for between the family of Sir Rice and that of the Duke there always had existed private feuds and the most implacable hatred, and they continually made predatory incursions into each other's territories. In one of the poems of Lewis Glyn Cothi there is an account of these inroads, in which he describes the Duke as advancing to attack Abermarlais, and relates how he was compelled through the valour of Sir Rice and his brethren to retreat. To gain over a man so powerful and wealthy as Sir Rice, must have been of the utmost consequence; for without his concurrence it would have been in vain for the Earl of Richmond to attempt a landing at Milford Haven, as had been fixed by the conspirators. It was therefore deemed necessary in the first place to devise means of reconciling these parties; but how this was to be effected was the question; for only a few days before, Sir Rice had sent the Duke a challenge to a deadly combat, stating that if he would not meet him at Caermarthen he might expect to see him before his castle at Brecknock. However, just as Sir Rice was putting on his armour, making himself ready to carry his threat into execution, Dr. Lewis, who had been sent by the Countess of Richmond, and who had not only been successful in his former mission, but also had been a tutor to Sir Rice, waited upon him and prevailed with him after much persuasion to accept the Duke's friendship. Dr. Lewis then hastened to Brecknock, and there also he was successful in gaining over the Duke to be on friendly terms with Sir Rice, so that they both in a short time afterwards met by appointment at Trecastle,* where they buried their animosities in oblivion.

In his interview with Sir Rice, Dr. Lewis, it is stated, did not acquaint him of the existence of an organised party to bring over the Duke of Richmond, thinking it best to leave that part of the business in the hands of their mutual friend, Morgan of Kidwely, who was, when a fit opportunity offered itself, to disclose to Sir Rice the whole affair, and at the same time to call to his mind Richard's tyranny, as well as the wickedness of his unjust usurpation; and then to state what great good to the kingdom might be

---

* Trecastle is about midway between Abermarlais and Brecknock.

expected from the union of the Houses of York and Lancaster, by the marriage of Richmond with the Princess Elizabeth; and lastly, to point out to him, among other things, what glory would redound to himself and his posterity from assisting in bringing about so desirable a consummation.

Sir Rice did not join the disaffected party until after he had been waited upon by commissioners sent by the King, to demand of him an oath of allegiance, and at the same time to deliver up his son Griffith Rice as a hostage and pledge of fidelity. He took the oath, but wrote a letter to the King excusing himself from delivering up the child on account of his tender age, he being then about five years old.[1]

Sir Rice was greatly nettled, as well as mortified by these proceedings, especially at the thought that the King should suspect him of disloyalty to his person, and finding also that others were served in a similar way, he was much grieved at the King's proceedings, which he deemed to be highly dangerous to the interests of the crown. From this time Sir Rice began to be discontented; which Morgan of Kidwely perceiving, thought it a fair opportunity of opening his mind to him. And as he had already gained over to his side the Bishop of St. David's and the Abbot of Tally, he got them also to speak to him. But it was a long time before they could induce him to declare himself favourable to Richmond's cause, especially as he had so recently renewed his allegiance to the King. However, the bishop, with the assistance of the abbot, in his endeavours to remove the scruples he had relative to the violation of his oath, did not finally succeed until Sir Rice himself perceived that the nation at large was disaffected to the government.

Soon after his coronation, King Richard made a Progress towards the west. He passed through Oxford to Gloucester, a city which had always been devoted to his family, and in which he was now received with great rejoicings. He reached Tewkesbury on the 4th of August, and thence passed on to Worcester, Warwick, Coventry, Leicester, Nottingham, Doncaster, and York, where he was extremely popular, and his arrival was welcomed with extraordinary splendour and festivities. Several of the towns through which he passed obtained new and favourable charters of their municipal liberties. He reached York about the end of August, and remained there nearly a fortnight. On his way to his capital, he received at Lincoln the news of the treacherous rebellion of the Duke of Buckingham.

The Borders of Wales had become of importance at this period, from the part taken by the powerful Welsh family of the Tudors, against the reigning dynasty. The Duke of Buckingham had also great power in Wales and in Shropshire, in which county he held the castle and estate of Caus, as the representative of the ancient family of Corbet. He raised his standard at his Castle of Brecknock, on the 18th of October, and immediately advanced towards Worcester; but at Weobly his progress was arrested by unusual floods, and he was kept so long at this place, that his Welsh followers, discouraged by the tidings of the King's preparations and approach, disbanded themselves and returned to their native mountains.

The officers of the crown, in Brecknockshire, who, by the King's order, had their eyes upon the Duke, took up arms the instant he left that country.[2] Richard was himself advancing from the north: we trace him from Lincoln,[3] Oct. 12, to Grafton in Northamptonshire, Oct. 19, ready, says Mr. Carte,[4] to move against the insurgents in the west, or against Buckingham, as he saw occasion. Here he probably received such intelligence of that nobleman's movements, as induced him to strike across the country for Shropshire, since we find him at Leicester, 23d, and Coventry, 24th. The Duke, thus pressed by his enemies, both in the front and rear, sought to pass the Severn, and join his confederates in the west. But the bridges on

<hr />

[1] See Letter, Camb. Reg., i. p. 91.

[2] Chron. Croyland, p. 568.

[3] From this city he writes to its bishop, Russel, his chancellor (and this, by the way, will correct the error of Dugdale, who, in his Series, fixes this prelate's appointment to that high post a year later). The king's letter is written in great haste: and a postscript in his own hand, which the historian of Salop had seen in the hands of the late Mr. Lysons, expresses the bitterest resentment against the duke, whom he calls "the most untrew creature lyvynge. Whom, with God's grace, we shal not be long tyl that we wyll be in that parties, and subdue his malys. Wee assure you there was never falser traitor purvayde for." Strype, from the original still extant. Compl. Hist. Engl. i. 532.

[4] Carte, vol. ii. p. 813.

that important river had been broken down by the vigilance of Humfrey Stafford;[1] and he was deprived of all hopes of crossing it, by a mighty flood,[2] which at that crisis descended from the mountains of Wales, and was long remembered by the name of "Buckingham's Water." In this emergency, he was quickly abandoned by his Welsh and English tenantry, who had been reluctantly drawn to his standard; and their fears were, probably, increased by the royal proclamation which had been issued from Leicester, Oct. 23, and which was directed to the sheriffs of Shropshire and of other counties. This singular instrument is preserved in Rymer.[7] After a furious invective against Thomas Dorset, late Marquis of Dorset, whom the King accuses of "holding the unshameful and mischiefous woman, called Shore's wife, in adultery;" he suddenly adverts to the conduct of "our rebel and traitor, the late Duke of Buckihgham, and offers one thousand pounds to the person who shall take him."

The Duke left Weobly, in disguise as a fugitive, and was concealed for a few days in the neighbourhood of Wem. However, much time did not elapse before the discovery and apprehension of this illustrious fugitive. He was, according to some historians, discovered by an unusual quantity of victuals being seen near the place of his confinement; whilst others assert that he was betrayed by a person named Banastre. All, however, argue that he was put to death without mercy. Sir Thomas Mytton, the Sheriff of Shropshire, a staunch adherent of the family of York, carried the Duke to Shrewsbury, and he was thence sent to Salisbury, where he was beheaded on the 2nd of November. Richard showed his gratitude to the town of Shrewsbury, for the fidelity it had shown to him on this occasion, by remitting a part of its fee-farm.

When Sir Rice ap Thomas heard of the Duke of Buckingham's disaster, and the summary manner in which he was executed, he began to be alarmed lest the friends of Richmond should, in consequence, become discouraged, and their cause weakened. He, therefore, summoned a meeting, at which were present the Bishop of St. David, the Abbot of Tally, Morgan of Kidwely, and the following experienced soldiers, Arnold Butler, Richard Griffith, and Sir John Morgan. At this meeting it was that Sir Rice came to the final resolution of espousing Richmond's cause; to whom he then wrote a letter, which was sent by Morgan of Kidwely, tendering his services. It was of great importance to the Earl, thus to gain the support of Sir Rice, who was not only a veteran in feats of arms, but also a person of great wealth, and of unbounded influence in the country. Among the Bards of that day, Gytto'r Glyn eulogises his character in glowing terms. He says that his power was "greater than any in Wales, having three counties under his command; that he was the greatest hero of his day, and successful in battle."

Immediately after what transpired at the meeting was made known, Sir Rice was joined by Sir Thomas Perrot, of Haroldson, near Haverfordwest; Sir John Wogan, of Wisten Castle, Pembrokeshire; and John Savage; and also by several gentlemen from North Wales. When Richard was informed of the state in which the country stood affected to him, he issued a proclamation,[8] dated 23rd of June, 1484, in which he addresses his subjects in the most artful manner; with a view to influence the minds, not only of the multitude, but also the peers, bishops, dignitaries, and great men, and to induce them to resist, with all their power, the attempts of the Earl of Richmond upon the Crown. Another proclamation was issued, Oct. 20, and signed De la Pole, Duke of Suffolk.

The zeal and fidelity manifested by our countrymen to the Earl during this important position of his affairs, were no less honourable to them than advantageous to his future fortunes. Having completed their plans and made all the necessary arrangements for elevating Richmond to the throne, the secret was entrusted to two gentlemen, one from North and the other from South Wales, Richard Kyffin, Dean of Bangor, and Hugh Conwy, both strenuous friends to the House of Lancaster, who transmitted, by means of a fishing boat, the glorious intelligence to the Earl of Richmond, then in Brittany, with assurances of all possible aid on the part of the Welsh.

[1] This was Sir Humfrey Stafford, of Grafton, in Worcestershire, who, with his brother Thomas, rebelled against Henry VII. in 1486, and was executed at Tyburn. Lord Bacon, sub. ann.

[6] Chron. Croyland, ut supra.
[7] Rymer's Fœdera, xii., p. 204.
[8] Paston's Letters, ii., pp. 319, 327, 331.

In the meantime, the Royal standard, the "Red Dragon of Wales," was planted on the top of several mountains in the Principality, and the fiery Cambrians in vast numbers rallied round it with fierce alacrity. One bard of that day alludes to this subject in the following couplet,—

> " Dichon gael hyd yn Maelawr
> Drugain mil, D'rogan mawr."

These events were too alluring for the Welsh Bards to continue silent; their poetic effusions were very serviceable to the cause; their mysterious songs and prophecies, "that a chieftain of Wales should liberate the nation from Saxon bondage," so allured and wrought upon the valour of our countrymen, that they flocked by thousands and enlisted under the banner of the heroes that met Richmond at Milford. Henry apprised of the state of the nation and of the fitting position it was in for his reception, lost no time, but set sail from Harfleur, in the month of August, 1485, with two thousand troops, which the Duke of Brittany had furnished him.

The Earl of Richmond, in the meantime, well knowing what preparations were going on for his reception, greatly exerted himself, and wrote letters to several of his friends, among others to John ap Meredith of Gwydir, Sir Owen Tudor's cousin. The following is a copy of this letter[9]:—

> " *Right Truly and Well-beloved John ap Meredith, We greete you well.*
> " *By the King.*

"WHEREAS it is so, that throughe the helpe of Almighty God, the assistance of our loveing and true subjects, and the grete confidence that we have to the nobles and commons of this our Principalitie of Wales, we be entred into the same, purposeing by the helpe above rehearsed in all haste possible to descend into our realme of England, not only for the adoption of the crowne unto us of right appertaining, but also for the oppression of that odious tyrant, Richard, late Duke of Gloucester, usurper of our said right; and moreover to reduce as well our said realme of England into its ancient estate, honour, and property, and prosperite, as this our said Principalitie of Wales, and the people of the same theirtor dearest liberties, delivering them of such miserable servitude as they have piteously long stood in. We desire and pray you, and upon your allegiance, strictly charge and command you, that immediately upon sight hereof, with all such power as you may make, defencibly arranged for the warre, ye addresse you towards us, without any tarrying upon the way, untill such time as ye be with us, wheresoever we shall bé, to our aide, for the effect above rehearsed, wherein ye shall cause us in time to be your singular good lord, and that ye faile not hereof, as ye will avoid our gracious displeasure, and answere it unto your perill. Given under our signet, at our, &c.[1]

> " To our trusty and well-beloved John ap Meredith ap Jevan ap Meredith."

The following account of the preparations for receiving the Earl of Richmond at Milford Haven, and their progress to Bosworth-field, is taken from an old manuscript, written about two hundred years ago :—

A.D. 1485.—"About this time, Hugh Conway returned out of Brittany with letters from Earl Henry, to the Countess of Richmond, and divers others who were the principal actors for him both in England and Wales, among whom one was to Rice ap Thomas, which he received by the handes of Morgan of Kidwelly, whoe likewise at that verie time and to the verie same effect receaved letters himself from one Evan Morgan, his neere cosen and intimate friend. This Evan was a man of antient and noble house, as anie gentleman in Monmouthshire, the chiefe of Tredegar and Machau, and the leneall descendant of Bledri, the greate lord of Kilsant and Gwinvay. He fledd with the Earle Jasper from Chepstowe to Pembrock, and thence

---

[9] The original, we were informed by Lord Willoughby de Eresby, the representative of John ap Meredith, is now lost, but it was seen in 1670 by the Bishop of Bangor, who states, " I have seen the original letter and perused it at Gwydir, in 1670.—H. BANGOR."

[1] The date and place from which this order is issued are omitted in the MS.

attended the Earle of Richmond, whom he served in Brittany, where he continued in high favour with his master, for his true love and faithfull service, untill they returned for Milford Haven, and soe followed him on to the battle of Bosworth. There were some of his worthie familie (the Bishop of St. David's, Morgan of Kidwelly, John Morgan, and this Evan, the topp of them all), who were speciall actors and contrivers of this business, for as much as concerned us in Wales, and the onlie men that wrought Rice ap Thomas to the partie, which must needes clapp a wide marke of honour upon the name, and not without injurie to be passed over in silence.

"Noe sooner was Rice ap Thomas his answeare written, but Morgan of Kidwellye posts the same away for France to the Earle of Richmond, signifying alsoe unto him with what alacritie and cheerfulness Rice ap Thomas had embraced his quarrell; howe readie he was and how able for service, what a choice selected band of soldiers he had in readinesse, the goodnesse of his armes, and the bravnesse of his cavallerie; there being nothing in the sight of man, save only his presence, to make them invincible, and therefore humblie besought his lordshipp to foresloe no time, but that he would take opportunitie by the forelocke, and not suffer these inflamed spiritts in their first heates through further delayes to be evaporated. The Earle having received Rice ap Thomas's answeare, with other joyful and comfortable advertisements from Morgan of Kidwellie, he was soe greatlie encouraged therewith that noe hopes of auxiliarie from the French king, or anie other necessaire provisions whatsoever could make him any longer disappoint his friendes and confederates with an expectation of his coming, and therefore with all convenient speed, furnishing himself with such men, monie, and munition, as he could readilie procure, he enshipped himself and wayed anchor from Harfleet, having butt two thousand men in all, and they (God wott) poorlie provided; and soe in seven days, with a prosperous gale, he landed at Milford.[2] In the interim, Rice ap Thomas stood all upon thornes, as conceiving there myght be some private compacte and underhande working between the usurper and the French king, whereby the just pretences of Richmond should be for ever confounded, and being somewhat entangled in a laberinth of doubtful cogitations, he sendes for Robert of the Dale, his prophett, to come unto him. This Robert, in those blinder times, was taken for a verie understonding man, as having wonne some fame in foretelling divers things, which accordinglie came to passe, by which meanes he had insinuated himself soe far into Rice ap Thomas his good opinion, that oftentimes he was made partaker even of his nearer touching secretts. Being nowe together, Rice ap Thomas desird him to deliver his opinion freely of Richmond, and what he thought would be the issue of those greate designs he had in hand: to which the prophet would make no answeare, excusing himself, that though he could speak something in that kind of inferior persons, yet he was carefull nott to looke too narrowlie into princes matters, as being dangerous withall. Rice ap Thomas taking his silence as a presage of ill-luck, still importuned him by prayers and promises of greate rewardes, that he would not conceale his knowledge of this businesse. The prophette seeing Rice so vehement, and thinking it best not to provoke his anger, which, by his countenance, he found him apt to fall into, and therefore delivered his mind unto him in this manner :—

> " Full well I wend
> That in the end,
> Richmond, sprung from British race,
> From out this land the boare shall chace ; "

All which might verie will be, and yet Rice ap Thomas nothing the wiser, unlesse the Earle continued in a resolution to land at Milford. For if he made his entree some other way noe parte of the glorie (which he

---

[2] The manuscript from which we extract this does not state the day of his arrival on the Welsh coast, and our old historians differ on the point. The Chronicle of Croyland expressly states the first of August, 1485. " Primo die Augusti in nominatissimo illo portu Milford juxta Pembrochiam prospero flatu, nulla inventa resistentia, applicuerunt," p. 673. Hall says that he sailed from Harflet (Harfleur) in the calends of August, and the seventh day after his departure arrived at Milford Haven in the evening. Later historians have read Hall as if he had written, " on the calends of August," i. e. the first day of that month, and therefore place Henry's landing, Rapin on the 6th, Carte on the 7th: but the calends of August commence on the 17th of July, and therefore it is plain that the earl set sail on the 25th of that month, and landed on the 1st of August. Buck correctly makes him " loose from Harfleur in the month of July."

soe gredilie thirsted after) was like to fall to his share, soe that all his endevours, and the infinite charges he had been at, vanished away *in fumo;* wherefore he falls upon his prophet againe, urging him to deliver his opinion touching the Earle's landing, and wheather he would come for Milford or noe. To give him satisfaction herein the prophett required a day to deliberate, which being granted, and the next day come, the prophett saluted Rice ap Thomas betimes, but without declaring himself, would faine have taken his leave; whereat Rice grew into a rage, threatening to hang him if he perform'd not his promise first; well then, replied the prophett, to save thee that labour,

> "Hie thee to the dale,
> I 'll to the vale
> To drink gude ale,
> And soe I pre, hav a care of us all."

Everie man concluding by his speech that the Earle would come for Milford and land at the dale, and that the lives and fortunes of them all were in Rice ap Thomas's hands, of which the prophett desired him to have a speciall care. Hereupon Rice ap Thomas musters up all his forces, calls all his friends about him, and where he found anie want among them, eyther of armes or other necessaries of war, he supplied with his own store, whereof he had sufficient, as well for ornament as in use; soe that in fewe dayes he had gathered together to the number of two thousand horse and upward of his own followers and retayners, bearing his name and liverie. His kinsman and friends who came besides with brave companies to doe him honour, were Sir Thomas Perrott,[3] Sir John Wogan,[4] and John Savage, a man of no lesse valiantness than activitie, and much employed by the Earle after he came to be king, in the wars of France and elsewhere; Arnold Butler, Richard Griffith, John Morgan and two of his own brothers, David, the younger, and John, all of them worthy soldiers and verie expert commanders, with divers others, *Qui omnes urgentur longâ nocte, quia caruêre vate sacro.* There came likewise of North Wales to this service manie worthie gentlemen both of name and note, especially of the Salisburies, under the conduct of Robert Salisburie, a fast friend to Rice ap Thomas in the French warrs, and whoe, for his well deserving there, was knighted in the field by Charles Brandon, Duke of Suffolk. These Salisburies were ever firmlie united to Rice and his family, whereby they purchased to themselves the name of *Salsbriaid y Brain,* (Friends to the Raven,)[5] which name was given them first at the battle of Pennal, where Thomas ap Griffith, father to Rice ap Thomas, lost his leif, and manie of this noble familie in the said quarrell, to the eternall praise of their true affection. Rice ap Thomas being in his brave equipage, encompass'd with most able commaunders, and furnish'd with all things necessarie as well for armour as horse, (whereof a hundred and upward were out of his owne stables,) word was brought him by his conspicillos or spies, whoe kept continuall watch on the coast for that purpose, that they had discried a small fleete of shippes making towards the Haven's mouth; whereupon incontinently he bate up his drum, putt his men in order, and mounted on a goodly courser call'd *Llwya Baxe,*[6] or *Grey Fetter Locks,* he set forth in most martial manner towards the Dale, as his prophett whilome had advised him, a place nott farr from his castle of Carew, from whence at that time he led his army, and there meeting with the Earle of Richmond, readie to take land, he receav'd him ashore, to whom he made humble tender of his service, both in his owne and in all their names who were there present; and laying him downe on the ground, suffer'd the Earle to pass over him, soe to make good his promise to King Richard, that none should enter in at Milford onlesse he came first over his bellie.[7]

---

[3] Sir Thomas Perrott was of Horoldstone, near Haverford West, Pembrokeshire, father to Sir John Perrott, Lord-Deputy of Ireland in the reign of Queen Elizabeth.

[4] Sir John Wogan, of Wilston Castle, Pembrokeshire, a man of immense possessions and command in that country in those days.

[5] Alluding to the armorial bearing of Rice ap Thomas's house.

[6] The word should be written *Bacfen,* but the orthography of the original has been observed throughout.

[7] There is a tradition in that country, which seems to contradict the fact as here stated; namely, that Rice ap Thomas did not literally suffer the Earl to pass over his belly, but that in consequence of the declaration he had made in his letter to Richard, as a salvo to his conscience, he went under the arch of a small bridge, called Mullock Bridge, near Dale, over which their passage lay, and there remained till Richmond had crossed it.

"Being overjoyed with so glorious a sight, and transported with such an auspicious beginning, the Earl of Richmond, after some pause, spoke thus :—

"'My deere cozen[s] and beloved countrymen, and fellowe souldiers, it is now upward of fourteene years since my uncle Jasper and myself escaped out of these partes, and hither at length we are returned againe.

The Earl of Richmond addressing the Welsh Chieftains, at Milford Haven.

I fledd *then* for my lief, I returne *now* for a crowne,—a crowne my undoubted right. My lief and my crowne are inseparable; I must eyther enjoy both or nyether. David Thomas, your noble brother, sir, as all men here present, and I shall ever acknowledge above, beyond all hope miraculously preserved my lief; and you, my deere cousin, with the assistance of these valourouse gentlemen under your discreete conduct, may serve as special instruments to help me to my crowne, injuriously withheld from me by a most tyrannical and bloodie usurpation. Perform you the latter, sir, which I am confident of, as he hath truly accomplished the former, and you have not the could curtesie equivalent to these to bestow upon me. Oh ! the miserable affliction and heavy calamities we have sustained since last I trod upon this earth ! It strikes me with horrour to think of them, and all neighbouring nations tremble at the reporte. What hath that cruel butcher, Richard, Duke of Gloucester, left unattempted, that might make way for his outrageous ambition ? How many of our nobles and others have perished by his bloody commands, without anie legal triale ? Five kings and princes of the bloode miserably murdered ; two virtuous queens basely traduced, and a third, even his own wife, empoysond ; insest likewise proposed, myself forced to live in the state of a pilgrim or banished man, to leave my fortune and my country and live upon the alms of strangers ; a price sett upon my head, and wicked ministers suborned to worke my confusion, and all to raise a stair to his ungracious promotion.

"'My deere countrymen, you are all assembled heere at this time for the same purpose. I reade it in your lookes ; 'tis your valour and virtue which I principally neade ; you are the men who add strength to good causes. Heere I am; come, fellow souldiers, more in your right than my own. What shall I say? Heere I stand before you, but what name to give myself I am alltogether to seeke. A private man I will not be called, seeing I am of the best of the nobility and gentrie of this kingdom ; yea, by all the world

[s] Sir Rees ap Thomas, a brave chieftain in South Wales, and ancestor to the present Lord Cawdor.

o o 2

besides, that have heard of my just title and pretence, allowed for a prince; and yett a prince you cannot well call me whilst another professeth my right; beside, a question may be raised whether you yourselves be traytours or true subjects, till it be decided what manner of man you have amongst you, a true, lawful prince, or an enemie. What remaineth, then, butt that we jointly use our best endeavours for the clearing of this point, and showe to all parties whenever wee come by an invincible demonstration of our prowess, that the Lord of Hostes is patrone of our cause. To second us, doubt ye nott. Continue, therefore, in that height of courage and resolution you nowe are, and lett us either in living together, procure the peace and wellfare of this common wealth, or by our death conclude our miseries; in both lett us have a care of the honour of our ancestrie and posteritie.'

"The Earle had no sooner finished his oration, but all flocked unto him in a confused manner, mingle mangle, without all order, as being transported with his eloquence, and ravished with his presence, some kissing his handes, some his feete, and some adoring the ground he trod upon, as if hee were some angelic creature and noe terrestriall personage: then beating up their drums, sounding their trumpets, winding their cornetts, and to expresse their inward joy and contentment, they fell to shouts and acclamations, clapping their hands and crying up to heaven, 'King Henrie, King Henrie! downe with the bragging white boare!' After this they betake them to their orisons, praising God, and saying, 'Now is the accepted time, now are those happie dayes come, will recover againe that deluge of blood spilt within our land; here is the pledge of our peace and welfare; 'tis but an adventure we are to make, to make all this good: let us goe on in God's name and St. David, and we shall prevail.' When they had for a while in these lowd plauses and sweetest jubilyes penetrated the aire and echoed forth their loving affections in the most pleasing manner of expressions, Rice ap Thomas when he saw his time drewe them backe, commanding every man to his colours, whereby the Earl might see in what order and obedience he held them to their places of service; than he made up to the Earle in a grave march, and in an humble straine thus spoke to him: 'My lord and master, you are heere (you see) with the generall applause of these my fellow soldiers in a kind of militarie election, or recognition, saluted king; and suite nowe is, you will take us to your protection; we are as yet but in a storme, and it much concernes both you and us speedilie to provide for each others saftie. While we have you at the helm, we are confident, sir, by God's helpe, and your wise discretion to arrive ere long at our wished port. Let us, therefore, if we meane to doe well and goe through, stick with our business, strike while the yron is hot. We have furniture of armes sufficient, and to spare; and I assure you our heartes are as well furnished within as our bodies without. God has given you the absolute commaunderie of both; with us remains onlie the glorie of obedience. Weare we nowe, sir, upon some private attempt of our owne, we could proceede, and stop, goe on, and come off at pleasure. With youe, my lord, who are designed for Emperie, it is otherwise; there being no middle course to run, a king or a beggar. You are, God be thanked, in a good way to put things out of doubt: goe on then, sir, and lose no time; it's ill dallying with edge tools. As for our well wishes towards the advancement of your service, I hope wee have satisfied you in wordes; action (the onlie thing we could be at) must nowe be the true touchstone to try us throughout; that will shew us whole unto you, whoe for the present you see but in parte. Let us then, sir, pray be a doing, and let us noe further boast ourselves at the buckling on our armour, but reserve ourselves untill we put off. Call then, my lord, for your French forces ashore, and let them take some ease and refreachment; examine what effects they may have in their armes, or otherwise, and according to our meanes we shall not be wanting to minister a supplie; then may you dispose of both them and us as shall best suite with your affaires; soe God prosper our proceedings.'

"Rice ap Thomas having made an end of what he would say, the Frenchman lying abord all this while were sent for to land; whoe upon their coming were *mavouslie* well and kindly received by the Welshmen, and entreated with all curtesie, each man striving (and indeede to do them but right, for that sole virtue of courtesie towards strangers, I thinke the Welsh goe beyond all the nations of the world), everie man, I say, striving to give them all contentment, and cheering them up with fresh victuals, or what other way they could devise, to encrease and continue this new begun acquaintance. The Earle of Richmond then entreated the Earles of Oxford and Pembroke to muster the French and take a view of their defects, whoe, upon enquirie, found they wanted both necessarie furniture of armes and other munition; besides that they were verie rawe and ignorant in shooting, handling of their weapons, and discharging the ordinarie dutie of souldiers; men, as it seemed, raised out of the refuge of the people, and clap'd upon the Earle to avoid his further importunities; which coming to Rice ap Thomas his eares, he was not soe wrath with the French king's former delayes, as now, with the poornesse of his supplies; yet containing himself, he for the present furnished them with all such things as he could spare, without the damage of his own particular, though in harte he wished them back againe in France, there nott being one man of quality among them to endeere future ages to make mention either of his name or service.

"This being done, after the Earle of Richmond had embraced and thanked Rice ap Thomas, for his forwardnesse in the affurthering his service, they both together, with the Earles of Oxford and Pembrock, drew aside to consider of their present state and condition, and what course was best to be taken for their putting forward. In fine they concluded that the Earle should shape his course by Cardigan. And Rice ap Thomas by Carmarthen, that soe going several wayes, the Welsh and the French might be kept asunder, to prevent such jarres and quarrels as commonlie arise betweene strangers, appointing Shrewsburie as their rendezvous and place of meeting againe. In the meane while Arnold Butler, Richard Griffith, and John Morgan, men forward in their charge, weare appointed to meet the Earle in severall places; soe to strengthen his party, if occasion were offered; to direct and convey him over those uncouth ways and fastnesses; to call in for such provisions as the countrie could afford, for the reliefe of his armie; and, lastlie, to inform the people as they went along, what side Rice ap Thomas meant to stick to; by which meanes a world of companie flocked unto him, not caring wheather they went, soe they went along with him.

"When all these things were thus in a readinesse, the Bishop of St. David's stepps up and makes a learned sermon to the whole armie, taking for his text that of the Psalmist, lxxv. 4:—'The earth is weak and all the inhabitants thereof; I bear up the pillars of it.' Pointing out to them in the fore part of the verse the wicked reign of King Saul, to whom he likened King Richard; and in the latter part of the verse, the happy succession of King David, whom he wished the Earle of Richmond to imitate, in re-establishing the pillars which Richard by his bloodie tyrannie had put out of frame; that is, that he would have a care, when he was in perfect authoritie, for the true worshiping of God, and the administration of justice; the two maine pillars, wherewith all good commonwelths are supported; that now having taken armes, however, for the regaining of his owne right, he should nott put his trust in chariotts or horses, or in the strength of man, butt in the name of the Lord, for by that way onlie David proved victorious: those examples he advised the Earle to followe; and then the next newes, said the Bishop, we shall hear, will be, ' *Our enemies are brought downe and fallen; but we are risen and stand upright.*' (Psalm xx. 8). Going on in this kind, with manie other profitable admonitions, both divine and morall; the Bishop concluded, praying, and wishing the Earle in all his wayes, the strength of Jacob, and the strength of Israel; of Jacob to prevail over men, and of Israel to prevail with God; that the Lord of Hosts would shewe himself *El nekamoth*, a God of vengeance against his enemy, and but a letter change, *El nechamoth*, a God of comfort unto this whole nation. When the sermon was ended every man buckeled on his armes, and betook him to his weapons, clapping their hands and crying out afresh, ' King Henrie, King Henrie,' none but Henrie should be their King; soe they fell upon their march, the Earle as was resolved before, towards Cardigan, and Rice ap Thomas to Carmarthen.

"The Earle having taken leverie and seisin of parte of his kingdom, and nowe in the waye of possessing himself of the whole, Rice ap Thomas forthwith commanded the beacons to be sett on fire, thereby to give notice to all the countries adjacent, of his landing, and withall to summon his friendes and kinsmen from all partes where his power was extended, to come in with their forces, and meete him, some in one place, and some in another, on his waye to Shrewsburie. By the time he came to Carmarthen his number was much increased, from thence to a place called Llanymddyfri he goes, his snoweball gathering more and more in the rolling, and soe to Brecknocke, where divers of the Vaughans and Gamses gave him the meeting, men of noble families and verie powerful in those countries, with many tall and able followers: some, as being his neare kinsmen and fast friends, doing him the honour to go along with him in his brave adventures.

"When Rice ap Thomas was come to Brecknocke, his traine was growne soe long, that it was high time to cut it shorter, the companie that followed him growing cumbersome: for 'tis almost incredible, with howe much earnest affection from all quarters they came to him, even women and children, to their power expressing as much courage and resolution as the tallest souldier there, to undergoe the service. Notwithstanding which, Rice ap Thomas was nothing inflated with these palpations and applauses of the giddie multitude, but heeding the work he had in hand, fell presently to examine his forces, that, as they were assembled, culling out the best of them, soe manie as made up his number full two thousand horse, well manned and well armed at all pointes, such and soe excellent, as which way soe ever they went, drew with a kind of ravishing delight the eyes of all beholders; and, indeed, all English writers, whenever they make mention of Rice ap Thomas, doe still annex some epithet of honore to his brave troupes of horse. Having thus made his provision for the war, he began to think of his own fortunes at home; and howe to secure that and make a safe retreat in case of extremitie. Therefore, to make good his stake, he made choice of five hundred more, out of the remainder and overplus of his armie, whom he recommended to the charge of his two brothers, David, the younger, and John, togither with the tuition of his onlie son, young Griffith Rice, commanding them to keep togither, and not lay by their armes until his pleasure was further signified; and, withall, that they would take care in his absence, to protect those from injurie, who come in so loving a manner to express their affections towards him. With the assurance hereof, the residue of his followers went away home well satisfied, yet shedding abundance of teares, and filling the aire with doleful lamentations at his departure. Being in this glorious equippage and soe stronglie provided on all handes, Rice ap Thomas made with all speed to Shrewsburie, and as he went, mette with the Earle of Richmond in his way, to whom he made humble obeyance, vowing to follow him through all dangers, to the utter subversion both of the tyrant and his wicked complices."

After a hospitable reception by Sir Rice ap Thomas at Carew Castle,[*] Richmond proceeded on his journey with his army on their way to Shrewsbury. Dafyd ap Evan, of Llwyn Dafydd, in the parish of Llandysilia, in Cardiganshire, had the honour to entertain the Earl and his army, which he did in that style of hospitality suited to the high rank of his guest. He was entertained the next night by Einian ap Dafydd Llwyd at Wern Newydd, in the parish of Llanarth, with that hearty welcome and hospitality so generally and justly attributed to the Welsh, which the Earl acknowledged by several valuable presents. And to Dafyd ap Evan the Earl presented a superb hirlas (drinking horn) richly mounted on a silver stand, which was afterwards presented to Richard, Earl of Carbery, and may still be seen at Golden Grove, the seat of Lord Cawdor, in Caermarthenshire.

> " Pride of feasts, profound and blue,
> Of the ninth wave's azure hue;
> The drink of heroes formed to hold,
> Which art enriched with lid of gold."—HOARE's GIRALDUS.

The next place we hear of the Earl is at Mathavarn, near Mchhynlleth, the residence of his friend and adherent, David Llwyd, who, in those days, was considered an eminent man; Henry naturally interrogated him about the issue of his hazardous adventure. David promised the Earl an answer on the morrow, but perplexed by the question he passed a sleepless night. His wife learned the cause, " Can you doubt,"

---

[*] This noble edifice is situated on a neck of land washed by the tide of two estuaries, with a gentle fall towards the water, and consists of a superb range of apartments, round a quadrangle, with an immense bastion at each corner, containing handsome chambers. The ground rooms of the north front may boast of windows, than which nothing more nobly magnificent is known in the kingdom, giving light to the great state room, 102 feet in length. On the east side, over a chimney-piece of no mean workmanship, there is an escutcheon bearing the royal arms, to commemorate the visit and accession of Henry the Seventh to the throne. This castle was formerly one of the royal demesnes belonging to the princes of South Wales.

said she, " what to reply ?   Tell him the event will be successful and glorious, and if your prediction be verified, you will receive honours and rewards: if he fails, he will never return to reproach you." The truth of this tale is attested by a Welsh proverb founded upon it :—

" Cynghor gwraig heb ei ofyn."
A wife's advice without being asked for.

" When the Earle of Richmond was in his way to Shrewsberrie, mett and saluted by Rice ap Thomas, with soe goodlie a band of Welchmen, it was no small joy unto him to receive a full assurance of aid and succour of so powerful a commaunder; for you must knowe, the Earle, all this while (notwithstanding all those reall promises made unto him at Milford) was much appalled and troubled in mind, not knowing well what to think of Rice ap Thomas, there being divers rumours dispersed up and down through his armie, that the said Rice ment to side with Richard; and for that purpose was readie to give him battaile, and to interrupt his passage, which rumour, indeede, Rice himselfe, out of policy, had caused to be blown abroad, to hoodwinkle the tyrant, until he were in his full strength.

"The Earl with all at his first meeting with Sir Rice was made acquainted with his view, which presently removed all jealousie and cause of distrust, and so together they march towards Shrewsbury."

Tradition alleges that the two armies met at Mynydd Digoll, in Montgomeryshire, called by the English " Long Mountain," on the confines of Shropshire, where all the North Wales chieftains with their forces met them. This is not improbable. The extensive plain which crowns the summit of the hill, was a convenient spot for that purpose. None of the troops were missing, and it is added, that the name of the mountain, " Cefn Digoll," was derived from this circumstance: this, however, is not the fact, as the mountain of Digoll (Di, *no*, goll, *loss*) is mentioned as long ago as the poems of Prince Llywarch Hen, who flourished in the sixth century.

Of all the " British Alps " none point to the eye of the traveller such dreary uninteresting scenes as " Mynydd Digoll," or the neighbouring heights of Plymlymon, and few, if any, with the exception of Snowdon, carry to the warm heart of a Cambrian so many interesting reminiscences of " olden time." On these celebrated hills were assembled, on many a trying occasion, the ancient British princes and their brave followers, when compelled to fight in defence of their native country. Llywarch Hen, in his poem called the Gorwynion, mentions " the hill of Digoll," which is supposed to be Cevn Digoll, near Montgomery. Gwalchmai, another ancient bard, in his elegy on Cadwallon, says, that the army of his hero encamped on the top of Digoll mountain (Digoll vynydd) for seven months, and that in this situation he had seven skirmishes every day. He adds in the following stanza, that the army of Cadwallon encamped on Havren (the Severn) and on the farther side of Dygen; which probably refers to Dygen Vreiddin (the Breddin hill near Welsh Pool) :—

" Mochddwyrĕawg huan hav, dyfestin
Maws llavar adar, mygyr hĕar hin.
Mi ydwyv eur-ddeddyv, ddiovyn yn nhrin ;
Mi ydwyv lew rhag llu, lluch vy ngorddin.
Gorwiliais nôs, yn achadw fin.
Gorloes rydiau dwvyr Dygen Vreiddin.
Gorlas gwellt didryv ; dwvyr neud iesin ?
Gorddyar ĕaws awdyl gynnevin.
Gwylain yn gware ar wely lliant,
Lleithrion eu pluawr, pleidiau eddrin." [1]

[1] Translated thus :—

" Rise, orb of day ! the eastern gates unfold,
And show thy crimson mantle, fringed with gold :
Contending birds sing sweet on every spray ;
The skies are bright; arise, thou orb of day !
I, Gwalchmai, call, in song, in war renowned,
Who, lion like, confusion spread around.
The livelong night, the hero and the bard,
Near Breiddin's rocks, have kept a constant guard;

Where cool transparent streams in murmurs glide,
And springing grass adorns the mountain side;
Where snow-white sea-mews in the currents play,
Spread their gay plumes, and frolic through the day."

We believe this translation is from the pen of the late Mr. Lloyd, of Caerwys, the learned and classical companion of Pennant in his Tour through Wales, and to whom Pennant was indebted for most of the valuable information which his Tour through North Wales

In other early periods of our Welsh history those dreary mountains were the scenes of many civil contentions, and many a bloody skirmish; and numerous heaps of Carneddau are still to be found upon these rugged hills, as well as the contiguous hills of "Caer Carodoc," where the brave Caractacus made his stand against Ostorius, the Roman General, in the first century. Traces of British encampments are very visible.

Here in somewhat later times that murderous affair carried on between Owain Cyveiliog and Hywel ap Cadwgan took place; and, last of all, here it was that the heroic Glyndwr, for a considerable time, fixed his camp, when struggling to regain the lost sovereignty of the land of his ancestors; nor could a better defensive position be chosen, ill-suited as were his followers for such warfare; many a gallant band of Henry IV.'s heavy armed horse and foot never returned from "the bottomless bogs of Plymlymon."

Here the forces encamped, and here they made their arrangements prior to their march towards Bosworth, where they so materially assisted in placing Henry on the throne of his ancestors. The great

The meeting of the North and South Wales Chieftains at the Breiddyn Hills, on their way to Bosworth-field.

Sir Rhys ap Thomas was at the head of the forces of South Wales, while those of North Wales and the interior were under the command of the following patriots: Mostyn[2] of Mostyn, in Flintshire, with his sixteen hundred miners and colliers well equipped for battle. The men of Arfon, under the High Sheriff, Gwilym ap Gruffydd ap Robin of Penrhyn,[3] and Cochchwilan; the men of Mona, under Rhys of Bodychan; while those of the interior uplands "y wlad uchaf," were under Sir Rhys[4] Fawr ap Maredydd of Yspytty. On this occasion, strange to say, all the Welsh were united and co-operating except Madoc

contains. He was the father of Miss Angharad Lloyd, the authoress of the History of Anglesea, &c. &c.

[2] Ancestor to the Hon. E. M. Lloyd Mostyn, the present M.P. for Flintshire, and lord-lieutenant for the county of Merioneth.

[3] Ancestors of the Penrhyn family; this place is now the property and residence of the Hon. Colonel Douglas Pennant, M.P. for Caernarvonshire.

[4] Ancestor, on the paternal line, of the Right Honourable Lord Willoughby De Eresby, hereditary Great Chamberlain of England, and lord-lieutenant of the county of Caernarvon. After Sir William Brandon was knocked down in a personal rencontre with Richard III. at Bosworth, Sir Rhys was appointed standard-bearer, which he carried triumphantly out of the field.

of Coetomor, to whom Richard III., after calling for a bowl of wine before the battle began, said, "Here's to thee, Madoc, the only true Welshman I have found," and rushed to meet his foe, where he at once lost his life and his kingdom.

The Earl of Richmond delayed his march to Shrewsbury till he was master of Forton and Monford-bridge; two points of main importance to his designs, as he was thus provided with a passage into the midland counties, even though that town should shut up her gates upon him. Having secured that bridge; which, if the Salopians had been hearty in the cause of Richard, they would have broken down; his army encamped upon Forton-heath, and he dispatched messengers to Shrewsbury, to surround the town. When they arrived at the foot of the Welsh bridge, they found the place in a posture of defence; the gates shut, the portcullis let down,' and the bailiffs within ready to give their answer. The senior of these magistrates was Thomas Mytton, Esq., who is described in our old chronicle as "a stout wise gentleman:" he made answer, that he knew the Earl for no king, but "only Kynge Rychard, whose lyffetenants he and hys fellowes weare; and before he should entre there, he should goe over his belly: meaning thereby," continues

Henry Earl of Richmond's (afterwards Henry VII.) entrance into Shrewsbury over the Mayor's body.

our authority, "that he would be slayne to the ground, and so to (be) roon over by him before he entryd, and that he protestyd vehemently upon the oath he had tacken." Much conversation, we may suppose, ensued: but Mr. Mytton continuing resolute, the Earl "retornyd," says our chronicle (from which we may infer that he had himself advanced to the end of Frankwell), "wyth hys companye backe agayne to

---

⁵ Leland, who visited Shrewsbury in 1539, describes it in his usual quaint style, "as the greatest, fayrest, and highest upon the stream, having six great arches of stone.' "This bridge," he further says, "standeth on the west side of the towne, and hath at the one ende of it a great gate to enter by into the towne, and at the other end, towardes Wales, a mighty stronge towre to prohibit enimies to enter on the bridge."

Forton," where we know that he passed the night in the house of one Hugh, who derived his name from the village. Some one of the party seems to have recollected that the ancient appellation of the place might indicate a prosperous issue of the daring enterprise in which they were engaged. Situations of danger have a natural tendency to engender feelings of superstition: and if Henry was himself superior to the weakness, the spirits of many a follower might be raised by the consideration that their leader was entertained "*in the mansion of Fortune.*"

On the following morning, the negotiation with the bailiffs of Shrewsbury was renewed; and the Earl assured the magistrates that he did not mean to hurt the town or its inhabitants, but only desired to pass on to try his right to the Crown. We are told that Mr. Mytton began to yield to these suggestions; but that, on account of the oath he had so lately taken to oppose the entrance of Richmond into Shrewsbury, he adopted the ingenious expedient of lying down on the ground, and permitting the Earl to step over him. Hereupon the portcullis was drawn up, the Earl and his retinue admitted within the gates, to the general joy of the inhabitants, and received, we are assured, "with an *Ave chaire*, and *God speed the wel!* the streets being strewed with hearbes and flowers, and their doores adorned with greene boughs, in testimony of a true hartie reception." But the Earl of Richmond received, at Shrewsbury, more solid marks of attachment than the acclamations of a multitude. The Corporation received him with all respect, and assisted in procuring certain soldiers to accompany him; leaving, however, the bailiffs to pay the wages.[6] The house in which he lodged during his short stay at Shrewsbury was known when Sir William Dugdale visited the town, in 1663; and that eminent antiquary has preserved a notice of certain armorial bearings, which were then remaining on stained glass in its windows.[7] Sir Richard Corbet, of Morton Corbet, who had been a stout Lancastrian, and had evinced his attachment to the Earl on a former occasion, by rescuing him from imminent danger at the battle of Banbury, joined him immediately upon his arrival at Shrewsbury. He even went the hazardous length of taking the oath of allegiance to him, as if he were already invested with the royal dignity; and collected a band of eight hundred gentlemen and others, with whom he accompanied him to the field of Redmore, or Bosworth. This we learn from his own petition to Henry, after he was invested with royal dignity.[8]

"*The Petition of Sir Richard Corbet to Kinge H. 7.*

"In most humble wise showeth unto your most noble highness . . . your true and faithful subject and liegeman Ric. Corbett knight for your bodie, to consider the true faithfull service that he hath doun and hereafter entendeth for to doe to the uttermost of his power . . .

"First: Pleaseth your Grace to call to your remembrance the first service, that after the death of the Lord Herbert after the field of Banbury, hee was one of them that brought your Grace out of the danger of your enemyes, and conveyed your Grace unto your towne of Hereford, and there delivered you in safety to your greate Uncle now Duke of Bedford:—and then at your comynge into England, hee was one of the first, to his poore power, that tooke your parte, and first came unto your Grace at the towne of Shrewesbury, and there was sworne your liegeman, and went from thence unto the field of Boseworth, and there jeoparted with your Grace his life, lands, and goods, and the gentlemen and others his friends that came with him in company, takinge your parte and rightwise quarrell to the number of 800 men; and at every field and jorney since hee hath byne reddy to do your Grace service to his great costs and charges, and hee, ne

---

[6] In the accounts of Tho. Mytton and Rog. Knyght, bailiffs of Salop, from Michaelmas 2 Richard III. to Michaelmas 1 Henry VII., is this entry:

"Et de iiiili. iiiis. xd. solut' p' div' cost' . . . . ville in temp'e advent' H. VII. Reg. v's' Rege' R. et p' . . . . div's' soldur' ip'o Regi conduct':"

[7] The house was on the right-hand side of the Wyle, going down to the bridge: three doors below the Lion Inn. It was for many years the residence of the family of Elisha: and the passage through it, leading to the Back-lane, is still called by the old people Elisha's Shut. The coats noticed by Dugdale are six in number: and are described by him, in his Visitation of Shropshire, 1663, as being "in an auncient house in Shrewsbury wherein K. Henry the 7th loged when he went to Bosworth field."

[8] See Owen and Blakeway's History of Shropshire.

non of his that were with him at your first fielde, or at any other insurreĉons or tumolts were never noe cravers for noe rewardes nor offices as yet. The which God knoweth best, and your Highness."

From Shrewsbury they marched to a small village, called Newport, where the example of Sir Richard was followed by other gentry of Shropshire, in particular by Humphrey Cotes, Esq., of Woodcote, who fell on the Earl's side at Bosworth, and Sir Gilbert Talbot, who joined him with two thousand tall men, vassals or dependants of the Earl of Shrewsbury, "which still gave him more encouragement, insomuch that he hoped his game hitherunto being soe fouelie plaid, he could not chuse but rise a winner in the end. After this, for Stafford they goe, thence to Letchfeild, and soe to Adderstone, where he and his father-in-lawe, the Lord Stanley, met and consulted touching the ordering of their affaires, and howe to give battle to King Richard, which done, they departed each to his charge.

"Richard, all this while relying on the fastnesses of his friends in Wales, lay carelesslye at Nottingham, where, it seemes, his intelligence was but poore, or his espials verie false and trecherouse; for the Earle was come beyond Shrewsburie before he had anie intelligence of his landing; soe as wee may easilie perceave all things did conspire the confusion of this monster. It was nott long ere he was advertized of the Earle's arrivall at Millford, and that all things necessarie for his enterprize were unprovided and verie weake, which made him rechlesse of what soe nearlie concerned him, as being confident that Sir Walter Herbert and Rice ap Thomas would soone defeate soe poore a company. I take it there is an error committed here by all our historiographers, in joyning Sir Walter Herbert and Rice ap Thomas together in this place; for although Sir Walter was a man of greate command in Glamorgan and Monmouthshires, yet, in those partes where Rice ap Thomas bore sway, he had nothing to doe. The report goes that these two noble gentlemen, being neere kinsmen and faithfull friendes, took severall sides, the one with Richard, the other with Richmond, and that they both (careful of their owne safeties, however the world went) did mutuallie compact to procure each other's pardon, what side soever prevailed; and this tradition I have been the more bold to sett down here, having heared the same allowed and confirmed by divers of that honourable familie. Nowe, to proceed, by and by a second message was brought to the King that the Earle was on his way beyond Shrewsburie, and that Rice ap Thomas attended him with all his power: at which name the tyrant startled, crying out for vengeance on him who, contrarie to his oath, had thus deceived him. Being thus affrighted, he began to think it high time to looke about him; therefore, in all haste, he sendes for his most trustie friendes, Norfolk, Northumberland, and others. And soe, raiseing a puisant armie, like an experte commander (as, indeed, in feates of armes, and matters of chivalrie, to give the devill his dewe, he was nothing inferior to the best), falls, forthwith, to dispose them with a great deal of judgement. Then calling for his horse, a goodlie white courser,[2] with as much speede as the downe-pressing plummets of his villanies would give leave, attended by his footmen, and guarded with wings of horse, with a meaguer and dreadful countenance, he comes to the towne of Leycester.

"By this time both armies were come within view, the one of the other, near the village of Bosworth. Richard committed the vauntguard of his armie to that approved chieftaine Northfolke; after him the King followed himself with the bodie of his armie, consisting of veteran souldiers and approved men of war, such as were like enough to have carried the day, and their hearts and bodies walked in the same course. Hereupon Richmond leads forth his men; his vauntguard was fronted with archers, over which the Earle of Oxford was in cheefe; the right wing Sir Gilbert Talbot had designed unto him, and Sir John Savage had the left; the Earle himself governed the battilion, having with him Jasper, Earle of Pembroke, and Rice ap Thomas, in whose brave cavalry the Earle reposed much confidence, for as yet the Stanleys stood aloof. And nowe the time was come appointed by God in his secret judgement, to determine for the garland, soe that without anie further delaye these two royal combatants by there prayers recommended themselves to the protection of the Highest, whitting the valerouse spiritts of their followers with cheerful orations, large

---

[2] "Saddle white Surrey for the field to-morrow."—*Shakspeare's Richard III.*

promises, and their owne personal braverie.   And soe upon summons of the death-menacing trumpett, they encounter and fall to blowes.

> " ' ———— Pede pes et cuspide cuspis
> Arma sonant armis, vir petiturque viro.'

" While the avantguards were in this hot chase, the one of the other, King Richard held nott his hands in his pockets; but grinding and gnashing his teeth, up and downe he goes in quest of Richmond, whoe no sooner espying him, than he, with the impetuosity of a tyrant, sensible that his all was at stake, rushed forward to the place where the Earl was stationed, and, according to the immortal Shakspeare, who puts the following words into his mouth, braves him to battle.

> " ' What ho ! young Richmond, ho ! 'tis Richard calls thee ;
> I hate thee, Harry, for thy blood of Lancaster !
> Now if thou dost not hide thee from my sword,
> Now while the angry trumpet sounds alarms,
> And dying groans transpierce the wounded air ;
> *Richmond,* I say, come forth, and singly face me ;
> Richard is hoarse with daring thee to arms ! '

And by the way, in his furie manfullie overthrewe Sir William Brandon, the Earle's standard-bearer, as also Sir John Cheney, both men of mightie force and knowne valiancie.   In Wales we say, that Rice ap Thomas, whoe from the beginning closlie followed the Earle, and ever had an eye on his person, seeing his partie begin to quaile and the King's gain ground, took this occasion to send unto Sir William Stanley giving him to understand the danger they were in, and entreating him to joyne his forces for the disengaging the Earle, who was not onlie in despair of victory but almost of his lief.   Whereupon (for it seems he understood not the danger before) Sir William Stanley made up to Rice ap Thomas, and joining both together rushed upon there adversaries and routed them, by which means the glorie of the day fell upon the Earle's side.   King Richard, as a just guerdon for all his actions and horrible murders, was slain in the field while combatting with a single gentleman, and Henry, amidst blood, slaughter, and acclamations of victory, was saluted King of England, by the title of Henry the Seventh."

HOUSE OF TUDOR.

THE Battle of Bosworth Field and the restoration of the British Dynasty in the person of HENRY THE SEVENTH,[1] was an important epoch in the history of this country, inasmuch as it was the first event that had any tendency to heal the lacerations of ages,—to conciliate foes,—and to soften and humanise the nations. And if the battle of Bosworth, which effected this happy change, was the last and the least of thirteen,[2] which had desolated the kingdom, and destroyed at least one hundred thousand of its inhabitants, during the contention of the Houses of York and Lancaster, it was the first and the greatest in its consequences; by the marriage of this Prince with the Heiress of York, it united the rival Houses—by that of his daughter with James IV. of Scotland, it united the rival nations— it associated the Rose of the South with the Thistle of the North, in this instance the *Carduus Benedictus*, and formed a great national *bouquet*, that promises a perennial verdure; finally, aboriginal rights,—the claims of connexion—and the pretensions of conquest are happily united, and *the Princes of Wales are still Heirs and Kings of Great Britain.*[3]

Henry was born at Pembroke Castle in South Wales, where he passed many years of his childhood with his mother, the Countess of Richmond.

This castle is built on a rocky prominence, and in boldness of situation, grandeur of appearance, and adaptation for defence, it may vie with any other similar structure in the kingdom, Windsor Castle only excepted. It is an interesting fact connected with this castle, which no other can boast of, that it gave birth to King Henry VII., the progenitor of the kings and queens of this country, a race which has continued in a direct line ever since, and from whom our present most gracious Majesty derives her high and ancient genealogy. "In one of the rooms of this singularly noble edifice," says old Leland, the very best authority, as living near the time, and seldom speaking from hearsay, "in the utter warde I sawe the

---

[1] This monarch was crowned October 30th, 1485, and his queen, Elizabeth, October 30th, 1487. The coronation of the latter was remarkable for the procession by water from the palace of Greenwich to the Tower instead of from Westminster, as was usual. The queen was escorted by the Lord Mayor, sheriffs, and the heads of the different Companies in their state barges, richly ornamented with silken pennons and streamers, and also with the banners of the different trades, on which their arms were embroidered in gold. One of these barges, called the bachelors' barge, contained an extraordinary pageant, an enormous red dragon which spouted streams of fire into the Thames. When the queen rode through the city on the following day, choirs of children dressed as angels were stationed in different places, who sang hymns and songs as she passed by.

[2] "The unjust aggression of Henry IV. was the cause of the long contest between the Houses of York and Lancaster, wherein from the 28th of Henry VI. to the 15th of Henry VII. there were thirteen fields fought, in which three Kings of England, one Prince of Wales, twelve Dukes, one Marquis, eighteen Earls, with one Viscount and twenty-three Barons, besides knights and gentlemen, lost their lives." Camden, p. 507.

[3] It was to this event, doubtlessly, Simon Tudor, one of the most celebrated Bards, alluded in his ode to Queen Elizabeth, where he thus exultingly exclaims :—

"Harri lân hir lawenydd,
Ywr hwn a'n rhoes ninnau'n rhydd;
I Gymru da vu hyd vedd
Goroni gwr o Wynedd."

"Our Henry, happy may he be,
The chief, that set his country free;
Blest be the day, of blissful date,
That saw him placed on Empire's seat."

chaumbre where Kyng Henri VII. was borne, in knowledge whereof a chymmeney is now made, with the
armes and badges of Kyng Henri VII."

Pembroke Castle, the Birth-place of Henry the Seventh.

Henry was only fifteen weeks old when his father died, on the 3rd of November, 1456. His
infancy was sickly, but he was carefully nursed by his mother. He was afterwards committed by
Edward IV. to the care of the lady of Sir William Herbert, to be educated in a state of friendly and liberal
custody; and he owed to her the foundation of his manly accomplishments.[4] The best instructors were
provided for him; his mind was active and his improvement rapid.[5] He acquired that attachment to
religion which never left him, and his behaviour was interesting. Herbert falling at Bunbury, in 1470, and
Jasper, the Prince's uncle, having obtained possession of his person, carried him to London and introduced
him to the King, who was pleased with his countenance, and expressed the idea of his possible elevation.
The battle of Tewkesbury compelling Jasper to fly, he thought it prudent that Henry, then in his fifteenth
year, should leave the country with him. His mother suggested that Wales had many castles in which
he would be safe, but his uncle advised her not to take the chance, as his life would be aimed at, and
he promised to regard him as his son. The education[6] of Henry had made him a mark of dangerous
attention, and the Countess consented to his temporary exile. Jasper intended to have made France his
asylum, as Henry's grandmother was the sister of the French king's father; but a storm driving them on
Bretagne, the Duke received them courteously, yet detained them. Here they remained for twelve years
as actual prisoners, but kindly treated. The efforts of Edward IV. to get them within his power had the
effect of making the Duke more vigilant in watching them, and also more alive to the policy of keeping
them in his dominions.

[4] Pol. Virg., p. 522. " Well and honourably educated ; in all kind
of civility brought up by Lady Herbert." Holt, p. 287.

[5] His preceptor, Andrew Scot, says that he never knew a boy of
that age so capable and so quiet of learning. MS. B. Andrew, p. 135.

[6] Comines, i. p. 514, states, " that the Earl of Richmond told me
that from the time he was five years old he had always been a
fugitive or a prisoner. I was at the Court of Duke Francis at the
time they were seized, and the Duke treated them very handsomely.

From this time history is silent about Henry's life, and gives no account of him for a number of years.

"It is observable," says Pennant, "that none of our historians attempt to narrate the incidents in Henry's life during the intermediate period, from his leaving France to his accession to the crown." From the following events, however, it is more than probable that, during this interval, he was secretly employed in strengthening his interest among the Welsh gentry, who were zealous partisans of the House of Lancaster, and who bore towards him particularly, an ardent attachment, from the circumstance of his being born amongst them, and, by direct descent, one of their countrymen.

It is a well authenticated historical fact that Wales had no inconsiderable share in bringing about the present happy establishment of Great Britain, nor should it be concealed that the "men of Flintshire" acted a prominent part in the accomplishment of this great national object. We feel an honest pride in being a descendant of some of those worthies, and we hope that we shall be excused if we attempt to relate some facts connected with this subject which are not now generally known.

Wales was united to England (by parchment only, as our friends across the water would say) in 1282, by Edward I., but the inhabitants were not permitted to enjoy the same privileges as their English neighbours for centuries afterwards, but on the contrary they were treated as "aliens in blood, feeling, and language;" as a proof of which we would remark that no less than fifteen distinct and cruel laws were enacted against them from the time of Edward I. to that of Henry VI. Suffering as they were under those oppressive laws, particularly those of Henry VI., they seized the first opportunity of delivering their country from that tyranny which had ever proved inimical to their liberty and happiness, and this opportunity offered itself when Richard III., by murder and usurpation, had forced his way to the throne of England.

To the Earl of Richmond, the head of the House of Lancaster, in whose veins the blood of the Cambrian princes freely flowed, the hopes of our dejected countrymen were directed, and by a well-concerted scheme, first formed by a few patriotic gentlemen assembled at Mostyn Hall, in Flintshire, that distinguished individual, then an exile in France, was brought over and lodged under the parental care of "*Richard ap Howel*," the then lord of Mostyn, and it was here the North Wales chieftains, in conjunction with those of the South, planned the overthrow of the House of York, which eventually led to the supremacy of the House of Lancaster, in the person of a grandson of Sir Owen Tudor, of Mona.

It was to Mostyn Hall, the ancient seat of the respected member for Flintshire, that several of the bards of that period alluded in their compositions, under the fictitious cognomen of the Lion, the Eagle, and the like, but in such terms as to conceal their precise meaning from the jealous eye of the reigning prince, the cruel Richard. That tyrant, however, eventually got an intimation of the meaning of these allusions, and conscious of the weakness of his own title to the throne, he put a price upon the head of Richmond, and sent emissaries to different parts of Wales in search of him. They heard that Richmond was concealed at Mostyn Hall, whither they sent to apprehend him. The Earl was then about to dine with the family, but being apprised of his danger, he had just time to make his escape through a window (which is to this day called the "*King's Hole*,") when King Richard's party made their appearance at the old entrance hall.[7]

Richard ap Howel, lord of Mostyn, afterwards joined Henry at the battle of Bosworth, with a large

---

[7] Tradition informs us that the following colloquy took place here between the leader of the party and the then lord of Mostyn. On his entrance to the dining-room, the strangers said, "My lord, we have come here in quest of Henry Earl of Richmond, who, we are informed, is now staying with you." "Your information is not correct," answered the worthy host, "for he has left here." Looking round, and perceiving the family ready to sit down to dinner, the officer observed, "How is this, my lord! I see you have more knives and forks laid on your table than you have company to dinner." "It is always my custom," replied his lordship, "to have an extra knife and fork on my table in case a friend should drop in; and as I cannot look upon you in any other light, I shall be happy if you will sit down along with us, and make use of them." Whether the stranger did so or otherwise, "further the deponent knoweth not;" but we have occasion to know that the good old-fashioned way of providing an extra knife and fork for a friend is still observed by this ancient family at their hospitable house.

number of loyal troops of the ancient British, and after the victory, received from the King, in token of gratitude for his preservation, the belt and sword he wore on that day. Henry VII., when quietly fixed on the throne, sent a gracious message to the lord of Mostyn, to invite him to dwell with him at court; but it was courteously declined, as we have already narrated.

King Henry was not slow in his acknowledgments to those who had assisted him in his late emergency; the people of Shrewsbury, among others, experienced his gratitude for the zeal they had manifested in his cause. In less than three months after the battle of Bosworth, he remitted to them, " of his special grace, and for the singular favour which he bore towards the same town, and the bailiffs, burgesses, men, community, and inhabitants of the same, and in consideration of the ruin, poverty, and decay thereof, ten marks annually for the thirty pounds of fee-farm, at which they held their town;" this remission to continue for the term of fifty years.

A.D. 1488.—Henry took frequent opportunities of visiting Shrewsbury. In this year we are told by Phillips that he went to Shrewsbury and stayed several days; and again in 1490, on which last occasion he was attended by his Queen and son, Prince Arthur, and kept the feast of St. George, April 23, in the collegiate church of St. Chad. Shrewsbury was the first place in England where Henry was proclaimed King, for which and other cogent reasons, he appears to have been very partial to that town, for we find him, in company with his eldest son, Arthur, making frequent visits to this place. The young prince was sent to reside in the Marches of Wales, and to hold his court at Ludlow Castle, which was appointed to be his chief residence, but from which he made frequent, in all probability, annual, visits to Shrewsbury. His earliest act in his new capacity bears date January 31, 1493-4; and we learn from the accounts of the bailiffs of Shrewsbury for the year commencing Michaelmas, 1494, that during that period he honoured it with his presence, accompanied by several eminent personages of his council.

Henry, both as a king and as a father, and he seems to have been an affectionate one, must have been anxious to ascertain the state of the country nominally administered by his son. In the following year, therefore, he repaired to Shrewsbury, accompanied by his mother, the venerable Countess of Richmond, his Queen, and the rest of his family. He appears to have been lodged in the abbey, and from thence to have proceeded to view the castle; and when the bailiffs of the town met him at the Abbey bridge for the purpose of waiting upon him to that ancient fortress, they endeavoured to interest him in their favour, with regard to the contested jurisdiction of Merivale. One of them, several years afterwards, thus records what passed upon the occasion :—

" John Gyttins, of the town of Shrewsbury, the elder, Draper, showeth,—That whereas it pleased the King's Grace that now is to be at the said town of Shrewsbury when the said John Gyttins and Lawrence Hosier were bailiffs of the same town, the said bailiffs doing their duties and attendances according unto their allegeance unto the King's Highness, bare the King's maces of the town aforesaid before the King's said Grace from the abbey of the town aforesaid unto the King's castle of the same town: and as the King's said Grace ascended a brugg called Staunbrugg, the said John Gyttins, which at that season rode before the King's Grace bearing the King's said mace, and saying these words, ' My Liege Lord, please your Grace to understand that here, in this place of the said Staunbrugg, where of old season was a cross of stone on the south part, and at this day a great ash groweth beside the said brugg on the other side, that is to witt on the north side of the said brugg, is the Mere of the franchises of the town of Shrewsbury towards the abbey of the same, the which we the said bailiffs been peaciably possessed of; howbeit, that the abbot and convent of the abbey aforesaid make title and claim unto parcell of our said Liberty, upon and by the said Staun brugg:' And the said King's Grace then and there redelivered unto the same John Gyttins the said mace in the name and to the use of his town of Shrewsbury, and commanded the same John Gyttins and Lawrence Hosier then bailiffs there, and their successors, to keep the same Liberty, which the said J. G. and L. H. kept during the time of their bailiwick. In witness whereof the said J. G. hath put to his seal the 18th day of January, the 18th year of K. Henry the 7th."

The King was feasted royally at Shrewsbury: the accounts of the bailiffs Gyttins and Hosier, for one year from Michaelmas 1495, contain full particulars of his hospitable reception. It seems that the prince preceded his father, and was at Shrewsbury ready to give him welcome.

The total charge of these expenses is 39*l*. 17*s*. 6*d*. Wheat appears to have been at that time pretty regularly 6*d*. a bushel; which would swell the cost of this royal entertainment, even at the present unusually low rate of 7*s*. a bushel, to the great sum of 558*l*. Large as it was, it was not, however, thrown away: before the end of the year, the King, pleased by the attention of the burgesses, to which he expressly refers, granted them a new charter, containing an extension of the boundaries of their liberties, with other valuable privileges, and a restoration of the most important of them all, their exemption from taxes.

A.D. 1494.—In the month of July, Henry VII. paid a visit to Hawarden Castle, Flintshire, where he stayed for some time, in order to enjoy the amusement of stag hunting; but his primary motive was to soothe the Earl of Derby, who had married the Countess of Richmond, Henry's mother, after the cruel execution of his brother, Sir William Stanley. That gentleman had rendered Henry most material assistance at the Battle of Bosworth, and he had with his own hands placed the crown on Henry's head on the battle field; but being suspected of aiding Perkin Warbeck in his rebellious attempt, he was tried and executed by the command of the King. Historians are not agreed as to Stanley's guilt or innocence; some say that he had actually assisted Warbeck, whilst others aver that the King availed himself of the accusations made against him by Clifford in order to possess himself of Stanley's great wealth. Be that as it may, Henry, immediately upon Stanley's execution, seized upon his Castle of Holt, where he found treasure to the amount of 40,000 marks in money, together with plate, jewels, &c., and a landed estate producing 3000*l*. a year.

A.D. 1495.—In June the King proceeded from Hawarden Castle, accompanied by several of his nobles, to Knowsley and Latham, in Lancashire, where he stopped about a month with his mother, the Countess of Richmond, and his stepfather, the Earl of Derby. From thence he returned to London.[8]

Henry VII.'s eldest son, Prince Arthur, and his Princess, Katherine of Arragon, resided and held their courts at Ludlow.

The marriage of the Prince of Wales with Katherine of Arragon took place, attended with great pomp,[9] at St. Paul's, London, on the 14th of November, 1501, Arthur had just completed his fifteenth year, and his young bride had not quite completed her sixteenth year. Prince Arthur endowed his lovely Princess at the high altar with one-third of his property, among which is enumerated the Crown rents of Caernarvon and Conway Castles, &c., &c., which, in all, amounted to 5000*l*. per annum;[1] at least, that was the sum ostensibly allowed her, afterwards, as Princess Dowager.

Shortly afterwards the young married couple, Prince and Princess of Wales, departed from the English Court for Ludlow Castle, in Shropshire, where they were to govern the Principality of Wales, holding a miniature court, modelled like that of Westminster. Katherine performed the journey to Ludlow on horse-

---

[8] The King and the Queen repeatedly visited Shrewsbury. The following items are from the bailiffs' books :—

"Sweet wine (vino molli) given to the queen, 2*s*. 8*d*.

"Wine given to the valet of the crown and the guard of our Lord the King, 14*s*. 10*d*."

The valets of the yeomen of the guard mentioned here were the company of *tall strongmen* ordained by Henry VII. at his coronation. They are alluded to by one of our Welsh bards in the following beautiful couplet :

"A gwyr tal yn ei ganlyn
Mil myrdd mewn gwyrdd a gwyn."

"He was followed in his train by tall men—a seemly sight—
Thousands all clad alike in green and white."

[9] For particulars of the marriage we would refer our readers to the Lives of the Queens of England, by Miss Strickland—a most interesting and amusing work, to which we are indebted for many interesting particulars.

[1] Katherine's own marriage portion was 200,000 crowns, half of which had been paid down with her. After the death of Prince Arthur, Henry VII. had an extreme desire to touch the rest of his daughter-in-law's dower. He, therefore, proposed a marriage between his surviving son Henry, then only five years old, which, after some demur on the part of Katherine, was at the proper time accomplished.

back, riding on a pillion behind her master of horse, while eleven ladies followed her on palfreys. When she was tired she rested on a litter borne between two horses. Such was the mode of travelling before turnpike roads had made the country traversable for wheeled carriages, for the horses which bore the litter made good their footing in paths where a wheel-carriage could not be kept upright.

It appears that Prince Arthur visited Oxford on the road to Ludlow, for in the memorials of that city are these particulars of his entertainment at Magdalen College:—"He was lodged in the apartments of the President; rushes were provided for the Prince's bed-chamber; he was treated with a brace of pike, and a brace of tench: both their Highnesses received presents of gloves, and were refreshed with red wine, claret, and sack."

The Prince and Princess[2] of Wales were decidedly popular at Ludlow, but their residence there was of short continuance; for the Prince, whose learning and good qualities made him the hope of England, was suddenly taken ill, and expired at this castle on the 2nd of April, 1502. Connected with Ludlow Castle is a proclamation of Henry VII., which, considering his own avarice, does him more credit than most of the things recorded of him. It was issued at the funeral of his eldest son, Prince Arthur, who, dying at the age of sixteen, in the castle, was buried there.[3] "After the funeral rites were over," says Leland, "there was ordained a great dinner; and in the morning a proclamation was made in that city, that if any man could show any victuals unpaid for in that county, that had been taken by any of that noble Prince's servants before that day, they should come and show it to the late steward, comptroller and cofferer, and they should be contented." To be sure, this was no more than common justice, but considering the character of Henry, and how frequently, in those times, much baser things were done than leaving the debts of a prince unpaid, I think it deserves mention. Some historians declare that he died of decline, others say that he was very firm and robust: among these conflicting opinions, it is worth while, perhaps, to quote the Spanish historian, whose information seems to have been derived from Katherine herself.

"Prince Arthur died of the plague a little while after his nuptials, being in the Principality of Wales, in a place they call *Pudlow* (Ludlow). In this house was Donna Catalina left a widow, when she had been married scarcely six months." This observation is completely borne out by an statement in the Herald's[4] Journal; for, after describing the whole detail of the magnificent progress of the Prince's funeral to the city of Worcester, where he was buried, it declares, that but few citizens were assembled in the cathedral because of the great sickness that prevailed in Worcester.[5]

Henry VII., early in his reign, issued a commission to Sir John Leiaf, priest, Guttin Owen, and a number of others, to make enquiry into his paternal descent; and they, from our Welsh chronicles, proved incontestibly that "he was lineally descended by issue male, saving one woman, from Brutus,

---

[2] Katherine of Arragon. The device of the pomegranate ornament in our ancient churches is due to Queen Katherine; she brought it along with her from Granada, the bright home of her childhood. This device is still to be seen among the ornaments of the well of Saint Winifrede at Holywell, Flintshire, to which building Katherine of Arragon was a benefactress.

[3] The herald present at the funeral wrote the journal in Leland's Collectanea. It is replete with curious costumes. "On St. Mark's day commenced from Ludlow. It was the foulest cold and windy day I have seen, and the road was so bad in some places, that the car with the Prince's body stuck so fast in the mud, that yokes of oxen were required to draw it out. Such was the progress to Worcester, where, with weeping, Prince Arthur was laid in the grave."

[4] A journey from Shrewsbury to London three centuries ago was a serious affair, and some of its details perhaps may amuse the reader; we present a few scenes, quite as well fitted as graver matters, to convey an idea of the progress of travelling.

"Memorandum the vth day of May the xxij yere of Kyng Harry

the vij[th] Ric' Lyster received of Ric' Egge oon of the six men of the town of Salop in money xiij.li. xiij.s. iiij.d. for the expences of the said R' L. & Roger Thornes *for the rydyng* abowt the bysynes by twixt the said town and the Abbott:—

"*Wensday.* Wher of spend for the hire of a horss for William Draper to Edward Onslow, 3s. 4d.

Item. Spend at Schefnall for vitall, 9d.

Hampton the seid nyght. Soper, 14d.; horse-meat, 16d.; wyn, 2d.; fyre and candall, 2d.

"*Thursday.* Byrmyncham. Dyner, 18d.

Coventre.

Dayntre. Soper, 15d.

"*Fryday.* Stony Strettford: dyner. Dunstapl. St. Alban's at night.

"*Saturday.* Barnet. Londer to dyner.

"*Sonday.*

"*Monday.* Bothyr to and fro Westmestre, 5d."

[5] See Bernaldus, p. 236.

grandson of Æneas the Trojan, and that he was son to Brute in five score degrees. I shall drop a little short of this long descent," says Mr. Pennant, "but Owen Tudor was assuredly of high blood. He was seventh in descent from Ednyfed Fychan, councillor and leader of the armies of Llywelyn the Great, and a successful warrior against the English. His origin was from Marchudd, one of the fifteen tribes. Ednyfed's wife was Gwenllian daughter of Rhys, Prince of South Wales; so that he might boast of two royal descents, and be the founder of a line of kings not unworthy of the British Empire."

The following is a return of a Commission sent into Wales by King Henry VII., to search out the pedigrees of Owen Tudor, extracted from Powell's Wales, first edition, 1584 :—

Henry the Seventh, King of England, &c., son of Edmund, Earl of Richmond, son of Owen ap Meredith, and of Queen Catherine, his wife, daughter to Charles the Sixth, King of France. This Owen was son of Meredith ap Tudor ap Gronw ap Tudor, ap Gronw, ap Ednyfed Fychan, Baron of Brinfeingle in Denbigh Land, Lord of Kriceth, Chief Justice and Chief of Council to Llewelyn ap Iorwerth Drwyndwn, Prince of all Wales. And in the time of Prince Llewelyn grew a variance between King John of England and the said Prince; whereupon Ednyfed came with the Prince's host, and men of war, and also a number of his own people, and met these English Lords in a morning, at what time these English Lords were hostied and slain; and immediately brought their heads, being yet bloody, to the said Prince Llewelyn. The Prince, seeing the same, caused Ednyfed Fychan, from thenceforth to bear in his arms or shield, three bloody heads in token of his victory, where he had born in his arms before a Saracen's Head; and so ever after this Ednyfed bore the said arms, his son, and his son's son, unto the time of Tudor ap Gronw, ap Tudor ap Gronw, ap Ednyfed Fychan. And after this, Ednyfed wedded one Gwenllian Daughter to Rhys, Prince of South Wales, and had issue by her Gronw: which Ednyfed Fychan had in Wales divers goodly houses, royally adorn'd with turrets and garrets; some in Anglesey, some other in Caernarvonshire, and some in Denbigh Land; but his chiefest manor-house was in the Commot of Crythin in Caernarvonshire, which was a royal palace, now decay'd for want of reparations. Also he builded there a chappel in the worship of our Lady, and had License of the Pope for evermore to sing divine service therein for his soul, and his ancestors' and progenitors' souls always; and had authority to give his tythes and offerings to his chaplain there starving [and serving]; which Ednyfed Fychan was son to Kyner ap Iers ap Gwgan, ap Marchudd, which was one of the fifteen tribes of North Wales, and son to Kynan ap Elfyn, ap Mor, ap Mynan, ap Isbwis Newintyrche, ap Isbwis ap Cadrod Calch fynyd, Earl of Dunstable and Lord of Northampton, ap Cywyd Cindion, ap Cynfelyn ap Arthuys, ap Morydd ap Cynnaw, ap Coel Godeboc, King of Britain, of whom King Henry the Seventh descended lineally by issue-male, and is son to the said Coel in the thirty-first degree, as it is approved by old chronicles in Wales. Which Coel was son of Tegfan ap Deheufraint, ap Tudbwyl, ap Urban, ap Gradd, ap Rhyfedel, ap Rhyderine, ap Endigant, ap Endeyrn, ap Enid, ap Endos, ap Enddolaw, ap Affalach ap Afflech, ap Beli mawr, King of Britain, of whom King Henry the Seventh descended by issue-male, and is son to him in forty-one degrees. Which Beli was son to Monnogon king, ap king Kaxor, ap king Pyr, ap king Sawl Benissel, ap Rhytherech king, ap Rydion king, ap Eidol king, ap Arthafel king, ap Seissilt king, ap Owen king, ap Caxho king, ap Bleuddyd king, ap Meirion king, ap Gwrgust king, ap Elydno king, ap Clydaws king, ap Ithel king, ap Urien king, ap Andrew king, ap Kereni king, ap Porrex king, ap Coel king, ap Cadell king, ap Geraint king, ap Elidr king, ap Morydd king, ap Dan king, ap Seisyllt king, ap Cyhelyn king, ap Gwrgan king (alias) Farfdrwch, ap Beli king, ap Dyfnwal king, ap Dodion king, ap Enyd, ap Kwrwyd, ap Cyrdon, ap Dyfnfrath Prydain, ap Aedd mawr, ap Antonius, ap Seisillt king, ap Rhegaw daughter and heir of King Lyr, and wife of Henwin Prince of Cornwall. This Lyr was son of Bleuddyd, ap Rhunbaladr brâs, ap Lleon, ap Brutus darian lâs, ap Efrog Cadarn, ap Mymbyr, ap Madoc, ap Locrine, ap Brutus which inherited first this land, and after his name was called Britain, and had three sons, Locrine, Kamber, and Albanactus. Locrine, the eldest, parted the isle with his brethren, and kept half the land for himself, and called it Loegria. Kamber, second son, had the land beyond Severn, and named it Kambria, in English, Wales. Albanactus had Scotland, which he then called Albania, after his own name. Of which Brute King Henry the Seventh is lineally descended by issue-male, saving one woman, and is son to Brute in five score degrees.

How OWEN, *grandsire to King Henry the Seventh, cometh of Beli Mawr by* ANGHARAD, *Mother to Ednyfed by issue-female.*
By Guttin Owen, and Sir John Leiaf's books.

The mother of Ednyfed was Angharad, daughter of Hwfa, ap Cyner, ap Rhywallon, ap Dinged, ap Tudor Trefor, ap Mymbyr, ap Cadfarch, ap Gwrgenaw, ap Gwaethiawc, ap Bywyn, ap Biordderch, ap Gwriawn, ap Gwnnan, ap Gwnfiw frych, ap Cadell Dehurnlluc, ap Pasgan, ap Rhydwf, ap Rhudd Fedel frych, ap Cyndeirn, ap Gwrtheirn Gwrthenau, called in English Vortigern, by whom King Henry the Seventh, by the aforesaid Angharad, mother to Ednyfed Fychan, and wife to

Cyner ab Iers, ap Gwgon, is son to the said Vortigern in thirty degrees. Which Vortiger was son to Rhydeyrn ad Dehufraint, ap Eidigant, ap Endeirn, ap Enid, ap Endos, ap Enddolau, ap Afallach, ap Affiech, ap Beli mawr, to whom King Henry the Seventh is son by Angharad, mother to Ednyfed Fychan in forty degrees.

How KING HENRY THE SEVENTH *cometh of Beli Mawr by* GWENLLIAN, *wife to Ednyfed Fychan, and daughter to the Lord Rhys, called Arglwydd Rhys, by issue-female.*

Owen ap Meredith ap Tudor ap Gronw, ap Tudor, ap Gronw, ap Gwenllian, daughter to Rhys Prince of South Wales, ap Gruffydh prince, ap Rhys prince, ap Tudor mawr prince, ap Cadell prince, ap Rodri mawr prince of all Wales. This Rodri had three sons, and divided the Principality of Wales between them in three parts; to Merfyn, his first son, Prince of North Wales, all North Wales, who died without issue; and Anarawd, Prince of Powys, and Cadell, Prince of South Wales, of whom King Henry the Seventh descendet, by Gwenllian, daughter to Prince Rhys, called Arglwydd Rhys, wife to Ednyfed Fychan; and the said King Henry the Seventh is son to Rodri mawr in the seventeenth degree; which Rodri mawr was son to Merfyn, first King of Man, which wedded Essillt, daughter and heir to Cynan Dyndaethwy.

This Merfyn frych was son to Gwriad ap Elidur, ap Handdear Alcwn, ap Tegid, ap Gwiar, ap Dwywc, ap Llywarch hên, ap Elidur Lydanwin, ap Meirchion, ap Grwst, ap Ceuaw, ap Coel Godeboc, King of Britain, as before. This Coel was King of Britain and Earl of Colchester, a right worthy King, to whom King Henry the Seventh is son, by the said Gwenllian, wife to Ednyfed Fychan, in the thirty-first degree, by the said Guttin Owen, and Sir John Leiaf's books.

How OWEN, *grandsire to King Henry the Seventh, cometh of Beli Mawr, by* ESSILLT, *daughter to Cynan Dyndaethwy.*

Owen ap Meredith ap Tudor ap Gronw, ap Tudor ap Gronw, ap Gwenllian, daughter of Prince Rhys, ap Gruffydh ap Rhys, ap Tudor mawr, ap Engion, ab Owen, ap Howel Dda, ap Cadell, ap Rodri mawr, ap Essillt, daughter of Cynan Dyndaethwy, and heir, Prince of Wales, ap Rodri Moelwynoc, ap Idwal iwrch, ap Cadwalader Fendigaid, King of all Britain, to whom King Henry the Seventh is son in the twenty-second degree. Cadwalader was son to Cadwallen king, ap Cadfan king, ap Iago, ap Beli, ap Rhun, ap Maelgwn Gwynedd king, ap Casswallan Lawhîr, ap Eineon Irth, ap Cynedda weledig, ap Edeirn, which wedded Gwawl, ferch Coel Godeboc king, which Edeirn was son to Padarn Peisrydd, ap Tegid, ap Iago, ap Genedawc, ap Cain, ap Gwrgain, ap Doli, ap Gwrtholi, ap Dufu, ap Gorddufu, ap Amwerid, ap Omwedd, ap Diwc Brichwain, ap Owen, ap Afallach, ap Affiech, ap Beli mawr, to whom King Henry the Seventh is son by the said Gwenllian in the fiftieth degree.

Owen ap Meredith ap Tudor ap Gronw, ap Tudor ap Gronw, ap Gwenllian, daughter to Arglwydd Rhys, son to Gwenllian, daughter of Gruffydh prince, ap Cynan, Prince of North Wales, son of Iago prince, ap Idwall prince, ap Meuric prince, ap Idwall Foel Prince, ap Anarawd prince, ap Rodri mawr, Prince of all Wales, to whom King Henry the Seventh is son by Gwenllian, mother to the Arglwydd Rhys, in the seventeenth degree.

Owen ap Meredith ap Tudor ap Gronw, ap Tudor ap Gronw, ap Gwenllian, ferch Rhywallon ap Cynfyn Prince of Powys, and Angharad, wife to Cynfyn, daughter and heir to Meredith, Prince of Powys, son of Owen, Prince of Powys and South Wales, son to Cadell prince there. Which Owen ap Howell Dda had two sons, Meredith and Eineon, and Owen their father gave the Principality of South Wales to Eineon his son, and the Principality of Powys to Meredith, his other son. Which Meredith had issue Angharad, that wedded Cynfyn, by whom he was Prince of Powys, which Cadell was son to Rodri mawr Prince of all Wales, Son to Merfyn frych, &c., to Beli mawr, as above written by Guttin Owen's book.

Owen ap Meredith ap Tudor ap Gronw, ap Tudor, ap Gronw, ap Gwenllian, ferch Arglwydd Rhys, ap Gruffydh, ap Rhys, ap Tudor, ap Eineon, ap Eineon, ap Howell Dda, ap Cadell, ap Angharad, wife to Rodri mawr, daughter to Meyric ap Dyfnwal, ap Arthen, ap Seissillt, ap Clydawc, ap Artholes, ap Arnothen, ap Brothan, ap Seirwell, ap Ussa, ap Caredic, ap Cwnedda weledic, ap Edeirn, ap Padarn Peisvydd, which Edeirn wedded Gwawl ferch Coel Godeboc, mother to Cynedda wledic, &c.

How OWEN *cometh of Meuryc, Lord of Gwent, by Morfydd's daughter, wife to Gronw ap Ednyfed Fychan.*

Owen ap Meredith ap Tudor ap Gronw, ap Tudor, ap Morfydd, ferch Meuryc L. of Gwent.

How OWEN *cometh of Rodri Mawr, by* ANGHARAD, *daughter to Ithel Fychan, ap Ithel Llwyd, and wife of Tudor ap Gronw, ap Ednyfed Fychan.*

Owen ap Meredith ap Tudor ap Gronw, ap Angharad, ferch Ithel Fychan, ap Ithel Llwyd, ap Ithel Gam, ap Meredith ap Uchdrud, ap Edwin King of Tegeingle in Flintshire.

How OWEN *cometh of Rodri Mawr by* ADLEIS, *wife to Ithel Fychan, daughter to Ricart.*

Owen ap Meredith ap Tudor ap Gronw, ap Angharad ferch Adleis, wife to Ithel Fychan, daughter to Ricart, ap

Cadwalader, ap Gruffydh, ap Kynan Prince of North Wales, ap Iago, ap Idwal Foel, ap Anarawd, ap Rodri Mawr, &c. All
this by Gyttin Owen's Book.

*How OWEN cometh of Beli Mawr by GWEFILL FERCH MADAWC, o'r hên dwr, wife to Gronw ap Tudor, ap Gronw,
ap Ednyfed Fychan.*

Owen ap Meredith ap Tudor ap Gwerfill ferch Madawc o'r hên dwr, ap Iers, ap Madawc, ap Meredith, ap Bleddyn
ap Kynfyn, Prince of Powys, &c., and so to Beli Mawr.

How OWEN cometh to Beli Mawr by the mother of the said Gwerfill ferch Madawc.

Owen ap Meredith, ap Tudor, ap Gwerfil ferch Madawc o'r hên dwr, ap Lleucu ferch Angharad, ferch Meredith,
ap Madawc, ap Gruffdh Maelor, Prince of Powis. This Madawc ap Gruffudh Maelor, builded the Abby of Valecrucis, in
Welsh, Manschlog Llan Egwestl, the year of our Lord 1200, and lyeth there buried, and this Gruffudh Maelor was son to
Madawc, ap Meredith, ap Bleddyn, ap Cynfyn, ap Gwestan, ap Gwalthfoed, ap Gwrydor, ap Cariadawc, ap Lles Llaw Ddeawc,
ap Edwal, ap Gwnnan, ap Gwynnawe Farf Sych, ap Keidic, ap Corf, ap Cadnawc, ap Tegonwy, ap Teon, ap Gwinof
Daufreuddwyd, ap Powyr lêw, ap Bywdec, ap Rhun rhudd baladr, ap Llary, ap Casfar Wledic, ap Lludd, ap Beli Mawr,
King of all England and Wales, to whom King Henry the Seventh is son this way by Ludd in thirty-six degrees.

How OWEN cometh to Beli Mawr by the mother's side of Gwersill ferch Madawc.

Owen ap Meredith, ap Tudor, ap Gwerfil ferch Eva, ferch Llewelyn ap Gruffydh, ap Gwenwynwin, ap Owen,
Cyfeilioc, ap Gruff, ap Madawc, ap Meredith of Powis, ap Bleddyn, ap Cynfin, &c. to Beli Mawr.

Owen ap Meredith ap Tudor ap Gwerfil ferch Eva, ferch Margret, ferch Meredith gôch, ap Meredith, ap Iers Fychan,
ap Iers gôch, ap Meredith ap Bleddyn, ap Cynfin, &c., to Beli.

Owen ap Meredith ap Tudor, ap Gwerfyl, ferch Eva, ferch Margret, ferch Meredith gôch, ap Christin, ap Bledrws,
ap Edwal Owen Bendew, one of the fifteen tribes of North Wales, son to Cynan Feiniard ap Gwalthfoed, ap Gwlyddien, ap
Gwridor, ap Caradawc, ap Lles Llaw ddeawc, ap Edwal, ap Gwnnan, ap Gwnnawc Farf sych, ap Ceidio, ap Corf, ap
Cadnawc, an Tegonwy, ap Teon, ap Gwinau dau Freuddwyd, &c., and so to Beli.

Owen ap Meredith, ap Margret ferch Tomas, ap Llewelin, ap Owen ap Meredith, Lord Iscoed, ap Owen, ap Gruffydh,
ap Rhys, Prince of South Wales, so to Rodri Mawr.

Owen ap Meredith, ap Margret, ferch Tomas ap Llywelin, ap Angharad, ferch Arglwydd Sion. John of Hasson by
William ap David ap Gruffydh. Dubium.

Owen ap Meredith, ap Margret, ferch Tomas ap Llewelyn, ap Angharad ferch Margret, ferch Philip, ap Isor Lord
Iscoed by William ap Gruffydh. Dubium.

Owen ap Meredith, ap Margret, ferch Tomas ap Llewelyn, ap Angharad, ferch Margret, ferch Angharad, ferch
Llewelyn ap Iers drwyndwn, Prince of all Wales. This Llewelyn wedded Iuet, daughter of King John, which was son to
Henry the Second, son to Mawd the Empress, daughter to Henry the First, son to William the Conqueror, son to Robert
Duke of Normandy.

Owen ap Meredith, ap Margret, ferch Tomas ap Elinor ferch . . . . . Lord Barre by Gyttin Owen, by information
of Dr. Owen Pool, and Mr. Lingham's wife by an old pedigree.

Owen ap Meredith, ap Margret, ferch Tomas ap Elinor, ferch Elinor, ferch Edward Longshanks, King of England.

Owen ap Meredith, ap Margret, ferch Tomas, ap Elinor ferch Elinor, ferch Elinor second son to King Edward
abovesaid. Dubium.

Owen ap Meredith, ap Margret, ferch Elinor ferch Meredith, ap Owen, ap Gruffydh, ap Rhys, Prince of South Wales,
by Madawc ap Llewelyn ap Howel his books.

Owen ap Meredith, ap Margret, ferch Elinor, ferch Catrin, ferch Llewelyn ap Gruffydh last Prince of Wales.

Owen ap Meredith, ap Margret, ferch Elinor, ferch Llewelyn ap Gruffydh, ap Tangwistl, ferch Llywarch gôch, ap
Lhowarch ap Pyll, ap Cynan, ap Einion ap Gwridor gôch, ap Helic, ap Glannawc, ap Gwgon Gleddyfrudd, ap Cariadawc
Freichfras, ap Elir Merini, ap Einion irth, ap Cunedda wledic.

Owen ap Meredith, ap Margret, ferch Elinor, ferch Caterin, ferch Elinor ap Gruffydh, ap Tangwistl, ferch Tangwistl,
ferch Llowarch, ap Bran, ap Dinawal, ap Efnydd, ap Alawe Alser, ap Tudwal, ap Rodri mawr: by Gyttin Owen.

Owen ap Meredith, ap Margret, ferch Elinor Fychan, ferch Simon Montford, Earl of Leicester: by Gyttin Owen.

Owen ap Meredith, ap Margaret, ferch Elinor, ferch Caterin, ferch Elinor Fychan, ferch Elinor, ferch John King
of England.

Hereafter followeth the ancient lineage of the said OWEN's mother, MARGARET, wife to Meredith ap Tudor :—

Owen ap Margaret, ferch Dafydd Fychan, ap Dafydd Llwyd, ap Cyner, ap Gronw, ap Cyner, ap Iers, ap Hwfa, ap Cwmus, ap Cillin, ap Maeloc dda, ap Gredef, ap Kwmus du, ap Cillin Ynad, ap Predur Teirnoe, ap Meilir Eryr, gwyr gorsedd, ap Tiday, ap Tyfodde, ap Gwybfyw, ap Marchwin, ap Bran ap Pill, ap Cerfyr, ap Meilir Melirion, ap Goron, ap Cunedda wledic, ap Gwawl ferch Coel Godeboc, as before.

Owen ap Margret, ferch Dafydd Fychan, ap Dafydd Clwyd, ap Cyner, ap Gronw, ap Cyner, ap Iers, ap Hwfa, ap Generis ferch Ednowain Bendew, ap Cynon Finiaid, ap Gwarthfoed, ap Gwridr ap Cradoc, ap Lles llaw ddeuawc, ap Edwal, ap Gwynnan : and so to Ludd, ap Beli mawr, as before by Gyttin Owen.

Owen ap Margret, ferch Dafydd Fychan, ap Dafydd Lhwyd ap Cyner, ap Llaysedd daughter to Sir William Twychet, Knight, by William. Indub.

Owen ap Margret, ferch Dafydd Fychan, ap Dafydd Lhwyd, ap Alis, ferch Robert, ap Turstan Holland Capitain of Harlech : by William.

Owen ap Margret, ferch Dafydd Fychan, ap Dafydd Lhwyd, ap Alis, ferch Margret, ferch Alan Norris, Knight, by William. Indub.

Owen ap Margret, ferch Dafydd Fychan, ap Angharad, ferch Howel ap Meredith, ap Iers, ap Cadwgan, ap Llywarch, ap Bran, as before, &c.

Owen ap Margaret ferch Dafydd Fychan, ap Angharad ferch Howell ap Meredith, ap Iers, ap Gwenllian, ferch Cynan ap Owen Gwynedd, ap Gruffydh ap Cynan, &c.

Owen ap Margret, ferch Dafydd Fychan, ap Angharad, ferch Owen ap Bleddin, ap Owen Brogennwn, ap Madawc, ap Meredith, ap Bleddin, ap Cynfin Prince of Powis ; these three by Gyttin Owen.

Owen ap Margret, ferch Dafydd Fychan, ap Angharad, ferch Gwladis, ferch Llewelin gethni, ap Edwal, ap Gruffydh, ap Meuric, ap Cadhayarn, ap Gwrydd, ap Rhys gôch, one of the fifteen tribes of North Wales ; which was son to Sandwr ap Iarddwr, ap Mor, ap Tegerin, ap Aelaw, ap Gredres, ap Cwmus du, ap Cilliu Ynad, &c., to Coel Godeboc.

Owen ap Margret, ferch Dafydd Fychan, ap Angharad, ferch Gwladus, ferch Mali Llwyd, ferch Iers ap Engion, ap Geraint, ap Tegwared, ap Cynfawr, ap Madawc diffaeth, which were rulers and great men in Pentraeth.

Owen ap Margret, ferch Nest, ferch Jermy, ap Gruffydh, ap Howell, ap Meredith, ap Engion, ap Gwgon, ap Merwydd, ap Golwyn, one of the fifteen tribes of North Wales, son to Tangno, ap Cadfael, ap Lludd, ap Llen, ap Llaminod Angel, ap Pasgen, ap Urien Rheged, ap Meirchion, ap Grwst, ap Cennaf, ap Coel godeboc King, as before.

Owen ap Margret, ferch Nest, ferch Jermy, ap Gwerfill, ferch Gwladus, ferch Edwal Fychan, as before.

Owen ap Margret ferch Nest, ferch Angharad, ferch Gruffydh, ap Dafydd gôch, ap Gruffydh, ap Llewelyn Prince of Wales.

Owen ap Margaret ferch Nest, ferch Angharad, ferch Gruffydh ap Dafydd gôch, ap Dafydd, ap Gruffydh, ap Tangwistl, ferch Llowarch gôch, ap Llowarch Holbwrch, ap Pill, ap Cynan, ap Gwridor gôch, ap Helic, ap Glannoc as before.

Owen ap Margret ferch Nest, ferch Angharad, ferch Gruffydh, ap Dafydd gôch, ap Rhanullt, ferch Rheinallt King of Man.

Owen ap Margret ferch Nest, ferch Angharad, ferch Gruffydh, ap Angharad, ferch Heylyn, ap Tudor, ap Ednyfed Fychan.

Owen ap Margret ferch Nest, ferch Angharad, ferch Gruffydh, ap Angharad, ferch Heylyn, ap Adleir, ferch Ricart, ap Cadwalader, ap Gruffydh, ap Cynan Prince. These four by Gyttin Owen.

Owen ap Margret ferch Nest, ferch Angharad, ferch Gruffydh, ap Angharad, ferch Heylyn, ap Adleis, ferch Ricart, ap Cadwalader, ap Gruffydh, ap Cynan, ap Afandrec wife to Iago, daughter to Gwayr, ap Pill, ap Cynan, ap Cynddelw gam, ap Elgudi, ap Grwyfnad, ap Diwgludd, ap Tegawc, ap Cyfnerth, ap Madoc Madogion, ap Sauddl bryd Angel, ap Llywarch hên, ap Elidor Ludanwin, ap Meirchion gûl, ap Erwst galedlwm, ap Cenaw, ap Coel godeboc King, as before.

Owen ap Margaret ferch Nest, ferch Angharad, ferch Marret, ferch Tudor, ap Iers, ap Ewrgwnon, ap Cyfnerth, ap Rhuon, ap Nefydd hardd, one of the fifteen tribes of North Wales.

Owen ap Margaret ferch Nest, ferch Angharad, ferch Margaret, ferch Tangwistl, ferch Madawc, ap Cyfnerth, ap Cyhelyn, ap Llywarch Fychan, ap Llywarch gôch, ap Llowarch Holbwrch, ap Pill, ap Cynon, ap Gwrydr gôch, ap Helic ap Glannoc, ap Gwgon gleddyfrudd, ap Cariadoc freich fras, ap Glir Meirini, ap Engion yrth, ap Cynedda wledic, by Gyttin Owen.

Abstracted out of the old Chronicles of Wales, by Sir John Leiaf, priest, Guttin Owen, Gruffydh ap Llewelyn ap Jermy, Fychan Madawc ap Llewelyn ap Howell, Robert ap Howell ap Thomas, John King, with many others, at the King's Majesty's costs and charges. The Abbot of Llanegwestle, and Dr. Owen Pool, Canon of Harf, Overseers.

The following short Pedigree will show at one view the descent of Henry VII. from Sir Owen Tudor:—

Owen Tudor, of Penmynydd, in Anglesea, = Katherine of France, widow of Henry V., and mother of Henry VII.

Jasper Tudor, Earl of Pembroke.

Edmund, Earl of Richmond, = Jane, only daughter and heir of John Beaufort, third Marquis of Dorset, Earl of Kendal, and Duke of Somerset.

Henry VII., = Elizabeth, daughter of Edward IV.

Henry VIII.

Henry may be considered as the great restorer of the Royal Line of England. He terminated the agitations and dangers which threatened the monarchy, which had almost become like a Polish sovereignty, an aristocracy of many petty kings; obeying the nominal and paramount sovereign no longer than they pleased; and choosing or deposing him, and changing the dynasty, as it chanced to gratify their passions or to suit their varied interests. Henry VII. put an end to this state of things. He established the monarchy on a firm basis; and though frequent attempts were made during his reign to renew those disorders, he crushed every incipient rebellion and kept his unruly nobles in due subjection to the throne. One of his greatest aims was to rescue the government from the dictatorial tyranny, both of the nobility and of the Church establishment, each of which had, at various periods, threatened and subverted it; and to rest it on the general interests and affections and prosperity of the country. He considered the whole nation as one great family, headed by himself, and he depressed the two classes that had so long maintained a disproportionate degree of power, to the prejudice of the universal improvement and comfort of all.

The carrying out of these plans necessarily produced much obloquy; yet, even in his own days, his merit was felt amid all the opposing interest and prejudices that attacked him; and so much was his wisdom esteemed by his contemporaries, that he was called a Second Solomon.[6] He was so respected abroad, that three popes elected him, before all the other reigning monarchs, as the chief "Defensor" of Christendom, and sent him, by three successive embassies, three swords, and caps of maintenance.[7] He conquered his numerous enemies by his great policy and wisdom, more than by the shedding of blood or cruel war.[8]

That Henry acted upon the principle of making the law the master of all, we see by the speech he caused to be made to the parliament in January, 1503, on the inestimable value to every state of justice and law. The Chancellor forced on their attention, that justice was the queen of virtues, and without it kingdoms were but great dens of robbers; that all estates were upheld by the laws, and that justice was their architect; that it was the most honourable, the most useful, and the most pleasant of all things. His eloquent oration, ending with this peroration from St. Austin; "Despise dungeons, despise bonds, despise exiles, despise death—but let all men love justice," is said to have had a wonderful effect in animating the distinguished hearers, to an ardent attachment to this great social virtue.[9] But the introduction of this improvement in our legislation, instead of being referred to his discerning policy, or to his philanthropy, has been imputed only to his avarice, and stigmatised as rapacity.[1] Yet the nation felt his value, became steadily attached to his family, and improved under their government, far more than under any prior dynasty. The direct male line ceased in Queen Elizabeth, but the descendants of his daughter Margaret succeeded in the person of the first Stuart. The superior Brunswick line, which has given stability to our civil and religious liberties, and advanced our natural progression and accomplishments, which is now represented by Her Most Gracious Majesty, Queen Victoria, is also a branch of Henry's descendants.

---

[6] Fabian, who lived at the time, says, "he may most congruly, above all earthly princes, be called the Second Solomon, for his great sapience and acts."

[7] Fabian, p. 537.   [8] See Parl. Rolls, vi. p. 440.
[9] See this speech in Parl. Rolls, vi. p. 520.
[1] Blackstone, iv. p. 422.

Though the Welsh had the strongest claim on Henry VII., as a countryman who owed his elevation to the throne in a great degree to their arms, their condition, as a nation, was but little ameliorated during his reign. Though no oppressive statutes were added, those already enacted by Henry IV. and Henry VI. were not repealed, and were of themselves sufficiently galling. The almost unlimited power of the Lords Marchers was still in existence, and exercised with the greatest severity.[2] Nevertheless Henry's mild reign and lenient measures prepared the way for brighter days and more equitable laws, which were enacted by his successor, Henry VIII.[3]

HENRY THE EIGHTH.—This sovereign, as far as we can discover, was never in Wales, but we find him occasionally on the Borders. With all his faults we will say, that to him belongs the distinguished honour of uniting England and Wales in the bonds of equal rights and equal justice. This Prince followed his father's steps in doing away with the power of the Lords Marchers, and instituting and passing other salutary acts, which did honour to his humanity and judgment. He acknowledged the loyalty of his Welsh subjects, recognised their just claims, and with the soundest policy united a refractory nation to the English dominions by a statute passed for that purpose, which enacted, "that his subjects in Wales shall for ever enjoy, and inherit, all singular freedom, liberties, rights, privileges, and laws, which his subjects elsewhere enjoy and inherit." Henry acted in this instance with the same generous feeling of triumph as was practised by the Republic of Rome itself, in admitting the vanquished provinces to partake of the privileges of Roman citizens. The effects and benefits of these means were immediate and permanent, and should be resorted to in every instance of the sort.

Though the policy of Edward I. had allowed the Welsh nation to enjoy their liberties, and to hold their estates by their ancient tenures, they had for a long period much reason to complain of the excessive rigour which had been exercised over them by the officers of justice, and the rapacity of the English barons who had settled in Wales.

The powers of the Lord Marchers were still in their full force, and were exercised with such severity upon the Welsh as to render an act of parliament necessary in the reign of Henry VIII. The statute is to the following purpose:—

"WHEREAS many robberies, murders, and other evil practices, have been daily committed in the county palatine of Chester, and Flintshire, in Wales; and also in Anglesey, Caernarvon, Merionydd, Cardigan, Caermarthen, Pembroke, and Glamorgan, because justice is not administered there in such form as in other places of this realm: for the remedy of this, it is enacted that the Lord Chancellor of England, or keeper of the great seal, shall nominate and appoint justices of the peace, justices of the quorum, and justices of the gaol delivery in the said counties, and that they shall have like power and authority as those in England."

This statute in some measure lessened the evils complained of, as it was the means of keeping offenders in awe, they not being able as before to escape, and to flee from one Lordship Marcher to another; it also placed the administration of justice on a more stable foundation. Another evil had likewise

[2] The records of barbarism cannot show a more heavy penalty, for a trifling offence, than forfeiting a joint of the hand for deviating a number of feet from the highway!

[3] "This monarch was extremely fond of pageantry, and he was particularly anxious about the ceremonials of his coronation. The Londoners seconded his desires, and when, after having created twenty-four knights of the Bath, he rode through London from the Tower, June 22, 1509, the streets were hung with tapestry and cloth of arras, and a great part of the south side of Cheap and part of Cornhill were hung with cloth of gold. The several companies and civic dignitaries lined the streets; and Hall tells us, "The gold-smiths' stall unto the end of the Old Change, being replenished with virgins in white, with branches of white wax; the priestes and clearkes in rich copes, with crosses and censers of silver, censing his grace and the queene also as they passed. The Queene Katherine was sitting in hir litter, borne by two white palfries, the litter covered and richlie apparelled, and the palfries trapped in white cloth of gold; hir person apparelled in white satin imbroidered, hir haire hanging downe to hir backe, beautifull and goodlie to behold, and on hir head a coronall set with manie rich orient stones. The coronation was celebrated with brilliant justs and turneies, which the king and queen witnessed from a faire house covered with tapestrie."—*Coronation Anecdotes.*

arisen which strongly marked the oppression of the times, for the remedy of which a succeeding statute was judged necessary, and was to the following effect:—

"WHEREAS, in Wales and in the Marches, there are many forests belonging either to the King or to the Lord Marchers, wherein sundry actions have been committed for a long time, contrary to the law of God and man; insomuch that if any person entered the said forests without a token given him by any of the foresters as a license to pass, or unless he was a yearly *tributer* or *cheuser,* he was forced to pay a grievous fine; and if he should chance to be found twenty-four feet out of the highway, he was then to forfeit all the gold or money which was found on his person, and likewise a joint of one of his hands, unless he was fined for the offence at the discretion of the forester or farmer of the same: and whereas, likewise, if any cattle strayed into the said forests it was the custom of the foresters to mark them for their own, with the mark of the forest, &c."

By this statute it was enacted that people should pass through these forests as freely as in other places; and that strayed cattle, within a year and a day, should be restored to the right owners, they only paying a compensation for the herbage.

These statutes, restraining the power of the Lord Marchers, were some years after succeeded by another act of parliament, which rendered these lords no longer the objects of terror, and entirely destroyed their judicial authority:—

"WHEREAS, by the gifts of the Kings of England, many of the most ancient prerogatives and authorities of justice appertaining to the imperial crown of this realm have been severed and taken from the same; it was then enacted, that no person should have power and authority to pardon or to remit treasons, murders, manslaughters, or any felonies, or their accessories in any part of England, Wales, or in the Marches of the same: likewise that no person should make justices of oyer, justices of assize, justices of peace, or justices of gaol delivery, but they should in future be made only by the King's letters patent, and that all original writs, judicial writs, and all manner of indictments for treason, felony and trespass, and all manner of process should be only made in the King's name, and that all offences committed against the peace, should be considered as offences committed against the King, and not against the peace of any other person, &c."

The excessive powers, which had been anciently invested in those persons who enjoyed counties palatine and *jura regalia* in Lordships Marchers, being thus taken away, a more regular and uniform course of justice was established, and, in consequence, the disorders continually occurring within these precincts, were, in a great measure, prevented.

Though these humane and salutary statutes had relieved the Welsh from many of their sufferings, the line of distinction was still preserved, and they yet remained as a separate people; a distinction contrary to all just ideas of government, and which could only serve to keep alive their national prejudices. But the Welsh themselves, and it may be recorded to their honour, solicited Henry VIII. that he would extend his liberal designs, and would give them a more salutary effect. The petition itself, which they sent to that monarch, will best show their extensive views and manly spirit, as well as the nature and justice of their claims:—

" MAY IT PLEASE YOUR HIGHNESS:—We, on the part of your Highness's subjects, inhabiting that portion of the island which our invaders first called Wales, most humbly prostrate at your Highness's feet, do crave to be received and adopted into the same laws and privileges which your other subjects enjoy: neither shall it hinder us (we hope) that we have lived so long under our own. For as they were both enacted by authority of our ancient lawgivers, and obeyed for many succession of ages, we trust your Highness will pardon us, if we thought it neither easy nor safe so suddenly to relinquish them. We shall not presume to compare them with those now used, and less shall we contest how good and equal in themselves they are. Only if the defence of them and our liberty against the Romans, Saxons, and Danes, for so many hundred years, and lastly against the Normans, as long as they pretended no title but the sword, was thought just and

R R

honourable, we presume it will not be infamous now; and that all the marks of rebellion and falsehood which our revilers would fasten on us, will fall on any sooner than those who fought for so many years, and with so many different nations, for our just defence, which also is so true that our best historians affirm the Christian religion to have been preserved only by us for many years, that the Saxons (being heathens), either attempted to possess or possessed this country. May your Highness then graciously interpret our actions, while we did but that duty which your Highness would have now done by your subjects on like occasion; for when any should invade this country henceforth, we know your Highness would have us behave ourselves no otherwise. Besides, had not the assailers found some resistance, they might have despised a country that brought none forth able enough to assert it; so that we crave pardon, sir, if we say it was fit for the honour of your dominions that some part of it should never be conquered. We then, in the name of whatsoever in your Highness's possession hath in any age held out against all invaders, do here voluntarily resign and humble ourselves to that sovereignty, which we acknowledge so well invested in your Highness. Nor is this the first time; we have always attended on occasion to unite ourselves to the greater and better part of the island.

"But as kings of this realm, weary of their attempts in person against us, did formerly give, not only our country to those who could conquer it, but permitted them *jura regalia* within their several precincts; so it was impossible to come to an agreement, while so many that undertook this work, usurped martial and absolute power and jurisdiction in all they acquired, without establishing any equal justice. And that all offenders flying from one Lordship Marcher (for so they were termed) to another, did both avoid the punishment of the law, and easily commit those robberies which formerly tainted the honour of our parts; so that until the rigorous laws, not only of the several conquerors of England, but the attempters on our parts were brought to an equal moderation, no union, how much so ever affected by us, could ensue.

"Therefore, and not sooner, we submitted ourselves to Edward I., a prince who made both many and more equal laws than any before him: therefore, we defended his son, Edward II., when not only the English forsook him, but ourselves might have recovered our former liberty had we desired it. Therefore, we got victories for Edward III., and stood firm during all the dissensions of this realm to his grandchild and successor, Richard II. Only, if some amongst us resisted Henry IV., your Highness may better suppose the reason than we tell it; though divers foreigners openly refused to treat with him as a sovereign and lawful prince, have sufficiently published it, we did not yet decline a due obedience to Henry V., though in doubtful times we cannot deny that many refractory persons have appeared. Howsoever we never joined ourselves with the English rebels, or took occasion thereby to recover our liberty, though in Richard II.'s time, and during all the civil wars between Lancaster and York, much occasion was given for adhering to the House of York, which we conceived the better title: we conserved our devotion still to the crown until your Highness's father's time, who (bearing his name and blood from us) was the more cheerfully assisted by our predecessors in his title to the crown, which your Highness does presently enjoy. And thus, sir, if we gave anciently proof of a generous courage in defending our laws and country, we have given no less proof of our loyal fidelity since we first rendered ourselves, in so much, that we may truly affirm, that after one acceptance of the condition given us by Edward I., we have omitted no occasion of performing the duty of loving subjects. Neither is there anything that comforts us more than all those controversies about succession (which so long wasted this land) are determined in your Highness's person, in whom we acknowledge both Houses happily united.

"To your Highness therefore we offer all obedience, desiring only that we may be defended against the insults of our malignant censurers; for we are not the offspring of runaway Britons (as they term us), but natives of a country which, besides defending itself, received all those who came to us for succour. Give us then, sir, permission to say that they wrong us much who pretend that our country was not inhabited before them, or that it failed in a due piety, when it was so hospitable to all that fled thither for refuge; which also will be more creditable when it shall be remembered that it furnished good beef and mutton, not only to all the inhabitants, but supply to England in great quantity. We humbly beseech your Highness, therefore, that this note may be taken from us. As for our language, though it seems harsh, it is that yet which was spoken anciently, not only in this island, but in France; some dialects whereof remain still in use amongst the *Bas-Bretons* there, and here in Cornwall. Neither will any man doubt it, when he shall find those words of the ancient Gaulish language repeated by the Latin authors, to signify the same thing amongst us at this day; nor shall it be a disparagement (we hope) that it is spoken so much in the throat, since the Florentine and Spaniard affect this kind of pronunciation, as believing words that sound so deep proceed from the heart: so that if we have retained this language longer than the more northern inhabitants of this island (whose speech appears manifestly to be a kind of English, and consequently introduced by the Saxons), we hope that it will be no imputation to us; your Highness will have but the more tongues to serve you; it shall not hinder us to study English, were it but to learn how we might better serve and obey your Highness, to whose laws we most humbly desire again to be adopted; and doubt not, but if in all countries the mountains have afforded as eminent wits and spirits as any other part, ours also by your Highness's good favour and employment may receive that esteem."

Henry having considered the loyalty of his Welsh subjects and the reasonable nature of their claim, ordered the following statute to be enacted in parliament, which entirely united Wales with his English dominions, regarding, no doubt, such union to be an object of sound policy :—

"THAT, as the dominion, principality, and country of Wales is a member and part of the temporal crown of this realm, whereof, therefore, the King is head and ruler; yet as it hath divers rights, usages, laws, and customs of this realm, and because the language of that country is different from that which is spoken here, and that many rude people hereupon have made distinction and diversity betwixt his Highness's other subjects and them, to the causing of much discord and sedition; his Highness, therefore, out of his love and favour to his subjects in Wales, *and for reducing them* to his laws, doth by advice and consent of his parliament ordain and enact that Wales shall *be united and incorporated henceforth with his realm of England*, and that his *subjects in Wales shall enjoy* and inherit all singular freedoms, liberties, rights, privileges, and laws *which his Highness's subjects* elsewhere enjoy and inherit. And, therefore, that inheritances shall descend after the manner of England, without division or partition, and not after *any tenure or form of Welsh laws or custom*. And forasmuch as there are divers Lordship Marchers within the said county or dominion in Wales, being no parcels of any other shires where the laws and due correction is used and had, and that in them and the counties adjoining, manifold murders, robberies, felonies, and the like have been done contrary to all law and justice, because the offenders, making their refuge from one lordship to another, were continued without punishment or correction; therefore it is enacted, that the said Lordship Marchers shall be united, annexed, and joined to divers shires specified in the said act."

This statute was put into immediate execution, the utility of which has been fully justified by the experience of more than three centuries.[8] During this time the genius of the Welsh nation has taken a different turn, has composed itself to rational obedience, and has been directed to those pursuits which tend to polish their manners, to enlarge their views, and to cultivate their minds; and, by consequence, to promote the happiness of individuals, as well as the best interest of the state.

A.D. 1538.—The following remarkable documents, written by one of our countrymen to Lord Cromwell, will give an idea of the scenes which took place during the suppression of the monasteries by Henry VIII.

From Ellis Price, Commissary-General of the Diocese of St. Asaph, to Lord Cromwell, A.D. 1538.

"RIGHT HONORABLE AND MY SYNGULAR GOODE LORDE AND MAYSTER.—All circumstauncys and thankes sett aside, pleasithe yt youre good lordeshipe to be advertisid, that where I was constitute and made, by youre honorable desire and commaundmente, Commissarie-Generall of the dyosese of Saynte Assaph, I have done my dylygens and dutie for the expulsinge and takynge awaye of certan abusions, supersticions, and ipocryses, usid within the said diosece of Saynte Assaph, accordynge to the Kynge's honorable acts and injunctions therin made. That notwithstondinge there ys an Image of Darvellgadarn, within the saide diosece, in whome the people have so greate confidence, hope, and trust, that they cumme dayly a pillgramage unto hym, some with kyne, other with oxen or horsis, and the reste withe money: in so muche that there was fyve or syxe hundredthe pillgrames to a man's estimacion, that offered to the saide Image the fifte daie of this presente monthe of Aprill. The innocente people hathe ben sore aluryd and entisid to worshipe the said Image, in so muche that there is a commyn sayinge as yet amongist them that who so ever will offer anie thinge to the said Image of Dervel Gadern, he hathe power to fatche hym or them that so offers oute of hell when they be dampned. Therfore for the reformacion and amendment of the premisses, I wolde gladlie knowe by this berer your honorable pleasure and will; as knowithe God, who ever preserve your lordeshipe longe in welthe and honor. Writen in Northe Wales."

The further history of the Image of Darvel Gadern is detailed in our Chronicles. It was brought to London and burnt with Friar Forest in Smithfield, of which Hall gives the following account.

"And a little before the execution, a huge and great image was brought to the gallows, which image was brought out of Wales, and of the Welshmen much sought and worshipped. This image was called Dervel Gadern, and the Welshmen

---

[8] Though this monarch was the stern and cruel son of a mild father, and was more intent upon gratifying the passions of human nature, than for promoting the advancement of literature, yet he did not refuse to the bards his smiles and favour. As an instance, we insert the following summons for holding an Eisteddfod, issued by this king's authority :—" BE IT KNOWN TO ALL PERSONS, both gentry and commonalty, that an Eisteddfod of the professors of Poetry and Music will be held in the town of Caerwys, in the county of Flint, the 2nd day of July, 1523, and the 15th year of the reign of Henry VIII. King of England, under the commission of the said king, before Richard ap Howel ap Joan Vaughan, Esq., by the consent of Sir William Griffith and Sir Roger Salisbri; and the advice of Griffith ap Joan ap Llewelyn Vaughan, and the chair-bard, Tudor Aled, and several other gentlemen and scholars, for the purpose of instituting order and government among the professors of Poetry and Music, and regulating their art and profession."

had a prophecy that this image should set a whole forest a fire, which prophecy now took effect, for he set this Friar Forest on fire and consumed him to nothing. This Friar, when he saw the fire come, and that present death was at hand, caught hold upon the ladder, which he would not let go, but so unpaciently took his death, that no man that ever put his trust in God never so unquietly nor so ungodly ended his life. If men might judge him by his outward man, he appeared to have little knowledge of God and his sincere truth, and less trust in him at his ending." [*]

From the following interesting particulars extracted by Messrs. Owens and Blakeway, from the Corporation records in Shrewsbury, we find the Court in frequent communication with that town.

" Michaelmas, 2 to 3 Hen. VIII., 1510—1511.

" Sol' in regardo dat' nuncio portanti rumores magni gaudii de nativitate Principis filii Regis."

" Paid in reward to a messenger bearing news of great joy of the birth of a Prince, son of the King, 10s."

The joy on this occasion was of short continuance. Queen Katherine was delivered of a prince on New Year's Day, and the event was celebrated with banquets, tournaments, and processions. He was baptised by the name of Henry, but lived only till the 23rd of February, or 21st of September following : for our historians differ on this point.

" Michaelmas, 7 to 8 Hen. VIII., 1515—1516.

" In regardo dato nuncio d'ni Reg' portanti & nuncianti eis novos & jocundos rumores de nativitate Principisae & filie dicti d'ni Reg'."

" Reward to a messenger of our Lord the King bearing and announcing to the bailiffs new and joyful rumours of the birth of a Princess and daughter of our said Lord the King, 6s. 8d."

The hopes of Henry, after being again defeated, A.D. 1514, by the death of another son, were at length in some degree gratified by the birth of a daughter (afterwards Queen Mary) on the 18th of February, A.D. 1516-17 : though Carte says on the 11th.

" In regardo dato Rogero Hamerton armigero clerico mercati hospitii d'ni R' pro favore suo."

" Reward to Roger Hamerton, Esq., clerk of the market of the hostel of our Lord the King for his favour, 20d."

A.D. 1521.—The following entry appears in the bailiff's book :

" Vino dat' Griffino Rees militi alio comiss' d'ni R'."

" Wine to Sir Griffin Rees, knight, another commissioner of our Lord the King, 10d." [1]

Sir Griffyth Ryce (as he is called on his monument) was son of Sir Rhys ap Thomas, of whom we have formerly made mention. He attended his sovereign in his interview with Francis I., on which pompous occasion he was one of the *sceurers* with light horse, and had an hundred men under his command.[*] Sir

---

[*] It is astonishing how apt the commonalty is, in its popular likings and dislikings, to express its feelings in doggrell. Upon the gallows was set up in great letters the following verses :—

" David Darvell Gatheren,
    As saith the Welshmen,
        Fetched outlawes out of Hell.
Now is he come with spere and shilde
In harnes to burn in Smithfelde,
    For in Wales he may not dwell.

" And Forest the Frier,
    That obstinate lyer,
        That witfully shall be dead !
In his contumacie
The Gospel doth deny
    The Kyng to be supreme head."

[1] A vintner's bill of the reign of Henry VIII. may be thought too trifling for these pages. Yet its solemn commencement will show how much the feelings, at least the forms, of religion, pervaded every department of society at that time :—

                                    " Jhu
    " Mr. Bales,
" Item, you send Thomas a Bromley a pottel of clartt wyne, 4d.

" Item, Ryc' Atkis dranke this same tyme the clartt wyne and sugar, 4d.
" Item, Mr. Bales dranke the wyne and sug^r on Sent Janys even und^r paradeysse, when you whent to Bewdley, 2s. 2d.
" Item, yow send Mr. Hanmer a pottell of Rum'ey, 6d.
" Item, yow send Mr. Thornys by ys servand a pottell of Malsy, 8d.
" Item, yow spend apon my lade prynssys pleyyears, 3s. 10d.
                                    " Per me MAKEWORTH.
        " Expenses at the Newport.
" A samon morte and a troute, 19d.
" Spende upon the commissioners at after none in wyne, ale, and sugar, 11d.
" For carriege of fyshe to Newport, 2d.
" For shewynge of Mr. Mitton's horse, 2d.
" Mr. Bales gave the lord of Aldmon Parke a gallon of gaskyne wyne und^r paradeysse, 8d.
" To Mr. Schereve a pottell of Ossey, 8d.
" Item, Mr. Bales spend upon ther breyke fast when my m^r whent to the councill.
                                    " Per me JOHN MAKEWORTH."
Paradise appears to have been a house of public entertainment.

[*] See the list printed by Dr. Ducarel at the end of his Anglo-Norman Antiquities, from a MS. in the Lambeth library.

Griffith increased that favour of the crown to which he was entitled from the services of his father, by marriage with a second cousin of the King, Katherine St. John of Bletsoe,[2] was made a Knight of the Bath at the creation of Arthur Prince of Wales, whose banner he bore at his funeral in the cathedral of Worcester; and deceasing in the life-time of his father, September 29th, 1522, in the forty-third year of his age, was interred in the same church under a "fair raised monument in the south cross aile, commonly called the Dean's chapel."

"Vino dat' Magistro Magno Doctori ac commissionario d'ni R' & sociis suis inquirentibz de tr'is & tenementis Edwardi nup' ducis Bukhyngh'm mortui."	"Wine given to Master Doctor Magnus, commissioner of our Lord the King, and his fellow, enquiring concerning the lands and tenements of Edward late Duke of Buckingham, deceased, 2d."

This great peer, whose father we have seen arrested near Shrewsbury and brought to a scaffold, himself fell a victim to the hatred of Wolsey, the timid suspicions of Henry, and his own indiscretion, and was beheaded, May 17th, 1521. But fear for the succession was not the King's only passion: rapacity constituted an equal portion of his character; though, as he lavished his treasures with profusion, the misdeeming world awarded to him the praise of liberality. The Duke's son, Henry Lord Stafford, the inoffensive, the unoffending, the learned and the pious, was stripped of nearly all the vast estates of his father, and Dr. Thomas Magnus, with others his associates, was sent, as we see, to assess the value of the forfeited property.

"From Michaelmas, 19 to 20 Hen. VIII, 1527—1528.

"Sol p' expensis ballivor' scrutancium p' frugibus & granis p' mandatum d'ni R'."	"Paid the expences of the bailiffs searching for corn and grain by command of our Lord the King, 6s. 5d."
"In regardo & vin' dat' nuncio d'ni R' portanti commissiones circa ordinem lanar' & libros *Martini Luter*."	"Reward and wine given to a messenger of our Lord the King bearing commissions touching the order of wools, and the books of *Martin Luther*, 2s. 1d."

Neither Fox nor Burnet mention any act of the English government in so early a year, respecting the greatest moral revolution which mankind has witnessed since the establishment of Christianity in the world; and therefore the above brief entry forms a contribution, however slender, to the Church history of the realm.

Rice Griffith, Esq., who had recently succeeded his grandfather, Sir Rice ap Thomas, suffered death this year on a series of charges, one of which was, that he had taken the new name of Rice ap Griffith fitz Urien. Urien was a king of the Cumbrian Britons, who fought under King Arthur against the Saxons. He stands at the head of the pedigree of the Rices: and this harmless display of family pride was interpreted by the venal and servile statesmen and lawyers of this period, as a proof that Mr. Rice aspired to sovereignty. An accusation worthy of a reign in which the gallant and accomplished Surrey was doomed to the scaffold, for bearing the Confessor's arms; on the evidence of a sister who deposed, that her brother put a crown on his arms "to her judgment much like to a close crown." Other articles against Mr. Griffith were, that he had conspired to depose the King, and place his nephew, James of Scotland, with whom Henry was now mortally offended, on the throne, and that he had mortgaged his lordships of Carew and Narbeth, in order to raise money for the purpose of conveying himself into Scotland. For these alleged offences he suffered death, and, as some assert, in this town. Holinshed, however, and Fabyan, and even our MS. Chronicle, are express that he was beheaded on Tower-hill, December 4th, 1531. The act for his attainder is among the private acts, 23rd Henry VIII.

"In vino expendito in societate clerici coquine Joh'is Exon' ep'i, d'ni p'sidentis consilii d'ni R' in m'chias Wallie & alior' s'vientiu' ejus c'ca comestionem unius gruis & alior' victualium."	"Wine spent in company of the clerk of the kitchen of John Bishop of Exeter, Lord President of the Council of our Lord the King in the Marches of Wales, and other his servants, about the eating of a crane and other victuals, 9d."

---

[2] Mrs. Katherine Griffith, wife to the son and heir of Sir Rice ap Thomas, was among the ladies sent to Gravesend in 1501, to attend the Princess Katherine of Spain to London. Hardwicke State Papers. i. p. 3.

A.D. 1534.—It was in this year that Sir William Skeffington was sent over lord deputy of Ireland, as lieutenant to the King's natural son, Henry, Duke of Richmond.   Sir William, who was ancestor to the Earls of Massareene, was called by the Irish, " the gunner, by cause hee was preferred from that office of the King, hys maister gunner, to governe them ;" and it seems probable that the artillery now passing through Shrewsbury was dispatched by him to Dublin, then in danger from the rebellious Fitzgeralds. It is observable that "great brass ordnance, as canon and culverin, were first cast in England in this year." John Owen was the founder.

| "Sol' p' vino expendit' sup' burgenses p'liamenti in exitu suo de Salop v's' London." | " Paid for wine spent upon the burgesses of the parliament on their departure from Salop towards London, 7d." |

This was the important parliament which assembled on prorogation, February 3rd, 1534-5, and annihilated the papal power in England.   The burgesses, or, as we now call them, the members of parliament for Shrewsbury, were Robert Dudley and Adam Mitton, Esquires.

Henry, with all the deformities of his character, seems to have had a real desire to reform the state of his clergy : nor, though much of the merit of this attempt may be attributed to his spleen against the Pope, and to the urgent representations of Cranmer, recently preferred to the metropolitan see, should the King be deprived of his share of praise; since nothing of the kind could have been set on foot without his concurrence.   One of these good designs, the appointment of suffragan bishops, received the sanction of the legislature in 1534.   Suffragans, so called, *quia suffragantur*, because they are assistant to the bishops of the dioceses, were very ancient in the primitive Church, under the name of chorepiscopi, or rural bishops.

The latter end of 1535, Shrewsbury was distinguished by an extraordinary concourse of nobility. "Three Ducks," says the MS. Chronicle, quoted by the Shropshire historians, " cam throughe Shrowsbery : to say, the Ducke of Rychemoond, the Ducke of Northefolke, and the Ducke of Suffolke, with a greate retynewe."   The Duke of Richmond was Henry, surnamed Fitzroy, son of Henry VIII., by a Shropshire lady, wife of the Lord Talbois, and daughter to Sir John Blount of Kinlet.   He was at this time a youth of sixteen years ; had been appointed Lord High Admiral of England, lieutenant-general and warden of the Scottish Marches ; and now visited Shrewsbury on his way to take possession of the Holt in Flintshire, formerly a place of great importance under the name of Castle Lyons.   He was accompanied by one of the most considerable subjects of the realm, the Duke of Norfolk, whose daughter he married; yet he was the great object of attention, and a roll of accounts, dated 1535, contains numerous entries of expenses, none of them, however, worthy of notice, bestowed "upon the Duke."   The accounts of the bailiffs, for a year, from Michaelmas, 1535, have these entries.   From the first it is plain that the corporation met the great men at some distance from the town.   Nothing is said of the Duke of Suffolk, who came, if he came at all, at a different time.

| "In regardo dat' Ric'o Clerke, barbur, equitanti ad cognoscend' perfecte de adventu duc' Rechemund & duc' Norfolc' in com' Salop." | " Reward given to Richard Clarke, barber, riding to know perfectly of the coming of the Duke of Richmond and the Duke of Norfolk into the county of Salop, 2s. 4d." |

The bailiffs were probably guided in their choice of Mr. Clarke for this purpose by a consideration of his occupation, which has always been deemed favourable for the collection and circulation of intelligence.

| "Sol' p' conductu vini dictor' duor' ducu' a villa Salop usq' vill' Osewestrie." | "Paid for carriage of the wine of the said two dukes from Shrewsbury to Oswestry, 20d." |

| "Sol' p' exhinn' dat' dc'is ducibz ut in uno hoggeshed vini, cignis, caponibus, bovibus, vitulis, cuniculis, castrimargiis, wafters, ypocras, p'.... speciebz, confect', & aliis div'sis rebus pro honestate ville Salop ; in una grossa sum'a compilat p'pt' brevitatem temporis." | " Paid for presents given to the said duke, as in a hogshead of wine, swans, capons, oxen, calves, conies, dainties, wafers, hipocras per.... spices, comfits, and divers other things, for the honour of the town of Salop ; put together in one gross sum on account of the shortness of the time, 5l. 18s. 2d." |

We cannot help smiling, amidst the splendour of ducal progresses, and the breaking up of the old order of things, by means of a high-handed monarch's passions and politics combined, to perceive such a minute and profuse attention paid to creature comforts, on the part of our worthy forefathers.

" Sol' servo cl'ici pac' com' Salop' portanti respons' l're ballivor' Sal' de d'nis cancellario & p'vati sigilli d'ni R' c'ca elecc'oem burgensiu' p' p'liament' d'ni Reg'."	" Paid a servant of the clerk of the peace for the county of Salop bearing an answer to the letter of the bailiffs of Salop from the Lord Chancellor and Lord Privy Seal, touching the election of burgesses for the parliament of our Lord the King, 2s. 6d."

The letter of these great officers of state referred to in the above entry, has not occurred to our researches, but it was probably not very dissimilar from the following, addressed by Henry himself to the corporation at an earlier period of his reign: and which is too curious to be omitted.

" *To our Trusty and Welbeloved the Bailliffs and Burgesses of oure Town of Shrewsbury.*

" *By the King.*

" TRUSTY AND WELBELOVED, WE GREETE YOU WELE. And wherreas we, by the advice of our counsaill, have appointed our p'liament to bee holden the vth daye of February next comying at o^r Palays of Westm^r. for the declarac'on of such doubtefull poynts and articles conteyned in the Act made at our last p'iament, as also for other matres touching the comen weale of this our Reame, ffor the declarac'on of whiche ambiguities expedient shall it bee to have those burgeisses nowe to be at this p'liament as were present at the debating and resonyng in the making of the said Acte, being wele expert in the same; Where as in case newe burgesses shuld bee nowe elect, not having experience nor clere knowlege of the said difficulties, the matiers mought be tracted with long delayes, withoute any spede or effectuall expedic'on; Therefore it is thought to Us and our counsaill most expedient and necessary to have those nowe elect and chosen burgeisses of that o^r towne as were present the making of the saide Acte in our last p'liament, Wherefore we wol and desire yo soo to cause the said burgeisses to be chose accordingly, as ye tender our pleasure and thaduancement of the saide matiers. Yeven undre o^r signet at o^r manoir of Grenewiche the furst daye of Decembre."

The expedient suggested by this letter was no unusual measure in that century, when the government was well pleased to command again the services of parliament-men, whose obedience had already been tried; in times when opposition was dangerous, and to be dreaded by the minions of a court, a new and untried man was, as much as possible, to be avoided. Among Mr. Gough's MSS. in the Bodleian, is a letter copied from the Shrewsbury corporation archives, dated Windsor, September 19th, 1586, and addressed by the lords of the council to the Earl of Pembroke, President of the Marches and the council, in which they are required " to call together the principal and fittest gentlemen of the counties within their jurisdiction, and to acquaint them of a new parliament to be held the 15th of October following, and to take care to have the same representatives for such counties, cities, or boroughs, as were in the last parliament, if not deceased, or in her Majesty's service beyond the seas; if so, then to see appointed discreet and well-affected persons as should be most fit in their rooms."

Even at a much later period, we find an interference with elections avowed, in a manner, of which, now that regal and aristocratical nomination has yielded to the influence of the press, we have little conception. " If your Majesty," writes Secretary Windebanke to Charles I., " at this assembly of the lords, shall resolve upon a parliament, some of my lords here do humbly beseech your Majesty to treat with the lord chamberlain and others that have burgesses in their disposal, to reserve as many places as they can for your Majesty."[4]

Such were the precautions adopted by the ministers of the Crown to pack a House of Commons, when any important measure was to be carried: and a most momentous one was in contemplation in the case now before us; for the parliament of the present year, which met June 8th, 1536, was convened to settle the succession to the Crown; and its obsequious members actually conferred upon their wayward sovereign the power of disposing of it by will![5]

---

[4] Clarendon's State Papers, i. p. 123. The reader will learn the small effect of this " treating," when he observes the date of this letter, Sept. 25th, 1640, scarcely a month before the meeting of the Long Parliament, which subverted the monarchy.

[5] Henry VIII. had, under the authority of Parliament, by his will, entailed the Crown, first, on his son Edward Prince of Wales, and his issue; in default of which, on his daughter, the Princess Mary, and her children; and if she died issueless, on his daughter,

The dissolution was now proceeding apace. That of the lesser monasteries had been enacted in the last year (February 4th, 1535-6); and before that, and as a preparatory to it, a visitation of them was set on foot. One Leigh, whose christian name was Thomas, with two other doctors, Leighton and London, were chiefly employed, though there were many other subordinate agents. It was their chief business to spy out the offences of the conventuals, and encourage them to accuse their governors and each other. The friaries were spared in this first dissolution; they were greater favourites with the people in general than the abbeys, and indeed the dissolution as yet scarcely touched the Borders; none nearer to Shrewsbury than Bildewas and Wombridge fell at present, and therefore we must not wonder to read such articles as the following :—

" Regardo Provinciali fratrum predicator' p'dicanti & p'nuncianti verbū Dei p' tota' ebdoma' rogaconu'."	" Reward to the Provincial of the Friars Preachers, preaching and pronouncing the word of God through the whole of the Rogation week, 10s."
" Sol' Priori fra' heremitar' ordi's S'c'i Augustini ville Salop ad rep'ac'oe' dom' sue ei concess' p' co'itate ville."	" Paid to the Prior of the Friars Eremites of the order of St. Austin of the town of Salop towards the repairs of his house, granted him by the commonalty, 4l."

The further insertion may be pardoned here of a few curious particulars respecting an order of things soon to be swept away :—

" From Michaelmas, 28 to 29 Hen. VIII., 1536—1537.

" Sol' p' tortis & wafurnes dat' Doctori Leigh, visitatori d'ni Regis per ballivos."	" Paid for tarts and wafers given by the bailiffs to Dr. Leigh, visitor of our Lord the King, 12d."
" Sol' p' vino dat' Doctori Wall, fratri minori, p'dicanti & declaranti verba divina coram co'itate ville."	" Wine to Dr. Wall, friar minor, preaching and declaring the word of God before the commonalty of the town, 5d."
" Vino expendit' super Abbatem de Llannegwyst & aliis."	" Wine spent upon the Abbot of Llanegwyst (i.e. Valle Crucis) and others, 2s. 5d."
" Vino dat' s'vientibz prioris de Wombruge."	" Wine given to the serjeants of the prior of Wombruge, 5d."

The MS. Chronicle mentions a great plague in the town this year, but no particulars of it are recorded.

An order on the books of the corporation of Shrewsbury this year shows the manner in which the council of Wales was received on their arrival :—

" Wednesday before the Feast of St. Mary Magdalen (21 July) 29 Hen. VIII.

" They be aggreed that all the aldermen beyng owt of the towne, shal be warned att theyre howses to prepare theym selffs to mete the king's commissioners; and also that all wardens of occupac'ons shal be in like manner warned to present unto Master Bailiffs or theire deputies, what able men they can make with horses, to meet the said commissioners. Item, they aggreed to present the said commissioners, with four dozen bredd, halfe an oxe, a hogeshed of wyne; and forther, att M. Bailiffs' discression."

" Sol' Thōe Bromley, recordatori, in resoluc'oe pecuniar' p' ip'm solut' in Scc'io d'ni R' tam p' scrutacoe recordor' quam p' aliis feodis id'm c'ca exon'ac'oem inhabitancium foren' lib'tatis ville de soluc'oe subsidii d'ni R'."	" Paid to Thomas Bromley, Recorder, in repayment of monies by him in the exchequer of our Lord the King, as well for the search of records as for other fees there, touching the exoneration of the inhabitants of the foreign of the liberty of the town from paying a subsidy of our Lord the King, 8s. 8d."

Prince Edward was born on the 12th of October. The Queen's letters to the corporation were, no doubt, similar to those sent in her name to the lords of the council, in which she informs them that, " By the inestimable goodnes and grace of Almighty God, wee be delivered and brought in child-bed of a prince, conceived in most lawful matrimony between my Lord the King's Majesty and us," and exhorts them to render thanks for so great a benefit, and to pray for the long continuance and preservation of the same.[*]

the Princess Elizabeth and her descendants; in the event of their decease without lawful issue, the royal dignity, was, contrary to the general rules of the succession, to descend to the children of his nieces, the daughters of his younger sister Mary, Queen Dowager of France, then the wife of Charles Brandon, Duke of Suffolk.—*Owen and Blakeway.*

[*] Sylloge Epist. ad calcem Livii Foro-Juliens. ed Hearne, p. 113.

"In regardo Humfrido Hulston nuncio d'ne Regine portanti l'ras suas ball'is ad nativitatem d'ni p'ncipis."

"Reward to Humfrey Hulston, messenger of our Lady the Queen, bearing her letters to the bailiffs at the birth of the Lord Prince, 6s. 8d."

At length arrived the general dissolution of abbeys, when those that had been spared three years before, fell in one indiscriminate wreck, and "all monasteries, abbaties, priories, nunneries, colleges, hospitals, and houses of friars," were given to the King by the parliament which met, April 28, 1539. An eminent writer[6] has amused himself with speculating on the aids which might have been derived to religion and learning, from a judicious application of part of the spoil: and good men, even in that age of terror, made a few ineffectual attempts towards so beneficial a design. Our ancestors, we know, engaged the services of an eminent barrister, their countryman, who drew up a supplication to be exhibited to the King, "for the erection of the house of the late monastery of Salop into a college, or free school."[7] This would have been feasible; and a noble foundation might have arisen on the ruins of the Abbey. But Henry had, or (for with a genius so fertile in pretexts to cloak his views, or to appease the clamours of his people, it is impossible to pronounce what were his real intentions), he pretended to entertain, more magnificent designs, and to be determined to apply the revenues of some of the dissolved abbeys to the erection of thirteen new bishoprics.[8] Burnet[9] had seen a list in the King's own hand of the sees he intended to found. The alterations which it would have introduced into the ecclesiastical division of the kingdom would have been judicious, and evince a considerable knowledge of the internal state of his dominions. Shrewsbury was to have become the seat of a bishop, who was to have been endowed with the revenues of the abbey, and to have comprised in his diocese the counties of Salop and Stafford. We are assured[1] that John Boucher, abbot of Leicester,[2] was actually nominated bishop of Shrewsbury: and hence, no doubt, the tradition, so gratifying to the pride of every true Salopian, that their forefathers had the offer of having their borough converted into a city, but that they preferred continuing to inhabit "the first of towns," in preference to being the last of cities.

Henry was succeeded on the throne by his youthful son, who swayed a gospel sceptre for a too brief period, under the title of KING EDWARD THE SIXTH. The troubles of that transitional time, the mighty work of Reformation then carried on under his auspices, and his early death, prevented this virtuous monarch from visiting the Principality or the neighbouring counties.[3]

[6] History of Whalley, p. 111.
[7] "Solut' pro una supplicacione per Robertum Broke jurisperitum concepta ad exhibendum domino Regi pro errecc'oe domus nuper monasterii Salop in collegium sive liberam scolam, 6s. 6d. Et solut' Humfrido Dickens clerico domini Regis pro scripcione ejusdem supplicac'onis in pergameno, 20d." Accounts of the bailiffs for a year from Michaelmas, 1542.
[8] This project had been entertained even before the Dissolution. In 1528, a bull issued to Cardinals Wolsey and Campeius, directing them to inquire what abbeys were fit to be erected into cathedrals; and this was repeated, with further powers, in the following year. "For some of the dioceses were thought too large, and wanted much to be reduced, that the bishops might better discharge their offices." Pref. to Tanner's Notitia.
[9] Hist. Reform., vol. i. p. 262. Strype's Memorials, vol. i. Append. pp. 273, 275.
[1] Willis.
[2] Few of his brethren evinced more courage at the Dissolution than this intended Bishop of Shrewsbury. He refused to surrender his abbey to the royal commissioners for a long time. They threatened to accuse him of fornication, and other grievous offences. That they were unable to prove these charges is plain, from the pension which he at last secured, 200l. a-year; more than twice as much as was given to the mitred abbot of Salop. Had he been

a man of the infamous character suggested, he would have been hanged without scruple, instead of being designed for one of the new prelates.
[3] Edward VI. was crowned February 20th, 1546. "He rode through London into Westminster," says Holinshed, "with as great roialtie as might be, the streets being hung, and pageants in divers places erected, to testifie the good willes of the citizens. As he passed on the south part of Paule's Churchyard, an Argosine came from the battlements of Paule's Church upon a cable, being made fast to an anchor by the deane's gate, lieing on his breast, aiding himselfe neither with hand nor foot, and having ascended to the middest of the cable, where he tumbled and plaied many prettie toies, whereat the king and the nobles had good pastime." At this coronation, when the three swords, for the three kingdoms, were brought to be carried before him, the king observed, that there was yet one wanting, and called for the Bible. "That," said he, "is the sword of the spirit, and ought in all right to govern us, who use these for the people's safety, by God's appointment. Without that sword we are nothing: we can do nothing. From that we are what we are this day:—we receive whatsoever it is that we at this present do assume. Under that we ought to live, to fight, to govern the people, and to perform all our affairs. From that alone we obtain all power, virtue, salvation, and whatsoever we have of divine strength."—*Coronation Anecdotes.*

Henry VIII. took great pains to show Charles V. in what light he regarded his daughter Mary, who was early betrothed to the French monarch, but who, in consequence of Henry's meditated divorce from his Queen, Katherine of Arragon, broke his betrothal with one, who if not actually Princess of Wales, as some authors[4] have affirmed, assuredly received honours and distinctions which have never either before or since been offered to any but the heir-apparent of England. A court was formed for her at Ludlow Castle, on a grander scale than those established for her uncle Arthur, or Edward of York, both acknowledged Princes of Wales, and heirs-apparent of England.

The officers and nobles who composed the Princess Mary's court at Ludlow were employed likewise in superintending the newly formed legislature of Wales, the natives of that Principality being, at last, by the tardy gratitude of the Tudors, admitted to participation in the privileges of English subjects. The Welsh had been long discontented with the absence of the royal family from any part of their territory, and the sojourn of the heiress of England was intended to conciliate their affections and sanction the new laws. Sir John Dudley was appointed chamberlain to the Princess Mary at her new court. Thomas Audley, afterwards lord-chancellor, and John Russel, were members of her council. The Countess of Salisbury resided with her, as she had done from her birth, as head of her establishment and state governess, an office always filled, till the time of James I., by a lady of the blood-royal. The Princess had besides no less than thirteen ladies of honour, and a crowd of lower functionaries, whose united salaries amounted, even at that day, to 741*l.* 13*s.* 9*d.*[5]

Mary took leave of her parents at the Palace of Langley, in Hertfordshire, in September, 1525, previous to her departure for Ludlow Castle. Dr. Sampson gives us a pleasing description of her person and qualities at this epoch. " My lady princess," he says, in a letter to Wolsey, " came hither on Saturday ; surely, sir, of her age, as goodly a child as I ever have seen, and of good gesture and countenance. Few persons of her age blend sweetness better with seriousness, or quickness with deference ; she is at the same time joyous and decorous in manner." In fact contemporaries and all portraitures represent Mary at this period of her life as a lovely child. But if human ingenuity had been taxed to the utmost, in order to contrive the most cruel contrast between her present and future prospects, it could not have been more thoroughly effected than by first placing her in vice-regal pomp and state, as Princess of Wales at Ludlow Castle, and then afterwards blighting her young mind by hurling her undeservedly into poverty and contempt. It was exceedingly probable that Henry meant fraudulently to force a high alliance for Mary before he disinherited her, and therefore took the deceitful step of placing her in a situation which had never been occupied excepting by an heir-apparent of England. It was in her court at Ludlow Castle that Mary first practised to play the part of a queen, a lesson she was soon compelled to unlearn with the bitterest results. Her education, at the same time, went steadily on, with great assiduity. Fresh instructions were given to her council regarding her tuition when she parted from her royal parents ; they emanated from the natural tenderness and good sense of her mother, Queen Katherine, whose earnest wish was evident to render her daughter healthy and cheerful, as well as learned and accomplished.

" First, above all other things, the Countess of Salisbury, being lady-governess, shall, according to the singular confidence that the King's highness hath in her, give most tender regards to all that concerns the person of the said princess, her honourable education and training in virtuous demeanour ; that is to say, to serve God, from whom all grace and goodness proceedeth. Likewise, at seasons convenient, to use

---

[4] Burnet and many English authors, who however use more general terms without entering into documents. We copy the following translation of a passage from Pollino, from the author of the interesting lives of the Queens of England :—" Mary was," (says the author), " declared heir of the realm by the King her father, and Princess of Wales which was the usual title of the King of England's eldest son. She likewise governed that province according to the custom of the male heir." The Italian then carefully explains that the Princes of Wales were in the same

position, in regard to the English crown, as the dauphins were to France. Pollino must have had good documentary evidence, since he describes Mary's court and council (which he calls a senate), exactly as if the privy council books had been open to him. He says four bishops were attached to this court.

[5] To the deep research of Sir Frederic Madden the public are indebted for these particulars of Mary's sojourn ; see his Ancient Demesne of the English heirs-apparent. See also for further particulars, " Privy-purse Expense of Mary," p. 37.

moderate exercise, taking open air in gardens, sweet and wholesome places and walks, (which may conduce unto her health, solace and comfort,) as by the said lady-governess shall be thought most convenient. And likewise to pass her time, most seasons, at her virginals, or other musical instruments, so that the same be not *too much*, and without *fatigacion*, or weariness; to attend her learning of Latin tongue and French. At other seasons to dance, and among the rest, to have proper respect to her diet, which is *meet* (proper) to be pure, well-prepared, dressed, and served with comfortable, joyous and merry communication, in all honourable and virtuous manner. Likewise the cleanliness and well-wearing of her garments and apparel, both of her chamber and person, so that everything about her be pure, sweet, clean, and wholesome, as to so great a princess doth appertain; all corruptions, evil airs, and things noisome and unpleasant to be eschewed."[6] With these instructions the Princess Mary and her court departed for Ludlow, which Leland describes as " a fair manor-place, standing in a goodly park, west of the town of Bewdley, on the very knob of the hill;" he adds, "the castle was built by Henry VII., for his son, Prince Arthur." It was probably repaired and decorated, but the castle was previously the grand feudal seat of the Mortimers, as Lords of the Marches; Richard, Duke of York, as heir of the semi-royal chiefs, resided there; and the young Prince of Wales, afterwards the unfortunate Edward V., was educated and kept his court there, as heir-apparent of England, for some years previous to the death of his father, Edward IV.

As a great concourse of people were expected at Ludlow Castle during the Christmas festivities, for the purpose of paying respect to the Princess, her council thought it requisite that she should "keep Christmas with princely cheer;" they, therefore, wrote to the Cardinal, intimating the articles requisite for the use of their young mistress's household. A silver ship or *nef*, (which was to hold the table napkin for the princess), an alms dish, and silver spice plates were among these requests; they wanted trumpets and a rebeck, and hinted a wish for the appointment of a lord of misrule, and some provision for interludes, disguisings, and plays at the feast, and for the banquet at Twelfth-night.

The residence of Mary at Ludlow lasted about eighteen months, varied with occasional visits to Tickenhill, and to the magnificent unfinished palace of the unfortunate Duke of Buckingham, at Thornbury, which had been seized by the King; her education meantime proceeded rapidly.[7]

The precise time of the withdrawal of the Princess Mary from her court at Ludlow Castle is not defined; it was probably to receive the French ambassadors, who had arrived for the purpose of negotiating her marriage with the second son of France.

At the period of Anne Boleyn's death, when she was in her twentieth year, Mary was described by a French gentleman who was then, A.D. 1537, in London, and had been acquainted with her habits, to have made reading the Scriptures, music, needle-work, and the study of foreign languages, her favourite occupations.[8] She had been treated as a favourite princess, till the contest about her mother's divorce consigned her to private life, when all state was discontinued to her, and she lived alone, cultivating her religion, and every innocent pastime.[9]

QUEEN MARY succeeded her brother, Edward VI., to the throne of these realms on the 19th of July, 1553.[1] Though a catholic, she promised not to interfere with or alter the reformed religion, but be content with the private exercise of her own. The public, however, not being satisfied with her

[6] MS. Cotton. Vitellius C. fol. 24. In Sir F. Madden's Privy-purse expenses, introductory memoir, this document may be seen in the original orthography, p. 12.

[7] The following curious items, extracted from the Household Book of Lady Mary, Royal MSS. Brit. Mus., in various years, from the 28th to the 36th of her father Henry VIII.'s reign, show the customs of royalty in those days:

" Item, geven to George Mountejoye drawing my Ladye's Grace to his Valentine, xl[s].

"Item, geven amongs the yeoman of the King's guard bringing a leke to my Ladye's Grace on Saynt David's Day, xv[s].

" Item, geven to Heywood playing an enterlude with his children before my Lady's Grace, xl[s].

" Item, payed for a yerde and a halfe of damaske for Jane the Fole, vij[s].

" Item, for shaving of Jane's hedde, iiij[d].

" Payed for a frontlet loste in a wager to my Ladye Margaret, iiij[s].

" Item, payed for a brekefast lost at bolling by my Lady Mary's Grace, x[s]."

[8] Crispin, the lord of Miberve.   [9] Crapelot, p. 188.

[1] " Mary was the first female sovereign of this realm, and was crowned on the 1st of October, 1553, by Stephen Gardiner, Bishop

assertion, the Duke of Northumberland and a strong party, caused Lady Jane Grey to be proclaimed in opposition to Mary. This nobleman soon afterwards lost his head, as did also Sir John Gates, and Sir Thomas Palmer, and the Lady Jane too, whose death was as much lamented as her life had been admired. Her father, and about fifty-eight noblemen suffered on the same account. Six hundred of the rabble were appointed to come with ropes about their necks, and beg the Queen's pardon. Persecution now commenced with unabated violence; an order was given to turn all heretics and married clergymen out of the Church. The ordination in King Edward's time was declared null and void.

Seven of the reformed bishops were turned out of their bishopricks, viz., the Archbishop of York, the Bishops of St. David's, Chester, and Bristol, for being married; and the Bishops of Lincoln, Gloucester, and Hereford, for having acted (as was pretended) contrary to the practice of the universal Church. Scorry, Bishop of Chichester, renounced his wife, and did penance for his marriage. In all there were sixteen new bishops made, and shortly afterwards the Catholic service was everywhere set up. It is supposed that twelve thousand of the clergy were deprived of their livings for having married, and most of them were judged upon common fame, without any proofs but a citation.

Queen Mary seems to have inherited the sanguinary temper of her father only where religion was concerned, and some even of that may be ascribed to the influence possessed over her by the inexorable Gardiner, and to the excesses of the brutal Bonner. It is at least certain that she commenced her reign with some acts of signal clemency; she pardoned the Duke of Suffolk, who had endeavoured to exclude her from the succession, and she granted a reprieve to his daughter, Lady Jane Grey, who had actually, though reluctantly, occupied the royal chair, thereby intimating her desire to spare the life of that amiable victim of the ambition of others. While affairs stood in this position, the rebellion of Wyatt broke out, in which the Duke, with the deepest ingratitude, engaged. The result was fatal to himself and his family. His brother, Lord Thomas, fled into Shropshire, and was taken at Oswestrie, in Wales, "Master Richard Mytton, of Shrosbery, being then baylyffe."[1]

If ever a sovereign has reigned who has exhibited the deteriorating and degrading effects of allowing a political priesthood, with persecuting principles, to take the direction of the state government, and to make the mind of the sovereign subservient to the compulsory impositions on others of the religious system, tenets, and speculations which they choose to maintain, MARY is the person, whose name stands on the rolls of English history, like the Pharos on the dark and dangerous rock, to warn every potentate and country of what must be timely discerned and shunned; if honour, fame, happiness, or national prosperity be worthy of a monarch's pursuits.

QUEEN ELIZABETH.—This great Tudor Princess is considered the chief founder of the progressive amplitude of our national greatness; and her reign may be marked as the period in which it engendered into a visible existence. Our commercial enterprises; the spirit of a distant navigation; our colonial

---

of Winchester, the Archbishops of York and Canterbury being then prisoners in the Tower. On the last day of September she went in state from the Tower to Westminster in an open chariot, drawn by six horses, covered with cloth of tissue. In a second chariot came the Princess Elizabeth and the Lady Ann Cleves; the ladies in waiting rode upon horses covered with trappings of crimson velvet and satin. These pageants were erected in Fenchurch-street by the Genoese, Easterling, and Florentine merchants. Among the city pageants, the most remarkable was that of St. Paul's Cathedral, thus described by Holinshed:—There was one Peter, a Dutchman, that stood on the weather-cock of Paule's steeple, holding a streamer in his hand of five yards long, and waiving thereof, stood sometimes on the one foot and shooke the other, and then kneeled on his knees, to the great marvell of all people. He had made two scaffolds under him, one about the crosse, having torches and streamers set on it, and another over the ball of the crosse, likewise set with streamers

and torches, which could not burn, the wind was so great. The said Peter had 16l. 13s. 4d. for his costes, and paines, and all his stuffe. The conduits ran with wine, and, when the civic authorities received the queene at Cheape, the chamberlain presented her with a purse of tissue containing a thousand marks in gold."—*Coronation Anecdotes.*

[1] MS. Chronicle of Shrewsbury. The ancient town of Shrewsbury appears even at that time, 1551, to have been a place much attached to royalty. The following items are extracted from the bailiffs' account :—

" Expended by the bailiffs' and given to the poor, on the day of the coronation of our Lady the Queen, at the processions, 29s.

"1554. Expended by the bailiffs' at the procession when King Philip entered into the kingdom of England at three several places of the town of Salop, 34s."

establishments; the consolidated and settled power of the state; its just foreign policy; its wiser internal arrangements; and its meliorating legislation; all date from the happy reign of this Princess. But the healthful fountain of all our national vigour, was that Reformation of which she became the efficacious supporter, and the most successful champion. The history of her reign is the history of the perils to which it was exposed; of the long warfare it had to endure; and of its secure establishment in those countries which have ever since preserved it. To have thus contributed to the continuation of that beneficial reformation among mankind, is the greatest glory of her lengthened and important reign, and that which has immortalised her name among the sovereigns of the earth.

This exceedingly popular Queen ascended the throne of these realms on the death of her sister Mary, in A.D. 1558. She was crowned the 25th of January, by Oglethorpe, Bishop of Carlisle, the see of Canterbury being vacant by the death of Cardinal Pole.[3]

Queen Elizabeth, priding herself, as she did, upon being " a Princess of the House of Tudor," was warmly attached to Wales and its inhabitants; a part of her Majesty's household generally consisted of some portion of the Welsh nobility, among whom we would particularise Sir Richard Bulkeley,[4] Knight, and Mrs. Blanche Parry.[5] She felt a deep interest in, and anxious solicitude for, the general and

---

[3] Speed's account of the procession of Queen Elizabeth contains some particulars too remarkable to be omitted. " All things in readiness, upon the 14th of January, with great triumphes and sumptuous shewes, shee passed thorow London, towards Westminster, to receive her imperiall crowne; but before shee entered her chariot in the Tower, acknowledged that the seat was God's into which shee was to enter, and shee his vicegerent to wield the English sceptre; in that royall assembly, with eyes and hands elevated to heaven, upon her knees, she prayed for his assistance, as Solomon did for wisedome when he tooke the like charge; with a thankfull remembrance unto God for his continued preservation, who had brought her thorow great dangers unto that present dignitie."

[4] Among the Welsh nobility who formed a part of Her Majesty's Household, were Sir Richard Bulkeley, Bart., and Mrs. Blanche Parry, both of whom seem to have been brought up in the court from their infancy, and, consequently, in great esteem with Her Majesty; so much so, that the Earl of Leicester, the Queen's favourite, began to be jealous of Sir Richard; and with a view of having him removed from court, he made an attempt to have him accused, upon false evidence, of treason. With this wicked design, the Earl of Leicester informed Her Majesty that the council had been examining Sir Richard Bulkeley, and that they found him a dangerous person; that he dwelt in a suspicious corner of the world, and should be committed to the Tower. " What! Sir Richard Bulkeley!" said the Queen; " he never intended us any harm; we have brought him up from a boy, and have had special trial of his fidelity; ye shall not commit him!" " We have the care of your Majesty's person," said the Earl, " and see more and hear more of the man than you do; he is of an aspiring mind, and lives in a remote place." " Before God," replied the Queen, " we will be sworn upon the Holy Evangelists he never intended any harm;" and then her Majesty ran to the Bible, and kissing it, said, " You shall not commit him; we have brought him up from a boy." Sir Richard, however, was too high-minded to suffer such an imputation to be laid to his character. He insisted on an enquiry, during which it appeared that Lord Dudley, Earl of Leicester, had been appointed a Ranger of the Royal Forest of Snowdon, which, in the Queen's time, included some portion of Merioneth and Anglesea. This nobleman's insolence to the inhabitants of the forest was more than could be brooked. He tried to bring many freeholders' estates within the boundary; juries were empanelled, but the Commissioners rejected their returns as unfavourable to the Earl; those honest jurors, however, persisted, and found a verdict for the country. But

in the year 1538, he succeeded by a packed jury, who appeared in his livery, blue, with ragged staves on the sleeves; men, who after this nefarious act, were stigmatised with the title of " The Black Jury who sold their country." Sir Richard Bulkeley, who, with Sir William Herbert, and others, superseded a prior Commission, resisted this oppression with great firmness, and laid those odious grievances before the Queen, whose regard for her loyal subjects in Wales, was evinced by the recalling of the first commission, by proclamation at Westminster in 1579. The Earl being worsted, sought the life of Sir Richard by having him charged as above. But this generous and patriotic nobleman, by his excellent and manly conduct, overthrew every malevolent design of his enemy, and came out of this fiery trial, as clear as the pellucid crystal of Snowdon.

[5] Dr. Powell, in his Historie of Wales, published in 1584, thus notices " the efforts of Mrs. Blanche Parry in forwarding the public weale." " The Historie of the Winning of Glamorgan, being delivered unto me by the Right Worshipful Mistress Blanche Parry, one of the gentlewomen of the Queen's Majesty Privie Chamber, a singular well-wisher and furtherer of the weale publike of that country, I thought good to insert here as followeth." Powell's Wales, p. 121.

" Queen Elizabeth was attended from her birth by Blanche Parry. This lady was a daughter of Harry Parry, and granddaughter of Milo ap Harry by his wife Jane Stradling. Milo Parry died in the year 1488, at Bacton, Herefordshire, where a splendid window of stained glass was erected to his memory, and another to the memory of Mrs. Blanche Parry, his granddaughter. These windows were removed by Mrs. Burton of Atcham, to Atcham Church, near Shrewsbury, in order to be better protected and preserved. Milo Parry was lineally descended from Sitric, King of the Danes of Dublin, who fought the battle of Clontarf, in which Brian Boroihme was slain. After that battle, Ideo, second son of Sitric, settled at Lhywel, in Wales, where he had a grant of a large estate for his successful services on behalf of Rhys ap Tudor. Ideo's second son, Moreiddig, married the Baroness Lacy, with whom he obtained very large possessions at Ewias Lacy and in other parts of Herefordshire, where some of the Parrys reside to this day, a branch of them being now represented by Mr. Wegg Prosser, formerly Haggitt, son of a Miss Parry (who married Dr. Haggitt), and Member for the county.

" Milo Parry was nearly related to some of the first noblemen of that age, as the Earl of Northumberland, Earl of Pembroke, Lord Greystock, Lord Lisle, Earl of Powis, Earl of Kent, and others; and, doubtless, it was such connections that led the way to

spiritual welfare of "her loyal subjects in Wales," and the incalculable boon she caused them to be supplied with will never be forgotten. It is to her Majesty that the Welsh are indebted for the first translation of the Scriptures into their ancient and vernacular language. The New Testament was translated into Welsh by William Salisbury, in 1567; and the Old Testament was translated by Dr. Morgan, in 1588. These invaluable works were warmly patronised, and, by express command, dedicated to her Gracious Majesty, of grateful memory.[6]

From the first dawn of the Reformation to the time of Queen Elizabeth (a period of about forty-five years), the Welsh sees were filled, as they are at present, with English bishops, ignorant alike of the language, manners, and spiritual wants of the people; and, during this period, they were in total spiritual darkness: not even a single copy of the Scriptures was to be found amongst them, except some portions in manuscript, which were handed down as heir-looms in different families.

"No sooner," says Bishop Davies, in his Preface to the Salisbury Testament, "did this wise and patriotic Princess ascend the throne, than she filled the Welsh bishoprics with native Welshmen—men to whom Wales, in fact, owes all the religious light she at present enjoys; and, but for whom, it is more than probable, it would have been at this moment a Popish country, exposed to the superstitions and miseries of a neighbouring and kindred people!"

the employment of Mrs. Blanche Parry about the person of the infant Princess Elizabeth. In her epitaph at Bacton Church she is made to say that she was brought up in Princes' courts:

"I. Parrye, his doughter Blanche, of New Court born,
    That *traenyd was in Pryncy's courts*, with gorgious wyghts,
    Wheare fleetynge honor sounds with blaste of horne
    Am lodgyd here.   *   *   *   *   *   *
    I lyvde allweys as handmaede too a queene,
    In *chamber chiff*, my tyme dyd to overpasse,
    Uncareful of my wealth there was I seen
    Whyllste I abode the ronnynge of my glasse,
    Not doubtynge want whyllst that my mystress lyvde
    In woman's state, *whose cradell saw I rockte*;
    Her servaunte then, as when shee her crowne attcheeved,
    And so remaened tyll deathe my doore had knockte."

"Mrs. Blanche Parry attended the queen in all her varieties of fortune and all her progresses. There is an account remaining in Lord Burleigh's own hand-writing, of his preparations to receive the queen at his country house, amongst which were especial provisions for the accommodation of Mrs. Blanche Parry, who was at that time Chief of the Privy Chamber to the Queen.

"In the 'Additional MSS.' in the British Museum are preserved accounts of the presents given and received between the Queen and Mrs. Blanche Parry and other ladies; a specimen or two of which are subjoined.

"1561-2.—By Mrs. Blanche Apparrey, one square piece of un-shorne vellat edged with silver lace.

"1561-2.—To Mrs. Blanche Apparry oone guilt stoupe with a cover, per oz. 16, dim. ¼ oz.

"1571-2.—Item, a fayre flower of gold, being a rose enamelled white and redd in the toppe, and other flowers, also all sett with three diamonds, three rubies, and one little perle in the midds, half an ounce and a farthing gold weight, geven by Mrs. Blanche Apparry.

"1577-8.—To the Queen. By Mrs. Blanche a Parry a littill box of gold to putt cumphetts in, and a little spone of gold, weying all 3 oz. 1 qr.

"1577-8.—By the Queen, to Mrs. Blanche Parry, in guilte plate keele, per oz. 18 oz. di.

"Mrs. Blanche Parry had the custody of the Queen's jewels, a list of which is given in the 'Additional MSS.' in the British

Museum, 6142; and most of the new year's gifts to the Queen were delivered to her care.

"Mrs. Blanche Parry died on the 12th February, 1590, in the 82nd year of her age. Her death is thus mentioned in a letter written by Thomas Markham to the Earl of Shrewsbury:

"*Right Honorable my Syngular good Lord.*

*   *   *   "On Thursday last, Mrs. Blanshe a Parrye dep'ted: blynde she was here on earthe, but I hope the joyes in heven she shall se. Her Matie, God be praysed, is in helthe.   *   *   *   From Westmyster the xvii of Februarye, 1589 (1590.)

"Your Lordshypps most bounde,

"THO. MARKHAM."

"Her will, proved 5th March, 1590, was written by Lord Burleigh. In it she disposes of a great number of diamonds; amongst others, she gives 'to the Queen my best diamonds;' 'to Sir Christopher Hatton, Knight, Lord Chancellor of England, one table diamond;' 'to Lord Burleigh, Lord High Treasurer of England, my second diamond;' 'to Lady Cobham, Lady Dorothie Stafforde, Lord Lumley, her niece Lady Frances Burghe, her cousin Katherine Knollys, Lady Blanche Somersett, and many others, she gives diamonds, money, gold chains, girdles,' &c. She gives her nephew Frances Vaughan and Hugh Bethel, 'all her manor lands and woods of Risse in York and Wheeldrake.' She directs her executors, Thomas Powell and Hugh Bethell, 'to purchase as much land as shall yield above all charges yearly, for ever, the number of seven score bushels of corn; namely, wheat and rye, to be bestowed and distributed yearly amongst the poor people of Bacton and Newton. The Dean and Chapter of Hereford to have the oversight of the bestowing and distributing of the said corn.'

"At the foot of this will Lord Burleigh wrote, 'I do affirm that my cousin, Mrs. Blanche ap Parrye, did confess this to be her last will, and required me to seal it up, which I did; and now, the 17th of February, I have opened it.

"WILLIAM BURLEIGHE."

The monument to the memory of Mrs. Blanche Parry at Bacton, for which she left in her will 300*l.*, represents her kneeling before Queen Elizabeth, and presenting a book to Her Majesty. There is another monument to her in the church of St. Margaret's, Westminster.

[6] By a mistake of the printer, this edition, a copy of which is in the possession of the writer, is dedicated "To the most virtuous and noble *Prince* Elizabeth," &c.

"In a word," says Arthur Johns, Esq., the author of the excellent Essay on the Cause of Dissent in Wales, "both the religious education and general education of the people of the Principality, has sprung from the most discouraged part of the clergy, and the efforts of the various bodies of Dissenters. What can be expected from such a state of things but dissent—deep-rooted dissent? The influence of the English bishops on all these good works, has been like that of a stream which flows through Bala Lake—but, as it is thought, without mingling with the waters!"[7]

In 1568, the Queen issued a Commission, addressed to the nobility and gentry in the Principality, to hold an Eisteddfod, or literary meeting, at Caerwys in Flintshire, for the purpose of regulating the laws of the ancient bards and minstrels of Wales. The proclamation for that purpose ran thus :—

"BY THE QUEEN,

"ELIZABETH by the Grace of God, of England, France, and Ireland, Queen, and Defender of the Faith, &c.; to our trusty and right well beloved Sir Richard Bulkely, Knight; Sir Rees Griffith, Knight; Ellis Price, Esq., Dr. in Civil Law, and one of our Council in the Marchesse of Wales; William Mostyn; Jeuan Lloyd, of Yale; John Salisbury, of Rhug; Rice Thomas, Maurice Wynne, William Lewis, Pierce Mostyn, Owen John ap Howel Fychan, John William ap John, John Lewis Owen, Morris Griffith, Symon Thelwall, John Griffith, Ellis ap William Lloyd, Robert Puleston, Harry ap Harry, William Glynn, and Rees Hughes, Esq., and to every of them greeting :—

"Whereas it is come to the knowledge of the Lord President, and other our council in the Marchesse of Wales, that vagrant and idle persons, naming themselves *Minstrels*, *Rythmers*, and *Bards*, are lately grown into such *intolerable multitude* within the Principality of North Wales, that not only gentlemen and others, by their *shameless disorders*, are oftentimes disquieted in their habitations, but also the *expert minstrels* and *musicians* in *Tonge* and *Camynge*, thereby much discouraged to travaile in the Eucipe and Practise of their knowledg, and also not a little hindred (of) livings and preferment; the reformation whereof and the putting these people in order, the said Lord President and Council, have thought very necessary: And knowing you to be men of both wisdom and upright dealing, and also of experience and good knowledg in the scyence, have appointed and authorised you to be commissioners for that purpose : and forasmuch as our said council of late travailing in some part of the said Principality, had perfect understanding by credible report that the accustomed place for the execution of the like commission hath been hithertofore at Cayroes, in our County of Flynt, and that William Mostyn, Esq., and his ancestors have had the gift and bestowing the *Sylver Harp*, appertaining to the *chief* of *that Faculty*, and that a *Year's warning* (at least) hath been accustomed of the *Assembly* and execution of the like commission; Our said council have, therefore, appointed the execution of this commission to be at the said town of Cayroes, the Monday next after the Feast of the Blessed Trinity, which shall be in the year of our Lord, 1568. And, therefore, we require and command you, by the authority of these presents, not only to cause *open Proclamation* to be made in all *Faires*, *Market Towns*, and other *places of Assembly* within our

---

[7] The following summary of the comparison of the utility of the Welsh bishops during forty years, and the English bishops in Wales during forty years, will show the working of the present unhallowed system :—

Welsh Prelates, 1601.

"They found a people immersed in Popery; they left a nation of Protestants."—*Dr. Davies's Address to his Countrymen, prefixed to the First Edition of the New Testament.*

"In the last century there was not one Welshman acquainted only with the Welsh language who professed the Roman Catholic Religion."— *Welsh Piety, by the Rev. Griffith Jones.*

"The period of Welsh bishops terminates with the Civil Wars, 1641, during which time North Wales was more faithful than any other part of the kingdom to the Crown and the Church."—*Rev. Walter Davis's Life of Hugh Morris, the Bard.*

English Prelates, 1761.

"They found a nation of Churchmen; they left a nation of Dissenters !

"In the present century, in most districts of Wales, there is hardly one Welshman acquainted only with the Welsh language who does not frequent the Dissenting Chapel oftener than the Church !

"The period of English bishops ends in 1700, with the general predominance of Dissent, which has continued to progress ever since, and, according to the present iniquitous system, no doubt, will still progress !"

Counties of Agleze, Carnarvon, Meryonydd, Denbigh, and Flynt, that all and every person and persons that intend to *maintain* their *living* by name or colour of *Minstrels, Rythmers,* and *Bards,* within the Talaith of Aberffraw, comprehending the said five shires, shall be and appear before you, the said day and place, to *show* their *Leanings* accordingly: But also that you twenty, nineteen, eighteen, seventeen, fifteen, fourteen, thirteen, twelve, eleven, ten, nine, eight, seven, or six of you, wherof you the said Sir Richard Bulkeley, Sir Rees Griffith, Ellis Price, and William Mostyn, Esqs., or three or four of you to be of the number, to repair to the said place the days aforesaid, and calling to you such *Expert* men in the said *Faculty* of the *Welsh Musick,* as by you shall be thought convenient, to proceed to the execution of the Premises, and to admit such and so many, as by your wisdom and knowlegdes you shall find *worthy,* into and under such degrees (*in use*) in scrutable sort to *use, exersise* and *follow* the *Sciences* and *Faculties* of their *Professions,* in such decent order as shall appertain to each of their degrees, and as your discretions and wisdoms shall prescribe unto them: Giving streight monition and commandment in our name and on our behalf to the rest not worthy, that they return to some honest labour and due exersise, such as they be most apt unto for maintenance of their living, upon pain to be taken as sturdy and idle vagabonds, and to be used according to the laws and statutes provided in that behalf; letting you with our said council look for advertisement, by certificates at your hands, of your doings to the execution of the said Premises; foreseeing in anywise, that upon the said assembly the peace and good order be observed and kept accordingly; ascertaining you that the said William Mostyn hath promised to see furniture and things necessary provided for that assembly, at the place aforesaid.

"Given under our signet at our City of Chester the twenty-third of October, in the ninth of our reign, 1567.

       (Signed)   " HER HIGHNESS'S COUNCIL IN THE MARCHESSE OF WALES." [8]

The following is the result of this commission which took place in the 10th year of Queen Elizabeth, and is translated from the original in Welsh:—

"KNOW ALL MEN, BY THESE PRESENTS, That there is a congress of bards and musicians to be held in the town of Caerwys, in the County of Flint, on the 26th day of May, in the tenth year of the reign of her Majesty Queen Elizabeth, before Ellis Price, Esq., Doctor of the Civil Law, and one of her Majesty's Council in the Marches; and before William Mostyn, Pyers Mostyn, Owen John ap Hywel Vaughan, John William ap John, John Lewis Owen, Morris Griffith, Simon Thelwall, John Griffith, Serjeant, Robert Pulesdon, Evan Lloyd of Jâl, and William Glyn, Esquires.

"And that we the said Commissioners, by virtue of the said Commission, being her Majesty's Council, do give and grant to Symwnt Vychan, Bard, the degree of Pencerdd; and do order that persons do receive and hospitably entertain him fit for him to go and come to receive his perquisites according to the princely statutes in that case made and provided. Given under our hands in the year 1568." [9]

As these meetings are connected with royalty, and, in the ancient days of yore, were presided over by the Princes of Wales, and, in modern days, patronised by Royalty, a short historical account of them will not be unacceptable to our readers, especially of the Principality : [1]—

"There is good reason for believing that the Bards and Minstrels were originally a constitutional appendage of the Druidical Hierarchy, which was divided into three classes, priests, philosophers and poets. At Llanidan, in Anglesey, formerly

[8] "This Commission was copied exactly from the original at Mostyn, 1693; where the *Silver Harp* also is.—Rev. Evan Evans, (Ieuan Brydydd Hir)."— The Commission has been missing for several years, but the Elizabethan Silver Harp still remains in the possession of the Hon. E. M. H. Mostyn, M.P., Mostyn Hall, Flintshire.—ED.

[9] In pursuance of this royal mandate, an Eisteddfod was held on the 26th of May, 1568. At this assemblage, the number of the poetical Bards was seventeen, and of their musical brethren thirty-eight; and at the same time William Llyn was admitted to the degree of Pencerdd, or Doctor; and Sion Tudor, William Cynval, and Huw Llyn, commenced *Disgyblion Pencerddiaid,* Masters of the art of Poetry. The prize was adjudged to Sion ap William ap Sion.

[1] For a full account of these interesting meetings, we beg to refer our readers to " Observations on the Music of Wales," by Mr. Jones, late Royal Harper (Bardd y Brenin).

inhabited by the druidical conventual societies, we, even to this day, find vestiges of Tre'r Dryw, the Arch-Druid's mansion, and near it, of Tre'r Beirdd, the Hamlet of the Bards.   Mr. Mason, in his Caractacus, has adopted the ancient distinction of three orders of Druids.   Having spoken of the Arch-Druid, he proceeds—

> " His brotherhood
> Possess the neighbouring cliffs :
>   On the left
> Reside the sage Ovates : yonder grots
> Are tenanted by Bards, who nightly thence
> Robed in their flowing vests of innocent white,
> Descend, with harps that glitter to the moon,
> Hymning immortal strains."

The disciples of the druidical Bards, during a noviciate of twenty years, learnt an immense number of verses, in which they preserved the principles of their civil and religious polity by uninterrupted tradition for many centuries.   Though the use of letters was familiar to them, they never committed their verses to writing, for the sake of strengthening their intellectual faculties, and of keeping their mysterious knowledge from the contemplation of the vulgar.   The metre in which these poetical doctrines were communicated, was called *Englyn Milwr*, or the Warrior's Song, which is a stanza of three lines, each of seven syllables, the first and second containing the general subject of the poem, and the third conveying some divine or moral precept, or prudential maxim.

When the Roman legions, after the invasion of Britain, and the conquest of the Gallic provinces, were recalled to oppose the power of Pompey in Italy, the exultation of the Bards, at recovering the secure possession and exercise of their ancient poetical function, is described in a very animated manner by Lucan :—

> " Ye, too, ye Bards, whom sacred raptures fire,
> To chaunt your heroes to your country's lyre ;
> Who consecrate in your immortal strain,
> Brave patriot souls in righteous battle slain,
> Securely now the tuneful task renew,
> And noblest themes in deathless songs pursue."

The Druids being expelled from Britain by the Roman legions, the Bards soon lost their sacred character, and began to appear in an honourable, though less dignified capacity, at the courts of the British kings.   But the sixth century may emphatically be termed the golden age of Welsh poetry, when the Bards resumed the harp with unusual boldness, to animate their country's last struggle with the Saxons.   To this era is Wales indebted for some of her brightest luminaries, among whom may be numbered Aneurin Gwawdrydd, Taliesin, Llywarch Hên, and Merddyn ab Morfryn; whose works are pregnant with feeling, with fancy and enthusiasm, and do honour to the nation that produced them.

From the era of Cadwaladr, history is obstinately silent concerning the Welsh music and poetry, to the middle of the tenth century, a period illuminated by the laws of Howel.   In these laws we do not find the musical or poetical establishment of the national bards; but they contain such injunctions respecting the Bard of the Palace, and the Chief Bard of Wales, as in some measure to compensate for that defect of information.—When the Chief Bard appeared at the court of the Welsh princes, he sat next to the judge of the palace.   None but himself and the Bard of the Palace were allowed to perform in the presence of the Prince.   When the Prince desired to hear music, the Chief Bard sang to his harp two poems, one in praise of the Almighty, the other concerning kings and their heroic exploits; after which a third poem was sung by the Bard of the Palace.   He accompanied the army when it marched into an enemy's country; and while it was preparing for battle, or dividing the spoils, he performed an ancient song, called *Unbennaeth Prydain*,—the Monarchy of Britain :

> " The Bard, who first adorn'd our native tongue,
> Tuned to his British lyre this ancient song ; "

and for his service, when the Prince had received his share of the spoils, was rewarded with the most valuable beast that remained.

About the year 1070, Prince Bleddyn ap Cynfyn, the author of another code of Welsh laws, established some regulations respecting the musical Bards, and revised and enforced those which were already made.

Towards the close of the eleventh century the great Prince Gryffudd ap Cynan invited to Wales some of the best musicians of Ireland; and being partial to the music of that island, and observing with displeasure the abuses and disorders of the Welsh Bards, created a body of Institutes for the amendment of their manners, and the correction of their art and practice.   This grand reformation was effected by dividing the Bards into classes and assigning to each class a distinct profession and employment.

The period that intervened between the reign of Gruffydd ap Cynan, and that of the last Prince, Llywelyn, is the brightest in the annals of Cambria: it abounds with perhaps the noblest monuments of genius, as well as valour, of which the Welsh nation can boast. Early in the twelfth century, harmony and verse had approached their utmost degree of perfection. Nor by the common fate of the arts in other countries did they suddenly fall from the eminence they had attained. The poets of these memorable times added energy to a nervous language, and the musicians called forth from the harp its loudest and grandest tones, to animate the ancient struggle of their brave countrymen for freedom and the possession of their parent soil. What was the success of their virtuous and noble purpose, the history of the eras when they flourished, can best explain. It is no slight proof of their influence, that when the brave but unfortunate Prince, Llywelyn the Last, after the surrender of his rights, and the sacrifice of his patriotism to his love, was treacherously slain at Buellt, "Edward I.," says Mr. Jones, "did not think himself secure in his triumph, till he had added cruelty to injustice and given the final blow to Welsh liberty in the massacre of the Bards." The massacre was general, and as some of their most eminent Bards must have perished, it is probable that many of their works, and of the remains of their predecessors, were also destroyed, and are for ever lost.

Though heroic poetry was afterwards no more attempted in Wales, a long series of Bards succeeded, who by their elegies and odes have made their names memorable for ages. Nor had the national instrument, though not strung to inspire martial deeds of daring, ceased to vibrate in its native vallies. The ingenious author of "Musical and Poetical Relics of the Welsh Bards," tells us that, about the end of Queen Elizabeth's reign, flourished Twm Bach (or Thomas Pritchard) who was the Orpheus on the harp at that time. He was born at Coity, in Wales; died (anno 1597) in London, and was buried in St. Sepulchre's Church. That poetry sympathised with the sister art for the loss, we may be convinced by the bipartite Englyn, written upon his death, of which the following is an English translation:—

> "Ah, see! our last, best lyrist goes,
> Sweet as his strain be his repose!
> Extinct are all the tuneful fires,
> And Music with *Twm Bach* expires;
> No finger now remains to bring
> The tone of rapture from the string."

In the reign of George II., Powell, a Welsh harper, who used to play before that monarch, drew such tones from his instrument that the great Handel was delighted with his performance, and composed for him several pieces of music, some of which are in the first set of Handel's concertos.[2] He also introduced him as a performer in his Oratorios, in which there are some songs, Harp Obligato, that were accompanied by Powell, such as "Tune your harps," and "Praise the Lord with cheerful voice," in Esther; and "Hark! he strikes the golden lyre," in Alexander Balus.

The Eisteddfod was a triennial assembly of the Bards. The places at which it was anciently held, were Aberffraw, formerly the royal seat of the Princes of North Wales; Dynevor, the royal castle of the Princes of South Wales, in Carmarthenshire; Mathrafal, the royal palace of the Princes of Powis; and in later times, Caerwys, in Flintshire, received that honourable distinction, being chosen for this purpose, in compliance with the ancient custom of the Welsh, because it had been the princely residence of Llywelyn the Last.

What served greatly to heighten the emulation of the Bards, if they wanted any additional incitement, was the presence of the Prince, who usually presided in these contests. Their compositions delivered upon these occasions are frequently upon historical subjects, and are valuable for their authenticity; for it was the business of the Eisteddfod, not only to give laws to poetry and music, but to discover falsehood and establish certainty in the relation of events.

All those among them who aspired to the honour of presiding over the Bards, came forward (as the statute prescribes) at the triennial assembly, and contested it with each other, and with the Chief Bard who already possessed it. The successful candidate was seated in a magnificent chair, and was hence called Bardd Cadeiriog, the Chaired-Bard. He was at the same time invested with a little silver or gold chair, which he wore on his breast as a badge of his office.

---

[2] In this sketch of the Welsh Bards and Minstrels, it must not be understood as if we were insensible of the claims which many of a later date, and of the present day, have to distinction. We shall not enter into a discussion on their respective merits: suffice it to say, that the revival of Welsh literature within the last thirty years, has drawn forth from the shades of obscurity a splendid exhibition of talent, which would reflect lustre upon the best days of old Cambria. For this favourable revolution in the annals of Welsh letters, the country is chiefly indebted to the re-establishment of the Eisteddfodau, which in days of yore had the merit of extending and keeping alive the national patriotism, as well as that love of Poetry and Music that so much distinguished the ancient Britons. The Eisteddfodau were the school in which the Welsh language was gradually improved, and brought at last to its unrivalled perfection. The Bards, says an ingenious critic, have been always considered by the Welsh as the guardians of their language, and the conservators of its purity.

Before the time of Gruffudd ap Cynan, the musical Bards were subject to the Chief Bard of the poets; but there are good reasons for believing that in his reign, and afterwards, they had a chair and a president of their own.

It has already been said, in the preceding history of the Bards, that in the twelfth century harmony and verse had approached their utmost degree of perfection in Wales. In the progress of the succeeding age, there were some visible symptoms of decay; but, says a late writer, "a remedy was so diligently applied by the skill of the Eisteddfod to the declining art, that they preserved their former vigour, and perhaps acquired new graces." From the twelfth to the close of the fifteenth century, however, we collect no traces of the Eisteddfodau, and but few national occurrences that called forth the martial spirit of the Awen or Welsh muse. The accession of Henry VII. led to the revival of these national institutions. If during several inauspicious reigns, the Eisteddfodau had been discontinued, they were re-established in this Prince's reign, and the Bards were employed in the honourable commission of making out from their authentic records the pedigree of their King.

From the days of Sir Richard Bassett, to the year 1819, the only efforts to restore this national usage appear to have been those made by the Gwyneddigion,[3] a society established in London, in 1771, for the cultivation of the Welsh language. Under their patronage, several Bardic meetings have taken place, at different periods, in North Wales, and prizes have been distributed by them to the successful candidates both in music and poetry. Of late years, however, a new era has dawned upon Wales, and societies have been formed in the four provinces[4] for the encouragement of the national literature. The nobility, gentry, and clergy connected with the Principality, with a commendable zeal, have patronised these assemblages, by which a considerable portion of native talent has been elicited, which would otherwise have remained hid in obscurity. These meetings have been held in the following order:—On the 8th of July, 1819, the Cambrian Society, in Dyved, held its first Eisteddfod at Carmarthen, on which occasion the Bishop of St. David's presided. On the 13th of September, in the following year, "The Cymmrodorion in Powys" had a similar meeting at Wrexham, under the auspices of Sir W. W. Wynn. To these succeeded two other Bardic Festivals, at Caervarvon and Brecon, on the 12th of Setember, 1821, and the 15th of the same month in the following year, at which the Marquis of Anglesea, and Sir Charles Morgan, Bart., were respectively Presidents. In 1823, a second meeting was held at Caermarthen, Lord Dynevor, President; and in September, 1825, a Congress met at Welshpool, under the auspices of the Cymmrodorion in Powys, patronised by Lord Clive. Brecon had a second similar meeting, 1826, when Lord Rodney presided.

In 1828, a grand Eisteddfod was held at Denbigh, under the presidency of Sir Edward Mostyn, Bart. This was patronised by the presence of his Royal Highness the Duke of Sussex. In 1832 another grand Eisteddfod was held at Beaumaris, under the munificent presidency of Sir Richard Bulkeley, Bart., MP. This was patronised by the distinguished presence of her Royal Highness the Duchess of Kent, and the PRINCESS VICTORIA, now QUEEN OF ENGLAND, who jointly presented and personally invested each of the successful candidates with a Royal Medal. The next Eisteddfod was at Liverpool, in 1839, under the presidency of the Honourable E. M. Lloyd Mostyn, M.P., when the Mayor of Liverpool, Sir Joshua Walmesley, gave a most splendid entertainment to the Welsh nobility, gentry, and others who were present at that Eisteddfod.

The nobility and gentry of South Wales, with their princely patronage, kept up those meetings annually for several years at Abergavenny, under the presidency of Sir Charles Morgan, Bart., M.P.; Sir Benjamin Hall, Bart., M.P.; Sir John Guest, Bart., M.P., &c., &c., which were attended with the most beneficial results to the sons of Awen. The last Eisteddfod took place at Aberffraw, in Anglesea, 1849, under the presidency of O. F. Meyric, Esq. But the forthcoming Eisteddfod, to be held at Rhuddlan Castle this year (1850), under the presidency of the Right Honourable the Lord Mostyn, and the distinguished patronage of HER MAJESTY THE QUEEN, the PRINCE ALBERT, the PRINCE OF WALES, and the principal nobility and gentry of Wales, promises to excel in greatness and real utility, every other that has taken place for the last century. To the able promoters of such meetings as these, we would emphatically say, in the words of Goronwy Owen to the Cymry of London:—

> "Llwydd ichwi eirweilch, llaw Dduw ich arwedd,
> Dilyth eginau, da lwythau Gwynedd;
> Bro eich tadau, a bri eich tudwedd,—a harddoch
> Y mae wyr ynoch, emau o rinwedd!"

The principal object of this meeting, like those of its predecessors, will be to explore the treasures of ancient British history, and to recover from the ravages of time such relics of antiquity as may illustrate the customs and manners of the Cymry; but more especially, to revive and cultivate the ancient poetry, music, and the general literature of the country. For the promotion of these valuable purposes, so dear to the hearts of every true son of Cambria, these national assemblages are admirably calculated.

---

[3] Natives of Gwynedd, or North Wales.   [4] Gwynedd and Powys, in North Wales; Dyved and Gwent, in South Wales.

Annexed is a representation of the Silver Harp, alluded to in the Royal Commission, which is still in the possession of the Hon. E. M. Lloyd Mostyn, M.P. for Flintshire, and which has been from time immemorial in the gift of his ancestors, to bestow on the *chief of the faculty*. This badge of honour is about five or six inches long, and furnished with strings equal to the number of the Muses. It was probably worn by the Chief Musician, as the silver chair was by the Chief Poet.

The Elizabethan Silver Harp at Mostyn Hall.

A.D. 1563.—Her Majesty (Queen Elizabeth) created Robert Dudley, Earl of Leicester, Baron Denbigh, and made a grant to that favourite of Denbigh Castle and its dependencies; viz., the great lordships of Denbigh, Bromfeild and Yale, consisting of seventeen manors and their several townships.

Pennant records, on authority, that Leicester constrained the tenants on the lordship to treble their rents, to the sum of 900*l.* per annum, although they had presented him with 2000*l.* by way of fine on his first entry. He also enclosed the waste, to their great detriment; on which they rose in a body, and levelled his fences. This was construed into rebellion against the crown, and two hopeful young men of the Salusburys of Lleweni were tried at Shrewsbury and suffered death. He had the insolence also to mortgage the lordship to some merchants in London, and, of course, tricked them of their money. In fine his conduct was such as obliged his royal mistress to interfere and confirm the quiet possession to the tenants. In the year 1572, it was his will and pleasure that the burgesses should choose one Henry Dynne to be their representative, but they were refractory, and returned Mr. Richard Candishe. Among the corporation papers is a letter sent on this occasion by the Earl of Leicester to the bailiffs, aldermen, and burgesses, blaming them for making choice of a burgess to parliament without his consent, and commanding them to alter their election, and to choose Henry Dynne. The letter is as follows :—

" I have been latlie advertised how small consideration you have had of the Lettre I wrote unto you for the nomynasion of yor burgess, whereat as I cannot but greatlie meruayle (in respect I am yor L. and you my tenaunts,) as also the manie good tournes and comodities wch I have bene allways willinge to procure you for the benefitte of your whole state, so do I take the same in so——, and will yt so unthankfullie, as yf youe do not uppon receite hereof presently revoke the same, and appointe such one as I shall nominate, namelie Henrie Dynne, be ye well assured never to loke for any ffriendshipe or fav^r at my hande in any yor affayres hereafter : not for any great accompt I make of the thinge, but for that I would not it shou'd be thought that I have so small regard borne me at yor hands, who are bounden to owe (as yor L.) thus much dutie as to know myne advice and pleasure; that will haplie be alleadged that your choice was made before the receipt of my l^{res}. In replie I would litle have thoughte that youe would have bene so forgetfull, or rather carelesse of me, as before yor deĉion not to make me privie therto, or at the least to have some desire of myne advise therein (having tyme ynoughe so to do) but as you have of yor selves thus rashlie proceeded herein, without myne assent, soe have I thought good to signifie unto youe that I mean not to take it anywise at yor hands, and therefore wysh you more advisedlie to consider hereof and to deale with me as maye continue my fav^r towards you, otherwise loke for no fav^r at my hands, and so fare ye well. From the court, this last day of Aprill, 1572.

R. LEYCESTER."

To quiet his conscience perhaps for his many bad deeds, here and elsewhere, and to make that sort of atonement for ill-gotten wealth and power which many oppressors had done before him,[3] Lord Leicester began a magnificent structure for a parish church in the style of architecture of that day, neither pure Grecian nor Gothic, the remains of which attempt are now visible near St. Hilary's Chapel. Its date is engraved on a corner stone, viz., 1st of March, 1579, on which day its foundation was laid in honour of the patron saint of Wales. A moral sentence in Latin is added. A little below this inscription are the initials G. A., probably Gulielmus Asaphensis, viz., William Hughes, Bishop of St. Asaph at that time. Pennant adds, from certain MSS. of the late Dr. Foulkes, an anecdote which shows how Denbigh suffered from both the royal favourites of that reign. The Earl of Essex passing through Denbigh, on his way to Ireland, borrowed from the corporation some thousands which had been raised for the completion of the work, which were never repaid, and the unfinished work was abandoned to its present ruin.

Among other interesting letters of this period, we observe one from Bishop Grindal, who was one of our earliest horticulturists. His grapes at Fulham are stated by Strype to have been esteemed of that value, and a fruit the Queen stood so well affected to, and so early ripe, that the bishop used every year to send her Majesty a present of them. In a postscript to his letter of the 9th of September, 1569, the bishop himself mentions them, and says, " My grapes[6] this yeare are not yet rype; abowt the ende off the nexte weeke I hope to sende to the Queene's Majestie;" i. e., about the middle of September.

A.D. 1573.—Among the Lansdowne MSS. in the Museum, No. 16, Art. 52, is " an estimate of the increase of the chardgies, in the time of Progresse, which should not be if her Majestie remeynid at her standing house within xx miles of London; collected out of the Creditors of the last Progresse, Anno xv. Reginæ Elizabeth." It is altered and corrected in Lord Burleigh's hand. The increase of charges caused by the Progress appears to have amounted in the whole to 1034l. 0s. 6d. Although not exactly bearing on our subject, we will cite from the letters a few facts illustrative of the feelings of some of Queen Elizabeth's subjects, when they heard that her Majesty had vouchsafed to honour them with a visit during her Progresses. Lord Keeper Bacon, it will be seen, rejoiced much at the report that her Majesty intended him so great an honour; but owned himself quite a novice in receiving royalty. We gather from some of the letters how inconvenient these Progresses must have been to other lords. The Earl of Bedford thought two nights and a day quite sufficient for the visit at Woburn to continue; and hinted to Lord Burleigh that he had made preparation for no longer time.

Archbishop Parkes was one of the few who seemed thoroughly pleased at one of these intended visits. A thought struck him to make it subservient to the promotion of the Protestant religion.

Queen Elizabeth, on more than one occasion, intended to have visited the Border towns. The following is extracted from the Bailiff of Shrewsbury's account for the year 1574:—

" Given to the Queen's herbinger, in gold, and spent upon her Grace's s'vaunts resorting to this towne sondrye tymes this yeare, concerninge her Grace's comyng to this towne, 2l. 7s. 10d."

She was entertained at Bristol in August, in honour of which the celebrated Churchyard, the Elizabethan bard, supplied his usual contingent " of frigid conceits and bald rhymes;" so much, however, to the taste of the court, that Sir Henry Sydney, one of his numerous patrons, recommended him for the same service to the good folks of Shrewsbury, the place of his birth.

" Given Mr. Churchard, in rewarde, being sent unto us by my lord p'sident with letters con'inge of the Queene's majestie to this towne by the assent of the aldermen and counsellors, 3l. 6s. 8d."

The proposed visit, however, did not take place, but it was intended again in the following year. The MS. Chronicle, quoted by the Shropshire historians, states: " This yeare, 1575, the Queene's majesty went a progresse towardes Shrowsbury; but because of death," (i. e. some pestilential disease) " wythin a four

---

[3] Henry VII. is said to have built the beautiful churches of Wrexham, Gresford and Mold, out of the wealth he acquired by the death of Sir John Stanley.

[6] In the time of Henry VII., fruit appears to have been very scarce. In an original MS. signed by the king himself, and kept in the Remembrancer's Office, it appears that apples were not less than 1s. and 2s. a piece, and that a red rose cost 2s.

myles of the same, she cam no further than Lychefield, and from thence went to Worcester, the whych cyty she lyckyd well."

Lord Leicester writing to the Earl of Sussex, in 1577, says, " We do what we can to persuade [her Majesty] from any Progress at all." It is quite evident that the Queen was fickle; and frequently gave but short notice as to what part of the country she chose to visit.

Lord Buckhurst, who expected to receive her Majesty at Lewes, in 1577, was so forestalled in respect of provisions, by other noblemen in Sussex and the adjoining counties, that he was obliged to send for a supply from Flanders.

It does not appear that Queen Elizabeth ever visited Chester, but her two great favourites, the Earls of Leicester and Essex, the former in 1583,[7] the later in 1598, were received with almost regal honours. The Earl of Essex was at Chester both on his road to Ireland, and on his return. About this time the influx of soldiers passing and re-passing, to and from Ireland, was so great, that the city was not able to maintain them, and many riots and disorders ensued.[8] The Earl of Tyrone, who had so long maintained a rebellion against the Queen was brought to Chester in 1603, and lodged at the Mayor's house.[9]

A.D. 1586.—The autumn of this year was distinguished by the trial of Mary, Queen of Scots, for concurring in Babington's plot or conspiracy to assassinate Queen Elizabeth. The MS. Chronicle, quoted before, states, " The 17th day of December, the sheriffe proclaymed in Salop, the Queene of Scotts traitor being tried by examination, to be in confederacy with the former conspirators, as Babington and his associates, for conspiringe hir Majestie's death, who were exicuted; and the sayd traitor, the Scottish Queene, hath judgment to dye, and for joye thereof the bayliffes and aldermen caused bony fires and bell ringings, with assemblyng themselves in their beest arraye in banquetting and rejoysinge the same, praysinge God with triumph and sounde of trumpet."

Queen Elizabeth died on the 24th of March, 1603, having reigned forty-four years, and in the seventieth year of her age, a duration of sovereignty to which no monarch of England, with the exception of George III., ever attained. She was the scourge of Spain, and the terror of Rome; the darling of her people, and the dread of her enemies; and so happy in the choice of her ministers, that success attended all her enterprises. In a word, her incomparable wisdom, and the unusual happiness of her reign, raised her to the esteem and envy of that age, and the wonder of posterity.

---

[7] A meeting of the corporation was held on the 13th of May, 1583, to settle how the Earl of Leicester should be entertained; it was proposed that there should be a banquet, and that for the present supply of money, all members of the corporation should lend from twenty shillings to 6s. 8d., according to their degree. This intention was afterwards given up, and it was determined to present the Earl with 40 angels in a gold cup, value 18l. Harleian MSS. No. 1989, fol. 392.

[8] Harleian MSS., No. 2125.   [9] Ibid.

HOUSE OF STUART.

PON the death of Queen Elizabeth, of Ever Glorious Memory, King JAMES THE SIXTH of Scotland was proclaimed King of England, by the name and title of JAMES THE FIRST; in whose reign England and Scotland were united under one Crown, and took the denominative appellation of *Great Britain*. He ascended the throne on the 24th of March, 1603, with the approbation of all orders of the State, because in him every claim of hereditary descent was reconciled and united.[1]

In 1617, the King made a tour through a portion of his dominions in England and Wales. The following anecdote is related of him whilst in Wales. It appears that several of our countrymen were formerly known to the King, and by way of showing their attachment and loyalty, a number of them formed themselves as his body guard, and escorted him to the City of Chester. The weather was very dry, the roads dusty, and the King almost suffocated; he did not know how to get rid of them civilly, when one of his attendants putting his head out of the carriage, said, " It is his Majesty's pleasure that those who are the best gentlemen should ride forward." Away scampered the Welsh; and one solitary man was left behind. " And so, sir," said the King, " and you are not a gentleman then?" " *Oh yes, and please your Majesty, hur is as good a shentleman as the rest; but hur ceffyl* (horse), *God bless hur, is not so good.*"

The following anecdotes, as connected with our countrymen, and the Royal passion for creating knights and baronets, are also recorded of King James. Sir Kenelm Digby tells us, " He (the King) hated a drawn sword, since the fright his mother was in, during her pregnancy, at the sight of the swords, with which David Rizzio, her secretary, was assassinated in her presence; and hence it came that her son had such an aversion all his life to a drawn sword. I remember," proceeds he, " when he dubbed me knight, in the ceremony of putting a naked sword on my shoulder, he could not endure to look upon it, but turned his face another way; insomuch that, in lieu of touching my shoulder, he had almost thrust the point into my eye, had not the Duke of Buckingham guided his hand aright." " I remember," says Yorke, " to have heard that when he knighted old Sir William Morice, of Clenenneu, in Caernarvonshire, and turning upon him, after he quitted his sword, ' By Christ," says the King, ' I fear I have knighted an old woman,' and Sir William's picture justifies the notion."

When James I. was at Shrewsbury the magistrates of that day paid the overstrained compliment of wishing " that his Majesty might reign as long as the sun, moon, and stars endured." Upon this James shrewdly remarked, " That if their wishes were fulfilled his son must reign by candle light."

" On the 23rd of August, 1617, the ancient and loyal city of Chester," says one of our old manuscripts, " was graced with the royal presence of our sovereign, King James, who being attended with many

---

[1] The ceremonial for the coronation of James I. was prepared under the superintendence of that monarch, and displays many marks of the pedantry and extravagant notions of the royal prerogative, which formed so large a portion of his character. He created two earls, ten barons, sixty-two knights of the bath, and conferred the honour of knighthood on about four hundred gentlemen.

honourable earls, right reverend bishops, and worthy knights and courtiers, besides all the gentry of the Shire, rode in state through the City, being met by sheriffs, peers, and the common council of the City, with his foot cloth well mounted on horseback. All the train soldiers of the City, standing without the Eastgate, and every company with their ensigns in seemly sort, did keep their stations on both sides of the

James the First's Entrance into the City of Chester.

Eastgate-street. The mayor and all the aldermen took their places on a platform, railed and hung about in green, and there in most grave and seemly manner, they attended the coming of his Majesty. At which time, after a learned speech delivered by the recorder, the mayor presented to the King a fair standing cup, with a cover double gilt, and therein an hundred jacobins of gold; and likewise the mayor delivered the City sword to the King, who gave it to the mayor again: and the same was borne before the King by the mayor, he being on horseback; and the sword of state was borne by the Right Hon. William, Earl of Derby, chief chamberlain of the county palatine of Chester. The King rode first to the Minster, where he alighted from his horse, and in the west aisle of the Minster he heard an oration delivered in Latin, by a scholar of the Free School. He went to the choir, and there, in a seat made for the King, at the higher end of the choir, he heard an anthem sung; and, after certain prayers, the King went from thence to the Pentice, where a sumptuous banquet was prepared at the expense of the citizens, which being ended, the King departed to the Vale Royal, and at his departure the order of knighthood was offered to the mayor (Charles Fitton, merchant), which was refused by the same."[2]

The materials of Welsh history of the reign of James are but few and scanty, and form but a petty prelude to the importance, the variety, and the tragical nature of those connected with his son, the unfortunate Charles the First.

[2] The Rev. Thos. Crane's MS. The same MS. states that ale and strong beer were sold at this time (1617), at Chester, for one penny per quart.

CHARLES THE FIRST.—This monarch ascended the throne in the year 1625, on the death of his father, James I. No King of England paid more frequent visits to the Principality and the border towns than the unfortunate Charles I., and the important consequences of these visits, as well as the issue of the contest which was then waging, add greatly to their interest. Charles passed a considerable portion of the period of the civil war in Wales and the bordering counties.[3]

The mass of matter relating to this eventful period is so formidable, and the contemporary written documents are so voluminous and contradictory, that it is almost impossible to give anything like a correct narrative of the awful proceedings that took place. The terror of the King's Bench and of the Star Chamber being removed, the press began to pour forth its swarms of Mercurius Aulicus, Perfect Diurnals, Perfect Occurrences, Perfect Passages, Weekly Accounts, England's Remembrancer, Select Passages,[4] &c., &c. Their contradictory statements are quite sufficient to perplex the judgment, to baffle the brain, and weary the patience of the most industrious and skilful historian. The most patient reader would revolt from so dull a compilation, and we have no alternative but to arrange and modify the great mass of materials which we have collected, as fairly as we can, and with as much brevity as is consistent with precision.

The last parliament (commonly called the Long Parliament) of Charles I. assembled at Westminster, on the 3rd of November, 1640, just six months after the dissolution of the former one of the same year. That ill-advised dissolution, ill-advised even in the opinion of Clarendon, had further indisposed men's minds against the court. When the new parliament met, it immediately displayed a temper much more hostile to royalty than that which preceded it. The whole of the preceding year, A.D. 1641, violent as were the proceedings of the House of Commons, may be regarded as only preparatory to the warfare that ensued. But after the King's return from Scotland, in autumn, it became evident from the unceasing demands of that assembly, that peace could be of no long continuance; and the Irish massacre, which took place soon after (in October), filled the nation with the most dismal apprehensions.

It was about this time, January 1642, that the King was driven from London. He arrived at York in March; and an appeal to arms became every day more apparently unavoidable. For the House had, as early as February, passed an ordinance, that certain persons therein named should have power to assemble all able men fit for the wars, in their respective counties, and declared that the same should become law in the ensuing March, whether the royal assent was given to it or not. The certainty of war thus becoming daily more evident, every man of ability was ordered to provide himself with arms, and the authorities of several towns appear to have made preparations for defence, though without any predilection for either of the great parties engaged in the contest. Whilst the King was at York, the following petition of the Gentry, Ministers, and Freeholders of the County of Flint, was presented to him :—

Petition of the Gentry, Ministers, and Freeholders of the County of Flint.

"SHOWETH,—That your Petitioners doe with all due submission, thankfulnesse, and joy of heart, acknowledge the happiness they have enjoyed of a long peace under your gracious government, and your goodnesse in yielding to a ready redresse of such grievance as have growne in that time of peace and security, and in enacting such lawes in this Parliament, as your Petitioners hope will prevent the like in future. They are further tenderly apprehensive of your Majestie's transendant goodnesse, in your free condescending to give your people so full and cleer an accompt of your actions and intentions, and rest thoroughly perswaded of the sincerity, and constancy of your Majestie's resolution to mayntayne the true Protestant religion in its true primitive purity, the lawes of the land in their genuine sence, the just priviledges, freedome,

---

[3] The coronation of Charles I. was delayed until the 5th of February, 1626, in consequence of the plague which then reigned in London. The principal novelty was the introduction of the following clause in one of the prayers : "Let him obtain favour for thy people, like Aaron in the tabernacle, Elisha in the waters, Zacharias in the temple. Give him Peter's key of discipline and Paul's doctrine."

[4] King George III. made a present of a splendid collection of these tracts and pamphlets to the British Museum, where we have spent much time in examining and collating. The reader will no doubt be surprised at the extent of this collection. It contains in all about 30,000 books and tracts, MSS. and printed, uniformly bound, consisting of 2000 volumes. The catalogue connected with this period alone makes twelve volumes folio ! They are so arranged, marked, and numbered, that any tract may be readily found. They contain the result of every day's occurrence from the beginning of the year 1641, to the commencement of the reign of King Charles II.

and frequency of Parliaments, with the property and liberty of the subject thereupon depending, and your Majestie's willingnesse to join with your great counsell, in granting or enacting any other lawes, that may be for the publike weale of your people; who, as they have ever flourished and been most happy, and secure in all acts and ordinances, passed by the three estates; and most peaceably governed under the known lawes of the land: So it is the humble prayer of us, your Majestie's most loyall subjects, prostrating at your Majestie's feet our persons and estates for protection, (according to your oath,) from those dangers we should be driven into, by being bound by any rule, order, or ordinance, whereunto your Majestie, with both Houses of Parliament shall not assent. We also further supplicate your Majestie, so to maintain us in that antient and necessary privilege as not to suffer us to be governed, but by the known and established lawes of the land.

"And your Petitioners, as in duty, and by the oath of allegiance and supremacy they conceive themselves bound, shall not only pray for the preservation of your Majestie's sacred person, honour, estate, and lawful prerogative, but shall always be ready to hazard their lives and fortunes, for the mayntenance and defence of the same, against all power and persons whatsoever.

"Subscribed by the hands of the Knights, Gentry, Justices of the Peace, Ministers, and Freeholders of the County of Flint."

Similar petitions were sent from the gentry, freeholders, and the inhabitants of the several counties of Denbigh, Anglesea, Glamorgan, and a general one from the whole Principality of Wales.[5]

His Majestie's Answer to the Petition of the County of Flint.

"His Majestie hath commanded me to return this answer to this Petition. That his Majestie is much pleased with the duty and affection expressed by the petitioners, and with so evident a testimonie, that the grievances he hath redressed, the laws he hath passed, and the declarations he hath made, have produced the effects for which they were intended; the satisfaction, gratitude, and confidence of his good subjects, which hee doubts not, but the whole course of his government will daily increase. That his Majestie is no lesse pleased to see them so sensible of what hath and ever will best preserve their happiness and security, and that therefore, they desire only to be governed by that rule, which he is resolved only to governe by, the known established laws of the land; assuring them that according to his oath, he will always protect them from the invasion of any other assumed arbitrary power whatsoever, as long as he shall be able to protect himselfe, being resolved of nothing more, than to stand and fall together with the law. And that he will not expect they should be any longer ready to expresse their duties to him by the hazard of themselves and fortunes for the preservation of his person, honour, estate, and lawful prerogative, against all persons and powers whatsoever, than his Majestie shall ever be mutually ready to discharge his duty towards them by the hazard of himself and fortune for the preservation and defence of the religion and laws established, of the just priviledges and freedome of parliament, and of the liberty and prosperity of his subjects, against whomsoever shall endeavour either to destroy or oppose them.

"Falkland."

"At the Court of York, August 4th, 1642."

A.D. 1642.—On the 22nd of August, the King erected his standard at Nottingham. From thence he despatched commissioners to his friends in various parts of the country, and among others he sent one to Mr. Ottley, who then resided in Shropshire, empowering him to raise two hundred foot, "and with all possible expedition conduct them into the town of Shrewsbury, where" (says Charles) "we doubt not you will be well received." And when his Majesty arrived at Derby, he heard, says Lord Clarendon, "from the loyalists of Shrewsbury, that the town was at his disposal. Therefore, because of its strong and pleasant situation, and by reason of the neighbourhood of North Wales, and the use of the river Severn, he determined to repair thither." The following letter from Sir Edw. Hyde, dated "Exiter this 18th of 7ber," is from the Ottley MSS.:—

"To my worthy frende Francis Ottly, Esq. I acquainted his Ma^ty with your very good letter, and [have] a speciall commaunde from him (besydes writinge to Mr. Mayor) to * * * * a particular addresse to you, as to a person his Ma^ty ownes the * * * ninge most services from, havinge bene before informed of your great * * * * and industry in his service: I assure you he hath a very greate sense * * * * * and that he may prevent any inconveniences which may prejudice t[he affec]tions of that place he hath so much reguarde of he resolves to visit * * * * sooner than he meant, that is, before he goes to Chester."

[5] See King George III., Tracts in the British Museum, A.D. 1642.

On the 15th of September his Majesty wrote from Derby to the sheriff and commissioners of array for Carnarvonshire,[6] directing them to raise the trained bands of that county, and such other volunteers as they could persuade to come, and with all possible speed to bring them to Shrewsbury, to our "royal standard there;" and with a view to kindle that national spirit which has blazed so ardently in the Principality, he intimates his intention, that those forces, with others from the several counties of his dominion of Wales, should be received into pay on their arrival in Shrewsbury, and serve for a guard to his son the Prince of Wales, afterwards King Charles II., at that time a youth of twelve years.

On the 30th of August the corporation of Shrewsbury assembled together and passed a resolution "against all unlawful force:" a phrase which Royalists and Parliamentarians would interpret in senses directly opposite: scarcely a fortnight after, viz., on the 15th of September, they "agreed that if the King's Majesty come to this town, he shall have free access into it, and the town will make the best enterteynment these troublesome times afforde."" Charles, as it should seem, only waited for this intelligence, to leave Derby: for we find him at Stafford on the 18th. On the day following he advanced to Wellington, and on his way thither drew "his whole small forces," consisting at this time of about four thousand horse and nearly as many foot, "to rendezvous," caused his military orders (now called the articles of war) to be read at the head of each regiment, and then forming them so as he might best be heard, he delivered that speech which is preserved by Lord Clarendon, and in the Collections of the times, together with the Protestation which follows: and the effect of which upon a band of gallant loyalists, may be more readily conceived than described:—

"I do promise, in the presence of Almighty God, and as I hope for His blessing and protection, that I will to the utmost of my power defend and maintain the true reformed Protestant religion established in the Church of England; and by the grace of God, in the same will live and dye.

"I desire to govern by all the known laws of the land, and that the liberty and property of the subject may be by them preserved with the same care as my own just rights. And if it please God, by his blessing upon this army, raised for my necessary defence, to preserve me from this rebellion, I do solemnly and faithfully promise in the sight of God, to maintain the just priviledges and freedom of parliament, and to govern by the known laws of the land to my utmost power; and particularly, to observe inviolably the laws consented to by me this parliament. In the mean while, if this time of war, and the great necessity, and straits I am now driven to, beget any violation of those, I hope it shall be imputed by God and man to the authors of this war, and not to me; who have so earnestly laboured for the preservation of the peace of this kingdom.

"When I willingly fail in these particulars, I will expect no aid or relief from any man, or protection from Heaven. But in this resolution, I hope for the cheerful assistance of all good men, and am confident of God's blessing."

On Tuesday, the 20th, he entered Shrewsbury, and took up his residence at the Council House.

Sept. 24.—The urgency of the King's affairs did not permit him to enjoy much repose in Shrewsbury. The Parliamentary agents had been very busy in Chester:[8] and it was deemed expedient that his Majesty should repair immediately to that city, for the purpose of counteracting their designs. Accordingly, after resting at the Council House two days, he set out on the 23rd and reached Chester that night; a distance of twenty-eight miles, as then computed.[9] As he intended to be absent only a very short time, he left the main body of his army behind at Shrewsbury.[1] From Chester we find him writing on the 25th to the commissioners of array for Caernarvonshire, directing them[2] to pay the money contributed for their trained

---

[6] Williams's Tourist Guide through Caernarvonshire; Appendix.

[7] Book of Orders; Shrewsbury Records.

[8] Clarendon, b. vi.   [9] Iter Carolinum.

[1] Carte, iv. p. 456. Mr. Burghah, the puritanical vicar of Aston, whose journal is printed in the Antiquities of Cheshire, 1778, says that the King "moved to Chester with his army." He probably took a troop or two for an escort, but certainly not his army.

[2] Caernarvonshire Tourist, Appendix.

bands into the hands of John Owen, Esq., of Cleneney, in that county, "one of our colonels" (the celebrated Sir John Owen of Porkington). His Majesty returned to Shrewsbury late at night on the 27th, having stopped at Wrexham, where he took occasion to harangue the inhabitants of the Counties of Denbigh and Flint[3] from the Town Hall. His Majesty's speech on this occasion was as follows :—

Charles the First at the Town Hall, Wrexham.

"GENTLEMEN,—I am willing to take all occasions to visit all my good subjects, in which number I have cause to reckon you of these two counties, and having lately had a good expression of your loyalty and affections to me by those levies which at your charge have been sent me from your parts (which forwardness of yours I shall always remember to your advantage), and to let you know how I have been dealt with by a powerful and malignant party in this kingdom, whose designs are no less than to destroy my person and crown, the laws of the land, and the present government both of church and state. The leaders of these men, by their subtlety and cunning practises, have so prevailed upon the meaner sort of people about London, that they have called them up into frequent and dangerous tumults, and thereby have chased from thence myself, and the greatest part of the members of both Houses of Parliament. Their power and secret plots have had such influence upon the small remaining part of both Houses, that under colour of orders and ordinances, made without the Royal assent (a thing never heard of before this Parliament), I am forbid and spoiled of my towns, forts, castles, and goods ; my navy forcibly taken from me, and employed against me ; all my revenue is stopt and seized upon, and at this time a powerful army is marching against me.—I wish this were all: they have yet further laboured to alienate the affections of my good people; they have most injuriously vented many false reproaches against my person and government ; they have dispersed in print many notorious false scandals upon my actions and intentions; and in particular have laboured to cast upon me some aspersions concerning the horrid, bloody, and impious rebellion in Ireland. They tell the people that I have recalled two ships, appointed for the guard of these seas: 'tis true, but they conceal that at the same time I sent my warrants to the Downs, commanding four as good ships to attend that service instead of those should be recalled ; which warrant, by their means, could not find obedience. They forgot that they then employed forty ships (many of them my own, and all of them set forth at the public charge of this and that kingdom), to rob and pillage me of my goods, to chase my good subjects, and maintain my own town of Hull against me. And that by the absence of those ships from the Irish seas, the rebels have had opportunity to bring store of arms, ammunition, and supplies to their succour ; to which we may justly impute the calamities which have overwhelmed my poor Protestant subjects there. They cry out upon a few suits of clothes, appointed, as they say, for Ireland, which some of my forces took ; but conceal that they were taken as entering into

[3] Husband, p. 618.

Coventry (then in open rebellion against me), where I had reason to believe they would have been disposed of amongst their soldiers, who then bore arms against me. They talk of a few horses which I have made use of for my carriages, concealing that they were certified to be useless for the service of Ireland; when they themselves have seized 100,000*l.*, particularly appointed by Act of Parliament for the relief of Ireland (where my army was ready to perish for want of it), and employed it, together with such part of the 40,000*l.* subsidy as they have received, to maintain an unnatural civil war at home. Neither have they used their fellow-subjects better than they have done me their King. By their power the law of the land (your birth-right), is trampled upon, and instead thereof they govern my people by votes and arbitrary orders. Such as will not submit to their unjust unlimited power are imprisoned, plundered, and destroyed; such as will not pay such exaction as they require towards this rebellion, are threatened to be put out of protection (as they call it), of the Parliament. Such as conscienciously remember their duty to me their Sovereign, are reviled, prosecuted, and declared traitors. Such as do desire to maintain the true Protestant religion, as it is established by the laws of the land, are traduced and called Popish and superstitious; and on the contrary, such as are known Brownists, Anabaptists, and public depravers of the Book of Common Prayer, are countenanced and encouraged. They exact and receive tonnage and poundage, and other great duties upon merchandize, not only without law, but in the face of an Act of Parliament to the contrary, passed this present Parliament, which puts all men into the condition of a *Præmunire* that shall presume so to oppress the people. If you desire to know who are the contrivers in these wicked designs you shall find some of their names in particular, and their actions at large, in my declaration of the 12th of August, to which I shall refer you. I wish this craft and power were not such, that few of those copies can come to the view of my good people. Since that time, these men so thirst after the destruction of this kingdom, that they have prevailed to make all my offers of treaty (which might bring peace to this kingdom, and beget a good understanding between me and my Parliament) fruitless. In this distress, into which these men have brought me and this kingdom, my confidence is in the protection of Almighty God and the affections of my people: and that you may clearly see what my resolutions are, I shall cause my voluntary protestation, lately taken, to be read to you: and I desire that the Sheriffs of these two counties will dispose copies of that and what I now deliver to you, having no other way to make it public: these men having restrained the use of my presses at London and the Universities."

After this he expedited a letter to the justices of Carnarvonshire to the same effect with that just quoted: and bringing back with him certain eminent Parliamentarians, Sir Thomas Delves, and Mr. Mainwaring of Peover,[4] whom he found at Chester under charge of the sheriff. These gentlemen attended there about three weeks in hopes of being dismissed.[5]

The King found, waiting his return, Mr., afterwards the well-known General Fleetwood, with a message from the Earl of Essex, requesting to know his Majesty's pleasure respecting the delivery of a petition with which he was charged from the Houses of Parliament. Essex himself could be at no very great distance; for the Earl of Dorset, the Queen's Lord Chamberlain, who answers his letter, after apologising for "not sooner returning this gentleman, an account of his Majesty's late arrival here last night," informs him, "that those whom he shall appoint to bring the petition, (so they be none of those whom the King hath by name accused of treason,) shall come and go very safely; so as they come hither to-day,[6] and send a trumpet before."" The Houses subsequently resolved, that it did not "stand with their honour and privilege," to deliver their petition under such restrictions; and in fact it never was presented.[7]

On the morrow after the King's return to Shrewsbury, the principal gentry of the county, having been convened by the sheriff, Henry Bromley, Esq., of Shrawardine Castle, waited upon his Majesty, and it is unnecessary to say, were most graciously received. If aught of stateliness or shyness had marked his former demeanour, which has been asserted, with what truth we know not, it would be his endeavour to

[4] Burghah, pp. 906, 911.
[5] Burghah, ut supra, p. 906. He adds, Sir Richard Wilbraham and Mr. Wilbraham of Darfold. But the first of these is certainly a mistake, and the last too, if his name was Roger. For among the Ottley Papers is a letter from Mr. Orlando Bridgeman to Sir Francis Ottley, dated Chester, Feb. 10, 1642 (i.e. 1642-3), in which he writes, "Sir Richard Wilbraham and Mr. Roger Wilbraham are seized on by order from hence, and sent to Chirk Castle from thence to Shrewsbury, where they are to stay till his Majesty's further pleasure bee knowne. You are written unto about it by the commissioners, and to morrow they will bee at Shrewsbury."

Sir Richard (who was of Woodhay, knt. and bart.) died here shortly after; and there is a pass among the same Papers, from Lord Capel, dated April 9, 1643, authorising thirty persons and their horses to convey the body from Shrewsbury to Acton in Cheshire, where he had desired to be interred among his ancestors. Hist. Salop.

[6] The Earl of Essex writes from Worcester on the 29th; but he must have advanced nearer to Shrewsbury when he dispatched Mr. Fleetwood: as otherwise this restriction imposed by the king would have amounted to a prohibition.
[7] Parl. Hist. xi. 439.

divest himself of it when he wished to conciliate the affections of his people.   He addressed these gentlemen in an animated speech, in which, after expressing " his satisfaction, that the insolences and misfortunes which drove him about his kingdom had brought him to so good and faithful a part of it ;"' and his hopes that they would not be great sufferers by the excesses of his soldiers, which he promised he would do his best to restrain, ("though," said the King, "I fear I cannot prevent all disorders,") he informs them that he had sent for a mint, and would melt all his plate, and sell or mortgage his land to diminish the pressure upon them ; he conjures them to advance him pecuniary assistance ; " and whilst these ill men sacrifice their money, plate, and utmost industry to destroy the commonwealth, be you no less liberal to preserve it ; that you may hereafter reflect with honour and comfort, that with some charge and trouble to yourselves, you did your part to support your King, and preserve your kingdom."

Lord Clarendon is very severe upon " the unthrifty retention of their money, which possessed the spirits of those who did really wish the King all the success he wished for himself."   This reflection is made before the course of his narrative has brought him into Shropshire, where a more liberal spirit displayed itself ; for the same author adds, that at Shrewsbury " such proportions of plate and money were voluntarily brought in, and that the army was fully and constantly paid.

The following are some of the contemporary accounts of the transactions of this period :[8]—

His Majesty came to Salop on Tuesday last with great strength both of men and arms, where he stayed till Friday, and then came to Whitchurch, and went to Chester.   I was one that was appointed to attend him thither, which I did, with many more gentlemen and freeholders.   His Majesty and the Prince dined at Whitchurch, and so went for Chester.   When we came to Milton Green, there was Mr. Richard Egerton, of Ridley, with some six hundred musketeers, and then we came to Hatton Heath, there was the Lord Rivers with all his forces, and my Lord Cholmley with horse and foot, very compleat beyond the other ; so they having displayed their colours, gave his Majesty a volley of shot, which being done, his Majesty having ridden once or twice about the army, taking notice of the sheriff and his company, with divers other gentlemen that were there, then came to Rowton Heath, where was Sir Thomas Aston with that company he had, which did show themselves as the other had done.   Then his Majestie set forwards for Chester ; at Boughton, where the liberty of the city beginneth, the two sheriffs of Chester, with all their company attended.   Then coming to the Barrs there attended the Maior and Aldermen, when the Maior delivered both mace and sword into his Majestie's hand, who received them and gave them to him again, and so he marched before the King, with all the Aldermen and Sheriffs with all the companies in town with their gowns, and all the trained bands of the city, with volunteers set on each side of the street, who discharged just as his Majestie passed by.   Thus was his Majestie attended to the court with all the bells ringing, drums and trumpets sounding.   Thus, for his Majestie going to Chester.

A true relation of his Majesty's coming to the town of Shrewsbury on the 20th of this instant, September, and his passage from thence, the 23rd day, to the city of Chester, with the manner of his entertainment there.   Together with the L. Grandison's surprising Nantwich, and the plundering of divers houses thereabouts.[9]

                                                                                              Chester, September, 24, 1642.

Yesterday night, about four or five o'clock, the King came into this City, attended by two troops of horse that came with him : and after his Majestie came Sir Thomas Aston with his troop ; the Maior and Aldermen standing on a platform in Eastgate-street, before Thomas Parnel's door : Serjeant Brerewood, the Recorder, made a speech, but there was such great shouting for joy, that I think his Majestie scarce heard him ; and all the companies standing with their arms in Eastgate-street to entertain his Majestie, and the Sheriffs and Sheriffs Peers, and such as have Leave-lookers rode out of town in scarlet (as they used to ride out at Midsummer) to meet his Majestie with all our trained bands.   The Maior rode before his Majestie,

---

[8] Heath, 38 ; Husband, 623 ; Clarendon, b. vi.   [9] London, printed for R. R., September 29, 1642.

carrying the sword from the platform to the bishop's palace. The Lord Dillon and another Irish lord, a great rebell, came with his Majestie into this Citie: Sir Richard Wilbraham met his Majestie and fell down on his knees to him, but his Majestie would not take notice of him: he and Sir Thomas Delves are committed to the Sheriffs, both of these knights declared themselves for the ordinance of the militia. It is thought there are warrants out for the apprehending of many other gentlemen. About two hours before his Majestie came a troop of the Lord Strange, his horse and eighty horse loads of muskets and bandaliers, and such like provision, which were laid in our common hall, and there are two hundred more of Lord Strange his horse that came from Newcastle. The Lord Strange hath delivered those arms that were taken from Papists in Lancashire to them again, and threatened the Maior of Leverpool to batter down the town, if he would not deliver them; it is said there are five thousand coming thorow Lancashire, which came out of the north for his Majestie. Yesterday at nine o'clock the Lord Strange came into this city with one or two troop of horse. This day all betwixt the age of sixteen and sixty years, of the trained bands of the county, are summoned to appear before his Majestie, at Hoole Heath, two miles from Chester. Upon Wednesday last the town of Nantwich was in some fear, lest they should be disarmed, and stood upon their guard, and some ayd came to help them; but that night following about one thousand horse cam there, the Lord Cholmley came with them, with the commission for the array; they were to have a parley, the town would have been delivered, so that they might have their arms and liberties; this while the other side got in at back gardens, and disarmed all, and plundered some houses. The day following they went to Sir Richard Wilbraham's, and Sir Thomas Delves', and disarmed them, took their horses, and three cart load of armour from them, and do further proceed doing much harm at many other places and houses. It is thought our Maior and Aldermen intend to give the King a sum of money.[1]

A.D. 1643.—The Mercurius Aulicus (a court journal of January 17, 1643), informs us that "some false brethren in Shrewsbury" communicated such intelligence to the garrison at Wem, that they were able to surprise a part of the King's forces at Ellesmere, together with Sir Nicholas Byron and Sir Richard Willis, who, in another paper,[2] is styled "Serjeant-major Willis, one of the prime commanders in Shrewsbury;" and we know that about the same time Sir Francis Ottley discovered a plot which had been concerted within these walls, for delivering up the town to the power of the parliament.[3] This appears by a letter to the Governor from Prince Rupert, who had recently (6th January) been appointed Captain-General under his Majesty of all the forces now raised, or being within this and the neighbouring counties and all North Wales.[4]

"SIR,

"His Matie is pleased to entrust to my care his army in Shropshyre and the countreyes adjacent, togather with his interests there. In which coṁand I cannot but with very much apprehension thinke uppon Shrewsburie in your government, and the safetie thereof. Especiallie since I understood of a late designe for the betraying thereof to the enemy, for which you have divers persons in prison, but I doe not hear they are brought to justice by any proceedings against them, soe that the punishment may goe to

[1] See George III.'s Pamphlets and MS. in the British Museum.

[2] Perfect Diurnal, Jan. 20, 1643-4.

[3] "You are full of suspicions here in the towne, I perceive," says Mr. Symmons, in his Military Sermon, "that you have treacherous persons among you, such as are better affected to the enemies then to the King: and many have been imprisoned upon jealousies and feares; and nothing that I can see yet can be proved against them; insomuch that perhaps they may prove honester men then some of those that have molested them."

[4] Papers communicated by J. Bickerton Williams, Esq. It has been also said that the Prince was appointed President of the Council of Wales. It is certain that the Earl of Bridgewater, who had filled that office, adhered to the Parliament, and the King might nominate his nephew to the place, in order to mark his resentment; but the council itself "fell to pieces by reason of the civil wars,"

(MSS. Salusbury of Erbistock) and if Prince Rupert enjoyed the title, it was all he did enjoy. How zealously the Welsh supported the royal cause will be seen by the following, which we extract from Lord Clarendon's History of the Rebellion:—

"We shall now visit the Principality of Wales, of which hitherto very little hath been said; and from the affection thereof, the King had from the beginning a very great benefit, it having supplied him with three or four good regiments of foot, in which many of their gentry were engaged before the Battle of Edge Hill."

The Marquis of Hertford drew with him out of Wales, and brought to Oxford about Christmas, near 2000 men, leaving Wales guarded only by the courage and fidelity of the gentry and inhabitants. After that, North Wales lying most convenient to back Chester and Shrewsbury, whilst the enemy was master of the field, received chief supplies of men and provisions from thence.

some, the example and terro^r to all. I must strictly require from you an accompt of that place, which is the head quarter of those countreyes, and where I intend to make my owne residence duringe the time of my stay in that cõmaund, and therefore must recomend to you the particulars followinge : and require you to call together the gentlemen and townesmen to assist you in such charges as will be requisite for the coveringe of the Castle of Shrewsbury, and the dividinge and disposinge thereof into roomes capable and fittinge to receive the stores; soe as such amunicõn as from time to time shall be sent into those parts for his Maties service there may lye drye and safe. I desire this be done with all possible speed, for I have this day sent awaie 50 barrels of powder to begin yor stores. Other proportions of that, and all other kind of amunicõn, will bee speedily brought thither, and for the better security of the stores, which are the sinewes of the King's busines, I pray you, by the advice of Sir John Mennes, to consider of an accommodacõn for such as shall be the guard of that place, by erecting of a courte of guard and hutts for the souldiers, for such numb^r of men, in such manner as you and Sr John Mennes shall think best for his Maties service. I have no more to say to you at present, but shall willingly receive yor Letters from time to time concerninge yor affaires, and you shall be sure of all possible assistance and encouragement from mee,

" Your very lovinge friend,
" RUPERT."

" Oxon, this 25th day of Januarie, 1643.
 " The Governo^r of Shrewsbury."

 The inhabitants of Shropshire were not less anxious for their own safety and the success of the royal cause than the general himself, as will appear from the following engagement and resolution of the principal gentlemen of the County of Salop, for raising and maintaining forces at their own charge, for the defence of His Majestie King Charles I., their country, and, more particularly, the fortunes, persons, and estates of the subscribers undernamed :—

 " WE, whose names are underwritten, do hereby engage ourselves each to other, and promise upon the faith and word of a gentleman, that we will doe our utmost endeavours, both by ourselves and friends, to raise, as well as for defence of our King and country, as our own particular safeties, one entire regiment of dragooneers, and with our lives to defend those men's fortunes and families that shall be contributors herein, to their abilities; and for the more speedy expedition of the said service, as also for the prevention of being surprised and plundered by our enemies, we have thought fit to intreat Sir Vincent Corbet, formerly Captain of the Horse for this County, to be our chief commander of the aforesaid regiment; and likewise we have appointed the day of our appearance for bringing in of every man's proportion of his horse and money, according to the subscription of his undertaking, to be the 20th day of December, 1643, all in battle field.

" HENRY BROMLEY, *Sheriff*.

" SIR RICHARD LEE, Baronet.	ROBERT CORBET DE HUMFREST, Esq.
PAUL HARRIS, Knight and Baronet.	PELHAM CORBET, Esq.
VINCENT CORBETT, Ditto.	ROGER KINASTON, Esq.
SIR WILLIAM OWEN.	EDWARD ACTON, Esq.
SIR ROBERT EGTON.	WILLIAM FOWLER, Esq.
EDWARD CRESSET, Esq.	EDWARD BAWDWIN, Esq.
WALTER PIGOTT, Esq.	THOMAS EDWARDS, Esq.
FRANCIS THORNES, Esq.	CHARLES BAWDWIN, Esq.
ARTHUR SANDFORD, Esq.	WALTER WARING, Esq.
THOMAS CORBET, Esq.	RICHARD OKELEY, Esq.
SIR JOHN WILDE.	HENRY BILLINGSLEY, Esq.
SIR FRANCIS OTTELEY.	RICHARD CHURCH, Esq.
SIR THOMAS SKRYVEN.	THOMAS PHILLIPS, Esq.
SIR THOMAS EGTON.	EDWARD STANLEY, Esq.
SIR THOMAS LYSTER.	LAWRANCE BENTHALL, Esq.
EDWARD KINASTON, Esq.	GEORGE LUDLOW, Esq."

 We are now getting deeper and deeper into the stirring history of those melancholy times, in which our Principality, its gentry, and its citizens, bore a noble and a loyal part.

Jan. 26.—There were taken and killed at Namptwich, Major-General Gibson, Sir Richard Fleetwood, Sir Michael Earnsley, Colonel Monk, Colonel Warren, Sir Francis Butler, Lieutenant-Colonel Gibbs, Major Hammond, Sir Ralph Done, 14 captains, 20 lieutenants, 26 ensigns, 2 cornets, 2 quarter-masters, 4 serjeants, 63 corporals, 26 gentlemen of Companies, 40 drummers, 20 carriages, 6 pieces of ordnance, 1500 soldiers. At an assembly of the Corporation of Chester, held upon the 3rd day of February, it was ordered that an assessment of five hundred pounds should be made, and forthwith collected, upon the citizens and inhabitants of the city and liberties thereof, for the making of fortifications for the defence of the place, and the defraying divers charges and expenses necessarily incident thereunto; and certain of the body corporate were nominated and authorised to be assessors, and collectors accordingly.

ATT an assemblie houlden in the Common-hall of Pleas upon Friday the third day of February—William Ince, Maior Civit. Cestr., Anno Domini 1643—*Anno Rex Caroli decimo octavo. Those marked with asterisks were present.*

* WILLIAM INCE, Maior.
JAMES EARL OF DERBY.
JOHN EARL OF RIVERS.
SIR THOMAS SMITH, Knt.
ROBERT BREREWOOD, Recorder of Chester.
WILLIAM GAMULL, Ald.
* NICHOLAS INCE, Ald.
RICHARD DUTTON, Ald.
* CHRISTOPHER BLEASE, Ald.
* CHARLES MALLORY, Ald.
* THOMAS BYRD, Ald.
* WILLIAM SPARKE, Ald.
* RANDLE HOLME, Ald.
FRANCIS GAMULL, Ald.
WILLIAM EDWARDS, Ald.
* THOMAS THROPPE, Ald.
ROBERT SPROSTON, Ald.
ROBERT HARVIE, Ald.
* THOMAS ALDERSEY, Ald.
* THOMAS COOPER, Ald.
ROBERT FLECHER, Ald.
* ROBERT LEYCESTER, Ald.
* RANDLE HOLME, jun, Ald.
* WILLIAM CROMPTON, } Sheriffs.
* JOHN JOHNSON, }
* HUGH WHITEHEAD.
THOMAS HUMPHREYES.
* JOHN ALDERSEY.

* ROBERT INCE.
* RICHARD BROSTER.
* WILLIAM JONES.
* WILLIAM PARNELL.
* ROBERT WRIGHT.
* RICHARD BYRD.
* EDWARD EVANT.
CALVIN BRUEN.
* EDWARD BRADSHAW.
* OWEN HUGHES.
THOMAS WESTON.
* WILLIAM WILCOCKE.
WILLIAM DRINKWATER.
* RICHARD BRADSHAW.
* JOHN WHITTLE.
* EDWARD HOLTON.
* THOMAS MOTTERSHEAD.
* HUGH LEIGH.
* EDW. HALLWOOD, } Leave-
WM. BENNETT, } lookers.
* PETER GOOSE.
* WILLIAM GREGORY.
* EDMUND WILLIAMS.
ALEXANDER BYRD.
WILLIAM HINCKS.
PETER INCE.
* CHRISTOPHER BERNEARD.
JOHN WILDINGE.
* PETER LEIGH.

WILLIAM HIGGNETT.
JOHN WHITBYE.
• JOHN LECKONBY.
• WILLIAM WHITTLE.
RANDLE DAVIES.
• RICHARD SPROSTON.
LAWRENCE MASSEY.
• RANDLE BURROUGHS.
JOHN BROOKES.
• THOMAS WRIGHT.
• EDWARD REYNOLDS.
HUMPHRIE PHILLIPS.
ROBERT ANYON.
GEORGE BENNETT.
LAWRENCE FLECHER.
• HUGH MOUSON.
• JOHN SPROSTON.
• RICHARD LEA.
LAWRENCE YONGE.
RANDLE RICHARDSON.
HENRY YONGE.
* SIMON LEA.
RICHARD DICKINSON.
* MILO PEMBERTON.
HUMPHRIE LLOYD.
GERRARD JONES.
* WILLIAM BALL.
* DANIEL GREATBATCH.
* JAMES RAVENSCROFT.

It is ordered by general consent that the sume of five hundred pounds shall be forthwith assessed and levied upon all the inhabitants of this cittie towards the making of fortifications for the defence thereof : And for all other publique charges requisite for the good of this cittie, and in default of payment the same to be levied by distresse, &c.

Assessors.	*Collectors.*
Mr. Ald. SPARKES.	Mr. WILLIAM JONES.
Mr. Ald. HOLME.	Mr. OWEN HUGHES.
Mr. RICHARD BROSTER.	Mr. EDWARD HULTON.
Mr. HUGH LEIGH.	Mr. THOMAS MOTTERSHEAD.
Mr. JOHN LECKONBY.	
Mr. WILLIAM WHITTLE.	

Feb. 16.—Colonel Mitton came over Bangor Bridge in the morning, and took Sir Gerard Eyton, Sir Robert Eyton, John Eyton, Sir John's brother, all in the house of Sir Gerard, and plundered it. Thence he went and took Mr. Edisbury and Mr. John Jefferies, Mr. Humphrey Dimock of Willington, and his son; Mr. Kyffin, Vicar of Bangor, and his brother, William Kyffin, of Llanvyllin, that came there to visit him.

These loyal proceedings being related to his Majesty, he considered (as Lord Clarendon tells us) that his faithful citizens at Chester had no officers of skill and experience to manage and direct that courage, which, at least, was willing to defend their own walls; which they were now like to be put to: he, therefore, sent thither Sir Nicholas Byron, of Norfolk, a soldier of very good command, with a commission of Colonel-General of Cheshire and Shropshire, and to be Governor of Chester; who, being a person of great affability and dexterity, as well as martial knowledge, gave great life to the designs of the well-affected there, and, with the encouragement of some gentlemen of North Wales, in a short time raised such a power of horse and foot, as made often skirmishes with the enemy; sometimes with notable advantage, and seldom with any signal loss.

The outworks and entrenchments were carried on with such vigour, that, in the beginning of the next summer, the mud walls, mounts, bastions, &c., were all completed. The outworks commenced at the alcove on the city walls, which lies between the Water-tower and the North-gate, and proceeded towards the stone bridge leading to Blacon; then inclining to the north-east, took in the utmost limits in the Further Northgate-street; then turning eastward, near Flookers-brook, encompassed Horn-lane and all that part of the town to Boughton; from whence the works were carried down to the edge of St. John's Dee.

Sir William Brereton, a gentleman of competent fortune in this county, and knight for the shire in Parliament (a man most notorious for an aversion to the government of the Church), came to Nantwich with a troop of horse and a regiment of dragoons, and fortified that place as the King's party did Chester; with the intention of protecting those who were of his party, and under that shelter to encourage them to appear.

July 18.—Sir William Brereton came with his forces before this city, and, on the 20th, made a violent attack on the works, which were so resolutely defended, that he was repulsed, and forced to retire: many of his men were killed and carried away in carts. The besieged had no loss, except that one person was shot, who was fool-hardy enough to stand upright, on the highest part of the works, in defiance of the enemy; and another was wounded under similar circumstances. Sir William then joined Sir Thomas Middleton, and besieged the Castle of Flint; Colonel Mostyn, Governor for the King, held out till all provisions, even to horses, failed; he then surrendered upon honourable terms.

During the time of this siege, the garrison of Chester were busily employed in pulling down the Spittal-Boughton Chapel, all the houses thereabouts, and many other houses and barns in that neighbourhood, to prevent the enemy from harbouring in them, to the great annoyance of the city.

Sept. 3.—At an assembly it was ordered that the sum of one hundred pounds per week, towards the maintenance of the garrison, should be assessed as follows :—The sum of sixty pounds per week to be paid by the citizens and ancient inhabitants of the city and the liberties thereof; and the remainder, being the sum of forty pounds per week, to be paid by the nobility, gentry, clergy, and others who had come for protection into the city, to be collected by such as the governor should appoint: and the assessors of the sixty pounds were ordered to assess such of the city soldiers as were able and wealthy, having especial regard to those citizens as had most gainful trades in the city, whereby the poor might be eased in their assessments; and that this assessment be continued for five weeks only.

We here present our readers with another narration of the same events, as possessing more interest and authority than if we had combined and fused together the several details :—

At this time his Majesty received such advices from several parts, as induced him to think it necessary to proceed to Chester, to secure that city in his interest, being of the utmost importance, as the key to Ireland. He, therefore, previous to his departure from Stafford for Shrewsbury, dispatched a courier to Chester with the following letter :—

" CHARLES R.

" TRUSTY AND WELL-BELOVED :—Wee greete you well. Whereas we have resolved to make repayre to our Citie of Chester, on Friday next; These are to will and require you, to warn all the trayne-bands of that our Citie, to be in readiness, and give their attendance to us, in our entrance into the same; and to take care that necessary provision be made for entertainment of us and our retinue, soe not doubting of your diligence therein, we bid you heartily farewell. Given at our Court at Stafford, 18th of September, 1642.

" To our Trusty and Well-beloved Thomas Cowper, Mayor of our Citie of Chester."

Accordingly, on Friday, 23rd of September, the King, attended by many of the nobility and gentry, approached the city of Chester; the train-bands, well accoutred, were regularly drawn up on each side of the Foregate-street. The several incorporated companies, with their respective colours and banners, were properly ranged along the Eastgate-street: the sheriffs, sheriffs' peers and common council in their gowns being well mounted, and their horses caparisoned, received his Majesty at Spittal-Boughton.

The mayor, recorder, and aldermen, in their proper habits, were on the south side of the Eastgate-street, upon a scaffold railed and hung round with tapestry.

Upon the King's arrival at the place, where the magistrates stood, the recorder addressed him in an appropriate speech, after which the mayor immediately came down from the stand, and, upon his knees, delivered the city sword to the King, who graciously returned it; when the mayor, bare-headed, carried the same before his Majesty to the Pentice, where he and his suit were entertained, and the mayor, in the name of the corporation, presented the King with two hundred pounds in gold, and one hundred pounds to the Prince of Wales, which were thankfully received.

A true and exact Relation of the King's entertainment in the city of Chester, with the Recorder's speech at his entering the City. Sent from a citizen of note in Chester, on purpose to be printed, to prevent false copies.[b]

THE King came to Chester from Salop upon Friday, about five of the clock, but he brought in with him no great company: the Lord Rivers, Lord Cholmley, and Sir Thomas Ashton, came each of them with a troop of horse to wait on his Majestie into the citie; besides those that came with him, there went out of the citie to Broughton about forty that had been sheriffs, and some others on horseback and foot-cloaths, and rid before him into the citie, and at the Hony Stayrs there was a scaffold made for the aldermen to stand, and receive him (as they had done his father before time), and they kneeled down, and the Recorder made a speech or oration to the King, not such a one as is conceived much to his credit. Your father promised to send you a copy, that you may print it to his shame; for, I take it, he is so full of malice and pride, and but an ignorant man in his owne profession; and so, for present, leave him. After the oration, our mayor gave the King the sword, the mace, and his staffe, and the King gave them again to him, and the mayor got on his horse and carryed the sword before the King unto Bishops Pallace, where he stayed till Tuesday, and departed towards Salop, taking Rexham in his way, and there dined with Master Lloyd, a lawyer, and the King's Attorney for Flintshire, and thence to Salop where he is.

Our Maior and his brethren presented him with 200*l.* in gold, and to the Prince, 100*l.* It was well taken; but, by the report of some, a greater sum was expected; but those know not our having: for I persuade myself, before it be collected amongst the citizens, it will be thought a very great sum. His stay amongst us was very peaceable, and his departure very cheerful. The maior and aldermen brought him out of the liberty on horseback. It is reported he left a garrison amongst us, but he left none; but only commanded that one hundred of the countrey souldiers were put into the castle; but what we shall have put upon us I know not; but all those that are not of the array are observed; for some of our country gentlemen, as Sir Richard Wilbraham, Sir Thomas Delves, M. Manwaring of Badley, M. Wilbraham of Darfot, M. Berkinhead, the premotory, and his son, are all commanded to wait upon the King, and went with him to Salop, where they are all yet. And I am informed that some have a commission to search our houses in Chester—what for, as yet, I know not; but I hear my house is set down for one to be searched: if they plunder not, I do not fear them. We have great store of souldiers billetted round about our city—what for, I fear not; but they are very unruly, and come into many honest men's houses, specially into ministers' houses, and take away, some all, and what they please of their goods.

Since the Sabbath-day last, Manchester hath been besieged by my Lord Strange, now Lord of Derby; for his father lieth dead at his little house under St. John's, but we do not know nor heare that he hath taken the town as yet, neither they yielded. This is all the passages that we have at present: so I end with my prayer to God to bring all these troubles to an end. So comitting you to God and rest.

Chester, October 1, 1642.

Mr. Recorder Brierwood's speech at the entertainment of the King and Prince at Chester, Sept. 23, 1642.

MOST GRACIOUS SOVERAIGN:—We, your Majestie's most humble and obedient subjects, the maior and citizens of this your most ancient city, do in all humility crave leave to take the boldnesse to bid your Majestie and our most noble Prince, our hoped Earl of Chester, welcome to this place; the ancient seat of your Majestie, and your Majestie's Royall progenitours,

---

[b] King George III. Pamphlets, 1642, No. 75, E 119, Article 25.

Earls of Chester.   This ancient city, the metropolis of this ancient County Palatine, though it hath been sometimes honoured by the residence of senior Earls thereof within it, yet it hath seldom (ever since) been so highly honoured as to lodge a King and Prince of this realme at once within it, though but one night.   The honour, then, with the accesses of your royall person, and of the person of our noble Prince at this time unto this city doth bring such, that it doth transcend all former of this kinde, and doth fill our hearts at once with a great deal of joy and security: for we are in great fears in regard of the rebellion in Ireland; as also, in regard of a malignant party that hath lately appeared amongst us.   But we are as sensible that your Majestie's presence expells all dangers, and renders us secure from the dangers abroad and distractions at home.   And it is, most mighty King, the satisfaction of all our hearts that your Majestie hath already sufficiently testified to all the world, your Majestie's indeered love unto all your subjects, and to the Protestant religion, whereof your Majestie is justly stiled the Great Defender; and we in this place, in thankfulnesse to the same, will be ever ready to adventure our lives and fortunes for the defence of your Majestie, in whose safety rested only our security.

And Mr. Maior of this city humbly prostrate upon his knees, doth, according to his duty, surrender and yield up to your excellent Majestie all the authority and jurisdiction he holdeth under your Majestie, and with it the sword of this city, the ensign thereof: and he and we all of this city shall ever pray, Long live King Charles, victorious over all his enemies.

His Majesty having received intimation that a number of arms and warlike stores had been privately brought into the city by some disaffected persons, thought proper to issue out the following mandate that evening :—

"CHARLES R.

"These are to will and require you and every of you, taking unto you and every of you, the assistance of the sheriffs of our city of Chester, and such other force of the said city as you, the said Mayor thereof, Earl of Derby, Earl Rivers, Lord Visc. Cholmondeley, Robert Brerewood, Recorder; William Gamul, Chas. Walley and Thomas Throppe, aldermen of our said citty; or every of you, as you shall thinke meete as soon as you conveniently may, to search the several houses of Sir William Brereton, Bart.; William Edwards and Thomas Aldersey, aldermen; the Red Lyon and Golden Lyon Inns, situate in our said citty, wherein you, or every of you, shall suspect to be any armes or ammunition, intended to be used against us, or any person or persons deriving authority from us; or against any of our loving subjects; and all such armes and ammunition, that you or any of you should find upon your said search, to seize and take into your custodies for the use of us, to be disposed as we shall appoint.

"Given at our Court at Chester, this 26th of September, in the eighteenth year of our reign."

His Majesty departed thence much sooner than he at first intended, owing to the arrival of a messenger from Prince Rupert, who informed him of the important advantage before Worcester, and presented him with the colours which had been taken from the enemy.

Nov. 11.—Sir William Brereton came with his forces to Hawarden Castle, five miles distant from Chester. Mr. Robert Ravenscroft of Bretton, and Mr. John Aldersey, being then in possession of that garrison, received Sir William and his party with every demonstration of joy.   Sir William now being in possession of this strong fortress, and likewise of the town of Hawarden, prevented the garrison of Chester from receiving coals, corn, and other provisions, from that neighbourhood, which proved a great inconvenience.

In the evening of the same day, Mr. Ravenscroft, pretending to be of the King's party, had the audacity to enter the city, and apply to the governor for a barrel of gunpowder, and a quantity of match, which, as he was unsuspected, were delivered to him by the storekeeper of the garrison.   Sir William Brereton, on the Thursday following, sent an authoritative summons, from the Castle of Hawarden, to Sir Abraham Shipman, then Governor of Chester, expressly requiring him to surrender that city, adding some severe threats in case of refusal.

The governor sent him word in answer, " That he was not to be intimidated by mere threats, and that Sir William must *win it and wear it.*"   The governor then thought proper to order Hand-bridge suburbs and Overleigh-hall to be burnt down, to prevent the enemy from sheltering themselves there, if they should come to attack the city; and the next day he likewise ordered Bache-hall and Flookersbrook-hall to be burnt down, for fear of affording a lodgment for the enemy from another quarter.

The situation of the families residing in the suburbs was truly deplorable, being forced to make a hasty retreat from their habitations, to seek shelter in the houses of the hospitable and humane, who dwelt within the walls; and to see their property destroyed, without the least prospect of redress; but these are few when compared to the many dreadful consequences attendant on civil discord.

The people within the walls were nearly in as distressed a situation, being in continual apprehension of an attack from Sir William, but were suddenly relieved, receiving information of the Castle of Hawarden being besieged by the King's party, who had landed at Mostyn, in their return from Ireland, on an expedition to quell the disturbances in that kingdom.

On the arrival of the King's troops before the Castle of Hawarden, Colonel Marrow sent them a verbal summons by a trumpeter, to which they in the garrison sent in return a long paper, drawn up in the puritanical style of those times, and concluding thus :—" We fear the loss of our religion more than the loss of our dearest blood, and being resolved to make it good, we put our lives into the hands of that God who can, and, we hope, will secure them more than our walls or weapons."

Colonel Marrow immediately sent the following reply :—

"GENTLEMEN,

"It is not to hear you preach that I am sent hither, but it is, in his Majesty's name, to demand the castle for his Majesty's use, as your allegiance binds you to be true to him; and not to inveigle those innocent souls that are within with you; I desire your resolution whether you will deliver the castle or not."

Nov. 21.—A rejoinder was sent from the castle, in much the same style as the former answer, intimating, "That they were satisfied of Colonel Marrow's dislike to preaching; that God would require blood from those who shed it; and that they relied upon the Lord of Hosts."

Nov. 22.—Sir Michael Ernley and Major-General Gibson arrived with some additional forces from Ireland, and sent another summons in form : but received a similar answer to the former.

The garrison not surrendering, it was thought necessary to apply to Chester for a reinforcement; the governor immediately called a council for that purpose, who, after some debate, came to the following resolution :—

"AT a council holden at the council-chamber, within his Majesty's castle at Chester, this first day of December, 1643. We, whose names are hereunto subscribed, having duly weighed and considered the application and request of Sir Michael Ernley, knight, and Major-General Richard Gibson, for aid and assistance, whereby to enable them to reduce the rebel garrison at Hawarden; it is hereby ordered, that on the morrow, by break of day, three hundred of the citizens and train-bands, with their proper officers, together with the companies of Captains Thropp and Morgell do march to the assistance of the King's forces now at Hawarden, and that this detachment shall be commanded by Lieutenant-Colonel John Robison.

(Signed)   "ABRAHAM SHARMAN, ROB. CHOLMONDELEY, WM. MANWAIRING,* ROBT. BREREWOOD, THO. COOPER, FRANCIS GAMULL, R. GROSVENOR, THO. THROPP, CHA. WALLEY."

Accordingly, this reinforcement came to Hawarden on the 2nd of December, and the next day a brisk attack being made upon the castle, the besieged, the day following, hung out a white flag.

---

* This worthy knight lost his life during the siege of Chester, but we have not been able to learn the particular circumstances of his death. Close to the north part of the communion rails, in the choir of Chester Cathedral, is a very handsome marble monument erected to his memory by his lady. The following is part of the inscription :—

"To the perpetual memory of the eminently loyal Sir William Manwairing, eldest son of Sir Edmund Manwairing, chancellor of the county palatine of Chester; of the ancient family of the Manwairings of Poever, in the said county. He died in the service of his prince and country, and in defence of Chester, wherein he merited singular honour, for his fidelity, courage, and conduct. He died honourably, but immaturely, in the 29th year of his age, October 9th, 1644."

Dec. 4.—They capitulated, and, early the next morning, the castle was surrendered to Sir Michael Ernley, on the following conditions: That they were to march out with half arms, two pair of colours, one flying the other furled, and to be safely convoyed either to Wem or Nantwich. Thus was this fortress, which it was expected would have been a most troublesome neighbour to this city, subdued in the very short space of three days.[7] The party that went to their assistance returned to Chester, without the loss of a single man.

Jan. 31, 1644.—It was ordered that one hundred pounds worth of the ancient city plate should be forthwith converted into coin, for the necessary use and defence of the city. At the same assembly it was ordered, that the sum of eight-score pounds should be assessed upon the city, to be collected at twenty pounds per week, for the perfecting of the works and maintaining thereof; also for making provision of matches, coals, and candles, for the use of the garrison: viz., fifteen pounds per week from the free citizens, and the remaining five from the nobility, gentry, and others, who had fled into the city for protection in this present rebellion.   CHARLES WALLEY, *Mayor.*

There was also an order made to present the sum of three hundred pounds to the King, and the same to the Prince of Wales.

Feb. 13.—A detachment sallied out from the garrison, to attack a party of the Parliament forces, who had made a lodgment at Christleton; the battle began near Great Boughton, but, after a bloody engagement, the Parliamentarians were forced to retire. In this skirmish there were slain near one hundred and forty officers and soldiers of the King's party, most of them Chester men. On the Wednesday following, Great Boughton was burnt down to prevent the enemy from harbouring there.

Prince Maurice, arriving in this city, thought proper to issue out a precept to the commissioners here, to tender the following protestation or test to the inhabitants:—

" *To the Mayor of the City of Chester, Sir Francis Gamull, Sir William Manwaring, Lieutenant-Colonel Robinson, Alderman Thomas Cowper, Lieutenant-Colonel Grosvenor, Colonel Mostyn, Captain Thomas Thropp, Captain Morgell, or to any two of them.*

" THESE are to will, authorise, and require you, or any two of you, to administer the protestation, hereunto annexed, lately made for the security of this city, to all the nobility, gentry, divines, citizens, and all other inhabitants of this city; and to all and every the officers, soldiers, and others, that shall come into, or have any commerce within, the said city: and in case any person or persons refuse, deny, and will not take the same, you are hereby required to give a list of the names of all and every person so refusing, unto me. Herein you are not to fail. Given at Chester, under my hand and seal at arms, this 4th day of March, 1644.

" MAURICE."

Colonel Jones, who commanded the foot, Adjutant-General Louthaine, who commanded the horse, under Sir William Brereton, about eight o'clock in the evening of Sept. 19, drew off a party of thirteen hundred horse and foot, and advanced by a still march to the garrison of Chester.

They arrived the next morning before daybreak, and immediately transmitted, with a flag of truce, the following authoritative summons:—

" *To the Mayor, Aldermen, and Comunalty of the City of Chester.*

" SUCH is our tender care of the preservation of this city from spoil, and to prevent the effusion of Christian blood, that we have sent a second summons to the commander-in-chief for the delivery of it for the use of the King and Parliament; that you may see our reality herein, we signify to you (that which is obvious to all men) your desperate condition—hopeless of reliefe—forasmuch as the King is beaten in the field, fled farre from you, not able to gather any considerable recruits. Also that God hath encouraged us with a late glorious victory and potent army—our batteryes are fixt, and nothing wanting for an immediate prosecution of this design, by the blessing of God; we desire you to ponder the premises, and to endeavour

---

[7] Hawarden being situated upon so great an eminence, and of so short a distance from the city, the enemy had a full view of all those works which were opposite to them: this made the above fortress a great acquisition to either party.

that the summons may find acceptance; which, if despised as the former, we stand cleare before God and the world of all such sad effects as necessarily will follow, by a hot storm of enraged soldiers, of which you have a sufficient premonition, by your Servants,

"MICH. JONES,

"JAMES LOUTHAINE."

Before the Mayor could remit an answer, they privately divided into four squadrons, stormed the out-works and got possession, in some parts, even before the garrison were aware of them; who erroneously placing confidence in the honour of the enemy, expected them to wait for the Mayor and citizens' reply.

The Mayor with indignant contempt at this traitorous proceeding, remitted the following laconic answer :—

"GENTLEMEN,—Before I could acquaint the aldermen and citizens of this city of Chester with your summons, the shooting of your cannons did prevent your Servant,

"CHARLES WALLEY."

The horrors of war, and the customs and stratagems of the besiegers, are most interestingly illustrated in the following document :—

A Letter tied to an Arrow, and so shot into the City of Chester.

"WHATSOEVER thou art, that readest these ensuing lines, I believe if thou be a Christian, thou wilt seriously consider of them, both for thine own good and the prosperity of the famous city of Chester, wherein thou art; and that thou mayest understand my meaning, I have reduced it into several heads.

"*Imprimis.* That thou mayest know that this army that hath besieged thee with thy fellow-soldiers, is raised and employed for the defence of the true Protestant religion, the King and Parliament, and for the bringing known offenders of the ancient lawes of this kingdom into a just trial and punishment; those being the persons that have seduced and divided his Majesty from his Parliament, and knowing themselves offenders, have fled from justice, and so have proved the occasion of this unnatural war.

"*2ndly.* Consider (if thou wilt not believe what I have said already) how destitute of relief thou art. The King's army (within the view of your city walls) being totally routed, most of the great commanders killed and taken, all the soldiers scattered, and no hopes of any considerable recruit. The besiegers, encouraged with this victory, and having possession of the suburbs, receive as good accommodation as can be in any garrison: and besides this, the forces of several neighbouring counties are coming daily for their assistance; and what hopes of mercy canst thou have, if thou holdest out to the last?

"*3rdly.* Consider the hazard that thou runnest: if the city be forced, thy life is at the mercy of enraged soldiers; thy family (if thou hast one) undone; and thou be guilty of the spoiling and ransacking so famous and antient a city, as also the shedding of so much Christian blood.

"*4thly.* Consider how thou hast been persecuted by those that thou esteemest thy best friends; how they have been masters of thy estate, have quartered soldiers upon thee, and given thee nothing in recompense but harsh language; have made thee a slave to receive all abuses, and knewest no remedy: add to this the loss of trading, without which thou canst not long subsist; and how thou art a partner with the rebels of Ireland in destroying and seeking the blood of godly and conscientious Protestants.

"*5thly.* Consider how thy commanders daily delude thee with hopes of relief from Scotland, from Montrose; when, if thou wilt believe a Christian, the army there is absolutely defeated, and most of the lords, knights, gentlemen, and commanders that sided with him, taken prisoners and slain; and since this great overthrow, Montrose himself, with those that escaped, are taken by Lieut.-Gen. David Lesly, in Douglas Castle: add to this the gallant condition of the city of Bristol, in now having the enjoyment of its antient liberties of trading, both by sea and land; with many other towns and cities in the like conditions that thou knowest, are reduced to the obedience of King and Parliament: and the city of Chester almost beggared with oppression, and, if God prevent not, likely to suffer the violence of fire and sword.

"*6thly.* Consider the many religious good men, with their wives and families, that have been turned out of the city; their estates, in an unlawful manner seized; and what several unwarrantable oaths have been pressed upon their consciences for that end; and let thyself judge, whether the advice of him (that seeks thy welfare) be unreasonable, and be sure that forthwith thou communicate what is herein written, to thy fellow-soldiers, and consider, then, to use your utmost endeavours for the surrender of the city, upon honourable conditions, that the miserable effects, which is likely to come, may be prevented, and that thou mayst be left inexcusable, if thou takest not this timely warning and advertisement, from

"THY FAITHFUL WELL-WISHER."

On the 7th of January, the correspondence again resumed; and though, perhaps, it may be deemed prolix, yet, as showing the nature of the times, we think it worthy of continuing.

"*For the Mayor of Chester, and the Lord Byron.*

"EXPERIENCE tells you on what foundation your hopes of relief were grounded : but that you may see my tender care of the preservation of the city and the lives and the estates of the inhabitants, once more I summon you to deliver the city, castle, and fort into my hands, for the use of the King and Parliament. Expecting your speedy answer, I rest your Servant,

"WM. BRERETON."

"Chester Suburbs, Jan. 7th, 1645."

"*To Sir Wm. Brereton, Bart.*

"WE are not convinced by experience of the groundless foundation of our hopes of relief; neither, indeed, is our condition such as to precipitate us to a prejudicial treaty. However, if within twelve days we be not assured of our relief, by a gentleman and a citizen, whom we shall send for that purpose, with a trumpet of ours, and a pass from you, we shall then be contented to enter into a treaty for the delivery of the city, castle, and fort, upon honourable and soldierly conditions, remaining your Servants,

"JOHN BYRON,
"CHARLES WALLEY, *Mayor.*"

The following letter came in as the other was sent out :—

"*For the Mayor of Chester, and the Lord Byron.*

"I PERCEIVE my desires to preserve the city encourage so great obstinacie, as though you expected as good conditions, when you can hold out no longer, as if you had treated when you received the last summons, which proceeded not from any fear of disturbance, for I cannot but believe you are hopeless of relief. But to prevent further misery, and the ruin of the city, which will be remediless, unless speedily surrendered; therefore, you are to expect no further treaty if your answer be not returned by three of the clock in the afternoon.   "Your Servant,

"WM. BRERETON."

"Foregate-street, 12th Jan., 1645."

To this an answer was sent, which it would appear was not satisfactory, from the immediate and peremptory nature of the reply.

"*For the Mayor of Chester, and the Lord Byron.*

"THE writing sent by the drum is no satisfactory answer to the summons; neither will I assent to your desires in any part of it. If you return not a positive answer before one of the o'clock to-morrow morning, expect no further treaty.   "Your Servant,

"WM. BRERETON."

"Foregate-street, 12th Jan., 1645."

A Letter thrown over the Walls of Chester.

"I DID this day deliver unto Sir Edmund Varney and Major Thropp, conditions, wherein I tendered to all Welsh soldiers and officers liberty to go and live at their own houses; to the Irish that have not taken part with the rebels, liberty to return into Ireland, or to march to any of the King's garrisons; to the citizens who were not Commissioners of Array, nor Members of Parliament, and had not borne arms, liberty of their persons, enjoyment of their estates, and freedom of trade, as all towns and cities under the Parliament's power and protection have; taking only the national covenant: this should have been performed, but they would not receive them, as was desired by

"WM. BRERETON."

"Chester Suburbs, Jan. 22, 1645."

The same week they entered Wrexham, in which they converted the church (which structure, for its elegance, stands unrivalled in this part of the country) *into a stable for horses.* Being informed that Ruthin was garrisoned with a number of the King's forces, they directed their march thither; but the garrison being apprised of their intentions, immediately guarded the castle, and sent a detachment to Denbigh, for fear of their surprising that fortress. They took possession of the town, and, of course, plundered the inhabitants, but did not remain long there, returning to Wrexham.

They next followed Prince Maurice, who had marched with his army towards Chirk Castle, but, fearful of his entering Cheshire, and raising the siege of Beeston, they gave up their pursuit.

Feb. 20.—The Prince, wishing to enter Chester, the Parliament army opposed him; he then retreated to Holt, made a bridge of boats over the river, under the walls of the castle, and, with about five hundred men, came over into Cheshire, but was soon repulsed by the enemy's superior force. He several times afterwards attempted it, but without success.

March 17.—Prince Maurice and Prince Rupert came with great force and relieved the garrison at Beeston, which had been for some time again besieged by the enemy. The following day the soldiers plundered the parish of Bunbury exceedingly, and set Beeston-hall on fire.

About this time the enemy by degrees surrounded Chester, placing garrisons at Hool, Rowton, Huntingdon, Eccleston, Iron-bridge, Upton, &c., and also about Beeston Castle, where they began to raise a large mount, encompassed by a deep ditch and ramparts thereon, which were almost finished, when there was a report that the King with his army was marching into this county, upon which the enemy fled to Nantwich. But his Majesty advanced no further than Drayton, which place he left, May 24, and directed his march towards Uttoxeter.

Sept. 26.—His Majesty arrived at Chirk Castle, and remained there with the forces during the night: and the next morning detached Sir Marmaduke Langdale with most of the horse, over Holt-bridge, that they might be on the Cheshire side of the River Dee; intending that Sir Marmaduke should come upon them in the rear, and that all the forces in the town should sally out, and so inclose them.

The King, with his guards, and Lord Gerard, with the remainder of the horse, marched this evening into the city, amidst the shouts and acclamations of the soldiers and citizens. His Majesty lodged at Sir Francis Gamull's, in the Lower Bridge-street, opposite St. Olave's Church.

In this battle many gentlemen and officers of distinction lost their lives, or were taken prisoners. By computation not less than six hundred men were killed on both sides.

His Majesty remained that night and the next morning in this city, and before his departure gave orders to Lord Byron, then governor, and to his commissioners, "If after ten days they saw no prospect of future relief, to treat for their own preservation." Though, at the same time, he imagined the city must surrender, even before he could secure his own person.

Sept. 28.—The King marched over Dee-bridge with five hundred horse, and, not without some danger, passed into Wales, and arrived that evening at Denbigh Castle, attended by Sir Francis Gamull, Captain Thropp, and Alderman Cowper.

They remained with the King two days, when these loyal citizens took a sad and final leave of their Sovereign; and, on their return to Chester, found it, if possible, in a more distressed situation than when

Y Y

they left it : for at four o'clock that morning, the enemy had again forced the works at Boughton (which at the last battle they were obliged to quit), and repossessed themselves of all that part of the town without the Eastgate. The citizens, though again confined within the narrow compass of their own walls, vigorously exerted themselves in defence of the city.

They refused nine several summonses ; nor till they had received undoubted assurance that there were no hopes of any succour, did they answer the tenth : then, and not till then, they consented to a treaty, previous to which the following letters passed between the commanders :—

"MY LORD,—I cannot send such propositions as have formerly been rejected, every day producing loss of blood and expence of treasure ; neither will I trouble myself with answering the particulars of your unparalleled demands ; to which, if I should suit mine, I should require no less than yourself and all the officers and commanders to be my prisoners, and the rest to submit to mercy. Yet to witness my desires for the preservation of the city, I have, upon serious consideration and debate, thought fit to tender these inclosed conditions, conceived conducible to the welfare of the city and countries adjacent ; for the perfecting whereof I am content commissioners meet, and have given commission to these gentlemen to receive your answer in writing to these propositions of mine herewith, touching which I shall not be so scrupulous as to demand their return, not valuing to what view they may be exposed : therefore, they are left with you, if you please, and I remain your Servant,

"WM. BRERETON."

"Chester Suburbs, Jan. 26, 1646."

To this my lord that day returned, that he could not at present give a full answer, in regard that he must consult the gentleman joined in the commission with him. However, the next day he sent this answer, thus :—

"SIR,—Those demands of mine, which you term unparalleled, have been heretofore granted by far greater commanders than yourself, no disparagement to you, to places in a far worse condition than, God be thanked, this is yet. Witness the Bosse, Breda, and Maestricht, and as many other towns as have been beleaguered either by the Spaniards or the Hollanders ; or, to come near York and Carlisle, and nearest of all, Beeston Castle ; and therefore you must excuse me, if, upon the authority of so many examples, I have not only propounded, but think fit to insist upon them, as the sense of all manner of people in the city. As far as your conceit in demanding of myself and the rest of the commanders and officers, to be your prisoners, I would have you know, that we esteem our honour above our lives, that no extremity whatsoever can put so mean thoughts into the meanest of us all. That to submit to your mercy is by us reckoned amongst those things that we intend never to make use of. I am, nevertheless, still content that the commissioners, whose names I formerly tendered unto you, meet with such as you shall appoint, in any indifferent place, to treat upon honourable conditions ; and desire you to assure yourself that no other will be assented unto, by your Servant,

"JOHN BYRON."

"Chester Castle, Jan. 27, 1646."

To which Sir William Brereton sent the following reply :—

"MY LORD,—I cannot believe that you conceive the war betwixt the Hollanders and Spaniards is to be made a specimen for us ; neither can I believe that such conditions as you demand were granted to the Bosse, Breda, or Maestricht. Sure I am, none such were given to York, Carlisle, or Beeston, though some of them were maintained by as great commanders as yourself, and no disparagement to you. I shall, therefore, offer to your consideration the example of Liverpool, Basing, and Latham, who, by their refusal of honourable terms when they were propounded, were not long after subjected to captivity and the sword. You may, therefore, in pity to all those innocents under your command, tender their safety and preservation of the city; for which end I have sent you fair and honourable conditions, such as are the sense of all the officers and soldiers with me; which being rejected, you may expect worse from

"Your Servant,

"WM. BRERETON.

"Chester Suburbs, Jan. 27, 1646."

The following curious account of the proceedings of the Royalist, as well as the Parliamentary forces in South Wales, are from some scarce tracts in the British Museum, and as they contain very interesting and minute particulars which are not detailed in either Rushworth or Whitelock, the reader, possibly, may not be displeased with its length.

"*A True Relation of the discomfitting and routing of the Earl of Carberry and his forces out of the County of Pembroke, manned and performed under God by the valiant and courageous Gentlemen, Colonel Rowland Langhame, John Poyer, Mayor of Pembroke, Esq., Major Thomas Langhorne, Simon Thellwall, and Arthur Owen, Esq., Captain Powell, and Captain Carrey, and other well-affected Commanders and Gentlemen, with the aid and assistance of the renowned Seamen, ordered by the Admiral to be landed out of the several ships for that service, under the command of Captain Peter Whitley, and John Green, Lieutenant.*

"The fleet consisting of five ships and a frigate, appointed by the Right Honourable Robert Earl of Warwick, Lord High Admiral of England for the service of the King and Parliament, for the guarding of the coast of Ireland, &c.:—

"*Names of the Ships.*—LEOPARD, Admiral, Capt. Richard Swanley; SHALLOW, Vice-Admiral, Capt. William Smith; PROSPEROUS, Capt. Nicholas Gottenby; PROVIDENCE, Capt. William Swanley; LEOPARD, Merchant, Capt. John Guilson; CRESCENT, Frigate, Capt. Peter Whitley.

"The squadron of ships arrived at Milford Haven on the 25th of February, 1643, and at the time the said Earl of Carberry, his Majesty's Lieutenant-General for those parts, had possession and command of the entire country and county of Pembroke (only part of the hundred of Castle Martin). His garrison towns and places were Tenby, Haverfordwest, Trefloine, Stackpool House, Carew Castle, Roch Castle, Pix Pill, and the Dale, all which were considerable places, well manned and fortified; the next after the arrival of the fleet, there came aboard the Admiral, the said Colonel and Captain Poyer, with some other gentlemen of Pembroke, who declared the sad, miserable, and deplorable state and condition of the well-affected Protestants of Pembroke and the country adjacent, and that the enemy gave out and reported, that they would kill the dogs and ravish the bitches, and root them out to the third and fourth generations; and how it pleased God, with his outstretched powerful arm and infinite mercy (maugre the Earl of Carberry's forces), with their infernal adherents had kept the town, and part of the hundred, being not above two hundred foot, and fifty horse; and with forcing impunity, not silencing their heavy pressure and weighty cares, prayed the aid and assistance of the fleet, presuming with God's help and mercies, and the furtherance of them, to expel the said Earl with his unworthy rabble. *Daming* boys of the country; and upon agitation it was agreed to land two hundred *seamen*, one demi culverin, one sacre, and one faulconet of brass, with powder, shot, match, &c. The 30th of January last, Colonel Langherne, with his sea and land forces, being about three hundred foot, and about fifty horse, with his artillery and ammunition, advanced to Stackpool House, about two miles from Pembroke, and approaching the enemy they played with their small shot incessantly upon them, and our ordnance at the house, but the walls thereof were so strong that they performed little execution; at last our men gaining some part of the outer works near the walls. The enemy seeing the place no longer wardable, and themselves hard beset, yielded upon quarter, which was granted and nobly performed. In this action, or assault, there were two of our men slain, eight or nine wounded; and some of the enemy fell, and were hurt also, there being sixty soldiers in the said house, all completely armed. The house being taken the Colonel left the garrison, and returned to Pembroke, where, after a short repose to refresh his men, they marched to Trefloyne House, where was a strong garrison of one hundred and fifty foot, and forty horse, with one piece of ordnance; our forces making their approaches, the enemy played their parts manfully, by playing their small shot, and using all martial endeavours in matter of defence and opposition; yet our men marched up to their walls, gained their out-houses, our ordnance playing upon them, having made an assaultable breach, the enemy without hope of relief, and seeing an impossibility of maintaining their hold without a present disengagement, and some loss of blood, desired quarter, which was granted and honourably performed. In this enterprise some few were killed and hurt on each side, and there were taken in the said house forty horse with their arms and furniture, and one hundred and fifty foot arms. All this while the said Earl durst not march out of his stronghold, which was at that time in Tenby, not above a mile from the said house, to show himself in the field; only himself with some of his forces faced ours, keeping a river betwixt them, upon which our gunners making some shot they retreated; the said Colonel slighting the walls thereof, retired to Pembroke to refresh his men; that done, seeing God had given such prosperous success and encouragement of their proceedings at the beginning, with unanimous consent and courageous hearts, resolved to go over on Roos side, passed then by the enemy, there to engage themselves and try their fortunes against them, upon which the said Colonel and Captain Poyer came aboard the Admiral, desiring further aid and assistance to set forward and advance the design, which was willingly condescended to, and the time agreed on to send up all the boats belonging to the fleet, with a great gabbard which God sent accidently out of Ireland, which stood in very great stead for transporting the soldiers and artillery, and, accordingly, on the 22nd, in the night, the boats went up to the place appointed, being near Pembroke ferry, and the Crescent frigate to guard and enable their landing; the 23rd, by eight in the morning, the forces and artillery were landed on the enemies side, and that morning the Admiral appointed Captain Gottenby and Captain Gilson to go to the eastward of the fort, the Admiral and Vice-Admiral on the west side, and Captain William Swanley to guard the vessels of ammunition. Part of our forces drawing up two pieces on a hill which commanded the enemy's works on the east side, were guarded all night, and the Colonel next morning with the rest of the forces, bringing up his men in two divisions, and coming near the enemy's ambuscadoes on the north side, after a small skirmish, routed the enemy and beat them into their fort, the ships then playing on them, and the two pieces on the east side flanking their works, the demi cannon on the south side, and our forces giving a gallant and fierce assault, the enemy dismayed as in a toil or labyrinth threw down their arms and cried for quarter; and there were taken in the said fort about two hundred and forty prisoners, whereof some of note and quality, whose names, with the ships lying in Pix Pill, near to their said works, then also taken, with a number of their ordnance, as in a schedule herein contained appears. Our forces being landed, intelligence thereof was brought to Sir Henry Vaughan, who was then in garrison at Haverfordwest, with two or three hundred horse and foot, garrisoned with ten pieces of ordnance, upon which he presently dispatched away Captain Richard Steele with a letter to the Admiral and the rest of the commanders and gentlemen, praying a parley, or treaty for peace; but before the messenger arrived the said fort was taken. News thereof being carried to Haverfordwest, the old knight and the rest were stricken with such horror and amazement in a palsy or aguish condition fearing our forces would also presently march thither, that they caused a strict watch or sentry to be duly kept to give notice of the enemy's approach, that when they saw them coming they may the more *facilly* make their escape; and at that time there was one Wheeler, a grazier, who had a herd of cattle grazing on the hills; the watch having a circumspect vigilant eye to perform their duty and charge, looking sharply forth in the evening, the said cattle then getting head and running towards the town, the watch conceived them to be the army, and cried, 'G—d d—m them, the round-head rogues were coming;' the which, struck such further terror into the said old knight and cavaliers, that happy was he that could run away first and fastest; by that means the town was freed and acquitted of them; and in their escape they endeavoured to have carried three or four barrels of powder along with them; but fearing the round-headed black coats, (as they termed them,) which were the beasts, cast the said powder into a river, leaving behind them ten pieces of ordnance, with a good quantity of provisions, and red coats made to clothe our soldiers. Thus had the great Jehovah, the Lord of Hosts, blessed our endeavours and proceedings hitherto, and made the wicked to flee when none pursued them, with all reverence, be ascribed all praise, glory, &c.

"The people of the town and country afore enslaved and tyrannically intreated, being heartily oppressed, declared great joy for this victory and deliverance; and by authority, summons issuing forth for the gentry and able inhabitants on a certain day to meet at the town aforesaid, with the rest of the country thereabouts, came in and presented their service to the Colonel, whereupon was placed a garrison in Haverfordwest, and the whole country, freed from the catterpillars or cavaliers, saving Tenby, and Carew Castle, which places are strongly fortified, as is informed. The Colonel and well-affected gentlemen, conceiving themselves in no safe condition till they had taken in Tenby and Carew Castle also; to extirpate and root the anti-christian malignant party out of the said country, desired the admiral's farther aid for the recovery of the aforesaid town, which would satisfy their religious warrantable desires, and reduce the whole country into a happy and peaceable condition and government, to the advancement of God's glory, the King's honour, and the country's safety, with the subject's liberty, which tended to a considerate debate, it was granted, and with all alacrity furthered: and the Admiral, for the better effecting of the design, sent a demi-cannon to Pembroke, with as many seamen more as could be well spared out of the fleet, with powder, shot, match, &c.: the same day sent away his vice-admiral, Captain Gottonby, and the Crescent frigate, into the Baldy Road, near to Tenby, there to do such service against the town as God in mercy should enable them. Upon Wednesday the 6th of this instant, March, Colonel Rowland Langham, with the rest of the commanders, drew their forces into the field, which consisted of about five hundred horse and foot or thereabouts, with a demi-cannon, demi-culverin, and a saker of brass, with other ordnance and ammunition, and marched to Tenby, where planting there ordnance, summoned the town on Thursday following, being the 7th, by a trumpet, to surrender the town to king and parliament's use, the which obstinately refused; the ordnance played at the town from sea and land, and the garrison of the town with great resolution defended the same; but after three days siege a great part of the town was beaten down, a breach made, and one of the chief commanders in opposition wounded, their courage was rebated, and our forces, making a gallant and desperate assault, entered the breach, gained the town by the sword, with the loss of one man, and some few hurt, where many of the enemy fell and were hurt also, and were took betwixt three and four hundred prisoners, whereof some commanders of note; as relation being had to the schedule may appear, eight pieces of ordnance, about three hundred foot-arms, with plunder for the soldiers, by gaining which town the whole entire county of Pembroke was reduced, saving Carew Castle, which the 10th of this present was, upon summons, surrendered upon quarter, which was to quit the said hold, and to leave their arms, and to have a convoy for a secure passage out of the country. &c."

The Schedule mentioned of the prisoners of note and quality, with the ordnance and arms, together with the ships then taken, &c., viz. :—

AT THE PILL.—Captain John Barlow, Master of the Ordnance, and Captain of a troop of horse, a church papist; Captain Edward Bradshaw Captain, John Bradshaw, Captain John Butler, Captain Arnold Butler, Captain William Marychurch; the Globe and Providence of Bristol.

The commanders' names that run away out of Haverfordwest, being thereto forced by the horned beasts, as before mentioned :—

Sir Henry Vaughan, Major-General of the three counties, Pembroke, Cardigan and Caermarthen; Sir Francis Lloyd, Major of the Horse; Sir John Stepney, Governor of Haverford west; Lieutenant-Colonel Butler, High Sheriff of the County of Pembroke; Captain John Edwards, Commissioner of Array in *quorum;* Captain Hall of Bristol; with one hundred seamen; who all run away and quitted the place, as afore declared.

Prisoners of note taken at Tenby :—

John Ewyn, Governor of Tenby; Colonel David Gwyn, Lieutenant-Colonel Thomas Butler, High Sheriff of the County of Pembroke, who ran away from Haverford west; Captain George Lewis; Captain Methol, Captain Rice Richard, Archdeacon Rudd, a malignant priest.

Particulars of the ordnance, arms, powder, taken, &c. :—

Taken at the Pill abord the ships, Haverford west, Tenby, Trefloyn, and Carew Castle, of ordnance, 53; arms for foot and horse, fixed and unfixed, 700; powder barrels, 6 or 7; seamen killed upon the service, 6; seamen wounded, 20.

RICHARD SWANLEY.

The following chronological account of the rebellion in Wales is taken partly from a manuscript kindly lent us by the Hon. E. M. Ld. Mostyn, M.P., and from a manuscript, formerly a part of the Penbedw Collection, and partly from the memorandum book of William Morris, Llansilin, in the possession of Sir Watkin William Wynne, Bart., M.P.; the Salusbury MSS. belonging to Lord Bagot, " Cwtta Cyfarwydd," by Peter Roberts, Bronwylfa, kindly lent us by Lord Mostyn, from various MSS. in the British Museum, some memoranda in the possession of the heir of the Wynns of Llwyn, and other documents never before published. The orthography of the original manuscripts has been followed where practicable, but owing to a confusion as to dates, &c., a rearrangement has been found necessary. From the difficulty attending this, it is hoped that the author may be acquitted of inattention, with respect to any inaccuracy that may occur.

A.D. 1643, *February* 16.—Colonel Mitton came over Bangor-bridge in the morning, and took Sir Gerard Eyton, Sir Robert Eyton, John Eyton, Sir John's brother, all in the house of Sir Gerard, and plundered it. Thence he went and took Mr. Edisbury and Mr. John Jeffreys, Mr. Humphrey Dimock, of Millington, and his son; Mr. Kyffin, vicar of Bangor, and his brother, William Kyffin, of Llanfyllin, that came there to visit him.

February 18.—Prince Rupert came to Shrewsbury.

February 23, or thereabouts.—The ships of the Parliament, with the men of Pembroke, took the Pill,[a] and all the King's ammunition there; they took Haverfordwest and Mr. Barlowe; Bradshaw, Butler, Marschurch, and more prisoners; they took besides two of the King's ships, and the high sheriff of the county. The Prince's men got Hopton Castle, with the loss of many of the King's men at several times, amongst whom Major Vaughan, of Paut-glas, was slain. A while after Brompton Brian was taken by the Parliament. The men of Pembrokeshire, and most of Carmarthen, to their side, took Cardigan town and castle, on Sunday, the — day of ——, and took some gentlemen prisoners; but upon coming of some of

---

[a] This is a place on the River Mawddach in Merioneddshire, called Hên gwrt Pill; it is where the ships go highest up the river. This is necessary to be known to the readers unversed in naval terms.

the King's men, under the conduct of Gerard, governor of those parts, they left Cardigan and retired to their holds.

April.—General Cromwell dispersed the Parliament.

September 1.—Mr. Vavasor Powell marched with eighty men to Machynlleth, bringing with them Thomas Owen and his wife; and bound them to appear at the next quarter sessions. Others were remanded and sent prisoners to Red Castle.

November 9.—Houlte-bridge was taken by Sir Thomas Myddelton. "After taking Houlte-bridge, William Salusbury, of Rûg (and Bachymbyd) fortified Denbigh Castle."—*W. Morris.* "He received his commission from the King at this time and repaired the castle at his own charge, assisted by his kindred."—*Symond's Diary.* William Salusbury is known by the appellation of *Hosannau gleision,* from wearing blue stockings, and was a most worthy and loyal man, as the following particulars will abundantly prove. He is thus recorded in a Welsh MS.: "William Salusbury, ceidwad dewr castell Dinbech yn erbyn milwr y senedd—yr oedd ef mor wresog o blaid y grêd ac yr oedd galonog o achos y Brenin. Efe a seiliodd ac a waddolodd capel Rûg:" *i. e.*, W. Salusbury, the brave defender of Denbigh Castle against the Parliament General—he was as zealous for his religion as hearty in the cause of his King. He founded and endowed Rûg chapel.

On the arrival of Sir Thomas Myddelton at Wrexham, after his success at Houlte, he wrote the following letter to Governor Salusbury, which, with the answer, is among the Salusbury MSS.

"THE former friendship and familiarity which hath passed betwixt us doth not only invite but also engage me to use all possible means not only to continue but alsoe to encrease the same, which on my parte being donne and offered, however things fall out hereafter, I am excusable before God and the world.—It hath pleased God by reason of all the distractions of the times, for the present to put us in a way of opposition one to the other; the causes being well understood, I doubt not but the issue would be a firmer union betwixt us than ever. Sir, through all opposition, God hath brought me with a considerable force to Wrexham, able both to defend myself and offend my foes; wherein I am by unquestionable power as well authorised to preserve the peace of this country from the violence of oppression used and exercised by the commanders of arrays and others, against the Parliament, as alsoe to protect and receive into grace and favour such as shall willingly come in and submitt to the obedience of King and Parliament. This power, by God's grace, I will labour to put in execution, and this is the intente of my coming into these parts. Sir, I understand that for the present you are in armes in Denbigh Castle, and governor thereof— and being formerly satisfied of your ingenious disposition, I cannot doubt but that your intentions and mine will agree, and on your part produce such accŏns as may conduce to your honour and safety, and the prosperity of these oppressed countryes: and therefore I doe hereby invite you and desire God that you may for your own good embrace it, that you would please to submit yourself to the power and obedience of the King and Parliament, lay down your arms, and deliver up that castle to mee, or those that I shall appoynt, to be disposed of for their service and for the public peace and safety of these parts; which if you shall doe, you shall not only be protected in person and estate by mee and my power, but also you shall approve yourself, as formerly you have been, a patriot and preserver of your country, a lover of religion, and an instrument of the publick good; and will be by the state taken notice of as an acceptable service. Sir, now I have discharged my conscience, desiring your speedy consideration and speedy resolution, and soe desire God to direct you, and remayne,

"Your ould and true friend and kinsman,

"THO. MYDDLETON."

Answer to Sir Thomas Middleton's Letter or Summons.

"In nomine Jesu.

"SIR,—I desire not to live longer than I approve myself true to my King and country, a true lover of the Protestant religion, and that yealde chearful and hearty obedience to my King and Parliament; and if the want of your obedience be your quarrell, or any part of the cause of your coming with force into these parts, it is an offence taken but not given. I am not soe jealous as to think you point att me as one that did exercise violence or oppression in this country; I pray God wee doe not see those things now began to be exercised, instedd of being preserved from those. But to be playne—to betraye soe great a trust as the keeping of Denbigh Castle, tho' upon never soe fayre pretences, may be acceptable to them that desire it, but in my opinion, in itself abominable; and must needs render him that shall doe it odious to God and all good men, and I will never account him my friend that should move mee to it. But I cannot say you doe soe, for I shall with all pleasure and willingnes yeald it up as you desire (that is) when I am commanded by my King and Parliament. And for the discharge of that trust in the meane time, and for noe other cause I have armed myself, as well as God did enable me; and those arms (with God's leave) I shall beare and use for the service of my King and country, and not to exercise violence and oppression. This is my answeare to you, and, with God's healpe, the firm and constant resolution of him that is your kinsman, and would be your true friend, as far as truth and loyalty will give him leave,

"WILLIAM SALESBURY.

Denbigh Castle, the 15th 9ris, 1643.

December 12.—Came the Speaker of the Parliament and one half of the parliament men to Whitehall, to Lord Cromwell, to ask him, by force of the authority they had given him, to make laws and rule the kingdom, and said that they understood that this parliament could not be serviceable in settling this kingdom.

December 16.—Oliver Cromwell was proclaimed Lord Protector.

A.D. 1644, *January* 26.—Sir Thomas Myddleton sent a company of soldiers to Machynlleth, who did some harm to some men of Penal; thence marched to Cardiganshire, as far as Llanbadarn, and thence plundered Trawscoed, and many other houses. During their abode at Llanbadarn, thirty men of the garrison of Aberystwith, thinking to surprise fifty of the Parliamenteers then at Llanbadarn, were repulsed, and some thirteen of them drowned in a mill pond near the town, whereof Lieutenant Powel was one. About the latter end of January, Sir Thomas and Sir William Brereton came over Dee to Wrexham. Prince Maurice came to Shrewsbury, and thence he went to Chester. Then the townsmen of Shrewsbury betrayed the town to Colonel Mitton, who, on the 21st of February, entered and got it without blows, taking prisoner Herbert Vaughan. Prince Rupert came to the Marches of Wales, and, together with his brother, came near Shrewsbury, and thence to the Forest of Dean. When the Princes were gone, then the Parliamenteers came and besieged Chester and Hawardine Castle, and after came from Woorral (Wirrall), by the fords to Flintshire, and did much harm. The King's men took some of the plunders about Wrexham. Colonel Garret came suddenly upon the besiegers of Emlyn Castle, and killed and took prisoners about five hundred. Those that kept Cardigan Castle burnt it and fled to Pembrock. Garret took Haverfordwest, and quitted all Pembrockshire but the town of Pembroke and Tenby, and obtained a rich booty. About —— the Pembrockians took Cardigan Castle and town, and shortly after the King's men recovered the town and castle; also the besieged was relieved by Langham.

February 15.—Colonel Carter, Captain Veinor, and others of the Parliament side, surprised on a sudden, and took prisoners, F. Oatley, knight, high sheriff of the county of Salop, Mr. Richard Fowler, of the Grange, Littleton, and others, to the number of fifteen, at Hinton, near Pontsbury.

June.—The King found it necessary on Sir William Waller's advance to Oxford, to quit that City. He determined to take refuge within the walls of Shrewsbury, marching for that purpose through Worcester on the 6th. Hereupon Waller broke up from Oxford, and hastened in the direction of Shropshire. On this intelligence, his Majesty suddenly returned upon his own footsteps, which of course drew Waller off from this county to pursue the royal army: and soon after ensued the battle of Cropredy bridge (June 29), in which the parliamentary leader was routed with considerable loss. But a week before this, an event had occurred of much nearer concernment to the town of Shrewsbury; one which no victory at a distance could compensate to them; and in comparison of which the fatal battle of Marston Moor (July 3) was to them of small importance. This was the fall of Oswestry, captured June 22nd by the Earl of Denbigh and Colonel Mytton; which greatly straitened the communication of this town with Wales, and the western parts of Shropshire. Encouraged by this success, the Earl, in the beginning of July, drew his forces towards Shrewsbury, "but received such a welcome," says our authority, "from Sir Fulk Hunks's foot, and Colonel J. Marrow's horse, that one hundred and twenty of his men were killed upon the place."[9]

On the 16th or 17th *of September* both parties met not far from Montgomery, and fought stoutly till the Cavaliers fled;

---

[9] Mercurius Aulicus, Tuesday, July 9, 1644:—This was the Court Gazette of the day, and there is reason to apprehend that the information was unfounded.

the foot, notwithstanding, fought till they were almost slain; My Lord Biron fled, and lay at Bala. On the King's side Colonel Broughton, Captain Morgan, Sir Thomas Finnealay, Major Williams, ... were taken prisoners, and about 400 slain on both sides. Sir Thomas Myddleton being left to govern the country and castle, summoned all the gentry and commonalty of Montgomeryshire to appear before him at Montgomery and Newtown, and on September 26th, Bant Price, George Devereux, William Penrhyn, Lloyd Pyer Price of Park, Esq., Morgan of Aberhavesp, and Gabriel Wynn of Dol Arddyn; and the commons of all the country, save Cyfeiliog, met at Newtown and became for the parliament. Not long after the Red Castle was taken by night by Sir Thomas Myddleton, and my Lord Biron taken prisoner. Afterwards Sir Thomas Myddleton took Ruthin without the castle, and after that 60 of his men were slain by them of the castle, he forsook the said town and country, being warned that the country about were in arms.

In September the royalists sustained another reverse. Montgomery Castle had been held for the Parliament, and the King's forces were besieging it: but on the 28th, Sir John Meldrum, a Scot, with Sir William Brereton and Sir Thomas Middleton succeeded in relieving it, and in taking thirty-seven barrels of powder, twelve of brimstone, and a great deal of match, which was coming from Bristol for the relief of Shrewsbury and other places. Hence this town is described as being "at the last gasp;" of which the Scot announced to the lords and others of the committee of safety for both kingdoms, that he should shortly make a trial: but in his postscript he adds, that having since had intelligence of a body of horse and Colonel Hunks's regiment of foot being marched hither, he has altered his resolution touching Shrewsbury; "to which, at the best," says he, "I had no other inducement but the hope of a party within the town, and the scarcity of soldiers there."

After this, the Parliamentary forces proceeded to Montgomery, where they laid siege to the castle, as will appear by the following letters from Sir William Brereton, Sir Thomas Myddelton, and Sir John Meldrum, relative to the great victory given them in raising the siege before Montgomery Castle, and how they routed, and totally dispersed, his Majesty's forces under the command of the Lord Byron; where they took all their carriages, arms, and ammunition, and made them fly to Shrewsbury and Chester, with a list of the names of all the commanders and officers taken and killed in the same service.[1]

" To the Right Honourable the Lords and others of the Committee of both Kingdoms, sitting at Derby House, in Westminster.

"RIGHT HONOURABLE,—That God who is most glorified by working by the weakest and unworthiest instruments, hath this day given a most glorious victory, and as much manifested his power therein as in any day I have been engaged since the beginning of these warres.

"We have relieved Montgomery Castle, wherein there was closely besieged, and much distressed, the Lord Herbert of Cherbury, Colonel Price, and most of Sir Thomas Myddelton's officers, and neere five hundred souldiers. We were so very hard-tasked by the multitude of our enemies (who did much exceed us in number), as that, if the commanders and souldiers had not engaged, and behaved themselves very gallantly, or if we had wanted any part of our forces, it might have hazarded our army, for it was very dubious and uncertaine which way the Lord would incline the victory. It came to push of pike, wherein they were much too hard for us, having many more pikes. Our horse, also, at the beginning of the battell, were worsted, and retreated; but there was, I doe believe, an unanimous resolution, both in horse and foot, to fight it out to the last man. Indeed, there could be no other hope or expectation of safety or escape, there remaining no other way of retreat, all passages being in the enemies' power (if masters of the field); and truly, if God had not infatuated them, they might easily have interrupted our passage, and made good divers passages against us. But our extremity was God's opportunity to magnifie his power; for when it was most dubious, the Lord so guided and encouraged our men, that, with one fresh and valiant charge, we routed and put to retreat and flight their whole army, pursued them many miles, when in the mountains, and did perform great execution upon them; slew (I doe believe) five hundred; wounded many more; tooke neere fifteen hundred prisoners, and amongst them Colonell Broughton and Colonell Tilesley, who they report to be General Majors. There were also taken lieutenant-colonells, majors, and captaines, more than twenty; and all their carriages, and neere twenty barrels of powder, wherein they were furnished

[1] Parl. Hist. xiii. pp. 285—292.

the night before the battell; we tooke also (as was conceived) neere 1500 or 2000 armes, most for foot. Most of their horse escaped towards Shrewsbury and Chester.

"The enemies' army, it was reported (and I doe believe it), was no less than four thousand; the Foot being the old Irish, who came out of Ireland with Col. Broughton, Warren, Tyllier, and some Col. Ellis, and some of Col. Sir Michael Woodhouse's, and Sir Michael Ernly's, Regiment, from Shrewsbury, Chester, and Ludlow. Our army consisted of about fifteen hundred foot, and fifteen hundred horse. We lost not forty men slaine, and I doe believe there was not sixty wounded. Our greatest loss was of Sir William Fairfax and Major Fitzsimons, most gallant men. Sir John Meldrum did with much judgement order and command these forces; and, therefore, deserves a large share in the honour of this daie's successe. But, indeed, the whole honour and glory is to be given, and ascribed to God, the giver of victories, and who is most deservedly stiled the Lord of Hosts.

"What remains further to be done in prosecution of this victory shall not be omitted; and if it please God that Newcastle be delivered, and some Scottish forces assigned to assist to the taking in of Chester, I hope, through God's mercy, there may be a good account given of all these parts of the kingdome. To effect which no man shall serve you with more faithfulnesse than your humble Servant,

"WILLIAM BRERETON."

"Mountgomery, September 18th, 1644."

"We know not how to dispose of these common prisoners, unless it would please you to order of them that will take the covenant to be shipped (if God gives us Liverpoole), and transported over into Ireland, to serve you there.

"We have left Sir Thomas Middleton in a good condition in Montgomery Castle, and the gentlemen of the country begin to come in unto him. Sir John Price is already come unto him, before I came thence. He and Herbert is come away with us towards Oswestry."

"To the Right Honourable the Committee for both Kingdomes, at Darby House, in Westminster.

"MY LORDS AND GENTLEMEN, — I formerly acquainted you of our coming hither, and of our proceedings in these parts; and also the good successe it pleased God to bestow upon us. Since which time the enemy hastened to come on us, before we could bring in provisions for our garrison; by reason whereof I was enforced to retreat, with my horse, unto Oswestry, with some small loss only of straglers that lay loytering behind, leaving all my Foot in the castle, and hastened into Cheshire to procure releife, and likewise into Lancashire to Sir John Meldrum, from whom I found a great deale of readinesse to releive us in our distresse, and to preserve what we had gotten from the enemy, being thirty-seven barrells of powder, and twelve of brimstone, both which they exceedingly wanted. Sir John Meldrum, with Sir William Brereton, and Sir William Fairfax, marched with three hundred horse and foot towards Mountgomery, and came thither on the 17th of this instant September, where we lay that night in the field that was most advantageous for us, which the enemy had possest themselves of before, and deserted at our coming thither, placing themselves upon the mountaine above the castle, a place of great advantage for them. Wee resolved not to goe to them, but to endeavour the victualling of the castle; whereupon we sent out parties for the bringing in of provisions; which the enemy perceiving, they marched downe in a body both horse and foot, both in number about five thousand, and came up to our ground, and gave us battell; wherein, after an houre's fight, it pleased God we obtained a glorious victory, having taken many officers, fourteen thousand common souldiers, slaine four hundred, and taken their ammunition, with a great part of their armes, and some few horse, the rest all flying away. The Lord Byron commanded in chief the enemie's forces, and Sir John Meldrum the Parliament's forces, who behaved himself most bravely and gallantly; and Sir William Fairfax, who had the command of the horse, did most valiantly set upon their horse, and engaged himself too far, so that he was taken prisoner, but presently fetcht off by

z z

the valour of our men, but sore wounded; our men issued also out of the castle, and fell upon the enemies in their trenches, and tooke divers of their officers and souldiers, which they had left to keepe their workes; Sir William Brereton, with the Cheshire foot, did most bravely behave themselves that day, and did beat the best foote in England, as they the very enemies confesse, being all Prince Rupert's foot, and the chosen foot of all their garrisons.   I shall make it still my humble suite, that you will please to afford me some speedie course for present money for the payment of my souldiers; for without that I shall not be able to keepe them together: and for the presente I shall take upon me the boldnesse to subscribe my selfe, my Lords and Gentlemen, your humble Servant,

"Thomas Myddleton."

Mountgomery Castle, Sept. 19, 1644."

"Since the writing of this letter, it hath pleased God to take to his mercy Sir W. Fairfax, who is even now dead."

"To the Right Honourable the Lords and others of the Committee of Safety for both Kingdomes.

"My Lords,—I have thought fit to give your lordships a breife account of some passages of business here in Wales, forbearing a larger relation, until I shall have a further time and larger subject, which in all probability, by God's assistance, may offer itself within a short time.   For as by the earnest invitations of Sir William Brereton and Sir Thomas Middleton easily concurre with them for the relieve of Montgomery Castle, besieged by the King's forces; I resolved to contribute my best endeavours in that expedition, as well in the regard of the importance of the service, as that Liverpoole was not to be attempted suddenly by such forces as I had (being in number inferior to the forces within the towne), whereupon I went with the Yorkshire, Lancashire, Cheshire, and Staffordshire forces, amounting to three thousand horse and foote, and marched to Mountgomery Castle, in Wales, which was, by a great deale of industry and resolution, taken in by Sir Thomas Middleton, together with a great deal of powder, match, and brimstone, which (coming from Bristol) was prepared for the relief of Shrewsbury, Chester, and Liverpool.   Upon our approach towards the Castle, the enemie did withdraw themselves in some disorder; the next day after, being the 18th of September, they did take advantage of the weaknesse of our quarters, the third part of our horse being employed abroad for victuals and forage, their horse and foot came on with greate courage, resolving to break through our forces and to make themselves masters of a bridge we had gained the night before, which would have cut off the passage of our retreat.   It pleased God to dispose of the issue of the business, that (by the resolution of the officers and souldiers of horse and foot) the enemy did lose the advantage they had in the beginning, and were shamefully routed, by the pursuit of the victorie, which continued for the space of three miles; there were found dead upon the place five hundred, besides many officers of quality killed and wounded, and twelve hundred prisoners.   Sir William Fairfax and Major Fitzsimons (who carried themselves most bravely) are deadly wounded, without great hope of their recovery, with some other captaines and officers of our horse.   The Cheshire foot, with their officers, carried themselves more like lyons than men, especially Major Lowthian, who commanded as major-general. The Castle is relieved with victuals; Sir Thomas Middleton's souldiers, who were before prisoners, are made free, together with the Lord Herbert, of Cherberie.   Amongst the prisoners, Major-General Tilliseley, Colonel Broughton, and divers lieutenant-colonels and majors, with many captains and lieutenants, so that by the blow given here, the best of their foot are taken away; Shrewsburie, Chester, and Liverpoole, unfurnished with ammunition; and North Wales (which formerly had been the nurserie for the King's armies,) in all likelihood will shake off that yoke of servitude which formerly did lie upon their necks, and will be reduced to the obedience of King and Parliament, by the example of Mountgomery Castle, which is one of the goodliest and strongest places I ever looked upon.   The personal carriage and endeavours of Sir William Brereton and Sir Thomas Middleton hath been exceeding greate in the advancement of this service.   There is good hope that Liverpoole, by famine, will be soone rendered, and that Shrewsburie and

Chester will be at the last gaspe, whereof, by God's assistance, there shall be a short triall made. So having no further for the present to impart to your lordships, I shall cherish all occasions wherein I may approve myself, your lordships' most humble Servant,

"JOHN MELDRUM."

"*Montgomerie Castle, September, 19, 1644.*"

"MY LORDS,—The intelligence which I have since the closing of my letter of a body of horse and Colonel Hunks's regiment of foot that are marched to Shrewsburie, and that the Lords Byron and Mullinax are gone backe to Chester. I have altered my resolution touching Shrewsbury, which at the best had no other inducement but the hope of a partie within the towne, and the scarcitie of souldiers there. I am, your lordships' most humble Servant,

"JOHN MELDRUM."

The subjoined documents of the period are also of great interest, and include the *Iter Carolinum*, and the Journal of the Royal Army.

About the 6*th of October*, 1644, letters were sent from Welshpool to London, which certified that the renowned Sir Thomas Middleton had taken Redcastle, a place of very great consequence, and one of the strongest of the enemies holds in North Wales. The manner of taking it was said to bee thus :—The enemy in the castle, (wherof the Lord Powis, a grand papist, and most desperate and devilish opposer of the Parliament, was governour and owner also,) did often oppose and interrupt them bringing of provisions into our forces at Montgomery Castle; whereupon Sir Thomas Middleton summoned the whole country thereabout to come in unto him, and presently upon it advanced from Mountgomery to Pool with 300 foot and 100 horse, where they quartered on Monday and Tuesday night following, and on Wednesday morning next at two of the clock, even by moonlight, Mr. John Arundell, the Master-Gunner to Sir Thomas Middleton, placed a petarre against the outer gate, which burst the gate quite in pieces, and, notwithstanding the many showers of stones thrown from the castle by the enemies, Sir Thomas Middleton's foot, commanded by Captain Hugh Massey and Major Henry Kett, rushed with undaunted resolution into the enemies works, got into the porch of the castle, and so stormed the castle gate, entered it, and so possessed themselves of the old and new castle, and of all the plate, provisions and goods therein, which was great store, which had been brought from all parts thereabouts; they also took prisoners therein, the Lord Powis and his brother, with his two sons, together with a seminary priest, 3 captains, 1 lieutenant, and 80 officers and common souldiers, 40 horse and 200 armes. The place is of much concernment; for, before the taking of it, it did much mischief to the country, and had almost blocked up the passages from Oswestry to Montgomery Castle, so that now the strongest posts in all North Wales are in the possession of the Parliament : this castle being conceived to be of strength sufficient to hold out a year's siege, and been able to keep out at least 10,000 men for a whole twelvemonth, it having at that present sufficient provision in it for all sorts of such a continuance of time. Besides, by this means, the noble Sir Thomas Middleton hath now the command of all North Wales, and can raise men there at his own pleasure.

Shrewsbury was the main support of the Royalists in these parts,[2] and in a state of the greatest exhaustion. The following representation, presented by the corporation to the governor about this time, forcibly paints the miseries of civil war, and the extremities to which a town once so flourishing, was now reduced.

In consequence, as it seems, of this representation, it was ordered at a sitting of the Commissioners of Prince Rupert His Highness.

November 1.—Present, the High Sheriff [Tho. Edwards, Esq.,] Sir Francis Ottley, Mr. Owen, Mr. Lacon, Mr. Smith, Sir Vincent Corbet, Mr. Sandford, Mr. Treves, "that all the rents of the Lord of Bridgewater that are unreceaved and to bee receaved within this county be received by Sir Fr. Ottley, for satisfaction of all arrears due to him and his officers bie former engagements for quartering and cloathing of his souldiers, and the future pay of himself, officers and souldiers, hee rendering an accompt thereof when he shall be thereunto required by Prince Rupert His Highness, or the Commissioners for this county."

But many of the estates out of which these rents were to issue, did not lie within the obedience of the King; and all that could be recovered would be little adequate to the purposes which it was destined to supply; so that the corporation

[2] The paper called Special Passages and Certain Information, Tuesday, Nov. 15, 1644, speaks of Shrewsbury and Bridgenorth being made by the marquiss [probably of Worcester] "places to receive the Welsh and Lancashire forces, and so to bring them to Oxford to assist the cavaliers."

were obliged, only four days later, to "agree that a cessment of 200*l.* be levyed upon the abler sorte of people, according to Prince Rupert his Highness Commissioners' order, for payment of the officers of this garrison."

About the 1*st of November* 60 horses of Myddleton came to Machynlleth for the contribution money, and the day following parted thence, and plundered Dolgiog, and came to Mathavern, and fearing to be overmatched, came that night and quartered at Mallwyd; the morrow after, being Sunday, the people of the country gathered themselves together to stop the passage to Dinas, which when they heard, some of them came to the bridge to rouse them, but were beaten with stones, and a cornet of theirs taken prisoner, and two or three of them shortly afterwards died of their wounds.

About the 22*nd of November* a great company of Sir Thomas's men plundered some castle in Radnorshire, and thence went to Cardiganshire, and met 500 Pembrochians at Llanbadarn, under the command of Colonel Bell; from thence they came to Llanbadarn, and thence to Gogerddan, where they did no harm, Sir Richard having fled to Merionethshire.

November 27.—They marched towards Machynlleth, and, not far from the town, were met by some forces out of Merionethshire, under the command of Major Hooks and Sir Richard Price; but these small forces were driven through the town, over Dyfi Bridge, and on the other side of the bridge made a stand and kept off as long as their ammunition lasted, and then fled, having lost one man and some taken prisoners, &c. Then the Parliamenteers plundered Machynlleth without mercy, and came the . . . day of November to Mathafarn and killed two men, and burnt the house to ashes, and thence by Llanbrynmair marched to Newtown.

About the same time Dolgelle drapers were robbed by Sir William Vaughan and the King's men of Shrawardine Castle, to the value of 140*l.* in money, besides commodities.

About the 5*th of December* Sir John Price brought some new men out of Radnorshire to Newtown, prisoners. Some few days before Christmas, Sir Thomas Myddleton advanced towards Chirk Castle, but was driven to retire, being beaten off with staves and *scalding water*.

About . . . . the Pembrochians took Cardigan Castle and town, and shortly after the King's men recovered the town, and the castle, also besieged, was relieved by Langhorne.

About . . . . Sir William Brereton kept Chester very strait, stopping all passages to the city, save only from Wales; whereupon my Lord Biron issued out with a company of horse and foot, and meeting with the Parliamenteers near the city, his horsemen fled, and he with his foot was compelled to retire with some loss of men, and Colonel Worthyn, Colonel Goff Vane, and many men of note were taken prisoners.

About the 7*th* day the Parliamenteers came to Machynlleth, to the number of two or three hundred, who sent warrants to the constables of Merioneth for a contribution of 200*l.* monthly, besides 100*l.* for the five months last past. Whereof Mr. William Owen, High Sheriff of the County, having notice, sent to Sir Marmaduke Langdale and his men to come to their aid, who came with one . . .; and when he remained there near a fortnight, during which time he retired to Ynys y Maengwyn, and began to fortify it.[3] Shortly after Sir Marmaduke and his company marched to Machynlleth by Towyn, and sent for the residue of his men, who were at Caernarvon and Anglesey.

1645, *January 2nd.*—Cardiganshire men came over to Merioneddshire, as far as Barmouth; and on Saturday night, being the third day, plundered that village, and so went away in their boats.

———— Captain John Vaughan, with a few soldiers, came in the night from Abermarchant to Penllyn, and the confines of the same, and Denbighshire; had a rich prey of clothes and money of Mr. Price of Rhiwlas, being discovered by one whom Mr. Price had instrusted to convey those things from Denbighshire to his tenants in Merioneddshire, to be privately kept.

February 4th.—These are to certify, whom it may concern, that what inroads were by any soldiers made in Montgomery and Merioneddshires, were without orders and command from me, and were done in my absence. Therefore, I desire a free and usual intercourse and correspondence to be carried on between the counties of my association and the said counties of Montgomery and Merionedd; promising that if hereafter any of my men commit the like offences, they shall be exactly punished according to the law of war.[4]   ROWLAND LANGHORNE.

February 20th.—Captain Thellwall, and forty horse, came from Llanrwst to Festiniog, and so to Dolgelle, and ye next day to Bala.

February 21st.—Mr. Gregory Jones of Castell-march, was taken out of bed by a man of war, and carried abroad to Ireland or somewhere else.

April 7th.—Before the break of day, about 120 and 30 firelocks out of Denbigh Castle fell upon Captain Richard Price's quarter within two miles of Ruthin, who being warned by his scout was in the field before they came, and

---

[3] The house then fortified is still called Y Garris; it is in the parish of Llanwddoyn, opposite Ffynonisa.

[4] The narrative is in the original much disjointed, and this certificate necessarily appears out of place.

so avoided the danger, and gave an alarm to Ruthin, and thereupon Colonel Carter, with the horse guards, and Captain Smikes, with the Major-general's own troops, being there on the guard in Ruthin, drew out and fell between them and Denbigh, and within half a mile of the garrison, met with them and charged, killing seven of them, as is said, upon the place, and in pursuit took 4 captains, 1 lieutenant, 2 cornets, divers troopers, and about 40 horse, with the loss of one man on the Parliament side.

April 8th.—Sir William Neal, governor of Hardin Castle, went to the King; and, as is reported, was by him permitted to deliver the said castle to the Parliament.

About . . . of . . . Colonel Watts, governor of Chirk Castle, forcing the county about to pay their contributions before-hand, delivered the castle well furnished with bread and beer, &c., into the hands of Sir Thomas Myddleton's daughter for her father's use. My Lord Biron came with his army from Chester to Conway.

"We append the following list of officers taken and slaine at the battell neere Montgomery, upon the 18th of September, 1644 :—Colonels Broghton and Sir T. Tilsley; Lieut.-Colonel Bradwell; Major Williams. Captains: Boulton, Edgerton, Bellamy, Floyd, Dolehn, Congrave, Bowman, Right, Morgan, Lieutenants: Scudney, Rowes, Griffith, Morgan, Thurland, Wilson, Floyd, Lewis, Bowen, Brickam, Hager, Minchle, Floyd, Olliver, Carauogh, Perkins, Aldersay. Quartermaster W. Snelling. Cornets: Persons, Hachkisson, Stagge. Ensigns: Wallis, Williams, Dutten, Lampley, Parr, Edwards, Clackstone, Harrison, Contrey, Hest, Lagden, Jones, Barker, Price, Roberts, Richardson, Prichard, Winn, Johnson, Roe, Right, Erwin."

ITER CAROLINUM, ANNO XVI. REGIS CAROLI; BEING THE JOURNAL OF THE MARCHES OF HIS MAJESTY KING CHARLES I. THROUGH SOUTH WALES.[5]

List of His Majesty's several Marches, beginning June, 1645.

	Nights	Miles
Sunday, 15th.—From Ashby-de-la-Zouche, the governor's in the close	1	12
Monday, 16th.—To Wolverhampton; Mrs. Barnsford a widow	1	12
Tuesday, 17th.—To Bewdley, Worcestershire, the Angel	2	13
Thursday, 19th.—To Bramyard, dinner; to Harriford (Hereford), supper	12	1¾
July, 1645.		
Tuesday, 1st.—To Campson; dinner, Mr. Pritchard's; to Abergavenny, supper Mr. Guncer's	3	15
Thursday, 3rd.—To Ragland; supper, the Marquis of Worcester's	12	7
Wednesday, 16th.—To Tredegar, dinner; Cardiff, supper, Sir T. Tirrell, defrayed at the county charge	1	20
Thursday, 17th.—To Tredegar; Sir William Morgan to bed	1	8
Friday, 18th.—To Ragland; dinner, &c. On *Tuesday*, the 22nd, to Mr. Moore of the Creek, near Black Rock, and came back to Ragland, supper; but came in so late as made us doubtful of His Majesty's return. The Scots approach, and our own causeless apprehension of fear, made us both demur and doubt on the first what to resolve, and in the latter how to steer our resolutions, which involved us in a most disastrous condition, &c. &c.	6	12
Thursday, 24th.—From Ragland, to Mr. Moore of the Creek, to pass over all the Black Rock for Bristol; but His Majesty sitting in council, and advising to the contrary, marched only with his servants and troops that night to Newport or Uske; lay at Mr. Pritty's	2	21
Friday, 25th.—To Rupare, Sir Philip Morgan	4	5
Tuesday, 29th.—To Cardiff, dinner, the governor at our own charge	4	7
His Majesty's Marches in August, 1645.		
Tuesday, 5th.—To Glancayha, Mr. Pritchard's dinner; at Brecknock, the governor, supper	1	29
Wednesday, 6th.—To Gurnevit, Sir Henry Williams, dinner; to Old Radnor, supper; a Yeoman's house; the Court dispersed	1	18
Thursday, 7th.—To Ludlow Castle; no dinner, Col. Wodehouse	1	14

The beginning of July, 1645, Sir Marmaduke Langdale, with . . . horsemen, came from Machynlleth to Dolgelly; from whence, after he staid two nights, he went towards Caernarvonshire.

August 2nd.—The Montgomeryshire forces invaded Merionyeddshyre, and lay for a time at Dolgelle. The same day the King's forces burnt Ynys-y-maengwyn, lest the Parliamenteers should find any harbour there. The same day E. V. founded a new garrison at Aber Marchand.

August 21st.—The Montgomeryshire forces invaded again Merionyddshyre, and lay for a week at Bala, untill they wer driven out of the country by Sir John Owen and the North Wales men. In this voyage the Parliamenteers burnt Caer Gai.[6]

---

[5] From the second volume of the " Collectanea Curiosa."

[6] Caer Gai, supposed to have been a Roman station, was at this time the seat of Rowland Vychan, Esq., a staunch royalist, who suffered much in the royal cause. See Cambro-Briton, No. 6281.

Second List of His Majesty's Marches from Oxford, on Saturday, the 30th of August, 1645.

	Nights.	Miles.
Saturday, 30th.—To Moreton in the Marsh, White Hart, Sunday the last, no dinner; supper at Worcester—*a cruel day*	3	24
September, 1645.		
Wednesday, 3rd.—Bramyard; Mrs. Baynham	1	10
Thursday, 4th.—To Hereford; dinner, Bishop's Palace	1	10
Friday, 5th.—To Lempster (Leominster); dinner at the Unicorn; to Webley, supper, the Unicorn	1	14
Saturday, 6th.—To Hereford; dinner, Bishop's Palace	1	7
Sunday, 7th.—To Ragland Castle; supper, 14 miles; *Thursday*, 11th, to Ragland, supper; Abergavenny, dinner, 14 miles	7	45

	Nights.	Miles.
Monday, 14th.—To Monmouth; dinner, the governor; to Hereford, supper. *Monday*, 14th, we marched half way to Bramyard, but there was *Leo in Itinere*, and so back to Hereford again	3	10
Wednesday, 18th.—The rendezvous was at Athurnstone; there dined, 10 miles; to Ham Lacy, supper; Lord Scudamore's	1	26
Thursday, 19th.—To a rendezvous five miles from Lacy, with intentions for Worcester, Poins, and Rocester; in the passage whereupon we marched towards Hereford, so to Leominster, then to Webley, thence Prestine; there halted at Mr. Andrew: this march lasted from six in the morning until midnight, &c.	1	28

JOURNAL OF THE ROYAL ARMY THROUGH SOME PARTS OF THE COUNTIES OF MONMOUTH AND HEREFORD HIS MAJESTY KING CHARLES BEING PERSONALLY PRESENT.[7]

1645, *Septembember 4th, Saturday,* came news that the Scots was returned out of the North and came back towards Worcester. The King knighted the Lieutenant-Governor of Hereford, Sir Nicholas Throckmorton, and Sir William Layton, the Lieutenant-Colonel of the King's Life Guards, Foot.

Friday.—The King went to Lancaster, com. Herf., and lay that night at Webley. His guards returned to their old quarters.

Saturday.—The King determined to goe to Abergavfeny, but it was altered, his guards to Letton, his Majesty to Hereford.

Sunday.—To Ragland, guards to Treargaire, near Ragland, &c.

September 11th, Thursday.—The King, attended with his guards, went to Abergaveny, and returned at night to Ragland; his business was to commit five chief hinderers of that county from relieving Hereford. He that day committed Sir Trevor Williams, but he was bayled; Mr. Morgan, of T.; Mr. Herbert, of Coalbrooke; Mr. Baker and Mr. ——. During the time, the King being at Ragland, when he first came, he sent Sir Marmaduke Langdale, with his horse, to Cardiff, with Lord Astley and one hundred foot out of Monmouth; . . . . foot out of Ragland, Chepstow, &c., to parley with the Glamorganshire peace army who were agane resen. Both armyes mett eight myle of Cardiffe in Glamorganshire. The peace army seeing Lord Astley's resolved to fight, though not considerable in numbers, agreed to lay down their armes and provide one thousand men and armes, with money for the King, &c., &c. The next day or two after they sent their amunition and armes by . . . loaded in Pembrokeshire. Then these rogues hearing of the loss of Bristol, joynd with the Pembrokeshire forces. Sir Marmaduke Langdale marched towards Brecknock.

September 12th, Friday.—In the afternoon his Majesty, attended with his guards, left Ragland, and marched towards Hereford, but returned the Guards to Abergaveny.

Saturday.—The King rested at Ragland.

Sunday 14th.—About noon his Majesty left Ragland and marched to Monmouth. Thence that night to Hereford.

Monday 15th.—His Majesty in the morning attended to his guards, marched some miles towards Bromyat, but by reason Gerrard's horse had not orders soon enough to appear at the rendezvous, his Majesty returned to Hereford, accompanied by Prince Maurice, &c. His Majesty read a copy of a lettter from Montrose of his victory in Scotland.

During the commotions of the reign of Charles I., the King frequently visited Ragland, and was magnificently entertained by Henry, the first Marquis of Worcester. The majestic remains of this castle form an interesting and beautiful object to the surrounding country; the remains occupy a tract of ground one-third of a mile in circumference. The citadel was a large hexagon, defended by bastions, surrounded by a moat, and connected with the castle by a drawbridge. A stone staircase leads to the top, which commands a fine view of the ruins, and a prospect over an extensive tract of country, bounded by

---

[7] From Symon's Notes, Harleian MSS. The author of these notes was Richard Symons, of Black Notley, Essex, gent., who was in the king's army during the civil war, writing memoirs of battles, actions, motions, and promotions of officers, from time to time, in small pocket-books. Eight or ten of these books are in the Harleian Collection in the British Museum; two more in Dr. Mead's library, and two or three in the Herald's Office.

the distant hills and mountains in the neighbourhood of Abergavenny. Round the citadel was a terrace the walls of which were ornamented with statues of the Roman emperors. The grand entrance is formed by a gothic portal, flanked by two massive towers, and the groove for the portcullis still remains. The stately hall dividing the two courts was probably built in the time of Queen Elizabeth, and contains the vestiges of hospitality and splendour; it is sixty feet in length and twenty-seven in breadth.

Most of the apartments of this splendid abode, were of good dimensions, and the communications easy and convenient. The strength of the walls is still so great, that if the parts yet standing were roofed and floored, it might even now be formed into a magnificent and commodious habitation.

From the second court, a bridge across the moat leads to the terrace, which was much admired by King Charles I. The south-western side forms a noble walk of three hundred feet long, sixty feet broad, commanding an extensive view. The outworks formed for the defence of the castle before the siege were too large for the garrison; their shape and dimensions may be traced by the remains of the bastions, stone-work, and trenches.

Ragland is the most modern of the ancient castles in Monmouthshire, as the architecture of the building is of the different styles used between the era of Henry V. and that of Charles I. The great extent of the castle, the grandeur and number of the appointments, give astonishing proofs of baronial magnificence and hospitality. In the records preserved of the grand establishments of the first Marquis of Worcester, the numerous officers of his household, retainers, and servants, appear like the retinue of a sovereign rather than a subject. He supported for a considerable time a garrison of 800 men in defence of his sovereign; and on his surrender to General Fairfax, in addition to his own family and friends, the officers who capitulated were four colonels, eighty-two captains, sixteen lieutenants, four ensigns, four quarter-quarters, besides fifty esquires and gentlemen. After the King's retreat it was invested by Sir Trevor Williams, who thus commenced the memorable siege which distinguished Ragland Castle in the annals of Monmouthshire. Colonel Morgan soon advanced from Worcester at the head of a formidable detachment, and on June 3rd, 1646, summoned the garrison to surrender. The Marquis of Worcester having refused to yield without the consent of the King, Sir Thomas Fairfax came from Bath to superintend the siege; but notwithstanding the vigour with which he passed his approaches, he was retarded by repeated sallies,

The Ruins of Ragland Castle, formerly the residence of the Marquis of Worcester.

and the gallant veteran did not surrender till the 17th of August. The Marquis, on his arrival in London, was committed to the custody of the Black Rod, notwithstanding the terms of his capitulation; but the period of his confinement was of short duration, for he died in December following, four months after the destruction of his house, at the advanced age of eighty-five.[s]

The losses of this family in support of the royal cause were very great. It has been moderately computed at 100,000*l*., besides at least as great a sum lent to Charles I. by the Marquis, and the

---

[s] Every reader of taste will receive with sorrow the information, when he is told, that the magnificent library, esteemed one of the first in Europe, was totally destroyed by the demon spirit of vandalism on this occasion.

maintaining the garrison at Ragland, and the raising and maintaining two several armies at his own expense, commanded by his son Edward, Earl of Glamorgan, and the sequestration from 1646, and afterwards the sale of that whole estate by the Rump [Parliament,] which amounted, as appears by that year's audit, to 20,000*l.* per annum; and was not restored till the restoration of King Charles II. in 1660, when Edward, the then Marquis of Worcester, had the possession delivered him of that part of the estate he had not during that necessitous time sold and passed away.

The page of history (says the biography of the first Marquis of Worcester), does not present a character, among the whole body of nobility, which time has handed down to us, from whose conduct and behaviour, in the hour of adversity, a finer and more useful lesson can be drawn, nor whose maxims are more worthy of our highest attention. It falls to the lot but of few individuals to enjoy the splendour of fortune which attended him for such a long course of years; and still fewer to possess, in so ample a degree, the friendship of their sovereign; but, though enjoying to the utmost this mark of distinction, and treating His Majesty when at Ragland with all possible respect, he never sacrificed his opinions at the expense of truth. Domesticated together in the most friendly manner, King Charles appears seated by his side, receiving the strong truths of his experience with admirable temper, well knowing that they proceeded from an unshaken and disinterested regard for his person and safety, as, in the course of his reign, he had given him convincing proofs.

The Marquis had a mind to tell the King (as handsomely as he could) of some of his (as he thought) faults; and thus he contrived his plot. Against the time that his Majesty was wont to give his lordship a visit, as he commonly used to do after dinner, his lordship had the book of John Gower lying before him on the table. The King casting his eye upon the book, told the Marquis that he had never seen it before. "Oh," said the Marquis, "it is the book of books, which if your Majesty had been well versed in, it would have made you a King of Kings." "Why so, my Lord?" said the King. "Why," said the Marquis, " here is set down how Aristotle brought up and instructed Alexander the Great in all the rudiments and principles belonging to a Prince." And under the persons of Alexander and Aristotle, he read the King such a lesson, that all the standers-by were amazed at his boldness; and the King, supposing that he had gone further than his text would have given him leave, asked the Marquis if he had his lesson by heart, or whether he spake out of the book. The Marquis replied: " Sir, if you could read my heart, it may be you would find it there; or if your Majesty please to get it by heart, I will lend you my book;" which latter proffer the King accepted of, and did borrow it. "Nay," said the Marquis, "I will lend it to your Majesty upon these conditions: first, that you read it; secondly, that you make use of it." But perceiving how that some of the new-made lords fretted and bit their thumbs at certain passages of the Marquis's discourse, he thought a little to please his Majesty, though he displeased them the more, who were so much displeased already. Protesting unto his Majesty that no one was so much for the absolute power of a King as Aristotle; desiring the book out of the King's hand, he told his Majesty that he could show him a remarkable passage to that purpose, turning to that place that has this verse:—

> " A King can kill, a King can save,
> A King can make a lord a knave ;
> And of a knave a lord also,
> And more than that a King can do."

There were divers new made lords who shrunk out of the room; which the King observing, told the Marquis, "My Lord, at this rate you will drive away all my nobility." The Marquis replied, "I protest unto your Majesty, I am as new a made lord as any of them all; but I was never called knave and rogue so much in all my life as I have been since I received this last honour, and why should they not bear their shares?"

To punish, or reflect on, the present generation, for the political opinions of their ancestors, is a species of injustice which every liberal mind will disavow. No doubt but that in other countries, as well as in this, there were families of distinction who favoured the Republican cause, and very essentially assisted it, or it would not have triumphed in the contest; but time has softened down the asperities which the politics of that day gave birth to. We insert another instance of the free and unreserved manner in which the Marquis delivered his sentiments on the King's actions in his presence :—

At the King's being at Ragland, there was some information given of some gentlemen of the county who were supposed to have done his Majesty many ill offices, by withdrawing the hearts of the people from his Majesty : these men thus accused were ordered to be laid hold of, and it was executed accordingly, and they being brought before his Majesty, it was moved by some, that they should be forthwith tried by a commission of Oyer and Terminer; others advised his Majesty they should be sent to Hereford, and there to be kept in safe custody, until further consultation might be had concerning them, they excusing themselves as well as they could. One of them protesting his innocency, with tears in his eyes, the King ordered that he should be released, being always prone to lean to pity rather than justice, and to favourable rather than rigid construction. The King coming back from Abergavenny, where this was put in execution, told the Marquis what he had done, and that when he saw them speak so honestly, he could not but give some credit to their words, so seconded by tears, and withal told the Marquis that he had only sent them to prison, whereupon the Marquis said, " What to do ? To poyson that garison ? Sir, you should have done well to have heard their accusations, and then to have showed what mercy you pleased." The King told him that he heard they were accused by some contrary faction, as to themselves, who out of distaste they bore to one another upon old grudges, would be apt to charge them more home than the nature of their offences had deserved. To whom the Marquis made this return, " Well, sir, you may chance to gain you the kingdom of heaven by such doings as these, but if ever you get the kingdom of England by such wayes, I will be your bondman."

These anecdotes are extracted from a book, called " Apophthegms," by the Marquis himself,[1] and is addressed to the King and the members of both Houses of Parliament. In his dedication, he thus nobly and patriotically expresses himself :—

" And the way to render the King to be feared abroad is to content his people at home, whothen with hand and heart are ready to assist him; and whatsoever God blesseth me with to contribute towards the increase of his revenues in any considerable way, I desire it may be employed to the use of his people ; that is, for the taking of such taxes or burthens from them as they chiefly grone under, and by a temporary necessity only imposed upon them; which being then supplied, will certainly best content the King and satisfie his people, which I dare say is the continual tenor of all your indefatigable pains, and all the perfect demonstrations of your zeal to his Majesty, and an evidence that the kingdom's trust is justly and deservedly reposed in you."

1646, *January* 19th.—Sir Richard Lloyd delivered Holt Castle to Colonel Pope, in the absence of General Mitton, by a former agreement.

The beginning (2nd or 3rd) of February, the city of Chester, after a long penury and scarcity, was yielded. After that General Mitton came with his forces from Chester, and laid siege to Ruthin Castle, which was manfully defended by the governor and those that were with him in it until the eighth day of April following, and for want of aid were obliged to deliver it, &c.

February 23rd.—The Montgomeryshire forces began to fortifie Llangollan Church for the straightninge and keepinge in of the Chirk Castle men, where Sir John Watts was governor, who, shortly after deserting the castle, and marching towards the King's army with all his garrison, were taken by the men of Montgomery Castle, after a hotte bickeringe in Church Stoke Church, the first day of March, 1646.

March 24th, (circ.)—The soldiers in Denbighshire did stir a mutiny, and coming to Wrexham, they lay hold of Colonel Jones, treasurer, and others of the committee, and imprisoned them, demanding their arrears, and a just account

---

[1] Let it be remembered, to his eternal honour, that the Steam Engine, so useful to mechanical powers, owes its invention to his ingenuity and talents.

of the money which the county had paid them. General Mitton being that morning come to town had some intelligence, and fled towards Holt Castle, the soldiers firing after him.

March 25th, (circ.)—A warrant from General Mitton, to demand 7*l.* 2*s.* for four weeks, came to the Constable of Uwch Cregynnan.

March 26th, (circ.)—High Arool was delivered to the Parliament forces. Colonel Wats marched from Chirk, as he pretended towards the King, to Pool; thence to Churchstoke, where he proposed to stay that night, but was surprised by the country people, and some soldiers out of both castles, and the waggons of his carriages taken.

The latter end of March the garrison of Holt Castle burnt about forty houses in town, and burnt the gardens which the firelocks of the Parliamenteers kept.

April 1st.—They of the castle sallied out of the castle, and fell upon Major Saddler's quarters, resolving to put all in the house to the sword, which they had been like to effect, had not a guard, which was placed in a mount erected three days before, relieved them. There fell on the Parliament side five men, and fourteen wounded: of the other party, Captain Cottingham, their commander, a Papist, a Lieutenant, and two more, and many wounded. There hath been never a day since but they sallied out constantly twice or thrice a-day, and as constantly beaten back.

Idem.—The Parliament forces went to Caernarvon, and lay before the town, and the Lord Biron, somewhat before they came, burnt the suburbs, and sent Mr. Spicer, with a company of soldiers, for provision, who robbed and took all the cattle they found, and returned, but Spicer was taken.

April 6th.—Between three and four hundred of Lord Biron's men, horse and foot, came to Dolgelle under the conduct of Colonel Vane.

April 9th.—In the morning one hundred of them marched to Mowddû, and robbed and plundered all their way, and returned with a rich booty by eleven o'clock. They then received 28*l.* 10*s.*, being one month's contribution; falling on Uwch Cregynnan, and demanded the second contribution to be paid in white cloth at the Harlech Castle on the 16th day of April, which was undertaken by the inhabitants. The day following, having plundered all the town, and many places in the country, retired to Trawsfynydd, and thence to Festiniog and Maentwrog.

April —th.—Colonel Whitely delivered the Castle of Aberystwith to the besiegers, and his men, about —— or more came to Harlech, and thence to Caernarvonshire; and they went to Llanwrst. From thence they marched to Denbigh, and between Whitchurch and the town some horsemen of the castle met with some of the Parliament forces, and fought with them, and hurt or killed one captain, and returned.

April —th.—General Mitton, having intelligence that Biron's forces were at Dolgelle, that they had plundered his tenants in Mowddû, sent a company of soldiers, under Colonel ——, to Bala; and, on Saturday morning, marched by Micnant to Festiniog and Maentwrog, thinking to overtake my Lord Biron's men, but they had knowledge of their coming, and fled over the water to Caernarvonshire. The Forlorn Hope of the Parliament quartered at Maentwrog and Festiniog that night, and betimes on Sunday morning went back to stay the army from coming forwards.

The Parliament forces went to Llandyrnog about the 17th of April. Shortly after they lay before Denbigh, and had some loss of men several times.

September 21, Sunday.—Over y° mountaynes, less barren than the day before, by S° Arthur Blayne's howse to Llanvyllyn, a borough towne in Montgomeryshire.

Monday 22nd.—Over such mountaynes to Chirke Castle, com. Denbigh, there the King lay . . . . Watts is governor. The Guards to Llangothlyn, a market towne com. Denbigh, three mile from Chirke. Newes this day that Col. Will. Legge, y° governor of Oxon, was comitted, that P. R. comission was declared null. That part of y° outworkes at Chester were betrayed to y° enemy by a capt. and lieft. both apprehended. The King sent to Watts to send to Lord Byron to Chester, to hold out.

Tuesday.—His Ma⁽ᵗⁱᵉ⁾ marched towards Chester, attended with Montague, Ea. of Lindsey, Earle of Corke, Ea. of Lichfield, Lord Digbie, Lord Ashley, Lord Gerard. His force with him were his own regiment of Life Guards, consisting of these troopes: The King's; the Queen's, comanded by S° Edw. Brett, y° major of y° regim⁽ᵗ⁾, Earle of Lichfield's, Leift.-Col. Gourdon Scott comanded it. They were most Scotts officers. S° Hen. Stradling's troope, wch came from Carlisle wth S° Tho. Glemham. Toto, about 200. Ld General Cha. Gerard was also then wth the K. wth his gallant troope of Life Guard, 140 men; S° Marmaduke Langdale's brigade; S° Tho. Blakeston's brigade. S° W^m. Vaughans brigade, and Gen^ll. Gerard's horse marched before all night toward Holt Castle, com. . . . . a garrison of y° King's, comanded by S° Richard Lloyd, where we have a passe of boates over y° river. Their business was to fall upon, or &c., those horse and foot that lay before Chester. The King went into Chester and lay at S° F° Gamuls howse, his guards watched in the streets. The enemy who were gotten into the out workes wch secur'd y° suburbs, had made a breach the day before and had entered had it not bin most gallantly defended.

September 24th, Wednesday.—Contrary to expectation Pointz his horse were come between Nantwiche and Chester, to relieve those forces of their party who were afore Chester and to fight y⁵ King, as appeared by his letter intercepted by Sʳ Rich. Lloyd, to this purpose (directed to Jones, who sometimes was student in Lincoln's Inn, and comanded yᵉ horse yᵗ besieged Chester), thanking them for keeping their ground notwᵗʰstanding the King's approach, and tells them a neare relacion or accompt of the King's strength, of his tired over marcht horse, of his number of dragoons, of his resolucōn to engage them if possible, &c. This morning, Sʳ Marma. Langdale, in Chester side of yᵉ river Dee, and not farr from Beeston Castle, charged Pointz his horse, beate in and tooke some cornetts. But they beate us agen for't. About twelve of the clocke, those horse wᶜʰ came wᵗʰ yᵉ King and 200 foot were drawn out of Chester.

Charles the First on the Walls of Chester witnessing the Defeat of his Army on Rowton Moor.

From the walls of Chester, the King beheld the fatal battle of Rowton Moor.² There is a tablet on the Phœnix Tower, near the Cathedral, with the following inscription :—

KING CHARLES I.

STOOD ON THIS TOWER, SEPT. 24, 1645, AND SAW HIS ARMY DEFEATED ON ROWTON MOOR.

None of the historians that have related the military operations of this day,³ have impugned the gallantry of the royal troops, or the conduct of their leader; nor has the failure of Sir Marmaduke Langdale's enterprise been generally stated. The fact, however, is indisputable, that the defeat resulted from the mismanagement of the King or his commanders in not supporting Sir Marmaduke. Probably the following statement may be found to be the most accurate account of the negligence of the royal officers. It was

---

² For the account of this battle, we are indebted to Sir Peter Shakerley, Bart.

³ The following lines were written by a citizen of Chester to commemorate the event :—

" Two hundred times around the glorious sun
Earth her unvaried course has swiftly run,
Since the first Charles that Britain's sceptre sway'd
Nigh Cestria's wall his armed host display'd;
Her marshy field where Rowton spreads afar,
There rose the tide of slaughter-breathing War;
Arms clash'd with arms amid th' embattled throng,

Steed press'd on steed, and man drove man along;
Charles through his optic glass from yonder tower
Th' ensanguin'd plain beheld in battle's hour:
Her golden scales how Vict'ry pois'd on high,
The thoughtful Monarch mark'd with anxious eye:
Long time in dubious state the contest hung,
While fitful flames Death's thund'ring engines flung:
At length ' his mounted scale aloft ' gave way;
All hope is gone ;—to Charles is lost the day !
Now Fear, now Flight, his scatter'd troops attend,
While yells of dark despair heaven's concave rend."

3 A 2

written on a blank leaf of Clarendon's History of the Rebellion (now in the library of Sir Charles Shakerley, Bart.), by the son of Sir Geoffrey Shakerley, who commanded a regiment of horse under Langdale.

" The heath upon which Sir Marmaduke Langdale was drawn up, carries the name of Rowton Heath, a mile beyond which, in the London road from Chester, is another heath, called Hatton Heath. The order which Sir Marmaduke had received from the King was to beat Poyntz back. Sir Marmaduke performed the same effectually, for, having marched his men over Holt Bridge undiscovered by the enemy, who had taken the outworks and suburbs of the city on the east side thereof, and Poyntz coming in a marching posture along the narrow lane between Hatton Heath and Rowton Heath, Sir Marmaduke, having lined the edges, fell upon him, and killed a great many of his men, and, having done so, ordered Colonel Shakerley, who was best acquainted with that country, to go the next way he could to the King, who lodged then at Sir Francis Gammil's house in Chester, and acquaint him that he had obeyed his orders in beating Poyntz back, and to know his Majesty's further pleasure. His Colonel executed his orders with better speed than could be expected, for he galloped directly to the River Dee, under Huntingdon House, got a wooden tub used for slaughtering of swine, and a batting staff, used for batting of coarse linen, for an oar, put a servant into the tub with him, and in this desperate manner swam over the river, his horse swimming by him (for the banks were then very steep, and the river very deep), and ordered the servant to stay there with the tub for his return. He was with the King in little more than a quarter of an hour after he left Sir Marmaduke, and acquainted the King that if his Majesty pleased to command further orders to Sir Marmaduke, he would engage to deliver them in a quarter of an hour, and told the King the expeditious method he had taken, which saved him going nine or ten miles about by Holt Bridge (for the boats at Eaton were then made useless), but such delays were made by some about the King, that no orders were sent, nor any sally made out of the city by the King's party till past three o'clock in the afternoon, which was full six hours after Poyntz had been beaten back; and so Poyntz, having all that time to recover their fright that they had been put into in the morning, Poyntz rallied his forces, and with the help of the Parliament forces, who came out of the suburbs of the city to his assistance (upon which the King's party in the city might then have successfully fallen), put all those of the King's to route, which was the loss of the King's horse, and of his design to join Montrose in Scotland, who was then understood to be in good condition. This is what my father, the said Colonel Shakerley (afterwards Sir Geoffrey Shakerley), hath often declared in my hearing, and since no mention is made of him in all this History (though he faithfully served the King in all his wars, was personally engaged in all the field battles for the King, sold part of his estate to support that service, and was for many years sequestered of all the rest), I thought it my duty, as his eldest son and heir, to do that justice to his memory, to insert this here, that it may be remembered to posterity.

" PETER SHAKERLEY."

Thursday 25th.—About 9 and 10 in ye morning ye King left Chester and went to Hardin Castle, governed by Sr Wm. Neale, and stayed three houres, and went that night to Denbigh Castle, Governor Colonel Salusbury. This fortress was repaired by him and his kinred at their owne cost. Colonel Salusbury had his commission from the King two years since.

Saturday 27th.—Was a genll rendesvouz three myles from Denbigh. Newes again that Montros had routed David Lesly, about Kelso, on ye Borders; yt Pr. Maurice was coming wth 1000 horse to us, and was at Chirke. All ours reanimated and expected to follow Pointz to ye North.

Sunday, 28th.—After sermon, about noone, came intelligence yt ye enemies horse were over ye river, a little afore we heard that they were gone toward Scarborough (so ill intelligence has ye K.), but they went but into fresh quarters about Nantwich to refresh. About one of ye clock afternoone, ye King marched thorough Ruthyn, where there is a large castle and fortified, to Chirke Castle, com. Denbigh. Here Pr. Maurice mett us wth his troope and those of Pr. Rupert'e horse y came from Bristoll, Lucas his horse, &c. Toto, 6 or 700.

Tuesday.—From thence early at day breake marched, leaving Shrewsbury three myle on ye left hand; that night late and teadiously to Bridgnorth. The rare gard gott to Wenlock Magna, com. Salop. In this march three or four alarmes by Shrewsbury horse, and five or six of ym crosst the way and killed and tooke some. After the battaile at Rowton Moor, com. Cestr., upon ye rendesvouz neare Denbigh, divers complaints came to ye K. and Gen^ll^ about horses taken that were agen found, some tooke away their horses where they found y^m^. It was thus ordered by ye King according to the opinion of Lord Ashley in this case. One of Sr M. Lang's soldiers was killed, his horse the enemy tooke, and anon one of Gen. Gerard's soldiers tooke ye horse away from the enemy, this horse was challenged at the rendesvouz, and t'was adjudged to y^e^ first owner, Sr M. Lang^s^ man. The reason was given, that unlesse y^e^ enemy had had so much possession of the horse as to carry him to his quarters, it was nothing of validity to say that he was taken from the enemy.

The Arrival of Charles the First and Prince Rupert at Chirk Castle, Denbighshire.

We here subjoin an account of that ancient and noble structure, Chirk Castle, together with some of the transactions that took place therein; it is now the property and residence of Robert Myddelton Biddulph, Esq., lord lieutenant of Denbighshire, colonel of the militia, and for some time representative of the county in parliament.[4] This castle is situated, like all structures of the period, on a commanding eminence, well adapted in those days for the discovery of an enemy's approach, and furnished with every convenience for hostile excursions. As seen from the principal entrance, or north approach, it appears to the eye as a large uninhabited pile of quadrangular shape, partly covered with ivy; and, as it thus presents itself to the visitor, is strikingly gloomy. The fancy is hurried back to days of feudal times; history and romance divide the empire of the mind; and for a time it rests with mute but intense interest on these castellated landmarks of Cambrian history. Approaching nearer, its grey and venerable towers have a solemn and imposing appearance; but the eye is pleased to find that these massive emblems of gone-by days, so intimately associated with times of peril, seem to have undergone very little change since their erection. Its severe simplicity, stately proportions, and immense thickness of walls, carry instant conviction of age, and at once class it among one of the least impaired and most interesting of the feudal dwellings of ancient England.

"The best and most solid mansions of our ancient nobility were like their characters—greatness, without elegance; strength, without refinement; but lofty, firm, and commanding." Nothing out of keeping with the solemn dignity derived from the weight of years has been permitted to appear;—the few necessary repairs have been conducted with judgment, and no unseemly patches upon the walls are observable. The

[4] We are indebted to the worthy owner of this venerable mansion for his kind assistance in supplying us with much curious information not before published.—Ed.

family have protected from injury this seat of their ancestors—restoring with skill and taste where injuries have resulted from years, but so as in no degree to impair its original character; neither adding to nor taking from its early and stately proportions. It may therefore be regarded as a perfect model of the "time-honoured castles of the ancient lords of the soil," and be classed among the most interesting and oldest inhabited buildings in the kingdom.

> " Thy towers,
> Unmodernised by tasteless art, remain
> Still unsubdued by time."

According to a paper communicated to the Antiquarian Society, the present castle was begun in 1011; but another account states that it was built in the time of Henry II., by Roger Mortimer. It continued in this family but a short time, being sold by his grandson John, to Richard, Earl of Arundel, who with his family possessed it for three generations; after which it passed to Thomas Mowbray, Duke of Norfolk, justice of North Wales, Chester, and Flint, in right of his wife, Elizabeth, elder sister to Thomas, Earl of Arundel. On the disgrace and exile of Mowbray in 1397, it was taken by the crown, and granted to William Lord Abergavenny, who married the other sister, in which family it remained until the reign of Henry VI. The next possessor we hear mentioned was the unfortunate Sir William Stanley. After his execution it became forfeited to his rapacious master. In 1534 it was bestowed, along with Holt Castle, by Henry VIII., on his natural son, Henry Fitzroy, Duke of Richmond and Somerset. By his early death it returned to the crown. Queen Elizabeth granted it, with the lordship, to her favourite Earl of Leicester. On his death, Chirk Castle became the property of Lord St. John, of Bletso, whose son, in 1595, sold it to Sir Thomas Myddelton, in whose family it still remains.

There were four Sir Thomas Myddelton's successively at Chirk Castle, the two former knights, and the two latter baronets. The first Sir Thomas was lord mayor of London, when his brother, the celebrated Hugh Myddelton, was knighted for bringing the new river to the metropolis. The second Sir Thomas served in parliament for the county of Denbigh, and took arms in its support when he was fifty-seven years old: for his services at Holt Castle, at Oswestry, and at Montgomery, in the years 1643-4, he received the thanks of the house.

In 1644, when Sir Thomas engaged in the service of the parliament, his own castle became garrisoned for the King, and the veteran knight was under the necessity of besieging it in due form. An occurrence during the siege is thus noticed in the " Mercurius Aulicus," a party paper, dated Feb. 1st, 1644 :—

" Sir Thomas Myddelton is extream melancholie, since his last entertainment, at his house at Chirk Castle, where his pretious engineer's brain was dashed out by a stone from the castle, which the rebels ever since call the Welsh grenedoes. This engineer's death has so damp'd the factious thereabouts that a lady sent this form of prayer to one Mr. Lloyd (a sufficient brother) :—' *O heare us, heare us, good Lord: how long art thou deafe? Why didst thou suffer thy servant Tobias to perish? Curse them, O Lord, and cursed be that creature which was the cause of Tobias' death. Why didst thou suffer that castle, which was the seat of holiness, to be possessed with profaneness and popery? O curse with a heavy curse that great devil of Shrawarden (Sir William Vaughan), which doth torment thy children; and let all the righteous and holy say, Amen. O Lord, bless Sir Thomas, thy holy servant, grant him that strength that he may overcome his enemies and obtain his castle with honour.*' "

It appears, however, from a MS. journal kept near the spot, that Chirk Castle remained in the custody of the royalists till the latter end of February, 1646, when Sir John Watts, the governor, quitted it, and marched with his garrison as far as Churchstoke, in Montgomeryshire, where, after " a hotte bickering in the churche," he and his men were taken prisoners by the men of Montgomery, the 1st March, 1646. It appears also that in the year 1648, the house had changed its principles, but the knight might have done also as well; and he is then found among the excluded members, and bound in a bond of 20,000l. not to disturb the government.

Sir Thomas was an active and a successful commander on the side of the parliament; but towards the end of his life, finding that he had undesignedly assisted in establishing a more intolerable tyranny than that which he had formerly opposed, his patience forsook him, and in 1659 we find him taking up arms with Sir George Booth, a Cheshire general, in order to restore the ancient constitution, and replace Charles II. on his throne. The royalists being fewer in number, and not so well disciplined as the republicans, were easily defeated by Lambert, who retook Chester, and made Sir George Booth prisoner in a few days after the dispersion of his troops. He shortly afterward laid siege to Sir Thomas Myddelton in his own castle, which, after a few days' resistance, was taken by the vigilant General Lambert, who, in his dispatches to the parliament, said, that he thought neither the man nor the place ought to be left behind him; he should therefore march into Wales after him. Sir Thomas, after making a show of resistance for a day or two, was constrained to surrender; and accepted such terms and conditions as he could obtain, observing that it was to no purpose for one man to oppose the whole kingdom, when all other persons appeared subdued.

In another letter from Lambert, dated Chirk Castle, Aug. 24, 1659, detailing the terms of the surrender of the castle, he says, "There were about 150 men in this place, great store of provision, both for men and horses for many months, one little piece of brass ordnance,[5] and competent quantity of ammunition. * * * It is the opinion of many of the chief officers of the army that this castle may be demolished, that it may no longer be an occasion of trouble and inconvenience to this country, as it hath often been."

In the parliamentary proceedings, 27th August, 1659, it was "resolved that Chirk Castle be demolished, and the Lord Lambert is to see it demolished accordingly." Cromwell dying the same year, this order was never carried into effect.

Such is a brief history of the several changes to which this ancient castle was subjected, from the earliest possessors of whom any mention is found. And not to diverge too much, we must unavoidably pass over much that is interesting in the records of this old fortress, and leave the achievements of its owners, their feudal scuffles, its various sieges, its hostile aggressions, its MSS. accounts of the quotas of horse and firelock men furnished to the different arrays of war, and only glance at the last time of its being used as a fortress, which occurred about the time of the usurpation, when it was twice dismantled, and the damage done was not repaired for less than 30,000l., besides the plunder of the personal estate by Lambert, which amounted to 80,000l.

Sir Thomas, the soldier, had a son of the same name, who was made a baronet at the Restoration. The son died in 1663, his father surviving him three years, when he died at the age of eighty years. His picture at Chirk Castle seems to have been taken when he was about seventy. His grandson, the fourth Sir Thomas and the second baronet, married twice; by his second wife, Charlotte, daughter of the Lord Keeper Bridgman, he had an only daughter, Charlotte, who married first to the Earl of Warwick, and then to Joseph Addison, Esq., the celebrated writer. Their daughter, Miss Addison, died unmarried. The baronetage became extinct at the death of Sir William, son of Sir Richard, brother to the last Sir Thomas; Sir William having died unmarried in 1718. The estate, by the entailment, came to Robert Myddelton, eldest son of Richard, the third son of Sir Thomas, the soldier. He dying without issue, was succeeded by his brother John, father of Richard, father of the late Richard Myddelton, Esq., M.P. for the Denbigh boroughs, who died unmarried in 1796. The estate has since been divided between his three sisters. The eldest, Mrs. Myddelton Biddulph, had for her share the ancient castle and its noble domain; and it is now in the possession of her eldest son, Robert Myddelton Biddulph, Esq., who has greatly improved the estate.

The present structure is supposed to be built on the site of an ancient British fortress, called by the Welsh "Castell Crogen," of which we have no account, and of which no portion is observable in the masonry.

[5] This cannon is still at Chirk.

The principal entrance to the castle is in the north front, under a high arch, which formerly contained a portcullis and gate of massive strength, flanked by two towers, and leading into a courtyard of quadrangular shape, forming an area of 160 feet long by 110 broad.

The north and east wings are occupied by the family, and the south and west given up to the offices. The most remarkable of the apartments are a saloon of 60 feet by 30, lighted by three large mullioned windows looking towards the court; a drawing-room, 30 feet square; and an oak gallery extending the whole length of the west wing, 100 feet by 22, leading to the chapel. The ceilings throughout are ornamented by rich plastic work, and the rooms are hung with a large collection of paintings. The gallery contains several old cabinets, the work probably of some Italian or French artists; one in particular is very handsome, and was a gift from Charles II. to Sir T. Myddelton.

Charles the First's Arrival at Denbigh Castle, and his reception by Col. Salesbury.

According to Peter Roberts, public notary of Bronwylfa, St. Asaph, the King arrived at Denbigh Castle on the 26th of September. The following is extracted from his MS. called "Cwtta Cyfarwydd," now in the possession of Lord Mostyn, who kindly lent us the MS. for that purpose.

Libera nos (Domine) à malo.
Amen.
The 24th, 25, and 26th daies of Aprill, 1645, the rebells, viz., Sir Wm. Brerton and Sir Tho. Myddleton, Kt., with their army, have plyndered St. Asaph's parish, except Wickwer, and made great spoyles, &c., and defiled the Churches there, &c.

Mem.—That upon Friday and Saturday, being the xxvith and xxviith daie of September, 1645, ——— Caroli & xxist of our said sovereigne Lord King Charles, &c., was in person at the Castle of Denbigh, whereof Mr. Wm Salusbury, of Rûg, was governor under his Majestie, &c. God save our King and realme. God send us peace in Christ Jesus our Lord. Amen.

Mem.—That upon Tuesday, being the third day ——— 1645, the Citie of Westchester (being besieged ——— latter end of September last by the p.——— was yielded up by the Lo. Biron and other ——— officers and their army, &c.

Sir Marmaduke Langdale's rendezvous was early this morning within two miles of Holt Castle. Friday, September 26th, rested. I saw a rainbow within a mile of Denbigh at five in the morning.

This phenomenon the good man probably interpreted fondly as an omen of approaching peace and safety to the Royal person, now secure from the general deluge of rebellion within this loyal fortress and arc of defence. The appearance had, probably, an happy effect in encouraging the cause of loyalty. We shall now make use of "Symond's Diary"[*] more at large, as it traces the King's personal progress through this part of his kingdom. After a series of disasters to his cause subsequent to the battle of Naseby, in June this year, the King employed himself in raising contributions in the loyal associated counties, and arrived in North Wales in September. The Diary informs us,

Sunday, 21*st September*, 1645.—The King arrived at Llanfyllin, and proceeds on Monday, the 22nd, to Chirk Castle. There the King lay, Watts is governor—the King's guards went to Llangollen.

Tuesday.—His Majesty marched towards Chester. Sir W. Vaughan's brigade and General Gerard's horse marched before all night towards Holt Castle, county of Denbigh, a garrison of the King's commanded by Sir Richard Lloyd, where we have a pass of boats over the river. The King went into Chester, and lay at Sir Arthur Gamel's house.

Wednesday, September, 24th.—Pointz's horse, contrary to expectation, were come between Nantwich and Chester to relieve those forces of their party that were afore Chester, and to fight the King, and were charged by Sir Marmaduke Langdale on Chester side of the river Dee, not far from Beeston Castle, beat in, and took some cornets, but they beat us again for it. About twelve of the clock, those horse which came with the King and two hundred foot were drawn out of Chester; nine hundred prisoners of ours taken and carried to Nantwich, whereof about twenty gentlemen of the King's own troop.

This is the celebrated defeat of Rowton Heath; after which, the King retreats to Denbigh, as previously stated.

On Monday the 29th, we left Oswestry, a garrison of the rebels, on the left hand, to Llandysilio and Llandrinio, co. Montgomery, where the army lay in the field—some chief in houses—thence to Bridgenorth and Litchfield—and on to Newark (not to London, as W. Morris says). Friday, October the 17th, intelligence that the King had left Newark and gone towards Scotland.

The fatal effect of this step is well known, and hence it appears, that North Wales was the last portion of the kingdom which offered protection to its unhappy monarch. "It is a very remarkable fact," says Pennant, "that, notwithstanding the orders of fallen Majesty in June for the general surrender of every garrison in England and Wales on fair and honourable terms, yet the first that yielded in North Wales held out above two months longer than the last English castle.

About the beginning of November, Cardiganshire men laid siege to Aberystwyth Castle: tow[ds] the latter end of this month the owner of Red Castle, &c., sent am[t] of their contribution, and after the Epiphany we of Dolgelle and Llanfachreth sent our money, and they took after the rate of 60l. on the country. They gave as their acq[tt] to the day of payment and protection.

December 8th, (circ.)—Colonel Jones of Nanteos, and ab[t] twenty souldiers came by night to Peniarth, and there took Lewis Gwyn, of Peniarth, and Mr. Francis Herbert, of Dolgiog, (who did here sojourn for fear of the Parliamenteers,) in their beds and carried them to Cardiganshire. Not long after Hereford town was taken by the Parliament.

December 31st.—About three o'clock in the morning, Mr. Edward Vaughan came with a company of souldiers and people of Montgomeryshire and surprised Captain John Ranney, Dd. Lloyd, his lieutenant in Dolgell, with all their horse, being between thirty and forty, and some soldiers, and plundered some houses in town, and parted about sun rising: one man killed.

January 2nd.—Caerdiganshire men came over Merionyddshire as far as Barmoth, and on Saturday night, being the 3rd day, plundered that village and so went away in their boats.

Our authority, Symonds, was probably in the army of Sir W. Vaughan, which, as recorded in the last

---

[*] "Symond's Diary" differs from Peter Roberts's book, "Cwtta Cyfarwyd;" but in order that our readers may have an opportunity of judging for themselves, we insert both accounts.

extract from W. Morris, was now advancing towards Denbigh. In confirmation of the defeat of Sir W. Vaughan, he proceeds.

October 26th.—Sir W. Vaughan came to Chirk. *We* marched to Mr. Thelwall's house (to Llanynys and to Plâs y Ward).

October 31st.—Came intelligence to Denbigh to Sir W. Vaughan that the enemy, under the command of Mitton, was advanced to Ruthin, both horse and foot.

Saturday at noon, November 1st, we had the alarm, for they were at Whitchurch below the town. Their approach was handsomely disputed both by our horse and foot, above an hour, in the hedges and lanes. Their number of foot, being fifteen hundred at least, made ours retreat to the town, which was not long disputed by reason of their forward advancing. Their horse was put to a disorderly retreat notwithstanding. Sir W. Vaughan drew many up upon a green near two miles off, but could not be made to stand. A party of Arcall horse charged the pursuers and were seconded by part of Prince Maurice's lifeguard. The foot were let into the castle by the governor. The horse got to Llanrwst that night, twelve miles distant (thro' Llangerniew, *W. Morris.*) The governor of Denbigh wrote, that the enemy was in his sight above double our number.

"*For Sir William Vaughan.*

"Sir,—I wish you to be as free from danger as I hope we are secure and in good condition here. On your foot being perceived under the castle wall I received them in, tho' I conceived I had no need of them for the defence of this place; yet having, I doubt not, provisions enough, their valour and good service withall meriting my compassion, I freely entertained them. I judge the enemy had a force that came the other way over the Green, equal in number or thereabouts to what you fought with. Mitton and the foot I am informed quarter in the town, and most of the horse in the country about: God bless us all!

"Your friend and servant,

"WILLIAM SALISBURY."

"Denbigh Castle, 1st Nov. 1646—7 at night."

"What you may resolve to take I leave to your own discretion."

November 4th, Tuesday.—Returned a trumpet from Denbigh sent by Sir W. Vaughan, and told that their rendevous was at Northop the day before; and this morning, being Tuesday, came our foot to us out of the castle to Llanrwst. A regiment of reformadoes against us in this business came from London under Mitton's command. Sir W. Vaughan's forces consisted of these regiments and companies:—Prince Maurice's life guard in part. Sir W. Vaughan's own regiment, with Arcall, Bridgenorth, Chirke, Colonel Butler of Huster that commanded the horse in Monmouthshire, in all 300; Colonel Werden, Shakerley, Lieutenant-Colonel, Colonel Sandys of Worcester, Colonel Randal Egerton, Major-General to Gerard; and Colonel Whitley, both 200; Colonel Grudge's regiment, General Gerard, and Colonel Davatrie's, 200; Lord Biron's regiment 100 horse; toto 700, (qu. 800?) Foot: Prince Maurice's firelocks in part, 150; Ludlow foot, 90; Arcall Dragoons, 20; Chirke firelocks, 20; in all 280.

Wednesday 5th.—Rested.

Thursday 6th.—To St. George parish, the rest quartered thereabouts.

November 7th, Friday.—Was a general rendevous on Denbigh Green. This night the head quarters was at Llanrhayader, Sir Evan Lloyd's house.

Saturday.—Marched to Llansaintffraid, same side the water, in Merionethshire.

Sunday.—To Llanfyllin, a town where the King lay about two months before, as he marched from Hereford to Chester. All, both horse and foot, lay there.

November 10th, Monday.—To Newtown.

The following particulars relative to the different castles and garrisons in Wales and the Border towns, with the names of the governors, are extracted from a MS. in the British Museum.

GARRISONS COM. DENBIGH.

K. Denbigh Castle, Mr. Salisbury, of that county, is Governor. King made him Governor.

K. Ruthyn Castle. Capt. Sword, made by P. R., is deputy Governor, under Col. Marke Trevor. Sᵣ. Tho. Middleton did own it.

K. Chirke Castle, Capt. Watts is Governor. Lord Capell made him Governor.

K. Holt Castle, Sᵣ. Richard Lloyd is Governor. King made him Governor.

GARRISONS IN FLINTSHIRE.

K. Hardin Castle, Sʳ. Wᵐ. Neale is Governor, made by P. R., yᵉ Earle of Derbyes house, & lived there some times.

K. Rudland Castle, 2 mile from St. Asaph. Gilbert Byron, brother to the Lord Byron, is Governor. Made by Lᵈ Byron yᵉ King's cost.

K. Flint Castle, Colonel Mostyn is Governor. Yᵉ Kings own Castle.

GARRISONS IN ANGLESEY.

K. Beaumaris, Lord Bulkeley is Governor, Irish baron, yᵉ Kings Castle.

GARRISONS IN MONTGOMERYSHIRE.

R. Montgomery Castle. This Castle was built by H. 3. Holinshed 6. H. 3. to prevent yᵉ rising of yᵉ Welchmen.

R. Red Castle. Hugh Price is Govʳ.

R. Welchpole. Sʳ. Tho. Middleton is Governor; Mason is in his absence. Tho. Farrer house, Red Castle, and W. are wᵗʰin halfe a mile.

R. Abermarchnant, a garrison made about the time yᵉ King marched from hence to Chester; tis Lewis Vaughan's house, 4 mile from Llan Vutlyn.

GARRISONS IN MERIONETHSHIRE.

K. Harlech Castle. Wᵐ. Owen is now Governor, and is Constable during life, and now Sheriff.

GARRISONS IN CAERNARVONSHIRE.

K. Conway Castle. Aᵇᵖ. of Yorke now Governor & Sʳ. John Owen.

K. Caernarvon Castle. John Bodnell is Governor. Onely these two.

GARRISONS IN COM. SALOP.—15 OCTOB., 1645.

K. Ludlow. Sʳ Michael Woodhouse, Governor, quond paz à Marq. Hamilton.

K. Bridgnorth, Sʳ. Lewis Kirke G. Sʳ. Tho. Woolrich was first Governor 3 years since, then Sʳ. Lewis K. 200 in the Castle. Leift. Go. Tho. Wyne, Sʳ. Robᵗ. W. son. Major Fr. Billingaley, Jun. Com. Salop.

K. High Arcall, yᵉ house of Sʳ. Rich. Newport, now Lᵈ. N. Armorer is Governor.

Friday, Octob. 31.—Came intelligence to Denbigh, to Sʳ. Wᵐ. V., that yᵉ enemy, under yᵉ command of Mitton, was advanced to Ruthyn, both horse and foot.

Satterday, at noone, wee had yᵉ alarm, for they were at Whitt Church, below yᵉ towne. Their approach was handsomely disputed by oʳ horse and foot above an howre in the hedges and lane. Their number of foot being 1500 at least, made oʳ retreat to yᵉ towne, wᶜʰ was not long disputed, by reason of their forward advancing. Our horse were putt to a disorderly retreat and flight, notwithstanding Sʳ. Wᵐ. V. drew many of them up upon a greene neare two myles off, but could not be made stand; a party of Arcall horse charg'd yᵉ persuers, and were seconded by pt of P. M. Life guard. The foot were lett into yᵉ Castle by the Governor. The horse got to Llanrwst that night, Com. Denbigh 12 miles distant.

Next morning dispers'd to quarters, yᵉ Governor of D. wrote that the enemy was in his sight above double oʳ number.

Tuesday, 4 *Nov.*—Return'd a trumpet from Denbigh, sent by Sʳ. W. V., & told that their Rendezvous was at Northop yᵉ day before, and this morning came oʳ foot to us, out of the Castle, to Llanrust. A Regᵗ of Reformades agᵗ us in this busines came from London, under Mitton's comand. Sʳ. W. V. forces consisted of these Regiments and companies. P. Maurice life guard in part. Sʳ. Wᵐ. V. owne Regᵗ wᵗʰ Arcall, Bridgenorth, Chirke, Col. Hunter yᵗ comanded yᵉ horse in Monmouth, Colonel Wordius Shakerly, Col. Sandys, of Worcester, all 200.

		Foot.	
Col. Randal Egerton, Majoʳ Genᶫ. to Gerard, Col. Whitley, both 200		P. Maurice fire locks in pt. 150	
Col. Gradyes Regᵗ. Genᶫ. Gerards, and Colonel Danaliers 200		Ludlow foot 90	
Lord Byrons Regᵗ. 100		Arcall Dragoons 20	
		Chirke firelocks . . . . 20 capt.	
Horse toto . . . 700		280	

Wednesday, 5°.—Rested.

Thursday, 6°.—To Sᵗ. George p'ish, yᵉ rest quartered thereabouts.

Friday, 7° *Nov.,* was Genᶫ. Rendesvouz on Denbigh Greene. This night yᵉ head Qʳ. was at Llancaydor, Sʳ. Evan Lloyds house.

Satterday.—Marched to Llansanfraid, some into yᵉ water in Merionethsh.

Munday, Nov. 10, to Newtowne. In this march a Leiftᵗ. of horse and a trooper fell out, and had a single combate in private about a horse; both fought on horse back, yᵉ Leiftᵗ. shot him in yᵉ thigh, and yᵉ trooper him in yᵉ shoulder, disarm'd the leift & tooke away his horse & pistolls. Here yᵉ Van of quartermʳˢ. tooke Captaine Vyner & 7 of his men prisoners; yᵉ rest of his troop were at the siege of Chester then.

Tuesday, to Knighton, a pretty towne; Com. Radnoʳ. Here Mr. Crowder, yᵉ sheriff of yᵉ shire, lives.

The country people of Merionethshire at this time besieged Aberystwyth. When Sir. W. Vaughan marched out of Denbighshire the enemy lay in this manner: three troops of horse and three troops of dragoons at Bretton, Welsh side, two miles from Chester. Colonel Jones lay at Darleston (qu. Dodleston?) with a regiment of 400 horse and of 400 firelocks, called Jones's regiment. They have a bridge over the Dee at Eccleston. More lie at Wrexham. They drew out of those garrisons to fight us, viz., Wem, Oswestry, Red Castle, Montgomery, Derby, Stafford, Viner's troop fifty besides. Mitton brought 500 horse and foot; Sir W. Vaughan then marched to Leominster.

March, 1646.—Colonel Whitley delivered the castle of Aberystwyth to the besieger and his men — about 100 or more came to Harddlech and thence to Carnarvonshire and Llanrwst, and from thence they marched to Denbigh, and between Eglwys Wen and the towne, some horsemen of the castle met with some of the Parliament forces and foughte with them, and hurte or killed one captaine and so returned. The Parliament forces went towards Llandyrnog about the 17th of April. Shortly after, they lay before Denbigh, and had some loss of men several times."—*W. Morris.*

March 25th, (circ.)—A warrant from General Mitton, &c., to demand 17*l.* 2*s.* for four weeks, came to the constable of Uwch Cwgennau.

March 26th, (circ.)—High Arcol was delivered to the Parliament forces. Colonel Watts marched from Chirk, as he pretended towards the King, to Pool, thence to Church Stoke, where he proposed to stay that night, but was surprised by country people and some soldiers out of both castles, and waggons of his carriages taken, &c.

The latter end of March, the garrison of Holt Castle burnt above forty houses in town, and burnt the garrison with the firelocks the Parliamenteers kept.

April 1st following, they of the castle sallied out, and fell upon Major Sadler's quarters, resolving to put all in that house to the sword, which they had been like to effect had not a guard which was placed in a mount, erected three days before, relieved them. Here fell on the Parliament side five men, and fourteen wounded of the other party, Captain Cottingham, their leader, a papist, one lieutenant, and two more. There hath been never a day since, but they sallied, and constantly twice or thrice a day, and as constantly beaten back.

The following particular is from an anonymous writer of a work entitled "Short Account of the Rebellion in North and South Wales," which we extract from our venerable friend the Archdeacon Newcombe's interesting account of the castles of Denbigh and Ruthin, for which he obtained the silver medal at the Royal Denbigh Eisteddfod in 1828:—

"April 7, 1646.—Before the brake of day 120 men and 30 firelocks out of Denbigh Castle fell upon Captain Richard Price's quarters within two miles of Ruthin, who being warned by his scouts, was in the field before they came and avoided the danger and gave an alarm to Ruthin;[7] thereupon Colonel Carter with the Horse Guards and Captain Simkies with the Major-General's own troop, being then on guard at Ruthyn, drew oute and fell between them and Denbigh, and within two miles and a half of the garrison met with them and charged, killing seven of them (as is sayde) upon the place, and in pursuit took four captains, one lieutenant, four cornets, divers troopers, and about forty horse, with the loss of one man on the Parliament side." This account is corroborated, except as to the number killed, by that interesting and valuable collection, the Salesbury Letters.

" General Mytton to Colonel Salesbury.

"Sɪʀ,—I have here inclosed a list of those that are brought prisoners here; how many are thyne I doe not yet know, but I am heartily sorry things doe grow soe high between us, and so are your friends at London. Sir, I beeseich you remember your country, yourself, and your posterity, and goe on no further in this way, to the undoeing of the first and extreme hazarding of the others. If you please

---

⁷ Viz., to the Parliament troops under General Mytton, who were then besieging Ruthin Castle.

to make use of me, as an instrument to make your peace with the Parliament, rest assured you shall engage the best endeavours of him that will show himself to be

"Your ould friend and humble Servant,

"THO. MYTTON."

"Ruthin, 7th Aprilis, 1646.

"Credit me, the King hath noe army left him in the field in any place in the kingdom."

"Colonel Salesbury in Answer.

"WORTHY SIR,—I acknowledge myself much obliged unto you for your kind expressions in your letter sent by my Drum, which I hope to requite in a most reall way before I die. Sir, I have been and am dayly robbed and spoiled, contrary to the law of God and this kingdom for noe other offence that I know but for my loyallty to my King. The Parliament (if I may soe call it) I have noe ways offended, unless (as before) in being loyall to my King, in observing his commands, as well by commission under his hand and seale as also by worde from his own mouthe, for the keeping of this place, his Majestie's own house; which (without regard to my own life, lands, or posterity) with God's assistance, I will endeavour to make good for him to my last gaspe, soe I rest your poore kinsman, and ould play fellow to serve you,

"WILLIAM SALESBURY."

"Denbigh Castle, this 8th day of April, 1646.

"I take the King's own person for a sufficient armey, and what armeys alsoe be in England should of right bee his. Upon my credit, noe more of this place but one man killed, and that, (as they say) after quarter given—one other's pate cutt slightly. Too much security hath lost many a fayre game at tennis as you know : and soe fared it with our men last day."

When so honourable a man as Colonel Salisbury asserts, "upon his credit," that no more than one man was killed, we should feel disposed to believe him, though other authentic accounts of the affair agree with the numbers of the author of "The Short Account," &c., previously given. A printed account in the British Museum, entitled "Three Victories in Wales," published by order of Parliament, April 4th, 1646, contains, together with the Articles of Capitulation of Ruthin Castle, an account of this engagement, in two separate letters to General Mytton, from Major Edward Moore, and Thomas Brooke, his secretary. Each gives the same account. The former informs us in a letter from Ruthin, 8th April, 1646, "Upon Tuesday last, at night, the enemy from Denbigh fell upon part of our quarters, but took neither horse nor men, which gave us an alarm here; whereupon a party of our horse went out and fell between them and home, and meeting them neare Denbigh, took Captain Wynne, Captain Hugh Morris, Captain Morgan,* (Brook calls him of Walgrave; qu. of Gwylgre, now Golden Grove?), and Captain Pickering, one lieutenant, and two cornets, with some gentlemen of this county, and killed seven.—Taken by Colonel Mitton's forces near Denbigh,

"Captaine Wynne, Cap. Hugh Morris, Cap. Morgan, Cap. Pickering, one serjeant, divers gent* and other souldiers, divers armes, seven slaine upon the place, forty horse taken."

In the same account ("Three Victories") is also a letter from General Mytton to Speaker Lenthal, announcing the surrender of Ruthin Castle, which also speaks of this victory as follows: "Yesterday (April 7th) before the break of day a party of the enemy out of Denbigh Castle, being about six score, and

---

* Tradition informs us that Captain Morgan (ancestor to the present Captain Morgan, of Golden Grove,) fought and fell near his house, called, to this day, Plas-Captain, situated midway between Newmarket and Holywell. He took a most active part on behalf of the King, and was buried on the edge of Willenlake (Llynhelig), where his grave is still to be seen. It is now surrounded by a large plantation. We recollect when a boy, hearing of an old man, of the name of Edward Booly, flushed with the hopes of finding treasure in the captain's coffin (which is of oak, and very entire), dug into the grave, but, greatly to his disappointment, found only the skeleton, and two nightcaps covering the cranium. The one was of silk, and is now preserved by the family; the other was of cotton, and was formerly in the possession of Mrs. Jones, better known as "Fanny, of the Cross-Keys Inn," Newmarket.

thirty mounted firelocks, fell upon Captaine Richard Price's quarters, within two miles of this town, but he was vigilant, and his scouts perform their duty so well that they were drawn into the field before they came upon them, which gave him opportunity to avoid them and causing the alarm to this town. And thereupon Colonel Carter, with a standing horse guard, which we are fain to keep in the field constantly to secure our out-quarters, and Captain Simkies with my own troop, which were then upon the guard in this town, drew out and fell between them and Denbigh, and within half a mile of their garrison met with them and charged them so gallantly that they broke in upon them, killed seven of them (as is said) upon the place, and in the pursuit took four captains, one lieutenant, two cornets, divers troopers, and about forty horse, with the losse of one man of our side.

"1646, April 12th, Ruthin Castle was surrendered to the Parliament party and a strong seige lay'd to Denbigh Castle."—W. Morris.

General Mytton's Summons to Denbigh Castle.

"Sir,—I can noe less than put you in mind of the losse of Christian blood, the undoing of this country, and the retarding of the work of reformation in these parts (soe happily by God's blessing) not only began, but in great measure perfected in most parts of this kingdome, that you soe much cause, and will be deeply guilty of, if you persiste in your way, of your forcibly keeping this Castle of Denbigh from being reduced to the obedience of the King and Parliament, having no hopes of reliefe. I doe therefore hereby summon you to deliver into my hands the Castle of Denbigh for the use of the King and Parliament, upon Monday next, by nine of the clocke in the morninge; assuring you that you may have better conditions both for yourselfe and the rest of the castle with you, if you refuse not this my first summons, than eyther you or they can expect hereafter if you doe refuse it, and thereby cause mee to desire the Parliament that the whoall charge of this seige may for the saving of this poor exhausted countrey from ruyne bee mantayned out of your and theire estates, which will certenly be prosecuted by him who rather desires to bee unto you, as heretofore,

"Your ould friend and Servant,

"Tho. Mytton."

"Denbigh town, 17th April, 1646.

"I expect your answer by nine of the clocke to-morrow morning."

Colonel Salesbury's Answer, 18th Aprilis, 1646.
"In nomine Jesu.

"I am sorry to see the ruine of my in'ocent native countrey, for theire loyallty to theire King, and sensible of the effusion of Christian blood, but upon whose account that which is, or shall be spilt in your attempt to force this castle from mee, being our King's own house—entrusted to mee, unsought, both by his Majestie's commission and verbal com'and, I will leave it to the Highest Judge;—and, in answere to your summons, I will say no more than that, with God's assistance, I doe resolve to make good this place till I receive our King's com'and and warrant of my discharge—to whome, under God, wee all are tyed by common allegiance; and, when I shall have need of relief, I shall undoubtedly expect it from my merciful God, who knows the justness of my cause, and soe rest

"Your ould friend and Servant,

"William Salesbury."

The stout and loyal governor was assailed on the one hand by entreaties to submit, and on the other by exhortations to hold out, as the two following productions from the same MSS. evince.

A Paper endorsed, "The Bumkins' Petition."

"Gentlemen,—We on beehalfe of ourselves and our poor and wasted countrey are enjoyned (by as many of the inhabitants thereof as are met here this day) to present unto you our deplorable condition.

Having such strong confidence in your publicke affec'on towards us, that wee cannot beelieve you delight in our ruine; it is a common and true saying, that the preservation of the people is the supreame law; and as you allways asserted your engadgements to be in order to that law, you cannot say but youre country's complyance with you hath bin very free, and their trust in you very greate. If by detayning this castle from the Parliament's possession, you engadge the forces that are against you to lye upon us, and expose soe much of our substance, as was comitted to your custody, to be made a prize and a prey for the souldiers, you recede from those principles that supreame rule points at, and from the practice of other gentlemen, engaged with you in this unhappy difference, entrusted with places of great comande, and of whose valour and resolution to promote that service they have given ample testimonys. Theire readiness to deny themselves, and preserve their country by a timely submission and surrender of those garrisons that were in theire possession, when it pleased God to withdraw from them all visible means of releife, must needs embalme theire memory to posterity; the fruits of whose wisdom in that acte the countreys of South Wales, Devonshire, and Cornwall have seasonably received; and it is the earnest expectation of our deare native countrey that you will noe longer occasion the continuance of these heavy and insupportable pressures upon us; and in thankfullness of your tenderness of us, wee shall humbly supplicate the honourable Houses of Parliament to receave your submission upon such moderate tearmes as shall bee consistant with your abilities to undergoe. If your countrey's present sufferings, and approaching ruine, be not by you prevented, having now in your hands means to redress them, you will give unto many thousand innocent and helplesse people cause to have you in bitter remembrance, as long as your name or interest in this countrey shall remayne amongst us; excuse our playnness with you, w'ch proceeds from the weight and smart of our grievances; and take our desire into your deepe and serious consideration.

"In assurance whereof, wee rest,

"Gentlemen,

"Your humble Servants."

"The effect of this I hartyly wish it may take; for the avoyding of spilling Christian blood, and the ruyne of many poor, and rich, by continuance of a seage for reducement of that castle.

"Symon Thelwall."

This petition is also signed by forty-seven persons.

Colonel Salesbury's Answer.
" In nomine Jesu.

"Cosin Thelwall,—And the rest of the subscribers to the letter sent to this castle the 8th of this instant May. —How I became interested in this place and command is very well knowne to the best of you; and with what moderation I have since managed it doth clerely appeare by the exhausting of my own estate for the supply of this castle, (but what hath bin plundered from mee by the parliament forces,) to avoyd any pressure upon the country; who cannot in justice complayne, if the practice of other garrisons be impartially looked upon; and if by the advance of this force your condition be rendered so deplorable as you mention, I am confident I shall stand acquitted before God, and every good man; seeing all I do is in mayntenance of my alliegence and in pursuance of the trust reposed in me by *My King,* (whom you doe not vouchcafe to take notice of,) which in my understanding I cannot bee absolved from by that principle of law you soe much insist on, since the attayning of any end (tho' never soe specious) cannot be warranted by indirect means; neyther can I discerne how the countrey can be preserved, or your charge lessened by the surrender of this castle; since others of noe lesse strength and consequence are continued in our King's obedience and command, will probably engage the same force, which will be mentayned by the same means; and since the scope of your desires proceed from your private interests, give me leave to take equal care of my loyallty and reputation, all which may be preserved by your mediation with the parliament or commander-in-chiefe; this force now before this castle may bee withdrawn from this countrey; I shall then undertake this castle shall be no further charge to you. And to conclude with your bitter pill; I will not deny, but as the most savoury meate tastes bitter to a distempered pallate, so my faythfullness to his Majestie's service may seeme bitter to those that are redy to fall from their allegiance, which if you and others had not done, this countrey and other parts of the kingdome had not bin in this miserable condition they are now in; neyther had there bin any occasion of this kind of intercourse beetweene you and your kindsman

" And the King's loyall subject,

" WILLIAM SALESBURY."

" Denbigh Castle, this 16th Maii, 1646."

On the other hand, his stout resolution to adhere to loyalty was encouraged by the following lines sent to Colonel Salesbury at the time :—

> " If soe, hould out (brave Denbigh) that just fame,
> That after-times may historize thy name;
> When this thy glorious Epithit shall bee,
> Denbigh, that saved England's Monarchie.[9]

In the beginning of June, (4th or 5th,) the Castle of Caernarvon was delivered to General Mytton.

They came before Conway the —th day of June, with whom joined the Archbishop of York and Barret Williams. The Parliament forces went to Caernarvon and lay before the town, and the Lord Biron, somewhat before they came, burnt the suburbs, and sent Mr. Spicer with a company of soldiers for provision, who robbed and took all the cattle they found, and returned, but Spicer was taken.[1]

The parliament cause being now triumphant, Caernarvon and Beaumaris castles having opened their gates, General Mytton renewed his persuasion by letter, as follows :[2]

" SIR,—I persuade myself you cannot be ignorant how the affaires of this kingdome stand at this time in generall, and in particular of North Wales; that the towne and castle of Carnarvon is surrendered for the use of the parliament, as likewise the castle of Beaumarish, and the whole island of Anglisey, submitted thereunto; soe that your houlding the castle of Denbigh from its due obedience (having no hope of releife) can produce noe other probable effect than the ruin of your country, which heretofore you have been accounted so good a patriot that you have been very tender of. For the prevention whereof and the shedding of christian blood, wishing you not to forget yourself and estate, which, I do assure you, if you persist but a few days more in the way you are in, will be put to the uttermost hazard, I doe hereby summon you once more to deliver into my hands the castle of Denbigh, for the use of the king and parliament. And that you may seriously consider of it, I do allow you time till Saturday noone to returne (and then I expect) your answere.

" Your servant,

" THO. MYTTON."

" Lleweny, 24th June, 1646."

An Answer to Mytton's Second Summons.

" In nomine Jesu.

SIR,—In answere to your letter of the 24th of June last, it cannot bee (being soe closely besieged) that I should bee altogether ignorant of the affayers of this kingdome in general, much more in the particulars, contrary to what you suppose. What the castle and town of Carnarvon, the castle of Beawmarish, with the whole Island of Anglisea have done, doth noething concern me; that must lye upon theire accomp who were therein entrusted by our king;—now for the houlding this castle, I doe hold it in its proper and due obedience to our king; and when I have use of reliefe (as I formerly wrote) I am confident my good God

<hr />

[9] This is literally true, for, as Pennant observes, the first castle that surrendered in North Wales held out about two months longer than the last English castle. The power of the monarch was therefore nearly confined to this fortress.

[1] " That upon Thursday, being the xvi[th] daie of Aprill, 1646, the towne and Castle of Denbigh were besieged by the p'liament men, &c. And the market upon the Wednesday next following was kept at the elme tree in the lower end of the towne above and neare the Lady Salusburye's house." Roberts's Cwtta Cyfarwyd, p. 153.

[2] Salesbury MS.

will assuredly send it mee, who hitherto hath mercifully protected me. As for the ruine of this innocent countrey, I am hartily sorry, that soe noble a gentleman, soe generally beloved, as yourselfe, of soe antient and soe worthey a stocke, should bee made the prime actor therein; contrary to the lawes of God, and the fundamentall lawes of this kingdome; but for further prevention of the losse of innocent christian blood (of which I am very sensible) doe you withdraw your forces from before this castle and countrey; I shall give you good assurance that this garrison shall neyther bee hurtful nor burthensome to the countrey; desiring your consent, that I may send two gentlemen to our king (whoe entrusted mee) to bee assured of his pleasure;[2] till when, with God's leave, I shall cherefully runne the extreamest hazards of war, as shall please God; lastly for your summons;—when I see the authority you have from our king, and his parliament, commanding mee to deliver this place to your hands, I shall, with God's helpe, returne you a speedy, honest, and playne answere, till then

> " Your wellwishing Servant,
>
> "WILLIAM SALESBURY."

" What ruine shall befall this countrey, I refer it to the Supreme Judge, from whome noe secritts are hid, soe I rest, and soe I am.—There is a God that judgeth the earth."

" To the Governor of Denbigh.

" SIR,—I can doe noe less than give you a true sight of the condition of the kingdome in generall, and what North Wales is like to come to, in perticular; to which end I have sent you both the printed, and my private intelligence, which you may be assured are both really true and intended. I hope you will not make your countery so miserable, in persisting any longer in houlding out this castle, which I have divers times written unto you, can produce noe other probable effect. I must desire your speedy answere, whither you will treat with mee for the delivery of it, or noe; my messenger being ready to go to the Parliament in answer to what is desired in the letter.

> " Your Servant,
>
> "THO. MYTTON."

" Denbigh, August 30th, 1646."

" I desire your particular answer to-morrow morning between 8 and 9 of the clocke."

" For General Mytton, this Present.
" In nomine Jesu.

" SIR,—I shall ever acknowledge your curtesies, though unable to requite. For the condition of our King and his kingdoms, if God have soe disposed, blessed be his name and welcome bee his will. In my answere to your second summons, I desired your consent to send a gentleman or two to our king, to know his pleasure; but I received noe answere from you therein as yeat; the same desire I doe now second, being confident I shall speed, as others, who had the like granted from you; expecting your answere,

> " I rest, your Servant,
>
> "WILLIAM SALESBURY."

" Sir,—I doe returne per this Drum, Sir John Trevour's Letter and the Diurnall."

" For the Governor of Denbigh Castle.

" SIR,—I receaved yours by your Drum, wherein you desire to send to the King. I doe assure you, above three months since I received command from the Parliament not to suffer any, upon any pretence whatever, to goe unto the King, which I have exactly performed. The same that you desired was likewise proposed unto Sir Thomas Ffayrfax, by several garrisons of Oxford, Worcester, Wallingford, Pendennis,

---

[2] King Charles I. had issued a proclamation for delivering up every castle in England and Wales on fair and honourable terms. This proclamation was issued only in this month of June, so that Col. Salesbury was probably ignorant of it.

3 c

Ragland, and divers others, unto whome it was denied, and is not in my power to grant you. Wherefore in regard I am to returne an account of the condition of North Wales with all speede to the Parliament, I desire your positive answere by three this afternoon.—Your Servant,

"THO. MYTTON."

"Denbigh, 31st August, 1646."

": For General Mytton.

"In nomine Jesu.

"SIR,—The coming of more forces to besiege this place will noe way move my resolution; who preferre noe ende to the acquitting of myself like an honest man in that trust which my King hath committed to mee, which I am fully satisfied can never be done before my King receave an accompt of my proceedings, and without that (to deale freely with you) I have such an agreement upon mee, that I will not entertayne any overture of this nature;—and since I must beleeve that your hands are tied, yeat I am so much concerned in this business, that I must apply myself to other means in that perticular for my satisfaction, which will take up some time; and if I must quit the place, I professe I had rather you had the honour of it than any other person in England of your party; though give me leave to tell you, that the addition of a new force, bee the consequence what it will, will add to my honour, which is all I have now left to care for.—I remayne your Servant,

"WILLIAM SALESBURY."

"Ult. Augti, 1646."

Another printed account in the British Museum, entitled "An Exact Relation of the whole of gallant Colonel Mytton in North Wales, as is assured under the hands of severall Commanders of Note," &c. observes, "We have closely besieged Holt Castle, Denbigh, Caernarvon, and Flynt, all places of exceeding great strength; our forces are so many that all the countries under our command will hardly afford us provision. We are put to use our utmost skill to get maintenance this way, then you may judge how hard it is with us for want of pay, without which our soldiers will not continue patiently to goe on in their hard and difficult duty that hitherto they have undergone, harder than which, we dare boldly say, hath not been in any place since these wars, and besides many of our souldiers are auxiliaries from Lancashire, who are most unreasonable men if they are disappointed of their pay.

*   .   *   *   *   *   *   *   *

"Each seidges have made works suitable to the condition of the places, our hopes must be of starving, not storming any of them.   Denbigh we laid seidge too, soone as wee took Ruthin, which now is six weeks since, its governor is a verie wilfull man, he hath verie nigh five hundred able fighting men in it, it hath in its situation all the advantages for strength that any castle can have; there are many gentrie in it and some riches in it; but it would do well that as they are notoriously refractorie, so they may be made notoriously exemplary by the justice of the Parliament upon them and their estates according to their demerits; the countries have improved their interests, and many other ways have bin used, but all ineffectual: their hearts are as hard as the very foundation of the castle itself, being an unpierceable rock; there are mounts raised round about it and approaches for battering of a tower, called the Goblin's Tower, hoping thereby to deprive them of the benefit of a well in that tower, which can we attaine, we may then soon expect the castle, thro' want of water; they having but one well more, which is usually, as is reported, dry in June or July every summer. . . Sir, you may perceive we neither have bin or are idle; we hope the Lord will continue to bless our endeavours, for which we begge your prayers. We rest your assured friends and servants,

"RICHARD PRICE,
THOMAS MASON,
GEORGE TWISTELON."

Undated, but six weeks after surrender of Ruthin, viz. end of May, 1646.

Feeling at length how unavailing was his loyal constancy, Governor Salesbury addressed his fallen sovereign in the following letter :—

" In nomine Jesu.

"MAY IT PLEASE YOUR MAJESTY,—I have presumed to make my humble address to you by this gentleman, Mr. Eubull Thelwall, to let your Majesty understand that this castle hath now for severall months byne closely besieged ; what matter of action hath in that time happen'd, I humbly refer your Majesty to his relation, wherein I do beseech your Majesty to give him credit ; praying for your Majesty's health and happiness, I remayne your Majestie's loyall subject,

"WILLIAM SALESBURY."

To this noble letter of a loyal subject, the King returned the following grateful reply :—

"CORONELL SALESBURY,—I heartily thank you for your loyall constancie, and assure you, that whensoever it shall please God to enable me to show my thankfullness to my friends, I will particularly remember you. As for your answer, I refer you to thease messengers, to whom I have clearly declared my minde ; commend me to all my friends. So I rest, your most assured friend,

"CHARLES R."

" Newcastle, the 13th of September, 1646."

The "King declared his mind" in the following publick document, sent by the same messengers as the preceding :—

" To our Trusty and Well-beloved Colonel William Salesbury, Governor of the Castle of Denbigh, in Wales.

"CHARLES R.,—Whereas, Wee have resolved to comply with the desires of our Parliament in everything which may bee for the good of our subjects, and leave noe means unassayed for removing all difference betwixt us—therefore wee have thought fitt, the more to evidence the reality of our intentions of settling a happy and firm peace, to authorise you upon honourable conditions, to quit and surrender the castle of Denbigh, entrusted to you by us, and to disband all the forces under your commands ; for which your soe doeing this shall bee your warrant. Given at Newcastle, the 14th of Sept., 1646."

The sad account, which Mr. Thelwall was charged to deliver by word of mouth, is thus revealed in the Memoranda of Wm. Morris, 28th Sept., 1646 :—" Mr. William Salusbury, of Rûg, after he hadd sente to the King to show in what case the countrey stood, and what misery they suffered by reason of the leaguer, and also how his souldiers in the castle were infected with divers diseases, was commanded by the King, and delivered up the castle to them upon the 26th Oct." The terms of capitulation were honourable both to the victor and to the vanquished. They are given at large in the Appendix to Pennant's Tour. The garrison marched out, as stipulated in the articles, with " colours flying, drums beating, matches light at both ends, bullet in the mouth, every souldier with twelve chardges of powder, match and bullet proportionable, with bag and baggage, &c." in short, bearing no resemblance to the vanquished.

What families of distinction in the neighbourhood suffered in this memorable siege are not entirely known, save that which is mentioned in the following extract from MSS. Memoranda in the possession of

---

In taking our leave of Governor Salesbury, we must observe that he seems to have been a strong adherent to his royal master. Lloyd, the Author of " The Memoirs," who was contemporary with the loyal persons he describes, says of William Salesbury, " He spake so plainly to his Majesty (when the king was at Denbigh Castle, perhaps,) for two hours in private, that the good king said, " Never did prince hear so much truth at once."

After the articles were signed, it is said the noble Blue Stocking Hero mounted the tower above the Goblin Well, and threw down the key of the castle, making use of a coarse proverb—" Chwi biau'r byd," &c., after which he retired to a farm-house of his own, called Bodtegyrn, in the parish of Llanfihangel, Glyn Myfyr. His royal master's promise of remembering his brave and devoted subject was performed to the best of his power, though not as such extraordinary merit would have been rewarded on a favourable issue to the royal cause. The noble descendant of Hosanau Gleision

the heir of Llwyn. "Edward Wynn, fourth son of Edward Wynn, the only son of Maurice Wynn of Gwydir and Catherine of Beren, by Blanch his wife, daughter of John Vychan of Blaen y Cwm, was captain of a company of foot in Denbigh Castle in the service of Charles I., was wounded in a sally made by the said garrison against the besiegers under Sir John Carter, and in three days after died of his wounds, and was interred with military honours at Llanrhaiadr,[6] being conducted by a part of the garrison as far as Ystrad Bridge, where he had three vollies, thence taken by a party of the Oliverians, who likewise conducted him to his grave after the same manner.

The fall of this castle by no means fulfilled the promise of restoring peace and happiness to the country.[7] Heavy contributions were levied on the inhabitants to support the parliament forces, and yet these were inadequate to their purpose, if indeed they ever reached their destination. W. Morris proceeds to inform us as follows: "About the 24th of March, 1646-7, the souldiers in Denbighshire did stir a mutiny, and coming to Wrexham, they layde holde on Colonel Jones, treasurer of the parliament, and others of the comittee, imprisoned them, demanding their arrears, and a just accounte of the money paid to them by the country. General Mytton, being that morning come to towne, hadd some intelligence, and fled towards Houlte Castle to Colonel Pope, the souldiers firing after him." The sums paid by the country towards the parliament cause were considerable, according to the same Memoranda, which record: "April, 1647. We of the county paide monthly contribution 260l., and in May following we payde another contribution, contrary to General Mytton's promise. We payde alsoe our part of 1200l. for disbandinge of souldiers, and were to give free quarters to the horse souldiers."

The spirit which actuated the late governor was still alive in the minds of a few for some time after, as W. Morris relates in the following particulars, which are the last he has preserved relating to this subject:—

1648.—About the end of June, Mr. Dolben and Mr. Chambers of Denbigh hadd a design to take the castle of Denbigh; they scaled it in the night, and aboute sixty men got into utter-ward, but they were discovered, and some of them taken; they both plundered, but escaped, as is said.[8]

July.—In this monthe, aboute the 16th, Dolben and Chambers with their companye came before Denbigh Castle, and, in a bravado, discharged their pistols and wente away.

The following is a letter from Chester of the design about surprising of Denbigh Castle for the King:—

"Noble Sir,—We find the King's party still very active in these parts; those in Anglesey that revolted will not accept of the indemnity, but resolve to keep the island for the King. Sir John Owen is acting in Denbigh Castle, where, with his confederates, the castle was very neare being surprised. On Monday night last, the captaine of the guard being gone to bed, they began to act their design. And there was engaged in this business for surprise of Denbigh Castle (where Sir John Owen is prisoner) a corporall and a sentinell belonging to the castle, of the parliament souldiers, who had (it seems) been wrought upon by those who carried on the design, to whom large promises were made. These men we have discovered, besides some others whom we cannot yet find out, to have been corrupted by Serjeant-Major Dolton, Captain

---

and inheritor of Bachymbyd and other estates, in an interesting work on the annals of his own ancient house, which he lately printed at his private press, and distributed among his friends, observes, that, "When Sir Walter Bagot married the heiress of Salesbury, he became possessed of an ancient cabinet, containing the letters (here quoted by permission of the owner,) together with other interesting and valuable relics. Among the latter is a scull cap, most constantly worn by Charles I., and sent, before his death, to his highly esteemed friend and faithful servant, Colonel Salesbury, as the only token of remembrance he had it in his power to bestow."

[6] His grave, with an inscription, is to be seen in this churchyard, at the east end of it, railed in, with many others of the same family.

[7] Such was the distress of the country during the siege, that a gallon of butter sold for twenty shillings. The market was kept at the elm tree, near Lady Salesbury's House. Mem. of Mr. Peter Roberts, Notary P. of St. Asaph, Temp. Ch. 1st.

[8] A more particular history of this design is to be seen in the British Museum, in a printed account, entitled, "Denbigh Castle surprised for the King by sixty cavaliers," &c. London, printed for the general satisfaction of all moderate men, 1646.

Cutler, Captain Parry,[1] Captain Charles Chambers,[1] and some others, who were the chief actors in this plot. There was a party of the cavaliers that came at night with scaling ladders, who came privily to the walls without giving any alarm at all, the corporall and the two sentinells of the guard being privy to their design and confederacy. And about some sixty of the cavaliers had scaled the walls, and had got over without any opposition at all, and were within the walls at least an hour before any alarm was given, and it was a hundred to one that we had not been all surprised and ruined, but we were miraculously delivered. The aforesaid three-score cavaliers that were got over were so near entrance into the inner ward of the castle that they had but only one horselock to break, which the corporall was ready to have assisted them in, to open one of the sally posts. It so pleased God that the captain of the guard could not sleep in his bed, but was much troubled, tho' he knew not for what, and at last he resolved to rise and to walk the rounds with his souldiers, for which purpose he did get up accordingly. When he had drawn out some souldiers to walk with him about the rounds, he went with them, untill at last he espied a party got over the walls, and scaling ladders upon the walls, whereupon the alarum was given to the castle, and the towne also by these means took the alarm. But they all yielded themselves prisoners at mercy, only some few that had got back again over the wall. And upon remark of the business, the corporal was discovered to be going with them to help them to open the gate. I hope this will be a sufficient warning to them all to look well about them both in that castle and also in other parts about us.

"Chester City, the 8th of July, 1646."

After its surrender, this castle must have been dismantled by order of the Government, for, as it sustained but little damage in its siege, it could hardly have exhibited such total ruin[2] as meets the eye at present.

The following Extracts from Whitelocke's "Memorials of English Affairs,"[3] during the reign of Charles I., the Commonwealth, and Charles II.'s time, will throw additional light on this cruel and unhappy period of our history.

1645.—The Castle of Flint was besieged by Sir William Brereton and Sir Thomas Middleton; the Governor of it for the King held it out till all provisions, even to horses, failing him, and then rendered it upon honourable terms.

Then the Parliament forces took Mostyn House, belonging to Colonel Mostyn, the Governor of Flint, and in Mostyn they took four pieces of ordance and some arms.

This Colonel Mostyn is my sister's son, a gentleman of good parts and mettle, of a very ancient family, large possessions and great interest in that country, so that in twelve hours he raised 1500 men for the King, and was well beloved there, living very nobly.

A regiment of Irish soldiers landed about Mostyn, in Flintshire, for the King's service.

Colonel Gerrard besieged Cardigan Castle, kept by Lieutenant-Colonel Poole, and by stratagem got into the town, and cut down the bridge to prevent relief coming to the Castle, where they wanted provisions.

Gerrard sent a summons to the Castle, *that if they did not surrender by a day, they should have no quarter.* Poole and his men returned answer, *that they had divers raw hides, which, when they wanted provisions, they would first eat, and when they were spent, then they would come out and fight for their lives, but he would not surrender the Castle.*

Letters from the committee at Wem, and from Sir William Brereton, informed that the committee, having several times attempted the taking of Shrewsbury, but failed therein; on the last Lord's Day about 1200 horse and foot, under Colonel Mitton, marched to Shrewsbury, and unexpectedly entered and surprised the town and castle.

Sir William Brereton began to mine at Hawarden Castle, and took Ewysanna House, and in it a captain and twenty-seven prisoners, and some officers, and from thence blocked up to Chester, on the Welsh side, gained Manly House, killed divers, and took a captain and many prisoners.

---

[1] Captain Parry was of Plas Llanrhaiadr, near Denbigh, a descendant of Bishop Parry, of St. Asaph, who translated the present version of the Welsh Bible, published in 1620; from him are descended the Parrys of Flintshire.

[1] Captain Chambers was probably a member of the ancient family of that name, of Plâs Chambres, near Denbigh. The family derived its name from being chamberlains to the Earl of Lincoln. Pennant

speaks of a grant from Henry de Lacy to John de la Chambre, *Camerario.*

[2] On visiting these ruins a singular effect is observed from below in a mass of the ruined wall of the west side of the castle court. It exhibits an exact profile of George II. in the flowing wig in which he is usually represented.

[3] Selected from his large work, 2 vols, folio, page by page.

Letters informed of the storming and taking of the outworks of Chester, wherin Colonel Jones, who commanded the Parliament's Horse, with Captain Louthan, who commanded the foot, drew off over night, and fell on the next morning early, and stormed before they were discovered.

Upon a petition from some Cheshire men, Sir William Brereton was appointed to command the forces which he formerly commanded, for four months longer, and ordered money for those forces.

Glamorganshire men declared themselves for the Parliament, and took, in Cardiffe Castle, sixteen pieces of ordnance, store of arms, and ammunition.

The King came to Ludlow, in order to relieve Chester, and Major-General Pointz followed him.

Letters informed that the King, with about five thousand horse and foot, advanced to relieve Chester; Major-General Pointz pursued close after the King, and within two miles of Chester engaged with the King's whole body, was at the first worsted, but made good his ground upon the retreat.

In the mean time, Colonel Jones, with five hundred horse, and Adjutant-General Louthian, came from the Leaguer before Chester, to the assistance of Pointz, giving notice of their coming by shooting off two great guns, and by that time Pointz had rallied his forces; there Pointz in the front and Jones in the rear charged, and utterly routed the King's whole body.

The King, with about three hundred horse, fled into Chester, and the pursuit was so violent, that he immediately left that town, and fled into Wales; the rest of his party were utterly dispersed, killed, and taken.

Colonel Parsons made a particular relation to the house of the late fight at Chester, and they gave him one hundred pound to buy him horses, and referred it to the committee of both kingdoms to prosecute this great victory.

Intelligence came that the King was in Denbighshire, gathering forces, and that Prince Maurice was to come to him to endeavour again the relief of Chester, that Major-General Pointz had sent some parties after the King, who had taken some of his men.

Major-General Pointz wrote for supplies, and five hundred horse; one thousand dragoons were ordered to march forthwith to him.

One thousand pounds ordered for the Nottingham Horse, who fought gallantly at the late fight at Chester, and other sums for other of his forces.

Sir William Middleton and Lieutenant-Colonel Mason fell upon a party of Prince Maurice's in Montgomeryshire, took Colonel Rouse, other officers, twenty-three prisoners, thirty horses and arms.

Sir Trevor Williams, and divers gentlemen of Glamorganshire and Monmouthshire, raised fifteen hundred men for the Parliament.

An attempt was made to storm Chester, which proved ineffectual. Colonel Venables was wounded, and forty slain.

News came of the taking of Chepstow Castle, and of the ordnance, arms, and ammunition there. The house ordered a letter of thanks to Colonel Morgan, and gave £10 to the messenger, and ordered that the ministers should give thanks unto God for it.

Letters informed the taking of Carmarthen by Major-General Langhorne, whereby the whole country was reduced, and so was Monmouthshire by taking of Monmouth town and Castle, by Colonel Morgan, in which they had seven pieces of ordnance, and store of ammunition. Orders for thanks to God for this success, and a letter of thanks to Colonel Morgan. Sir Trevor Williams was made Governor of Monmouth.

The garrison of Chester made divers resolute sallies upon the besiegers, and were beaten back, and the forces of Major-General Poyntz slew many of them in the street.

Sir William Byron (the Lord Byron's brother) got together about four hundred horse about Holt Castle, upon notice whereof Colonel Jones drew out a party of horse from before the Leaguer, fell upon the enemy in the field, who worsted the Forlorn Hope of Jones; but he rallied them, and, after a sharp dispute, routed them, took Sir William Byron and others of quality prisoners, divers troopers, slew forty, and took forty horse.

Letters from Colonel Mitton, Colonel Jones, and Colonel Louthaine, informed that one thousand seven hundred horse, and seven hundred foot, under Sir William Vaughan, designing to relieve Chester, the council of war of the besiegers ordered to draw forth a party to meet them, before they came near to Chester.

1646.—Mr. Edward Vaughan, with a small party in Merionethshire, fell upon a hundred of the King's forces, who were fortifying at Dolgethly, took their Captain, eighteen prisoners, and divers horses and arms.

January 31.—Sir William Brereton intercepted a letter from Lord Byron to Oxford, that if they had not relief by the last of January, then of necessity they must surrender Chester.

February 4.—Reference to a committee to consider of propositions for reducing North Wales.

Feb. 5.—Letters came to the Speaker from Sir William Brereton.

That in case of preserving Chester, the most considerable city in those parts, from ruin, invited him to entertain a treaty, which was continued ten days, and delayed by the enemy hoping for relief, for which there were strong preparations' by conjunction of Ashley, Vaughan, and the Welsh and Irish forces, and those Irish newly landed.

Orders for settling of that garrison, and that Alderman Edward, of Chester, be Colonel of a regiment of that city.

Holt Castle, Ruthen Castle, and Hawarden Castle, besieged by the Parliament's forces.

27.—Letters from Major-General Langhorne confirmed the defeat of the King's forces at Cardiffe, that there were slain of them two hundred, and eight hundred prisoners, store of arms, and all their bag and baggage, and their design frustrated of recruits in Wales, and of the Irish landing there.

1645, *March* 16.—Hawarden Castle was surrendered to Major-General Mitton, and he besieged Holt Castle.

April 30.—Letters from Colonel Mitton informed that the Archbishop of York, Dr. Williams, had betaken himself to his house at Purin, near Conway, put a garrison therein, and fortified it, protesting against the King's party, and persuading the country against payment of contribution to Conway.

That the Lord Byron, upon notice of the Bishop's revolt, sent out a party from Conway to besiege him, and the Bishop sending for assistance to Major-General Mitton, he drew out a party to interpose.

The Lord Byron surrendered Caernarvon Castle to Major-General Mitton upon articles.

June 10.—Colonel Glyn voted to be Governor of Caernarvon Castle.

June 22.—Sir William Brereton being come into the house, the Speaker, by order, gave him thanks for his good services, particularly for that of Chester.

June 25.—Beaumaris town and castle surrendered to Major-General Mitton, and he was voted to be governor there. Orders for money, and for a ship at Anglesey.

July 2.—Letters from Major-General Mitton informed the readiness of Bishop Williams to promote the Parliament's affairs, and particularly for reducing the Castle of Conway, giving his advice, and being very active in that and all other matters for the Parliament.

August 18.—Major-General Mitton took Conway town by storm, and killed and wounded divers, took many officers, twenty-two soldiers, and fifty townsmen, in arms, one great gun, arms, ammunition, and provisions; many Irishmen who were tied back to back, and thrown into the water.

A copy of the articles sent up of the surrender of Ragland Castle; there were in the castle seven hundred officers and soldiers, twenty pieces of ordnance, and a thousand arms.

August 25.—Order to make Ragland Castle untenable; Colonel Fortescue appointed Governor of Pendennis Castle.

August 26.—Letters informed that when the officers and soldiers marched out of Ragland Castle, not the least injury or incivility was offered by Sir Thomas Fairfax's army to any of them, but they were courteously used, and not a tittle of their articles broken.

August 26.—That Sir Thomas Fairfax had much conference with the Marquis with all respect, and there being rich store of furniture and goods in the castle, the General caused the commissioners of the army to make an inventory of them, and to proclaim that if any of them belonged to any well-affected in the country, that they should be restored.

October 5.—Beaumaris Castle, in Anglesey, was surrendered to the use of the Parliament upon articles.

October 20.—Order that Colonel Mitton offer reasonable conditions to those garrisons in Wales not yet reduced, which if they refuse within twenty days, that then they shall not be received to mercy, and referred to a committee to consider of employing those forces in Ireland after the rest of the garrisons should be reduced, and a letter sent to Colonel Mitton to acquaint him of these votes.

October 27.—The city of Chester choose Mr. Recorder Glyn to be an Alderman of that city, instead of the Earl of Derby.

October 28.—Three ministers sent to preach in Wales.

November 18.—Conway Castle surrendered to the Parliament.

December 15.—A Scotch minister preached boldly before the King at Newcastle, and after his sermon called for the fifty-second psalm, which begins "*Why didst thou, tyrant, boast thyself, thy wicked works to praise?*" His Majesty thereupon stood up and called for the fifty-sixth, which begins, "*Have mercy, Lord, on me, I pray, for men would me devour.*"

The people waved the minister's psalm, and sung that which the King called for.

May 30, 1647.—Harleigh Castle, the last in Wales, surrendered to Colonel Mitton, whose soldiers put a guard upon Colonel Jones for their pay.

April 13.—The soldiers in North Wales mutinied for money, kept some of the committee men prisoners in Wrexham Church, and say they will have money before disbanding.

Cromwell began now to mount still higher, and carried his business with great subtlety.

An impeachment was against his enemies in parliament, and the business of the army, guided by his son-in-law, Ireton, and others under Cromwell.

July 2nd.—Reference to the committee of Cheshire, about pay and lessening the garrison of Chester.

April 15th, 1648.—Reference and power given to the Committee of Monmouth and Glamorgan, to apprehend such as are guilty of tumults and insurrections there.

Lieutenant-General Cromwell ordered by the General to go into South Wales, with two regiments of horse and three regiments of foot.

The General likewise acquainted the house of his sending Lieutenant-General Cromwell to Wales, and with the non-payment of assessments, whereby the soldiers would be obliged to take free quarters. The house passed instructions to the Committee of the Army and officers to rectify it.

Letters that Lieutenant-General Cromwell came to Chepstow, where they drew out some forces against them, but Colonel Pride's men fell upon them so furiously that they gained the town and beat the soldiers into the castle, which being strongly fortified and provided, Cromwell sent to Bristol for some great guns.

May 20th.—Lieutenant-General Cromwell possessed Carmarthen, the forces being drawn into Pembroke Castle, where Langhorne, Powel, and Poyer were, but some differences reported to be among them there.

Letters from Cromwell's success in Wales.

June 19th.—The county and city of Chester raised forces for the Parliament, and desired that Captain Carter might command those of the city, which the house granted.

A battery made against Pembroke Castle; an assault was attempted, but the Parliament's forces were repulsed with the loss of three-and-twenty men, and but four of the garrison.

June 20th.—Letters from Lieutenant-General Cromwell, that the garrison of Pembroke began to be in extreme want of provisions, that they mutinied, and crying out that we shall be starved for two or three men's pleasures, better it were that we should throw them over the walls.

July 4th.—Letters from Pembroke Leaguer, that 120 in the town laid down their arms, and Poyer and Langherne told them *that if relief came not within five days they should hang them;* that they have only rain water and a little bisket left; that Cromwell shot stones into the town with mortar pieces, which killed divers.

July 10th.—Letters from Wales of a design to betray Denbigh Castle prevented.

July 15th.—Letters from Lieutenant-General Cromwell to the General and Committee of Derby House, that the 11th July last the town and castle of Pembroke were surrendered to him upon articles.

The town, castle, arms, ammunition, and provisions to be delivered up to Lieutenant-General Cromwell for the use of the Parliament.

July 26th.—Sir John Owen was sent to Windsor Castle, upon a charge of high treason and murder against him, for the business of North Wales.

August 1st.—An order to send Major-General Mitton into North Wales, to suppress the insurrections there.

August 6th.—Letters from Chester, that the Lord Byron was out with three hundred men, and advanced towards Anglesea.

August 18th.—The Prince sent a letter to the Lord General Fairfax for moderation to be used towards Major-General Langherne, Colonel Power, and Colonel Poyer, and others, who acted by commission from him, otherwise he should be necessitated to proceed contrary to his intentions against such as should fall into his hands.

    (Subscribed)   Your loving friend,
                                                                    CHARLES P.

The General returned answer, that he had acquainted the houses with his Highness's letter, it not being in his power to act farther, the Parliament having ordered the way in which the prisoners should be proceeded against, not so much for hostility as for breach of the trust they reposed in them to the engaging the nation again in war and blood.

    (Subscribed)   Your Highness's most humble Servant,
                                                                    FAIRFAX.

September 20th.—Letters from Anglesey of the Lord Bulkely and the Lord Byron; that the island is in an uproar, and that Colonel Mitton, with a strong power, is marching towards them.

October 2nd.—Letters from Anglesey, of the taking of it, by Major-General Mitton, by storm; that the Lord Byron and Lord Bulkely were escaped by flight.

November 10th.—Vote that the Lords Goring, Capel, and Loughborough, the Earl of Holland, Major-General Langherne, and Sir John Owen, shall be banished out of the kingdom.

April 21st, 1649.—The General sent an order for Major-General Langherne, Colonel Powel, and Colonel Poyer, to draw lots which of them should die, the other two to be spared their lives. In two of the lots were written, *Life given by God,* the third lot was a blank. The prisoners were not willing to draw their own destiny, but a child drew the lots and gave them; and the lot fell to Colonel Poyer to die.

June 11th.—Order for demolishing Montgomery Castle, and allowance for his damage thereby, out of his fine.

An act passed for altering the original seals of Carmarthen, Pembroke, and Cardigan.

June 30th.—Letters from Cheshire, that Ormond had besieged Dublin with 14,000 men, and doubted not but to carry it in a short time, and that divers ministers in Cheshire did pray publicly for restoring Charles II. to his father's crowns and honours.

August 15th.—The act published for the composition of the delinquents of North Wales, for 24,000*l.*

September 27th.—Order for speedy bringing in the fines of delinquents, and for 20,000*l.* fine upon North Wales, to be paid to the committee of the army for the service of the army.

February 6th.—An act passed for propagating and preaching of the gospel, and for the maintainance of the ministers and schoolmasters in Wales.

March 4th.—Letters from Shrewsbury, that the ministers preach much against the present government, and to encourage the people to sedition, and to raise for their King.

March 5th.—Letters from Chester, of the ministers in that country bitterly exclaiming against the engagement, and condemning all that take it *to the Pit of Hell.*

March 11th.—From Beaumaris, that Major-General Mitton and other officers, upon intelligence that Ormond had given a commission to Colonel Robinson to garrison the Isle of Bardsey, they sent thither Ensign Aspinall, with thirty men, who, three days after his landing there, seized upon Colonel Gerrard, Mr. Conwy, and six gentlemen more who landed there to surprise the island, took their boat and sent them prisoners to Caernarvon, and the pirate fled away also who had set them on shore, and was an Irishman.

March 13th.—Letters from Chester, that O'Neal's army was in great want about Caernarven. That as soon as supplies should come Sir Charles Coot intended to take the field.

June 5th, 1650.—From Denbigh, that the committee for propagating the gospel in Wales ejected many malignant and scandalous ministers.

June 15th.—Letters of a very solemn keeping of the fast day at Shrewsbury, and of the militia settled in Herefordshire.

July 2nd.—Letters that the plague had broken out in Shrewsbury.

July 24th, 1651.—Letters of a rising in Cardiganshire, of four hundred horse and foot got together in a body and intending to march Northwards.

October 18th.—Letters that Captain Benboe was shot to death at Shrewsbury, according to the sentence of the court martial; and that the Earl of Derby was beheaded at Bolton the same day.

May 13th, 1658.—Sir Roger Mostyn was secured, and a prisoner to Colonel Carter, at Conway.

May 15th.—I procured Sir Roger Mostyn's liberty upon his parole, to be at his own house at Mostyn, engaging to do nothing to the present government.

The following Account is extracted from another MS. in the Mostyn Collection, kindly lent to the author by the Honourable E. M. Lloyd Mostyn, M.P., who can boast of one of the best collections of ancient MSS. in the Principality.

About the beginning of March, 1647, the soldiers were disbanded in Merioneddshire.

March 13.—The articles for the delivery of Harleoh Castle were signed. The next day, Mr. Robert Folks, being in the castle, died, and was buried at Llanfair. The 16th day, being Tuesday, the Governor, Mr. William Owen, delivered the keys of the castle to General Mitton.

There were in the castle, of gentlemen, the Governor, Sir Hugh Blayney, Knight; Mr. Folks; Mr. John Edwards of Chirk, who, being somewhat aged, died in February; Captain William Edwards, his son; Lieutenant Roger Arthur; Lieutenant Roberts; John Hanmer, son of Richard Hanmer of Pentre Pant; William Edwards of Cefn y Wern; Ancient William Williams was shot in the hand about Allhallowtide, and died 19th of January; Meredith Lloyd, of Llanfair, in Caer Einion; Roger Burton; Francis Mason; Peter Simon; William Thomas; and Thomas Arthur, the Governor's man.

Besides these there were twenty-eight common soldiers; their duty was performed as follows:

Squadron 1.—The Governor, and Lieutenant Arthur.

    2.—Captain William Edwards, and John Hanmer.

    3.—Meredith Lloyd, and William Edwards. These went the round by turns, and Burton went to the guard on the new wall.

2. Squadron 1.—Ancient William Williams, by himself.

    2.—Lieutenant John Roberts, and Thomas Arthur.

    3.—Francis Mason, and Peter Simon. William Thomas on the new wall.

These went the rounds every other night; they were on the guard appointed.

Seven centries stood every night, wherein were fourteen soldiers; their relief was hourly, and their duty every other night.

3 D

We of Merioneddshire paid of monthly contribution, 360*l.* April, 1647, we paid the last. May following we paid another contribution, contrary to General Mitton's promise. We paid also our part of 1200*l.* for disbanding of soldiers, and were to give free quarters to the horse soldiers.

June 22.—The Earl of Denbigh, and Colonel Mitton, came before Oswestry, and, without any loss on any side, got it.

Colonel Mason, with three thousand or more, as is said, beset the town of Oswestry about. The Earl of Denbigh came to raise the siege, and the King's men encountering with him, he gave ground, whereupon the King's men followed them, thinking they had fled indeed; but they had belayed the edges with musketeers, who slew no small number of them; the rest fled.

The Earl of Denbigh and Colonel Mitton went before Shrewsbury, but they were beaten back with some loss.

Sir Thomas Myddleton came to Pool, with Colonel Mitton, in the night time, and took two hundred horse and some men. Sir Thomas Dalison escaping very narrowly; and took Captain Grace prisoner.

After Michaelmas the soldiers in Caernarvonshire forced the inhabitants to give them free quarters and other necessaries, a company of them coming to Capel Carrig were beaten back by the neighbours thereabouts, and they came from thence to Llyn, and the countrymen did rise against them and pursued them, but they turn'd upon the countrymen, and they fled; then the soldiers did plunder Penllach and did much harm thereabouts; twenty-seven of them that had risen against the soldiers in those parts were taken and imprisoned in Carnarvon Castle, and suffered much misery, and had likely perished, but that the Lady Williams, of Vaenol, did weekly relieve them with meat, drink, and other necessaries.

About the 12th of May following, the foot soldiers under Captain Callant, Pickin, and Dawson were disbanded. We paid, in Merioneddshire, 360*l.* of disbanding money.

After Allhallowtide a strong body of Colonel Jones's soldiers enter'd into Penrhyn House, wherein Humphrey Jones, sometime King's receiver, a very rich man, dwell'd, and demanded. But the Gentleman spake them fair, and caused them to be brought to the celler to drink, and in the meantime, the neighbours, who to the number of forty came there, and the soldiers and them began to jar, and at last fell to blows, but the soldiers being more in number and better arm'd, kill'd one; but the countrymen took thirty-six of them and sent them prisoners to Carnarvon Castle. But Captain Glyn, that did govern the castle, did let them all go away, who went to Conway, from whence they came.

At the same time, Thomas Glynllifon, Esq., Governor of Carnarvon Castle, and John Bodwrda, Esq., died.

Sir Thomas Myddleton came to Newtown and took twenty-six barrels of powder of the Prince's, and then went to Llandiloes and took Sir Thomas Grace and most of his troop prisoners at Newtown.

Sir Thomas came before Montgomery Castle, and the lord of Cherbury delivered the same unto him without blows. A day or two after, Sir Thomas, with a company of soldiers went to Oswestry. Colonel Broughton, with the foot forces of Shropshire, and all the power he could levy, came before the Castle of Montgomery; and Sir William Vaughan and Sir Thomas Dalison led the horse.

When Sir William Vaughan and Sir Thomas Dalison came before Montgomery Castle; then Sir Thomas Myddleton sent soldiers out of the castle to skirmish with them between Hêndommen and the Park, whilst he himself got away; then the King's men beat the Castleleers into their hold, and, having intelligence that Sir Thomas was fled, they followed to Pont y Cymhe, and there took thirty-six prisoners; but Sir Thomas very narrowly escaped.

And after him, Lord Biron, with two thousand men from Chester, came thitherwards, by Llansilin, and so to Llanfyllin, and thence to Berrien, and quartered at Vaugnor; he begins to intrench himself and his men not far from Montgomery the 16th of September.

Friday before the battle he came to the Leaguer. The battle was to be the Wednesday following.

The other side, Sir William Brereton, Sir Thomas Fairfax, Watlesborough Heath.

The said Lord Biron sent the commissioners of array in Merioneddshire and the adjacent counties commanding them to make ready trained bands, and all able men besides, and send them to ———, there to rest until they should hear more from him.

We proceed to illustrate the history of this period, in what we consider the most interesting and efficacious manner, by reference to the numerous private documents in the possession of our ancient families.

The following are particulars of the rising which took place in Anglesey, in 1648, and the taking of the castle by General Mytton.[4]

In the beginning of 1648, the good people of the land, groaning under the oppressions of a rebellious parliament and army, resolved upon some attempts to set the King at liberty (then a prisoner in the castle of Carisbrook, in the Isle of Wight) and to vindicate themselves from slavery and tyranny, whereupon

---

[4] From the MS. of the Rev. Mr. Williams, schoolmaster, of Beaumaris, in 1669.

several risings broke out: the Kentish men, under Goring, Earl of Norwich; Essex men, under Lucas and Lisle: those of South Wales, under Langhorne, Powell, and Poyer; North Wales, under Sir John Owen; and the Scots, under the Duke of Hamilton; therefore the islanders of Anglesey having as good claim to their King, and being as desirous of their antient liberties under monarchy as any of their fellow-subjects, would not be backward in their endeavors for a restoration, and so took up arms under Thomas Lord Bulkeley, Colonel Richard Bulkeley (his son) and other worthy gentlemen of the country; with whom joined Captain Thomas Symkys, governor of Beaumaris Castle, and all the garrison except some few private soldiers. It was thought fit, by a council of war, that a declaration should be drawn, to which all the islanders, from sixteen to sixty, should subscribe, for the better cementing the gentry, commonalty, and soldiers, together, and for manifesting their loyal principles to the world; but by what fate, I know not, the penning of this declaration was referred to two ministers, Mr. Michael Evans, chaplain to Lord Bulkeley, and Mr. Robert Morgan, rector of Llanddyfnan, who had skill enough to draw it in high swelling words and bitter language, and subtletie sufficient to impose it upon a well-meaning gentry and soldiery, yet wanted discretion to pen it in that wary way, and prudent style, as the state of affairs at that time did require: it followeth in these words:—

"WE, the inhabitants of the Isle of Anglesey, whose names are hereunto subscribed, after mature consideration, and hearty invocation of the name of God for directions and assistance, do remonstrate and declare to our fellow subjects and neighbours whom it may concern, That, we having, according to our bounden duty and allegiance, preserved the said island in due obedience to our most dread sovereign, Lord King Charles, during the time of this intestine war and rebellion, and, by God's blessing upon our careful endeavours, defended the same until the enemy had over-mastered the whole kingdom (a few strong holds only excepted) this being the only county of England or Wales, for two months together kept entire, under his Majesty's authority and command; and being then, through the vast number of men and horse threatened to be poured in upon us (finding no possible expectance of relief) enforced to submit to the then prevailing power; do now, out of conscience towards God, and loyalty towards his anointed, with all humbleness prostrate ourselves, our lives and fortunes, at his Majesty's feet, resolving, with the utmost exposal of all that we are or have, to preserve the said island, together with the castle and houlds therein, in due obedience to his sacred Majesty, his heirs and lawful successors, against all rebellious opposers and invaders whatsoever; and do also, with sincerity of heart, profess that we will, according to our several degrees, places and callings, maintain the true Protestant religion by law established, his Majesty's royal prerogative, the known laws of the land, just privileges of parliament, together with our own and fellow-subjects legal properties and liberties. And we also do further declare and protest, that we shall and will account all those that do, or shall stand, in opposition hereunto, to be enemies and traitors to their King and country, and accordingly to be proceeded against, being most ready to contribute our best abilities for their reducement, and reinstating our gracious sovereign (who hath long endured the tyranny and oppression of his barbarous and bloody enemies) to his rights, dominions, and dignity, according to the splendour of his most illustrious progenitors. Given under our hands the 14th day of July, 1648.

(Subscribed) "BULKELEY."

"RICHARD BULKELEY.	OWEN ARTHUR.	THOMAS SYMKYS.
WILLIAM GRYFFYTH.	JOHN YOUNG.	HENRY WYNNE.
JOHN BODVEL.	JOHN PRICE.	WM. WYNNE.
HENRY OWEN.	WILLIAM LEWIS.	ROWLAND JONES.
OWEN HOLLAND.	ROWLAND WHITE.	WILLIAM LLOYD.
RICHARD MEYRICK.	OWEN LEWIS.	WILLIAM OWEN.
HENRY LLOYD.	GODFREY PRYTHERGH.	RICHARD BODYCHEN.
RICHARD ROBERTS.	JOHN ROBINSON.	JOHN WYNNE.
HUGH OWEN.	WILLIAM BULKELEY.	HENRY JONES.
WILLIAM OWEN.	RICHARD WILLIAMS.	HENRY OWEN.
JO. TURBRIDGE.	JOHN LLOYD.	HENRY LLOYD.
OWEN GRYFFYTH.	ROWLAND BULKELEY.	RICHARD WYNNE."

3 D 2

After subscribing this high declaration, the whole island armed and mustered, and many gentlemen of other countries, with men, horses, and arms, flocked thither: as Sir Arthur Blaney and others out of Montgomeryshire; Major John Dolben, Captain Charles Chambers, Captain Robert Hughes, Captain William Eyton, Mr. Richard Parry, and others, from Denbighshire; Major H. Pennant, Mr. Thomas Griffith, Mr. Thomas Davenport, and others, from Flintshire; Captain John Morgan, and others, from Merionethshire; Lieut.-Colonel Hugh Hooks, and others, from Caernarvonshire; Sir Faithful Fortescue, Bart., Samuel Singleton, and many more, came from other places into Anglesey, as into a city of refuge. A rendezvous of all the forces in the island was appointed at Talwrn Mawr, a large common near the centre of the island. The declaration rendered in the Welsh tongue to the Welsh people by Mr. Robert Morgan aforesaid, and enforced with a long exhortation. Great acclamations and shoutings, and promises made to stand unanimously for the King's cause, and in defence of the island against all invaders.

The Parliament in the mean time were not negligent about the reducement of the island, but appointed five commissioners to manage that service, viz., Sir Thomas Myddleton, Bart., Major-General Mytton, Thomas Myddelton, Esq., Symon Thelwall, Esq., and Colonel John Jones.

These commissioners brought forces together, and rendezvoused at Conway, where they provided boats, and got one Major Richard Chedle, an Anglesey man, to guide the said boats by sea to Bangor, the body of their party (being about fifteen hundred men, horse and foot) marching by land. As soon as the boats and army appeared at Penmaen Mawr, within sight of Beaumaris Green, the Anglesey people began to bustle: the drums beat—the trumpets sounded—great volleys of small shot were given on Beaumaris Green—and all the ordnance upon the castle discharged, which the enemies took little or no notice of. That night the enemies came to Bangor, and quartered there for four or five days, and then wafted over to Cadnant, in Anglesey, about Sept. 15, 1648, near the fall of night; John Wiggins, of the town of Bangor, being their guide.

There was little or no resistance made to their landing, only Major Hugh Pennant appeared with his troop near Cadnant, but the enemies pouring shot upon him from the hedges and rocks he was forced to retreat. At Porthaethwy, about a quarter of a mile from Cadnant, there was a strong guard of foot, under the command of two officers, but they both quitted their posts most shamefully, not without strong suspicion of treachery, for it was afterwards currently famed, that one of them had received 50l. from General Mytton, before hand, for betraying the island, and that 50l. more were promised him after he should betray it, but never paid, as all traitors are commonly cheated by those that employ them; it being a maxim among enemies themselves, to love the treason, but hate the traitors.

Now Cadnant afore-mentioned being a Welsh word, comes from Nant y Gâd, the "Dingle of the Army," where it seems that some army, in former times, either landed or encamped, and this army too chose to land in the same place, or very near it.

On the next day, after landing at Cadnant, they made their rendezvous at Orsedd Migin, and thence marched towards Beaumaris, the way of Red-hill Park, and drew in battalia upon the hill; the islanders, commanded by Colonel Bulkeley as General, and Colonel Roger Whitely as Major-General, drew up in the fields below the hill, viz., on St. Mary's Fields; Colonel Bulkeley's regiment of foot on the Harp Field; the towne's company commanded by one Captain Sanders, and some others, on Red-hill Fields. The horse were scatteringly drawn: some in the way to the alms-house, some at Mr. R. Vaughan's house (Tros yr Afon), some in the lands of the towne and elsewhere.

About three o'clock in the afternoon the enemy made the onset, and were stoutly repulsed by Captain Sanders and the towne's company, from the hedges in the Harp Field, but the foot in the other fields did all betake themselves to flight in disorder. Major Pennant and his troop charged the enemy, in the lane coming down from the park towards Mr. Richard Vaughan's house, and was like to take Colonel Louthian prisoner; Sir Arthur Blaney and his troop charged in the back lands, and was dangerously wounded in the arm, his elbow being shattered to pieces. Colonel Bulkeley his own troop, consisting of gentlemen, made a valiant charge upon Brickes Fields, encountering with Captain Benbow, but being overpowered by far greater numbers, were forced to retreat to the barricades near Mary Ned's house, and there another charge happened, when, on the Roundhead party, Captain Benbow and Vavasor Powell (a military preacher) were wounded, and on the cavalier side, not far from the same place, one Mr. Price, vicar of Bettws Abergele, in the county of Denbigh, got his mortal wound; at the same time one Captain Lloyd, of Penhwnllys, being commanded to guard the church, he locked up his men in it, and ran himself away, taking the key in his pocket, whereupon he was called Captain Church to his dying day. These men, from the steeple and church leads, and some others from Court Mawr garden, played very hotly upon the enemies, and killed several, especially Captain Hancock of Colonel Louthian's regiment, his Lieutenant and Ensign, in the clay pits and back lanes. The islanders were so full of disorder and confusion in this fight (and indeed it might be called an affray or scuffle rather than a fight) that they were easily routed and dispersed, Colonel Bulkeley, Colonel Whitely, and most of the commanders retiring into the castle; but let it be understood, that a great party of the island forces being the men of Talybolion and Llison, the two remotest comotes of the island under the command of Colonel John Robinson, were not come to the place of battle this day, but in their march, about Traeth Coch, hearing of the defeat of their friends at Beaumaris, returned to their own houses. Of the enemy were killed this day about forty, and of the islanders about thirty, but near four hundred taken prisoners; and now General Mytton having routed the field, and entered the towne of Beaumaris, he sent a drum to the castle, to demand the body of Colonel Bulkeley and Colonel Whitely, which, if refused to him, he would put all the prisoners taken that day to death; upon which the two colonels surrendered themselves, to save more effusion of Christian blood, and lay prisoners at the Old Place till they were ransomed.

The island forces were then scattered; the gentlemen of the country saw no other remedy but submission to General Mytton and the other commissioners, and therefore they all hastened to Beaumaris, and agreed upon these following articles, Oct. 2, 1648 :—

Entered into, concluded, and agreed upon, the 2nd day of Oct. 1648, between Sir Thomas Myddelton, Knight, Major-General Mytton, Thomas Myddelton, Esq., Simon Thelwall, Esq., and Colonel John Jones, of the one part; and Thomas Viscount Bulkeley, Hugh Owen, Owen Wood, Dr. Robert Whyte, Richard Prytherch, Dr. William Gryffydd, Rowland Bulkeley, Owen Holland, William Bold, Richard Owen, Owen Wynn, Henry Owen, Richard Meyrick, Pierce Lloyd, John Bodville, William Bulkeley, Esq., Henry Wynne, Jno. Williams, Randulph Wally, Jno. Owen, and Howell Lewis, gentlemen, on behalf of themselves and the rest of the inhabitants of the Isle of Anglesey, on the other part.

Imprimis—It is agreed by and between the said parties, that the Viscount Bulkeley, &c., doe, on behalf of themselves and the Island of Anglesey, engage and promise to pay to Colonel George Twistleton, treasurer, appointed for the present service, the sum of 7000*l.* of current English money, within fourteen days next ensuing, towards satisfaction of two months pay to the officers and soldiers employed in this

<hr/>

[a] The first governor of Beaumaris Castle appointed by the founder (Edward I.) was Sir William Pickmore, a Gascon, and the same person (in one instance excepted[b]) was always constable of the castle, and captain of the town; his annual fee, as constable, was 40*l.*; as captain, 12*l.* 3*s.* 4*d.*; and the porter at the town gate (*porth mawr*) 9*l.* 2*s.* 6*d.* The town and castle had a guard of twenty-four men, at 4*d.* a day each. But out of every one's pay there was a proportionate deduction every month towards letters and intelligence; and, as the sage historian adds, " for the gratification of itinerant preachers who did use to come at certayne times from Caernarvonshire, Denbighshire, Montgomeryshire, and other places, to pray and teach." The garrison was withdrawn in the reign of Henry VII., in the constableship of Sir Rowland Villeville. The Earl of Dorset being constable in 1642, his deputy (Thomas Chedle, Esq.[†]) furnished it with men and ammunition, but Thomas the first (Lord Bulkeley) succeeding in 1643, Colonel Thomas Bulkeley (his son) and the country gentlemen, held it for the King till 1648, when it was given by Major-General Mytton, whose deputy was Captain Evans.

[b] In the reign of Henry VI. Sir John Boteler was governor of the castle, and Thomas Norris, Esq., Alderman of Beaumaris (mentioned as a feoffee in the records of Kyghley) was captain of the town. The Norrises of Hafodty Ardderch (an antient mansion, situated at a short distance north-east of Trefawr, the residence of H. Thomas, &c.), were a branch of the family of Speke, in Lancashire. The curious arched mantel-piece in the once festive hall of this house, is still entire, decorated with heraldic ornaments, and a pious motto, in well executed relievo characters : the fee-farm of this property was afterwards disposed of by Sir William Norris.

† Of the Lleiniog family.

present expedition, and other charges incidental. In consideration whereof, they, the said Thomas Myddelton, &c. doe engage themselves effectually to mediate with the Parliament, that the personal estates of all the inhabitants within the said island be freed and acquitted from sequestration, and from any tax for the 25th part, &c., as touching the real estates of such of the said inhabitants as come within the ordinance of sequestration : they, the said Sir Thomas Myddelton, &c., do likewise engage themselves effectually to mediate with the Parliament, that they be admitted to compound for the same after the rate of two years value, for all estates of inheritance and proportionably for all other lesser estates. In witness whereof we have hereunto interchangeably put our hands, this 9th day of October, 1648.

1648.—About the same time, Thomas Llynligon, Esq., governor of Caernarvon Castle, and John Bodwrda, Esq., died.

Poyer, governor of Pembroke Castle, declared that he kept the said castle to the King's use, and about Easter, or rather before, issued out, and fell on the Parliament soldiers near unto him, killed some, and took forty, or thereabouts, prisoners, to whom he gave an oath never to bear arms against the King, and gave them 30d. a-piece and let them go. Captain Rhys Powel, governor of Tenby, declared himself likewise for the King.

The Duke of York escaped to Holland, as also did General Latham from London to Pembroke Castle.

In the latter end of April some three hundred of the Parliamenteers, under the conduct of Captain Fleming and Captain Jones, did set on the Pembrokians, who were far greater in number, but country fellows ; they brake their array and were like to have routed, but that Major Rhys Powel and Captain Adish, being there, suffered their enemies to pass till they had compassed them in ; then they played upon them on all sides, and killed a great many of them. At last Captain Jones by the swiftness of his horse, escaped hurt, and Captain Fleming, with some six score soldiers, took the church of Llandirlofawr upon them ; but the Pembrokians broke in upon them, and made, as they say, a slaughter of them ; Captain Fleming, as they say, having taken an oath before Poyer not to bear arms against the King, and then shot himself with a pistol, and died.

Great scarcity there is in Pembrokeshire of all kind of victuals.

May 8th.—The Pembrokians did very fiercely set on and assail Horton and the Parliament army, who had fortified themselves many days before, choosing a place fit to receive their enemy's charge, and to assail them with deal of advantage ; but after an hour's fighting, the Pembrokians, being on the lower ground, were feign to retire, and were warned by the general to shift every man for himself. This battle was fought at St. Fagan's parish, not far from Llandaff.

May 17th.—Sir John Owen came to Dolgelle, having about one hundred reformads in his company, all of them almost being commanders, amongst whom was Colonel Lloyd of Llwyn y Maen, Colonel Scriven, Colonel Lee, Mr. Morgan Herbert, Captain Edward Herbert, his son, Captain Blodwst, Captain Kynaston, Captain Phillips, &c., where they quartered two nights, and at their departure paid for their quarters, and did no man harm ; from whence they went to Dyffnyn Ardydwy ; from whence they went to Caernarvonshire ; and on Monday following they came back to Ardydwy.

Monday, in the evening, about one hundred horse of the Parliamenteers came to Dolgelle, under Twisleton and Captain Soutley. These, having some intelligence that some foot came over Dyfy from Sir Richard Price to Sir John Owen, took their horse and went to Penal, and from thence to Towyn ; and at Llwyn-gwril overtook some of those footmen ; who, thinking they had been some of their own men, made no resistance nor shift for themselves ; and, therefore, about forty-eight were taken prisoners, among whom were Captain Vaughan, Henry Vaughan's son, of Golden Grove ; one Captain Lloyd, of * * * and * * * and returned to Dolgelly at six o'clock in the evening. Tuesday ; and when it was about midnight, they took their prisoners, and went their way to Bala, and so towards Denbigh. Sir Thomas Owen having intelligence from Bala that the Parliamenteers were marched towards Dolgelle, returned back to Ardydwy late in the evening. Monday, intending to be at their quarters at Dolgelle ; but having intelligence, as it seems, that * * * was very vigilant they altered their purpose, and retired back into Caernarvonshire.

In the month of May, 1648, some attempts being then on foot in the north for restoring the King's power, the fortifications at Chester were put in complete repair.

In the month of August following, Captain Oldham formed a plan for seizing the city and castle for the use of the King ; but the design being discovered, they both suffered death.

In the beginning of June, a party of Sir John Owen's men scouting abroad, met William Lloyd, sheriff of Caernarvonshire, who had * * * with carbines, in his company, where he was hurt and taken.

On Monday, the 5th of June, Sir John and his men marched towards Bangor, carrying along the sheriff in a litter ; they took a messenger of the Parliamenteers who had a letter to them that were in Caernarvon, to come on the * * * * of Sir John, affirming that they were but few. Sir John, fearing lest if the Caernarvon men should not be able to encounter them, made haste to meet the Parliament soldiers, who were, by three o'clock on Tuesday, before them, thinking those to be but few. Presently they were discovered to march towards Llandegai; then Sir John carried his foot over the river, and presently met them. Sir John's forlorn hope was led by Lieutenant-General Scriven, who did quite beat the forlorn hope of the Parliament; the second charge the Parliament side got the better. The foot of the cavaliers did at first prevail with good success, yet the Parliament house kept a close body, so that at the end of half an hour, they began to break through the cavaliers, and routed them, taking Sir John Owen and his son, Colonel Lloyd, of Llwyn y Maen, and some fourteen gentlemen, and about forty of the foot. Here died of the cavaliers Captain Sanderson, and a few more of the Parliament side.

Sir John's army was not three hundred horse and foot; the Parliament had * * * * *

Sir Arthur Blaenay, Lieutenant Scriven, Herbert Vaughan, and many others, escaped.

The sheriff of Caernarvonshire being left in his litter when they went to fight, died the day after, about the 10th of June * * *

Sir William Brereton and Sir Thomas Myddleton came to Wrexham and got it, and shortly left it, and returned over Dee, by reason that * * * Irishmen landed near Mostyn. Captain Robinson kept Holt Castle from them all the while they were in Wrexham.

Mr. Ravenscroft delivered Hardin Castle to the enemies, and shortly after fled unto them, and not long afterwards they forsook the castle.

About the latter end of June, — Dolben and — Chambers, of Denbigh, had a design to take the same castle; they scaled it in the night, and about sixty men got into the outer ward; but they were soon discovered, and some of them taken; they both plundered * * * escaped, as is said.

Lieutenant-Colonel Hughes, Captain Morgan, Captain Brynkir, and others, to the number of twelve, kept still in a body after the Battle of Bangor, which drew Captain Soutley and twenty-two soldiers more to come into the country, to scatter or take them, in the beginning of July.

Whilst Soutley and his men were in Dolgelle, in July, certain men in Anglesey, notwithstanding that a company of Parliament lodged at Bangor, came over in the night, and in the morning took of them between thirty and forty about Aber. Soutley and his men went towards Bala on Sunday morning, July 16th.

The same time Dolben and Chambers, with their company, came before Denbigh Castle and Chirk Castle, and, in a bravado, discharged their pistols and went their way.

In Caernarvonshire the soldiers of the Parliament did plunder Clynenne, and a great many gentlemen of Cevnydo and Llynn.

Shortly after, Anglesey men came over to Caernarvon, and took some men and horses about Chyrmog; and hearing that General Mitton and Colonel Jones were at Pwhelli, they made that way; but those men having intelligence of their purpose, went their way and returned to Anglesey.

About the midst of August, Sir Harry Lingen, Knight, of Herefordshire, came with horse and foot, and advanced towards North Wales, intending to join with Anglesea men, but being narrowly watched by the troops of the counties adjacent, who gave General Horton intelligence of Lingen's design. Whilst they followed after him, Horton came from Pembroke crosswise, and met Lingen's men near Llanidloes, took Sir Harry sore hurt, and * * * prisoners. The rest fled, whereof about thirty horse, and some few men came to Mallwyd, 17th day, and lay there that night; the morrow they came to Dolgelle, where they rested till the morrow, being Saturday, for they were bruised; and thither came Sir Arthur Blaeney, and they went to Harlech, and so to Anglesey.

Another company of them (or from the north), to the number of sixty, came to Bala, intending to go to Anglesey, but they had no sooner lighted, but Colonel Jones and * * * soldiers came after them, and, after some struggling, they took about fifty of Lingen's men; some few escaped. It is reported they had 300l. in money and booty.

---

* Sir John was sent prisoner to Walmer Castle, and was put on his trial with the Duke of Hamilton, Lords Holland, Goring, and Cope. Sir John showed a spirit worthy of his country; he told his judges that "He was a plain gentleman of Wales, who had always been taught to obey the King: that he had served him honestly during the war, and finding many honest men endeavoured to raise forces whereby they might get him out of prison, he did the like." He was condemned to lose his head; for which, with a humorous intrepidity, he made the court a low reverence, and gave his humble thanks. A byestander asked what he meant? He replied aloud: "*It was a great honour to a poor gentleman of Wales to lose his head with* such noble lords; for, by G—, he was afraid they would have hanged him!*" Sir John was deprived of "the honour" he felt so flattered with; strong remonstrances were made in parliament on behalf of the noble lords; but finding no one speak in favour of Sir John, Ireton proved his advocate: he told the house, "there was one person for whom no one spoke a word, and therefore he requested that he might be saved by the sole motive and goodness of the house." He was pardoned, and retired to Wales, where he died in 1666. Lady Owen built several almshouses in London as a thankful remembrance to Almighty God for saving her husband's life. A monument was erected to his memory at Penmorfa Church, Caernarvonshire.

Colonel Horton followed as far as Pool, and returned; and on his return burnt Havod Uchtryd, Morgan Herbert's house, for that one of his had been there murdered by Morgan Herbert's men, with the privity of Morgan, who was there.

September 26th.—At night the Parliament forces entered Anglesey, and with fifty or sixty boats put over both horse and foot the 27th day.

In the month of August King Charles and his host * * * to England, and went to Manchester and to Chester, and to Wem, and by Shrewsbury, and thence to Caer Mangen (Worcester).

July, 1649.—Colonel Dunkenfield was appointed governor of Chester.

In the month of August there was a battle between the Earl of Derby and Colonel Lilburn, and the Earl lost the field.

The month of September came some men of Denbigh to Merioneddshire; namely, Captain Wynn and others, to raise horses and muskets, or 17l. 18s. instead of the horse, and a month of pay; and 2l. 13s. instead of * * * and a month of pay, to be had again in taxes beforehand.

> "*The Humble Petition of many Thousands in the Six Counties of North Wales.*

"SHOWING that (since the ejecting of ministers from their churches, and silencing of them, and sequestring of tythes by colour of the act made the 22nd of February, 1649, for propagation of the gospel in Wales,) divers parishes are left vacant, without any minister to officiate, to minister the sacrament of Baptism or the Lord's Supper, to marry, or to visit the sick in them, for two years past, to the scandal and decay of religion among us, the consideration whereof we humbly present to your honours—

> "Beseeching not only that our tythes may be accounted for (which we hope your honours will look into), but that the health of our souls, which we value above earthly things (by setting of pious and able ministers in our parishes) may speedily be provided for according to the real intent of the said act.

> "And we shall ever pray," &c.

An act for the Propagation of the Gospel in Wales.—In April Poyer was shot.

Duke Hamilton[2] and Earl Holland were beheaded, and Lord Capel; and, by the grace of God, Lord Goring and Sir John Owen were preserved.

A tax was given towards supporting the war in Ireland, and to the Lord Fairfax in England; namely, 90,000l. a-month, to begin the 25th of March, 1649, for three months; and of this 47l. 7s. 3d. fell upon Merioneddshire, and 165l. a-month for six months more.

About the middle of March, 1650, men were placed in Castell y Waen,[7] and Sir Thomas Myddleton went as a *sculker* to England. At the same time soldiers came to Merioneddshire, and took Rowland Vaughan, of Caer Gai; young William Wynn, of Glyn; Mr. William Owen, of Elynnone; Colonel Mostyn; Wynn, of Bodsgallan;[8] 500 volunteers who * * * from Wales to Ireland.

In the month of December an act came out to raise a tax on the kingdom, of 120,000l. for the war, to continue for four months; that is to say, a tax of 853l. 9s. 8d. a-month every month, for these four months.

The following particulars are from another of our documents, and translated from the original Welsh MS. They remarkably elucidate and confirm each other.

1649.—This year a tax was levied in support of the Irish War, and Lord Fairfax in England, amounting to 9000l. a month, which caused our contribution in Merionethshire to be raised from 47l. 7s. 3d. to 165l. per month, for the ensuing six months.

1650.—About the middle of March this year soldiers were placed in possession of Chirk Castle, and Sir Thomas Myddleton was obliged to leave for England.

In the same month a party of soldiers came to Merionethshire and took Rowland Vaughan, Caer Gai;[9] William Wynn, Junior, of Glynn; William Owen, of Clenenna: Colonel Mostyn, of Mostyn; Mr. Wynne, Bodysgallen, with five hundred volunteers went to Ireland.

In December this year, 1650, another act was passed to raise 160,000l. per month, to support the Irish war for the four months following; the portion allotted to be raised by our county was 853l. 6s 8d., which continued monthly from the 25th of March for the six months following.

1650-1.—Several of our churches in Wales were empty, no service performed, and our clergy had nought to support them.

---

[7] Chirk Castle.   [8] Bodysgallen, near Conway.

[9] Castell Rhôs, in this parish, belonged anciently to Torwetrh ap Owen; for except this and Llanvrihengel Castle in Pengwern, the whole of Cardiganshire was taken from him by Cadell Meredydd and Rhys in the year 1150. Eight years afterwards it was fortified by the Earl of Clare.

In June this year fifty men were pressed in Merionethshire to go to Ireland, all the counties in England and Wales were obliged to send a number of men according to the population of each county.

In the month of August this year King Charles came with his army to England, marched to Manchester and Chester, from thence to Wem and Shrewsbury on their way to Caerwrongan, where a battle took place the beginning of September.

From the 26th of March, 1651; for six months more, is 120,000*l*.

Many churches in Wales were empty, without service, and the priests without anything to live upon.

A press of fifty men of Merioneddshire, beginning of June, 1651, and in proportion this number through Wales and England to go to Ireland.

The 14th of the same month a battle in Cardiganshire, Llan Rhystyd,[1] and twenty men of the country were killed.

In 1651 the Earls of Derby and Lauderdale were both prisoners in the Castle of Chester. When Sir George Booth put himself at the head of a formidable insurrection against the three ruling powers, in the year 1659, he took possession of Chester, and appointed Colonel Croxon, Governor, who, after Sir George's defeat at Northwich, on the 16th of August, surrendered it to General Lambert on his first summons.[2]

The private life of the unfortunate Charles was free from reproach; and whatever might have been the imperfections or the errors of his public conduct, his dignified demeanour at the hour of death was unspeakably touching. A fine tribute is paid to it by that incorruptible patriot, Andrew Marvell, in an ode to Cromwell. Alluding to the execution of that monarch, he says:—

> " While round, the armed bands
> Did clasp their bloody hands,
> He nothing common did or mean
> Upon the memorable scene :
> But with his keener eye
> The axe's edge did try ;
> Nor called the gods, with vulgar spite,
> To vindicate his helpless right,
> But bowed his comely head
> Down, as upon a bed."

OLIVER CROMWELL, although not a royal person, may in some respects be looked upon as such. During the civil war in the time of Charles I., most of the Welsh chieftains took arms on the side of their Royal master, and although the war was there carried on with vigour, under less renowned generals, we do not hear of Cromwell being much in Wales during these troublesome times. We have, however, an account of his besieging, in person, the castles of Pembroke and Tenby in 1648. Tenby surrendered at discretion, on the 26th of May in that year, but Pembroke held out until the 11th of July, not, however, until its inmates were reduced to the greatest possible straits. A curious letter is still extant, written by the celebrated Hugh Peters, complaining of the hardships of the campaign. We have a tradition that Cromwell subsequently paid a friendly visit to his friend and adherent, Colonel Carter, whilst he resided at Kinmel Park, in Denbighshire, now the residence of Lord Dinorben. Before the old hall was taken down there was one room there, called "Cromwell's parlour."

Cromwell, although it is not generally known, was a Welshman by descent, deriving his pedigree from Bleddyn ap Cynfyn, Prince of Powys, and great grand-son of Morgan Williams of New Church in Glamorganshire. His pedigree may be seen in the work of Sir John Prestwich of Prestwich which is also corroborated by the Lion of Powys on the centre of his coins.

The following is the Pedigree, as given in the "Banners Displayed," written at the time of his installation, in 1657 :—

Genealogical Line or Paternal Descent of His Highness, the Most Serene and Most Illustrious Oliver Cromwell, Supreme Chief or Lord Protector of the Common Wealth of England, Scotland, and Ireland, and the Dominions, Islands, and Territories thereunto belonging.

I. Bleddyn ap Cynfyn.—II. Madoc ap Bleddyn.—III. Meredith ap Madoc.—IV. Griffith Maylor.—V. Cadwgan ap Gryffydd.—VI. Owen ap Cadwgan, Lord of Kibian.—VII. Alan ap Owen.—VIII. Madoc ap Alan.—IX. Howel ap

---

[1] Perfect Diurnal, Sept. 29th, 1651.   [2] See Lord Clarendon, and Heath.

Madoc.—X. Morgan ap Howel.—XI. John ap Morgan.—XII. Morgan ap John.—XIII. William Morgan, of New Church, in Glamorganshire, married ..... daughter of Walter Crumwell, sister to Thomas Crumwell, Earl of Essex.—XIV. Sir Richard Williams, Knt., surnamed Cromwell, Gentleman of the Privy Chamber to King Henry VIII., Constable of Berkeley Castle, and Captain of Horse.—XV. Sir Henry Cromwell, of Hinchingbroke, in Huntingdonshire, had issue two sons.—XVI. Sir Oliver Cromwell, Knight of the Bath at the coronation of King James.—XVII. Oliver Cromwell, Lord Protector of England, Scotland, and Ireland.

The following is another account of Cromwell's descent :—

The genealogy of this remarkable man is thus traced by our late friend, Sir Samuel Rush Meyrick, in a light which, we are sure, is perfectly new to most of our readers.

Oliver Cromwell was descended from a very ancient and highly allied family of WELSH origin, sprung from Cadwgan, second son of Bleddyn ab Cynvyn, Prince of Powis, the founder of one of the Royal tribes of Wales. His great great grandfather was William ab Jevan, who held an honourable office in the household of Jasper Tudyr, Earl of Bedford, one of whose sons, Morgan ap William, was also Morgan Williams, and he lived at a house named Cwm Castell, in the parish of Newchurch, Caermarthenshire. This Williams married a sister of Thomas, Lord Cromwell, created Earl of Essex in 1540; and his eldest son, out of respect to his uncle's memory, obtained the Royal license to assume the name of Cromwell. Sir Henry Cromwell, the son and heir, resided in Cambridgeshire, and was the father of Sir Oliver Cromwell, created Knight of the Bath in 1603, who died without issue; and of Robert Cromwell, Esq., who settled in the town of Huntingdon, and relieved the scantiness of his patrimony by engaging in the business of a brewer. Robert Cromwell married the widow of William Lynne, of Basingbourne, Cambridgeshire, daughter of Sir Robert Stewart, a Knight of the city of Ely, and they became, on the 25th of April, 1599, the parents of Oliver, so named after his uncle. Through his maternal ancestry he sprang from the same stock as King Charles I., but as the fact is very curious, I shall give it in detail.

Alexander Stuart, died in 1286.

Year		Year	
1298.	John Stuart	. . . . .	Andrew Stuart.
1320.	Walter Stuart	. . . .	Alexander Stuart.
1390.	Robert II., King of Scotland	. .	John Stuart.
1406.	Robert III.	. . . . .	John Stuart.
1437.	James I.	. . . . . .	Thomas Stuart.
1460.	James II.	. . . . .	Richard Stuart.
1488.	James III.	. . . .	Nicholas Stuart.
1513.	James IV.	. . . . .	Nicholas Stuart.
1542.	James V.	. . . . . .	William Stuart.
1567.	Mary, Queen of Scots	. .	Elizabeth Stuart.
1626.	James VI., of Scotland	. .	Elizabeth, married to Robert Cromwell.
1646.	Charles I., King of England	. .	Oliver Cromwell, Protector.

The following anecdote is related in the genealogical history of the Cromwell family, but strange to say, has never been noticed by historians. On the death of Queen Elizabeth, James the Sixth of Scotland was no sooner proclaimed King of England, than it was understood that his route, which was marked out by the government, would take its course through the county of Huntingdon, when Sir Thomas Stewart, Bart., who resided in the county and possessed large estates, lost no time in forwarding an invitation to the King to pass some days at his mansion on his journey to England; this the King accepted, and in the regular course of time found himself comfortably lodged in the mansion of the baronet; the King was at this period accompanied by his son, the Prince of Wales, afterwards the unfortunate King Charles the First.

It appears that Oliver Cromwell was at this time on a visit to his uncle, Sir Thomas Stewart, his mother being sister to Sir Thomas, and was about the same age with the Prince; the two boys soon became familiar, and were allowed to play daily in the grounds about the mansion; while all was enjoyment in the royal circle, the Prince one day suddenly made his appearance *with a bloody nose and his face much disfigured*; this operated as a thunderbolt for the moment on the mind of the King and Sir Thomas Stewart; it was soon discovered that the Prince and Oliver Cromwell got into a dispute in the shrubbery, which ended in this tragical affair. Oliver was immediately dispatched home to his father, with a letter from Sir Thomas Stewart stating what had occurred, with directions to chastise his son well; that he had violently assaulted the Prince of Wales, having repeatedly struck him while playing in the shrubbery. It appears that Oliver was well flogged by his father on the occasion, but the impression which such an occurrence made on his mind continued for months after to disturb the peace of his family, by getting up in his bed in the middle of the night, and putting his bed-curtains aside, *when he would exclaim aloud, that he would be King of England, and on each occasion did his father flog him.*[3]

Oliver received his education in the Free School of Huntingdon, whence he was removed to Cambridge.

His son, Richard Cromwell, who was of a peaceful disposition, retired to Chertsey, in Surrey, to the quietude which he loved, and was permitted to enjoy it.

A.D. 1651.—The last bloody conflict in the cause of Charles was sustained at Worcester on the 2nd of September. Still attached to the Royal House of Stuart, though the city was garrisoned by Cromwell's troops on the approach of Charles II., the common council ordered the gates to be thrown open and to admit his Majesty; he accordingly entered; next day he was proclaimed King. The number of royal forces did not exceed 10,000 Scotch, and 2000 English, while those of Cromwell amounted to 60,000.

On the 28th of August, Cromwell arrived at Red-hill, one mile from Worcester,[4] and fixed his head-quarters at Spetchley, at the house of Judge Berkeley. The day after hostilities commenced. On the 29th, Cromwell, with a great body of horse and foot appeared on Red-hill, but did nothing. On the 30th, the King's forces made a most gallant sally which would have had a most extraordinary effect had not the design been discovered by the treachery of one Guyes, a tailor, of Worcester, who had betrayed the King's signals to the enemy; being detected he was hanged the day following. September 3rd was the fatal day. The King held a council of war upon the top of College Church steeple; from whence, perceiving a kind of skirmish at Powis Bridge, he commanded his men to march thither, and accompanying them, after securing the pass he returned to the city, and resolved to engage Cromwell himself, and charged him with so much fury, that Cromwell's invincible Life Guards were compelled to give ground. His Majesty in person led the Highlanders, charging with so much courage and gallantry that Cromwell could not help applauding his intrepid valour. The fight continued for three or four hours with great fierceness, during which the King had his horse shot twice under him, and rallied the infantry himself; but being overpowered by number, their ammunition expended, and compelled to sustain the fight with the butt end of their muskets, and giving every proof of loyalty and bravery, the King's troops were at length overpowered and put to flight. The King was the last in the field, and could hardly be persuaded to outlive the day. Seeing his troops throw down their arms, he cried out, "I had rather you should shoot me than keep me alive to see the effect of this fatal day."

The King entered the city on foot; a sort of defence was made by a small party of brave Royalists at Sudbury gate, which, by delaying the entrance of the enemy, afforded an opportunity for the King to escape out at St. Martin's gate. It is said that the King would certainly have been taken by Cromwell's cavalry notwithstanding, had not one of the inhabitants purposely drawn a load of hay into the gateway which blocked up the passage so as no horse could enter. The King crept under the hay and so escaped. About half a mile out of Worcester, at Barbon's Bridge, the King, with a handful of brave followers, made several stands and faced about, but perceiving that all was lost, his party desired his Majesty to make his escape in the best manner he could. In the meantime Cromwell was butchering all he could in the streets. Meeting with sharp resistance at the Fort Royal, he put all the defenders, fifteen hundred, to the sword. Other cruelties and enormities, plunders, robberies, &c., were committed.

There fell on the King's side Duke Hamilton and many loyal gentlemen, with four thousand soldiers; a great number of officers and privates were made prisoners, to the number, including inhabitants of the

---

[3] We are indebted to Captain Stuart of the Charter House, a descendant of the royal house of Stuart, for this interesting anecdote, which he says he extracted from an old MS. genealogy some years ago.

[4] Worcester, according to John Speed, " is the Branonium mentioned by Antonine and Ptolomie, called by the Britons Caerwrangon, by Minius Caerquorcon, by the Old Saxons, Ager-na Ceastre."

city who had some arms, of about seven thousand. So total was the route that few of the Royal army made their escape. The King was conducted from Worcester to Boscobel.

Cromwell in his letter to the Parliament states the number of the King's troops to have been sixteen thousand, and that his own loss did not exceed two hundred men. On leaving Worcester he ordered the walls to be pulled down and levelled to the ground.[5]

During his Protectorship he caused an edition of the Welsh Bible to be printed, which, at that time, was exceedingly scarce. The edition to this day is called Cromwell's Bible. He also caused a law to be passed for the more general propagation of the Gospel in North Wales. Cromwell was a potent prince and the world stood in awe of him; and though Great Britain and Ireland were within his power for several years, there is *neither pension, palace, or place, attached to his name!*

A.D. 1655.—The following couplet was written under the Lord Protector's Picture beyond sea.

> " He treads upon his foes amain,
> Kings and Princes bear his train."

This was ill resented by the great ones in France and elsewhere * * * * orders taken for the putting out of those verses * * * * the perfect account * * * * adjournal.

During the Protectorate the Welsh still at times manifested their loyalty to their rightful sovereigns, as will appear from the following address of the County of Flint, to the Parliament, on the subject of loyal manifestations, which had made their appearance :—

" *At the Great Sessions of the Countie of Flint, held at Flint, the 23rd day of April*, 1655.

"WE, who have been returned to serve of the Great Inquest for the bodie of this countie, attended at the same Sessions, being trewley informed of the late suddaine and dangerous designs of divers ould and inveterate enemies to raise a new war on behalf of the sonne of the late King, and to make unlawful insurrections in the several parts of the Commonwealth, to the hazard of reviving and introducing again the miseries of the former wars, and involving us in bloud, doe with all thankfulness humbly acknowledge the goodness and mercies of God so seasonably and kindly preventing the same, &c., and having seen the results of the neighbouring counties of Denbigh and Montgomery, at their several sessions immediately preceding ours— we do, &c., to the utmost of our ability promise to oppose the plotts, designs, and attempts of those who shall endeavour to maintain any of the family or ward of the Stewarts within this nation—patiently waiting upon the Lord till he shall in his due time confirme and settle the just rights and liberties of the people of this Commonwealth—the overthrow whereof hath been (and we have reason to foresee) still is, the unwearied wish and endeavour of that partie who idolise that family, against whom and whose tyrannies and bloodsheds the Lord hath given such testimonies of his wrath, and gloriously appeared in the behalf of the Parliament and good people of this Commonwealth, adhering to them and their righteous cause.

" DAVID GRIFFITH.	JNO. THOMAS AP THOMAS.	WM. LEDSHAM.
EDW. JOHN ROBERTS.	REES AP EDWARDS.	THOS. DAVIES.
JOHN EDWARDS.	WILLIAM EDWARDS.	ANDREW BITHELL.
THOS. AP RICHARD AP THOS.	THOS. VAUGHAN.	ROGER AP WILLIAMS.
EDW. MORGAN.	THOS. ELLIS.	HENRY PARRY."

The circumstances attending the remarkable and interesting escape of King Charles II., after the battle of Worcester, have been often before the public, and in a variety of forms, yet there are many particulars upon record which have never yet been embodied as a whole. The following narrative is condensed, partly from Mrs. Anne Wyndham's edition of " A Complete History of the Miraculous Preservation of King Charles II.," and partly from other rare sources and authorities.

" From the disastrous battle of Worcester, in the year 1651, which afforded Cromwell what he called his ' crowning mercy,' King Charles retreated in disguise, and arrived that night at the house of Mr. Thomas Harris in Leominster, when being introduced to a chamber in which his royal father had reposed six years before, he abandoned himself to the bitterest reflections on the instability of human greatness, the precarious state of royal grandeur, the slippery and perilous state of princes. Unable to compose himself to sleep, he renewed his flight, resolving to trust himself to the mountains

---

[5] Chambers's Worcester.

and the tried loyalty of Wales. Having proceeded on his journey about half way to Presteign, he was informed that his person was discovered, and that a detachment of troops was in pursuit of him, on which he immediately changed his route to Shropshire.

"At a house one mile beyond Stonebridge, his Majesty drank water and eat a crust of bread, the house in which he was entertained affording no better fare. Here the King was informed of the Earl of Derby's secure concealment at Boscobel; he therefore accepted Mr. Giffard's proposal to carry him first to White Ladies, where he had a seat, and which was only half a mile from Boscobel. To this place the King was safely conducted, when Mr. Giffard sent for the Pendrills, William and Richard. Richard came first, and was immediately sent back to bring a suit of his own clothes for the King, and by the time he returned, William came, and both were brought into the parlour where the Earl of Derby and the King were. The Earl, addressing William Pendrill, said, ' William, thou must have a care of him, and preserve him as thou didst me.' Mr. Giffard also gave strict charge to Richard, but these loyal brothers required no charge to stimulate them to their duty. His Majesty was then advised to rub his hands upon the back of the chimney, and with them his face, for a disguise. The King also submitted to have his hair cut and disfigured by one of the party, and, for better disguise, his Majesty put on a coarse noggen shirt, borrowed of Edward Martin, who lived in the house, and Richard Pendrill's green suit and leathern doublet. There being a troop of rebels quartered at Cotsal, but three miles distant, to prevent a sudden surprise, Richard Pendrill, unknown to most of the company, conducted the King to Spring Coppice, or Boscobel Wood.

"His Majesty being thus, as the loyal party hoped, in a place of security, the Duke of Hamilton, the Earl of Derby, Earl of Lauderdale, Lord Talbot, and the rest, being then about forty horse, of which number the King's pad-nag was one, and ridden by Mr. Richard Lane, marched from White Ladies by way of Newport, hoping to meet General Lesley, with the main body of the Scotch horse. As soon as they were got into the road, Lord Leviston, who commanded his Majesty's life-guards, overtook them, pursued by a party of rebels under the command of Colonel Blundel; another party of rebels, under Colonel Lilburn, met them in front; the loyal party being overpowered, the Earl of Derby, Lord Lauderdale, Mr. Giffard, and others were taken prisoners, and carried first to Whitechurch, and from thence to an inn at Bunbury, in Cheshire, where Mr. Giffard found means to escape, but the Earl of Derby was conveyed to Chester, where he was tried and sentenced to death on the 1st of October, 1651, and thence carried to Bolton, in Lancashire. The people, as he passed along the road, cried, 'O sad day, O woeful day, shall the good Earl of Derby, the ancient honour of our country, die here!' When arrived at Bolton a carpenter could not be obtained for a long time, nor any one that would lift a hammer to strike a nail in the erection of the scaffold. One was however finally erected, and, on the 15th of October, after a tumult among the soldiers and the people, on a sign given twice to the executioner, his head was severed from his body, and being thrown into his coffin, it was carried off the scaffold with hideous cries and lamentations of all spectators. Into his coffin was thrown the following couplet:—

> " ' Bounty, wit, courage, all here in one lie dead;
> A Stanley's hand, Vere's heart, and Cecil's head.'

"The Earl of Lauderdale, with several others, were carried prisoners to the Tower, and afterwards to Windsor Castle, where they continued many years. Duke Hamilton, Lord Leveston, Colonel Blayne, Mr. Marmaduke Darcey, and Mr. Hugh May got to Bloore Park, near Cheswardine, where they received some refreshment at a very obscure house of Mr. George Burlow's, and afterwards they met with two honest labourers to whom they communicated their distress, and finding them likely to prove faithful, the Duke changed his dress with one of the men, and, after some days' concealment, was conveyed by one Nicholas Mathews, a carpenter, to the house of Mr. Hanley, at Bilstrop in Nottinghamshire; the others shifted for themselves as well as they could. Mr. May was forced to live twenty-one days in a hay-mow belonging to Mr. John Bold, who lived at Sondley; this honest loyal man being compelled at the same time to keep in his house a party of rebels. The Lord Talbot hasted to his father's house at Longford, and was for four or five days confined in one of the out-houses, the rebel soldiers being frequently very near the place of his concealment. The venerable Earl of Cleveland escaping from the defeat at Worcester, had travelled twenty-one days on a very poor horse, and taken refuge at Woodcot in Shropshire; here he was taken near Mr. Broughton's house, and carried prisoner to Stafford, and from thence to the Tower of London. To return to Boscobel: by the time Richard Pendrill had carried the King to the thickest part of the wood it was sunrising, and the heavens wept bitterly at the sight of these calamities, insomuch that the thickest tree in the wood could not keep his Majesty dry. Richard Pendrill therefore borrowed a blanket of Francis Yates for his Majesty to sit on, the good wife Yates in the mean time prepared a mess of milk with butter and eggs. The King was startled at the sight of her, and not knowing whether the Pendrills had intrusted her with the secret, he said cheerfully to her, 'Good woman, can you be faithful to a distressed cavalier?' she answered, 'Yes, sir, I would rather die than discover you.' On Tuesday night, when it was quite dark, his Majesty resolved to proceed to Wales, and take Richard Pendrill with him for his guide. Having completely disguised himself, his name was agreed to be William Jones; they began their journey that night to Madely, where lived a zealous loyalist, Mr. Francis Woolf. They had but six or seven miles to go, but the night was very dark, and they passed Evelyn Mill, two miles from Madeley; Richard permitting a gate to clap too loudly, brought out the miller, who asked in a haughty tone where they were going at that unseasonable hour; on his bidding them to stand, Richard ran through the water, the King following by the sound of his calf-skin breeches. The darkness prevented the miller's pursuit; had he overtaken the fugitives, what would have been his feelings in taking into custody that sacred person, for whom he would have willingly sacrificed his life, having then under his care and protection in the mill several Royalists who escaped from the bloody field of Worcester? When they arrived at Madeley, Richard goes to Woolf's house; they were all invited; Mr. Woolf's daughter came to the door and received the King. There being so many soldiers belonging to the Parliament party in the neighbourhood, it was considered unsafe for the King to remain in the house; he therefore retired to the Barn, and there lay on a hay-mow all the day following. Finding himself in great danger, he returned to Boscobel House, where he met with Colonel Careless, who had seen the last man killed at the battle of Worcester, and who then returned into his own neighbourhood.

"Richard having acquainted the Colonel where the King was, that faithful officer accompanied William and Richard Pendrill to his Majesty, who was seated on the root of a tree; glad to see the Colonel he accompanied them into the house, where he heartily partook of plain bread and cheese; William's wife also made a kind of posset of skimmed milk and small beer. His Majesty's shoes being very wet, the good wife put some hot cinders in them to dry them.

"After this refreshment the King and Colonel returned to the wood, where the Colonel made choice of a thick leaved oak, which being ascended, the King rested his head in the Colonel's lap. In the evening the King returned to the house, and was secreted in the same place where the Earl of Derby had been secured. Being now in a hopeful security he permitted William Pendrill to shave him and cut his hair quite close at the top, as the scissors would do it, but leaving some about the ears as was the country mode. The King bade William to burn the hair, but in this instance he was disobedient, for he kept a great part of it, which was afterwards divided into portions, and greatly valued by his friends.

"Saturday night Humphrey Pendrill went to pay taxes to Shiffnall, where a Colonel of the rebels laid before him the danger of concealing the King, which was death without mercy, and pleaded the advantage of a thousand pounds reward if he discovered his retreat. This being told to his Majesty he was determined to leave Boscobel. This night, the good wife, whom the King called Dame Joan, provided some chickens for his supper, a dainty he had not lately been acquainted with. The King spent the Sunday in reading and prayers, and retired to a pretty arbour in Boscobel garden, which grew on a mount, and where there was a stone table and seats around it, and having understood from John Pendrill that Lord Wilmot was at Mr. Whitegrave's house at Moseley, he was determined to go thither. Upon this intelligence Lord Wilmot delayed his journey to Bristol. Moseley, in Staffordshire, was about five miles distant from Boscobel, and near the midway from thence to Bentley. It was therefore concluded that the King should ride upon Humphrey Pendrill's mill horse, for Humphrey was miller of White Ladies' Mill; thus his Majesty was mounted, and thus he rode towards Moseley. After he had travelled some distance the King complained that '*it was the heaviest, dull jade, he ever rode on,*' to which the miller replied, '*My liege, can you blame the horse going so heavily when it has the weight of three kingdoms on its back!*' His Majesty arrived at Mr. Whitegrave's, where he was much comforted by Mr. Huddleston, a Catholic priest. The King's attire at this time was a leather doublet, with pewter buttons, a pair of stirrups, stockings lent him at Moseley, an old grey greasy hat, and a noggen shirt; his hands and face made a variety of colours by the help of soot and walnut leaves. Mr. Huddleston very kindly supplied his Majesty with a finer linen shirt, and some other articles.

"On Monday his Majesty and my Lord Wilmot sent John Pendrill to Colonel Lane, at Bentley Hall, Walsall, to make way for his Majesty's reception there, designing to go Westward, under the protection of Mrs. Jane Lane's pass. At this time Mr. Whitegraves was in great danger as well as the King. A party of soldiers came to the house while the King lay on Mr. Huddleston's bed, intending to take Mr. Whitegraves, as one who had fought for the King at Worcester. The fidelity of Mr. Whitegrave's servants, and his own boldness, saved his life, and probably that of his royal master. While here, also, some rebels came to White Ladies in search of the King, and put a pistol to the breast of Mr. George Gifford, declaring they would instantly shoot him if he did not disclose the place of the King's retreat. They used the same threats with great promises, to Mrs. Anne Andrew, who had custody of some of the King's clothes, but all in vain.

"On Tuesday, 9th of September, between twelve and one o'clock, the Lord Wilmot sent Colonel Lane to attend his Majesty to Bentley. The night was both dark and cold, and the King's clothing thin. Mr. Huddleston therefore lent his Majesty his cloak, which the King sent carefully back.

"The King arrived safely at Bentley; he stayed there only a short time, but taking advantage of Mrs. Lane's pass he rode before her to Bristol, the Lord Wilmot attending at a distance. From thence he proceeded amidst great dangers, and experiencing unchanging fidelity and numerous interferences of divine Providence, to Brighthelmstone in Sussex; and on the 15th October, 1651, took shipping, and landed securely in France next morning.

"The day after Charles left Boscobel, a party of soldiers plundered the house of what was portable, and one of them presented a pistol at William Pendrill, and much frighted poor Dame Joan, yet both parties maintained their fidelity. Boscobel House was afterwards the asylum, in 1659, of Lord Brereton."

The Earls of Northampton, Peterborough, and Northumberland, Sir Edward Griffin, Colonel Griffin taken; Sir William Owen, Roger Owen, Edward Owen, apprehended in Shrewsbury; many more in all parts of the kingdom.

In North Wales, Sir John Owen, Lewis Lloyd, Esq., of Rhiwaedog, Edmund Meyric, and Rowland Vaughan, were prisoners at Chester.

Copy of a Letter from Major-General Jones, one of the leading men in Oliver Cromwell's forces, to Captain Wray, Lieutenant of Beaumaris Castle.

"CAPTAYNE WRAY,—I had no time by the last post to write unto you as touching the two men you mention to be continued in prison for stealing the leads of the Castle. I have advised with the Advocate-General, and he tells me they cannot be tried by martial law, without being sent up hither with witnesses; so that the way to proceed against them is putting them out of the list, and then cause them to be indicted and proceeded against at the sessions, and likewise those that bought the lead of them. But if you conceive them to be penitent, and there is any hope of their reducement to a civil life, you may let them return to their duty and continue the list upon their good behaviour, and forbear further proceedings against them. This I leave to your discretion. I intend to allow Edward Gregory for his encouragement to remain in the garrison, 10*l.* per annum, to be paid him quarterly, and the first 50*s.* to be paid him now in May, which I intreat you to pay him. I understand likewise that there be some few people in your town that meet often together to seek the Lord, and to improve each other in the knowledge and fear of God. I would have you to pay them 50*s.*, to be by them at their meeting distributed as they shall judge fit, either for the relief of their poor or otherwise, as shall be most conducible to the advancement of that good practice. I would have you likewise to pay to the hands of Cornet Jeffrey Parry, who dwells near Pwllheli, in Caernarvonshire, 5*l.*, which is to be distributed by him and those that walk in the fellowship of the Gospel in that county, in such a way as may be most for the encouragement of such as carry on the work of the Gospel there, whether it be by relieving their poor or otherwise; and 20*l.* more I would have you to pay unto such persons as shall come for it, and appointed to receive it by a note under Mr. Morgan Lloyd's hand, which is intended for the like use in other places where there is need. There will be, as I take it, 12*l.* remaining in your hands, besides the two men's pay, which I leave with you, till things be better settled or an opportunity given me to come to visit the garrison. I have no more to trouble you. Your assured friend,

"JOHN JONES."

April 28th, 1657.

N.B.—J. Jones succeeded Courtney in the governorship of Beaumaris Castle, after the death of General Mytton. Jones was also succeeded by Sir John Carter,[6] of Cymel (Kimmel), in Denbighshire, by commission from General Monk. Jones was a native of Merionethshire, and was born at a farm house called Maes y Garnedd, between Harlech and Barmouth. He was sent up to London to be settled in some trade, but was placed as a servant to a gentleman, and afterwards by some means got into some employment under Sir Thomas Middleton, Lord Mayor of London, with whom he lived many years. At the beginning of the war he sided with the rebels, and had a captain's place of foot for his first post, and his factious spirit recommending him to Cromwell's party, he was made a Member of Parliament, and an instrument in all his plots and treasons against the King; for a reward of which service he was raised through several successive employments, till he was made one of the Commissioners of Parliament for the government of Ireland; and in this post he is said to have conducted himself in a most arbitrary and oppressive manner.

From the time of Sir Rowland Villeville, *alias* Brittayne, reputed base son of Henry VII., and Constable of Beaumaris Castle, the garrison was withdrawn till the year 1641, when Thomas Cheadle, Deputy to the Earl of Dorset, then Constable, put into it men and ammunition. In 1643, Thomas Bulkeley, Esq., soon after created Lord Bulkeley, succeeded. His son, Colonel Richard Bulkeley, and several gentlemen of the country, held it for the King till June, 1646, when it surrendered on honourable terms to General Mytton, who made Captain Evans his Deputy-Governor. In 1658 the annual expense of the garrison was 1703*l.*

The following transactions of the civil wars at Chester are extracted principally from Randle Holme's[7] collection, amounting to two hundred and sixty-eight volumes in MS., now in the British Museum.

The first interruption of the peace which happened to Chester,[8] after the commencement of the war between Charles I. and his parliament, was on the 18th of August, 1642, when a drum was beaten for the parliament by the order of William Brereton; the loyal citizens, who appear to have composed by far the more numerous party, rose in consequence in arms, and

---

[6] Colonel Carter before mentioned, who succeeded Jones, married Miss Holland, the heiress of Kinmael, and, it was jocularly observed on this occasion, that the Colonel had chosen the best bit of Holland in the country. Kinmael had more anciently belonged to the Lloyds of the tribe of Marchudd; and it is recorded that one Alice Llwyd, the heiress of the place, left 20*s.* to her ghostly father, Sir John ap Ellis, the Parson of Cegidog (or St. George's), the neighbouring church.

[7] There were three Randle Holmes, mayors, and sheriffs of Chester; and it is more than probable that several of the records of that ancient city were taken away by some parties who had the charge of them at that time: hence the great scarcity of historical papers connected with this and other periods which now remain in the archives of that city.

[8] Randle Holme's Narrative of the Siege of Chester.

Sir William Brereton, who was afterwards commander-in-chief of the parliamentary forces in this county, and to whose repeated assaults the city, after a long siege, was at length compelled to yield, was, at the intercession of the Mayor (William Ince, Esq), with much difficulty saved from the fury of the populace.[9]

Not long after this the King came to Chester for the purpose of securing that city in his interest, and was staying there when Sir Richard Crane came from Prince Rupert with tidings of some successes obtained by his forces before Worcester, and presented to him the colours taken on that occasion.[1] The King and the Prince remained at the bishop's palace[2] at Chester from the 23rd to the 27th of September; when, having given orders for fortifying the city, he returned through North Wales to Shrewsbury. The corporation presented the King with 200l. and the Prince with 100l., and attended him on his road to Wrexham.[3]

The beginning of the next summer, by the "advice of Colonel Ellis and Major Sydney, and other skillful engineers, a trench was cut, and mud walls made from the Dee side without the Bars, to Dee side at the New Town; the walls repaired and lined with earth, the New Gate and the New Tower Gate mured up, divers pieces of cannon placed in convenient places, both for offence and defence; drawbridges at the North gate, East gate bridge and castle, made, and turnpikes at all outworks, as Bars, Cow Lane end, without the North gate, and at the mouth of Dee Lane end, by Little St. John's, besides several mounts, pitfalls and other devices to secure the outworks and annoy the enemy's approach to the city."[4]

The outworks are described as beginning "about the middle part of the city walls, which is between the New Tower, (looking towards Hawarden), and the North gate, and proceeding towards the stone bridge leading towards Blacon; inclining then to the north-east, and taking in the utmost limits of the further North Gate Street; then turning eastward, near Hooker's Brook, and encompassing Horn Lane, the justing croft, and all that part of the town to Boughton, from where the works were carried to the brink of the river.

Sir Nicholas Byron was sent by the King to be Colonel-General of Cheshire and Governor of Chester,[5] in which situation he appears to have continued until he was taken prisoner by the parliamentary forces between Chester and Nantwich in January, 1644;[6] it appears, nevertheless, that Sir Abraham Shipman acted as Governor of Chester in November and December, 1643. Sir William Legge, Lieutenant-General of the Ordnance, was made Governor of Chester in May, 1644, and continued in that situation in the month of August following;[7] in the latter month Colonel Marrow either succeeded Sir William Legge, or acted as Lieutenant-Governor. During the latter part of the siege Lord Byron, son of Sir Nicholas, had the government of the garrison.

On the 18th of July, Sir William Brereton came with his forces before Chester, and on the 20th made a violent assault on the works, but was repulsed.[8] Soon afterwards Spital Boughton Chapel was pulled down, and several houses and barns in the neighbourhood, to prevent their affording harbour to the besiegers. In the month of November following, Sir William Brereton being then at Hawarden, and renewing his threats against the city, the suburbs of Handbridge, Over Legh Hall, Bache Hall, and Hooker's-brook Hall were burnt down, by order of the Governor, for the same purpose.[9] In February, 1644-5, Great Boughton shared the same fate, and the hospital and chapel of St. John without the North gate was razed to the ground, a party of the parliamentary forces being then stationed at Christleton. Prince Rupert having been appointed Generalissimo of Cheshire and Lancashire, arrived at Chester on the 11th of March, being received with much joy and entertained with public feasts: in the month of June following the city works were very much improved by the Prince's engineers, the mud walls were heightened, several new mounts made, and trenches cut.[1] On the 18th of August Colonel Mavron, the Governor, received his death wound in a skirmish with a party of Sir William Brereton's forces; Prince Rupert was then in the garrison, and the next day made an unsuccessful sally with two regiments of horse.[2] In the month of October, 1644, Chester was blockaded by Sir William Brereton.[3] Prince Maurice was at Chester in the months of February and March, 1645, and caused a protestation or test to be tendered to the inhabitants. After the Prince was gone, the parliamentary army came again from Wales; and fixing their quarters so near the city as Nether Legh, made an attack upon it from Handbridge, but were repulsed. After this attack Handbridge was again burned by the citizens, together with all the

[9] Clarendon's Hist. Rebellion, 8vo, ii. p. 34.
[1] Harl. MSS. No. 2125. [2] Ibid.
[3] Randle Holme's MS. Narrative of the Siege of Chester.
[4] Clarendon, ii. pp. 146, 850. [5] Whitelock, p. 76.
[6] Harl. MSS. No. 2135, fol. 22 and 60.
[7] Narrative of the Siege of Chester.
[8] We have seen it stated that the entire moneys raised by the Commonwealth in England and Ireland from 1640 to 1659, amounted to the sum of 96,608,393l. 18s. 6d.; but we cannot vouch for its correctness.
[9] Besides these, Brewer's Hall, on the other side of the Dee;

Nun's Hall, Sir William Brereton's, Dutton Hall in Upper Northgate Street, Mr. Jolley's Hoole Hall, Mr. Banbury's, Lord Cholmondeley's Hall in John's Churchyard, and the houses of Mr. Gammul and Mr. Weeden, were all destroyed, some by the besiegers, but mostly by the besieged, for the purpose above mentioned. The cathedral and St. Thomas's Church sustained great injury, the whole damage being estimated at 200,000l. The burning of Handbridge, as Randle Holme observed, caused the ruin of some hundreds of people. Harl. MSS. No. 2155.
[1] Randle Holme's Narrative. [2] Ibid.
[3] Whitelock, ibid.

glovers' houses under the walls, and houses without Water Gate. On the 20th of May, 1645, Sir William Brereton drew off his forces from Chester, the siege was raised, and the town relieved by the King's forces.

On the 19th, Colonel Jones having drawn off a large party of his forces from the siege of Beeston Castle, marched by night to Chester, and stormed the outworks before day-break.

The attack was so sudden, that they not only possessed themselves of Boughton, but St. John's Church, the steeple of which they turned into a battery; [4] and a great part of the suburbs, with the mayor's house, (where they seized the sword and mace,) before the garrison were well prepared for their defence, but no impression was made on the city itself, before the King, who was on his march thither, when he heard of Colonel Jones's success, arrived at Chester on the 23rd of September. His Majesty lodged at Sir Francis Gammul's house, near the bridge; on the 25th the battle of Rowton Heath was fought between Sir Marmaduke Langdale, who had the command of the forces which accompanied the King for the relief of Chester, and Major Poyntz, who came to the relief of the besiegers. This battle, which proved fatal to his cause, the King had the mortification of seeing, first on the leads of the Phœnix Tower, and afterwards from St. Werburgh's Steeple, where a shot from some of the assailant's works killed an officer with whom he was conversing by his side. [5] His Majesty was attended by the mayor, Sir Francis Gammul, and Alderman Cowper; he remained that night in Chester, and on the morrow, not without some danger, escaped, with five hundred horse, to Denbigh Castle, whither he was attended by Mr. Cowper and Sir Francis Gammul.

The King, before he quitted Chester, commissioned Lord Byron to surrender the garrison if he saw no hopes of assistance within eight days; the brave governor defended it nevertheless for four months. The besiegers now repossessed themselves of the suburbs, and on the 29th made a breach in the walls near the New Gate, but were prevented from forcing an entrance; from the 1st to the 9th of October the besiegers made various unsuccessful attempts upon the walls; on that day Sir William Mainwaring and Captain Adlington were killed in the street.

"By this time," says Randle Holme, "our women were all on fire, striving through a gallant emulation to outdo our men, and will make good our yielding walls, or lose their lives to show that they dare attempt it. The work goes forward, and they, like so many valliant Amazons, do outface death and dare danger, though it lurke in every basket; seven are shot and three are slain, yet they scorn to leave their matchless undertaking, and thus they continue for two day's space, possessing the beholders that they are immortal. Our ladies, likewise, like so many exemplary goddesses, create a matchless forwardness in the meaner sorts by their dirty undertakings, that he who saw them would have thought them a hundred suns eclipsed, at leastways clouded with our loyal dust, had he been in that place, which they wipe off with such a pleasing smile, that they seem silent solicitors of a new deformity, than willing partners with that purchased honour. [6] " About this time the besiegers made a bridge of boats, which the citizens made several ineffectual attempts to destroy; the Dee mills and the water tower were several times attacked by the besiegers, and the citizens were kept in perpetual alarm by renewed assaults, and by the explosion of hand grenades, the effects of which are minutely described by Randle Holme. [7]

On the 8th of December, Colonel Booth, with the Lancashire forces, joined Sir William Brereton in his blockade of Chester, when such dispositions were made, "that the city was quite encompassed, nor was ever any place more straitly beleaguered," so that the town and garrison were obliged to feed on horses, dogs, and cats; notwithstanding this distress they refused nine several summonses, nor did they answer the tenth until they had received undoubted appearance that there was no hope of any succours.

No shot was fired after the 25th of December, when a treaty was set on foot, which was carried on for several weeks by commissioners on each side; the result was, that the city and castle were surrendered on the 3rd of February, 1646, upon terms equally honourable to the besiegers and to the besieged. Sir William Brereton immediately took possession of the castle, with its ordnance and arms, the county palatine seal, sword and records; pursuant to one of the articles of the treaty, two thousand stand of arms and five hundred and twenty head-pieces were brought into the castle court; the sword and mace were restored to the city, but, contrary to the terms of the treaty, the parliamentary army pulled down the high cross, defaced the choir of the cathedral, destroyed the organ, broke the painted glass in all the church windows, and demolished all the fonts.

---

[4] Randle Holme's Narrative.

[5] Randle Holme's Narrative.   [6] Ibid.

[7] Some of his descriptions are expressed in a very whimsical manner, ill according with the nature of the scenes which he describes. The following may serve for a specimen; speaking of the mischief caused by the bursting of some granadoes, December 10: he says :—" Two houses in Watergate-street skip joint from joint, and create an earthquake; the main posts jostle against each other while the frighted casements fly for fear; in a word, the whole

fabrick lively set forth in this metamorphosis; the grandmother, mother, and three children, are struck starke dead, and buried in the ruins of this humble edifice. About midnight they shoot seven more; one of these lights in an old man's bed chamber almost dead with age, and sends him some days sooner to his grave than perhaps was given him. The next day (December 11), six more breake in upon us, one of which persuades an old woman to bear the old man company to heaven because the times were evil." Harl. MSS., 2155, fol. 112.

Randle Holme, who was an eye-witness to the devastation, having been mayor in the year 1643, gives the following detailed account of the damage the city received:[a]

Thus the most aunchante and famouse citie of Chester in times past, but now beholde and marke the ruins of it in these present times within these few years, viz., from 1643—1645, the particular demolitions of it now most grievous to the spectators, and more woefull to the inhabitants thereof.

Imprimis. Without the barrs of the chapelle of Spittle, with all the houses, and gardens, and edifices there.

Item. All the houses, barnes, and buildings, near the Barrs, with Great Boughton and Christleton.

Item. In the Forgate-street, Cow-lane, St. John's-lane, with other houses in the same street, all burnt to the ground.

Item. Without the Forgate, from the said gate to the last house, Jolly's Hall, all burnt and consumed to the ground, with all the lanes in the same, with the chappelle of Little St. John, not to be found.

Item. From the Dee Bridge, over the water, all that long street called Handbridge, with all the lanes, barnes, and buildings about it, ruinated to the ground.

Item. All the Glovers' houses under the walles of the citie, all pulled down to the ground.

Item. All the buildings and houses at the Watergate, upon the Roode, pulled down to the ground.

Item. Besides all the famous houses of gentlemen in the same citie, and near unto adjoining, viz., the Bashe Hall, Mr. Whitbie's, those of Sir William Brereton, Sir Randal Crewe, Sir Thomas Smith, Bretton Hall, (and others which he enumerates). The Water-tower, the mills, and other property destroyed; the Lord Cholmondeley's Hall, in St. John's Churchyard, with the ruins of the said church.

Item. The destruction of divers of the houses in the citie, with granadoes too tedious to recite.

Item. The ruins of stalls, porticos, doors, trees, and barns, in divers lanes and places in the citie.

Item. The destroying of the Bishop's Palace, with stables in the barne-yard, and the ruins of the great church.

Item. The drawing dry of the citie stocks, plates, rents, and collections, not knowne; all which losses, charges, and demolishments, in opinion of most, will amount to two hundred thousand pounds at the least, so far hath the God of Heaven humbled this citie.

Immediately after the surrender of Chester, orders were issued by the Parliament, for its future regulations. One of the aldermen was appointed mayor, and the sword and mace were restored to the citizens; but, contrary to the 10th article of the treaty, which enacted, that "no church within the city, or evidence or writings, belonging to the same, shall be defaced," the bigotry of the Parliamentary forces led them to pull down the high cross, break the stained glass, and remove the fonts from most of the churches, and also to injure the organ and other parts of the cathedral.

Upon the execution of Charles I., his son was proclaimed traitor, at the principal public places in Chester. The Royal arms were removed from the County Hall, &c., by Bradshaw, Chief Justice of Chester, and two years afterwards the Bishop's Palace, with all the furniture, were sold for 1059l.

CHARLES II., having been invited to Scotland by the Presbyterians, was crowned at Scone, January 1st, 1651.[b]

We do not hear of this monarch ever having been in Wales in the capacity of King, but it would appear that he was grateful to the loyal inhabitants of that country for the great assistance they afforded his father. The following is a list of the gentry of North and South Wales who were deemed "fit and qualified to be made Knights of the Royal Oak," with the value of their estates, A.D. 1660, taken from a manuscript of Peter le Neve, Esq. This order was intended by King Charles II. as a reward to several of his followers, and the knights of it were to wear a silver medal, with a devise of the King in the oak, pendant to a ribbon, about their necks: but it was thought proper to lay it aside, least it might create heats and animosities, and open those wounds afresh, which at that time were thought prudent should be healed; and, as no list of them was ever published, we thought such a curiosity would be acceptable to the public, though not immediately relating to the order of baronets.

---

[a] MS. in the British Museum.

[b] "On this occasion a most extraordinary sermon was preached by 'Master Robert Douglas, minister at Edinburgh, moderator of the General Assembly, from 2 Kings xi., verses, 12—17.' The preacher delivered a fierce philippic against the young King's father and mother, the latter of whom he compared to the wicked Athaliah. When the ceremony was concluded, 'the minister spoke to him a word of exhortation;' that is to say, a long oration, scarcely less offensive than the sermon."

KNIGHTS OF THE ROYAL OAK.[1]

Anglesey.

John Robinson, Esq.	£800[2]
William Bould, Esq.	1000
Thomas Wood, Esq.	600
— Bodden, Esq.	1000
Pierce Lloyd, Esq.	1000

Brecknock.

Richard Gwynn, Esq.	600
Wilbourne Williams, Esq.	600
John Jefferys, Esq.	600
Walter Vaughan, Esq.	700

Cardigan.

John Jones, Esq.	800
Edward Vaughan, Esq.	1000
Thomas Jones, Esq.	600
Reynold Jenkins, Esq.	700
James Lewis, Esq.	700

Carmarthen.

— Vaughan, Esq.	1000
Philip Vaughan, Esq.	600
Henry Maunsell, Esq.	700
Rewland Gwynn, Esq.	800
Charles Vaughan, Esq.	600
William Gwynn, Esq.	700
Nicholas Williams, Esq.	1000
Richard Gwynn, Esq.	700

Carnarvon.

Sir John Owen's heire	1500

Denbigh.

Charles Salisburie, Esq.	1300
Eubal Thelwall, Esq.	600
Foulke Middleton, Esq.	600
John Wynn, Esq.	600
Sir Thomas Middleton, Knt. (of Chirk Castle, of Westminster after, spent most of his estate)	600
Bevis Lloyd, Esq.	600
John Lloyd, Esq.	800

Flintshire.

Sir Roger Mostyn, Knt. of Mostyn, Bart.	4000
Sir Edward Mostyn, Knt.	1500
— Salisbury, of Bachegrag, Esq.	600
Robert Davis, Esq.	2000
John Puliston, Esq.	2500
John Hanmer, Knt. Bart.	3000
William Hanmer, Esq.	1500

Glamorganshire.

Sir — Esterlinge, Knt.	£2000
Herbert Evans, Esq.	1500
David Jenkins, Esq.	1500
Thomas Mathews, Esq.	1100
William Bassett, Esq.	800
William Herbert, Esq.	1000
Edmund Lewis, Esq.	800
David Mathews, Esq.	1000

Merioneth.

William Salisbury, Esq.	800
William Price, Esq.	1500
William Vaughan, Esq.	1200
Howell Vaughan, Esq.	800
— Anwyl, of Parke, Esq.	1500
Lewis Owen, Esq.	600
John Lloyd, Esq.	600

Monmouth.

William Morgan, Esq.	4000
William Jones, of Lanarthe, Esq.	1000
Thomas Lewis, Esq.	1000
Charles Vaughan, Esq.	800
Walter Rumsey, Esq.	600
William Jones, of Lantrisent, Esq.	600
— Milbourne, Esq.	800

Montgomery.

John Pugh, Esq.	1000
— Owen, Esq. of Ruserton	1000
— Blaney, Esq.	1000
Roger Lloyd, Esq.	800
Richard Owen, Esq.	800
Richard Herbert, Esq.	700
Sir Edward Lloyd	1200
Edmund Wareinge, Esq.	700

Pembrokeshire.

Tho. Langhorne, Esq.	800
Lewis Wogan, Esq.	1000
Hugh Bowen, Esq.	600
Essex Merricke, Esq.	600
Sir John Lort, Knt. (Bart. after)	2000

Radnorshire.

George Gwynn, Esq.	1500
Evan Davies, Esq.	600
— Price, Esq.	1000

In the Cambrian Quarterly Magazine there are some very interesting accounts of these families by our late learned and much respected friend, the Rev. Walter Davies, author of " Surveys of North and South Wales," and one of the distinguished Chaired Bards of Wales. He was one of those who gave a new life and interest to the poetical genius of his country, in the re-establishment of the Eisteddfodau.

By permission of Sir R. Williams Bulkeley, Bart., who in the handsomest manner has given us access to a valuable collection of MSS. connected with the history of Wales, in his possession at Baron Hill, we are enabled to publish the following highly curious document[3] with respect to the destruction of Caernarvon

[1] The original orthography is used in the list.
[2] At this period, 4000l. would be equal to about 18000l. of the present day, the value of money having increased nearly 450 per cent.
[3] Archæologia Cambrensis.

Castle. It will be seen by it that the first time when any extensive injury was done in cool blood to that magnificent monument of the first Edward's military skill and taste, was the comparatively peaceful epoch of the Restoration; and that the perpetrator of the Vandalism was no other than King Charles II. Doubtless his Majesty had never seen the castle, or, we think, any man, even of the coldest heart, would have hesitated ere he touched a stone of so grand a building; and, from the names mentioned in the warrant, we are inclined to suspect that the measure was suggested to the royal mind by persons who had pecuniary motives for giving such bad advice. When such a warrant as this had been issued, we may well be surprised that any portion of the castle, still more of the town walls, should now be standing; and we should be very curious to know what were the local circumstances that occurred to hinder the royal mandate from taking full effect. Possibly some light might be thrown upon this subject by the archives of the town of Caernarvon. We now cease to wonder at the needy and profligate Earl of Conwy following his royal master's example, and dismantling Conwy Castle for the sake of the timber and lead, just as a corrupt corporation of Ludlow, at a later period, did their best to ruin what they ought to have preserved at all cost and hazard.

We transcribe this warrant literally. The King's name is in his own hand-writing; a seal, formerly at the left hand upper corner of the paper, has been removed. The document is endorsed in a hand of the same date, " Demolishing of Caernarvon Castle."

CHARLES R.

WHEREAS for good causes & consideracõns us thereunto moving, We have resolved & determined that the Castle and Town-Wall of Our Town of Caernarvon shall be forthwith dismantled & demolished, We do therefore hereby impower, authorise, & require you or either of you, to take care that the same be dismantled and demolished accordingly at the charge of the Country, so as they may be made untenable for the future; And you are to dispose of and improve the materialls that belong unto the same towards the defraying of the said charge which the Country shall be at in demolishing the same. And for so doing this shall be your sufficient Warrant & discharge in that behalf. Given at our Court at Whitehall, the 24th day of October, 1660, in the twelfth year of our Reigne.

By his Maᵗⁱᵉˢ Comãand,

WILL. MORICE.

To Our Trusty & Wellbeloved Sir John Carter Knt. & William Griffiths of Llyn, Esqʳ; or to either of them; *and* in their absence to Griffiths Bordurda, Esqʳ.

JAMES THE SECOND[4] succeeded to the throne on the death of his brother Charles II. His attachment to the Catholic religion had made him unpopular with the great majority of his subjects, and he had not been long on the throne when a formidable rebellion broke out under the Duke of Monmouth, who claimed to be heir to the crown. The rebellion was after a little time suppressed, and a series of the most barbarous executions followed.

These cruelties still further increased the King's unpopularity; and he, in order to strengthen his hands, and gain over as many friends as he could throughout the country, determined to make a tour through various parts of the kingdom. He visited Ludlow on the 23rd of August, 1687, on his way to Shrewsbury,[5] and took up his residence at the castle, where he was magnificently entertained; at least, as much so as time and circumstances would permit; but the sovereign was so rapid in his movements, that time was not allowed for all the preparations he might otherwise have expected; added to which his popularity was on the decline. James II. paid a visit to the town of Shrewsbury, and kept his court at the council-house on the 24th of August, 1687. Those sentiments of loyal attachment, for

[4] " James's coronation, April 23, 1685, was celebrated with so much splendour, that it rendered him for a considerable time popular in London. The most remarkable anecdote connected with the solemnity is, that on the King's return from the Abbey, the crown tottered upon his head, and would have fallen off, had not the Honourable Henry Sidney supported it, saying, " This is not the first time our family have supported the crown."—*Coronation Anecdotes.*

[5] The following appears to have been his Majesty's route on this occasion : The King left Windsor on the 16th, went first to Portsmouth, from hence to Bath, and then through Gloucester, Worcester, Ludlow, Shrewsbury, and Whitchurch to Chester.

which Shrewsbury has ever been conspicuous, burst forth on this occasion with chivalrous enthusiasm. They blazed forth in bonfires and illuminations; torrents of wine are said to have run literally through the streets.

A.D. 1687.—In the month of August, His Majesty made his entrance into the city of Chester. The following particulars of this visit are extracted from Thomas Cartwright's,' then Bishop of Chester, own diary, lately published by the Camden Society:—

27th.—His Majesty came to the palace of Chester about four in the afternoon. I met him at the palace gates, attended by the Dean and Prebends, and about forty more of the clergy, and afterwards introduced them to kiss his hand; Mr. Dean making an excellent speech to him. Then his Majesty went and viewed the choir; after that the castle, to which he walked; and then returned to supper, and I waited at his cushion till I saw him in bed.

James the Second, Bishop Cartwright, and William Penn, the Quaker, taking leave of each other at the western door of Chester Cathedral.

28th.—I was at his Majesty's levée, from whence at 9 o'clock I attended him into the choir, where he healed three hundred and fifty persons. After which he went to his devotions in the Shire Hall, and Mr. Penn' held forth in the Tennis Court, and I preached in the cathedral. His Majesty returned to dinner, on whom I attended, having introduced the Mayor and Recorder of Wigan, to whom he recommended their two former members, and also the Mayors of Preston and Lancaster; then I dined

⁶ Bishop Burnet gives the following account of Thomas Cartwright, Bishop of Chester : " The two other bishopricks were less considerable ; so they resolved to fill them with the two worst men that could be found out. Cartwright was promoted to Chester. He was a man of good capacity, and had some progress in learning : he was ambitious and servile, cruel and boisterous ; and by the great liberties he allowed himself, he fell under much scandal of the worst sort. He set himself long to raise the King's authority above law, which he said was the only method of government, to which Kings might submit as they pleased ; but their authority was from God, absolute and superior to law, which they might exert as oft as they found it necessary, for the ends of government. So he was looked upon as a man that would more effectually advance the designs of popery, than if he should turn over to it. And, indeed, bad as he was, he never made that step in the most desperate of his affairs."— *History of our own Times,* vol. iii. p. 136.

⁷ " This celebrated Quaker, who was much about the King at this time, attended him in his progress, and when at Chester he held forth in the open air, as the bishop relates."—*Hunter's Notes.*

with my lord president, and went to evening prayers, as his Majesty did again to the castle. After his Majesty had gone to bed, I supped with my Lord Feversham in his chamber, having entertained Mr. William Stevens, Mr. Ware, and the Bishop of Man, in the study.

29th.—I was at the King's levée at six in the morning; brought my Lord Feversham, Lord Churchill, and Lord Tyrconnell to drink coffee in the study; I then attended his Majesty to his horse half an hour before seven, who went to heal and dine at Holywell;[a] from whence he returned to Chester at five at night, and took me into his closet for half an hour, where I gave him an account of what he had entrusted with me, which he graciously accepted, and assured me I should hear from my Lord President before he called a parliament, and have sufficient instructions how to serve him. I recommended the recorder, Mr. Livesdy, to him, as a person fit to serve him in the next parliament; and Mr. Dean, for better encouragement, because he was daily affronted for his zeal in his service by the Whigs, and told him of my Lord Cl's letter. I waited on him at supper, and afterwards supped with my Lord Castlehaven, and Mr. Rider, and Mr. Griffiths. Mr. Williams and his son dined with me.

The following very laughable anecdote concerning the King is related by Messrs. Owen and Blakeway, the Salop historians, relative to this royal tour through that county. It appears that the loyal and good people of S hrewsbury, being anxious to know in what state or manner the King had been received at Gloucester and Worcester, dispatched two gentlemen to make the necessary inquiries; when the corporation came to the resolution that the conduits should run with wine on the day of his Majesty's entrance. The officers of this corporation met under the market-house for the purpose of rehearsing their parts. This was rendered necessary, from the timidity and caution of some of the proposed speakers, and from some blunders made by other municipal officers on like occasion, particularly by the Mayor of Winchester, who being remarkably illiterate, dull, and incapable of reading or remembering an address, "it was settled therefore," says the story, "that the Recorder should stand behind him to set him right if he happened to be out." When they were ushered into the royal presence, and the chief magistrate was about to commence his harangue, as he appeared somewhat sheepish and embarrassed, his friendly monitor whispered in his ear, "Hold up your head, sir, and look like a man." Mistaking this for the beginning of his speech, he boldly stared the King in the face, and audibly repeated, "*Hold up your head, sir, and look like a man.*" The Recorder chagrined, again whispered, "What the D——l do you mean?"

[a] St. Winifred's Well is one of the most remarkable springs in the kingdom, and to this day continues to excite surprise and curiosity. The legend told of this well is singular and curious:—In the seventh century lived a vestal, named Winifred; her father's name was Thewith, a powerful lord over the parts where Holywell now stands; her mother's Wenlo, sister to St. Beuno. Beuno was of a pious disposition; he built a church and founded a convent at Clynog, in Caernarvonshire, after which he repaired to his relations to Holywell, obtained from his brother-in-law the spot on which stands the present church-yard, erected on it a church, and undertook the care of his niece Winifred. Caradog, son of King Alen, fascinated with the beauty of Winifred, made repeated overtures to her, which were as repeatedly rejected. Caradog, enraged, pursued her, drew his sabre, and cut off her head. The severed head rolled down the hill and stopped at the bottom. Beuno, being apprised of the act, ran to the head, took it up, carried it to the corpse, and miraculously reunited it to the body! On this being effected, a stream burst forth with wonderful impetuosity from the spot where the head rested. It is said that the valley through which the stream runs was previously called *Sychnant*, from its dryness, and that then it assumed the name of Fullbrook; that the moss on the sides of the Well miraculously diffuses an odoriferous scent; that the blood stained the stones at the bottom of the Well, which have, at certain periods, colours different from their natural ones; that the town is called Holywell, in consequence of this miracle, and that the water is sanative through divine intercession alone. One

circumstance asserted of this spring, which to some may seem incredible, may at any time be demonstrated to the curious. By the gauge, the basin will hold about two hundred and forty tons of water, which, when emptied, is filled again in less than two minutes. The experiment was tried for a wager, on Tuesday, July 12th, 1731: Mr. Price, the rector of Holywell, Mr. Williams, Mr. Wynne, Dr. Taylor, and several other gentlemen, were present; when, to the surprise of the company, the Well filled in less than two minutes, which proves that St. Winifred's spring rises more than one hundred tons of water in a minute. The basin is six feet deep, and yet the water is so clear that a pin may be seen at the bottom.

St. Winifred died in Gwytherin, in Denbighshire, where her bones rested till the reign of King Stephen; when, after divine admonition, they were surrendered to the Abbey of St. Peter and St. Paul, at Shrewsbury. The memory of these two great events is celebrated, that of her decapitation, on the 22nd of June, and that of her translation on the 3rd of November. After the death of St. Winifred, her sanctity was shown by numerous miracles. The waters are almost as sanative as those of the Pool of *Bethesda*: all infirmities incident to the human body meet with relief by bathing in them. The votive crutches, the barrow, and other proofs of cures, remain to this moment as evidences pendant over the Well.

"Fair life and precious health
Adorn these living springs:
Without them what's all wealth
Of Princes, Lords, and Kings?"

This was likewise repeated with proper emphasis. The Recorder, out of all patience, muttered, " By heavens ! sir, you will ruin us all." *His worship still taking this to be a continuance of his speech, and still staring his Majesty full in the face, and, with a still louder voice, repeated, " By heavens ! sir, you will ruin us all."* James, conscious how little his measures were approved by some of his subjects, now rose in much anger, but being informed of the cause of this rough address, passed it off with a smile.

King James II. payed a visit to St. Winifred's Well on the 29th of August, 1686. " The King," says Bishop Cartwright, " went to heal and dine at Holywell, and received as a reward a present of the very shift in which his great grandmother, Mary Stuart, lost her head." This monarch gave in the course of his Progress, as marks of his favour, golden rings with his hair plaited beneath a crystal. Mr. Pennant saw one which he had bestowed on a Roman Catholic priest of a neighbouring family.

St. Winifred's Well, Holywell. James the Second healing persons afflicted with the King's evil.

30th.—I was at his Majesty's levée, and obtained a promise from him to make Mr. John Warburton, M.A. of Brasen Nose, fellowship in All Souls ; after that he had mass in the presence chamber, where he eat. From thence I attended him to the choir, where he healed four hundred and fifty people ; from thence to the Pent House, where he breakfasted under a stall, and from thence took horse about ten of the clock ; from whence I returned to prayers, having taken leave of the Lord Tyrconnell. The King told me that he had given a severe reprimand to the governor for not promoting the address, and that he said it would not pass; to which the King replied, " Let me know what alderman opposed, and I will turn him out," whereas in truth he never showed it to them at all. The King commanded me to enquire out a chapel in the city where it might be best spared, and give notice of it to my Lord Sunderland, to whom I sent my coach to go as far as Whitechurch. William Pen gave me a visit, and promised to remember William Fanshaw.

When his Majesty was at Chester, he sent for Sir Thomas Grosvenor, who was at that time M.P. for Chester, when he promised him in a private audience, that if he, Sir Thomas, would support in the House the bill for the repeal of the penal laws against the papists, and the " Test Act," *that he would give him a regiment and a peerage ; but he refused, preferring the religion and liberty of his country to all the honour and power, so likely at the same time to be attended with popery and slavery.*

" The following presents," says Bishop Cartwright, " were sent to me when the King was at Chester :— Sir Thomas Delves sent me a stag, which I gave half to the King, and half to the Lord President; Lord Brandon, half a buck ; Colonel Howard, half a buck ; Lord Molineux, one buck ; Sir Thomas Stanley of Alderley, half a buck ; Sir John Crewe, six couple rabbits and twelve pigeons ; Mr. Tilsley, a buck ; and fruit from Colonel Whitley's. The King left 20*l.* for the house servants."

The royal family of the Stuarts stands unprecedented in the history of this country for their unfortunate end, as the following account will testify :—

<hr>

[9] Hunter's Notes to Bishop Cartwright's Diary.

The first of the Scottish kings, whose name was James, after having been eighteen years a prisoner in England, was assassinated with his wife, by his own subjects. James II. (his son) was killed at the age of twenty-nine, in fighting against the English. James III. was thrown into prison by his people, and afterwards perished in a battle against the revolters. James IV. was defeated and slain. Mary Stuart, his granddaughter, driven from her throne, became a fugitive in England, and after having languished eighteen years in confinement, was condemned to die by Engligh judges, and beheaded.

Charles I., (grandson of Mary,) King of England and Scotland, sold by the Scotch, was adjudged to death by the English, and perished on the scaffold. James, his son, the seventh of the name in Scotland, and the second in England, was driven from his three kingdoms, and, to add to his misfortunes, even the legitimacy of his son was disputed.[1] The attempt of James II.'s son to ascend the throne of his ancestors was productive only of the death of his friends by the hand of the executioner. If anything can justify those who believe in an irresistible fatality, it is the continued misfortunes that persecuted the House of Stuart for the space of three hundred years.

WILLIAM AND MARY.—For the first time in England both the King and the Queen were crowned as sovereigns.[2] It does not appear that either of these monarchs ever visited Wales; but the King, in the year 1689, passed through Cheshire on his way to Ireland. On the 4th of March he embarked with his army at Hoylake, near Chester. He arrived at Kinsale on the 12th, and entered Dublin on the 24th. A few years ago, as one William Hughes, stonemason, was removing some rubbish in search of a stone quarry, on Windle Hill, near Parkgate, the instrument he was using struck against a cask, which, we are informed, was found to contain coins of William III. to the amount of 8000l. King William's army is known to have been stationed there for several weeks on his expedition to Ireland. It is therefore surmised that some of his commissioners had deposited the money at that place, and were prevented by death from removing it.

In 1696, King William III. granted a patent, under the great seal, to William Earl of Portland, for the lordships of Denbigh, Bromfield, and Yale.[3] Some of the Welsh representatives objecting to such a grant, which encroached upon the properties and privileges of the subject, disclosed their grievances to the honourable House of Commons, who after some consideration, resolved (*nemine contradicente*) that a petition should be presented to his Majesty by the body of the whole house, to request him to recall his grant to the said Earl of Portland, which was accordingly done in the following manner:—

"MAY IT PLEASE YOUR MOST EXCELLENT MAJESTY,—We, your Majesty's most dutiful and loyal subjects, the knights, citizens, and burgesses in Parliament assembled, humbly lay before your Majesty, that whereas there is a grant passing to William Earl of Portland, and his heirs of the manors of Denbigh, Bromfield, and Yale, and divers other land in the Principality of Wales, together with estates of inheritance enjoyed by your Majesty's subjects by virtue of ancient grants from the crown:

"That the said manors, with large and extensive royalties, powers, and jurisdictions to the same

---

[1] It was said that James II 's son was carried in a warming-pan into Queen Mary's bed-chamber, and afterwards imposed upon the nation as the son of her Majesty and King James—a story long ago consigned to the credit of those usually told in the nursery. But, thank God, the title of the present reigning successor to the crown is not founded upon the certainty or uncertainty of the birth of James II.'s son. It stands upon a much firmer foundation—a succession established by the consent of the people, confirmed by an Act of Parliament, and [supported by the warm attachment and affection of her subjects.

[2] The ceremonial was very stately and cold; it took place on the 11th of April, 1689, the Bishop of London officiating instead of the Archbishop of Canterbury (Sancroft), who scrupled to place the crown upon the head of sovereigns who claimed it by a parliamentary title, and not by hereditary descent, and what he called 'divine right.'"—*Coronation Anecdotes.*

[3] The lordship of Denbigh, together with the forests, as they are legally deemed, of Bromfield and Yale, still form a part of the landed possessions belonging to the crown. What the rights of the lordship were in remote times might be discovered by any one who could decipher an ancient document in the British Museum, entitled "Extenta Castri et honoris de Denbigh facta per Hugon deme Beckele," 8 Edward III. (1334) Harl. Miscel. 3622. Mr. Gough says, "Mr. J. Rawlinson had a fine copy of this, formerly belonging to Dudley, Earl of Leicester."

belonging, are of great concern to your Majesty and the crown of this realm, and that the same have been usually annexed to the Principality of Wales, and settled onthe Princes of Wales for their support ; and that a great number of your Majesty's subjects, in those parts, hold their estates by royal tenure, under great and valuable compositions, rents, royal payments, and services to the crown and Princes of Wales, and have by such tenures great dependance on your Majesty and the crown of England, and have enjoyed great privileges and advantages with their estates under such tenure.

"We, therefore, most humbly beseech your Majesty to put a stop to the passing of this grant to the Earl of Portland, of the said manors and lands, and that the same may not be disposed from the Crown, but by consent of Parliament."

This caused warm debates in Parliament on resisting these claims, the particulars of which may be read in Rapin and other English historians. In fine the grant was withdrawn in order to allay the ferment. Baron Price, that able and upright judge, afterwards Justice of the Common Pleas, was one of the most determined opponents to the grant of the great Welsh lordships by King William III. to the Earl of Portland. His famous speech in the House of Commons against it, called "Gloria Cambria," or the speech of the "Bold Briton against a Dutch Prince of Wales,"[4] will ever testify to his love of country ; and his speedy promotion by King William does equal credit to his Majesty and Mr. Price ; since the former, however grievous to him might be the opposition to his will, could not be induced by any consideration to permit his subjects to lose the benefit of a magistrate so able and so honest as he knew our countryman to be. The Baron was ably supported by Sir William Williams, Sir Roger Puleston, and Sir Robert Cotton. Lord Godolphin, and other Lords of the Treasury, after hearing their arguments, stated, "You have offered many weighty reasons, and we shall represent them to his Majesty."

The King shortly afterwards sent the following answer to the Commons, in reply to the memorial against his grant of the lordship of Denbigh to his favourite, the Earl of Portland :—

"Gentlemen,—I have a kindness for my Lord Portland, which he has deserved of me, by long and faithful services, but I should not have given him these lands if I had imagined the House of Commons could have been concerned. I will, therefore, recall the grant, and find some other way of showing my favour to him.[5]

"William Rex."

In this reign an estate in Caernarvonshire changed hands in a somewhat unusual manner. Sir William Williams, Bart., of Vaynol, who though married, led a most profligate life, and had no issue, in a drunken fit devised his large property to King William. After Sir William's death, Mr. Smith, of Tedworth in Hampshire, took possession of it by virtue of a grant to his ancestor, a commissioner of the Salt Office ; and at present the estate, to the amount of 4000l., independent of the vast slate quarries at Llanberis, which brings in a princely income, is enjoyed by his great nephew, Thomas Assheton Smith, Esq.

On the 9th of September, 1682, the Duke of Monmouth, the natural and favourite son of Charles II., came to Chester. "He was accompanied by a train of one hundred horse. The inhabitants went out of the city to welcome him and salute him with loud acclamations of 'God save the Protestant Duke!' On entering the city he alighted at the mayor's house, where he was received by his worship and the recorder, Mr. W. Williams, the late Speaker of the House of Commons. At night his Grace supped at the Feathers Inn ; the streets were illuminated with flambeaux and bonfires, and the bells of the different churches loudly proclaimed his welcome. Next Sunday the mayor and corporation went with him to church, the mayor and sword-bearer walking immediately before him. The sermon was preached by the Rev. Dr. Fogge, which much galled the Duke's enemies, the papists, non-jurors, &c., so much so that they repented that he did not pray for the queen ; he was attended to the Feathers Hotel by the mayor, &c., who, in the evening, again conducted him to the cathedral. He then went to the mayor's house, attended by so

---

[4] See Vol. xi. of Lord Somer's Tracts ; Sir Walter Scott's edition.   [5] Wynne's History of Wales, p. 303.

great a crowd as almost to render the streets impassable. Mrs. Mayoress having been lately brought to bed, the child was that evening christened Henrietta, his Grace being godfather. On the Monday the Duke, followed by a numerous suite of gentry, went to Wallasey races (Wirral) where he was received with every testimony of joy. He there rode his own horse, won the plate, and presented it to his goddaughter the same evening.[6] The populace seem to have evinced a singular mode of showing their respect for the Duke, as they pelted the doors of the houses of gentlemen in the city with stones, and otherwise damaged the same; they furiously forced the doors of the cathedral, and destroyed most of the painted glass, burst open the little vestries and cupboards, where were the surplices and hoods belonging to the clergy, which they rent to rags, and beat to pieces the baptismal font, pulled down some monuments, attempted to demolish the organ, committed other most enormous outrages, published a most seditious placard, and they did not cease till several of the Duke's attendants were arrested, and security taken for their appearance and good behaviour, notwithstanding the assertion of several writers that these disturbances were very trifling, that the city presented a vast field of joy, alloyed only by the puerile attempts of the disaffected of the Church establishment, who beat the boys in the streets and put out the bonfires: they were, however, soon obliged to desist.[7] It is evident that they must have been of considerable importance, for, on the 17th of September, the grand jury of the county presented, that security of the peace be demanded from all concerned in promoting the aforesaid seditious address, or in aiding the riotous reception of the Duke of Monmouth and his confederates, and all frequenters of conventicles, and harbourers or countenancers of any non-conformist ministers, and particularly from the four baronets, Mainwaring, Cotton, Aston, and Bellot, and about sixty other parties, many of high respectability, amongst whom were Whitmore of Wellaston, Glegg of Gayton, and others, at or near to whose residences the Duke had been during his short sojourn at Wirrall."

We do not find that either of the next three monarchs were ever in Wales, nor even on the Borders.

ANNE was crowned April 23rd, 1702; her husband, Prince George of Denmark, was present, but took no prominent part in the ceremony. The Queen gave the kiss of peace to the archbishop and the other prelates; but when the temporal peers did their homage, they only seemingly kissed her majesty's left cheek. As the parliament was sitting, galleries were provided for members of the House of Commons, both in the Hall and the Abbey, and a sumptuous dinner was prepared for them in the Exchequer Chamber.[8]

[6] Observations on the landed revenues of the Crown, pp. 114, 122.   [7] Henshall, p. 165.   [8] Coronation Anecdotes.

HOUSE OF HANOVER.

EORGE THE FIRST was crowned at Westminster, October 20th, 1714, with the usual solemnities. The King did not understand English, and few of those around him could speak German, so that the ceremonies had to be explained to his majesty in such Latin as those near him could command: this gave rise to the popular jest, that much *bad language* had passed between the King and his ministers on the day of the coronation.[1]

GEORGE THE SECOND and Queen Caroline were crowned, October 11th, 1727, with the usual solemnities, but nothing occurred to give any variety or interest to the scene.

GEORGE THE THIRD and QUEEN CHARLOTTE were crowned the 22nd of September, 1761.[2]

We cannot learn that this great monarch ever visited Wales or the Border Counties, but he showed his affectionate care for his loyal subjects in those parts by the appointment of his brother, the Duke of Gloucester, to be Governor of Chester and North Wales, during the commencement of the French war. This Prince, with his son Prince William Frederick, visited the ancient and loyal City of Chester, on military duty, on the 8th of August, 1803. Their Royal Highnesses left Liverpool that morning, and were met at Backford by the First Troop of Western Cheshire Volunteer Cavalry, who escorted them through this City to the Roodee, where they arrived at twelve o'clock, and were received by the Royal Chester Volunteers with presented arms; they then inspected the corps by passing down and up the line; and having taken their station in front, the regiment passed in review, first in slow, and then in quick time; the regiment then wheeled into line and advancing a few paces, the review finished by a general salute. Their Royal Highnesses, in the most handsome manner, complimented Colonel Barnston on the steadiness, military appearance, and discipline of the corps.

General Burton, arrived on the ground about nine o'clock, and was received in line by a general

---

[1] Coronation Anecdotes.

[2] In the "Gentleman's Magazine" for 1764, p. 28, is an extract from a letter addressed to the Duke of Devonshire, which contains the following singular anecdote:—"The young Pretender himself was in Westminster Hall during the coronation, and in town two or three days before and after it, under the name of Mr. Brown. A gentleman told me so, who saw him there, and who whispered in his ear, 'Your Royal Highness is the last of all mortals whom I should expect to see here.' 'It was curiosity that led me,' said the other: 'but I assure you,' added he, 'that the person who is the cause of all this pomp and magnificence is the man I envy the least!' When the champion cast down his gauntlet for the last time, a white glove fell from one of the spectators, who was in an elevated situation; on its being handed to the champion, he demanded ' Who was his fair foe ?' The glove was said to have been thrown by the young cavalier, who was present in female attire."

salute; after reviewing them in this position, the regiment was thrown into open column, and marched past the General in ordinary and quick time; they were then wheeled into line, and the review finished with another general salute. The General expressed in the warmest terms to Colonel Barnston his approbation of the very steady and soldierlike appearance of the regiment, which would have done honour to the most veteran corps under the crown. When the review was over, they were mustered and inspected by Lieutenant-Colonel Cuyler, the inspecting field-officer for this district; after which fifty-six waggons and one cart, which were to convey them in case of invasion, were also mustered and inspected, having previously the seats slung across them for the accommodation of the troops; in which the regiment proceeded through the city to Vicker's-cross, and returned through Littleton and Christleton to Foregate-street, where they got out, and were dismissed.' The Roodee was crowded with beauty and fashion, as were the windows of the streets through which they passed, all eager to behold a band of patriots in which the fair of the city had such an interest, thus come forward in the defence of their country; and we could proudly boast that should the Usurper of France and his minions have ever dared to set their unhallowed feet on this land of freedom, the Royal Chester Volunteers would have been the foremost in repelling them, or, as the Bard of Snowdon sang, " fill one great and glorious grave."

After the review, their Royal Highnesses and suite, at the invitation of the Bishop, partook of an elegant cold collation at the palace, to which place they were escorted as before, where his Royal Highness the Duke of Gloucester graciously received an address from the Lord Bishop, the Dean and Chapter, and the Clergy of the City.

The Mayor, Aldermen, Sheriffs, and Common Council, then delivered an address, which his Royal Highness received with the utmost affability and condescension, and graciously accepted the freedom of the city.

The Prince replied in a speech of considerable length, and in a style most engaging, eloquent, and energetic. His Royal Highness expressed his extreme satisfaction on being placed over a district where loyalty and patriotism so universally prevailed, and in terms of the highest encomium complimented the inhabitants of the city on their known firm attachment to their King and Constitution at all times, more particularly as displayed at that momentous crisis. The Prince was graciously pleased to accept of the freedom of the city, and after conversing with the Mayor and several other members of the Corporation, for some time, with the most pleasing affability, they withdrew under a deep and lasting impression of his Royal Highness's amiable manners and condescension.

His Royal Highness on Saturday in the forenoon, took a view of the city, and in the afternoon dined with Colonel Barnston. On Sunday morning, his Royal Highness inspected the Volunteers on the Roodee, and accompanied them to the Cathedral, where a most impressive discourse was delivered by the Lord Bishop—with whom the Prince retired to dine privately, at his lordship's seat at Christleton.

On Monday evening, his Royal Highness Prince William of Gloucester arrived at Mold, and the following morning, after inspecting, with evident satisfaction, the Volunteers of the town, six hundred in number, he set off on a visit to Sir W. W. Wynn, Bart., at Wynnstay.—On Wednesday, his Royal Highness honoured the Wrexham Gentlemen and Yeomanry Cavalry with an inspection, and afterwards retired with their commander, Sir Foster Cunliffe, Bart., from whose seat his Royal Highness returned to Chester. The Chester corps of Volunteers were reviewed on the succeeding day by this august personage, and on Sunday he took his departure for Liverpool, the head-quarters of the district.

' The officers in the evening dined together at the Hotel, when Colonel Barnston, in the name of the officers, presented an elegant silver vase, embellished with the arms of the regiment on one side, and on the other with an appropriate inscription, to Capt. Henderson, for the services he had rendered the corps as Adjutant; and another, equally elegant, to Lieut. Samuel Humphryes, as a small testimony of the sense they entertained for the faithful discharge of his duty as secretary; Mr. Thomas Taylor, sergeant-major, was likewise presented with two silver goblets, and Mr. Howell, second sergeant, with one, for their meritorious services, when embodied at Ellesmere and Oswestry.

On Sunday evening, his Royal Highness Prince William Frederick arrived at Lleweny Hall, the seat of the Right Hon. Lord Viscount Kirkwall, where his Royal Highness was entertained with the most splendid hospitality. On the following morning, the Aldermen, Bailiffs, and capital Burgesses of the Borough of Denbigh, attended by their inferior officers, went in procession to Lleweny Hall, and presented the Prince with a loyal address: to which his Royal Highness replied in a speech replete with energy and elegance. It is impossible to do justice to the terms in which the Prince delivered himself; suffice it therefore to say, that his reply completely won the hearts of all who had the honour of being present, and made an impression on their minds which can never be erased. The Freedom of the Corporation was then, in a neat and appropriate speech, presented to his Royal Highness by the Recorder. The Prince received that mark of respect in a manner highly flattering to the members of the Body Corporate, assuring them, that he considered it an honour to be enrolled among the burgesses of the ancient and loyal borough of Denbigh. The above ceremony being concluded, the Prince withdrew, and the Body Corporate were ushered into a room, where they partook of a most sumptuous and elegant cold collation, and wines of the choicest flavour. At noon, his Royal Highness reviewed the Volunteers of Denbigh and its vicinity, who were drawn out in the Town Parks, and consisted of a troop of cavalry, and upwards of twelve hundred infantry. The appearance of so many ancient Britons, all anxious to bear arms in defence of their King and country, collected from a district of comparatively small extent, must have been grateful to every loyal beholder; and his Royal Highness was pleased to commend the soldier-like appearance of the men, and to express to their commanders, Lord Viscount Kirkwall, and Richard Willding, Esq., his entire satisfaction at their behaviour on the occasion. The business of the day being over, his Royal Highness was conducted by Lord Kirkwall to the Castle of Denbigh, to behold the incomparable prospect which that venerable ruin commands.[4]

During this time his Royal Highness paid a visit to, and spent several days, with the late Sir Richard Puleston, Bart., at Gennal, Flintshire, and made himself most agreeable. As a proof that his Royal Highness liked his visit, he proposed to come again the next year.

Oak Tree planted by the Prince of Wales, afterwards George IV., on his First Visit to the Principality.

It is a fact not generally known that his Royal Highness George, Prince of Wales, and his brother William, Duke of Clarence, afterwards Kings of England, paid a friendly but flying visit to the Principality. In 1806, they were the guests of Sir Robert Leighton, Bart., of Lotton Park, Shropshire, for a few days, during which time they received the loyal addresses of the corporation of Shrewsbury, and visited the nearest point of the Principality, about a mile from Lotton, on the road to Llandrino, where they were received with loud acclamations of the gentry, to whom only the intention of the visit was made known.

The Prince of Wales went through the ceremony of planting a young oak on the spot where he and his royal brother first trod upon Welsh ground. The tree is now in a flourishing state, and is called the "Prince's Tree." It is enclosed within a handsome railing, and a brass plate is fixed thereon with a suitable inscription commemorating the event. When the business was over, the Prince of Wales plucked

<hr />

[4] This subject ought not to be dismissed without observing, that the very affable demeanour of His Royal Highness, added to the consideration of his being so near a relative to our good old King, caused the populace to greet His Royal Highness with almost incessant huzzas—a certain predication of heartfelt respect, when proceeding from the exulting Sons of Liberty, as on the above joyful occasion.

a branch of the tree and placed it in his hat, and then returned, on which occasion he was greeted by a goodly number of truly loyal Welshmen, who were proud to see their Prince among them.

We are indebted for the following additional particulars, to the politeness of the late Dowager Lady Puleston, as well as for the drawing of the Oak Tree :—

"The 8th of September, 1806, Sir Robert Leighton, Bart., had the honour of receiving his Royal Highness the Prince Regent as his guest for a few days, at his place, Lotton Park, in Shropshire. The following morning it was proposed that Sir Richard Puleston, the only Welsh gentleman present, who had been asked to meet his Royal Highness, should have the honour of introducing his Royal Highness into the Principality. Sir Richard, in a very appropriate speech, addressed the Prince on the occasion, at the same time presenting his Royal Highness with a sprig of an Oak Tree, which the Prince most graciously accepted, and said it was the proudest ornament he had ever worn.

"This took place in Montgomeryshire, about a mile from Lotton, on the road to Welshpool, where the tree now stands, with a brass plate on it to commemorate the event.

"Sir Richard Puleston, from an early period of his life, had the honour of enjoying the friendship of both his Royal Highness the Prince Regent, and his Royal Highness the Duke of Clarence.

"His Royal Highness the Prince Regent was pleased to signify his pleasure that Sir Richard Puleston, Bart., should, in testimony of his Royal Highness's regard and esteem, and in commemoration that on the 9th day of September, 1806, he had enjoyed the distinguished honour of introducing his Royal Highness into the Principality of Wales, bear as a crest of honourable augmentation, an Oak Tree, pendant therefrom an escocheon charged with three ostrich feathers within a coronet, in allusion to the badge of his Royal Highness as Prince of Wales.

"Present at his Royal Highness's introduction into his Principality :—His Royal Highness Duke of Clarence, Lord Viscount Petersham, Sir R. Leighton, Bart., C. Forester, Esq., M.P., R. Heathcote, Esq., Major-General Sir Benjamin Bloomfield."[6]

In 1809, his Majesty George III. reached the fiftieth year of his reign. On this occasion the inhabitants of the Principality were among the first to show their attachment and loyalty to their King by a large subscription for the purpose of erecting a monument to commemorate the unusual event of a British King's reign extending to fifty years. At a meeting of the inhabitants of the counties of Flint and Denbigh, to celebrate the Jubilee, it was unanimously resolved to erect a monument on an advantgeous site, as a lasting testimonial of that event. "Moel y Fammau," the highest part of the Clwydian range of hills, was selected from its being so conspicuous to the surrounding country, as the site of the monument. The design was by that eminent architect, the late Mr. Harrison, of Chester. It is a rough stone pyramidal mass of masonry, one hundred and fifty feet in height, and sixty feet in diameter at the base. The first stone was laid by the Right Hon. Lord Kenyon, on the 25th of October, 1810. His lordship placed a variety of coins under the stone and afterwards addressed the company, and explained to the loyal sons of Cambria the occasion of the meeting. Sir Watkin Williams Wynn, Bart., M.P., came also from Ruthin with five hundred of the Denbighshire volunteers.

We have been favoured with the following list of subscribers to the Jubilee Tower by our venerable and learned friend, Rev. H. Parry, Vicar of Llanasa.

	£.	s.	d.		£.	s.	d.
His Royal Highness the Prince of Wales	105	0	0	Sir Stephen Glynne, Bart., Hawarden Castle	20	0	0
Sir Thomas Mostyn, Bart., M.P., Mostyn Hall	52	10	0	Sir Thomas Hanmer, Bart., Battisfield-park.	10	10	0
F. R. Price, Esq., Bryn y Pys, High Sheriff for Flintshire	21	0	0	Mostyn Edwards, Esq., Nannerch Hall	10	10	0
				Lord Kenyon, Greddinton-park	52	10	0
Sir Edward Lloyd, Bart., Pengwern	25	0	0	William Shipley, Esq., Bodrydden	10	10	0
The Rev. W. W. Davies	26	5	0	Thomas Hanmer, Esq.	10	10	0
Sir John Williams, Bart., Bodelwydden	21	0	0	David Pennant, Esq., Downing	25	0	0

The subscribers of one guinea were very numerous.

---

[5] Afterwards created Lord Forester, of Willey, Shropshire.　　　　[6] Afterwards created Baron Bloomfield.

Pillars and monuments have been the record of the great in all ages; and to the memory of none of them could one more fitly be erected, than to that of the Bible King.

"Beibl i bawd o bobl y byd." [7]

Jubilee Monument on Moel Vammau to commemorate the 50th year of the reign of George the Third, 1809.

The following lines, written by the celebrated Mrs. Piozzi, on the monument,[8] are, we believe, their first appearance in print, and were communicated to us by our late venerable friend and townsman, Dr. Thackeray :—

" Perchance some future stranger, wand'ring near,
Shall ask, why soars this monumental pier !
Hence let him learn that Heaven's paternal power
Our country saved in Fate's tempestuous hour.

---

[7] A bible for each inhabitant of the earth.

[8] The height of the hill is 1845 feet from the level of the sea, and the views from it are very extensive and varied. The celebrated Vale of Clwyd is seen from one end to the other, and appears like a map laid out before the spectator. The Derbyshire hills, the Wrekin in Shropshire, Snowdon and Cader Idris, in Wales, as well as the Cumberland hills, and even the Isle of Man, are seen from this elevated spot. We are sorry to learn that this monument is in a very dilapidated state; and unless it is soon repaired, will, in all probability, tumble down. Surely this is a subject well worthy of the attention of the nobility, gentry, and magistrates of the counties of Flint and Denbigh, at whose expense it was originally erected.

Hence let him learn that still, by Heaven's decree,
Britain shall flourish, glorious, great, and free !
While land surrounding prove that here alone
The people's weal, the virtues of a throne,
Mark out the favoured soil, by freedom trod,
By Fame adorned, and cherished by its God ! "

A.D. 1819.—Prince Leopold, now King of Belgium, paid a visit to Eaton Hall, Chester, and the Principality. There are so many amiable traits in the character of this virtuous Prince—so much of the Englishman in his composition, that he has endeared himself to the country, and found as it were a home, by the fire-side of every Briton.—The loss which the nation and himself sustained in the death of her who was its pride and boast, gives additional interest to this illustrious individual; and the way in which he sustained the great calamity, created a sympathetic participation in his grief by all classes, perhaps unequalled in the history of this empire.—Under all these considerations, it might be expected, that his reception would be everywhere as warm as the hearts of those who have adopted him for their countryman.

His Royal Highness arrived on Saturday afternoon; and as the hour approached, the crowd in the streets accumulated prodigiously. The Eastgate was fully occupied by two o'clock, and the hotel and the street presented a vast mass of people. The rows on each side Eastgate-street, and the windows, exhibited a delightful assemblage of the beauty and fashion of Chester. His Royal Highness was in a close dark-green travelling carriage, (accompanied by his aide-de-camp, Sir Robert Gardiner,) which stopped at the hotel amidst incessant cheering. The bells of the cathedral immediately commenced ringing, and were followed by those of the other churches. The carriage was quickly surrounded by the multitude, all wishing to see one of whom they had heard so much. His Royal Highness alighted, and showed himself from the windows of the Royal Hotel to the surrounding thousands, who again greeted him with loud huzzas! His stay in the hotel was but short; but he received there the complimentary welcome of several of the gentry of the city and county. A passage was with some difficulty obtained from the hotel to the carriage, which the Prince ascended, and drove slowly through the city, on his way to Eaton, the seat of Earl Grosvenor, amidst the most enthusiastic shouts, and waving of hats and handkerchiefs.—At the Lodge, near Iron Bridge, immediately within the city, nearly three hundred of the tenantry of the noble earl on horseback, were drawn up, who saluted the Prince as the carriage passed the line, and followed it. At the entrance to the park, Lord Belgrave, Lord Wilton, and the Honourable Mr. Grosvenor, met the carriage, and complimented the Prince; preceded by the noble Lords, the cavalcade arrived at Eaton House. The bugles of the 71st regiment were stationed in the centre of the lawn, and the horsemen formed round it. On alighting from the carriage, the Prince was received under the portico on the steps leading to the great hall, by the noble host and hostess, and many personages of distinction, and conducted to the saloon, the organ playing " God Save the King."

On Sunday morning His Royal Highness attended divine service in the parish church of Eccleston; and the Rev. James Ireland had the honour of preaching before the Prince. The discourse was appropriate and excellent. The church was much crowded, as was the church-yard also, with persons from many miles round the country.—Amongst the noble and distinguished persons present, were the Earl and Countess Grosvenor, Lord and Lady Elizabeth Belgrave, Lord Wilton, Lord F. L. Gower, Sir Watkin and Lady Harriet Wynn, the Hon. Mr. Cust, the Baron Hardenbrok, Wilbraham Egerton, Esq., M.P., and lady, the Hon. Robert Grosvenor, Mr. and Mrs. Thomas Cholmondeley of Vale Royal, &c., &c.—The Prince returned from church in Earl Grosvenor's carriage.

On Monday morning at eleven o'clock, the Mayor and Corporation of Chester, proceeded in state to Eaton, to pay their respects to His Royal Highness, and signify that they had voted to him the freedom of the city. The procession consisted of twenty carriages.

On arriving at Eaton, the body were received in the great hall by Alderman Earl Grosvenor and Lord Belgrave, who preceded them to the grand dining-room, at the upper end of which stood His Royal

Highness Prince Leopold, attended by General Lord Hill, and the gentlemen of his suite, on his right hand, and behind him, the principal nobility and gentry of the neighbourhood. The Mayor advanced towards His Royal Highness, followed by the other gentlemen of the corporation, and paid his respects to the Prince; when the Town Clerk, John Finchett, Esq., read the Address, to which His Royal Highness returned the following reply :—

"Mr. Mayor and Gentlemen,—I beg you to receive the assurances of my heartfelt thankfulness for this proof of your attention and regard.

" I recur with great happiness, to the instances of kindness I have on more than one occasion received from the City of Chester,—and believe me, the affectionate and kind manner in which you have now welcomed me into your county will ever be deeply borne in my recollection.—I am soon, I hope, to meet you in your Town Hall, and in receiving the franchise you offer, I trust you will believe, that I must ever remember, with equal pride and sense of your kindness, that my name is enrolled in its ancient and distinguished records."

His Royal Highness here expressed a wish to be introduced personally to every individual of the Corporation, and the introduction accordingly took place. After partaking of refreshments, of wines and cake in the great hall, the Mayor and Corporation returned to Chester in the same order in which they left it; gratified at once with their gracious reception and the condescending affability of the Prince.

Soon after the departure of the corporation, the Prince, in Earl Grosvenor's carriage, drawn by six beautiful brown horses, and accompanied by the noble earl, the Lords Hill, Belgrave, Wilton, and F. L. Gower, Baron Hardenbrok, the Hon. Robert Grosvenor, General Grosvenor, Sir Robert Gardiner, &c., set off to Chester, to visit the castle, county gaol, &c. The castle yard afforded a truly pleasing *coup d'œil :* on the battery in the upper ward proudly waved the Union flag of England, and nearly sixty colours, belonging to various corps of militia, and volunteers, ornamented the summits of the tower called after Julius Cæsar, the battlements, the great gateway, the armoury, &c. The weather was fine, and the sun shone brilliantly. On the approach of the Prince to the castle yard, a royal salute was fired, and the guard presented arms. The Prince passed through the great gateway, and went along the castle ditch to the walls of the city, the delightful prospects from which, particularly between the Watergate and the Northgate, frequently elicited His Royal Highness's admiration; and he spoke highly of that excellent institution, the Infirmary. The Prince descended from the walls at the Northgate, and proceeded direct to the Exchange, in order to take the oaths, as a freeman of Chester.

Every accommodation was provided by the city treasurers (Aldermen Broster and Williamson) for the ladies who graced the hall with their presence. Exactly at a quarter before three o'clock, His Royal Highness, preceded by the Mayor, Alderman Earl Grosvenor, the Lords Hill, Belgrave, Wilton, &c., entered the hall through the private door leading to the council chamber; the band playing " God Save the King," the audience standing up, and testifying their joy by the loudest acclamations. The usual oaths were then administered by the town clerk, and the Prince's enfranchisement was the signal for a repetition of heartfelt cheering. The Prince returned his thanks in a low, but clear tone of voice, rendered almost inaudible by the buzz of admiration which prevailed throughout the hall; we understood him, however, to say that " he offered his warmest thanks for the honour conferred upon him; and he assured the citizens of Chester, that he should at all times feel particularly proud and happy, if he could in the least contribute to the prosperity and welfare of this ancient and respectable city." His Royal Highness and suite, after leaving the town hall, remained some time in the council chamber, which was thronged to excess, and then proceeded to the banquetting-room, where an elegant and varied déjeûné was prepared : wines of every description were laid on the board, of which the royal and noble guest partook.

In about half an hour they proceeded to the diocesan palace, where the Prince was received by the estimable bishop with his usual dignified urbanity, and conducted through the cathedral, preceded by the two vergers, the organ playing " God save the King." The architecture of that venerable edifice claimed the particular observation of the royal visitors, and especially the beautiful gothic vestibule and interior of the chapter-house, where the Prince extended his stay to nearly twenty minutes, examining the contents of the valuable library, the sculptured relics there preserved, &c. On returning to the palace through the private door from the broad aisle, the royal and noble visitors partook of refreshments, laid out in the drawing-room in a style of neatness and elegant simplicity which we have seldom seen equalled. His Royal Highness seemed highly pleased with the attention paid to him by the bishop and his lady, who accompanied him to the door of the palace, where he ascended Earl Grosvenor's carriage and six, and with some difficulty (for the area of the palace yard was completely crowded) proceeded down Northgate-street to St. John's Church, through which he walked, and with great interest contemplated the venerable ruins of the ancient choir and chancel. His Royal Highness also inspected the ruins of the Priory, the Free Schools of Earl and Countess Grosvenor, where nearly five hundred children of both sexes receive gratuitous education in the pure principles of the Established Church.

It was past five o'clock before the illustrious party left Chester for Eaton, where a sumptuous dinner was served up in the grand dining-room, in all the gorgeous magnificence of the house. The party consisted of about thirty nobles and gentry; and in addition to the personages we have before mentioned, were present Lord and Lady Dungannon, Lord L. Gower, Sir Thomas and Lady Stanley, Sir R. Brooke, Bart. and family, Sir F. Cunliffe, Bart. and family, General and Mrs. Glegg, G. Brooke, Esq., and Miss Brooke, &c. The Mayor and town-clerk of Chester also dined with the party, by social invitation.

Every mode calculated to give His Royal Highness a hearty welcome was resorted to: the Holyhead mail coach, the horses and drivers decorated with the royal colours, followed the carriages of the Prince and suite through the streets; the guards firing off their blunderbusses. The British flag was hoisted on Mr. Mellor's shot tower, and the bells were rung throughout the day. The Prince appeared much pleased with the antiquities of the city, and particularly its ancient walls of Roman foundation; and expressed his sense of the very kind reception he had met with, in terms of unqualified approbation.

On Tuesday morning, the Prince, accompanied by Earl Grosvenor, Lords Hill, Belgrave, Wilton, F. L. Gower, and other distinguished personages, honoured Lady Glynne with their company to breakfast, at her beautiful and romantic seat at Hawarden Castle. His Royal Highness remained there a considerable time; and proceeded on his way to Holywell races, escorted by a squadron of the Hawarden and Mold hussar yeomanry cavalry, commanded by Lieutenant Boydell. The Prince expressed his high satisfaction at this mark of attention from so respectable a body of men. He was everywhere received with the utmost demonstration of joy and affection: at Halkin, the miners and others in the employ of Earl Grosvenor, dressed in their holiday clothes, to the number of nearly seven hundred, saluted and cheered him as he passed. On the race-course his presence was greeted with the same marked attention. After the races, His Royal Highness visited Holywell, and walked down the principal street to view that great natural wonder, the Well of St. Winifred. The Prince returned the same evening to Eaton.

On Wednesday morning, His Royal Highness and suite quitted Eaton, to the great regret of his noble hosts, expressing his warm thanks for the cordial and welcome reception which he had met. His Royal Highness passed through Chester about twelve o'clock, on his way to Trentham, the seat of the Marquis of Stafford; from thence he paid a visit to the Marquis of Anglesea, at Beaudesart. The Prince then passed through Oxford on his way to London.

GEORGE IV.—This monarch succeeded to the throne on the death of his father, George III. He was crowned at Westminster, on the 19th of July, 1821; this coronation was the most splendid ever celebrated in England.[s] Soon after, His Majesty determined upon paying a visit to Ireland and his loyal subjects

---

[s] The account of this coronation given by Sir Walter Scott is so graphic and lively, that we think it will gratify our readers to insert an abridgment of it:—" The effect of the scene in the Abbey was beyond measure magnificent. The altar surrounded by the fathers of the church—the King encircled by the nobility of the land and the councillors of his throne, and by warriors, wearing the honoured marks of distinction bought by many a glorious danger—add to this, the rich spectacle of the aisles crowded with waving plumage and

in Wales. His Majesty embarked at Portsmouth, on the 1st of August, 1821, in the Royal George yacht, which had the Royal Marine band on board. The day was ushered in with merry peals from the bells; at eight the signal was given, and the royal yacht got under way; she passed the platform, under a salute from every gun, standing out towards St. Helen's, when she tacked, and run through Spithead, at which place the royal standard was seen at every point, and the busy hum of the assembled multitude formed a grand and pleasing sight. As she passed along, the respective ships forming the royal escort unmoored, the spectacle became grand beyond conception, the sea for miles was covered with craft of every description. The superb appearance of the royal yacht was particularly striking; the whole squadron stood away towards Cowes, consisting of—*The Royal Yacht*, Commander Sir C. Paget; *Royal Sovereign Yacht*, Capt. Adam; *Liffey Frigate*, Hon. Capt. Duncan; *Active Frigate*, Sir J. Gordon; *Hind Sloop*, Sir Charles Burrand; *Lee Brig*, Capt. Blacker; *Cameleon Brig*, Capt. Mingay; *Wolf Brig*, Capt. Yeoman; *Starling Cutter*, Lieut. Reeves; *Emerald Yacht*, tender to the *Royal George; Pearl Yacht*, belonging to the Marquis of Anglesea; *Louisa*, Lord Craven's; *Falcon*, Hon. Mr. Belhaven's. With numerous others belonging to the yacht clubs, forming a gay summer squadron. His Majesty was accompanied in his voyage by a suite consisting of Admiral Sir E. Nagle, General Sir Hilgrove Turner, Sir William Keppel, Colonel Thornton, Sir Andrew Bernard, Mr. Douglas, &c.

The King's reception at Portsmouth must have been particularly gratifying to him; the usual rapid movement through the town in a close carriage was much regretted; every place was thronged to excess with ladies and gentlemen, anxious to behold the King and to testify their loyalty to him. His Majesty's condescension when on board his yacht made amends for this, for he appeared on deck, when he was loudly cheered by a more numerous assemblage of all ranks than ever was seen before in that harbour.

The wind having turned round to the eastward, the royal squadron set off, and made way on their voyage to Holyhead Harbour, where the King arrived on the 16th of August, at four o'clock in the afternoon, unattended with any military guard or escort whatever. He was received with the loudest acclamations of loyalty and affection that a loyal people could bestow.

This Royal Visit may be considered one of the most auspicious of any we have had to record. The first King of England who visited the Principality inspired terror among the inhabitants, and their bards invoked "ruin on his ruthless head," but this monarch came amongst them with the olive branch. The warm reception which he universally met with on that occasion must have been very gratifying to his feelings. Every preparation was made that a truly loyal and devoted people had it in their power to effect.

The conduct of Sir John T. Stanley, Bart., (now Lord Stanley of Alderley,) on the arrival of His Majesty, was a theme of general admiration; the whole arrangements for the royal reception were admirably conceived, and executed with astonishing promptitude and regularity. A splendid triumphal arch was erected on the pier, and tastefully ornamented with festoons of laurel and flowers intermixed. The arch was surmounted with a regal crown, supported on either side by a Welsh harp; other appropriate devices were placed on the structure, and the following inscription was encompassed with a wreath of laurel immediately under the crown, "ANRHYDEDD I'R BRENIN," *Honour to the King.* Commodious steps were fixed on the outside of the jetty, covered with red baize, for the greater convenience of His Majesty's landing, and a

coronets, and caps of honour, and the sun, which brightened and saddened as if on purpose, now beaming in full lustre on the rich and varied assemblage, and now darting a solitary ray, which caught, as it passed, the glittering folds of a banner, or the edge of a group of battle-axes or partisans, and then rested full on some fair form, ' the cynosure of neighbouring eyes,' whose circlet of diamonds glistened under its influence. Imagine all this, and then tell me if I have made my journey of four hundred miles to little purpose. The box assigned to the foreign ambassadors presented a most brilliant effect, and was perfectly in a blaze with diamonds. When the sunshine lighted on Prince Esterhazy, in particular, he glimmered like a galaxy. An honest Persian was also a remarkable figure, from the

dogged and impenetrable gravity with which he looked on the whole scene, without ever moving a limb or a muscle during the space of four hours. Like Sir Wilful Witwoud, I cannot find that your Persian is orthodox, for, if he scorned everything else, there was a Mahometan paradise extended on his right hand along the seats which were occupied by the peeresses and their daughters, which the Prophet himself might have looked on with emotion. But, in truth, the only interesting spectacle connected with this feast was the challenge of the champion, which is now not only unmeaning but illegal; for it is directly contrary to the statute abolishing wager of battle in all cases whatsoever."

temporary platform was erected in front of the lighthouse, and such other arrangements were made for the accommodation of the public as were deemed best calculated to preserve that order and regularity which the occasion required; the activity of the magistrates was such, and so very judicious was their arrangement of the police, that every individual knew the particular post he was to repair to on a signal being given.

On Monday evening, August the 6th, about half-past five o'clock, the long looked-for signal was made from the top of the mountain, to the indescribable joy of all the inhabitants. It was hailed with the thunder of artillery from the Salt Island, to announce to the surrounding neighbourhood the near approach of His Majesty.

> " The King appears ! The news proclaim !
> See safe on Mona's land the monarch move :
> How glorious such a sovereign's name,
> Whose body-guard—his people's *love !* "

So soon as the royal standard was hauled down on board the royal yacht, as a signal that his Majesty was in his barge, the yards of the royal squadron were manned, and royal salutes fired, which added much

George the Fourth landing at Holyhead, and Sir John (now Lord) Stanley presenting his Majesty with a loyal Address.

to the grandeur of the scene, and a few minutes brought him to the steps prepared for his landing, accompanied by all the captains of the squadron, in their respective barges, when he was received by Sir John Stanley, Bart., and the magistrates and gentlemen appointed to accompany him with the address; His Majesty was assisted to land from his barge by two gentlemen, who handed the ropes to him, and he ascended the steps without difficulty, and landed on the shores of Cambria, greeted by the most enthusiastic cheers and waving of handkerchiefs from many thousands of the inhabitants of this and the adjoining counties. The following address was read and presented by Sir John Stanley :—

" To the King's Most Excellent Majesty.

"MAY IT PLEASE YOUR MAJESTY,—We, your dutiful and loyal subjects, the magistrates, clergy, gentlemen, freeholders, and other inhabitants, of the town of Holyhead and its neighbourhood, humbly approach your Majesty, to offer you our sincere congratulations on your safe arrival within our harbour, and to express our heartfelt joy at beholding our gracious and beloved sovereign in the midst of us.

"In tendering our homage, we can assure your Majesty, that in no part of your dominions, however splendid may be the reception your Majesty may meet with, can purer loyalty, a stronger sense of duty, or a more sincere and lively wish for your prosperity and happiness be felt, than in this remote corner of your kingdom : and we cannot refrain from adding, that we shall ever feel proud in the recollection, that it has been our peculiar good fortune to belong to that town and neighbourhood in the Principality of Wales, which has been first honoured with the august presence of your Majesty."

In answer to which, his Majesty was most graciously pleased to express himself to the following effect :—

That he wished that all he felt on the occasion could be known,—that to be received with such proofs of attachment was highly grateful to him,—that his heart was indeed warmed in witnessing such a show of loyalty and affection on his landing in a country which was, and always would be, dear to him ; and of which he had borne the title since his birth, and for the greatest period of his life.

While the ceremony lasted, as much silence was observed by the vast multitude as their enthusiasm would permit, but no sooner had his Majesty pronounced the last word than the cheering was resumed by every individual present. His Majesty remained some time on the pier, and bowed most graciously to the enraptured assembly. The Royal Marine band stood near the spot, playing " God save the King."

Three of the Marquis of Anglesea's carriages were in readiness on the Pier, to convey his Majesty and suite to Plas Newydd ; the carriage in which was the King, passed at a walking pace from the end of the pier to Spencer's Hotel, a distance of nearly a mile, through an immense concourse of people, who continued cheering till the carriage was out of sight.

His Majesty arrived at the Marquis of Anglesea's beautiful mansion of Plâs Newydd,[9] about half-past six on Tuesday evening ; upon which a royal salute was fired from the terrace, and the guns of the *Cheerful* revenue cutter, Captain Greet, then at anchor in the Straits of Menai, whilst the band of the 7th Hussars played " God save the King," and the populace assembled in the park rent the air with acclamations. The King was accompanied by the Marquis, Lord F. Conyngham, and Sir C. Paget, in the same carriage ; in other carriages were the Lord Graves, Lord Amelius Beauclerk, Sir Hilgrove Turner, and Sir Andrew Bernard. At eight o'clock this distinguished party sat down to a sumptuous dinner with the Marquis of Anglesea's family. His Majesty did not appear to be in high spirits, as the news of the Queen's illness had been previously communicated to him.

---

[9] Plâs Newydd is situated on the banks of the Menai, rising, as it were, out of the Straits, and backed by an extensive forest of oaks of unknown date, every one of which talks to intelligence of other times—
"Of Druid haunts, and Mona's hallow'd shores."
Within a few yards of the house are to be seen two vast cromlechs. The upper stone of one is twelve feet seven inches long, twelve broad, and four thick, supported by five tall stones. The other, barely separated from the first, is almost a square of five feet and a half, and supported by four stones. These are the largest and most massy known, and the highest from the ground ; for a middle-sized horse may easily pass under the largest. Howel, a descendant of Llywarch ab Brân, Lord of Cwmwd Menai, sold his patrimony of Plâs Newydd, Plâs Gwyn, &c., to William Gruffydd Vychan, Esq., of

Penrhyn, chamberlain of North Wales.—Plâs Newydd continued in this line till the marriage of Elin, heiress of Edward Gruffydd, to Sir Nicholas Bagnall, knight-marshal of Queen Elizabeth's armies in Ireland. His daughter and heiress married Dr. Lewis Bayley, Bishop of Bangor in 1616, who purchased Corswen in Caer-Rhûn. This exemplary prelate wrote the " Practice of Piety." His grandson, Edward Bayley, was made a baronet of Ireland in 1730. And his son, Sir Nicholas Bayley, who sat in parliament for Anglesea about 1760, married Caroline, daughter and heiress of Thomas Paget, Esq., and eventually succeeded to the estates of his brother, the last Earl of Uxbridge of that family. And her son by the said Thomas Paget, was Henry Bayley Paget, father of the present Marquis of Anglesea, Lord Lieutenant of the county.

On Wednesday morning deputations arrived from the corporate and other bodies of Anglesea and Caernarvonshire, to present loyal addresses to the King. His Majesty received them in the grand

Plâs Newydd, the seat of the Marquis of Anglesea : George IV., 1821; Princess Victoria, 1832.

saloon, in the following order, due arrangements having been made for their introduction, according to the established forms :—first, from the Lord Bishop and the Clergy of the Diocese of Bangor; from the High Sheriff and Gentlemen of the County of Anglesea ; from the High Sheriff and Gentlemen of the County of Caernarvon ; from the Mayor, Bailiffs, and Burgesses of the Borough of Beaumaris ; from the Mayor, Bailiffs, and Burgesses of the Borough of Caernarvon ; and from the body of Calvinistic Methodists.

His Majesty's gracious manner, and the dignified tone of voice and action with which the answers to the addresses were delivered, imparted to all present the warmest admiration. The Lord Bishop of Bangor, who remained in the room during the whole ceremonial, engaged much of His Majesty's attention; and it was grateful to observe the King's conferring distinction, by his notice of all around him. Joseph Huddard, Esq., the High Sheriff of Caernarvonshire, received the honour of knighthood upon this occasion.

An elegant collation was provided for the gentlemen of the deputations under marquees, erected for that purpose in the park; and the noble Marquis gave orders also for a plenteous regale of bread and beef and ale to a numerous population assembled in the grounds.

His Majesty returned to Holyhead on Wednesday afternoon, about four o'clock, and was received at the entrance of the town, and conducted to his barge, which was in readiness for his reception at the end of the pier, with similar attention and marks of respect and loyalty as were evinced the day previous on his landing; royal salutes were fired from the stations on shore at his embarkation, in the same order as was observed at his landing, and the squadron also manned their yards and fired royal salutes; the town was again illuminated.

From this time till Sunday morning the wind was contrary for Ireland, during which period the royal squadron remained in the bay. The wind still continuing adverse, on Sunday morning his Majesty was pleased to remove from the *Royal George* yacht, to the *Lightning* post-office steam packet, and departed immediately for Ireland. He landed at Howth at five o'clock in the afternoon.

The following are further particulars relative to this interesting occasion :—

Holyhead, Saturday, August 12th, 1821.

At ten o'clock this morning, his Majesty's yacht, the *Royal George*, was moved from our pier after a stay of nearly six days. The royal squadron was first seen from the signal station on Holyhead mountain at about six p.m. of Monday. The crowds who thronged to the pier were of course disappointed for that night, and contented themselves with illuminating the town in the most brilliant manner.

The morning of Tuesday (7th) was extremely fine, and the appearance of the whole squadron particularly beautiful; but it was understood that it was his Majesty's intention not to land or visit the Marquis of Anglesea, at Plas Newydd, according to his original plan. Shortly however after the arrival of the steam-packet with dispatches from Dublin, and not long after the return of the Marquis, who had landed and gone to Plas Newydd during that night, it was announced that the King was about to land. The head of the pier was immediately crowded to excess, but the utmost order was preserved, and a wide passage kept clear down its whole length by a body of special constables, consisting of upwards of two hundred tenants of Sir J. T. Stanley, Bart., nearly the same number of labourers belonging to the works, and several of the other inhabitants of the town. At the foot of the lighthouse near the temporary flight of steps, were ranged tier above tier of well-dressed ladies, and near them stood the Royal Marine band, which had been put on shore for the occasion. At four p.m. His Majesty quitted the *Royal George* and stepped into his barge, under a salute from the *Liffey* and *Active* frigates, and numerous other vessels belonging to the squadron, now riding off the mouth of the harbour.

The moment of his setting his foot on the pier was likewise announced by a discharge of artillery from the Custom-house quay and the battery of Penrhos, the band at the same time played "God save the King," but the sound of the national air was overpowered by that more grateful music to a monarch's ear—the hearty and united shout of a loyal and affectionate people. At the top of the steps stood a deputation of the inhabitants with the address, which they obtained leave to present. On His Majesty's landing, the King walked firmly up the steps, and on reaching the top looked round in a most graceful manner upon the assembled multitude. He seemed surprised at the beauty and extent of the pier, as well as deeply affected by the enthusiastic cheers which resounded in every direction. Sir J. Stanley now stood forward at the head of the deputation, and was preparing to read the address, when the King took his hand and said in a low tone of voice, that " he could not forbear expressing how deeply he was affected by the reception," and then added that " it gave him additional pleasure as coming from a country whose name he had borne during so long a period of his life." The address [already inserted] was then read.

Upon the conclusion of the address, the band again played, and the shouts were renewed with additional vehemence, whilst the King giving his arm to Lord Anglesea, walked forward and got into the Marquis's carriage, and followed by a suite of carriages prepared for them, drove at a slow pace along the pier under a temporary arch erected at the end, and through the upper street, till he arrived opposite to the inn at the entrance of the town, where the horses quickened their pace and hastened on to Plas Newydd. In the evening there was a ball at the National School for the company who had come into the town from all parts of the country. Wednesday morning was wet and squally, but by the dawn of day all was again fair, and soon after four p.m., his Majesty returned from Plâs Newydd. He was met by a crowd of people at the entrance of the town, drove at a slow pace along the lower road, alighted from his carriage near the end of the pier, and was attended by the same deputation to the head of the stairs, where he descended into his barge, under a salute of all the guns, both those on shore and those of the vessels in the bay, which had now anchored much nearer the pier head. The yards were also manned both days, and the effect of the whole scene was most magnificent. The salute was repeated when he entered his yacht, and the royal standard was again unfurled at the mast-head. In the evening the wind began to blow hard from the west, and the Commodore, Sir C. Paget, instead of sailing for Ireland, turned the royal yacht in close to the pier-head. Brilliant illuminations closed the night.

Such an event as a king's visit in Wales was not a circumstance to pass by unnoticed. A handsome subscription was soon set on foot, for the purpose of erecting a splendid monument to commemorate the arrival of His Majesty, who, as we have said, landed at Holyhead, on the 7th of August, 1821. This triumphal arch is a chaste and elegant structure in the Doric style, formed of Mona marble, and erected on the very spot where his Majesty first placed his foot when he landed. It consists of a central carriage way, separated on each side by two handsome pillars, from a foot-way enclosed exteriorly by a wall, ornamented at the extremities by *antæ* of corresponding character. The gate is twenty feet high, surrounded by masonry, forming a platform. Over the carriage way, on each side, are empaneled inscriptions in Welsh and Latin, commemorative of the event.

Thursday morning the wind continued high enough to render the swell unpleasant, but the royal yacht was by this time moored within the pier, and His Majesty thus enjoyed the full benefit of this admirable public work.

Triumphal Arch at Holyhead to commemorate the visit of George the Fourth.

Before noon a king's messenger brought intelligence of the decease of the Queen, and a council was immediately held on board the *Royal George;* amongst other members of the council were the Marquises

3 i

of Londonderry and Anglesea. From that period up to the departure of the squadron, His Majesty did not appear on deck, and it was understood that he dined each day by himself, without any company.

Friday morning the wind still continued adverse; the flags were hoisted half-mast high, and the gaiety of the preceding days was mournfully contrasted by the silence and solemnity that reigned throughout the squadron.

On Saturday, the wind still continuing high, the yacht still remained in harbour, but towards evening it grew more calm, and it was generally understood that the squadron would sail for Dublin in the morning. Accordingly, at ten A.M. on Sunday morning they got under weigh, and by noon were completely out of sight. His Majesty's stay in this harbour was most remarkable, both as forming his visit to the Principality, and as connected with his visit to Ireland, and moreover marked by the death of his Royal Consort, and by quitting on his birthday. All these circumstances have given to this place an interest and importance in the eyes of the nation and in the page of history. His Majesty sailed in the post-office steam-boat, in the hope of landing privately in Ireland, before the arrival of the royal yacht.

On his return from Ireland his Majesty paid a visit to the loyal and ancient town of Milford; the following account is extracted from one of the journals of the day :—

"The inhabitants of this place have experienced a surprise of a most agreeable nature. Little did they expect, two hours ago, to be delighted with a visit from their sovereign. It appears, however, that in order to avoid the heavy sea at the turning of the Land's End, where the whole pressure of the Atlantic falls into a small compass, and large black rocks render the navigation difficult, even in the most favourable weather, His Majesty determined upon putting into this port, where he is now arrived in perfect health and spirits. At the moment in which I write to you, the royal yacht, with the standard flying at the mast head, is at anchor in the harbour, exactly opposite to the Nelson Hotel, where thousands are assembled in expectation of shortly witnessing the landing of their beloved Sovereign. It is utterly impossible for us to describe the bustle and anxiety which are depicted upon every countenance. We need not say that we are *all* loyal here, for who can doubt the loyalty of a Welshman? Our King, our own Prince, is amongst us, and we are happy. Old and young, halt and lame, man, woman, and child, all rejoice at the arrival of their Sovereign. There is some selfishness, however, in the elder part of the population; but it is a selfishness with which the King will not be displeased. A gentleman, nearly ninety years of age, resting upon his crutches, and viewing with delight the royal yacht as she majestically sailed into the harbour, exclaimed with enthusiasm, 'The King is coming! Shout, my boys, shout! Milford will be a town again.'"[1]

[1] George IV. was particularly attached to the Principality of Wales, and was a warm supporter of her institutions, particularly the Welsh Charity School in London, as the following address from the honourable and loyal Society of Ancient Britons,* in London, which was presented to his Majesty by Sir W. W. Wynn, Bart., President, will show :—

"To the King's most Excellent Majesty,—May it please your Majesty, We, the society of Ancient Britons, originally instituted at the auspicious period of the first accession of the House of Hanover† to the British throne, and founded in commemoration of the birthday of the first princess of that illustrious house, it is our pride to acknowledge, with sentiments of gratitude and attachment, that from the cradle of our late gracious monarch, we have experienced his unabated patronage and his liberal protection.

"For sixty-five years did his Majesty extend to us, not only the

* George IV. presided at the 114th anniversary festival of the Ancient Britons, on St. David's day, 1830.

† The line of descent from Egbert, in 828, to William IV. 1830, by marriages and intermarriages, may be traced, On the death of Queen Anne in 1714, the Elector of Hanover was called to the British throne as George I., in virtue of the Act of Settlement, he being the nearest Protestant descendant of James I.

encouragement of his munificent personal contributions, but the still more valuable boon of his unvarying public countenance under which the Welsh charity school, from the education of only twelve boys in 1762, has increased to the entire maintenance, clothing, and support of not less than one hundred boys and fifty girls.

"For benefits so generously conferred, we are desirous of offering this last, but zealous, tribute of our gratitude and acknowledgment to the memory of our late Royal Patron; and, at the same time, we crave permission to congratulate your Majesty upon your accession to that crown which your Majesty's ancestors have worn from the earliest period to which the most remote tradition can extend, and to express our anxious hopes that we may still experience the same patronage with which your Majesty has already honoured us, by presiding at our annual festival, and that your Majesty will be convinced that the sentiments of loyalty and attachment to your Majesty's sacred person and government, though they pervade every class of the subjects of these realms, are no where more warmly cherished than in the breasts of the society of Ancient Britons.

"Signed at the request, in the name, and on the behalf of the Honourable and Loyal Society of Ancient Britons.

"WATKIN WILLIAMS WYNN, *President.*"

This society was instituted in 1714. When our late beloved monarch was only three years old, he received an address from the

His Royal Highness the Duke of Sussex, son of George III., visited the Principality annually for several years, and spent several weeks at Kinmel Park, the hospitable mansion of his old and valued friend, Lord Dinorben. Whilst on one of his visits there, His Royal Highness patronised and attended an Eisteddfod, or a meeting of the Welsh bards, which took place within the precincts of the ancient castle of Denbigh, under the princely presidency of Sir Edward Mostyn, Bart., of Talacre. The proceedings commenced on Wednesday morning, the 17th of September, 1828. The weather was delightfully fair and clear, which caused a very large company; in fact the town was literally crammed. At eight o'clock the bards were summoned to the town hall, where the successful poems and essays were read with admirable effect, and much applauded. At the time appointed for the visit of the Duke of Sussex, the corporation left the town to meet His Royal Highness, and proceeding to the confines, in the following order, awaited his arrival :—

Band.—Members of three Friendly Societies, two and two.—Royal Denbigh Band.—The Bards and Minstrels.—The harp, decorated with ribbons and borne by two men.—Members of the Denbigh Literary Society, with banner, staves, and rosettes.—Members of the Cymmrodorion Society, banner, staves, and rosettes.—The Corporation of Denbigh.—Beadle.—Mace-bearers.—Capital Burgesses, two and two.—John Copner Williams, Esq., Deputy-Recorder.—Thos. Hughes, Esq., Bailiff.—David Hughes, Esq., Bailiff.—John Hughes, Esq., Alderman.—John Parry, Esq., Alderman.—The Recorder, J. Wynne Griffith, Esq.—Members of the Committee, two and two. — R. P. Jones, Esq., M.D., Honorary Secretary.—The PRESIDENT, Sir E. Mostyn, Bart., supported by the Vice-Presidents, Sir W. W. Wynn, Bart., and John Heaton, Esq.—A long train of Gentlemen, two and two.—Carriages, &c.

On His Royal Highness's approach, the Recorder addressed him in the following terms :—

"MAY IT PLEASE YOUR ROYAL HIGHNESS.—As Recorder of this Borough I am deputed by the aldermen, bailiffs, and capital burgesses, to present to your Royal Highness their dutiful and loyal address, upon your Royal Highness's visit to the Principality, and to express to your Royal Highness how highly they appreciate your condescension in honouring them with your presence at the national festival this day. With your Royal Highness's permission, I will read the Address.

" To His Royal Highness the Duke of Sussex.

"SIR,—We, the Aldermen, Bailiffs, and Capital Burgesses, of the Borough of Denbigh, assembled by special Convocation, beg leave to congratulate your Royal Highness upon your arrival in the Principality. Anxious upon all occasions to testify our loyalty and attachment to the House of Brunswick, under whose mild and constitutional sway we have enjoyed so many blessings, we eagerly embrace the opportunity which your Royal Highness's visit to us has fortunately afforded, to present your Royal Highness, in the most respectful terms, the Freedom of our ancient Corporation, as the most appropriate token of personal regard for so distinguished a member of the Royal Family we have it in our power to confer.

"It would have been particularly gratifying to us upon any occasion to have marked your Royal Highness's visit to our ancient Borough with every possible respect, but under the peculiar circumstances which now occur, we feel imperatively bound to acquit ourselves of that obligation by an ardent feeling of gratitude for the truly courteous and liberal spirit in which your Royal Highness has condescended to honour our national Festival,[2] or Eisteddfod, with your presence, and by

society, a copy of which, ornamented at the top with a drawing representing the Prince of Wales receiving the deputation, is preserved at the Welsh school in Gray's-Inn-lane road. From that early period to the 1st of March last, his late Majesty gave the munificent donation of a hundred guineas annually, and, in 1820, when he ascended the throne, he presented the charity with an extra hundred guineas, making a total of more than 7000*l.*

[2] We avail ourselves of this opportunity of illustrating the Welsh literary meeting held at Denbigh by the following account of the eminent characters who were born within or near its walls. The sons of Richard Myddelton, governor in the reigns of Edward VI.,

Mary, and Elizabeth, whose monument on a brass plate, representing himself and wife kneeling each at an altar with their nine sons and seven daughters ranged behind each respectively, is to be seen in the porch of the parish church at Whitchurch, first claim notice. The third son, William, was an eminent sea captain, and still more eminent, at least in Wales, as a poet. By his skill and prowess our fleet which was sent to the Azores in 1501, under the command of Lord Thomas Howard, to intercept the Spanish galleons, was saved from destruction by an overpowering force. As a Welsh poet, he stood high. It was he who first composed the Welsh Psalms in metre. He also wrote a work on Barddoniaeth, or the Art of Welsh Poetry; the

that means so powerfully contributing to increase in splendour and effect those popular attractions which must ensure its eventual success, and thus promote the combined objects for which this and other meetings of a similar kind have been really revived.

"Signed and passed under the seal of the Corporation, at the Council Chamber of and in the said Borough, the tenth day of September, 1828.

(Signed)   "J. W. GRIFFITH, *Recorder.*"

The learned Recorder, then proceeded:

"I am also instructed by the members of the Convocation to convey to your Royal Highness their warmest acknowledgments for this high mark of your Royal Highness's respect, and to present your Royal Highness in this box the freedom of this ancient borough, which is the highest compliment they have in their power to confer. I feel particularly proud that I have been selected to address your Royal Highness upon the present occasion, as it gives me an opportunity of testifying my respect for your Royal Highness, by personally expressing the high sense I entertain of your Royal Highness's public and private virtues."

The Recorder then presented His Royal Highness with the freedom of the borough in an elegant gold box, upon which was engraved the following Englyn :—

"*Ar ymweliad ei Riawl Uchelder, Dug Sussecs, yn Eisteddfod Dinbych, ar y 16eg, 17eg, a 18fed o fis Medi, 1821.*

"Trwydd Dinbych, dêg anrhegiad,—gwiw estyn.
I AUGUSTUS benllad,
Am ei haelaf ymweliad
A Gwledd barddoni ein gwlâd."

His Royal Highness then read the following reply :—

"ALDERMEN, BAILIFFS, AND CAPITAL BURGESSES OF THE BOROUGH OF DENBIGH.—Gentlemen, I thank you for your congratulations on my arrival in the Principality.

"I am fully sensible of the compliment paid to my person by conferring on me the freedom of your ancient Corporation, accompanied with the assurances of your loyalty to our most gracious Sovereign, (whom may God long preserve!) and of your attachment to the House of Brunswick.

"Born and educated in those principles which placed my family upon the throne of these realms, it has ever been my most anxious wish to mix with my fellow subjects, and to participate with them in all those festivities that tend to commemorate and keep up a spirit of liberty and national independence, which we have sworn to maintain with our lives.

"Among the many institutions of this kind, the Eisteddfod is the most ancient; and therefore I am delighted in being permitted to witness a scene which must be highly interesting to all well-wishers of their country, and most particularly gratifying to the inhabitants of the Principality, amongst whom I have the peculiar happiness to find myself upon the present occasion.

(Signed)   "AUGUSTUS FREDERICK."

The procession then returned through the town, with the band playing "God save the King," and proceeded to the Bowling Green in the castle, amidst the waving of handkerchiefs from the ladies in the windows, and the shouts of the multitude which lined the streets. His Royal Highness kept his hat off all the time, bowing most condescendingly to all around. On ascending the platform, His Royal Highness was again greeted by the waving of hats and handkerchiefs for several minutes, and was conducted to his seat by the President, Sir Edward Mostyn.

---

first he published in 1503, and the latter in 1543. His other works are known by his Bardic name, "Gwilym Ganoldref," (Middleton). The fourth son, Thomas, became Lord Mayor of London, and purchasing Chirk Castle, became the founder of that eminent family. Charles, the fifth son, succeeded his father as governor of Denbigh. But the most eminent of all was Hugh, the sixth son, made a baronet in 1622, who, as a benefactor to the metropolis in bringing the New River to supply its wants, is too generally known to need further mention here. He represented the boroughs in 1603-14-20-23-25 and 28, and presented silver cups to the corporations of Denbigh and Ruthin, being a burgess of both towns; these cups are preserved, as is another given by him to the head of his family at Gwaenynog. It is sad to be told that this New River scheme, which was a blessing to thousands, was the ruin of his own fortune, and that the sole recompense he received on the completion of his work was the empty honour of being attended on its opening day by the King and court, and the corporation of London, among whom was his brother, the Lord Mayor elect.

The proceedings commenced by Mr. Parry (Bardd Alaw) singing his celebrated national song, " *Oh, let the kind minstrel,*" with the following additional stanza, in honour of the Royal Duke :—

" Long life to the Prince from whose generous heart
The stream of sweet charity silently flows ;
Who fosters the progress of Science and Art,
Whose presence a lustre on Cambria bestows :
In strains of past ages, Oh ! let us all sing,
Till *Clwyd's* mighty mountains responsively ring,
To welcome the brother of Britain's good King."

His Royal Highness appeared to be highly gratified with this out-pouring of Cambrian gratitude and loyalty, and bowed repeatedly while it was being sung, all the company joining in the chorus. Mr. Parry presented the royal visitor with a copy of the song, which His Royal Highness was pleased to receive most graciously.

The following Pennill on the occasion, by Robert Davies, the celebrated Bard of Nantglyn, was also recited :—

" Balch yw Cymru weled Llin
Ei Brenin ar ei bronydd,
Yn talu têg ymweliad da
Eisteddfod bena'r gwledydd :
Ei Enw fydd ar ucha'r fainc
Tra chof, tra chainc, tra Phrydydd."[3]

Among the various prizes offered for competition at the Eisteddfod, a handsome medal and a premium was offered for the best Englynion (epigrammatic verses) on the Royal Duke's visit. The following by Catwg was considered best ; they were recited by the author, Mr. Griffith Williams, of Llandegai.

" Y bàn a difalch bendefig—astud,
Sef Augustus Ffrederic ;
Rhydd y daeth, heb arwydd dig,
I noddi 'r iaith Wyneddig.

" Croesaw, mawr groesaw i'r grasol—Funer,
A fo yn feunyddiol ;
Ei glôd am ryddid gwladol
Erys yn wir oesau 'n ol.

" Wele, yn awr yn ein Blaenorion—Sior,
A'i siriol frawd tirion,
Dueddiad i'w henwlad hon,
Ac i noddi Gwyneddion.

" Ha ! gwir aerod i goron !—ein ceraint,
Ac ein carwŷr ffyddlon,
Dianach o waed union,
Tewdwr, a meib *Tudur* Môn." [4]

The reading was followed by a burst of applause, and the bard presented the Englynion to the Royal Duke, who expressed his acknowledgments.

And now came on the contest for the silver harp. The competitors were as under :—

Richard Pugh, of Dolgellau, who played *Difyrwch y Brenin*, or the King's Delight.—Edward Jones, of Llangollen (blind) who played *Pen Rhaw*. [During his performance, the Duke of Sussex emphatically said, " How beautiful ! "] — Hugh Pugh, of Dolgellau, *Nôs Galan*, with variations.—John Roberts, Mold, *Difyrwch y Brenin.*—Edward Humphreys, Welshpool, *Merch Megan*, or Margaret's Daughter.—Richard Jones, Llangollen, *Sweet Richard.*

After a fair trial of skill, Edward Jones (the blind harper), was declared victor, and was invested with the medal by Lady Mostyn.

The judges to decide on the merits of the performers in this prize, as well as the one following, were

[3] Translated thus :—" Wales is proud to behold a relative of her King honouring her Grand Eisteddfod with his presence ; his name will be cherished while memory lasts, song records, or bard exists."

[4] Translated thus :—" The exalted but condescending Prince, the literary Augustus Frederic. Free he comes, where rancour is banished, to patronise the language of Gwynedd.

" Let us proclaim our loftiest welcome to the gracious lord ; let future ages tell his love of constitutional liberty.

" See, now, our own chiefs—George and his brother, in whom kindness smiles. They have an inclination to this their ancient country, and to cherish the choice things of Gwynedd.

" Right heirs of the crown—our own relations—our faithful friends ! Spotless from *Tewdwr's* noble blood—sons of Mona's Tudor ! "

the Hon. Mrs. Cunliffe, Mr. Aneurin Owen Pugh, and Mr. Parry, who concurred in recommending that a medal should be presented to Hugh Pugh, and Richard Jones, two boys of very great promise.

The Rev. T. Price, of Crickhowel, Radnorshire, in announcing the contest for the gold harp, took occasion to address the meeting at considerable length. The Rev. gentleman commenced with a warm panegyric upon the powers and sweetness of this national instrument. "He had heard the light and airy vibrations of the guitar of the south—the war-song of 'the Wolf' of the northern nations—'Come to me

Contest for the Gold Harp at the Royal Denbigh Eisteddfod, before H. R. H. the Duke of Sussex, 1828.

and I'll give you flesh'—the inspiriting pibroch of Donald Ddû, and the highland clans;—the martial drums and trumpets of England: but none had the soul-stirring powers of the Welsh Harp, in rousing to deeds of valour, or kindling a poetic fire in the breasts of all who heard it. Even the melodies of Erin, breathed 'in dying sounds her green hills among,' and in which the prevalence of the minor third and the flat seventh cast a shade of melancholy over even her liveliest strains;—even those were less plaintive, and less calculated to calm the ruffled passions and soothe the soul to peace, than were the 'native woodnotes wild' of Cambria's lyre, touched by the skilful hand of her minstrels. The thrilling tones of the Welsh Harp now heard within the ancient walls of Denbigh Castle,[5] and in the presence of a member of the Royal

---

[5] The following is a short history of this fortress. The castle which stands on the slope of a great rock, inclosing a part of the town, took in a considerable space, and was defended by strong walls and towers; the last are chiefly square, and do not exhibit that beautiful appearance, as those at Caernarvon and Conway. It was erected in the beginning of the reign of Edward I., from whom David, in defiance of his brother Llewelyn, chose to hold his lordship, together with the cantred of Dyffryn Clwyd. He made it his residence till the conquest of the country; soon after which he was taken near the place, loaded with irons, to the English monarch at Ruddhlan. Edward gave the lordships hereabouts to Henry Lacy, Earl of Lincoln, who built the castle, and inclosed within a wall the small town found there. Among other

family, were calculated, at once, to revive in the mind of every Welshman the recollection of the ancient glories of Cambria in the days of her Owens, her Llywelyns, and her Tudors: and to contrast her situation then with what it was at present under the mild and constitutional sway of the House of Brunswick. Cambrians were ever grateful for the blessings they enjoyed under the dominion of that Royal House; and their loyalty to it ever was, and ever would be, firm and unshaken. Thus it was, that while some of the other portions of the British Empire continued to be rent with intestine broils, and presented a scene of tumult and confusion bordering upon rebellion, the sons of Cambria were contented and happy, engaged in singing Penillion—reviving their national festivals—and cultivating the language and literature of the ancient Britons. He congratulated his countrymen upon an occupation at once so peaceable and so rational

privileges, he gave his vassals liberty of killing and destroying all manner of wild beasts, excepting in certain parts reserved out of the grant. In the time of Edward VI., he constituted Owen Tudor ranger of five parks in this lordship. On the death of Lacy, it descended to Thomas, Earl of Lancaster, who married his daughter: after the fatal end of that favourite, it was given by Edward III. to the equally unfortunate Roger Mortimer, Earl of Salisbury, who died in 1333, and at the reversal of the attainder of the Earl of March, it was restored to his grandson Roger, and by the marriage of Anne, sister to the last Earl of March, with Richard Plantagenet, Earl of Cambridge, it came to the House of York, and so unto the crown.

Here stands the chapel, called St. Hillary's, formerly belonging to the garrison, but now the place of worship for the town. In old times, on every Sunday, here were masses said for the souls of Lacy and Percy. Not far from it are the remains of an unfinished church, a hundred and seventy-five feet long, and seventy-one broad, and designed to have been supported by two rows of pillars. This noble building was begun in 1579, as appears by a date on the foundation stone. This church was begun under the auspices of Leicester, but it is said he left off his buildings in Wales, by reason of the public hatred he had incurred on account of his tyranny. A sum was afterwards collected, in order to complete the work, but it is said, when the Earl of Essex passed through Denbigh on his Irish expedition, he borrowed the money destined for the purpose, which was never repaid; and by that means the church had been left unfinished. The castle crowns the summit of the hill, one side of which is quite precipitous. The entrance is very magnificent, beneath a gothic arch, over which is the statue of Henry Lacy, sitting in stately flowing robes; on each side of the gateway stood a large octagonal tower. The breaches in it are vast and awful; they serve to discover the ancient manner of building. A double wall appears to have been built, with a great vacancy between, into which is poured all sorts of rubbish, stone, and hot mortar, which time has consolidated into a stony hardness. This part, as Leland says, was never completed, the work having been deserted by the Earl on the loss of his eldest son, who was accidentally drowned in the well, whose opening is still seen in the castle yard. Charles I. lay here on the 23rd September, 1645, after his retreat from Chester, in a tower called "Siamber y Brenhin," or the King's tower. The prospect through the broken arches is extremely fine, extending in parts over the whole vale of Clwyd, and all its eastern hills from Moelenlli to Diserth rock; a rich view, but deficient in water, the river Clwyd being too small to be seen, but in great rains so furious as to overflow a great space of the meadowy tract. Leland says, that Edward IV. was besieged in it, and that he was permitted to retire, on condition that he should quit the kingdom for ever; but this is doubted. Jasper Tudor, Earl of Pembroke, had, in the year 1459, possessed this place and several others in the Principality, in behalf of his weak half-brother Henry VI., but they were wrested from him by the Yorkists in the following year. In 1468 he returned, was

joined by two thousand Welsh, and burnt the town. In the beginning of November, 1645, the Parliament army obtained near this town a most important victory over the Royalists.

In searching British annals for accounts from which to infer whether any fortification existed on the Caledfryn yn Rhôs (the more ancient name of Denbigh), we meet with the following, which not only illustrates the foregoing remark on the character of feudal times, but may satisfy us that the site of Denbigh Castle contained a strong hold to the ruler of some of the adjoining cantreds of Dyffryn Clwyd, Rhôs, and Rhyfoniog.* "1115 Y bu ryfel rhwng Howel ab Ithel, yr hwn oedd yn cynnal Rhôs a Ryfoniog, a meibion Owain ab Edwyn o Degaingl, Ririd a Llowarch a'u brodyr ereill. Ac yna anvon y mae Howel ab Ithel ab Ririd ab Bleddyn, am Meredydd ab Bleddyn ei ewythr, a meibion Cadwgan ab Bleddyn yn borth iddo, canys hwynt hwy oedd yn cynnal y rhannau hynny o'r wlâd y gan Owain ab Edwyn. Ac wynt a ddoethant i Dyffryn Clwyd a'u llu, canys y wlâd honno oedd eiddo Owain ab Edwyn. A gwedi glowed o veibion Owain ab Edwyn oedd Howel a Meredydd a meibion Cadwgan yn dyfod, wynt a gynnullasant gyda meibion uchtryd i'w cefnderw i holl allu ar Ffrancod o Gaerlleon, ac a doethant yn i erbyn ac ymladd yn wychdir greulon o bob parth, ac o'r diwedd y ffoes meibion Owain ab Edwyn, ac y llâs Llowarch ab Owain ab Edwyn, a Iorwerth ab Meredydd, gwr da anrhydeddus, a llawer gyda hynny. Howel ab Ithel a vrathwyd, ac yn y seithfed wythnos y bu farw o'r brath." i.e. "In the year 1115, there was war between Howel ab Ithel, who held Rhôs and Rhyfoniog, and Ririd and Llowarch and their brethren, the sons of Owain ab Edwyn of Degaingl. Hereupon Howel ab Ithel ab Ririd ab Bleddyn sends for Meredydd ab Ririd ab Bleddyn his uncle, and the sons of Cadwgan ab Bleddyn, to his assistance, for they held those parts of the country from Owain ab Edwyn. Then they came to Dyrffyn Clwyd with their forces, for that country belonged to Owain ab Edwyn. And when the sons of Owain ab Edwyn heard that Howel and Meredydd and the sons of Cadwgan had arrived, they, together with their sons, joined their cousin with all their forces and the Normans of Chester, and came against him, and the fight was sharp and cruel on both sides. At last, the sons of Owain ab Edwyn fled, and Llowarch, the son of Owain ab Edwyn, was slain, and also Iorwerth, the son of Meredydd, a good and honourable man, and many with him. Howel ab Ithel was stabbed, and, seven weeks after, died of his wound." This feudal scuffle affords a specimen of the barbarity of the times before described, and a fair presumption there was a strong post or rallying point adjoining the contending territories; and if so, where more likely than the Caledfryn yn Rhôs!

* From *Llyfr Basing* (the Book of Basinwerk Abbey), written by Gyttyn Owen, a Monk there in the time of Edward IV., and now in the possession of Thomas Griffith, Esq., of Wrexham.

as that in which they were now engaged; and he was of opinion that the aristocracy and gentry of the country were promoting its best interests in giving encouragement to these national meetings." The Rev. gentleman concluded an eloquent and effective address, in the course of which he was often interrupted by the loud plaudits of the assembled multitude, by pronouncing the following Englyn on the Harp, which obtained the prize on a former occasion :—

> " Plethiadan tannau tynnion—Y delyn
> I'r dileag feddylion,
> Odlau Saint yw adlais hon,
> Llais neu fawl llfa nefolion."

The grand contest for the gold harp now took place, for which there were only two competitors, viz., Richard Jones, of Liverpool, who played " Codiad yr Ehedydd," or the *Rising of the Lark*; and Richard Roberts of Caernarvon, who played " Sweet Richard." This was a most delightful performance, and afforded great satisfaction to the lovers of the national instrument. The prize was well and ably contested for, but victory was awarded to Richard Roberts, who had his honours conferred by the hands of the Royal Duke, to whom the successful minstrel acknowledged his obligations.

In order to give every possible eclât to the royal visitor, and to afford an opportunity to the " fair maids of Cambria," to pay their respects to the distinguished stranger, a ball was held on the evening of Thursday, September 27th. On that occasion the town hall was brilliantly illuminated, and crowded with a most elegant company, including a long list of the nobility and gentry of the six counties of North Wales. About ten o'clock the Royal Denbigh band struck up " God save the King," which was no sooner heard than all was in motion; the ladies, superbly dressed, formed two columns, and left an opening for His Royal Highness the Duke of Sussex to pass. As he entered, cheers, waving of handkerchiefs, and clapping of hands ensued, and the royal visitor appeared highly pleased; he remained about two hours, when he departed, expressing the very great delight he had experienced, and passing a high but deserved compliment on the beauty of Cambria's fair daughters. So crowded was the town hall, that it was with difficulty sufficient room could be found for the dance. The orchestra was occupied by Mr. Stephenson's excellent quadrille band, over which the three concluding lines from Mr. Parry's additional stanza were inscribed :—

> " In strains of past ages, Oh! let us all sing,
> Till *Clwyd's* mighty mountains responsively ring,
> To welcome the brother of Britain's good King."

Upon the arrival of the Royal Duke and his party, from Kinmel, His Royal Highness was received at the entrance door by the Recorder, J. W. Griffith, Esq., R. P. Jones, Esq., M.D., Honorary Secretary, and the gentlemen belonging to the committee, bearing wands, and conducted to the upper end of the room, where a carpet was spread, on which was placed a chair for the royal visitor. After the departure of His Royal Highness, a good part of the company, which consisted of upwards of four hundred persons, continued the festive dance.

Letters were received by R. P. Jones, Esq., M.D., the Hon. Secretary, from the following distinguished writers, regretting their inability to attend on this interesting occasion—Sharon Turner, Esq., Sir Walter Scott, Bart., Robert Southey, Esq., Thomas Moore, Esq., and William Wordsworth, Esq.

The following ladies and gentlemen were invested with silver medals as a reward for their prize poems, essays, &c. :—Mr. Robert Davies, Nantglyn; Rev. R. Newcome, Ruthin: Rev. E. Hughes, Bodfary; Rev. J. Blackwell; Miss Angharad Llwyd, Caerwys; H. Maxwell, Esq., Denbigh; Edw. Parry, Chester; Rev. Mr. Probart, of Bolton; Mr. Samuel Evans, Caerwys; Rev. Samuel Roberts, Llanbrynmair; Rev. William Rees, Llansanan; Mr. Absalon Roberts, Llanrwst; and though last, not least, the Rev. Evan Evans, of Chester, who on this occasion gained the premier prize, the Bardic Chair of Gwynedd. He was installed by proxy (in the person of the Rev. John Blackwell, his fellow collegian), according to the ancient manner of the Britons, by laying of hands, &c., &c., by those only who were entitled, they having obtained the chair before at some previous meeting. One of these gentlemen pronounced the verdict of the judges,

"YNGWYNEB HAUL, AC YN LLYGAID GOLEUNI," by reciting the following Englyn, composed by the late Rev. Walter Davies, A.M. :—

" Credwch chwi feib Cyridwen,—fryd uchel
Na fradychwydd Awen ;
Cadeiriwyd mewn coed derwen,
Y Bardd a farnwyd yn ben ! "

The Royal Denbigh Eisteddfod was one of the most splendid meetings that ever took place up to that period. It was attended by nearly the whole of the nobility and gentry of Wales, whose numbers and high respectability added very considerably to the great attractions of this national fête. It took place on the bowling-green, in the month of September, 1828 ; the weather being remarkably fine, so much so that one of the bards, when he saw the glorious sun shining with its transcendent beams on the meeting, after he had recited his verses, exclaimed, with all his might,

" Rwy'n chwenych d'weud gair y chawneg,
Mawr—hawn ein Duw, am yr hin deg."

The Denbigh bowling-green is one of the most enchanting spots we know of, and commands a most splendid view of the celebrated Vale of Clwyd (Dyffryn Clodfawr Clwyd), extending about twenty miles in length by ten in width. The green is situated on a considerable elevation in the interior of the interesting remains of Denbigh Castle.

The Duke of Sussex visited Eaton Hall, the mansion of Earl Grosvenor, from Kinmel Park, Denbighshire, the seat of Colonel Hughes, where His Royal Highness had been staying for some time in a delicate state of health. The freedom of the city of Chester, and a congratulatory address, having been voted on Monday, the mayor and corporation proceeded to Eaton Hall on Tuesday, and presented the same. The Royal Duke expressed his high satisfaction at the distinction conferred on him, and regretted that the state of his health prevented him from receiving the franchise in person in their hall, but hoped, at some future and not distant period, he should again visit the hospitable roof under which he then resided, when he should be proud and happy to enrol his name in the books of their ancient and loyal city. The mayor, aldermen, sheriffs, and several members of the common council, in official costume, proceeded to Eaton Hall in a long cavalcade of carriages. They were received in the saloon of the Noble Earl and Lord Belgrave, accompanied by Sir W. W. Wynn, all three in their civic robes. They then proceeded in procession through the magnificent suite of rooms to the drawing-room, at the extremity of which the royal guest was seated, surrounded by the Countess Grosvenor, the Countess of Wilton, Lady Elizabeth Belgrave, Lord and Lady Delamere. Having been introduced to his Royal Highness, and presented the address, the Mayor and Corporation retired, completely gratified by their reception on the interesting occasion.

WILLIAM THE FOURTH.—This monarch succeeded to the throne of these realms on the death of his brother, George IV., in 1830. We cannot learn that he ever was in Wales or on the Borders on the capacity of King, but we have already alluded to his having visited it as Duke of Clarence. The arrangements for the coronation of William IV. and Queen Adelaide were of a plain and simple character, in accordance with their dispositions. The procession from the Hall to the Abbey, and the coronation feast in the Hall, were omitted. The popular enthusiasm was greater, however, than on any former occasion. The new entrance to St. James's Park was opened for the first time, and in the evening the metropolis was universally illuminated. The very lanes and alleys tenanted by the poorer classes were lighted to testify the loyal affection of even the humblest for " the Sailor King."

3 K

ER MOST GRACIOUS MAJESTY QUEEN VICTORIA succeeded to the throne of her ancestors on the death of her uncle, William IV. The only daughter of the Duke of Kent,[1] fourth son of George III., and of the Duchess of Kent, sister of Leopold, King of the Belgians, she was born on the 24th of May, 1819, and had reached the age (eighteen) required by law, before she could assume the reins of government, in the month previous to her accession to the throne. Her Majesty was crowned on the 20th of June, 1837, Queen of this mighty empire.[2]

> " ALL hail, Queen Victoria ! all hail to this day,
>   So teeming with promise—we welcome it here !
> As the bright stream of glory pursues its glad way,
>   And the blessing of thousands ascends in that cheer!
>
> But if thousands on thousands are happy before thee,
>   Saluting thy favours, and catching thy smiles ;
> Oh ! think of the millions of hearts that adore thee—
>   For this day is a Jubilee over the Isles !

> Not alone o'er the Isles—but Hindostan afar,
>   Doth our jubilee spread—in the West, the poor slave,
> As he prays for thy mercy, " Fair Liberty's star !
>   " Be the Queen of the Free, as the Queen of the Brave."
>
> Let the African joy, for his freedom is nigh ;
>   Our Queen would not reign but o'er happy and free :
> Let that thunder attest it—your banner on high—
>   The Banner of glory o'er land and o'er sea !

> Bear witness, ye nations ! the homage we pay,
>   The pride that we feel, and the love we declare ;
> For the Queen of our hearts is, on this happy day,
>   Not alone of the Brave—but the Queen of the Fair !

Till her accession to the throne Her Majesty led a retired life under the care of her mother, who, giving up her native land, devoted herself most assiduously to the education of her child, in order to make Her Majesty worthy of the high station to which she was born. Her Majesty is, undoubtedly, to be reckoned among the most accomplished ladies in her dominions. She is mistress of the modern languages, in which she expresses herself with grace and fluency. Her love of music developed itself at a very early age ; she plays with taste and expression on several instruments, and has inherited her royal grandfather's predilection for the organ. She is said to evince a decided preference for Italian music, and takes delight in the compositions of Beethoven and Mozart. Her voice is *mezzo soprano*. She inherits her numerous talents, not only from the Royal Family from whom her descent is paternally derived, but also from her illustrious mother.

---

[1] On her first memorable appearance before the council on the day of her accession, her Majesty said,—" I have learned from my infancy to respect and love the constitution of my native country." Stepping from the privacy of domestic life to the discharge of her high functions, she so demeaned herself as to cause general approbation. " She inspired," said the late Sir Robert Peel, " a confident expectation that he was destined to a reign of happiness for her people and of glory to herself." " There is something," he added, " which art cannot make nor lessons teach, and can only be suggested by a high and generous nature." Her Majesty has completely realised the hopes with which her careful education, and her demeanour on her accession to the throne inspired all her subjects.

[2] The following anecdote deserves to be mentioned as, beyond

The Queen's talents for drawing are so remarkable, that one of her masters, before her accession to the throne, when speaking of his Royal pupil, said: "The Princess Victoria would have made the best female artist of the age, if she had not been born to wear a crown." She told this gentleman that her pencil was a source of great delight to her; and that, when fatigued by severer studies, it was a refreshment to devote an hour to drawing. So affable was this amiable Princess in her deportment to her instructors, that she was beloved by them all. One of her drawing-masters, Mr. Westall, ventured to make known to her, that a lady whom he knew had expressed the most ardent desire to possess something sketched by her hand. "Indeed," replied her Royal Highness, with a smile; "I wish it were in my power to gratify the wish of every one so easily;" and dipping a pen in the standish she rapidly executed a free sketch of a horse's head, in the style called etching, and kindly presented it to him for his friend. The lady was astonished at the beauty of the execution, but observed that no one would believe it was really the work of the Princess Victoria unless it were distinguished by her autograph.

When this remark was repeated to the Princess, she very good-humouredly completed the happiness of the fortunate possessor of this valued drawing by adding her autograph.

In September, 1832, Her Most Gracious Majesty (when Princess Victoria), accompanied by her august and amiable mother, the Duchess of Kent, paid a visit to the Northern Principality and the Border Counties; they made a stay of some months at Plâs Newydd, on the banks of the Menai, in Anglesea, the beautiful marine residence of the Marquis of Anglesea.

This friendly and unostentatious visit of their Royal Highnesses was hailed as an event of no ordinary importance, and were accompanied by results most beneficially effective and durable, tending powerfully to direct the feeling of the Welsh to the present Royal Family, whom they themselves had in a great measure appointed to rule over the destinies of Britain.[3] Their Royal Highnesses were delighted with the truly loyal reception they received while travelling through the country. The dignified demeanour of the Royal strangers, coupled with their kind condescension; the happiness they evinced on viewing the garlands, triumphal arches, bonfires, and holiday clothes (in compliment to the future Queen of these realms) of an artless and affectionate people, has done much to cement and preserve inviolate, the good

measure, honourable to the Duke of Kent, that he deeply felt the great importance of diffusing the blessings of instruction among the lower orders of the people. The improved system of education enjoyed his steady, warm, and unceasing patronage, and that at a time when he had to labour in the sacred cause, almost alone, and unassisted. He introduced it into the army, having attached a school to his own regiment:—The school consisted of the children of the privates, and amounted to two hundred and twenty! A young man, a sergeant in the regiment, was trained as schoolmaster at the Borough-road, and the school was instituted at Maldon in Essex, where the regiment was then quartered. The Lieutenant-Colonel, and other officers, co-operated with their royal commander in his benevolent design. The regiment removed its quarters to Dunbar, where the establishment was carried on. By permission of the Duke, a number of the boys went to Edinburgh to illustrate the system, in a lecture which was delivered on the occasion in the city. On joining the Duke's regiment, if a recruit was found incapable of reading, he was sent to the school, and as a powerful stimulus to exertion, those who made a good proficiency in learning, were promoted as duplicate non-commissioned officers.

[3] It is a fact not generally known, that the *Hanoverian Succession* was secured to England by the vote of two Welsh members of the House of Commons, who decided the question of establishing George I. on the throne, in preference to other families of the royal blood. The following are the particulars of this transaction:—On the memorable day that the Hanoverian Succession Bill passed the House of Commons, in the beginning of Queen Anne's reign, Sir Arthur Owen, Bart., Member for Pembrokeshire, and Griffith

Rice, Esq., Member for Carmarthenshire, prevented the friends of the present Royal Family from being left in a minority.

The particulars known now but to few, as related by the posterity of these families, are: Sir Arthur Owen and Mr. Rice, on that day, met accidentally in the lobby, when the Tory administration were stealing the question through the House, at an early hour, when a majority of their friends attended by design, and when many of the Whigs were absent, not thinking it would come on till the usual hour. When the house was about to divide, one of the Whig members, seeing a seeming majority in favour of the House of Stuart, exclaimed, that the whole was an infamous proceeding. He immediately ran out of the house, almost frantic, in search of some of his partisans, to give a turn to the question in favour of the Elector of Hanover. Perceiving Sir Arthur Owen and Mr. Rice, as he came out, walking earnestly about the lobby, he addressed them thus with much vehemence—"What do you mean, gentlemen, staying here when the Hanoverian Succession Bill is going to be thrown out of the house!" "When I heard that," Sir Arthur used often to relate, "I made but one step into the house and my voice made the number equal for the bill, 117, and the Tories had no more. Mr. Rice, with great gravity, coming after me, had the honour of giving the casting vote in favour of the Hanoverian Succession! "Had it not" added Sir A. "been for the warmth of my zeal, being then a young man, this honour would have been mine; for as Mr. Rice was my senior, I might have followed him into the house." Sir A. Owen was the ancestor of Sir John Owen, Bart., the present M.P. for Pembroke. Mr. Rice was the ancestor of the Right Hon. Lord Dynevor.

3 K 2

understanding that should exist, between our Sovereign Lady the Queen, and the truly loyal inhabitants of the Principality.

The Arrival of their Royal Highnesses the Duchess of Kent and Princess Victoria at Shrewsbury.

Her Royal Highness the Duchess of Kent and the Princess Victoria arrived at the Talbot Hotel, Shrewsbury, accompanied by Lady Catherine Jenkinson, the Baroness Lehzen, Sir John Conroy, and Lady Conroy. Their entrance into the town, and progress through it, were greeted with enthusiastic cheers. At the Talbot, they were met by Viscount Clive and the Hon. Robert Clive, who introduced the Mayor, Archdeacons Butler and Bather, and the other members of the corporation; when the following address was read by the Deputy-Recorder:—

"Madam,—We, the Mayor, Aldermen, and assistants of the town of Shrewsbury, in common council assembled, humbly beg leave to express our high gratification at having the honour to see your Royal Highness and the Princess Victoria, for the first time, in this ancient and loyal borough. We most heartily wish your Royal Highness health and enjoyment in the beautiful and interesting scenes you are about to visit; and most respectfully hope that your Royal Highness will be pleased graciously to accept, on the part of ourselves and the rest of the inhabitants of this borough, our humble, but deep-felt expressions of personal respect to yourselves, and of duty and loyalty to our most gracious Sovereign and the august House of Brunswick."

Her Royal Highness the Duchess of Kent returned the following answer:—

"Mr. Mayor and Gentlemen,—I have to offer you my warmest thanks for the sentiments you have just expressed to the Princess and myself. We are highly gratified with the reception we have met with in your ancient borough; the inhabitants of which, distinguished for loyalty to our King, have received us as members of his family, so cordially, it will ever be my care that the recollection of such attachment be indelibly impressed on the memory of the Princess; as the happiness of her future life must depend on her identifying herself with the feelings of all classes in this great and free country."

Her Royal Highness then desired the Mayor to introduce to the Princess and herself each of the gentlemen present, by name, which being done, several other introductions took place, amongst which were the High Sheriff of the county, Sir Rowland Hill, and W. Ormsby Gore, Esq., M.P.

The honour of an invitation was then given to the Right Hon. the Lord Clive, the Hon. Henry Clive, and to the Mayor, to partake of dinner with the Princesses, when their Royal Highnesses again expressed the high gratification they had experienced at the warm testimonies of respect and loyalty which had been so fully evinced by the inhabitants during their stay within it; and, through the Mayor, they begged to make known to the inhabitants the high sense of gratitude and delight they felt at their zealous manifestations of attachment and goodwill.

The unaffected simplicity of the youthful Princess, her condescension and affability, won her the hearts of all who approached her. She frequently appeared at the windows of the Talbot, and bowed to the populace, who were assembled in a dense crowd in the street, and greeted her appearance with enthusiastic cheers. The Mayor presented her with a box of "Shrewsbury Cakes," made by Mr. Pidduck, of which her Royal Highness partook, and solicited her mother to join her. Another cake, the manufacture of Mr. Davies, the King's confectioner, was likewise presented; and elegant prints of the free schools and other public buildings of the town, were graciously accepted. The young Princess looked particularly hearty and well, and seemed greatly delighted with the homage and attentions of her visitors and future subjects.

The *cortège* then departed for Powis Castle, on the confines of Montgomeryshire; and on their first entrance into Wales, they were met by a portion of the Montgomeryshire yeomanry cavalry, commanded by Captain Corrie. The inhabitants of Pool had appointed a committee, and entered into a subscription for celebrating the day, and had erected various arches, and adorned their houses with oak, laurel, and flowers. A large assemblage of gentlemen of the town and neighbourhood, and a squadron of the Montgomeryshire yeomanry cavalry, formed themselves into a cavalcade, and met the royal visitors at Buttington. By a well-conducted arrangement, the committee had placed signals in various places, which gave the neighbouring inhabitants an opportunity of viewing the procession. From Buttington, the procession moved onwards through Pool to Powis Castle.

Standards were placed on the steeple and Town Hall, and also on the old tower of Powis Castle. The guns of Powis Castle, taken at Seringapatam, were used upon the occasion, under the direction of experienced artillery men; and those, with the ringing of the bells and loyal shouts of the spectators, made the scene a truly grand one. The royal visitors appeared to feel intensely their complimentary reception. About ninety gentlemen sat down in the evening to an excellent dinner at the Royal Oak, provided by Mrs. Whitehall, in her usual good style; Major Pugh, of Llanerchydol, in the chair. The president read a letter, conveying the thanks of the royal party to the gentlemen, civil and military, who had attended a deputation of the corporation and inhabitants of Pool. On the following morning (Friday), the Mayor and Corporation of Welshpool waited upon Her Royal Highness at Powis Castle, and presented an address, which was most graciously received. The following is an extract:—" As Welshmen, devotedly attached to our most gracious sovereign and the illustrious House of Brunswick, we feel the distinguished honour conferred upon us by the appearance among us of your Royal Highness; and in behalf of ourselves and the inhabitants of the ancient and loyal town of Pool, we most gladly embrace this opportunity of expressing our profound and devoted attachment to your Royal Highness and the Princess Victoria, to which we humbly venture to add our hearty wishes and earnest prayers for the health and happiness of your Royal Highness, trusting that you will be graciously pleased to accept this testimony of our respect with your accustomed favour and condescension."

The answer of her Royal Highness was as follows :—

" GENTLEMEN,—It has been for some time my wish to visit, with the Princess, the Principality.   But I was unprepared to enter it in the agreeable manner that so cordially marked our reception in Welshpool—

Powis Castle, the seat of the Right Hon. the Earl of Powis.

a reception so loyal to the King, so gratifying to us as members of his family.   I, therefore, seize this occasion to assure you, and the inhabitants of Welshpool, how deeply we feel the attention shown to us yesterday by all classes on our coming into Wales."

In the evening the treasurer of the schools was presented with a letter from Sir John Conroy, inclosing from her Royal Highness the Duchess of Kent a donation of 100*l.* in aid of the schools.

Their Royal Highnesses arrived at Oswestry about four o'clock.   They were escorted to Llanymynach by a party of the Montgomeryshire Cavalry, where the Oswestry squadron of N. S. Cavalry, under the command of Captain Croxon, were in attendance to receive the royal party.   Nothing could exceed the manifestation of attachment to the illustrious travellers which was displayed along the " Marches " by the " Borderers ; " the road was literally lined to catch a glance of the heiress apparent.   The rockmen welcomed them across the River Verniew with a royal salute of twenty-one rounds from the hill ; houses, gates, were decorated at this place as were those at Pant, Sweeney and Morda on the road to Oswestry. At that town the illustrious visitors were received at the turnpike by the High Steward (the Hon. Thomas Kenyon), the deputy mayor, the coroner, and other members of the corporation, in their robes, and a great number of gentlemen and tradesmen of the town, with white staves, together with an immense multitude from the town and country.   Lord Clive descended from the carriage in which he had accompanied Sir John Conroy, and proceeded with the corporation on foot to the Wynnstay Arms, at a slow pace ; the carriage, in which was Sir John, the Princess's carriage, and the attendants in a third, following one another, gave the people an opportunity of seeing those distinguished personages.   An address had been prepared by the corporation; but an express had been sent off the previous evening to the deputy-mayor from Powis Castle, to say that Her Royal Highness could not vary from her usual practice, in not receiving addresses from places where she did not stop.   This importunate etiquette prevented its delivery, and the Princess remained a short time in their carriage opposite the Wynnstay Arms, while changing horses. In the midst of the acclamations of the people, the Hon. Thomas Kenyon, High Steward, congratulated the royal visitors in the name of the corporation; and in conclusion was commanded by the Duchess to inform the "good people of Oswestry" of "the very great satisfaction she felt at the manner in which she was received by the inhabitants of the town and neighbourhood; and that she felt obliged by their loyal and affectionate feeling manifested

Wynnstay Park, the seat of Sir Watkin Williams Wynn, Bart., M.P

towards herself and the Princess Victoria." "The History of Oswestry," compiled by Mr. Minshull, Oswestry, was presented to them as they sat in the carriage, and was most graciously accepted. The horses having been put to, the carriages moved on, the corporation, and gentlemen, walking slowly before, through the town, stopping at intervals, to gratify the eager gaze of the well-dressed thousands in the town. The streets of Oswestry presented in appearance, avenues of oak and laurel, with innumerable flags, streamers with appropriate inscriptions, the ladies waving their handkerchiefs.   The corporation and gentlemen conducted the cavalcade to the Beatrice Gate, and the Oswestry squadron continued to escort it to Chirk Bridge; Captain Croxon riding on one side of the royal carriage, and Cornet Nicholls on the other.   Here they were met by Sir W. W. Wynn, in his splendid uniform of aid-de-camp to the King, and a body of the Denbighshire cavalry were in waiting to receive them, with a multitude of honest Cambrians rending the air with shouts; Lord Clive and Sir J. Conroy then descended from their carriage, and introduced Captain Croxon to the Duchess. Sir Watkin then took charge of his illustrious visitors (having been previously introduced by his lordship), when the Duchess expressed her high opinion of the officers and gentlemen of the Oswestry squadron under his command.

The roar of cannon from the castle announced the arrival at Chirk; which place they passed through, greeted by the inhabitants. The scene at the bridge was very imposing; the two bodies of cavalry meeting on the confines of England and Wales; the sun darting his rays on the helmets of the cavalry; the assembly of the people; the roar of the cannons, presented a spectacle not easily to be forgotten. At Newbridge, a royal salute was fired from four nine-pounders on the royal approach by the staff of the Royal Denbighshire Militia, under the command of Captain Jones; the party turned to the right at the bridge, and proceeded under the new entrance of the Dee into Wynnstay Park, the princely residence of Sir W. W. Wynn. The royal party attended Ruabon church on Sunday, where the service was performed by the Rev. Rowland Wingfield, A.M.

Their Royal Highnesses on the Monday following visited the aqueduct at Pontcyssyllte, accompanied by Sir W. W. Wynn, Bart., and Mr. Stanton, and inspected that great work for nearly an hour. Thence they proceeded to Llangollen, and changed horses at the King's Head (now Royal Hotel). The inhabitants decorated their houses with festoons and laurels, evergreens, and flowers. The portico over the door of the above hotel was highly ornamented, over which was placed a royal crown; a very large triumphal arch was also thrown over the street, about twenty yards from the door, highly decorated as above. The royal party remained about half an hour, during which time the dense crowd occasionally complimented them with deafening acclamations of " God bless her Royal Highness Princess Victoria and her amiable mother."

The windows of the Hand Hotel, and of the King's Head, were full of ladies waving their handkerchiefs. Every one was delighted with the affability and condescension of their Royal Highnesses.

The royal visitors arrived in safety at Bangor, inspected the Suspension Bridge, accompanied by Mr. W. Provis, and terminated their journey for a day or two at Beaumaris, Anglesey. Soon after crossing the Menai Bridge, the guns of the Craig-y-don yachts fired a royal salute, and upon the cavalcade entering Beaumaris the royal ladies were most enthusiastically greeted by the loud acclamations of the whole population. The royal standard was hoisted upon the battlements of the ancient castle of Beaumaris, and in front of the Bulkeley Arms Hotel; the vessels in the bay displayed their colours; and festoons of ribands, flowers, and evergreens, were hung across the main street leading to the hotel. It is one of the strange revolutions of history, that here, in this very spot, where it is supposed the bards of Wales were massacred by order of Edward I., now, in the reign of William IV., and in the presence of the heir apparent, the representatives and descendants of these very bards should be the subjects of honour, and looked upon with pride and veneration, by the nobility and gentry of the land.[4]

On reaching the Bulkeley Arms Hotel, the royal party were waited upon by the landlady, Mrs. Bicknell, who had been indefatigable in making every requisite preparation for the suitable reception of her illustrious

---

[4] Beaumaris Castle was the last of the three great fortresses erected by Edward I. to hold in awe his new and unwilling subjects on both sides of the Menai. For this purpose, he fixed upon a flat near the water side, with a view of surrounding it with a fosse, for the double purpose of defence, and bringing small craft to unload their cargoes under its walls; part of which canal, called Llyn-y-Green, was, till lately, remaining; and the large iron ring, to which the craft were fastened, is still in its place at the great east gate. Within the Castle is an area or square of 190 feet, with obtuse corners; on the right is the chapel—an admirable piece of masonry, and the only entire room in all Edward's buildings; its stone arched roof having saved it from the general dilapidation. Opposite to the south-east entrance is the Great Hall, 70 feet long, and 23 broad, having a range of five elegant windows, and forming a front (its turreted angles excepted) that has rather a modern appearance; and though, upon the whole, a fortress of prodigious magnitude, yet its low situation, and the great diameter of its nearly circular towers, takes off considerably from its height and appearance.

> " Ah! what avails it that the lordly tower
> Attracts the thoughtless stare, and vacant hour!
> If ev'ry Bard with indignation burns,
> When to the tragic tale the eye returns;
> If for his haunted race, to distant times,
> There 's still reserv'd a vengeance for his crimes."—LLWYD.

The massacre of the bards is an act of cruelty imputed to Edward without evidence, and inconsistent with his temper, which fitted him for what stern policy required, but was not infected by wanton ferocity. It is one of those traditions of which the long prevalence attests the deep-rooted hatred of a nation towards conquerors.

guests. Within a few minutes after their arrival, the Duchess appeared upon the portico, leading by the hand the youthful Princess. They were received with deafening shouts of applause from the immense multitude which filled the street in front of the hotel. The young Princess at once displayed all the buoyancy of spirit, so beautifully characteristic of her time of life, and the bloom of healthful beauty. On Tuesday afternoon the royal ladies walked across the green of the landing-place, where a ten-oared barge belonging to the yacht waited for them. The barge crew received them with the appropriate naval honours, and with the Royal standard displayed at the stern. They were rowed along side the royal yacht, and immediately on their coming on board, the standard of England was hoisted at the main, and the yacht getting under weigh stood down as far as Puffin Island, and returned to her anchorage at half past three o'clock, when the barge was manned, and the royal party were rowed to shore with the same ceremonies which had attended their embarkation. A great number of the respectable inhabitants and visitors of Beaumaris were assembled on the green, whose respectful salutations were returned by the Duchess and the Princess with condescension and affability.

On Wednesday morning a meeting of the Mayor, Bailiffs, and Capital Burgesses of Beaumaris was held at the council chamber; where it was resolved to present a congratulatory address to the Duchess and Princess on the occasion of their visit to Beaumaris. The address was moved by T. P. Williams, Esq., M.P., seconded by W. W. Sparrow, Esq., and unanimously adopted by the meeting. On Thursday morning, the Mayor, (Rowland Williams, Esq.,) and a deputation waited on the Duchess at the Bulkeley Arms Hotel; when the following address was read by the Mayor :—

"WE, the Mayor, Bailiffs, and Burgesses of the ancient and loyal borough of Beaumaris, beg to express the sincere pleasure and gratification afforded us by the presence of your Royal Highness in this island; as well as our grateful sense of the distinguished honour conferred upon the borough, by your Royal Highness having condescended to make choice of it as a place of residence for yourself and your illustrious daughter. United as we are by the bonds of duty, loyalty, and attached to our most gracious Sovereign and every member of his illustrious house, we entreat your Royal Highness will accept our strongest assurance of respect and attachment towards yourself and your illustrious daughter, and sincerely hope that your Royal Highness may enjoy lengthened years of uninterrupted health and happiness.

"Signed in the Council Chamber in the name and on the behalf of the Corporation of Beaumaris, this eighth day of August, 1832.

"ROWLAND WILLIAMS, *Mayor.*"

The following was her Royal Highness's answer to the address :—

"MR. MAYOR AND GENTLEMEN.—I have to thank you, most warmly, for the Princess and myself, for the manner in which you express yourselves, on our visit to this charming place. We receive with much gratification your assurances of good feeling to us, dictated as they are by your loyal attachment to the King; and which has led you to receive us with so much attention."

A most numerous meeting of the inhabitants and visitors of the town, was also held in the Guildhall, on Wednesday afternoon, at one o'clock, pursuant to a requisition, for the purpose of deciding upon the best mode of testifying their respect for her Royal Highness the Duchess of Kent and her illustrious daughter: when it was resolved, that an address, drawn up and presented by the Rev. Dr. Howard, and

---

From the death of Llewelyn, one of the most ancient branches of the Celtic race lost their national character. For two centuries more Wales suffered all the evils of anarchy and misrule. The Marches were governed by arbitrary maxims; in the interior the people suffered alike from banditti and from tyrannical magistrates. It was not till the reign of the Tudors, "Britannia's issue," that wise attempts were made to humanise them by equal laws. Their language withheld many of them from contributing to English literature; and yet their small numbers, their constant disorder, and their mul- tiplied links of dependence, repressed a genius which might have otherwise assumed a national form. If considered, as they now should be, as a part of the people of England, their contributions have been by no means inadequate to reasonable expectations. But the mental produce of a nation has been inconsistently expected from a people robbed of national character, and who are only now re-appearing on a footing of legal and moral equality with all other Englishmen."— *Sir James Mackintosh.*

seconded by the Lord Bishop of Dromore, should be presented to her Highness by a deputation, consisting of the Lord Bishop of Dromore, Richard Armit, Esq., —— Gresley, Esq., Francis Pendergast, Sir Daniel Bailey, Rowland Williams, Mayor, Rev. Dr. Howard, John Wright, Esq., William P. Poole, Esq., Llywellyn Jones, M.D., Rev. Mr. Bold, Mr. Archdeacon Saurin, Leonard Naisteck, Esq., W. Molineux, Esq., Andrew Gresley, Junior, Esq., Thomas Peers Williams, M.P., Esq., Edmund Meyrick, Esq., Mr. Redding, Mr. Thomas, John Williams, Esq., Richard Howard, Rev. Bulkeley Williams, and Mr. Balley.

The deputation accordingly waited upon her Royal Highness at the hotel on Thursday morning; when the following address was presented and read by the Rev. Dr. Howard:—

"WE, the undersigned, the inhabitants and visitors of the town of Beaumaris, anxious to manifest the high consideration we entertain for your royal person and the regard in which we hold your character and virtues, beg leave to express the gratification we feel in seeing your Royal Highness and the Princess Victoria in the island of Anglesea. With that loyal attachment which has so long characterised our country, we hail the arrival of your Royal Highness amongst us with a respectful and affectionate welcome; and offer our most ardent hopes, that an excursion which has conferred on us so much honour and delight, may prove to your Royal Highness and the Princess Victoria, a source of health, pleasure, and agreeable remembrance."

Their Royal Highnesses the Duchess of Kent and Princess Victoria's entrance into Caernarvon Castle, the birth-place of Edward the Second.

The royal visit to Caernarvon was intended to be private, but it became known, on the morning of the 9th of August, 1832, that such an event was to occur, and, notwithstanding the shortness of the time that intervened, the most active preparations were set on foot to give the presumptive heiress to the throne, and her august mother, a reception worthy the acceptance of royalty, and becoming the loyalty of the free and independent burgesses of Caernarvon to bestow.

A yacht had been put in readiness to reconvey the illustrious party to Beaumaris, and Mr. Parry, the landlord of the Uxbridge Arms, upon a short notice, received orders to prepare a luncheon.

The burgesses were hastily summoned to the Guildhall. The deputy-ranger, William Roberts, Esq., and the senior bailiff, Dr. O. O. Roberts,' being out of town when the news arrived, Mr. Edward Parry, the junior bailiff, presided. An address was prepared, and, after the programme had been arranged, all hands set to work: flags were hoisted, guns were loaded, and every one had his throat cleared, preparatory to giving true lusty British cheers and huzzahs, to welcome the visit of Britain's future Queen, and her august mother.

At half-past twelve, a procession of the burgesses and inhabitants, headed by the two bailiffs and the corporate officers, in their robes and the insignia of their respective offices, moved from the Uxbridge Arms Hotel to meet the royal cavalcade. The Bangor road presented a most animated appearance: flags floated in every direction, and the hedges and trees on both sides of the road were crowded.

When the royal party arrived at the place where the procession was, the royal cavalcade halted; and Sir John Conroy introduced the two bailiffs as the two chief corporate officers to their Royal Highnesses. When the procession had fallen into line, and began to move towards the town, a royal salute was fired by the *Paul Pry* steamer.

Upon the arrival of the Duchess's party at the Hotel, a royal salute was fired from the guns at Twthill, to which the immense crowd assembled in the large open space in front of the Hotel, responded with such cheering acclamations as must have convinced the royal party that the people of Wales had hearts worthy the character of ancient British loyalty. When the Duchess presented her royal daughter at the front window of the Hotel, the acclamations were repeated with, were it possible, greater energy.

The sweetness and modesty which characterised the demeanour of the young Princess in making her acknowledgments, excited universal admiration; and she seemed highly pleased and gratified, as she repeatedly appeared at the window, at the cordial and respectful reception which she experienced.

Sir John Conroy having announced that the Duchess was ready to receive the deputation, the corporate officers, attended by a number of burgesses and other inhabitants, proceeded into their Royal Highness's apartment.

The Duchess and her august daughter received them with great urbanity, and stood in front of their attendants, while the senior bailiff, Dr. O. O. Roberts, read the following address:—

" MADAM,—We, the deputy-mayor, the bailiffs, burgesses, and other inhabitants of the ancient and loyal borough of Caernarvon, humbly beg to approach your Royal Highness and the Princess Victoria, with sincere congratulations on your arrival in the Principality, but more especially to express our high gratification at the honour now done to our town, the birthplace of the Royal Edward.

" We avail ourselves of this opportunity to express our warmest feelings of loyalty to our most Gracious Sovereign, and humbly to request your Royal Highness to accept the assurance of our highest esteem and respect."

As soon as the reading of the address had been concluded, her Royal Highness made, in a distinct and emphatic tone, the following answer:—

" MR. MAYOR AND GENTLEMEN,—The Princess and myself were not aware that this visit, of which you could hardly have been apprised, would have permitted you to show us this attention. But the loyalty of your ancient borough to the King, has led you to hasten to offer us, as members of his family, the demonstrations of attachment that have marked our reception here to-day; and for which we are most grateful."

The royal party, after having partaken of the luncheon hastily prepared for them, a little after two o'clock entered an open barouche in which they travelled, and were escorted by the corporate officers and

---

' We are indebted to Dr. O. O. Roberts for this interesting account of the Royal Visit to the ancient town of Caernarvon.

an immense crowd, whilst they proceeded, through Porth Mawr, into High-street and up Castle-street, to the principal entrance into the castle called the King's-gate, to visit the castle.

When the royal party arrived at the Castle-gate, the crowd, with that sense of propriety seldom to be met with in other places, fell back, and very few individuals, excepting those in office, intruded with their presence in the castle.

The royal party having entered, they appeared much struck with the sense of propriety manifested by the immense crowd of the people assembled, as well as with astonishment at the grandeur and extent of the ruins, which they examined with minute attention.

Whilst the Princess Victoria was being escorted up the spiral steps to the top of the Eagle Tower, by Sir John Conroy, and two or three of the attendants, the Duchess of Kent remained below in the castle-yard, attended by the two bailiffs and the officers of the corporation.

The Princess Victoria, led by Sir John Conroy from the apartment in which Edward II. was born, appeared upon that parapet of the castle which adjoins it; the Duchess at this moment displayed considerable emotion; the senior bailiff, Dr. O. O. Roberts, observed to her Royal Highness how many mighty changes had taken place in the kingdom, during the nearly five centuries and a half that had elapsed since the last appearance of an heir to the throne upon that wall.

The Princess having descended to the castle yard, the royal party proceeded to examine the "Queen's Gate," at the opposite extremity of the area, through which Eleanor, Queen of Edward I., entered, previous to giving birth to the first Prince of Wales of the Saxon line, which, by permanently uniting England and Wales, has been productive of so many blessings to the Principality.

Having re-entered their carriages, the royal party proceeded to *Porth yr Aur*, where, under a royal salute, they embarked in a boat waiting to convey them on board the royal yacht.

Early in the morning of the day proposed, it was known at Caernarvon that their Royal Highnesses would pass through the town, on their visit to the romantic lake of Llanberis. Accordingly, the fires lighted on the previous evening on Torhil and on the Elidir mountain, in honour of the Duchess's birthday, were scarcely extinct, when Caernarvon was all in a bustle of preparation to display yet further proofs of attachment to the royal visitors. The day was such as the morning promised, clear and refreshing. The Uxbridge Arms Hotel was tastefully decorated with evergreens and flags. The streets leading to Llanberis road from the hotel were profusely decorated; the neighbouring woods seemed to have been dismantled of their branches to supply the fronts of the houses with foliage. Flags, with appropriate inscriptions, were hoisted opposite the houses in the Bangor road, and in many places in the town. The children of the National Schools were drawn up, girls and boys separately, in front of the hotel, headed by benevolent individuals and their teachers. A little after twelve o'clock the royal carriage arrived in front of the hotel. It was soon perceived that the Princess Victoria was not present, and a feeling of anxiety pervaded the people to learn the cause. It was understood that her Royal Highness was slightly indisposed, on account of the fatigues of the preceding day, and it had not been deemed advisable that she should leave home. The Duchess seemed much pleased with the children, and, after changing horses, the party proceeded in the direction of Llanberis amid the loud greetings of the assembled inhabitants. The road to Llanberis pursues its course chiefly along an elevated ridge at the foot of the Leiont, winding over its rugged bed, guiding the eye to its origin in the lake of Llanberis. The cavalcade stopped at a temporary pier, erected for the embarkation of the royal party, near the northern extremity of the lake, a few hundred yards from the ruins of the hall of Llywelyn, where, tradition informs us, King Edward I. embarked to attack the Welsh when they made their last stand. Here her Royal Highness and suite entered the boat of T. A. Smith, Esq., provided for their reception, at the stern of which floated the royal standard for the first time on the lake since the days of Edward I. The cortège was increased by the arrival of a number of carriages from Caernarvon, which kept pace with the boat as it proceeded up the lake, and pedestrians lined the roads and rocks. As the boat proceeded slowly along, the royal visitor was greeted by salutes from above two thousand rock cannon, a species of artillery which will require some description : in convenient parts of the rock, holes are bored to a sufficient depth, and being charged with gunpowder, are connected by means of trains, so that upon the application of a match countless successive explosions take place, which reverberate in a fearful manner among the mountains. The royal party landed at the ruins of Dolbadarn, one of the ancient British castles which guarded the pass, where they were escorted by several hundred members of the Benefit Societies of the vale to the new inn just erected by Mr. Smith, and now called the Royal Victoria, where the royal banner was displayed opposite the Hill of Council, where the barons of Snowdon encamped when they made with Edward the treaty which united England and Wales. Considerable disappointment was felt when it became known that the young Princess, or, as the quarry-men called her, " Y Frenines fach," (the little queen) was not of the party. After partaking of refreshments, the royal party proceeded to visit the ancient castle, and Mr. Smith's beautifully situated cottage on the lake; they then set out on their return by land, receiving as they went a thundering farewell from the mountain cannons, which the Llangciau Eryri (lads of Snowdon) had reloaded.

Never was there witnessed such an intensity of feeling as that which was displayed on the anniversary of the Duchess's natal day. Bonfires were kindled on Penman Mawr, Snowdon, Glydir, Garth Point, and several other mountains and eminences. At Beaumaris, the thunder of artillery and the merry pealing of the bells ushered in the morning of the 17th, and as the day progressed the town presented the most animated appearance. Triumphal arches crossed some of the principal streets, which were thronged with well-dressed and respectable people, and flags and banners, bearing appropriate devices, floated on all the public edifices, and on the habitations of numbers of private individuals. About twelve o'clock, public notices were posted about the town, intimating Sir R. Bulkeley's request that the two friendly societies (the Druid and St. David,) established in the town, should meet at the castle at six o'clock in the evening, and walk thence in procession to the green, for the purpose of drinking her Royal Highness's health in good Welsh ale. This announcement collected not only the members of the societies, but also an immense concourse of the residents and visitors of the town in the castle yard at the appointed hour. On the arrival of the worthy and esteemed baronet and his lovely bride within the castle, deafening cheers echoed through that ancient building. The two societies then formed in order of procession, headed by Sir Richard and Lady Bulkeley, and a numerous party of their friends, and proceeded to the front of the Williams Bulkeley Arms, where they halted, and immediately her Royal Highness and her august daughter appeared in front of the portico, accompanied by Sir John Conroy, and others of their suite. Their Royal Highnesses appeared highly gratified by this mark of public attention, and expressed their sense of it in the most courteous and condescending manner.

A circle having been formed, Sir Richard, placing himself in an elevated position, announced the health of the King; he then gave the health of her Royal Highness the Duchess of Kent. He alluded to her great and munificent charities, to her kindness and condescension, and then to the great and high charge of guarding, from infancy to maturity, the future Queen of this mighty kingdom; a charge, which he very justly observed, could hardly be placed in better hands. Every word he said appeared to give the deepest satisfaction to the vast crowd around him, and no health was ever given or pledged with greater sincerity and gratitude. Sir Richard then took his leave, cautioning all to be temperate in their festivities, and return early to their respective homes.

In the river the pleasure yachts and other vessels were gaily attired in their holiday uniform, and peculiar honour was paid to the day by Mr. James Watson, of Liverpool, who, in his splendid yacht, the Zephyr, fired repeated royal salutes, the reverberating echoes of which, amongst the neighbouring mountains, had the most imposing effect. During the night this beautiful vessel was illuminated in such a manner as, from the shore, to present a blazing mass of blue light.

At Bangor, on Thursday, a meeting of the clergy and principal inhabitants was held in the Chapter Room of the Cathedral. The Lord Bishop of Bangor honoured the meeting with his presence, and took the chair; and an address was adopted. A deputation consisting of the Lord Bishop of Bangor,

G. H. D. Pennant, Esq., T. A. Smith, Esq., Captain Walker, Rev. J. H. Cotton, Rev. J. Hamer, Rev. R. R. P. Mealy, J. H. Cottingham, Esq., Rev. H. Price, and P. Berthon, Esq., was appointed to present the address at Beaumaris on Friday, with instructions that at their interview with the royal visitors they should use every respectful endeavour to induce them to honour the city of Bangor with their presence in the course of the day; as the inhabitants of all classes, from the highest to the lowest, were most anxious to have an opportunity of displaying on that auspicious day their loyalty and attachment to the illustrious Princesses. The address was presented accordingly, and a most gracious answer returned by her Royal Highness, who was also pleased to intimate her intention to visit Bangor, in company with her interesting daughter, between two and four o'clock in the afternoon. The deputation then withdrew, and upon their return with the glad intelligence that the royal visitors would certainly be at Bangor in the afternoon, every face brightened, and every hand was exerted to perfect the preparations for their reception, which had been commenced the previous evening. A battery of seven four pounders was procured from Conway, and planted on the mountain which overlooks the city; carpenters were set to work to form triumphal arches; woodmen, by permission of the proprietors, laid the axe to the branches of the oaks in the neighbouring forests; flowers were liberally supplied from the gardens; and the civic population, both male and female, were busied in devising and executing banners with appropriate mottoes for the occasion.

About three o'clock the royal cavalcade was seen approaching the head of the town by the road leading from the Menai Bridge, the cry of "They are coming," ran through the city in an instant.

The royal visitors, with their attendants entered the town in two open carriages, which were followed by three gentlemen on horseback. In compliment to the fair maids of Cambria, the Duchess and Princess wore the head-dress of the country, the Welsh hat, and we may venture to add, without fear of contradiction, that they well became the national costume which they honoured by wearing. This delicate token of respect to the country was acknowledged by all, especially by the female part of the spectators, with admiration. After parading the town to the delight of the assembled multitude, the horses were urged to a brisk trot, which speedily brought the royal party to Vaynol, the hospitable seat of T. A. Smith, Esq., by whom, and his amiable and accomplished lady, the Duchess, the Princess, and the ladies and gentlemen of their suite, were entertained to dinner. In the evening the royal party returned by the Menai Bridge to the Bulkeley Arms Hotel, Beaumaris.

On Monday the royal party visited Conway. On arriving within the Castle, their Royal Highnesses were received by the Lord Bishop of St. Asaph and his lady, Mr. and Mrs. Assheton Smith, and the Rev. John Owen, Vicar of Conway; at the head of a numerous deputation of gentlemen appointed to present an address of the inhabitants to her Royal Highness the Duchess of Kent.

Having minutely inspected the beautiful ruins of the castle, the party proceeded to the terrace, at the south end, where the address was presented and read by the Rev. John Owen, and a most gracious answer returned by her Royal Highness. After partaking of a collation, the royal party promenaded the town, and during their progress they received from all ranks and classes the most evident marks of respect and attachment, of which they showed their feeling in the most amiable and condescending manner.

About three o'clock the royal party left Conway in their carriages, and returned by Aber, Bangor, and the Menai Bridge, to Beaumaris. All along their route they were received by all classes with the highest respect.

On Friday the gentlemen of the town and neighbourhood of Conway dined at the Castle Hotel, in honour of the day, being anxious to show every mark of respect to a lady whose extreme affability and high character made her really beloved. The chair was taken by Sir John Hilton, who made an admirable president. When the health of her Royal Highness and also the health of the interesting Princess Victoria was proposed, nothing could surpass the enthusiasm manifested. Royal salutes were fired at Deganwy and Conway Castles.

All the population of the surrounding districts went forth to welcome the royal visitors. In the course of the day, the *Palmerston* steamer arrived from Bristol, bringing four carriages and fifteen horses for the use of the Duchess during her stay, and this vessel, as well as the *Emerald* cutter, in attendance on the Duchess, fired a royal salute as the cortège entered the town. The Princess seemed greatly delighted, and showed herself several times at the windows to an admiring populace. The sons of Mona seemed to be in raptures with the blooming appearance and prepossessing manners of the young and interesting Princess, testifying their approbation, in their own expressive language, with the remark, "*Y mae hi yn beth bach anwyl.*" "Oh, she is a dear little creature."

On Tuesday, her Royal Highness, accompanied by Sir John Conroy and Lady Conroy, took an excursion round Puffin Island, in the *Emerald* cutter. Off Friars, Lady Williams, in the *Prince Llewelyn*, from Liverpool, came up with the royal party and fired a royal salute, amidst the cheers of passengers and crew. Her Royal Highness and the Princess acknowledged the compliment by standing forward in the cutter. The *Llewelyn* kept in the wake of the *Emerald* until they arrived at Beaumaris, where the illustrious visitors landed. On going ashore, the passengers in the *Llewelyn* joined the assembled crowd in three times three cheers. The distinguished objects of the compliment turned round and graciously made their acknowledgments.

On Thursday they went to view the Menai Bridge, after which they proceeded to visit Caernarvon. They were received by the corporation and the inhabitants with all possible honour.

On their return under the Menai bridge a salute was fired from cannon placed on the pillars, which was answered from the *Paul Pry* and *Llewelyn* steamers below. The effect was grand. The hills on each side were covered with people, and the Craig-y-don yachts were dressed out in all the finery of colours. The *Paul Pry* was filled with ladies and gentlemen belonging to the Principality. Among them was Mr. Finchett Maddock, the member for Chester. The tide being against them, the *Paul Pry* took the *Emerald* in tow, and the party arrived at Beaumaris to dinner, at seven.

On Friday, the Princess Victoria partook of an early dinner with T. A. Smith, Esq., of Vaenol, and his lady, on board of that gentleman's magnificent steam-vessel, the *Menai*.

Since their arrival at Beaumaris, the illustrious strangers were visited at the hotel by most of the people of distinction now resident in this quarter of the country. The local charities have greatly benefited by the bounty of the benevolent Duchess. Sir John Conroy has intimated to the mayor and rector of Beaumaris, that it was her Royal Highness's command to make the following donations in her name :—

Her Royal Highness the Duchess of Kent has given at Beaumaris, to the Society of Antient Druids, 25*l.*; the Caernarvonshire and Anglesey Dispensary, 50*l.*; the Ladies' Society of Beaumaris, 25*l.*; the National Schools of Beaumaris, 50*l.*; to aid in building a school-room, 50*l.* At Bangor, for the relief of the widows and orphans of clergymen, and disabled and necessitous clergymen, 25*l.*; the National Schools, 50*l.*; the Female Friendly Society, 25*l.*; the Lying-in Charity, 25*l.*; the Penny Club, 25*l.*; the Infant School, 50*l.* At Conway, to the Conway Charity Schools, 30*l.* At Pwllheli, in aid of the subscription for the new church, 25*l.*; in aid of the National School built at Bryngwran for the benefit of the three parishes of Llechylched, Ceirchriog, and Llanbeulan, in the County of Anglesea, 26*l.* The last public act of their Royal Highnesses in the Principality was laying the foundation of the school for boys, in the parishes of Llanedwen and Llanfair pwll gwyn gyll, to which they had munificently contributed, and the land for which, (to the extent of an acre,) was liberally granted by the Rev. Henry Rowlands of Plas-gwyn. The ceremony was performed by their Royal Highnesses jointly, and an appropriate prayer was offered up by the Rev. Henry Rowlands. A grateful and affectionate address from the inhabitants of these two parishes was presented on the occasion, and most graciously received.

Their Royal Highnesses the Duchess of Kent and the Princess Victoria, during their stay at Plas Newydd, the seat of the Marquis of Anglesea, visited Holyhead, unexpectedly, and were received with the same demonstrations of loyalty to the reigning family, and personal respect and attachment to these individual members of it, which had marked the progress of the royal visitors in other parts of the Principality. A royal salute was fired from Sir John Stanley's battery, at Penrhos, and at a very short notice the worthy baronet, at the head of a deputation of the inhabitants of the borough and neighbourhood, waited upon the royal party on board the *Emerald* yacht, to present an address of congratulation. The deputation was presented by Sir John Conroy, and most graciously received, as were Lady Maria and the Misses Stanley, and some other ladies, who availed themselves of this opportunity of paying their dutiful respects to the royal visitors.

The following is the answer of her Royal Highness to the address, from which it will be seen that she had higher and more worthy motives than mere curiosity, or relaxation from the fatigue incidental to a life at court, for an excursion into the Principality, and bringing her infant daughter, the future sovereign of these realms, into immediate contact with the people:—

" GENTLEMEN,—We are very sensible of the attention that has led you, at hardly any notice, to receive us with so much good feeling on our landing here. It marks your loyal attachment to the King.

" I was anxious to show the Princess a harbour, erected to promote a safe and speedy intercourse between England and Ireland—as everything that can tend to their mutual advantage must be viewed with the deepest interest."

After the presentation of the address, the royal party and suite landed, under a salute from Captain Evan's temporary battery, and the hearty cheers of the assembled multitude; and having got into their carriages, which were in waiting on the pier, drove off on their return to Plas Newydd.

Previous to her departure, her Royal Highness the Duchess of Kent, with that spirit of charity and benevolence which has so eminently characterised her sojourn in the Principality, entrusted to the Rev. Mr. Jones, incumbent of Holyhead, the sum of 25*l.* for distribution amongst the charitable institutions, and the poor of the borough.

The royal ladies were so much pleased with Wales, that they prolonged their stay for several months. They resided at Plas Newydd, the beautiful mansion of the Right Hon., the Marquis of Anglesea. The many acts of kindness, condescension, and munificence conferred by them on the neighbouring inhabitants, have impressed the memory of their residence here indelibly on their hearts.

During their stay in Wales, the Princess Victoria and her royal mother patronised an Eisteddfod, one of the ancient meetings of the bards and minstrels of Wales, which took place under the presidency of Sir Richard Williams Bulkeley, Bart., M.P., at the beautiful town of Beaumaris, which was converted into a theatre of fashionable gaiety for four days.

The company was very numerous and highly respectable, comprising a large portion of the gentry, nobility, and clergy of North Wales, and the bordering English counties. We observed Lord Robert Grosvenor, M.P. and Lady Grosvenor; Lord and Lady Mostyn; Lady Helena Cooke; Hon. E. M. Lloyd Mostyn, M.P., and Lady; Lord and Lady Fingal; Lord Archbishop of Tuam; Lord Bishop of Bangor; Lord Bishop of Dromore; Lord Boston; Sir W. W. Wynn, Bart., M.P.; Sir Edward Mostyn, Bart. and Lady Mostyn; Sir S. R. Glynne, Bart., M.P.; Sir R. Vivian, Bart. M.P.; Sir John Jennings, Bart.; Sir John and Major Hilton; John Jervis, Esq., M.P.; J. Maddock, Esq., Glan-y-Wern; P. York, Esq., Erddig; W. O. Stanley, Esq., Penrhos; Pierce Mostyn, Esq.

On Tuesday morning, about twelve o'clock, a procession was formed at the Town Hall, which headed by a band of music, escorted the president, Sir R. B. W. Bulkeley, to the castle, in the area of which was erected a spacious and commodious platform, surrounded by seats for the accommodation of the company. Sir Richard, on taking the chair, was most enthusiastically greeted.

The heralds having advanced to the front of the platform, and sounded their trumpets three times, in order to command attention and silence while the proclamation was read, the president, Sir Richard Bulkeley, Bart., M.P., stepped forward, and following the example of presidents on former occasions, made a most excellent and appropriate address, which was delivered in a very graceful and animated manner, and received with loud applause.

The awarding of the various prizes, and investing the successful candidates, occupied the first day, and in the evening a splendid concert took place in the Town Hall. The following day the town appeared all alive, in order to give their Royal Highnesses the Duchess of Kent and Princess Victoria a cordial and loyal reception. The heralds perambulated the streets, and ever and anon sounded their trumpets, by way of reminding the bards and other personages of the important business of the day. As the weather continued unfavourable, it was intimated that the company would assemble in the Town Hall; every place was in consequence literally crammed.

At half-past twelve o'clock, Sir R. B. W. Bulkeley entered, and stated he had received a letter from Sir John Conroy, which he would read. The letter was expressive of the regret of her Royal Highness that the state of the weather prevented her intended presence at the Eisteddfod, and announced her intention of being at Baron Hill in the evening, at four o'clock, when the Princess and herself would invest the successful candidates, and present each with an extra royal medal. Sir Richard then proceeded to say, that as the room would not hold one-third of the ladies and gentlemen who wished to be present, it was proposed to adjourn to the castle; and that he should be happy to see such of the company as wished to be witnesses of the investiture of the successful competitors with medals by their Royal Highnesses, at Baron Hill, at four o'clock in the evening. These announcements were received with loud cheers, and the company began to move towards the castle.

A little before one o'clock the band announced the arrival of the President, by striking up a national air.

The President, upon entering, advanced to the front of the platform, amid loud cheers, and repeated the information respecting the intentions of their Royal Highnesses which he had previously given in the Town Hall. The Rev. Henry Parry, of Llanasa, opened the proceedings of the morning with an appropriate address, giving an historical account of the Eisteddfodau.

Among the various prizes offered for competition on this occasion was a handsome gold medal for the best Englynion on "The honour conferred by the presences of their Royal Highness Princess Victoria and the Duchess of Kent at our national festival." The successful candidate was the venerable old Bard of Nantglyn, who was invested by the Lady Harriot Lloyd Mostyn.

> " I Dduges Caint, braint i'n bro,—bid mawl mawr,
>   Bid mil a myrdd croeso,
>   Ail seren drylen deg dro,
>   Hoen ddiwrnod i'n haddurno.
>
> " Teyrnwaed Tudurwaed, da dirion,—oreu
>   Aeres Prydain goron,
>   Derchafid yn dra chyfion
>   O blanwydd Penmynydd, Mon.
>
> " Mal cenedl, grym hawl cynhes,—i'n tirion
>   Victoria, D'wysoges,
>   Mae ynom o wraidd mynwes
>   Galon yn wreichion o wres."

About four o'clock in the afternoon, a large concourse of persons assembled at Baron Hill,[6] the splendid seat of Sir R. Bulkeley, to witness the ceremony of investing the successful candidates with silver medals, by their Royal Highnesses the Duchess of Kent and Princess Victoria. Baron Hill is situated about one mile from Beaumaris, at the head of an extensive lawn, sloping down to the town and castle, and screened and backed with umbrageous woods, which form great embellishments to this part of the Island. The house was first built by Sir Richard Bulkeley, a distinguished character in the reign of Elizabeth and James I.,[7] but it has since that period been rebuilt in an elegant style by the present worthy baronet. The

---

[6] This place has been in possession of the Bulkeley family from the date of the second Charter of the corporation of Beaumaris, procured in the reign of Elizabeth. The first house was built in the next reign— altered, improved, and the grounds laid out after the manner of our day, by the late Viscount, who willed it with his estates on both sides of the Menai, to the present proprietor, paternally descended from the celebrated Ednyved Vychan, of the Penrhyn branch of the

Tudor family. Ednyved was counsellor to Llywelyn ab Iorwerth, Prince of Wales, in 1200, and leader of his forces, who having defeated a detachment of the Palatine Earl of Chester's army, near Abergele, wherein three of the leading captains fell, Llywelyn ordered him in future to bear *gules, a chevron ermine between three Saxon heads bleeding,* (*tri phen Sais yn gwaedu,*) as an honourable trophy.

[7] See page 317, text and note.

grounds surrounding this charming residence are richly diversified by nature, and variegated by art; the lawns, groves, and bridges, are finely dispersed, and the numerous walks and rides judiciously laid out. But the view from the hill far surpasses all, and is justly the boast of the Island.

Her Majesty investing the Welsh Bards with Royal medals, at Baron Hill, the seat of Sir Richard Bulkeley, Bart., M.P.

The spot chosen for investing the bards and other successful candidates with the medals, was the terrace in front of Baron Hill. The literary arrangements were under the direction of the active Secretary, William Jones, Esq., (Gwrgant,) and the musical ones under that of Mr. Parry. Upon the entry of their Royal Highnesses, attended by Sir Richard and Lady Bulkeley, the band struck up the national air, "God save the King." Mr. Parry sung the following stanza, to the national song of "Mewn awen fwyn lawen," the chorus being joined by the whole company:—

> " Far, far from the pomp and the splendour of court,
> To Cambria's sweet valleys the Royal resort;
> Oh ! let us our love and our gratitude show,
> To those who such honour on Wallia bestow.
> Ye bards and ye minstrels your voices combine,
> To welcome a Princess of Tudor's famed line.
> *Gogoniant a moliant i'r Seren lwys gain.*" [8]

After the cheering had subsided, the active Secretary, William Jones, Esq., (Gwrgant,) and Mr. Parry of London, the managers, were requested to introduce each of the successful candidates to their Royal Highnesses, who presented each of them with a silver medal, with the royal arms, as a special mark of their favour and encouragement to Welsh literature. Each candidate had the high honour and felicity of being invested by her Most Gracious Majesty herself.

[8] Glory and honour to the lovely young star.

The following are the names of those who received this distinguished honour:—Rev. John Blackwell, Holywell; Miss Angharad Llwyd, of Caerwys; Mr. John Williams, of Oswestry; Rev. William Williams, Caernarvon; Mr. Aneurin Pugh, Egryn; Mr. Edward Parry, of Chester; Rev. Dr. Williams, of Clynog; Mr. Robert Davies, of Nantglyn; Mr. William Edwards, of Ysgeifiog; Mr. T. Jones, Holywell; the veteran harper, Mr. Roberts, of Caernarvon; and the Rev. J. Jones, Holywell. Their Royal Highnesses then presented Mr. Jones, the Secretary, and Mr. Parry with a medal each.

At the conclusion of the ceremony, their Royal Highnesses retired, and shortly afterwards sat down to dinner in a capacious room, erected for the occasion. At the table her Royal Highness the Princess Victoria sat on the right of her parent; Lady Bulkeley on the right of the Princess Victoria, and Sir Richard Bulkeley on the left of the Duchess of Kent. The Hon. E. Mostyn Lloyd Mostyn, M.P., was at the head of the table, and Brice Pierce, Esq., at the bottom. Many distinguished individuals were present; among them were Lord and Lady Robert Grosvenor. About seven o'clock their Royal Highnesses took their departure for Plas Newydd. Thus ended one of the most interesting and imposing meetings we ever recollect. It is impossible to describe the feelings of a Welshman at a meeting of an Eisteddfod, for his very soul seems absorbed in the proceedings of the day, particularly when the thrilling tones and trembling strings of the ancient harps of the Cymru are put in motion. To all such meetings we would say, most emphatically, "*Esto perpetua!*"

The following is an account of the departure of their Royal Highnesses from Wales, and their progress from Plâs Newydd, through part of Caernarvonshire, Denbighshire, and Flintshire, on their way to Eaton Hall and Chester.

Their Royal Highnesses, the Duchess of Kent and the Princess Victoria, attended by Sir John Conroy, Lady Catherine Jenkinson, and suite, took leave of the hospitable mansion of Plâs Newydd, and bade adieu to the Principality, on Monday morning, October 15th, 1832, on their progress to Claremont. The royal visitors carried along with them the best wishes of the inhabitants of Gwynedd for their future health and happiness; and left behind them a grateful recollection of their munificent bounty to the different local charities, and an affectionate remembrance of the condescension and affability that invariably marked their intercourse with the people. Afterwards the royal party proceeded on their way to Abergele, into which town they were escorted by a troop of the Denbighshire cavalry, under the command of Captain Heaton, where they were received with every demonstration of respect by the inhabitants of the town and neighbourhood. The church bells rang a merry peal, and a royal salute of twenty-one guns was fired from a rising ground about the town, the residence of the Vicar, the Rev. Richard Jackson. Triumphal arches were erected at the Bee Inn, and in the centre of the town, and most of the windows were decorated with laurel and wreaths of flowers. The children of the National School, and the members of the Benefit Society, were drawn up on both sides of the street, and the garden opposite the Bee Inn afforded the ladies and gentlemen an admirable opportunity of obtaining a full view of the royal visitors in the carriage, as they changed horses. From Abergele the royal party, still escorted by the Yeomanry, proceeded to Kinmel Park, the seat of Lord Dinorben, where they partook of a collation, in company with his Royal Highness the Duke of Sussex, who was guest at that mansion, and afterwards proceeded on their route.

The reception of their Royal Highnesses in Flintshire was of the same cordial character that marked their Progress through the other parts of the Principality. They were met on the borders of that county by Sir John Williams, Bart., of Bodelwyddan, at the head of a vast concourse of persons. Cannon were fired, and triumphal arches composed of garlands were thrown across the road.

The royal cavalcade was met on the Elwy Bridge at St. Asaph, by Sir Henry Brown, the Dean of St. Asaph, the gentry and clergy of the neighbourhood, the members of the Benefit Societies, and a large body of the inhabitants of that ancient city. They were conducted into and through the city, which was gaily decorated for the occasion, preceded by a band of music, and most enthusiastically cheered on their departure.

At Holywell the Princess Victoria and her royal mother were received with every demonstration of loyalty and respect. A detachment of the Flintshire Yeomanry cavalry, under the command of

Major Jones, of Wepre Hall, was in attendance.   Both sides of the road for miles were lined with anxious spectators to see their future queen, who was welcomed with loud and reiterated huzzas.   During the time of changing horses at the White Horse Hotel, the royal party was again received with the loudest acclamations and loyal attachment by the inhabitants of the town and those of the surrounding country who had assembled to pay their respects on the occasion.   Triumphal arches were erected in the streets, and the waving of flags, handkerchiefs, &c., were seen from every window and avenue, all of which were graciously acknowledged, and elicited the continued smiles of the royal strangers, who were afterwards escorted by another party of the Royal Flintshire Yeomanry Cavalry to Northop, of which the Earl Grosvenor was commandant.

At Northop the reception of their Royal Highnesses was no less flattering and loyal.   Triumphal arches were erected, one at each end of the village.   The inhabitants, even to the humblest cottagers, seemed to vie with each other in their endeavours to evince their loyalty and respect.   Crowds of gaily dressed persons flocked from the neighbouring places, all anxious to catch a glimpse and to hail the appearance of their future queen.   At three o'clock the Mold troop of cavalry, under the command of Captain Wynne Eyton, took position near the entrance of the village from Holywell; and near the spot were stationed several carriages, containing the beauty and fashion of the neighbourhood.   Among them were the Hon. Lloyd Mostyn, M.P., Colonel Phillips, Mrs. Wynne Eyton, Miss Gatacre, J. Eyton, Esq., Mr. and Mrs. Garmons, Rev. J. C. Conwy, and party, Mrs. Jones, Wepre Hall; and the Misses Danes; Rev. J. Husband, Miss Jones, Miss Coates, Rev. Henry Jones, Mrs. Jones, J. Pemberton, Esq., J. Mather, Esq., J. Lewis, Esq., &c.   About four o'clock the approach of the royal party was announced by a military *avant-courier* from the Holywell troop of Yeomanry, and in a few minutes they arrived, preceded and escorted by Major Jones and his troop, who on entering the village were relieved by Captain Wynne Eyton, and his troop.   The cavalcade proceeded slowly on amidst the deafening cheers of the assembled multitude, the bells ringing a merry peal.   When the procession reached the extremity of the village, their Royal Highnesses, after acknowledging their enthusiastic reception by bowing to the individuals assembled round the carriage, proceeded on their journey, evidently highly gratified by the sincere exhibition of the loyal feelings of the inhabitants of the village of Llanergain.

At Hawarden Castle their Royal Highnesses were received, in the absence of Sir Stephen Glynne, by the Hon. and Rev. George Neville Grenville and the Lady Charlotte.

Having consented to honour the the Most Noble the Marquis of Westminster with their company for a few days at Eaton Hall, the necessary preparations were made to receive the royal visitors with the honour befitting their rank and station, and to entertain them, during their stay, with that splendid hospitality for which this magnificent residence is so justly celebrated.   Early in the afternoon, carriages with four horses were dispatched from Eaton to meet the royal carriage at Hawarden; and at three o'clock the Border Troop of the Flintshire Yeomanry Cavalry, under the command of Captain Lord Robert Grosvenor, Captain French, and Lieutenant G. Brooke, in their scarlet uniforms, mustered at the hall to the sound of " the shrill trumpet," in all " the pride, pomp, and circumstance of glorious war."

> " All the lawn
> Covered with thick embattled squadrons, bright
> Carbines, and flaming swords, and fiery steeds,
> Reflecting blaze on blaze."

The " neighing steeds," the elegant accoutrements and the fine stature of the men, gave the whole a very imposing and soldier-like appearance.   After the troop had gone through various cavalry evolutions, in a manner highly creditable to their own industry, the zeal of their noble commander, and the assiduity of the serjeant-major of the corps, a detachment, comprising an escort and guard of honour, was dispatched to meet the royal visitors at Bretton Lodge (the Hawarden troop having escorted them to that point), and conduct them to Eaton, where the remainder of the corps had drawn up to receive them on the lawn.   At a quarter to six o'clock the royal *cortège* approached through the long avenue, and advanced to the lawn, amid the salute of the cavalry and the enthusiastic plaudits of a multitude of the tenantry and the inhabitants of the surrounding villages, who had assembled on the occasion. The noble host and hostess met the royal visitors at the portal. The band struck up "God save the King" as they alighted from the carriages, and the royal standard of England was hoisted on the top of the mansion, in lieu of the Union Jack which usually floats on the breeze during the residence of the family at Eaton. The weather, which had hitherto during the day been unpropitious, now became overcast and lowering; the rain fell in torrents, and continued with little intermission until nearly midnight.

A select party of eighteen sat down to dinner at seven o'clock in the principal *salle à manger*, in which the table was laid in a style of more than Eastern magnificence, and any attempt at description would fall far short of the reality. The party consisted of H.R.H. the Duchess of Kent, Lady Catherine Jenkinson, and Sir John Conroy; Lord Bagot, the Hon. Mr. Bagot, Mr. and Mrs. Newton Lane, and the Hon. Miss Bagot; Sir Philip and Lady Grey Egerton, Mr. G. Brooke, and the Rev. Mr. Ayckbowm. The members of the family present, were the Marquis and Marchioness, the Countess of Wilton, Earl and Countess Grosvenor, and Lord Robert Grosvenor. The young Princess was too much fatigued by her journey to join the dinner party; and she therefore dined in a separate apartment with the Baroness Lehzen.

On Tuesday morning the corporation of the ancient city of Chester, distinguished in all ages for loyalty to the throne and devoted attachment to the reigning dynasty, proceeded to Eaton in fifteen carriages, to present an address to their Royal Highnesses adopted in full assembly on the Friday previous. On the Mayor entering the great hall, the Yeomanry on duty, as a guard of honour, under the command of Captain Lord Grosvenor, in full uniform, presented arms, and did not "recover" until the whole body had passed into the ante-room. Here they were met by the Alderman, the Marquis of Westminster, and Earl Grosvenor, in their civic robes, by whom they were conducted into the presence of the Duchess, the Princess, and the ladies of the family. The young Princess at that time, strongly resembled the illustrious family of her departed sire, and irresistibly reminded the beholder of the late Princess Charlotte. From our recollection of the features of that much lamented Princess, even in her more mature years, the resemblance was, to our eyes, as complete as it could be between persons with their disparity of ages.

The Recorder (R. Tyrwhitt, Esq.,) then proceeded to read the following address:—

"*To Her Royal Highness, the Duchess of Kent.*

"MAY IT PLEASE YOUR ROYAL HIGHNESS,—We, the Mayor, Recorder, Aldermen, Sheriffs and Common Council of the City of Chester, most humbly beg to approach your Royal Highness and your illustrious daughter, the Princess Victoria, to offer our dutiful congratulations upon the arrival of your Royal Highness in the vicinity of our ancient city, and to express our anxious wish for the long continued enjoyment by your Royal Highness of health and everything that heaven can bestow.

" We beg to assure your Royal Highness of our loyalty and devoted attachment to the House of Brunswick, and to express the pride and satisfaction we feel in the opportunity now afforded us of making that assurance, in person, to the members of that illustrious family, so distinguished as your Royal Highness and the presumptive heiress to the throne of these realms."

Her Royal Highness in a clear and distinct tone of voice, and with less of a foreign accent than might have been expected, delivered the following most gracious reply:—

"MR. MAYOR AND GENTLEMEN,—The Princess and myself are exceedingly sensible of the attention that leads you to come here to convey to us, with so much good feeling, your congratulations on our arrival in the vicinity of your ancient city. It shows your loyal attachment to the King, receiving us as members of his family in this manner.

"We hope to be able to visit your ancient city to-morrow. I am naturally anxious to seize every opportunity to bring under the Princess's observation those things that may tend to make her acquainted with all that is interesting,—your city is particularly so,—and to connect her with the country, by mixing with all classes in it, so as to identify herself with their interests."

The Marquis of Westminster then presented the Mayor, (George Harrison, Esq.,) Mr. Alderman Larden, (the father of the corporation,) and some others of the Aldermen, to her Royal Highness. The body then retired a few paces to make way for Lord Robert Grosvenor and Mr. Finchett Maddock, the members for the city, to present the address from the inhabitants at large, adopted by acclamation at a public meeting, held for that purpose in the Town Hall, on Monday. The address was read by Lord Robert, and was in these words:—

" To Her Royal Highness the Duchess of Kent.

"MAY IT PLEASE YOUR ROYAL HIGHNESS :—We, the inhabitants of the ancient and loyal city of Chester, gladly avail ourselves of your arrival in this vicinity, to offer to your Royal Highness and your illustrious daughter our dutiful homage and respectful congratulations, and to testify our deep sense of the amiable virtues and the shining excellencies by which you have always been distinguished as a wife and mother.

"We beg leave also to express our devoted attachment to the illustrious House of Brunswick, and if, in the progress of time, and by permission of Divine Providence, your royal daughter should be called to the government of these realms, we indulge in the hope that, treading in the steps of her ancestors, she will sustain abroad the high destinies of this great nation, and preserve at home, inviolate, those institutions which have been the admiration and example of surrounding countries."

Her Royal Highness and the young Princess repeatedly bowed during the delivery of this address; and the Duchess, as well as some of her immediate attendants, appeared to be much affected at the allusion to the probability that her infant daughter would one day sway the British sceptre. Her Royal Highness with considerable emotion delivered the following very gracious reply :—

"GENTLEMEN :—I cannot sufficiently express to you how much the Princess and myself feel the sentiments conveyed to us from the inhabitants of the city of Chester; we are deeply alive to them.

"The inhabitants of Chester, distinguished always for their loyalty to the King, seize this occasion to evince it by this attention to us, as members of his family.

"To-morrow, I trust, we shall be able to visit your city, the inhabitants of which have already a claim on our warm feelings, which will tend to confirm my most anxious desire that the Princess should be so brought up, as to identify herself with all classes in this great and free country; for the usefulness and happiness of her future life, if it be spared, must depend on her doing so."

The corporation then retired to the ante-room. Here Lady Elizabeth, (the name of the amiable Countess Grosvenor, still more familiar to our ears,) entered, leading young Hugh Lupus, the representative of a long line of Norman ancestors,[9] and two or three of her interesting little girls, and conversed familiarly

---

[9] Perhaps there is no family in Great Britain that can boast of such ancient associations with the history of this country as that of the Grosvenor family, now represented by the Most Noble the Marquis of Westminster, the present Lord High Steward of Her Majesty's household. At the period of the conquest, the Earldom of Chester was given by William to Gherbard, a Flemish nobleman, and on his decease the grant was transferred to the Conqueror's nephew, Hugh Lupus (the Wolf); and the Palatinate jurisdiction of the Earl was in every respect (but title) invested with regal authority. The stronghold and seat of the Earl was the castle of Chester.

The family name of Grosvenor had its origin in the office to which he who came over with the Conqueror was appointed — that of Gros-veneur, or the great hunter—a place similar to that now held by the "Master of the Queen's Horse;" and to his son Robert were assigned Over Lostock, Farndon, Little Budworth, &c., &c. Others of the Grosvenors were settled in the different parts of the Palatinate,

and several of them held high offices in the royal and Palatinate armies.

In 1102, we find Ulger Grosvenor, with Roger Fitzcorbet and Robert Neville, taking an active part with their neighbour, the Earl of Shrewsbury, in the troublesome transactions of that period.

In 1135, we find that Henry le Grosvenor took part with the Empress Maude against King Stephen.

In 1190, Robert le Grosvenor followed Cœur de Lion to Palestine; and his descendant, Sir Robert le Grosvenor, served under Edward III. in the French wars, and was killed at the siege of Calais.

During the Commonwealth we find several members of the Grosvenor family stedfast to their loyal principles, espousing and fighting for the cause of the unfortunate King Charles.

In 1687, when his Majesty James II. was at Chester, Sir Thomas Grosvenor was then M.P. for Chester. The King sent a message to

with the Mayor, the venerable Alderman Larden, and several other members of the body, whom she graciously recognised.

The corporation, after partaking of a splendid *déjeûner à la fourchette*, returned to Chester, and the royal visitors took a drive through the beautiful grounds and plantations of Eaton before dinner. The dinner party this day consisted of the Duchess of Kent and the Princess Victoria and suite, the Marquis and Marchioness of Westminster, the Countess Wilton, the Earl and Countess Grosvenor, Lord Robert Grosvenor, Sir Philip and Lady Egerton, Mr. and Lady Ann Wilbraham, Lord Bagot, the Hon. Mr. Bagot and Miss Bagot, Mr. and Mrs. Newton Lane, the Rev. Richard Massie, and the Rev. F. Ayckbowm.

The following address, adopted by the Chester Cambrian Society, was transmitted by the Secretary to Lord Robert Grosvenor :—

To Her Royal Highness the Duchess of Kent.

"MAY IT PLEASE YOUR ROYAL HIGHNESS,—We, the members of the Cambrian Society, residing in the city of Chester, (but natives of Wales,) strongly participating in the loyal feelings so universally manifested by our countrymen in the Principality towards your Royal Highness and your illustrious daughter, beg permission to avail ourselves of the royal visit to the ancient city of Chester, to present to your Royal Highness the expression of our ardent and devoted regard. Attached as we are from principle and affection to the Royal House of Brunswick, with which your Royal Highness is intimately connected, it cannot but inspire us with the most gratifying feelings to behold you personally amongst us ; especially when accompanied by a Princess, in whose preservation and welfare are concentrated the hopes and interest of a great empire.

"That your Royal Highness may long live to be the guardian and example of the presumptive heiress of these realms, is a prayer in which the Cambrian Society most cordially unite.

(Signed on behalf of the Society)   "EDWARD PARRY."

Chester, October 18th, 1832.

Lord Robert was pleased to return the following reply :—

"SIR,—The expression of the wishes of the Cambrian Society by their Secretary needed no apology to me ; I had the greatest pleasure in being the instrument of conveying to her Royal Highness the loyal sentiments of that society, and I now beg leave to enclose to you the answer.

"I am, Sir,
"Your obedient servant,
"*To Edward Parry, Esq., Hon. Secretary.*"   "R. GROSVENOR."

"SIR,—The Duchess of Kent has received, with the greatest pleasure, the expressions of good feeling, which the loyalty of the members of the Cambrian Society, resident in the city of Chester, so kindly conveyed to their Royal Highnesses on the occasion of their visit to its neighbourhood.

"I have the honour to be, Sir,
"Your most obedient servant,
"*To Edward Parry, Esq., Hon. Secretary.*"   "JOHN CONROY."

Sir Thomas, wishing to have a private audience with him, the purport of which was to secure Sir Thomas's services in parliament on behalf of the Catholics. The King said, "If you will support a bill which will be brought into the House for the repeal of the penal laws against the papists and the 'Test Act,' I'll give you a regiment and a peerage ;" but he refused, "preferring the religion and liberty of his country to all the honour and power, so likely at that time to be attended with popery and slavery."

From that time, in less troublesome periods, we find them always advocating principles calculated to support the throne, and to pre-serve and protect the rights and privileges of the people. The late Marquis of Westminster, that enlightened and liberal minded statesman, did much to forward religious liberty. Throughout his extended life, it was one noble career of aiding the vanquished and oppressed. The Catholics and Jews have cause to remember him as their earliest and firmest supporter in assisting them to establish their civil and religious position ; and the poor of this country never had a more unflinching, liberal, or zealous defender of such a line of policy, as would place within their reach, at a moderate cost, the staff of life. Peace to the manes of that illustrious and enlightened statesman !

Nothing could exceed the enthusiasm of the inhabitants in their endeavours to give all possible *éclat* to the happy occasion that procured for their ancient city the honour of a visit of the heiress presumptive to the throne, and the exemplary lady, her mother, who has richly deserved the gratitude of the nation, for the truly English and constitutional course of education which she laid down for the future sovereign of the vast British Empire. It was a perfect *jour de fête:* the shops were closed and all care and business were by common consent postponed to the morrow. The houses, windows, and even the " posts " of our unique rows, were tastefully decorated with laurels and garlands of flowers, interspersed with flags, inscribed, " HEALTH AND LONG LIFE TO THE PRINCESS VICTORIA," " HAIL STAR OF BRUNSWICK," and a variety of other appropriate inscriptions and tasteful devices. It would be invidious to particularise in this respect, when in fact all classes of citizens seemed to vie with one another in their endeavours to do all possible honour to the day.

> " Let labour cease ; with laurel wreath your posts,
> And strew with flowers the pavement. Rejoice :
> To pomp and triumph give this happy day ! "

The national standard waved from the tops of the steeples of the several churches in the city, and was prominently conspicuous at the castle, the summit of the shot-towers at the Mount, and several other places. The exterior of the armonry was tastefully hung with the flags of the various new corps of the local militia therein deposited ; and over the centre of that stupendous work of art, the bridge, was erected a magnificent triumphal arch, surmounted by a crown, and the royal arms.

At twelve o'clock the garrison (part of the 18th Royal Irish), and the artillery, under the command of Captain Dunn, were drawn up in the castle-yard, and two guns were manned, ready to fire a royal salute upon a signal, to be communicated from the bridge, of the approach of the royal visitors.

Precisely at one o'clock, the expected signal was given, and the *cortège* approached the bridge under a royal salute of twenty-one guns from the castle-yard. Lord Robert Grosvenor led the way on horseback, followed by Mr. Wilbraham, M.P., and Lady Anne Wilbraham, in one carriage, Lord Bagot and family in another, Sir John Conroy, the Baroness Lehzen, Lady Catherine Jenkinson, members of the royal suite, in a third ; Earl and Countess Grosvenor, and the Countess of Wilton in a fourth ; and last came a coach and six, containing the illustrious visitors and the Marquis and Marchioness of Westminster.

When the carriage, containing the royal visitors, reached the triumphal arch, the royal standard was hoisted on its summit, and the Right Worshipful the Mayor presented himself to their Royal Highnesses to take their pleasure as to naming the bridge. The interesting young Princess promptly replied,—

" I seize the opportunity, being one of the first persons to pass over this magnificent arch, to lend myself to the feeling that prevails, and at once name it ' Grosvenor Bridge.' "

This announcement of the young Princess was received with long and continued applause. The cavalcade then passed over and entered the castle-yard, amid the salute of the military, the most enthusiastic plaudits from the most respectable, and perhaps the most numerous, assemblage of persons ever congregated within the walls. The royal party having alighted, visited the magnificent Court of Justice, and the Shire Hall.

Their Royal Highnesses appeared to be highly pleased with all they saw, and the benevolent Duchess left 25*l.* for the comfort and consolation of the poor debtors. The royal party then proceeded to the Armoury, to which alone it was originally supposed their inspection would have been limited. They were received by Captain Henderson, and shown the ample store of the weapons of death and destruction (about 30,000 stand of arms) there deposited, ranged however in so tasteful a manner as to banish all recollection of the purposes for which they were made—and kept in the admirable order and condition, for which the master armourer, Mr. Alcock, is so justly praised by all who visit the place.

The royal party now entered their carriages and left the castle-yard, amid the renewed plaudits of the multitude.

> " The shouting cries
> Of pleased people rend the vaulted skies."

The *cortége* then proceeded through Nicholas-street, up Watergate-street, and Northgate-street, to the west entrance of the cathedral. An immense concourse of people lined the streets, rows, and windows, as they passed along.

The royal visitors were met at the great western door of the Cathedral by the Lord Bishop, the Rev. Prebendary Bromfield, the Rev. Chancellor Raikes, the Rev. Joseph Eaton, Precentor, the Rev. J. Halton, and other dignitaries of the Cathedral. The fine-toned organ struck up that beautiful anthem of Handel, " Zadoc the Priest," as the royal party entered the broad aisle.

> " And as the slow procession paced along
> Still to th' anthem, as if in sympathy,
> The regular foot-fall sounded."

The sacred edifice was nearly filled with the children of the Charity Schools, and vast numbers of persons, of the first respectability, were admitted by tickets. As the royal party passed along in procession, through the motley crowd in the broad aisle, the scene had a very lively and animated appearance.

The royal party were conducted along the broad aisle, and through the cloisters to the Chapter House, where the Lord Bishop, as the spokesman of his reverend brethren, delivered the following address, with much feeling and fervour :—

"MAY IT PLEASE YOUR ROYAL HIGHNESS,—The Dean and Chapter of this Cathedral Church, together with the clergy of the city and neighbourhood, desire to act as their representative on this occasion, when they have the unexpected honour of receiving your Royal Highness within the walls of this Cathedral.

" We rejoice in the opportunity thus given us of offering to your Royal Highness, and to the illustrious Princess your daughter, the humble but sincere assurance of our loyalty. And we rejoice no less in the opportunity afforded to the people of this land of becoming personally acquainted with the character and virtues of those whom their religion requires them to honour. It must ever be regarded as an especial blessing to the country, when the character of those who are most elevated in rank and station, command by their character the veneration which is due to their persons. When they who are on the throne, or nearest to the throne of this kingdom, set an example in their own conduct of that piety towards God, and charity towards mankind, which is the only sure foundation of individual happiness, or national prosperity. With this imperfect expression of our sentiments, we beg to welcome the visit of your Royal Highness to the cathedral of this ancient city."

Her Royal Highness received this address most graciously, and made the following reply :—

"MY LORD BISHOP AND REV. GENTLEMEN,—The Princess and myself cannot fail to be highly sensible of the attention that has led you to assemble here on this occasion to receive us on entering this venerable cathedral.

"This mark of your loyal attachment to the King, we duly appreciate, as members of his family. I cannot better allude to your good feeling towards the Princess, than by joining fervently in the wish, that she may set an example in her conduct, of that piety towards God, and charity towards man, which is the only sure foundation of individual happiness or national prosperity. May that happiness and prosperity be interwoven, if it be the will of Providence she should be called to discharge higher duties, at a very distant day, I sincerely trust, is my constant aim in bringing her up."

The Rev. Prebendary Bromfield, the Rev. Chancellor Raikes, and the Rev. W. Richardson, Vicar of St. John's, were then presented to her Royal Highness the Duchess of Kent, by the Marquis of Westminster.

3 N

The royal party were now conducted to the choir, and the Chapel of St. Mary, which they no sooner entered than the organ struck up the National Anthem. The well-trained band of tuneful choristers,

> " Swelling now
> Their voices in one chorus, loud and deep,
> Rang through the echoing aisle ; and, when it ceased,
> The silence of that huge and sacred pile
> Fell on the heart."

The royal party entered the bishop's palace through the private passage from the cathedral; and after

The Procession through Bridge-street, Chester, in honour of the visit of their R.H. the Duchess of Kent and Princess Victoria.

partaking of an elegant collation, set out on their return for Eaton, at three o'clock, under another royal salute from the castle. The return route was through Bridge-street, where,

> " You would have thought the very windows spake,
> So many greedy looks of young and old
> Through casements darted their desiring eyes."

When the procession arrived at the High Cross, and on their way down Bridge-street, the plaudits which were repeated at intervals, now swelled into one universal peal, and " Long live the Princess Victoria," resounded from every side.

> " Long live Victoria !
> Be this the general public voice sent up to heaven,
> And every public place repeat, VICTORIA ! "

When passing over the old bridge they were cheered by the members of the " Royal Yacht Club," and the boats crews on the river, and through Hand-bridge, which (humble as is the neighbourhood) was not the least gaily decorated part of the city, nor the least enthusiastic in its demonstrations of respect for the royal party on this occasion.

We must not omit to state, that before the royal party left the town this day, Sir John Conroy put the following letter into the hands of the Right Worshipful the Mayor, inclosing the munificent donation of one hundred pounds in aid of the drooping funds of the Chester Infirmary :—

" Eaton Hall, 17th October, 1832.

" Sir,—The Duchess of Kent finds a difficulty in making selections from the many and well-supported charitable institutions, the benevolence of the inhabitants of Chester leads them to maintain ; therefore her Royal Highness feels she may have the happiness of serving more effectually the Infirmary, which must always be of such importance to the poorer class of society ; and particularly at this time, when every medical and personal care should be within their reach, to avert the disease that has so awfully prevailed. I have therefore received her Royal Highness's commands to forward herewith an order on her bankers for one hundred pounds, as a donation to the funds of the Infirmary.

" I have the honour to be, Sir,

" Your most obedient Servant,

" The Mayor of Chester."

" JOHN CONROY."

It is impossible to withhold our admiration of the benevolent spirit that could dictate a long series of liberal donations to the various local charities of the country through which she passed, like those that marked the progress of this amiable lady. The selection of the Infirmary, as the peculiar object of her bounty in this city was most judicious; and the donation proved very acceptable in the then reduced state of the funds of that most excellent charity.

The admission of the infant daughter of Lord and Lady Robert Grosvenor within the pale of the Christian Church, took place on Wednesday evening, in the music saloon, in the presence of all the company then visiting with the family. The ceremony was performed by the Lord Bishop of Chester, assisted by the Rev. W. Massie. Their Royal Highnesses the Duchess of Kent and the Princess Victoria, were the female sponsors ; and the noble grandsires, Lord Cowley, by proxy, and the Marquis of Westminster, in person, were the godfathers on this interesting occasion.

The noble infant was called Victoria Charlotte ; Victoria after the Princess, and Charlotte after the family name of her noble mother. Her Royal Highness the Duchess of Kent took from her own neck a superb gold chain and locket, and placed it on that of Lady Robert, as a baptismal present for the little Christian.

The dinner party was the same this day as on Tuesday, with the exception of Mr. and Lady Anne Wilbraham, who took their departure this morning, and with the addition of Lord and the Hon. Miss Kenyon, (who arrived in time to accompany the royal party to Chester,) Major Pratt, of the 18th Regiment, and Captain Dunn, of the Artillery, from the Chester garrison.

In order to give every *éclat* to this visit of the heir apparent, the Marquis of Westminster determined to institute an archery meeting on the occasion. The primitive pastime of archery [2] appears to be on the decline throughout the country, although several societies of bowmen exist in England, and the delightful and healthful exercise is still continued.

" Hurrah ! the bow, the British bow,
The stately, firm, old English bow,
What souls with freedom's spirit glow,
That love not the heroic bow."

Among the most distinguished of these is that of the Royal British Bowmen, who held their last meeting,

---

[2] The long bow was introduced into England at the invasion, and to this weapon was the Conqueror indebted for his victory at Hastings. From this period the English adopted the long bow as their national weapon, and expressed the strongest antipathy to the cross-bow, as well as the universal practice of drawing the shaft to the breast instead of the eye, or rather the ear—a mode of shooting never used amongst ancients or moderns.

for that season, at Eaton Hall. The day was most anxiously looked forward to by the inhabitants of the city and the neighbourhood, as well as by all the rank and fashion of the surrounding country, who were included in the invitations to Eaton.

The Royal Bow-Meeting at Eaton Hall, the seat of the Most Noble the Marquis of Westminster.

We attended upon this interesting occasion, and were pleased with the sport of the gentlemen, but delighted with that of the ladies, who made some very excellent shots. The ladies, like Love, are the best archers after all, and we understood that they made good their claims to this distinction at the several meetings throughout the season, as well as in this instance.

"Such troops as these, in shining arms were seen,
When Theseus met in fight the maiden Queen."

It is a noble sight to behold the rank and beauty of our land among the green fields of nature; they have an appearance then truly English, and recall to us the days of Robin Hood, when Maid Marian was the Queen of Sherwood.

Two marquees were pitched in the lawn, for the accommodation and refreshment of several hundreds of respectable inhabitants of the city and neighbourhood, who were especially invited to witness the day's sports. A military band (that of the Royal Denbighshire Militia) was stationed on the lawn, and played several military and favourite pieces during the day.

The immense multitude outside the lawn was plentifully regaled with strong ale and cold beef, the orders of the Noble Marquis being, that refreshments should be served indiscriminately to all that chose to partake of them.

Besides the vast numbers who were specially invited to partake of the hospitality of the Hall this day, covers were laid in the library for two hundred and fifty to dinner at six o'clock, including the visitors to the family, together with the venerable Earl of Derby, who arrived in time for dinner; the members of the Bow Meeting, their immediate friends, and the gentry of the surrounding country.

The appearance of the dining-room, or rather suite of three rooms, in which the tables were laid, was magnificent in the extreme. On a slight elevation above the floor, at the top of the room, was placed a table for the royal visitors and the members of the family, and double sets of tables ran along the length of the rooms for the remainder of the party.

A superb plateau of gold, richly chased and embossed, (worth at least three thousand guineas,) occupied the middle of the cross table almost from one extremity to the other. The centre piece, a beautiful vase, was filled with a bouquet of choice flowers of the brightest hues; and at intervals at each side of the vase were placed some elegant gold cups, the glittering prizes borne off by the Eaton stud in many a severe and well-contested race.

At either end of the table stood a massive gold candlestick, that might vie in beauty and exquisite workmanship with those in the far-famed Temple of Solomon. The whole dinner service was of gold and silver, and the ample sideboard groaned under its load of gorgeous gold plate.

Among the variety of ornaments on the table was an ingenious miniature of the celebrated illuminated revolving Temple of Concord, erected in the Green Park, in August, 1814, at the Jubilee for Peace. It was a perfect fac-simile, (upon a small scale,) and was executed in pastry composition, and painted by Mr. Allen of Eaton.

The beautiful proportions of the rooms, lighted up by superb candelabras, and numerous additional lights, reflected from several mirrors, gave the *tout ensemble* more the appearance of a fairy scene, than a mundane entertainment.

About one hundred and thirty of the members of the society of "Royal British Bowmen," assembled on the lawn about noon on Thursday. Foremost among the ladies was Mrs. Wynne Eyton, the Lady Paramount for the year. Next came Mrs. Lloyd of Rhaggatt, the lady patroness. Then followed a train of lovely nymphs, of whom Diana herself might have been justly proud.

In the absence of Sir Stephen Richard Glynne, Bart., the President (who was unavoidably absent), the gentlemen were led out by Colonel Phillips, the Vice-president.

The gentlemen were appropriately equipped in caps and suits of "forest green;" the ladies in fawn-coloured dresses, turned up and trimmed *en echellons*, with light green. Some hundreds of the friends of the members and others specially invited to witness the sport, promenaded the lawn inside the fence, while several thousands of pedestrians and equestrians, from the ancient city of Chester and the neighbourhood, assembled outside, but near enough to have a perfect view of the company and progress of the sport. The whole had a very pleasing and highly picturesque appearance. Nothing could have been more favourable than the weather this day. The following was the result of the day's sport:—*Ladies' Target*—Miss Anna Kenyon, first medal, of the value of 15*l.*: Mrs. Dod, of Cloverly, second ditto, 10*l.*; Miss Louisa Eyton, best gold shot ditto, 5*l.*; Mrs. Dod, of Cloverly, best gold shot for a prize given by the Marquis of Westminster (a handsome book of the views of Eaton). *Gentlemen's Target.*—Mr. B. Townsend, first medal, 15*l.*; Mr. T. Mainwaring, second ditto, 10*l.*; Mr. Dod, of Cloverly, best gold shot, 5*l.*

In the course of the afternoon the royal visitors and suite, conducted by the noble host and hostess, made their appearance on the green, and were hailed by the respectful greetings of the company within the railings, and the enthusiastic plaudits of the multitude without. Their Royal Highnesses repeatedly acknowledged these spontaneous effusions of loyalty and personal respect and regard; the young Princess in particular was conspicuous for her anxiety to return the salutations of the delighted multitude. As she bowed condescendingly to all around, it was impossible not to exclaim,

> "Is she not
> As harmless as the turtles in the woods,
> Fair as the summer beauty of the fields,
> As opening flowers, untainted yet by winds."

At six o'clock nearly three hundred individuals, comprising nearly all the rank and fashion of the surrounding country, sat down to dinner in a suite of rooms appropriated to the library. A recent domestic calamity in the Wynnstay family, prevented the presence of Sir Watkin and Lady Harriet Wynn, and Lord and Lady Delamere. The entertainment was in every way worthy of the splendid hospitality of the noble host, and in perfect accordance with the chaste magnificence of the mansion. The galaxy of beauty and fashion they contained, and the additional lights themselves, were reflected in the mirrors, and reflected a hundred-fold, until the whole seemed to be a representation of, not one, but *mille cafés de milles colonnes*. The noble host proposed the health of the King, the Queen, the Duchess of Kent, and the Princess Victoria, with a few words of appropriate preface to each. The Noble Marquis subsequently proposed " the Church," which was warmly applauded by the company.

Lord Kenyon then, in the name of the company, proposed the health of the noble host and hostess, with an eulogium, equally warm and well merited, upon the splendid hospitality of the day. Shortly afterwards (at a quarter to nine o'clock) the royal visitors and the company at the upper end of the table withdrew, and were quickly followed by the remainder.

At eight o'clock on Friday morning the royal visitors and suite took leave of their noble host and hostess at Eaton, with expressions of high gratification at the distinguished hospitality they had experienced at the Hall, and their enthusiastic reception by the inhabitants of the ancient city of Chester. Previous to their departure, her Royal Highness the Duchess of Kent presented Hugh Lupus, Viscount Belgrave,[3] with a gold knife, and the female children of the Earl and Countess Grosvenor, each with a neat emerald brooch, as a souvenir of the royal visit.

About half-past eight the royal *cortège* drove up to the Royal Hotel under an escort of the Flintshire Cavalry. Here, Earl Grosvenor and Lord Robert Grosvenor, with the main body of the troop, and Major Pratt, with a detachment of the 18th regiment from the castle, were drawn up in readiness to receive them with a royal salute. The front of the hotel was profusely decorated with laurel and flags, and on each side of the entrance were two smaller ones in white satin, inscribed: " HEALTH AND LONG LIFE TO THE PRINCESS VICTORIA,"—" HEALTH AND LONG LIFE TO THE DUCHESS OF KENT."

Both their Royal Highnesses repeatedly bowed to the plaudits of the crowd in front of the hotel, and appeared highly gratified with the loyal demonstrations of the inhabitants of the ancient city of Chester.

Having thus commemorated the visits of Queen Victoria to the Principality in the days of her youth, and while she was as yet but the hope of the nation, we proceed with our account from the period of her accession.

HER MOST GRACIOUS MAJESTY QUEEN VICTORIA succeeded to the throne of these realms on the death of her uncle, William IV., June 20th, 1837. Her Majesty is right heir in lineal succession to the British, Cambro-British, Anglo-Saxon, Anglo-Norman, English, and Scottish kings.[4]

Her Majesty gave her hand in marriage, on the 10th of February, 1840, to his Royal Highness,

[3] Now Earl Grosvenor, who, in conjunction with the Honourable William Owen Stanley, represents the City of Chester in parliament.

[4] THE FOLLOWING IS A CORRECT GENEALOGICAL ACCOUNT OF HER MAJESTY'S DESCENT :—Queen Victoria is the only daughter of Edward Duke of Kent, brother of George IV. and William IV., who were the sons of George III., the eldest son, by Augusta of Saxe Gotha, of Frederick, Prince of Wales, the son of George II., the son of George I., the son of Ernest Augustus, Elector of Hanover, by Sophia, the daughter of Frederick Elector Palatine, and Elizabeth, the daughter of James I., the son of Lord Darnley and Mary, Queen of Scotland, the daughter of James V., the son of James IV., by Margaret, the eldest daughter of Henry VII., by Elizabeth, the eldest daughter of Edward IV., the eldest son of Richard Duke of York, the son of Richard of Conisburg, Earl of Cambridge, by Anne, daughter and heiress of Roger, Earl of March, the son of Edmund, Earl of March, by Philippa, daughter and sole heiress of Lionel,

Duke of Clarence, the third son of Edward III. This Edmund was the son of Edmund Mortimer, the son of Roger, the first Earl of March of this family, the son of Edmund, the son of Roger, the son of Ralph, by Gwladys Ddu, or the Black, the heiress of her brother Dafydd ap Llywelyn, the son of Llywelyn ap Iorwerth, or Leolinus Magnus, Prince of North Wales, the eldest son of Iorwerth drwyn-dwnn, the eldest son of Owain Gwynedd, the son of Gruffudd ap Cynan, the son of Cynan, the son of Iago or James, the son of Idwal, the son of Meurig, the son of Idwal foel, the son of Anarawd, the eldest son of Rodri fawr, or Roderick the Great, the son of Merfyn frych and Esyllt, the daughter and heiress of the last Prince Cynan Tindaethwy, the son of Rodri Molwynog, the son of Idwal iwrch (or the Roe) the son of Calwaladr, the last King of the Britons, who abdicated, and died at Rome in 688. This genealogy extends over the space of eleven hundred and sixty-two years.

Albert,[4] Duke of Saxe Coburg and Prince of Gotha, K.G., C.B. By that marriage are the following issue:—His Royal Highness the Prince of Wales,[5] Her Royal Highness the Princess Royal, Her Royal Highness the Princess Alice, His Royal Highness Prince Alfred, Her Royal Highness Princess Helena, Her Royal Highness Princess Louisa, His Royal Highness Prince Arthur Patrick.

His Royal Highness the Prince of Wales was born on the 9th of November, 1841. The birth of the heir-apparent to the British throne is an event probably involving in it the future destiny of the vast empire over which, if Providence spares his life, he may be called to rule. And, we may say, the event may also include it the peace and happiness of the whole world. We hailed the birth of this illustrious Prince as one of the most joyful events that could have happened, and as one which diffused the most delightful feelings amongst all the Queen's most loyal subjects in every quarter of her vast dominions.

The christening of the young Prince of Wales took place in St. George's Chapel, Windsor, on the 25th of January, 1842; His Majesty Frederick William IV., King of Prussia, being one of the six royal sponsors; all relations of Her Majesty. The King of Prussia it appears is descended from the same maternal great-grandmother as our beloved Queen. The Archbishop of Canterbury received the royal infant "into the congregation of Christ's Flock," saying in a most impressive manner, "ALBERT EDWARD, I baptise thee in the name of the Father, and the Son, and the Holy Ghost."

The ceremony throughout was performed in a most solemn manner; and amidst the unrivalled splendour of the occasion, it is said, there was observable among the royal and illustrious personages present, the most serious attention and solemnity of feeling. The royal infant, the delight and admiration of every one, was attired in a white satin slip, over which was an elegant lace dress. Their Royal Highnesses the Duchesses of Kent and Cambridge, and all the other ladies present, were in dresses of British manufacture. It was observed that Her Majesty and her royal mother wore shawls of the

[4] His Royal Highness the Prince Albert Francis Augustus Charles Emanuel, born the 26th of August, 1819. The intelligent Duke Ernest of Saxe-Coburg and Gotha, devoted much care and attention to the education of his sons from their earliest youth. They where brought up in the Castle of Ehrenberg, were they received the instructions of distinguished preceptors. Prince Albert lost his mother when only eleven years of age, which circumstance induced the Duke to place his son for some time under the care of his sister, the Duchess of Kent. Here in the grounds of Kensington and Claremont, Prince Albert became the play-fellow of his cousin, the Princess Victoria, and the choice which the Queen of Great Britain made of the companion of her childhood for the husband of her youth, shows that the seeds of affection, which were so early sown in their young hearts, took deep root; that years of absence had not power to eradicate them.

In his seventeenth year Prince Albert entered the University of Bonn, devoted himself to study with great zeal and success, and won the affections of those who came in contact with him by his kindness and generosity. In 1838, when the crown of England devolved upon the head of his youthful cousin, he attended the august ceremony of the coronation in company with his father. That they met with a warmer welcome from her Majesty than she was pleased to grant to the generality of her distinguished guests, was proved by the prolonged period of their stay. After his return, the Prince visited Italy; and the following year saw him again in England enjoying the society of the friend of his earliest years. On the 23rd of November, 1839, Queen Victoria announced to the privy council her intention of bestowing her hand on Prince Albert of Saxe-Coburg and Gotha, a decision which she felt certain would secure her domestic felicity: and he has proved such, for he is universally acknowledged to be "Good without effort, great without a foe!"

[5] Since the conquest of Wales by King Edward I. there have been eighteen Princes of Wales and Earls of Chester, including the young Prince, as will appear from the following list, each being heir-apparent to the British throne, embracing a period from the time of Edward I. to the present, of 566 years:—

Edward Plantagenet having been born at Caernarvon Castle, was presented to the Welsh as a genuine Welshman, and as such was submitted to by the subjects of his Principality. Edward the Black Prince was also created Earl of Chester and Duke of Cornwall. Richard Plantagenet same title as the preceding. Henry Plantagenet same titles, and also Duke of Acquitaine. Edward Plantagenet same titles as Edward the Black Prince, murdered 1471. Edward Plantagenet same titles as the preceding. Edward Plantagenet Earl of Salisbury, and titles as preceding. Arthur Tudor of Welsh pedigree, eldest son of Henry VII., same titles as preceding, and Earl of Flint, died before his father. Henry Tudor, brother of the last, same titles, and also Duke of York. Edward Tudor, son of the above, Prince of Wales, Earl of Chester, and Duke of Cornwall. Henry Frederick Stuart, of Scottish pedigree, same titles as the preceding, and also Duke of Rothsay, Earl of Carrick, and Baron Renfrew, of Scotland, K.G. Charles Stuart, Duke of York, Duke of Albany, and titles of his brother the preceding Prince. Charles Stuart II., declared, but never created, Prince of Wales, same titles as Henry Frederick Stuart. George Augustus, first of the Guelph or Brunswick line, the usual titles of Henry Frederick Stuart, and also Duke of Cambridge. Frederick Lucas, Duke of Gloucester, Edinburgh, and with usual titles as Henry Frederick Stuart. George William Frederick, son of the above, Marquis of Ely, Earl of Eltham, Viscount Launceston, and Baron Snowdon, with the usual titles. Grandfather of the present young Prince. George Augustus Frederick, eldest son of the preceding, the usual titles as Henry Frederick Stuart only. The present heir-apparent, created by his royal mother, December 8th, Prince of Wales, having also the titles of Earl of Chester, Duke of Cornwall and Rothsay, Earl of Carrick, Baron of Renfrew, Lord of the Isles, and Great Steward of Scotland: *Whom God Preserve!*

manufacture of Paisley, with a view to encourage the trade of that place. The Dukes of Wellington, Sutherland, Rutland, Richmond, and other illustrious Knights of the order of the Garter, were present.

> " O Lord in bounty shed
>   Joys round young ALBERT's head :
>   Thy love evince !
>   Hear now a nation's prayer,
>   Guard England's youthful heir,
>   Make him thy special care—
>   God save the PRINCE !
>
> " Oh, Lord, by day and night,
>   Bid guardian angels bright
>   Their care evince !
>   With strength the Prince sustain,
>   With health infuse each vein,
>   Till he shall age attain,
>   God save the PRINCE ! "

In speaking of the Noble Order of the Garter, it may be here a fitting opportunity, now that we have a Prince of Wales, to suggest the propriety of establishing another Order, connected especially with the Principality. Why should not Wales be placed in the same position as Scotland, Ireland, and England ? Loyalty is the foundation of those Orders, and the Principality may proudly take its place amongst other countries for fidelity to the throne, and indomitable perseverance in sustaining and upholding its rights and privileges. In the time of George IV., such an order was to have been created ; in proof of which we give the names[*] of the then promised Knights of St. David ; and if a childless monarch could deem such a creation necessary, how much more should it be deemed requisite when we have a Prince of Wales.

The Guelphic order, we believe, is no longer at the disposal of the Sovereign of Great Britain. We, therefore, beg most humbly to suggest to Her Majesty's gracious consideration the claim of a British Saint and Champion, who has been sadly overlooked. We have St. George, and the Most Noble Order of the Garter, for England ; St. Andrew, with the Most Noble Order of the Thistle, for Scotland ; and St. Patrick, with his Most Illustrious Order, for Ireland ; but Wales, the fourth gem of the British Crown, that gives a title to its heir, that gave a title to the Black Prince, the land of Arthur and Llywelyn, the country of the Bards, the soil of the royal tree of Tudor, has not only been excluded from representation in the arms[7] of every British sovereign since Elizabeth, but the Patron Saint of Wales has been denied the honours of that chivalric fellowship which have been lavished on those other holy and renowned champions of Christendom.

---

[*] The following is the list :—The Sovereign, two Princes of the blood royal, the Marquis of Anglesea, the Viscount Bulkeley, the Earl of Cardigan, the Viscount Dungannon, Sir Watkin Williams Wynn, Bart., the Lord Milford, the Earl of Powis, the Lord Kenyon, the Lord Gwydir, the Lord Dynevor. Prebend of the Order, the Lord Bishop of St. Asaph ; Chancellor, the Lord Bishop of Bangor ; Registrar, Rhys Jones, Esq. ; Genealogist, R. Richards, Esq. ; Pursuivant, Heralds, Gentleman Usher, &c., at the disposal of the Earl Marshal. Ribband, Light Green, edged with white. Motto, " CREANTUR FORTIBUS ET BONIS." In adopting Green with a border of White as the ribbon of the Order, there happens to be a correctness that we conceive is purely accidental, for we can hardly suppose that the following Englyn, descriptive of one of the temporary residences of the Prince of Wales at Rhôs Vair, in Anglesey, was ever in the contemplation of the gentlemen, whose province it is to settle these matters :

> " Mae llys yn Rhôs Vair, mae llyn,
>   Mae aur gylch, mae Arglwydd Llewelyn,
>   A gwyr tâl yn ei ganlyn,
>   Mil, myrdd Mewn gwyrdd a Gwyn."

It, however, clearly ascertains, that the retainers of the Princes of Wales were clad in these colours, and the point is further confirmed by an historical fact ; for Henry VII., sensibly appealing to that union of local attachment, innate honour, and perhaps prejudice, which constitutes what is called nationality—displayed the Red Dragon of the Ancient Britons on a banner of green and white silk, at the decisive battle of Bosworth ; but when Sir William Brandon, his standard-bearer, fell in a personal contest with King Richard, Henry judiciously gave it to Rhys Vawr ap Mereydd of Hiraethog, a man of great personal strength and prowess, whose effigies is still to be seen in the church of Ysputty Evan, in Denbighshire.

[7] It is unaccountable how the arms of the Principality happen to be omitted in the royal escutcheon with those of England, and also how it is that the Red Dragon, the ancient banner of the Princes of Wales, has been forgotten in the state processions of the late reign ; especially as Henry VII. instituted the heraldic degree of " Rouge Dragon," expressly to commemorate the victorious standard of Bosworth.

With regard to the Guelphic order above alluded to, the preamble states, that it has been instituted "to reward faithful servants of the State, individuals devoted to His Majesty's exalted person, distinguished services to the country, and the undoubted proofs of unshaken fidelity shown by all classes of our beloved German subjects, particularly their never-to-be-forgotten fame obtained at the Battle of Waterloo," &c.

Now, surely, if the above qualifications are to be considered as forming a claim to royal notice, few of Her Majesty's subjects can assert a stronger title to this honourable distinction than the natives of Wales. Whether we look to their unshaken loyalty at home, or their bravery in the field, from the arduous and protracted struggle in the Peninsula to the fierce and decisive conflict of Waterloo, nowhere shall we find more illustrious instances of devotedness and valour than amongst the Welsh. At the last-named battle, so well established was the high character of one of the heroes of Cambria in the mind of his formidable antagonist, that on the morning of that day one of Napoleon's first inquiries was, " *Où est la division de Picton ?* " Should Her Majesty, with the advice of her Privy Council, be pleased to institute a new order of distinction in favour of our patron Saint, St. David, it would be hailed with the greatest reverence by her loyal subjects of the Principality, and would ever redound to her honour and glory!

In the month of August, 1847, Her Majesty paid to a visit to her Scottish dominions, and it was generally expected she would have landed for a short time in Caernarvon on her way thither. During the entire week, previous to Her Majesty's starting, great preparations had been made at Caernarvon to give a cordial meeting to the royal party. A committee of the principal inhabitants had been formed— a subscription entered into to defray the necessary expenses—communications with Lord Willoughby d'Eresby, the Lord High Chamberlain, the Marquis of Anglesey, the constable of the Castle, and the Admiralty entered into—signals agreed upon by which to telegraph the arrival; and flags and guns put in instant requisition. The result of the various communications from head quarters led to a general belief that the royal squadron would pass over Caernarvon Bar on the morning of Saturday; and, accordingly, the *Prince of Wales*, steamer, Liverpool, (having made the requisite arrangements induced by previous instructions,) entered the harbour at eleven o'clock full of passengers from Liverpool, with the intention of following in the wake of the royal party. The town wall, pierhead, and entire quay frontage, were crowded with eager expectants; and continued to be so for many hours.

At one o'clock in the afternoon of Sunday, a glimpse of the royal squadron was obtained at Llandwyn —the pilot station off the bar. The fact that the vessels were in Caernarvon Bay was instantly telegraphed from the light house, and as readily announced on the Guildhall Tower, by the signals agreed upon. The movements of the squadron now became matter of deep interest: and telescopes were being plied from every elevated position, the Twt Hill, the Castle turret, Guildhall Tower, &c. At length a signal was hoisted that the squadron had parted, and that one portion would round the island, and another proceed up the straits. These proved to be the *Fairy* and the *Garland*. The signal was answered from the tower of the Guildhall. The next intimation of the approach of the steamers was the firing of the guns of Belan, Lord Newborough's fort. His Lordship, Lady Newborough, and Master Wynne, were on the battery to greet Her Majesty as she passed by. Her Majesty waved her handkerchief in acknowledgment. As the royal party came near the town, flags were hoisted on the Eagle Tower of the venerable castle, on the Victoria Pier, on Coed Helen Hill, at the Custom House, and on the walls of several private residences by the water side; and, at the same time, royal salutes were fired from the Victoria Pier, from Coed Helen Summer House, and from Mr. Edwards's grounds, at the Uxbridge Arms Hotel. The royal steamers "lay to" opposite to the town, where they remained twenty minutes. In the town itself all was excitement. A large proportion of the inhabitants, of all classes, immediately hastened to the shore, and nothing could surpass in effect the imposing scene which presented itself. The fine esplanade at the foot of the Town Hall, the wall itself, the quay, and every point in the neighbourhood which could command a view of the Straits, were thronged with anxious and delighted spectators, "all in their Sunday attire," while the beautiful *Fairy* steamer, with her precious freight, had the appearance of a radiant gem on the bosom of the water.

A pilot was put on board the *Fairy*, and in the boat which conveyed him from the shore, were Mr. Thomas Turner, Mayor of Caernarvon, Mr. William Roberts, Deputy-constable of the Castle, and Mr. John Hughes, Comptroller of the Customs. These gentlemen were courteously received by Earl Grey, Minister of State in waiting upon Her Majesty. The mayor begged to know the pleasure of Her Majesty as to landing and as to receiving an address of welcome from the inhabitants of the town. Lord Grey said that it was not the Queen's intention to land, and that if the address were intrusted to him, he should have much pleasure in communicating it to Her Majesty. Prince Albert then appeared, and expressed, on the part of the Queen, how much gratified she had been by the magnificence of the scenery, and by the delightful voyage which she had had along the coast. He observed that Her Majesty would be most happy to go on shore, but the tide was ebbing fast, and if there were any delay, it would be impossible for the steamers to pass through the Swellies. His Royal Highness introduced the Prince of Wales. "May we be allowed the pleasure," said Mr. William Roberts, "of shaking hands with *our* Prince?" "Most certainly," was the reply. The three gentlemen immediately availed themselves of the honour. Just as the *Fairy* was departing, the national air was most tastefully played by a band on the quay. Under such peculiar circumstances, it harmonised with a thousand feelings, which no language can describe.

At five o'clock in the afternoon, the Mayor and the Deputy-constable of the Castle, proceeded to the neighbourhood of Beaumaris, for the purpose of presenting the address. They were accompanied by Mr. David Williams, Collector, and Mr. John Hughes, Comptroller of the Customs, Mr. Bransby, Mr. Owen Jones, Mr. John Turner, and Mr. Robert Williams, jun. The address, which had been very neatly printed on white satin, was as follows:—

"Most Gracious Sovereign,—We, your dutiful and loyal subjects, the inhabitants of this ancient town, most humbly approach your Majesty, to give utterance, as far as we are able, to our feelings of exulting joy at your presence among us, and to tender the homage of our sincerest gratitude, attachment, and respect.

"We speak from our hearts; but we cannot express to your Majesty how thankful we are, that your Majesty is accompanied to our shores by your illustrious Consort, whose virtues have endeared him to all classes of your Majesty's subjects; and that you bring with you your interesting son, who derives his distinctive title from this portion of your Majesty's dominions, where one vast realm of natural wildness and grandeur spreads itself before us, and all the tales of enchantment that we read seem to have been truly told.

"It is our earnest prayer that a life so important and so inestimable as your Majesty's, may be protracted through many, many years; that the sweetest light of heaven may be shed upon your path; and that, under your benignant sceptre, Great Britain may rise to an eminence of prosperity and glory, unexampled in the annals of the world."

The *Fairy* lay at anchor a little above Garth-point, awaiting the arrival of Prince Albert, who after having walked over the Menai Bridge and returned to the steamer, had gone ashore with Lord Grey and two other gentlemen of the royal party, for the purpose of seeing Penrhyn Castle.

In about half an hour His Royal Highness and his attendants came to the steamer in a beautiful eight-oared boat, which was steered by Captain Beechy. The Prince was welcomed with the most respectful cordiality by those who were around the *Fairy*. Preparations were instantly made for getting the steamer under weigh. Without loss of time the Mayor placed the address in the hands of Lord Grey, who stated, with much affability of manner, that he would take care to lay it before her Majesty. Mr. Hughes then respectfully requested that his lordship would do him the honour of presenting for him to Her Majesty, a large paper copy of "A Description of Caernarvon and the Neighbouring District," most elegantly bound in morocco, and illustrated with a number of exquisite engravings. Lord Grey said that he would be sure to present it to the Queen. The Mayor and his fellow-townsmen then took their leave, and returned home, highly pleased with the privilege which they had enjoyed. While they were alongside the *Fairy*, a boat arrived from Caernarvon with a basket of fruit, a basket of flowers, and some of the purest and most beautiful honey in the comb, a present from Lady Newborough to the Queen.

Several Liverpool steamers followed in the wake of the *Fairy* and *Garland*, having large pleasure parties on board. The firing from the batteries continued until the royal vessels had passed far up the Straits.

The booming of the heavy guns at Caernarvon, coming down the Straits on the wings of the wind, spread far and wide the intelligence of Her Majesty's arrival in the Menai, and threw the city in a whirl of excitement. The inhabitants immediately deserted the city, some making their way to the Menai Bridge, others wending their road to Garth, and all taking up favourable positions for viewing the royal yachts.

The *Fairy* dropped anchor off St. George's pier, to give Prince Albert an opportunity of inspecting the Menai Bridge. His Royal Highness was rowed to the Caernarvonshire shore, and landed at the pier under the George Hotel, whence he walked to and over the bridge, concerning which he put various questions. The Prince then returned to the *Fairy*, which came down the Straits in beautiful style, followed by a train of passenger steamers, coming to an anchor nearly opposite Bangor. Prince Albert was immediately rowed ashore, and was received with deafening acclamations, which were gratefully acknowledged. His Royal Highness availed himself of Mr. Francis of Brynderwen's phaeton, which luckily happened to be at the Point, and was driven by that gentleman to Penrhyn Castle[s] over which magnificent structure he and the gentlemen who accompanied him were shown, returning in Mr. Wyatt's carriage, and attended by that gentleman. His Royal Highness, when at the castle, expressed his admiration of it and the surrounding scenery. The Prince was accompanied in his visit by his Serene Highness the Prince of Leiningen, Earl Grey, and Captain Gordon (a relative of the Hon. Colonel D. Pennant). During the absence of the Prince, the *Fairy* was surrounded by boats, all of which were suffered to approach close to the royal yacht, and thousands of loyal hearts were gratified with a very good view of our Most Gracious Sovereign, who was seated to the rear of the pavilion, sketching, and occasionally playing with the Princess Royal and the Prince of Wales. Her Majesty now and then acknowledged by a smile or friendly nod the loyal cheers of her subjects, who were further gratified by a sight of the Prince of Wales and the Princess Royal. Captain Warren, of the *Prince of Wales*, who conveyed all his passengers in the steamer's boat, in turn, to the *Fairy*, addressing Lord Adolphus Fitzclarence, said he had the honour of commanding *a Prince of Wales*, and should like to be honoured with a sight of *the* Prince of Wales. Her Majesty assenting, Lord Adolphus held up his little Royal Highness, who was tremendously cheered, as was also the Princess Royal. The Prince of Wales wore a glazed hat, blue jacket, white trowsers,—a miniature British tar. The Princess Royal appeared in a straw bonnet, tunic, and salmon-coloured dress, and, with her royal brother, looked the very picture of health and contentment.

During Prince Albert's absence, the tide had ebbed considerably, and his Royal Highness had to rough it along the causeway, to his great discomfort, as all who have gone through the ordeal of the weed, mud, and water will readily acknowledge. He was rowed to the yacht, as before, by eight lusty tars, and steered by Captain Beechy. The *Fairy* dropped anchor at four o'clock, and got under weigh at half-past seven, steaming right on.

Royal salutes were fired from the batteries at Craig-y-don, Port Penrhyn, and Beaumaris. The

---

[s] Penrhyn Castle, the property and residence of the Hon. Col. Douglas Pennant, M.P.

> " Abode of native Chiefs, of Bards the theme,
>   Here princely Penrhyn soars above the stream,
>   And Phœnix like, in rising splendour drest,
>   Shows on its wide domain a regal crest:
>   Here Cambria opes her tome of other days,
>   And, with maternal pride, the page displays—
>   Dwells on the glorious list, and loves to trace
>   From Britain's genuine kings—her noblest race."

Penrhyn was the residence of Roderic Molwynog, Prince of Wales, in 720, and of several succeeding Princes, till 1230, when Llywelyn dignified Iarddur ab Trahaearn with the office of Great Forester of Snowdon; and at the same time, with the liberality of a Prince, bestowed upon him the whole hundred of Llechwedd uchav. Eva, fourth daughter and heiress of Gruffydd, fourth in descent from Iarddur, afterwards conveyed this property into the family of the celebrated Ednyved Vychan, by her marriage with Gruffydd ab Heylin, ab Sir Tudor, ab Ednyved Vychan; and a Bard of 1450, speaking of the then resident, adds,

> " Un llîn a'i Frenhin fu'r âch."
> " His descent is the same as that of his sovereign."

steamers, merchantmen, and yachts displayed their full force of flags, and the American vessels which were anchored in the straits joined heartily in the general demonstration of respect and welcome.

As the *Fairy* approached the U.S. ship, *Josiah Quincy*, Captain Grazier; the barque *John Parker*, Captain Cumming; and the barque *Juniatta*, Captain Childs; the British flag was displayed forward, the American flag at the peak; and as the royal yacht glided past, the American flag was hauled down, and the British flag run up, which marks of courtesy were acknowledged by the exhibition of the flag of America on the quarter deck of the *Fairy*, Her Majesty standing by. As Prince Albert rowed off in his barge, he was met by Captain Childs of the *Juniatta*, in his gig, the crew of which gave three cheers—whereupon the Prince stood up, uncovered, and bowed his acknowledgments.

The *Prince of Wales, Taliesin, Ayrshire Lassie, Snowdon,* and other passenger steamers were in requisition. We noticed likewise the *Jenny Lind* steam yacht (T. A. Smith, Esq.), with a party on board, and a German steam yacht, attached to the royal convoy. Mr. Beaver's yacht, the *Zoe*, made a brilliant display of the flags of all nations, and added much to the general effect.

WELCOME TO HER MOST GRACIOUS MAJESTY, QUEEN VICTORIA, AND TO HER MAJESTY'S ROYAL CONSORT, PRINCE ALBERT;

ON THEIR PASSING THROUGH THE MENAI STRAITS IN THEIR PROGRESS TO SCOTLAND, AUGUST 15TH, 1847.

HARP of our everlasting hills—
    Of Cambria's wild, romantic shore,
The home of cataracts and rills,
    Where storms are nursed, and rave, and roar—
    Haste loyal harp, thy numbers pour,
And welcome to our steep and rocky strand
VICTORIA, Cambria's Queen, Queen of our mountain land.

Hail Britain's gem !—Hail Britain's boast !
    Hail Queen of many a region wide,
From distant India's glowing coast
    To lands laved by each polar tide !
    But chiefly thou 'rt our joy and pride
(Though on thy realms the sun unsetting smiles),
And honour'd most as Queen of Britain and her isles.

Queen of the Isles, we offer thee
    The homage of a loyal race :
In all else poor, save loyalty.—
    O Queen enriched by every grace,
    In thee the TUDOR line we trace—
Of Cambria's ancient kings the royal line—
Hence thrice we bow the knee, and pray for thee and thine !

Lo ! Arvon's sons and daughters fair,
    With Mona's join'd—a joyous band—
Rush from their misty homes, mid-air,
    And crowd upon the shingly strand,
    To welcome to their rugged land,
And hail thine advent, O most gracious Queen ;
An advent such as thine, their shores have seldom seen !

The bosoms of our mountaineers
    To day with other feelings swell,
Than those which roused the battle cheers,
    A crown'd invader to repel :
    All strive each other to excel,
With welcomes warm in many a wild huzza,—
'Tis joy that fills all hearts on this auspicious day.[9]

The Queen being expected in the lively and picturesque town of Beaumaris on Saturday, the good people were eagerly looking out for her arrival. The *Prince of Wales* packet left the pier (with a great number of genteel people on board) at nine o'clock, expecting to meet the royal squadron, but returned at nine in the evening to the Menai Bridge, without having obtained a glimpse of the regal voyagers. The green was crowded the whole day with anxious spectators. Flags were displayed from all parts of the town; a great number of cutters which had arrived for the occasion, were beautifully decorated. There were various reports in circulation as to the route by which her Majesty would arrive. On Sunday, at three o'clock, the news came that her Majesty was at Caernarvon. The town was again all excitement; many thousands of people assembled on the green and pier. At a quarter to eight o'clock her Majesty passed Beaumaris at a

---

[9] A copy of the above elegant verses, which were composed by John Morris Jones, written upon vellum, was forwarded for presentation to the Queen, by the then Mayor of Caernarvon (T. Turner, Esq.). Sir Denis le Marchant acknowledged the receipt, and said that her Majesty was graciously pleased to accept the same.

rapid rate; and, owing to the duskness of the evening, few people had the gratification of seeing her, excepting those on the pier: the Queen came on deck with the Prince of Wales. The strength of the pier was well tested, there being thousands of persons on it; amongst whom we noticed Sir Richard and Lady Bulkeley, the four Masters Bulkeley, Lady Stanley, Sir A. and Lady Aston, &c., &c.

Her Majesty's yacht joined the other vessels forming the royal escort, at the cross-roads at Penmon, where they had arrived about seven o'clock, and the squadron passed the night in the roads. The address from the Mayor and Corporation of Beaumaris was delivered to Lord Grey, after the yacht had reached the cross-roads. At four o'clock on Monday morning Her Majesty proceeded on her route.

On board the royal yacht were Her Majesty, Prince Albert, the Prince of Wales, the Princess Royal, and the Prince of Leiningen, with the Duke and Duchess of Norfolk, lord and lady in waiting; the Viscountess Jocelyn, lady in waiting; Earl Grey, Secretary of State; and Sir James Clarke, Baronet, physician to the Queen. On board the *Black Eagle* were Major-General Wemyss and the Honourable Captain Gordon, equerries to Prince Albert, and seventy-two servants and carriages. In the *Garland* were the Queen's messengers; Angus M'Kay, the Queen's piper, &c.

Rev. Mr. Williams (*Caledfryn*) of Caernarvon, composed a beautiful descriptive poem of the welcome the people of Wales gave to Her Majesty, Prince Albert, the Prince of Wales, and the rest of the royal family, on their visit to the Cambrian shore; but as the poem is written in the Welsh language and unintelligible to the English reader, we will insert the argument[1] of the poem in their own language, and a few verses as a specimen in the ancient language of the Cymry.

DONAU'R môr cydunwch,—ar ein hanwyl
　　Frenhines na wgwch ;
　　Chwi awelon trymion, trwch,
　　Yn Arfon na chynhyrfwch.

Na roddwch rwystr iddi,
　　Wynt na môr, tra llwybro'r lli'.

Suwch a rhowch groesawiad—i enwog
　　Frenhines pedeir gwlad,
　　Gyda'i gwr,—o gydgariad—ysblenydd,
　　At dir y moelydd, dd'ont ar ymweliad.

Mae y wlad oddiyma i L'yn,—a Chonwy
　　Yn chwenych ei derbyn ;
　　Yn Mon deg, p'le mae un dyn,
　　Na hoffai ei hamddiffyn.

Wele dorf o wlad Arfon,
　　A gwyr mawr o gyrau Mon,
　　Cor eirian Llanciau'r 'Ryri,
　　Golud a nerth ein gwlad ni,
　　A rhif o deg wyryfon,
　　Fwyned ynt, ar fin y dòn ;
　　Pawb a'i wên ar ei enau,
　　Oll un wedd yn llawenhau.

Rhuog anadl twrw y gynau—mawr,
　　Fel myrdd o daranau ;
　　Arwyddant i bob graddau,
　　A'u swn, ei bod yn nesáu.

Ochrau'r bryniau'n llawn i'w cribau
　　O bersonau mewn brys hynod,
　　Gan fawr draserch, am ei hanerch,
　　Wych ŏonferch hardd, a'i chanfod.

Bwriwn gangau ar ei llwybrau,
　　A sidanau res a daener ;
　　Porffor leni, aur a phali,
　　'Nawr, heb oedi, na arbeder.

Rhes o bendefigesau—a'u dwylaw
　　Yn dwyn dail a blodau,
　　O lin Elen, lân aeliau,
　　I fyn'd dan fyrdd o fwliau.

Down a grawn o dan eu gwrid,
　　A'r aeron, lliw'r myrierid,
　　Llawenyched, gwaedded gwyr
　　Yn groew nes rhwygo'r awyr.

Boed rhuadan y cerbydau,
　　A'r meirch hwythau mor chwai, weithion,
　　Yn eu nwyfiant nes bo'r palmant
　　Llawu a rychant oll yn wreichion.

---

[1] THE ARGUMENT.—The winds and waves are conjured not to be inauspicious to Her Majesty and her Royal Consort whilst visiting our shores—The inhabitants of Mona and Arfon full of anxiety with regard to the event—The great guns to give the signal of her approach—All the surrounding hills crowded with spectators waiting with the most exhilarating sensations—The utmost determination evinced to gain an early view of the squadron at a distance—The flags waving on the Castle towers—The multitude moving to and fro on the banks of the Menai—The walls of our turrets filled with gazers congratulating each other—A number of boats and yachts gliding on the Menai—The shades of the trees and bushes lining the sides of the beautiful crystal-like stream—Victoria represented as moving along amidst the waves without any fear or alarm—Armed men not required on the shores to protect Her Majesty's person—Her defence is in the warm hearts of the natives. A monarch never more respected by persons of every age and condition—Even the print of her foot held in high estimation—A desire that her paths should be paved with marble, decorated with satin, crimson, velvet, and gold

On the evening of the 27th of August, 1847, the Rev. Mr. Price, vicar of Cwmdû, one of the most eminent antiquaries of Wales, submitted to Her Majesty and his Royal Highness Prince Albert at Buckingham Palace, the beautiful Welsh harp, described in the engraving, as a present to the Prince

A fac-simile of the Ancient Welsh Harp presented
to His Royal Highness the Prince of Wales.

of Wales. The Queen was graciously pleased to permit the Prince of Wales to accept the present; and two Welsh harpers, who attended by the royal command, performed upon the beautiful instrument. Mr. Price also explained to Her Majesty and the Prince the peculiar construction of the harp:[2] it is in the ancient and picturesque form of the national instrument of the Principality; stands about six feet high: it is elaborately carved in solid wood, the base of the pillar being supported by the leek, entwined with mistletoe and oak leaves; a wreath of oak leaves goes up the pillar, which terminates in the Prince of Wales's plume, supported by sprays of oak, whence depend three labels, on which are carved, in antique characters, "Albert, Tywysawc Cymru" (or Albert, Prince of Wales). On the side of the comb of the harp is likewise carved, in old characters, the following line from one of the Welsh bards:—"Iaith enaid ar ei thannau" (*The language of the soul is on its strings*). On the sounding-board are emblazoned the arms of Wales, four lions passant, or, and gules counterchanged, with the red dragon of Wales supporting the shield, and the coronet and plume of the Prince of Wales. *Her Majesty, while examining the harp, observed to Mr. Price that she was not a stranger to the tones of the Welsh harp, having heard it during her visit to the Principality, at the great national festival of the Eisteddfod, in 1832.* The harpers afterwards performed both on the Prince of Wales's harp, and also on their own instruments, several of the finest old Welsh melodies, singly and in duets, with which the royal party were much gratified. On the following day the harpers were presented with 20*l.* by Her Majesty's command, in testimony of her approbation. They were attired in the picturesque costume of their country, with the silver harp and medals gained in the various trials of skill in which they had been engaged.

It has always been a custom, from time immemorial, for the Prince of Wales to have his harper, and we are happy to find that Her Majesty has not forgotten that ancient custom: she has been pleased to appoint that exquisite player,

—Bands of musicians and harpers invited to fill the air with their melody—A number of ladies, beautiful as Helen, invoked to bear garlands and flowers, and to advance in procession under a thousand triumphal arches—Chariots and horses, their rumbling described, the sparks from the wheels of the chariots, and the hoofs of the horses—Aged females full of astonishment, forgetting their infirmities, shouting and greeting their Queen—A veteran, with his silvery locks, who has been a loyal subject ever since the reign of George III., and who could unfold many a tale of woe—The times of George III.—The horrors of war exemplified—The peaceful reign of Victoria—The visit will long be remembered and blessed—Nature and art ready to pay homage—The picturesque scenery along the banks of the Menai—Our determination to conspire with Nature—The bonfires and roaring of cannon expected—The times of Edward I.—His cruelty to the Welsh bards.—A bard flying for refuge into the caves—The contrast—Our Queen, the Queen of peace—An allusion to the royal medal received by the author, and the medals received by other successful candidates, at the Beaumaris Eisteddfod, in 1832, from their Royal Highnesses the Duchess of Kent and Princess Victoria—The value the author places upon this token of royal favour—An allusion to the great and important event of suspending, and ultimately repealing, the corn laws, which clogged the commerce of ages—The kind-heartedness of our beloved Queen in listening to the cry of her people—The repeal of obnoxious laws, one of the most brilliant gems in her crown, which event will be commemorated a thousand generations hence—An ejaculation for the prosperity of her offspring, with a desire that they may remain an unbroken chain till the end of time.

[2] This beautiful Welsh triple harp has been made expressly for His Royal Highness the Prince of Wales, by Mr. Basset Jones, of Cardiff.

Mr. Ellis Roberts (*Eos Meirion*) of London, harper to his Royal Highness the Prince of Wales. The following note was received by Mr. Roberts, announcing his appointment:—

> "*Osborne House, August 8th*, 1850.
>
> "THIS is to certify that Mr. Ellis Roberts was, by the authority of Her Majesty the Queen, appointed harper to His Royal Highness the Prince of Wales, upon the 28th of August, 1849.
>
> "C. B. PHIPPS,
> "*Treasurer and Cofferer to the Prince of Wales.*"

No appointment could possibly have given greater satisfaction, for it is universally acknowledged by all who have had the pleasure of hearing Mr. Roberts,[2] that he has reached the top of his profession. He has frequently played before Her Majesty, as well as the principal nobility in England and Wales. In the latter place he has always carried away the premier prizes for the best performance on the harp at the royal and provincial Eisteddfodau, where he has frequently been invested with gold and silver medals, silver harps, &c., &c. When Mr. Roberts touches the "trembling strings" of his fine instrument, presented to him by his countrymen in London, he creates quite a sensation. Well might the poet sing to the old Welsh air,—

> Hark! the harp to rapture sounding,
> *Ar hyd y nos.*
> Hark! the hills and vales rebounding,
> *Ar hyd y nos.*
> Eye to eye its gladness telling,
> Heart to heart, with rapture swelling,
> Cambria's harps all harps excelling,
> *Ar hyd y nos.*

The last visit Her Majesty paid to the Border counties was on the 31st of September, 1848, when Her Majesty, Prince Albert, the Prince of Wales, and all the royal family and suite, paid an unexpected visit, and domiciled for the night at the Crewe Hotel, Cheshire, which is proverbially known, under the able and efficient management of the landlord and his lady (Mr. and Mrs. Edwards), to be one of the best hotels in the country. The following account of this visit is from a friend who was present: we adopt his own words:—

CREWE, *2nd Oct.* 1848.—On Saturday evening last, this place (Crewe) was the scene of considerable excitement in consequence of the unexpected arrival and temporary sojourn of the Queen, Prince Albert, and suite, on their route to town, from Scotland.

Arrangements had, as it is known, been made for Her Majesty's proceeding directly by sea to Portsmouth from Aberdeen, but adverse and stormy weather induced the royal squadron to put back into Aberdeen harbour, and, as there was no prospect of better weather, the Queen (albeit Her Majesty is no mere fresh-water sailor) determined on proceeding to town by land. Her Majesty's intention to halt at Crewe having only preceded her, twenty minutes, by telegraph, very few were assembled to receive her. She was escorted to the Crewe Arms Hotel, by Mr. and Mrs. Edwards, who were in attendance.

Having inspected the apartments selected for their reception, the Queen signified her intention to remain for the night, and arrangements were made accordingly. Dinner was served at half-past eight to Her Majesty, Prince Albert, and suite, which consisted of Lady Gainsborough, Sir George Grey, Mr. and Mrs. Anson, Captain Gordon, and Sir James Clarke. Her Majesty returned to the drawing-room at ten o'clock, where coffee was served. The Prince of Wales, the Princess Royal, and Prince Alfred had tea at eight o'clock, which seemed to afford them great refreshment after the fatigue of their journey. The Queen retired to rest at eleven, after which hour, the house, under the surveillance of Mr. Edwards, remained in perfect quietness.

---

[2] Mr. Roberts's execution is very neat and brilliant, and his *sons étouffés* and harmonics are most perfect; his *pianissimos* and *expressivos* very beautiful; and he has the good taste to eschew, to a great extent, the detestable "rip and tear" of the modern school. His selection of Welsh melodies is in fine taste; and the various effects peculiar to them and the instrument of their expression, he gives with great excellence; whilst his occasional touchings upon the difficulties of modern harpists show him to be possessed of a musician's, as well as of a mere lyrist's, knowledge.

The suite were in motion at four A.M., and her Majesty rose at five. Breakfast was served at six, half an hour after which, the royal party departed by special train for London. The managing engineer at Crewe, Mr. Trevethick, had made every arrangement for facilitating Her Majesty's comfort on the journey to town without delay or annoyance. A pilot engine was despatched at four o'clock, with guards, to see everything clear, and make the necessary signals on approach of Her Majesty's train, which means were perfectly effective. The Queen and Prince Consort both appeared in perfect health and in excellent spirits. The royal children were somewhat fatigued by their land and sea voyage, so much so that some difficulty was experienced by their attendants in rousing them at the early hour at which Her Majesty departed.

The Queen, Prince Albert, and suite were pleased to express their high satisfaction to Mr. and Mrs. Edwards, for their kind attention and the comfortable manner they were entertained at the Crewe Hotel.

In the month of December, 1848, His Royal Highness Prince George of Cambridge paid a visit to Sir Richard B. W. Bulkeley, Bart., M.P., at Baron Hill, accompanied by the Hon. St. George Foley, Sir C. F. Smith, K.C.B., Hon. James McDonald, and Captain Williams. On Saturday, December 16th, his Royal Highness and party visited the Baron Hill covers, and in spite of wind and weather, killed two hundred and fifty head of game.

In the month of September, 1849, His Royal Highness the late Duke of Cambridge and suite, paid a friendly visit to the Principality, and made some stay at Plas Newydd, the beautiful marine residence of the Marquis of Anglesea. The royal party visited most of the attractive and wonderful scenes in that part of the country, but they were so pleased with the celebrated pass of Llanberis, at the foot of Snowdon, that they signified their intention of again honouring Llanberis with a visit; and, accordingly, early on Wednesday morning, the Duchess of Cambridge and the Princess Mary, the Grand Duchess of Mecklenburg Strelitz, and Prince George of Cambridge, attended by the Baron Knesebeck, crossed over to Port Dinorwic, where they were met by Mr. Owen Roberts, and Mr. John Millington, jun., (the agents of T. Assheton Smith, Esq.,) and proceeded to Llanberis by the Padarn Railway, in open slate waggons, which had been fitted up for the occasion. On their arrival at Llanberis they visited Mr. Assheton Smith's extensive slate quarries; having inspected the steam saw-mill, where they were much interested with the operation of sawing and planing slabs, they ascended five steep inclines to the Raven Rock quarry, where they saw some large blocks quarried from the mountain side. Each of the royal party here took chisel in hand, and with a little assistance split a slate. After descending from the quarries and partaking of lunch at Glanybala Cottage, they visited the Waterfall and Dolbadarn Castle, and returned to Plas Newydd by the same route in the evening, evidently much gratified with the excursion.

On Tuesday, the 25th of September, the royal party, consisting of his Royal Highness the Duke of Cambridge, Prince George of Cambridge, and Princess Mary, with the Grand Duke and Duchess of Mecklenburg Strelitz, paid a visit to Bodorgan, the seat of Owen Fuller Meyrick, Esq. In the absence of Mr. Meyrick, the royal party were conducted over the gardens, grounds, and house, by Mr. Ewing. In the gardens the royal party were first conducted through the orchidaceous house, which contains many of the rarest species of air-plants recently introduced into Europe. They then proceeded through the pineries, vineries, exotic plant-houses, and flower-garden. Their Royal Highnesses were graciously pleased to express admiration at all they saw, intimating that the gardens equalled anything that they had ever before seen, and passed high enconiums upon the spirited proprietor. They subsequently visited Mr. Ewing's house, where they remained half an hour, and familiarly conversed with his family. They were afterwards shown through Bodorgan House, the principal apartments of which they examined. They made particular enquiry about the family paintings, some of which are by Sir Joshua Reynolds and Sir W. Beechy. One by the former artist was particularly admired, viz., a portrait of General Elliott, afterwards Lord Heathfield, who gained a European fame by his noble defence of Gibraltar. In the meantime the cannons from Bodorgan battery were pouring forth a loud salute in honour of the visit. As the royal party drove through the park gate, the workmen of the demesne gave a hearty demonstration of loyal feeling which was condescendingly acknowledged.

Their Royal Highnesses the Duke and Duchess of Cambridge, accompanied by their Serene Highnesses the Duke and Duchess of Mecklenburg Strelitz and the Princess Mary, attended by Baron Knesebeck, &c., left Plas Newydd, on Saturday, September 29, for Heaton Park, near Manchester, the seat of the Earl and Countess of Wilton.

It is with much pleasure we learn that her Royal Highness the Duchess of Cambridge intends to honour the Isle of Anglesea, by making it her future residence. Arrangements are about to be made for her permanent residence, and Plas Newydd, the beautiful seat of the Marquis of Anglesea, is to be her royal abode.

We would now sum up our observations by taking a retrospective but quaint review of the most remarkable scenes and actions of our patriotic countrymen in defending their native land. We trust that we have given sufficient instances of their heroic conduct, to excite interest and respect in the minds of those who are capable of appreciating the brave and patriotic conduct of the Cymry, or can learn a lesson from the mutations of time and nature. We have endeavoured to describe the land where the Aborigines of this island sought and found a refuge; we have traced the fields where our great ancestors warred successfully against Roman, Saxon, and Norman powers; and we have given some account of the ruined walls of those fortresses which were intended by the powers that were, to hold in subjection the oppressed patriarchs and patriots of the land, if not to extirpate both language and people, but which are now only monuments of the impotency of human will, and prove more strongly than all histories that neither

> " Stony tower, nor walls of beaten brass,
> Nor airless dungeon, nor strong links of iron,
> Can be retentive to the strength of spirit."

In the prophetic language of Taliesin, notwithstanding the political mutations which the people of Cambria have been subjected to,

> " Their God they still worship,
> Their language remains,
> Though the children of strangers
> Dwell on their green plains :
> Yet the mother of mountains still clasps to her breast,
> Of her offspring the eldest, the bravest, the best."

The feudal and the gavel laws no longer contend with each other in dire hostility; they have been blended and moulded anew, and all are governed by the same just and equitable code. The strong Norman castle, with its dread portcullis and deep dungeons, no longer exists but in ruins; the modest and comfortable gentleman's seat rises in its stead, and peace reigns upon the mountains, in the vales, and upon all the frontiers. The traveller or the tourist can now proceed from north to south, and from south to north, without carrying arms for his defence, sure of meeting with kindness and the most generous hospitality. The glare of the beacon, the burning of towns, the foraging of hostile bands, are no longer seen; security and confidence reign on every side, whilst prosperity and affluence attend upon the great and the noble; and health, peace, and contentment, cheer the humble cottage of the virtuous and industrious poor.

From the annexation of the Principality of Wales to the crown and realm of England, the Ancient Britons, even in the most turbulent times, have been as remarkable for their allegiance, as they had before been tenacious of their rights and liberties. A proof of this will be found in the following historical facts. No less than 6700 Cambro-Britons joined the Black Prince at Portsmouth, in his expedition to France, and he commanded 5800 of them at the Battle of Cressy. The success of that day, the 26th August, 1346, was entirely owing to this corps of Britons.[*] Again: at the Battle of Poictiers, in 1356, the majority of the forces were Welsh; at which battle Sir Howel y Fwyall took the French king prisoner, and did great

---

[*] See Carte, ii., 462.

acts of prowess with his battle-axe, &c. This event is recorded by one of our ancient bards in the following distich :—

> " Pan roddodd
> Y ffrwyn ymhen Brenin Ffrainc."

> " When on the head of royal France
> A bridle strong he placed."

The Black Prince, son of Edward III., seems to have been so sensible of Howel's services, that he knighted him on the field of battle, gave him the rent of the Dee Mills at Chester for life, and the constableship of the castle of Criccieth, where he afterwards resided ; added his battle-axe to his coat of arms, and ordered that a mess of meat should be served before it daily, for ever, to preserve in memory the uncommon prowess of its master. The King appointed eight yeomen, at eight-pence a day each, to guard the mess, and see it regularly served before the axe. After the death of Howel, the mess was given to the poor for his soul's sake, till the reign of Queen Elizabeth, when the establishment was abolished.

At the Battle of Agincourt, in 1415, where a glorious victory was obtained over the French, Henry V. selected our countryman, David Gam, to reconnoitre the enemy before the battle, whose numbers were 100,000, being ten times the number of Henry's force. He returned and told the prince, "*An't please you, my liege, there are enough to be killed, enough to be taken prisoners, and enough to run away.*" The King was pleased with the reply ; and in the battle, David, his son-in-law, Roger Vychan, and his relation, Walter Lloyd, rescued his Majesty when surrounded by his foes (viz. eighteen French cavaliers), whose life they saved at the expense of their own, and killed fourteen of the enemy. The King, after the victory, approached the spot where they lay in the agonies of death, and bestowed on them the only reward that could be then paid to their valour, the honour of knighthood ! Shakspeare designates Sir David Gam by the name of Fluelin.

When the plausible, yet delusive tenets of republicanism were over-running the land, we find them uniformly attached to the throne ; and in the perilous times of Charles I.,[5] impenetrable to its importunities, brave in defence of that unhappy monarch ; ever loyal, ever sincere. In a more recent revolution, in which Great Britain was necessitated to act a more conspicuous and successful part ; when politics and levelling had rendered Europe mad with insubordination, Wales still remained true to her post, and shed her best blood in crushing democracy. In former days she furnished England with courageous soldiers to fight her battles, and brave generals to command her armies. Need we mention a few of our gallant heroes ? Our Picton ! our Anglesea ! ! our Combermere ! ! ! In these days of Indian warfare, we still claim a portion of the brilliant and glorious victories of our armies in China, Hyderabad, and Scinde. Our Nott, our Lloyd, our Edwardes, and the better half of our brave and distinguished Generals, Napier[6] and Sale ! Gen. Sir William Nott, K.G.C.B., the hero of Ghuznee and Cabul, was a native of Caermarthen, and entered the army in 1798. By his consummate judgment and indomitable courage, he extricated the British army under his command, from the toils and treachery which surrounded it in Affghanistan ; and after several brilliant exploits, such as the capture of Ghuznee, the release of the British captives,[7] and the advance on Cabul, he succeeded, in

[5] During one of our perambulations out of the metropolis in the month of Sept., 1850, we visited Windsor Castle, the residence of our beloved Queen. We inspected the Royal Chapel of St. George, and the ancient cloisters thereof. In the latter we discovered a small brass monument, with the following inscription :—

" Neare this place lieth the bodie of Capt. Richard Vaughan, of Pantglâs, in the county of Caernarvon, who behaved himself with great courage in the service of King Charles I., of blessed memory, in the civil warrs, and thereupon lost his eyesight, in recompense thereof he was, in July, 1663, made one of the poor knights of this place (Windsor), and died the 5th day of June, 1700, in the 80th yeare of his age."

[6] When General Napier resided, as general of the district, in Chester, he was in the habit of calling upon the author, and has often said that "he would sooner go to battle than sit down to dinner ;" and finding that he was acquainted with the Welsh language, the General said that Lady Napier was a native of Wales. The next time the General came, he brought his lady with him, who entered into a long conversation with the writer in the ancient British language. Her ladyship spoke fluently and humorously.

[7] Among these captives was the heroic Lady Sale, who is also a native of Wales. Her ladyship's work on the Indian war has lately been published, and is full of interesting events. The following anecdote is related of her : When General Nott was advancing on the town where the British captives were imprisoned, some of the chiefs made a proposition to Lady Sale—that if she would write to

conjunction with General Pollock, in regaining the Indian territory with safety and honour. For his services in India, General Nott received from the hand of his sovereign, Queen Victoria, the highest honour it was in the power of Her Majesty to bestow, viz. that of being created a knight of the Grand Cross of the Order of the Bath. He also received the thanks of both Houses of Parliament, and the East India Company granted him a pension of 1000*l*. a-year for life, for his brave and extraordinary services in the East, which pension, alas! he only lived to enjoy about six months. He died in January, 1845.

The following evidence of the Judges of the North Wales Circuit, is a sufficient proof of the honesty and moral conduct of the people of Wales, notwithstanding the vindictive heaps of calumny imposed upon them by the authors of the "*Blue Books.*"

The inhabitants of the Principality may well lay claim to the character of "honest Welshmen." Theft and fraud will always be practised to a certain extent, in every country; but in Wales these vices are comparatively of rare occurrence, and are generally confined to the worst portion of society. The very few cases of this kind, which have to be tried at our assizes, attest the honesty of the Welsh population. Often, very often, are our prison-doors thrown open; there being no malefactors within, when the judges go on their circuit. The result of two of our recent assizes will justify these assertions.

At the Montgomeryshire assizes there was not a single prisoner for trial, and only two civil causes; at the Merionethshire assizes only two prisoners, and two civil causes; at the Caernarvonshire assizes there was not a single case of any kind to be tried; at the Anglesea assizes, only one prisoner, and one civil cause; at the Denbighshire assizes, only two prisoners and a few civil causes; and at the Flintshire assizes, only one prisoner and one civil cause!

No wonder, then, that the judge, Baron Vaughan, should congratulate the grand juries in each of the six counties in North Wales, upon the happy and peaceful state of the country. The following extract is from the Baron's charge to the grand jury at Ruthin :—

"It was particularly gratifying to him, who had travelled all the circuits in England, and who had seen crime abounding to an extent so frightful in many districts there, that last winter he alone tried nearly three hundred prisoners—it was most gratifying to him, to reflect that he had hitherto tried only three prisoners on this circuit. In travelling through this beautiful Principality, he had been delighted to observe the religion, morality, and loyalty of its inhabitants, and those happy results which flowed from them—peace, contentment, and good order."

Another instance, equally creditable to Wales and Welshmen, recently took place in Anglesea. We quote the following extract from Mr. Justice Coleridge's address to the grand jury at Beaumaris :—

"Gentlemen, I have nothing whatever to charge you with. There are no depositions of any kind before me, nor am I aware of any bills to be brought before you. There is no calendar, and there is not a criminal prisoner in the gaol. There is not even a civil cause entered to engross the attention of the court; a state of things unprecedented not only during my judicial career, but I can also say during the entire of my professional life. Allow me most heartily to congratulate you upon the occurrence. You must not, gentlemen, imagine that your attendance has thereby become a mere form. It is not so. The external sanctities of justice are essential to her influence and well-being, and your attendance here this day will not be lost upon the moral feelings of the community. Most heartily do I congratulate you upon the circumstances under which we have met. There is nothing in the flourishing state either of agriculture or commerce that can teem with greater blessings than those that flow from laws judiciously enforced and regularly obeyed. These facts, gentlemen, are mentioned by me, not to induce you to relax, but rather to persevere in your endeavours to promote the good character of your county. Passing, as I have this day

General Nott, to request him *not to advance*, the lives of all the captives should be spared. Her ladyship wrote in the same quaint style as William the Fourth once did to Admiral Sir Edward Codrington, " Go it, Ned :" she said, "*Advance, Nott !*" which might be interpreted either way; the General understood it, and soon relieved the prisoners.

done, the most stupendous monument of modern art, and gazing with delight upon the vast, the beautiful and magnificent amphitheatre of hills, by which your broad Menai is circled, I feel still more vividly the grandeur of the scenery by finding its deep repose in unison with the peace and harmony of the people. Gentlemen, you will retire for a brief period, and if no bill comes before you, I shall most gladly discharge you forthwith."

The sheriff distributed white gloves amongst the officers of the court.

The foreman of the jury, the Hon. W. O. Stanley, M.P., having returned to inform his lordship, that no bill had been presented, the jury were discharged, and the assizes terminated.

The following gratifying result transpired at the conclusion of a recent investigation into the mendicity of London, by a committee of the House of Commons. It appeared that there were at least 15,249 individuals, consisting of Irish, Scotch, parochial, and some foreign beggars, who daily infest the vast capital, "seeking whom they may deceive:" but in this mass of profligacy and deception, hear it, ye natives of Cambria, and rejoice, not a Welshman was found!

With regard to the great beneficial results of the union of England with Wales, Sir James Mackintosh, the philosophical English historian, has fairly and generously admitted, that Wales had contributed her full share to the general wealth and prosperity of the kingdom; it is therefore unnecessary to enumerate every instance, we shall be content by naming a few.

While we are willing to admit the important advantages Wales has derived from her incorporation with England, we must also contend that the blessings of the annexation have been reciprocal. In many respects the English nation has acquired several essential benefits from its union with the Cymry.

In popular discontents and political commotions, our countrymen have maintained a uniform loyalty to the throne—equally firm in their attachment to the prince, as they were formerly tenacious of their liberty and independence. In war we have supplied the national armies with brave and courageous soldiers and sailors; and whether in peace or in war, have cheerfully contributed our quota to the national burthens: nor, under any circumstance, have our peaceful population required the presence or incurred the expense of military force. Their staunch fidelity to the throne and the altar, when the security of both were so seriously menaced, will ever remain a proud distinction in their national character!

The surplus of our agricultural produce is constantly poured into the English markets, which, in years of scarcity, contributes to mitigate the distresses of famine, and in seasons of plenty tends to correct the high price of the necessaries of life. Our native mountains abound with metals of every description, and the very bowels of our earth are replete with the most useful and valuable minerals, which, when transported into England, supply labours for her machines, furnish useful commodities to her community, and serve to fill the sails of her commerce. In a word, if the proverbial adage be true, that the Emerald Isle is the right hand of the British empire, surely those who know the character and importance of Old Cambria, will not deny her that station in the body politic which is usually termed the left hand.

But in noticing the benefits our neighbours and fellow-subjects enjoy from their connection with us, forbid it, every sentiment of patriotism, that we should mention them for any invidious purpose, or concede them with a grudging feeling. On the contrary, we could wish from our hearts, that our capabilities of advantaging the English nation were infinitely greater than they are, because the increased prosperity of any part of our united community brings with it an addition to the prosperity of every part. While England flourishes, our country, identified with her by laws and reciprocity of interest, can never be depressed.

By this happy union of Wales with England, a peaceful country and a tranquil mind was restored to the Welsh, and England benefited by the result, when they became subject to sovereigns of their own race;[a] kings lineally descended from their own royal blood, whose interest it was to promote their comfort

[a] Henry VII., and the Tudor family.

and safety, rather than to molest and oppress them. When, we say, this reformation was effected, the Welsh began to turn their attention to different objects, and to more beneficial pursuits; to a mode of life more pleasing to their rulers, and more conducive to their own welfare. Instead of training up their sons for war and turmoils, they prepared them to be more useful members of the community, and more dutiful subjects to their government; instead of sharpening and multiplying their swords and spears, there was henceforth nothing hammered on their anvils but their ploughshares and scythes; their priests and their bards, instead of preaching and poetising ferocity and contention into the minds of their countrymen, now employed their talents to compose orations on religion and immortality, and odes on domesticity and agriculture; instead of building castles and digging entrenchments to withstand their enemies, they turned to erect and repair the temples of their God, and the seminaries of their literati, and the re-establishment of their Eisteddfodau.

Before the union of Wales and England, the inhabitants of the former were designated by the latter as a ferocious and barbarous nation, but since their union they have become civilised and mild, and their general character is that of a moral and happy people. Instead of being rustic and ignorant, they became skilful and learned; instead of being infatuated and superstitious, they became religious and devotional; yea, we say, in their conjunction with the English, the Welsh nation are become as eminent in science, literature, and piety, as any people on the face of the globe. Who more devoted to their God? Who more loyal to their Queen? Who more affable to their fellow-subjects, and to one another? Who more hospitable to strangers? Who more submissive to their superiors? And who more charitable to the distressed? What part of the kingdom is troubled with less disturbances? In what counties in this realm are there fewer law disputes to adjust? And what prisons are so scantily inhabited with criminals? Yea, year after year, have their gaol doors been thrown open, having no longer a malefactor to be confined!

Land of our fathers! sincerely do we rejoice that the storms of foreign invasion, of domestic factions, and of civil wars, which formerly darkened thy bright horizon, have passed away, and that thou art now blessed with halcyon days, when we can range thy mountains and thy vales in safety, *and listen to the thrilling tones of thy divine telyn.*

The blessings that have resulted to Wales from her incorporation with England are not less numerous than valuable. So long as the countries were divided by separate interests, governed by different laws, and distinguished by varied usages and habits, they were each actuated by national prejudices and animosities, which were not only sources of hostile conflicts, but also of internal feuds and commotions. How often have our fine valleys been drenched with the blood of our countrymen, and the clamour of war heard on our mountains! How often have the fatherless children cried for their parents, and the widow lamented for the husband who fell in battle! But those scenes of horror are no longer known, save in the page of history. Conflicting interests and broils no longer distract and disturb our population; and we behold no other competition but a peaceful rivalry among the people of both countries,—which shall conduce most essentially to the common good—which shall be most useful to the arts, and best affected to our beloved Queen and government.

By the union of the two countries, we are now made one with a people who may truly be denominated the greatest in the world—a people whose learning and science diffuse all the blessings of civilisation and polished refinement; and whose courage and strength are capable of shielding from insult and invasion every portion of her immense dominion. In her commerce, Great Britain visits every continent, island, and creek known to navigation, and the four winds of heaven waft her richly laden vessels on the bosom of every sea. Conscious of her own strength, she presents an undaunted front to all the nations of the earth, and in return, receives from each the homage of reverence and honour! In herself but an island, —comparatively a speck rising on the ocean,—she has encompassed in the arms of conquest, extensive possessions in both hemispheres, and numbers among her subjects the inhabitants of the antipodes! Thus holding in her hand the destinies of scores of millions of the human family!

But great and splendid as is the glory of England in these particulars, she shines with still greater lustre when viewed through the medium of her inimitable constitution and government. Her political institutions are founded in wisdom, and sanctioned by the approval of experience. Her mixed monarchy contains all the excellences, and provides against the evils of the three sorts of government of which it is compounded. Its excellence does not lie in any one of its component parts, but in a nice union of the three, which union is then perfect, when it prevents any one from preponderating and rendering the other two subservient to itself. Thus they distribute equally the duties and honours of the state with the blessings of personal liberty and security to all; protecting the property of the rich, and shielding the rights of the poor!⁹

By our union with England, we are blessed with a permanent security against oppression and licentiousness: and by the establishment of that great paladium of freedom—"trial by jury," we are protected against all assaults, arbitrary power, and violence. This generous and much-admired system of law is universally administered, and holds the life, liberty, and property of every individual in the realm sacred. In short, our constitution is the "glory of Britain, and the admiration of the world!" Of all the nations of Europe, *here only are all men free.* But to crown all, we are united to a people whose religion is Christianity;¹ who enjoy the blessings of Christianity in its incorrupt and purest state—blessings in comparison of which all others of a temporal nature sink into insignificance. This, in truth, is the last best gift of God to man!

In a word, whatever privileges and immunities pertain to England, are enjoyed by Wales; in her greatness we are great, and her strength is our security. There is not a gem in the British crown that we are not interested in preserving; under the shadow of the constitution, we are guarded from all violence, and there is not a peasant in our mountains or valleys who is not as securely protected by our salutary laws as the first nobleman in the land.

Identified with Englishmen in their privileges, we cheerfully submit ourselves to their duties; partaking of their blessings, we claim a right to share in their burdens; and allied to them, not only by political compact, but also by interest and affection, with undissembled sentiments we exclaim, *May this great compacted nation, the aggregate of kingdoms once rivals and foes, but now so happily concentrated and entwined together, endure in never-fading verdure;—may they continue as long as their rivers rush to their subject-ocean;—and may the youth and vigour of all flourish, until our native mountains fail to raise their hoary heads to the sky!*

Our history of the Royal Visits and Progresses, and their happy result, is now brought to a close We will conclude our remarks by calling the attention of our readers, as concisely as possible, to a brief summary of the leading events of Her Majesty's glorious reign—the great and progressive improvements of her legislative enactments, the wonderful discoveries in arts and sciences, the prodigious inventions, the steam-engine on land and sea, the electric telegraph—the tubular bridges that span the waters of the Menai, (the last achievement of the scientific engineer, rivalling the triumphs of the Pharaohs and the Ptolemies, &c., &c., which are calculated for the intellectual, moral, and social improvement of her loyal and devoted subjects throughout her vast dominions.

Though the times in which we live appear to be destitute of romance, and utilitarianism to be its feature, yet, in truth, the history of the reign of HER MAJESTY QUEEN VICTORIA has been one more fertile in

⁹ An ancient sage of the law, Sir John Fortescue, Chief Justice of England, has affirmed (see his *Laudibus Legum Angliæ*) that our admirable system of jurisprudence, the present laws of England, were first instituted by Dyfnwal Moelmud, a Welshman. He also says that no material changes have taken place in that system, either by the Romans, the Saxons, or the Normans. This is corroborated by Judge Blackstone, who states that Edward I. made some alterations in the Welsh laws, so as to bring them nearer the English standard, but still they retain much of their original polity.

¹ This part of the world is indebted to a Welshman—Bran, the father of Caractacus—for first introducing Christianity into this country: and what is more remarkable, the scriptures were first translated into three out of four of the languages of the British isles, English, Welsh, and Manks, by Welshmen—Tindal, Salusbury, and Phillips—forming a noble and honourable triad of translators.

wonders than that of any of her predecessors. The age of faith has gone, it is true, but the age of facts has come; and the wonders of fairy-land and the gorgeous imaginings of romance sink into common-place when compared with realities.

It is during this reign that the astonishing system of iron roads which everywhere mark the face of the country, has sprung up to the completeness and perfection which it has attained. It is true, that even previously the experiment had been tried, and plans matured which assured success for such undertakings; but it was reserved for the wealth and power of England at this period to produce the enterprise and the spirit of adventure which enabled and urged on companies of private capitalists to gather together armies of labourers, and to undertake works from which, in other times, princes and potentates, with the power and riches of empires at their backs, would have started in dismay.[2]

And while sturdy arms and thoughtful brains were at work preparing the mechanical means by which miles were to be transmuted into minutes, abstract science was planning to effect the transmission of thought with greater speed than that possessed by thought itself,—to make Heaven's own messenger the errand-boy of man; and now, while the bodies of men are sped to remote distances at the rate of a hundred miles in the hour, the minds of men, mocking the tardiness of the utmost speed of gross materiality, flash by them at the lightning's own pace, as thought vibrates along the electric wires which stretch nerve-like along the trunk line of every railway. What is magic itself to this? But the crowning triumph of the lightning-thought-carrier has yet to be consummated. It is not only that it can make London and Liverpool as one place, so far as thought is concerned, but it may, nay will, make all mankind near neighbours. The depths of the sea have heard the faint whisper of thought as it passes through the long-drawn wires trailing along the bottom of the Channel. What a wonderful imagination that, of the mind of the world glancing along these subtle life-endowing wires in all the tongues of Europe! The Babel of tongues come again, but translated from confusion into intelligence. Possibly too, ere long, the link will span the broad Atlantic, and through its agency British accents from the far West will greet a kindred language in our own isles; and, despite of adverse winds and roaring waves, of perils by flood and field, men from the uttermost ends of the earth will speak together as brother speaketh unto brother.[3]

All this would seem to be enough for a few short years; but another wonder as great, though at present not so important in its practical utilitarianism as those just mentioned; we have succeeded in making the sun itself a portrait-painter. Daguerre in France, and Talbot in England, have mastered the light of heaven

[2] A deservedly popular foreign writer, (Lamartine,) who visited England in the month of September, 1850, after an absence of nearly twenty years, thus expresses himself on the wonderful improvement that has taken place :—It is impossible for me not to be dazzled by the immense progress made in England, not only in population, in riches, industry, navigation, railroads, extent, edifices, embellishments, the charitable institutions of the country, but the real religious and fraternal associations and comfort of the people;—all as if it were prospering, not by the brutality of the police, but by the arm of public virtue, which gives to England, at the present moment, an incontestable predominance over the rest of Europe !"

Speaking of London, he says :—" The metropolis has vastly changed its appearance since the time I last saw it. It presents a vast image of opulence, of comfort, and of industry; it has enlarged its issues, widened its streets, ennobled its monuments, extended and beautified its suburbs, and made them more healthy. In the country districts, and secondary towns, the same transformation is observable. The innumerable railways which run in every direction, have covered the soil with stations, coal depôts, viaducts, bridges, &c. &c. The justice which all classes of the English population render to each other, the readiness of all to co-operate, each according to his means and disposition, in advancing the general good,—the employments, comforts, instruction, and morality of the people; in a word, a mild and serene air is breathed throughout the land, which has established

the equilibrium of England in the natural atmosphere. In this way the people can come to an understanding with itself; in this way they can live, last, prosper, and improve for a long time. Had I my residence on this soil, I should not any longer tremble for my hearth."

[3] The public are indebted for this most wonderful and extraordinary invention to W. F. Cooke, Esq., who sacrificed a large fortune in experiments in bringing it to a practical and successful issue; and we are glad to find that he now enjoys the fruit of his labours, contrary to the generality of such bold adventurers. We would instance our highly-talented countryman, Sir H. Middleton, who, at the expense of his own ruin, brought the New River to London, for the benefit of its inhabitants. The wonderful effect of the Electric Telegraph may be instanced from the following rapid communication between London and Edinburgh. We were present on one occasion when a message was sent from one place to the other; and to our astonishment, a reply was received, a distance, including to and from, of nearly eight hundred miles, in the short space of twenty-two seconds ! But its usefulness is yet in its infancy. When the Submarine Telegraph is completed between France, England, and other Continental powers, we shall be able to communicate with the whole of Europe in an equally wonderful short space of time.

analysed it, separated it, taken ray from ray, even as we might separate the woven threads of a web, and made it their agent. Shadows in the hands of these magicians of the modern world are no longer fleeting. Caught in their aërial unsubstantiality they are fixed upon the enchanted plate.

We cannot pass without a notice the progress of that great branch of the Anglo-Saxon race, perpetuating our language and our modes of thought throughout another hemisphere. Connected with this topic there is another striking feature of this reign. We mean the great tide of emigration, which, setting in from the East to the West, is taking the surplus nerve, and sinew, and mind, from the old world to confer the blessings of an extended and enlightened civilisation on the new, a tide which rolls ceaselessly onward, and destined, in the dispensation of Providence and the history of the philosophy of nations, to bring back a rich freight and reflux of blessings to ourselves.

We would point also to the spirit of enquiry of the time, as evinced in the researches of Mr. Layard, at Nineveh, where the ruins of an ancient empire are being explored under the auspices of government; so that the history of the past, which enshrines so many wonders, may be unrolled to modern eyes: to the explorations of Dr. Richardson and his companions into the interior of Africa: to the Arctic voyages of Parry, Ross, and Franklin; and of that adventurous band, who are seeking to release the latter voyager from his icy prison: nor can we forget the educational efforts on the part both of people and their rulers, but all these things mark, as we have stated, the reign of our present sovereign as an era of progress unparalleled in time.

It is our earnest prayer that a life so important as Her Majesty's, may be prolonged through many, many years; that the sweetest light of heaven may be shed upon its path; and that under the long-continued shadow of her benignant sceptre, Great Britain may rise to a still greater eminence of prosperity, usefulness, and glory, unexampled in the annals of the world!

AND NOW OUR LABOURS ARE ENDED, OUR TASK HAS BEEN FULFILLED. WITH MUCH TROUBLE AND ANXIETY WE HAVE ACCOMPLISHED THE OBJECT OF OUR LONG-CHERISHED DESIRE; AND WE WOULD HUMBLY OFFER IT ON THE SHRINE OF OUR LOYALTY TO OUR QUEEN, AND OUR LOVE TO THAT LAND OF WHICH IT IS THE HISTORY—TO CAMBRIA, THE COUNTRY OF OUR BIRTH. MAY THY PROSPERITY, THY HONOUR, AND THY LIBERTY LAST FOR EVER!

INDEX.

3 Q

THE END.

LONDON:
BRADBURY AND EVANS, PRINTERS, WHITEFRIARS.

LIST OF SUBSCRIBERS.

—————+—————

LARGE THICK ROYAL PAPER, ILLUMINATED WITH SPLENDID COLOURED DRAWINGS FROM ANCIENT MSS. IN THE BRITISH MUSEUM, NUMEROUS STEEL PLATES, AND A PROFUSION OF HISTORICAL AND PICTORIAL WOOD ENGRAVINGS, ELEGANTLY BOUND, £3 3 0.

HER MOST GRACIOUS MAJESTY THE QUEEN	10 Copies.
HIS ROYAL HIGHNESS PRINCE ALBERT	5 „
HIS ROYAL HIGHNESS THE PRINCE OF WALES	5 „
HER ROYAL HIGHNESS THE PRINCESS ROYAL	2 „
HER ROYAL HIGHNESS THE PRINCESS ALICE	2 „
HIS ROYAL HIGHNESS PRINCE ALFRED	2 „
HER ROYAL HIGHNESS THE PRINCESS HELENA	2 „
HER ROYAL HIGHNESS THE PRINCESS LOUISA	2 „
HIS ROYAL HIGHNESS THE DUKE OF CAMBRIDGE	2 „
HER ROYAL HIGHNESS THE DUCHESS OF KENT	3 „

	Copies.
Most Noble the Marquis of Anglesea, K.G., Beaudesart, Staffordshire, Plâs Newydd, Anglesey	2
Most Noble the Marquis of Westminster, Eaton Hall	2
Right Hon. Earl of Powis, Powis Castle	2
Right Hon. Earl of Shrewsbury, Alton Towers	2
Right Hon. Earl Grosvenor, M.P., Grosvenor House	2
Right Hon. Earl of Abergavenny, 58, Portland Place, London	2
Right Hon. Earl of Derby, K.G., Knowsley Park, Preston	2
Right Hon. Lord Viscount Combermere, Combermere Abbey	2
Right Hon. Lord Berwick, Cronkhill Park, Salop	1
Right Hon. Lord Boston, Hedsor, Marlow, Bucks	2
Right Hon. Lord Dinorben, Kinmel Park	2
Right Hon. Lord Fielding, Downing, Flintshire	1
Right Hon. Lord Dynevor, Berrington Park, Burford, Oxon	2
Right Hon. Lord Robert Grosvenor, M.P., Moor Park	1
Right Hon. Lord Kenyon, Greddington Park	2
Right Hon. Lord Mostyn, Pengwern, St. Asaph	2
Right Hon. Lord Alfred Paget, M.P., Berkeley Square	1
Right Hon. Sir Robert Peel, Bart., M.P.	2
Right Hon. Lord John Russell, M.P.	1
Right Hon. Lord Willoughby d'Eresby, Gwydir House	2
Right Hon. Lord Viscount Hill, Hawkstone	1
Right Hon. Admiral Dundas, M.P.	1
Right Hon. Sir John Jervis, Chief Justice of the Common Pleas	1
Right Rev. the Lord Bishop of St. Asaph	1
Right Rev. the Lord Bishop of St. David	1
The Right Rev. the Lord Bishop of Chester	1
The Very Rev. the Dean of Bangor	1
The Very Rev. the Dean of Chester	1
Hon. Thomas Kenyon, Pradoe, Salop	1
Hon. Thomas Price Lloyd, Pengwern	1
Hon. F. R. West, M.P., Ruthin Castle	2

	Copies.
Hon. Col. Douglas Pennant, M.P., Penrhyn Castle, Bangor	2
Hon. E. M. Ll. Mostyn, M.P., Mostyn Hall	2
Hon. William Owen Stanley, M.P., Penrhose, Anglesey	1
Sir Harford J. Jones Brydges, Bart., Boultibrook, Hereford	1
Sir Richard B. Williams Bulkeley, Bart., M.P., Baron Hill	2
Sir Andrew Vincent Corbet, Bart., Acton Reynald	1
Sir Robert Cunliffe, Bart., Acton Park	1
Sir Stephen R. Glynne, Bart., Hawarden Castle	1
Sir Benjamin Hall, Bart., M.P., Llanover Court	1
Sir John Hanmer, Bart., M.P., Bettisfield Park, Overton	2
Sir Richard Jenkins, D.C.L., F.R.S., India House	1
Sir John R. Kynaston, Bart., Hardwick, Salop	1
Sir Francis Lawley, Bart., M.P., 18, Grosvenor Square	1
Sir Pyers Mostyn, Bart., Talacre, Holywell	1
Sir John Owen, Bart., M.P., Orielton Park, Pembroke	2
Sir Charles John Salisbury, Bart., Llanwern House, Monmouth	1
Sir Edward Samuel Walker, Chester	1
Sir J. Hay Williams, Bart., Bodelwyddan	1
Sir Watkin Williams Wynn, Bart., M.P., Wynnstay	2
Sir William Wynne, Knight, Maes-y-neuadd	1
Lady Edwardes, Sansaw, Salop	1
The Dowager Lady Puleston, Albrighton Hall, Shrewsbury	1
Lieut.-Gen. Sir Love P. Jones Parry, Madryn Park	1
Major-General Sir Charles Felix Smith, K.C.B., Pen Dyffryn	1
William Bulkeley Hughes, Esq., M.P., Plâs Côch, Anglesey	1
Colonel Powell, M.P., Nanteos, Cardigan	1
R. A. Slaney, Esq., M.P., Walford Manor, Salop	1
John Williams, Esq., M.P., Bronwylfa, St. Asaph	2
Stevenson, Robert, Esq., M.P., 34, Gloucester-square, London	1
Thomas Peers Williams, Esq., M.P., Craig-y-don	2
Aldersey, S., Esq., Aldersey Hall, Cheshire	1
Barker, Richard, Esq., Solicitor, Chester	1

3 U

LIST OF SUBSCRIBERS.

	Copies.
Bate, Edward, Esq., Kelsterton	1
Bennett, Thomas, Esq., Chester	1
Bennion, Miss, Wrexham Fechan, near Wrexham	1
Bicknell, Mr. Henry, Penrhyn Arms Hotel, Bangor	1
Biddulph, R. M., Esq., Chirk Castle	1
Bowen, Mrs. Webb, Pope Hill, Haverfordwest	1
Brassey, Thomas, Esq., Adam Street, London	1
Brindley, Doctor, Tarvin Hall, Cheshire	1
Broster, John, Esq., F.A.S.E., Chester Cottage, Sandown Bay, Isle of Wight	1
Brown, Mrs., Victoria Terrace, Beaumaris	1
Bryant, J. B., Esq., Dr. Johnson's Hotel, London	1
Buckley, F. R., Esq., Chester	1
Clarke, Ambrose, Esq., Chester	1
Cooke, P. Davies, Esq., Gwysaney, Mold	1
Cludde, Mrs., Orleton, Wellington	1
Darby, Francis, Esq., Coalbrookdale, Salop	1
Davies, T., Esq., 19, Hanover Street, Hanover Square, London	1
Dutton, Charles, Esq., Chester	1
Eaton, John, Esq., Garden Lane, Chester	1
Eaton, Peter, Esq., Chester	1
Edgeworth, Thomas, Esq., Wrexham	1
Edwardes, Rev. J. C., 64, Russell Square, London	1
Edwards, Mrs. Williams, Cerrig Llwydion, Ruthin	1
Evans, David, Esq., New Hall, Cheshire	1
Evans, Jeremiah, Esq., 33, King William Street, London	1
Evans, John E., Esq., Bond Street, London	1
Eyton, John P., Esq., Llanerch-y-môr	1
Feilding, John, Esq., Mollington Hall, Cheshire	1
Folliott, George, Esq., Vicar's Cross, Chester	1
Fletcher, Thomas, Esq., Chester	1
Ford, Rev. Frederick, M.A., Chester	2
Forde, Col. Hilton, Chester	1
Foster, Samuel B., Esq., 33, Roscommon Street, Everton, Liverpool	1
Foulkes, John, Esq., Ashfield, Wrexham	1
Gerrard, Enoch, Esq., Chester	1
Henderson, J. B., Esq., Bern House, Forfarshire	1
Hesketh, Lloyd Hesketh Bamford, Esq., Gwrych Castle	1
Hope, John Thomas, Esq., Nettley, Donnington, Salop	1
Hughes, Hugh Robert, Esq.	1
Hughes, Robert, Esq., Birkenhead	1
Humberston, P. Stapleton, Esq., Chester	1
James, Rev. D., Kirkdale, Liverpool	1
Johnes, Arthur James, Esq., Garthmyl, Welshpool	1
Jones, F. Walker, Esq., Mayor of Caernarvon	1

	Copies.
Jones, John, Esq., Newcastle, Staffordshire	1
Jones, Rev. H. Wynn, Chancellor, Bangor, and Rector of Aberffraw.	1
Jones, Thomas, Esq., Admiralty, Somerset House, London	1
Jones, William, Esq., Crosby-square, London	1
Jones, William, Esq., (Gwrgant,) St. Mildred's-court, London	1
Lawrence, Freeling, Esq., Greenwich	1
Leche, John Hurleston, Esq., Carden Park, Cheshire	1
Lewis John, Esq., Solicitor, Wrexham	1
Lloyd, Cynric, Esq., Pontriffith	1
Lloyd, John, Esq., Earl's Terrace, Kensington	1
Lloyd, Morgan, Esq., Chester Square, London	1
Lloyd, Mrs., Aston Hall, Oswestry	1
Madock, Edward John, Esq., Glan-y-wern	1
Morris, George, Esq., Old Bank, Shrewsbury	1
Morgan, Wm., Esq., Moorgate-street, London	1
Mayer, Joseph, Esq., F.S.A., Liverpool	1
Myers, John, Esq., Chester	1
Nanney, John, Esq., Eton College	1
Oldfield, T., Esq., Farm, Betws, Abergele	1
Ormerod, George, Esq., F.R.S., F.S.A., Sedbury Park, Chepstow	1
Parkins, James, Esq., Wepre Hall	1
Parkins, William Trevor, Esq., 79, Cadogan Place, London	1
Parry, E. Jones, Esq., Aberdunant, Tremadoc	1
Peers, Joseph, Esq., Plâs-newydd, Ruthin	1
Penson, T. K., Esq., Architect, Chester	1
Prichard, Robert, Esq., Bangor	1
Price, John, Esq., Llanrhaiadr Hall, Denbigh	1
Rees, Evans, Esq., 1, Southampton Row, Russell Square	1
Richards, John, Esq., Treiorwerth, Anglesey	1
Roberts, Miss, George Hotel, Bangor Ferry	1
Robertson, Henry, Esq., C.E., Chester	1
Royle, John, Esq., Chester	1
Saunderson, John, Esq., Druid's-lodge, Anglesey	1
Seller, Edward Russell, Esq., Sheriff of Chester	1
Smith, William, Esq., Cop Farm, Sealand	1
Thackeray, William M., Esq., M.D., Chester	1
Thomas, John Evan, Esq., F.S.A., 7, Belgrave-place, London	1
Tomkins, —, Esq., Victoria Terrace, Beaumaris	1
Vincent, G. Giles, Esq., Dean's Yard, Westminster	1
Wardell, William, Esq., Banker, Chester	1
Wedge, Thomas, Esq., Sealand, Cheshire	1
Whitley, Robert, Esq., Rockcliffe, Flint	1
Williams, Robert Wynne, Esq., Temple, London	1
Wynne, John Lloyd, Esq., Coed Côch	1
Wynne, Robert, Esq., Tower Buildings, Liverpool	1
Yorke, P. Wynne, Esq., Dyffryn Aled	1

LARGE ROYAL PAPER, ILLUSTRATED WITH NUMEROUS STEEL PLATES AND A PROFUSION OF HISTORICAL AND PICTORIAL WOOD ENGRAVINGS, HANDSOMELY BOUND, £2 2 0.

Right Hon. Lord Dinorben, Kinmel Park, (additional)	2
The Venerable Archdeacon Williams, Llandovery	1
Bage, F., Esq., Surgeon, Chester	1
Beattie, William, Esq., Warwick Street South, Liverpool	1
Blomfield, Rev. Canon, Chester	1
Brittain, William W., Esq., Chester	1
Brooks, Charles, Esq., Walsall	1
Casson, George, Esq., Blaen-y-ddôl, Ffestiniog	1
Churton, H., Esq., Coroner, Chester	1
Darby, Miss M., Dale House, Coalbrook Dale	1
Darton, J. M. Esq., London	1

Davies, Griffith, Esq., Bangor	1
Davies, Rev. Walter, A.M., Llanrhaiadr, Oswestry	1
Dawson, John, Esq., Gronant	1
Dixon, Thomas, Esq., Littleton, Chester	1
Dixon, William James, Esq., Chester	1
Drury, Mr. Robert, Chester	1
Edwards, Mr. John, Chester	1
Ellis, W. T., Esq., Cornist Hall, near Flint	1
Evans, Edward, Esq., Eyton Hall, Leominster	1
Evans, Rev. Evan, Ince, Cheshire	1
Evans, R. D., Esq., Holyhead	1

LIST OF SUBSCRIBERS.

	Copies.
Grey, John, Esq., Chester	1
Hawkins, Edward, Esq., British Museum	1
Hill, Mr. John, Castle Street, Chester	1
Hughes, John, Esq., Bodfor, Rhyl	1
Huxley, Mr. John, Chester	1
Hughes, Rev. Joseph, (Carn Ingli,) Meltham, Huddersfield	1
Hughes, Thomas, Esq., Ystrad, Denbigh	1
James, J., Esq., (Ioan Meirion,) Secretary to the Royal Society of Ancient Britons, London	1
James, Rev. Thomas, Hetherthong, Huddersfield	1
Johnston, Mr., Royal Hotel, Chester	1
Jones, Mr., Dinorben, Abergele	1
Jones, Edward, Esq., Pendre, Holywell	1
Jones, John, Esq., Liverpool	1
Jones, Rees, Esq., Salop	1
Jones, Robert, Esq., Chester	1
Jones, Robert, Britannia Buildings, Liverpool	1
Kennedy, Rev. Dr., F.R.S., Shrewsbury	1
Lloyd, Mr. C. J., Wynnstay Arms, Machynlleth	1
Lloyd, John, Esq., Maentwrog	1
Lloyd, Sir William, Knt., Brynestyn	1
Lloyd, Mr., Wynnstay Hotel, Oswestry	1
Maddock, Thomas F., Esq., Chester	1
Massie, Rev. William, Chester	1
Morgan, Edward, Esq., Golden Grove	1
Nichol, Mr. I. F., Wolverhampton	1
Nicholson, Mr., Bank, Chester	1
Nixon, Robert, Esq., Gwersyllt	1
Owen, Rev. H. D., D.D., Beaumaris	1
Owen, Rev. W. Hicks, A.M., Rhyllon, St. Asaph	1
Painter, Mr., Wrexham	1
Palin, Mr. John, Chester	1
Parry, Edward, Esq., St. Alkmond's Square, Shrewsbury	1
Parry, F. C., Esq., Manor House, Drayton Green, Ealing	1
Parry, Mr. Llywelyn, Shrewsbury	1
Parry, Mr. R. Griffith, Chester	1

	Copies.
Parry, Mr. Goronwy Hughes, Chester	1
Parry, Miss J. G., Uxbridge, Middlesex	1
Patchett, William, Esq., Shrewsbury	1
Peters, Mr. Edward, Chester	1
Prescot, Mr., Temple Place, Liverpool	1
Price, John, Esq., Cadnant, Anglesey	1
Raffles, Rev. Thomas, D.D., Liverpool	1
Rees, Mr. James, Caernarvon	1
Rees, Mr. William, Bookseller, Llandovery	2
Roberts, Dr. O. O., Castle Hill, Bangor	1
Roberts, Mr. Robert, Bank Buildings, Liverpool	1
Roberts, Thomas Q., Esq., Chester	1
Roberts, Mr., Royal Hotel, Holyhead	1
Rosson, John, Esq., Moor Hall, Lancashire	1
Rowland, Owen, Esq., London	1
Salisbury, E. G., Esq., London	1
Scoltock, S., Esq., Shrewsbury	1
Seller, William John, Esq., Chester	1
Smith, John, Esq., Chester	1
Soorn, Mr. Samuel, Chester	1
Thomas, O. Wynne, Esq., London	1
Topham, E. W., Esq., Chester	1
Topham, Mr., York	1
Truss, Thomas, Esq., Chester	1
Turner, Robert, Esq., Chester	1
Vaughan, John, Esq., Penmaen, Machynlleth	1
Vicars, Rev. Archdeacon, Chelten Rectory, Bridgenorth	1
Walker, Henry, Esq., Chester	1
Walker, John, Esq., Chester	1
Welsby, W. Newland, Esq., Recorder of Chester	1
Whaley, Mr., Albion Hotel, Chester	1
Wheeler, Herbert, Esq., Wolverhampton	1
Williams, John, Esq., Furnival's Inn, London	1
Williams, Rev. Rowland, Ysceifiog	1
Williams, William, Esq., Chester	1
Wyatt, Charles E., Esq., St. Asaph	1

SMALL PAPER, ILLUSTRATED WITH NUMEROUS HISTORICAL AND PICTORIAL WOOD ENGRAVINGS, £1 1 0.

Anderson, Mr. John G., Chester	1
Axon, Mr. William, jun., Chester	1
Barnett, Mr. G. J., Shrewsbury	1
Bell, G. Angelo, Esq., C.E., Chester	1
Bland, Mr. Robert, Crown Inn, Denbigh	1
Bloor, Mr., May Cottage, Chester	1
Boden, Mr. Henry, Chester	1
Boydell, Francis, Esq., Chester	1
Brereton, Mr. A. Jones, New Street, Mold	1
Brooks, J., Esq., Brymbo, near Wrexham	1
Brown, Mr. Samuel, Heraldist, Chester	1
Brown, Rev. T. L., Flint	1
Burr, George, Esq., Shrewsbury	1
Carter, Mr. James, Chester	1
Clark, Mr. Isaac, Ruthin	1
Davies, William, Esq., Mostyn	1
Davies, George, Esq., Cyffty, Llanrwst	1
Davies, Mr. James, Jun., Shrewsbury	1
Davies, Mr. Richard, Bold Square, Chester	1
Debrisey, Colonel, Chester	1
Denton, J. W., Esq., M.D., Newbold, Cheshire	1
Edisbury, John, Esq., Bersham, Wrexham	1

Edwards, Mr., Penrhôs, Anglesey	1
Edwards, Mr. T., Cutler, Chester	1
Ellis, Mr., Binder, Chester	1
Evans, Rev. Edward, A.M., Newmarket	1
Evans, John, Esq., Stoney Down, Walthamstone	1
Evans, Rev. John, Gelliog, Pwllheli	1
Evans, Mr. Joseph, Flint	1
Evans, Robert, Esq., Flint	1
Eyton, Edward, Esq., Pistill, Holywell	1
Eyton, Miss, Pistill Hall, Holywell	1
France, Mr., Warrington	1
Friend Cymro, (by Mr. Francis Tuck Parry)	1
Gardner, Mr. Samuel, Chester	1
Glanville, George, Esq., Christleton	1
Griffith, Mr. C., Stockport	1
Griffith, Mr. Edwin, Whitford	1
Griffith, Mr. Robert, Pwllheli	1
Griffith, Mr., Sealand, Flintshire	1
Griffith, Rev. Thomas, Llanvawr Vicarage, near Bala	1
Griffith, Thomas, Esq., Trevalyn Hall	1
Gwynne, Mrs., 9, Beacon Terrace, Torquay	1
Hughes, E. S., Esq., Custom House, Chester	1

LIST OF SUBSCRIBERS.

	Copies.
Hughes, F. Bond, Esq., London	1
Hughes, Mr. Josiah, Chester	1
Hughes, Rev. Morgan, Corwen	1
Humphreys, Mr. John, Birkenhead	1
Jones, John, Esq., (Talhaiarn,) London	1
Jones, Jonathan, Esq., Chester	1
Jones, Mr. Hugh, (Erfyl,) Chester	1
Jones, Mr. John, Tower Royal, London	1
Jones, Mr. Joseph, New Street, Mold	1
Jones, Mr. Robert, Ludlow	1
Jones, Mr., Saracen's Head, Chester	1
Jones, Mr. Thomas, Denbigh	1
Jones, Mr. Theophilus Henry, Manchester	1
Jones, Mr. William, Market Square, Northampton	1
Jones, R. Phillips, Esq., M.D., Chester	1
Jones, Rev. John, Llanllyfni	1
Jones, Rev. J., (Tegid,) Preb. St. David's, Haverfordwest	1
Jones, Thomas, Esq., Wood Street, Liverpool	1
Kearsley, Mr. John, Chester	1
Lawrence, Benjamin, Esq., Doctor's Commons, London	1
Leake, Mr. J. H. Shrewsbury	1
Lloyd, Edward Watson, Esq., Chester	1
Lloyd, Rev. C. A. A., Whittington, Oswestry	1
Lloyd, Rev. J. Vaughan., A.M., Hope	1
Lloyd, Rev. R., Wilneaston, near Tamworth	1
Lowe, Mr. John, Goldsmith, Chester	1
Maddock, Mr. Henry, Chester	1
Mainwaring, Townsend, Esq., Marchwiail	1
Manley, Mr. William, Chester	1
Morrall, Edward, Esq., Plas Warren	1
Massey, F. W., Esq., Chester	1
McVennels, Mr. Little, Chester	1
Morgan, Rev. Augustus Henry, Golden Grove	1
Morris, Mr. Joseph, Shrewsbury	1
Mortimer, Wm. William, Esq., Birkenhead	1
Moss, Mr. John, Crane, Chester	1
Newcome, Rev. Archdeacon, Cloisters, Ruthin	1
Nicholl, Mr. J. F., Wolverhampton	1
Nicholls, Mr., 4, Gore Piazzas, Liverpool	1
Owen, Edward, Esq., Hoole, Chester	1
Owen, Robert, Esq., New Bond Street, London	1
Parry, Rev. H., Vicar of Llanasa	1
Parry, Mr. Bernard, Newmarket	1
Parry, Mr. Dashwood, Old Rhyddyn, Hope	1
Parry, Mr. Edwin Vickers, Chester	1
Parry, Mr. Francis Tuck, Chester	1
Parry, Mr. Henry, Holyhead	1
Parry, Mr. John, Newmarket	1
Parsonage, Mr. John, Shrewsbury	1
Parsons, Mr. John, Shrewsbury	1
Pickering, Mr., Chester	1
Pierce, John, Esq., 180, Albany Road, London	1
Pierce, William, Esq., Clement's Inn	1

	Copies.
Poole, Mr. Samuel, Shrewsbury	1
Price, William, Esq., Llanffoist, Abergavenny	1
Prichard, Mr. William, Caernarvon	2
Pugh, David, Esq., Dolgelly	1
Ralphs, Simon, Esq., Saighton, Chester	1
Rees, Mr. R. O., Bookseller, Dolgelley	3
Rees, Mr. William, Bookseller, Llandovery	2
Rees, Rev. W. J., Cascob, Radnorshire	1
Richardson, Captain, Chester	1
Roberts, Mr. Ellis, Harper to H.R.H. the Prince of Wales	1
Roberts, Mr. Thomas, Bodidris	1
Roberts, Rev. Gabriel Lloyd, Ruthin	1
Robinson, Mr. William, Feathers Hotel, Chester	1
Rogers, Edward, Esq., Stennage Park, Ludlow	1
Rogers, Mr. Joseph, Chester	1
Roussell, Mr., Chester and Holyhead Railway, London	1
Roy, Robert, Esq., Chester	1
Rutter, Mr. Samuel, Chester	1
Sheffer, Mr., Denbigh	1
Smith, Mr. G., Wrexham	1
Smith, Mr. John Russell, London	1
Stephens, Mr. R., Brook Street, Chester	1
Taylor, George, Esq., Eccleston	1
Thelwall, Bevis, Esq., Chester	1
Thomas, George, Esq., London	1
Thomas, William, Esq., Bryn Merllyn	1
Tiltson, Edward, Esq., Chester	1
Twemlow, John, Esq., Hatherton, Nantwich	1
Twigg, Mrs., Churchfield House, Hackney	1
Vaughan, Mr., Cross Keys, Shrewsbury	1
Wheatley, Hewitt, Esq., Hereford	1
Whitley, Edward, Esq., Broncoed, Mold	1
Whitmore, Mr., Shrewsbury	1
Whittakers, Mr., London	1
Whittell, Mr. Thomas, Chester	1
William, W. Wynn, Esq., Menai-fron, near Caernarvon	1
Williams, Mr. Benjamin, White Chapel, Liverpool	1
Williams, Mr. D., Bangor	1
Williams, Rhys, Esq., 34, Mornington Place, Hampstead Road	1
Williams, David, Esq., 20, Hemingford Terrace, Barnsbury Park	1
Williams, Mr. D., Pwllheli	1
Williams, Mr. Dyer, Chester	1
Williams, Mr. John, (Ioan Madoc,) Port Madoc	1
Williams, Mr. W., Glan-y-wern, Denbigh	1
Williams, Rev. J. Lloyd, Llandudno	6
Williams, Rev. John, Duke Street, Chester	1
Williams, Rev. John, A.M., Llan yn Mowddwy	1
Williams, Rev. Rowland, A.M., Vice-principal St. David's College	1
Williams, Rev. W., (Caledfryn,) London	1
Williams, Richard, Esq., Denbigh	1
Williamson, Samuel, Esq., Holywell	1
Woolrich, Mr., Cholmley, near Nantwich	1
Wyatt, Rev. Mr., Dyserth	1

CPSIA information can be obtained
at www.ICGtesting.com
Printed in the USA
BVHW060033121218
535350BV00005B/61/P